THE CLARENDON EDITION OF THE
NOVELS OF GEORGE ELIOT

General Editor: GORDON S. HAIGHT

————

ADAM BEDE

GEORGE ELIOT

ADAM BEDE

EDITED BY
CAROL A. MARTIN

CLARENDON PRESS · OXFORD

OXFORD
UNIVERSITY PRESS

Great Clarendon Street, Oxford OX2 6DP

Oxford University Press is a department of the University of Oxford.
It furthers the University's objective of excellence in research, scholarship,
and education by publishing worldwide in

Oxford New York

Athens Auckland Bangkok Bogotá Buenos Aires Cape Town
Chennai Dar es Salaam Delhi Florence Hong Kong Istanbul Karachi Kolkata
Kuala Lumpur Madrid Melbourne Mexico City Mumbai
Nairobi Paris São Paulo Shanghai Singapore Taipei Tokyo Toronto Warsaw
with associated companies in Berlin Ibadan

Oxford is a registered trade mark of Oxford University Press
in the UK and in certain other countries

Published in the United States
by Oxford University Press Inc., New York

British Library Cataloguing in Publication Data

Data available

Library of Congress Cataloging in Publication Data
Eliot, George, 1819–1880
Adam Bede / George Eliot ; edited by Carol A. Martin.
p. cm.—(The Clarendon edition of the novels of George Eliot.)
Includes bibliographical references.
1. Women clergy—Fiction. 2. Infanticide—Fiction. 3. Carpenters—Fiction. 4. England—Fiction.
I. Martin, Carol A., 1941–
PR4656.A2 M37 2001   823'.8–dc21   00–049114
ISBN 0-19-812595-X

Typeset by Kolam Information Services Pvt. Ltd, Pondicherry, India
Printed in Great Britain
on acid-free paper by
Biddles Ltd,
Guildford and King's Lynn

ACKNOWLEDGEMENTS

My first and foremost debt of gratitude is to Professor David Carroll, without whose support I would not have come to this project and without whose encouragement and good advice my task would have been much more difficult. I wish also to thank the staff at the British Library, London, for the assistance and unfailing courtesy of too many individuals to mention; the staff in Manuscripts and Rare Books at the National Library of Scotland, especially Iain G. Brown and Olive Geddes; Richard W. Oram, Pat Fox, John Kirkpatrick, and Jeanne Peterson at the Harry Ransom Humanities Research Center, University of Texas at Austin; H. G. Carron, Curator of the Library of Emmanuel College, Cambridge; the staff at the Bodleian Library, Oxford University, and at the Beinecke Rare Books and Manuscript Library, Yale University.

I wish also to thank Frances Whistler, my editor at Oxford University Press, with whom it has been a great pleasure to work, and the following individuals who have read the manuscript in its various stages and have given invaluable advice: William Baker, Robert Colby, Margaret Harris, J. C. Ross, Joseph Wiesenfarth, Elizabeth Winston, Hugh Witemeyer, and Michael Wolff. Jonathan G. Ouvry, great-great-grandson of George Henry Lewes, has been gracious and helpful not only in granting permissions needed but in sharing his enthusiasm for the works of George Eliot and offering encouragement to me as the project proceeded.

I am grateful to the National Endowment for the Humanities for providing a Research Fellowship, the Idaho State Board of Education for a research grant, and Boise State University for a sabbatical leave, all of which provided time necessary for completion of this project. I am also grateful to the Boise State University Office of Research Administration for assistance with travel expenses. For her invaluable assistance in proofreading, I wish to thank Pamela J. Peterson. And for his patience and encouragement over the past five years of my preoccupation with *Adam Bede*, I thank my husband, Lonnie Willis.

C.A.M.

GENERAL CONTENTS

ILLUSTRATIONS

REFERENCES AND ABBREVIATIONS

Ashton	Rosemary Ashton, *George Eliot: A Life* (London, 1996)
Cunningham	Valentine Cunningham, *Everywhere Spoken Against: Dissent in the Victorian Novel* (Oxford, 1975)
Haight	Gordon S. Haight, *George Eliot: A Biography* (New York, 1968)
Handley	Graham Handley, *George Eliot's Midlands: Passion in Exile* (London, 1991)
Hughes	Kathryn Hughes, *George Eliot: The Last Victorian* (London, 1998)
JGE	*The Journals of George Eliot*, ed. Margaret Harris and Judith Johnston (Cambridge, 1999)
JGHL	The Journals of George Henry Lewes, MS Vault George Eliot. Section VI. George Henry Lewes Writings. Beinecke Rare Books and Manuscript Library, Yale University
Letters	*The George Eliot Letters*, ed. Gordon S. Haight, 9 vols. (New Haven, 1954–78)
LGHL	*The Letters of George Henry Lewes*, ed. William Baker, 3 vols. (Victoria, BC, 1995, 1999)
NLS	National Library of Scotland
OED	*Oxford English Dictionary*, 1st edition
Pinney	*Essays of George Eliot*, ed. Thomas Pinney (New York, 1963)
Smiles	Samuel Smiles, *The Life of George Stephenson: Railway Engineer* (London, 1857)
Wiesenfarth	Joseph Wiesenfarth, *George Eliot's Mythmaking* (Heidelberg, 1977)
Witemeyer	Hugh Witemeyer, *George Eliot and the Visual Arts* (New Haven, 1979)
A Writer's Notebook	*George Eliot: A Writer's Notebook, 1854–1879, and Collected Writings*, ed. Joseph Wiesenfarth (Charlottesville, Va., 1981). Material on *Adam Bede* was originally published as 'George Eliot's Notes for *Adam Bede*', *Nineteenth-Century Fiction*, 32 (1977), 127–65

INTRODUCTION

Adam Bede is George Eliot's first full-length work of fiction, but it is not the work of a novice. In a review in the London *Times* E. S. Dallas called it 'a first-rate novel [whose] author takes rank at once among the masters of the art'.[1] The identity of that author was unknown, he wrote, 'Nobody seems to know who is Mr. George Eliot,' and he asked rhetorically, 'can this be a young author? Is all this mature thought, finished portraiture, and crowd of characters the product of a 'prentice hand and of callow genius? If it is, the hand must have an extraordinary cunning, and the genius must be of the highest order.' Eliot's genius was 'of the highest order', but she was neither an apprentice nor young. She was 39 when *Adam Bede* was published in February 1859, and she had prepared herself for writing fiction by serving as *de facto* editor of the *Westminster Review* in the early 1850s, by writing book reviews for the *Westminster* and other leading periodicals, and by publishing one work of fiction that was well, if quietly, received—a series of three novellas that appeared under what Dallas called 'the modest title of "Scenes" '.

Scenes of Clerical Life was first published serially in *Blackwood's Edinburgh Magazine*, beginning with 'The Sad Fortunes of the Reverend Amos Barton', in January and February 1857. Although anonymous publication was customary in many British periodicals in 1857 including *Blackwood's*, what was uncommon was the fact that even its publisher, John Blackwood, did not know who his new author was. George Henry Lewes, Eliot's companion from 1854 to his death in 1878, and himself a contributor to 'Maga', as *Blackwood's* was called, submitted the story on behalf of a 'friend', who Blackwood, as Lewes intended, inferred was a man, probably a clergyman, given the title and contents of 'Amos'. Blackwood was initially reluctant to begin a 'series' with only one story in hand, but Lewes's comments about the discouraging effect of this decision on the author determined Blackwood to proceed. It was the beginning of a long and productive partnership between Eliot and the firm of William Blackwood & Sons, interrupted only by the publication of *Romola* by Smith Elder.

'Amos' was followed by 'Mr. Gilfil's Love Story', in four instalments from March to June, and 'Janet's Repentance', in five instalments, July to November 1857. Eliot had intended to continue the series with one or two more stories, but John Blackwood's preference for idealistic portrayals of

---

[1] 12 Apr. 1859, 5.

character and events increasingly conflicted with the author's insistence on realism. Blackwood had expressed doubts about the impulsive, emotional heroine in 'Mr. Gilfil's Love Story',[2] but the next story disturbed him even more. Although he praised the cleverness of the first instalment of 'Janet's Repentance', he confessed that 'I should have liked a pleasanter picture. Surely the colours are rather harsh for a sketch of English County Town life only 25 years ago.'[3] By early July, after receiving Blackwood's criticism of the next instalment of 'Janet',[4] Eliot made up her mind to end *Scenes of Clerical Life* after this story. Her journal entry 'How I came to write Fiction' (6 December 1857) recalls Lewes's approval of 'Janet's Repentance' as 'almost better than the other stories', and her 'disappointment [that] Blackwood did not like it so well, seemed to misunderstand the characters, and be doubtful about the treatment of clerical matters'. As a result, she 'wrote at once to beg him to give up printing the story if he felt uncomfortable about it, and he immediately sent a very anxious, cordial letter, saying the thought of putting a stop to the series "gave him quite a turn"—"he didn't meet with George Eliots every day"—and so on'.[5] Although Blackwood 'came round to admiration at the third part' of 'Janet's Repentance',[6] she could anticipate that he would be less enthusiastic about instalments 4 and 5, which depict the abused wife's struggle with her own alcoholism and her husband's death from *delirium tremens*. Their disagreement on the nature of fiction was exacerbated by the fact that Eliot was barely keeping up with each month's magazine deadline; therefore Blackwood received the stories one instalment at a time, forcing him to comment on each part before he saw the story as a whole.

On 5 September Eliot conveyed her decision to Blackwood, mentioning her plan for a longer work, 'I have a subject in my mind which will not come under the limitations of the title "Clerical Life," and I am inclined to take a large canvas for it, and write a novel.'[7] She left open the possibility that the new novel might appear first as a serial in *Blackwood's Edinburgh Magazine*, but she was determined not to send him one instalment at a time: 'In case of my writing fiction for Maga again, I should like to be considerably beforehand with my work, so that you can read a thoroughly decisive portion before beginning to print.'[8]

---

[2] See *Letters*, II. 297 and 308.   [3] 8 June 1857; *Letters*, II. 344.

[4] 'Your Bishop is doubtless a true sketch, but I wish he had been a better sample of the cloth,' Blackwood wrote. He also called for 'Some allusion to the solemn and affecting sight that a confirmation ought to be' (*Letters*, II. 360).

[5] *JGE* 291.   [6] *JGE* 291.

[7] *Letters*, II. 381. Haight calls this 'The first reference in the letters to *Adam Bede*' (*Letters*, II. 381 n. 6).

[8] *Letters*, II. 381.

There is no record of any response from Blackwood until 15 October 1857. Six letters between 25 July and 6 October from Major Blackwood in Edinburgh to his brother suggest that John was at St Andrews, as was often the case from late July well into October.[9] Nonetheless, extant letters from other years show the latter conducting business despite the call of the links. Perhaps he wished to avoid further comment—and conflict. In any case, when he sent proofs of the last instalment of 'Janet's Repentance', he mingled his praise of her 'bold choice of a plot' for 'Janet's Repentance' and his affirmation of the subject of alcoholism as 'legitimate material for the writer of Fiction' with doubts about the propriety of its graphic depiction in the final number: 'Should there be so much of Dempster's delirium?'[1] This same letter also contains his first recorded response to her proposal for what would become *Adam Bede*:

> I rejoice to think that you are going to devote your powers to a Tale on a great scale. With a larger canvass your exquisite little sketches of character will all come into full life and take their legitimate share in the story.
>
> It will give me much pleasure to hear anything about this new story and to know how soon there is any chance of it being transferred from your head to paper.[2]

Eliot wrote by return post: 'My new story haunts me a good deal, and I shall set about it without delay. It will be a country story—full of the breath of cows and the scent of hay. But I shall not ask you to look at it till I have written a volume or more, and then you will be able to judge whether you will prefer printing it in the Magazine, or publishing it as a separate novel when it is completed.'[3]

On 28 October, Blackwood notes the advantage another story would have given to *Scenes of Clerical Life*, but otherwise is content with the new plan: 'I wish the Series had been long enough to make the statutory 3 vols. as that would have afforded time to fix your reputation more firmly and *familiarly* in the public mind and given the reprint a better chance of a start at first. With this view I would have suggested a prolongation of the Series had I not thoroughly agreed in the opinion that you require a broader canvass and freedom from the trammels of your Clerical Title.'[4] He concludes this letter with a cordial wish, 'I shall miss the series very much but I trust soon to see you in the field with your new Tale. Pray let me know if you begin to make way.'[5]

---

[9] NLS MS 4122.

[1] *Letters*, II. 386–7. His tact to Eliot is apparent when contrasted with his blunt comments to Lewes on 28 October, just before the appearance of the last part of 'Janet's Repentance': 'I daresay it would have been no use, but I wish I had pressed George Eliot more to curtail or to indicate more delicately the Delirium Tremens scene. It is too naked and the shudder with which one turns from the picture is too much akin to disgust' (*Letters*, II. 394).

[2] 15 Oct. 1857; *Letters*, II. 387.   [3] 17 Oct. 1857; *Letters*, II. 387–8.

[4] *Letters*, II. 393.   [5] *Letters*, II. 394.

Writing to John Blackwood on 20 November 1857, Joseph Munt Langford, the firm's London manager, also laments the end of the series of
Scenes and the impact on sales. After discussion of book sales being 'dull',
Langford contrasts them with 'the sales of Maga [which] are very good we
have but 63 left of the months number, and there continues a dripping sale
of numbers for the year. It is a great pity we can have no more Clerical
Experiences which are only just getting known.'[6] However, Eliot's mind
was made up and *Adam Bede* was under way. The divergence of opinion
between author and publisher was not over, however: their differing
perspectives on the acceptable level of realism in fiction would determine
the form in which readers first encountered the new story as well.

GENESIS

'It had always been a vague dream of mine that some time or other I might
write a novel,' Eliot records in 'How I came to write Fiction', 'and my
shadowy conception of what the novel was to be, varied, of course, from one
epoch of my life to another. But I never went farther towards the actual
writing of the novel than an introductory chapter describing a Staffordshire
village and the life of the neighbouring farm houses.... My "introductory
chapter" was pure description though there were good materials in it for
dramatic presentation.' She apparently thought this chapter worth preserving, for she had it 'among the papers I had with me in Germany [in
1854–5] and one evening at Berlin, something led me to read it to George'.[7]
Although there is no extant text of this chapter to prove a connection, it is
possible to see in the 'Staffordshire village and the life of the neighbouring
farm houses' the earliest reference to *Adam Bede*. Not on paper, but in her
mind, were two other narratives that made their way into *Adam Bede*, both
of which might have appeared as short stories if Blackwood's response had
not discouraged Eliot from continuing *Scenes of Clerical Life*. One was a
story she had heard from the wife of her uncle Samuel Evans, and the other
she referred to as the 'Clerical Tutor'.

In her 'History of "Adam Bede"' recorded 30 November 1858, Eliot
recalls telling Lewes, in December 1856 just before the first instalment of
Scenes was published, a story that she had heard from her 'Methodist Aunt
Samuel', of a young girl condemned to death for child murder. Lewes
'remarked that the scene in the prison would make a fine element in a
story.... At first I thought of making the story one of the series of
"Scenes", but afterwards, when several motives had induced me to close
these with "Janet's Repentance", I determined on making what we always
called in our conversations "My Aunt's Story", the subject of a long novel:
which I accordingly began to write on the 22nd of October 1857.'[8] Her

---

[6] NLS MS 4125, fos. 67–70.   [7] *JGE* 289.   [8] *JGE* 296–7.

'Aunt's Story' had a powerful effect upon the adolescent, Evangelical Mary Ann Evans. This aunt, Mrs Samuel Evans, the wife of Robert Evans's younger brother, was visiting in 1839

when it occurred to her to tell me how she had visited a condemned criminal, a very ignorant girl who had murdered her child and refused to confess—how she had stayed with her, praying, through the night and how the poor creature at last broke out into tears and confessed her crime. My Aunt afterwards went with her in the cart to the place of execution, and she described to me the great respect with which this ministry of hers was regarded by the official people about the gaol. The story, told by my aunt with great feeling, affected me deeply, and I never lost the impression of that afternoon and our talk together.[9]

Eliot 'afterwards began to think of blending this and some other recollections of my aunt in one story with some points in my father's early life and character'.[1]

In a letter to Sara Sophia Hennell on 7 October 1859, Eliot expanded this account of her aunt's story. Her letter was published in the *Pall Mall Budget* on 7 January 1881, two weeks after her death, with a prefatory note in which Hennell gave as her reason for publication 'signs of a renewed controversy on the source from which George Eliot drew the beautiful character of Dinah in "Adam Bede"'.[2] The original impetus for the letter was Eliot's annoyance that Charles Holte Bracebridge, a Warwickshire man with whom Eliot and Sara Hennell's sister Caroline (Cara) Hennell Bray had dined in 1845,[3] claimed to have identified the originals of many of *Adam Bede*'s characters. He had also promulgated the notion that a Warwickshire native, Joseph Liggins, was the author of *Scenes of Clerical Life* and *Adam Bede*. Eliot and Lewes received Bracebridge's claims through Sara's brother-in-law and Eliot's longtime Coventry friend Charles Bray, and the resulting correspondence in the second half of September 1859 reveals the tension in her relationship with Cara Bray and Sara Hennell, whose disapproval of Lewes five years earlier had strained their relationship with Eliot.[4] Several letters in early October from Eliot to Sara Hennell or Cara Bray signal an effort to return to their earlier amity. These efforts partly account for the 7 October letter, but Eliot may have had posterity in mind as well. In a letter to Cara Bray tentatively dated 3 October 1859, Eliot considered possible falsehoods stemming from a future ' "investigator" of the Bracebridge order [who] will arise after I am dead, and revive the story—and perhaps posterity will believe in Liggins'.[5] In her letter to Sara Hennell, Eliot wishes to establish an accurate record: 'Perhaps I am doing a superfluous thing in writing all this to you—but I am prompted to do it by the feeling that in future years "Adam Bede" and all that concerns

---

[9] *JGE* 296.   [1] *JGE* 296.   [2] *Letters*, III. 174 n. 2.
[3] *Letters*, I. 188, 188 n. 2.   [4] See Ashton, 114–18, 180–1; and Hughes, 212–15.
[5] *Letters*, III. 170–1.

it, may have become a dim portion of the past, and I may not be able to recall so much of the truth as I have now told you.'[6] Such concerns probably prompted Hennell to offer her letter for publication after the author's death.

The truth as Eliot recalls it in autumn 1859 is detailed in seven lengthy paragraphs that not only refute Bracebridge but illuminate the spirit in which Eliot first met her aunt and heard her story of the young girl hanged for child murder. In her childhood, Eliot had met other 'northerly relatives' on her father's side, that is, those from Staffordshire and Derbyshire, 'but *not* my uncle and aunt Samuel, so far as I can recall the dim outline of things'. However, when she was 17, her father visited his brother and sister-in-law, and finding the latter in ill health, invited her for a visit, 'telling her that *I* should be very, very happy to have her with me for a few weeks. I was then strongly under the influence of Evangelical belief, and earnestly endeavouring to shape this anomalous English-Christian life of ours into some consistency with the spirit and simple verbal tenor of the New Testament.' Eliot acknowledges that she '*was* delighted to see my aunt', and, even though she 'had only heard her spoken of as a strange person, given to a fanatical vehemence of exhortation in private as well as public, I believed that we should find sympathy between us'.[7] In the 'History of "Adam Bede" ', Eliot describes that sympathy as something unique in her family experience: 'I was very fond of her, and enjoyed the few weeks of her stay with me greatly. She was loving and kind to me, and I could talk to her about my inward life, which was closely shut up from those usually round me.'[8] In both the 'History' and the letter to Sara Hennell, Eliot describes her aunt's appearance and temperament in similar ways. Given Eliot's practice of referring back to her journals, it is likely that the account to Sara draws from this journal entry, which describes her aunt as

a very small, black-eyed woman, and (as I was told, for I never heard her preach) very vehement in her style of preaching. She had left off preaching when I knew her, being, probably, sixty years old, and in delicate health; and she had become, as my father told me, much more gentle and subdued than she had been in the days of her

---

[6] *Letters*, III. 177.   [7] *Letters*, III. 174–5.

[8] *JGE* 297. Michael Wolff speculates that Eliot used Aunt Samuel as a sympathetic mother figure in *Adam Bede* because she had played that role in Eliot's own life. He notes that Aunt Samuel offered a 'motherly ear to the adolescent Mary Ann at a time when she was by her own account cut off from any sharing of her inner life with her own mother and indeed with anyone in her immediate family', and adds that the need for someone to fill 'this gap—the lack of an effective mother—was a chronic one for Mary Ann, one which began long before her mother's death', that is, before the 17-year-old Mary Ann met Aunt Samuel the year after Christiana Pearson Evans's death, when Mary Ann was 16 ('Adam Bede's Families: At Home in Hayslope and Nuneaton', *George Eliot–George Henry Lewes Studies*, 32–3 (Sept. 1997), 61–2).

active ministry and bodily strength, when she could not rest without exhorting and remonstrating in season and out of season.[9]

In her letter to Sara Hennell, her aunt, when Eliot knew her, was a

tiny little woman, with bright, small dark eyes, and hair that had been black, I imagine, but was now grey—a pretty woman in her youth, but of a totally different physical type from Dinah. The difference . . . was not *simply* physical: no difference is. She was a woman of strong natural excitability, which I know, from the description I have heard my father and half-sister give, prevented her from the exercise of discretion under the promptings of her zeal.

In her late years, however, 'she was very gentle and quiet in her manners—very loving—and (what she must have been from the very first) a truly religious soul, in whom the love of God and love of man were fused together'.[1] In temperament and character, the elderly Elizabeth Evans seems very like the young Dinah Morris.

Unlike Dinah, who in the Epilogue of *Adam Bede* quietly gave up preaching when the Society forbade women to preach,[2] Elizabeth Tomlinson Evans left the Society and joined the New Wesleyans, as Seth, at the end of *Adam Bede*, feels he and Dinah should have done. Like Seth too, Eliot's aunt was an Arminian, and her then 'strong Calvinist' niece engaged with her in 'little debates about predestination', debates in which her aunt's 'superiority came out'. Eliot recalls 'her telling me one sunny afternoon how she had, with another pious woman, visited an unhappy girl in prison, stayed with her all night, and gone with her to execution'. But of the prison scene itself, Eliot remembers

no word she uttered—I only remember her tone and manner, and the deep feeling I had under the recital. Of the girl she knew nothing, I believe—or told me nothing—but that she was a common coarse girl, convicted of child-murder. The incident lay in my mind for years on years, as a dead germ, apparently—till time had made my mind a nidus in which it could fructify; it then turned out to be the germ of 'Adam Bede'.[3]

Another story, among the 'one or two accounts of supposed miracles in which [her aunt] believed', was '*the face with the crown of thorns seen in the glass*', which figures in Dinah's sermon in Chapter II.[4] Eliot met her aunt on

---

[9] *JGE* 297.   [1] *Letters*, III. 175.

[2] Joseph Wiesenfarth points out that George Eliot in her notebook does not 'give exactly correct information': 'It was the "opinion" of the conference (Manchester, 25 July 1803) that women "in general" ought not to preach. "But if any woman among us think she has an extraordinary call from God to speak in public . . . we are of the opinion she should, in general, address her <u>own sex</u>, and <u>those only</u>" ' (*A Writer's Notebook*, 161 n. 9). In the Epilogue Eliot's inexact information is conveyed in Adam's voice in the discussion of Dinah's having given up preaching.

[3] *Letters*, III. 176.   [4] *Letters*, III. 175–6.

only two other occasions, by which time Eliot's own religious faith had undergone change, which perhaps made their meetings 'less interesting', she writes. 'This is all I remember distinctly, as matter I could write down, of my dear aunt, whom I really loved. You see how she suggested Dinah; but it is not possible you should see as I do how entirely her individuality differed from Dinah's. How curious it seems to me that people should think Dinah's sermon, prayers, and speeches were *copied*—when they were written with hot tears, as they surged up in my own mind!'[5]

Writing to John Blackwood a few days later, she refers to the 'supposition' that the author could not have invented Dinah's sermon, prayers, and speeches as 'a proof of the low conceptions of art that are prevalent, and the narrow, ignorant views of religious history and religious life. *Truth* in art is so startling, that no one can believe in it as art; and the specific forms of religious life which have made some of the grandest elements in human history are looked down upon as if they were not within the artist's sympathy and veneration and intensely dramatic reproduction.'[6] Many years later, Lewes emphatically denied, on Eliot's behalf, an identification of literal truth and artistic truth in the characterization of Dinah. Guy Roslyn (a pseudonym for George Barnett Smith) had written to Eliot explaining that his 'papers on Elizabeth Evans (the Dinah of Adam Bede) will appear in all probability in the *Gentleman's Magazine*', the editor of which 'wishes me to ask you if you have any objection to the course I am taking. He would be sorry for me to reveal anything in his pages that might offend you.'[7] Lewes replied that Eliot objected on 'grounds not personal but artistic [and] she begs you to understand that *Dinah Morris was never intended to be a representation of Mrs. Elizabeth Evans*; and that any identification of the two (or of any other characters in Adam Bede with real persons) would be protested against as not only false in fact and tending to perpetuate false notions about art, but also as a gross breach of social decorum'.[8] Lewes had made the same point in a letter to Bracebridge on 19 September 1859.[9] But as Graham Handley points out, 'Local tradition felt differently.' On a 'memorial tablet to Elizabeth Evans in Ebenezer Wesleyan Chapel, Wirksworth (the Snowfield of the novel)', is an inscription that describes Evans as 'KNOWN TO THE WORLD AS "DINAH BEDE"'.[1]

Eliot's truth in art was firmly grounded in historical knowledge, both personal and general. She not only drew upon her aunt's experience for

---

[5] *Letters*, III. 176.   [6] 16 Oct.; *Letters*, III. 185.   [7] *Letters*, V. 338–9.
[8] *Letters*, V. 339. The articles were not published in *Gentleman's Magazine*. Instead, they 'appeared eventually in *London Society*, 27 (1875), 311–319, 439–451; and 28 (1875), 20–27', and 'were reprinted as *George Eliot in Derbyshire: A Volume of Gossip about Passages and People in the Novels of George Eliot*, by Guy Roslyn, with intro. by George Barnett Smith, 1876' (*Letters*, V. 338 n. 6).
[9] *Letters*, III. 158–60.   [1] Handley, 48.

Dinah's character, but she also read Robert Southey's *The Life of Wesley; and Rise and Progress of Methodism.* 'Southey supplied data, reinforced what she knew already and what she had learned from her Methodist aunt. Reading the *Life of Wesley* may even have given George Eliot the name Hetty: Southey discusses at some length the unhappy love life of Wesley's sister Hetty (Mehetabel).'[2] Cunningham points to numerous details in Dinah's dress and demeanour that Eliot drew from Southey. He notes, for instance, that 'Dinah's abstemiousness... is in line with Wesley's instructions to his preachers ("Do you eat no flesh suppers? no late suppers?..."; "Breakfast on nettle or orange-peel tea").' Although the 'work-discipline' of Methodism 'paid... any material advantage was incidental; holiness was an end in itself. The unworldly ideal (Dinah's gravity and self-sacrifice, Seth's repugnance for Wiry Ben's "wicked songs," his refusal to join the dancing at Arthur's coming-of-age celebration) was less the manifestation of gloom than the results of optimistically striving for perfection.'[3]

Dinah's visit to Hetty in prison in Chapter XLV represents 'a central and characteristic function [of early Methodists]. Their literature and hymns reflected this orientation and their awareness that conversions effected in prison were an appropriate acting out of New Testament metaphor: salvation was a release from the bondage and captivity of sin.'[4] Although the general outlines of Dinah's ministration to Hetty match Methodist experience, Cunningham notes significant differences. Instead of an overnight conversion, the 'Nottingham Methodists, including Elizabeth Tomlinson, persuaded Mary Voce [the original for Hetty] to confess her guilt only after weeks of effort'.[5] And in contrast to Hetty's journey to the gallows, where she and Dinah are alone in the cart, praying with their eyes closed, 'Mary Voce had gone to the gallows accompanied by "above one hundred voices singing penitentiary hymns on the way to and at the gallows, and three or four persons attending voluntarily in the cart, administering comfort and consolation"'.[6]

In her notebook, Eliot recorded other details from Wesley's experiences that she included in the novel: Dinah preaches 'while standing on a wall', she believes in opening the Bible at hazard, she elicits strong emotional responses in her audience.[7] Sometimes small details inspired the author to create a whole fictional scene. Eliot noted a letter to Wesley from 'one of his female disciples', who writes that she 'can heartily bless [God] that he has made me just what I am, a creature capable of the enjoyment of himself. If I go to the window & look out, I see the moon & stars: I meditate awhile on the silence of the night.'[8] In Chapter XV, Dinah, who 'delighted in her

---

[2] Cunningham, 149.   [3] Cunningham, 150.   [4] Cunningham, 167.
[5] Cunningham, 168.   [6] Cunningham, 167.
[7] *A Writer's Notebook*, pp. xxii and 24–8.   [8] *A Writer's Notebook*, 23.

bedroom window', looks out on the 'peaceful fields beyond which the large moon was rising' and thinks of her work in Snowfield, to which she is about to return. Eliot's notebook also records Wesley's preaching while 'A row of children sat under the opposite wall, all quiet & still.'[9] Dinah has a similar power. In Chapter LI, Seth describes to Adam a scene on the Common, in which Dinah was 'speaking with power this forenoon from the words, "I came not to call the righteous, but sinners to repentance" ', when

a little thing happened as was pretty to see. The women mostly bring their children with 'em, but to-day there was one stout curly-headed fellow about three or four year old, that I never saw there before. He was as naughty as could be at the beginning while I was praying, and while we was singing, but when we all sat down and Dinah began to speak, th' young un stood stock still all at once, and began to look at her with's mouth open, and presently he run away from's mother and went up to Dinah, and pulled at her, like a little dog, for her to take notice of him. So Dinah lifted him up and held th' lad on her lap, while she went on speaking; and he was as good as could be till he went t' sleep—and the mother cried to see him.

Seth's story helps to counter Adam's belief that Dinah's 'heart's so taken up with other things [that] She's one o' those women that feel no drawing towards having a husband and children o' their own' (Chapter L).

'My Aunt's Story' provided two of the five essential dramatis personae of *Adam Bede*—the child-murderer and the female Methodist preacher. The eponymous hero also came from Eliot's family life, sharing, as the author notes in the 'History of "Adam Bede" ', 'some points in my father's early life and character'.[1] Robert Evans began his working life as an apprentice in carpentry to his father, later becoming 'agent to Francis Parker, a landowner who inherited the large estate centred on Arbury Hall' in Warwickshire, and who 'took the name Newdigate' after the death of his cousin, Sir Roger Newdigate, in 1806. Robert Evans 'surveyed land and buildings, found respectable tenants for the various farms on Newdigate's land, collected rents, discussed and oversaw repairs, negotiated for the sale and purchase of land, and was actively involved in the arrangements for road-building, timber-cutting, and the coal-mining which went on beneath the estate'.[2] By the end of volume II, the ambitious Adam Bede, at the age of 26, plans and oversees building repairs and manages the woods on the Donnithorne estate.

In a letter to Charles Bray on 19 September 1859, Eliot acknowledged that she 'could never have written Adam Bede if I had not learned something of my father's early experience', but again she asserts the role that imagination played in developing the fictional character: 'no one who knew my father could call Adam a portrait of him—and the course of Adam's life

[9] *A Writer's Notebook*, 26.   [1] *JGE* 296.   [2] Ashton, 11.

is entirely different from my father's.'[3] In terms of inward qualities, Graham Handley connects Adam's 'growing self-awareness' with the character of Robert Evans. Adam comes to recognize

his intolerance of those morally weaker than himself, and ultimately this means he comes to genuine humility and acquires the capacity for forgiveness. One can't help feeling that the traits seen here in part at least derived from Robert Evans, and that his daughter experienced the severity of his moods during the three and a half years when she nursed him, and equally definite, much earlier, when she refused to go to church.[4]

Handley also points out that Adam shares her father's 'practicality of planning' and his work-ethic.[5]

A second influence on the development of Adam's character comes from nineteenth-century history, in particular Eliot's reading of Samuel Smiles's *The Life of George Stephenson: Railway Engineer*. In her journal of the visit she and Lewes made to Jersey in June and July 1857, just when friction with Blackwood over 'Janet's Repentance' was most intense, Eliot records 'long rambles and long readings. But our choice of literature has been rather circumscribed in this out of the way place. The Life of George Stephenson has been a real profit and pleasure.'[6] Wiesenfarth identifies commonalities between Adam and Stephenson in their physical strength (Robert Evans shared this as well), Stephenson's undertaking extra work to make it possible for him to marry a servant in a nearby farmhouse just as Adam takes on extra work in hopes of marrying Hetty, and both men's attending night school to gain knowledge for their future work.[7] Stephenson's second schoolmaster, Andrew Robertson, was 'a skilled arithmetician' under whose tutelage Stephenson made rapid progress, using a method similar to that which Bartle Massey in Chapter XXI recommends to two recalcitrant pupils: 'if you're to know figures, you must turn 'em over in your own heads, and keep your thoughts fixed on 'em.' Stephenson learned more rapidly than another of Robertson's pupils because of 'his perseverance. He worked out his sums in his bye-hours, improving every minute of his spare time by the engine-fire, solving the arithmetical problems set for him upon his slate by the master. In the evenings he took to Andrew Robertson the sums which he had thus "worked," and new sums were "set" for him to study out the following day.' As a result, 'Robertson became somewhat proud of his scholar' and even moved his night school when Stephenson and other workers were forced by a pit closure to find work in another location;[8] Bartle Massey, in his own curmudgeonly fashion, calls Adam 'the only scholar I've had in this stupid country that ever had the will or the head-piece for mathematics' (Chapter

---

[3] *Letters*, III. 155.   [4] Handley, 42–3.   [5] Handley, 43.   [6] *JGE* 281.
[7] *A Writer's Notebook*, 163 n. 1.   [8] Smiles, 19.

XL). Stephenson is a capable, though generally reluctant fighter;[9] Adam will fight only when there is no other way to deal with a 'scoundrel' (Chapter XVI). And Stephenson maintained infirm parents after his father was blinded by a blast of steam;[1] Adam began to support his family when his father became an alcoholic years before the novel opens. Stephenson used his entire savings to pay for a substitute when he was 'drawn for the militia' during the Napoleonic Wars;[2] Adam pays his savings for his brother Seth's substitute. Even a small detail in the first chapter, Adam's praise for the working man who makes an oven for his wife, may have been inspired by Smiles's account of Stephenson's building an oven for his cottage.[3] Adam's dog Gyp seems modelled on Stephenson's dog, which was 'so sagacious that he performed the office of a servant, in almost daily carrying his [Stephenson's] dinner to him at the pit' in a tin,[4] just as Gyp carries Adam's dinner in a basket in Chapter I. However, the name Gyp came from Eliot's travels the previous spring to Ilfracombe and Tenby. Lodging in the house she and Lewes stayed in at Ilfracombe were a family named Webster: 'Little Gyp, Mrs. Webster's dog, ... we had made our pet.'[5]

Eliot also drew on family memories for Mrs Poyser. Biographer Kathryn Hughes suggests that she is modelled on Christiana Pearson Evans, George Eliot's mother, who died when her daughter was 16: 'The dairy, which is Mrs Poyser's pride and joy, was likewise the centre of Mrs Evans's prestige and influence at Griff House. The stream of pithy sayings which pour from Mrs Poyser's mouth are not, as [Eliot] was quickly indignant to point out to Blackwood, local and general turns of phrase. . . . But while the specifics may have been her own, it is hard to imagine where else she could have got that voice except from the sharp-tongued Christiana Evans and her trio of formidable Pearson sisters.'[6] However, a literary source, Sir Walter Scott's *Heart of Midlothian*, suggested one detail, the illness that keeps Mrs Poyser confined to her room throughout January in Chapter XXXV. Like Mrs Saddletree in Scott's novel, Mrs Poyser is the one person in the household who might have noticed Hetty's pregnancy, had not illness—so conveniently for the plot—prevented her from exercising her usual sharp-eyed scrutiny of the household.

A second story intended for *Scenes of Clerical Life* provided two more of the essential dramatis personae in *Adam Bede*. In 'How I came to write Fiction' Eliot explains that 'I had meant to carry on the series beyond Janet's Repentance, and especially I longed to tell the story of the Clerical Tutor.'[7] She does not describe its plot, but the title suggests that it is an embryonic version of the story of Arthur Donnithorne and Mr Irwine. *Adam Bede* contains several reminders of their former relationship as pupil

[9] Smiles, 26.   [1] Smiles, 35.   [2] Smiles, 36.   [3] Smiles, 48.
[4] Smiles, 20.   [5] *JGE* 271.   [6] Hughes, 280.   [7] *JGE* 291.

and tutor. In Chapter XVI, Arthur, intending to confess his passion for Hetty Sorrel in hopes of creating a bulwark against temptation, arrives on the pretext of breakfasting with the Rector: ' "It was a tempting morning for a ride before breakfast," said Arthur; "and I used to like breakfasting with you so when I was reading with you." ' The word *pupil* occurs later in the same chapter when Mr Irwine discusses his mother's view that 'your lady-love will rule you as the moon rules the tides. But I feel bound to stand up for you, as my pupil, you know. . . . So mind you don't disgrace my judgment.' Allusion to their pupil–tutor days recurs in Chapter XXII, when Mr Irwine, covering Arthur's momentary embarrassment at being caught out in his vanity, says, 'I don't like to admit that I'm proud of my pupil when he does graceful things,' and again in Chapter XXIV at the health-drinking, where Mr Irwine recalls that he had had 'the pleasure of being his tutor for several years'. A final reminder of their early relationship appears in the Epilogue: Mr Irwine will keep Arthur 'under [his] old tutor's thumb' until he regains his health. Combining the 'Clerical Tutor' and 'My Aunt's Story' resolved Eliot's problem of how 'to make the unhappy girl [accused of infanticide] one of the chief *dramatis personae* and connect her with the hero'.[8] Just as she later blended two separate works to create *Middlemarch*, so Eliot blended the two stories in *Adam Bede*.

For details about the period and about Hetty, Arthur, and Mr Irwine, Eliot turned to printed sources. As already noted, Southey's *Life of Wesley* provided details from Methodist history. But details from Mary Voce's life, apart from her conversion, did not easily lend themselves to creation of a sympathetic character. A married woman who was unfaithful to her husband, Voce had poisoned her child, and in any case Eliot had learned from her aunt only that she was 'a common coarse girl'. Robert Colby suggests that the character of Hetty was influenced by a literary source, Dinah Mulock's *A Woman's Thoughts about Women*, published in 1858, in which the author urges sympathy rather than condemnation for '*the illiterate village lass, who thinks it so grand to be made a lady of* ',[9] which, of course, is precisely Hetty's foolish dream. Colby notes that Mulock and George Eliot have similar attitudes 'towards the "straying" woman . . . a sternness which refuses to gloss over the sin, tempered by pity for human frailty and a charitable disposition to forgive'.[1] Although readers have sometimes regarded Eliot's treatment of Hetty as harsh, her wanderings in Chapters XXXVI and XXXVII stimulate the sympathy of those she encounters as well as that of the narrator—and Eliot's readers.

---

[8] *JGE* 296–7.

[9] Robert Colby, 'Miss Evans, Miss Mulock, and Hetty Sorrel', *English Language Notes*, 2.3 (Mar. 1965), 208.

[1] Ibid. 210–11.

In the *Gentleman's Magazine* Eliot found useful details for the celebration of Arthur Donnithorne's twenty-first birthday. Although the Duke of Rutland's coming-of-age celebration in January 1799 was on a grander scale and at a cold and dark time of year, Eliot drew on her notes from the account of it for details in various parts of the novel. Wiesenfarth makes several connections between material in Eliot's notes and details from the novel, including the echoing of place names in Mr Irwine's being rector of Broxton, and an unnamed 'Rector of South Croxton' who gives an entertainment on the occasion of the Duke's birthday.[2] The transparencies of Pitt directing Britannia's spear and the medallion referring to the 'generous youth' at the Duke of Rutland's festivities are only slightly transformed in Irwine's description of the birthday fête of Arthur's colonel at the end of Chapter XVI.[3]

Several other details from the *Gentleman's Magazine* found their way into *Adam Bede* even though they are not recorded in *A Writer's Notebook*. The Duke of Rutland's festivities included three feasts in which bullocks, oxen, and/or sheep were roasted whole. When Arthur mentions that his grandfather has limited his expenditure despite promising him carte blanche, Mr Irwine assures him that 'it sounds very grand to say that so many sheep and oxen were roasted whole . . . but in the end it generally happens that no one has had an enjoyable meal' (Chapter XXII). For the Duke's fête, 'A detachment of the Leicestershire militia also kept watch at each tent, where the workmen were regaled; and at the approach of night, though the multitude were warmed with the good liquor, there was scarcely the least approach towards riot.'[4] In keeping with his more modest celebration, Arthur has gotten 'Casson and Adam Bede, and some other good fellows, to look to the giving out of ale in the booths, and to take care things don't go too far' (Chapter XXII). In one detail, though, Arthur could match the Duke: both wear their regimentals for the evening dance, although the Duke's guests are not farm tenants, but titled men and women, including the Prince of Wales.[5] The February 1799 number of *Gentleman's Magazine* contains a summary of news from Ireland, including an address to the Duke of Rutland from the officers of his regiment in Ireland, with the dateline '*Dublin, Dec.* 18 [1798]' and another report datelined 'Dublin, Jan. 20 [1799]': 'This day the House of Commons voted thanks to the British militia and fencible regiments which tendered their services in Ireland during the late rebellion.'[6] Eliot sends Arthur's regiment to Ireland in early February 1800, thereby accounting for his absence from Windsor, where Hetty expected to find him, and giving him a slower and more uncertain return journey, which

---

[2] *A Writer's Notebook*, 29, 162 n. 4.
[3] *A Writer's Notebook*, 29; *Gentleman's Magazine*, 85 (Jan. 1799), 74.
[4] *Gentleman's Magazine*, 85 (Jan. 1799), 74.   [5] Ibid. 73.
[6] Ibid. 85 (Feb. 1799), 155.

heightens the drama of the chapters centring on the trial. But an unintended effect is that the Loamshire militia is anachronistically late in helping to quell the Irish Rebellion of 1798. Finally, the April number may have provided the family name for Arthur and his grandfather: in the column noting the Duke of Rutland's marriage is also recorded the marriage of one Isaac Donnithorne.[7]

COMPOSITION

The rapidity with which Eliot went from completing her final story in *Scenes of Clerical Life* to composing *Adam Bede* is indicative of their close linkage in her mind and the long-existing presence of the new story in her imagination. On 9 October 1857, her diary records, 'Finished "Janet's Repentance" '.[8] Less than two weeks later, she began *Adam Bede*. Progress during the autumn and winter was slow. On 5 November, sending the first sixteen pages of proofs for the two-volume *Scenes* along with a reference to his earlier plan to print only 'a short number', Blackwood asked: 'What of the new Tale? I shall miss you much each month.'[9] Eliot's response reflects her disappointment that more copies were not being printed. Although he had told her in his 5 November letter not to let the fact of the short number 'discourage you', it inevitably had done so:

> My new story is in progress—slow progress at present. A little sunshine of success would stimulate its growth, I daresay. Unhappily, I am as impressionable as I am obstinate, and as much in need of sympathy from my readers as I am incapable of bending myself to their tastes. But if I can only find a public as cordial and agreeable in its treatment of me as my editor, I shall have nothing to wish. Even *my* thin skin will be comfortable then.[1]

Her skin became more 'comfortable' as good news on *Scenes* began to appear. Lewes reported to Blackwood on 5 December 1857 that the new novel benefited as a result: 'G.E. has come to stay at Richmond and is writing his new story with a fresh influx of confidence (much needed) from having heard of a rector of a large parish having "cried like a child" over Janet's Repentance. If a few more rectors would be equally tearful I think E. would at last really begin to believe in his power.'[2]

On 17 December, Eliot's diary records: 'Read my new story to G. this evening as far as the end of the third chapter. He praised it highly.'[3] In manuscript, the chapter number 4 is written over an original number 3; the 'third chapter' mentioned in Eliot's diary corresponds to Chapter IV of the published text.[4] What Lewes heard, then, on 17 December were the

---

[7] Ibid. 85 (Apr. 1799), 346.   [8] *JGE* 70.   [9] *Letters*, II. 399.
[1] *Letters*, II. 399–400.   [2] *Letters*, II. 406.   [3] *JGE* 71.
[4] The chapter published as III was written after 'Home and its Sorrows', published as Chapter IV. See p. 38.

contents of a projected first instalment of *Adam Bede*, from the opening in
the workshop through the long night in which Adam makes the coffin that
his father has neglected and takes it with Seth's help to Broxton, and the
brothers return to find their father's body in the Willow Brook. At the end
of this section of the manuscript is the notation 'End of part I', pencilled in
Eliot's hand. Two days later, perhaps with Lewes's praise still in her mind,
she contemplates the past year and her entrance into fiction-writing:

Alone this evening, with very thankful solemn thoughts—feeling the great and
uphoped for blessings that have been given me in life. This last year especially has
been marked by inward progress and outward advantages.... I have written the
Scenes of Clerical Life—my first book—and though we are uncertain still whether
it will be a success as a separate publication, I have had much sympathy from my
readers in Blackwood, and feel a deep satisfaction in having done a bit of faithful
work that will perhaps remain like a primrose root in the hedgerow and gladden and
chasten human hearts in years to come.[5]

The sentiments reflect the imagery of the novel she was immersed in. Adam
too is described in terms of the faithful workman whose work, he hopes,
will outlive him and be a good to human beings. The primrose in the
hedgerow suggests the rural scenes that she loved from her childhood and
celebrates in *Adam Bede*.

   The 'encouragement' of a positive review of *Scenes of Clerical Life* in *The
Times*, Lewes reported to Blackwood on 3 January 1858, 'will materially
help [Eliot] in his new story'.[6] Her diary that month records progress
despite illness. On 6 January 1858 she 'Finished chapter 4 of my novel',[7]
that is, Chapter V, 'The Rector', as published. The next day Blackwood
wrote to offer further encouragement. Sending optimistic predictions
about the success of the republication of *Scenes*, he adds, 'How does the
new Tale progress? I think you should be in good feather about it now.'[8]
Eliot replied that the 'subscription [for *Scenes*] far exceeds my highest
hopes'. As for *Adam Bede*,

   My new story goes on with a pleasant andante movement. I have read the early
chapters to Lewes, who is a safer test than Molière could find in his housekeeper, I
imagine, and he pronounces them to be better than anything I had done before.
That is the best thing I have to tell you about it, and the next best is, that my heart is
in the story. But I fear this last has been the case with very poor writers and very poor
stories.[9]

Her optimism continued. On 'Sunday' [17 January], she writes: 'Cold
and sore throat, but enjoying the writing of my 5th chapter'; this is
published Chapter VI. She also refers to works she and Lewes were reading, including 'the Eumenides, having finished the Choephoræ. We are

[5] 19 Dec. 1857; *JGE* 71.   [6] *Letters*, II. 416.   [7] *JGE* 73.
[8] 7 Jan. 1858; *Letters*, II. 418.   [9] 9 Jan. 1858; *Letters*, II. 419.

reading Wordsworth in the evenings—at least G. is reading him to me.' On 2 and 3 February, she records the Wordsworth reading more specifically: 'G. has finished The Excursion, which repaid us for going to the end by an occasional fine passage even to the last. He has now begun the other poems of Wordsworth. This morning I finished the Eumenides.'[1]

The influence of both Wordsworth and Aeschylus is evident throughout *Adam Bede*. Eliot drew the epigraph from the *Excursion* (book VI, 'The Churchyard among the Mountains', lines 651–8),[2] and *Lyrical Ballads* is among the books Arthur Donnithorne receives from his London bookseller (Chapter V). Going beyond the obvious connection with Wordsworth, manifest in Eliot's choice of rural, working-class characters who speak in a local dialect, Stephen Gill has demonstrated how thoroughly she had read and studied the poet and how closely her knowledge is interwoven in the themes and motifs of *Adam Bede*. Arthur's dismissal of most of *Lyrical Ballads* as 'twaddling stuff', Gill notes, 'marks the axes on which the novel moves. Like *Lyrical Ballads*, *Adam Bede* emphasizes feeling as the fundamental connective between human beings, between themselves and their environment, and between their sense of present and past. Key sequences of the novel recapitulate *Lyrical Ballads* and *The Excursion* on this theme.' In Arthur's case, his failure to appreciate *Lyrical Ballads* signals 'a potential fault-line in his relation to other human beings, especially to women and those beneath him in rank'.[3] *The Oresteia* appears in Mr Irwine's explicit references to Aeschylus in Chapters XVI and XXII and in the communal impact of the tragedy and the treatment of private vengeance vs. civilly established law and judge and jury, with Mr Irwine's higher power in place of Aeschylus' Athena as the final arbiter. These stories from Greek myth are part of the novel's presentation of 'the ethos of Victorian society: the idea that life is a struggle in which a man succeeds by practicing virtue and working hard'. From Greek myth too comes the concept of Nemesis, voiced in Mr Irwine's 'Consequences are unpitying' in Chapter XVI.[4] Eliot's imaginative transformation of Wordsworth and Greek myth as well as of biographical details from her own experience was an essential part of the creative process, as she insisted when objecting to the view that her father, her aunt, and others were simply 'portraits'.

---

[1] *JGE* 73.

[2] Eliot misquotes Wordsworth in the first line of her epigraph, which she gives as *So that ye may have* instead of *so that ye shall have*. (See *The Poetical Works of William Wordsworth*, ed. E. de Selincourt and Helen Darbishire (Oxford, 1949), V. 206, line 651.) William Baker, in *The Libraries of George Eliot and George Henry Lewes* (English Literary Studies (University of Victoria, 1981), 120, catalogue items 999–1001), cites Eliot's preference for Edward Moxon's 1845 edition of the poems, but notes that she and Lewes also owned seven other volumes: *Poetical Works* in 6 vols. (1841) and *Earlier Poems* (1857), as well as a separate edition of 'The Prelude'.

[3] *Wordsworth and the Victorians* (Oxford, 1998), 156.   [4] Wiesenfarth, 84–5.

On 20 January, Eliot recorded in her diary a letter from Charles Dickens (dated 18 January) and also reading 'aloud the additional dialogue in the chapter of "The Hall Farm". G. admired it very much.'[5] Dickens's praise for the 'extraordinary merit' of *Scenes*,[6] we learn from her letter to Blackwood on 21 January, moved her 'deeply': 'There can hardly be any climax of approbation for me after this.'[7] Writing progressed rapidly in the next week and a half. Her diary for 31 January notes that she 'Finished Chapters 7 and 8—the dialogue between Dinah and Mr. Irwine, and the rest up to the arrival of the Rector and Captain at Adam's cottage.'[8] These are Chapters VIII and IX as published.[9]

Even Dickens's enthusiastic letter and another from Jane Carlyle on 21 January[1] could not, in the face of illness, sustain her cautious optimism. Her diary on 31 January adds, 'Headachy since yesterday,' and on 2 and 3 February she laments, 'Unable to work still, so that I have lost 3 days.'[2] Not surprisingly, on 5 February, Lewes reports to Blackwood that 'G.E. is again "down in the mouth." ' He attributes this not to illness, but to the author's distress that 'his book does not sell and all his old misgivings come over him in spite of Dickens's letter which raised his spirits for a time. I preach a sanguine philosophy, but half the prosperity of a sermon lies in the audience, and here my audience is painfully deaf. If you hear of any *good* critical notices mention them when you write. They will make his new story (which I think surpassingly fine) evolve itself more pleasantly.'[3]

Blackwood again responds with encouragement: although they have not, as he expected, 'got through the edition [of *Scenes*] at once ... there is no call to feel disappointed. On the contrary the sale is a good sale.' He asks about the 'new Tale': 'Is it at all in such a state that you could send me a portion to read? I feel a very warm interest in it on your account as also partly on my own.'[4] This letter was written on 10 February, the same day that her diary marks the completion of Chapter IX (i.e. published Chapter X).[5]

Despite illness, Eliot took time in early February to write to Bessie Rayner Parkes, explaining her inability to contribute to the *Englishwoman's Journal*:

My negative about the writing has no special relation to the 'Englishwoman's Journal,' but includes that and all other Reviews.... I have not written for the Westminster since the last Christmas but one—that is, just a year ago—and ... I have been obliged to say 'No' to all [John Chapman's] requests for contributions. I

---

[5] *JGE* 73. [6] *Letters*, II. 423. [7] *Letters*, II. 424. [8] *JGE* 73.
[9] The 'rest' includes Dinah's telling Mrs Poyser of Thias Bede's drowning and her plan to go to the cottage to offer comfort, along with Hetty's response and the narrator's commentary in 'Hetty's World', published as Chapter IX.
[1] *Letters*, II. 425–6. [2] *JGE* 73. [3] *Letters*, II. 432. [4] *Letters*, II. 433.
[5] *JGE* 73.

have given up writing 'articles,' having discovered that my vocation lies in other paths. In fact *entre nous*, I expect to be writing *books* for some time to come. Don't speak of that at all: but I tell it you that you may not in the least misapprehend my negatives. If it were a mere question of a little more or less of effort, I should have contrived to write an article for Mr. Chapman for old friendship's sake. But it is not that. It is a question whether I shall give up building my own house to go and help in the building of my neighbour's garden wall.[6]

Behind this is her apprehension that her friends will wonder what she is doing and inadvertently add to public speculation about the identity of the author of *Scenes of Clerical Life*.

'Building [her] own house' was going so well that on 12 February 1858 Eliot wrote to Blackwood that she 'hope[d] to send [him] the first volume of my new novel shortly'.[7] However, completion of Chapter IX (i.e. X as published) was the extent of her progress for nearly a week: 'Wretched with headache for several days since the 10th and my work has been almost at a stand still.'[8] Lewes wrote to Blackwood on 25 February, 'G.E. has not yet *quite* finished the part he wants to show you, so that it must remain till you come to Richmond, if you *do* come, and go by post, if you don't.'[9] Blackwood did come, and on Sunday, 28 February, the identity of his new author was revealed. It was, as he wrote to his wife, 'the Mrs. Lewes whom we suspected'.[1] Eliot's progress had slowed so much, however, that it was not until 'the following Friday' (5 March) that he called again and she gave him 'the MS. of my new novel to the end of the second scene in the wood [Chapter XIII]. He opened it, read the first page, and smiling, said, "This will do."'[2]

---

[6] 3 Feb. 1858; *Letters*, II. 431.   [7] *Letters*, II. 434.   [8] 16 Feb.; *JGE* 73.
[9] *Letters*, II. 435.
[1] *Letters*, II. 436. The Blackwoods had already made the connection between 'Mrs Lewes' and 'George Eliot'. Eliot's journal for 10 Dec. 1857 records: 'Major Blackwood called—an unaffected agreeable man. It was evident to us when he had only been in the room a few minutes that he knew I was George Eliot' (*JGE* 71). Ashton suggests that John Blackwood may have 'guessed straight away' who George Eliot was, but 'was wise enough to keep the conjecture to himself' (172). The way Blackwood phrased his question on 28 February, 'Well, am I to see George Eliot this time?' (*JGE* 295), also suggests that all involved acknowledged the charade but were willing to maintain it until the author was comfortable revealing herself. On his next visit, Blackwood told Eliot that 'Mrs. Blackwood is *sure* [the stories in *Scenes of Clerical Life*] are not written by a woman' (*JGE* 295), even though his letter to his wife shows that she too was party to the brothers' accurate guess.
[2] *JGE* 295. Eliot's diary for 1854–61 gives 4 March as the date of this second visit, with similar wording: 'I gave him my M.S. to the end of the second scene in the wood.' However, one suspects her dating is off by a day. The next entry is dated 7 March: 'We went into town again and did errands. I wrote my will, and signed it in the presence of Mr. Chapman and Mr. Birt.' In 1858, 4 March was a Thursday, and 7 March, a Sunday, not a day for errands or legal business to have been transacted. If Eliot made her diary entry later, she may have calculated the date for 'Friday' and the following Monday by adding 29 February to a year in which February had only 28 days (*JGE* 74).

Eliot and Lewes, as well as John Blackwood, anticipated that the novel would appear first in *Blackwood's Edinburgh Magazine*, and for that purpose it may have been unfortunate that the publisher did not receive the entire volume at once. Before the arrival of the last part of volume I, Chapters XIV to XVI, emphasizing the moral rectitude of Adam, Dinah, and Mr Irwine (though Chapter XVI ends with Arthur's failure to confess), Blackwood had three weeks in which to ponder Chapters XII and XIII, whose imagery and action anticipate the seduction to come. With Chapters I to XIII in hand, Blackwood feared that *Adam Bede* might prove unsuitable for magazine serialization. Writing to Lewes on 11 March, he asks him to 'Tell George Eliot that I think Adam Bede all right, most lifelike and real.' With this rather equivocal beginning, he continues disingenuously to protest that he is so 'overpowered with business that cannot be postponed that I may not for a little get the *mental* leisure necessary to do justice to a second perusal. For the first reading it did not signify how many things I might have had to think of. I would have hurried through it with eager pleasure.' He merely writes 'to allay all anxiety in [*sic*] the part of G.E. as to my appreciation of the merits of this most promising opening of a picture of life'. But he asks, 'Is there much more written or is it merely blocked out?',[3] a question he repeats more insistently later in the month.

Lewes begins his response on 13 March with a playful private joke and reassures the publisher generally that all is well, but he declines to give details about what is planned but as yet unwritten:

> By a strange coincidence G.E. was with me when your letter arrived with its checque (for which thanks) and he was greatly relieved and inspirited by your approbation, for with his customary misgivings he had no belief in anybody's feeling the sort of delight in his personages he feels, or in any one (I, of course, counting as nobody!) liking the story. Your hearty letter made him quite comfortable and he will doubtless write with fresh confidence—till the next desponding fit comes....
>
> He bids me say that no more is yet *written*; although all is laid out; but before he goes away he will send m.s.s for another *part*.[4]

In fact, although writing was slow, by 8 March Eliot records: 'Wrote Chapter 14 up to the going to bed.'[5] Two weeks later Blackwood wrote to Lewes:

> George Eliot will think that I am forgetting him but I am not. I think a good deal about Adam Bede every day. There being no absolute necessity for hurry in the reperusal, I have thought it better both for him and me to delay until I was a little out of my present turmoil of occupation. Tomorrow night the Magazine will be off my hands for the month, and in a few days I shall be able to write at length about the excellent Adam.[6]

---

[3] *Letters*, VIII. 197.   [4] *Letters*, II. 439–40.   [5] *JGE* 74.
[6] 25 Mar.; *Letters*, VIII. 199.

Eliot apparently saw nothing amiss. On 27 March she promised to send
him 'a small packet of M.S. forming the fourth part of "Adam Bede," if he
is destined to appear in parts, which your last pleasant letter has made me
regard as probable'.[7]

With *Blackwood's* put to bed and Lewes and Eliot anticipating an
extended visit to Germany, the exchange of letters between Edinburgh
and London increases apace. Blackwood wrote to Eliot on 31 March, to
Lewes on 2 April, and again to Eliot on 3 April. Letters to Edinburgh
include one from Eliot on 1 April, and two from Lewes, on 1 and 3 April,
although the former does not mention Eliot or *Adam Bede*.

The first in this sequence, which determined the fate of *Adam Bede* as a
serial, is John Blackwood's long-deferred letter.[8] *Adam Bede* promises to be
'a very remarkable story', he writes, praising the scenes in the carpenter's
workshop and on the Green, Dinah's 'beautiful' sermon, and the scene at
Adam's cottage in Chapter IV. But he suggests softening some of the
reflections on relations at the beginning of Chapter IV, and he continues
to find Eliot's clergy less than ideal. Although the 'Vicar is a capital fellow
and the visit to the sick room is very touching', he wishes 'for the sake of my
Church of England friends he had more of "the root of the matter in him"',
but he hopes Irwine 'is to sublime [*sic*] as the story goes on'. He also
hints that 'the passage page 53 about the identity of Love, religious
feeling, and Love of Art would be better modified a little'.[9] There are no
variants in the first edition that indicate Eliot took his advice on any of these
points.

A desire that Irwine be heard to utter some morally uplifting advice
seems to underlie Blackwood's comment, 'Does it not seem inconsistent
with the minute reality of the story to say nothing of the Vicar's visit to the
cottage after the death.' Blackwood liked his Church of England clergymen
to be more ideal, and his Methodists soft-spoken and moderate in evangelical enthusiasm. He had also felt 'doubtful about [Dinah's] direct address
to poor Bess [Cranage] and her throwing down the ear rings' in Chapter II,
but he approves her visit to Lisbeth Bede in Chapters X and XI. 'Dinah's
soothing influence on her is exquisitely painted—the influence of real
religion and good feeling with no cant or methodism about it. Dinah's is
indeed an angel visit.' He calls Mrs Poyser 'first rate', but is more equivocal
about the 'Captain's inquiries as to Hetty walking in the Chase [which] are
direct enough. Dinah and the clergyman are good together and Hetty is
certainly very attractive.' The phrases 'direct enough' and 'certainly very
attractive' are faint praise at best. The only objection that Eliot acted

[7] *Letters*, II. 442.   [8] *Letters*, II. 444–6.
[9] MS 1. ⟨50⟩/53. Foliation is given for numbers in Eliot's hand. It does not include foliation
added later when the British Museum acquired the manuscript. Volume number precedes
folio numbers only when necessary for clarity.

upon—and then not until the first edition proofs—is his observation that 'there is rather too much of [Lisbeth Bede], or rather of her dialect'. Lewes was also concerned about the dialect, and a comparison of the manuscript and the first edition reveals extensive emendation as Eliot sought to preserve the dialect but make it intelligible to a wide readership. Blackwood's principal problem with the novel, however, is the love affair between Arthur and Hetty: 'The Captain's unfortunate attachment to Hetty will I suppose form a main element in the Tragic part of the story. I am not quite sure how far I like the scenes in the wood and I hope things will not come to the usual sad catastrophe!'[1] No naive reader, Blackwood is aware that Victorian reticence about sexuality does not signify its absence, and 'the scenes in the wood' are charged with imagery suggestive of the sexual relationship to come. As a result, he rephrases the query he had made obliquely in his 11 March letter, this time asking directly, 'When you send down the two other parts you mention will you give me a sketch of the rest of the story?' He concludes with what is probably unintentional ambiguity: 'I look *anxiously* for more of Adam Bede.'[2]

Eliot's response was what Blackwood feared, but may also have, at least subconsciously, wished for. She wrote immediately, with one brief paragraph thanking him for his 'appreciatory criticism of "Adam Bede"' and four longer ones addressing his concerns. A touch of humour in her analogies is accompanied by a vigorous defence of her views.

But I entertain what I think is well-founded objection against telling you in a bare brief manner the course of my story. The soul of art lies in its treatment and not in its subject. If a dramatist were to tell a manager that he had a fine tragedy in preparation, the subject of which was a man with a sore foot on a desert island, it is probable the manager would not feel any very brilliant hopes. Yet the Philoctetes is one of the finest dramas in the world.

It is true my theme is not so meagre as a sore foot, nor am I Sophocles; but the mere skeleton of my story would probably give rise in your mind to objections which would be suggested by the treatment *other* writers have given to the same tragic incidents in the human lot—objections which would lie far away from my treatment. The Heart of Midlothian would probably have been thought highly objectionable if a skeleton of the story had been given by a writer whose reputation did not place him above question. And the same story told by a Balzacian French writer would probably have made a book that no young person could read without injury. Yet what girl of twelve was ever injured by the Heart of Midlothian? Of artistic writing it may be said pre-eminently—'to the pure writer all things are pure.'[3]

With her experience from *Scenes* still fresh, Eliot read Blackwood's reservations as a reluctance to serialize. She points out that she is 'not arguing against your hesitation to publish "Adam Bede" in Maga, but simply

[1] *Letters*, II. 446.   [2] 31 Mar.; *Letters*, II. 446; emphasis added.
[3] *Letters*, VIII. 201.

stating my reasons for objecting to tell more of the story than I have already told you—namely, that it is partly tragic', adding that 'you can certainly not be more solicitious [*sic*] about the moral spirit of what you publish in the Magazine, than I am about the moral spirit of what I write'. Consequently, she suggests, 'it will perhaps be better definitively to give up the idea of monthly publication, and await the printing of the book in three volumes'. Despite the 'definitively', she leaves room for further negotiations when she promises to send 'the amount of another part' the next day, 'the perusal of [which] may in some degree modify your views'.[4]

Her readiness to abandon serialization must have alarmed Blackwood, who wasted no time in reading the new instalment and writing enthusiastically to its author on 3 April; his letter survives in a Blackwoods' Letter Book:

> I have just finished the perusal of the 4th part of Adam Bede which arrived a few hours ago.
>
> It is capital. Hetty Strutting about in her room is one of the most vivid pictures I ever read or rather looked at, for one Seems to be present and to hear the utterance of her Swelling thoughts. You have painted the charm of the Baggage with such a force of reality that one is excessively sorry for her and does not wonder at [space left for word 'Dinah's' which the copyist apparently could not make out] anxiety for so fair a waif but wish her success on her rather uphill missionary enterprise. The annoyance I feel at the heartlessness of the little monkey is an excellent illustration of the truth of your admirable reflections on the way men look upon things so fair and Bright as Hetty.

As for Arthur Donnithorne, his 'feelings and struggles are depicted to the life. . . . I like the Rector. Adam with Arthur is very good and there is a dim foreshadowing of the mischief between the two friends.' And he anticipates their later understanding: 'I hope however to see them friends in their old age.'

Picking up Eliot's theme in her 1 April letter, Blackwood finds 'an atmosphere of genuine religion and purity that fears no evil about the whole opening of the Story'. Apparently he still wants it for Maga: 'I think It must go into the Magazine. It will be the best thing for both parties. I would not wish to commence for some months so I was glad to hear that you were not anxious for early publication. Send me more M.S. when you can.'[5]

Even before receiving Chapters XIV to XVI, Blackwood had apparently decided to pour oil on the turbulent waters by writing to Lewes as well, knowing that any positive comments would be conveyed immediately to the author. He writes first about Lewes's own articles, but includes a final

---

[4] *Letters*, VIII. 202.

[5] Qtd. in Carol A. Martin, 'Two Unpublished Letters from John Blackwood on the Serialization of *Scenes of Clerical Life* and *Adam Bede*', *Publishing History*, 37 (1995), 55–6.

comment on the 'admirable letter' he had received that day from Eliot. Acknowledging that he 'knew that he [Eliot] would fear to give me a sketch of the rest of the Story lest he should give me a wrong impression and I very nearly said so when I made the request', he temporizes, attempting to lighten the mood by applying her argument in his editorial duties:

On the whole I think he is right. What he says of the treatment of a subject being the essence of art is very true and a more elegant rendering of my constant reply to fellows sending lists of subjects for articles, 'that any subject being suitable entirely depends upon how it is handled.' I shall steal his expression the next time I wish to choke off any anxious enquirer as to the probable acceptability of his proposed 'little paper.'

Finally, he anticipates receiving the new manuscript material 'in time to congratulate George on its merits before he leaves England'.[6]

The next day, Lewes reassures Blackwood while also reminding him of Eliot's sensitivity: 'I will give G.E. your message. You are the right sort of person to deal with him, for you perceive his Pegasus is tender in the mouth, and is apt to lay back his ears in a restive ominous style if even the reins be shaken when he is at work. Some people's Pegasus seems to have the mouth (as well as the *pace*,) of a cart horse; but your thoroughbred—all bone and nerve—requires other treatment.'[7]

Blackwood's earlier treatment of his thoroughbred author appears, however, to have settled decisively the publication plans for *Adam Bede*. Only two letters are on record for the rest of April, a brief one from Munich on 14 April from Lewes to Blackwood making no reference to *Adam Bede*, and one from Blackwood to Lewes dated 30 April from which one might infer some additional correspondence on the subject:

Give my best regards to George Eliot and tell him that he will find me quite ready to meet his wishes by the publication of Adam Bede as a separate work at once. In whatever form the Tale first sees the light I am sure it will be an excellent thing both for the pocket and for the reputation of the author.

I am very anxious to hear how it gets on and shall be delighted to see more of the MS when ready. I would write to G.E. but I am desperately busy, having run myself into a corner for time. This you will readily imagine when I mention that I leave for England tomorrow.[8]

This must be the letter referred to in Eliot's journal entry for 4 May 1858: 'Letter from Blackwood today, in which he appears to fall in rather with the idea of separate publication for Adam Bede than of publication in the Magazine.'[9] At a glance, the decision appears to have been Eliot's, and there may have been another letter, no longer extant, in which she reiter-

---

[6] 2 Apr. 1858; *Letters*, II. 447–8.   [7] 3 Apr.; *Letters*, II. 448.
[8] *Letters*, VIII. 203.   [9] *JGE* 315.

ated her, or as Blackwood writes *his*, wishes[1] for separate volume publication, wishes that Blackwood is 'quite ready to meet'. On the other hand, it is possible that Blackwood, after nearly a month in which to reflect on the matter, continued to doubt the story's suitability for Maga, and either forgot, or chose to forget, her equivocation of 1 April and his own statement of 3 April that 'it must go into the Magazine'. In the absence of any further evidence, it is impossible to be certain. Given her difficulties with deadlines and Blackwood's objections to parts of *Scenes of Clerical Life*, Eliot may have been relieved to accept Blackwood's 'fall[ing] in', although she and Lewes would have known that this meant losing the ready market that a major periodical like *Blackwood's Edinburgh Magazine* provided. Furthermore, John Blackwood's information on the slow sales of *Scenes*, which caused concern on its own account, may also have made them uneasy about how well *Adam Bede* would succeed on its own, without prior magazine publication.

Eliot and Lewes's arrival in Munich on Sunday, 11 April, followed a brief visit to Nuremberg, whose architecture so excited Eliot that Lewes opined to Blackwood, 'Who knows but some day we may have a Nürnberg novel, as the product?'[2] But at the moment, the author's resumption of the novel in hand was shaped and stimulated more by the art galleries of Munich than by anything in Nuremberg. According to the 'History of "Adam Bede"', she 'began the second volume in the second week of my stay at Munich, about the middle of April'.[3] That is, on 20 or 21 April, she began Chapter XVII, which argues for realism in fiction by analogy with the Dutch school of painting. Eliot's journal for this period records frequent visits to Munich galleries as well as conversations with German acquaintances about art. One entry notes that up to 'Friday the 16th, we have reason to be content [with Munich]. We have been taking sips of the Glyptothek,[4] and the two Pinacotheks, in the mornings, not having settled to work yet.'[5] Her enthusiasm for dramatic, realistic portrayal in art dominates her journal, although it contains more specific references to Rubens and to religious pictures than to works of Dutch realism.[6] The

---

[1] Probably because they knew that others besides Blackwood would see the Eliot–Lewes correspondence, all three of the principal parties kept up the fiction of a male author, using the third person singular masculine pronoun. As Blackwood had written to his wife, the authorship 'is to be kept a profound secret, and on all accounts it is desirable, as you will readily imagine.... I am not to tell Langford the secret even' (*Letters*, II. 436).

[2] *Letters*, II. 449.   [3] *JGE* 298.

[4] At the Glyptothek, Eliot saw the Medusa Rondanini, which made its way into the imagery of volume III of *Adam Bede*, as discussed in the Explanatory Notes for Chapter XXXVII.

[5] *JGE* 310.

[6] For instance, at the Glyptothek on 'Friday [April] 23' where they went, 'Not being well enough to write, we ... delighted ourselves anew with the Sleeping Faun, The Satyr and Bacchus, and the Laughing Faun.' They went on to the Alte Pinakothek, 'where we looked at

Samson and Delilah in the Rubens-Saal at the Alte Pinakothek prompted an enthusiastic comment in her journal,[7] and on Saturday, 17 April, she described to Sara Hennell the power of Rubens's 'real, breathing men and women—men and women moved by passions, not mincing and grimacing and posing in mere apery of passion!'[8] Lewes's journal for the next day reports that, in addition to revisiting Rubens, 'Several of the Dutch pictures claimed our admiration.'[9]

Writing to Sara in mid-May, Eliot mentions one Dutch artist in particular: 'It is an unspeakable relief, after staring at one of [Wilhelm von Kaulbach's[1]] huge pictures' instead 'to sweep it all out of one's mind . . . and call up in your imagination a little Gerard Dow [sic] that you have seen hanging in a corner of one of the cabinets.'[2] In Chapter XVII, she calls up this painting for her readers. Gerard Dou's

> the *Betende Spinnerin* at Munich is clearly the model for Eliot's 'old woman . . . eating her solitary dinner, while the noonday light, softened perhaps by a screen of leaves, falls on her mob-cap, and just touches the rim of her spinning-wheel, and her stone jug.' . . . The details of this description correspond exactly with those of the painting, and show how attentively Eliot could look at a picture that interested her.[3]

The narrator in Chapter XVII affirms that 'It is for this rare, precious quality of truthfulness that I delight in many Dutch paintings.' On 14 May, Eliot records that 'After writing we went for an hour to the Pinacothek and looked at some of the Flemish pictures,' but she offers no details.[4] Her use of 'Flemish' as a generic term here may explain a cancellation in Chapter XVII, in which she wrote heavily, in a different pen, the word *Dutch* over the original word *Flemish* in the sentence quoted above.[5] Her continued interest in both is evident in her recollections of Dresden, completed on 27 October, almost two months after her return, when she describes frequent visits to art galleries, where she 'did not half satisfy [her] appetite for the rich collection of Flemish and Dutch pictures here—for Teniers, Ryckaert, Gerard Dow, Terburg, Mieris and the rest'.[6]

Albert Dürer's portrait again, and many other pictures among which I admired a group by Jordaens: "A Satyr eating with a peasant shows him that he can blow hot and cold at the same time"; the old grandmother nursing the child, the father with the key in his hand with which he has been amusing baby, looking curiously at the Satyr, the handsome wife still more eager in her curiosity, the quiet cow, the little boy, the dog and cat—all are charmingly conceived' (*JGE* 313).

[7] *JGE* 311.　　　[8] *Letters*, II. 451.　　　[9] JGHL X, 1858.
[1] In her journal entry for 24 April, Eliot refers to Kaulbach's 'complex, wearisome symbolical style' (*JGE* 313).
[2] 13 May; *Letters*, II. 455.　　　[3] Witemeyer, 108.　　　[4] *JGE* 316.
[5] Eliot did, however, use the term 'Dutch school' in a letter to William Blackwood on 4 Feb. 1857, discussing realism in her work in terms of painting (*Letters*, II. 292).
[6] *JGE* 326.

Two letters from Lewes to Blackwood on 5 and 15 May make no mention of the new novel, and Blackwood's letter on 23 May merely asks, 'How does Adam Bede get on?'[7] Eliot and Lewes both wrote on 28 May, but only Lewes's letter mentions *Adam Bede*. He assumes that the decision not to serialize is final:

'Adam Bede' gets on steadily and vigorously. As it is not to appear in Maga, the new edition of C.S. (whenever you think it desirable to bring one out) will be the best possible advertizement it can have. If 'Adam' does not produce a profound sensation I will hold my tongue as critic for ever after, and say that I have grown 'out of joint with the time.'[8]

The novel had indeed been getting on well. By 15 May, she was able to read Chapter XVIII to Lewes (there is no record of when she might have read Chapter XVII aloud, if she did[9]) and on 26 May, Chapter XX.[1] On 10 June she records that she is 'at the end of chapter 21 and am this morning going to begin chapter 22'. Illness slowed this pace, however. It was not until 13 June that she was 'This morning at last free from headache and able to write. I am entering on my history of the Birthday with some fear and trembling.'[2] Her progress overall, she wrote to John Blackwood on 28 May, came despite the difficulties posed by Munich's weather and dining habits: the 'inconvenience of climate, with the impossibility of dining (well) at any other hour than one o'clock, is not friendly to the stomach—that great seat of the imagination'. She will 'never advise an author to come to Munich except *ad interim*—when he is writing nothing, and only gathering materials for a picture of society where it is held a recreation to drink tea without flavour and tell jokes without point'.[3] Eliot and Lewes left Munich on 7 July, passing through Salzburg, Ischl, and Linz on their way to Vienna,[4] where they remained until 17 July, travelling then to Prague and Dresden. Lewes wrote to Blackwood on 19 July that they had left Munich with 'pleasant memories' of the people if not the place, but were glad to settle in 'the most habitable of German towns', Dresden, adding that Eliot 'says he has seen so much beauty this last fortnight, and such fine works that he feels it shameful not to have spent less time in Munich, and more in the Tyrol or elsewhere. The *Bedesman* ought to profit by such a journey.'[5]

---

[7] *Letters*, II. 459.   [8] *Letters*, II. 461.

[9] It is possible that Lewes's journal for 13 May recording Eliot's reading a newly completed chapter refers to Chapter XVII and not XVIII (JGHL X, 1858). If so, she must have drafted both XVII and XVIII and then, after revising each one, read Chapter XVII on 13 May and Chapter XVIII on 15 May, since she could not have written the extremely long Chapter XVIII in two days. Lewes's journal for 15 May, when Eliot records reading Chapter XVIII, does not mention any reading from her *Adam Bede* manuscript. It is also possible that she simply confused her dates, or that both entries refer to reading Chapter XVIII, which, given the chapter's length, could easily have taken two days.

[1] *JGE* 316, 317.   [2] *JGE* 318.   [3] *Letters*, II. 460.   [4] *JGE* 321–4.
[5] *Letters*, II. 469.

Settled in comfortable, spacious lodgings in Dresden ('a whole apart-
ment of six rooms all to ourselves for s18/- per week!'), Eliot records that
'Here I wrote the latter half of the second volume of Adam Bede, in the long
mornings that our early hours—rising at six o'clock—secured us.'[6] The
'History of "Adam Bede"' modifies this slightly: in Dresden she 'nearly
finished the second volume—all, I think, but the last chapter, which I wrote
here in the old room at Richmond in the first week of September'.[7]
Undoubtedly her travels through the countryside of Catholic regions in
Germany and Austria influenced this 'last chapter' (Chapter XXXV), in
which the responses of Eliot the traveller are again conflated with those of
Adam Bede's narrator. Describing Hetty's suicidal despair amidst nature's
early signs of 'the beautiful year [that] is all before one', the narrator
recalls 'foreign countries' where the landscape resembles 'our English
Loamshire'—but for one non-English detail, 'an image of great agony—
the agony of the Cross', which might seem 'strangely out of place in
the midst of this joyous nature' if one knew nothing of suffering like
Hetty's.

From Dresden on 16 August, Lewes responded to John Blackwood's
good news about sales of *Scenes of Clerical Life*:

G.E. is vastly pleased to hear of a revival of the clerical interest. White neck-
cloths for ever! Bedesman is in training, and will make a splendid run if he does not
win the Derby. I have faith in that horse and will back him to any reasonable
amount.

E. begs his kindest regards to his best and most encouraging of jockeys, and says
he will let Bedesman show some of his paces directly we return to Richmond (NB.
this will be the 1 September) when E. will also write to that successful and cheering
jockey.[8]

On 5 September Lewes wrote Blackwood that he 'will see Mr. Simpson and
consult with him about the C.S. [Clerical Scenes] and give him also the 2d
volume of Bedesman to take back with him. We are not a little curious to
hear your impressions thereof'.[9] On 11 September Lewes wrote that 'Mr.
Simpson takes volume 2 of Bedesman with him [to Edinburgh].'[1] After a
holiday in Wales and a working visit to London, Simpson returned to
Scotland on Monday, 13 September. That day William Blackwood wrote
to his brother, 'Simpson has returned in great force. He got Adam Bede Vol
II from Lewes which I send herewith.'[2] Despite receiving the manuscript
so expeditiously, John Blackwood wrote nothing to Eliot or Lewes for
nearly four weeks. Two brief letters to Major Blackwood reveal that John

---

[6] *JGE* 324–5.   [7] *JGE* 298.   [8] *Letters*, II. 474.   [9] *Letters*, II. 479.
[1] *Letters*, II. 481.
[2] NLS MS 4129, fos. 160–1. An undated letter from Simpson, headed 'Tuesday', says he
'returned yesterday' (NLS MS 4133, fos. 95–6). This letter can be dated based on Major
William Blackwood's letter to John, headed [Monday,] 13 Sept.

Blackwood began the new portion of the work immediately, but they also indicate a somewhat equivocal response. The first letter is headed 'St. Andrews, Tuesday Ev^g' and must have been written immediately after he received the manuscript on 14 September:

> I am glad to hear of Simpsons return in good force & tell him we shall be happy to see him here on Friday or Saturday. I wish either him or [?Birt] or both to come. Tell them so—& if you are so disposed I hope you will come with them.
>
> I do not intend to golf tomorrow & will dispose of George Eliot & any other business. I have read the first chapter of G.E. admirable.[3]

Internal evidence suggests that his second letter was written two days later, on 16 September. Headed simply 'St. Andrews, Thursday Ev^g', it is more equivocal: 'Adam Bede does not move quite enough but is very good. I have not read the whole yet.'[4]

Tentativeness is the keynote of the letter John Blackwood finally wrote to the author on 4 October. 'You would feel that I could not do otherwise than like the second volume of Adam Bede otherwise I should not have been guilty of so long a silence as to its merits, although my house has been so full of visitors during the last few weeks that I have had the greatest difficulty in finding any time to read, think, or write.' He calls the story 'a very striking one' and 'cannot recollect anything at all of the same kind', but, as he was six months earlier, Blackwood remains apprehensive about the direction the story will take, 'long[ing] to see how you will work it out'.[5] Chapters XXVII and XXVIII provoked extended comment:

> I have thought a great deal over the encounter between Adam and Arthur, indeed I daresay it is pondering over that scene which has prevented me from sooner sitting down to write to you. The picture of Adam's feelings before he gets the fatal glimpse of the scene in the wood is perfection. The point is worked up to with wonderful skill. It is very difficult to imagine what would happen between any two men brought so suddenly into such a total revulsion of feelings and change of relative positions as happens to Adam and Arthur, but on the whole I think you have hit the mark and sustained in a very trying climax the characters of the two men you are drawing. I am ashamed of myself for not feeling more sorry for Adam, but I have no doubt the sympathies will gather round him keenly when the full force of his affliction comes upon him and the tender and stern fibres in his heart of oak fairly begin to struggle.[6]

Lewes too had been concerned about the characterization of Adam. Eliot relates that 'George expressed his fear that Adam's part was too passive throughout the drama, and that it was important for him to be brought into more direct collision with Arthur. This doubt haunted me, and out of it grew the scene in the Wood between Arthur and Adam: the fight came to

[3] NLS Letterbook 30011, fos. 281–2.   [4] Ibid. 283–4.   [5] *Letters*, II. 483.
[6] *Letters*, II. 484.

me as a *necessity* one night at the Munich Opera when I was listening to *William Tell*.'[7] Eliot's journal records that they heard Rossini's opera on 30 May, by which time she had completed Chapter XX.[8]

The fight was not, however, an entirely new idea, which perhaps is why Eliot emphasizes the word *necessity* in her phrase 'came to me as a *necessity*'.[9] The fight is foreshadowed in Chapter XVI, which was in Blackwood's hands in March. There, with a touch of ironic self-deprecation, Adam tells Arthur that although he 'used to fight for fun', he will 'never fight any man again, only when he behaves like a scoundrel. If you get hold of a chap that's got no shame nor conscience to stop him, you must try what you can do by bunging his eyes up.' Arthur, who is riding to Mr Irwine's to make the confession he has promised himself, is too 'preoccupied' to laugh. In Chapter XXVII, 'A Crisis', Arthur is again preoccupied, but this time he is the one who, misreading Adam, at first tries to 'laugh the whole thing off'. The reader, however, can hardly miss Adam's reiterated accusation that Arthur is a 'scoundrel' and its connection with Adam's description two months earlier of the man whose eyes he would 'bung up'. But Lewes's advice and the visit to *William Tell* on 30 May may have produced another foreshadowing of events to come in Chapter XXVII. Late in Chapter XXI, written between 26 May and 10 June, Bartle Massey reminds Adam of his inclination to condemn others hastily and to use physical force to achieve what Adam considers justice:

You must learn to deal with odd and even in life, as well as in figures. I tell you now, as I told you ten years ago, when you pommelled young Mike Holdsworth for wanting to pass a bad shilling, before you knew whether he was in jest or earnest— you're over-hasty and proud, and apt to set your teeth against folks that don't square to your notions. It's no harm for *me* to be a bit fiery and stiff-backed: I'm an old schoolmaster, and shall never want to get on to a higher perch. But where's the use of all the time I've spent in teaching you writing and mapping and mensuration, if you're not to get for'ard in the world, and show folks there's some advantage in having a head on your shoulders, instead of a turnip? Do you mean to go on turning up your nose at every opportunity, because it's got a bit of a smell about it that nobody finds out but yourself?

Bartle's speech humanizes Adam, counterbalancing his idealization by the narrator in Chapter XIX by a critique of his tendency to angry self-righteousness. At the same time, the speech reminds readers that Adam will not sit by quietly when wrong is done 'in earnest' and not 'in jest', although Arthur attempts to pass off his relationship with Hetty as a specimen of the latter. Blackwood's letter of 4 October also repeats by

---

[7] *JGE* 298.   [8] *JGE* 317, 318.
[9] In her 'History of "Adam Bede"', Eliot recalls that this was one of two scenes that Lewes 'recommended me to "space out" a little'. The other one was the 'first scene at the Farm' (*JGE* 298).

chance an image cancelled by the author in volume I. Blackwood wrote: 'Hetty is a wonderful piece of painting. One seems to *see* the little villain. She is painted in such irresistible colours that I am very sorry for the well intentioned Arthur. One feels that there is no chance of escape for any youth of his age unless he takes to his heels.'[1] Flight is precisely what Mr Irwine advises Arthur, in a sentence and a half cancelled at the end of Chapter IX. In their first and only conversation about Arthur's attraction to Hetty, Irwine suggests that he take no more notice of her, illustrating with an analogy to himself:

When I've made up my mind that I can't afford to buy a tempting dog, I take no notice of him, because if he took a strong fancy to me, and looked lovingly at me, the struggle between arithmetic and inclination might become unpleasantly severe. I pique myself on my wisdom there, Arthur, and as an old fellow to whom wisdom has become cheap, I bestow it upon you.

The manuscript originally continued with this addition in Irwine's voice: 'It's a fine thing to conquer oneself, but I have always preferred running away. One gets more secure in that way, & what is better, one leans now in another.' Instead of completing the sentence with a word like 'direction', Eliot cancelled it, and in its place Arthur turns the conversation with 'Thank you. It may stand me in good stead some day, though I don't know that I have any present use for it. Bless me! how the brook has overflowed. Suppose we have a canter, now we're at the bottom of the hill.'[2] In fact, Arthur does try 'running away', first to his friend Gawaine for lunch, and then to Eagledale for a few days' fishing, but both visits only postpone the seduction. Ironically, underlying the confession scene itself is a potential conversation about Hetty from which *both* Irwine and Arthur run away. When Irwine asks a direct question, instead of taking the opportunity to confess his attraction to her, Arthur suddenly retreats. Although it occurs to Irwine that perhaps Arthur wants to speak of Hetty, he too quickly dismisses the thought, and, reluctant to probe another man's secrets, turns the conversation.

Despite his enthusiasm for the fight scene, for Hetty, and for the Poysers, Blackwood was reluctant to come to terms: 'There can be no doubt that the book will be successful but the degree of success will depend very much upon the third volume, so I think the best plan will be to leave our final arrangements for publication, number of copies to be printed, etc. etc. until the book is finished.'[3] At the start of his letter, Blackwood had assured the author that 'You may be sure that I shall sit down to the

---

[1] *Letters*, II. 484.
[2] It is unlikely Blackwood got his image from the cancellation. Not only does the passage occur in volume I, which he had read six months earlier, but it is heavily cancelled and requires persistent study to be deciphered.
[3] *Letters*, II. 484.

third volume the moment I get the M.S. and you shall have no cause for impatience to hear from me about it.'[4] Blackwood's letter to Lewes three days later suggests that he was apprehensive about the effect of his words:

George Eliot would I daresay show you what I said of Adam Vol. 2. It is very difficult indeed to judge of a second volume as one does not read it with the eager curiosity with which one opens the first, or the rapid haste with which one rushes on to the finish, as for example had Vols. 2 and 3 been before me I am sure that I would have read them in less time than I took to Vol. 2 by itself. There can be no mistake about the merits however and I am not sure whether I expressed myself sufficiently warmly. But you know that I am not equal to the abandon of expression which distinguishes the large hearted school of Critics.[5]

Lewes responded: 'That is a delicious touch in your note about the *largehearted* critics—an awful race. E. was extremely gratified by the praise and the *kind* of praise in your letter.' He predicts that when Blackwood receives volume III he might 'rush even into largehearted emphasis, only that it will be *sincere* emphasis and not mere typography'. Although Lewes advised Eliot 'to send you the m.s. which concludes the tragedy', she 'is disposed to wait till the whole is completed before sending you any. What do *you* think? If you agree with me write him word.' Knowing Blackwood's predilection for a happy ending, Lewes reveals that 'After the winding up of Hetty's story [i.e. 'the tragedy'] nothing but peaceful sunshine and happiness will come.'[6] With these hints, the publisher may have felt it wisest to leave Eliot to work in her own way; there is no record of a follow-up letter such as Lewes suggests. In the event, Eliot did send Blackwood a large section of volume III before the whole was finished. Her journal of the trip to Germany records that 'tonight, the 27th of October, as I am finishing this fragmentary story of our travels, I am not far off the end of my third volume'.[7] Two days later, her diary notes: 'George took the M.S. of the third volume up to p. 216 to town, to be dispatched to Edinburgh.'[8] Volume III's manuscript folio 216, which contains only a line and half of writing, stops midway through Chapter LII, with Adam having proposed to Dinah. She has refused, at least until the Divine Will has been made clear to her, but indications of future happiness appear in the final paragraph on folios 215 and 216, as Adam and Dinah go out from the Hall Farm to meet the Poyser family returning from afternoon church. Dinah takes his arm for the first time, and the narrator concludes, 'no sadness in the prospect of her going away—could rob the sweetness from Adam's sense that Dinah loved him. He thought he would stay at the Hall Farm all that evening. He would be near her as long as he could.' Even without Lewes's assurance of the

[4] *Letters*, II. 483–4.   [5] 7 Oct.; *Letters*, VIII. 211.
[6] 8 Oct. 1858; *Letters*, II. 488.   [7] *JGE* 326.   [8] *JGE* 74.

ending in 'peaceful sunshine and happiness', no reader, much less the astute Blackwood, could imagine that Eliot would lead Adam, the hero who has suffered and learned so much, to recognize his new love and then have it taken from him.

Eliot's dependence on Blackwood's response and her sense of its relationship to her future career is suggested by her diary entry for 1 November:

> I am alone to-night, G. being gone on one of his rare visits to town. I have begun Carlyle's Life of Frederic the Great, and have also been thinking much of my own life to come. This is a moment of suspense, for I am awaiting Blackwood's opinion and proposals concerning Adam Bede.[9]

Fortunately for posterity, Blackwood responded quickly and enthusiastically. On 3 November he wrote to both Eliot and Lewes, describing the third volume to Lewes as 'wonderful'.[1] In his letter to the author he is more specific: he read the manuscript in one afternoon, and 'I am happy to tell you that I think it capital. I never saw such wonderful effects worked out by such a succession of simple and yet delicate and minute touches.' He 'shuddered' for Hetty in her 'night in the fields' which he calls 'marvellous', adding, 'I do not think the most thoughtless lad could read that horrible picture of her feelings and hopeless misery without being deeply moved.' He is satisfied now with Adam: his 'going to support her at the Trial is a noble touch. You really make him a gentle Man by that act,' for which Blackwood finds a suitably manly analogy, 'It is like giving him his spurs.'[2]

As Eliot and Lewes would have expected, he anticipates the ending, calling Dinah 'a very striking and original character, always perfectly supported and never obtrusive in her piety. Very early in the book I took it into my head that it could be "borne in upon her" to fall in love with Adam.' Although Arthur Donnithorne 'is the least satisfactory character' he is 'true too' and 'The picture of his complacent happy feelings before the bomb shell bursts upon him is very good.'[3] This comment must have been especially gratifying to the author, who had rearranged her final volume to intensify the impact of Arthur's complacent assurance that Providence had continued to treat him well. Manuscript foliation indicates that Chapter XLIV, 'Arthur's Return', was originally to have followed Chapter XL, 'The Bitter Waters Spread'. Although a powerful contrast would have been effected by setting Arthur's patronizing thoughts and his refusal to accept moral responsibility against the first pictures of the suffering of Adam, his mother and brother, and the Poyser family in Chapters XXXIX and XL, the altered placement of 'Arthur's Return' immediately after the judge condemns Hetty 'to be hanged by the neck till you be dead' produces an

---

[9] *JGE* 74. [1] *Letters*, VIII. 212. [2] *Letters*, II. 492.
[3] *Letters*, II. 492.

even stronger dramatic effect.[4] Eliot's journal records her receipt of this letter: 'November 4. Received a letter from Blackwood containing warm praise of my 3rd volume and offering £800 for the copyright of Adam Bede for four years. I wrote to accept.'[5] Her relief is apparent in her response to Blackwood the next day. She thanks him 'once more for writing me such cordial words of admiration. I *was* rather desponding, now I am singing "Viva la joia, fidon la tristessa." '[6]

Blackwood's 3 November letter enclosed his formal offer, which the *George Eliot Letters* states has not been found.[7] However, a copy exists in the Blackwoods' Letter Book for 1857 and 1858, in the National Library of Scotland:

Edinburgh Nov[br] 3. 1858

Dear Sir

We beg to offer you for the copyright of Adam Bede for four years from this date the sum of Eight Hundred Pounds (L800) payable in two instalments by cash or bill at six and nine months from date of publication.

> We are Dear Sir
> Yours very truly
> (signed) W[m] Blackwood and Sons[8]

On 16 November, Eliot 'Wrote the last word of Adam Bede, and sent it to Langford. *Jubilate!*'[9] The next day Lewes wrote to Blackwood, 'Yesterday I placed the concluding portion of the m.s.s. of "Adam Bede" in Langford's hands, who undertook to forward it in the next parcel.'[1]

On 23 November Blackwood sent his congratulations on this final part, 'which is very beautiful. The supper party at the Poyser's [*sic*] is delightful and Martin's preternatural shrewdness made me laugh. The meeting between Adam and Dinah on the hillside is picturesque and touching. I should have liked to *see* the meeting between Adam and Arthur, but I daresay you were wisest only to indicate it.'[2] Eliot responded, 'Your praise of my ending was very warming and cheering to me in the foggy weather. I'm sure if I have written well, your pleasant letters have had something to do with it.'[3] Despite his occasional early misgivings, those pleasant feelings became even stronger as Blackwood began to reread in proof. Writing to Langford, 22 December, he observed, 'As to Adam Bede I am very confident. It is a very remarkable book. In all my unlimited novel reading I can recollect nothing of the same kind at all. It is a singular proof of the hold it takes that in reading the proofs I remember the impression made not

---

[4] The change in the position of Chapter XLIV is discussed in detail in the Manuscript section below.

[5] *JGE* 74.

[6] *Letters*, II. 493. Haight's note on this passage reads: 'Quoted from *Tristram Shandy*, VII, 43, where Sterne writes the Provençal "Fi donc" as "Fidon" ' (*Letters*, II. 493 n. 6).

[7] *Letters*, II. 492–3 n. 5.   [8] MS 30,358, fo. 370.   [9] *JGE* 75.

[1] *Letters*, II. 497–8.   [2] *Letters*, II. 499.   [3] 25 Nov.; *Letters*, II. 500.

merely by each scene but almost by each turn of phrase when I read the M.S.'[4] Eliot, however, remained uncertain about the public response. In the 'History of "Adam Bede"', she reflects that 'I love it [the book] very much and am deeply thankful to have written it, whatever the public may say to it—a result which is still in darkness, for I have at present had only four sheets of the proof.'[5]

PUBLICATION

In his letter of 3 November, Blackwood reported that the preliminaries to publication were already under way: 'We have been trying pages so as to start with the printing immediately. The extent is not so great as I imagined and I cannot help thinking that our people have rather underestimated the quantity.'[6] He included a specimen page, which Eliot describes as 'look[ing] shabby by the side of the pages of Clerical Scenes'.[7] Blackwood's letter does not mention a publication date or any delay, but when Eliot responded on 5 November, she was 'rather disappointed to find that a delay was desirable'.[8]

Publication timelines had been a matter of concern to Eliot and Lewes at least since early September. Sending volume II to Blackwood and wishing it were volume III, Eliot emphasized that 'it is important to use every means of saving time, and it will be some saving if you will be so good as to read this portion at your earliest convenience'. Her urgency was dictated by Lewes's view that 'I shall lose a considerable advantage if the book does not appear in the Christmas season, and I shall work with the hope of being ready in time for that. I suppose the three volumes could be printed in six weeks, when the preliminaries were once arranged?'[9] But members of the firm differed on how to position *Adam Bede* relative to Edward Bulwer-Lytton's *What will he do with it?* whose serialization in *Blackwood's Edinburgh Magazine* was nearly completed. In a letter to John Blackwood on 14 September, Simpson favoured postponing *Adam Bede* until late January: 'You have received, I hope Vol 2 of Adam Bede. M[r]. Eliot whom I did not see is desirous to have it published before Christmas. I trust you will have it postponed till the end of January, as I should like to let "What will he do with it" have the Christmas demand all to itself.'[1] Langford, however, argued that *Adam Bede* should appear before Christmas, even if that meant delaying *What will he do with it?* On 27 September, he wrote to John Blackwood, 'Mudie seems to think well of the tale of "What will he do with it?" I am rather indisposed to publish it before completion in Maga— and I should be inclined to hurry on Adam Bede so as to publish it before

---

[4] NLS MS 4129, fos. 106–7.   [5] *JGE* 298.   [6] *Letters*, II. 492.
[7] *Letters*, II. 493.   [8] *Letters*, II. 493.   [9] *Letters*, II. 480.
[1] NLS MS 4133, fos. 95–6, 'Tuesday' [14 Sept.].

Christmas and if even by keeping out of Maga one month to hold Bulwers [*sic*] book till the end of January.'[2]

No extant letter indicates how the final decision was reached, but by November Simpson's opinion had prevailed. Eliot records in her 'History of "Adam Bede"' that the novel 'would have been published at Christmas, or rather, early in December, but that Bulwer's "What will he do with it?" was to be published by Blackwoods at that time, and it was thought that this novel might interfere with mine'.[3] Despite her disappointment, Eliot defers to John Blackwood's 'experience and judgment' on both appearance and publication date, adding that she has 'no motive for haste that would outweigh your opinion as to what is best for the book'.[4] Blackwood's next letter, ten days later, affirms that 'The printers were, as I expected, all wrong in their calculation of the extent, and you will speedily see as full and handsome a page as you could wish.' He adds that he 'thought some sheets would have been ready by this time, but in a day or two I shall be able to write with them'.[5] By the time he sent his congratulations on the final part on 23 November, Blackwood was able to enclose the first two proof sheets.[6] Eliot returned them on 25 November with a letter expressing the hope that 'the sheets will come rapidly and regularly now, for I dislike lingering, hesitating processes'.[7] This hope, like her hopes for a pre-Christmas publication date, was to be disappointed. The interference of Bulwer-Lytton's novel took a more pressing practical shape than envisioned in Simpson's letter of 14 September, which raised the question of simultaneous appearance in terms of public reception. By November, both works were being set in type—unfortunately, the same type—and Bulwer-Lytton was slow in returning proof. On 26 November John Blackwood wrote to Eliot: 'We are rather puzzled to get on just at present as "Adam" and "What will He do with it" are printing in the same type and from a want of return of proofs of the last there is about a ton and a half of Type locked up. This difficulty will however be overcome immediately.'[8]

This delay increased the anxiety of the already diffident author, as she feared her incognito could not be maintained. On 5 November Herbert Spencer had dined with Eliot and Lewes and 'brought the unpleasant news that [John] Chapman had asked him point blank if I wrote the Clerical Scenes'. Eliot 'wrote at once to the latter to check further gossip on the subject'.[9] In her letter, she pointed out to Chapman that if the rumours were true, her not having informed friends of her authorship would be 'evidence that I regarded secrecy on such subjects as a matter of importance'.[1] She explained her anxiety to Blackwood on 1 December:

---

[2] NLS MS 4132, fos. 121–2.   [3] *JGE* 298.   [4] *Letters*, II. 493.
[5] 15 Nov.; *Letters*, II. 496.   [6] *Letters*, II. 499.   [7] *Letters*, II. 500.
[8] *Letters*, VIII. 214.   [9] *JGE* 74.   [1] *Letters*, II. 494.

I am very nervous about the preservation of the incognito, for I have reason to believe that some rumour of the authorship of C.S. has escaped from a member of my own family, who, however, could only speak on *suspicion*.

This makes me anxious that the publication of 'Adam' should not be delayed longer than is necessary after the Christmas Holidays, for I wish the book to be judged quite apart from its authorship.[2]

The next day Lewes returned to the question of *Adam Bede*'s appearing simultaneously with Bulwer-Lytton's novel.

G.E. is very uncomfortable about the delay in printing. He thinks—and I agree with him—that *mystery* as to authorship will have a great effect in determining critical opinion, and although when once a success has been made, the knowledge of the authorship cannot affect it, it might have a prejudicial influence if the rumour to which he alluded in his letter to you should spread—as spread of course it will. The evil consequences of the mystery being disclosed before the book appears seem to him, and to me, far greater than any disadvantage of contemporaneous appearance with 'What will he do with it'—the more so as that book having already been for 18 months in the mouths of men, will necessarily be less of a novelty, less *talked* about, than if it were now first appearing. Under these circumstances don't you think it very desirable to crowd all sail?[3]

Desirable, but it was difficult to crowd sail when another crew member was not cooperating. However, by 9 December, Blackwood reported that they were back on schedule:

I have been quite vexed about the delay in the printing, but it was one of those unexpected fixes which will arise in the best regulated establishments. I am thankful to say that we have now got a release of Type and your Bedes or rather pearls will be strung as fast as you could wish now. I expect to have the whole in Type by the end of the year so that in reality no time will have been lost.

He also discussed American arrangements, which Langford was making with 'Low and Co. who wish us to name a price'. He suggests £50, although he doubts 'whether we will get more than £30', and adds that 'Sampson Low, the American agent, asked to see some of the sheets of Adam, but I consider this a farce.'[4] Eliot wrote the next day,

à propos of the American business. I think we had better not *ask* more than £30, American publishers being very narrow-necked jars indeed. Farcical enough—that Sampson Low should want to see some sheets of Adam! In order to form a critical judgment, I suppose? That is a little too far to descend for £30;—though I acknowledge myself to be a very sordid author, with some love for money as well as for mankind.

She added that she found the 'present type of "Adam" . . . very satisfactory—one reads it without thinking about it, which is the best of all

---

[2] *Letters*, II. 505. [3] 2 Dec.; *Letters*, II. 506. [4] *Letters*, II. 507.

recommendations for type'.[5] By Christmas more than a volume had been set, and Langford, Eliot reported in a letter of 22 December, 'has gained £30 for me from the American publisher, and I think myself fortunate'.[6]

The 'evil consequences' of the authorship being revealed before reviews had appeared would, she feared, be exacerbated by the sexual nature of the book's central plot. Perhaps recalling Blackwood's reactions nine months earlier, Eliot proposed in her 22 December letter that a 'Remonstrance' be prefixed to *Adam Bede*. She had 'written it rather against the grain—although the evil in question is one that used to excite some indignation in me long before I became a novelist myself—for I have a strong disinclination to place anything in the shape of preface or personal speech with the public, before my novels. Still, I should feel (metaphorically) flayed alive, if the story of "Adam" were to be told in all the variety of bad journalistic styles.'[7] In their March–April epistolary debate she had refused to give Blackwood her own summary of the plot, arguing that the 'treatment', which is 'the soul of art', made all the difference.[8] Plot summaries in 'bad journalistic styles' would not have been an improvement.

If the connection with their earlier debate occurred to Blackwood, he did not mention it, but tactfully took up her request for his opinion:

> What you say by way of Preface is excellent in itself and I cordially sympathise with your feelings, but I decidedly advise against the publication of such a preface. It might raise a nest of hornets about you. Consider that probably one half of the small deer who will sit down to review you are constantly guilty of the very crime you reprobate and would consequently come to the book with highly irritated feelings after seeing themselves so justly shown up.[9]

He acknowledges Lewes's expertise but in this case, 'I am sure I am right.'[1] Words of encouragement follow this negative response. 'I have read the first volume in print and am delighted to tell you that I am more confident than ever. Your characters are wonderfully individual and lifelike.' He praises especially the humour in the depiction of Mrs Poyser: 'While laughing over her quaint reflections on Hetty's want of feeling, I was positively affected at the illustration she gave of Hetty's supposed strong indifference to the child she had handled from its cradle.'[2] He was also reminded of his manuscript reading of Mrs Poyser's 'passage at arms with Bartle' in Chapter LIII, which he terms 'a wonderful performance'. Near the end of the letter, he reverts to the 'Remonstrance', asking tactfully

[5] *Letters*, II. 508.   [6] *Letters*, II. 509.   [7] *Letters*, II. 509.
[8] *Letters*, VIII. 201.   [9] *Letters*, II. 509–10.   [1] *Letters*, II. 510.
[2] Blackwood refers to Mrs Poyser's comment in Chapter XV, beginning, 'She's no better than a peacock.'

whether Eliot thinks of 'reviewing or writing miscellaneous papers. Your preface would come in capitally in a review.'[3]

On one point Blackwood is less tactful than usual. Waiting to begin volume II 'to let the proofs accumulate so as to read it more in a mass', he acknowledges that 'I had more doubt about the latter half of second volume [*sic*] than any other part of the book.'[4] He does not explain why, but given his squeamishness, this part, which focuses upon Hetty's pregnancy, is likely to have made him uncomfortable about the details that reveal her condition. Early reviews in the *Saturday Review* and the *Examiner* demonstrate the reaction he feared. The former called the novel part of the 'literature of pregnancy' with which readers 'seem to be threatened. . . . Hetty's feelings and changes are indicated with a punctual sequence that makes the account of her misfortunes read like the rough notes of a man-midwife's conversations with a bride. This is intolerable. Let us copy the old masters of the art, who, if they gave us a baby, gave it us all at once. A decent author and a decent public may surely take the premonitory symptoms for granted.'[5] The *Examiner* felt 'bound to protest against the depiction in a novel of the stages of childbirth, related with almost obstetric accuracy of detail'.[6] The modern reader may find it difficult to detect even 'premonitory symptoms' much less 'obstetric accuracy of detail', but these reviews demonstrate that Blackwood's fears were not unreasonable.

If Eliot recognized those fears, she does not say so directly. And, although her response assures Blackwood that she agrees with him on the preface and has 'anticipated the very effects you predict',[7] Lewes, and possibly Eliot, had apparently not abandoned the idea of something like the Remonstrance. Before Lewes departed for his customary Christmas visit with his friend Arthur Helps, he asked her to ' "Ask Mr. Blackwood what he thinks of putting a mere advertisement at the beginning of the book to this effect: As the story of Adam Bede will lose much of its effect if the development is foreseen, the author requests those critics who may honour him with a notice, to abstain from telling the story." ' Transmitting this question, Eliot also asks Blackwood not to read volume II 'until it is all in print. There is necessarily a lull of interest in it to prepare for the crescendo.' She is 'delighted' with his praise for Mrs Poyser: 'I'm very sorry to part with her and some of my other characters—there seems to be so much more to be done with them. Mr. Lewes says she gets better and better as the book goes on, and I was certainly conscious of writing her dialogue with heightening gusto. Even in our imaginary worlds there is the sorrow of parting.'[8]

[3] *Letters*, II. 510.   [4] *Letters*, II. 510.
[5] David Carroll (ed.), *George Eliot: The Critical Heritage* (New York, 1971), 76.
[6] 5 Mar. 1859, 149.   [7] 28 Dec. 1858; *Letters*, II. 512.   [8] *Letters*, II. 512.

Enclosing a cheque for £100 for the first part of *Physiology of Common Life* then running in *Blackwood's Edinburgh Magazine*, Blackwood wrote to Lewes on 31 December: 'It is not like so knowing a party as you to suggest so dangerous a preface as that proposed for G.E. The single sentence is fully as doubtful a step as the larger preface.'[9] This closed the matter of any Remonstrance, long or short, but the episode illustrates how Eliot's general diffidence was exacerbated by worry that her authorship could not remain concealed much longer.

On New Year's Day, Eliot 'corrected the last sheets of the second vol. of Adam Bede'.[1] Additional proofs were slow in coming from Edinburgh. On 6 January 1859, Lewes wrote to Blackwood that 'G.E. wishes me to tell you that he has had no proofs this week; a fact he thinks you ought to know, in case the negligence of printers should be in fault—or their new year's jollifications.'[2] Eliot's diary for 12 January records a 'Letter from Blackwood today speaking of renewed delight in Adam Bede, and proposing 1st February as the day of publication.'[3] Lewes responded: 'G.E. says that if 1 February is the earliest day on which it can *conveniently* appear nothing more is to be said; but in his opinion every day that can be gained before the rumour [of authorship] may chance to reach critical circles would be in his favor.'[4] Proofs must have come before or along with Blackwood's letter, because Eliot's diary for 15 January records that she 'corrected the last sheets of Adam Bede', after which she and Lewes 'walked to Wimbledon to see our house, which we have taken for seven years'.[5]

Adam Bede was published on 1 February 1859. It was advertised in the *Athenaeum* on 22 and 29 January, and weekly advertisements continued throughout February. The *Publishers' Circular and General Record of British and Foreign Literature* listed it among the books published between 31 January and 14 February. The day before publication Eliot thanked Blackwood and his brother, Major William Blackwood, for their encouragement, which 'counterbalances, in some degree, the depressing influences to which I am peculiarly sensitive. I perceive that I have not the characteristics of the "popular author," and yet I am much in need of the warmly expressed sympathy which only popularity can win.'[6] She was soon to know that popularity in full measure.

Eliot was apprehensive that there might be design rather than chance in the founder of Mudie's library Charles Edward Mudie's 'almost always' leaving *Scenes of Clerical Life* 'out of his advertised list'.[7] However, there was good news about *Adam Bede*. Blackwood wrote to Lewes on 4 February that Mudie had abandoned his attempt 'to beat us down [by] taking only 50 at first' and had 'finally succumbed, taking 500 at our terms 10 per cent off sales'. Although the 'other subscription was not good, about . . . 230 in all',

---

[9] *Letters*, II. 513.   [1] *JGE* 76.   [2] *Letters*, III. 4.   [3] *JGE* 76.
[4] *Letters*, III. 5.   [5] *JGE* 76.   [6] *Letters*, III. 6.   [7] *Letters*, III. 7.

Blackwood asked Lewes to 'Tell G.E. that I am neither surprised nor disappointed by this', noting that *Scenes of Clerical Life* had established 'a reputation with readers and men of letters...but not a public general reputation, so the orders for the book would not be in the hands of the [Paternoster] Row houses, which is the only guide they have in subscribing'. He assures them that when reviews appear and people begin to talk about the book 'the movement will take place'. Furthermore, we 'are leaving nothing untried to get up the steam by sending copies to the Press in all directions'.[8] He also offers anecdotal encouragement, relating a story in which Eliot 'will be interested and amused'. George Simpson had taken home proof sheets, which 'his brother, a Cabinet Maker, read... with great admiration. He maintains that the writer must have been bred to the business or at all events passed a great deal of time in the workshop listening to the men.' By the date of Blackwood's letter, 4 February, copies had not yet arrived in Edinburgh, 'but I suppose they will arrive tomorrow'.[9]

The story of the cabinetmaker seems to have had the desired effect, for Lewes wrote the following day that Eliot 'was both greatly amused and greatly gratified at the Cabinet Maker's verdict. Having already been a clergyman of puseyite tendencies and large family, he is now a carpenter and doubtless will soon be a farmer and methodist. It is a great compliment when a writer's dramatic presentation is accepted as actual experience.'[1] On 11 February, Blackwood reported that 'the murmur of opinion regarding Adam Bede which begins to reach me is as favourable as we could possibly wish'. Assuring her that 'we are all right and the wiseacres of the Row will speedily be buying fast', Blackwood enclosed 'a communication from "a worshipper of genius" here [Dr John Brown, author of *Rab and his Friends*] who has been raving to me about Adam and raving sensibly, which is not always the case in the worthy Doctor's enthusiastic fits'.[2] In a letter on 13 February Eliot asked Blackwood to send her thanks to Brown for the copy of his book that he sent as a tribute to the author of *Adam Bede*.[3] The day before, in her journal, she referred to the packet from Dr Brown as the 'First agreeable token'.[4] Blackwood's letter 'full of real encouragement' was especially welcome to Lewes, who had seen the *Statesman* review, which 'was laudatory throughout; but the kind of laudation was fatal. "One of the best novels we have read for a long time." The nincompoop couldn't see the distinction between Adam and the mass of novels he had been reading.'[5]

---

[8] *Letters*, III. 8–9. The printing and sales ledger MS 30,859 at the National Library of Scotland shows sixty-six copies of the first edition were delivered to newspapers.
[9] *Letters*, III. 9.   [1] *Letters*, III. 10.   [2] *Letters*, III. 11.   [3] *Letters*, III. 13.
[4] *JGE* 299.   [5] GHL Journal, 12 Feb. 1859; qtd. in *Letters*, III. 12.

More valued tributes began to arrive. On 17 February, Lewes forwarded to Blackwood a 'charming letter' from Richard Owen to Eliot, thanking her for his presentation copy.[6] Jane Welsh Carlyle wrote that 'It was as good as *going into the country for one's health*, the reading of that Book was!'[7] On 23 February Blackwood wrote that the Scottish preacher John Caird was an hour late to an appointment to meet Mrs Blackwood, having been 'so fascinated with Adam Bede as to forget time altogether'. Blackwood also predicted that the 'real demand for Adam will I think begin within the next week or ten days' and sent separately a packet of newspaper notices.[8] Eliot thanked him for his encouraging letter: 'I needed your letter very much, for when one lives apart from the world, with no opportunity of observing the effect of books except through the newspapers, one is in danger of sinking into the foolish belief that the day is past for the recognition of genuine truthful writing.' Both ruefully and wryly lamenting the 'wretched weakness of my nature to be so strongly affected by these things', she articulates her sense of writing as a vocation:

and yet, how is it possible to put one's best heart and soul into a book and be hardened to the result—be indifferent to the proof whether or not one has really a vocation to speak to one's fellow-men in that way? Of course one's vanity is at work; but the main anxiety is something entirely distinct from vanity. You see, I mean you to understand that my feelings are very respectable, and such as it will be virtuous in you to gratify with the same zeal as you have always shown.[9]

When the promised packet arrived, it evoked both pleasure and indignation as Lewes, to whom she refers as her 'friend at my elbow', read selections from the notices to Eliot. Just as Mrs Poyser and her sayings had amused Mr Irwine *in* the novel, so she continued to amuse readers *of* the novel. The *Edinburgh Courant*, which 'has the ring of sincere enjoyment in its tone', Eliot wrote with pleasure, is mistaken, however, in 'supposing that Mrs. Poyser's original sayings are remembered proverbs! I have no stock of proverbs in my memory, and there is not one thing put into Mrs. Poyser's mouth that is not fresh from my own mint.'[1] But Eliot worried that the puffing comments highlighted by 'certain threatening marks in ink' next to 'stock sentences . . . from such authorities as the Sun or Morning Star or other orb of the newspaper firmament' signalled material for future advertisements. She asks Blackwood,

Am I taking a liberty in intreating you to keep a sharp watch over the advertisements that no hackneyed puffing phrase of this kind may be tacked to my book? . . . it would gall me as much as any trifle could, to see my book recommended by such an authority as the writer in Bell's Weekly Messenger who doesn't know how to write decent English.[2]

---

[6] *Letters*, VIII. 222.   [7] 20 Feb.; *Letters*, III. 17.   [8] *Letters*, III. 20.
[9] *Letters*, III. 23–4.   [1] *Letters*, III. 25.   [2] *Letters*, III. 25.

How much more might it have galled her had she seen the extreme of trivialization in *Bell's Life in London* a year later when a horse named 'Adam Bede' was listed as one of the 'Horses Struck out of their engagements' at the Nottingham Handicap.[3]

John Blackwood, however, might have been amused. He employs a racing metaphor himself in a hasty letter (before going to golf) on 7 March, reporting the appearance of that 'real demand' he had so confidently and presciently predicted less than two weeks earlier: 'I write a line to say that we may now consider the Bedesman fairly round the corner and coming in a winner at a slapping pace. Which being interpreted means that Adam Bede is moving rapidly. Mudie had 100 a few days ago and another 100 yesterday and there are other dropping sales both in London and here.'[4] In just over a month, Mudie's had taken 700 copies, as William Blackwood wrote Lewes, adding, 'In the circulating libraries the subscribers are all yelling for it and the librarians are not sufficiently philanthropic to take the proper means for adequately meeting the public appetite.' Although 'the movement in the sale . . . has been a little longer in commencing than I anticipated yet I feel very confident now that it will equal our most sanguine expectations'.[5]

The slow growth in demand for *Adam Bede* probably stemmed from two causes: first, the fact that *Scenes of Clerical Life* had not made, as John Blackwood had observed on 4 February, 'a public general reputation',[6] and, second, the fact that most reviews did not appear until late February or early March. Early notices in the *Press* and the *Statesman* on 12 February were followed by a more perceptive review in the *Edinburgh Evening Courant* on 15 February. The *Illustrated Times* included a brief item on 19 February, the *Daily News*, one on 24 February. But not until the last Saturday of the month, 26 February, were there reviews in the influential *Athenaeum* and *Saturday Review*, the *Literary Gazette*, and the *Leader*, the first three of which Eliot called 'Very laudatory'.[7] They were followed in March by notices in the London *Guardian* (2 March), the *Examiner* (5 March), and the *Morning Post* (16 March). Although the superficial comparisons of *Adam Bede* to the general run of novels annoyed Eliot and Lewes, these enthusiastic notices sent readers rushing to the libraries. Only the *Morning Chronicle*, on 28 February, contained a negative notice, with

[3] 26 Feb. 1860, 4. I am indebted to Pamela J. Peterson, MA, Boise, Idaho, for bringing this race listing to my attention.

[4] 7 Mar.; *Letters*, III. 29. Blackwood and Lewes were both fond of horseracing metaphors. In his letter from Germany on 16 Aug. 1858, quoted above, Lewes wrote: 'Bedesman is in training, and will make a splendid run if he does not win the Derby. I have faith in that horse and will back him to any reasonable amount' (*Letters*, II. 474). Years later, Blackwood repeated Lewes's image after Eliot had accepted his offer for *Felix Holt*: 'I most heartily respond to the feelings expressed in your gratifying note and do rejoice in resuming old relations with you. It quite takes me back to the days when Adam Bede won the Derby' (26 Apr. 1866; *Letters*, IV. 244).

[5] 9 Mar.; *Letters*, III. 31.   [6] *Letters*, III. 9.   [7] *JGE* 76.

the premiss that 'A high-minded peasant cannot be made a very interesting being.'[8] Readers and other reviewers apparently disagreed, and March saw the beginning of the movement the firm had been anticipating.

William Blackwood wrote on 12 March to quote Langford's report that Mudie's had taken a total of 1,000 copies and that ' "Everyone is talking of the book." '[9] Other letters continued to register its growing popularity. Elizabeth Gaskell wrote to John Blackwood on 9 March: 'One of Mrs. Poyser's speeches is as good as a fresh blow of sea-air, and yet she is a true person, and no caricature.'[1] And J. A. Froude, whose letter on *Scenes of Clerical Life* had pleased Eliot, wrote a 'very feeling letter'.[2] Lewes's trip 'into town' ten days later yielded

a budget of good news. . . . Mr. Langford says that Mudie thinks he must have another hundred or two of Adam—has read the book himself and is delighted with it. Charles Reade says it is 'the finest thing since Shakspeare'—placed his finger on Lisbeth's account of her coming home with her husband from their marriage—praises enthusiastically the style—the way in which the author handles the Saxon language. Shirley Brooks also delighted—John Murray says there has never been such a book. Mr. Langford says there must be a second edition in 3 vols. and they will print 500: whether Mudie takes more or not they will have sold all by the end of a month. Lucas delighted with the book and will review it in the Times at the first opportunity.[3]

Reviews in the monthlies and quarterlies that appeared at the beginning of April (*Blackwood's*, the *Westminster Review*, the *Critic*) undoubtedly stimulated sales, and when E. S. Dallas's long and highly laudatory review appeared in *The Times* on 12 April, *Adam Bede*'s popular success was assured. On 17 April, Eliot 'left off recording the history of Adam Bede, and the pleasant letters and words that come to me—the success has been so triumphantly beyond anything I had dreamed of, that it would be tiresome to put down particulars'.[4] The enthusiasm of the public for *Adam Bede* was also beyond the expectations of members of the firm of William Blackwood and Sons, as demonstrated in the seven printings during its first year of publication and the continuing demand during her lifetime for the work that became the benchmark for all her future novels.

EDITIONS

Overview

Adam Bede went through more editions[5] and sold more copies during Eliot's lifetime than any of her other works. The three-volume *Adam*

[8] *Morning Chronicle*, 6.   [9] *Letters*, VIII. 226.   [1] *Letters*, VIII. 225.
[2] 16 Mar.; *JGE* 300.   [3] *JGE* 300.   [4] *JGE* 300.
[5] The firm used the term 'edition', until 1862, to indicate any new print run. All printings from the 1st edition in 1859 to the 10th in 1862 involved a resetting of at least two-thirds of the

Bede at 31*s.* 6*d.* went through three separate editions between 1 February
and early May 1859. These were followed by a cheaper, two-volume
edition in June 1859, at 12*s.*, which was called the 'Fourth Edition' on the
title page. It was followed by four resettings in the same format between
July 1859 and June 1860 (called the 'Fifth' to the 'Eighth' editions).
Another small edition of the same format, called the 'Ninth', appeared in
June 1861. None of these was stereotyped. The following table taken from
figures in Blackwoods' publication ledgers, NLS MSS 30,859 (the first to
the eighth editions) and 30,860 (ninth edition), gives press orders, press
runs, and publication dates:

Edition	Number ordered to print	Number printed	Month/year of publication
1 (3 vols.)	2,000	2,101	February 1859
2 (3 vols.)	750	788	April 1859
3 (3 vols.)	500	527	May 1859
4 (2 vols.)	3,000	3,150	June 1859
5 (2 vols.)	3,000	3,150	July 1859
6 (2 vols.)	2,000	2,100	September 1859
7 (2 vols.)	2,000	2,124	November 1859
8 (2 vols.)	1,000	1,004	June 1860
9 (2 vols.)	500[6]	502	June 1861
TOTAL	14,750	15,446	

By April 1861, with the publication of *Silas Marner*, Eliot had four works in
print. This number was sufficient to lead Blackwoods to plan a series of her
works that would include a one-volume *Adam Bede* at 6*s*. The title page
called this the 'Tenth Edition'. It was published 31 January 1862; 3,000
copies were ordered and 3,018 printed.[7] This edition was stereotyped and
electrotyped, and from that point until the Cabinet edition of 1878 the
firm's use of 'edition' refers to impressions from the plates.[8] The tenth
edition was followed by two more at the same price, 6*s.*, in 1864 and 1866,
with the following print runs:

type. In most cases, the entire text was reset. The exceptions are the 3rd edition, which used a
quantity of type left standing from the 2nd, and the 5th, which used 112 pages of type left
standing from the 4th.

[6] This number is not stated in the ledger but can be inferred from the details on cost. The
actual number printed, 502, *is* listed in NLS MS 30,860.

[7] NLS MS 30,860, fo. 213, shows October 1861 as the date when the print order
was made and the copies printed. However, the firm did not receive Eliot's corrected
copy of the 8th edition until late October, and the new edition did not appear until January
1862.

[8] In correspondence as well as on the title page of the 1867 illustrated edition, Blackwoods
used the term *stereotyped* to include both stereotyping and electrotyping. Where the term
stereotyped is used below, it should be understood to include both.

Edition	Number ordered to print	Number printed	Month/year of publication
10 (1 vol.)	3,000	3,018	January 1862
11 [9]	1,000	1,008	March 1864
12	500	500	August 1866
TOTAL	4,500	4,526	

In 1866, after Eliot returned to the firm with *Felix Holt*, following publication of *Romola* by Smith Elder, Blackwoods projected a new, even cheaper series of her works. The plates from 1862 were used again, this time for the seven parts of a serialized, illustrated *Adam Bede*, the first part of which appeared in April 1867. Although the serial publication at 6*d*. per number was a failure, the sheets were bound and sold for years afterward as an illustrated one-volume edition at 3*s*. 6*d*. Blackwoods' publication ledger MS 30,861 gives no annual breakdown of sales either of parts or of the one-volume illustrated edition for the years 1867 to 1874. It does show, however, that a total of 41,881 individual numbers of the thirty illustrated parts of *Adam Bede* and the other four works were sold during this period. The printing record indicates that 33,281 parts out of 56,069 printed were parts of *Adam Bede*, although it does not necessarily follow that over half the sales were of that novel. The number of copies of *Adam Bede* printed dropped from 13,000 for part 1 to 3,500 by part 3, and 2,000 by parts 6 and 7. Even assuming that early buyers were more numerous than 2,000 and some simply failed to complete their sets with the final numbers, the sales for *Adam Bede*'s seven parts altogether probably did not exceed 20,000, although there is no way to be certain.

As one volume in cloth at 3*s*. 6*d*., the illustrated *Adam Bede* fared better, selling 17,299 copies, including exports of 878 volumes, from 1867 to the middle of 1874. In addition, another 764 were sold in sheets for binding by individuals. The number actually printed is difficult to compute from the records, because some of the unsold sheets intended for part issue were used in bound volumes. From 1 July 1874, however, records are again available year by year, and the part-issue figures of 1,174 on hand are simply carried over until after Eliot's death in December 1880.

---

[9] I have been unable to locate a copy of the 1864 reimpression, which the firm evidently regarded as the 11th 'edition', given that the next reprint, in 1866, is called the 'Twelfth Edition' on the title page. Bibliographer J. C. Ross believes that the 1864 printing used the title page of the 10th, since the firm's ledger books list no costs that would indicate setting of a new title page, nor can this printing be found in library data bases (J. C. Ross, private e-mail correspondence with editor of the Clarendon *Adam Bede*). In contrast, the records for the 1866 impression include 'Electroing New Titlepage' (NLS MS 30,860, fo. 430). This title page not only specifies the 'Twelfth Edition', but also bears a new date, MDCCCLXVI.

Sales of the 3s. 6d. edition from 1867 to the close of the fiscal year[1] in June 1881 are:

Year (July–June)		Printed[2]	To boarding[3]	Sales in cloth[4]	Sales in sheets[5]
1867–74		[?18,063][6]	17,650	17,299	764
1874–5		2,100	3,041	2,808	
1875–6	June[7]	2,100			
	Dec.	2,100	2,800	3,109	190
1876–7	Sept.[8]	1,050			
	Nov.	1,575			
	Feb.	3,150	5,773	5,662	293
1877–8	Oct.	4,200	4,125	3,846	321
1878–9	Oct.78	3,150			
	Aug. 79	3,150	3,750		
			1,350	5,499	72
1879–80	Apr.	3,150	3,285	2,827	154
1880–1	Nov.	3,150	2,907[9]		
	Feb.	4,200			
	Mar.	4,200	8,975	12,016	470
Total 1867–74		[?18,063]	17,650	17,299	764
Total 1874–81		37,275	36,006	35,767	1,500

[1] The 'year' in Blackwoods' ledgers runs from 1 July to 30 June. After 1866, edition numbers for the stereotyped reprints are no longer given, and the title pages do not bear dates. The 1867 edition's title page includes the words 'Stereotyped Edition'. When the title page was redone for the 1873 cheap edition (2s. 6d.), this designation was replaced by 'A New Edition', which was also used on subsequent illustrated editions at 3s. 6d. The number printed in a given year is generally stated in the ledger as 'Since printed' or 'Printed Since'; the boarding and sales figures give an idea of peaks of demand and are included on this chart.

[2] This is given in the ledger book as number of 'Imp', or impressions from the stereo plates.

[3] The number for boarding is sometimes higher than the number printed because the year's inventory began with copies on hand. For example, 1,042 copies are listed as 'Onhand' in July 1874, with 2,100 'Printed Since'.

[4] This figure includes both domestic and export sales.

[5] This is, of course, distinct from sales in instalments; sales in sheets were made to purchasers who wished to have the book bound specially rather than in the standard cloth covers generally used. No figure for sales in sheets is given for 1874–5.

[6] This figure, 18,063, is the total of the number sold in volumes (17,299) and the number sold in sheets (764). The exact number printed cannot be determined, because the records for the period 1867 to 1874 are not as detailed as those of some other years, but obviously it had to be at least 18,063. The number given for boarding and the sales figures help to place the period 1867 to 1874 in the context of other printing and sales records.

[7] Months are listed here according to the order they appear in the ledger entry for the year, not, as in this case, according to the chronological sequence of months from 1 July to 30 June. It is possible that the reference to 'June' indicates June of 1875. The ledger books are not always exact in listing all relevant data under the correct heading. For example, an impression of 3,150 copies is given as 'Aug 79' under the heading 'Eliot's Works 1878–9' on p. 101 of this ledger.

[8] The success of Daniel Deronda, appearing in parts February to September 1876, stimulated demand, just as Middlemarch led to the 2s. 6d. edition of Adam Bede in 1873.

[9] No date is listed for the two instances of 'Boarding' in 1880–1. However, given the number of new impressions printed, one can surmise that the first figure accompanied the

Figures for sales of the 3s. 6d. edition during Eliot's lifetime cannot be determined precisely, because there is no record of sales as of 22 December 1880. Of the 12,016 sold in cloth and the 470 sold in sheets for 1880–1, the majority were obviously purchased after the author's death on that date. Some of the 2,907 boarded in November may have been taken up in the Christmas trade, but, since the first two printings of 1881 (4,200 each) were not run until February and March, there were probably some bound copies remaining in early 1881 to satisfy immediate demand.

To the stereotyped edition's sales figures for the period 1867–80 must be added those of another edition from the plates of 1862. What was called 'A New Edition' of 3,150 copies was printed from these same plates in 1873. Without the illustrations, and printed on cheaper paper, it sold for 2s. 6d., alongside the 3s. 6d. illustrated edition.

Adam Bede appeared for the last time during the author's life as volumes IV and V of the Cabinet edition, in March and April 1878, with an initial print run of 1,050 copies. Another 525 copies were printed in May 1879 for a total print run of 1,575.

The printing figures for *Adam Bede* in volumes from 1859 to 1880 are:

Year(s)	Format	Editions (title page listing)	Price	Number printed
1859	3 vols.	1, 2, 3	31s. 6d.	3,416
1859–61	2 vols.	4, 5, 6, 7, 8, 9	12s.	12,030
1862–6	1 vol.	10, [?11], 12	6s.	4,526
1867–74	1 vol.	—	3s. 6d.	[18,063][1]
1874–80	1 vol.	—	3s. 6d.	37,275
1873	1 vol.	'A New Edition'	2s. 6d.	3,150
1878–9	2 vols.	'Cabinet'	10s.	1,575
Total copies printed:				80,035

The First Edition: *Adam Bede* in Three Volumes

Despite the predictions and assurances that John and William Blackwood made to the author, the rapidity of sales took the firm by surprise. As a result, they were uncertain how soon to issue a cheaper edition in two volumes. On 16 March John Blackwood reported to Eliot that 2,090 copies of the first edition were printed:[2] 'with the aid of the insatiable Mudie we have disposed of upwards of 1800, so a second edition is now a certainty.[3]

printing of November 1880. Eliot's death on 22 December obviously stimulated sales so that two print runs of 4,200 each correspond roughly to a boarding figure (also including sheets already on hand) of 8,975 in March 1881.

[1] Inferred from sales records, as discussed above.

[2] The records of the firm show a print order of 2,000 for the 1st edition, with 2,101 actually printed (NLS MS 30,859).

[3] William Blackwood wrote to Langford on 28 Mar. 1860 that Mudie had taken 1,500 copies of the three-volume editions of *Adam Bede*, including 225 in May, i.e. of the 3rd edition (NLS MS 4146, fos. 164–5).

The question is in what form should it be: 2 volumes small 8° 12/ or another short edition in the present shape. The two vol. 12/- must be the form one day even as intermediate to a people's edition for which I have a strong inclination so I think we had better set about printing the two volume edition at once to be ready.'[4]

Both Eliot and Lewes responded on 17 March. She is tentative: 'As to the question of the editions, I am not a good opinion—but I enclose the suggestions of a more experienced judge. I concur in what he says, only that I attach more weight to the possibility of the present edition vanishing too quickly for the immediate production of the cheaper one. Still, I really know nothing about it.'[5] Lewes is firm, and more precise:

> Respecting the edition or editions, as I am referred to, I suggest this. By all means print the 2 volumes at 12/—that will be ready, and is certain to be wanted sooner or later. But as printing small editions is very expensive—a ruinous proceeding in most cases—I should only do that if the demand made it imperative. My view of the case is this: with a history, or biography, which is purchased by private persons, there is an obvious unfairness to the purchasers of the first expensive edition, in rapidly bringing out a cheap edition—or rather there is the *appearance* of unfairness, since in point of fact a publisher is at liberty to affix his own price. But in the case of a novel, almost exclusively purchased by the libraries, this does not obtain. The libraries *prefer* three volumes, and they never take a copy more than they are forced to take. Many libraries can't afford 31/6, which would gladly give 12/- and thus accommodate subscribers. Then too private persons gladly purchase a book which has delighted them, if at 12/-. *Voilà!*[6]

Once again the typesetting became part of the deliberations. In a letter to Langford on 14 March, John Blackwood had written, 'We are puzzling as to how we should reprint if that becomes necessary immediately. It must either be in the present form or 2 vols. ⟨poss⟩ sm. 8° 12/. I had ordered the type to be kept up but it was required & taken down but the setting of a 3 vol novel does not come to much.'[7] Even as late as 25 March he seems doubtful as to whether another three-volume edition will be needed, writing again to Langford that 'The present [i.e. first] edition of Adam Bede will I suspect last until we can bring out a 12/- edition.'[8] On 27 March he wrote to Eliot and Lewes that 'If the dregs of the first edition go off very quickly I suppose we must treat the public to another 3 volume edition.'[9]

---

[4] *Letters*, III. 33.   [5] *Letters*, III. 34.   [6] *Letters*, III. 36.

[7] NLS MS 4135, fos. 164–5. The part of this letter quoted here is reproduced, with slight variation, in *Letters*, III. 33 n. 7.

[8] NLS MS 4135, fos. 168–9.

[9] *Letters*, III. 33. Stereotyping was already in use by Blackwoods, but John and William Blackwood undoubtedly knew that it would have been a risk to stereotype the first three-volume novel of a relatively unknown author. The method was more frequently used for educational books, including scientific and philosophical works for which moderate demand might continue for months and years. John Blackwood, for instance, had proposed it to Lewes

Blackwood had made up his mind by 30 March. Sending Eliot a copy of Maga's review of *Adam Bede*, he informed her:

The demand for Adam goes on and we have decided to print a short edition in the present form. Mudie wishes 100 more but Mr. Langford has only given him 50 as the stock is running low. The Magazine Review is calculated to tell on the circulation more than any puff, however enthusiastic. From what I hear too I expect that there will be Reviews in other influential quarters, so on the whole I think it was best to reprint in the present form.

Tell Lewes however that I perfectly agree with his views about the reprints of books according to their character. Indeed his views are identical with my own.[1]

Eliot responded immediately, asking that Blackwood 'convey my gratitude to your reviewer' and showing that, despite her purported unwillingness to read reviews, she knew what they contained: 'The review in the "Universal" is better written than usual, and contains some good critical remarks. It will help the sale of the second edition, if the magazines and quarterlies will take up the book, and I shall be anxious to know that the new five hundred move off the shelves.'[2] Eliot's journal for 26 March records a conversation that Lewes had with Langford, who said 'they will print 500 [copies]: whether Mudie takes more or not they will have sold all by the end of a month'.[3] This number was increased to a print order of 750, with a print run of 788, according to the publications ledger.[4] The edition was advertised as the 'second' in the *Athenaeum* on 16 April (No. 1642, p. 529) and listed in the *Publishers' Circular* among the books published between 14 and 30 April.

Issuing another 'edition' in three volumes meant a hurried resetting, with the inevitable introduction of errors. Since the type from the first edition had been taken down, the second printing was not simply a new impression but a new typesetting that the firm called the 'second edition' on the title page. This 'second edition' differs from the first in numerous variants. Some are errors that compositors introduced, including the use of *vale* for *veil* in Chapter IX[5] and *here* for *hear* in Chapter XVIII.[6] Compositors also corrected errors in the first edition, altering, for instance, *hairbrained* to the correct spelling, *harebrained*, in Chapter XVI.[7]

---

on 15 November 1858 for *The Physiology of Common Life*: 'We propose to stereotype the book as selling in numbers; the stock would not otherwise be kept square, but when a new and revised edition was called for, we would break up the plates' (*Letters*, VIII. 213). Having come to recognize Eliot's selling power, the firm did, however, stereotype both the first three-volume edition of her next work, *The Mill on the Floss*, and the first two-volume edition.

[1] *Letters*, III. 39–40.   [2] *Letters*, III. 40–1.   [3] *JGE* 300.
[4] NLS MS 30,859, fos. 380–1.
[5] MS I. ⟨143⟩/156: *veil*. 1st edn., I. 183: *veil*. 2nd and 3rd edns., I. 183: *vale*.
[6] MS II. 26: *hear*. 1st edn., II. 33: *hear*. 2nd and 3rd edns., II. 33: *here*.
[7] MS I. 262: *hare-brained*. 1st edn., I. 309: *hairbrained*. 2nd and 3rd edns., I. 309: *harebrained*.

After E. S. Dallas's review appeared in *The Times* on 12 April, John Blackwood wrote to Eliot that its

> effect on the second edition was instantaneous. Mr. Langford who has been bewailing my recklessness in printing 750, now writes wildly to send up the whole impression. What the exact sale is I do not know. I fancy over 400, but Lewes who has been in the Row will have seen. The demand seems so brisk that we have given orders to reprint again. There is about a volume in type.[8]

That same day Major William Blackwood wrote to Langford about plans for a third edition in three volumes:

> The accounts of the demand for Adam Bede are very gratifying, and there can be little doubt but that edition number 2 will be out of print very soon. We have got the type of one volume standing, and have ordered the remainder to be set up again immediately. When the public attention is once fairly attracted to such a book its sale must be very great. I have not heard of a single person who has read it who has not expressed perfect satisfaction with it. [James] Syme the eminent Surgeon here and Professor [James Y.] Simpson are as warm in their eulogy of it as Theodore Martin, so that we may calculate on every reader who is attracted to the book by the Times still further extending it's [*sic*] reputation.[9]

The order may have been given, but as late as 22 April, when Major Blackwood wrote again to Langford, the firm was still hesitating:

> We have not yet put the 3d edition of Adam Bede to press and are in some doubts about it, ⟨The⟩ so if you can give any further information tomorrow it will be very acceptable. Though its readers will be as numerous as those of 'What Will,' my brother feels that the libraries have had much more time with Adam & that one copy of it will have done much duty.[1]

Perhaps recognizing that John Blackwood's doubt whether libraries would buy more copies in three volumes was behind the firm's hesitation, Langford replied that

> Adam Bede is still vigorous in sale. Hamiltons have had 10 and Whittakers 6 to day we have sold ⟨altoget⟩ about 90 this week. I think the present form will go 500 more, indeed I do not know why we should not sell 3500 in 3 vols. I would however get a cheap edition ready at once in whatever form you may decide upon—it would sell immensely at 6/- like Lady Lee—and publish it as soon as Mudie puts the book on his cheap list.[2]

On 26 April, he wrote again to Major Blackwood that the sale 'continues with unabated vigour'.[3] This report seems to have settled the question. 'The sale of Adam goes on and the 750 are pretty well exhausted now. 500 more are being got ready to supply the public appetite which it is to be

---

[8] 16 Apr. 1859; *Letters*, III. 51.   [9] *Letters*, VIII. 231–2.
[1] NLS MS 4136, fos. 9–10.   [2] 23 Apr.; NLS MS 4140, fos. 82–3.
[3] Ibid. 86–7.

hoped will continue healthy and good,' John Blackwood reported to Eliot on 27 April.[4] The print order for the third edition was 500 copies; the actual print run was 527.[5] The *Athenaeum* advertised it as 'now ready' on 7 May (No. 1645, p. 624), and the *Publishers' Circular* listed it among the books published between 30 April and 14 May. William Blackwood wrote to Eliot that it was published on 2 May.[6] John Blackwood had earlier referred to this print run as a reprint, but both advertisements and the title page call it the Third Edition. With nearly a volume remaining in type, this was a hybrid, partly an impression of the second edition and partly a resetting.

Adam Bede in Two Volumes

In the same letter to Eliot on 27 April announcing a third edition in three volumes, John Blackwood informed her that a two-volume edition to meet new demand would be published when the three-volume copies were exhausted.[7] He therefore asked her to let him know 'if you wish to make any alterations or corrections'.[8] Eliot responded:

There is *one* alteration or rather one addition—merely of a sentence—that I wish to make in the 12s/. edition of 'Adam Bede.' It is a sentence in the chapter where Adam is making the coffin at night, and hears the willow wand. Some readers seem not to have understood what I meant, namely—that it was in Adam's peasant blood and nurture to believe in this, and that he narrated it with awed belief to his dying day. That is not a fancy of my own brain, but a matter of observation, and is in my mind an important feature in Adam's character.[9]

The passage from Chapter IV that she wished to alter reads in the first edition: 'yet he believed in dreams and prognostics, and you see he shuddered at the idea of the stroke with the willow wand.'[1] Eliot added, 'There is nothing else I wish to touch. I will send you the sentence some day soon, with the page where it is to be inserted.'[2] She was reminded of the promised correction when she received William Blackwood's letter of 5 May, reporting that 'the sale of Adam still goes on to admiration. We published another edition, the 3d, of 500 copies on Monday [2 May] and have disposed of almost 400. This makes a total sale of over 3000, a result which should assure even your self distrusting spirit of the value of your

---

[4] *Letters*, III. 57.   [5] NLS MS 30,859.   [6] *Letters*, III. 65.

[7] In retrospect the firm realized that they had acted too hastily. William Blackwood acknowledged to Langford on 28 Mar. 1860 when the firm was considering publication plans for *The Mill on the Floss*: 'We published the 12/ edition of Adam Bede sooner than we think we should have done for our own interest, having then only the comparatively limited sale of the author's previous work Clerical Scenes to guide us. We cannot however see that Mr. Mudie suffered by our doing so; the large numbers he took of the 12/ edition showed that he had not near enough of the 3 vol. edition wherewith to supply his readers' (*Letters*, III. 283).

[8] *Letters*, III. 58.   [9] 29 Apr.; *Letters*, III. 60.

[1] *Adam Bede*, 1st edn., I. 87. The altered version first appeared in the 4th edition, I. 68–9.

[2] *Letters*, III. 60.

work.'[3] The day she must have received this letter, 6 May, she sent William, rather than John, her customary correspondent, the 'correction for the two-volume edition of "Adam"—which I unhappily forgot until this morning'.[4] Beginning with the fourth edition, the first in two volumes, the substituted passage reads: 'yet he believed in dreams and prognostics, and to his dying day he bated his breath a little when he told the story of the stroke with the willow wand. I tell it as he told it, not attempting to reduce it to its natural elements: in our eagerness to explain impressions, we often lose our hold of the sympathy that comprehends them.'

John Chapman's notice in the *Westminster Review*, the only one to question the willow wand incident before Eliot's letter of 29 April, probably led her to make this alteration. Discussing the novel's 'faithful realism', Chapman observes that 'The introduction of the supernatural incident on the night when Thias Bede was drowned is, in our opinion, a disfigurement.'[5] Chapman, of course, knew Eliot's espousal of realism in fiction from the many essays she published in the *Westminster Review* from 1851 to 1857. And, although Eliot and Lewes were displeased that he had spread the rumour about the identity of 'George Eliot' in autumn 1858 and was now taking advantage of his special knowledge by pretending, in this *Westminster* notice, to detect the woman writer, they would have recognized the validity of Chapman's opinion.[6] Eliot's alteration clarifies the relationship of this passage to her theory of realism. The willow wand incident represents not the novelist's endorsement of a supernatural incident but Adam's complexity as a character. In keeping with his peasant roots, he believes in folk superstitions, and in keeping with his trade as carpenter and builder, he is a practical, forward-looking man with a head for mathematics.

On 18 May, John Blackwood sent a specimen sheet for the two-volume edition,[7] and soon afterward arrived in London himself. He dined with Eliot and Lewes on 27 May and 'brought an amusing correspondence about the authorship of Adam Bede, which is the great literary mystery of the day. It appears that subscriptions of money have actually been set on foot [for] Liggins, the supposed author. Blackwood urged that the secret [of the authorship] should stedfastly be kept, at least until after the next book.'[8] The Liggins matter proved to be anything but amusing. Joseph Liggins, 'son of a baker at Attleborough, who had been rusticated from Cam-

---

[3] *Letters*, III. 65.   [4] *Letters*, III. 66.   [5] NS 15 (Apr. 1859), 510.
[6] In a letter to John Blackwood on 1 April, Lewes 'observe[d] the West. Rev. has a long article on "Adam Bede." The more the merrier' (*Letters*, VIII. 230). From the light-hearted nature of his comment, it is evident that when he wrote to Blackwood he had not yet read it. His journal records that he 'looked over' this review at breakfast on 1 April. He 'read' it the next day (JGHL XI, 1859–66). Years later Chapman's conduct still rankled. See Eliot's letter to Sara Hennell, 23 Apr. 1862 (*Letters*, IV. 26).
[7] *Letters*, III. 67.   [8] GHL Journal, qtd. in *Letters*, III. 73.

bridge',[9] had first been put forward as the author of *Scenes of Clerical Life* in June 1857, as readers in Warwickshire recognized the locale and the originals of some of the characters. After *Adam Bede* appeared, a letter from one of his supporters, Henry Smith Anders, was published in *The Times* on 13 April 1859. Lewes responded with a denial in Eliot's name, which was published on 16 April.[1] But neither Lewes's letter nor one from William Blackwood & Sons[2] could lay the imposture to rest in summer 1859, largely because Liggins's claim was taken up by Charles Holte Bracebridge, whom Haight calls 'a muddle-headed magistrate of Atherstone',[3] and who did not renounce his belief in Liggins until October.[4] By July Eliot had declared herself sick of it, and asked her correspondent, Charles Bray, to 'Take no more trouble about me—and let every one believe—as they will in spite of all your kind efforts—*what they like to believe*.'[5] Meanwhile, the true identity of the author was becoming known in literary London, and Eliot and Lewes were confronted with a difficult decision, to acknowledge her authorship or to try to keep it secret as the Blackwoods urged them to do.

Despite the excellent sales of the three-volume editions and Langford's expectations of a 'rapid sale' for the new two-volume edition,[6] George Simpson was cautious about sales in this cheaper 12s. format. He believed that by the autumn *Adam Bede* would go into a cheaper, 5s. edition: 'for my part I incline to 2 vols & think 1000 copies should be the basis of your agreement [with Eliot], because as soon as we issue a five shillings Adam Bede the Sale of the other Book will stop, & a 5/- A.B. will I fancy appear early in Autumn. I am on tenter-hooks to hear the result of the Sub^{crt} [subscription, for the two-volume edition].'[7] John Blackwood sent a note to Eliot on 10 June, 'You will be delighted to hear that the opening of the subscription to the new edition of Adam Bede is very promising nearly 1000 on the Row. I have ordered some copies to be sent to you and hope you will like the appearance of the book.'[8]

The print order for this edition, called the fourth on the title page, was 3,000 copies; the actual number printed was 3,150. It was first advertised in the *Athenaeum* on 4 June 1859, as a 'CHEAPER EDITION In Two Volumes, price Twelve Shillings' (No. 1649, p. 756). The *Publishers' Circular* included it among books published from 31 May to 14 June. This edition too sold with greater rapidity than anticipated. Within two weeks, 2,000 of the 3,150 copies were gone. The edition was not stereotyped, but 112 pages were still in forme when the firm realized they had underestimated demand. On 20 June William Blackwood wrote to his brother, in London:

[9] Haight, 244.   [1] *Letters*, III. 50.
[2] Published in *The Times* on 6 June 1859; reprinted *Letters*, III. 74–5.
[3] Haight, 284.   [4] See *Letters*, III. 179.   [5] *Letters*, III. 110.
[6] 3 June 1859; NLS MS 4140, fos. 91–2.   [7] 8 June 1859; NLS MS 4143, fos. 20–1.
[8] *Letters*, III. 81.

Mr. Simpson thinks we ought to get ready another edition of 2000 of Adam Bede, and that this is Langford's opinion too. By the latter's letter to me of Friday 2000 were accounted for as gone here and in London and I thought the remaining 1000 would keep us in hand for a time. However as it will take 3 weeks to get an edition ready with comfort to the printing office it is a matter for consideration to go to press at once, especially as 112 pp. of the last are still in form and keeping them up interferes with the new edition of Clerical Scenes.[9] If the demand has been continued today in London I should think we are quite safe in another edition.[1]

William wrote again on 23 June: 'You have said nothing about a new edition of Adam Bede. From the demand today from Langford we think we are safe in going for another 2000 & so releasing the ⟨sheets⟩ types now set & have ordered accordingly.'[2] His brother responded immediately, 'I thought I had said to go on printing Adam[3]—I think you may venture on 3000. Hamiltons offered today to take any number we liked if we would give 25/24 to this half. I told Langford to indulge them and he will probably tell you the number. I am going out to see the author tomorrow.'[4] This edition, called the fifth on the title page, was the second in two volumes; again the print order was 3,000, with 3,150 copies printed.[5] It was advertised as 'A New Edition, being the FIFTH' in the *Athenaeum* on 16 July 1859 (No. 1655, p. 93), and was included in the *Publishers' Circular* list of books published from 15 to 30 July.

In a letter 23 July, after she and Lewes returned from Switzerland, Eliot told Blackwood that she had 'carried away with me the comfort of knowing

---

[9] Plans for the two-volume *Adam Bede* included a companion volume of *Scenes of Clerical Life*, whose sales, it was anticipated, would be stimulated by the success of *Adam Bede*. On 8 June William Blackwood sent his brother calculations for *Scenes* 'uniform in two volumes with Adam Bede' and also 'in one volume of the same size'. William adds, however, that he does not think the one-volume format 'will do—it leaves so small a profit and will not make a nice volume. I think the two volumes should do, but after the subscription for the two volume edition of Adam Bede we shall be able to judge better. Slip leaf announcing this edition of Clerical Scenes should be put in every copy of the other book, Mr. Simpson says. This should be got ready in London' (*Letters*, III. 80).

[1] *Letters*, III. 89.   [2] NLS MS 4136, fos. 54–5.

[3] This comment probably refers to John's undated 1859 letter to his brother, headed 'P.N. Row Friday', in which the former wrote, 'Adam Bede is going so fast that I think we shall need to reprint' (NLS MS 4135, fos. 303–4). Internal evidence suggests that this letter was written on Friday, 17 June 1859. The letter refers to Simpson's legal business in London on behalf of the firm: John has not 'seen Simpson today but [I] understand from Langford that he is in great feather and expects to finish everything with Dobie [counsel for the firm] today'. William Blackwood's 20 June letter indicates that Simpson was back in Edinburgh by then. John Blackwood also 'project[s] a visit to Wimbledon' (Lewes and Eliot) 'today' and refers to 'a glorious day yesterday' about which his wife Julia may have written—probably a reference to Ascot, which they attended on 16 June. If such a visit occurred on 17 June, it is not mentioned in Eliot's or Lewes's journals. It is possible that Blackwood was prevented from going. Lewes's journal does note the visit on 25 June to which Blackwood refers in his letter of the previous day (III. 92): 'Blackwood came to lunch full of the novels, of course' (JGHL XI, 1859–66).

[4] 24 June 1859; *Letters*, III. 92.   [5] NLS MS 30,859, fos. 380–1.

that 5000 of Adam had gone in a fortnight'.[6] Her elation at this figure is
evident in two other letters she wrote that day, one to Barbara Bodichon
('The 4th edition of "Adam Bede" (5000) sold in a fortnight!'[7]) and the
other to Charles Bray ('The fourth edition of Adam Bede (5000) was sold in
a fortnight, and the publishers were scouring London for spare copies to
meet pressing orders while the 5th edition was being prepared'[8]). The
figure came from Lewes, whose journal for 9 July records: 'Before leaving I
learned from Langford the amazing news that the 4th edition of "Adam
Bede" was already out of print—5,000 copies in a fortnight—and the fever
still at its height.'[9] The number 5,000 does not correspond to any figure in
the firm's ledgers or letters. Lewes must have conflated Langford's discussion of sales of the fourth edition with his expectations of sales of the
fifth. Later in the year this misunderstanding was to exacerbate friction
between Eliot and Lewes and the firm.

Sales continued vigorously. If there were any readers who had not yet
heard *Adam Bede*'s praises, Anne Mozley's thoughtful and enthusiastic
review in *Bentley's Quarterly Review* for July probably sent them to buy or
borrow the new, cheap edition. By August it was obvious that yet another
edition would be necessary. On 13 August Langford wrote that 'You are
quite right to reprint Adam Bede, selling as it is at present,'[1] and ten days
later he noted that 'Both Adam Bede and Clerical Scenes are doing
excellently indeed the former seems to be moving beyond the ⟨b⟩ libraries
as well as ever and your next 2000 will be speedily wanted.'[2] On 3 September Langford reported 'unabated' demand: 'we shall have a good subscription for the new edition.'[3] A print order of 2,000 produced 2,100 copies of
the sixth edition.[4] This edition was not advertised in the *Athenaeum*. The
explanation can be found in Langford's letter of 13 September: 'You will
see that I am not advertising Adam Bede. The sale is going on so well that it
seems really not worthwhile to spend money on it—particularly as there
must be a good many of the fifth edition about the retail trade and
advertising the sixth might injure the sale of those. In a week or two it
will be as well perhaps to have a round of advertisements.'[5] In fact, no
further advertisement appears in the *Athenaeum* until 17 December. Continued strong sales made advertising an unnecessary expense, and the
controversy over the incognito and Eliot's (lack of) response to the firm's
offer of an extra payment for *Adam Bede* cooled relations between the
Blackwoods and Eliot in autumn 1859. The sixth edition was listed in

[6] *Letters*, III. 118.   [7] *Letters*, III. 119.   [8] *Letters*, III. 120.
[9] *Letters*, III. 118 n. 4. Eliot's journal for 21 July records the same information: 'Before we
set off we had heard the excellent news that the fourth edition of Adam Bede (5000) had all been
sold in a fortnight.' Her entry adds, 'The fifth edition appeared last week' (*JGE* 79).
[1] NLS MS 4140, fos. 99–100.   [2] 23 Aug.; NLS MS 4140, fos. 103–4.
[3] Ibid. 105–8.   [4] NLS MS 30,859.   [5] NLS MS 4140, fos. 109–10.

the *Publishers' Circular* among books published from 31 August to 14 September.

As autumn approached, the truth about the authorship was spreading. As early as May and June, the firm was apprehensive about rumours. On 31 May 1859 William Blackwood wrote to his brother, 'I am not surprised at G.E.s secret having leaked out but as long as he does not let on himself rumours are not of much consequence. People wont believe them either. It is ⟨only⟩ an absurd story like that of Liggins gets the most general credence.'[6] Langford wrote to William Blackwood on 13 June[7] that 'Mr Crawley [who worked for the firm] heard a curious story in the City about the authorship—that these books were written by a lady who lives with Mr Lewes "a very clever woman." I should be sorry for such a notion to get about.'[8] By September, Langford noted, 'The Adam Bede secret seems to be known by every body. It is a great pity they could not keep it,'[9] but ten days later he was reassured about the effect on sales: 'The authorship of Adam seems now pretty generally known in London but the avidity of the public is evidently not at all diminished and the present edition [i.e. the sixth] will I have no doubt go rapidly out of print.'[1]

Relations between Eliot and the Blackwoods were not going as well as sales of *Adam Bede*. John Blackwood proposed to publish Eliot's next novel, *The Mill on the Floss*, anonymously in *Blackwood's Edinburgh Magazine*, suggesting that anonymous publication would provide the 'excitement of uncertainty',[2] a tactless comment which reached Eliot and Lewes in the midst of continued harassment by Liggins supporter Charles Holte Bracebridge. Eliot rejected Blackwood's proposal.[3] On their part, John and William Blackwood felt that Eliot was unappreciative of the extra payment they planned to give her because of *Adam Bede*'s unexpected success. Underlying these anxieties was disagreement about revealing the true authorship. Nonetheless, after William Blackwood advised that they had only 450 copies to meet 'an order from Paternoster Row for more Adam Bede' and suggested they 'go to press with 2000 more',[4] his brother wrote diplomatically to Eliot and Lewes, 'I am happy to tell you that Adam Bede still goes on selling and we have ordered another edition of 2000 to be printed. It is a grand success and a deserved one.'[5] The publication ledger and the title page call this the seventh edition; 2,000 copies were ordered and 2,124 printed in November 1859.[6] The *Publishers' Circular*

---

[6] NLS MS 4136, fos. 23–4.

[7] This letter is torn in the lower left corner of the last page, so that only 'Blackwood' shows; the addressee is likely to be William rather than John, since the former was the recipient of most of Langford's letters and John Blackwood is usually followed by Esq.

[8] NLS MS 4140, fos. 95–6.   [9] 3 Sept.; NLS MS 4140, fos. 105–8.

[1] Ibid. 109–10.   [2] *Letters*, III. 161.   [3] *Letters*, III. 161–2.

[4] 5 Oct. 1859; *Letters*, III. 172.   [5] 14 Oct.; *Letters*, III. 182.

[6] NLS MS 30,859, fos. 380–1.

lists this edition among the books published from 31 October to 14 November.

The prospect of this edition was probably the impetus for Eliot to call to John Blackwood's attention additional errors in the early editions:

> The other day, happening to take up the 2 volume edition of 'Adam,' I read on a good way, and shuddered not a little, every now and then, to find how many misprints had crept even into this first of the 2 volume editions. Unless something can be done to refresh the official Reader's care, the text will become corrupt to an extent that will really mar many passages of the book. Conceive an author's feelings at finding such changes as 'vale' for 'veil,' making him guilty of bad metaphors! Will you 'sharpen it into' the right persons, that in correcting the press a copy of the *first 3* volume edition must be used, and that great care must be taken of the dialect, though this is less vital than nouns and verbs. Still it is a blemish, to see such things as 'theed'st' constantly printed for 'thee'dst.'[7]

John Blackwood replied that 'The printers have been sorely reprimanded for the blunders in the recent editions of Adam of which I was sorry to hear. You may rely upon them all being put straight now. The blunders in the "dialect" arise no doubt from the compositors thinking that there is no "dialect" in the world except Scotch.'[8]

Eliot's letter of 16 October was the first one Blackwood received with the signature 'Marian Evans Lewes', a sign that the authorship was no longer to be a secret. She had written three briefer notes to Langford on 6, 10, and 13 October with this signature, but these seem not to have come to William Blackwood's notice. Forwarding her letter to his brother, William commented 'I am rather sorry to see the change of signature', and, showing how sales and the authorship question were linked in their minds, added 'On the whole I think you may be as well without the new tale for Maga.'[9] But this revelation did not alter the brothers' determination to treat the author fairly. On 27 October John Blackwood informed her of their intention to pay not £400 but £800 as her 'further pecuniary share in the triumph of Adam',[1] doubling the amount he had promised in May,[2] when she had replied with a warm acknowledgement of their 'fine integrity which makes part of my faith in you'.[3] Her response in October was more subdued.[4] Even John Blackwood, her strongest supporter and friend in the firm, referred to his 'disgust' at her '*cool* note',[5] and George Simpson, writing to Langford in November, expressed unguardedly his disapprobation for her 'inordinately greedy' disposition, her 'insatiable greed', and her 'avaricious soul'.[6] Lewes and Eliot's response was coloured by their misunderstanding of Langford's report in July, which led them to believe that 5,000

[7] 16 Oct.; *Letters*, III. 184.   [8] 27 Oct.; *Letters*, III. 190.
[9] *Letters*, III. 188.   [1] *Letters*, III. 190.   [2] See *Letters*, III. 67–8.
[3] *Letters*, III. 69.   [4] See *Letters*, III. 191–2.   [5] 30 Oct.; *Letters*, III. 192.
[6] *Letters*, III. 194, 200, 205.

copies of the fourth edition had been sold. With three more two-volume editions published or in press, Blackwood's generosity did not seem extraordinary.[7] Amity returned following Eliot's frank letter to John Blackwood on 30 November,[8] and his visit to the Leweses in London in December, after which he wrote to his brother for 'a memo of the exact numbers printed of Adam Bede I think they have an over estimate of this. They think there was an edition of 5000 but I do not.'[9]

In the midst of the tension, the firm continued to seek new ways of putting *Adam Bede* before the public. On 12 November, Simpson wrote Langford: 'Be prepared to advise whether cheap Edition shall be 6/, 5/ or 2/6. I am hankering for another 2000 in 2 volumes as a Library Edition à la Bulwer.'[1] The question seems to have been mooted when Blackwoods and Eliot reached agreement on *The Mill on the Floss*. Although Eliot urged John Blackwood to publish a cheap edition of *Scenes of Clerical Life* before the cheap edition of *Adam Bede*,[2] he decided to delay both to avoid interfering with sales of *The Mill on the Floss*. Instead, the firm planned another 12s. edition of *Scenes of Clerical Life*, despite its being a poor plan 'pecuniarily' for them:

but considering the large interests both you and we have in the other books, we think it is the wisest course. A 6/- Clerical Scenes would naturally lead to the expectation of a 6/- Adam and that again to a 6/- edition of the new novel, which might be very fatal to the 12/- edition. When we come to have the three books there will really be something to be made out of a uniform edition of them at 6/-. They will help instead of hurt each other.[3]

Occupied with writing the final volume of *The Mill on the Floss*, Eliot responded simply that 'Your plan about the Clerical Scenes is thoroughly satisfactory to me,' not mentioning *Adam Bede* at all.[4]

The 12s. *Adam Bede* continued to sell. On 6 March 1860 Lewes wrote to Barbara Bodichon that it was still 'selling at the rate of 200 a month',[5] information that he probably received after visiting Langford on 1 March.[6] On 24 March, Eliot and Lewes left for three months abroad, during which correspondence related principally to the sales and reception of the new novel, which was published on 4 April 1860. John Blackwood, in a halting sentence befitting such secondary news, did inform them on 25 May of a

---

[7] Eliot wrote of 16,000 copies sold in a letter to Charles Bray, 25 November, in which she regrets parting with the copyright (*Letters*, III. 214) and also of 16,000 to Barbara Bodichon, 5 December (*Letters*, III. 226). Her estimate to François D'Albert-Durade on 18 October, before the 2,124 copies of the 7th edition had been printed, was 14,000 (III. 186). Lewes gives the more moderate estimate of 10,000 copies in a letter to Émile Montégut on 1 December (*Letters*, VIII. 253).

[8] *Letters*, III. 217–19.   [9] 12 Dec.; *Letters*, III. 234.   [1] *Letters*, III. 200.
[2] 3 Jan. 1860; *Letters*, III. 240–1.   [3] 6 Jan.; *Letters*, III. 244.
[4] *Letters*, III. 246.   [5] *Letters*, III. 270.
[6] GHL Journal; qtd. in *Letters*, III. 268.

new edition of *Adam Bede*: 'I think [Adam] is . . . in a new edition in which you have interest although I am not quite certain still I feel pretty sure it is.'[7] This edition, called the 'eighth' on the title page, is listed in the firm's ledger book as printed June 1860, with printing and paper calculations for an edition of 1,000 copies; 1,004 were printed.[8] It was advertised in the *Athenaeum* as 'ADAM BEDE. Eighth Edition' on 23 June 1860 (No. 1704, p. 865), but was not listed in the *Publishers' Circular* for 1860.

The last of this series of two-volume, 12s. editions appeared a year later. A letter from Eliot to John Blackwood on 23 March 1861 refers to another new edition in a way that suggests he might have raised the matter in a letter no longer extant:

> I would on no account publish a 6/. edition of the books until the 12/. edition of the Mill has had a fair chance of disappearing from the shelves. And pray print the smallest practicable number of Adam at 12/., for I have a great dread of having my books printed to lie in warehouses. I suppose the types of the 6/. edition whenever it is printed will serve for all cheaper editions, by altering the paper and narrowing the edges. But let us wait.[9]

Blackwood had probably been taking stock of supplies of *Adam Bede*, anticipating that sales of *Silas Marner*, to be published on 2 April, might stimulate new demand for her earlier works. He or another member of the firm must have written again, for Eliot wrote to Blackwood in April, 'We had not heard of Mudie's new demand for 500, and I am particularly glad to know of the prudent limitation as to printing.'[1] The sentence addresses two different subjects, the first clause referring to *Silas Marner*, and the second, to the proposed reprinting of *Adam Bede*. The publications ledger closed out after the death of Major Blackwood on 8 April 1861 shows 109 copies of *Adam Bede* on hand on that date.[2] Low inventory obviously prompted Blackwoods to issue a small, final two-volume edition in June 1861, called the 'Ninth Edition' on the title page. The new ledger to which the data were transferred repeats the number on hand, 109, and adds '502 [copies] since printed'. Paper and printing costs are based on a print run of 500, the 'smallest practicable number'. Only a few were left to 'lie in warehouses' after the author's death: when the new ledger was closed out in 1873, 211 copies remained on hand; a later notation gives 141 copies 'Sold [as] Waste' in 1880.[3]

---

[7] *Letters*, III. 298.

[8] NLS MS 30,859, fo. 381. A memorandum in Simpson's hand lists 1,002 copies of *Adam Bede* printed on 21 May 1860, with 273 still on hand on 31 Dec. 1860 (*Letters*, III. 371), instead of the 1,004 given in the publications ledger.

[9] *Letters*, III. 392.   [1] 15? Apr.; *Letters*, III. 405, reprinted *Letters*, VIII. 278.

[2] NLS MS 30,859, fo. 381.   [3] NLS MS 30,860, fo. 213.

Adam Bede in One Volume

The cheap edition that Simpson anticipated for autumn 1859 was finally to make its appearance in 1862, though not without further deliberation during the summer and autumn of 1861. On 13 June 1861 William Blackwood Jr., known as 'Willie', who since his father's death was assuming a more active role in the firm, wrote to his uncle in London: 'Will you remember when you see George Eliot to ask her if she wishes to make any alterations in the text of "Adam" & "The Mill on the Floss" for the 6/- edition so that the printers may begin to set it up & let us publish in August or Sept'. I do not think you require any data but what they can give you in the Row as regards sales & the agreement is already made.'[4] There is no record of John Blackwood's answer, and by August there was still no sign of a cheap edition. Even the form and the price remained unresolved. William, who was in London then, reported that Eliot and Lewes were inclined to a '2/6 Ed. but I do not fancy it yet. They the Novels[5] I think certainly stand 6/- & if stereotyped we can print small & bring out a 2/6 ed later in the same form but they are quite willing to do whatever you advise. They say the 2/6 ed. of Jane Eyre sold 25,000. Lewes thinks there is not a large market at 6/- & that the 12/ ed. will have exhausted it. I do not think so.'[6]

Lewes had apparently come to agree with 'Willie' by 12 September, when Eliot wrote to John Blackwood about 'the new edition of my books. Mr. Lewes's suggestion is, that a 6/. edition might be published in moderate numbers, which, if stereotyped, might be reproduced on thinner paper as the 2/6 edition—one set of types thus serving for two editions. You, of course, will weigh the merits of this suggestion against those of any other plan you may have in your mind.'[7] By 23 September Blackwood had 'told Mr. Simpson to be making calculations for cheap editions etc. He rather inclines to the cheap edition at once now, and so do I. The 12/- editions must have cut into the 6/- class passengers.' But he plans 'to have some further talk with Mr. Simpson and Willie before coming to a definite decision'.[8] Their decision was to proceed, although on 21 October William Blackwood suggested to his uncle that *Silas Marner* rather than *Adam Bede* lead off the series: 'In case you may make tomorrow a business day & be writing to George Eliot I drop you a line to suggest that Silas Marner be the first to come out of the 6/- series of the novels. Simpson thinks we should sell nearly 3000 of it & you should go for that No. for first impression.'[9]

In the meantime, Eliot began to reread and correct *Adam Bede* and *The Mill on the Floss*. By 25 September, she had completed her work:

[4] NLS MS 4157, fos. 31–3.
[5] William Blackwood inserted 'the Novels' above the line.
[6] 8 Aug. 1861; NLS MS 4157, fos. 95–8.   [7] *Letters*, VIII. 289.
[8] *Letters*, III. 453–4.   [9] NLS MS 4157, fos. 166–7.

I have read carefully all through 'Adam Bede' and 'The Mill' and have marked all the *errata* I have discovered. I hope the new editions will be carefully printed after these corrected copies, which I shall presently send. I have also marked in the Clerical Scenes some corrections which Mr. Lewes noted when he last read them. But I cannot read these and Silas Marner through, as I have done the other two books—I find this reading excite me too much and carry me away from the present. I am very glad, however, that I have given the needful time to 'Adam' and 'The Mill,' for there were several mistakes which affected the sense in an important manner. It has moved me a good deal—reading the books again after a long interval, but it has done me good, for I can say a full Amen to everything I have written. I shall await your letter about the new editions and then send the corrected copies.[1]

For *Adam Bede*, Eliot marked her corrections on a copy of the 'Eighth Edition' published in two volumes in June 1860. This copy, now at the Harry Ransom Humanities Research Center of the University of Texas, Austin, bears an endorsement by George Simpson 'Corrected by Author Nov. 1861.' Simpson's date refers to the firm's receipt of the corrected copies, which probably arrived in Edinburgh the last week of October. On 26 October, a Saturday, Lewes wrote that Eliot was 'laid up in bed with a violent cold & is forced to use my pen to thank you for your last letter. As to beginning with a 6/- edition, she agrees with me that it may be desirable.' He repeats his idea, which Eliot had conveyed earlier, that 'the same ster[e]otypes would do for the 2/6', and adds that 'Mrs. Lewes has gone carefully through *all* the books, & corrected them. I will take them to Langford next week.'[2] There is no indication in the *Letters* of the precise date on which Langford received and forwarded the corrected copies, but

---

[1] *Letters*, VIII. 291.

[2] *LGHL* II. 27. Always alert to changes that affected costs, Lewes notes that Blackwood's 'offer of '59 was made ⟨during⟩ before the removal of the paper duty'. He suggests that Blackwood has not calculated that, because two of the works are much shorter than a three-volume novel, they would cost less to produce. Therefore, 'Mrs. Lewes was led to expect that as she received 200 £ per thousand for Silas at 12/- with paper duty she would not receive less than 100 £ per thousand at 6/- without duty. Perhaps you will look again into the data of the calculation, & let her know the result' (*LGHL* II. 27). On 31 October, Blackwood wrote to explain that he did not have 'the data here [at Strathtyrum, St Andrews] to enable me to answer your note with precision, but you may rely upon it that Mrs. Lewes will have all the benefit that the repeal of paper duty or the difference in the expense of producing the shorter works can give'. He added that the 'difference will not I should think be so great as you imagine', citing the binding costs and the need to 'print the shorter works [*Silas* and *Scenes*] on a sparser page and probably thicker paper' so that they are uniform with the longer ones (*Letters*, III. 461). Writing to Lewes from Edinburgh on 15 November, Blackwood explained the costs in detail, and Eliot responded on 18 November: 'Your explanatory letter to Mr. Lewes leaves, I think, nothing more to be discussed about this long-agitated business of the new editions. I agree with you that the £4. saved on the paper will be best applied in improving the binding. We can hardly expect a very large sale of the 6s/. editions, so it will be wisest to proceed on the basis of modest hopes in the printing. Let us understand, then, that I ⟨expect⟩ accept the proposition of £60 per thousand for all the four books in their 6s/. edition i.e. if you at length decide on fixing "Silas" at that price' (*Letters*, VIII. 292–3).

on 2 November William Blackwood wrote to his uncle, 'Have you written to Lewes yet? The corrected copies of all George E's works have come down. We should not lose time as the stock of Silas is almost nothing.'[3] In a letter to Lewes on 15 November, John Blackwood 'propose[d] to begin with Adam. Suppose we start that on the first of January.'[4] The firm's ledger lists '1861 Oct' as the date 'To printing', with 3,000 copies ordered. The actual number printed, after Eliot's corrections were received in November, was 3,018. Called the 'Tenth Edition' on the title page, it appeared at the end of January 1862, and was partly stereotyped, partly electrotyped so that it could be reprinted as demand for the series developed.[5] It was first advertised in the *Athenaeum* on 25 January: 'On the 31st inst. will be published A CHEAP EDITION OF ADAM BEDE' (No. 1787, p. 128). The *Publishers' Circular* lists the edition among the books published from 14 to 31 January.[6]

This edition, while showing steady sales, was not likely to require reprinting for some time. John Blackwood reported on 21 October 1862 that 'we printed 3000 of the 6/- edition of Adam Bede and of these there are still about 900 on hand. They are pretty sure to go however, and I have now the pleasure of inclosing you a cheque £180 in acknowledgment of this edition being at the rate of £60 per thousand as agreed upon.'[7] Blackwood was less optimistic three months later, after the one-volume *Adam Bede* had been out nearly a year and a third volume in the 6s. series, including both *Silas Marner* and *Scenes of Clerical Life*, was projected for Eastertime 1863:

Of the Mill at 6/- there are about 950 sold including 200 to Australia so I think we shall only print 1000 of the next volume in the first instance. This edition is stereotyped, so that if there is a run on the three volumes when published together we will be ready to meet it. Of the 6/ edition of Adam there are about 650 on hand.

This 6/ edition is not doing what we hoped, and I see that up to midsummer last we had spent 85£ on advertising it (and only Adam was published at that time) so we are not neglecting it in that way indeed. The proposition is too heavy, as much as we had calculated on a sale of 5000. I wish I had a more flourishing account of sales to give but we must hope that the 3 volumes will go together.[8]

Having the three volumes in print did not alter what Blackwood termed the 'failure of this 6/ edition', which he found 'very annoying', as he wrote to Lewes on 10 November 1863.[9] Sending Lewes an account of sales on 7 March 1864, Blackwood commented that *Adam Bede* 'goes on' but he

    [3] NLS MS 4157, fos. 174–5.
    [4] *Letters*, III. 464.   [5] NLS MS 30,860, fo. 231.
    [6] The *Letters* gives 15 February as the publication date (III. 465 n. 5) based on an advertisement that day in the *Publishers' Circular*. Like those in the *Athenaeum* on 1 and 15 February, the *Circular*'s advertisement employs the sometimes fictional formula 'This day is published', despite contradictory information elsewhere.
    [7] *Letters*, IV. 61.   [8] 17 Jan. 1863; *Letters*, IV. 73–4.   [9] *Letters*, IV. 113.

wishes that he 'had a more flourishing account of sales to show' and would have written 'long ago if I had been able to give cheery news'.[1] *Adam Bede*, however, was flourishing well enough that a reprinting of 1,000 copies was ordered in Feburary 1864 from the plates of the earlier edition; 1,008 copies was the actual print run.[2] More than a year later, Eliot wrote that 'Probably further reprints of the 6/- edition will not be required, and Mr. Lewes thinks that it will be well to defer a cheaper edition until I have published another book.'[3] By the time *Felix Holt* appeared in June 1866, sales of the one-volume *Adam Bede* had exhausted the supply, and a further reprinting of 500 copies was ordered in August 1866, nearly 400 of which were sold between August 1866 and June 1867;[4] only 37 remained 'on hand' in 1874.

Illustrated Edition of *Adam Bede*

Adam Bede finally got its opportunity to appear in serialized form in a new and even cheaper edition of Eliot's works in 1867. Given the moderate success of the one-volume editions of the early novels and the slow sales of *Felix Holt* in three volumes, John Blackwood felt that there was little promise of success for this new work as a one-volume addition to the cheap series that began with *Adam Bede* in 1862. After some debate, members of the firm, along with Eliot and Lewes, finally decided upon a two-volume *Felix Holt* at 12s.[5] But even before this question was settled, the firm was looking to a still cheaper *Adam Bede*. William Blackwood reminded his uncle, 'The next time you come over we must decide something about cheaper ed^{ns} of Adam Bede & Felix—& you must write to George Eliot.'[6] On 25 September he raised the question again: 'Simpson asks me to remind you about your letter to George Eliot as to the Illus^{td} cheap Ed^{n} of her works. We are anxious to have it decided one way or another.'[7] In late October when William was in London, he visited Eliot and Lewes and they discussed the new edition about which John Blackwood had not yet written. On 2 November, Eliot wrote to him:

---

[1] *Letters*, IV. 137.   [2] NLS MS 30,860, fo. 213.

[3] 4 May 1865; *Letters*, VIII. 337.   [4] NLS MS 30,860, fo. 430.

[5] Langford indicated that his preference for a new edition of *Felix Holt* was for 'an edition (not a large one) in 2 vols. and then a 6/ one uniform with the others' (25 Aug.; NLS MS 4210, fos. 154–7). Simpson, as John Blackwood communicated to Eliot on 10 Sept. 1866, 'at first was in favour of trying a one volume edition' but now opted for two volumes at 12s., which is what Blackwood himself had 'first thought of' (*Letters*, IV. 307). With the firm in agreement, Blackwood solicited Eliot's and Lewes's opinions. Their concurrence, in a letter dated 11 September, settled the matter (*Letters*, IV. 308). On the 13th, John Blackwood wrote to his nephew: 'I enclose a nice letter from George Eliot which send on to Simpson & let the 2 vol. 12/- edition proceed' (NLS MS 4206, fo. 212). The two-volume edition of *Felix Holt* did not, however, turn out to be a great commercial success; see Fred C. Thomson (ed.), 'Introduction', *Felix Holt, the Radical* (Oxford: Clarendon Press, 1980), p. xxix.

[6] 31 Aug. 1866; NLS MS 4207, fos. 54–5.   [7] NLS MS 4207, fos. 58–9.

According to Mr. William Blackwood, whom we had the pleasure of seeing the other day, you have been saying that you ought to have written to me. Pray consider, therefore, that this letter is a fire-douche on your head.

I think the project of publishing an illustrated edition of the books—which Mr. William tells me you are entertaining—is a wise one, as likely to assist in their circulation. In the abstract I object to illustrated literature, but abstract theories of publishing can no more be carried out than abstract theories of politics. The form in which books shall appear is a question of expediency to be determined chiefly by public taste and convenience, not by private preference. I am not inclined to be sturdy except about the *matter* of my books, and I shall be glad if a satisfactory plan can be matured for an illustrated edition.[8]

More than a month later, on 13 December, John Blackwood added a postscript to a letter enclosing payment for *Felix Holt*: 'I intended to have written another letter along with this about the cheap illustrated edition of your works, but I have been so much interrupted that I could not make it out. I shall do so tomorrow however.'[9] 'Tomorrow' extended to 21 December, when John Blackwood described the matured plan: 'After many consultations and much dubiety the opinion we have formed here is that the best plan will be to try the cheap illustrated edition of your Novels in sixpenny numbers of which Adam, The Mill, Scenes, Silas, and Felix would make 30, ultimately to form four volumes selling at 3/6 each.' Blackwood proposed 30,000 copies of seven parts, with seven illustrations, each part selling for 6*d*. 'Thirty thousand is a large number to put down for Adam Bede, and it is a very great chance whether we do sell so many, but I think we should.' He offered either an outright payment or a percentage of profits, as the author preferred. Although using the stereo plates of the one-volume edition would reduce costs, he considered the venture a 'speculation', adding that 'The 6/- editions of the works have been a disappointment. They produce so little that they are hardly worth considering.'[1] The next day Eliot accepted his offer of £1,000 for her interest in the five works for the next ten years, with an additional payment of £500 'in case of success according to your estimate'.[2]

Adam Bede was the logical choice to lead off the illustrated series, as it had the cheap, one-volume novels in 1862, where its sales had outpaced those of others in that series. By 29 December Blackwood had seen two illustrations, both of which proved unacceptable: 'I got a cold bath this morning in the shape of two specimen illustrations of Adam. They are both returned as unsuitable.'[3] Almost three months later, the illustrations remained a problem, as Blackwood explained on 20 March 1867:

---

[8] *Letters*, IV. 313.   [9] *Letters*, IV. 318.   [1] *Letters*, IV. 320–1.
[2] 22 Dec. 1866; *Letters*, VIII. 393.   [3] *Letters*, IV. 327.

I intended to have sent along with this a copy of the first part of the cheap edition of the novels, but Mr. Simpson has not yet got an impression of the cover and illustration thrown off to please his critical eye. The cover I think you will like, as it seems to me neat. The first illustration seems to me the worst of the lot, but some of them are really very good. I found it was no use fighting with the illustrators and that they must be allowed to have their own way in choice of subjects, and they assert that figures are the only things to tell. Some of the illustrations will, I doubt not, give you 'a turn' but on the whole they are much better than I expected, and Mr. Cooper has certainly spared no pains or trouble.[4]

Although she had not yet seen them, Eliot was resigned about the illustrations: 'I have adjusted my hopes so as to save myself from any great shock. When I remember my own childish happiness in a frightfully illustrated copy of the Vicar of Wakefield, I can believe that illustrations may be a great good relatively, and that my own present liking has no weight in the question.'[5]

The first 6d. part of *Adam Bede* was published on 1 April 1867 with a pale green cover printed in black. Medallions in the four corners contain the following illustrations (clockwise, from upper left to lower left): (1) a carpenter's workshop with workbench, tools lying on and hanging above it, and wood shavings on the floor; (2) a mill, showing the mill-wheel in the centre and part of the building to which it is attached, with bare, wintry trees in background; (3) a weaver's loom; and (4) a graveyard with tombstone engraved 'AMELIA | XXXV. | BARTON.' This part-issue was advertised in the *Publishers' Circular* on 1 April 1867, page 193: 'IN SIXPENNY NUMBERS, AN ILLUSTRATED EDITION OF THE NOVELS OF GEORGE ELIOT The First Number of ADAM BEDE Is now Published, and may be had of all Booksellers.' By 5 April Eliot had received her copy and was evidently satisfied with it, for on 8 April, John Blackwood responded to a letter no longer extant, 'I was glad to receive your pleasant note about the first part of the illustrated edition of the Novels which Mr. Simpson feels as a peculiar grace to himself. The figure of Adam is hard and their making it so sinuous as well as sinewy irritated me, but the accessories are good.'[6]

The front matter for part 1 bears the statement, 'Each number will contain a highly-finished Engraving, executed, under the direction of Mr J. D. Cooper, by a selection of able Artists.' In fact, all six of the part-issue illustrations within the text were done by a single 'able artist', whose name appears on each drawing, 'W. Small'. William Small (1843–1929) was an illustrator whose work appeared in more than a dozen prominent periodicals, including the *Argosy*, the *Boy's Own Magazine*, *Good Words*, the

---

[4] *Letters*, IV. 352. Gordon Haight adds, 'James Cooper (1823–1904) engraved the illustrations for this edition of the novels. Blackwood's fear was justified' (*Letters*, IV. 352 n. 1).

[5] 21 Mar. 1867; *Letters* IV. 354.   [6] *Letters*, IV. 357.

Graphic, *Once a Week*, and the *Sunday Magazine*, and who 'became the highest paid illustrator of his time, earning sixty guineas for each drawing for the *Graphic*'.[7] He also illustrated more than fifty books, including fiction, poetry, and children's stories. All of his magazine work catalogued in Goldman and most of his book illustrations date from the 1860s and 1870s. Goldman, who calls him a man of 'immensely varied talents' and 'a gifted artist',[8] includes a checklist of his illustrated books[9] and an index of his magazine illustrations.[1] In the former, he lists *Adam Bede* as 'n.d.' because the illustrated edition bore no date on the title page. The cover was designed by John Leighton (1822–1912), whose name appears at bottom centre of the green paper covers. 'Artist, illustrator, book decorator and designer of ex-libris', Leighton was 'a founder proprietor of *The Graphic* in 1869 and designed their title page which remained in use until 1930'.[2]

The first part of *Adam Bede* includes two illustrations, the first showing the 'sinewy' Adam to which Blackwood refers. It runs opposite page 2 and bears a quotation from Chapter I, 'In his tall stalwartness Adam Bede was a Saxon, and justified his name.' The second illustration faces page 117 and shows Arthur kissing Hetty, although its caption, 'In the wood', is misleading. It refers to the title of Chapter XII, in which Arthur slips his arm around Hetty's waist, but it is not until Chapter XIII, titled 'Evening in the Wood', that he kisses her for the first time. Parts 2 and 3 contain no illustrations. Part 4, like part 1, includes two. The first, facing page 261, shows Adam kneeling above the prostrate Arthur after giving him the blow that Adam fears has been fatal. Its quotation comes from the final paragraph of Chapter XXVII: 'The horror that rushed over Adam completely mastered him. He made not a single movement, but knelt like an image of despair.' Facing page 300, the second illustration in this number shows Squire Donnithorne's retreat from the Hall Farm in Chapter XXXII, with the quotation ' "You may run away from my words, Sir," continued Mrs Poyser.' Part 5 contains no illustrations. The fifth and sixth illustrations appear in part 6. The first of these, facing page 390, depicts Dinah and Hetty in the prison in Chapter XLV: 'Slowly, while Dinah was speaking, Hetty rose, took a step forward, and was clasped in Dinah's arms.' The second, facing page 442, shows Adam confessing his love to Dinah in Chapter LII : ' "Dinah," he said suddenly, taking both her hands between his.'[3]

[7] Rodney Engen, *Dictionary of Victorian Wood Engravers* (1985), 240, qtd. in Paul Goldman, *Victorian Illustration: The Pre-Raphaelites, the Idyllic School and the High Victorians* (Aldershot, 1996), 140.

[8] Goldman, *Victorian Illustration*, 140.   [9] Ibid. 142–4.   [1] Ibid. 307–11.

[2] Simon Houfe, *The Dictionary of 19th Century British Illustrators and Caricaturists* (Woodbridge, 1996), 210.

[3] The only copy of the original part-issue *Adam Bede* that I have seen is at the British Library. In this copy, the title page and other front matter appear to have been included with

The uneven distribution of the illustrations, in contradiction of the statement in the front matter, cannot be attributed to uncertainty about how the text would divide up, since the 1867 illustrated edition was printed from the 1862 plates. Undoubtedly, despite the plan to have an illustration per part, the artist selected subjects that were not evenly distributed.[4] The size of the parts varied: number 1 contains 8 signatures; numbers 2 to 6, 4 signatures each; and number 7, 1 signature plus 3 leaves. As a reading text, the individual part-issue of this illustrated edition had limitations. Unlike nineteenth-century serial fiction generally, these parts did not end with a climactic moment, or even with the conclusion of a paragraph or a sentence. Instead, as in eighteenth-century works such as encyclopedias, dictionaries, and scientific and religious works issued in fascicle to permit gradual purchase, but intended ultimately for binding as a whole, the serial breaks of the illustrated novels were determined by signatures, so that breaks could, and do, occur in mid-sentence.

The distribution of signatures, pages, and illustrations for *Adam Bede*, and the stamped British Museum accession dates, are as follows:

Letters and number of signatures	Pages	British Museum accession date	Illustrations: BM accession date
1 $A-H^8$; 8	1–128	1–64, 15 AP 67; 65–128, 3 JY 67	(1) 15 AP 67 (2) 3 JY 67
2 $I-M^8$; 4	129–92	3 JY 67	None
3 $N-Q^8$; 4	193–256	3 JY 67	None
4 $R-U^8$; 4	257–320	12 NO 67	(3) 3 JY 67 (4) 12 NO 67
5 $X-2A^8$; 4	321–84	12 NO 67	None
6 $2B-2E^8$; 4	385–448	12 NO 67	(5) 3 JY 67
7 $2F^8 2G^4$ (−2G4); 1+3 leaves	449–70	12 NO 67	(6) 12 NO 67[5]

the first number, although 'The Hall Farm' is stamped '12 NO [November] 67'. This copy, like the British Library copies of the other four novels issued in parts, has been bound, but the original green covers are retained. However, Eliot's correspondence suggests that she did not see the vignette of 'The Hall Farm' until she received her copy of the one-volume edition on 30 May (*Letters*, IV. 366). If 'The Hall Farm' had been part of the first number, one might expect her to have noticed it when she received that instalment on 5 Apr. 1867 (*JGE* 129).

[4] This is also true of the other four novels in the 6*d*. series. Each of the four has at least one instalment with no illustration, and three of the four have at least one instalment with two illustrations. Furthermore, the advertised number of illustrations and the number included in *Adam Bede* and *The Mill on the Floss* differ. Apparently, the firm changed the number after advertising had gone out.

[5] Clearly there is something anomalous about the date stamping. What is bound as number 6 includes text that is date stamped only once: 12 NO 67. However, the illustration of Dinah with Hetty in the prison is stamped 3 JY 67, whereas the next one, of Adam proposing to Dinah, is stamped 12 NO 67. One can only guess that some dates were stamped on parts after receipt, and some stamps must have been introduced later. The series title page bears the Museum's stamp, dated 12 NO 67 on the verso.

It may have been a deliberate commercial choice that the parts are arranged so that the first is twice the length of any other. In 1875 Blackwood reassured Eliot about the uneven length of instalments of *Daniel Deronda*: 'Practically if there is to be a difference in the thickness of the volumes it is well that the two first should have the preponderance, and in this case unless I am utterly mistaken by the time the public have reached the third volume they will be too happy to take and pay for whatever you give.'[6] The example of uneven lengths in the part issue of *Adam Bede* in 1867 is probably predicated on the belief that if readers purchased the thicker early parts, they would complete their set by buying the thinner, later ones. And, of course, a long first part would make them feel they were getting value for money, in this case their 6*d*. As Blackwood had written Lewes in 1858 regarding the unequal length of parts in the serialization of his *Physiology of Common Life*, 'it is no disadvantage to have the early parts portly'.[7]

Publication in parts, even for Eliot's most popular novel, was soon recognized as a failure. On publication day for part 1 of *Adam Bede*, Langford expressed his disappointment in the subscription: 'I enclose a memorandum of what we have done with Part 1 of the Geo Eliot Tales. My expectations were as you know very moderate but I am greatly disappointed by the small demand in London. However we can form no accurate estimate of the actual sales in parts for two or three months. In fact I am inclined to think that the greatest demand will be for the volumes.'[8] Three days later, however, he was more positive:

> The sale of G. Eliot is going on tolerably well and I by no means despair of it. Smith & Sons preferred to order it as they want it 'not liking onepenny things.' They have had a further supply. Vickers has really no means of pushing such a thing—he is merely a medium for supplying what the public want and from the very nature of his business can give no especial attention to any one thing. Mr Glass saw them and gave them 5 per cent extra.[9]

Writing to Eliot on 8 April, John Blackwood was cautious: it is too early to 'tell yet how the series is going to do but although the first demand has not been so good as I expected, I hope that it will go on steadily improving. I feel that it should do.'[1] But by the next month news was again dispiriting. On 6 May, William forwarded a letter from London to his uncle at St Andrews:

---

[6] *Letters*, VI. 185–6.

[7] *Letters*, II. 513. *The Mill on the Floss*, the second in the series, does not support this theory. Its first part is the smallest, with only 2 signatures. But by the time it began to appear in November 1867, the part-issue experiment was acknowledged by Blackwood to have been a failure.

[8] 1 Apr. 1867, to William Blackwood; NLS MS 4222, fos. 32–3. Langford was right. As a series of one-volume novels, the illustrated edition experienced steady sales throughout the next decade.

[9] NLS MS 4222, fos. 36–9.   [1] *Letters*, IV. 357.

'Inclosed is a letter from Langford & his report of Sale of Pt II Adam Bede is very depressing.'[2]

The firm's publications ledger for this period shows the optimism with which the illustrated edition in parts began: 13,000 of the first part were 'done up'. That number dropped to 6,981 for number 2; 3,500 each for parts 3 and 4; 2,300 for part 5; and 2,000 each for parts 6 and 7, the final instalments of *Adam Bede*. Numbers for the other novels continue to diminish over the course of publication, reaching a low of 550 copies each for the last two parts of *Felix Holt*, which concluded the series. Of the total of 56,069 parts printed, more than half—33,281—were the seven parts of *Adam Bede*. For the total of 30 parts in the series, the ledger records that 1,321 were 'Delivered' (as copies to the author, press, and others), 11,693 were withdrawn for binding in volumes, and 41,881 were sold,[3] leaving 1,174 on hand in 1874.[4] With the 41,881 sold through dealers, 13 as 12, at 4½ d. each, it is easy to understand Blackwood's discouragement at the return.

Adam Bede in One Volume, at 3*s*. 6*d*.

William Blackwood's assessment on 6 May, based on Langford's 'depressing' report, combined with the announcement of 'a cheaper ed^n of Charles Dickens' works', led them to decide that it was time to proceed with the projected new series of Eliot's works including, for the first time, *Felix Holt*. Using the same stereo plates and engravings as the illustrated part-publication, this series would also begin with *Adam Bede*. William reported, 'Simpson & I resolved to get the vol ready for publication at once & so be in the field first ⟨so⟩ and from this poor report [of part-publication sales] I think we were quite right to try our chance in vol shape without further delay. I trust it will be more successful. Specimen bindings came down this morn^g but they are beastly & another lot are written for.'[5]

The one-volume *Adam Bede* appeared in late May and was advertised in both the *Athenaeum* (25 May 1867, No. 2065, p. 705) and the *Publishers' Circular* (1 June, p. 322); the latter included it under the list of new works published from 15 to 31 May. Receiving a copy on 27 May, John Blackwood wrote to his nephew, 'I have just got your note & copy of Adam Bede. If such a book does not sell at such a price the country is disgraced.'[6] Eliot's copy also arrived before the end of the month, and she wrote enthusiasti-

---

[2] NLS MS 4218, fos. 11–12.

[3] This sounds like a large number until one realizes that 41,881 is the total for the 30 instalments; sales therefore averaged only 1,396 copies per instalment.

[4] NLS MS 30,861, fos. 97–8, summarizing the years 1867 to 1874. The 1,174 copies were carried over in the ledger each year until 1880–1 when '1174 On hand' at the start of the year (1 July 1880) became 'Since sold as Waste' at the bookkeeping year's end, July 1881, following Eliot's death.

[5] 6 May 1867; NLS MS 4218, fos. 11–12.   [6] NLS MS 4217, fos. 164–5.

cally to John Blackwood on 30 May about the illustration of 'The Hall
Farm' that appeared on the series title page: 'I must tell you how pleased I
was to receive two copies of the really handsome volume containing Adam
Bede. The vignette on the title-page is perfect—almost exactly as I saw the
Hall Farm eight years ago in my mind's eye.'[7] This vignette of 'The Hall
Farm' was the work of Edmund Morison Wimperis (1835–1900), whose
monogram EMW is visible in the lower right of the frontispiece illustration. Wimperis exhibited nearly 300 watercolours between 1873 and 1900,
but he began by studying wood engraving and took up magazine and book
illustration early in his career.[8]

By 15 July it was this edition that gave hope for the illustrated novels.
John Blackwood regretted that 'The new edition of the Novels . . . is not
selling as I calculated upon at all. The sale in numbers is a failure.'
However, he noted that, of the one-volume *Adam Bede*, 'we have sold
about 3000, and I think it is going on steadily. I fear however that there is no
chance whatever of the payment contingent to you on the sale of a certain
number of this present edition becoming due, which is a disappointment
and loss to us both.'[9] Eliot responded that she 'care[d] comparatively little
about profiting further by [the new edition] myself, but I am seriously
anxious that the speculation should not prove ultimately an undesirable
one for you'.[1] Simpson reported to John Blackwood on 27 July that 'Adam
Bede is swinging into a sale', with Paternoster Row ordering its ninth 500
copies in cloth. He expects this format to 'sell regularly at this price for
years'.[2] This edition did indeed 'sell regularly . . . for years'. In fact, it
proved to be the largest-selling single edition of *Adam Bede* during
the author's lifetime and immediately after her death. Blackwoods'
publications ledger MS 30,861 records reprintings throughout the
1870s, with 53,066 sold in volumes and 2,264 sold in sheets for binding between June 1867 and March 1881, three months after the author's
death.

[7] *Letters*, IV. 366.
[8] 'Edmund Morison Wimperis, R.I. Water-Colour Painter', *Walker's Quarterly*, 4 (July
1921), 28 and *passim*.
[9] *Letters*, IV. 372–3.   [1] *Letters*, IV. 373.
[2] NLS MS 4226, fos. 53–4. Blackwood conveyed his disappointment again on 7 November:
'Adam Bede goes on steadily but not brilliantly. I must confess to heavy disappointment at the
non success of the works as a serial, and I cannot understand it. Next to predicting who will win
the Derby I think foretelling how many of a book will sell is about the most difficult problem
going' (*Letters*, IV. 394). Eliot's experience led her to regard the results of the experiment as
part of the uncertainties of publishing: 'I am vexed by the non-success of the serial. It is not,
heaven knows, that I read my own books or am puffed up about them, but I have been of late
quite astonished by the strengthening testimonies that have happened to come to me, of people
who care about every one of my books and continue to read them—especially young men, who
are just the class I care most to influence. But what sort of data can one safely go upon with
regard to the success of editions?' (9 Nov. 1867; *Letters*, IV. 397).

The 'New' Edition of 1873, at 2s. 6d.

Adam Bede continued to be the benchmark for Eliot's novels. In October 1871, Lewes advised Alexander Main, who was preparing the first edition of the *Wise, Witty, and Tender Sayings of George Eliot*, 'to reduce the extracts from "Adam Bede" rather than from the other works because that has been so much more widely read and reread'.[3] In the 1870s, reviewers of *Middlemarch* and *Daniel Deronda* referred to these two works as 'by the author of *Adam Bede*'. The popularity of *Middlemarch*, which appeared in eight instalments from December 1871 to December 1872, led John Blackwood to query Eliot about a new, even cheaper edition of her works:

> The success of Middlemarch has given a good stimulus to the sale of the Works, and for some time Mr. Simpson has been talking to me about a reduction in price, making Adam Bede 2/6 and so on in proportion, and meeting the change of price so far by a cheaper paper with less margin and also a cheaper binding with the omitting of the blessed illustrations. Will Lewes and you turn this over in your minds and let me know what you think? I am doubtful myself.

Blackwood viewed the question as one of 'large sales at 2/6 or . . . modest sales at 3/6', the latter being the price of the stereotyped, illustrated series of her works first issued in 1867. The sales of this edition, he added,

> have been good and steady but never anything like what we calculated we might hope for. They stand about something as follows: Adam 14500; The Mill 8500; Felix 5800; Scenes 5000; Silas 5300. During the past year and half [*sic*] the influence of Middlemarch has been distinct and Adam has been moving at the rate of something like 2000 copies a year and the others in a like lesser proportion. This is something like a half more than had been selling during the recent previous years.[4]

Although there is no extant letter from Eliot to indicate her preference for the 2s. 6d. or the 3s. 6d. edition, the publications ledger shows that a 2s. 6d. edition was sent 'To Printing' in June 1873, with a print order of 3,150 copies. Their disposition includes 1 copy delivered to the press, 1 to the 'B Museum', 2,781 sold '25 as 24' at the trade sales rate of 1s. 9d., and an

---

[3] *Letters*, V. 205.

[4] 28 Apr. 1873; *Letters*, V. 407. These figures may be estimates based on a record I have not discovered. NLS MS 30,861, the third of three publications ledgers recording printing and sales figures for *Adam Bede* during Eliot's lifetime, provides only a summary of 'Eliot's Works 1867–74' on fos. 97–8. Sales of *Adam Bede* in cloth at 3s. 6d. (retail) are given as 16,421 domestic sales plus 878 export, for a total of 17,299 during the eight years and one month between the appearance of the 3s. 6d. *Adam Bede* in late May 1867 and the close of the fiscal year 1873–4 on 30 June 1874. With sales averaging more than 2,100 per year, Blackwood's (or Simpson's) estimate on 28 Apr. 1873 is well founded.

additional 367 sold 'Export'.[5] The 'edition' is another one printed from the 1862 stereotype plates. The 1867 illustrations were omitted, and the title page, which bears no date, calls it 'A New Edition'. The British Museum (now British Library) copy is stamped with the accession date '12 AU 1873'.[6] The *Athenaeum* for 2 August 1873 includes in its 'LIST OF NEW BOOKS' 'Adam Bede, by Geo. Eliot, new edit. cr. 8vo. 2/6 cl.' (No. 2388, p. 146). The *Publishers' Circular* lists among its new works published from 16 to 30 August 'Adam Bede. New Edition. 12mo. Pp. 470, cloth, 2s.6d.' Apparently Eliot had neither seen the advertisements nor received a copy by 19 September: 'I wonder whether you have abandoned—as you seemed to agree that it would be wise to do—the project of bringing out my other books[7] in a cheaper form than the present 3/6—which, if it were not for the blemish of the figure illustrations, would be as pretty an edition as could be, and perhaps as cheap as my public requires.'[8] A delay in sending her a copy might explain this letter, but another letter five months later is difficult to account for:

I have been compunctious lately about my having sprinkled cold water on the proposal suggested by Mr. Simpson, of bringing out my novels in a cheaper way—on thinner paper and without illustrations. The compunction was roused by my happening, in looking at old records, to alight on some letters, one especially, written by a working man, a certain E. Hall, more than 10 years ago, begging me to bring out my books in a form cheap enough to let a poor man more easily get 'a read of them.' Hence if you and Mr. Simpson see good to revive the design in question I am perfectly in accord.[9]

Of interest as a publishing experiment, the illustrated and the 'New' editions are textually of little consequence, since they were printed from plates of the first one-volume edition (1862).

---

[5] NLS MS 30,861, fo. 370.

[6] Blackwoods' publications ledger MS 30,861 includes an account of this edition in two different places. Fo. 97, left-hand column, under the heading 'Eliot's Works 1867–74', gives 3,150 copies of 'Adam Bede 2/6'; but below this entry is another one, undated, that seems to refer to the same edition, but which includes costs for illustrations. The British Library copy of the 2s. 6d. edition verifies that illustrations were omitted from this edition, as Blackwood indicated would be the case. On fo. 370, a fuller entry, under the heading 'Eliot's Adam Bede 2/6', matches more closely the information in his letter. This entry also records 3,150 copies 'To Printing' and the same number 'Printed', both dated '1873 June'. The sales column shows 367 sold export, the same as on fo. 97, right-hand column, but 2,781 sold 25 as 24 for 1s. 9d., a higher figure than the 2,400 given in the summary on fo. 98, right-hand column. The more explicit and methodical nature of the details on fo. 370 suggests that the entry on fo. 97 is the one in error.

[7] That is, books before *Middlemarch*. This paragraph follows a discussion of responses to that novel.

[8] *Letters*, V. 441.   [9] 20 Feb. 1874; *Letters*, VI. 22.

The Cabinet Edition of *Adam Bede*

By autumn 1876, following the publication of *Daniel Deronda*, earlier frictions were long past, and author and publisher felt a mutual loyalty and friendship strengthened by their awareness of increasing age and ill health. A warm letter from Eliot on 8 October (unfortunately lost) 'move[d] and gratif[ied]' Blackwood, as he wrote on 12 October.[1] A week later, anticipating the renewal of the lease on her works, he expressed himself 'ready to meet any suggestions for alterations [in their publication arrangements] as I am bent upon continuing your publisher as well as friend through life', adding, 'We have a long career of successive triumphs to look back upon and I hope there is much yet before us.'[2]

Beyond adding *Romola* to the cheap one-volume series of Eliot's works, the principals were uncertain about the format for a complete new edition. On 27 February 1877 Lewes wrote to Blackwood proposing 'a new and uniform edition of the works of G.E.' using 'the type of the present edition . . . but a larger margin and a new cover', with the argument 'that the public is always attracted by a novelty—be it only that of the binding!—and that six shillings would be just as freely paid as 2/6 by a great many people'.[3] Not until 19 March did John Blackwood respond, explaining that both illness and 'being very much puzzled what to advise about the Novels' had caused him to

put off writing from day to day.

I feel that there is too little being made out of those admirable books and we must try something to give a semblance of novelty to a complete edition of George Eliot's Works.

After many talks with Simpson and Willie I think we all point to something very like what you propose viz. a 6/- edition beginning with Romola in the same type as the present edition but printed on larger and finer paper which being adopted with the other volumes would make them like entirely new editions and fully worth 6/- except of course Silas Marner. As long as Middlemarch continues to sell as it is doing it will be advisable to keep it at 7/6 and Deronda the same. These two are so much larger than the other volumes that the difference in price could not reasonably be objected to. Deronda we may I think start at 7/6 in Spring some time. We would propose to cancel the illustrations to the present edition and give in each volume an engraved vignette frontispiece like what we have in Middlemarch. We would continue the 3/6 edition or at all events be guided by circumstances as we found how the two editions worked abreast.[4]

At this point Blackwood seems to have taken his cue from Lewes in assuming another edition from the existing plates. But by the time Blackwood responded, Eliot, undoubtedly with Lewes's concurrence, had a new

---

[1] *Letters*, VI. 294–6. [2] 19 Oct.; *Letters*, VI. 297.
[3] *Letters*, VI. 345. [4] *Letters*, VI. 349.

suggestion: 'I was enjoying the fine octavo page of an edition of Fielding which we possess when it occurred to me that I should like my own books to be published in *eight* volumes of like size with fine type and paper.... Mr. Lewes thinks that each volume should not cost more than 7/6' but that she 'had been thinking of 10/'.[5] Blackwood in turn asked her to 'refer us to the edition of Fielding you possess or send down a volume to guide us', but added that 'It is difficult to get novels of length such as yours into one volume octavo at once portable and with an open readable page. 1 would be inclined to go in for 10/- volumes if we fix upon 8vo but uniformity in price would not be necessary.'[6] By the time Blackwood wrote, Eliot had changed her mind again. Searching for a new edition of Tennyson 'the other day ... rather in a hurry, because the poet was coming to read to us', she wanted a 'rather grand' one and 'asked first for the Library Edition', but the volume recommended by a bookseller to meet this description proved heavy and unmanageable: 'Since then I have been feeling the advantage of your former idea, that our new edition should have the existing type printed on finer, tinted paper, with more margin and with a nice bit of landscape to each volume.' She adds that there is no hurry to reach a decision: 'There is no shame in being shilly-shally before any practical step has been taken, and being in committee we shall all do well to consider and reconsider.' She proposes olive green for the cover 'to distinguish the new edition from the cheaper', and suggests that 'to my fancy it does not answer to put the vignette of the title-page in gold on the outside. The little *tondi*[7] on the covers of the 3/6 edition are charming.'[8]

On 30 April John Blackwood wrote,

After much puzzling and consideration we have pretty well come to the old conclusion that the handiest and most handsome form for your works will be an edition in 19 or 20 volumes somewhat similar to the 2 volume edition of Adam and Felix. We have been further assisted to this conclusion by looking at a set of your novels which had been bound and cut to as near as might be a uniform size to catch the eye of some of your worshippers here.

Enclosing calculations from Simpson, he added that the 'only other form would be the novels in one volume octavo but it is impossible to make that a handy volume to read by the fireside'.[9] Discussion of the new edition continued through the summer, sometimes by letter, sometimes

---

[5] 20 Mar. 1877; *Letters*, VI. 351.   [6] 27 Mar.; *Letters*, VI. 357.

[7] The 3*s*. 6*d*. editions include on the front cover a centre medallion blocked in gold and utilizing, in the case of *Adam Bede*, the same drawing of the carpenter's workshop found in the upper left-hand corner of the paper covers of the illustrated part-edition of 1867. The Bodleian Library copy shows such a tondo.

[8] 29 Mar.; *Letters*, VI. 358–9.   [9] *Letters*, VI. 366.

undoubtedly in person as John Blackwood visited Eliot and Lewes in their new home, The Heights, at Witley, in Surrey.[1]

By October, details were settled. In a letter to his nephew on 15 October, John Blackwood reflected in an almost elegiac tone that 'This edition must be the permanent one of these works and the publisher of it the natural successor to all the people's editions which surely will come. The Lewes's have I think our calculations of the printing and will feel that we are doing what we can for them as well as presenting her works in the handsomest possible shape. Write what Simpson and you think of this.'[2] The firm's formal offer for the Cabinet edition was made on 25 October in two letters to Lewes: 19 volumes, 17 of the fiction and 2 of the poems, will sell for 5s. each, with 'a lordship of 1/1½ on each copy of every volume sold after the first 500'.[3] Blackwood's cover letter observes that 'although a large sale cannot be looked for at first, my hope is that there will be a quiet but steady sale which will gradually bring in a steady little income. The book will I think be as handsome as well could be and form I hope a permanent and creditable presentment of George Eliot's Works.'[4] On 5 November, Eliot expressed her pleasure that 'we have settled together on a satisfactory standing form for the series of books. And though I have little confidence in a great sale for such an edition in this un-book-buying world, I trust that there will be enough to hinder any regret.'[5] Eliot approved the cover design on 22 November: 'The design for the cover we like very much. I had thought of a rich olive green for the colour—a hue which sets off well both the gold and the black. But Mr. Simpson promises to let us see specimens. Is it not desirable to omit any numbering of the volumes *according to the series?*—for two reasons: first, because the order of publication is not the chronological, in which they should ultimately be ranged, and secondly, because it would be a disadvantage for the independent sale of the several works.'[6]

Eliot's care for the external appearance of these 'grown-up children', as she called her works in the renegotiation of her copyrights, did not, however, manifest itself in the text of *Adam Bede* within these covers. The many unique variants in both substantives and accidentals shared by the tenth and the Cabinet editions show that the former was used as the base text for the Cabinet edition, but there is no evidence that she read either a copy of the tenth or proofs of the Cabinet. Busy family and social lives, renovation of The Heights, where Eliot and Lewes hoped to spend their later years, work on new projects, and recurring illness left her little time for correcting or proofreading. And in any case, she probably regarded her 1861 revision as sufficient.

---

[1] See *Letters*, VI. 390, 396–7.   [2] *Letters*, VI. 405.   [3] *Letters*, VI. 412.
[4] *Letters*, VI. 410.   [5] *Letters*, VI. 414.   [6] *Letters*, VI. 422–3.

Adam Bede appeared as volumes IV and V in the Cabinet edition. They were published on 1 April and 1 May 1878 respectively; 1,050 copies were printed of each volume. The first volume is included on the *Publishers' Circular* list of new works published between 1 and 15 April: 'Eliot, (G.)—Adam Bede. New edit. Vol. 1. 12mo. pp. 444, 5s.' The second volume is listed as published between 1 and 15 May: 'Eliot, (George)—Works. Cabinet edit. Adam Bede. Vol. 2. 12mo. 6s.' (*sic*; the correct price was 5s. for each volume). The firm continued to advertise the cheap edition, and the *Athenaeum* for 11 May 1878 shows an advertisement for the Cabinet edition next to one for the works of George Eliot 'Each Complete in One Volume' including the illustrated *Adam Bede* at 3s. 6d. (No. 2637, p. 616).[7]

THE MANUSCRIPT

The three-volume autograph manuscript of *Adam Bede* was returned by the publisher to George Eliot. It was the first of the 'row of Russia backs', i.e. her bound manuscripts, about which she wrote to William Blackwood on 13 January 1880: 'Mr. Lewes had set his mind on their going after our death to the British Museum.'[8] The Museum received the manuscript on 8 May 1891, and it is now in the British Library (Add. MSS 34,020–2). The three volumes consist of 285, 318, and 265 folios respectively. Volume I contains Book I, Chapters I to XVI; volume II, Books II to IV, Chapters XVII to XXXV; and volume III, Books V and VI, Chapters XXXVI to LV plus the Epilogue. The manuscript is foliated at least twice: in Eliot's numbering and in numbers added by the British Museum. Each folio contains at least one set of numbers in the author's hand, often a second set, and occasionally a third set as well. The author's numbering sometimes includes superscripts, signalling the addition and/or rearrangement of folios. Eliot's numbers are centred at the top of each folio, except for the first folio in a chapter, where the number appears in the upper right. The opening folio in volume I is inscribed by Eliot with a dedication to George Henry Lewes. Folios 2 to 4 contain a list of the books and chapter titles, also in Eliot's hand. The text of the novel begins on the folio numbered 5 by the British Museum, which was left unnumbered by the author. In volumes II and III, the text of the novel begins on the first folio.

The manuscript is written on blue-lined paper, with twenty-three ruled lines per page. The writing is on one side only, except for occasional insertions written on the verso. On some occasions Eliot wrote below the

---

[7] *Adam Bede* had the opportunity for a final appearance in the author's lifetime in an entirely new guise. Eliot turned down a proposal for a dramatized version in January 1879: 'Letter from Wells the dramatist asking my sanction for dramatising Adam Bede on behalf of Mrs. Hare and the Court Theatre. Wrote refusal for Charles to copy' (Saturday, 18 Jan. 1879; *JGE* 158).

[8] *Letters*, VII. 245.

lines, and in a few sections where portions of the text have been recopied, pages are only partially filled. There are occasional marks by or for the compositors, whose names were sometimes added when the manuscript was divided up for typesetting, along with marks indicating new signatures. Page size is 18.5 × 22.7 cm. The manuscript was bound in reddish-brown leather by the publisher before he returned it to the author. The binding is 18.9 × 24 cm, with the top edges of the folios trimmed and gilded; occasionally portions of page numbers, including superscripts, were lost in the process. New spine binding was added by the British Museum.

Eliot's diary for 23 March 1859 notes the receipt of the manuscript from Edinburgh: 'The M.S. of Adam Bede came this morning from Blackwood, who has had it bound in russia, before sending it to George in answer to his request.'[9] On 26 March Lewes wrote his thanks: 'I thought myself lucky when the news came that the m.s. of the Bedesman had not gone the way of the m.s.,[1] but of course never had any idea of receiving it in that superb shape—c'est faire noblement les choses, Monsieur! and I wish your good nature could have had the gratification of witnessing the pleasure with which G.E. turned over the pages, and recalled the feelings with which they were written.'[2]

The manuscript of *Adam Bede* was the first to be returned to the author; John Blackwood wrote to Eliot on 30 March, 'I had great pleasure in sending the M.S. of Adam. I have kept the M.S. of Clerical Scenes for myself. . . . It is one of the strongest practical marks of my admiration for the Scenes that from the first I had ordered the M.S. to be set aside for me.'[3] Eliot's inscription to Lewes on the first folio of volume I reads:

Marian Lewes
March 23. 1859

To my dear husband, George Henry Lewes, I give this M.S. of a work which would never have been written but for the happiness which his love has conferred on my life.

Below the inscription is a paragraph describing the novel's composition:

The first volume was written at Richmond, the second at Munich & Dresden, the third at Richmond again. The work was begun on the 22^d. October 1857, & finished on the 16th. November 185⟨7⟩8. A large portion of it was written twice, though often scarcely at all altered in the copying; but other parts only once, & among these the description of Dinah & a good deal of her sermon, the love scene between her &

[9] *JGE* 77.

[1] What Lewes probably means is that he considered it lucky that the manuscript of *Adam Bede* had not gone the way that manuscripts usually go; that is, that it had not been discarded.

[2] *Letters*, III. 38–9.

[3] *Letters*, III. 40. The manuscript for *Scenes of Clerical Life* was purchased by J. P. Morgan in 1911 (*Scenes of Clerical Life*, ed. Thomas A. Noble (Oxford, 1985), p.xxi) and is now in the Pierpont Morgan Library in New York City.

Seth, 'Hetty's World,' most of the scene in the Two Bedchambers, the talk between Arthur & Adam, various parts in the second volume which I can recal [*sic*] less easily, & in the third, Hetty's journeys, her confession & the cottage scenes.

George Eliot's recollection in 'The History of "Adam Bede"' is that 'Throughout the book, I have altered little.'[4] This phrase does not, however, accurately describe the state of the manuscript. Perhaps Eliot was recalling volume III, which had been completed only two weeks earlier. But, while that volume exhibits fewer alterations than other volumes, even it does not contain so few as to justify the phrase 'altered little'. In fact, throughout the manuscript, there is evidence of rearrangement of chapters and sections of chapters; renumbering of folios as a result of expansion or contraction of material; cancellations consisting of words, phrases, and paragraphs, sometimes heavily scored through; insertions; and transpositions. Volume III contains the fewest cancellations, volume II the most numerous and extensive. In all three volumes, some cancellations are made lightly with a pen, but many are heavily blotted in black ink. Most of these have been deciphered for the Clarendon edition, although a few remain impenetrable; others that are probable, but not certain, are marked as such.

Eliot's handwriting is generally legible, although, as was inevitable, compositors occasionally misread it, producing variants which, in some instances, were never restored by the author to their manuscript form. These variants and the handling of them in the Clarendon *Adam Bede* are discussed in the Emendations section.

Volume I

Foliation in the manuscript of volume I signifies the expansion of some sections after they were first drafted, as well as three instances of belated chapter division, in which Chapters III, IX, and XV were divided from the preceding chapters of which their text had been a part. All three begin part-way down a folio, with the chapter titles squeezed in above the line. The first eighteen folios of text (all of Chapter I and the first four folios of Chapter II) were recopied and the next four folios renumbered,[5] suggesting that the early part of Chapter II was expanded to provide a fuller description of Mr Casson, landlord of the Donnithorne Arms, in both his person

---

[4] *JGE* 298.
[5] Folio numbers refer to those in Eliot's hand; they do not include the British Museum number, added in 1891. Where more than one number appears, the first represents Eliot's original foliation, the second (and occasionally a third), her refoliation. When two numbers are given, the original number is in angle brackets (⟨⟩) and the number that replaced it follows. Likewise, where chapter numbers have been cancelled and new ones substituted, the cancelled number is in angle brackets (⟨⟩), followed by the replacement number. Eliot also refoliated Chapters I to XIII in pencil shortly before she gave the manuscript for those chapters to John Blackwood, in March 1858. The numbers for this refoliation are not included unless specifically noted.

and his assumed superiority to the evils of dialect speech. The remainder of Chapter II proceeds without a break in folio sequence.[6]

Eliot's memory of the composition process is verified by the appearance of the last part of Chapter II, which carries the reader through 'the description of Dinah and a good deal of her sermon', which the author's dedication states was written only once. However, on early folios of the sermon itself, handwriting and partially filled or over-filled folios indicate recopying. Much of Dinah's speech contains no cancellation, although late in the chapter, a proper name, Mary Allen, is cancelled and replaced by an anonymous 'servant of God in the days of her vanity' who 'one day . . . put her new cap on & looked in the glass [and] saw a bleeding face crowned with thorns' (fo. 40; p. 30 below). The author's letter recounting her aunt's story of this 'supposed miracle' names no individual;[7] if Eliot recalled a name while writing manuscript Chapter II, she obviously changed her mind about including it there. However, in Chapter III Dinah mentions a 'sister Allen, who is in a decline, [and] is in need of me' as a reason for returning to Snowfield (p. 32).

Handwriting style and alterations in foliation and chapter numbers provide evidence for the composition history of Chapter III. Chapter II concludes on line 8 of folio 43. Chapter III, 'After the Preaching', starts on line 9, with the title squeezed between the ruled lines. Its handwriting is smaller and more upright than that with which Chapter II concludes. The remaining folios in Chapter III are numbered 44 to 53. The foliation in 'Home and its Sorrows', published as Chapter IV, shows what happened. Chapter IV's original chapter number was III, and its original foliation was 44 to 68, with no superscripts or other breaks in the sequence. Later, Eliot wrote the scene describing Seth's proposal and Dinah's refusal, and at some point detached this new material as Chapter III. Rather than refoliating Chapter ⟨III⟩IV, Eliot simply attached superscript letters to the folios whose numbers were duplicated in the new Chapter III. Thus, Chapter ⟨III⟩IV's folios 44 to 53 became 44^a to 53^a. On folio 54 in Chapter ⟨III⟩IV, numbers without superscripts resume. The impetus behind the changes can be deduced from the 'History of "Adam Bede"' in which Eliot records Lewes's suggestion to expand Dinah's role:

Dinah's ultimate relation to Adam was suggested by George, when I had read to him the first part of the first volume: he was so delighted with the presentation of

---

[6] The exception is folio ⟨33⟩36^a, a fair copy with fifteen filled lines. Its foliation is puzzling. In renumbering the folios in Chapters I to XIII as she prepared to give them to John Black-wood, Eliot probably missed the partially filled ⟨33⟩36^a, and later added 36^a rather than again renumbering. Similar anomalies occur in Chapter III (folios ⟨52⟩55 and ⟨53⟩55^a), Chapter VII (folios ⟨123⟩137 and ⟨124⟩137^a), and at the beginning of Chapter IV (⟨44⟩⟨44^a⟩56) and Chapter VIII (⟨125⟩138). In Chapter V, where ⟨88⟩100 is followed by ⟨89⟩102, she apparently skipped a number in her final refoliation.

[7] *Letters*, III. 175–6.

Dinah and so convinced that the readers' interest would centre in her, that he wanted her to be the principal figure at the last. I accepted the idea at once, and from the end of the third chapter worked with it constantly in view.[8]

In writing the 'History', Eliot consulted not only her memory, but also her journal entries. In this instance, the relevant one is 17 December 1857: 'Read my new story to G. this evening as far as the end of the third chapter. He praised it highly.'[9] At this point in the composition of the 'first part of the first volume', Seth's interest in Dinah had obviously been decided upon: Chapters I and II refer to his 'coortin'' (as Wiry Ben calls it) of the female preacher. A connection between Dinah and Seth would have seemed obvious to Eliot: Adam is partly modelled on her father, whose brother Samuel married the original for Dinah. Perhaps to give Dinah sufficient moral authority as well as suggest greater propriety in her travelling alone, Eliot originally conceived of her as a *widder-woman*, as she is described by Wiry Ben on folio 25 (p. 22). This uncancelled manuscript phrase must have been altered on proofs to *preacher-woman* after Eliot, having accepted Lewes's suggestion, realized that a widowed love interest for the hero of a novel was too unconventional. (It mattered less when Seth, a minor character, was Dinah's only wooer.) The same change in plan probably explains a variant between manuscript and first edition in Chapter I, where Adam is only 'four an' twenty' in manuscript, but 'six-an'-twenty' in the first edition. The extra two years make him a more appropriate partner for Dinah who, though no longer characterized as a widow, is a mature woman known not only in Snowfield but in Leeds as a successful Methodist preacher. Furthermore, the new role for Adam required a fuller clarification of Seth's relationship to Dinah. If Seth is to be an *unsuccessful* wooer, Eliot needed to establish, as she does in the new Chapter III, Dinah's firm refusal and the inevitability of Seth's disappointment, so that Adam does not lose readers' sympathy by displacing his brother in Dinah's affections.

It is impossible to know exactly when Eliot wrote the new material, but chapter numbering demonstrates that she did not separate it from Chapter II until several more chapters were written: cancelled chapter numbers in the manuscript show that Chapters IV to X were originally numbered III to IX.[1] It is possible that the new material, 'After the Preaching', was not

___

[8] *JGE* 297.   [9] *JGE* 71.

[1] Each of these chapters except Chapter VII bears a cancelled number, from 3 to 9, which was replaced by a number from 4 to 10 after Chapter III, 'After the Preaching', was created. The first folio in Chapter VII is numbered 130 in Eliot's hand, a number belonging to the set added just before she gave Blackwood the first thirteen chapters. Foliation in Eliot's initial sequence would have given it the number 116. Anomalously, 130 is written in pen, not in pencil as are other numbers in the final set. Either the folio was damaged in some way, or Eliot felt that cancellations were such that compositors would find them hard to decipher. Taking up a pen to recopy, she used it to renumber this folio as well.

composed until after Chapter ⟨IX⟩X, although there is no way to be certain. But the chapter numbering makes it clear that Chapter III did not take on a separate existence until Chapter ⟨IX⟩X was at least under way, if not completed.

The manuscript shows only minor alterations in Chapters ⟨IV⟩V and ⟨V⟩VI, but in the latter, two cancellations are significant in showing how vividly Eliot visualized the Hall Farm. With the reader positioned to peer through the gates, a pair of cancellations moves the walnut-trees from the left to the right and the 'gorse-built hovel' from the right to the left (p. 67). If 'George Eliot had Griff House in her mind' when she wrote about the Hall Farm,[2] that association would account for the seemingly unnecessary precision of detail indicated by these cancellations—unnecessary, that is, unless the setting had a particular personal significance for the author. The view described is pictured, with attention to details right and left, in the frontispiece to the stereotyped edition of 1867, the only illustration in that edition to gain Eliot's approbation.

The principal change in Chapter ⟨V⟩VI is the addition of material, equivalent to about one folio, after the chapter was written. In her journal for 17 January 1858, Eliot records 'enjoying the writing of my 5th [i.e. 6th] chapter', and on 20 January she 'Read aloud the additional dialogue in the chapter of "The Hall Farm". G. admired it very much.' In her 'History of "Adam Bede"', Eliot recalls that 'Throughout the book, I have altered little, and the only cases, I think, in which George suggested more than a verbal alteration, when I read the M.S. aloud to him, were the first scene at the Farm and the scene in the Wood between Arthur and Adam, both of which he recommended me to "space out" a little, which I did.'[3] Sometime between 17 and 20 January, she must have read Chapter ⟨V⟩VI to Lewes, and then, following his advice, expanded and recopied the conversation between Dinah and her Aunt Poyser. Folios 97 to 110 are new copies, but folios 110[a] and 111 are part of the earlier set. Recopied folio 108 shows no cancellations in two references to 'aunt Rachel', but on folio 111 *Rachel* overwrites *Susan* (p. 74): ' "Nay, dear aunt ⟨Susan⟩ Rachel," said Dinah gently.' This is the only trace in the manuscript of an earlier given name for Mrs Poyser.

Chapter ⟨VII⟩VIII, 'A Vocation', originally included some of what was published as Chapter IX, 'Hetty's World'. When Eliot decided to make the latter a separate chapter, she divided a single long paragraph and revised what became the chapter's opening sentence: '⟨As⟩ {While} she adjusted the broad ⟨green⟩ leaves... I am afraid ⟨she⟩ Hetty was thinking a great deal more of the looks Captain Donnithorne had cast at her than of Adam &

---

[2] William Mottram, *The True Story of George Eliot in Relation to 'Adam Bede'* (London, 1905), 71. Griff House was Eliot's home from infancy to age 21.

[3] *JGE* 73, 298.

his troubles' (p. 91). This chapter division occurred soon after composition. Eliot's journal for 31 January records: 'Finished Chapters 7 and 8—the dialogue between Dinah and Mr. Irwine, and the rest up to the arrival of the Rector and Captain at Adam's cottage.'[4] The dialogue and its aftermath, Dinah's departure to visit Lisbeth Bede, is represented in what was, at the time of the journal entry, Chapter VII. The 'arrival of the Rector and Captain at Adam's Cottage' concludes 'Hetty's World', which by then must have been separated from the first part of Chapter VII, to become Chapter VIII (and later Chapter IX). These two chapters provide the first contrast between Dinah and Hetty, Dinah looking outward as she describes her calling to preach and minister to the poor and then visits Lisbeth Bede, Hetty looking inward as she comments absently on the death of Adam's father and then contemplates her power over men, especially Arthur Donnithorne. The only anomalous foliation in Chapter ⟨VIII⟩IX, folio ⟨145⟩146, suggests that the description of Hetty's reflections on the relative desirability of Adam and Arthur was expanded from an earlier, briefer text, after which old folio 145 was renumbered as 146.

The next chapter, 'Dinah's Visit to Lisbeth', was also renumbered in manuscript, ⟨IX⟩X. Manuscript cancellations and revised foliation show how Eliot restructured this chapter to foreshadow Adam's future relationship to Dinah. Foliation begins with 149 and proceeds without anomalies to 157. The next three folios, with two sets[5] of numbers (⟨154⟩158, ⟨155⟩159, and ⟨156⟩160), were renumbered after Eliot introduced new material represented on fair copied folios 153 to 157. This reworking altered the original sequence of events in which Dinah arrives at the cottage while Adam is still downstairs.

Manuscript cancellations reveal the old and new arrangements. Folio ⟨156⟩160 concludes with Lisbeth Bede's response to Dinah's visit: ' "Nay, nay, angered? who said I war angered? It war good on you to come. An' Seth, why donna ye get her some tay? Ye war in a hurry to get some for mey, as hed no need, but ye donna think o' gettin' 't for them as wants it. Sit ye down, sit ye down["]' (p. 105). The speech ends here in the published versions, but in manuscript a cancelled passage follows: 'an' I'll goo an' see arter Adam, for I canna think where hey's gotten, an' I want him to goo upstairs wi' me afore it's dark. ⟨⟨"⟩⟩ An' it's fittin' yey should go too, Seth, for th' minutes to look at th.'[6] Folio ⟨156⟩160 ends abruptly; the sentence was probably completed on another, no longer extant, folio. In the original

---

[4] *JGE* 73.

[5] Not including the final set with which Eliot numbered Chapters I to XIII before giving the manuscript to John Blackwood in March 1858.

[6] Here as elsewhere in this section, the manuscript version of the text is given, including Lisbeth's occasional manuscript use of *hey*, *mey*, and *yey* for *he*, *me*, and *ye*, as discussed in the Dialect section below.

plan, immediately after Dinah arrives, the family visits the upstairs room where the body lies. The new arrangement postpones her arrival, so that Adam, who remains upstairs and goes to bed early after his sleepless night, is unaware of her presence. The cancelled sentence quoted above is repeated, in a slightly altered version, in new material which now describes events *before* Dinah appears. Thus, on new 154, the restructured text reads: 'I'll goo an' see arter Adam, for I canna think where hey's gotten, an' I want him to goo upstairs wi' me afore it's dark, for the minutes to look at the corpse is like the meltin' snow' (p. 101).

The reorganization is also evident in the uncancelled repetition of a transitional sentence. On recopied folio 153, Lisbeth refuses Seth's offer of tea, and he retires to the back kitchen. The final two lines on 153 read: 'But after Lisbeth had been rocking herself & moaning for some minutes, she suddenly paused, & said aloud to herself,'. New folio 154 opens: 'I'll goo an' see arter Adam' (p. 101). When Lisbeth enters the workshop, Gyp's bark awakens Adam. New folios 154, 155, and 156 describe his dreams, his awaking, and Lisbeth's lengthy complaint. New folio 157 briefly notes the visit of mother and sons to the corpse and Adam's going to bed, and ends with Lisbeth's beginning 'to cry & moan & rock herself as before . . . [while Seth] went into the *back kitchen again to tend his little fire, hoping that he should presently induce her to have some tea*' (p. 103). The words emphasized here by italics, amounting to one and a half lines, are squeezed in below the last ruled line on 157.

Squeezed in above the ruled line on the next folio, ⟨154⟩158, is a transitional sentence introducing Dinah: *Lisbeth had been rocking herself in this way for more than five minutes, giving a low moan with every forward movement of her body, when she* (italics mine). The sentence continues on the ruled lines: 'suddenly felt a hand placed gently on hers, & a sweet treble voice said to her, "Dear Sister, the Lord has sent me to see if I can be a comfort to you" ' (p. 103). The italicized passage above is nearly identical to the sentence preceding Lisbeth's decision to look for Adam on folio 153. The rearrangement of Dinah's arrival resulted in the repetition of the scene of Lisbeth's crying and rocking and Seth's retirement to the back kitchen.

Except for Lisbeth's complaints on folio 156 and the top of 157, the material on new folios 154 to 157 focuses on Adam's relationship to Hetty and Dinah and the contrast between the two women. On folios 154 and 155, after noting Adam's exhaustion, the narrator describes his dream, in which his attachment to Hetty and his mother's objections to her are mingled. His desire for Hetty manifest in this dream reappears in Chapter XI, 'In the Cottage', when he imagines Dinah's 'light' step to be Hetty's, a thought that he knows is 'foolish', but that he hesitates to dispel by encountering 'the clear proof that it was some one else' (p. 110). The rearrangement in Chapter ⟨IX⟩X enables the novelist to dramatize the encounter between Adam and Dinah the following morning in Chapter XI, instead of depicting their meeting in the presence of his mother and brother. In Adam's conversation with Seth in the workshop after breakfast, his observation that Dinah has 'a face like a lily' and is 'made out of stuff with a finer grain than most o' the women', and his affirmation that he 'can't think she'll fall short of 'em in loving', are prophetic, but not in reference to Seth's love (fos. 192–3; p. 116). Part of the novel's pattern of parallel scenes, this first encounter anticipates Dinah and Adam's morning meeting in Chapter L.

Foliation in Chapter ⟨XI⟩XII and cancellation of its original chapter number reveal that Eliot wrote Chapter ⟨XI⟩XII before she inserted 'In the Cottage' as Chapter XI. After the manuscript alterations described above, Eliot's numbering in Chapter ⟨IX⟩X is sequential until folios 179 and 179ᵃ.[7] These pencilled numbers are part of the final sequence of numbers she added just before she gave Blackwood Chapters I to XIII. Following Chapter XI's final folio, whose only number in Eliot's hand is 193, Chapter ⟨XI⟩XII's opening folio also shows only one number, 194. Both 193 and 194 are part of Eliot's final sequence. But the second folio of Chapter ⟨XI⟩XII shows a double set of numbers by the author, the first of which is 168, from the original sequence; the second, 195, from the later sequence. The first folio in Chapter ⟨XI⟩XII was [167], its original number having been for some unknown reason omitted. A cancellation in the opening sentence confirms that folio [167] was written before a new Chapter XI was inserted; this cancellation adjusts the time sequence to accommodate the new chapter. Chapter I opens in 'The Workshop' on Tuesday, 18 June 1799; Chapters II to IV span the evening, night, and early morning of the next day, Wednesday, 19 June. Chapter IV ends that morning with the discovery of Thias Bede's body. Chapters V to X take place the same day, in the late afternoon of which Dinah arrives at the Bedes' cottage. Chapter ⟨XI⟩XII originally opened with the words 'The next morning', i.e. Thursday, 20 June. But when the Thursday morning scene in the cottage was added as Chapter XI, the first words of Chapter ⟨XI⟩XII were revised from 'The next morning' to 'That same Thursday morning' (p. 117).[8] This opening folio of Chapter ⟨XI⟩XII also establishes the *terminus ad quem* for Chapter III's separate existence: old Chapters III–IX were renumbered as IV–X before Eliot wrote Chapter ⟨XI⟩XII, 'In the Wood', to follow 'Dinah Visits Lisbeth', Chapter ⟨IX⟩X. When she inserted 'In the Cottage', whose title emphasizes the contrasts between Dinah and Hetty, Adam

---

[7] As the following discussion demonstrates, fos. 179 and 179ᵃ must have been recopied from a single fo. 166, probably when Eliot prepared to give John Blackwood the first thirteen chapters in March 1858.

[8] This alteration not only confirms the order of composition; it also indicates that the first folio of Chapter XII was not recopied after Eliot wrote Chapter XI, despite the absence of a number in the original sequence. If the opening folio had been recopied, evidence of the revision of 'The next morning' would have disappeared.

and Arthur, and duty and self-indulgence, 'In the Wood' became Chapter XII.[9]

Given the close relationship between the scenes of Hetty and Arthur 'In the Wood' (Chapter ⟨XI⟩XII) on Thursday afternoon and again on Thursday evening (Chapter XIII, 'Evening in the Wood'), it is probable that Eliot wrote these chapters at the same time, before returning to Adam, Dinah, Seth, and Lisbeth 'In the Cottage'. But there is no way to be certain. Because Eliot recopied Chapter XIII when she introduced the second set of numbers, the chapter contains no traces of earlier foliation that might have made the order of composition clear.

After giving Blackwood Chapters I to XIII on 5 March 1858, Eliot completed Chapter XIV three days later: 'Wrote Chapter 14 up to the going to bed.'[1] The 'going to bed' describes the end of Chapter XIV, which she resumed on the folio on which she had left off. When she realized that the continuation required a separate chapter, she squeezed the chapter number and title in above line 5 on folio 234.

Manuscript Chapters XIV to XVI show only occasional cancellations and insertions, and one sign of expansion, none of rearrangement. Part-way through Chapter XV, folios numbered 243 and 243[a] indicate addition of material developing the image of Hetty as rootless. In particular, this section emphasizes Hetty's indifference to the children she has tended since their birth and to young animals and 'hatching' in general, foreshadowing the infanticide to come. Handwriting, cancellations, and foliation in the early part of Chapter XVI support Eliot's memory in her inscription that 'the talk between Arthur and Adam' was written 'only once'.

Volume II

Writing all but the final chapter of volume II on their trip to Germany from early April to early September 1858, Eliot found both distraction and inspiration in the art, music, reading, and socializing that occupied much of her and Lewes's time, in a country where Lewes's biography of Goethe had made him a sought-after guest and the couple's extralegal union was no barrier to Eliot's inclusion on social occasions, as was the case in England. As a result, she did less recopying, and the manuscript shows heavier and more frequent cancellations than in volumes I or III. Rearrangements such as those in volume I that resulted as she determined on Adam's relationship to Dinah are absent from volume II. After the opening chapter, 'In Which the Story Pauses a Little', events unfold smoothly from Thias Bede's funeral to intimations of Hetty and Arthur's developing relationship to the birthday celebration and its aftermath—the discovery by Adam,

---

[9] If this chapter had been written before 'After the Preaching' became Chapter III, it would originally have been numbered X, not XI.

[1] *JGE* 74.

Arthur's departure, the betrothal, and Hetty's flight. Alterations in the initial foliation of Chapters XVIII and XIX and on the final folio in Chapter XXXI signal additions in the voice of the narrator. A slight expansion in Chapter XXVI increases tensions in the Arthur–Hetty–Adam relationship and prepares for the fight in the next chapter.

The lightly revised Chapter XVII contains two renumbered folios, ⟨11⟩12 and ⟨12⟩13, which signal an expanded commentary on Mr Irwine's efficacy as a clergyman, an issue raised by John Blackwood in his letter of 31 March 1858. In the first part of Chapter XVII, the narrator begins his discussion of realism in art by addressing a putative lady reader's objection to the portrayal of Mr Irwine. The narrator's generalized discussion of realism vs. idealism in art concludes on folio 7, whose last two lines begin a new paragraph, 'And so I come back to Mr Irwine, with whom I desire you to be in perfect charity' (p. 168). After quoting Adam's views on Mr Irwine's kindness and good example (folios 8 to 10), the narrator raises the question of his preaching, in what seems a response to Blackwood's 'hope' that the Rector 'is to sublime as the story goes on', advice connected with his wish that Eliot had depicted Mr Irwine's visit to the Bede cottage.[2] The narrator becomes a devil's advocate for Blackwood's point of view, and Adam, 'to whom [the narrator] talked of these matters in his old age', is Mr Irwine's defender (p. 169). Folios 7 to 11, which record their conversation, are fair copies, making details of the expansion impossible to recover.

Refoliation in Chapter XVIII signals an alteration late in Chapter XVII. The dialogue between Adam and the narrator ends near the bottom of ⟨12⟩13 with Adam's '& that's enough for me' (p. 171). Handwriting suggests that Chapter XVII originally concluded here, and that Eliot later added the paragraph beginning, 'Adam, you perceive, was ⟨rather⟩ a warm admirer perhaps a partial judge of Mr Irwine', on the last three lines of folio ⟨12⟩13 and continued her address to the reader on folio 14 and part of 15.[3] The additional material in Chapter XVII concludes the discussion of realism and returns to the narrator–reader dialogue with which the chapter began.

'Adam Visits the Hall Farm' was originally the title of Chapter XIX, but when Eliot decided to focus on Adam as a common man in Chapter XIX and postponed his visit to the Hall Farm until the next chapter, she cancelled this title and replaced it with 'Adam on a Working Day'. Her

---

[2] *Letters*, II. 445. Blackwood is diplomat enough to place his advice in the context of Eliot's desire for realism, but the advice is of a piece with his concern about the unspiritual Bishop in 'Janet's Repentance' (*Letters*, II. 360).

[3] Chapter XVIII originally began with folios numbered 14 and 15, later renumbered as 14ᵃ and 15ᵃ. Because the upper edges of the folios were trimmed and gilded, probably by Blackwoods when the manuscript was bound for Lewes, the superscript letter is not visible on 14ᵃ, although Eliot's usual underline indicates it was part of her numbering. Folio 15ᵃ shows the underline and the superscript letter fully.

attempt to balance Adam as the common man at work with his status as a
hero is evident in two separate additions to the end of Chapter XIX, made
after Chapter XX was written.[4] The first, starting on folio 61, expands the
narrator's discussion of the way in which Adam is both ordinary and
exceptional.

> Adam, you perceive,[5] was by no means a marvellous man, nor, properly speaking,
> a genius, yet I will not pretend that his was ⟨a common⟩ an ordinary character
> among workmen, & it would not be at all a safe conclusion that the next best man you
> may happen to see with a basket of tools over his shoulder & a paper cap on his head
> has the strong conscience & the strong sense, the blended susceptibility & self-
> command of our friend Adam. (p. 200)

The final words produce a sense of closure. However, a shift to smaller,
tighter handwriting after 'our friend Adam' (folio 62, line 6) signals that
Eliot later made a second addition, 'He was not an average man. Yet such
men as he are reared here & there in every generation of our peasant
artizans.' The chapter concludes on folio 63 with an elegy for 'such men',
of whom Adam is only one example.

The next five chapters, XXI to XXV, mix fair copies with folios showing
occasional cancellations. Foliation in Chapter XXI shows only two anomalies: a single folio numbered '110 & 111', condensing two earlier folios, and
the two final folios, 115 and 115ª. In the first, the text is fitted into twenty-
four lines, constituting part of Adam's narrative about the cause of Squire
Donnithorne's hostility—their dispute over payment for the screen Adam
made for the Squire's daughter. Handwriting and ink colour show that the
text on the second half of folio 109, folio '110 & 111', and folio 112, was
written at one time, beginning with Adam's explanation, 'O, it was a bit o'
nonsense' (p. 229). The scene shows both Adam's respect for the gentry,
which the narrator emphasizes in Chapter XVI, and his refusal to defer to
them on matters of principle, foreshadowing his reaction to Arthur in
Chapters XXVII and XXVIII. Highlighting the blend of deference and
independence in his character, this revision in Chapter XXI addresses
Lewes's concern that Adam 'was too passive'.[6] Adam's diction is similar

---

[4] Chapter XIX is numbered without interruption from 53 to 63. The first folio of Chapter
XX exhibits two numbers in the author's hand, 62ª and 63ª, which must have been originally
62 and 63; on the second folio of Chapter XX, an original 63 is cancelled and replaced by 64.
This pattern continues from ⟨63⟩64 to ⟨71⟩72, after which the next five folios, all fair copies,
are numbered 73 to 76ª. From this foliation early in Chapter XX, one can infer that two folios
were added, one at a time, to Chapter XIX after most or all of Chapter XX was written. When
revision added folio 62 to Chapter XIX, the first folio of Chapter XX, which had been 62,
became 62ª. Further expansion and revision in Chapter XIX resulted in new folio 63, so that
folio 62ª in Chapter XX became 63ª and the following folios, 63 to 71, were renumbered 64 to
72.

[5] As noted above, this locution also begins the expanded material in Chapter XVII.

[6] JGE 298.

in Chapters XXI and XXVIII: 'I didn't mean to be disrespectful, & I spoke as polite as I could; but I can give in to no man, if he wants to make it out as I'm trying to overreach him' (fo. 112, Chapter XXI; pp. 229–30), and 'I dont [*sic*] forget what's owing to you [Arthur] as a gentleman—but in this thing we're man & man, & I can't give up' (Chapter XXVIII; p. 293). Recopying the last three folios (113 to 115) after Chapter XXII was under way probably led to the anomalous folio 115ᵃ.

Cancellations and refoliation[7] in Chapter XXII indicate Eliot's careful development of the description of Hetty's preparations for the birthday celebration. This bedroom scene is the first hint of her intimacy with Arthur since their meetings in Chapters XII and XIII. The presents of earrings and locket and the description of her physical person and her attire for the dance signal to readers the danger of which Hetty herself is unconscious. The delicacy required in describing the arrangement of the locket concealed in Hetty's bosom led to a lengthy cancellation on folio ⟨119⟩121.

Foliation also indicates that the Adam–Arthur–Hetty relationship was expanded from an earlier version in Chapter XXVI. Since Arthur and Hetty's meetings after Chapter XIII occur 'off-stage', nothing of Arthur's internal struggle has been visible in volume II except his 'twinge of conscience during Mr Poyser's speech' at the health-drinking in Chapter XXIV, followed by his self-congratulatory 'another man . . . would have acted much worse' (p. 249), giving the reader a fairly exact measure of how far things have gone. Chapter XXVI returns the reader to his struggles of conscience and the question of how far things might yet go.

After Chapter XXVI was first drafted, four new folios, 176 to 179, resulted from the expansion of material originally on two folios.[8] Unrecopied folio 175 includes five heavily cancelled passages describing the dance, ending with two lines at the top of new folio 176, concluding Mr Poyser's decision to give 'his face up to hilarity unchecked by moral judgments'. This new folio and three additional ones numbered 177 to 179 replace earlier folios 176 and 177, which are not extant. With unrecopied folio ⟨178⟩180, opening 'the glass [of the locket] was not broken', it is clear that the earlier 177 must have been occupied with the complex set of manœuvres leading to Totty's breaking the beads holding the locket, a description that could not have occupied much less space in the ur-text than it does in the revision. Thus, the original 176 has been expanded to nearly three new folios.[9] This expanded section, which describes Arthur's

---

[7] Two folios are renumbered: ⟨119⟩121 and ⟨120⟩122, indicating that two original folios, 117 and 118, became four, 117 to 120.

[8] Refoliation involves three folios: original 178, 179, and 180 are renumbered as 180, 181, and 182.

[9] The manœuvres leading to the breaking of the beads fill lines 21 to 25 on new folio 178 and all of new folio 179.

passion for Hetty in the long paragraph beginning 'How Hetty's heart beat', his second 'twinge' of guilt that day when he responds to Mrs Poyser's assurances that Hetty has saved a dance for him (p. 269), and Adam's daydreams about Hetty as his wife, contrasts the motives of the two men and prepares for their angry words and blows in the next chapter.

Eliot did not begin her 'history of the Birthday' until 13 June, four days before Lewes went to Hofwyl to visit his sons, but she had been pondering this section and the fight scene for some time. As she writes in the 'History of "Adam Bede"', the fight between Adam and Arthur in Chapter XXVII 'came to me as a *necessity* one night at the Munich Opera when I was listening to *William Tell*', an event her journal dates 'Sunday [May] 30'.[1] The birthday chapters lead up to it carefully. At the health-drinking, Arthur has been acting the gracious benefactor toward Adam. In other events of the birthday celebration, Adam is mostly off-stage, the loyal retainer assigned by Arthur to help maintain order. At the birthday dance their competing passion for Hetty is foregrounded.[2] If the fight was a 'necessity', Eliot also needed to portray the feelings of each man for the beautiful girl whose sleeves and neckerchief are put aside for the evening dance. The expanded text in Chapter XXVI indicates, as far as Victorian reticence allowed, their competing passion. Arthur 'would have given up three years of his youth for the happiness of abandoning himself without remorse to his passion for Hetty' (fo. 177; p. 268), and Adam imagines himself married and 'coming home from work, & drawing Hetty to his side & feeling her cheek softly pressed against his' (fo. 178; p. 269). The intensity of their desire in Chapter XXVI anticipates the violence of their hostility in Chapter XXVII.

Lewes suggested Eliot ' "space out" a little' the 'scene in the Wood between Arthur and Adam',[3] probably when she read her manuscript to him on 25 June, the day after his return.[4] Chapter XXVII includes numerous heavily corrected folios and one alteration in foliation, ⟨217⟩216, suggesting a condensing of the text. Emphasizing the focus on Adam and Arthur's relationship, Chapter XXVII's original title, 'In the Wood Again', was cancelled in manuscript, and 'A Crisis' substituted. Instead of connecting Chapter XXVII with Chapters XII and XIII, 'In the Wood' and 'Evening in the Wood', the new title pairs Chapter XXVII with Chapter XXVIII, 'A Dilemma', where the peasant Adam insists on equality 'in this matter' with the heir of the Squire.

---

[1] *JGE* 298, 318.

[2] Neither, of course, is aware that the other is a rival. Arthur cannot be a suitor, and Adam does not imagine him as a seducer, and Arthur, misled by Mr Irwine's belief that there is 'a kindness' between Adam and Mary Burge (Chapter IX), has no notion of Adam's feeling for Hetty.

[3] *JGE* 298.   [4] *JGE* 318–19.

Cancellations in volume II show Eliot paying close attention to historical detail.[5] In Chapter XVII, as already noted, she substituted *Dutch* for *Flemish* when she realized that the painting she describes most precisely was by a Dutch artist. She read and took notes from the *Gentleman's Magazine*, recording details of the weather in summer 1799, particularly the rains that brought floods and crop failure throughout England and a rise in the price of bread. In *Adam Bede* Chapter XXII, before writing the title (which is squeezed in above the insertion), she inserted a lengthy clause after the opening six-word sentence, in which the date is altered twice: 'The ⟨thirtieth⟩ ⟨twenty fifth⟩ thirtieth of July was come⟨.⟩ {& it was one of those ⟨hot⟩ {half dozen warm} days which sometimes occur in the middle of a rainy English summer.}' (p. 233). The author selected 30 July as the date for the birthday,[6] then moved it back to 25 July, perhaps to allow more time between the birthday fête and Arthur's departure. But the *Gentleman's Magazine* shows the weather of 25 July 1799 unpropitious for outdoor events. For 24 July, Eliot recorded 'Severe lightning in the evening', and for 25 July 'Loud thunder with a heavy shower of rain, previous to which the throstle poured fourth his song with a degree of violence.'[7] In fact there was little to choose from; July 1799 was a wet month in a wet summer. Holt's Meteorological Diary in the *Gentleman's Magazine* shows only six days in July with fine, clear weather: 1, 9, 16, 21, 26, and 30 July. The first three occur too early in the month to have allowed sufficient time to pass for the change in Adam's prospects and the development of Arthur and Hetty's relationship. Of the last three, 21 July was a Sunday and 26 July, a Friday. With church and the 'Treddles' on market-day' (held on Fridays, see Chapter VI) precluding these dates, only 30 July, a Tuesday, remained. Chapter XXII's account of the weather is almost accurate:

No rain had fallen for the last three or four days, & the weather was perfect for that time of the year: there was less dust than usual on the dark green hedgerows & {on} the wild camomile that starred the road side, yet the grass was dry enough for the little children to roll on it, & there was no cloud but a long dash of light, downy ripple, high, high up in the far-off blue sky. (fo. 116; p. 233)

Holt's Diary describes the preceding four days as 'clear, sun, and pleasant' (26 July), 'overcast' (27th), and 'gloomy' (28th); only the 29th is recorded as having 'showers', which might be assumed to have fallen elsewhere than in Hayslope.

---

[5] Nonetheless, she missed the anachronism regarding Bartle Massey's use of the Lucifer match, as discussed below.

[6] Eliot had given 30 July as the date for Arthur's birthday as early as Chapter VII, and repeated it in Chapter XVIII. Neither of these manuscript chapters shows any sign of an altered date.

[7] *A Writer's Notebook*, 30.

The opening paragraphs in Chapter XXVII also attempt to locate events in their historical context:

It was {beyond} the middle of August—{nearly} three weeks after the birthday feast. The reaping of the wheat had begun in our north midland county of Loamshire, but the harvest was likely still to be retarded by the heavy rains which were causing inundations & much damage throughout the country. From this last trouble the Broxton & Hayslope farmers, on their pleasant uplands & in their brook-watered valleys had not suffered, & as I cannot pretend that they were such exceptional farmers as to love the general good better than their own, you will infer that they were not in very low spirits about the rapid rise in the price of bread[8] so long as there was hope of gathering in their own corn undamaged. And occasional days of sunshine {& drying winds} flattered this hope. (fo. 186; p. 277)

A cancellation in the next paragraph changes another date, 'The ⟨fifteenth⟩ eighteenth of August was one of these days.' Eliot's only note on August weather in *A Writer's Notebook* reads: 'August seems to have been a rainy month. 29. Reaping oats—still near the sea, Liverpool.' Nonetheless, the change of date, from the 15th to the 18th, fits the weather discussed by Holt: 'heavy rain, P.M.' on the 15th, whereas on 18 August there was simply 'rain', followed by a day on which Arthur, in Chapter XXIX, could easily ride out in comfort to contemplate his course of action: Holt's Diary for 19 August records 'after slight showers, clears up'. This weather is also a metaphor for Arthur's temperament: the 'problem' is a slight shower, which clears up after his ride.

However, in making the change from 15 to 18 August, Eliot placed events on a Sunday, a day on which Hetty *might* have gone after church with the upper servants from the Chase and contrived to meet Arthur later, but not one on which Adam would have been walking home from work. Eliot also erred in dating the betrothal in Chapter XXXIV. It takes place on 'a dry Sunday, & really a pleasant day, for the second of November'. But the first Sunday in November in 1799 was the 3rd, not the 'second', which is written out in manuscript and therefore could not have been mistaken by compositors, who set it as '2d'.

Volume III

George Eliot began volume III in Richmond, after sending volume II to Blackwood in early September.[9] By late October she had finished 216 folios,[1] and the remainder were completed on 16 November.[2]

---

[8] In *A Writer's Notebook* Eliot notes the rise in the price of bread: 'Price of the quartern loaf in 1799, 13d; whereas in 1798 it was 8d. Weight of penny loaf in 1799, 5 oz. 5 dr. In 1798, 8 oz. 11 dr.' (32).

[9] *JGE* 74.

[1] *JGE* 298. That is, 216 by Eliot's numbering; superscript folios increase the actual number to 220, as the British Museum numbering shows.

[2] *JGE* 75.

This volume contains fewer cancellations, insertions, and rearrangements than volumes I and II. The most significant alteration revealed
in the manuscript is a rearrangement that moved the chapter called
'Arthur's Return' from its original place as Chapter XLI to a new position
as Chapter XLIV.

In the 'History of "Adam Bede"', Eliot recalls that 'The opening of the
third volume—Hetty's journeys—was, I think written more rapidly than
the rest of the book, and was left without the slightest alteration of the first
draught.'[3] The appearance of Chapters XXXVI and XXXVII, however,
suggests otherwise. There are fewer alterations than in parts of volume II,
but there are still more than six dozen cancellations and insertions in
Chapters XXXVI and XXXVII, mostly in the latter. Slight expansions
are indicated by foliation in Chapters XXXVIII, XXXIX, and XL, but for
only one is it possible to speculate on the nature of the expansion. The text
preceding folio 46[a] in Chapter XXXVIII was expanded and recopied on
folios 45 and 46, probably to provide an explanation of why Adam fails to
consider that Hetty might have gone to Windsor.

The final folio of Chapter XL signals the most important single
change in the manuscript of volume III, the repositioning of the chapter
titled 'Arthur's Return'. Eliot's original plan envisioned three related
chapters in which characters react to news of Hetty's imprisonment:
Adam in Chapter XXXIX, the Poysers and their neighbours in
Chapter XL, and Arthur in Chapter XLI. In the new arrangement, Chapter XLI, 'Arthur's Return', became Chapter XLIV, following 'The Verdict', which concludes with the death sentence and Hetty's collapse in
court.

Changes in foliation and chapter numbering reveal the process. Chapter
XL in an early draft concluded on folio 75; 'Arthur's Return' began on folio
76. When recopying Chapter XL produced an extra folio, numbered 76,
Eliot added a superscript a to the folio 76 with which 'Arthur's Return', still
Chapter XLI, began. Later she made 'Arthur's Return' Chapter XLIV by
overwriting the chapter's original number, XLI, and renumbering folios
⟨76⟩76[a] to 81 as 101 to 106.[4]

Eliot's journal does not mention repositioning 'Arthur's Return', much
less a reason for it, but the new placement makes excellent dramatic sense.
After Chapters XXXIX to XLII focus on Adam and his family, the
Poysers, and their friends, Chapter XLIII divides the emphasis between

---

[3] *JGE* 298.

[4] The foliation of new Chapter XLI, 'The Eve of the Trial', is puzzling. It also opens on fo.
76[a], although, if it were written after 'Arthur's Return' was moved (when the recopying had
already occurred), it should start on fo. 77. If 'Arthur's Return' had been written but *not* moved
when 'The eve of the trial' was composed, the latter would originally be Chapter XLII and
foliation would follow the original sequence in 'Arthur's Return'.

Adam and Hetty, who appears for the first time since her arduous journeys in Chapters XXXVI and XXXVII. At the end of Chapter XLIII, she collapses as the sentence is pronounced, and readers' attention shifts to the complacent Arthur, journeying comfortably in a chaise and anticipating his new life in the certainty that a benevolent Providence has arranged his escape from the consequences of his affair with Hetty. The shock of the revelation is like that in Greek drama, whose audience knows before the hero the Nemesis that awaits him.

Following Chapter XLIV, there are only a few breaks in foliation and no extensive cancellations. However, the manuscript does reveal two significant variants from the first edition, one an omission and the other an addition. The omission occurs at the end of Chapter L, where a long paragraph in manuscript is reduced to two sentences in the first edition (p. 458), probably because the author decided that realism had been treated sufficiently in Chapter XVII. All that remains are the first and last parts, including the narrator's phrase 'your lady friends', which seems to address male readers rather than female, in contrast to Chapter XVII, where the narrator in manuscript and first edition[5] imagines an objection from 'one of my lady readers' whom he addresses as 'my fair critic'. In Chapter L, the manuscript phrase 'all your lady friends' is altered in the first edition to 'all your feminine friends', a style that suggests a female addressee more than does the phrase 'your lady friends'.

At the end of Chapter LIII, two published paragraphs are *not* part of the manuscript, which concludes with Bartle Massey's misogynist description of Mrs Poyser as ' "a terrable woman—made of needles, made of needles" ', and his concession that Martin Poyser is ' "a cushion made on purpose for 'em" ' (fo. 241). The first edition, however, contains two additional paragraphs in which Adam defends Mrs Poyser as ' "a downright good-natur'd woman, for all that, . . . and as true as the daylight. . . . If her tongue's keen, her heart's tender: I've seen that in times o' trouble. She's one o' those women as are better than their word." ' Bartle gets the last word, but it is a softened one. He concedes, ' "I don't say th' apple isn't sound at the core; but it sets my teeth on edge, it sets my teeth on edge" ' (p. 489). In reading proofs, Eliot probably realized that leaving Bartle's speech unanswered would have made Adam seem unfeeling toward Mrs Poyser, and neglectful of Dinah's wisdom in Chapter L, that 'we must learn to see the good in the midst of much that is unlovely'.

The manuscript for volume III, perhaps because more folios have been recopied, shows less evidence of alteration in dates, weather, and other realistic details, and there is no evidence, external or internal to the manuscript, that Eliot consulted the weather tables or the assizes calendar in the *Gentleman's Magazine* when she scheduled Hetty's journey to Windsor,

---

[5] Eliot cancelled the gendered references in the marked 8th edition.

Adam's journey to Snowfield and Stoniton in search of her, or the trial and execution dates. In the event, she mismatches days and dates in 1800. The novel gives both day and date for the birth of the child (Saturday, 27 February, according to the testimony of Sarah Stone at the trial, Chapter XLIII), Adam's journey to Snowfield (Sunday, 'the last morning in February', Chapter XXXVIII), and the day scheduled for Hetty's execution (Monday, 15 March, which is also the day Hetty and Adam were to be married, Chapters XXXIX, XLV, and XLVI). However, Eliot's calendar is off by two days: 27 and 28 February were on Thursday and Friday in 1800, not Saturday and Sunday, and 15 March was a Saturday, not a Monday. Perhaps she did not consult any calendar—or perhaps she consulted a calendar for 1802, the year in which Mary Voce, the 'original' for Hetty, was executed; the days and dates match for that year. Eliot comes close, but still misses the dates of Lenten assizes in 1800. Graham Handley states that the town of Stoniton is 'based on Derby', although Mary Voce was tried and executed in Nottingham.[6] According to the Circuits of the Judges calendar in the February number of *Gentleman's Magazine*, the 'Lent Circuit' for Midland district in 1800 included 'Nott & Town' on 'Thursda [sic] 13' March, and 'Derby' on 'Monday 17' March.[7] Hetty's trial falls between the two, Friday, 12 March,[8] according to Eliot's calendar for 1800.

The only manuscript evidence showing the author's struggle with the time sequence involves several cancellations in passages referring to Hetty's expected return from Snowfield. In Chapter XXXVIII, *fortnight* replaces *week* in six places, usually in some variant of 'Friday was a ⟨week⟩ fortnight.'[9] These references to a week represent an earlier stage of the manuscript, in which Eliot had not yet projected the timelines precisely.

One further confusion of dates occurs in the Epilogue, in the calculation of the number of years that have passed from the opening of the story to the final meeting of Adam and Arthur. The Epilogue begins:

It is near the end of June, in 1807. The workshops have been shut up half an hour or more in Adam Bede's timber yard, which used to be Jonathan Burge's, & the mellow evening light is falling on the pleasant house with the buff walls & the soft grey thatch, very much as it did when we saw Adam bringing in the keys on that June evening nine years ago. (p. 498)

However, calculating from 18 June 1799, when the novel opens, to late June 1807 gives eight years, not nine. On folio 255, Seth says that 'it's getting on towards eight year since they parted'. Adam is closest to the time when he

[6] Handley, 91.   [7] *Gentleman's Magazine*, 87 (Feb. 1800), 176.
[8] Again the day/date is off by two days; the Friday between the two court dates was the 14th in 1800.
[9] The first three folios of Chapter XXXVIII have been recopied; consequently, the opening folio, 34, uses the later term *fortnight* without showing a cancellation to *week*.

tells Dinah that Arthur has asked whether she has changed: 'I told him "no," . . . only a bit plumper, as thee'dst a right to be after seven year.'[1] The manuscript shows evidence of alteration in only one of these three dates—and that in the direction of imprecision. The final paragraph on manuscript folio 255 reads:

> 'Ay, they'd have a deal to say to one another', said Seth. 'And the meeting 'ud touch 'em both pretty closish. ⟨Why,⟩ Why, it's ⟨seven year & a quarter as nigh as can be⟩ getting on towards eight year, since they parted.' (p. 499)

Perhaps Eliot intended to characterize the absent-minded, or unworldly, Seth through the vague phrase 'getting on towards eight year'. But there is nothing in the manuscript to indicate, or explain, the opening paragraph's miscount.

The inconsistencies in the chronology outlined here have been allowed to stand in the Clarendon edition of *Adam Bede*. Attempting to put them right would not add to the integrity of the text, which does not depend on the correspondence of day and date in 1799 and 1800, or on the passage of time in the Epilogue.

DIALECT

More than for any of her other novels, in *Adam Bede* George Eliot sought to represent precisely the dialect of her regional characters. Grounded in her theory of realism articulated in Chapter XVII, her handling of dialect individualizes the working people of Loamshire and Stonyshire, registering their place, socially and educationally, within the community. In some cases, it marks her characters as outsiders. Graham Handley calls dialect 'the distinguishing mark in her sure sense of place'.[2] Although there would have been regional dialectal differences among the more educated, upper-class characters as well, Eliot does not attempt to represent the speech of the gentry—Mr Irwine, Arthur Donnithorne, and their family members—in distinctive configurations of pronunciation, grammar, or lexicon. In its written representation in *Adam Bede*, their speech could be that of Eliot, Lewes, or even the Scotsman John Blackwood.

Chapter XVII argues for the importance of 'faithful representing of commonplace things' in art, especially 'common, coarse people'. In writing and rewriting the dialect of the farmers and artisans, Eliot consulted her memory of the speech she had heard her father and his brothers use among themselves, the dialects of Staffordshire and Derbyshire, where Robert Evans had lived before moving to Warwickshire. Having only an aural

---

[1] The meeting between Adam and Arthur in Chapter XLVIII occurs the day after Hetty was to have been executed, that is, 16 March 1800 by Eliot's calendar. Thus the meeting in the Epilogue occurs seven years and three months later.

[2] Handley, 4.

experience of these dialects, Eliot had to develop an orthography that would represent speech that she and her readers had never seen in written form and that most of her readers would be unfamiliar with in spoken form as well.[3] From the standpoint of the textual editor, the result is a complex set of variants produced when the author altered dialect within the manuscript, on the proofs for the first edition, and on the copy of the eighth edition that she corrected in 1861.

Eliot's dilemma lay in the conflict between representation and readability. Years later she described her intentions to W. W. Skeat, who founded the English Dialect Society in 1873:

It must be borne in mind that my inclination to be as close as I could to the rendering of dialect, both in words and spelling, was constantly checked by the artistic duty of being generally intelligible. But for that check, I should have given a stronger colour to the dialogue in 'Adam Bede,' which is modelled on the talk of N. Staffordshire and the neighbouring part of Derbyshire. The spelling, being determined by my own ear alone, was necessarily a matter of anxiety, for it would be as possible to quarrel about it as about the spelling of Oriental names.

Adam Bede was the only novel in which she attempted to reproduce a specific dialect closely and accurately:

in all my other presentations of English life, except 'Adam Bede,' it has been my intention to give the general physiognomy rather than a close portraiture of the provincial speech as I have heard it in the Midland or Mercian region. It is a just demand that art should keep clear of such specialities as would make it a puzzle for the larger part of its public; still, one is not bound to respect the lazy obtuseness or snobbish ignorance of people who do not care to know more of their native tongue than the vocabulary of the drawing-room and the newspaper.[4]

---

[3] In representing the dialect of ordinary people, Eliot had, of course, the model of Sir Walter Scott, who was in her mind as she composed the early parts of *Adam Bede*, as her reference to *The Heart of Midlothian* in her letter to John Blackwood quoted above shows. But Scott could serve only as an affirmation of this *kind* of verisimilitude. Blackwood commented humorously on the dialect issue and his countrymen, the compositors, in a letter also quoted earlier: 'The blunders in the "dialect" arise no doubt from the compositors thinking that there is no "dialect" in the world except Scotch' (27 Oct. 1859; *Letters*, III. 190).

[4] Dated tentatively 1872; *Letters*, IX. 39. Almost twenty years after she wrote *Adam Bede*, Eliot also explained her views on dialect in responding to a letter from the poet William Allingham: 'Mr. Lewes feels himself innocent of dialect in general and of Midland d[ialect] in especial. Hence I presume to take your reference on the subject as if it had been addressed to me. I was born and bred in Warwickshire, and heard the Leicestershire, North Staffordshire and Derbyshire dialects during visits made in my childhood and youth.

'These last are represented (mildly) in "Adam Bede." The Warwickshire talk is broader and has characteristics which it shares with other Mercian districts.

'Moreover dialect, like other living things, tends to become mongrel, especially in a central fertile and manufacturing region attractive of migration: and hence the Midland talk presents less interesting relics of elder grammar than the more northerly dialects' (8 Mar. 1877; *Letters*, VI. 347). A postscript gives the pronunciations of numerous sounds in Warwickshire dialect,

The alterations that Eliot made in the dialect of *Adam Bede* represent her negotiations between that desirable 'stronger colour' and the 'specialities as would make [art] a puzzle'. As a publisher, John Blackwood was especially desirous to avoid such puzzles. From the first, he expressed concern about the quantity of dialect in the manuscript. On 31 March 1858, he wrote: 'Lisbeth is a very perfect picture but there is rather too much of her, or rather of her dialect.'[5] Lisbeth Bede is the most prominent of several minor characters who share the most distinctive Loamshire dialect in the novel. She plays a significant role in three of the thirteen chapters that Blackwood had read by that date (Chapters IV, X, and XI). However, in responding on 1 April Eliot does not mention dialect,[6] and in volumes II and III Lisbeth continues to use the dialect forms found in the first volume.

Blackwood did not raise the question again until the novel was being set in type in November 1858. His silence resulted not only because he feared to discourage his diffident author, but also because, until Chapters L and LI, Lisbeth's speaking role is minimal, although when she does speak, her dialect in manuscript is just as distinctive. However, sending Eliot 'the two front sheets of the book,[7] which I have read with great pleasure', he ventured a tactful hint: 'If the provincial dialect was not so exceedingly good, I would be inclined to say that there should be less of it.'[8] This time Eliot acknowledged his objections and, in returning these first proofs, agreed that

The dialect must be toned down all through in correcting the proofs, for I found it impossible to keep it subdued enough in writing. I am aware that the spelling which represents a dialect perfectly well to those who know it by the ear, is likely to be unintelligible to others. Mr. Lewes is a good test, being innocent of dialects, and he is good enough to run over the proofs for the sake of checking unintelligibility.[9]

but ends by advising Allingham that 'Perhaps, however, these imperfect indications may only determine you to reject all but the faintest signs of dialect in your well-to-do farmers who have been to London' (*Letters*, VI. 348). Gordon Haight adds: 'A pencil note signed W.A. says that this [subject] refers "to a dialogue in verse 'Old Master Grunsey and Goodman Dodd, Stratford-on-Avon, AD 1597,'" found in Allingham's *Songs, Ballads and Stories*, 1877, pp. 186–190' (*Letters*, VI. 347 n. 4).

[5] *Letters*, II. 445. His objection was not new. In 'Mr. Gilfil's Love Story', Blackwood thought 'that the patois of Daniel and Dorkis. [*sic*] stands too prominently forward in the scenes where the feelings are so highly wrought up' (*Letters*, II. 323).

[6] *Letters*, VIII. 201.

[7] Taking the 'two front sheets' to refer to the first two signatures, the dialect that Blackwood read in proof did not include Lisbeth Bede's. The first line of signature C as printed (first edition: I. 33) reads: 'teazin' him iver sin' we've been workin' together' (which is part of Wiry Ben's praise of Seth in Chapter II). The dialect to this point occurs in the workshop and in the conversations on the Green preliminary to Dinah's sermon. Lisbeth does not speak until I. 68; signature E begins on I. 65.

[8] 23 Nov.; *Letters*, II. 499.   [9] *Letters*, II. 500.

Although the proofs have not survived, the number and systematic nature of variants in the first edition show that Eliot and Lewes subdued not only Lisbeth's dialect, but that of minor characters, beginning in Chapter I.

The hundreds of variants in the dialect of Lisbeth, Mr and Mrs Poyser, Wiry Ben, and other working people reveal significant modification of the dialect for the first edition. One frequently used manuscript word, *alys*, appears consistently as *allays* in the first edition. Other words are altered so that the dialect is eliminated. The most frequent of these is the manuscript's use of *y* added to subject pronouns to produce *mey*, *wey*, *yey*, *hey*, and *shey*. With one exception, perhaps a deliberate one, the first edition shows *me*, *we*, *ye*, *he*, and *she*.[1] The exception is a comic commentary on dialect, in which Mr Casson, landlord of the Donnithorne Arms, explains to the stranger on horseback in Chapter II that

> I'm not this countryman, you may tell by my tongue, sir. They're cur'ous talkers i' this country, sir; the gentry's hard work to hunderstand 'em. I was brought hup among the gentry, sir, an' got the turn o' their tongue when I was a bye. Why, what do you think the folks here says for 'hevn't you?'—the gentry, you know, says, 'hevn't you'—well, the people about here says 'hanna yey.' It's what they call the dileck as is spoke hereabout, sir. That's what I've heared Squire Donnithorne say many a time; it's the dileck, says he.

Mr Casson apparently has not noticed that in published versions of *Adam Bede* the Hayslope inhabitants no longer say 'yey'. But then neither has he noticed his own 'dileck', which in this conversation includes such non-Loamshire forms as *hout*, *hoaks*, *hage*, *'ay-'arvest*, *hexcuse*, and *somethink*.

Less often but not infrequently, dialect forms are introduced in the first edition where they had not existed in manuscript. A passage in Chapter XXVI illustrates the movement toward increased dialect usage. The first edition reads:

> 'Nonsense!' said Mr Poyser. 'Why, everybody's goin' [MS: going] to dance to-night, all but th' old Squire and Mrs Irwine. Mrs Best's been tellin' [MS: telling] us as Miss Lyddy [MS: Lydia] and Miss Irwine 'ull [MS: are going to] dance, an' the young Squire 'ull [MS: squire's going to] pick my wife for his furst [MS: first] partner, t' open the ball [MS: to lead the dance]: so she'll be forced to dance, though she's laid by ever sin' the Christmas afore [MS: before] the little un was born. You canna [MS: cant] for shame stand still, Adam, an' you a fine young fellow, and can dance as well as anybody.'

The variants are of several kinds, but all increase the use of dialect. Only one, the word *furst* in the first edition, was rejected by Eliot when she marked her copy of the eighth edition in 1861, probably because *furst* is not generally used by the dialectal speakers in *Adam Bede*. The increase in dialect in Mr Poyser's speech here and in his wife's speech at the end of

---

[1] The manuscript form for third person plural, *the'*, becomes *they* in the first edition.

Chapter XXVI heightens the distinction between the honest farmer and dairy woman, who respond with simple frankness to their honours at the ball or the lateness of the hour, and the double-speaking Arthur Donnithorne, who expresses concern for Mrs Poyser's welfare at one moment and, in the next, wishes he could seduce her husband's niece without compunction.

Blackwood was pleased with the alterations on the first two proof sheets. He responded immediately to Lewes, 'Tell G.E. that the sheets arrived safely and are sent to press. I think it is wise to lessen the quantity of the local dialect.'[2] Writing to Langford on 24 January 1859, a week before *Adam Bede* was published, Blackwood applauded the authenticity and effect of the modified dialect: 'The book is so good and so thoroughly novel. . . . What a perfect picture it is of English Country Life and as in Scotts Scotch there is not a tinge of vulgarity about the dialect. Mrs Blackwood tells me it is perfect Nottinghamshire.'[3] One reader who disagreed was the novelist Edward Bulwer-Lytton. On 23 February 1860, Eliot wrote to Blackwood that Bulwer-Lytton had called the day before: 'He thinks the two defects of "Adam Bede" are the dialect and Adam's marriage with Dinah; but of course I would have my teeth drawn rather than give up either.'[4]

Eliot's passion about the dialect is evident in the insistent tone of letters calling John Blackwood's attention to compositor errors.

> While I think of it, let me beg of you to mention to the superintendent of your printing office, that in case of another reprint of 'Adam,' I beg the word 'sperrit' (for 'spirit') may be particularly attended to. Adam never ⟨says⟩ said 'speerit,' as he is made to do in the cheaper edition, at least in one place—his speech at the birthday dinner [Chapter XXIV]. This is a small matter, but it is a point I care about.[5]

The objectionable spelling appeared in the second edition in Chapter LIII and in the Epilogue, but it was not until the fourth edition ('the cheaper edition') that a compositor introduced it in the birthday dinner speech, at which time it came to Eliot's attention. Another letter, quoted above, describes the misprint 'theed'st' as 'constantly printed',[6] although it appears only three times in the publication history of *Adam Bede*. But for an author whose representation of common people included accurate presentation of their dialect, three instances were sufficient to elicit a strong remonstrance.

The dialect continued to be a subject for discussion months, even years, after *Adam Bede* was first published. In a postscript to Charles Bray 19 September 1859, dismissing Bracebridge's claims to know the originals of

[2] 26 Nov. 1858; *Letters*, VIII. 214.   [3] NLS MS 4135, fos. 158–9.
[4] *Letters*, III. 264.   [5] 23 July 1859; *Letters*, III. 118.
[6] 16 Oct. 1859; *Letters*, III. 184.

characters in *Scenes* and *Adam Bede*, Eliot cited the dialect to support her point that the characters were developed by her imagination from slight suggestions given by actual people such as her father or her aunt:

The people (readers of 'Adam') who know Derbyshire and the adjacent counties all say, 'This is just the way the people talk there.' Now, I never knew any Derbyshire people, or Staffordshire either, except my father and his brothers. His brothers I never saw so many times as I could count fingers, and my visits to those counties were not more than four or five altogether— none of them for more than a few days. Yet, I imagine, no one will go to the length of saying that the dialect was put in for me.[7]

She made a similar point less than two years later during a visit from John Blackwood, who described to his wife Eliot's

distinction between what is called the real and the imaginative. It amounted to this, That you could not have the former without the latter and greater quality. Any real observation of life and character must be limited, and the imagination must fill in and give life to the picture. . . . The dialect of Lisbeth in 'Adam Bede' arose from her occasionally hearing her father when with his brothers revert to the dialect of his native district, Derbyshire. She could not tell how the feeling and knowledge came to her, but when Lisbeth was speaking she felt it was a real language which she heard.[8]

This facility of a speaker like Robert Evans to change dialects according to context is well represented in Adam's speech. Even in Chapter I, his speech is distinct from that of the other carpenters in containing fewer dialectal features, as might be expected of the foreman who is a 'favright' (as Wiry Ben says) of Mr Irwine and the young heir. But when he feels close emotionally to his mother, his speech 'reverts' to forms more like hers. In Chapter IV, the narrator recognizes Adam's linguistic flexibility:

'Dunna thee sit up, mother,' said Adam in a gentle tone. He had worked off his anger now, & whenever he wished to be especially kind to his mother he fell into his strongest native accent & dialect with which at other times his speech was less deeply tinged. 'I'll see to father when he comes home; may be, he wunna come at all tonight. I shall be easier if thee't i' bed.'[9]

Eliot's early experiences listening to her father had taught her that speakers adjust pronunciation, grammar, and lexicon according to context. Along with the dialectal *dunna* and *wunna* (altered in the first edition to *donna* and *wonna*), Adam uses, in both manuscript and first edition, the familiar second person pronoun *thee*. But he never uses the manuscript pronouns ending in *y*, such as *hey*, which are employed so frequently by his mother, Wiry Ben, and others.[1]

---

[7] *Letters*, III. 157.   [8] [15] June 1861; *Letters*, III. 427.   [9] MS I. 51[a].
[1] In manuscript the author sometimes forgot Adam's folk speech. In Chapter XI, he uses *your* and *you* in addressing his mother, ' "Very well, mother, if that's your wish, I'll make the

In contrast to his 'strongest native accent and dialect' usually spoken with his mother, when he addresses Arthur or Mr Irwine, Adam comes close to assuming theirs. Such fluidity is especially common to those whose economic and social status is in flux, as is the case with Adam. Eliot's sensitivity in using dialect as part of her characterization is apparent in manuscript/first edition variants in Adam's conversation with Arthur in Chapter XVI. The scene is replete with markers of difference: the narrator's disquisition on Adam's respect for the gentry and his feeling 'the honour keenly' when Arthur condescends to shake hands with him, which Arthur 'never [does] with any of the farmers'; Arthur's college learning and Adam's night schooling with Bartle Massey; the physical arrangement of the scene, with Adam walking, Arthur on horseback. In manuscript Adam uses colloquial diction (*reckon, kin*) and addresses Arthur as 'sir'. Otherwise, their speech is not particularly distinct. Both men use contractions common to informal speech of gentlemen and workmen (*we're, we'll, he'll, I'm, you're, they've, can't*, etc.).

But in proofreading the first edition, Eliot apparently decided there was insufficient difference between Adam's and Arthur's speech. Twenty-three words in Adam's speech in the first edition are variants that increase his dialect usage. Eighteen signal pronunciation changes in pronouns, verbs, adverbs, prepositions, or articles (*ones/uns*; *would/'ud*; *will/'ull*; *have/ha'*; *always/allays*; *to/t'*; *of/o'*; *in/i'*; *the/th'*). Three change *that* to *as* to open a clause (including one instance of *that's* altered to *as is*), and two adjust the pronunciation of nouns: *Treddleston/Treddles'on* and *fellow-creatures/fellow-creaturs*. These forms are common to other dialect speakers as well as Adam, and none is likely to pose a problem for readers.

Though minor individually, these changes in the direction of linguistic difference stress Adam's place as the working man whose social distance from Arthur cannot be erased by Adam's adoption of some of the gentry's forms of speech. In Chapters XXVII and XXVIII, Adam's consciousness of social and linguistic difference underlies his insistence that he be treated as an equal in the matter of Hetty. Going 'man to man', he defeats Arthur both physically, knocking him down, and rhetorically, winning the argument in the Hermitage that forces Arthur to write the letter to Hetty.[2] In Chapter XXX, reflecting on Hetty's loving Arthur rather than himself, Adam knows that class difference makes him the lesser man in Hetty's eyes: ' "Her head was allays likely to be turned," he thought, "when a gentleman, with his fine manners, and fine clothes, and his white hands,[3] and that way

---

coffin at home, but I thought you wouldn't like to hear the work going on" ' (fo. 190). In the 1st edition, the familiar *thy* and *thee* replace *your* and *you*.

[2] Physical power helps here too, as Adam blocks the door until Arthur accepts his terms.

[3] In correcting the 8th edition, Eliot cancelled the adjectives in the references to Arthur's 'white jeweled' hands and 'white' right hand, perhaps to avoid *over*stressing the class difference.

o' talking gentlefolks have, came about her, making up to her in a bold way, as a man couldn't do that was only her equal." ' Language—'that way o' talking gentlefolks have'—is as significant and unchangeable a marker of class as Adam's work-worn hands. At the same time, in keeping with the novel's emphasis on depicting the common man and woman, the manuscript, in a passage in Chapter L that was omitted from the first edition, defends Adam's speech by associating it with another arbitrary social marker, dress:

That is a simple scene, I confess; & now I have written it, I am alarmed at the recollection that these 'immense nothings' of a growing, half-conscious love have seldom been thought worth writing or reading, unless they have had the adjuncts of expensive upholstery & millinery, & *very refined language*, if not abundant literary allusion. But after all, reader, if you had demanded these conditions of interest, you would long ago have ceased to follow Adam Bede's fortunes.... Since you have come with him so far, you must care more for the man than for his clothes or *his grammar*, & drapery, whether of the tailoring or *literary* kind must be a small thing in your esteem.[4]

Realism requires the reader, unlike Hetty, to accept a hero in working dress and diction.

Eliot's dialect alterations on the first proofs are evidence that although she expected her readers to move beyond 'the vocabulary of the drawing-room and the newspaper', she knew that the differences could be so great that readers might be unable to negotiate the gap. She demonstrates this through the character of Lisbeth Bede, who seldom converses even with people of her own class. In Chapter XL, Lisbeth cannot allow Seth to go in search of Dinah himself because she cannot understand Mr Irwine's reports of Adam in Stoniton: 'Nay, nay, I canna spare thee. Thee must go an' see thy brother, an' bring me word what he's a-doin'. Mester Irwine said he'd come an' tell me, but I canna make out so well what it means when he tells me.' If Lisbeth's speech, especially in its manuscript form, posed problems for readers like John Blackwood, the speech of her upper-class neighbours posed problems for her.

The linguistic diversity of the Loamshire community is treated comically in another scene involving Mr Casson, who seeks to identify a stranger in Chapter XXXII:

'... And I stood still till he come up, and I says, "Good morning, sir," I says, for I wanted to hear the turn of his tongue, as I might know whether he was a this-country-man; so I says, "Good morning, sir: it'll 'old hup for the barley this morning, I think. There'll be a bit got hin, if we've good-luck." And he says, "Eh, ye may be raight, there's noo tallin'," he says; and I knowed by that'—here Mr Casson gave a wink—'as he didn't come from a hundred mile off. I dare say he'd

---

[4] MS III. 184–5 (emphasis added).

think me a hodd talker, as you Loamshire folks allays does hany one[5] as talks the right language.'

Bartle Massey is contemptuous of Casson's claims to the 'right language': 'You're about as near the right language as a pig's squeaking is like a tune played on a key-bugle.' Casson argues for his (supposed) class credentials as at least equal to the claims of education, even as his speech undercuts his pretensions: 'Well, I don't know. . . . I should think a man as has lived among the gentry from a by, is likely to know what's the right language pretty nigh as well as a schoolmaster.' Bartle responds to Casson, 'you talk the right language for *you*. When Mike Holdsworth's goat says ba-a-a, it's all right—it 'ud be unnatural for it to make any other noise', and, the narrator concludes, the 'rest of the party being Loamshire men, Mr Casson had the laugh strongly against him'.

   Like Casson and the stranger, the characters Hetty meets on her journeys in Chapters XXXVI and XXXVII are set apart from Loamshire men and women through a few distinctive dialect features. For example, the waggoner who gives Hetty a lift outside Stoniton in Chapter XXXVI uses the long *o* in *wooant, dooant, coom*, and *doog*, a form not found among Loamshire speakers in the printed editions, although Eliot did include it in some manuscript speeches for Wiry Ben and Lisbeth Bede. The waggoner also says *fawst* (fast) and *furder* (further) and *puck* (picked), forms unknown in Loamshire speech. Sometimes Eliot did not distinguish an outsider in the manuscript, but introduced a distinctive variant in the first edition. Thus, in Chapter XXXVI, the landlord of the Green Man uses *I doubt* in manuscript, as do the inhabitants of Loamshire when they mean *I fear* or *I suspect*. The replacement of the landlord's *I doubt* with *I suspect* in the first edition suggests a deliberate effort to give him a distinctive speech form. In contrast, there is little dialectal differentiation in the speech of witnesses at Hetty's trial. Sarah Stone, a poor Dissenting widow and the first of the two witnesses whose testimony is 'quoted' at length in Chapter XLIII, says, 'I was dreadful frightened', but otherwise tells her story without distinctive regional or class speech patterns. John Olding, the labourer who found the dead infant, refers to 'a bit of a haystack' and 'bits of openings'. But these phrases and '*em* and *a-sitting* are as close to dialect as his speech gets. The narrative style of their testimony—it is given without pauses, repetitions, dislocations of time sequence, or interruption for questions, such as one might expect in a narrative of any length at a trial for murder—indicates that, although it is placed in quotation marks and uses first person

---

[5] The word *one* is written as *wonn* in manuscript and 1st to 8th editions. Eliot apparently decided that this form did not fit the dialect she establishes for Casson, or that it was too difficult for the reader, and altered it in correcting the 8th edition, so that the stereotyped and Cabinet editions read *one*.

pronouns, it represents a narrator's summary rather than the expression of their individual voices.

The speech of the two main female characters is also remarkably spare in representative dialect. Hetty and Dinah seldom show the distinctive pronunciation, grammar, or lexicon that Eliot gives to other characters similarly placed in the social and educational hierarchy. In the case of Hetty, the landlady at the Green Man hears what readers seldom do, a distinctive regional speech, which disposes her favourably toward the unfortunate girl. 'She's not a common flaunting dratchell, I can see that. She looks like a respectable country girl, and she comes from a good way off, to judge by her tongue. She talks something like that ostler we had that come from the north: he was as honest a fellow as we ever had about the house.' But elsewhere, unawareness of Hetty's distinctive speech is ominous. In Chapter XII the narrator notes that 'While Arthur gazed into Hetty's dark beseeching eyes, it made no difference to him what sort of English she spoke,' and connects the conventions of speech with those of costume: 'and even if hoops and powder had been in fashion, he would very likely not have been sensible just then that Hetty wanted those signs of high breeding.' These class signifiers in Hayslope and environs are invisible in the mythical world of the Chase, where Arthur sees Hetty only as an idealized beauty, not as a speaking individual. But in the realistic texture of the novel, Hetty and Arthur ignore at their peril speech and costume as signifiers of their place in the community and of the distance between them.

Hetty's lack of connection with the other working people is also represented through speech—or the absence of direct speech. In most of the chapters in which she is the centre of attention, her thoughts are mediated by the narrator.[6] Even Hetty's longest speech and the one in which we are to believe she is most sincere, her confession 'In the Prison', Chapter XLV, is more connected and non-dialectal than one might expect under the circumstances. A few dialect forms common to the Poyser household are evident,[7] but by and large this is the speech of a young, distraught girl from anywhere.

One of the first to raise the question of Dinah's speech in terms of dialect usage was William A. Axon, in the *English Dialect Society, Miscellanies* for 1880: 'It may be asked why Dinah Morris, . . . although on the same social and educational plane as the dialect-speaking characters of *Adam Bede*, is rarely represented as employing any provincial words or phrases.' His answer is that 'such intensely religious natures nurturing mind and soul upon the pure English of the Bible have their entire diction permeated by the influence of its words'. He argues that Eliot 'would have been justified in not putting dialect words into the mouth of her fair saint. When we see

---

[6] See especially Chapters IX, XV, XXII, XXXI, and XXXV to XXXVII.
[7] For example, *daredn't, o', 'em, 'ud, allays*.

any one possessed of and possessed by a spirit of intense religious earnestness and seeking for the good of others, we do not notice the strange or
uncouth fashion in which their message may be delivered. The accidents of
speech and manner are burned up like dross in the fire of their zeal.'[8]
Cunningham places Dinah's speech more precisely in the context of
Methodist history. Noting several parallels between Dinah's life and that
of the early Methodist preacher Mary Bosanquet Fletcher, whose *Life* Eliot
had borrowed from her aunt Elizabeth Tomlinson Evans in 1839, Cunningham points out the linguistic parallels between the two women and
argues against scholars 'who complain about her Methodist idiom': 'if
Dinah spoke differently she would be less truly Methodist.' Such scholars
'have taken an unwise cue from the "canting jargon" tradition, neither
apprehending the necessity of this ideolect if Dinah is truly to represent
Methodism, nor perceiving its wholly serious nature, the real communication by means of it, and its indication of the life lived in, as it were, the light
of the Scripture'.[9] In her sermon in Chapter II, instead of using the
colloquial speech of other working people, Dinah employs the rhythms
and diction of the Bible and prayer, suited to one whose vision through
much of the novel is directed heaven-ward rather than toward the soil and
trees of Loamshire. Cunningham notes that Dinah's speech employs the
typical features of the Methodist sermon. Her 'sermon is characteristic in
form and content, as well as in effect. Her text (Luke 4: 18), "The spirit of
the Lord is upon me, because he hath anointed me to preach the Gospel to
the poor", was Wesley's . . . in his first sermon in the fields, and, with a sure
sense of occasion, took the statement with which Christ initiated His public
ministry. Dinah claims to follow "That man of God . . . Mr. Wesley."' The
techniques they share include 'Particularization ("Here Dinah turned to
Bessy Cranage . . .") . . . [And] Wesley and Whitefield would dramatically
invoke Christ: "Thus look unto Jesus! . . . Look yonder."' Dinah does
likewise: ' "See!" she exclaimed, turning to the left, with her eyes fixed
on a point above the heads of the people—"see where our blessed Lord
stands and weeps."' Elements of her sermon style are also found in her
private conversations, e.g. to Seth in Chapter III, to Mr Irwine in Chapter
VIII, to Lisbeth in Chapter X, and, as might be expected given the
occasion, to Hetty in prison in Chapter XLV.

There may also be a second rationale related to verisimilitude. Like
Hetty, Dinah is rootless, at least until the end of the novel. She returns to

---

[8] 'George Eliot's Use of Dialect', rpt. in Stuart Hutchinson (ed.), *George Eliot: Critical
Assessments*, vol. I (Mountfield, 1996), 604. Other, more recent discussions of Dinah's speech
include Kathleen Watson's 1971 essay 'Dinah Morris and Mrs Evans: A Comparative Study of
Methodist Diction', originally published in *Review of English Studies*, reprinted in *Critical
Assessments*, III. 33–45, and K. C. Phillipps's discussion of Dinah's 'Nonconformist Usage', in
Language and Class in Victorian England (Oxford, 1984), 118.

[9] Cunningham, 161.   [1] Cunningham, 151–2.

Snowfield, spends time in Leeds, but has no specificity in either place. If, as Eliot said in her letter to William Allingham, mobility results in 'mongrel' speech, then speech relatively unmarked by regional dialect is appropriate to her.

The complexities of dialect usage pose problems for the textual editor. Inconsistencies abound in the distribution of variants. Some are the result of inconsistency on the part of the author in manuscript. Some must have originated on proofs for the first edition or in the setting of the edition itself. Others result from changes introduced by compositors after the first edition.

The word *cliver* (including four instances with affixes, *cliverer* (twice), *cliverness, cliverish*) might be selected as the exemplar for the complexities of variant history in *Adam Bede* and the problem the textual editor faces in making decisions about whether to restore manuscript or first edition variants in the interests of consistency. *Cliver* is used eleven times in manuscript: (1) Wiry Ben in Chapter I: 'some o' your kin, as is mayhap cliverer'; (2) Mr Casson in Chapter II: Adam is 'an uncommon cliver stiddy fellow'; (3) Lisbeth Bede in Chapter IV: Thias was 'a cliver workman, an' taught thee thy trade'; (4) Mrs Poyser in Chapter XV: Hetty has 'cliver fingers of her own'; (5) Mr Poyser in Chapter XVIII: 'There's maybe a workman now an' then, as isn't over cliver at 's work, takes to preachin' an' that, like Seth Bede';[2] (6) Lisbeth to Dinah in Chapter L: Seth 'isna cliver enough for thee, happen';[3] (7) Lisbeth in Chapter L: Adam would make 'a fine husband, . . . so looked-on an' so cliver';[4] (8) Lisbeth in Chapter LI: 'Thee't made to be loved—for where's there a straighter, cliverer man?'; (9) Mr Craig in Chapter LIII: 'you talk o' Bony's cliverness'; (10) Mr Craig in Chapter LIII, Bonaparte 'may be a bit cliver'; and (11) Mr Craig again in Chapter LIII: 'I like a cliverish woman.' Of these eleven manuscript examples, seven are unaltered in the published texts. The transmission history of the other four illustrates the complex patterns of variant distribution in *Adam Bede*.

[2] This passage also illustrates the role of the compositors in variants *niver/never*. The manuscript reads: '"Nay," said Mr Poyser, . . . "It's on'y tradesfolks as turn Methodists; you niver knew a farmer bitten wi' them maggots. . . . But you see Adam, as has got one o' the best head-pieces hereabout, knows better; he's a good Churchman, else I'd niver encourage him for a sweetheart for Hetty."' The manuscript reads *niver* in both instances. The editions also read *niver* in the first instance. However, only the 1st and the 7th read *niver* in the second instance; the 2nd, 4th, 5th, 6th, 8th, 10th, and Cabinet read *never*, a variant whose origin Eliot could not have authorized, although she did not mark the inconsistency when she corrected the 8th edition.

[3] In Lisbeth's statement to Dinah in Chapter L, the manuscript first read: Seth 'isna good enough for thee, happen', but Eliot cancelled *good* and wrote *cliver* above, probably realizing as she wrote that Seth's goodness is never in question, but that it is precisely in their cleverness that the brothers differ, as is clear in Lisbeth's comments in examples 7 and 8.

[4] Eliot also used it in a continuation of Lisbeth's speech that she cancelled in manuscript: 'I know I did. I liked Thias 'cause he was cliver at things' (MS III. 187/191).

Examples 3 and 5 demonstrate the role of compositors in the uneven distribution of variants. In example 3, Lisbeth's *cliver* appears in editions 1, 2, and 7; *clever* appears in 4, 5, 6, and 8. In example 5, Mr Poyser uses *over-cliver* in editions 1, 2, 4, and 5; *over cliver* in 6 and 7, and *over clever* in 8. In neither case did Eliot alter the variant when she read the eighth edition; as a result, *clever* continues in 10 and Cabinet. The two instances have different textual history, but both are ascribable to compositors, since the only edition Eliot proofread was the first. In correcting 8 in 1861, she altered more than 120 dialect forms, but no instances of *clever* or *cliver*.

The case of *clever* also illustrates inconsistency in the manuscript and editions, where *clever* is not distributed strictly along class lines. Mr Irwine, Arthur, the old Squire, and the narrator use it in manuscript and all editions, but so also do dialect-speaking characters: *cleverness*, by Lisbeth in Chapter XI and Bartle Massey in Chapter LIII; *clever* by Adam in Chapter XXVII, Dinah in Chapter XLIX, and Mrs Poyser, twice in Chapter XLIX.

Mr Craig's use of the term *cliver* in examples 9, 10, and 11 illustrates both authorial inconsistency and the difficulty of determining the role of the author in first edition variants. Examples 9 and 10 use *cliver* in manuscript and all editions. In example 11, *cliverish* appears in manuscript, *cleverish* in all editions. If Eliot made the alteration between manuscript and first edition, why did she not also replace *cliver* in the two instances nearby? Alternatively, if *clever* were a compositor error, did she not notice it when she read first edition proofs? The question of authority arises again in Chapter II when Mr Casson uses *cliver* in the manuscript but *clever* in the first and subsequent editions in referring to Adam. With proofs no longer extant, it is impossible to know whether the first edition variant originated with the author or the compositor.

Another inconsistently used form is the suffix *-in'* in dialect usage in place of *-ing* in the formation of participles and gerunds. This dialect form was unlikely to pose comprehension problems for readers, and perhaps for that reason it was altered several times on first edition proofs in the direction of increased dialect usage. For example, at the end of Chapter XXVI, Mrs Poyser's speech to her husband reads in manuscript:

Eh! . . . I'd sooner ha' *brewing* day & *washing* day together than one o' these *pleasuring* days. There's no work so *tiring* as *dangling* about an' *starin'* an' not rightly *knowin'* what you're *goin'* to do next; ⟨&⟩ an' *keepin'* your face i' *smilin'* order ⟨because⟩ like a grocer o' market-day, ⟨because⟩ for fear people shouldna think you civil enough. An' you've *nothing* to show for 't when it's done, if it isn't a yallow face wi' *eating* things as disagree.[5]

---

[5] MS II. 184–5, emphasis added.

Of the seven words ending in -*ing* in manuscript, all but *nothing* end in -*in'* in the first edition. It is likely that these changes to -*in'* originated with the author but whether she simply missed making all dialect forms consistent, or felt that there was sufficient flavour of the dialect, cannot be known. Perhaps both. For a non-dialect speaker, writing in dialect requires constant vigilance. At times, Eliot undoubtedly slipped into her own speech patterns, and in reading proof noticed some examples and missed others. This inconsistent mixture of dialect and non-dialect speech poses a particular challenge to the textual editor, as discussed below.

CHOICE OF TEXT

Of the eleven separate typesettings of *Adam Bede* during the author's lifetime,[6] the first ten editions, as Blackwood & Sons called them on the title pages, were published between February 1859 and January 1862, and were entirely reset except for portions of the third and the fifth editions, as noted above. The tenth edition, the first in one volume, was stereotyped and electrotyped,[7] and the plates were used for all subsequent editions in Eliot's lifetime except the Cabinet *Adam Bede* in 1878. The texts in which the author had a hand in writing, editing, and/or proofing are the manuscript, the first edition, the fourth edition (where her role was limited to the revision of the willow wand passage in Chapter IV), and the eighth edition corrected by the author in 1861. This marked eighth edition was used to set the 'Tenth Edition'. The two-volume Cabinet edition of 1878 was the last edition published during the author's lifetime. The manuscript and these five editions were considered in selecting the copy text.

The manuscript is, of course, the only text free from variants introduced by compositors, although it cannot be said to be solely the work of the author, given George Henry Lewes's role in suggesting alterations as Eliot read him the novel in progress. The manuscript is, however, an unsuitable choice for copy text. It represents the author's first design for a novel that she wrote and rewrote over the course of four years, from the time she began the manuscript of Chapter I in October 1857 to her correction of the eighth edition in autumn 1861.

Even as she wrote and revised her manuscript, Eliot was aware that she would make further alterations on proofs for the first edition, particularly

---

[6] This number does not include Tauchnitz or American editions, in none of which the author participated in proofreading and correcting. The American editions' failure to keep abreast of authorial correction is indicated by the fact that Harper's second American edition, dated 1860, fails to include the correction to Chapter IV which the author sent to William Blackwood in May 1859, and which appeared in the first two-volume edition published the next month.

[7] The Blackwoods ledger that contains the print order for the 10th edition gives 'Electrotyping 281pp' and 'Stereo 192pp' (NLS MS 30,860, fo. 213). In correspondence and on the title page of the 1867 edition, the firm used the term 'stereotyped'.

in the dialect. Since these proofs are not extant, it is impossible to be certain precisely which of the variants in substantives or accidentals were initiated by the author and which resulted from compositor error or the application of house style. It is clear, however, from the edition itself and from letters in which Eliot declared her intentions, that many first edition variants were authorized changes. Eliot's effort to mediate between the conflicting demands of representation and readability in the dialect usage has been discussed above. More than 900 dialect variants exist between manuscript and first edition. A majority systematically lessen the dialect, but a significant number change one dialect form to another without a noticeable change in readability, and many introduce dialect usage where it had not existed. Instances of the last are, however, usually forms readily intelligible to readers who are like Lewes in being 'innocent of dialect'. For example, *and* becomes *an'*, or a preposition drops a final letter (*to* becomes *t'*, or *of*, *o'*), or a word ending in *-ing* is altered to end in *-in'*. In addition, dialect variants excluded, more than 500 other substantive variants exist between manuscript and first edition, including a long manuscript paragraph omitted at the end of Chapter L in the first edition and two paragraphs added at the end of Chapter LIII.

Apart from the revision in Chapter IV that Eliot sent to William Blackwood on 6 May 1859, the author had no role in preparing the fourth edition, nor did she proofread any of the three other two-volume editions in 1859, although she continued to call John Blackwood's attention to their unauthorized variants.

The author's only thorough and systematic revision of *Adam Bede* after the first edition was made in autumn 1861, in preparation for a new edition in one volume. Called the 'Tenth' on the title page, this edition seems at first the likely choice for copy text, because it is the first to incorporate changes Eliot made in correcting her copy of the eighth edition. However, there is no evidence that she read proofs of the 'Tenth', and it introduces new substantive variants and new house style which, in contrast to that of the first edition, the author did not read in proof and therefore had no opportunity to approve or alter.

Because of its position chronologically, the Cabinet edition came to be regarded as the standard edition, or, as Blackwood expressed it, the 'permanent form for her works'.[8] But again, there is no evidence that the author edited or proofread it. Furthermore, although it corrects egregious typographical errors in the tenth/stereotyped editions, the Cabinet follows the tenth edition in many of its new variants as well as introducing new unauthorized readings and the house style peculiar to the Cabinet series, in which, for example, *Oh* replaces *O*, dashes replace commas or colons to introduce speeches, and new variants in capitalization are common. In

[8] *Letters*, VI. 410.

addition to hundreds of variants in accidentals, the Cabinet edition includes significant variations in the dialect, consistently in the direction of regularizing the forms, for instance, *instead* in place of *istead* (Chapter VI), *poisoned* for *pisoned* (Chapter XXII), *was* for *wast* (Chapter L), *ran* for *run* and *talking* for *talkin'* (Chapter LI), *manufactures* for *manifactures* (Chapter LIII). Other substantive variants present alternative readings that are possible, and therefore might not be readily apparent to a reader, e.g. 'frighten the *cows*' for 'frighten the *crows*' (Chapter XVIII), *produced* for *produce* (Chapter XXXVI), *dozen* for *dozing* (Chapter XXXVII), and *trust* for *thrust* (Chapter XL).

THE CORRECTED EIGHTH EDITION

The last authorized revision, Eliot's corrected eighth edition (8), an amalgam of printed text and handwritten authorial corrections, has been selected as the copy text. Substantive variants in the two other significant authorized versions, the manuscript (MS) and first edition (1), are included in the textual apparatus, as are variants from the Cabinet edition (Cabinet), because of its frequent use as the basis for modern reprints.

The corrected eighth edition contains more than 200 authorial revisions of substantives, of which nearly two-thirds are variants in dialect usage. Others include a significant revision of the opening paragraphs of Chapter XVII, correction of an anachronism pointed out by a reviewer, and correction of inconsistencies existing since the manuscript in place and personal names. Not until the marked eighth edition did Eliot notice and revise all the inconsistencies that resulted when she changed names or spellings in the course of composition. Thus, the nearby town is variously *Drosseter*[9] and *Rosseter*; Mr Irwine's butler is both *Carroll* and *Carrol*;[1] and Dinah's aunt is variously *Mary* and *Judith*.[2] In marking the eighth edition, Eliot regularized the forms in all instances as *Rosseter*, *Carroll*, and *Judith*. Furthermore, on the first edition proofs, the author failed to notice a compositor's literal representation of an incompletely cancelled phrase in manuscript Chapter XXXII. As a result, all the three- and two-volume editions give the nonsensical reading 'come next Michaelmas Lady Day'. Eliot changed the text to *Michaelmas* in the marked eighth edition.

---

[9] *Drosseter* appears only in volume I in manuscript. In the 1st edition, it is corrected to *Rosseter* in Chapters VI and XI, but an instance of *Drosseter* remained in Chapter II until Eliot noted it on the marked 8th edition.

[1] The history of *Carroll/Carrol* is more complex than that of *Drosseter*, as the textual notes demonstrate. Compositors changed the name variously to *Carrol* and *Carroll* in editions up to and including the 8th.

[2] *Judith* is used in volume I and *Mary* in volumes II and III in manuscript. In volume II, Chapter XVIII, *Judith* must have replaced *Mary* on proofs for the 1st edition, but *Mary* remained in Chapter XL until Eliot noted the inconsistency on her copy of the 8th edition.

The author's correction of the eighth edition included a significant rewriting of the opening of Chapter XVII. This revision marks another stage in her debate with John Blackwood on realism vs. idealism in fiction. Roland F. Anderson in 1973 argued persuasively that after Eliot received Blackwood's objections to *Adam Bede* in spring 1858, she realized she needed to make 'a more emphatic and detailed statement of her position'[3] and that she did so by writing Chapter XVII. Anderson quotes the chapter's opening sentence, ' "This Rector of Broxton is little better than a pagan!" I hear one of my readers exclaim!' and adds, 'John Blackwood, no doubt!'[4] But Anderson, in citing an undated Cabinet edition, fails to observe that the original form of this passage is ' "This Rector of Broxton is little better than a pagan!" I hear one of my *lady* readers exclaim!' (emphasis added). Anderson is surely correct in viewing Chapter XVII as a veiled address to Blackwood, but if he had recognized that early and late editions differ, he could have taken his argument one step further by positing that Eliot included the spectre of '*lady* readers'[5] in the manuscript and early editions to prevent Blackwood from recognizing himself as the principal addressee.

The change from *lady readers* to *readers* marks the change in Eliot's professional position between 1858 and 1861. When she wrote Chapter XVII in April and May 1858, Eliot had published one work of fiction, a series of three stories, which had received positive but limited critical attention and achieved moderate sales. It had appeared under a pseudonym because the writer's identity as the scandalous Marian Evans, living with a married man, had to be concealed. By autumn 1861, when she corrected the eighth edition, her reputation as a novelist was established. Blackwood had seen edition after edition of *Adam Bede* sell to an eager public, *The Mill on the Floss* and *Silas Marner* had solidified her reputation and validated her belief in realism, the revelation of the authorship had not noticeably affected her popularity, and her relationship with the Blackwood firm was cordial. By then, Eliot no longer needed to dress her reader in female clothes to disguise the male publisher underneath. In the marked eighth

---

[3] Roland F. Anderson, 'George Eliot Provoked: John Blackwood and Chapter Seventeen of *Adam Bede*', *Modern Philology*, 71 (Aug. 1973), 46.

[4] Ibid.

[5] This spectre was, of course, a Victorian cliché. Lewes had had his own exchange with Blackwood a year earlier, when Blackwood objected to a detailed discussion of marine life in Lewes's 'Seaside Studies' as 'distasteful, especially to ladies who form a large section of the readers of such papers' (*Letters*, II. 322). Lewes agreed to 'cut out the objectionable fæces altogether', adding 'But you must confess it is an awful wet blanket on a writer's shoulders, that terror of lady readers, and what they will exclaim against.' The next sentence in his letter humorously expresses his belief in writing for posterity, a sentiment that Eliot shared, although she probably would not have phrased it quite as irreverently as Lewes does: 'I am tempted to exclaim with Charles Lamb "Hang up the ladies! I will write for antiquity" ' (*Letters*, II. 325 and 325 n. 9).

George Eliot's revision of the opening of Chapter XVII in her corrected copy of the eighth edition.

edition, she not only eliminates the gendered reference, but also makes her narrative persona a more confident, powerful figure. The narrator does not 'creep servilely after nature and fact' as in the early editions, but boldly asserts that his 'strongest effort' is to avoid 'arbitrary pictures' that present life as readers prefer it rather than as it is. Realism is the 'highest vocation of the novelist'.

Other substantive changes were made for historical accuracy. In manuscript and first edition, Mr Poyser, in his toast in Chapter XXIV, says in reference to Arthur's birthday ale, that 'we warna goin' to taste it till we'd drunk your health in it'. Eliot alters the phrase 'warna goin' to' to 'couldna well' to describe more accurately what protocol on the occasion would have allowed. Another alteration removes an anachronism noted by E. S. Dallas in the London *Times*:[6]

For the sake of introducing a fair young Methodist who has the gift of preaching, the date of the incidents is thrown to the end of the last century, but the time is not strictly observed, and we are not very much surprised to be informed that Bartle Massey 'lighted a match furiously on the hob,' which is far from being the only anachronism in the tale.

This review, which Eliot and Lewes eagerly awaited (Lewes reported to Blackwood that 'G.E. is most anxious about the Thunderer'[7] and Blackwood in turn noted the 'instantaneous' effect on sales of the second edition[8]), led her to revise Chapter XXI two and a half years later. Realizing that she had anticipated by thirty years the invention of the Lucifer match, Eliot substituted 'striking a light furiously' for the manuscript and first edition phrase, 'lighting a match furiously against the hob'.[9] Another inconsistency, in Chapter XXX, where Adam performs the same action twice in the manuscript and early editions, was removed when Eliot cancelled the first of two references to Adam's 'throwing off his coat'. However, without rewriting much of volume III, Eliot could not eliminate the anachronism in which the Loamshire Militia goes to Ireland more than a year after the Rebellion of 1798 has been put down; she let this anachronism stand.

TREATMENT OF THE COPY TEXT

Emendation

In the absence of corrected proofs for the first edition, it is impossible to be certain which variants between manuscript and first edition originated with

---

[6] 12 Apr. 1859, 5.   [7] 15 Apr. 1859; *Letters*, III. 49.   [8] *Letters*, III. 51.

[9] Eliot avoided another anachronism by cancelling in manuscript a passage in Chapter XLVIII in which Arthur Donnithorne, in March 1800, anticipates the Peace of Amiens: ⟨Whatever they may say about this peace, it is sure not to last long & there will be harder service for our army than ever⟩ (p. 436 n. 3). Peace negotiations began in August 1800; the treaty was signed in March 1802, according to *Gentleman's Magazine*, 91 (Apr. 1802), 358.

the author and which resulted from compositor misreadings. Eliot read carefully the proofs for the first edition, and she had a second chance to review its variants when she corrected the eighth edition in 1861. The Clarendon edition has for the most part accepted substantive variants from the manuscript that persisted from the first to the eighth edition. The exceptions involve variants where compositors misread Eliot's handwriting and where the manuscript reading is preferable, for reasons such as those outlined below. Either Eliot failed to notice the new reading, or, in one case, she altered the reading on the marked eighth edition but instead of restoring the manuscript variant, which she had apparently forgotten, she inserted a new variant.

The Clarendon edition replaces the less precise first and eighth edition variant *strikes* with the manuscript reading *thrills* in Chapter II: 'as a melody thrills us with a new feeling when we hear it sung by the pure voice of a boyish chorister.' In the same chapter, *retired* is replaced by *stirred*, which more exactly describes the situation: 'Yet no one had stirred, except the children and "old Feyther Taft," who being too deaf to catch many words, had some time ago gone back to his ingle-nook.' Even though the children may be restless, it is only Feyther Taft who leaves the otherwise spell-bound crowd. In Chapter V the Clarendon edition restores the manuscript reading *Mrs* in Joshua Rann's reference to Dinah as 'Mrs Poyser's own niece'. The compositor for the first edition misread *Mrs* as *Mr*, and the author overlooked the error in the first and eighth editions. In Chapter XIV the singular *door* of the manuscript is restored in the passage reading 'The heavy wooden bolts began to roll in the house door', where the compositor mistook the comma after *door* for a plural. The singular form is consistent with Mrs Poyser's usage in the preceding paragraph.

The manuscript form *towards*, used almost universally in *Adam Bede* in manuscript and editions, is restored in the sentence beginning, 'And there were liberal touches of crimson towards the chancel' in Chapter XVIII, as well as in Hetty's speech, 'I can't afford to go by the coach; do you think there's a cart goes towards Ashby in the morning?' in Chapter XXXVI. In Chapter XXVIII, the manuscript reading *your* is restored in Arthur's statement, 'Say no more about your anger, Adam.' The compositor's misreading of Eliot's handwriting is understandable, when one notes that the *y* on *your* is attached to *about* and followed by a space, so that the manuscript appears to read *abouty our*. The manuscript reading is consistent with Arthur's tendency to excuse himself and condescend to Adam. The singular *trouble*, used commonly in *Adam Bede*, is restored in Chapter XXXVIII, where the compositor missed the author's manuscript cancellation of the final *s* in 'his trouble⟨s⟩ pressed upon him with a new weight'. And in Chapter XLIV, the manuscript reading gives Arthur Donnithorne a view of 'yapping curs of mysterious pedigree'. The first and subsequent editions read 'gaping curs of mysterious pedigree'. The manuscript reading is more plausible, and *yapping* is restored in the Clarendon *Adam Bede*. In Chapter L, the narrator, in the first and eighth editions, says that 'the new sensibilities bought by a deep experience were so many new fibres' in Adam's connection with others. The manuscript reads *brought*, which is more plausible than the commercial metaphor *bought* for Adam's growing sympathy with others. The Clarendon restores *brought*.

A variant that appears in other Eliot novels also occurs in Chapter XX of *Adam Bede*: the manuscript reading *county*, the customary nineteenth-century usage in this context, is restored in the Clarendon edition in Adam's speech to Mrs Poyser: 'may you always have strength to look after your own dairy, and set a pattern to all the farmers' wives in the county.'[1] In Chapter XXI, Eliot caught an obviously erroneous first edition variant when she proofread the eighth edition, but instead of restoring the manuscript reading, she created a new variant. The manuscript version of Bartle Massey's diatribe against women reads: 'you might as well say adders & wasps & bugs & wild beasts, are a blessing.' In the first edition, the compositor's misreading replaced *bugs* with *hogs*. Correcting the eighth edition, but apparently forgetting the manuscript word, Eliot replaced *hogs* with *foxes*, hogs obviously not belonging in the company of adders, wasps, and wild beasts—especially in an agricultural novel. The manuscript reading, *bugs*, has been restored in the Clarendon *Adam Bede*.

The Clarendon edition restores three readings shared by the manuscript and first edition, where Eliot failed to notice a variant introduced by compositors between the second and eighth editions. In Chapter XX, the manuscript and first edition reading *let* replaces the unauthorized *led*; *let* fits the description that follows, in which the horses are being driven, heads down, with 'many "whups" from Tim the ploughman, as if the heavy animals who held down their meek, intelligent heads, and lifted their shaggy feet so deliberately, were likely to rush wildly in every direction but the right'. In Chapter XXX, the manuscript/first edition variant *round* replaces the eighth edition's *around* ('and all round her was the dark unknown water where Arthur was gone') in consistency with the use of *round* elsewhere in the novel. And the manuscript/first edition reading *afternoon sun* is restored in Chapter X, in place of the awkward *afternoon's sun*, which came into use with the two-volume editions.

Dialect speech is the largest single category of substantive variant between manuscript and first edition. As discussed above, Eliot attempted to represent the lexicon, syntax, and phonology of speech she had heard but never seen printed. Her experimentation with the dialect began in 1857–8 within the manuscript, whose cancellations show her effort to arrive at the 'right' form, and it continued to autumn 1861, when she altered more than

---

[1] The word *county* is also clear in the adjacent manuscript cancellation in Chapter XX.

120 dialect forms in correcting her copy of the eighth edition for a new edition in one volume.

The dialect varies most between the manuscript and the first edition, and the relative responsibility of author and compositors in introducing first edition variants can be inferred by comparing the number and systematic nature of manuscript/first edition dialect variants with the unauthorized dialect variants that entered the text from the second to the eighth editions, all of whose variants from the first were unauthorized, since the author did not proofread any of these intervening editions.[2] The variant patterns between the first and the eighth edition are complex: compositors corrected the occasional variant from the manuscript and first edition to address the author's objections to specific errors, but they also continued to adopt unauthorized variants from earlier editions and to introduce, in each new edition, new variants. Nonetheless, there are over 900 dialect variants between manuscript and first edition, in contrast to fewer than 50 dialect variants between the first and the eighth editions. Even allowing for the greater difficulty in setting type from handwriting rather than from a printed text, this difference suggests that most of the 900 dialect variants in the first edition originated with the author.

Of course, compositors also played a role. At least some first edition variants normalizing dialect forms are likely to have originated with compositors; normalization is the usual direction of compositor-introduced variants in the unauthorized editions after the first. Some of the variants they introduced were undoubtedly accepted by the author, who, not having the manuscript by her when she read proof, did not realize that there had been a change. Later, when Eliot corrected her copy of the eighth edition, she sometimes restored forms from the first edition, at other times, forms from the manuscript. One example of the complexity of variant patterns occurs in Chapter XXX, where the manuscript uses non-dialectal *make you*, the first edition reads *make y'*—whether introduced by author or by compositor it is impossible to know. By the eighth edition, a compositor had turned *make y'* into *mak y'*. Eliot not only corrected the unauthorized *mak* in this edition, but changed *y'* as well, returning the usage to the undialectal *make you* found in manuscript.

If decisions about restoration of other substantive variants sometimes require fine distinctions on the part of the textual editor, decisions to restore manuscript or first edition dialect forms present a still greater challenge. As Eliot recognized, dialect is idiosyncratic and difficult to represent because it is usually part of an oral rather than a written tradition. Therefore, apart from a few instances in which a form found only in manuscript seems clearly desirable, the restoration of dialect forms in the Clarendon edition is limited to those cases in which consistency in the

---

[2] She did, of course, write to Blackwood objecting to the dialect errors *theed'st* and *speerit*.

context calls for restoration of forms that appear in both the manuscript and the first edition. Three manuscript restorations involve compositor mis-readings of Eliot's handwriting. In Chapter XXXI, the manuscript's ampersand was misread as *to* in 'go to be a lady's-maid'; *and* is restored in the Clarendon. In Chapter XXXIV, a misreading of the manuscript resul-ted in *Hetty* instead of *welly*, in Mr Poyser's speech, 'I'm as wishful to have you settled well as if you was my own daughter, & so's your aunt, I'll be bound, for she's done by you this seven year welly as if you'd been her own.' The reading 'welly' gives emphasis to Mr Poyser's declaration, and is more plausible than the appositive, given the speaker and the context. In Chapter LII, the Clarendon restores the manuscript reading where the compositor misread Eliot's handwritten *them* as *those*, in Mrs Poyser's 'I'm not one o' them as can see the cat i' the dairy, an' wonder what she's come after.'

The Clarendon edition also restores dialect forms shared by manuscript and first edition where clusters of similar forms exist and where composi-tors from editions 2 to 8 regularized one or more instances of either *an'* to *and* or the suffix *-in'* to *-ing*. Eliot's practice in the first edition was often to increase the usage of the dialect form, as in Mrs Poyser's final speech in Chapter XXVI, although she was not entirely consistent herself and, as noted above, let the word *nothing* stand amidst several other changes from *-ing* to *-in'*. The first edition variants suggest authorial changes on proof to achieve consistency (even though the author apparently missed, or chose not to alter, one example). In marking the eighth edition, she sometimes failed to note when compositors had caused her text to revert to *-ing*, as in Chapter XI, where several words end with *-in'* in manuscript and all editions, but two others in the same section, Lisbeth Bede's *likin'* and *mislikins*, were altered by compositors between the first and the eighth editions to the unauthorized variants *liking* and *mislikings*. The manu-script/first edition variants *likin'* and *mislikins* are restored in the Claren-don edition. Another example in which context calls for the restoration of the manuscript/first edition variant is the dialect form *an'* in Chapter XXIV.[3] Mr Poyser uses *an'* eighteen times in his birthday toast in the manuscript and first edition, vs. one instance of *And*, which starts a sentence. One of those eighteen examples appears as the unauthorized *and* in the eighth edition; *an'* is restored in the Clarendon edition. These and other dialect forms restored in the Clarendon edition are included in the list of substantive emendations below.

Finally, inconsistencies in descriptive details that are common to the manuscript and all editions should be noted, although they are not altered

---

[3] Eliot used three forms to represent the coordinating conjunction *and* in manuscript: ampersand, *and*, *an'*. The ampersand generally appears as *and* in the first edition, but occasionally as *an'*. The latter is probably the result of a correction on 1st edition proofs. In such cases, *an'* is treated as a substantive variant and is included in the textual apparatus.

in the Clarendon edition. These inconsistencies involve grandfather Poyser's age, the colour of Seth Bede's eyes and hair, the 'kerchief' Hetty leaves in the Hermitage, and Seth's whereabouts in Chapter LI. Old Martin Poyser's age diminishes as the book progresses: he is 75 in Chapter XVIII, but only 72 in Chapter XL, eight and a half months later. Seth Bede's eyes are grey in Chapters I, III, and IV, but blue in Chapter L. His hair is black like Adam's in Chapter I, but 'thin wavy [and] brown' in Chapter L. Hetty's discarded attire in Chapter XXVIII is 'a woman's little pink silk neckerchief', but in Chapter XLVIII it has become 'the little pink silk handkerchief'.[4] And in Chapter LI, the narrator describes Seth as having gone 'to chapel at Treddleston'. But when Adam asks if Seth will return for Sunday dinner, Lisbeth answers that 'He isna gone to Treddles'on' but to the 'Common'. Obviously, there is no way to know what alteration Eliot might have made had she noted these inconsistencies, and it is impossible for a textual editor to make that decision for her. Common in long Victorian novels, they stand as a record of the writing process in which authors forgot minor details from earlier sections of a work, which might already be in the publisher's hands, as in the case of *Adam Bede*, or in the hands of readers, as with serialized novels.

The following is a list of substantive emendations, with the Clarendon reading first and the reading that has been emended following:

Page	Clarendon reading	Corrected eighth edition
16	heared	heard
17	an'	and
21	lookin'	looking
26	thrills	strikes
27	stirred	retired
40	cliver	clever
40	iverythin'	everythin'
43	niver	never
55	fould	fold
55	o'	of
56	Mrs. Poyser's own niece	Mr. Poyser's own niece
56	heared	heard
99	afternoon sun	afternoon's sun
114	likin'	liking
114	mislikins	mislikings
133	desarvin'	desarving
139	door	doors

---

[4] The form *neck-handkerchief* is used in *The Heart of Midlothian*, a text that was on Eliot's mind as she wrote *Adam Bede*; this form is recognized in other examples in the *Oxford English Dictionary*, 1st edition. If Eliot recalled it from Scott, she might not have considered the words *neckerchief* and *handkerchief* to be as inconsistent as they seem to modern readers.

Page	Clarendon reading	Corrected eighth edition
183	towards	toward
192	folks's	folk's
192	th'	the [twice]
195	th'	the
195	gets	get
203	an'	and [thrice]
204	an'	and
205	an'	and [twice]
205	county	country
211	let	led
226	bugs	⟨hogs⟩ foxes
248	an'	and
265	an'	and
291	your anger	our anger
303	round	around
318	go to be a lady's-maid	go and be a lady's-maid
341	welly	Hetty
349	towards	toward
360	jew'llery	jewellery
376	trouble	troubles
390	an'	and [twice]
414	yapping	gaping
442	an'	and
454	brought	bought
459	bendin'	bending
460	th'	the
464	th'	the
466	comin'	coming
466	a-lookin'	a-looking
475	them	those

Treatment of Accidentals

Altogether, more than 8,000 variants in accidentals exist between the manuscript and the corrected eighth edition, most of them beginning with the first edition. The majority are changes in punctuation. While the manuscript's light punctuation, especially its use of commas rather than semicolons, produces a flowing, modern style, the manuscript punctuation is inconsistent, particularly in its use of apostrophes, dashes, ellipses, upper and lower case, hyphenation, and spacing between words. In cancelling or inserting material, Eliot sometimes failed to adjust the existing punctuation to suit the new syntax. Though generally legible, her handwriting sometimes makes it difficult to distinguish between commas and periods and between upper and lower case letters, and her habit of running together two or three words led to compositor misreadings.[5] On occasion, compositors also misread question marks as exclamation points, because of Eliot's habit of closing completely the upper part of the former.

There is no evidence in letters that Eliot objected to the house style of the first edition, although she may have introduced changes in accidentals on the proofs, just as she did in marking her copy of the eighth edition. House styling generally reduced her use of dashes,[6] replaced commas with semicolons in long sentences, and added hundreds of commas elsewhere. It regularized somewhat her handling of upper and lower case, ellipses, and apostrophes, although no edition is entirely consistent in these matters. At least some of the systematic changes in terminal punctuation may have originated with the author on proofs rather than with compositors.

The punctuation of the marked eighth edition has generally been followed in the Clarendon edition. In correcting the eighth edition, Eliot made more than sixty alterations to accidentals, often to variants introduced by compositors after the first edition. The Clarendon edition incorporates these alterations as well as other accidentals of the eighth edition, except in a few instances where the usage of the manuscript or the first edition is to be preferred for clarity. Restorations, which total no more than fifty, are indicated in the textual apparatus.

In addition to punctuation variants, compositors introduced hundreds of variants in capitalization, hyphenation, and spelling in the first edition, most of which remained in later editions as well, although, inevitably, some further variants appeared as the text was repeatedly reset. Determining variants in capitalization is complicated by Eliot's handwriting habits, in which certain letters, C and S in particular, can in some instances be read as either upper or lower case. Nonetheless, within the printed editions and within the manuscript, handling of capitalization is fairly consistent, although between manuscript and print several hundred variants exist. A large proportion of these variants appear in two words that are used frequently: *Sir* (MS)/*sir* (print) and *squire* (MS)/*Squire* (print). *Sir* is used by the working people, usually in addressing Arthur Donnithorne or Mr Irwine, except in Chapter XXXII, where Arthur's grandfather is the addressee, and in Chapters II (Casson to the stranger on horseback) and XLV (Dinah to the same man, who turns out to be a magistrate). *Squire*

---

[5] Eliot usually wrote the word *daresay* as two words, *dare say*, but, in several instances, joined them by an ambiguous long penstroke. With one exception in the 1st edition, house style converted Eliot's usage to the single word *daresay*. In this exception, in Chapter XVII, her habit of running words together produced *Idaresay* in manuscript, which the compositor divided into three words in the 1st edition. By the 2nd edition, house style had prevailed here as well.

[6] In one case at least, Eliot was probably the person who eliminated the dash. In Chapter XXVII, the manuscript reads: Adam's 'eyes fell on—two figures', a rather melodramatic touch that, one suspects, the author decided against on 1st edition proofs.

refers to either Arthur or his grandfather (the 'old Squire'), most often the latter, since Arthur through most of the novel is only the prospective Squire. Of the other variants, the largest number (more than fifty) are religious references, the majority of which alter lower case letters to capitals. For instance, the manuscript's lower case *divine*, *one* (as in 'there's one above', Chapter XL), and *word* were capitalized by compositors. However, Eliot used the upper case *Abbey* twice to refer to the building that had once been a religious establishment but has become part of the Donnithorne estate; compositors altered it to *abbey*. For terms of relationship or reference, e.g. *aunt*, *godmamma* or *godmother* (Mrs Irwine), *captain* (Arthur), *grandfather* (the old Squire or grandfather Poyser, who is also referred to by Totty as *Dandad* in MS Chapter XVIII, *dandad* in print), the manuscript generally uses upper case, and the printed text, lower case. Eliot apparently accepted the compositors' alterations, and most of the printed forms have been allowed to stand in the Clarendon edition. One exception occurs in Chapter II, where lower case *green* is used once for the location of Dinah's sermon, amidst several instances of upper case *Green*. The Clarendon edition replaces the anomaly with the manuscript's *Green*. Among the religious references, the most frequent inconsistency lies in the handling of pronouns *He* and *Him* in references to Jesus or God. Among the dozen inconsistencies in both directions (upper case in MS, lower in print, and vice versa), where the manuscript's capitals have been altered to lower case in print, manuscript usage has been silently restored in accordance with the majority of the novel's pronoun references to the Deity.

Eliot's hyphenation in manuscript was also, on occasion, idiosyncratic and inconsistent. She was erratic in inserting hyphens in dialect words that begin with the prefix *a-*, such as *a-going*, *a-praying*, *a-stannin'*, *a-collectin'*. Compositors usually introduced hyphens where they were omitted in the manuscript. On the other hand, compositors omitted manuscript hyphens in typesetting words like *farm-yard* and *farm-house*, *board-wage* and *ear-rings*, or hyphenated or left spaces between syllables, in words like *upstairs* and *downstairs*, which Eliot usually ran together. In these cases and others where the manuscript form corresponds to that preferred in the *Oxford English Dictionary*, manuscript usage has been silently restored. Otherwise, the Clarendon edition follows the usage of the corrected eighth edition.

The manuscript for *Adam Bede* contains numerous spelling inconsistencies along with the use of archaic or idiosyncratic forms favoured by the author. Many of these were altered by compositors between the manuscript and the first edition. Eliot seems to have accepted these alterations for the most part, although when she felt strongly, she did not hesitate to insist upon her preference—even when she had been inconsistent herself, as two examples from the corrected eighth edition demonstrate.

The first involves variants *chestnut/chesnut*. In Chapter IX the manuscript form, which is also used in all early editions, is *chesnut*. When Eliot corrected a copy of the eighth edition in autumn 1861, she cancelled the *t* in *chestnut*. However, in Chapter LI, her manuscript form, *chesnut*, was altered by compositors to *chestnut* in the first edition, and this form continued to the eighth edition where Eliot, perhaps because she failed to notice it in correcting her copy, let *chestnut* stand. One is left, then, with the anomalous situation in which the manuscript form *chestnut* in Chapter IX has been corrected to *chesnut* in the eighth edition, but the manuscript's *chesnut* in Chapter LI, altered to *chestnut* by the compositor, is retained in the corrected eighth edition. The Clarendon edition uses *chesnut* in both places, given Eliot's expression of a marked preference in Chapter IX of the corrected eighth edition.

A second example also demonstrates both Eliot's ability to insist upon a preferred form and her habit of inconsistency. At the top of the first text page of the corrected eighth edition, she wrote: 'To the printer – "Unmistakeable" is to be spelt with an e.' However, in manuscript three years earlier she had written *unmistakable* in Chapters XIV, XVII, and XX, and *unmistakeable* in Chapters IX and XV. The *OED* preferred form, *unmistakable*, was substituted by compositors in the first edition, and apparently Eliot made no objection, although no proofs exist to confirm this supposition.[7] Given Eliot's explicit direction in the corrected eighth edition, the Clarendon edition adopts *unmistakeable*.

Eliot's manuscript spelling also includes the *z* in words such as *agonize*, *harmonize*, *neutralize*, *patronize*, *recognize*, *scandalize*, *theorize*, and *vocalize*, for which compositors substituted an *s*. The Clarendon edition restores the manuscript usage where it coincides with forms preferred by the *Oxford English Dictionary*, first edition. Other manuscript forms restored on the same principle include *connexion, inflexions, dispatch, lacquered, oneself*, and *slyly*. The Clarendon retains *surprise* and *tease* from the printed editions, although, as the following table shows, compositors were not entirely consistent with the latter, nor Eliot with the former. As is the practice in other Clarendon editions of George Eliot's works, a few archaic forms preferred in manuscript have been restored: *burthen, drest, gaol, lanthorn*, and *quire*.

Two commonly used words show considerable variation in manuscript: *good-bye/good bye/goodbye/goodby/good by/goodbys* and *aye/ay*. For the first group, the situation is complicated by the uncertainty of whether Eliot's

---

[7] Eliot's direction to include the *e* was followed in all instances in the 10th edition, which was set from the marked 8th, but by the Cabinet (set from the 10th), compositors had restored the *OED* preferred form, *unmistakable*, in three places and let stand Eliot's preferred form, *unmistakeable*, in two others. This distribution happens to correspond with that of the manuscript. However, since Eliot had long had the bound manuscript in her possession, the correspondence has to have been a coincidence.

handwriting was signalling one or two words. For the most part, Eliot included the *e* (*good bye* or *goodbye*) in the first twenty chapters, and after Chapter XX omitted it. The preferred *OED* form, the hyphenated *good-bye*, is used only once in manuscript. The corrected eighth edition is consistent in using *good-by* (including Totty's version, *Dood-by*, in Chapter XVIII), except for *good-byes* in Chapter XLIX. In the case of *aye* and *ay*, the *OED* notes that, apart from 'Aye' when it is used in voting in the House of Commons, the words *aye* and *ay* are 'dialectal or nautical', and are 'not used for "yes" in modern educated speech or writing, except as an archaism'. *Aye* and *ay* are used in *Adam Bede* exclusively by the working-class characters, but their variant spellings appear to indicate no phonetic distinction and are not included as dialect variants in the textual apparatus. Except for the first four chapters, where manuscript usage was generally *aye*, after Chapter IV *ay* was the common manuscript form; *ay* was used in most editions until the tenth (stereotyped) and Cabinet. The spellings in the eighth edition, *good-by* and *ay*, are followed in the Clarendon edition.

The spelling *O* is the usual form for this exclamation in the manuscript and early editions. With the Cabinet edition, *Oh*, which was seldom used by Eliot, was introduced generally with the new house style adopted in that series. In three instances, however, compositors altered the manuscript's *O* to *Oh* or *oh* by the eighth edition; the manuscript form has been restored. In two other examples, *Oh* is the form in manuscript and all editions and is retained in the Clarendon edition.

Apart from *ay/aye* (discussed above) and *teazin'* in Chapter II (which is included in both the textual apparatus and the spelling table below), dialect words, which as a matter of course involve spelling variants, are treated as substantives and are included in the textual apparatus rather than in the spelling table.

Below is a list of Eliot's manuscript spellings and the variant spellings found in the eighth edition, with page references to the Clarendon edition. Where Eliot spelled words in different ways in manuscript, examples are included of the unvaried forms. Words that appear frequently, such as *show*, are indicated by selective instances in which the manuscript and the eighth edition agree. Asterisks indicate manuscript spellings that have been restored to the text.

MS	Clarendon (*page*)	Corrected eighth edition
agonized*	401	agonised
agonizing*	373	agonising
ancle	79, 273	ankle
ancles	226	ankles
artizan	48, 92	artisan
artizans	200, 227	artisans

MS	Clarendon (page)	Corrected eighth edition
asthetic	167	aesthetic
aye	8, 10, 13, 16, 17, 39, 44, 154, 172	ay
baritone	199	barytone
befal	128, 241, 346, 472	befall
befall	151	bcfall
benefitting	249	benefiting
burden	197	burden
burthen*	151, 351	burden
burthen	51, 102, 307, 381, 389, 422, 453	burthen
burthened	196	burthened
burthens	357	burthens
by and bye	53, 103, 147, 198, 250, 313, 334, 345, 349, 404, 407, 411	by-and-by
by the bye	77, 81, 87, 160	by the by
chequered*	212, 225	checkered
chesnut*	466	chestnut
chestnut	92	ches⟨t⟩nut
chimnies	66	chimneys
cieling	263	ceiling
civilization*	152	civilisation
cognizant*	63	cognisant
connexion*	32	connection
curtsey	80, 123, 272, 325, 480	curtsy
curtseyed	83, 88, 185, 267, 324, 480	curtsied
curtseying	75, 185	curtsying
curtseys	185, 259	curtsies
disburthened	88	disburthened
disburthenment	116	disburthenment
dispatch*	70	despatch
Dood bye	175	Dood-by
drest*	29	dressed
drest	53	drest
drily	225, 487	dryly
dropped	259	dropped
dropt	259	dropped
embarass	153	embarrass
embarassed	175, 252, 290	embarrassed
embarassment	86, 331	embarrassment
entrusted*	182, 500	intrusted
favorite	17	favourite

MS	Clarendon (page)	Corrected eighth edition
fidgettiness	388	fidgetiness
fidgetting	229	fidgeting
fidgetty	231	fidgety
fillys	322	fillies
fullness*	311, 494	fulness
further*	221, 374	farther
gaol*	393, 400, 404, 418	jail
gaoler*	419	jailer
gaoler's*	419	jailer's
glass full	288	glassful
good-bye	82	good-by
good bye[8]	87, 88, 125, 157, 177, 193, 202	good-by
good bys	448	good-byes
harmonized*	65	harmonised
honourable*	248	honorable
hoydenish*	258	hoidenish
inflexions*	27	inflections
intreaty	440	entreaty
lacquered*	268	lackered
lacquey	67	lackey
lanthorn*	419	lantern
lightening	213	lightning
loth	32	loth
loth	132, 291, 331	loath
lovable	172	lovable
loveable	167	lovable
moveable	217, 238	movable
neutralized*	390	neutralised
O*	425	oh
O*	421, 457	Oh
Oh	193, 326	Oh
oneself*	61	one's-self
page-full	223	pageful
pannelling	7	panelling
pannels	8, 9, 11, 196	panels
patronize*	60	patronise
patronized*	60	patronised

---

[8] Eliot's handwriting habit of connecting two or three words with a sweeping penstroke made many instances of *good bye* appear to be *goodbye*. These uncertain forms are treated as *good bye*.

MS	Clarendon (page)	Corrected eighth edition
patronizing*	162, 283	patronising
pease	91	peas
pendent*	173	pendant
potatoe	310	potato
potatoe beds	231	potato-beds
potato ground	370	potato-ground
quire*	187	choir
recognize*	13	recognise
recognized*	153, 370, 419	recognised
sate	452	sat
scandalized*	80	scandalised
scandalizing*	118	scandalising
shew	230, 234	show
shewed	82	showed
shewing	94	showing
show	223	show
showed	82, 236	showed
slyly*	78	slily
soubriquet	221	sobriquet
staid	377	stayed
staid	109, 175, 180, 181, 418	staid
sta⟨i⟩yed	138	stayed
straight	309	straight
strait	374, 375	straight
straitened	12	straightened
stupefied*	316	stupified
stupefied	430	stupefied
surprised	55	surprised
surprising	476	surprising
surprize	8, 22, 36, 55, 88, 103, 111, 123, 147, 179, 184, 215, 241, 252, 278, 282, 288, 316, 319, 330, 334, 339, 368, 378, 390, 445, 450, 464, 470, 475	surprise
surprized	53, 121, 152, 260, 283, 304, 325, 347, 383, 444, 457, 468	surprised
surprizing	145, 147, 172, 304, 333, 415, 416	surprising
sweetbriar	112, 456	sweetbrier
sybils	166	sibyls
teaze	209, 451	tease

MS	Clarendon (page)	Corrected eighth edition
teazing	146	teasing
teazin⟨g⟩'	22	teazin'
theorizing*	477	theorising
trowsers	118	trousers
tyrannized*	498	tyrannised
unmistakable	139, 167, 211	unmistak{e}able
unmistakeable	91, 149	unmistak{e}able[9]
unrecognized*	162	unrecognised
unsympathizing*	186	unsympathising
vallies	344	valleys
violincello	20, 187	violoncello
vocalization*	488	vocalisation
wainscoating	7	wainscoting
wofully	187	woefully

Recording of Variants

All substantive variants in manuscript and the first edition are recorded, along with variants in the corrected eighth edition where its usage has been rejected in favour of the manuscript or first edition. Cabinet variants are noted when they are anomalous. As the textual notes show, the manuscript includes heavily cancelled chapters and chapters with minimal cancellations. Because of the extensive revision of the dialect on proofs for the first edition, chapters in which dialect speakers, especially Lisbeth Bede, appear are heavily annotated. Eliot's alterations of both substantives and accidentals in the corrected eighth edition are indicated in the textual apparatus as well.

Cancelled words, phrases, and sentences are given in angle brackets (⟨⟩). Cancellations within cancellations are indicated by double angle brackets (⟨⟨⟩⟩). Where there is strong evidence, but not certainty, for a reading, the uncertain words are placed within square brackets and preceded by a question mark (⟨...[?...]...⟩). Indecipherable words are indicated in square brackets with a notation of the apparent number of words in the indecipherable part of the cancellation, e.g. ⟨...[two words]...⟩. The following cancellation in Chapter XX (p. 216 n. 5) includes an uncertain word and two indecipherable words in addition to parts of the cancellation that could be deciphered:

day, ⟨& folks [two words] [?this] dark world sometimes⟩ & loves you the best when you're most i' need on't." MS

---

[9] As noted above, Eliot insisted on *unmistakeable* in a note on the first text page of the corrected 8th edition. The braces are inserted here to indicate that preference, even though she did not mark the insertion on each individual instance of *unmistakable*, the form regularly used in the 8th edition and the preferred *OED* form.

In a few cases, the passage was so heavily blotted as to remain impenetrable despite repeated efforts. If all words in the cancellation are indecipherable, it is not recorded. Such cases amount to less than 1 per cent of the cancelled words.

In recording deletions, the last unrevised word before the deletion is given, with the superscript following this word in the text, then the deleted word or passage in angle brackets, and then the first word after the deletion if that word follows on the line in the manuscript. To give the Clarendon reader a clearer idea of how the text has evolved, when the replacement text is inserted above the line rather than on the line immediately following the cancellation, the entirety of the replacement text is given (in abbreviated form, using ellipses, when it is especially lengthy). Sequential deletions indicate that the author was testing more than one possibility; these are indicated by a series of angle brackets (⟨⟩ ⟨⟩ . . .), as in this example from Chapter XXII (p. 235 n. 4):

she ⟨may keep⟩ ⟨might⟩ may make her uncle & aunt wait⟨ing⟩. She *MS*

The text that precedes and follows cancellations is given in its manuscript form (including ampersands and manuscript punctuation), which may differ from that of published editions. The exceptions to the inclusion of cancellations in the textual apparatus are cancellations at the start of a new folio that merely repeat the final word(s) of the previous folio, cancellations of single letters, and cancellations that occurred when the author recognized and corrected forms that resulted from homonym interference.[1]

Additions made as part of a cancellation are indicated by braces ({ }), as in Chapter XXIX (p. 299 n. 7):

& ⟨encourage⟩ {lull her} in{to} dream⟨s⟩{ing on}. A *MS*

In a few cases where the manuscript includes cancellations and the affected or immediately adjacent passage also contains material added in the first and retained in the eighth edition, a different presentation may be required, with the text of the Clarendon edition followed by a single square bracket (]), after which the manuscript reading is given. In this case, the note number appears in the text following the last word of the Clarendon text. Thus in Chapter LIV (p. 491 n.1), the manuscript includes the phrase *for a man* inserted above the line; the words *with cataract* do not appear until the first edition. The Clarendon edition shows the reading of the first, eighth, and Cabinet editions before the single square bracket, with the manuscript form, including an addition, after the bracket:

possible for a man with cataract to] possible {for a man} to *MS*

---

[1] For example, in the sentence 'Here Vixen tucked her tail between her legs' in Chapter XXI, *tail* overwrites *tale*.

An example from Chapter XXII shows the variant found in published editions before the square bracket, and Eliot's manuscript experimentation with dialect after the bracket (p. 237 n. 6):

hanna] ⟨ha'nt⟩ hadn't *MS*

Additions, transpositions, and other manuscript changes in the order of the text sometimes require clearer demonstration than brackets and braces provide. In these cases, the Clarendon text is followed by a single square bracket, after which the phrase *revised in MS from* is followed by the original manuscript text.

The author also inserted words, phrases, and sentences above the line, in the margins, and occasionally on the verso of manuscript folios. When these are separate from changes involving deletions, the inserted word or phrase is given, followed by a single square bracket (]) and the phrase *added in MS*. Such insertions occasionally indicate copying errors, but usually they represent substantive changes that are afterthoughts by the author to create a more subtle or specific meaning. Very occasionally, a sequence of related additions is indicated by a series of braces ({ }), as in Chapter XXVII (p. 281 n. 8):

two trees {wedded together}, but {only} one. {For the rest of his life} He *MS*

Author's corrections in the marked eighth edition are indicated in the notes by giving first the text of the Clarendon, followed by a single square bracket (]), followed by the manuscript and first edition form(s), then the cancelled text from the eighth edition in angle brackets (⟨ ⟩) followed by the correction. The following example from Chapter XXVII shows a text in which the manuscript and first edition variants are followed by the correction in the marked eighth edition (p. 283 n. 8):

affair. Arthur] affair. Confound the fellow!—Arthur *MS* affair. Confound the fellow! Arthur *1* affair. ⟨Confound the fellow!⟩ Arthur *8*

Another example shows the restoration of the non-dialect form in Chapter XXX (p. 306 n. 8):

to his] *MS* t's *1* ⟨t's⟩ to his *8*

In the case of accidentals altered in the corrected eighth edition, the format is like that of changes in substantives. In Chapter XXXIII, two commas added in the eighth edition set off a phrase which was inserted above the line in manuscript without commas to accompany the new material; Eliot apparently did not observe their absence on proofs for the first edition (p. 335 n. 2):

nature, we must consider, it] nature {we must consider} it *MS* nature we must consider it *1* nature{,} we must consider{,} it *8*

Where words, phrases, and sentences were added above lines, in margins, and on the verso of manuscript folios, the text is presented, followed by a single square bracket (]), and the phrase *added in MS*. Occasionally the manuscript shows cancellations within an addition; these are indicated along with other features of the manuscript form of the text, as in Chapter XX (p. 216 n. 6).

¶ Mrs. Poyser, you perceive, was aware that nothing would be so likely to expel the comic as the terrible {.} <, & the necessity for recovering her dignity>] *added on verso of MS II. 86*

Otherwise, presentation of cancellations and additions in the textual apparatus is not necessarily representative of their appearance in manuscript, although this is shown when it is possible to do so without affecting clarity.

Throughout the textual apparatus, the source of the reading is the corrected eighth edition unless otherwise noted.

DESCRIPTIVE LIST OF EDITIONS
1859–1878

1 *First Edition, 3 volumes octavo,* 20 × 12.5

ADAM BEDE | BY | GEORGE ELIOT | AUTHOR OF | "SCENES OF CLERICAL LIFE" | [motto:] "So that ye may have | Clear images before your gladden'd eyes | Of nature's unambitious underwood | And flowers that prosper in the shade. And when | I speak of such among the flock as swerved | Or fell, those only shall be singled out | Upon whose lapse, or error, something more | Than brotherly forgiveness may attend." | WORDSWORTH. | IN THREE VOLUMES | VOL. I. (II. III.) | WILLIAM BLACKWOOD AND SONS | EDINBURGH AND LONDON | MDCCCLIX | *The Right of Translation is reserved.*

Collation
VOL. I. π^4 A–U^8 X^4 (−X4); pp. viii + 326
VOL. II. π^4 A–O^8 [P]^8 Q–Z^8 2A^2 2B^2 (−2B2); pp. viii + 374
VOL. III. π^4 (−π4) [A]^8 B–U^8 X^8 (−X8) ; pp. vi + 334

VOL. I.
[i] half-title; [ii] blank; [iii] title page; [iv] blank; [v] CONTENTS OF THE FIRST VOLUME.; [vi] blank; [vii] sub-half-title: BOOK FIRST; [viii] blank; [1]–325 text | END OF THE FIRST VOLUME. | PRINTED BY WILLIAM BLACKWOOD AND SONS, EDINBURGH.; [326] blank.

VOL. II.
[i] half-title; [ii] blank; [iii] title page; [iv] blank; [v] CONTENTS OF THE SECOND VOLUME.; [vi] blank; [vii] sub-half-title: BOOK SECOND; [viii] blank; [1]–374 text | END OF THE SECOND VOLUME. | PRINTED BY WILLIAM BLACKWOOD AND SONS, EDINBURGH.

VOL. III.
[i] half-title; [ii] blank; [iii] title page; [iv] blank; [v] CONTENTS OF THE THIRD VOLUME.; [vi] blank; [1] sub-half-title: BOOK FIFTH; [2] blank; [3]–333 text | THE END. | PRINTED BY WILLIAM BLACKWOOD AND SONS, EDINBURGH.; [334] blank.

Binding: Brownish-orange cloth, diagonal fine wave pattern, ornamental frame blocked in blind on back and front covers; ornamental bands top and bottom and lettering blocked in gold on spine: ADAM | BEDE | BY | GEORGE ELIOT | —— [ruled line in gold] | VOL. I. (II.) (III.) | [gold ornament] | W$^{\underline{M}}$ BLACKWOOD & SONS | EDINBURGH & LONDON. Pale yellow endpapers. Inside the back cover of volume I pasted rectangular label 1.4 × 2 cm: BOUND BY | EDMONDS & REMNANTS.| LONDON.

Publication: 1 February 1859, 31*s*. 6*d*.

Copies: (1) Beinecke Rare Books and Manuscript Library, Yale University: presentation copies sent by author to Mrs. Thomas Carlyle, James Anthony Froude, and the Revd. Charles Kingsley (all original binding); (2) Harry Ransom Humanities Research Center, University of Texas, Austin: Hugh Renton copy in Robert Lee Woolf collection (original binding) and Miriam Lutcher Stark copy (rebound); (3) Bodleian Library (rebound); (4) British Library (rebound, front leaves disarranged); (5) National Library of Scotland (rebound, front leaves disarranged); (6) editor.

Notes: (1) On title page, WILLIAM BLACKWOOD AND SONS is followed by a comma after SONS in volume III, but not in volumes I and II; (2) on title page, *reserved* in *The Right of Translation is reserved.* is lower case in volumes I and II, and upper case in volume III; (3) in the Carlyle and Kingsley copies at the Beinecke, the Woolf collection copy at the Ransom Center, and the editor's copy, a 16–page publisher's catalogue is added in at the end of volume III; in the Froude copy at the Beinecke, the centre four leaves are missing; this catalogue is missing from Bodleian, British Library, and National Library of Scotland copies.

2   *Second Edition, 3 volumes octavo,* 20 × 12.5

ADAM BEDE | BY | GEORGE ELIOT | AUTHOR OF | "SCENES OF CLERICAL LIFE" | [motto:] "So that ye may have | Clear images before your gladden'd eyes | Of nature's unambitious underwood | And flowers that prosper in the shade. And when | I speak of such among the flock as swerved | Or fell, those only shall be singled out | Upon whose lapse, or error, something more | Than brotherly forgiveness may attend." | WORDSWORTH. | IN THREE VOLUMES | VOL. I. (II. III.) | SECOND EDITION | WILLIAM BLACKWOOD AND SONS | EDINBURGH AND LONDON | MDCCCLIX | *The Right of Translation is reserved.*

Collation
VOL. I. π^4 A–U^8 X^4 (–X4); pp. viii + 326

VOL. II. π^4 A–O^8 [P]^8 Q–Z^8 2A^2 2B^2 (−2B2); pp. viii + 374
VOL. III. π^4 (−π4) [A]^8 B–U^8 X^8 (−X8); pp. vi + 334

VOL. I.
[i] half-title; [ii] blank; [iii] title page; [iv] blank; [v] CONTENTS
OF THE FIRST VOLUME.; [vi] blank; [vii] sub-half-title: BOOK
FIRST; [viii] blank; [1]–325 text | END OF THE FIRST VOLUME. |
PRINTED BY WILLIAM BLACKWOOD AND SONS,
EDINBURGH.; [326] blank.

VOL. II.
[i] half-title; [ii] blank; [iii] title page; [iv] blank; [v] CONTENTS OF
THE SECOND VOLUME.; [vi] blank; [vii] sub-half-title: BOOK
SECOND; [viii] blank; [1]–374 text | END OF THE SECOND
VOLUME. | PRINTED BY WILLIAM BLACKWOOD AND SONS,
EDINBURGH.

VOL. III.
[i] half-title; [ii] blank; [iii] title page; [iv] blank; [v] CONTENTS OF
THE THIRD VOLUME.; [vi] blank; [1] sub-half-title: BOOK
FIFTH; [2] blank; [3]–333 text | THE END. | PRINTED BY WILLIAM
BLACKWOOD AND SONS, EDINBURGH.; [334] blank.

Binding: Brownish-orange cloth, diagonal fine wave pattern, ornamental
frame blocked in blind on front and back covers; ornamental bands top and
bottom and lettering blocked in gold on spine: ADAM | BEDE | BY |
GEORGE ELIOT | —— [ruled line in gold] | VOL. I. (II.) (III.) | [gold
ornament] | *Second Edition* [in script] | W$^{\underline{M}}$ BLACKWOOD & SONS |
EDINBURGH & LONDON. Pale yellow endpapers. Inside the back
cover of volume I pasted rectangular label 1.4 × 2 cm: BOUND BY |
EDMONDS & REMNANTS.| LONDON.

Publication: April 1859, 31s. 6d.

Copies: (1) Beinecke Rare Books and Manuscript Library, Yale University;
(2) Harry Ransom Humanities Research Center, University of Texas,
Austin; (3) British Library.

Note: Volume I contains 16–page advertiser headed: WORKS
PUBLISHED | BY | MESSRS BLACKWOOD & SONS |
EDINBURGH AND LONDON.

3   *Third Edition, 3 volumes octavo,* 20 × 12.4

ADAM BEDE | BY | GEORGE ELIOT | AUTHOR OF | "SCENES OF
CLERICAL LIFE" | [motto:] "So that ye may have | Clear images before

your gladden'd eyes | Of nature's unambitious underwood | And flowers that prosper in the shade. And when | I speak of such among the flock as swerved | Or fell, those only shall be singled out | Upon whose lapse, or error, something more | Than brotherly forgiveness may attend." | WORDSWORTH. | IN THREE VOLUMES | VOL. I. (II. III.) | THIRD EDITION | WILLIAM BLACKWOOD AND SONS | EDINBURGH AND LONDON | MDCCCLIX | *The Right of Translation is reserved.*

Collation
VOL. I. π^4 A–U^8 X^4 (−X4); pp. viii + 326
VOL. II. π^4 A–O^8 [P]^8 Q–Z^8 2A^2 2B^2 (−2B2); pp. viii + 374
VOL. III. π^4 (−π4) [A]^8 B–U^8 X^8 (−X8); pp. vi + 334

VOL. I.
[i] half-title; [ii] blank; [iii] title page; [iv] blank; [v] CONTENTS OF THE FIRST VOLUME.; [vi] blank; [vii] sub-half-title: BOOK FIRST; [viii] blank; [1]–325 text | END OF THE FIRST VOLUME. | PRINTED BY WILLIAM BLACKWOOD AND SONS, EDINBURGH.; [326] blank.

VOL. II.
[i] half-title; [ii] blank; [iii] title page; [iv] blank; [v] CONTENTS OF THE SECOND VOLUME.; [vi] blank; [vii] sub-half-title: BOOK SECOND; [viii] blank; [1]–374 text | END OF THE SECOND VOLUME. | PRINTED BY WILLIAM BLACKWOOD AND SONS, EDINBURGH.

VOL. III.
[i] half-title; [ii] blank; [iii] title page; [iv] blank; [v] CONTENTS OF THE THIRD VOLUME.; [vi] blank; [1] sub-half-title: BOOK FIFTH; [2] blank; [3]–333 text | THE END. | PRINTED BY WILLIAM BLACKWOOD AND SONS, EDINBURGH.; [334] blank.

Binding: Brownish-orange cloth, diagonal fine wave pattern, ornamental frame blocked in blind on back and front covers; ornamental bands top and bottom and lettering blocked in gold on spine: ADAM | BEDE | BY | GEORGE ELIOT | —— [ruled line in gold] | VOL. I. (II.) (III.) | [gold ornament] | *Third Edition* [in script] | W$^{\underline{M}}$ BLACKWOOD & SONS | EDINBURGH & LONDON. Pale yellow endpapers. Inside the back cover of volume I pasted rectangular label 1.4 × 2 cm: BOUND BY | EDMONDS & REMNANTS. | LONDON.

Publication: May 1859, 31*s*. 6*d*.

Copy: Beinecke Rare Books and Manuscript Library, Yale University.

4   *Fourth Edition, 2 volumes octavo,* 17.2 × 10.7

ADAM BEDE | BY | GEORGE ELIOT | AUTHOR OF | "SCENES OF CLERICAL LIFE" | FOURTH EDITION | IN TWO VOLUMES | VOL. I. (II.) | WILLIAM BLACKWOOD AND SONS | EDINBURGH AND LONDON | MDCCCLIX | *The Right of Translation is reserved.* [motto on verso of half-title:] "So that ye may have | Clear images before your gladden'd eyes | Of nature's unambitious underwood | And flowers that prosper in the shade. And when | I speak of such among the flock as swerved | Or fell, those only shall be singled out | Upon whose lapse, or error, something more | Than brotherly forgiveness may attend." | WORDSWORTH.

Collation
VOL. I. π^4 A–Q^8 R^2 (−R2) [2]R^8 S–2C^8 2D^8 (−2D8); pp. viii + 432 (430 plus 2 unpaginated pages between 256 and [257])
VOL. II. π^4 (−π4) A–Z^8 2A^8 (−2A8); pp. vi + 382

VOL. I.
[i] half-title; [ii] motto; [iii] title page; [iv] blank; [v]–vi CONTENTS OF THE FIRST VOLUME.; [vii] sub-half-title: BOOK FIRST; [viii] blank; [1]–429 text | END OF THE FIRST VOLUME. | PRINTED BY WILLIAM BLACKWOOD AND SONS, EDINBURGH.; [430] blank.

VOL. II.
[i] half-title; [ii] motto; [iii] title page; [iv] blank; [v]–vi CONTENTS OF THE SECOND VOLUME.; [1] sub-half-title: BOOK FOURTH; [2] blank; [3]–382 text | THE END. | PRINTED BY WILLIAM BLACKWOOD AND SONS, EDINBURGH.

Binding: Brownish-orange cloth, diagonal fine wave pattern, rectangular frames blocked in blind on front and back covers. Gold band and ornament at top and gold band at bottom on spine; lettering blocked in gold: ADAM | BEDE | BY | GEORGE ELIOT | —— [ruled line in gold] | VOL. I. (II.) | [gold ornament] | W$^{\underline{M}}$ BLACKWOOD & SONS | EDINBURGH & LONDON; pale yellow endpapers; pasted inside the recto endpaper at the end of volume I a rectangular label: BOUND BY | EDMONDS & REMNANTS. | LONDON.

Publication: June 1859, 12s.

Copies: (1) Bodleian Library, Oxford University; (2) editor.

Notes: (1) Volume II includes a 16–page publisher's catalogue following the text; (2) the Bodleian copy is missing the right-hand front endpaper in volumes I and II (endpapers are intact at the ends of both volumes) and the leaf containing pages 419–20 in volume I; (3) the editor's copy includes a half-sheet advertising 'A New and Cheaper Edition' of *Scenes of Clerical Life* '*In preparation*' pasted between the front endpapers of volume 1.

5 *Fifth Edition, 2 volumes octavo*, 17 × 10.5

ADAM BEDE | BY | GEORGE ELIOT | AUTHOR OF | "SCENES OF CLERICAL LIFE" | FIFTH EDITION | IN TWO VOLUMES | VOL. I. (II.) | WILLIAM BLACKWOOD AND SONS | EDINBURGH AND LONDON | MDCCCLIX | *The Right of Translation is reserved*.
[motto on verso of half-title:] "So that ye may have | Clear images before your gladden'd eyes | Of nature's unambitious underwood | And flowers that prosper in the shade. And when | I speak of such among the flock as swerved | Or fell, those only shall be singled out | Upon whose lapse, or error, something more | Than brotherly forgiveness may attend." | WORDSWORTH.

Collation
VOL. I. π^4 A–2D^8; pp. viii + 432
VOL. II. π^4 (−π4) A–Z^8 2A^8 (−2A8); pp. vi + 382

VOL. I.
[i] half-title; [ii] motto; [iii] title page; [iv] blank; [v]–vi CONTENTS OF THE FIRST VOLUME.; [vii] sub-half-title: BOOK FIRST; [viii] blank; [1]–431 text | END OF THE FIRST VOLUME. | PRINTED BY WILLIAM BLACKWOOD AND SONS, EDINBURGH.; [432] blank.

VOL. II.
[i] half-title; [ii] motto; [iii] title page; [iv] blank; [v]–vi CONTENTS OF THE SECOND VOLUME.; [1] sub-half-title: BOOK FOURTH; [2] blank; [3]–382 text | THE END. | PRINTED BY WILLIAM BLACKWOOD AND SONS, EDINBURGH.

Binding: Brownish-orange cloth, diagonal fine wave pattern, rectangular frames blocked in blind on front and back covers. Gold band and ornament at top and gold band at bottom on spine; lettering blocked in gold: ADAM | BEDE | BY | GEORGE ELIOT | —— [ruled line in gold] | VOL. I. (II.) | [gold ornament] | W$^{\underline{M}}$ BLACKWOOD & SONS | EDINBURGH & LONDON; pale yellow endpapers; pasted inside the recto endpaper at the end of volume I a rectangular label: BOUND BY | EDMONDS & REMNANTS. | LONDON.

Publication: July 1859, 12s.

Copies: (1) British Library; (2) editor.

Notes: (1) Editor's copy has new endpapers and is missing binder's sticker; (2) British Library copy is smaller in horizontal dimension by 2 cm.

6   *Sixth Edition, 2 volumes octavo,* 17.2 × 10.7

ADAM BEDE | BY | GEORGE ELIOT | AUTHOR OF | "SCENES OF CLERICAL LIFE" | SIXTH EDITION | IN TWO VOLUMES | VOL. I. (II.) | WILLIAM BLACKWOOD AND SONS | EDINBURGH AND LONDON | MDCCCLIX | *The Right of Translation is reserved.*
[motto on verso of half-title] "So that ye may have | Clear images before your gladden'd eyes | Of nature's unambitious underwood | And flowers that prosper in the shade. And when | I speak of such among the flock as swerved | Or fell, those only shall be singled out | Upon whose lapse, or error, something more | Than brotherly forgiveness may attend." | WORDSWORTH.

Collation
VOL. I. π^4 A–2D^8; pp. viii + 432
VOL. II. π^4 (–π4) [A]^8 B–Z^8 2A^8 (–2A8); pp. vi + 382

VOL. I.
[i] half-title; [ii] motto; [iii] title page; [iv] blank; [v]–vi CONTENTS OF THE FIRST VOLUME.; [vii] sub-half-title: BOOK FIRST; [viii] blank; [1]–431 text | END OF THE FIRST VOLUME. | PRINTED BY WILLIAM BLACKWOOD AND SONS, EDINBURGH.; [432] blank.

VOL. II.
[i] half-title; [ii] motto; [iii] title page; [iv] blank; [v]–vi CONTENTS OF THE SECOND VOLUME.; [1] sub-half-title: BOOK FOURTH; [2] blank; [3]–382 text | THE END. | PRINTED BY WILLIAM BLACKWOOD AND SONS, EDINBURGH.

Binding: Brownish-orange cloth, diagonal fine wave pattern, rectangular frames blocked in blind on front and back covers. Gold band and ornament at top and gold band at bottom on spine; lettering blocked in gold: ADAM | BEDE | BY | GEORGE ELIOT | —— [ruled line in gold] | VOL. I. (II.)| [gold ornament] | W$^{\underline{M}}$ BLACKWOOD & SONS | EDINBURGH & LONDON; pale yellow endpapers; pasted inside the recto endpaper at the end of volume I a rectangular label: BOUND BY | EDMONDS & REMNANTS. | LONDON.

Publication: September 1859, 12s.

Copies: (1) British Library; (2) editor.

Notes: (1) Volume II includes a 16–page publisher's catalogue; (2) British Library copy is missing binder's sticker.

7   *Seventh Edition, 2 volumes octavo, 17.2 × 10.7*

ADAM BEDE | BY | GEORGE ELIOT | AUTHOR OF | "SCENES OF CLERICAL LIFE" | SEVENTH EDITION | IN TWO VOLUMES | VOL. I. (II.) | WILLIAM BLACKWOOD AND SONS | EDINBURGH AND LONDON | MDCCCLIX | *The Right of Translation is reserved.* [motto on verso of half-title:] "So that ye may have | Clear images before your gladden'd eyes | Of nature's unambitious underwood | And flowers that prosper in the shade. And when | I speak of such among the flock as swerved | Or fell, those only shall be singled out | Upon whose lapse, or error, something more | Than brotherly forgiveness may attend." | WORDSWORTH.

Collation
VOL. I. π^4 A–L^8 [M]^8 N–2D^8; pp. viii + 432
VOL. II. π^4 ($-\pi4$) [A]^8 B–Z^8 2A^8 ($-$2A8); pp. vi + 382

VOL. I.
[i] half-title; [ii] motto; [iii] title page; [iv] blank; [v]–vi CONTENTS OF THE FIRST VOLUME.; [vii] sub-half-title: BOOK FIRST; [viii] blank; [1]–431 text | END OF THE FIRST VOLUME. | PRINTED BY WILLIAM BLACKWOOD AND SONS EDINBURGH.; [432] blank.

VOL. II.
[i] half-title; [ii] motto; [iii] title page; [iv] blank; [v]–vi CONTENTS OF THE SECOND VOLUME.; [1] sub-half-title: BOOK FOURTH; [2] blank; [3]–382 text | THE END. | PRINTED BY WILLIAM BLACKWOOD AND SONS EDINBURGH.

Binding: Brownish-orange cloth, diagonal fine wave pattern, rectangular frames blocked in blind on front and back covers. Gold band and ornament at top and gold band at bottom on spine; lettering blocked in gold: ADAM | BEDE | BY | GEORGE ELIOT | —— [ruled line in gold] | VOL. I. (II.) | [gold ornament] | W$^{\underline{M}}$ BLACKWOOD & SONS | EDINBURGH & LONDON; pale yellow endpapers in volume I, faded ivory in volume II; pasted inside the recto endpaper at the end of volume I a rectangular label: BOUND BY | EDMONDS & REMNANTS. | LONDON.

Publication: November 1859, 12*s*.

Copy: British Library.

Notes: (1) In volume I, signature M is absent on page 177, a text page partway through Chapter XI. The notation 'Vol. I' appears below the line in the usual place, but no M is visible to the right of it; (2) punctuation after PRINTED BY WILLIAM BLACKWOOD AND SONS on the final page of text is missing in both volumes.

8   *Eighth Edition, 2 volumes octavo,* 17.2 × 10.7

ADAM BEDE | BY | GEORGE ELIOT | AUTHOR OF | "SCENES OF CLERICAL LIFE" | EIGHTH EDITION | IN TWO VOLUMES | VOL. I. (II.) | WILLIAM BLACKWOOD AND SONS | EDINBURGH AND LONDON | MDCCCLX | *The Right of Translation is reserved.*
[motto on verso of half-title:] "So that ye may have | Clear images before your gladden'd eyes | Of nature's unambitious underwood | And flowers that prosper in the shade. And when | I speak of such among the flock as swerved | Or fell, those only shall be singled out | Upon whose lapse, or error, something more | Than brotherly forgiveness may attend." | WORDSWORTH.

Collation
VOL. I. π^4 A–2D^8; pp. viii + 432
VOL. II. π^4 (−π4) [A]^8 B–Z^8 2A^8 (−2A8); pp. vi + 382

VOL. I.
[i] half-title; [ii] motto; [iii] title page; [iv] blank; [v]–vi CONTENTS OF THE FIRST VOLUME.; [vii] sub-half-title: BOOK FIRST; [viii] blank; [1]–431 text | END OF THE FIRST VOLUME. | PRINTED BY WILLIAM BLACKWOOD AND SONS, EDINBURGH.; [432] blank.

VOL. II.
[i] half-title; [ii] motto; [iii] title-page; [iv] blank; [v]–vi CONTENTS OF THE SECOND VOLUME.; [1] sub-half-title: BOOK FOURTH; [2] blank; [3]–382 text | THE END. | PRINTED BY WILLIAM BLACKWOOD AND SONS, EDINBURGH.

Binding: Brownish-orange cloth, diagonal fine wave pattern, rectangular frames blocked in blind on front and back covers. Gold band and orna-ment at top and gold band at bottom on spine; lettering blocked in gold:

ADAM | BEDE | BY | GEORGE ELIOT | ———— [ruled line in gold] | VOL.
I. (II.) | [gold ornament] | W$\underline{M}$ BLACKWOOD & SONS | EDINBURGH
& LONDON; pale yellow endpapers.

Publication: June 1860, 12*s*.

Copies: (1) editor; (2) Harry Ransom Humanities Research Center.

Note: The copy in the Harry Ransom Humanities Research Center, which
is the copy text for the Clarendon *Adam Bede*, was pulled apart in the
typesetting and the front matter disarranged in the subsequent reassembly
and rebinding.

9   *Tenth Edition*, 1 *volume octavo*, 18.4 × 12.2

ADAM BEDE | BY | GEORGE ELIOT | AUTHOR OF | "SCENES OF
CLERICAL LIFE" | TENTH EDITION | WILLIAM BLACKWOOD
AND SONS | EDINBURGH AND LONDON | MDCCCLXII

Collation
π^4 $(-\pi 4)$ A–2F^8 2G^4 $(-2G4)$; pp. vi + 470

[i] half-title; [ii] motto ["So that ye may have | Clear images before your
gladdened eyes | Of nature's unambitious underwood | And flowers
that prosper in the shade. And when | I speak of such among the flock as
swerved | Or fell, those only shall be singled out | Upon whose lapse,
or error, something more | Than brotherly forgiveness may attend." |
WORDSWORTH.]; [iii] title page; [iv] blank; [v]–vi CONTENTS; [1]–
470 text | THE END. | PRINTED BY WILLIAM BLACKWOOD AND
SONS, EDINBURGH.

Publication: January 1862, 6*s*.

Copy: British Library (trimmed and rebound).

Note: The one-volume edition begins the use of *gladdened* in the motto
instead of *gladden'd*.

9*b*   *Twelfth Edition*, 1 *volume octavo*, 19 × 12.5

ADAM BEDE | BY | GEORGE ELIOT | AUTHOR OF | 'SCENES OF
CLERICAL LIFE' | [motto:] "So that ye may have | Clear images before
your gladdened eyes | Of nature's unambitious underwood | And flowers
that prosper in the shade. And when | I speak of such among the flock as
swerved | Or fell, those only shall be singled out | Upon whose lapse, or

error, something more | Than brotherly forgiveness may attend." | WORDSWORTH. | TWELFTH EDITION | WILLIAM BLACKWOOD AND SONS | EDINBURGH AND LONDON | MDCCCLXVI

Collation
π^4 $(-\pi 4)$ A–2F^8 2G^4 $(-2G4)$; pp. vi + 470

[i] half-title; [ii] publisher's announcement: *BY THE SAME AUTHOR* | THE MILL ON THE FLOSS. 6s. | SCENES OF CLERICAL LIFE. | SILAS MARNER. | In One Volume, 6s. | FELIX HOLT, THE RADICAL. Three Volumes, | 31s. 6d.; [iii] title page; [iv] blank; [v]–vi CONTENTS; [1]–470 text | THE END. | PRINTED BY WILLIAM BLACKWOOD AND SONS, EDINBURGH.

Binding: Brownish-orange cloth, fine wave pattern, ornamental interlocking diamond pattern inside rectangular frame blocked in blind on front and back covers. Spine with interlocking diamond pattern blocked in blind, lettering blocked in gold: | WORKS | OF | GEORGE ELIOT | ADAM | BEDE | W$\underline{M}$ BLACKWOOD & SONS | EDINBURGH & LONDON. Pale yellow endpapers.

Publication: August 1866, 6s.

Copy: National Library of Scotland.

Note: Publisher's advertising catalogue, consisting of two separate units (pages 1–4, and 1–[20]), added in following the text.

9c   *Stereotyped Edition, issued in 7 parts*, 18.3 × 12.5

Part-issue title pages:
No 1 [2, 3, 4, 5, 6, 7] SIXPENCE | THE | NOVELS | & | TALES | OF | GEORGE ELIOT | ADAM BEDE | W. BLACKWOOD & SONS. | EDINBURGH | & LONDON. | ILLUSTRATIONS | J. D. COOPER

Collation: Part 1, A–H^8; Part 2, I–M^8; Part 3, N–Q^8; Part 4, R–U^8; Part 5, X–2A^8; Part 6, 2B–2E^8; Part 7, 2F^8–2G^4 $(-2G4)$.

Binding: Apple green paper wrappers. *Front cover*: frame in black with rounded corners, enclosing medallions in each corner, depicting (clockwise, from upper left to lower left): (1) a carpenter's workshop with workbench, tools lying on and hanging above it, and wood shavings on the floor; (2) a mill, showing the mill-wheel in the center and part of the building to which it is attached, with bare, wintry trees in background; (3) a weaver's loom; and (4) a graveyard with tombstone engraved 'AMELIA | XXXV. | BARTON.' *Back cover*: NOVELS AND TALES | OF | GEORGE ELIOT | Illustrated Edition | [ornamental line with berries] | This Edition will be published in | Monthly Numbers, price SIX-| PENCE. | Each Number will contain a | highly-finished Engraving, executed, | under the direction of Mr J. D. | Cooper, by a selection of able Artists.

Publication: 7 monthly parts from April to October 1867, 6*d*. per part.

Copy: British Library (bound).

Note: Bound in with the part issue covers and text in the British Library copy is the front matter of the one-volume stereotyped edition. Its collation is $\pi 4$ ($-\pi 4$) with the following sequence: [i] title page; [ii] blank; [iii] List of Illustrations; [iv] publisher's advertisement: THE SECOND VOLUME | WILL CONTAIN | THE MILL ON THE FLOSS. | WITH EIGHT ILLUSTRATIONS. | Price 3s. 6d.; [v]–vi CONTENTS; the series title page precedes these pages and is engraved with the illustration of the Hall Farm and printed on heavier paper stock; it matches the description given for 9*d*, *Stereotyped Edition*.

9*d*   *Stereotyped Edition*, 1 *volume octavo*, 18.2 × 12.2

Series title page (blank on verso):
NOVELS | OF | GEORGE ELIOT | VOL. I. | ADAM BEDE | WITH ILLUSTRATIONS | [vignette of Hall Farm exterior with stone wall and iron gate in foreground] | THE HALL FARM | WILLIAM BLACKWOOD AND SONS | EDINBURGH AND LONDON

Volume title page:
ADAM BEDE | BY | GEORGE ELIOT | [motto:] "So that ye may have | Clear images before your gladdened eyes | Of nature's unambitious underwood | And flowers that prosper in the shade. And when | I speak of such among the flock as swerved | Or fell, those only shall be singled out | Upon whose lapse, or error, something more | Than brotherly forgiveness may attend." | WORDSWORTH. | STEREOTYPED EDITION | WILLIAM BLACKWOOD AND SONS | EDINBURGH AND LONDON

Collation: π^4 ($-\pi 4$) A–2F^8 2G^4 (-2G4); pp. vi + 470

[i] title page; [ii] blank; [iii] LIST OF ILLUSTRATIONS; [iv] publisher's announcement of Volume II; [v]–vi CONTENTS.; [1]–470 text |

THE END. | PRINTED BY WILLIAM BLACKWOOD AND SONS, EDINBURGH.

Publication: 1867, 3s. 6d.

Copies: (1) Bodleian Library, Oxford University; (2) editor.

Notes: (1) The stereotyped edition was first issued in 1867 without a date on the title page; it continued to be issued thus until 1873 when a new title page called new printings from the stereo plates 'A NEW EDITION'; (2) two cognate leaves on heavier paper stock precede [i]; facing pages are engraved with the drawing of Adam Bede in the workshop on the verso of the first leaf and the series title page with the drawing of the Hall Farm on the recto of the second leaf; this drawing of Adam in the workshop faces page 2 in the part issue and in later printings of the illustrated edition called 'A New Edition' (see 9e and 9f); (3) both copies can be dated 1867 by the advertiser on page [iv] announcing: 'THE SECOND VOLUME | WILL CONTAIN | THE MILL ON THE FLOSS | WITH EIGHT ILLUSTRATIONS. | Price 3s.6d.'; (4) both copies have been trimmed and rebound.

9e   *'A New Edition'*, 1 *volume octavo*, 18.2 × 12.1

ADAM BEDE | BY | GEORGE ELIOT | [motto:] "So that ye may have | Clear images before your gladdened eyes | Of nature's unambitious underwood | And flowers that prosper in the shade. And when | I speak of such among the flock as swerved | Or fell, those only shall be singled out | Upon whose lapse, or error, something more | Than brotherly forgiveness may attend." | WORDSWORTH. | A NEW EDITION | WILLIAM BLACKWOOD AND SONS | EDINBURGH AND LONDON

Collation: π^4 ($-\pi4$) A–2F^8 2G^4 ($-$2G4); pp. vi + 470

[i] blank; [ii] blank; [iii] title page; [iv] blank; [v]–vi CONTENTS; [1]–470 text | THE END. | PRINTED BY WILLIAM BLACKWOOD AND SONS, EDINBURGH.

Publication: June 1873, 2s. 6d.

Copy: British Library (trimmed and rebound).

Notes: (1) This edition was issued from the stereo plates of the 10th edition, the same ones used for the 1867 illustrated edition; this cheaper edition, however, contains none of the illustrations found in the 'Stereotyped' edition or the later copies also labelled 'A New Edition' on the title page, described as 9*f*; (2) the date of publication is verified in Blackwoods ledger MS 30,861, folios 97 and 370, and by the stamped British Museum accession date: '12 AU 73'.

9*f* '*A New Edition*', 1 volume octavo, 19 × 12.7

ADAM BEDE | BY | GEORGE ELIOT | [motto:] "So that ye may have | Clear images before your gladdened eyes | Of nature's unambitious underwood | And flowers that prosper in the shade. And when | I speak of such among the flock as swerved | Or fell, those only shall be singled out | Upon whose lapse, or error, something more | Than brotherly forgiveness may attend." | WORDSWORTH. | A NEW EDITION | WILLIAM BLACKWOOD AND SONS | EDINBURGH AND LONDON

Collation: π^4 $(-\pi_4)$ A–2F^8 2G^4 $(-2G_4)$; pp. vi + 470

[i] title page; [ii] blank; [iii] LIST OF ILLUSTRATIONS; [iv] blank; [v]–vi CONTENTS; [1]–470 text | THE END. | PRINTED BY WILLIAM BLACKWOOD AND SONS, EDINBURGH.

Binding: Red cloth, sand grain, with ornamental rectangular frame blocked in blind on front and back covers. Medallion of Adam's workshop (repro-ducing the medallion on paper covers of the 1867 part-issue) blocked in gold on front cover. Very dark brown endpapers. Spine lettering in gold, with top and bottom gold rules enclosing text: *ADAM | BEDE | BY | GEORGE | ELIOT* | W$^{\underline{M}}$ BLACKWOOD & SONS | EDINBURGH & LONDON

Publication: from 1873–, 3*s*. 6*d*.

Copies: (1) Bodleian Library, Oxford University; (2) editor.

Notes: (1) Series title page (blank on verso): NOVELS | OF | GEORGE ELIOT | VOL. I. | ADAM BEDE | *WITH ILLUSTRATIONS* | [vignette of the Hall Farm exterior with stone wall and iron gate in foreground] | THE HALL FARM | WILLIAM BLACKWOOD AND SONS | EDINBURGH AND LONDON; (2) publication dates were omitted on the title pages of this edition. The Bodleian catalogue gives 1876 for its copy, a date supported by works in the publisher's advertiser added before the series title page, which includes on the verso the WORKS OF GEORGE ELIOT, including the 4–volume *Daniel Deronda* and the 7*s*. 6*d*. *Middlemarch*, as well as works by other authors. The editor's copy can be dated *c*.1880, based on the advertiser for the Cabinet edition from *Romola* to *Theophrastus Such*; later in the 1880s an edition bearing the same title page was reset and issued in the same binding with a new advertiser.

Cabinet Edition, 2 volumes octavo, 17.6 × 11.3.

THE WORKS | OF | GEORGE ELIOT | ADAM BEDE | VOL. I. (II.) |
WILLIAM BLACKWOOD AND SONS | EDINBURGH AND
LONDON | MDCCCLXXVIII | *All Rights reserved*
[motto on verso of series title page:] "So that ye may have | Clear images
before your gladdened eyes | Of nature's unambitious underwood | And
flowers that prosper in the shade. And when | I speak of such among the
flock as swerved | Or fell, those only shall be singled out | Upon whose lapse,
or error, something more | Than brotherly forgiveness may attend." | ——
WORDSWORTH.

Collation
VOL. I. π^4 [A]^8 B–2D^8 2E^4; pp. viii + 440
VOL. II. π^4 [A]^8 B–Z^8 2A^6; pp. viii + 380

VOL. I.
[i] blank; [ii] publisher's advertisement; [iii] series title page; [iv] motto; [v]
title page; [vi] blank; [vii]–'vi' CONTENTS OF THE FIRST
VOLUME.; [1] sub-half-title: BOOK I.; [2] blank; [3]–438 text |
END OF THE FIRST VOLUME. | PRINTED BY WILLIAM
BLACKWOOD AND SONS; | [439–40] blank.

VOL. II.
[i] blank; [ii] publisher's advertisement; [iii] series title page; [iv] motto; [v]
title page; [vi] blank; [vii]–'vi' CONTENTS OF THE SECOND
VOLUME.; [1] sub-half-title: BOOK IV.; [2] blank; [3]–379 text | THE
END. | PRINTED BY WILLIAM BLACKWOOD AND SONS.; [380]
blank.

Binding: Olive green cloth, diagonal fine rib grain, rectangular frame
enclosing reversed J pattern of leaves and berries blocked in black;
WORKS | OF | GEORGE ELIOT blocked in black in upper right on
front cover; rectangular frame enclosing circle of leaves and berries blocked
in black on back cover; spine blocked in gold and black: —— [ruled line] |
WORKS | OF | GEORGE ELIOT | [ornamental leaves and berries] | ——
[ruled line] | ADAM BEDE | I. (II.) | —— [ruled line] | [ornamental leaves
and berries] | CABINET | EDITION | —— [ruled line]; chocolate brown
endpapers.

Publication: April (vol. I) and May (vol. II) 1878, 5*s*. per volume.

Copies: (1) Emmanuel College, Cambridge. (2) British Library (rebound).

Notes: (1) Volume I of the Emmanuel College copy has the original binding; volume II has been rebacked with new endpapers pasted onto the boards over the original brown endpapers; (2) the publisher's advertiser reveals the evolution of Blackwoods' plan for the Cabinet edition. In *Adam Bede*, volume I, p. [ii], the advertiser lists *Scenes of Clerical Life* as '1 vol.', but in volume II, p. [ii], the advertiser lists it as '2 vols.' The first instance is not a typographical error; in the Cabinet *Romola*, several works are given without a specified number of volumes, as the matter was still being decided.

OVERSEAS EDITIONS

Several overseas editions of *Adam Bede* were issued during George Eliot's lifetime. Two American editions, each in a single duodecimo volume, were issued by Harper & Brothers, New York, in 1859 and 1860. Both were based on the three-volume editions, since neither Harper's first nor second edition contains the correction Eliot made in Chapter IV, regarding Adam and the willow wand, which she sent to Blackwoods in May 1859, and which was published in June 1859 in the first two-volume edition, called the 'Fourth' on the title page. The copyright English edition for the Continent was published in 1859 in Leipzig by Bernhard Tauchnitz, in two volumes, numbers 482 and 483 in the Tauchnitz Collection of British Authors series; this edition, which included the revised willow-wand passage in Chapter IV, was based on an early two-volume edition. A French translation by George Eliot's friend François d'Albert-Durade was published in Paris and Geneva in 1861, in two volumes. This edition includes a letter from Eliot to d'Albert-Durade, dated 7 February 1860: 'I have much pleasure in authorizing you to translate *Adam Bede*, and it is desirable that you should prefix this authorization to your translation of the work, in order to apprize the public that yours is the only French translation which has received my sanction.' This letter appears immediately after the title page, with a French translation following on a new page. The French translation of *Adam Bede* includes the revised willow-wand passage in Chapter IV. A German edition in two volumes, translated by Julius Frese, appeared in 1860, published in Berlin by Franz Drucker. Despite its date, this translation did not adopt the correction to Chapter IV. All these editions were authorized, but the author read proofs for none of them.

ADAM BEDE

"So that ye may have
Clear images before your gladden'd eyes
Of nature's unambitious underwood
And flowers that prosper in the shade. And when
I speak of such among the flock as swerved
Or fell, those only shall be singled out
Upon whose lapse, or error, something more
Than brotherly forgiveness may attend."

WORDSWORTH.

ADAM BEDE

BY

GEORGE ELIOT

AUTHOR OF

"SCENES OF CLERICAL LIFE"

EIGHTH EDITION

IN TWO VOLUMES

VOL. I.

WILLIAM BLACKWOOD AND SONS
EDINBURGH AND LONDON
MDCCCLX

CONTENTS OF THE FIRST VOLUME.

CONTENTS OF THE SECOND VOLUME.

[1] In the table of contents in both the 1st edn. and the 8th edn., the title of Chapter XXIII is given as 'THE DINNER'. However, in the text the manuscript title is uniformly used: 'DINNER-TIME'.

BOOK FIRST

*

CHAPTER I.

THE WORKSHOP.

With a single drop of ink for a mirror, the Egyptian sorcerer undertakes to reveal to any chance comer far-reaching visions of the past. This is what I undertake to do for you, reader. With this drop of ink at the end of my pen, I will show you the roomy workshop of Mr Jonathan Burge, carpenter and builder in the village of Hayslope, as it appeared on the eighteenth of June, in the year of our Lord 1799.

The afternoon sun was warm on the five workmen there, busy upon doors and window-frames and wainscoting. A scent of pine-wood from a tent-like pile of planks outside the open door mingled itself with the scent of the elder-bushes which were spreading[1] their summer snow close to the open window opposite; the slanting sunbeams shone through the transparent shavings that flew before the steady plane, and lit up the fine grain of the oak panelling which stood propped against the wall. On a heap of those soft shavings a rough grey shepherd-dog had made himself a pleasant bed, and was lying with his nose between his fore-paws, occasionally wrinkling his brows to cast a glance at the tallest of the five workmen, who was carving a shield in the centre of a wooden mantelpiece. It was to this workman that the strong barytone belonged which was heard above the sound of plane and hammer singing—

> "Awake, my soul, and with the sun
> Thy daily stage of duty run;
> Shake off dull sloth . . . ."

Here some measurement was to be taken which required more concentrated attention, and the sonorous voice subsided into a low whistle; but it presently broke out again with renewed vigour—

> "Let all thy converse be sincere,
> Thy conscience as the noonday clear."

Such a voice could only come from a broad chest, and the broad chest belonged to a large-boned muscular man nearly six feet high, with a back so flat and a head so well poised that when he drew himself up to take a more distant survey of his work, he had the air of a soldier standing at ease. The[2]

---

[1] spreading] shedding *MS*   [2] The sleeve⟨s⟩ rolled up above ⟨an⟩ the *MS*

sleeve rolled up above the elbow showed an arm that was likely to win the
prize for feats of strength; yet the long supple hand, with its broad finger-
tips, looked ready for works of skill. In his tall stalwartness Adam Bede was
a Saxon, and justified his name; but the jet-black hair, made the more
noticeable by its contrast with the light paper cap, and the keen glance of the
dark eyes that shone from under strongly marked, prominent and mobile
eyebrows, indicated a mixture of Celtic blood. The face was large and
roughly hewn, and when in repose had no other beauty than such as belongs
to an expression of good-humoured honest intelligence.

It is clear at a glance that the next workman is Adam's brother. He is
nearly as tall; he has the same type of features, the same hue of hair and
complexion; but the strength of the family likeness seems only to render
more conspicuous the remarkable difference of expression both in form
and face. Seth's broad shoulders have a slight stoop; his eyes are grey;
his eyebrows have less prominence and more repose than his brother's;
and his glance, instead of being keen, is confiding and benignant. He
has thrown off his paper cap, and you see that his hair is not thick and
straight, like Adam's, but thin and wavy, allowing you to discern the
exact contour of a coronal arch that predominates very decidedly over
the brow.

The idle tramps always felt sure they could get a copper[3] from Seth; they
scarcely ever spoke to Adam.

The concert of the tools and Adam's voice was at last broken by Seth,
who, lifting the door at which he had been working intently, placed it
against the wall, and said—

"There! I've finished my door to-day, anyhow."

The workmen all looked up; Jim Salt, a burly red-haired man,[4] known as
Sandy Jim, paused from his planing, and Adam said to Seth, with a sharp
glance of surprise—

"What! dost think thee'st finished the door?"

"Ay, sure," said Seth, with answering surprise, "what's awanting[5] to't?"

A loud roar of laughter from the other three workmen made Seth look
round confusedly. Adam did not join in the laughter, but there was a slight
smile on[6] his face as he said, in a gentler tone than before—

"Why, thee'st forgot the panels."

The laughter burst out afresh as Seth clapped his hands to his head, and
coloured over brow and crown.

"Hoorray!" shouted a small lithe fellow, called Wiry Ben, running
forward and seizing the door. "We'll hang up th' door at fur end o' th'
shop an' write on't,[7] 'Seth Bede, the Methody, his work.' Here, Jim, lend's
hould o' th' red-pot."

---

³ a copper] something *MS*   ⁴ man] man *MS 1* ⟨men⟩ man *8*
⁵ awanting] wanting *MS*   ⁶ on] in *MS*   ⁷ on't,] *MS 1* on't *8*

"Nonsense!" said Adam. "Let it alone, Ben Cranage. You'll mayhap be making such a slip yourself some day; you'll laugh o' th' other side o' your mouth then."

"Catch me at it, Adam. It'll be a good while afore my head's full o' th' Methodies," said Ben.

"Nay, but it's often full o' drink, and that's worse."

Ben, however, had now got the "red-pot" in his hand, and was about to begin writing his inscription, making, by way of preliminary, an imaginary S in the air.

"Let it alone, will you?" Adam called out, laying down his tools, striding up to Ben, and seizing his right shoulder. "Let it alone, or I'll shake the soul out o' your body."

Ben shook[8] in Adam's iron grasp, but, like a plucky small man as he was, he didn't mean to give in. With his left hand he snatched the brush from his powerless right, and made a movement as if he would perform the feat of writing with his left. In a moment Adam turned him round, seized his other shoulder, and pushing him along, pinned him against the wall. But now Seth spoke.

"Let be, Addy, let be. Ben will be joking. Why, he's i' the right to laugh at me—I canna help laughing at myself."

"I[9] shan't loose him, till he promises to let the door alone," said Adam.

"Come, Ben, lad," said Seth in a persuasive tone,[1] "don't let's have a quarrel about it. You know[2] Adam will have his way. You may 's well try to turn a waggon in a narrow lane. Say you'll leave the door alone, and make an end on't."

"I binna frighted at Adam," said Ben, "but I donna mind sayin' as I'll[3] let 't alone at your[4] askin', Seth."

"Come, that's wise of you, Ben," said Adam, laughing and relaxing his grasp.

They all returned to their work now; but Wiry Ben, having had the worst in the bodily contest, was bent on retrieving that humiliation by a success in[5] sarcasm.

"Which was ye thinkin' on, Seth," he began—"the pretty parson's face or her sarmunt, when ye forgot the panels[6]?"

"Come and hear her, Ben," said Seth, good-humouredly; "she's going to preach on the Green to-night; happen[7] ye'd get something to think on yourself then, instead[8] o' those wicked songs ye're[9] so fond on. Ye might get religion, and that 'ud be the best day's earnings y' ever made."

[8] shook] turned white MS   [9] I ⟨shanna⟩ shan't MS
[1] tone, "⟨donna⟩ don't MS   [2] know ⟨you may's well try⟩ Adam will have MS
[3] I'll ⟨let tha 't alone for⟩ let MS   [4] your] yare MS I ⟨yare⟩ your 8
[5] a success in] added in MS   [6] panels] pannels MS panel I ⟨panel⟩ panels 8
[7] happen ⟨you'd⟩ ye'd MS   [8] instead] istead MS   [9] ye're] you're Cabinet

"All i' good time for that, Seth; I'll think about that when I'm a-goin' to settle i' life; bachelors doesn't want such heavy earnins. Happen I shall do the coortin' an' the religion both together, as *ye*[1] do, Seth; but ye wouldna ha' me get converted an' chop in atween ye[2] an' the pretty preacher, an' carry her aff?"

"No fear o' that, Ben; she's neither for you nor for me to win, I doubt. Only you come and hear her, and you won't speak lightly on her again."

"Well, I'n half a mind t' ha' a look at her to-night, if there isn't good company at th'[3] Holly Bush. What'll she take[4] for her text? Happen ye can tell me, Seth, if so be as I shouldna come up i' time for't. Will 't be,—What[5] come ye out for to see? A prophetess? Yea, I say unto you, and more than a prophetess—a uncommon pretty young woman."

"Come, Ben," said Adam, rather sternly, "you[6] let the words o' the Bible alone; you're going too far now."

"What! are *ye*[7] a-turnin' roun', Adam? I thought ye war dead again th' women preachin', a while agoo?"

"Nay, I'm not turnin'[8] noway. I said nought about the women preachin'[9]: I said, You let the Bible alone: you've got a jest-book, han't you, as you're rare and proud on? Keep your dirty fingers to that."

"Why, y'are gettin' as big a saint as Seth. Y'are goin' to th' preachin' to-night, I should think. Ye'll do finely t' lead the singin'. But I don'[1] know what Parson Irwine 'ull say at his[2] gran' favright Adam Bede a-turnin' Methody."

"Never do you bother yourself about me, Ben. I'm not a-going to turn Methodist any more nor you are—though it's like enough you'll turn to something worse. Mester Irwine's got more sense nor to meddle wi' people's doing as they like in religion. That's between themselves and God, as he's said to me many a time."

"Ay, ay; but he's none so fond o' your dissenters, for all that."

"Maybe; I'm none so fond o' Josh Tod's[3] thick ale, but I don't hinder you from making a fool o' yourself wi't."

There was a laugh at this thrust of Adam's, but Seth said, very seriously,

"Nay, nay, Addy, thee mustna[4] say as anybody's religion's like thick ale. Thee dostna believe but what the dissenters and the Methodists have got the root o' the matter as well as the church folks."

"Nay, Seth, lad; I'm not for laughing at no man's religion. Let 'em follow their consciences, that's all. Only I think it 'ud be better if their consciences

---

[1] *ye*] yey *MS*   [2] ye] yey *MS*   [3] th'] the *MS*
[4] take] tek *MS 1* ⟨tek⟩ take *8*
[5] be,—What] be—'What *MS* be, 'What *1* be,{—} What *8*
[6] you] *MS 1* ⟨you⟩ ⟨&⟩ you *8*   [7] *ye*] yey *MS*
[8] turnin'] turning, *MS*   [9] preachin'] preaching *MS*
[1] don'] dun *MS 1* ⟨dun⟩ don' *8*   [2] at his] at 's *MS 1* ⟨at 's⟩ at his *8*
[3] Tod's] Todd's *MS*   [4] mustna] munna *MS*

'ud let 'em stay quiet i' the church—there's a deal to be learnt there. And there's such a thing as being over-speritial; we must have something beside Gospel i' this world. Look at the canals,[5] an' th' aqueducs, an' th' coal-pit engines, and Arkwright's mills there at Cromford; a man must learn summat beside Gospel to make them things, I reckon. But t' hear some o' them preachers, you'd think as a man must be doing nothing all's life but shutting's eyes and looking what's a-going on inside him. I know a man must have the love o' God in his soul, and the Bible's God's word. But what does the Bible say? Why, it says as God put his sperrit into the workman as built the tabernacle, to make him do all the carved work and things as wanted a nice hand. And this is my way o' looking at it: there's the sperrit o' God in all things and all times—weekday as well as Sunday—and i'[6] the great works and inventions, and i' the figuring and the mechanics. And God helps us with our head-pieces and our hands as well as with our souls; and if a man does bits o' jobs out o' working hours—builds a oven for 's wife to save her from going to the bakehouse, or scrats at his bit o' garden and makes two potatoes grow istead o' one, he's doing more good, and he's just as near to God, as if he was running after some preacher and a-praying and a-groaning."

"Well done, Adam!" said Sandy Jim, who had paused from his planing to shift his planks while Adam was speaking; "that's the best sarmunt I've heared this long while. By th' same token, my wife's been[7] a-plaguin' on me to build her a oven this twelvemont."

"There's reason in what thee say'st, Adam," observed Seth, gravely. "But thee know'st thyself as it's hearing the preachers thee find'st so much fault with as has turned[8] many an idle fellow into an industrious[9] un. It's the preacher as empties th' alehouse; and[1] if a man gets religion, he'll do his work none the worse for that."

"On'y he'll[2] lave the panels out o' th' doors sometimes, eh, Seth?" said Wiry Ben.

"Ah, Ben, you've got a joke again me as 'll last you your life. But it isna[3] religion as was i' fault there; it was Seth Bede, as was allays[4] a wool-gathering chap, and religion hasna[5] cured him, the more's the pity."

"Ne'er heed me[6], Seth," said Wiry Ben, "y' are a downright good-hearted chap, panels or no panels; an' ye[7] donna set up your bristles at every[8] bit o' fun, like some o' your kin, as is mayhap cliverer."

[5] canals, ⟨and⟩ an' th' aqueducs, ⟨an'⟩ and the coal-pit engines, ⟨an'⟩ and *MS*
[6] i'] in *MS*   [7] been] a-bin *MS* *1* ⟨a-bin⟩ been *8*
[8] fault with as has turned] fault with has turned *Cabinet*
[9] an industrious] a{n} industrous *MS*   [1] alehouse; and] alehouse. And *MS*
[2] he'll] hey'll *MS*   [3] isna] t'eent *MS*   [4] allays] always *MS*
[5] hasna] hesn't *MS*   [6] me] mey *MS*   [7] ye ⟨dunna⟩ donna *MS*
[8] every] ivery *MS*

"Seth, lad," said Adam, taking no notice of the sarcasm against himself, "thee mustna[9] take me unkind. I wasna driving at thee in what I said just now. Some 's got one way o' looking at things and some 's got another."

"Nay, nay, Addy, thee mean'st me no unkindness," said Seth, "I[1] know that well enough. Thee't like thy dog Gyp—thee bark'st at me sometimes, but thee allays[2] lick'st my hand after."

All hands worked on in silence for some minutes, until the church clock began to strike six. Before the first stroke had died away, Sandy Jim had loosed his plane and was reaching his jacket; Wiry Ben had left a screw half driven in, and thrown his screw-driver into his tool-basket; Mum Taft, who, true to his name, had kept silence throughout the previous conversation, had flung down his hammer as he was in the act of lifting it; and Seth, too, had straightened his back, and was putting out his hand towards his paper cap. Adam alone had gone on with his work as if nothing had happened. But observing the cessation of the tools, he looked up, and said, in a tone of indignation,

"Look there, now! I can't abide to see men throw away their tools i' that way, the minute the clock begins to strike, as if they took no pleasure i' their work, and was afraid o'[3] doing a stroke too much."

Seth looked a little conscious, and began to be slower in his preparations for going, but Mum Taft broke silence, and said,

"Ay, ay, Adam lad,[4] ye talk like a young un. When y' are six-an'-forty[5] like me[6], istid o' six-an'-twenty[7], ye wonna be so flush o' workin' for nought[8]."

"Nonsense," said Adam, still wrathful; "what's age got to do with it, I wonder? Ye[9] arena getting stiff yet, I reckon. I hate to see a man's arms drop down as if he was shot, before the clock's fairly struck, just as if he'd never a bit o' pride and delight in 's work. The very grindstone 'ull go on turning a bit[1] after you loose it."

"Bodderation, Adam!" exclaimed Wiry Ben. "Lave a chap aloon, will 'ee? Ye[2] war a-finding[3] faut wi' preachers a while agoo—y' are fond enough o' preachin' yoursen. Ye[4] may like work better nor play, but I like play better nor work; that'll 'commodate ye—it laves ye th' more[5] to do."

With this exit speech, which he considered effective, Wiry Ben shouldered his basket and left the workshop, quickly followed by Mum Taft and

[9] mustna ⟨think⟩ take *MS*
[1] Seth, "I] Seth. "I *MS*   [2] allays] alys *MS*   [3] o'] of *MS*
[4] lad, ⟨yer⟩ ye *MS*   [5] six-an'-forty] four an' forty *MS*   [6] me] mey *MS*
[7] six-an'-twenty] four an' twenty *MS*   [8] nought] noght *MS*
[9] wonder? Ye] wonder. Y' *MS*   [1] a bit] *added in MS*
[2] 'ee? Ye] *MS* 'ee. Ye *1* 'ee⟨.⟩? Ye *8*   [3] a-finding] afindin' *MS*
[4] Ye] Yey *MS*   [5] more] moor *MS 1* ⟨moor⟩ more *8*

Sandy Jim. Seth lingered, and looked wistfully at Adam, as if he expected him to say something.

"Shalt go home before thee go'st to the preaching?" Adam asked, looking up.

"Nay; I've got my hat and things at Will Maskery's. I[6] shan't be home before going for ten. I'll happen see Dinah Morris safe home, if she's willing. There's nobody comes with her from Poyser's, thee know'st."

"Then I'll tell mother not to look for thee," said Adam.

"Thee artna[7] going to Poyser's thyself to-night?" said Seth, rather timidly, as he turned to leave the workshop.

"Nay, I'm going to th' school."

Hitherto Gyp had kept his comfortable bed, only lifting up his head and watching Adam more closely as he noticed the other workmen departing. But no sooner did Adam put his ruler in his pocket, and begin to twist his apron round his waist, than Gyp ran forward and looked up in his master's face with patient expectation. If Gyp had had a tail he would doubtless have wagged it, but being destitute of that vehicle for his emotions, he was like many other worthy personages, destined to appear more phlegmatic than nature had made him.

"What, art ready for the basket, eh, Gyp?" said Adam, with the same gentle modulation of voice as when he spoke to Seth.

Gyp jumped and gave a short bark, as much as to say, "Of course." Poor fellow, he had not a great range of expression[8].

The basket was the one which on workdays held Adam's and Seth's dinner; and no official, walking in procession, could look more resolutely unconscious of all acquaintances than Gyp with his basket, trotting at his master's heels.

On leaving the workshop Adam locked the door, took the key out, and carried it to the house on the other side of the wood-yard. It was a low house, with smooth grey thatch and buff walls, looking pleasant and mellow in the evening light. The leaded windows were bright and speckless, and the door-stone was as clean as a white boulder at ebb tide[9]. On the door-stone stood a clean old woman, in a dark-striped linen gown, a red kerchief, and a linen cap, talking to some speckled fowls which appeared to have been drawn towards her by an illusory expectation of cold potatoes or barley. The old woman's sight seemed to be dim, for she did not recognize Adam till he said,

"Here's the key, Dolly; lay it down for me in the house, will you?"

"Ay, sure; but wunna ye come in, Adam? Miss Mary's i' th' house, an' Mester Burge 'ull be back anon; he'd be glad[1] t' ha' ye to supper wi'm, I'll be's warrand."

---

[6] I ⟨shanna⟩ shan't *MS*   [7] artna] wiltna be *MS*
[8] he had not a great range of expression] his voice had not a great range *MS*
[9] at ebb tide] between tides *MS*   [1] glad ⟨to⟩ t' *MS*

"No, Dolly, thank you; I'm off home. Good evening."

Adam hastened with long strides, Gyp close to his heels, out of the work-yard, and along the high road leading away from the village and down to the valley. As he reached the[2] foot of the slope, an elderly horseman, with his portmanteau strapped behind him, stopped his horse when Adam had passed him, and turned round to have another long look at the stalwart workman in paper cap, leather breeches, and dark-blue worsted stockings.

Adam, unconscious of the admiration he was exciting, presently struck across the fields, and now broke out into the tune which had all day long been running in his head:

> "Let all thy converse be sincere,
> Thy conscience as the noonday clear;
> For God's all-seeing eye surveys
> Thy secret thoughts, thy works and ways."

[2] the ⟨bot⟩ foot *MS*

CHAPTER II.

THE PREACHING.

About a quarter to seven there was an unusual appearance of excitement in the village of Hayslope, and through the whole length of its little street, from the Donnithorne Arms to the churchyard gate, the inhabitants had evidently been drawn out of their houses by something more than the pleasure of lounging in the evening sunshine. The Donnithorne Arms stood at the entrance of the village, and a small farm-yard and stack-yard which flanked it, indicating that there was a pretty take of land attached to the inn, gave the traveller a promise of good feed for himself and his horse, which might well[1] console him for the ignorance in which the weather-beaten sign left him as to the heraldic bearings of that ancient family, the Donnithornes. Mr Casson, the landlord, had been for some time standing at the door with his hands in his pockets, balancing himself on his heels and toes, and looking towards a piece of unenclosed ground, with a maple in the middle of it, which he knew to be the destination of certain grave-looking men and women whom he had[2] observed passing at intervals.

Mr Casson's person was by no means of[3] that common type which can be allowed to pass without description. On a front view it appeared to consist principally of two spheres, bearing about the same relation to each other as the earth and the moon: that is to say, the lower sphere might be said, at a rough guess, to be thirteen times larger than the upper, which naturally performed the function of a mere satellite and tributary. But here the resemblance ceased, for Mr Casson's head was not at all a melancholy-looking satellite, nor was it a "spotty globe," as Milton has irreverently called the moon; on the contrary, no head and face could look more sleek and healthy, and its expression, which was chiefly confined to a pair of round and ruddy cheeks, the slight knot and interruptions forming the nose and eyes being scarcely worth mention, was one of jolly contentment, only tempered by that sense of personal dignity which usually made itself felt in his attitude and bearing.[4] This sense of dignity could hardly be considered excessive in a man who had been butler to "the family" for fifteen years, and who, in his present high position, was necessarily very much in contact with his inferiors. How to reconcile[5] his dignity with the satisfaction of his curiosity by walking towards the Green, was the problem that Mr Casson

---

[1] well] *added in MS* [2] had] *added in MS* [3] of ⟨an⟩ that *MS*
[4] bearing. ⟨It⟩ This sense of dignity *MS* [5] reconcile ⟨this⟩ his *MS*

had been revolving in his mind for the last five minutes; but when he had
partly solved it by taking his hands out of his pockets, and thrusting them
into the armholes of his waistcoat, by throwing his head on one side, and
providing himself with an air of contemptuous indifference to whatever
might fall under his notice, his thoughts were diverted by the approach of
the horseman whom we lately saw pausing to have another look at our
friend Adam, and who now pulled up at the door of the Donnithorne Arms.

"Take off the bridle and give him a drink, ostler," said the traveller to the
lad in a smock-frock, who had come out of the yard at the sound of the
horse's hoofs.

"Why, what's up in your pretty village, landlord?" he continued, getting
down. "There seems to be quite a stir."

"It's a Methodis preaching, sir; it's been gev hout as a young woman's
a-going to preach on the Green," answered Mr Casson, in a treble and
wheezy voice, with a slightly mincing accent. "Will you please to step in,
sir, an' tek somethink?"

"No, I must be getting on to Rosseter[6]. I only want a drink for my horse.
And what does your parson say, I wonder, to a young woman preaching just
under his nose?"

"Parson Irwine, sir, doesn't live here; he lives at Brox'on, over the hill
there. The[7] parsonage here's a tumble-down place, sir, not fit for gentry to
live in. He comes here to preach of a Sunday afternoon, sir, an' puts up his
hoss here. It's a grey cob, sir, an' he sets great store by 't. He's allays[8] put up
his hoss here, sir, iver since before I hed the Donnithorne Arms. I'm not
this countryman, you may tell by my tongue, sir. They're cur'ous talkers i'
this country, sir; the gentry's hard work to hunderstand 'em. I was brought
hup among the gentry, sir, an' got the turn o' their tongue when I was a bye.
Why, what do you think the folks here says for 'hevn't you?'—the gentry,
you know, says, 'hevn't you'—well, the people about here says 'hanna yey.'
It's what they call the dileck as is spoke hereabout, sir. That's what I've
heared[9] Squire Donnithorne say many a time; it's the dileck, says he."

"Ay, ay," said the stranger, smiling. "I know it very well. But you've not
got many Methodists about here, surely—in this agricultural spot?[1] I
should have thought there would hardly be such a thing as a Methodist
to be found about here. You're all farmers, aren't you? The Methodists can
seldom lay much hold on *them*."

"Why, sir, there's a pretty lot o' workmen round about, sir. There's
Mester Burge as owns the timber-yard over there, he underteks a good bit
o' building an' repairs. An' there's the stone-pits not far[2] off. There's
plenty of emply i' this country-side, sir. An' there's a fine batch o' Meth-

[6] Rosseter] Drosseter *MS* *1* 〈Drosseter〉 Rosseter *8*   [7] there. The] there—the *MS*
[8] allays] al'ys *MS*   [9] heared] *MS* heard *1* *8*   [1] spot?] spot. *MS* *1*
[2] far] fur *MS*

odisses at Treddles'on—that's the market town about three mile off—
you'll maybe ha' come through it, sir. There's[3] pretty nigh a score of 'em
on the Green now, as come from there. That's where our people gets it from,
though there's only two men of 'em in all Hayslope: that's Will Maskery, the
wheelwright, and Seth Bede, a young man as works at the carpenterin'."

"The preacher comes from Treddleston, then, does she?"

"Nay, sir, she comes out o' Stonyshire, pretty nigh thirty[4] mile off. But
she's a-visitin' hereabout at Mester Poyser's at the Hall Farm—it's them
barns an' big walnut-trees, right away to the left, sir. She's own niece to
Poyser's wife, an' they'll be fine an' vexed at her for making a fool of herself
i' that way. But I've heared as there's no holding these Methodisses when
the maggit's once got i' their head: many of 'em goes stark starin' mad wi'
their religion. Though this young woman's quiet enough to look at, by what
I can make out; I've not seen[5] her myself."

"Well, I wish I had time to wait and see her, but I must get on. I've been
out of my way for the last twenty minutes, to have a look at that place in the
valley. It's Squire Donnithorne's, I suppose?"

"Yes[6], sir, that's Donnithorne Chase, that is. Fine hoaks there,[7] isn't
there, sir? I should know what it is, sir, for I've lived butler there a-going
i' fifteen year. It's Captain Donnithorne as is th' heir, sir—Squire Donnithorne's grandson. He'll be comin' of hage this 'ay-'arvest, sir, an' we shall
hev fine doins. He owns all the land about here, sir, Squire Donnithorne
does."

"Well, it's a pretty spot, whoever may own it," said the traveller,
mounting his horse; "and one meets some fine strapping fellows about
too. I met as fine a young fellow as ever I saw in my life, about half an hour
ago, before I came up the hill—a carpenter, a tall broad-shouldered fellow
with black hair and black eyes, marching along like a soldier. We want such
fellows as he to lick the French."

"Ay, sir, that's Adam Bede, that is, I'll be bound—Thias Bede's son—
everybody[8] knows him hereabout. He's an uncommon clever[9] stiddy
fellow, an' wonderful strong. Lord bless you, sir—if you'll hexcuse me
for saying so—he can walk forty mile a-day, an' lift a matter o' sixty ston'.
He's an uncommon favourite wi' the gentry, sir: Captain Donnithorne an'[1]
Parson Irwine meks a fine fuss wi' him. But he's a little lifted up an'
peppery-like."

"Well, good evening to you, landlord; I must get on."

"Your servant, sir; good evenin'."

The[2] traveller put his horse into a quick walk up the village, but when he
approached the Green, the beauty of the view that lay on his right hand, the

[3] sir. There's] Sir—there's *MS*   [4] thirty] twenty *MS*   [5] seen] see *MS*
[6] Yes] Yis *MS*   [7] there, ⟨Sir?⟩ isn't *MS*   [8] everybody] ivery body *MS*
[9] clever] cliver, *MS*   [1] an'] *MS 1* and *8*   [2] The ⟨horseman⟩ traveller *MS*

singular contrast presented by the groups of villagers with the knot of
Methodists near the maple, and perhaps yet more, curiosity to see the
young female preacher, proved too much for his anxiety to get to the end of
his journey, and he paused.

The Green lay at the extremity of the village, and from it the road
branched off in two directions, one leading farther up the hill by the church,
and the other winding gently down towards the valley. On the side of the
Green that led towards the church, the broken line of thatched cottages was
continued nearly to the churchyard gate; but on the opposite, north-
western side, there was nothing to obstruct the view of gently-swelling
meadow, and wooded valley, and dark masses of distant hill. That rich
undulating district of Loamshire to which Hayslope belonged, lies close to
a grim outskirt of Stonyshire, overlooked by its barren hills as a pretty
blooming sister may sometimes be seen linked in the arm of a rugged, tall,
swarthy brother; and in[3] two or three hours' ride the traveller might
exchange a bleak treeless region, intersected by lines of cold grey stone,
for one where his road wound under the shelter of woods, or up swelling
hills, muffled with hedgerows and long meadow-grass and thick corn; and
where at every turn he came upon some fine old country-seat nestled in the
valley[4] or crowning the slope, some homestead with its long length of barn
and its cluster of golden ricks, some grey steeple looking out from a pretty
confusion of trees and thatch and dark-red tiles. It was just such a picture as
this last that Hayslope church had made to the traveller as he began to
mount the gentle slope leading to its pleasant uplands, and now from his
station near the Green he had before him in one view nearly all the other
typical features of this pleasant land. High up against the horizon were the
huge conical masses of hill, like giant mounds intended to fortify this region
of corn and grass against the keen and hungry winds of the north; not
distant enough to be clothed in purple mystery, but with sombre greenish
sides visibly specked with sheep, whose motion was only revealed by
memory, not detected by sight; wooed from[5] day to day by the changing
hours, but responding with no change in themselves—left for ever grim
and sullen after the flush of morning, the winged gleams of the April
noonday, the parting crimson glory of the ripening summer sun. And
directly below them the eye rested on a more advanced line of hanging
woods, divided by bright patches of pasture or furrowed crops, and not yet
deepened into the uniform leafy curtain[6] of high summer, but still showing
the warm tints of the young oak and the tender green of the ash and lime.
Then came the valley, where the woods grew thicker, as if they had rolled
down and hurried together from the patches left smooth on the slope, that
they might take the better care of the tall mansion which lifted its parapets,

and sent its faint blue summer smoke among them. Doubtless there was a large sweep of park and a broad glassy pool in front of that mansion, but the swelling slope of meadow would not let our traveller see them from the village Green. He saw instead a foreground which was just as lovely—the level sunlight lying like transparent gold among the gently-curving stems of the feathered grass and the tall red sorrel, and the white umbels of the hemlocks lining the bushy hedgerows. It was that moment in summer when the sound of the scythe being whetted makes us cast more lingering looks at the flower-sprinkled tresses of the meadows.

He might have seen other beauties in the landscape if he had turned a little in his saddle and looked eastward, beyond Jonathan Burge's pasture and wood-yard towards the green cornfields and walnut-trees of the Hall Farm; but apparently there was more interest for him in the living groups close at hand. Every generation in the village was there, from old "Feyther Taft" in his brown worsted night-cap, who was bent nearly double, but seemed tough enough to keep on his legs a long while, leaning on his short stick, down to the babies with their little round heads lolling forward[7] in quilted linen caps. Now and then there was a new arrival; perhaps a slouching labourer, who, having eaten his supper, came out to look at the unusual scene with a slow[8] bovine gaze, willing to hear what any one had to say in explanation of it, but by no means excited enough to ask a question. But all took care not to join the Methodists on the Green,[9] and identify themselves in that way with the expectant audience, for there was not one of them that would not have disclaimed the imputation of having come out to hear the "preacher-woman,"—they had only come[1] out to see "what war a-goin' on, like." The men were chiefly gathered in the neighbourhood of the blacksmith's shop. But do not imagine them gathered in a knot. Villagers never swarm; a whisper is unknown among them, and they seem almost as incapable of an undertone as a cow or a stag. Your true rustic turns his back on his interlocutor, throwing a question over his shoulder as if he meant to run away from the answer, and walking a step or two farther off[2] when the interest of the dialogue culminates. So the group in the vicinity of the blacksmith's door was by no means a close one, and formed no screen in front of Chad Cranage, the blacksmith himself, who stood with his black brawny arms folded, leaning against the door-post, and occasionally sending forth a bellowing laugh at[3] his own jokes, giving them a marked preference over the sarcasms of Wiry Ben, who had renounced the pleasures of the Holly Bush for the sake of seeing life under a new form. But both styles of wit were treated with equal contempt by

[7] forward] forwards *MS*   [8] slow ⟨&⟩ bovine *MS*
[9] Green, ⟨or to⟩ {&} identify themselves with *MS*
[1] had only come] had come *MS*   [2] off] *added in MS*
[3] at ⟨the⟩ {his own} jokes{,} ⟨of⟩ {giving them a marked preference ⟨to⟩ {over} the sarcasms} of Wiry *MS*

Mr Joshua Rann. Mr Rann's leathern apron and subdued griminess can leave no one in any[4] doubt that he is the village shoemaker; the thrusting out of his chin and stomach, and the twirling of his thumbs, are more subtle indications, intended to prepare unwary strangers for the discovery that they are in the presence of the parish clerk. "Old Joshway," as he is irreverently called by his neighbours, is in a state of simmering indignation; but he has not yet opened his lips except to say, in[5] a[6] resounding bass undertone, like the tuning of a violoncello, "Sehon, King of the Amorites: for His mercy endureth for ever; and Og the King of Basan: for His mercy endureth for ever,"—a quotation which may seem to have slight bearing on the present occasion, but, as with every other anomaly, adequate knowledge will show it to be a natural sequence. Mr Rann was inwardly maintaining the dignity of the Church in the face of this scandalous irruption of Methodism, and as that dignity was bound up with his own sonorous utterance of the responses, his argument naturally suggested a quotation from the psalm he had read the last Sunday afternoon.

The stronger curiosity of the women had drawn them quite to the edge of the Green, where they could examine more closely the Quaker-like costume and odd deportment of the female Methodists. Underneath the maple there was a small cart which had been brought from the wheelwright's[7] to serve as a pulpit, and round this a couple of benches and a few chairs had been placed. Some of the Methodists were resting on these, with their eyes closed, as if wrapt in prayer or meditation. Others chose to continue standing, and had turned[8] their faces towards the villagers with a look of melancholy compassion, which was highly amusing to Bessy Cranage, the blacksmith's buxom daughter, known to her neighbours as Chad's Bess, who wondered "why the folks war a-makin'[9] faces a that'ns." Chad's Bess was the object of peculiar compassion, because her hair, being turned back under a[1] cap which was set at the top of her head,[2] exposed to view an ornament of which she was much prouder than of her red cheeks, namely, a pair of large round ear-rings with false garnets in them, ornaments contemned not only by the Methodists, but by her own cousin and namesake[3] Timothy's Bess, who, with much cousinly feeling, often wished "them ear-rings" might come to good.

Timothy's Bess,[4] though retaining her maiden appellation among her familiars, had long been the wife of Sandy Jim, and possessed a handsome set of matronly jewels, of which it is enough to mention the heavy baby she

[4] one in any] *added in MS*   [5] say, in] say in *MS* *1* say {,} in *8*
[6] a ⟨sonorous⟩ resounding bass *MS*   [7] wheelwright's] wheelwright{s'} *MS*
[8] turned] *added in MS*
[9] a-makin'] a meckin' *MS* a-mekin' *1* ⟨a-mekin'⟩ a-makin' *8*
[1] a] *added in MS*
[2] head, ⟨allowed a full⟩ {exposed to} view ⟨of⟩ an *MS*
[3] & namesake] *added in MS*   [4] Bess ⟨retained⟩ though retaining *MS*

was rocking in her arms, and the sturdy fellow of five in knee-[5]breeches and red legs, who[6] had a rusty milk-can round his neck by way of drum, and was very carefully avoided by Chad's small terrier. This young olive-branch,[7] notorious under the name of Timothy's Bess's Ben, being of an inquiring disposition, unchecked by any false modesty, had advanced beyond the group of women and children, and was walking round the Methodists, looking up in their faces with his mouth wide open, and beating his stick against the milk-can by way of musical accompaniment[8]. But one of the elderly women bending down to take him by the shoulder, with an air of grave remonstrance, Timothy's Bess's Ben first kicked out vigorously, then took to his heels and sought refuge behind his father's legs.

"Ye[9] gallows young dog," said Sandy Jim, with some paternal pride, "if ye donna[1] keep that stick quiet, I'll tek it from ye. What d'ye mane by kickin' foulks?"

"Here! gie him[2] here to me, Jim," said Chad Cranage; "I'll tie him[3] up an' shoe him[4] as I do th' hosses. Well, Mester Casson," he continued, as that personage sauntered up towards the group of men, "how[5] are ye[6] t' naight? Are ye coom t' help groon? They[7] say folks allays[8] groon when they're[9] hearkenin' to th' Methodys, as if they[1] war bad i' th' inside. I mane to groon as loud as your[2] cow did th' other naight, an' then the praicher 'ull think I'm i' th' raight way."

"I'd advise you not to be up to no nonsense, Chad," said Mr Casson, with some dignity; "Poyser wouldn't like to hear as his wife's niece was treated any ways disrespectful, for all he mayn't be fond of her taking[3] on herself to preach."

"Ay, an' she's a pleasant-looked[4] 'un too," said Wiry Ben. "I'll stick up for the pretty women preachin'; I know they'd persuade me over a deal sooner nor[5] th' ugly men. I shouldna wonder if I turn Methody afore the night's out, an' begin to coort the preacher, like Seth Bede."

"Why, Seth's lookin'[6] rether too high, I should think," said Mr Casson. "This woman's kin wouldn't like her to demean herself to a common carpenter."

[5] knee-] added in MS [6] who ⟨was⟩ had MS
[7] olive-branch, ⟨rejoiced in the complex⟩ notorious under the MS
[8] accompaniment ⟨, until⟩. But MS [9] Ye] Yey MS
[1] donna] dunna MS 1 ⟨dunna⟩ donna 8 [2] gie him] gie 'm MS 1 ⟨gie 'm⟩ gie him 8
[3] tie him] tie 'm MS 1 ⟨tie 'm⟩ tie him 8
[4] shoe him] shoe 'm MS 1 ⟨shoe 'm⟩ shoe him 8 [5] how] hoo MS
[6] ye] yey MS [7] They] The' MS 1 ⟨The'⟩ They 8
[8] allays] al'ys MS [9] they're] the're MS [1] they] the' MS 1 ⟨the'⟩ they 8
[2] your] yare MS [3] taking] tecking MS
[4] pleasant-looked] pleasant-lookst MS [5] nor ⟨an⟩ th' MS
[6] lookin'] MS 1 looking 8

"Tchu!" said Ben, with a long treble intonation, "what's folks's kin got
to do wi't?—Not a chip. Poyser's wife may turn her nose up an' forget
bygones, but this Dinah Morris, they[7] tell me, 's as poor as iver she was—
works at a mill, an's much ado to keep hersen. A strappin' young carpenter
as is a ready-made Methody, like Seth, wouldna be a bad match for her.
Why, Poysers make as big a fuss wi' Adam Bede as if he war a nevvy o' their
own."[8]

"Idle talk! idle talk!" said Mr Joshua Rann. "Adam an' Seth's two men;
you[9] wunna fit them two wi' the same last."

"Maybe," said Wiry Ben, contemptuously, "but[1] Seth's the lad for me[2],
though he war a Methody twice o'er. I'm fair beat wi' Seth, for I've[3] been
teazin'[4] him iver sin' we've[5] been workin' together, an' he bears me no more
malice nor a lamb. An' he's a stout-hearted feller too, for when we saw[6] the
old tree all a-fire, a-comin' across the fields one night, an' we thought as it
war a[7] boguy, Seth made no more ado, but he[8] up to't as bold as a constable.
Why, there he comes[9] out o' Will Maskery's; an' there's Will hisself, lookin'
as meek as if he couldna knock a nail o' the[1] head for fear o' hurtin 't. An'
there's the pretty preacher-woman[2]! My eye, she's got her bonnet off. I[3]
mun go a bit nearer."

Several of the men followed Ben's lead, and the traveller pushed his
horse on to the Green, as Dinah walked rather quickly, and in advance of
her companions, towards the cart under the maple-tree. While she was near
Seth's tall figure, she looked short, but when she had mounted the cart, and
was away from all comparison, she seemed above the middle height of
woman, though in reality she did not exceed it—an effect which was due to
the slimness of her figure, and the[4] simple line of her black stuff dress. The
stranger was struck with surprise as he saw her approach and mount the
cart—surprise, not so much at the feminine delicacy of her appearance, as
at the total absence of self-consciousness in her demeanour. He had made
up his mind to see her advance with a measured step, and a demure
solemnity of countenance; he had felt sure that her face would be mantled
with the smile of conscious saintship, or else charged with denunciatory
bitterness. He knew but two types of Methodist—the ecstatic and the
bilious. But Dinah walked as simply as if she were going to market, and
seemed as unconscious of her outward appearance as a little boy: there was

[7] they] the' *MS 1* ⟨the'⟩ they *8*
[8] Why, Poysers make as big a fuss wi' Adam Bede as if he war a nevvy o' their own."] Why,
Poyser's wife's all for hevin' Adam Bede marry Hetty, carpenter as he is." *MS*
[9] you ⟨wont⟩ wunna *MS*   [1] but ⟨I like⟩ Seth's *MS*   [2] me] mey *MS*
[3] I've] I'n *MS*   [4] been ⟨teazing⟩ teazin' *MS*   [5] we've] we'n *MS*
[6] saw ⟨the tree a-⟩ {th' old ⟨oak⟩ tree all} afire *MS*   [7] a ⟨buggat⟩ boguy *MS*
[8] he ⟨went⟩ up *MS*   [9] comes ⟨wi' the little wid⟩ out *MS*   [1] the] th' *MS*
[2] preacher-woman] widder-woman *MS*   [3] off. I] aff—I *MS*
[4] the ⟨uniform⟩ simple *MS*

no blush, no tremulousness, which said, "I know you think me a pretty woman, too young to preach;" no casting up or down of the eyelids, no compression of the lips, no attitude[5] of the arms, that said, "But you must think of me as a saint." She held no book in her ungloved hands, but let them hang down lightly crossed before her, as she stood and turned her[6] grey eyes on the people. There was no keenness in the eyes; they seemed rather to be shedding love than making observations; they had the liquid look which tells that the mind is full of what it has to give out, rather than impressed by external objects. She stood with her left hand towards the descending sun, and leafy boughs screened her from its rays; but in this sober light the delicate colouring of her face seemed to gather a calm vividness, like flowers at evening. It was a small oval face, of a uniform transparent whiteness, with an egg-like line of cheek and chin, a full but firm mouth, a delicate nostril, and a low perpendicular brow, surmounted by a rising arch of parting between smooth locks[7] of pale reddish hair. The hair was drawn straight back behind the ears, and covered, except for an inch or two, above the brow, by a net Quaker cap. The eyebrows, of the same colour as the hair, were perfectly horizontal and firmly pencilled; the eyelashes, though no darker, were long and abundant; nothing was left blurred or unfinished. It was one of those faces that make one think of white flowers with light touches of colour on their pure petals. The eyes had no peculiar beauty, beyond[8] that of expression; they looked so simple, so candid, so gravely loving, that no accusing scowl, no light sneer could help melting away before their glance. Joshua Rann gave a long cough, as if he were clearing his throat in order to come to a new understanding with himself; Chad Cranage lifted up his leather skull-cap and scratched his head; and Wiry Ben wondered how Seth had the pluck to think of courting her.

"A sweet woman," the stranger said to himself, "but surely nature never meant her for a preacher."

Perhaps he was one of those who think that nature has theatrical properties,[9] and, with the considerate view of facilitating art and psychology, "makes up" her characters, so that there may be no mistake about them. But Dinah began to speak.

"Dear friends," she said, in a clear but not loud voice, "let us pray for a blessing."

She closed her eyes, and hanging her head down a little, continued in the same moderate tone, as if speaking to some one quite near her:—

"Saviour of sinners! when a poor woman, laden with sins, went out to the well to draw water, she found Thee[1] sitting at the well. She knew Thee not;

---

[5] attitude] posing *MS*   [6] her ⟨mild⟩ grey *MS*
[7] of parting between smooth locks] of white strand parting smooth locks *MS*
[8] beauty, beyond] beauty except *MS*
[9] properties, & {,} ⟨"makes up" her characters⟩ with *MS*   [1] Thee] Thee *MS*

she had not sought Thee; her mind was dark; her life was unholy. But Thou didst speak to her, Thou didst teach her, Thou didst show her that her life lay open before Thee, and yet Thou wast ready to give her that blessing which she had[2] never sought. Jesus! Thou art in the midst of us, and Thou knowest all men: if there is any here like that poor woman—if their minds are dark, their lives unholy—if they have come out not seeking Thee, not desiring to be taught; deal with them according to the free mercy which Thou didst show to her. Speak to them, Lord; open their ears to my message; bring their sins to their minds, and make them thirst for that salvation which Thou art ready to give.

"Lord! Thou art with Thy people still: they see Thee in the night-watches, and their hearts burn within them as Thou talkest with them by the way. And Thou art near to those who have not known Thee: open their eyes that they may see Thee—see Thee weeping over them, and saying,[3] 'Ye will not come unto me that ye might have life'—see Thee hanging on the cross and saying, 'Father, forgive them, for they know not what they do'—see Thee as Thou wilt come again in Thy glory to judge them at the last. Amen."

Dinah opened her eyes again and paused, looking at the group of villagers, who were now gathered rather more closely on her right hand.

"Dear friends," she began, raising her voice a little, "you have all of you been to church, and I think you must have heard the clergyman read these words: 'The spirit of the Lord is upon me, because he hath anointed me to preach the gospel to the poor.' Jesus Christ spoke those words—he said he came *to preach the Gospel to the poor:* I don't know whether you ever thought about those words much; but I will tell you when I remember first hearing them. It was on just such a sort of evening as this, when I was a little girl, and my aunt as brought me up, took me to hear a good man preach out of doors, just as we are here. I remember his face well: he was a very old man, and had very long white hair; his voice was very soft and beautiful, not like any voice I had ever heard before. I was a little girl, and scarcely[4] knew anything, and this old man seemed to me such a different sort of a man from anybody[5] I had ever seen before, that I thought he had perhaps come down from the sky to preach to us, and I said, 'Aunt, will he go back to the sky to-night, like the picture in the Bible?'

"That man of God was Mr Wesley, who spent his life in doing what our blessed Lord did—preaching the Gospel to the poor—and he entered into his rest eight years ago. I came to know more about him years after, but I was a foolish thoughtless child then, and I remembered only one thing he told us in his sermon. He told us as 'Gospel' meant 'good news.' The Gospel, you know, is what the Bible tells us about God.

---

[2] had ⟨not⟩ never *MS*   [3] saying,] *MS 1* saying *8*
[4] scarcely ⟨understood⟩ knew *MS*   [5] anybody] any body *MS*

"Think of that now! Jesus Christ did really come down from heaven, as I, like a silly child, thought Mr Wesley did; and what he came down for, was to tell good news about God to the poor. Why, you and me, dear friends, are poor. We have been brought up in poor cottages, and have been reared on oat-cake and lived coarse; and we haven't been to school much, nor read books, and we don't know much about anything but what happens just round us. We are just the sort of people that want to hear good news. For when anybody's well off, they don't much mind about hearing news from distant parts; but if a poor man or woman's in trouble and has hard work to make out a living, they like[6] to have a letter to tell 'em they've[7] got a friend as will help 'em[8]. To be sure, we can't help knowing something about God, even if we've never heard the Gospel, the good news that our Saviour brought us. For we know everything comes from God: don't you say almost every day, 'This and that will happen, please God'; and 'We shall begin to cut the grass soon, please God to send us a little more sunshine'?[9] We know very well we are altogether in the hands of God: we didn't bring ourselves into the world, we can't keep ourselves alive while we're sleeping; the daylight, and the wind, and the corn, and the cows to give us milk— everything we have comes from God. And he gave us our souls, and put love between parents and children, and husband and wife. But is that as much as we want to know about God? We see he is great and mighty, and can do what he will: we are lost, as if we was struggling in great waters, when we try to think of him.

"But perhaps doubts come into your mind like this: Can God take much notice of us poor people? Perhaps he only made the world for the great and the wise and the rich. It doesn't cost him much to give us our little handful of victual and bit of clothing; but how do we know he cares for us any more than we care for the worms and things in the garden, so as we rear our carrots and onions? Will God take care of us when we die? and has he any comfort for us when we are lame and sick and helpless? Perhaps, too, he is angry with us; else why does the blight come, and the bad harvests, and the fever, and all sorts of pain and trouble? For our life is full of trouble, and if God sends us good, he seems to send bad too. How is it? how is it?

"Ah! dear friends, we are in sad want of good news about God; and what does other good news signify if we haven't that? For everything else comes to an end, and when we die we leave it all. But God lasts when everything else is gone. What shall we do if he is not our friend?"

Then Dinah told how the good news had been brought, and how the mind of God towards the poor had been made manifest in the life of Jesus, dwelling on its lowliness and its acts of mercy.

---

[6] they like] he likes *MS 1* ⟨he likes⟩ they like *8*
[7] 'em they've] him he's *MS 1* ⟨him he's⟩ 'em they've *8*
[8] 'em] him *MS 1* ⟨him⟩ 'em *8*   [9] sunshine'?] *MS* sunshine.' *1* sunshine?' *8*

"So you see, dear friends," she went on, "Jesus spent his time almost all in doing good to poor people; he preached out of doors to them, and he made friends of poor workmen, and taught them and took pains with them. Not but what he did good to the rich too, for he was full of love to all[1] men, only he saw as the poor were more[2] in want of his help. So he cured the lame and the sick and the blind, and he worked miracles[3] to feed the hungry, because, he said, he was sorry for them; and he was very kind to the little children, and comforted those who had lost their friends; and he spoke very tenderly to poor sinners that were sorry for their sins.

"Ah! wouldn't you love such a man if you saw him—if he was here in this village? What a kind heart he must have! What a friend he would be to go to in trouble! How pleasant it must be to be taught by him.[4]

"Well, dear friends, who *was* this man? Was he only a good man—a very good man, and no more—like our dear Mr Wesley, who has been taken from us?.... He was the Son of God—'in the image of the Father,' the Bible says; that means, just like God, who is the beginning and end of all things—the God we want to know about. So then, all the love that Jesus showed to the poor is the same love that God has for us. We[5] can understand what Jesus felt, because he came in a body like ours, and spoke words such as we speak to each other. We were afraid to think what God was before—the God who made the world and the sky and the thunder and lightning. We could never see Him; we could only see the things he had made; and some of these things was very terrible, so as we might well tremble when we thought of him. But our blessed Saviour has showed us what God is in a way us poor ignorant people can understand; he has showed us what God's heart is, what are his feelings towards us.

"But let us see a little more about what Jesus came on earth for. Another time he said, 'I came to seek and to save that which was lost;' and another time, 'I came not to call the righteous, but sinners to repentance.'

"The *lost!*.... *Sinners!*.... Ah, dear friends, does that mean you and me?"

Hitherto the traveller had been chained to the spot against his will by the charm of Dinah's mellow treble tones, which had a variety of modulation like that of a fine instrument touched with the unconscious skill of musical instinct. The simple things she said seemed like novelties, as a melody thrills[6] us with a new feeling when we hear it sung by the pure voice of a boyish chorister; the quiet depth of conviction with which she spoke seemed in itself an evidence for the truth of her message. He saw that she had thoroughly arrested her hearers. The[7] villagers had pressed nearer to her, and there was no longer anything but grave attention on all faces. She

[1] all ⟨people⟩ men *MS*   [2] more] most *MS*   [3] miracles] *MS 1* miracles, *8*
[4] him.] him! *MS 1*   [5] us. We] us; we *MS*   [6] thrills] *MS* strikes *1 8*
[7] hearers. The] hearers: the *MS*

spoke slowly, though quite fluently, often pausing after a question, or
before any transition of ideas. There was no change of attitude, no gesture;
the effect of her speech was produced entirely by the inflexions of her voice,
and when she came to the question, "Will God take care of us when we
die?" she[8] uttered it in such a tone of plaintive appeal that the tears came
into some of the hardest eyes. The stranger had ceased to doubt, as he had
done at the first glance, that she could fix the attention of her rougher
hearers, but still he wondered whether she could have that power[9] of
rousing their more violent emotions, which must surely be a necessary
seal of her vocation as a Methodist preacher, until she came to the words,
"Lost!—Sinners!" when there was a great change in her voice and manner.
She had made a long pause before the exclamation, and the pause[1] seemed
to be filled by agitating thoughts that showed themselves in her features.
Her pale face became paler; the[2] circles under her eyes deepened, as they do
when tears half gather without falling; and the mild loving eyes took an
expression of appalled pity, as if she had suddenly discerned a destroying
angel hovering over the heads of the people. Her voice became deep and
muffled, but there was still no gesture. Nothing could be less like the
ordinary type of the Ranter than Dinah. She[3] was not preaching as she
heard[4] others preach, but speaking directly from her own emotions, and
under the inspiration of her own simple faith.

But now she had entered into a new current of feeling. Her manner
became less calm, her utterance more rapid and agitated, as she tried to
bring home to the people their guilt, their wilful darkness, their state of
disobedience to God—as she dwelt on the hatefulness of sin, the Divine
holiness, and the sufferings of the Saviour by which a way had been opened
for their salvation. At last it seemed as if[5], in her yearning desire to reclaim
the lost sheep, she could not be satisfied by addressing her hearers as a body.
She appealed first to one and then to another, beseeching them with tears to
turn to God while there was yet time; painting to them the desolation of
their souls, lost in sin, feeding on the husks of this miserable world, far away
from God their Father; and then the love of the Saviour, who was waiting
and watching for their return.

There was many a responsive sigh and groan from her fellow Methodists, but the village mind does not easily take fire, and a little smouldering
vague anxiety, that might easily die out again, was the utmost effect Dinah's
preaching had wrought in them at present. Yet no one had stirred[6], except
the children and "old Feyther Taft," who being too deaf to catch many

---

[8] she ⟨spoke⟩ uttered it *MS*   [9] power ⟨over⟩ of *MS*
[1] pause ⟨was⟩ seemed *MS*   [2] the ⟨lines⟩ circles *MS*
[3] Dinah. She] Dinah⟨'s⟩: she *MS*   [4] she heard] she had heard *MS*
[5] if {, in} her yearning desire to reclaim the lost sheep {, she} could *MS*
[6] stirred] *MS* retired *1 8*

words, had some time ago gone back to his ingle-nook. Wiry Ben was feeling very uncomfortable, and almost wishing he had not come to hear Dinah; he thought what she said would haunt him somehow. Yet he couldn't help liking to look at her and listen to her, though he dreaded every moment that she would fix her eyes on him, and address him in particular. She had already addressed Sandy Jim, who was now holding the baby to relieve his wife, and the big soft-hearted man had rubbed away some tears with his fist, with a confused intention of being a better fellow, going less to the Holly Bush down by the Stone Pits, and cleaning himself more regularly of a Sunday.

In front of Sandy Jim stood Chad's Bess, who had shown an unwonted quietude and fixity of attention ever since Dinah had begun to speak. Not that the matter of the discourse had arrested her at once, for she was lost in a puzzling speculation as to what pleasure[7] and satisfaction there could be in life to a young woman who wore a cap like Dinah's. Giving up this inquiry in despair, she took to studying Dinah's nose, eyes, mouth, and hair, and wondering whether it was better to have such a sort of pale face as that, or fat red cheeks and round black eyes like her own. But gradually the influence of the general gravity told upon her, and she became conscious of what Dinah was saying. The gentle tones, the loving persuasion, did not touch her, but when the more severe appeals came she began to be frightened. Poor Bessy had always been considered a naughty girl; she was conscious of it; if it was necessary to be very good, it was clear she must be in a bad way. She couldn't find her places at church as Sally Rann could, she had often been tittering when she "curcheyed" to Mr Irwine, and[8] these religious deficiencies were accompanied by a corresponding slackness in the minor morals, for Bessy[9] belonged unquestionably to that unsoaped, lazy class[1] of feminine characters with whom you may venture to "eat an egg, an apple, or[2] a nut." All this she was generally conscious of, and hitherto had not been greatly[3] ashamed of it. But now she began to feel[4] very much as if the constable had come to take her up and carry her before the justice for some undefined offence. She had a terrified sense that God, whom she had always thought of as very far off, was very near to her, and that Jesus was close by looking at her, though she could not see him. For Dinah had that belief in visible manifestations of Jesus, which is common among the Methodists, and she communicated it irresistibly to her hearers;

---

[7] pleasure ⟨there⟩ & MS

[8] & ⟨as to her domestic character ⟨⟨disposition it⟩⟩ it had often been briskly summed up⟩ these MS

[9] slackness in the minor morals, for Bessy] slackness ⟨of⟩ {in domestic} morals, {for} Bessy MS

[1] that unsoaped, lazy class of feminine characters] that class of feminine character MS

[2] or] & MS

[3] greatly] much MS   [4] feel ⟨as⟩ {very} much ⟨terrified⟩ as MS

she made them feel that he was among them bodily, and might at any moment show himself to them in some way that would strike anguish and penitence into their hearts.

"See!" she exclaimed, turning to the left, with her eyes fixed on a point above the heads of the people—"see where our blessed Lord stands and weeps, and stretches out his arms towards you. Hear what he says: 'How often would I have gathered you as a hen gathereth her chickens under her wings, and ye would not!' . . . and ye would not," she[5] repeated, in a tone of pleading reproach, turning her eyes on the people again. "See the print of the nails on his dear hands and feet. It is your sins that made them! Ah, how pale and worn he looks! He has gone through all that great agony in the garden, when his soul was exceeding sorrowful even unto death, and the great drops of sweat fell like blood to the ground. They spat upon him and buffeted him, they scourged him, they mocked him, they laid the heavy cross on his bruised shoulders. Then they nailed him up. Ah! what pain! His lips are parched with thirst, and they mock him still in this great agony; yet with those parched lips he prays for them, 'Father, forgive them, for they know not what they do.' Then a horror of great darkness fell upon him, and he felt what sinners feel when they are for ever shut out from God. That was the last drop in the cup of bitterness. 'My God, my God!' he cries, 'why hast Thou forsaken me?'

"All this[6] he bore for you! For you—and you never think of him; for you—and you turn your backs on him; you don't care what he has gone through for you. Yet he is not weary of toiling for you: he has risen from the dead, he is praying for you at the right hand of God—'Father, forgive them, for they know not what they do.'[7] And he is upon this earth too; he is among us; he is there close to you now; I see his wounded body and his look of love."

Here Dinah turned to Bessy Cranage, whose bonny youth and evident vanity had touched her with pity.

"Poor child! poor child! He is beseeching you, and you don't listen to him. You think of ear-rings and fine gowns and caps, and you never think of the Saviour who died to save your precious soul. Your cheeks will be shrivelled one day, your hair will be grey, your poor body will be thin and tottering! Then you will begin to feel that your soul is not saved; then you will have to stand before God drest in your sins, in your evil tempers and vain thoughts. And Jesus, who stands ready to help you now,[8] won't help you then: because you won't have him to be your Saviour, he[9] will be

---

[5] not!'. . . and ye would not," she] not!' And ye would not!" she *MS* not!' . . . and ye would not!" *1*

[6] this] that, *MS*   [7] do.' ⟨Yet⟩ And *MS*

[8] now, ⟨will not⟩ wont help you then: ⟨he will be⟩ because *MS*

[9] Saviour, he] *MS 1* Saviour{,} he *8*

your judge. Now he looks at you with love and mercy, and says, 'Come to me that you may have life;' then he will turn away from you, and say, 'Depart from me into everlasting fire!' "

Poor Bessy's wide-open black eyes began to fill with tears, her great[1] red cheeks and lips became quite pale, and her face was distorted like a little child's before a burst of crying.

"Ah! poor blind child!" Dinah went on, "think if it should happen to you as it[2] once happened to a servant of God in the days of her vanity. *She* thought of her lace caps, and[3] saved all her money to buy 'em; she thought nothing about how she might get a clean heart and a right spirit, she only wanted to have better lace than other girls. And one day when she put her new cap on and looked in the glass, she saw a bleeding Face crowned with thorns. That face is looking at you now,"[4]—here Dinah pointed to a spot close in front of Bessy.—"Ah![5] tear off those follies! cast them away from you, as if they were stinging adders. They *are* stinging you—they are poisoning your soul—they are dragging you down into a dark bottomless pit, where you will sink for ever, and for ever, and for ever, further away from light and God."

Bessy could bear it no longer: a great terror was upon her, and wrenching her ear-rings from her ears, she threw them down before her, sobbing aloud. Her father, Chad, frightened lest he should be "laid hold on" too, this impression on the rebellious Bess striking him as nothing less than a miracle, walked hastily away, and began to work at his anvil by way of reassuring himself. "Folks mun ha' hoss-shoes, praichin' or no praichin': the divil canna lay[6] hould o' me for that," he muttered to himself.

But now Dinah began to tell of the joys that were in store for the penitent, and to[7] describe in her simple way the divine peace and love with which the soul of the believer is filled—how the sense of God's love turns poverty into riches, and satisfies the soul, so that no uneasy desire vexes it, no fear alarms it: how, at last, the very temptation to sin is extinguished, and heaven is begun upon earth, because no cloud passes between the soul and God, who is its eternal sun.

"Dear friends," she said at last, "brothers and sisters, whom I love[8] as those for whom my Lord has died, believe me I know what this great blessedness is; and because I know it, I want you to have it too. I am poor, like you: I have to get my living with my hands; but no lord nor lady can be so happy as me, if they haven't got the love of God in their souls. Think

---

[1] great ⟨round⟩ red *MS*

[2] it {once} happened to ⟨Mary Allen⟩ a servant of God in the days of her vanity. *MS*

[3] & ⟨she⟩ saved {all her} money *MS*   [4] now," {—} ⟨said⟩ {here} Dinah *MS*

[5] Bessy.—"Ah!] Bessy—ah, *MS* Bessy.—"Ah, *1*   [6] lay] ley *MS*

[7] to ⟨explain⟩ describe *MS*

[8] I love ⟨because you are poor sinners like myself & because our Lord has died for you & me & all sinners⟩ as those for whom my Lord has died *MS*

what it is—not to hate anything but sin; to be full of love to every creature; to be frightened at nothing; to be sure that all things will turn to good; not to mind pain, because it is our Father's will; to know that nothing—no, not if the earth was to be burnt up, or the waters come and drown us—nothing could part us from God who loves us, and who fills our souls with peace and joy, because we are sure that whatever he wills is holy, just, and good.

"Dear friends, come and[9] take this blessedness; it is offered to you[1]; it is the good news that Jesus came to preach to the poor. It is not like the riches of this world, so that the more one gets the less the rest can have. God is without end; his love is without end—

> 'Its streams the whole creation reach,
> So plenteous is the store;
> Enough for all, enough for each,
> Enough for evermore.' "

Dinah had been speaking at least an hour, and the reddening light of the parting day seemed to give a solemn emphasis to her closing words. The stranger, who had been interested in the course of her sermon, as if it had been the development of a drama—[2] for there is this sort of fascination in all sincere unpremeditated eloquence, which opens to one the inward drama of the speaker's emotions—now turned his horse aside[3] and pursued his way, while Dinah said, "Let us sing a little, dear friends;" and[4] as he was still winding down the slope, the voices of the Methodists reached him, rising and falling in that strange blending of exultation and sadness which belongs to the cadence of a hymn.

---

[9] come &] *added in MS*   [1] offered to you] offered you *MS*
[2] drama—⟨watching the phases of feeling through which her mind ⟨⟨past⟩⟩ passed⟩ ⟨unwilling to leave until he had seen every phase of feeling⟩ for *MS*
[3] aside] *MS 1* aside, *8*   [4] & ⟨while⟩ as *MS*

CHAPTER III.

AFTER THE PREACHING.

In less than an hour from that time Seth Bede was walking by Dinah's side along the hedgerow-path that skirted the pastures and green cornfields which lay between the village and the Hall Farm. Dinah had taken off her little quaker bonnet again, and was holding it in her hands that she might have a freer enjoyment of the cool evening twilight, and Seth could see the expression of her face quite clearly as he walked by her side, timidly revolving something he wanted to say to her. It was an expression of unconscious placid gravity—of absorption in thoughts that had no con-nexion with the present moment or with her own personality: an expression that is[1] most of all discouraging to a lover. Her very walk was discouraging: it had that quiet elasticity that asks for no support. Seth felt this dimly; he said to himself, "She's too good and holy for any man, let alone me," and the words he had been summoning rushed back again before they had reached his lips. But another thought gave him courage: "There's no man could love her better, and leave her freer to follow the Lord's work." They had been silent for many minutes now, since they had done talking about Bessy Cranage; Dinah seemed almost to have forgotten Seth's presence, and her pace was becoming so much quicker, that the sense of their being only a few minutes' walk from the yard-gates of the Hall Farm at last gave Seth courage to speak.

"You've quite made up your mind to go back to Snowfield o' Saturday, Dinah?"

"Yes," said Dinah, quietly. "I'm called there. It was borne in upon my mind while I was meditating on Sunday night, as sister Allen, who's in a decline, is in need of me. I saw her as plain as we see that bit of thin white cloud, lifting up her poor thin hand and beckoning to me. And this morning when I opened the Bible for direction, the first words my eyes fell on were[2], 'And after we had seen the vision, immediately we endeavoured to go into Macedonia.' If it wasn't for that clear showing of the Lord's will I should be loth to go, for my heart yearns over my aunt and her little ones, and that poor wandering lamb, Hetty Sorrel. I've been much drawn out in prayer for her of late, and I look on it as a token that there may be mercy in store for her."

"God grant it," said Seth. "For I doubt Adam's heart is so set on her, he'll never turn to anybody else; and yet it 'ud go to my heart if he was to

---

[1] is ⟨the least encouraging⟩ most of all discouraging *MS*   [2] were] was *MS*

marry her, for I canna think as she'd make him happy. It's a deep mystery—
the way the heart of man turns to one woman out of all the rest he's seen i'
the world, and makes it easier for him to work seven year for *her*, like Jacob
did for Rachel, sooner than have any other woman for th' asking. I often
think of them words, 'And Jacob served seven years for Rachel; and they
seemed to him but a few days for the love he had to her.' I know those words
'ud come true with me, Dinah, if so be you'd give me hope as I might win
you after seven years was over. I know you think a husband 'ud be taking up
too much o' your thoughts, because St Paul says, 'She that's married careth
for the things of the world,[3] how she may please her husband;' and may
happen you'll think me over-bold to speak to you about it again, after what
you told me o' your mind last Saturday. But I've been thinking it over again
by night and by day, and I've prayed not to be blinded by my own desires, to
think what's only good for me must be good for you too. And it seems to me
there's more texts for your marrying than ever you can find against it. For
St Paul says as plain as can be in another place, 'I will that the younger
women marry, bear children, guide the house, give none occasion to the
adversary to speak reproachfully;' and[4] then,[5] 'two are better than one;' and
that holds good with marriage as well as with other things. For we should be
o' one heart and o' one mind, Dinah. We[6] both serve the same Master, and
are striving after the same gifts; and[7] I'd never be the husband to make a
claim on you as could interfere with your doing the work God has fitted you
for. I'd make a shift, and fend indoor and out, to give you more[8] liberty—
more than you can have now, for you've got to get your own living now, and
I'm strong enough to work for us both."

When Seth had once begun to urge his suit, he went on earnestly, and
almost hurriedly, lest Dinah should speak some decisive word before he
had[9] poured forth all the arguments he had prepared. His cheeks became
flushed as he went on, his mild grey eyes filled with tears, and his voice
trembled as he spoke the last sentence. They had reached one of those very
narrow[1] passes between two tall stones, which performed[2] the office of a
stile in Loamshire, and Dinah paused as she turned towards Seth and said,
in her tender but calm treble notes—

"Seth Bede, I thank you for your love towards me, and if I could think of
any man[3] as more than a Christian brother, I think it would be you. But my
heart is not free to marry. That is good for other women, and it is a great and
a blessed thing to be a wife and mother; but[4] 'as God has distributed to

---

[3] world,] *MS 1* world *8*   [4] reproachfully;' and] reproachfully." And *MS*
[5] then,] *MS 1* then *8*   [6] Dinah. We] Dinah; we *MS*
[7] gifts; and] gifts. And *MS*   [8] more ⟨time &⟩ liberty *MS*
[9] had ⟨uttered⟩ poured forth *MS*   [1] narrow ⟨passages⟩ passes *MS*
[2] performed] perform *MS*
[3] think of any man] *MS* think any man *1* think {of} any man *8*
[4] mother; but] mother. But *MS*

every man, as the Lord hath called every man, so let him walk.' God has called me to minister to others, not to have any joys or sorrows of my own, but to rejoice with them that do rejoice, and to weep with those that weep. He has called me to speak His word, and he has greatly owned my work. It could only be on a very clear showing that I could leave the brethren and sisters at Snowfield, who are favoured with very little of this world's good; where the trees are few, so that a child might count them, and there's very hard living for the poor in the winter. It has been given[5] me to help, to comfort, and strengthen the little flock there, and to call in many wanderers; and[6] my soul is filled with these things from my rising up till my lying down. My life is too short, and God's work is too great for me to think of making a home for myself in this world. I've not turned a deaf ear to your words, Seth, for when I saw as your love was given to me, I thought it[7] might be a leading of Providence for me to change my way of life, and that we should be fellow-helpers; and I spread the matter before the Lord. But whenever I tried to fix my mind on marriage, and our living together, other thoughts always came in[8]—the times when I've prayed by the sick and dying, and the happy hours I've had preaching, when my heart was filled with love, and the Word was given to me abundantly. And when I've opened the Bible for direction, I've always lighted on some clear word to tell me where my work lay. I believe what you say, Seth, that you would try to be a help and not a hindrance to my work; but[9] I see that our marriage is not God's will—He draws my heart another way. I desire to live and die without husband or children. I[1] seem to have no room in my soul for wants and fears of my own, it has pleased God to fill my heart so full with the wants and sufferings of his poor people."

Seth was unable to reply, and they walked on in silence. At last, as they were nearly at the yard-[2]gate, he said—

"Well, Dinah, I must seek for strength to bear it, and to endure as seeing Him who is invisible. But I feel now how weak my faith is. It seems as if, when you are gone, I could never joy in anything any more. I think it's something passing the love of women[3] as I feel for you, for I could be content without your marrying me if I could go and live at Snowfield, and be near you. I trusted as the strong love God had given me towards you was a leading for us both; but it seems it was only meant for my trial.[4] Perhaps I

---

[5] given {me} to help {to} comfort & strengthen *MS*
[6] wanderers; and] wanderers. And *MS*   [7] it] that *MS*
[8] in ⟨& pushed that out⟩—the {blessed}⟨blessed⟩ times ⟨I've had praying⟩ when I've prayed *MS*
[9] work; but] work. But *MS*   [1] children. I] children: I *MS*
[2] yard-] *added in MS*   [3] women ⟨that⟩ as *MS*
[4] trial. ⟨You wouldn't be displeased with me if things turned out so as I could leave my work here & go to live at Snowfield?⟩ Perhaps *MS*

feel more for you than I ought to feel for any creature, for I[5] often can't help saying of you what the[6] hymn says,—

> 'In darkest shades if she appear,
>   My dawning is begun;
> She is my soul's bright morning-star,
>   And she my rising sun.'

That may be wrong, and I am to be taught better. But you wouldn't be displeased with me if things turned out so as I could leave this country and go to live at Snowfield?"

"No, Seth; but I counsel you to wait patiently, and not lightly to leave your own country and kindred. Do nothing without the Lord's clear bidding. It's a bleak and barren country there, not like this land of Goshen you've been used to. We mustn't be in a hurry to fix and choose our own lot; we must wait to be guided."

"But you'd let me write you a letter, Dinah, if there was anything I wanted to tell you."

"Yes, sure; let me know if you're in any trouble.[7] You'll be continually in my prayers."

They had now reached the yard-gate, and Seth said, "I won't go in, Dinah, so farewell." He paused and hesitated after she had given him her hand, and then said, "There's no knowing but what you may see things different after a while. There may be a new leading."

"Let us leave that, Seth. It's good to live only a moment at a time, as I've read in one of Mr Wesley's books. It isn't for you and me to lay plans; we've nothing to do but to obey and to trust. Farewell."

Dinah pressed his hand with rather a sad look in her loving eyes, and then passed through the gate, while Seth turned away to walk lingeringly home. But instead of taking the direct road, he chose to turn back along the fields through which he and Dinah had already passed; and I think his blue linen handkerchief was very wet with tears long before he had made up his mind that it was time for him to set his face steadily homewards. He was but three-and-twenty, and had only just learned what it is to love—to love with that adoration which a young man gives to a woman whom he feels to be greater and better than himself. Love of this sort is hardly distinguishable from religious feeling. What[8] deep and worthy love is so? whether of woman or child, or art or music. Our caresses, our tender words, our still rapture under the influence of autumn sunsets, or pillared vistas, or calm majestic statues, or Beethoven symphonies, all bring with them the consciousness that they are mere waves and ripples in[9] an unfathomable ocean

---

[5] I ⟨could say of you⟩ often cant help *MS*   [6] the] th' *MS*
[7] trouble. ⟨I shall bear you in mind always⟩ You'll *MS*
[8] feeling. What] feeling: what *MS*   [9] in] on *MS*

of love and beauty: our emotion in[1] its keenest moment passes from expression into silence, our love at its highest flood rushes beyond its object, and loses itself in the sense of divine mystery. And this blessed gift of venerating love has been given to too many humble craftsmen since the world began, for us to feel any surprise that it should have existed in the soul of a Methodist carpenter half a century ago, while there was yet a lingering after-glow from the time when Wesley and his fellow-labourer fed on the hips and haws of the Cornwall hedges, after exhausting limbs and lungs in carrying a divine message to the poor.

That after-glow has long faded away; and the picture we are apt to make of Methodism in our imagination is not an amphitheatre of green hills, or the deep shade of broad-leaved sycamores, where a crowd of rough men and weary-hearted women drank in a faith which was a rudimentary culture, which linked their thoughts with the past, lifted their imagination above the sordid details of their own narrow lives, and suffused their souls with the sense of a pitying, loving, infinite Presence, sweet as summer to the houseless needy. It is too possible that to some of my readers Methodism may mean nothing more than low-pitched gables up dingy streets, sleek grocers, sponging preachers, and hypocritical jargon—elements which are regarded as an exhaustive analysis of Methodism in many fashionable quarters.

That would be a pity; for I cannot pretend that Seth and Dinah were anything else than Methodists—not indeed of that modern type which reads quarterly reviews and attends in chapels with pillared porticoes; but of a very old-fashioned kind. They believed in present miracles, in instantaneous conversions, in revelations by dreams and visions; they drew lots, and sought for Divine guidance by opening the Bible at hazard; having a literal way of interpreting the Scriptures, which is not at all[2] sanctioned by approved commentators; and it is impossible for me to represent their diction as correct, or their instruction as liberal. Still—if I have read religious history aright—faith, hope, and charity have not always been found in a direct ratio with a sensibility to the three concords; and it is possible, thank Heaven! to have very erroneous theories and very sublime feelings. The raw bacon which clumsy Molly spares from her own scanty store, that she may carry it to her neighbour's child to "stop the fits," may be a piteously inefficacious remedy; but the generous stirring of neighbourly kindness that prompted the deed, has a beneficent radiation that is not lost.

Considering these things, we can hardly think Dinah and Seth beneath our sympathy, accustomed as we may be to weep over the loftier sorrows of[3] heroines in satin boots and crinoline, and of heroes riding fiery horses, themselves ridden by still more fiery passions.

---

[1] in] at *MS*   [2] at all] *added in MS*   [3] of ⟨ladies⟩ heroines *MS*

Poor Seth! he was never on horseback in his life except once, when he was a little lad, and Mr Jonathan Burge[4] took him up behind, telling him to "hold on tight;" and instead of bursting out into wild accusing apostrophes to God and destiny, he is resolving, as he now walks homeward under the solemn starlight, to repress his sadness, to be less bent on having his own will, and to live more for others, as Dinah does.

[4] Burge ⟨had⟩ took *MS*

CHAPTER IV.[1]

HOME AND ITS SORROWS.

A green valley with a brook running through it, full almost to overflowing with the late rains; overhung by low stooping willows. Across this brook a plank is thrown, and over this plank Adam Bede is passing with his undoubting step, followed close by Gyp with the basket; evidently making his way to the thatched house, with a stack of timber by the side of it, about twenty yards up the opposite slope.

The door of the house is open, and an elderly woman is looking out; but she is not placidly contemplating the evening sunshine; she has been watching with dim eyes the gradually enlarging speck which for the last few minutes she has been quite sure is her darling[2] son Adam. Lisbeth Bede loves her son with the love of a woman to whom her first-born has come late in life. She is an anxious,[3] spare, yet vigorous old woman, clean as a snow-drop. Her grey hair is turned neatly back under a pure linen cap with a black band round it; her broad chest is covered with a buff neckerchief, and below this you see a sort of short bed-gown made of blue-checkered linen, tied round the waist and descending to the hips, from whence there is a considerable length of linsey-wolsey petticoat. For Lisbeth is tall, and in other points too there is a strong likeness between her and her son Adam. Her dark eyes are somewhat dim now—perhaps from too much crying—but her broadly-marked eyebrows are still black, her teeth are sound, and as she stands knitting rapidly and unconsciously with her work-hardened hands, she has as firmly-upright an attitude as when she is carrying a pail of water on her head from the spring. There is the same type of frame and the same keen activity of temperament in mother and son, but it was not from her that Adam got his well-filled brow and his expression of large-hearted intelligence.

Family likeness has often a deep sadness in it. Nature, that great tragic dramatist, knits us together by bone and muscle, and divides us by the subtler web of our brains; blends yearning and repulsion; and ties us by our heartstrings to the beings that jar us at every movement. We hear a voice with the very cadence of our own uttering the thoughts we despise; we see eyes—ah! so like our mother's—averted from us in cold alienation; and our[4] last darling child startles us with the air and gestures of the sister we

---

[1] CHAPTER IV.] Chapter ⟨3⟩ 4. *MS*   [2] darling] *added in MS*
[3] life. She is an anxious,] life: an anxious, *MS*   [4] our] *added in MS*

parted from[5] in bitterness long years ago. The father to whom we owe our best heritage—the mechanical instinct, the keen sensibility to harmony, the unconscious skill of the modelling hand—galls us, and puts us to shame by his daily errors; the long-lost mother, whose face we begin to see in the glass as our own wrinkles come, once fretted our young souls with her anxious humours and irrational persistence.

It is such a fond anxious mother's voice that you hear, as Lisbeth says,

"Well, my lad, it's gone seven by th' clock. Thee't allays[6] stay till the last child's born. Thee wants thy supper, I'll warrand. Where's Seth? gone arter some[7] o's chapellin', I reckon?"

"Ay, ay, Seth's at no harm, mother, thee mayst[8] be sure. But where's father?" said Adam quickly, as he entered the house and glanced into the room on the left hand, which was used as a workshop. "Hasn't he done the coffin for[9] Tholer? There's the stuff standing just as I left it this morning."

"Done the coffin?" said Lisbeth, following him, and knitting uninterruptedly, though she looked at her son very anxiously. "Eh, my lad, he went aff to Treddles'on this forenoon, an's niver come back. I doubt he's got to th' 'Waggin Overthrow' again."

A deep flush of anger passed rapidly over Adam's face. He said nothing, but threw off his jacket, and began to roll up his shirt-sleeves again.

"What art goin'[1] to do, Adam?" said the mother, with a tone and look of alarm. "Thee wouldstna go to work again, wi'out ha'in' thy bit o' supper?"

Adam, too angry to speak, walked into the workshop. But his mother threw down her knitting, and, hurrying after him, took hold of his arm, and said in a tone of plaintive remonstrance—

"Nay, my lad, my lad, thee munna go wi'out thy supper; there's the taters wi' the gravy in 'em, just as thee lik'st 'em. I saved[2] 'em o' purpose for thee. Come an' ha' thy supper, come."

"Let be!" said Adam impetuously, shaking her off, and seizing one of the planks that stood against the wall. "It's fine talking about having supper when here's a coffin promised to be ready at Brox'on by seven o'clock tomorrow morning, and[3] ought to ha' been there now, and not a nail struck yet. My throat's too full to swallow victuals."

"Why, thee canstna get the coffin ready," said Lisbeth. "Thee't work thyself to death. It 'ud take[4] thee all night to do 't."[5]

"What signifies how long it takes me? Isn't the coffin promised? Can they bury the man without a coffin? I'd work my right hand off sooner than

[5] sister we parted from] sister from whom we parted MS   [6] allays] al'ys MS
[7] some ⟨of his⟩ o's MS   [8] thee mayst] you may MS
[9] for ⟨? Bills⟩ Tholer MS   [1] goin'] gooin' MS
[2] 'em. I saved] 'em—I saved MS 'em. I sav'd 1   [3] and] an' MS
[4] take] tek MS   [5] night to do 't."] night welly to do 't." MS

deceive people with lies i' that way. It makes me mad to think on't. I shall overrun these doings before long. I've stood enough of 'em."

Poor Lisbeth did not hear this threat for the first time, and if she had been wise she would have gone away quietly, and said nothing for the next hour. But one of the lessons a woman most rarely learns, is never to talk to an angry or a drunken man. Lisbeth sat down on the chopping bench and began to cry, and by the time she had cried enough to make her voice very piteous, she burst out into[6] words.

"Nay, my lad, my lad, thee wouldstna[7] go away an' break thy mother's heart[8], an' leave thy feyther to ruin. Thee[9] wouldstna ha' 'em carry me to th' churchyard, an' thee not to follow me. I shanna rest i' my grave if I donna[1] see thee at th' last, an' how's they to let thee know[2] as I'm a-dyin', if thee't gone a-workin' i' distant parts, an' Seth belike gone arter thee, and[3] thy feyther not[4] able t' hold[5] a pen for 's hand[6] shakin', besides not[7] knowin'[8] where thee art[9]. Thee mun forgie thy feyther—thee munna be so bitter again' him. He war a good feyther to thee afore he took to th' drink. He's a cliver[1] workman, an' taught thee thy trade, remember, an's niver gen me a blow nor so much as an ill word—no, not even[2] in 's drink. Thee wouldstna ha 'm go to the workhus[3]—thy own feyther—an' him as was a fine-growed man an' handy at iverythin'[4] amost[5] as thee[6] art thysen, five-an'-twenty 'ear ago[7], when thee wast a babby[8] at the[9] breast."

Lisbeth's voice became louder, and choked with sobs: a sort of wail, the most irritating of all sounds where[1] real sorrows are to be borne, and real work to be done. Adam broke in impatiently.

"Now, mother, don't cry, and talk so. Haven't I got enough to vex me without that? What's th' use o' telling me things as I only think too much on every day? If I didna think on[2] 'em, why should I do[3] as I do, for the sake o' keeping things together here? But I hate to be talking where it's no use: I like to keep my breath for doing istead[4] o' talking."

---

[6] into ⟨broken sobs⟩ words ⟨and sobs,⟩. *MS*

[7] wouldstna] wotna *MS*   [8] break thy mother's heart] break mother's heart *MS*

[9] Thee ⟨wotnt⟩ wouldstna *MS*   [1] donna] dunna *MS*

[2] how's they to let thee know] hoo's the' to let thee knoo *MS*   [3] and] an' *MS*

[4] not] noot *MS*   [5] t' hold] to hoald *MS* to hold *Cabinet*   [6] hand] han' *MS*

[7] not] noot *MS*   [8] knowin'] ⟨knooing⟩ knooin' *MS*   [9] art] bin *MS*

[1] cliver] *MS 1* clever *8*   [2] even] aven *MS*

[3] ha 'm go to the workhus] ha 'm goo to th' workhus *MS* ha 'm go to th' workhus *1*

[4] iverythin'] *MS 1* everythin' *8*   [5] amost] a'most *MS*

[6] thee ⟨art thyself⟩ ⟨atn thyself⟩ art thysen *MS*   [7] ago] agoo *MS*

[8] babby] baby *Cabinet*   [9] the] th' *MS*

[1] sobs: a sort of wail, the most irritating of all sounds where] sobs—a wailing sound of all others the most irritating where *MS*

[2] didna think on] didn't think of *MS*

[3] why should I do] do you think I should do *MS*   [4] istead] istid *MS*

"I know thee dost things as nobody else 'ud do, my lad.[5] But thee't allays[6] so hard upo' thy[7] feyther, Adam. Thee think'st nothing[8] too much to do for Seth: thee snapp'st me up if iver I find faut wi' th' lad. But thee't so angered wi' thy feyther, more nor wi' anybody else."

"That's better than speaking soft, and letting things go the wrong way, I reckon, isn't it? If I wasn't sharp with him, he'd sell every bit o' stuff i' th' yard, and spend it on drink. I know there's a duty to be done by my father, but it isn't my duty to encourage him in running headlong to ruin. And what has[9] Seth got to do with it? The lad does no harm as I know of. But leave me alone, mother, and let me get on with the work."

Lisbeth dared not say any more; but she got up and called Gyp[1], thinking to console herself somewhat for Adam's refusal of the supper she had spread out in the loving expectation of looking at him while he ate it, by feeding Adam's dog with extra liberality. But Gyp was watching his master with wrinkled brow and ears erect, puzzled at this unusual course of things; and though he glanced at Lisbeth when she called him, and moved his fore-paws uneasily, well knowing that she was inviting him to supper, he was in a divided state of mind, and remained seated on his haunches, again fixing his eyes anxiously on his master. Adam noticed Gyp's mental conflict, and though his anger had made him less tender than usual to his mother, it did not prevent him from caring as much as usual for his dog. We are apt to be kinder to the brutes that love us than to the women that love us. Is it because the brutes are dumb?[2]

"Go, Gyp; go, lad!" Adam said, in a tone of encouraging command; and Gyp, apparently satisfied that duty and pleasure were one, followed Lisbeth into the house-place.

But no sooner had he licked up his supper than he went back to his master, while Lisbeth sat down alone to cry over her knitting.[3] Women who are never bitter and resentful are often the most querulous; and if Solomon was as wise as he is reputed to be, I feel sure that when he compared a contentious woman to a continual dropping on a very rainy day, he had not a vixen in his eye—a fury with long nails, acrid and selfish. Depend upon[4] it, he meant a good creature, who had no joy but in the happiness of the loved ones whom she contributed to make uncomfortable, putting by all the tid-bits for them, and spending nothing on herself. Such a woman as Lisbeth for example—at once patient and complaining, self-renouncing and exacting, brooding the livelong day over what happened yesterday, and what is likely to happen to-morrow, and crying very readily both at

---

[5] nobody else 'ud do, my lad.] nobody else welly 'ud do. *MS*
[6] allays] al'ys *MS*   [7] thy ⟨father⟩ feyther *MS*   [8] nothing] nothin' *MS*
[9] what has] what's *MS*   [1] called Gyp] called to Gyp *MS*
[2] us. Is it because the brutes are dumb?] us: perhaps because the brutes are dumb. *MS*
[3] knitting. ⟨It is the w⟩{W}omen *MS*   [4] upon] *added in MS*

the good and the evil. But a certain awe mingled itself with her idolatrous love of Adam, and when he said, "Leave me alone," she was always silenced.

So the hours passed, to the loud ticking of the old day-clock and the sound of Adam's tools. At last he called for a light and a draught of water (beer was a thing only to be drunk on holidays)[5], and Lisbeth ventured to say as she took it in, "Thy supper stans ready for thee, when thee lik'st."

"Donna[6] thee sit up, mother," said Adam, in a gentle tone. He had worked off his anger now, and whenever he wished to be especially kind to his mother, he fell into his strongest native accent and dialect, with which at other times his speech was less deeply tinged. "I'll see to father when he comes home; maybe he wonna[7] come at all to-night. I shall be easier if thee't i' bed."

"Nay, I'll bide till Seth comes. He wonna[8] be long now, I reckon."

It was then past nine by the clock, which was always in advance[9] of the day, and before it had struck ten the latch was lifted and Seth entered. He had heard the sound of the tools as he was approaching.

"Why, mother," he said, "how is it as father's working so late?"

"It's none o' thy feyther[1], as is a-workin'—thee might know that well anoof[2] if thy head warna full o' chapellin'—it's thy brother as does iverything, for there's niver nobody else i' th' way to do nothin'."

Lisbeth was going on, for she was not at all afraid of Seth, and usually poured[3] into his ears all the querulousness which was repressed by her awe of Adam. Seth had never in his life spoken a harsh word to his mother, and timid people always[4] wreak their peevishness on the gentle. But Seth, with an anxious look, had passed into the workshop and said—

"Addy, how's this? What![5] father's forgot the coffin?"

"Ay, lad, th' old tale; but[6] I shall get it done," said Adam, looking up, and[7] casting one of his bright keen glances at his brother. "Why, what's the matter with thee? Thee't in trouble."

Seth's eyes were red, and there was a look of deep depression on his mild face.

"Yes, Addy, but it's what must be borne, and can't be helped. Why, thee'st never been to the[8] school, then?"

"School? no; that screw can wait," said Adam, hammering away again.

"Let me take my turn now, and do thee go to bed," said Seth.

---

⁵ & a draught of water (beer was a thing only to be drunk on holidays)] *added in MS*
⁶ Donna] Dunna *MS*   ⁷ maybe he wonna] may be, he wunna *MS*
⁸ wonna] wunna *MS*   ⁹ always in advance] always long in advance *MS*
¹ feyther] father *MS 1*   ² might know that well anoof] mut knoo well enoof, *MS*
³ Seth, and usually poured] Seth & poured *MS*   ⁴ always] *added in MS*
⁵ What!] What, *MS*   ⁶ tale; but] tale. But *MS*   ⁷ & ⟨fixing⟩ casting *MS*
⁸ the] th' *MS*

"No, lad, I'd rather go on, now I'm in harness. Thee't help me to carry it to Brox'on when it's done. I'll call thee up at sunrise. Go and eat thy supper[9], and shut the door, so as[1] I mayn't hear mother's talk."[2]

Seth knew that Adam always meant what he said, and was not to be[3] persuaded into meaning anything else. So he turned, with rather a heavy heart, into the house-place.

"Adam's niver touched a bit o' victual sin' home he's come," said Lisbeth. "I reckon thee'st hed thy supper at some o' thy Methody folks."

"Nay, mother," said Seth, "I've had no supper yet."

"Come, then," said Lisbeth, "but donna[4] thee ate the taters, for Adam 'ull happen ate 'em if I leave 'em stannin'. He[5] loves a bit o' taters an' gravy. But he's[6] been so sore an' angered, he[7] wouldn't ate 'em, for all I'd putten 'em by o' purpose for him. An' he's[8] been a-threatenin' to go[9] away again," she went on, whimpering, "an' I'm fast sure he'll go[1] some dawnin' afore I'm up, an' niver let me know[2] aforehand, an' he'll niver come[3] back again when once he's gone[4]. An' I'd better niver ha' had[5] a son, as is like no other[6] body's son for the[7] deftness an' th' handiness, an' so[8] looked on by th' grit folks, an' tall an' upright like a poplar tree, an' me[9] to be parted from him, an' niver see 'm no more[1]."

"Come, mother, donna[2] grieve thyself in vain," said Seth, in a soothing voice. "Thee'st not half so good reason to think as Adam 'ull go away as to think he'll stay with thee. He may say such a thing when he's in wrath—and he's got excuse for being wrathful sometimes—but his heart 'ud never let him go. Think how he's stood by us all when it's been none so easy—paying his savings to free me from going for a soldier,[3] an' turnin' his earnins into wood for father, when he's got plenty o' uses for his money, and many a young man like him 'ud ha' been married and settled before now. He'll never turn round and knock down his own work, and forsake them as it's been the labour of his life to stand by."

"Donna talk to me[4] about's marr'in'," said Lisbeth, crying afresh. "He's[5] set's heart on that Hetty Sorrel, as 'ull niver save a penny,[6] an' 'ull toss up her head at's old mother. An' to think as he might ha'[7] Mary

---

[9] supper {but get me} ⟨but get me⟩ & MS   [1] door, so as] door, as MS
[2] talk." ⟨But get me a drop of hot yill⟩ ¶ Seth MS   [3] be] *added in* MS
[4] donna] dunna MS   [5] He] Hey MS   [6] he's] hey's MS
[7] he] hey MS   [8] he's] hey's MS   [9] go] goo MS
[1] he'll go] hey'll goo MS   [2] know] knoo MS
[3] he'll niver come] *1* hey'll niver coom MS he'll never come *8*
[4] he's gone] hey's goon MS   [5] had] hed MS   [6] no other] noo oother MS
[7] the] th' MS   [8] so] soo MS   [9] me] mey MS
[1] see 'm no more] sae 'm no moor MS   [2] donna] dunna MS
[3] soldier, ⟨and⟩ an' MS   [4] "Donna talk to me] "⟨Dont t⟩ Dunna talk t' mae MS
[5] He's] Hey's MS
[6] as 'ull niver save a penny,] as niver saves a penny of her wage MS
[7] he might ha'] he mut ha⟨e⟩{'} MS

Burge, an' be took partners, an' be a big man wi' workmen under him[8], like Mester Burge—Dolly's told me so o'er an'[9] o'er again—if it warna as he's[1] set's heart on that bit of a wench, as is o' no more use nor the gillyflower on the wall. An' he[2] so wise at bookin' an' figurin', an' not to know[3] no better nor that!"[4]

"But, mother, thee know'st we canna love just where other folks 'ud have us. There's nobody but God can control the heart of man. I could ha' wished myself as Adam[5] could ha' made another choice, but I wouldn't reproach him for what he can't help. And I'm not sure but what he tries to o'ercome it. But it's a matter as he doesn't like to be spoke to about, and I can only pray to the Lord to bless and direct him."

"Ay, thee't allays[6] ready enough at prayin', but I donna[7] see as thee gets much wi' thy prayin'. Thee wotna get double[8] earnins o' this side Yule. Th' Methodies 'll niver make[9] thee half[1] the man thy brother is, for all they're a-makin'[2] a preacher on thee."

"It's partly truth thee speak'st there, mother," said Seth mildly; "Adam's far before me, an's done more for me than I can ever do for him. God distributes talents to every man according as He sees good. But thee mustna undervally prayer. Prayer mayna bring money, but it brings us what no money can buy—a power to keep from sin, and be content with God's will, whatever he may please to send. If thee wouldst pray to God to help thee, and trust in His goodness, thee wouldstna be so uneasy about things."

"Unaisy? I'm i' th' right[3] on't to be unaisy. It's well seen on *thee* what it is niver to be unaisy. Thee't gi' away all thy earnins, an' niver be unaisy as thee'st nothin' laid up again' a rainy day. If Adam had been as aisy as thee, he'd niver ha' had[4] no money to pay for thee. Take[5] no thought for the morrow—take[6] no thought—that's what thee't allays[7] sayin'; an' what comes on't? Why,[8] as Adam has to take[9] thought for thee."

"Those are the words o' the Bible, mother," said Seth. "They don't mean as we should be idle. They mean we shouldn't be over-anxious and worreting ourselves about what'll happen to-morrow, but do our duty, and leave the rest to God's will."

"Ay, ay, that's the way wi' thee: thee allays makes[1] a peck o' thy own words out o' a pint o' the Bible's. I donna[2] see how thee't to know as

---

[8] under him] under 'm *MS*   [9] an'] and *Cabinet*   [1] he's] hey's *MS*
[2] he] hey *MS*   [3] know] knoo *MS*   [4] that!"] that." *MS*
[5] Adam ⟨had⟩ could *MS*   [6] allays] al'ys *MS*   [7] donna] dunna *MS*
[8] double ⟨wage⟩ earnins *MS*   [9] make] ma'e *MS*   [1] half] hafe *MS*
[2] a-makin'] a ma'in' *MS*   [3] right] raight *MS*   [4] had] hed *MS*
[5] Take] ⟨Teck⟩ Tae *MS*   [6] morrow—take] morrer—tae *MS*
[7] allays] al'ys *MS*   [8] Why,] *MS 1* Why *8*   [9] has to take] hes to tae *MS*
[1] allays makes] al'ys meks *MS*   [2] donna] dunna *MS*

'take³ no thought for the morrow' means⁴ all that. An' when the Bible's such a big book, an' thee canst read all⁵ thro't, an' ha' the pick o' the⁶ texes, I canna think why thee dostna pick better words as donna mean⁷ so much more nor they⁸ say. Adam doesna pick a that'n; I can understan' the tex as he's allays⁹ a-sayin', 'God helps them as helps theirsens¹.' "

"Nay, mother," said Seth, "that's no text o' the Bible. It comes out of a book as Adam picked up at the stall at Treddles'on. It was wrote by a knowing man, but over-worldly, I doubt. However, that saying's partly true; for the Bible tells us we must be workers together with God."

"Well, how'm I to know²? It sounds³ like a tex. But what's th' matter wi' th' lad? Thee't hardly atin' a bit o' supper. Dostna mean⁴ to ha' no more⁵ nor that bit o' oat-cake⁶? An' thee lookst as white as a flick o' new bacon. What's th' matter wi' thee?"

"Nothing to mind about, mother; I'm not⁷ hungry. I'll just look in at Adam again, and see if he'll let me go on with the coffin."

"Ha' a drop o' warm⁸ broth," said Lisbeth, whose motherly feeling now got the better of her "nattering" habit. "I'll set two-three sticks a-light in a minute."

"Nay, mother, thank thee; thee't very good," said Seth, gratefully; and encouraged by this touch of tenderness, he went on: "Let me pray a bit with thee for father, and Adam, and all of us—it'll comfort thee, happen, more than thee thinkst."

"Well, I've⁹ nothin' to say again' it."

Lisbeth, though disposed always to take the negative side in her conversations with Seth, had a vague sense that there was some comfort and safety in the fact of his piety, and that it somehow relieved her from the¹ trouble of any spiritual transactions on her own behalf.

So the mother and son knelt down together, and Seth prayed for the poor wandering father, and for those who were sorrowing for him at home. And when he came to the petition that Adam might never be called to set up his tent in a far country, but that his mother might be cheered and comforted by his presence all the days of her pilgrimage, Lisbeth's ready tears flowed again, and she wept aloud.

When they rose from their knees, Seth went to Adam again, and said, "Wilt only lie down for an hour or two, and let me go on the while?"

"No, Seth, no. Make mother go to bed, and go thyself."

³ take] Tae ⟨Teck⟩ MS   ⁴ morrow' means] morrer' manes MS
⁵ all] added in MS   ⁶ the] th' MS   ⁷ donna mean] dunna mane MS
⁸ they] the' MS   ⁹ allays] al'ys MS   ¹ theirsens] thersens MS
² know] knoo MS   ³ sounds] souns MS   ⁴ mean] mane MS
⁵ more] moor MS   ⁶ oat-cake] cake MS   ⁷ I'm not] I binna MS
⁸ warm ⟨yill⟩ broth MS   ⁹ I've] I'n MS   ¹ the ⟨necessity⟩ trouble MS

Meantime Lisbeth had dried her eyes, and now followed Seth, holding something in her hands. It was the brown-and-yellow platter containing[2] the baked potatoes with the gravy in them, and bits of meat which she had cut and mixed among them. Those were dear times, when wheaten bread and fresh meat were delicacies to working people. She set the dish down rather timidly on the bench by Adam's side, and said, "Thee canst pick a bit while thee't workin'. I'll bring thee another drop o'[3] water."

"Ay, mother, do," said Adam kindly, "I'm getting very thirsty."

In half an hour all was quiet; no sound was to be heard in the house but the loud ticking of the old day-clock, and the ringing of Adam's tools. The night was very still: when Adam[4] opened the door to look out at twelve o'clock, the only motion seemed to be in the glowing, twinkling stars; every blade of grass was asleep.

Bodily haste and exertion usually leave our thoughts very much at the mercy of our feelings and imagination; and it was so to-night with Adam. While his muscles were[5] working lustily, his mind[6] seemed as passive as a spectator at a diorama: scenes of the sad past, and probably sad future, floating before him, and giving place one to the other in swift succession.

He saw how it would be to-morrow morning, when he[7] had carried the coffin to Broxton and was at home again, having his breakfast: his father perhaps would come in, ashamed to meet his son's glance—would sit down, looking older and more tottering than he had done the morning before, and hang down his head, examining the floor-quarries; while Lisbeth would ask him how he supposed the coffin had been got ready, that he had slinked off and left undone—for Lisbeth was always the first to utter the word of reproach, although[8] she cried at Adam's severity towards his father.

"So it will go on, worsening and worsening," thought Adam; "there's no slipping uphill again, and no standing still when once you've begun to slip down." And then the day came back to him when he was a little fellow and used to run by his father's side, proud to be taken out to work, and prouder still to hear his father boasting to his fellow-workmen how "the little chap had an uncommon notion o' carpentering." What a fine active fellow his father was then! When people asked Adam whose little lad he was? he had a sense of distinction as he answered, "I'm Thias Bede's lad"—he was quite sure everybody knew Thias Bede: didn't he make the wonderful pigeon-house at Broxton parsonage? Those were happy days, especially when Seth, who was three years the[9] younger, began to go out working too, and Adam began to be a teacher as well as a learner. But then came the days of

---

[2] containing] full of *MS*   [3] o' ⟨drink⟩ water *MS*
[4] Adam ⟨looked⟩ opened *MS*   [5] were ⟨moving⟩ working *MS*
[6] mind ⟨was⟩ seemed *MS*   [7] he ⟨should⟩ had *MS*
[8] although] though *MS*   [9] the] *added in MS*

sadness, when Adam was some way on in his teens, and Thias began to loiter at the public-houses, and Lisbeth began to cry at home, and to pour forth her plaints in the hearing of her sons. Adam remembered well the night of shame and anguish when he first saw his father quite wild and foolish, shouting a song out fitfully among his drunken companions at the "Waggon Overthrown." He had run away once when he was only eighteen, making his escape in the morning twilight with a little[1] blue bundle over his shoulder, and his "mensuration book" in his pocket, and saying to himself very decidedly that he could bear the vexations of home no longer—he would go and seek his fortune,[2] setting up his stick at the crossways[3] and bending his steps[4] the way it fell. But by the time he got to Stoniton, the thought of his mother and Seth, left behind to endure everything without him, became too importunate, and his resolution failed him. He came back the next day, but the misery and terror his mother had gone through in those two days had haunted her ever since.

"No!" Adam said to himself to-night, "that must never happen again. It 'ud make a poor balance when my doings are cast up at the last, if my poor old mother stood o' the wrong side. My back's broad enough and strong enough; I should be no better than a coward to go away and leave the troubles to be borne by them as aren't half so able. 'They that are strong ought to bear the infirmities of those that are weak, and not to please themselves.' There's a text wants no candle to show't; it shines by its own light. It's plain enough you get into the wrong road i' this life if you run after this and that only for the[5] sake o' making things easy[6] and pleasant to yourself. A pig may poke his nose into the trough and think o' nothing outside it; but if you've got a man's heart and soul in you, you can't be easy a-making your own bed an' leaving the rest to lie on the stones.[7] Nay, nay, I'll never slip my[8] neck out o' the yoke, and leave the load to be drawn by the weak uns. Father's a sore cross to me, an's likely to be for many a long year to come. What then? I've got th' health, and the limbs, and the sperrit to bear it."

At this moment a smart rap, as if with a willow wand, was given at the house door, and Gyp, instead of barking, as might have been expected, gave a loud howl. Adam, very much startled, went at once to the door and opened it. Nothing was there; all was still, as when he opened it an hour before; the leaves were motionless, and the light of the stars showed the placid fields on both sides of the brook quite empty of visible life. Adam

---

[1] little] *added in MS*   [2] fortune, ⟨as Tom [?Nelson] did⟩ setting *MS*
[3] crossways] cross ways *MS*
[4] steps ⟨in the direction⟩ the way it fell. But ⟨when⟩ by the time *MS*
[5] the ⟨op⟩ sake o' *MS*   [6] easy] *added in MS*
[7] stones. ⟨Life's a workin' day, as far as I can make out: we've got our work cut out for us & we must set to and do 't.⟩ Nay *MS*
[8] Nay, nay, I'll never slip my] Nay, nay, Adam Bede! You shall never slip your *MS*

walked round the house, and still saw nothing except a rat which darted into
the woodshed as he passed. He went in again, wondering; the sound was so
peculiar, that the[9] moment he heard it, it called up the image of the willow
wand striking the door. He could not help a little shudder, as he remembered how often his mother had told him of just such a sound coming as a
sign when[1] some one was dying. Adam was not[2] a man to be gratuitously
superstitious; but he had the blood of the peasant in him as well as of the
artisan, and a peasant can no more help believing in a traditional superstition than a horse can help trembling when he sees a camel. Besides, he
had that mental combination which is at once humble in the region of
mystery, and keen in the region of knowledge: it was the depth of his
reverence quite as much as his hard common sense, which gave him[3] his
disinclination to doctrinal religion, and he often checked Seth's argument-
ative spiritualism by saying, "Eh, it's a big mystery; thee know'st but little
about it." And so it happened that Adam[4] was at once penetrating and
credulous. If a new building had fallen down and he had been told that this
was a divine judgment, he would have said, "May be; but the bearing[5] o' the
roof and walls wasn't right, else it wouldn't ha' come down;" yet he
believed in dreams and prognostics,[6] and to his dying day he bated his
breath a little when he told the story of the stroke with the willow wand. I
tell it as he told it, not attempting to reduce it to its natural elements: in our
eagerness to explain impressions, we often lose our hold of the sympathy
that comprehends them.

But he had the best antidote against imaginative dread in the necessity
for getting on with the coffin, and for the next ten minutes his hammer was
ringing so uninterruptedly that other sounds, if there were any, might well
be overpowered. A pause came, however, when he had to take up his ruler,
and now again came the strange rap, and again Gyp howled. Adam was at
the door without the loss of a moment; but again all was still, and the
starlight showed there was nothing but the dew-laden grass in front of the
cottage.

Adam for a moment thought uncomfortably about his father; but of late
years he had never come home at dark hours from Treddleston, and there

---

⁹ peculiar that the] peculiar, the *MS*
¹ when ⟨anybody in the family⟩ some one *MS*
² Adam was not] Adam, you perceive clearly enough, was not *MS*
³ him ⟨a⟩ his *MS*
⁴ Adam ⟨who could look through & through⟩ was at once penetrating & credulous: if *MS*
⁵ bearing] bearings *MS*
⁶ prognostics, and to his dying day he bated his breath a little when he told the story of the
stroke with the willow wand. I tell it as he told it, not attempting to reduce it to its natural
elements: in our eagerness to explain impressions, we often lose our hold of the sympathy that
comprehends them.] prognostics & you see he shuddered at the idea of the stroke with the
willow wand. *MS* prognostics, and you see he shuddered at the idea of the stroke with
the willow wand. *1*

was every reason for believing that he was then sleeping off his drunkenness at the "Waggon Overthrown." Besides, to Adam, the conception of the future was so inseparable from the painful image of his father, that the fear of any fatal accident to him was excluded by the deeply-infixed fear of his continual degradation. The next thought that occurred to him was one that made him slip off his shoes and tread lightly upstairs, to listen at the bedroom doors. But both Seth and his mother were breathing regularly.

[7]Adam came down and set to work again, saying to himself, "I won't open the door again. It's no use staring about to catch sight of a sound. Maybe there's a world about us as we can't see, but th' ear's quicker than the[8] eye, and[9] catches a sound from't now and[1] then. Some people think they get a sight on't too, but they're mostly folks whose[2] eyes are not much use to 'em at anything else. For my part, I think it's better to see when your perpendicular's true, than to see a ghost."

Such thoughts as these are apt to grow stronger and stronger as daylight quenches the candles and the birds begin to sing. By the time the red sunlight shone on the brass nails that formed the initials on the lid of the coffin, any lingering foreboding from the sound of the willow wand was[3] merged in satisfaction that the work was done and the promise redeemed. There was no need to call Seth, for he was already moving overhead, and presently came downstairs.

"Now, lad," said Adam, as Seth made his appearance, "the coffin's done, and we can take it over to Brox'on, and be back again before half after six. I'll take a mouthful o' oat-cake[4], and then we'll be off."

The coffin was soon propped on the tall shoulders of the two brothers, and they were making their way, followed close by Gyp,[5] out of the little wood-yard into the lane at the back of the house. It was but about a mile and a half to Broxton over the opposite slope, and their road wound very pleasantly along lanes and across fields, where the pale woodbines and the dog-roses were scenting the hedgerows, and the birds were twittering and trilling in the tall leafy boughs of oak and elm. It was a strangely-mingled picture—the fresh youth of the summer morning, with its Eden-like peace and loveliness, the stalwart strength of the two brothers in their rusty working clothes, and the long coffin on their shoulders[6]. They paused for the last time before a small farm-house outside the village of Broxton. By six o'clock the task was done, the coffin nailed down, and Adam and Seth were on their way home. They chose a shorter way homeward, which would take them across the fields and the brook in front of the house.

[7] ⟨Again⟩ Adam *MS*   [8] the] th' *MS*   [9] and] an' *MS*   [1] and] an' *MS*
[2] whose] as their *MS*   [3] was ⟨quenched⟩ merged *MS*   [4] oat-cake] cake *MS*
[5] followed close by Gyp,] *added in MS*
[6] shoulders ⟨with the initials glistening on the top⟩. They *MS*

Adam had not mentioned to Seth what had happened in the night, but he still retained sufficient impression from it himself to say—

"Seth, lad, if father isn't come home by the time we've had our breakfast, I think it'll be as well for thee to go over to Treddles'on and look after him, and thee canst get me the brass wire I want. Never mind about losing an hour at thy work; we[7] can make that up. What dost say?"

"I'm willing," said Seth. "But see what clouds have gathered since we set out. I'm thinking we shall have more rain. It'll be a sore time for th' haymaking if the meadows are flooded again. The brook's fine and full now: another day's rain 'ud cover the plank, and we should have to go round by the road."

They were coming across the valley now, and had entered the pasture through which the brook ran.

"Why, what's that sticking against the willow?" continued Seth, beginning to walk faster. Adam's heart rose to his mouth: the vague anxiety about his father was changed into a great dread. He[8] made no answer to Seth, but ran forward, preceded by Gyp, who began to bark uneasily;[9] and in two moments he was at the bridge.

This was what the omen meant, then! And the grey-haired father, of whom he had thought with a sort of hardness a few hours ago, as certain to live to[1] be a thorn in his side, was perhaps even[2] then struggling with that watery death. This was the first thought that flashed through Adam's conscience, before he had time to seize the coat and drag out the tall heavy body. Seth was already by his side, helping him, and when they had it on the bank, the two sons in the first moments knelt and looked with mute awe at the glazed eyes, forgetting that there was need for action—forgetting everything but that their father lay dead before them. Adam was the first to speak.

"I'll run to mother," he said, in a loud whisper. "I'll be back to thee in a minute."[3]

Poor Lisbeth was busy preparing her sons' breakfast, and their porridge was already steaming on the fire. Her kitchen[4] always looked the pink of

[7] work; we] work. We *MS*
[8] mouth: the vague anxiety about his father was changed into a great dread. He] mouth. He *MS*
[9] preceded by Gyp, who began to bark uneasily;] *added in MS*   [1] to] & *MS*
[2] even ⟨at that moment⟩ then *MS*
[3] him, and when they had it on the bank, the two sons in the first moments knelt and looked with mute awe at the glazed eyes, forgetting that there was need for action—forgetting everything but that their father lay dead before them. Adam was the first to speak. ¶ "I'll run to mother," he said, in a loud whisper. "I'll be back to thee in a minute."] him, & the moment they had it on the bank, Adam said, ¶ "I'll run to mother, & be back to thee in a minute." *MS*
[4] kitchen ⟨was⟩ always *MS*

cleanliness, but this morning she was more than usually bent on making her hearth and breakfast-table look comfortable and inviting.

"The lads 'ull be fine an' hungry," she said, half aloud, as she stirred the porridge. "It's a good step to Brox'on, an' it's hungry air o'er the[5] hill—wi' that heavy coffin too. Eh! it's heavier now, wi' poor Bob Tholer in't. Howiver, I've[6] made a drap more porridge[7] nor common this mornin'. The feyther 'ull happen come in arter a bit. Not as he'll[8] ate much porridge. He[9] swallers sixpennorth o' ale[1], an' saves a hap'orth[2] o' porridge—that's his way o' layin' by money, as I've told[3] him many a time, an' am likely to tell him again afore the day's out. Eh! poor mon, he takes[4] it quiet enough; there's no denyin' that."

But now Lisbeth heard the heavy "thud" of a running footstep on the turf, and, turning quickly towards the door, she saw Adam enter, looking so pale and overwhelmed that she screamed aloud and rushed towards him before he had time to speak.

"Hush, mother," Adam said, rather hoarsely, "don't be frightened. Father's tumbled into the water. Belike we may bring him round again. Seth and me are going to carry him in. Get a blanket, and make it hot at the fire."

In reality Adam was convinced that his father was dead, but he knew there was no other way[5] of repressing his mother's impetuous wailing grief than by occupying her with some active task which[6] had hope in it.

He ran back to Seth, and the two sons lifted the sad burthen in heart-stricken silence. The wide-open glazed eyes were grey, like Seth's,[7] and had once looked with mild pride on the[8] boys before whom[9] Thias had lived to hang his head in shame. Seth's[1] chief feeling was awe and distress at this sudden snatching away of his father's soul; but Adam's mind rushed back over the past in a flood of relenting and pity. When death, the great Reconciler, has come, it is never our tenderness that we repent of, but our severity.

---

[5] air o'er the] air ⟨over⟩ o'er th' *MS*   [6] I've] I'n *MS*
[7] porridge] parridge *MS*   [8] he'll] hey'll *MS*
[9] porridge. He] parridge. Hey *MS*   [1] ale] yill *MS*   [2] hap'orth] happorth *MS*
[3] I've told] I'n tould *MS*   [4] takes] taes *MS*   [5] way] *added in MS*
[6] which] that *MS*   [7] Seth's{,} ⟨; the⟩ & had *MS*   [8] the ⟨two⟩ boys *MS*
[9] whom ⟨he had⟩ Thias *MS*
[1] Seth{'s} ⟨had no⟩ {chief} feeling ⟨but sorrow⟩ was *MS*

CHAPTER V.[1]

THE RECTOR.

Before twelve o'clock there had been some heavy storms of rain, and the water lay in deep gutters on the sides of the gravel-walks in the garden of Broxton Parsonage; the great Provence roses had been cruelly tossed by the wind and beaten by the rain, and all the delicate-stemmed border flowers[2] had been dashed down and stained with the wet soil. A melancholy morning—because it was nearly time hay-harvest should begin, and instead of that the meadows were likely to be flooded.[3]

But people who have pleasant homes get indoor enjoyments that they would never think of but for the rain. If it had not been a wet morning, Mr Irwine would not have been in the dining-room playing at chess with his mother, and he loves both his mother and chess quite well enough to pass some cloudy hours very easily by their help. Let me take you into that dining-room, and show you the Rev. Adolphus Irwine, Rector of Broxton, Vicar of Hayslope, and Vicar of Blythe, a pluralist at whom the severest Church-reformer would have found it difficult to look sour. We will enter very softly, and stand still[4] in the open doorway, without awaking the glossy-brown setter who is[5] stretched across the hearth, with her two puppies beside her[6]; or the pug, who is dozing, with his black muzzle aloft, like a sleepy president.

The room is a large and lofty one, with an ample mullioned oriel window at one end; the walls, you see, are new, and not yet painted; but the furniture, though originally of an expensive sort, is old and scanty, and there is no drapery about the window[7]. The crimson cloth over the large dining-table is very threadbare, though it contrasts pleasantly enough with

---

[1] CHAPTER V.] Chapter ⟨4⟩5. *MS*

[2] border flowers] border plants *MS* border-flowers *1*

[3] likely to be flooded.] likely to be flooded. One of the great calamities of the country in those times were the floods; people were known to look on in terror while coach-horses had to swim their way over a bridge; & the precious crops stood out in the fields till the young grain sprouted, or else were floated on the broad waters in the sight of the hungry labourer standing in forced idleness. Thinking of such things, it is doubly pleasant to see the heaps of bright red draining tiles lying on the green grass, & the long channels of dark earth ready dug to receive them. *MS*

[4] still ⟨at the door⟩ in the open doorway *MS*   [5] is ⟨restless⟩ stretched *MS*

[6] with her two puppies beside her] *added in MS*

[7] & there is no drapery about the window] *added in MS*

the dead hue of the plaster on the walls; but on this cloth there is a massive silver waiter with a decanter of water on it, of the same pattern as two larger ones that are propped up on the sideboard with a coat of arms conspicuous in their centre. You suspect at once that the inhabitants of this room have inherited more blood than wealth, and would not be surprised to find that Mr Irwine had a finely-cut nostril and upper lip; but at present we can only see that he has a broad flat back and an abundance of powdered hair, all thrown backward and tied behind with a black ribbon—a bit of conservatism in costume which tells you that he is not a young man. He will perhaps turn round by-and-by, and in the mean time we can look at that stately old lady, his mother, a beautiful aged brunette, whose rich-toned complexion is well set off[8] by the complex wrappings of pure white cambric and lace about her head and neck. She is as erect in her comely embonpoint as a statue of Ceres; and her dark face, with its delicate aquiline nose, firm proud mouth, and small intense black eye, is so keen and sarcastic in its expression that you instinctively substitute a pack of cards for the chess-men, and imagine her telling your fortune. The small brown hand with which she is lifting her queen is laden with pearls, diamonds, and turquoises; and a large black veil is very carefully[9] adjusted over the crown of her cap, and falls in sharp contrast on the white folds about her neck. It must take a long time to dress that old lady in the morning! But it seems a law of nature that she should be drest so: she is clearly one of those children of royalty who have never doubted their right divine, and never met with any one so absurd as to question it.

"There, Dauphin, tell me what that is!" says this magnificent old lady, as she deposits her queen very quietly and folds her arms. "I should be sorry to utter a word disagreeable to your feelings."

"Ah! you witch-mother, you sorceress! How is a Christian man to win a game of you? I should have sprinkled the board with holy water before we began. You've not won that game by fair means, now, so don't pretend it."

"Yes, yes, that's what the beaten have always said of great conquerors. But see, there's the sunshine falling on the board, to show you more clearly what a foolish move you made with that pawn. Come, shall I give you another chance?"

"No, mother,[1] I shall leave you to your own conscience, now it's clearing up. We must go and plash up the mud a little, mustn't we, Juno?" This was addressed to the brown setter, who had jumped up at the sound of the voices and laid her nose in an insinuating way on her master's leg. "But I must go upstairs first and see[2] Anne. I was called away to Tholer's funeral just when I was going before."

---

[8] is well set off] added in MS   [9] carefully ⟨placed⟩ adjusted MS
[1] "No, mother,] "No, you unnatural mother, MS   [2] see ⟨poor⟩ Anne MS

"It's of no use, child; she can't speak to you.[3] Kate says she has one of her worst headaches this morning."

"O she likes me to go and see her just the same; she's never too ill to[4] care about that.[5]"

If you know how much of human speech is mere purposeless impulse or[6] habit, you will not wonder when I tell you that this identical objection had been made, and had received the same kind of answer, many hundred times in the course of the[7] fifteen years that Mr Irwine's[8] sister Anne had been an invalid. Splendid old ladies, who take a long time to dress in the morning, have often slight sympathy with sickly daughters.

But while Mr Irwine was still seated, leaning back in his chair and stroking Juno's head, the servant came to the door and said, "If you please, sir,[9] Joshua Rann wishes to speak with you, if you're at liberty."

"Let him be shown in here," said Mrs Irwine, taking up her knitting. "I always like to hear what Mr Rann has got to say. His shoes will be dirty, but see that he wipes them, Carroll[1]."

In two minutes Mr Rann appeared at the door with very deferential bows, which, however, were far from conciliating Pug, who gave a sharp bark, and ran across the room to reconnoitre the stranger's legs; while the two puppies, regarding Mr Rann's prominent calf and ribbed worsted stockings from a more sensuous point of view, plunged and growled over them in great enjoyment. Meantime, Mr Irwine turned round his chair and said:

"Well, Joshua, anything the matter at Hayslope, that you've come over this damp morning? Sit down, sit down. Never mind the dogs; give them a friendly kick. Here, Pug, you rascal!"

It is very pleasant to see some men turn round; pleasant as a sudden rush of warm air in winter, or the flash of fire-light in the chill dusk. Mr Irwine was one of those men. He bore the same sort of resemblance to his mother that our loving memory of a friend's face often bears to the face itself: the lines were all more generous, the smile brighter, the expression heartier. If the outline had been less finely cut, his face might have been called jolly; but that was not the right word for its mixture of bonhommie and distinction.

"Thank your reverence," answered Mr Rann, endeavouring to look[2] unconcerned about his legs, but shaking them alternately to keep off the puppies; "I'll stand, if you please, as more becoming. I hope I see you and Mrs Irwine well, an' Miss Irwine—an' Miss Anne, I hope's as well as usual[3]."

---

[3] you. ⟨Carrol⟩ Kate *MS*   [4] to ⟨know⟩ care about *MS*
[5] that. ⟨I take her hand & kiss her.⟩ ⟨It matters.⟩" *MS*
[6] or] or *MS 1* ⟨of⟩ or *8*   [7] the ⟨twenty⟩ fifteen *MS*
[8] Mr Irwine's ⟨younger⟩ sister *MS*
[9] Sir, ⟨Mr. Rann, the parish clerk⟩ Joshua *MS*
[1] Carroll] Carrol *MS 1*   [2] look ⟨as⟩ unconcerned *MS*   [3] usual] usal *MS*

"Yes, Joshua, thank you. You see how blooming my mother looks. She beats us younger people hollow. But what's the matter?"

"Why, sir, I had to come to Brox'on to deliver some work, and I thought it but right to call and let you know the goins-on as there's been i' the village, such as I hanna seen[4] i' my time, and I've lived in it man and boy sixty year come St Thomas, and collected th' Easter dues for Mr Blick before your reverence come into the parish, and been at the ringin' o' every[5] bell, and the diggin' o' every[6] grave, and sung i' the quire long afore Bartle Massey come from nobody knows where, wi' his counter-singin' and fine anthems, as puts everybody[7] out but himself[8]—one takin'[9] it up after another like sheep a-bleatin' i' th' fould[1]. I know what belongs to bein' a parish clerk, and I know as I should be wantin' i' respect to your reverence, an' church, an' king, if I was t' allow such goins-on wi'out speakin'. I was took by surprise, an' knowed nothin' on it beforehand, an' I was so flustered[2], I was clean as if I'd lost my tools. I hanna slep more nor four hour this night as is past an' gone; an' then it was nothin' but nightmare, as tired me worse nor wakin'."

"Why, what in the world is the matter, Joshua? Have the thieves been at the church lead again?"

"Thieves! no, sir,—an' yet[3], as I may say, it *is* thieves, an' a-thievin' the church, too. It's the Methodisses as[4] is like to get th' upper hand i' th' parish, if your reverence an' his honour, Squire Donnithorne, doesna think well to say the word an' forbid it. Not as I'm a-dictatin' to you, sir; I'm not forgettin' myself so far as to be wise above my betters. Howiver, whether I'm wise or no, that's neither here nor there, but what I've got to say I say—as the young Methodis woman, as is at Mester Poyser's, was a-preachin' an' a-prayin' on the Green last night, as sure as I'm a-stannin' afore your reverence now."

"Preaching on the Green!" said Mr Irwine, looking surprised but quite serene. "What, that pale pretty young woman I've seen at Poyser's? I saw she was a Methodist, or Quaker, or something of that sort, by her dress, but I didn't know she was a preacher."

"It's a true word as I say, sir," rejoined Mr Rann, compressing his mouth into a semicircular form, and pausing long enough to indicate three notes of exclamation. "She preached on the Green last night; an'[5] she's laid hold o'[6] Chad's Bess, as the girl's[7] been i' fits welly iver sin'[8]."

"Well, Bessy Cranage is a hearty-looking lass; I dare say she'll come round again, Joshua. Did anybody else go into fits?"

"No, sir, I canna say as they did. But there's no knowin' what'll come, if we're t' have[9] such preachins as that agoin' on ivery week—there'll be no

---

[4] seen] saen *MS*   [5] every] ivery *MS*   [6] every] ivery *MS*
[7] everybody] iverybody *MS*   [8] himself] hisself *MS*   [9] takin'] teckin *MS*
[1] fould] *MS 1* fold *8*   [2] flustered] fluthered *MS*   [3] yet] yit *MS*
[4] as ⟨are⟩ is *MS*   [5] night; an'] night. An' *MS*   [6] o'] *MS 1* of *8*
[7] girl's] gell's *MS*   [8] iver ⟨since⟩ sin' *MS*   [9] have] hev *MS*

livin' i' th' village. For them Methodisses make folks believe as if they take a mug o' drink extry, an' make theirselves a bit comfortable, they'll have[1] to go to hell for't as sure as they're born. I'm not a tipplin' man nor a drunkard—nobody can say it on me—but I like a extry quart at Easter or Christmas time, as is nat'ral when we're goin' the rounds a-singin', an' folks offer't you for nothin'; or when I'm a-collectin' the[2] dues; an' I like a pint wi' my pipe, an' a neighbourly chat at Mester Casson's now an' then, for I was brought up i' the[3] Church, thank God, an' ha' been a parish clerk this two-an'-thirty year: I should know what the church religion is."

"Well, what's your advice, Joshua? What do you think should be done?"

"Well, your reverence, I'm not for[4] takin' any measures again' the young woman. She's[5] well enough if she'd let alone preachin'; an'[6] I hear as she's a-goin' away back to her own country soon. She's Mrs[7] Poyser's own niece, an' I donna wish to say what's anyways disrespectful o' th' family at th' Hall Farm, as I've measured for shoes[8], little an' big, welly iver sin' I've been a shoemaker. But there's that Will Maskery, sir, as is the rampageousest Methodis as can be, an' I make no doubt it was him as stirred up th' young woman to preach last night, an' he'll be a-bringin' other folks to preach from Treddles'on, if his comb[9] isn't cut a bit; an' I think as he should be let know as he isna t' have[1] the makin' an' mendin' o' church carts an' implemens, let alone stayin' i' that house an' yard as is Squire Donnithorne's."

"Well, but you say[2] yourself, Joshua, that you never knew any one come to preach on the Green before; why should you think they'll come again? The Methodists don't come to preach in little villages like Hayslope, where there's only a handful of labourers, too tired to listen to them. They might almost as well go and preach on the Binton Hills. Will Maskery is no preacher himself, I think."

"Nay, sir, he's no gift at stringin' the words together wi'out book; he'd be stuck fast like a cow i' wet clay. But he's got tongue enough to speak disrespectful about's neebors, for he said as I was a blind Pharisee;—a-usin' the Bible i' that way to find nicknames for folks as are his elders an' betters!—and[3] what's worse, he's been heared[4] to say very unbecomin' words about your reverence; for I could bring them as 'ud swear as he called you a 'dumb dog,' an' a 'idle shepherd.' You'll forgi'e[5] me for sayin' such things over again."

"Better not, better not, Joshua. Let evil words die as soon as they're spoken. Will Maskery might be a great deal worse fellow than he is. He used

---

[1] comfortable, they'll have] comfortable, they'⟨er⟩{ll} ⟨goin post to⟩ hev *MS*
[2] the ⟨Easter⟩ dues *MS*   [3] the] th' *MS*   [4] for ⟨techin'⟩ takin' *MS*
[5] woman. She's] woman—she's *MS*
[6] preachin'; an'] preachin'. An' *MS* preaching,' an' *1*   [7] Mrs] *MS* Mr *1 8*
[8] measured for shoes, little] misured {for} shoes ⟨for⟩, little *MS*
[9] comb ⟨eent⟩ isn't *MS*   [1] have] hev *MS*   [2] say] *added in MS*
[3] betters!—and] betters! An' *MS*   [4] heared] *MS* heard *1 8*   [5] forgi'e] forgi' *MS*

to be a wild drunken rascal, neglecting his work and beating his wife, they told me; now he's thrifty and decent, and he and his wife look comfortable together. If you can bring me any proof that he interferes with his neighbours, and creates any disturbance, I shall think it my duty as a clergyman and a magistrate to interfere. But it wouldn't become wise people, like you and me, to be making a fuss about trifles, as if we thought the Church was in danger because Will Maskery lets his tongue wag rather foolishly, or a young woman talks in a serious way to a handful of people on the Green. We must 'live and let live,' Joshua, in religion as well as in other things. You go on doing your duty, as parish clerk and sexton, as well as you've always done it, and making those capital thick boots for your neighbours, and things won't go far wrong in Hayslope, depend upon it."

"Your reverence is very good to say so; an' I'm sensable as, you not livin' i' the[6] parish, there's more upo' my shoulders."

"To be sure; and you must mind and not lower the Church in people's eyes by seeming to be frightened about it for a little thing, Joshua. I shall trust to your good sense, now, to take no notice at all of what Will Maskery says, either about you or me. You and your neighbours can go on taking your pot of beer soberly,[7] when you've done your day's work, like good churchmen; and if Will Maskery doesn't like to join you, but to go to a prayer-meeting at Treddleston instead, let him; that's no business of yours, so long as he doesn't hinder you from doing what you like. And as to people saying a few idle words about us, we must not mind that, any more than the old church-steeple minds the rooks cawing about it. Will Maskery comes to church every Sunday afternoon, and does his wheelwright's business steadily in the weekdays, and as long as he does that he must be let alone."

"Ah, sir, but when he comes to church, he sits an' shakes his head, an' looks as sour an' as coxy when we're a-singin', as I should like to fetch him a rap across the jowl—God forgi'e[8] me—an' Mrs Irwine, an' your reverence,[9] too, for speakin' so afore you. An' he said as our Christmas singin' was no better nor the cracklin' o' thorns under a pot."

"Well, he's got a bad ear for music, Joshua. When people have wooden heads, you know, it can't be helped. He won't bring the other people in Hayslope round to his opinion, while you go on singing as well as you do."

"Yes, sir, but it turns a man's stomach t' hear the Scripture[1] misused i' that way. I know as much o' the words o' the Bible as he does, an' could say the Psalms right through i' my sleep if you was to pinch me; but I know better nor to take 'em to say my own say wi'. I might as well take the Sacriment-cup home and use it at meals."

"That's a very sensible remark of yours, Joshua; but, as I said before—"

[6] the] th' *MS* [7] soberly,] *added in MS* [8] forgi'e] forgi' *MS*
[9] an' your reverence,] *added in MS* [1] Scripture] Scriptur *MS*

While Mr Irwine was speaking, the sound of a booted step[2], and the clink of a spur, were heard on the stone floor of the entrance-hall, and Joshua Rann moved hastily aside from the doorway to make room for some one who paused there, and said, in a ringing tenor voice,

"Godson Arthur;—may he come in?"

"Come in, come in, godson!" Mrs Irwine answered, in the deep half-masculine tone which belongs to the vigorous old woman, and there entered a young gentleman in a riding-dress, with his right arm in a sling; whereupon followed that pleasant confusion of laughing interjections, and hand-shakings, and "How are you's?" mingled with joyous short barks and wagging of tails on the part of the canine members of the family, which tells that the visitor is on the best terms with the visited. The young gentleman was[3] Arthur Donnithorne, known in Hayslope, variously, as "the young squire," "the heir," and "the captain." He was only a captain in the Loamshire Militia; but to the Hayslope tenants he was more intensely a captain than all the young gentlemen of the same rank in[4] his Majesty's regulars—he outshone them as the planet Jupiter outshines the Milky Way. If you want to know more particularly how he looked, call to your remembrance some tawny-whiskered, brown-locked, clear-complexioned young Englishman whom you have met with in a foreign town, and been proud of as a fellow-countryman—well-washed, high-bred, white-handed, yet looking as if he could deliver well from the left shoulder, and floor his man: I[5] will not be so much of a tailor as to trouble your imagination with the difference of costume, and insist on the striped waistcoat, long-tailed coat, and low top-boots[6].

Turning round to take a chair, Captain Donnithorne said, "But don't let me interrupt Joshua's business—he has something to say."

"Humbly begging your honour's pardon," said Joshua, bowing low, "there was one thing I had to say to his reverence as other things had drove out o' my head."

"Out with it, Joshua, quickly!" said Mr Irwine.

"Belike, sir, you havena heared as Thias Bede's dead—drownded this morning, or more like[7] overnight, i' the Willow Brook, again' the bridge right i' front o' the house."

"Ah!" exclaimed both the gentlemen at once, as if they were a good deal interested in the information.

"An' Seth Bede's been to me this morning to say he wished me to tell your reverence as his brother Adam begged of you particular t' allow his father's grave to be dug by the White Thorn, because his mother's set her

---

[2] step ⟨was⟩ & *MS*   [3] was ⟨M^r.⟩ Arthur *MS*   [4] in ⟨her⟩ His *MS*
[5] man: I] man. I *MS*
[6] low top-boots] *MS* low-top boots *1* low⟨-⟩top{-}boots *8*
[7] like] liker *MS*

heart on it, on account of a dream as she had; an'[8] they'd ha' come theirselves to ask you, but they've so much to see after with the crowner, an' that; an' their mother's took on so, an' wants 'em to make sure o' the spot for fear somebody else should take it. An' if your reverence sees well and good, I'll send my boy to tell 'em as soon as I get home; an' that's why I make bold to trouble you wi' it, his honour being present."

"To be sure, Joshua, to be sure, they shall have it. I'll ride round to Adam myself, and see him. Send your boy, however, to say they shall have the grave, lest anything should happen to detain me. And now, good morning, Joshua; go[9] into the kitchen and have some ale."

"Poor old Thias!" said Mr Irwine, when Joshua was gone. "I'm afraid the drink helped the brook to drown him. I should have been glad for the load to have been taken off my friend Adam's shoulders in a less painful way. That fine fellow has been propping up his father from ruin for the last five or six years."

"He's a regular trump, is Adam," said Captain Donnithorne. "When I was a little fellow, and Adam was a strapping lad of fifteen, and taught me carpentering, I used to think if ever I was a rich sultan, I would make Adam my grand-vizier. And I believe now, he would bear the exaltation as well as any poor wise man in an Eastern story. If ever I live to be a large-acred man,[1] instead of a poor devil[2] with a mortgaged allowance of pocket-money, I'll have Adam for my right-hand. He shall manage my woods for me, for he seems to have a better notion of those things than any man I ever met with; and I know he would make twice the money of them that my grandfather does, with that miserable old Satchell to manage, who understands no more about timber than an old carp. I've mentioned the subject to my grandfather once or twice, but for some reason or other he has a dislike to Adam, and *I* can do nothing. But come, your reverence, are you for a ride with me? It's splendid out of doors now. We can go to Adam's together, if you like; but I want to call at the Hall Farm on my way, to look at the whelps Poyser is keeping for me."

"You must stay and have lunch first, Arthur," said Mrs Irwine. "It's nearly two. Carroll[3] will bring it in directly."

"I want to go to the Hall Farm too," said Mr Irwine, "to have another look at the little Methodist who is staying there. Joshua tells me she was preaching on the Green last night."

"O, by Jove!" said Captain Donnithorne, laughing. "Why, she looks as quiet as a mouse. There's something rather striking about her, though. I

---

[8] Thorn, because his mother's set her heart on it, on account of a dream as she had; an'] Thorn, ⟨i' the churchyard⟩ {because his mother's set her heart on it, upo' 'count of a dream as she had.} An' *MS*

[9] Joshua; go] Joshua. Go *MS*   [1] man,] *MS* 1 man *8*   [2] devil] *MS* devil, *1 8*

[3] Carroll] Carrol *MS 1*

positively felt quite bashful the first time I saw her: she was sitting stooping over her sewing in the sunshine outside the house, when I rode up and called out, without noticing that she was a stranger, 'Is Martin Poyser at home?' I declare, when she got up and looked at me, and just said, 'He's in the house, I believe;[4] I'll go and call him,' I felt quite ashamed of having spoken so abruptly to her. She looked like St Catherine in a quaker dress. It's a type of face one rarely sees among our common people."

"I should like to see the young woman, Dauphin," said Mrs Irwine. "Make her come here on some pretext or other."

"I don't know how I can manage that, mother[5]; it will hardly do for me to patronize a Methodist preacher, even if she would consent to be patronized by an idle shepherd, as Will Maskery calls me. You should have come in a little sooner, Arthur, to hear Joshua's denunciation of his neighbour Will Maskery. The old fellow wants me to excommunicate the wheelwright, and then deliver him over to the civil arm,[6] that is to say, to your grandfather,[7] to be turned out of house and yard. If I chose to interfere in this business, now, I might get up as pretty a story of hatred and persecution as the Methodists need desire to publish in the next number of their magazine. It wouldn't take me much trouble to persuade Chad Cranage and half-a-dozen other bull-headed fellows, that they would be doing an acceptable service to the Church by hunting Will Maskery out of the village with rope-ends and pitchforks; and[8] then, when I had furnished them with half a sovereign to get gloriously drunk after their exertions, I should have put the climax to as pretty a farce as any of my brother clergy have set going in their parishes for the last thirty years."

"It is really insolent of the man, though, to call you an 'idle shepherd,' and a 'dumb dog,' " said Mrs Irwine: "I should be inclined to check him a little there. You are[9] too easy-tempered, Dauphin."

"Why, mother, you don't think it would be a good way of sustaining my dignity to set about vindicating myself from the aspersions of Will Maskery? Besides, I'm not so sure that they *are* aspersions. I *am* a lazy fellow, and get terribly heavy in my saddle; not to mention that I'm always spending more than I can afford in bricks and mortar, so that I get savage at a lame beggar when he asks me for sixpence. Those poor lean cobblers, who think they can help to regenerate mankind by setting out to preach in the morning twilight before they begin their day's work, may well have a poor opinion of me. But come, let us have our luncheon. Isn't Kate coming to lunch?"

"Miss Irwine told Bridget to take her lunch upstairs," said Carroll; "she[1] can't leave Miss Anne."

   [4] believe;] *MS 1* believe: *8*   [5] mother] queen-mother *MS*
   [6] arm,] *MS* arm,—*1 8*   [7] grandfather,] *MS* grandfather,—*1 8*
   [8] pitchforks; and] pitch-forks. And *MS*   [9] You are] You're *MS 1*
   [1] Carroll; "she] Carrol. "She *MS* Carrol; "she *1*

"O, very well. Tell Bridget to say I'll go up and see Miss Anne presently. You can use your right arm quite well, now, Arthur," Mr Irwine continued, observing that Captain Donnithorne had taken his arm out of the sling.

"Yes, pretty well; but Godwin insists on my keeping it up constantly for some time to come. I hope I shall be able to get away to the regiment, though, in the beginning of August. It's a desperately dull business being shut up at the Chase in the summer months, when one can neither hunt nor shoot, so as to make oneself pleasantly sleepy in the evening. However, we are to astonish the echoes on the 30th of July. My grandfather has given me *carte blanche* for once, and I promise you the entertainment shall be worthy of the occasion. The world will not see the grand epoch of my majority twice. I think I shall have a lofty throne for you, godmamma, or rather two, one on the lawn and another in the ball-room, that you may sit and look down upon us like an Olympian goddess."

"I mean to bring out my best brocade, that I wore at your christening twenty years ago," said Mrs Irwine. "Ah, I think I shall see your poor mother flitting about in her white dress, which looked to me almost like a shroud that very day; and[2] it *was* her shroud only three months after; and your little cap and christening dress were buried with her too. She had set her heart on that, sweet soul! Thank God you take after your mother's family, Arthur.[3] If you had been a puny, wiry, yellow baby, I wouldn't have stood godmother to you. I[4] should have been sure you would[5] turn out a Donnithorne. But you were such a broad-faced, broad-chested, loud-screaming rascal, I knew you were every inch of you a Tradgett."

"But you might have been a little too hasty there, mother," said Mr Irwine, smiling. "Don't you remember how it was with Juno's last pups? One of them was the very image of its mother, but it had two or three of its father's tricks notwithstanding. Nature is clever enough to cheat even you, mother."

"Nonsense, child! Nature never makes a ferret in the shape of a mastiff. You'll never persuade me that I can't tell what men are by their outsides. If I don't like a man's looks, depend upon it I shall never like *him*. I don't want to know people that look ugly and disagreeable, any more than I want to taste dishes that look disagreeable. If they make me shudder at the first glance, I say, take them away. An ugly, piggish, or fishy eye, now, makes me feel quite ill; it's like a bad smell."

"Talking of eyes," said Captain Donnithorne, "that reminds me, that I've got a book I meant to bring you, godmamma. It came down in a parcel from London the other day. I know you[6] are fond of queer, wizard-like

[2] day; and] day. And *MS*   [3] Arthur.] Arthur! *MS 1*
[4] to you. I] to you; ⟨but you⟩ I *MS*   [5] would ⟨have been⟩ turn out *MS*
[6] you ⟨like⟩ are fond of *MS*

stories. It's a volume of poems, 'Lyrical Ballads:' most of them seem to be twaddling stuff[7]; but the first is in a different style—'The Ancient Mariner' is the title. I can hardly make head or tail of it as a story, but it's a strange, striking thing. I'll send it over to you; and there are some other books that *you* may like to see, Irwine—pamphlets about Antinomianism and Evangelicalism, whatever they may be. I can't think what the fellow means by sending such things to me. I've written to him, to desire that from henceforth he will send me no book or pamphlet on anything that ends in *ism*."

"Well, I don't know that I'm very fond of *isms* myself;[8] but I may as well look at the pamphlets; they let one see what is going on. I've a little matter to attend to, Arthur," continued Mr Irwine, rising to leave the room[9], "and then I shall be ready to set out with you."

The little matter that Mr Irwine had to attend to took him up the old stone staircase (part of the house was very old), and made him pause before a door at which he knocked gently. "Come in," said a woman's voice, and he entered a room so darkened by blinds and curtains that Miss Kate, the thin middle-aged lady standing by the bedside, would not have had light enough for any other sort of work than the knitting which lay on the little table near her. But at present she was doing what required only the dimmest light—sponging the[1] aching head that lay on the pillow with fresh vinegar. It was a small face, that of the poor sufferer; perhaps it had once been pretty, but now it was worn and sallow. Miss Kate came towards her brother and whispered, "Don't speak to her; she can't bear to be spoken to to-day." Anne's eyes were closed, and her brow contracted as if from intense pain. Mr Irwine went to the bedside, and took up one of the delicate hands and kissed it; a slight pressure from the small fingers told him that it was worth while to have come upstairs for the sake of doing that. He lingered a moment, looking at her, and then turned away and left the room, treading very gently—he had taken off his boots and put on slippers before he came upstairs. Whoever remembers how many things he has declined to do even for himself, rather than have the trouble of putting on or taking off his boots, will not think this last detail insignificant.

And Mr Irwine's sisters, as any person of family within ten miles of Broxton could have testified, were such stupid uninteresting women! It was quite a pity handsome, clever Mrs Irwine should have had such common-place daughters. That fine old lady herself was worth driving ten miles to see, any day; her beauty, her well-preserved faculties, and her old-fashioned dignity, made her a[2] graceful subject for conversation in turn

[7] be twaddling stuff] be precious twaddling stuff *MS*
[8] myself; ⟨" said Mr. Irwine, rising. "But⟩ {but} I *MS*
[9] to leave the room] *added in MS*   [1] the ⟨poor worn fore⟩ {aching} head *MS*
[2] her a] her quite a *MS* 1 her ⟨quite⟩ a *8*

with the King's health, the sweet new patterns in cotton dresses, the news from Egypt, and[3] Lord Dacey's law-suit, which was fretting poor Lady Dacey to death. But no one ever thought of mentioning the Miss Irwines, except the poor people in Broxton village, who regarded them as deep in the science of medicine, and spoke of them vaguely as "the gentlefolks." If any one had asked old Job Dummilow who gave him his flannel jacket, he would have answered, "the gentlefolks, last winter;" and widow Steene dwelt much on the virtues of the "stuff" the gentlefolks gave her for her cough. Under this name, too, they were used with great effect as a means of taming refractory children, so that at the sight of poor Miss Anne's sallow face, several small urchins had a terrified sense that she was cognizant of all their worst misdemeanours, and knew the precise number of stones with which they had intended to hit farmer Britton's ducks. But for all who saw them through a less mythical medium, the Miss Irwines were[4] quite superfluous existences; inartistic figures crowding the canvas of life without adequate effect. Miss Anne, indeed, if her chronic headaches could have been accounted for by a pathetic story of disappointed love, might have had some romantic interest attached to her; but no such story had either been known or invented concerning her, and the general impression was[5] quite in accordance with the fact that[6] both the sisters were old maids for the prosaic reason, that they had never received an eligible offer.

Nevertheless, to speak paradoxically, the existence of insignificant people has very important consequences in the world. It can be shown to affect the price of bread and the rate of wages, to call forth many evil tempers[7] from the selfish, and many heroisms[8] from the sympathetic, and, in other ways, to play no small part in the tragedy of life. And if that handsome, generous-blooded clergyman, the Rev. Adolphus Irwine, had not had these two hopelessly-maiden sisters, his[9] lot would have been shaped quite differently: he would very likely have taken a comely wife in his youth, and now, when his hair was getting grey under the powder, would have had tall sons and blooming daughters—such possessions, in short, as men[1] commonly think will repay them for all the labour they take under the sun. As it was—having with all his three livings no more than seven hundred a year, and seeing no way of keeping his splendid mother and his sickly sister, not to reckon a second sister, who was usually spoken of without any adjective, in such lady-like ease as became their birth and habits, and at the same time providing for a family of his own—he remained, you see, at the age of eight-and-forty, a bachelor, not making any merit of that renunciation, but saying laughingly, if any one alluded to it, that he made

---

[3] & ⟨poor⟩ Lord *MS*   [4] were ⟨regarded⟩ quite *MS*   [5] was ⟨in⟩ quite *MS*
[6] fact that {both}⟨Miss⟩ sisters *MS*   [7] tempers ⟨in⟩ from *MS*
[8] heroisms ⟨in⟩ from *MS*   [9] his ⟨life⟩ lot *MS*
[1] men ⟨usually⟩ commonly *MS*

it an excuse for many indulgences which a wife would never have allowed him. And perhaps he was the only person in the world who did not think his sisters uninteresting and superfluous; for his was one of those large-hearted, sweet-blooded natures that never know a narrow or a grudging thought; epicurean, if you will, with no enthusiasm, no self-scourging sense of duty; but yet, as you have seen, of a sufficiently subtle moral fibre to have an unwearying tenderness for obscure and monotonous suffering. It was his large-hearted indulgence that made him ignore his mother's hardness towards her daughters, which was the more striking from its contrast with her doting fondness towards himself: he held it no virtue to frown at irremediable faults.

See the difference between the impression a man makes on you when you walk by his side in familiar talk, or look at him in his home, and the figure he makes when seen from a lofty historical level, or even in the eyes of a critical neighbour who thinks of him an an embodied system or opinion rather than as a man. Mr Roe, the "travelling preacher" stationed at Treddleston, had included Mr Irwine in a general statement concerning the Church clergy in the surrounding district, whom he described as men given up to the lusts of the flesh and the pride of life; hunting and shooting, and adorning their own houses; asking what shall we eat, and what shall we drink, and wherewithal shall we be clothed?—careless of dispensing the bread of life to their flocks, preaching at best but a carnal and soul-benumbing morality, and trafficking in the souls of men by receiving money for discharging[2] the pastoral office in parishes where they did not so much as look on the faces of the people more than once a year. The ecclesiastical historian, too, looking into parliamentary reports of that period, finds honourable members zealous for the Church, and untainted with any sympathy for the "tribe of canting Methodists," making statements scarcely less melancholy than that of Mr Roe. And it[3] is impossible for me to say that Mr Irwine was altogether belied by the generic classification assigned him. He really had no very lofty aims, no theological enthusiasm: if I were closely questioned, I should be obliged to confess that he felt no serious alarms about the souls of his parishioners, and would have thought it a mere loss of time to talk in a doctrinal and awakening manner to old "Feyther Taft," or even to Chad Cranage the blacksmith. If he had been in the habit of speaking theoretic-ally, he would perhaps have said that the only healthy form religion could take in such minds was that of certain dim but strong emotions, suffusing themselves as a hallowing influence over the family affections and neigh-bourly duties. He thought the custom of baptism more important than its doctrine, and that the religious benefits the peasant drew from the church where his fathers worshipped and the sacred piece of turf where they lay buried, were but slightly dependent on a clear understanding of the

---

² discharging] *added in MS*   ³ it ⟨would be⟩ is *MS*

Liturgy or the sermon. Clearly, the Rector was not what is called in these days an "earnest" man: he was fonder of church history than of divinity, and had much more insight into men's characters than interest in their opinions; he was neither laborious, nor obviously self-denying, nor very copious in alms-giving, and his theology, you perceive, was lax. His[4] mental palate, indeed, was rather pagan, and found a savouriness in a quotation from Sophocles or Theocritus that was quite absent from any text in Isaiah or Amos. But if you feed your young setter[5] on raw flesh, how can you wonder at its retaining a relish for uncooked partridge in after life? and[6] Mr Irwine's recollections of young enthusiasm and ambition were all associated with poetry and ethics that lay aloof from the Bible.

On the other hand, I must plead, for I have an affectionate partiality towards the Rector's memory, that he was not vindictive—and some philanthropists have been so; that he was not intolerant—and there is a rumour that some zealous theologians have not been altogether free from that blemish; that although he would probably have declined to give his body to be burned in any public cause, and was far from bestowing all his goods to feed the poor, he had that charity which has sometimes been lacking to very illustrious virtue—he was tender to other men's failings, and unwilling to impute evil. He was one of those men, and they are not the commonest, of whom we can know the best only by following them away from the market-place, the platform, and the pulpit,[7] entering with them into their own homes, hearing the voice with which they speak to the young and aged about their own hearthstone, and witnessing their thoughtful care for the everyday wants of everyday companions, who take all their kindness as a matter of course, and not as a subject for panegyric.

Such men, happily, have lived in times when great abuses flourished, and have sometimes even been the living representatives of the abuses. That is a thought which might comfort us a little under the opposite fact— that it is better sometimes *not* to follow great reformers of abuses beyond the threshold of their homes.

But whatever you may think of Mr Irwine now, if you had met him that June afternoon riding on his grey cob, with his dogs running beside him— portly, upright, manly, with a good-natured smile on his finely-turned lips as he talked to his dashing young companion on the bay mare, you must have felt that, however ill he harmonized with sound theories of the clerical office, he somehow harmonized extremely well with that peaceful land-scape.

See them in the bright sunlight, interrupted every now and then by rolling masses of cloud,[8] ascending the slope from the Broxton side,

---

[4] His ⟨literary⟩ mental *MS*
[5] setter] carnivorous animal *MS*
[6] life? and] life? And *MS*
[7] pulpit, ⟨&⟩ entering *MS*
[8] cloud,] *MS 1* cloud *8*

where the tall gables and elms of the Rectory predominate over the tiny white-washed church. They will soon be in the parish of Hayslope; the grey church-tower and village roofs lie before them to the left, and farther on, to the right, they can just see the chimneys of the Hall Farm.

CHAPTER VI.[1]

THE HALL FARM.

Evidently that gate is never opened: for the long grass and the great hemlocks grow close against it; and if it were opened, it is so rusty, that the force necessary to turn it on its hinges would be likely to pull down the square stone-built pillars, to the detriment of the two stone lionesses which grin with a doubtful carnivorous affability above a coat of arms, surmounting each of the pillars. It would be easy enough, by the aid of the nicks in the stone pillars, to climb over the brick wall with its smooth stone coping; but by putting our eyes close to the rusty bars of the gate, we can see the house well enough, and all but the very corners of the grassy enclosure.

It is a very fine old place, of red brick, softened by a pale powdery lichen, which has dispersed itself with happy irregularity, so as to bring the red brick into terms of friendly companionship with the limestone ornaments surrounding the three gables, the windows, and the door-place. But the windows are patched with wooden panes, and the door, I think, is like the gate—it is never opened: how it would groan and grate against the stone floor if it were! For it is a solid, heavy, handsome door, and must once have been in the habit of shutting with a sonorous bang behind a liveried lackey, who had just seen his master and mistress off the grounds in a carriage and pair.

But at present one might fancy the house in the early stage of a chancery suit, and that the fruit from that grand double row of walnut trees on the[2] right hand of the enclosure would fall and rot among the grass, if it were not that we heard the booming bark of dogs echoing from great buildings at the back. And now the half-weaned calves that have been sheltering themselves[3] in a gorse-built hovel against the[4] left-hand wall, come out and set up a silly answer to that terrible bark, doubtless supposing that it has reference to buckets of milk.

Yes, the house must be inhabited, and we will see by whom; for imagination is a licensed trespasser: it has no fear of dogs, but may climb over walls and peep in at windows with impunity. Put your face to one of the glass panes in the right-hand window: what do you see? A large open fireplace, with rusty dogs in it, and a bare-boarded floor; at the far end, fleeces of wool stacked up; in the middle of the floor, some empty corn-bags. That is the

[1] CHAPTER VI.] Chapter ⟨5⟩6. *MS*   [2] the ⟨left⟩ right *MS*
[3] themselves ⟨against the⟩ in *MS*   [4] the ⟨right⟩ left *MS*

furniture of the dining-room. And what through the left-hand window? Several clothes-horses, a pillion, a spinning-wheel, and an old box wide open, and stuffed full of coloured rags. At the edge of this box there lies a great wooden doll, which, so far as mutilation is concerned, bears a strong resemblance to the finest Greek sculpture, and especially in the total loss of its nose. Near it there is a little chair, and the butt-end of a boy's leather long-lashed whip.

The history of the house is plain now. It was once the residence of a country squire, whose family, probably dwindling down to mere spinster-hood, got merged in the more territorial name of Donnithorne. It[5] was once the Hall; it is now the Hall Farm. Like the life in some coast-town that was once a watering-place, and is now a port, where the genteel streets are silent and grass-grown, and the docks and warehouses busy and resonant, the life at the Hall has changed its focus, and no longer radiates from the parlour, but from the kitchen and the farmyard.

Plenty of life there! though this is the drowsiest time of the year, just before hay-harvest; and it is[6] the drowsiest time of the day too, for it is close upon three by the sun, and it is half past three by Mrs Poyser's handsome eight-day clock. But there is always a stronger sense of life when the sun is brilliant after rain; and now he is pouring down his beams, and making sparkles among the wet straw, and lighting up every patch of vivid green moss on the red tiles of the cow-shed, and turning even the muddy water that is hurrying along the channel to the drain into a mirror for the yellow-billed ducks, who are seizing the opportunity of getting a drink with as much body in it as possible. There is quite a concert of noises: the great bull-dog, chained against the stables, is thrown into furious exasperation by the unwary approach of a cock too[7] near the mouth of his kennel, and sends forth a thundering bark, which is answered by two fox-hounds shut up in the opposite cow-house; the old top-knotted hens, scratching with their chicks among the straw, set up a sympathetic croaking as the discomfited cock joins them; a sow with her brood, all very muddy as to the legs, and curled as to the tail, throws in some deep staccato notes; our friends the calves are bleating from the home croft; and, under all, a fine ear discerns the continuous hum of human voices.

For the great[8] barn-doors are thrown wide open, and men are busy there mending the harness, under the superintendence of Mr Goby the "whit-taw," otherwise saddler, who entertains them with the latest Treddleston gossip. It is certainly rather an unfortunate day that Alick, the shepherd, has chosen for having the whittaws, since the morning turned out so wet; and Mrs Poyser has spoken her mind pretty strongly as to the dirt which the extra number of men's shoes brought into the house at dinner-time.

Indeed, she has not yet recovered her equanimity on the subject, though it is now nearly three hours since dinner, and the house-floor is perfectly clean again; as clean as everything else in that wonderful house-place, where[9] the only chance of collecting a few grains of dust would[1] be to climb on the salt-coffer, and put your finger on the high mantel-shelf on which the glittering brass candlesticks[2] are enjoying their summer sine-cure; for at this time of year, of course, every one goes to bed while it is yet light, or at least light enough to discern the outline of objects after you have bruised your shins against them. Surely nowhere else could an oak clock-case and an oak table have got to such a polish by the hand: genuine "elbow polish," as[3] Mrs Poyser called it, for she thanked God she never had any of your varnished rubbish in her house. Hetty Sorrel often took the oppor-tunity, when her aunt's back was turned, of looking at the pleasing reflec-tion of herself in those polished surfaces, for the oak table was usually turned up like a screen, and was more for ornament than for use; and she could see herself sometimes[4] in the great round pewter dishes that were ranged on the shelves above the long deal dinner-table, or in the hobs of the grate, which always shone like[5] jasper.

Everything was looking at its[6] brightest at this moment, for the sun shone right on the pewter dishes, and from their reflecting surfaces pleasant jets of light were thrown on mellow oak and bright brass;—and[7] on a still pleasanter object than these; for some of the rays fell on Dinah's finely-moulded cheek, and lit up her pale red hair to auburn, as she bent over the heavy household linen which she was mending for her aunt. No scene could have been more peaceful, if Mrs Poyser, who was ironing a few things that still remained from the Monday's wash, had not[8] been making a frequent clinking with her iron, and moving to and fro whenever she wanted it to cool; carrying the keen glance of her blue-grey eye from the kitchen to the dairy, where Hetty was making up the butter, and from the dairy to the back-kitchen, where Nancy was taking the pies out of the oven. Do not suppose, however, that Mrs Poyser was elderly or shrewish in her appear-ance; she was a good-looking woman, not more than eight-and-thirty, of fair complexion and sandy hair, well-shapen, light-footed: the most con-spicuous article in her attire was an ample checkered linen apron, which almost covered her skirt; and nothing could be plainer or less noticeable than her cap and gown, for there was no weakness of which she was less tolerant than feminine vanity, and the preference of ornament to utility. The family likeness between her and her niece, Dinah Morris, with the contrast between her keenness and Dinah's seraphic gentleness of expres-

---

9 where ⟨your⟩ the *MS*   1 would ⟨have been⟩ be *MS*
2 candlesticks ⟨were⟩ are *MS*   3 as] *added in MS*   4 sometimes] *added in MS*
5 like ⟨jet⟩ jasper *MS*   6 looking at its] looking its *MS*
7 brass;—and] brass. And *MS*   8 had not {been} ⟨made⟩ making *MS*

sion, might have served a painter as an excellent suggestion for a Martha and Mary.[9] Their eyes were just of the same colour, but a striking test of the difference in their operation was seen in the demeanour of Trip,[1] the black-and-tan terrier, whenever that much-suspected dog unwarily exposed himself to the freezing arctic ray of Mrs Poyser's glance. Her tongue was not less keen than her eye, and, whenever a damsel came within earshot, seemed to take up an unfinished lecture, as a barrel-organ takes up a tune, precisely at the point where it had left off.

The fact that it was churning-day was another reason why it was inconvenient to have the "whittaws," and why, consequently, Mrs Poyser should scold Molly the housemaid with unusual severity. To all appearance Molly had got through her after-dinner work in an exemplary manner, had "cleaned herself" with great dispatch, and now came to ask, submissively, if she should sit down to her spinning till milking time. But this blameless conduct, according to Mrs Poyser, shrouded a secret indulgence of unbecoming wishes, which she now dragged forth and held up to Molly's view with cutting eloquence.

"Spinning, indeed! It isn't spinning as you'd be at, I'll be bound, and let you have your own way. I never knew your equals for gallowsness. To think of a gell o' your age wanting to go and sit with half-a-dozen men! I'd ha' been ashamed to let the words pass over my lips if I'd been you. And you, as have been here ever since last Michaelmas, and I hired you at Treddles'on[2] stattits, without a bit o' character—as I say, you might be grateful to be hired in that way to a respectable place; and you knew no more o' what belongs to work when you come here than the mawkin i' the field. As poor a two-fisted thing as ever I saw, you know you was. Who taught you to scrub a floor, I should like to know? Why, you'd leave the dirt in heaps i' the corners—anybody 'ud think you'd never been brought up among Christians. And as for spinning, why, you've wasted as much as your wage i' the flax you've spoiled learning to spin. And you've a right to feel that, and not to go about as gaping and as thoughtless as if you was beholding to nobody. Comb the wool for the whittaws, indeed! That's what you'd like to be doing, is it? That's the way with you—that's the road you'd all like to go, headlongs to ruin. You're never easy till you've got some sweetheart as is as big a fool as yourself: you think you'll be finely off when you're married, I dare say, and have got[3] a three-legged stool to sit on, and never a blanket to cover you, and a bit o' oat-cake for your dinner, as three children are a-snatching at."

"I'm[4] sure I donna want t' go[5] wi' the whittaws," said Molly, whimpering, and quite overcome by this Dantean picture of her future, "on'y we allays[6] used to comb the wool for 'n at Mester Ottley's; an' so I just axed ye.

[9] Mary. ⟨There was⟩ Their *MS*   [1] Trip,] *added in MS*
[2] Treddles'on] Treddleston *MS*   [3] and have got] and have a got *MS*
[4] I'm] I've *MS*   [5] go] goo *MS*   [6] we allays] wey alys *MS*

I donna want[7] to set eyes on the whittaws again; I wish I may never[8] stir if I do."

"Mr Ottley's, indeed! It's fine talking o' what you did at Mr Ottley's. Your missis there might like her floors dirtied wi' whittaws, for what I know. There's no knowing what people *wonna*[9] like—such ways as I've heard[1] of! I never had a gell come into my house as seemed to know what cleaning was; I think people live like pigs, for my part. And as to that Betty as was dairymaid at Trent's before she come to me, she'd ha' left the cheeses without turning from week's end to week's end, and the dairy thralls, I might ha' wrote my name on 'em, when I come downstairs after my illness, as the doctor[2] said it was inflammation—it was a mercy I got well of it. And to think o' your knowing no better, Molly, and been here a-going i' nine months, and not for want o' talking to, neither—and what are you stanning there for, like a jack as is run down, istead[3] o' getting your wheel out? You're a rare un for sitting down to your work a little while after it's time to put by."

"Munny, my iron's twite told; pease put it down to warm."

The small chirruping voice that uttered this request came from a little sunny-haired girl between three and four, who, seated on a high chair at the end of the ironing-table, was arduously clutching the handle of a miniature iron with her tiny fat fist, and ironing rags with an assiduity that required her to put her little red tongue out as far as anatomy[4] would allow.

"Cold, is it,[5] my darling[6]? Bless your sweet face!" said Mrs Poyser, who was remarkable for the facility with which she could relapse from her official objurgatory tone to one[7] of fondness or of friendly converse. "Never mind! Mother's done her ironing now. She's going to put the ironing things away."

"Munny, I[8] tould 'ike to do into de barn to Tommy, to see de whittawd."

"No, no, no; Totty 'ud get her feet wet," said Mrs Poyser, carrying away her iron. "Run into the dairy, and see cousin Hetty make the butter."

"I tould 'ike a bit o' pum-take," rejoined Totty, who seemed to be provided with several relays of requests; at the same time, taking the opportunity of her momentary leisure, to put her fingers into a bowl of starch, and drag it down, so as to empty the contents with tolerable completeness on to the ironing-sheet.

"Did ever anybody see the like?" screamed Mrs Poyser, running towards the table when her eye had fallen on the blue stream. "The child's

[7] axed ye. I donna want] ast yey. ⟨I wish I may niver stir if⟩ I {donna} want *MS*
[8] never] niver *MS*   [9] *wonna*] wont *MS*   [1] heard] heared *MS*
[2] doctor] doctors *MS*   [3] istead] instead *Cabinet*
[4] anatomy] anatomical facts *MS*   [5] it,] *MS 1* it *8*   [6] darling] dilling *MS*
[7] objurgatory tone to one] objurgatory to one *Cabinet*   [8] I ⟨could⟩ tould *MS*

allays[9] i' mischief if your back's turned a minute. What shall I do to you, you naughty, naughty gell!"[1]

Totty, however, had descended from her chair with great swiftness, and was already in retreat towards the dairy with a sort of waddling run, and an amount of fat on the nape of her neck, which made her look like the metamorphosis of a white sucking-pig.

The starch having been wiped up by Molly's help, and the ironing apparatus put by, Mrs Poyser took up her knitting, which always lay ready at hand, and was the work she liked best, because she could carry it on automatically as she walked to and fro. But now she came and sat down opposite Dinah, whom she looked at in a meditative way, as she knitted her grey worsted stocking.

"You look th' image o'[2] your aunt Judith, Dinah, when[3] you sit a-sewing.[4] I could almost fancy it was thirty years back, and I was a little gell at home, looking at Judith as she sat at her work, after she'd done th'[5] house up; only it was a little cottage, father's was, and not a big rambling house as gets dirty i' one corner as fast as you clean it in another; but for all that, I could fancy you was your aunt Judith,[6] only her hair was a deal darker than yours, and she was stouter and broader i' the shoulders. Judith and me allays[7] hung together, though she had such queer ways, but your mother and her never could agree. Ah! your mother little thought as she'd have a daughter just cut out after the very pattern o' Judith, and leave her an orphan, too, for Judith to take care on, and bring up with a spoon when *she* was in the graveyard at Stoniton. I allays[8] said that o' Judith, as she'd bear a pound weight any day, to save anybody else carrying a[9] ounce. And she was just the same from the first o' my remembering her; it made no difference in her, as I could see, when she took to the Methodists, only she talked a bit different, and wore a different sort o' cap; but she'd never in her life spent a penny on herself more than keeping herself decent."

"She was a blessed woman," said Dinah; "God had given her a loving, self-forgetting nature, and he perfected it by grace. And she was very fond of you too, aunt Rachel. I've often heard her talk of you in the same sort of way. When she had that bad illness, and I was only eleven years old, she used to say, 'You'll have a friend on earth in your aunt Rachel, if I'm taken from you; for she has a kind heart;' and[1] I'm sure I've found it so."

"I don't know how, child; anybody 'ud be cunning to do anything for you, I think; you're like the birds o' th' air, and live nobody knows how. I'd ha' been glad to behave to you like a mother's sister, if you'd come and live i'

    [9] allays] alys *MS*   [1] gell!"] gell?" *Cabinet*   [2] th' image o'] the image of *MS*
    [3] when] *MS 1* ⟨whom⟩ when *8*
    [4] a-sewing {.} ⟨& I was a little gell at home looking⟩ I *MS*   [5] th'] the *MS*
    [6] Judith, ⟨but⟩ only *MS*   [7] allays] alys *MS*   [8] allays] alys *MS*
    [9] a] an *MS*   [1] heart;' and] heart.' And *MS*

this country, where there's some shelter and victual for man and beast, and folks don't live on the naked hills, like poultry a-scratching[2] on a gravel bank. And then you might get married to some decent man, and there'd be plenty ready to have you, if you'd only leave off that preaching, as is ten times worse than anything your aunt Judith ever did. And even if you'd marry Seth Bede, as is a poor wool-gathering Methodist, and's never like to have a penny beforehand, I know your uncle 'ud help you with a pig, and very like a cow, for he's allays[3] been good-natur'd to my kin, for all they're poor, and made 'em welcome to th'[4] house; and 'ud do for you, I'll be bound, as much as ever he'd do for Hetty, though she's his own niece. And there's linen in the[5] house as I could well spare you, for[6] I've got lots o' sheeting and table-clothing, and towelling, as isn't made up. There's[7] a piece o' sheeting I could give you as that squinting Kitty spun—she was a rare girl to spin, for all she squinted, and the children couldn't abide her; and, you know, the spinning's going on constant, and there's new linen wove twice as fast as th' old wears out. But where's the use o' talking, if you[8] wonna[9] be persuaded, and settle down like any other woman in her senses, istead o' wearing yourself out with walking and preaching, and giving away every penny you get, so as you've nothing saved against sickness; and all the things you've got i' the world, I verily believe, 'ud go into a bundle no bigger nor[1] a double cheese. And all because you've got notions i'[2] your head about religion more nor what's i'[3] the Catechism and the Prayer-book."

"But not more than what's in the Bible, aunt," said Dinah.

"Yes, and the Bible too, for that matter," Mrs Poyser rejoined, rather sharply; "else[4] why shouldn't them as know best what's in the Bible—the parsons and people as have got nothing to do but learn it—do the same as you do? But, for the matter o' that, if everybody was to do like you, the world must come to a standstill; for if everybody tried to do without house and home, and with poor eating and drinking, and was allays[5] talking as we must despise the things o' the world, as you say, I should like to know where the pick o' the stock, and the corn, and the best new-milk cheeses 'ud have to go.[6] Everybody 'ud be wanting bread made o' tail ends, and everybody 'ud be running after everybody else to preach to 'em, istead o' bringing up their families, and laying[7] by against a bad harvest. It stands to sense as that can't be the right religion."

[2] a-scratching] a scratting *MS*   [3] allays] al'ys *MS*   [4] th'] the *MS*
[5] the] th' *MS*   [6] you, for] you enough, for *MS*
[7] up. There's] up—there's *MS*   [8] you] ye *Cabinet*   [9] wonna] wont *MS*
[1] nor] than *MS*   [2] i'] in *MS*   [3] i'] in *MS*
[4] Prayer-book." ¶ "But not more than what's in the Bible, aunt," said Dinah. ¶ "Yes, and the Bible too, for that matter," Mrs Poyser rejoined, rather sharply; "else] *revised in MS from* prayer-book—the Bible too, for that matter; else
[5] allays] al'ys *MS*   [6] go.] go? *MS 1*   [7] laying ⟨up⟩ by *MS*

"Nay, dear aunt, you never heard me say that all people are called to forsake their work and their families. It's quite right the land[8] should be ploughed and sowed, and the precious corn stored, and the things of this life cared for, and right that people should rejoice in their families, and provide for them, so that this is done in the fear of the Lord, and that they are not unmindful of the soul's wants while they are caring for the body. We can all be servants of God wherever our lot is cast, but he gives us different sorts of work, according as he fits us for it and calls us to it. I can no more help spending my life in trying to do what I can for the souls of others, than you could help running if you heard little Totty crying at the other end of the house; the voice would go to your heart, you would think the dear child was in trouble or in danger, and you couldn't rest without running to help her and comfort her."

"Ah," said Mrs Poyser, rising and walking towards the door, "I know it 'ud be just the same if I was to talk to you for hours. You'd make me the same answer at th'[9] end. I might as well talk to the running brook, and tell it to stan' still."

The causeway outside the kitchen door was[1] dry enough now for Mrs Poyser to stand there quite pleasantly and see what was going on in the yard,[2] the grey worsted stocking making a steady progress in her hands all the while. But she had not been standing there more than five minutes before she came in again, and said to Dinah in rather a flurried, awe-stricken tone,

"If there isn't Captain Donnithorne and Mr Irwine a–coming into the yard! I'll lay my life they're come to speak about your preaching on the Green, Dinah; it's you must answer 'em, for I'm dumb. I've said enough a'ready about your bringing such disgrace upo' your uncle's family. I wouldn't ha' minded if you'd been Mr Poyser's own niece—folks must put up wi'[3] their own kin, as they put up wi' their own noses—it's their own flesh and blood. But to think of a niece o' mine being cause o' my husband's being turned out of his farm, and me brought him no fortin[4] but my savins—"

"Nay, dear aunt[5] Rachel," said Dinah gently, "you've no cause for such fears. I've strong assurance that no evil will happen to you and my uncle and the children from anything I've done. I[6] didn't preach without direction."

"Direction! I know very well what you mean by direction," said Mrs Poyser, knitting in a rapid and agitated manner. "When[7] there's a bigger maggot than usial[8] in your head you call it 'direction;' and then nothing

[8] right the land] right that the land *MS*   [9] th'] the *MS*
[1] was ⟨quite⟩ dry *MS*   [2] yard, ⟨while⟩ the *MS*   [3] wi'] with *MS*
[4] fortin] fortune *MS*   [5] aunt ⟨Susan⟩ Rachel *MS*   [6] I ⟨don't⟩ didn't *MS*
[7] manner. "When] manner, "when *MS*   [8] than usial] nor usual *MS*

can stir you—you look like the statty o' the[9] outside o' Treddles'on[1] church, a-starin' and a-smilin' whether it's fair weather or foul. I hanna[2] common patience with you."

By this time the two gentlemen had reached the palings, and had got down from their horses: it was plain they meant to come in. Mrs Poyser advanced to the door to meet them, curtsying low, and trembling between anger with Dinah and anxiety to conduct herself with perfect propriety on the occasion. For in those days the keenest of bucolic minds felt a whispering awe[3] at the sight of the gentry, such as of old men felt when they stood on tip-toe to watch the gods passing by in tall human shape.

"Well, Mrs Poyser, how are you after this stormy morning?" said Mr Irwine, with his stately cordiality. "Our feet are quite dry; we shall not soil your beautiful floor."

"O, sir, don't mention it," said Mrs Poyser. "Will you and the Captain please to walk into the parlour?"

"No, indeed, thank you, Mrs Poyser," said the Captain, looking eagerly round the kitchen, as if his eye were seeking something it could not find. "I delight in your kitchen. I think it is the most charming room I know. I should like every farmer's wife to come and look at it for a pattern."

"O, you're pleased to say so, sir. Pray take a seat," said Mrs Poyser, relieved a little by this compliment and the Captain's evident good-humour, but still glancing anxiously at Mr Irwine, who, she saw, was looking at Dinah and advancing towards her.

"Poyser is not at home, is he?" said Captain Donnithorne, seating himself where he could see along the short passage to the open dairy-door.

"No, sir, he isn't; he's gone to Rosseter[4] to see Mr West, the factor, about the wool. But there's father i' the barn, sir, if he'd be of any use."

"No, thank you; I'll just look at the whelps and leave a message about them with your shepherd. I must come another day and see your husband; I want to have a consultation with him about horses. Do you know when he's likely to be at liberty?"

"Why, sir, you can hardly miss him, except it's o' Treddles'on market-day—that's of a Friday, you know. For if he's anywhere on the farm we can send for him in a minute. If we'd got rid o' the Scantlands we should have no outlying fields; and I should be glad of it, for if ever anything happens he's sure to be gone to the Scantlands. Things allays[5] happen so contrary, if they've a chance; and[6] it's an unnat'ral thing to have one bit o' your farm in one county and all[7] the rest in another."

"Ah, the Scantlands would go much better with Choyce's farm, especially as he wants dairy-land and you've got plenty. I think yours is the

[9] the] th' *MS*   [1] Treddles'on] Treddleston *MS*   [2] hanna] haven't *MS*
[3] awe ⟨of⟩ at the sight of *MS*   [4] Rosseter] Drosseter *MS*   [5] allays] alys *MS*
[6] chance; and] chance. And *MS*   [7] all] added in *MS*

prettiest farm on the estate, though; and do you know, Mrs Poyser, if I were going to marry and settle, I should be tempted to turn you out, and do up this fine old house, and turn farmer myself."

"O, sir," said Mrs Poyser, rather alarmed, "you wouldn't like it at all. As for farming, it's putting money into your pocket wi'[8] your right hand and fetching it out wi'[9] your left. As fur as I can see, it's raising victual for other folks, and just getting a mouthful for yourself and your children as you go along. Not as you'd be like a poor man as wants to get his bread: you could afford to lose as much money as you liked i' farming; but it's poor fun losing money, I should think, though I understan'[1] it's what the great folks i' London play at more than anything. For my husband heard[2] at market as Lord Dacey's eldest son had lost thousands upo' thousands to the Prince o' Wales, and they said my lady was going to pawn her jewels to pay for him. But you know more about that than I do, sir. But as for farming, sir, I canna[3] think[4] as you'd like it; and this house—the draughts in it are enough to cut you through, and it's my opinion the floors upstairs are very rotten, and the rats i'[5] the cellar are beyond anything."

"Why, that's a terrible picture, Mrs Poyser. I think I should be doing you a service to turn you out of such a place. But there's no chance of that. I'm not likely to settle for the next twenty years, till I'm a stout gentleman of forty; and my grandfather would never consent to part with such good tenants as you."

"Well, sir, if he thinks[6] so well o' Mr Poyser for a tenant, I wish you could put in a word for him to allow us some[7] new gates for the Five Closes, for my husband's been asking and asking till he's tired, and to think o' what he's done for the farm, and's never had a penny allowed him, be the times bad or good. And as I've said to my husband often and often,[8] I'm sure if the Captain had anything to do with it, it wouldn't be so. Not as I wish to speak disrespectful o' them as have got the power i' their hands, but it's more than flesh and blood 'ull bear sometimes, to be toiling and striving, and up early and down late, and hardly sleeping a wink when you lie down[9] for thinking as the cheese may swell, or the cows may slip their calf, or the wheat may grow green again i' the sheaf—and after all, at th' end o' the year, it's like as if you'd been cooking a feast and had got the smell of it for your pains."

Mrs Poyser, once launched into conversation, always sailed along without any check from her preliminary awe of the gentry. The confidence she felt in her own powers of exposition was a motive force that overcame all resistance.

---

[8] wi'] with *MS*   [9] wi'] with *MS*   [1] understan'] understand *MS*

[2] heard] heared *MS*   [3] canna] cant *MS*   [4] think] *added in MS*

[5] i'] in *MS*   [6] thinks ⟨as my husband⟩ so well o' Mr Poyser *MS*

[7] some ⟨timber for⟩ new gates *MS*   [8] often, ⟨if⟩ I'm *MS*

[9] you lie down] you do lie down *MS*

"I'm afraid I should only do harm instead of good, if I were to speak about the gates, Mrs Poyser," said the Captain, "though I assure you there's no man on the estate I would sooner say a word for than your husband. I know his farm is in better order than any other within ten miles of us; and as for the kitchen," he added, smiling, "I don't believe there's one in the kingdom to beat it. By the by, I've never seen your dairy: I must see your dairy, Mrs Poyser."

"Indeed, sir, it's not fit for you to go in, for Hetty's in the middle o' making the butter, for the churning was thrown late, and I'm quite ashamed." This Mrs Poyser said blushing, and believing that the Captain was really interested in her milk-pans, and would adjust his opinion of her to the appearance of her dairy.

"O, I've no doubt it's in capital order. Take me in," said the Captain, himself leading the way, while Mrs Poyser followed.

CHAPTER VII.

THE DAIRY.

The dairy was certainly worth looking at: it was a scene to sicken for with a sort of calenture in hot and dusty streets—such coolness, such purity, such fresh fragrance of new-pressed cheese, of firm butter, of wooden vessels perpetually bathed in pure water; such soft colouring of red earthenware and creamy surfaces, brown wood and polished tin, grey limestone and rich orange-red rust on the iron weights and hooks and hinges. But one gets only a confused notion of these details when they surround a distractingly pretty girl of seventeen, standing on little pattens and rounding her dimpled arm to lift a pound of butter out of the scale.

Hetty blushed a deep rose-colour when Captain Donnithorne entered the dairy and spoke to her; but it was not at all a distressed blush, for it was inwreathed with smiles and dimples, and with sparkles from under long curled dark eye-lashes; and while her aunt was discoursing to him about the limited amount of milk that was to be spared for butter and cheese so long as the calves were not all weaned, and the[1] large quantity but inferior quality of milk yielded by the short-horn, which had been bought on experiment, together with other matters which must be interesting to a young gentleman who would one day be a landlord, Hetty tossed and patted her pound of butter with quite a self-possessed, coquettish air, slyly conscious that no turn of her head was lost.

There are various orders of beauty, causing men to make fools of themselves in various styles, from the desperate to the sheepish; but there is one order of beauty which seems made to turn the heads not only of men, but of all intelligent mammals, even of women. It is a beauty like that of kittens, or very small downy ducks making gentle rippling noises with their soft bills, or babies just beginning to toddle and to engage in conscious mischief—a beauty with which you can never be angry, but that you feel ready to crush for inability to comprehend the state of mind into which it throws you. Hetty Sorrel's was that sort of beauty. Her aunt, Mrs Poyser, who professed to despise all personal attractions, and intended to be the severest of mentors, continually gazed at Hetty's charms by the sly, fascinated in spite of herself; and after administering such a scolding as naturally flowed from her anxiety to do well by her

---

[1] the] a *Cabinet*

husband's niece—who had no mother of her own to scold her, poor thing!—she would often confess to her husband, when they were safe out of hearing, that she firmly believed, "the naughtier the little huzzy behaved, the prettier she looked."

It is of little use for me to tell you that Hetty's cheek was like a rose-petal, that dimples played about her pouting lips, that her large dark eyes hid a soft roguishness under their long lashes, and that her curly hair, though all pushed back under her round[2] cap while she was at work, stole back in dark delicate rings on her forehead, and about her[3] white shell-like ears; it is of little use for me to say how lovely was the contour of her pink-and-white neckerchief, tucked into her low plum-coloured stuff boddice, or how the linen butter-making apron, with its bib, seemed a thing[4] to be imitated in silk by duchesses, since it fell in such charming lines, or how her brown stockings and thick-soled buckled shoes lost all that clumsiness which they must certainly have had when empty of her foot and ankle;—of[5] little use, unless you have seen a woman who affected you as Hetty affected her beholders, for otherwise, though you might conjure up the image of a lovely woman, she would not in the least resemble that distracting kitten-like maiden. I might mention all the divine charms of a bright spring day, but if you had never in your life utterly forgotten yourself in straining your eyes after the mounting lark, or in wandering through the still lanes when the fresh-opened blossoms fill them with a sacred, silent beauty like that of fretted aisles, where would be the use of my descriptive catalogue? I could never make you know what I meant by a bright spring day. Hetty's was a spring-tide beauty; it was the beauty of young frisking things, round-limbed, gambolling, circumventing you by a false air of innocence—the innocence of a young star-browed calf, for example, that, being inclined for a promenade out of bounds, leads you a severe steeple-chase over hedge and ditch, and only comes to a stand in the middle of a bog.

And they are the prettiest attitudes and movements into which a pretty girl is thrown in making up butter—tossing movements that give a charming curve to the arm, and a sideward inclination of the round white neck; little patting and rolling movements with the palm of the hand, and nice adaptations and finishings which cannot at all be effected without a great play of the pouting mouth[6] and the dark eyes. And then the butter itself seems to communicate a fresh charm—it is so pure, so sweet-scented; it is turned off the mould with such a beautiful firm surface, like marble in a pale yellow light! Moreover, Hetty was particularly clever at making up the butter; it was the one performance of hers that her aunt allowed to pass

---

[2] her round] *added in MS*   [3] her ⟨ears⟩ white *MS*

[4] thing ⟨for duchesses⟩ to *MS*   [5] ankle;—of] ancle. Of *MS*

[6] mouth] *MS 1* mouth, *8*

without severe criticism; so[7] she handled it with all the grace that belongs to mastery.

"I hope you will be ready for a great holiday on the thirtieth of July, Mrs Poyser," said Captain Donnithorne, when he had sufficiently admired the dairy, and given several improvised opinions on Swede turnips and short-horns. "You know what is to happen then, and I shall expect you to be one of the guests who come earliest and leave latest. Will you promise me your hand for two dances, Miss Hetty? If I don't get your promise now, I know I shall hardly have a chance, for all the smart young farmers will take care to secure you."

Hetty smiled and blushed, but before she could answer, Mrs Poyser interposed, scandalized at the mere suggestion that the young squire could be excluded by any meaner partners.

"Indeed, sir, you are very kind to take that notice of her. And I'm sure, whenever you're pleased to dance with her, she'll be proud and thankful, if she stood still all the rest o' th' evening."

"O no, no, that would be too cruel to all the other young fellows who can dance. But you will promise me two dances, won't you?" the Captain continued, determined to make Hetty look at him and speak to him.

Hetty dropped the prettiest little curtsy, and stole a half-shy, half-coquettish glance at[8] him as she said,

"Yes, thank you, sir."

"And you must bring all your children, you know, Mrs Poyser; your little Totty, as well as the boys. I want all the youngest children on the estate to be there—all those who will be fine young men and women when I'm a bald old fellow."

"O dear sir, that 'ull[9] be a long time first," said Mrs Poyser, quite overcome at the young squire's speaking so lightly of himself, and think-ing how her husband would be interested in hearing her recount this remarkable specimen of high-born humour. The Captain was thought to be "very[1] full of his jokes," and was a great favourite throughout the estate on account of his free manners. Every tenant was quite sure things would be different when the reins got into his hands—there was to be a millennial abundance of new gates, allowances of lime, and returns of ten per cent.

"But where is Totty[2] to-day?" he said. "I want to see her."

"Where *is* the little un[3], Hetty?" said Mrs Poyser. "She came in here not long ago."

---

[7] so] *added in MS*   [8] at ⟨Captain⟩ him *MS*   [9] 'ull] will *MS*
[1] thought to be "very] thought "very *MS*
[2] where is Totty] where *is* Totty *MS 1* where ⟨is⟩ is Totty *8*
[3] "Where *is* the little un] "Where is the little un *MS 1* "Where ⟨is⟩ *is* the little un *8*

"I don't know. She went into the brewhouse to Nancy, I think."

The proud mother,[4] unable to resist the temptation to show her Totty, passed at once into the back kitchen,[5] in search of her, not, however, without misgivings lest something should have happened to render her person and attire unfit for presentation.

"And do you carry the butter to market when you've made it?" said the Captain to Hetty, meanwhile.

"O no, sir; not when it's so heavy; I'm not strong enough to carry it. Alick takes it on horseback."

"[6]No, I'm sure your pretty arms were never meant for such heavy weights. But you go out a walk sometimes these pleasant evenings, don't you? Why don't you have a walk in the Chase sometimes, now it's so green and pleasant? I hardly ever see you anywhere except at home and at church."

"Aunt doesn't like me to go a-walking only when I'm going somewhere," said Hetty. "But I go through the Chase sometimes[7]."

"And don't you ever go to see Mrs Best[8], the housekeeper? I think I saw you once in the housekeeper's room."

"It isn't Mrs Best[9], it's Mrs Pomfret, the lady's-maid, as I go to see. She's teaching me tent-stitch and the[1] lace-mending. I'm going to tea with her to-morrow afternoon."

The reason why there had been space for this *tête-à-tête*[2] can only be known by looking into the back kitchen, where Totty[3] had been discovered rubbing a stray blue-bag against her nose, and in the same moment allowing some liberal indigo drops to fall on her afternoon pinafore. But now she appeared holding her mother's hand—the end of her round nose rather shiny from a recent and hurried application of soap and water.

"Here she is!" said the Captain, lifting her up and setting her on the low[4] stone shelf. "Here's Totty! By the by, what's her other name? She wasn't christened Totty."

"O sir, we call her sadly out of her name. Charlotte's her christened name. It's a name i' Mr Poyser's family: his grandmother was named Charlotte. But we began with calling her Lotty, and now it's got to Totty. To be sure it's more like a name for a dog than a Christian child."

"Totty's a capital name. Why, she looks like a Totty. Has she got a pocket on?" said the Captain, feeling in his own waistcoat pockets.

---

[4] mother, ⟨entirely possessed by the pleasure of having⟩ {unable to resist the temptation to show} her Totty ⟨asked for⟩, passed *MS*   [5] back kitchen, ⟨not how⟩ in *MS*

[6] "⟨No, indeed,⟩ No, *MS*

[7] the Chase sometimes] the Chase when I'm going to see M[rs]. Clay at the Chase Farm *MS*

[8] Best] Brett *MS*   [9] Best] Brett *MS*   [1] the] th *MS*

[2] *tête-à-tête*] tête-à-tête *MS*   [3] Totty ⟨is⟩ had been *MS*

[4] low] *added in MS*

Totty immediately with great gravity lifted up her frock, and showed a tiny pink pocket at present in a state of collapse.

"It dot notin in it," she said, as she looked down at it very earnestly.

"No! what a pity! such a pretty pocket. Well, I think I've got some things in mine that will make a pretty jingle in it. Yes! I declare I've got five little round silver things, and hear what a pretty noise they make in Totty's pink pocket." Here he shook the pocket with the five sixpences in it, and Totty showed her teeth and wrinkled her nose in great glee; but[5] divining that there was nothing more to be got by staying, she jumped off the shelf and ran away to jingle her pocket in the hearing of Nancy, while her mother called after her, "O for shame, you naughty gell! not to thank the Captain for what he's given you. I'm sure, sir, it's very kind of you; but she's spoiled shameful; her father won't have her said nay in anything, and there's no managing her. It's being the youngest, and th' only gell."

"O, she's a funny little fatty; I[6] wouldn't have her different. But I must be going now, for I suppose the Rector is waiting for me."

With a "good-by," a bright glance, and a bow to Hetty, Arthur left the dairy. But he was mistaken in imagining himself waited for. The Rector had been so much interested in his conversation with Dinah, that he would not have chosen to close it earlier; and you shall hear now what they had been saying to each other.

---

[5] glee; but] glee. But *MS*   [6] fatty; I] fatty. I *MS*

CHAPTER VIII.[1]

A VOCATION.

Dinah, who had risen when the gentlemen came in, but still kept hold of the sheet she was mending, curtsied respectfully when she saw Mr Irwine looking at her and advancing towards her. He had never yet spoken to her, or stood face to face with her, and her first thought, as her eyes met his, was "What a[2] well-favoured countenance! O that the good seed might fall on that soil, for it would surely flourish." The agreeable impression must have been mutual, for Mr Irwine bowed to her with a benignant deference, which would have been equally in place if she had been the most dignified lady of his acquaintance.

"You are only a visitor in this neighbourhood, I think?" were his first words, as he seated himself opposite to her.

"No, sir, I come from Snowfield, in Stonyshire. But my aunt was very kind, wanting me to have rest from my work there, because I'd been ill, and she invited me to come and stay with her for a while."

"Ah, I remember Snowfield very well; I once had occasion to go there. It's a dreary bleak place. They were building a cotton-mill there; but that's[3] many years ago now: I suppose the place is a good deal changed by the employment that mill must have brought."

"It *is* changed, so far as the mill has brought people there, who get a livelihood for themselves by working in it, and make it better for the tradesfolks. I work in it myself, and have reason to be grateful, for thereby I have enough and to spare. But it's still a bleak place, as you say, sir—very different from this country."

"You have relations living there probably, so that you are attached to the place as your home?"[4]

"I had an aunt there once; she brought me up, for I was an orphan. But she was taken away seven years ago, and I have no other kindred that I know of, besides my aunt Poyser, who is very good to me, and would have me come and live in this country, which to be sure is a good land, wherein they eat bread without scarceness. But I'm not free to leave Snowfield, where I was first planted, and have grown deep into it, like the small grass on the[5] hill-top."

---

[1] CHAPTER VIII.] Chapter ⟨7⟩8.   [2] a ⟨goodly⟩ well-favoured *MS*
[3] that's ⟨a good⟩ many *MS*   [4] home?"] home." *MS*   [5] the ⟨hard⟩ hill-top *MS*

"Ah, I dare say you have many religious friends and companions there; you are a Methodist—a Wesleyan, I think?"

"Yes, my aunt at Snowfield belonged to the Society, and I have[6] cause to be thankful for the privileges I have had thereby from my earliest childhood."

"And have you been long in the habit of preaching?—for[7] I understand you preached at Hayslope last night."

"I first took to the work four years since, when I was twenty-one."

"Your Society sanctions women's preaching, then?"

"It doesn't forbid them, sir, when they've a clear call to the work, and when their ministry is owned by the conversion of sinners, and the strengthening of God's people. Mrs Fletcher, as you may have heard about, was the first woman to preach in the Society, I believe, before she was married, when she was Miss Bosanquet; and Mr Wesley approved of her undertaking the work. She had a great gift, and there are many others now living who are precious fellow-helpers in the work of the ministry. I understand there's been voices raised against it in the Society of late, but I cannot but think their counsel will come to nought. It isn't for men to make channels for God's Spirit, as they make channels for the watercourses, and say, 'Flow here, but flow not there.'"

"But don't you find some danger among your people—I don't mean to say that it is so with you, far from it—but don't you find sometimes that both men and women fancy themselves channels for God's Spirit, and are quite mistaken, so that they set about a work for which they are unfit, and[8] bring holy things into contempt?"

"Doubtless it is so sometimes; for there have been evil-doers among us who have sought to deceive the brethren, and some there are who deceive their own selves. But we are not without discipline and correction to put a check upon these things. There's a very strict order kept among us, and the brethren and sisters watch for each other's[9] souls as they that must give account. They don't go every one his own way and say, 'Am I my brother's keeper?'"

"But tell me—if I may ask, and I am really interested in knowing it—how you first came to think of preaching?"

"Indeed, sir, I didn't think of it at all—I'd[1] been used from the time I was sixteen to talk to the little children and teach them, and sometimes I had had my heart enlarged to speak in class, and was much drawn out in prayer with[2] the sick. But I had felt no call to preach; for when I'm not greatly wrought upon, I'm too much given to sit still and keep by myself: it seems as if I could sit silent all day long with the thought of God overflowing my

---

6 have ⟨a⟩ cause *MS*   7 preaching?—for] preaching? For *MS*
8 & ⟨so⟩ bring *MS*   9 other's] others' *MS*
1 all—I'd] all. I'd *MS*   2 with] by *MS*

soul—as the pebbles lie bathed in the Willow Brook. For thoughts are so great—aren't they, sir? They seem to lie upon us like a deep flood; and it's my besetment to forget where I am and everything about me, and lose myself in thoughts that I could give no account of, for I could neither make a beginning nor ending of them in words. That was my way as long as I can remember; but sometimes it seemed as if speech came to me without any will of my own, and words were given to me that came out as the tears come, because our hearts are full and we can't help it. And those were always times of great blessing, though I had never thought it could be so with me before a congregation of people. But, sir, we are led on, like the little children, by a way that we know not. I was called to preach quite suddenly, and since then I have never been left in doubt about the work that was laid upon me."

"But tell me the circumstances—just how it was, the very day you began to preach."[3]

[4]"[5]It was one Sunday I walked with brother Marlowe, who was an aged man, one of the local preachers, all the way to Hetton-Deeps—that's a village where the people get their living by working in the lead-[6]mines, and where there's no[7] church nor preacher, but they live like sheep without a shepherd. It's better than twelve miles from Snowfield, so we set out early in the morning, for it was summer-time; and I had a wonderful sense of the Divine love as we walked over the hills, where there's no trees, you know, sir, as there is here, to make the sky look smaller, but you see the heavens stretched out like a tent, and you feel the everlasting arms around you. But before we got to Hetton, brother Marlowe was seized with a dizziness that made him afraid of falling, for he overworked himself sadly, at his years, in watching and praying, and walking so many miles to speak the Word, as well as carrying on his trade of linen-weaving. And when we got to the village, the people were expecting him, for he'd appointed the time and the place when he was there before[8], and such of them as cared to hear the Word of Life were assembled on a spot where the cottages was thickest, so as others might be drawn to come. But he felt as he couldn't stand up to preach, and he was[9] forced to lie down in the first of the cottages we came to. So I went to tell the people, thinking we'd go into one of the houses, and I would read and pray with them. But as I passed along by the cottages and saw the aged trembling[1] women at the doors, and the hard looks of the men, who seemed to have their eyes no more filled with the sight of the Sabbath

[3] But, Sir, we are led on, like the little children, by a way that we know not. I was called to preach quite suddenly, & since then I have never been left in doubt about the work that was laid upon me." ¶ "But tell me ⟨just how it was—⟩ the circumstances—just how it was, the very day you began to preach."] *added on verso of MS I. 128/141*

[4] *No paragraph division in MS.*   [5] ⟨But⟩ ⟨o⟩One {"It was one} Sunday *MS*
[6] lead-] *added in MS*   [7] no ⟨preacher⟩ church nor *MS*
[8] when he was there before] *added in MS*   [9] was ⟨obliged⟩ forced *MS*
[1] aged trembling] aged and trembling *Cabinet*

morning than if they had been dumb oxen that never looked up to the sky, I
felt a great movement in my soul, and I trembled as if I was shaken by a
strong spirit entering into my weak body. And I went to where the little
flock of people was gathered together, and stepped on the low[2] wall that was
built against the green hill-side, and I spoke the words that were given to me
abundantly. And they all came round me out of all[3] the cottages, and many
wept over their sins, and have since been joined to the Lord. That was the
beginning of my preaching, sir, and I've preached ever since."

Dinah had let her work fall during this narrative, which she uttered in
her usual simple way, but with that sincere, articulate, thrilling treble, by
which she always mastered her audience. She stooped now to gather up her
sewing, and then went on with it as before. Mr Irwine was deeply interested. He[4] said to himself, "He must be a miserable prig who would act the
pedagogue here: one might as well go and lecture the trees for growing in
their own shape."

"And you never feel any embarrassment from the sense of your youth—
that you are a lovely young woman on whom[5] men's eyes are fixed?" he said
aloud.

"No, I've[6] no room for such feelings, and I don't believe the people ever
take notice about that. I think, sir, when God makes his presence felt
through us, we are like the burning bush: Moses never took any heed
what sort of bush it was—he only saw the brightness of the Lord. I've
preached to as rough ignorant people as can be in the villages about
Snowfield—men that looked[7] very hard and wild; but they never said an
uncivil word to me, and often thanked me kindly as they made way for me to
pass through the midst of them."

"*That* I can believe—that I can well believe," said Mr Irwine emphatically. "And what did you think of your hearers last night, now? Did you find
them quiet and attentive?"

"Very quiet, sir; but I saw no signs of any great work upon them, except
in a young girl named Bessy Cranage, towards whom my heart yearned
greatly, when my eyes first fell on her blooming youth, given up to folly
and vanity. I had some private talk and prayer with her afterwards, and
I trust her heart is touched. But I've noticed, that in[8] these villages where
the people lead a quiet life among the green[9] pastures and the still waters,
tilling the ground and tending the cattle, there's a strange deadness to the
Word, as different as can be from the great towns, like Leeds, where I once
went to visit a holy woman who preaches there. It's wonderful how rich is
the harvest of souls up those high-walled streets, where you seem to walk

---

² low] *added in MS*   ³ all] *added in MS*   ⁴ interested. He] interested: he *MS*
⁵ on whom] on whose *MS 1* on ⟨whose⟩ whom *8*   ⁶ I've] I have *MS*
⁷ looked] look *MS 1*   ⁸ noticed, that in] noticed as in *MS*
⁹ green] *added in MS*

as in a prison-yard, and the ear is deafened with the sounds of worldly toil. I think maybe it is because[1] the promise is sweeter when this life is so dark and weary, and the soul gets more hungry when the body is ill at ease."

[2]"Why, yes, our farm-labourers are not easily roused. They take life almost as slowly as the sheep and cows. But we have some intelligent workmen about here. I dare say you know the Bedes; Seth Bede, by the by, is a Methodist."

"Yes, I know[3] Seth well, and his brother Adam a little. Seth is a gracious young man—sincere and without offence; and Adam is like the patriarch Joseph, for his great skill and knowledge, and the kindness he shows to his brother and his parents."

"Perhaps you don't know the trouble that has just happened to them?[4] Their father, Matthias Bede, was drowned in the Willow Brook last night, not far from his own door. I'm going now to see Adam."

"Ah, their poor aged mother!" said Dinah, dropping her hands, and looking before her with pitying eyes, as if she saw the object of her sympathy. "She[5] will mourn heavily; for Seth has told me she's of an anxious, troubled heart. I must go and see if I can give her any help."

As she rose and was beginning to fold up her work, Captain Donnithorne, having exhausted all plausible pretexts for remaining among the milk-pans, came out of the dairy, followed by Mrs Poyser. Mr Irwine now rose also, and advancing towards Dinah, held out his hand, and said—

"Good-by. I hear you are going away soon; but this will not be the last visit you will pay your aunt—so we shall meet again, I hope."

His[6] cordiality towards Dinah set all Mrs Poyser's anxieties at rest, and her face was brighter than usual, as she said—

"I've never asked after Mrs Irwine and the Miss Irwines, sir; I[7] hope they're as well as usual[8]."

"Yes, thank you, Mrs Poyser, except that Miss Anne has one of her bad headaches to-day. By the by, we all liked that nice cream-cheese you sent us—my mother especially."

"I'm very glad, indeed, sir. It is but seldom I make one, but I remembered Mrs Irwine was fond of 'em. Please to give my duty to her, and to Miss Kate and Miss Anne. They've never been to look at my poultry this long while, and I've got some beautiful[9] speckled chickens, black and white, as Miss Kate might[1] like to have some of amongst hers."

"Well, I'll tell her; she must come and see them. Good-by," said the Rector, mounting his horse.

[1] maybe it is because] it is maybe because MS   [2] "⟨Ah,⟩ Why {yes} our MS
[3] know ⟨both⟩ Seth {well} & his brother Adam ⟨well⟩ {a little}. Seth MS
[4] them?] them. MS   [5] She ⟨has⟩ will MS   [6] His] This MS
[7] sir; I] Sir. I MS   [8] usual] usial MS
[9] beautiful ⟨spotted⟩ speckled MS   [1] might ⟨look⟩ like MS

"Just ride slowly on, Irwine," said Captain Donnithorne, mounting also. "I'll overtake you in three minutes. I'm only going to speak to the shepherd about the whelps. Good-by, Mrs Poyser; tell your husband I shall come and have a long talk with him soon."

Mrs Poyser curtsied duly, and watched the two horses until they had disappeared from the yard, amidst great excitement on the part of the pigs and the poultry, and under[2] the furious indignation of the bull-dog, who performed a Pyrrhic dance, that every moment seemed to threaten the breaking of his chain. Mrs Poyser delighted in this noisy exit; it was a fresh assurance to her that the farm-yard was well guarded, and that no loiterers could enter unobserved; and it was not until the gate had closed behind the Captain that she turned into the kitchen again, where Dinah stood with her bonnet in her hand, waiting to speak to her aunt, before she set out for[3] Lisbeth Bede's cottage.

Mrs Poyser, however, though she noticed the bonnet, deferred remarking on it until she had disburthened herself of her surprise at Mr Irwine's behaviour.

"Why, Mr Irwine wasn't angry, then? What did he say to you, Dinah?[4] Didn't he scold you for preaching?"

"No, he was not at all angry; he was very friendly to me. I was quite drawn out to speak to him; I hardly know how, for I had always thought of him as a worldly Sadducee. But[5] his countenance is as pleasant as the morning sunshine."

"Pleasant! and[6] what else did y' expect[7] to find him but pleasant?" said Mrs Poyser, impatiently, resuming her knitting. "I should think his countenance *is* pleasant indeed! and him a gentleman born, and's got a mother like a picter. You[8] may go the country round, and not find such another woman turned sixty-six. It's summat-like to see[9] such a man as that i' the desk of a Sunday! As I say to Poyser, it's like looking at a full crop o' wheat, or a[1] pasture with a fine dairy o' cows in it; it makes you think the world's comfortable-like. But as for such creaturs as you[2] Methodisses run after, I'd as soon go to look at a lot o' bare-ribbed runts on a common. Fine folks they are to tell you what's right, as look as if they'd never tasted nothing better than bacon-sword and sour-cake i' their lives. But what did Mr Irwine say to you about that fool's trick o' preaching on the Green?"

"He only said he'd heard of it; he didn't seem to feel any displeasure about it. But, dear aunt, don't think any more about that. He told me something that I'm sure will cause you sorrow, as it does me. Thias Bede

---

[2] under] *added in MS*   [3] for ⟨Adam's⟩ Lisbeth Bede's *MS*
[4] Dinah?] Dinah. *MS*
[5] for I had always thought of him as a worldly Sadducee. But] *added in MS*
[6] "Pleasant! and] "Pleasant! And *MS*   [7] y' expect] you expect *MS*
[8] picter. You] picter; you *MS*   [9] see a {such} man ⟨like⟩ as *MS*
[1] a ⟨dairy⟩ pasture *MS*   [2] you ⟨Methodists⟩ Methodisses *MS*

was drowned last night in the Willow Brook, and I'm thinking that the aged mother will be greatly in need of comfort. Perhaps I can be of use to her, so I have fetched my bonnet and am going to set out."

"Dear heart, dear heart! But you must have a cup o' tea first, child," said Mrs Poyser, falling at once from the key of B with five sharps, to the frank and genial C. "The kettle's boiling—we'll have it ready in a minute; and the young uns 'ull be in and wanting theirs directly.[3] I'm quite willing you should go and see th' old woman, for you're one as is allays[4] welcome in trouble, Methodist or no Methodist; but, for[5] the matter o' that, it's[6] the flesh and blood folks[7] are made on as makes the difference. Some cheeses are made o' skimmed milk and some o' new milk, and it's no matter what you call 'em, you may tell which is which by the look and the smell. But as to Thias Bede, he's better out o' the way nor in—God forgi' me for saying so—for he's done little this ten year but make trouble for them as belonged to him; and[8] I think it 'ud be well for you to take a little bottle o' rum for th' old woman, for I dare say she's got never a drop o' nothing to comfort her inside.[9] Sit down, child, and be easy, for you shan't stir out till you've had a cup o' tea, and so I tell you."

During the latter part of this speech, Mrs Poyser had been reaching down the tea-things from the shelves, and was on her way towards the pantry for the loaf (followed[1] close by Totty, who had made her appearance on the rattling of the tea-cups), when[2] Hetty came out of the dairy relieving her tired arms by lifting them up, and clasping her hands[3] at the back of her head.

"Molly," she said, rather languidly, "just run out and get me a bunch of dock-leaves: the butter's ready to pack up now."

"D' you hear what's happened, Hetty?" said her aunt.

"No; how should I hear anything?" was the answer, in[4] a pettish tone.

"Not as you'd care much, I dare say, if you did hear; for you're too feather-headed to mind if everybody was dead, so as you could stay upstairs a-dressing yourself for two hours by the clock. But anybody besides yourself 'ud mind about such things happening to them as think a deal more of you than you deserve. But Adam Bede and all his kin might be drownded for what you'd care—you'd be perking at the glass the next minute."

[3] & the young uns 'ull be in and wanting theirs directly.] *added in MS*
[4] allays] alys *MS*   [5] but, for] *MS 1* but {,} for *8*
[6] that, it's] *MS 1* that {,} it's *8*   [7] blood folks] blood as folks *MS*
[8] him; and] him. And *MS*
[9] And I think it 'ud be well for you to take a little bottle o' rum for th' old woman, for I dare say she's got never a drop o' nothing to comfort her inside.] *added in MS*
[1] loaf (followed] loaf, followed *MS 1* loaf⟨,⟩ {(} followed *8*
[2] tea-cups), when] tea-cups, when *MS 1* tea-cups{)}, when *8*
[3] hands {at} ⟨behind⟩ the back of *MS*   [4] in ⟨ra⟩ a *MS*

"Adam Bede—drowned?" said Hetty, letting her arms fall, and looking rather bewildered, but suspecting that her aunt was as usual exaggerating with a didactic purpose.

"No, my dear, no," said Dinah, kindly, for Mrs Poyser had passed on to the pantry without deigning more precise information[5]. "Not Adam. Adam's father, the old man, is drowned. He was drowned last night in the Willow Brook. Mr Irwine has just told me about it."

"O, how dreadful!" said Hetty, looking serious, but not deeply affected; and as Molly now entered with the dock-leaves, she took them silently and returned to the dairy without asking further questions.

[5] for Mrs Poyser had passed on to the pantry without deigning more precise information] *added in MS*

CHAPTER IX.[1]

HETTY'S WORLD.

[2]While she adjusted the broad[3] leaves that set off the pale fragrant butter as the primrose is set off by its nest of green, I am afraid[4] Hetty was thinking a great deal more of the looks Captain Donnithorne had cast at her than of Adam and his troubles. Bright, admiring glances from a handsome young gentleman, with white hands, a gold chain, occasional regimentals, and wealth and grandeur immeasurable—those were the warm rays that set poor Hetty's heart vibrating, and playing its little foolish tunes over and over again. We do not hear that Memnon's[5] statue gave forth its melody at all under the rushing of the mightiest wind, or in response to any other influence divine or human than certain short-lived sunbeams of morning; and we must learn to accommodate ourselves to the discovery that some of those cunningly-fashioned instruments called human souls have only a very limited range of music, and will not vibrate in the least under a touch that fills others with tremulous rapture or quivering agony.

Hetty was quite used to the thought that people liked to look at her. She[6] was not blind to the fact that young Luke Britton of Broxton came to Hayslope Church on a Sunday afternoon on purpose that he might see her; and that he would have made much more decided advances if her uncle Poyser, thinking but lightly of a young man whose father's land was so foul as old Luke Britton's, had not forbidden[7] her aunt to encourage him by any civilities. She[8] was aware, too, that Mr Craig, the gardener at the Chase, was over head and ears in love with her, and had lately made unmistakeable avowals in luscious strawberries and hyperbolical peas. She knew still better, that Adam Bede—tall, upright, clever, brave Adam Bede—who carried such authority with all the people round about, and whom her uncle was always delighted to see[9] of an evening, saying that "Adam knew a fine sight more o' the natur o' things than those as thought themselves his betters"—she knew that this Adam, who was often rather stern to other people, and not much given to run after the lasses, could be made to turn

---

[1] CHAPTER IX.] Chapter ⟨8⟩9. *MS*   [2] ⟨As⟩ While *MS*
[3] broad ⟨green⟩ leaves *MS*   [4] afraid ⟨she⟩ Hetty *MS*
[5] Memnon's ⟨harps played⟩ statue gave forth its ⟨music⟩ melody *MS*
[6] She ⟨knew⟩ was not blind to the fact *MS*
[7] forbidden ⟨his wife to ask him⟩ {her aunt to ⟨invite⟩} encourage *MS*
[8] She ⟨knew⟩ was aware *MS*   [9] see ⟨if he would come in⟩ of *MS*

pale or red any day by a word or a look[1] from her. Hetty's sphere of comparison was not large, but she couldn't help perceiving that Adam was "something like" a man; always knew what to say about things, could tell her uncle how to prop the hovel, and had mended the churn in no time; knew, with only looking at it, the value of the chesnut[2] tree that was blown down,[3] and why the damp came in the walls, and what they must do to stop the rats; and wrote a beautiful hand that you could read off, and could do figures in his head—a degree of accomplishment totally unknown among the richest farmers of that country-side. Not at all like that slouching Luke Britton, who, when she once walked with him all the way from Broxton to Hayslope, had only broken silence to remark that the grey goose had begun to lay. And as for Mr Craig, the gardener, he was a sensible man enough, to be sure, but he was knock-kneed, and had a queer sort of[4] sing-song in his talk; moreover, on the most charitable supposition, he must be far[5] on the way to forty.

Hetty was quite certain her uncle wanted her to encourage Adam, and would be pleased for her to marry him. For those were times when there was no rigid demarcation of rank between the farmer and the respectable artisan, and on the home hearth, as well as in the public house, they might be seen taking their jug of ale together; the farmer[6] having a latent sense of capital, and of weight in parish affairs, which sustained him under his conspicuous inferiority in conversation. Martin Poyser was not a frequenter of public houses, but he liked a friendly chat[7] over his own home-brewed; and[8] though it was pleasant to lay down the law to a stupid neighbour who had no notion how to make the best of his farm, it was also an agreeable variety to[9] learn something from a clever fellow like Adam Bede. Accordingly, for the last[1] three years—ever since he had superintended the building of the new barn—Adam had always been made welcome at the Hall Farm, especially of a winter evening, when the whole family, in patriarchal fashion,[2] master and mistress, children and servants, were assembled in that glorious kitchen, at well-graduated distances from the blazing fire. And for the last two years[3], at least, Hetty had been in the habit of hearing her uncle say, "Adam Bede may be[4] working for wage now, but he'll be a master-man some day, as sure as I sit in this chair.

---

[1] look ⟨any⟩ from *MS*   [2] chesnut] chestnut *MS 1* ches⟨t⟩nut *8*
[3] knew, with only looking at it, the value of the chesnut tree that was blown down,] *revised in MS from* knew the value of the chestnut tree that was blown down, with only looking at it
[4] of ⟨hum⟩ sing-song *MS*   [5] far] *added in MS*   [6] farmer ⟨with⟩ having *MS*
[7] chat {with a neighbour} ⟨with a neighbour⟩ over his {own} home-brewed *MS*
[8] & ⟨he had acuteness enough to prefer Adam Bede's company⟩ though it was pleasant to lay down the law to a stupid *MS*
[9] to ⟨have the society of⟩ learn something from *MS*   [1] last ⟨four⟩ three *MS*
[2] fashion, ⟨from the⟩ master *MS*   [3] last two years] *revised in MS from* last year
[4] be ⟨a⟩ working ⟨man⟩ {for} wage *MS*

Mester Burge[5] is in the right on't to want him to go partners and marry his daughter, if it's true what they say;[6] the woman as marries him 'ull have a good take, be't Lady Day or Michaelmas[7],"—a[8] remark which Mrs Poyser always followed up with her cordial assent. "Ah," she would say, "it's all very fine having a ready-made rich man, but mayhappen he'll be a ready-made fool; and it's no use filling your pocket full o' money if you've got a hole in the corner. It'll do you no good to sit in a spring-cart o' your own, if you've got a soft to drive you: he'll soon turn you over into the ditch. I allays[9] said I'd never marry a man as had got no brains; for where's the use of a woman having brains of her own if she's[1] tackled to a geck as everybody's a-laughing at? She might as well dress herself fine to sit back'ards on a donkey."

These expressions, though figurative, sufficiently indicated the bent of Mrs Poyser's mind with regard to Adam; and though[2] she and her husband might have viewed the subject differently if Hetty had been a daughter of their own, it was clear that they would have welcomed the match with Adam for a penniless niece. For what could Hetty have been but a servant elsewhere, if her uncle had not taken her in and brought her up as a domestic help to her aunt, whose health since the birth of Totty had not been equal to more positive labour than the superintendence of servants and children? But[3] Hetty[4] had never given Adam any steady encouragement. Even in the moments when she was most thoroughly conscious of his superiority to her other admirers, she[5] had never brought herself to think of accepting him. She liked to feel that this strong, skilful, keen-eyed man was in her power, and would have been indignant if he had shown the least sign of slipping from under the yoke of her coquettish tyranny, and attaching himself to the gentle Mary Burge, who would have been grateful enough for the most trifling notice from him. "Mary Burge, indeed! such a sallow-faced girl: if she put on a bit of pink ribbon, she looked as yellow as a crow-flower, and her hair was as straight as a hank of cotton." And always when Adam stayed away for several weeks from the Hall Farm, and otherwise made some show of resistance to his passion as a foolish one, Hetty took care

---

[5] Burge ⟨may⟩ is MS

[6] say; ⟨and it'll be a good take for the woman that marries him⟩ the woman as marries him 'ull have a good take, MS

[7] be't Lady Day or Michaelmas] revised in MS from be't ⟨at⟩ Michaelmas or Lady Day

[8] Michaelmas,"—a] Michaelmas." A MS   [9] allays] al'ys MS

[1] she's ⟨got to walk to church of a Sunday wi'⟩ {tackled to} a MS

[2] though ⟨they⟩ she & her husband MS

[3] welcomed ... children? But] MS reads welcomed ⟨him as a husband⟩ {the match with Adam} for a penniless niece who must have been a servant elsewhere if her uncle had not taken her in {as a domestic help to her aunt whose health since the birth of Totty had not been equal to more positive labour than ⟨that of superintendence over⟩ superintendence of servants & children. But

[4] Hetty ⟨, even in the moments in⟩ had never given Adam MS   [5] she] added in MS

to entice him back into the net by little airs of meekness and timidity, as if
she were in trouble at his neglect. But as to marrying Adam, that was a very
different affair! There was nothing in the world to tempt her to do that. Her
cheeks never grew a shade deeper when his name was mentioned; she felt
no thrill when she saw him passing along the causeway by the window, or
advancing towards her unexpectedly in the footpath across the meadow;
she felt nothing when his eyes rested on her, but the cold triumph of
knowing that he loved her, and would not care to look at Mary Burge: he
could no more stir in her the emotions that make the sweet intoxication of
young love, than the mere picture of a sun can stir the spring sap in the
subtle fibres of the plant. She saw him as he was—a poor man, with old
parents to keep, who would not be able, for a long while to come, to give her
even such luxuries as she shared in her uncle's house. And[6] Hetty's dreams
were all of luxuries: to sit in a carpeted parlour and always wear white
stockings;[7] to have some large beautiful ear-rings, such as were all the
fashion; to have Nottingham lace round the top of her gown, and something
to make her handkerchief smell nice, like Miss Lydia Donnithorne's when
she drew it out at church; and not to be obliged to get up early or be scolded
by anybody. She thought, if Adam had been rich and could have given her
these things, she loved him well enough to marry him.

But for the last few weeks a new influence had come over Hetty—vague,
atmospheric, shaping itself into no self-confessed hopes or prospects, but
producing a pleasant narcotic effect, making her tread the ground and go
about her work in a sort of dream, unconscious of weight or effort, and
showing[8] her all things through a soft, liquid veil, as if she were living not in
this solid world of brick and stone, but in[9] a beatified world, such as the sun
lights up for us in the waters. Hetty had become aware that Mr Arthur
Donnithorne would take a good deal of trouble for the chance of seeing her;
that he always placed himself at church[1] so as to have the fullest view of her
both sitting and standing; that he was constantly finding reasons for calling
at the Hall Farm, and always would contrive to say something for the sake
of making her speak to him and[2] look at him. The poor child no more
conceived at present the idea that the young squire could ever be her lover,
than a baker's pretty daughter in the crowd, whom a young emperor
distinguishes by an imperial but admiring smile,[3] conceives that she shall
be made empress. But the baker's daughter goes home and dreams of the
handsome young emperor, and perhaps weighs the[4] flour amiss while she is
thinking what a heavenly lot it must be to have[5] him for a husband: and so

---

[6] house. And] house:—and *MS*   [7] stockings;] *1* stockings, *MS* stockings: *8*
[8] effort, and showing] effort, ⟨making⟩ shewing *MS*   [9] in ⟨the⟩ a *MS*
[1] at church] *added in MS*   [2] & look⟨ing⟩ at *MS*
[3] smile, ⟨dreams⟩ conceives *MS*   [4] the ⟨flower⟩ flour *MS*
[5] have ⟨the⟩ him *MS*

poor Hetty had got a face and a presence haunting her waking and sleeping dreams; bright, soft glances had penetrated her, and suffused her life with a strange, happy languor. The eyes that shed those glances were really not half so fine as Adam's, which sometimes looked at her with a sad, beseeching tenderness; but they had found a ready medium in Hetty's little silly imagination, whereas Adam's could get no entrance through that atmosphere. For three weeks, at least, her inward[6] life had consisted of little else than living through in memory the looks and words Arthur had directed towards her—of little else than recalling[7] the sensations with which she heard his voice outside the house, and saw him enter, and became conscious that his eyes were fixed on her, and then became conscious that a tall figure, looking down on her with eyes that seemed to touch her, was coming nearer in clothes of beautiful texture, with an odour like that of a flower-garden borne on the evening breeze. Foolish thoughts! but[8] all this happened, you must remember, nearly sixty years ago, and Hetty was quite uneducated—a simple farmer's girl, to whom a gentleman with a white hand was dazzling as an Olympian god. Until to-day, she had never looked farther into the future than to the next time Captain Donnithorne would come to the Farm, or the next Sunday when she should see him at church; but now she thought, perhaps he would try to meet her when she went to the Chase[9] to-morrow—and if he should speak to her, and walk a little way, when[1] nobody was by! That had never happened yet; and now her imagination, instead of retracing the past, was busy fashioning what would happen to-morrow—whereabout in the Chase she should see him coming towards her, how she should put her new rose-coloured ribbon on, which he had never seen, and what he would say to her to make her return his glance—a glance which she would be[2] living through in her memory, over and over again, all the rest of the day.

In this state of mind, how could Hetty give any feeling to Adam's troubles, or think much about poor old Thias[3] being drowned? Young souls, in such pleasant delirium as hers, are as unsympathetic as butterflies sipping nectar; they are isolated from all appeals by a barrier of dreams—by invisible looks and impalpable arms.

While Hetty's hands were busy packing up the butter, and her head filled with these pictures of the morrow, Arthur Donnithorne,[4] riding by

[6] inward] *added in MS*

[7] her—of little else than recalling] her: in recalling *MS*

[8] Foolish thoughts! but] Foolish thoughts! you see; having nothing at all to do with the love felt by sweet girls of eighteen in our days; but *MS* 1 Foolish thoughts! ⟨you see; having nothing at all to do with the love felt by sweet girls of eighteen in our days;⟩ but *8*

[9] she went to the Chase] she passed through the Chase *MS*

[1] way, when] way with her when *MS*

[2] be ⟨imagining⟩ living through in her memory *MS*

[3] Thias ⟨Bede's⟩ being *MS*   [4] Donnithorne, ⟨was⟩ riding *MS*

Mr Irwine's side towards the valley of the Willow Brook, had also certain indistinct anticipations,[5] running as an under-current in his mind while he was listening to Mr Irwine's account of Dinah;—indistinct[6], yet strong enough to make him feel rather conscious when Mr Irwine suddenly said,

"What fascinated you so in Mrs Poyser's dairy, Arthur? Have you become an amateur of damp quarries and skimming-dishes?"

Arthur knew the Rector too well to suppose that a clever invention would be of any use, so he said, with his accustomed frankness,

"No, I went to look at the pretty butter-maker, Hetty Sorrel. She's a perfect Hebe; and if I were an artist, I would paint her.[7] It's amazing what pretty girls one sees among the farmers' daughters, when the men are such clowns. That common round red face one sees sometimes[8] in the men—all cheek and no features,[9] like Martin Poyser's—comes out in the[1] women of the family as the most charming phiz imaginable."

"Well, I have[2] no objection to your contemplating Hetty in an artistic light, but I must not have you feeding her vanity, and filling her little noddle with the notion that she's a great beauty, attractive to fine gentlemen, or you will spoil her for a poor man's wife—honest Craig's, for example, whom I have seen bestowing soft glances on her. The little puss seems already to have airs enough to make a husband as miserable as it's a law of nature for a quiet man to be when he marries a beauty. Apropos of marrying, I hope our friend Adam will get settled, now the poor old man's gone. He will only have his mother to keep in future, and I've a notion that there's a kindness between him and that nice modest girl, Mary Burge,[3] from something that fell from old Jonathan one day when I was talking to him. But when I mentioned the subject to Adam he looked uneasy, and turned the conversation. I suppose the love-making doesn't run smooth, or perhaps Adam hangs back till he's in a better position. He has independence of spirit enough for two men—rather an excess of pride, if anything."

"That would be a capital match for Adam. He would slip into old Burge's shoes, and make a fine thing of that building business, I'll answer for him. I should like to see him well settled in this parish; he would be ready then to act as my grand-vizier when I wanted one. We could plan no end of repairs and improvements together. I've never seen the girl, though, I think—at least I've never looked at her."

---

[5] anticipations ⟨about seeing Hetty in the Chase⟩ running as an under-current in his *MS*

[6] Dinah;—indistinct] Dinah. Indistinct *MS*

[7] Hebe; and if I were an artist, I would paint her.] Hebe; it's a pity she shouldn't be painted. *MS*

[8] sometimes] *added in MS*   [9] features,] *MS 1* features— *8*

[1] the ⟨men of⟩ women *MS*   [2] I have] I've *MS*

[3] Burge, ⟨&⟩ ⟨I think⟩ from *MS*

"Look at her next Sunday[4] at church—she[5] sits with her father on the left of the reading-desk. You needn't look quite so much at Hetty Sorrel then. When I've made up my mind that I can't afford to buy a tempting dog, I take no notice of him, because if he took a strong fancy to me, and looked lovingly at me, the struggle between arithmetic and inclination might become unpleasantly severe. I pique myself on my wisdom there, Arthur, and as an old fellow to whom wisdom has become cheap, I bestow it upon you."[6]

"Thank you. It may stand me in good stead some day, though I don't know that I have any present use for it. Bless me! how the brook has overflowed. Suppose we have a canter, now we're at the bottom of the hill."

That is the great advantage of dialogue on horseback;[7] it can be merged any minute into a trot or a canter, and one might have escaped from Socrates himself in the saddle. The two friends were free from the necessity of further conversation till they pulled up in the lane behind Adam's cottage.

---

[4] Sunday ⟨then⟩ at *MS*   [5] church—she] church. She *MS*

[6] upon you.⟨" It's a fine thing to conquer oneself, but I have always preferred running away. One gets more secure in that way, & what is better, one leans now in another⟩ {¶ "Thank you. It may ⟨serve⟩ stand me in good stead someday though I dont know that I have any present use for it. Bless me! How the brook has overflowed}. *MS*

[7] horseback; ⟨you⟩ {one} ⟨one⟩ {it} can {be} merge{d} ⟨it⟩ any *MS*

CHAPTER X[1].

DINAH VISITS LISBETH[2].

At five o'clock Lisbeth came downstairs with a large key in her hand: it was the key of the chamber where her husband lay dead. Throughout the day, except in her occasional outbursts of wailing grief, she had been in incessant movement, performing the initial duties to her dead with the awe and exactitude that belong to religious rites. She had brought out her little store of bleached linen, which she had for long years kept in reserve for this supreme use. It[3] seemed but yesterday—that time so many midsummers ago, when she had told Thias where this linen lay, that he might be sure and reach it out for her when *she* died, for she was the elder of the two. Then there had been the work of cleansing to the strictest purity every object in the sacred chamber, and of removing from it every trace of common daily occupation. The small window which had hitherto freely let in the frosty moonlight or the warm summer sunrise on the working man's slumber, must now be darkened with a fair white sheet, for this was the sleep which is as sacred[4] under the bare rafters as in ceiled houses. Lisbeth had even mended a long-neglected and unnoticeable rent in the checkered[5] bit of bed-curtain; for the moments were few and precious now in which she would be able to do the smallest office of respect or love for the still corpse, to which in all her thoughts she attributed some consciousness. Our dead are never dead to us until we have forgotten them: they can be injured by us, they can be wounded; they know all our penitence, all our aching sense that their place is empty, all the kisses we bestow on the smallest relic of their presence. And the aged peasant-woman most of all believes that her dead are conscious. Decent burial was what Lisbeth had been thinking of for herself through years of thrift, with an indistinct expectation that she should know when[6] she was being carried to the churchyard, followed by her husband and her sons; and now she felt as if the greatest work of her life were to be done in seeing that Thias was buried decently before her—under the white thorn, where once, in a dream, she had thought she lay in the coffin, yet all the while saw the sunshine above, and smelt the white blossoms that were so thick upon the thorn the Sunday she went to be churched[7] after Adam was born.

---

¹ CHAPTER X.] Chapter ⟨9⟩ 10. *MS*   ² Dinah⟨'s⟩ Visit{s} ⟨to⟩ Lisbeth *MS*
³ use. It] use: it *MS*   ⁴ sacred ⟨as⟩ under *MS*
⁵ checkered ⟨window⟩ bit of *MS*   ⁶ when ⟨her⟩ she *MS*
⁷ churched ⟨when⟩ after *MS*

But now she had done everything that could be done to-day in the chamber of death—had done it all herself, with some aid from her sons in lifting[8], for she would let no one be fetched to help her from the village, not being fond of female neighbours generally; and her favourite Dolly, the old housekeeper at Mr Burge's,[9] who had come to condole with her in the morning as soon as she heard of Thias's death, was too dim-sighted to be of much use. She had locked the door, and now held the key in her hand, as she threw herself wearily into a chair that stood out of its place in the middle of the house floor, where in ordinary times she would never have consented to sit. The kitchen had had none of her attention that day; it was soiled with the tread of muddy shoes, and untidy with clothes and other objects out of place. But what at another time would have been intolerable to Lisbeth's habits of order and cleanliness, seemed to her now just what should be: it was right that things should look strange and disordered and wretched, now the old man had come to his end in that sad way: the kitchen ought not to look as if nothing had happened. Adam, overcome with the agitations and exertions of the day after his night of hard work, had fallen asleep on a bench in the workshop; and Seth was in the back kitchen making a fire of sticks that he might get the kettle to boil, and persuade his mother to have a cup of tea, an indulgence which she rarely allowed herself.

There was no one in the kitchen when Lisbeth entered and threw herself into the chair. She looked round with blank eyes at the dirt and confusion on which the bright afternoon[1] sun shone dismally; it was all of a piece with the sad confusion of her mind—that confusion which belongs to the first hours of a[2] sudden sorrow, when the poor human soul is like one who has been deposited[3] sleeping among the ruins of a vast city, and wakes up in dreary amazement, not knowing whether it is the growing or the dying day—not knowing[4] why and whence came this illimitable scene of desolation, or why he too finds himself desolate in the midst of it.

At another time Lisbeth's first thought would have been, "Where is Adam?" but the sudden death of her husband had restored him in these hours to that first place in her affections which he had held six-and-twenty years ago: she had forgotten his faults as we forget the sorrows of our departed childhood, and thought of nothing but the young husband's kindness and the old man's patience. Her eyes continued to wander blankly until Seth came in and began to remove some of the scattered things, and

---

[8] with some aid from her sons in lifting] *added in* MS
[9] Burge's, {who had come to condole with her in the morning as soon as she heard of Thias's death, was} ⟨being⟩ too MS
[1] afternoon] MS *1* afternoon's *8*   [2] a ⟨new⟩ sudden MS
[3] like one who has been deposited] like a man {who has been} deposited MS
[4] knowing ⟨the⟩ why MS

clear the small round deal table that he might set out his mother's tea upon it.

"What art goin' to do?" she said, rather peevishly.

"I want thee to have a cup of tea, mother," answered Seth, tenderly. "It'll do thee good; and[5] I'll put two or three of these things away, and make the house look more comfortable."

"Comfortable! How canst talk o' ma'in' things comfortable? Let a-be, let a-be. There's no comfort for me[6] no more," she went on, the tears coming[7] when she began to speak, "now[8] thy poor feyther's gone, as I'n washed for and mended, an' got's victual for him[9] for thirty 'ear, an' him allays[1] so pleased wi' iverything I done for him[2], an' used to be so handy an' do the jobs for me when I war ill an' cumbered wi' th' babby, an' made me the posset an' brought it upstairs as proud as could be, an' carried the lad as war as heavy as two children for five mile an'[3] ne'er grumbled, all the way to Warson[4] Wake, 'cause I wanted to go an' see my sister, as war dead an' gone the very next[5] Christmas as[6] e'er come. An' him to be drownded in the brook as we[7] passed o'er the day we[8] war married an' come home together, an' he'd[9] made them lots o' shelves for me[1] to put my plates an' things on, an' showed 'em me[2] as proud as could be, 'cause he know'd[3] I should be pleased. An' he[4] war to die an' me[5] not to know[6], but to be a-sleepin' i' my bed, as if I caredna nought[7] about it. Eh! an' me[8] to live to see that! An' us as war young folks once, an' thought we[9] should do rarely when we[1] war married. Let a-be, lad, let a-be! I wonna ha' no tay: I carena if I ne'er ate nor drink no more. When[2] one end o' th' bridge tumbles down, where's th' use o' th' other stannin'? I may's well die, an' foller my old man. There's no knowin' but he'll want me[3]."

Here Lisbeth broke from words into moans, swaying herself backwards and forwards on her chair. Seth, always timid in his behaviour towards his mother, from the sense that he had no influence over her, felt it was useless to attempt to persuade or soothe her, till this passion was past; so he contented himself with tending the back-kitchen fire, and folding up his father's clothes, which had been hanging out to dry since morning; afraid to move about in the room where his mother was, lest he should irritate her further.

[5] good; and] good. And *MS*   [6] me] mey *MS*   [7] coming ⟨now⟩ when *MS*
[8] now ⟨your⟩ thy *MS*   [9] him] 'm *MS 1* ⟨'m⟩ him *8*   [1] allays] alys *MS*
[2] him] 'm *MS 1* ⟨'m⟩ him *8*   [3] an' ⟨niver⟩ ne'er *MS*
[4] Warson] War'son *MS 1* War⟨'⟩son *8*   [5] next] *added in MS*
[6] as ⟨ever⟩ e'er *MS*   [7] we] wey *MS*   [8] we] wey *MS*   [9] he'd] hey'd *MS*
[1] me] mey *MS*   [2] me] mey *MS*   [3] he know'd] hey knoo'd *MS*
[4] he] hey *MS*   [5] me] mey *MS*   [6] know] knoo *MS*
[7] nought] noght *MS 1* ⟨noght⟩ nought *8*   [8] me] mey *MS*   [9] we] wey *MS*
[1] we] wey *MS*   [2] When] Whan *MS*   [3] he'll want me] hey'll want mey *MS*

But after Lisbeth had been rocking herself and moaning for some minutes, she suddenly paused, and said aloud to herself,

"I'll go[4] an' see arter Adam, for I canna think where he's[5] gotten; an' I want him to go[6] upstairs wi' me afore it's dark, for the minutes to look at the corpse is like the meltin' snow."

Seth overheard this, and coming into the kitchen again, as his mother rose from her chair, he said,

"Adam's asleep in the workshop, mother. Thee'dst better not wake him. He was o'erwrought with work and trouble."

"Wake him? Who's a-goin' to wake him? I shanna wake him wi' lookin' at him. I hanna seen[7] the lad this two hour—I'd welly forgot as he'd[8] e'er growed up from a babby when's feyther carried him."

Adam was seated on a rough bench, his head supported by his arm, which rested from the shoulder to the elbow on the long planing-table in the middle of the workshop. It seemed as if he had sat down for a few minutes' rest, and had fallen asleep without slipping from his first attitude of sad, fatigued thought. His face, unwashed since yesterday, looked pallid and clammy; his hair was tossed shaggily about his forehead, and his closed eyes had the sunken look which follows upon watching and sorrow. His brow was knit, and his whole face had an expression of weariness and pain. Gyp was evidently uneasy, for he sat on his haunches resting his nose on his master's stretched-out leg, and dividing the time between licking the hand that hung listlessly down, and glancing with a listening air towards the door. The poor dog was hungry and restless, but would not leave his master, and was waiting impatiently for some change in the scene. It was owing to this feeling on Gyp's part, that when Lisbeth came into the workshop, and advanced towards Adam as noiselessly as she could, her intention not to awake him was immediately defeated; for[9] Gyp's excitement was too great to find vent in anything short of a sharp bark, and in a moment Adam opened his eyes and saw his mother standing before him. It was not very unlike his dream, for his sleep had been little more than living through again, in a fevered delirious way, all that had happened since daybreak, and his mother with her fretful grief was present to him through it all. The chief difference between the reality and the vision was, that in his dream Hetty was continually coming before him in bodily presence— strangely mingling herself as an actor in scenes with which she had nothing to do. She was even by the Willow Brook; she made his mother angry by coming into the house; and he met her with her smart clothes quite wet through as he walked in the rain to Treddleston, to tell the coroner. But wherever Hetty came, his mother was sure to follow soon; and when he opened his eyes, it was not at all startling to see her standing near him.

"Eh, my lad, my lad!" Lisbeth burst out immediately, her wailing impulse returning, for grief in its freshness feels the need of associating its loss and its lament with every change of scene and incident, "thee'st got nobody now but thy old mother to torment thee and be a burthen to thee: thy poor feyther 'ull ne'er anger thee no more; an'[1] thy mother may's well go arter him—the sooner the better—for I'm no good to nobody[2] now. One old coat 'ull do to patch another, but it's good for nought[3] else. Thee'dst like to[4] ha' a wife to mend thy clothes an' get thy victual, better nor thy old mother. An' I shall be nought[5] but cumber, a-sittin' i' th' chimney-corner. (Adam winced and moved uneasily; he dreaded, of all things, to hear his mother speak of Hetty.)[6] But if thy feyther had lived, he'd ne'er ha' wanted me[7] to go to make room for another, for he[8] could no more ha' done wi'out me[9] nor one side o' the[1] scissars[2] can do wi'out th' other[3]. Eh, we[4] should ha' been both flung away together, an' then I shouldna ha' seen[5] this day, an' one buryin'[6] 'ud ha' done for us both."

Here Lisbeth paused, but[7] Adam sat in pained silence: he could not speak otherwise than tenderly to his mother to-day; but he could not help being irritated by this plaint. It was not possible for poor Lisbeth to know how it affected Adam, any more than it is possible for a wounded dog to know how[8] his moans affect the nerves of[9] his master. Like all complaining women, she complained in the expectation of being soothed, and when Adam said nothing, she was only prompted to complain more bitterly.

"I know[1] thee couldst do better wi'out me[2], for thee couldst go[3] where thee likedst, an' marry them as thee likedst. But I donna want to say thee nay, let thee bring home who thee wut[4]; I'd ne'er open my lips to find faut, for when folks is old an' o' no use, they may think theirsens well off to get the bit an' the sup, though they'n to swallow ill words wi't. An' if thee'st set thy heart on a lass as'll bring thee nought[5] and[6] waste all, when thee mightst ha' them as 'ud make a man on thee, I'll say nought[7], now thy feyther's dead an' drownded, for I'm no better nor an old haft[8] when the blade's gone."

---

[1] more; an'] more. An' *MS*   [2] nobody] noobody *MS*
[3] nought] noght *MS 1* ⟨noght⟩ nought *8*   [4] to] t' *MS 1* ⟨t'⟩ to *8*
[5] nought] noght *MS 1* ⟨noght⟩ nought *8*
[6] (Adam winced, & moved uneasily: he dreaded, of all things, to hear his mother speak of Hetty.)] *added on verso of MS I. 156/169*
[7] me] mey *MS*   [8] he] hey *MS*   [9] me] mey *MS*   [1] the] th' *MS*
[2] scissars] scithers *MS 1* ⟨scithers⟩ scissars *8*
[3] wi'out th' other] wi'out the tother *MS 1* ⟨wi'outt he tother⟩ wi'out th' other *8*
[4] we] wey *MS*   [5] seen] saen *MS*   [6] buryin'] bur'in' *MS*
[7] Here Lisbeth paused, but] *added in MS*   [8] how ⟨its⟩ his *MS*
[9] the nerves of] *added in MS*   [1] know] knoo *MS*   [2] me] mey *MS*
[3] go] goo *MS*   [4] wut] wot'st *MS*   [5] nought] noght *MS 1* ⟨noght⟩ nought *8*
[6] and] an' *MS*   [7] nought] noght *MS 1* ⟨noght⟩ nought *8*
[8] haft ⟨now⟩ when *MS*

Adam, unable to bear this any longer, rose silently from the bench, and walked out of the workshop into the kitchen. But Lisbeth followed him.

"Thee wutna go[9] upstairs an' see thy[1] feyther, then? I'n done everythin' now, an' he'd[2] like thee to go[3] an' look at him[4], for he[5] war allays[6] so pleased when thee wast mild to him[7]."

Adam turned round at once, and said, "Yes, mother; let us go upstairs. Come, Seth, let us go together."

They went upstairs, and for five minutes all was silence. Then the key was turned again, and there was a sound of footsteps on the stairs. But Adam did not come down again; he was too weary and worn-out to encounter more of his mother's querulous grief, and he went to rest on his bed. Lisbeth no sooner entered the kitchen and sat down than she threw her apron over her head, and began to cry and moan, and rock herself as before. Seth thought, "She will be quieter by-and-by, now we have been upstairs;" and he went into the back-kitchen again to tend his little fire, hoping that he should presently induce her to have some tea.

Lisbeth had been rocking herself in this way for more than five minutes, giving a low moan with every forward movement of her body, when she suddenly felt a hand placed gently on hers, and a sweet treble voice said to her, "Dear sister, the Lord has sent me to see if I can be a comfort to you."

Lisbeth paused, in a listening attitude, without removing her apron from her face. The voice was strange to her. Could it be her sister's spirit come back to her from the dead after all those years? She trembled, and dared not look.

Dinah, believing that this pause of wonder was in itself a relief for the sorrowing woman, said no more just yet, but quietly took off her bonnet, and then[8], motioning silence to Seth, who, on hearing her voice, had come in with a beating heart, laid one hand on[9] the back of Lisbeth's chair, and leaned over her, that she might be aware of a friendly presence.

Slowly Lisbeth drew down her apron, and timidly she opened her dim dark eyes. She saw nothing at first but a face—a pure, pale face, with loving grey eyes, and it was quite unknown to her. Her wonder increased; perhaps it *was* an angel. But in the same instant Dinah had laid her hand on Lisbeth's again, and the old woman looked down at it. It was a much smaller hand than her own, but it was not white and delicate, for Dinah had never worn a glove in her life, and her hand bore the traces of labour from her childhood upwards. Lisbeth looked earnestly at the hand for a moment, and then[1], fixing her eyes again on Dinah's face, said, with something of restored courage, but in a tone of surprise,

---

[9] go] goo *MS*   [1] thy ⟨father⟩ feyther *MS*   [2] he'd] hey'd *MS*
[3] go] goo *MS*   [4] at him] at'n *MS* at 'm *1* ⟨at 'm⟩ at him *8*   [5] he] hey *MS*
[6] allays] al'ys *MS*   [7] to him] to'n *MS* to 'm *1* ⟨to 'm⟩ to him *8*
[8] then] *added in MS*   [9] on ⟨Lis⟩ the *MS*   [1] then ⟨looking up⟩ fixing *MS*

"Why, ye're a workin' woman!"

"Yes, I am Dinah Morris, and I work in the cotton-mill when I am[2] at home."

"Ah!" said Lisbeth slowly, still wondering; "ye[3] comed in so light, like the shadow[4] on the wall, an' spoke i' my ear, as I thought ye[5] might be a sperrit. Ye've[6] got a'most[7] the face o' one as is a-sittin' on the grave[8] i'[9] Adam's new Bible."

"I come from the Hall Farm now. You know Mrs Poyser—[1]she's my aunt, and she has heard of your great affliction, and is very sorry; and[2] I'm come to see if I can be any help to you in your trouble; for I know your sons Adam and Seth, and I know you have no daughter[3], and when the clergyman told me how the hand of God was heavy upon you, my heart went out towards you, and I felt a command to come and be to you in the place of a daughter in this grief, if you will let me."

"Ah! I know[4] who y' are now; y' are a Methody, like Seth; he's[5] tould me on you," said Lisbeth, fretfully, her overpowering sense of pain returning, now her wonder was gone. "Ye'll[6] make it out as trouble's a good thing, like *he*[7] allays[8] does. But where's the use o' talkin' to me[9] a-that'n? Ye[1] canna make the smart less wi' talkin'. Ye'll[2] ne'er make me believe[3] as it's better for me[4] not to[5] ha' my old man die in 's bed, if he[6] must die, an' ha' the parson to pray by him[7], an' me[8] to sit by him[9], an' tell him ne'er to mind th' ill words I've gi'en[1] him sometimes when I war angered, an' to gi' him[2] a bit an' a sup, as long as a bit an' a sup he'd[3] swallow. But eh! to die i' the[4] cold[5] water, an' us close to him[6], an' ne'er to know[7]; an' me[8] a-sleepin', as if I ne'er belonged to him[9] no more nor if he'd[1] been a journeyman tramp from nobody knows[2] where."

Here Lisbeth began to cry and rock herself again; and[3] Dinah said,

"Yes, dear friend, your affliction is great. It would be hardness of heart to say that your trouble was not heavy to bear. God didn't send me to you to make light of your sorrow, but to mourn with you, if you will let me. If you

---

[2] I am] I'm *MS*   [3] wondering; "ye] wondering. "Yey *MS*

[4] shadow] shadder *MS*   [5] ye] yur *MS* you *1* ⟨you⟩ ye *8*   [6] Ye've] Yey've *MS*

[7] a'most] welly *MS*   [8] a-sittin' on the grave] *added in MS*   [9] grave ⟨in⟩ i' *MS*

[1] Poyser—⟨she is⟩ she's *MS*   [2] sorry; and] sorry. And *MS*

[3] & I know you have no daughter] *added in MS*   [4] Ah! I know] Ah, I knoo *MS*

[5] he's] hey's *MS*   [6] Ye'll] Yey'll *MS*   [7] *he*] hey *MS*   [8] allays] al'ys *MS*

[9] me] mey *MS*   [1] Ye] Yey *MS*   [2] Ye'll] Yey'll *MS*

[3] me believe] mey belave *MS*   [4] me] mey *MS*   [5] to] t' *MS*

[6] he] hey *MS*   [7] him] 'm *MS 1* ⟨'m⟩ him *8*   [8] me] mey *MS*

[9] him] 'm *MS 1* ⟨'m⟩ him *8*   [1] I've gi'en] I'n gen *MS 1* ⟨I'n gen⟩ I've gi'en *8*

[2] him] 'm *MS 1* ⟨'m⟩ him *8*   [3] he'd] hey'd *MS*   [4] the] th' *MS*

[5] cold] could *MS 1* ⟨could⟩ cold *8*   [6] him] 'm *MS 1* ⟨'m⟩ him *8*

[7] know] knoo *MS*   [8] me] mey *MS*   [9] him] 'm *MS 1* ⟨'m⟩ him *8*

[1] he'd] hey'd *MS*   [2] nobody knows] noobody knoos *MS*

[3] again; and] again. And *MS*

had a table spread for a feast, and was making merry with your friends, you would think it was kind to let me come and sit down and rejoice with you[4], because you'd[5] think I should like to share those good things; but I should like better to share in your trouble and your labour, and it would seem harder to me if you denied me that. You won't send me away?[6] You're not angry with me for coming?"

"Nay, nay; angered![7] who said I war angered? It war good on you to come. An' Seth, why donna ye get her some tay? Ye war in a hurry to get some for me[8], as had[9] no need, but ye donna think o' gettin' 't for them as wants it. Sit ye down; sit ye down.[1] I thank ye kindly for comin', for it's little wage ye get by walkin' through the wet fields to see an old woman like me[2] . . . . Nay, I'n got no daughter o' my own—ne'er had[3] one—an' I warna sorry, for they're poor queechy things, gells is; I allays wanted to[4] ha' lads, as could fend for theirsens. An' the lads 'ull be marryin'[5]—I shall ha' daughters eno'[6], an' too many. But now, do ye make the tay as ye like it, for I'n got no taste i' my mouth this day—it's all one what I swaller—it's[7] all got the taste o' sorrow wi't."

Dinah took care not to betray that she had had her tea, and accepted Lisbeth's invitation very readily, for the sake of persuading the old woman herself to take the food and drink she so much needed after a day of hard work and fasting.

Seth was so happy now Dinah was in the house that he could not help thinking her presence was worth purchasing with a life in which grief incessantly followed upon grief; but the next moment he reproached himself—it was almost as if he were rejoicing in his father's sad death. Nevertheless the joy of being with Dinah *would* triumph: it was like the influence of climate, which no resistance can overcome. And the feeling even suffused itself over his face so as to attract his mother's notice, while she was drinking her tea.

"Thee may'st well talk o' trouble bein' a good thing, Seth, for thee thriv'st on't. Thee look'st as if thee know'dst[8] no more o' care an' cumber nor when thee wast a babby a-lyin' awake i' th' cradle. For thee'dst allays[9] lie still wi' thy eyes open, an' Adam ne'er 'ud lie still a minute when he wakened. Thee wast allays[1] like a bag o' meal as can ne'er be bruised,

[4] you ⟨; but now I want to mourn with you⟩ because you would think I should like *MS*
[5] you'd] you would *MS* 1 ⟨you would⟩ you'd 8   [6] away?] away. *MS*
[7] angered!] angered? *MS*   [8] me] mey *MS*   [9] had] hed *MS*
[1] down{.} ⟨an' I'll goo an' see arter Adam, for I canna think where hey's gotten, an' I want him to goo upstairs wi' me afore it's dark.⟨⟨"⟩⟩ An' it's fittin' yey should go too, Seth, for th' minutes to look at th⟩ I *MS*
[2] me] mey *MS*   [3] had] hed *MS*   [4] allays wanted to] alys wanted t' *MS*
[5] marryin'] marr'in' *MS* marryin 1 marryin' 8   [6] eno'] enoo *MS* 1 ⟨enoo⟩ eno' 8
[7] swaller—it's] swaller. It's *MS*   [8] know'dst] knoo'dst *MS*   [9] allays] alys *MS*
[1] allays] alys *MS*

though, for the matter o' that, thy poor feyther war just such[2] another. But *ye*'ve[3] got the same look too" (here Lisbeth turned to Dinah). "I[4] reckon it's wi' bein' a Methody. Not as I'm a-findin' faut wi' ye for't, for ye've[5] no call to be frettin', an' somehow ye[6] looken sorry too. Eh![7] well, if the Methodies are fond o' trouble, they're like to thrive: it's a pity they canna ha't all, an' take[8] it away from them as donna like it. I could ha' gi'en 'em plenty; for when I'd gotten my old man I war worreted from morn till night; and[9] now he's gone[1], I'd be glad for the worst o'er again."

"Yes," said Dinah, careful not to oppose any feeling of Lisbeth's, for her reliance, in her smallest words and deeds, on a divine guidance, always issued in that finest woman's tact which proceeds from acute and ready sympathy—"yes; I remember, too, when my dear aunt died, I longed for the sound of her bad cough in the nights, instead of the silence that came when she was gone. But now, dear friend, drink this other cup of tea and eat a little more."

"What![2]" said Lisbeth, taking the cup, and speaking in a less querulous tone, "had ye got no feyther[3] and mother, then, as ye[4] war so sorry about your aunt?"

"No, I never knew a father or mother; my[5] aunt brought me up from a baby. She had no children, for she was never married, and she brought me up as tenderly as if I'd been her own child."

"Eh, she'd fine work wi' ye, I'll warrant[6], bringin' ye up from a babby, an' her a lone woman—it's ill bringin' up a cade lamb. But I dare say ye[7] warna franzy, for ye[8] look as if ye'd[9] ne'er been angered i' your life. But what did ye do when your aunt died, an' why didna ye come to live i'[1] this country, bein' as Mrs Poyser's your aunt too?"

Dinah, seeing that Lisbeth's attention was attracted, told her the story of her early life—how she had been brought up to work hard, and what sort of place Snowfield was, and how many people had a hard life there—all the details that she thought likely to interest Lisbeth. The old woman listened, and forgot to be fretful, unconsciously subject to the soothing influence of Dinah's face and voice. After a while she was persuaded to let[2] the kitchen be made tidy; for Dinah was bent on this, believing that the sense of order and quietude around her would help in disposing Lisbeth to join in the prayer[3] she longed to pour forth at her side. Seth, meanwhile, went out to

---

[2] war just such] war such *MS*   [3] *ye*'ve] yey've *MS*
[4] too" (here Lisbeth turned to Dinah). "I] too," here Lisbeth turned to Dinah, "I *MS*
[5] ye've] yey've *MS*   [6] ye] yey *MS*   [7] Eh!] Eh, *MS* Eh! *1* Eh⟨?⟩ {!} *8*
[8] take] ta'e *MS*   [9] and] an' *MS 1*   [1] now he's gone] noo hey's goon *MS*
[2] "What!] "What, *MS 1*   [3] feyther] father *MS*   [4] ye] yey *MS*
[5] mother; my] mother. My *MS*   [6] warrant] warrand *MS*   [7] ye] yey *MS*
[8] ye] yey *MS*   [9] ye'd] yey'd *MS*   [1] i'] in *Cabinet*
[2] let ⟨Dinah put⟩ the kitchen {be put} ⟨be put⟩ ⟨in order⟩ be *MS*
[3] prayer ⟨Dinah⟩ she *MS*

chop wood; for he surmised that[4] Dinah would like to be left alone with his mother.

Lisbeth sat watching her as she moved about in her still quick way, and said at last, "Ye've[5] got a notion o' cleanin' up. I wouldna mind ha'in'[6] ye[7] for a daughter, for ye[8] wouldna spend the lad's wage i' fine clothes an' waste. Ye're[9] not like the lasses o' this country-side. I reckon folks is different at Snowfield from what they are here."

"[1]They have a different sort of life, many of 'em," said Dinah; "they work at different things—some in the mill, and many in the mines, in the villages round about. But the heart of man is the same everywhere, and there are the children of this world and the children of light there as well as elsewhere. But we've many more Methodists there than in this country."

"Well, I didna know[2] as the Methody women war like ye[3], for there's Will Maskery's wife, as they say's a big Methody, isna pleasant to look at, at all. I'd as lief look at a[4] tooad. An' I'm thinkin' I wouldna mind if ye'd[5] stay an' sleep here, for I should like to see ye i' th' house i' th' mornin'. But may-happen they'll be lookin' for ye at[6] Mester Poyser's."

"No," said Dinah, "they don't expect me, and I should like to stay, if you'll let me."

"Well, there's room; I'n[7] got my bed laid i' th' little room o'er the back kitchen, an' ye[8] can lie beside me. I'd be glad to ha' ye wi' me to speak[9] to i' th' night[1], for ye've[2] got a nice way o' talkin'. It puts me i' mind o' the swallows as was under the thack last 'ear, when they fust begun to sing low an' soft-like i' th' mornin'. Eh, but my old man war fond o' them birds! an' so war Adam, but they'n ne'er comed again this 'ear. Happen *they*'re[3] dead too."

"There," said Dinah, "now the kitchen looks tidy, and now, dear[4] mother—for I'm your daughter to-night, you know—I should like you to wash your face and have a clean cap on. Do you remember what David did, when God took away his child from him? While the child was yet alive he fasted and prayed to God to spare it, and he would neither eat nor drink, but lay on the ground all night, beseeching God for the child. But when he knew it was dead, he rose up from the ground and washed and anointed himself, and changed his clothes, and ate and drank; and[5] when they asked him how it was that he seemed to have left off grieving now the child was

---

[4] that ⟨it would be better to leave⟩ Dinah {would like to be left} alone *MS*

[5] Ye've] Yey've *MS*   [6] ha'in'] ha'in *MS*   [7] ye] yey *MS*   [8] ye] yey *MS*

[9] Ye're] Yey're *MS*

[1] "⟨No, much the same⟩ They have a different sort of life, many of 'em," *MS*

[2] know] knoo *MS*   [3] ye] yey *MS*   [4] a ⟨toad⟩ tooad *MS*

[5] ye'd] yey'd *MS*   [6] at ⟨M^r⟩ Mester *MS*   [7] room; I'n] room. I'n *MS*

[8] ye] yey *MS*   [9] speak] spake *MS*   [1] night] naight *MS*

[2] ye've] yey've *MS*   [3] *they*'re] they'n *MS* they're *1* ⟨they're⟩ they're *8*

[4] now, dear] *MS 1* now {,} dear *8*   [5] drank; and] drank. And *MS*

dead, he said, 'While the child was yet alive, I fasted and wept; for I said, Who can tell whether God will be gracious to me, that the child may live? But now he is dead, why⁶ should I fast? can I bring him back again? I shall go to him, but he shall not return to me.' "

"Eh, that's a true word,⁷" said Lisbeth. "Yea, my old man wonna come back to me, but I shall go to him—the sooner the better. Well, ye⁸ may do as ye like wi' me: there's a clean cap i' that drawer, an' I'll go i' the back kitchen an' wash my face. An' Seth,⁹ thee mayst reach¹ down Adam's new Bible wi' th' picters in, an' she² shall read us a chapter. Eh, I like them words—I shall go to him, but he³ wonna come back to me⁴."

Dinah and Seth were both inwardly offering thanks for the greater quietness of spirit that had come over Lisbeth. This was what Dinah had been trying to bring about, through all her still sympathy and absence⁵ from exhortation. From her girlhood upwards she had had experience among the sick and the mourning, among minds hardened and shrivelled through poverty and ignorance, and had gained the subtlest perception of the mode in which they could best be touched, and softened into willingness to receive words of spiritual consolation or warning. As Dinah expressed it, "she was never left to herself; but it was always given her when to keep silence and when to speak." And do we not all agree to call rapid thought and noble impulse by the name of inspiration? After⁶ our subtlest analysis of the mental process, we must still say, as Dinah did, that our highest thoughts and our best deeds are all given to us.

And so there was earnest prayer—there was faith, love, and hope pouring itself forth that evening in the little kitchen. And poor aged fretful Lisbeth, without grasping any distinct idea, without going through any course of religious emotions, felt a vague sense of goodness and love, and of something right lying underneath and beyond all this sorrowing life. She couldn't understand the sorrow; but, for these moments, under the subduing influence of Dinah's spirit, she felt that she must be patient and still.

⁶ why] wherefore *Cabinet*   ⁷ word,] word! *MS 1*   ⁸ ye] yey *MS*
⁹ Seth, ⟨ye⟩ thee *MS*   ¹ reach] raich *MS*   ² she] shey *MS*
³ he] hey *MS*   ⁴ me] mey *MS*   ⁵ absence] abstinence *MS*
⁶ After ⟨the⟩ our *MS*

CHAPTER XI.

IN THE COTTAGE.

It was but half past four the next morning, when Dinah, tired of lying awake listening to the birds, and watching the growing light through the little window in the garret roof, rose and began to dress herself very quietly, lest she should disturb Lisbeth. But already some one else was astir in the house, and had gone downstairs, preceded by Gyp. The dog's pattering step was a sure sign that it was Adam who went down; but Dinah was not aware of this, and she thought it was more likely to be Seth, for he had told her how Adam had staid up working the night before. Seth, however, had only just awaked at the sound of the opening door. The exciting influence of the previous day, heightened at last by Dinah's unexpected presence, had not been counteracted by any bodily weariness, for he had not done his[1] ordinary amount of hard work; and so when he went to bed, it was not till he had tired himself with hours of tossing wakefulness, that drowsiness came, and led on a heavier morning sleep than was usual with him.

But Adam had been refreshed by his long rest, and with his habitual impatience of mere passivity, he was eager to begin the new day, and subdue sadness by his strong will and strong arm. The white mist lay in the valley; it was going to be a bright, warm day, and he would start to work again when he had had his breakfast.

"There's nothing but what's bearable as long as a man can work," he said to himself: "the natur[2] o' things doesn't change, though it seems as if[3] one's own life was nothing but change. The square o' four is sixteen, and[4] you must lengthen your lever in proportion to your weight, is as true when a man's miserable as when he's happy; and the best o' working is, it[5] gives you a grip hold o'[6] things outside your own lot."

[7]As he dashed the cold water over his head and face, he felt completely himself again, and with his black eyes as keen as ever, and his thick black hair all glistening with the fresh moisture, he went into the workshop to look out the wood for his father's coffin, intending that he and Seth should

---

[1]   his ⟨usual⟩ ordinary *MS*   [2]   natur] nature *MS*
[3]   if ⟨our lives was⟩ one's own life was *MS*
[4]   and ⟨a long lever will lift more than a short one⟩ you must lengthen your lever in proportion to your weight *MS*
[5]   is, it] is as it *MS*   [6]   o'] of *MS*   [7]   ⟨He⟩ As *MS*

carry it with them to Jonathan Burge's, and have the coffin made by one of
the workmen there, so that his mother might not see and hear the sad task
going forward at home.

He had just gone into the workshop, when his quick ear detected a light
rapid foot on the stairs—certainly not his mother's. He had been in bed
and asleep when Dinah had come in,[8] in the evening, and now he wondered whose step this could be. A foolish thought came, and moved him
strangely. As if it could be Hetty! She was the last person likely to be in the
house. And yet he felt reluctant to go and look, and have the clear proof
that it was some one else. He stood leaning on a plank he had taken hold
of, listening to sounds which his imagination interpreted for him so
pleasantly, that the keen strong face became suffused with a timid tenderness. The light footstep moved about the kitchen, followed by the sound
of the sweeping brush, hardly making so much noise as the lightest
breeze that chases the autumn leaves along the dusty path; and Adam's
imagination saw a dimpled face, with dark bright eyes and roguish
smiles looking backward at this brush, and a rounded figure just leaning
a little to clasp the handle. A very foolish thought—it could not be
Hetty; but the only way of dismissing such nonsense from his head was
to go and see *who* it was, for his fancy only got nearer and nearer to belief
while he stood there listening. He loosed the plank, and went to the kitchen
door.

"How do you do, Adam Bede?" said Dinah, in her calm treble, pausing
from her sweeping, and fixing her mild grave eyes upon him. "I trust you
feel rested and strengthened again to bear the burthen and heat of the day."

It was like dreaming of the sunshine, and awaking in the moonlight.
Adam had seen Dinah several times, but always at the Hall Farm, where he
was not very vividly conscious of any woman's presence except Hetty's,
and he had only in the last day or two begun to suspect that Seth was in love
with her, so that his attention had not hitherto[9] been drawn towards her for
his brother's sake. But now her slim figure, her plain black gown, and her
pale serene face, impressed him with all the force that belongs to a reality
contrasted with a preoccupying fancy. For the first moment or two he made
no answer, but looked at her with the concentrated, examining glance
which a man gives to an object in which he has suddenly begun to
be interested. Dinah, for the first time in her life, felt a painful self-
consciousness; there was something in the dark penetrating glance of this
strong man so different from the mildness and timidity of his brother Seth.
A faint blush came, which deepened as she wondered at it. This blush
recalled Adam from his forgetfulness.

---

[8] in, {in} the evening ⟨before⟩, & *MS*   [9] hitherto] *added in MS*

"I was quite taken by surprise; it was very good of you to come and see my mother in her trouble," he said, in a gentle grateful tone, for his quick mind told him at once how she came to be there. "I hope my mother was thankful to have you," he added, wondering rather anxiously what had been Dinah's reception.

"Yes," said Dinah, resuming her work, "she seemed greatly comforted after a while, and she's had a good deal of rest in the night, by[1] times. She was fast asleep when I left her."

"Who was it took the news to the Hall Farm?" said Adam, his thoughts reverting to some one there; he wondered whether *she* had felt anything about it.

"It was Mr Irwine, the clergyman, told me, and my aunt was grieved for your mother when she heard it, and wanted me to come; and so is my uncle, I'm sure, now he's heard it, but he was gone out to Rosseter[2] all yesterday. They'll look for you there as soon as you've got time to go, for there's nobody round that hearth but what's glad to see you."

Dinah, with her sympathetic divination, knew quite well that Adam was longing to hear if Hetty had said anything about their trouble; she was too rigorously truthful for benevolent invention, but she had contrived to say something in which Hetty was tacitly included. Love has a way of cheating itself consciously, like a child who plays at solitary hide-and-seek; it is pleased with assurances that it all the while disbelieves. Adam liked what Dinah had said so much that his mind was directly full of the next visit he should pay to the Hall Farm, when Hetty would perhaps behave more kindly to him than she had ever done before.

"But you won't be there yourself any longer?" he said to Dinah.

"No, I go back to Snowfield on Saturday, and I[3] shall have to set out to Treddleston early, to be in time for the Oakbourne[4] carrier. So I must go back to the farm to-night, that I may have the last day with my aunt and her children. But I can stay here all to-day, if[5] your mother would like me; and her heart seemed inclined towards me last night."

"Ah, then, she's sure to want you to-day. If mother takes to people at the beginning, she's sure to get fond of 'em; but she's a strange way of not liking young women. Though, to be sure," Adam went on,[6] smiling, "her not liking other young women is no reason why she shouldn't like you."

Hitherto Gyp had been assisting at this conversation in motionless silence, seated on his haunches, and alternately looking up in his master's face to watch its[7] expression, and observing Dinah's movements about the kitchen. The kind smile with which Adam uttered the last words was

---

[1] night, by] *MS* night by *1* night {,} by *8*   [2] Rosseter] Drosseter *MS*
[3] I ⟨must⟩ shall have to *MS*   [4] Oakbourne] Stoniton *MS*
[5] to-day, if] to-day if *MS 1* to-day{,} if *8*   [6] on,] *MS* on *1 8*   [7] its] it's *MS*

apparently decisive with Gyp of the light in which the stranger was to be regarded, and as she turned round after putting aside her sweeping-brush, he trotted towards her, and put up his muzzle against her hand in a friendly way.

"You see Gyp bids you welcome," said Adam, "and he's very slow to welcome strangers."

"Poor dog!" said Dinah, patting the rough grey coat, "I've a strange feeling about the dumb things as if they wanted to speak, and it was a trouble to 'em because they couldn't. I can't help being sorry for the dogs always, though perhaps there's no need. But they may well have more in them than they know how to make us understand, for we can't say half what we feel, with all our words."

Seth came down now, and was pleased to find Adam talking with Dinah; he wanted Adam to know how much better she was than all other women. But after a few words of greeting, Adam drew him into the workshop to consult about the coffin, and Dinah went on with her cleaning.

By six o'clock they were all at breakfast with Lisbeth in a kitchen as clean as she could have made it herself. The window and door were open, and the morning air brought with it a mingled scent of southernwood, thyme, and sweetbrier from the patch of garden by the side of the cottage. Dinah did not sit down at first, but moved about, serving[8] the others with the warm porridge and the toasted oat-cake, which she had got ready in the usual way, for she had asked Seth to tell her just what his mother gave them for breakfast. Lisbeth had been unusually silent since she came downstairs, apparently requiring some time to adjust her ideas to a state of things in which she came down like a lady to find all the work done, and sat still to be waited on. Her new sensations seemed[9] to exclude the remembrance of her grief. At last, after tasting[1] the porridge, she broke silence:

"Ye[2] might ha' made the parridge worse," she said to Dinah, "I can ate it wi'out its turnin' my stomach. It might ha' been a trifle thicker an' no harm, an' I allays[3] putten a sprig o' mint in mysen; but how's ye t' know[4] that? Th'[5] lads arena like to get folks as 'ull[6] make their parridge as I'n made it for 'em; it's well if they get onybody as 'll make parridge at all. But ye[7] might do, wi' a bit o' showin'; for ye're a stirrin' body in a mornin', an' ye've[8] a light heel, an' ye've[9] cleaned[1] th' house well enough[2] for a ma'-shift."

[8] about, serving] about serving *MS 1* about{,} serving *8*
[9] seemed ⟨for the time⟩ to *MS*   [1] after tasting] having tasted *MS*
[2] Ye] Yey *MS*   [3] allays] alys *MS*   [4] how's ye t' know] hoo's yey t' knoo *MS*
[5] Th'] The *Cabinet*   [6] 'ull] 'll *Cabinet*   [7] ye] yey *MS*
[8] ye've] yey'n *MS*   [9] ye've] yey'n *MS*   [1] cleaned ⟨the⟩ th' *MS*
[2] enough] anoof *MS* enoof *1* ⟨enoof⟩ enough *8*

"Makeshift, mother?" said Adam. "Why, I think the house looks beautiful. I don't know how it could look better."

"Thee dostna know?—nay; how's thee to know?[3] Th' men ne'er know[4] whether the floor's cleaned or cat-licked. But thee'lt[5] know[6] when thee gets thy parridge burnt, as it's like enough to be when[7] I'n gi'en o'er makin[8] it. Thee'lt[9] think thy mother war good for summat then."

"Dinah," said Seth, "do come and sit down now and have your breakfast. We're all served now."[1]

"Ay, come an' sit ye down—do," said Lisbeth, "an' ate a morsel[2]; ye'd[3] need, arter bein' upo' your legs[4] this hour an' half a'ready. Come,[5] then," she added, in a tone of complaining affection, as Dinah sat down by her side,[6] "I'll be loath for ye t' go[7], but ye canna stay much longer, I doubt. I could put up wi' ye i' th' house better nor wi' most folks."

"I'll stay till to-night if you're willing," said Dinah. "I'd stay longer, only I'm going back to Snowfield on Saturday, and I must be with my aunt to-morrow."

"Eh, I'd ne'er go back to that country. My old man come from that Stonyshire side, but he[8] left it when he[9] war a young un, an' i' the right[1] on't too; for he[2] said as there war no wood there, an' it 'ud ha' been a bad country for a carpenter."

"Ah," said Adam, "I remember father telling me when I was a little lad, that he made up his mind if ever he moved it should be south'ard. But I'm not so sure about it. Bartle Massey says—and he knows the South—as the northern men are a finer breed than the southern, harder-headed and stronger-bodied, and a deal taller. And then he says, in some o' those counties it's as flat as the back o' your hand, and you can see nothing of a distance, without climbing up the highest trees. I couldn't abide that: I like to go to work by a road that'll take me up a bit of a hill, and see the fields for miles round me, and a bridge, or a town, or a bit of a steeple here and there. It makes you feel the world's a big place, and there's other men working in it with their heads and hands besides yourself."

"I like th'[3] hills best," said Seth, "when the clouds are over your head, and you see the sun shining ever so far off, over the Loamford way, as I've

---

[3] "Thee dostna know?—nay; how's thee to know?] "Thee dostna knoo? Nay, hoo's thee t' knoo? *MS* "Thee dostna know. Nay: how's thee to know? *1* "Thee dostna know⟨.⟩{?—} ⟨N⟩{n}ay: how's thee to know? *8*

[4] know] knoo *MS*   [5] thee'lt] thee't *MS 1* ⟨thee't⟩ thee'lt *8*   [6] know] knoo *MS*

[7] as it's like enough to be when] as thee't like to ha 't when *MS* as thee't like to ha' it when *1* as {it's} ⟨thee't⟩ like {enough} to ⟨ha' it⟩ {be} when *8*

[8] makin'] ma'in' *MS*   [9] Thee'lt] Thee't *MS 1* ⟨Thee't⟩ Thee'lt *8*

[1] served now."] served." *MS*   [2] morsel] mossel *MS 1* ⟨mossel⟩ morsel *8*

[3] ye'd] yey'd *MS*   [4] legs ⟨a⟩ this *MS*   [5] Come,] Coom *MS*

[6] as Dinah sat down by her side,] *added in MS*   [7] go] goo *MS*

[8] he] hey *MS*   [9] he] hey *MS*   [1] the right] th' raight *MS*

[2] he] hey *MS*   [3] th'] the *MS*

often done o' late, on the stormy days: it seems to me as if that was heaven where there's always joy and sunshine, though this life's dark and cloudy."

"O, I love the Stonyshire side," said Dinah; "I shouldn't like to set my face towards the countries where they're rich in corn and cattle, and the ground so[4] level and easy to tread; and to turn my back on the hills where the poor people have to live such a hard life, and the men spend their days in the mines away from the sunlight. It's very blessed on a bleak cold day, when the sky is hanging dark over the hill, to feel the love of God in one's soul, and carry it to the lonely, bare, stone houses, where there's nothing else to give comfort."

"Eh!" said Lisbeth, "that's very well for ye[5] to talk, as looks welly like the snowdrop-flowers[6] as ha' lived for days an' days when I'n gethered 'em, wi' nothin' but a drop o' water an' a peep o' daylight; but th' hungry foulks had better leave th' hungry country. It makes less mouths for the scant cake. But," she went on, looking at Adam, "donna thee talk o' goin' south'ard or north'ard, an'[7] leavin' thy feyther an'[8] mother i' the[9] churchyard, an' goin' to a country as they know[1] nothin' on. I'll ne'er rest i' my grave if I donna see thee i' th'[2] churchyard of a Sunday."

"Donna[3] fear, mother," said[4] Adam. "If I hadna[5] made up my mind not to go, I should ha'[6] been gone before now."

He had finished his breakfast now, and rose as he was speaking.

"What art goin' to do?" asked Lisbeth. "Set about thy feyther's coffin?"

"No, mother," said Adam; "we're[7] going to take the wood to the village, and have it made there."

"Nay, my lad, nay," Lisbeth burst out in an eager, wailing tone; "thee wotna let nobody[8] make thy feyther's coffin but thysen? Who'd[9] make it so well? An' him as know'd[1] what good work war, an's got a son as is th'[2] head o' the village, an' all Treddles'on too, for cleverness."

"Very well, mother, if that's thy[3] wish, I'll make the coffin at home[4]; but I thought thee wouldstna[5] like to hear the work going on."

"An' why shouldna I like 't? It's the right thing to be done. An' what's likin'[6] got to do wi't? It's choice o' mislikins[7] is all I'n got i' this world. One

---

⁴ ground so] ground is so *MS*   ⁵ ye] yey *MS*

⁶ snowdrop-flowers] snowdrop flowers *MS 1* snowdrop{-}flowers *8*

⁷ But," she went on, looking at Adam, "donna thee talk o' goin' south'ard or north'ard, an'] *revised in MS from* But donna thee talk o' goin' south'ard or north'ard," she went on, looking at Adam, "an'

⁸ an'] and *Cabinet*   ⁹ the] th' *MS*   ¹ know] knoo *MS*

² th'] the *Cabinet*   ³ Donna] Dont *MS*

⁴ mother," said] mother, dont fear," said *MS*   ⁵ hadna] hadn't *MS*

⁶ ha'] have *MS*   ⁷ Adam; "we're] Adam. "We're *MS*

⁸ nobody ⟨ma'⟩ make *MS*   ⁹ Who'd ⟨ma 't⟩ make it *MS*

¹ know'd] knoo'd *MS*   ² th'] the *Cabinet*   ³ thy] your *MS*

⁴ at home] *added in MS*   ⁵ thee wouldstna] you wouldn't *MS*

⁶ likin'] *MS 1* liking *8*   ⁷ mislikins] *MS 1* mislikings *8*

morsel's[8] as good as another when your mouth's out o' taste. Thee mun set about it now this mornin' fust thing. I wonna[9] ha' nobody to touch the coffin but thee."

[1]Adam's eyes met Seth's, which looked from Dinah to him rather wistfully.

"[2]No, mother," he said, "I'll not consent but Seth shall have a hand in it too, if it's to be done at home. I'll go to the village this forenoon, because Mr Burge 'ull[3] want to see me, and Seth shall stay at home and begin the coffin. I can come back at noon, and then he can go."

"Nay, nay," persisted Lisbeth, beginning to cry, "I'n[4] set my heart on't as thee shalt[5] ma' thy feyther's coffin. Thee't so stiff an' masterful, thee't ne'er do as thy mother wants thee. Thee wast[6] often angered wi' thy feyther when he[7] war alive; thee must be the better to him, now he's gone. He'd[8] ha' thought nothin' on't for Seth to ma's coffin."

"Say no more, Adam, say no more," said Seth gently, though his voice told that he spoke with some effort; "mother's[9] in the right. I'll go to work, and do thee stay at home."

He passed into the workshop immediately, followed by Adam; while Lisbeth, automatically obeying her old habits, began to put away the breakfast things, as if she did not[1] mean Dinah to take her place any longer. Dinah said nothing, but presently used the opportunity of quietly joining the brothers in the workshop.

They had already got on their aprons and paper caps, and Adam was standing with his left hand on Seth's shoulder, while he pointed with the hammer in his right to some[2] boards which they were looking at. Their backs were turned towards the door by which Dinah entered, and she came in so gently that they were not aware of her presence till they heard her voice saying, "Seth Bede!" Seth started, and they both turned round. Dinah looked as if she did not see Adam, and fixed her eyes on Seth's face, saying with calm kindness,

"I won't say farewell. I shall see you again when you come from work. So as I'm at the farm before dark, it will be quite soon enough."

"Thank you, Dinah; I should like to walk home with you once more. It'll perhaps be the last time."[3]

---

[8] morsel's] mossel's *MS 1* ⟨mossel's⟩ morsel's *8*   [9] wonna] wunna *MS 1* ⟨winna⟩ wonna *8*

[1] ⟨"Nay"⟩ Adam's *MS*   [2] "⟨Nay⟩ No *MS*   [3] 'ull] will *MS*
[4] cry, "I'n] cry. "I'n *MS*   [5] shalt] sha't *MS*   [6] wast] wart *MS*
[7] he] hey *MS*
[8] him, now he's gone. He'd] 'm noo hey's goon. Hey'd *MS* 'm, now he's goen. He'd *1* ⟨'m⟩ him, now he's ⟨goen⟩ gone. He'd *8*
[9] effort; "mother's] effort. "Mother's *MS*   [1] did not] didn't *MS*
[2] some ⟨wood⟩ boards *MS*   [3] time." ⟨There was a little⟩ ¶ There *MS*

There was a little tremor in Seth's voice. Dinah put out her hand and said, "You'll have sweet peace in your mind to-day, Seth, for your tenderness and long-suffering towards your aged mother."

She turned round and left the workshop as quickly and quietly as she had entered it. Adam had been observing her closely all the while, but she had not looked at him. As soon as she was gone, he said,

"I don't wonder at thee for loving her, Seth. She's got a face like a lily."

Seth's soul rushed to his eyes and lips: he had never yet confessed his secret to Adam, but now he felt a delicious sense of disburthenment, as he answered,

"[4]Ay, Addy, I do love her—too much, I doubt. But she doesna[5] love me, lad, only as one child o' God loves another. She'll never love any man as a husband—that's my belief."[6]

"Nay, lad, there's no telling; thee mustna lose heart. She's made out o'[7] stuff with a finer grain than most o' the women; I can see that clear enough. But if she's better than they are in other things, I canna[8] think she'll fall short of 'em in loving."

No more was said. Seth set out to the village, and Adam began his work on the coffin.

"God help the lad, and me too," he thought, as he lifted the board. "We're like enough to find life a tough job—hard work inside and out. It's a strange thing to think of a man as can lift a chair with his teeth, and walk fifty mile on end, trembling and turning hot and cold at only a look from one woman out of all the rest i' the world. It's a mystery we can give no account of; but no more we can of the sprouting o' the seed, for that matter."

---

[4] "⟨Ad⟩ Ay *MS*   [5] doesna] doesn't *MS*

[6] belief." ⟨There's [one word]⟩ ¶ "Nay *MS*   [7] o'] of *MS* *1* ⟨of⟩ o' *8*

[8] canna] can't *MS*

CHAPTER XII.[1]

IN THE WOOD.

[2]That same Thursday morning, as Arthur Donnithorne was moving about in his dressing-room, seeing his well-looking British person reflected in the old-fashioned mirrors, and stared at, from a dingy olive-green piece of tapestry, by Pharaoh's daughter and her maidens, who ought to have been minding the infant Moses, he was holding a discussion with himself, which, by the time his valet was tying the black silk sling over his shoulder, had issued in a distinct practical resolution.

"I mean to go to Eagledale and fish for a week or so," he said aloud. "I shall take you with me, Pym, and set off this morning; so[3] be ready by half past eleven."

The low whistle, which had assisted him[4] in arriving at this resolution, here broke out into his loudest ringing tenor, and the corridor, as he hurried along it, echoed to his favourite song from the "Beggar's Opera,"[5] "When the heart of a man is oppressed with care." Not an heroic strain; nevertheless Arthur felt himself very heroic as he strode towards the stables to give his orders about the horses. His own approbation was necessary to him, and it was not an approbation to be enjoyed quite gratuitously; it must be won by a fair amount of merit. He had never yet forfeited that approbation, and he had considerable reliance on his own virtues. No young man could confess his faults more candidly; candour was one of his favourite virtues; and how can a man's candour be seen in all its lustre unless he has a few failings to talk of? But he had an agreeable confidence that his faults were all of a generous kind—impetuous, warm-blooded, leonine; never crawling, crafty, reptilian. It was not possible for Arthur Donnithorne to do anything mean, dastardly, or cruel. "No! I'm a devil of a fellow for getting myself into a hobble, but I always take care the load shall fall on my own shoulders." Unhappily there is no inherent poetical justice in hobbles, and they will sometimes obstinately refuse to inflict their worst consequences on the prime offender, in spite of his loudly-expressed wish. It was entirely owing to this deficiency in the scheme of things that Arthur had ever brought any one into trouble besides himself. He was nothing, if not

---

[1] CHAPTER XII.] Chapter ⟨11⟩ 12. *MS*   [2] ⟨The next⟩ That same Thursday *MS*
[3] morning; so] morning. So *MS*   [4] him] *added in MS*
[5] Opera— "⟨O [three words] all those endearing young charms [three words]⟩ When the heart of a man is oppressed with care *MS*

good-natured; and all his pictures of the future, when he should come into the estate, were made up[6] of a prosperous, contented tenantry, adoring their landlord, who would be the model of an English gentleman—mansion in first-rate order, all elegance and high taste—jolly housekeeping—[7] finest stud in Loamshire—purse open to all public objects—in short, everything as different as possible from what was now associated with the name of Donnithorne. And one of the first good actions he would perform in that future should be to increase Irwine's income for the vicarage of Hayslope, so that he might keep a carriage for his mother and sisters. His hearty affection for the Rector dated from the age of frocks and trousers. It was an affection[8] partly filial, partly fraternal;—fraternal enough to make him like Irwine's company better than that of most younger men, and filial enough to make him[9] shrink strongly from incurring Irwine's disapprobation.

You perceive that Arthur Donnithorne was "a good fellow"—all his college friends thought him such: he[1] couldn't bear to see any one uncomfortable; he would have been sorry even in his angriest moods for any harm to happen[2] to his grandfather; and his aunt Lydia herself had the benefit of that soft-heartedness which he bore towards the whole sex. Whether he would have self-mastery enough to be always as harmless and purely beneficent as his good nature led him to desire, was a question that no one had yet decided against him: he was but twenty-one, you remember; and we don't inquire too closely into character in the case of a handsome generous young fellow, who will have property enough to support numerous peccadilloes—who, if he should unfortunately break a man's legs in his rash driving, will be able to pension him handsomely; or if he should happen to spoil a woman's existence for her, will make it up to her with expensive *bon-bons*[3], packed up and directed by his own hand. It would be ridiculous to be prying and analytic in such cases, as if one were inquiring into the character of a confidential clerk. We use round, general, gentlemanly epithets about a young man of birth and fortune; and ladies, with that fine intuition[4] which is the distinguishing attribute of their sex, see at once that he is "nice." The chances are that he will go through life without scandalizing any one; a sea-worthy vessel that no one would refuse to insure. Ships, certainly, are liable to casualties, which sometimes make terribly evident some flaw in their construction, that would never have been discoverable in smooth water; and many a "good fellow," through a disastrous combination of circumstances, has undergone a like betrayal.

---

[6] made up] *added in MS*   [7] housekeeping—] *MS 1* housekeeping, *8*

[8] affection ⟨blended ⟨⟨compounded⟩⟩ of the⟩ {partly} filial ⟨& {the}⟩ {partly} fraternal; {it was} ⟨it was⟩ fraternal *MS*

[9] him shrink⟨ly⟩ strongly *MS*   [1] such: he] such: why, he *MS*

[2] happen ⟨even⟩ to *MS*   [3] *bon-bons*] bon-bons *MS*

[4] intuition ⟨for⟩ which *MS*

But we have no fair ground for entertaining unfavourable auguries concerning Arthur Donnithorne, who this morning proves himself capable of a prudent resolution founded on conscience. One thing is clear: Nature has taken care that he shall never go far astray with perfect comfort and satisfaction to himself; he will never get beyond that border-land of[5] sin, where he will be perpetually harassed by assaults from the other side of the boundary. He will never be a courtier of Vice, and wear her orders in his button-hole.

It was about ten o'clock, and the sun was shining brilliantly; everything was looking lovelier for the yesterday's rain. It is a pleasant thing on such a morning to walk along the well-rolled gravel on one's way to the stables, meditating an excursion. But the scent of the stables, which, in a natural state of things, ought to be among the soothing influences of a man's life, always[6] brought with it some irritation to Arthur. There[7] was no having[8] his own way in the stables; everything was managed in the stingiest fashion. His grandfather persisted in retaining as head groom an old dolt whom no sort of lever could move out of his old habits, and who was allowed to hire a succession of raw Loamshire lads as his subordinates, one of whom had lately tested a new pair of shears by clipping an oblong patch on Arthur's bay mare. This state of things is naturally embittering; one can put up with annoyances in the house, but to have the stable made a scene of vexation and disgust, is a point beyond what human flesh and blood can be expected to endure long together without danger of misanthropy.

Old John's wooden, deep-wrinkled face was the first object that met Arthur's eyes as he entered the stable-yard, and it quite poisoned for him the bark of the two bloodhounds that kept watch there. He could never speak quite patiently to the old blockhead.

"You must have Meg saddled for me and brought to the door at half past eleven, and I shall want Rattler saddled for Pym at the same time. Do you hear?"

"Yes, I hear, I hear, Cap'n," said old John, very deliberately, following the young master into the stable. John considered a young master as the[9] natural enemy of an old servant, and young people in general as a poor contrivance for carrying on the world.

Arthur went in for the sake of patting Meg, declining as far as possible to see anything in the stables, lest he should lose his temper before breakfast. The pretty creature was in one of the inner stables, and turned her mild head as her master came beside her. Little Trot, a tiny spaniel, her inseparable companion in the stable, was comfortably curled up on her back.

"Well, Meg, my pretty girl," said Arthur, patting her neck, "we'll have a glorious canter this morning."

[5] of ⟨wrong-doing⟩ sin *MS*   [6] always ⟨suggested⟩ brought *MS*
[7] Arthur. There] Arthur: there *MS*   [8] having ⟨one's⟩ his own way ⟨there⟩ in *MS*
[9] the ⟨naturally⟩ natural *MS*

"Nay, your honour, I donna see[1] as that can be[2]," said John.

"Not be? Why not?"

"Why, she's[3] got lamed."

"Lamed, confound you! what do you mean?"

"Why, th' lad took her too close to Dalton's hosses, an' one on 'em flung out at her, an' she's[4] got her shank bruised o' the near fore-leg."

The judicious historian[5] abstains from narrating precisely what ensued. You understand that there was a great deal of strong language, mingled with soothing "who-ho's" while the leg was examined; that John stood by with quite as much emotion as if he had been a cunningly-carved[6] crab-tree walking-stick, and that Arthur Donnithorne presently repassed the iron gates of the pleasure-ground without singing as he went.

He considered himself thoroughly disappointed and annoyed. There was not another mount[7] in the stable for himself and his servant besides Meg and Rattler. It was vexatious; just when he wanted to get out of the way for a week or two. It seemed culpable in Providence to allow such a combination of circumstances. To be shut up at the Chase with a broken arm, when every other fellow in his regiment was enjoying himself at Windsor—shut up with his grandfather, who[8] had the same sort of affection for him as for his parchment deeds! And to be disgusted at every turn with the management of the house and the estate! In such circumstances a man necessarily gets in an ill humour, and works off the irritation by some excess or other.[9] "Salkeld would have drunk a bottle of port every day,"[1] he muttered to himself; "but[2] I'm not well-seasoned enough for that. Well, since[3] I can't go to Eagledale, I'll have a gallop on Rattler to Norburne this morning, and lunch with Gawaine."

Behind this explicit[4] resolution there lay an implicit one. If he lunched with Gawaine and lingered chatting, he should not reach the Chase again till nearly five, when Hetty would be safe[5] out of his sight in the house-keeper's room; and when she set out to go home, it would be his lazy time after dinner, so he should keep out of her way altogether. There really would have been no harm in[6] being kind to the little thing, and it was worth dancing with a dozen ball-room belles only to look at Hetty for half an hour.

---

[1] see] ⟨see⟩ sae MS   [2] be] be{y} MS   [3] she's] shey's MS
[4] she's] shey's MS   [5] historian ⟨pass⟩ abstains MS
[6] cunningly-carved] added in MS
[7] mount {in the stable} for himself and his servant ⟨in the stable⟩ besides MS
[8] who ⟨cared about⟩ had the same MS   [9] other. ⟨Gawain⟩ "Salkeld MS
[1] "Salkeld would have drunk a bottle of port every day,"] "Salkeld would have smoked a box of cigars in a ⟨day⟩ week" MS
[2] but ⟨I don't smoke⟩ I'm MS   [3] Well, since] Well! Since MS
[4] explicit] added in MS
[5] safe {out of his sight} in the housekeeper's room, ⟨out of his sight⟩. And MS
[6] in ⟨flirting with⟩ being kind to the little thing {& it was worth dancing with a dozen ball-room belles only to look at Hetty for half an hour};, [sic] but MS

But perhaps he had better not take any more notice of her; it might put notions into her head, as Irwine had hinted; though Arthur, for his part, thought girls were not by any means so soft and easily bruised; indeed, he had generally found them twice as cool and cunning as he was himself. As for any real harm in Hetty's case, it was out of the question: Arthur Donnithorne accepted his own bond for himself with perfect confidence.

So the twelve o'clock sun saw him galloping towards Norburne; and by good fortune Halsell Common lay in his road, and gave him some fine leaps for Rattler. Nothing like "taking" a few bushes and ditches for exorcising a demon; and it is really astonishing that the Centaurs, with their immense advantages in this way, have left so bad a reputation in history.

After this, you will perhaps be surprised to hear, that although Gawaine was at home, the hand of the dial in the courtyard had scarcely cleared the last stroke of three, when Arthur returned through the entrance-gates, got down from the panting Rattler, and went into the house to take a hasty luncheon. But I believe there have been men since his day who have ridden a long way to avoid a rencontre, and then galloped hastily back lest they should miss it. It is the favourite stratagem of our passions to sham a retreat, and to turn sharp round upon us at the moment we have made up our minds that the day is our own.

"The Cap'n's been ridin' the devil's⁷ own pace," said Dalton the coachman, whose person stood out in high relief as he smoked his pipe⁸ against the stable wall, when John brought up Rattler.

"An' I wish he'd⁹ get the devil¹ to do's grooming for'n," growled John.

"Ay; he'd hev a deal haimabler² groom nor what he has³ now," observed Dalton; and the joke appeared to him so good⁴, that, being left alone upon the scene, he continued at intervals to take his pipe from his mouth in order to wink at an imaginary audience, and shake luxuriously with a silent, ventral laughter; mentally rehearsing the dialogue from the beginning, that he might recite it with effect in the servants' hall.

When Arthur went up to his dressing-room again after luncheon, it was inevitable that the debate he had had with himself there earlier in the day should flash across his mind; but it was impossible for him now to dwell on the remembrance—impossible to recall the feelings and reflections which had been decisive with him then, any more than to recall the peculiar scent of the air that had freshened him when he first opened his window. The desire to see Hetty had rushed back like an ill-stemmed current; he was amazed himself at the force with which this trivial fancy seemed to grasp him: he was even rather tremulous as he brushed his hair—pooh! it was

⁷ devil's] divil's *MS*   ⁸ as he smoked his pipe] *added in MS*
⁹ he'd] hey'd *MS*   ¹ devil] divil *MS*
² haimabler] hamabler *MS 1* ⟨hamabler⟩ haimabler *8*   ³ has] hes *MS 1* ⟨hes⟩ has *8*
⁴ so good] *MS reads* so marrowy & unctuous

riding in that break-neck way. It was because he had made a serious affair of
an idle matter, by thinking of it as if it were of any consequence. He would
amuse himself by seeing Hetty to-day, and get rid of the whole thing from
his mind. It was all Irwine's fault. "If Irwine had said nothing, I shouldn't
have thought half so much of Hetty as of Meg's lameness." However, it was
just the sort of day for lolling in the Hermitage, and he would go and finish
Dr Moore's[5] *Zeluco* there before dinner. The Hermitage stood in Fir-tree
Grove—the way Hetty was sure to come in walking from the Hall Farm. So
nothing could be simpler and more natural: meeting Hetty was a mere
circumstance of his walk, not its object.

Arthur's shadow flitted rather faster among the sturdy oaks of the Chase
than might have been expected from the shadow of a tired man on a warm
afternoon, and it was still scarcely four o'clock when he stood before the tall
narrow gate leading into the delicious labyrinthine wood[6] which skirted
one side of the Chase, and which was called Fir-tree Grove, not because the
firs were many, but because they were few. It was a wood of beeches and
limes, with here and there a light, silver-stemmed birch—[7] just the sort of
wood[8] most haunted by the nymphs: you see their white sunlit limbs
gleaming athwart the boughs, or peeping from behind the smooth-
sweeping outline of a tall lime; you hear their soft liquid laughter—but if
you look with a too curious sacrilegious eye, they vanish behind the silvery
beeches, they make you believe that their voice was only a running brooklet,
perhaps they metamorphose themselves into a tawny squirrel that scam-
pers away and mocks you from the topmost bough. It was not a grove[9] with
measured grass or rolled gravel for you to tread upon, but with narrow,
hollow-shaped, earthy paths, edged with faint dashes of delicate moss—
paths which look as if they were made by the free-will of the trees and
underwood, moving reverently aside to look at the tall queen of the white-
footed nymphs.

It was along the broadest of these paths that Arthur Donnithorne passed,
under an avenue of limes and beeches. It was a still afternoon—the golden
light was lingering languidly among[1] the upper boughs, only glancing
down here and there on the purple pathway and its edge of faintly-
sprinkled moss: an[2] afternoon in which destiny disguises her cold awful

[5] Dr. Moore's] *added in MS*   [6] wood ⟨that⟩ which *MS*
[7] It was a wood of beeches and limes, with here and there a light, silver-stemmed birch—] It
was a wood of {silver} beeches & limes— *MS*
[8] wood ⟨that the nymphs haunt most⟩ most haunted by the nymphs *MS*
[9] bough. It was not a grove] bough. Not a ⟨wood⟩ grove *MS* bough. Not a grove *1* bough.
{It was n}⟨N⟩ot a grove *8*
[1] avenue of limes and beeches. It was a still afternoon—the golden light was lingering
languidly among] avenue of limes. You see it all—the afternoon stillness, the golden light
lingering languidly among *MS*
[2] moss: an] moss. An *MS*

face behind a hazy radiant veil, encloses us in warm downy wings, and poisons us with violet-scented[3] breath. Arthur strolled along carelessly, with a book under his arm, but not looking on the ground as meditative men are apt to do; his eyes *would* fix themselves on the distant bend in the road, round which a little figure must surely appear before long. Ah![4] there she comes: first, a bright patch of colour, like a tropic bird among the boughs, then a tripping figure, with a round hat on, and a small basket under her arm; then a deep-blushing, almost frightened, but bright-smiling girl, making her curtsy with a fluttered yet happy glance, as Arthur came up to her. If Arthur had had time to think at all, he would have thought it strange that he should feel fluttered too, be conscious of blushing too—in fact, look and feel as foolish as if he had been taken by surprise instead of meeting just what he expected. Poor things! It was a pity they were not in that golden age of childhood when they would have stood face to face, eyeing each other with timid liking, then given each other a little butterfly kiss, and toddled off to play together. Arthur would have gone home to his silk-curtained cot, and Hetty to her home-spun pillow, and both would have slept without dreams, and to-morrow would have been a life hardly conscious of a yesterday.

Arthur turned round and walked by Hetty's side without giving a reason. They were alone together for the first time. What an overpowering presence that first privacy is! He actually dared not look at this little butter-maker for the first minute or two. As for Hetty, her feet rested on a cloud, and she was borne along[5] by warm zephyrs; she had forgotten her rose-coloured ribbons[6]; she was no more conscious of her limbs than if her childish soul had passed into a water-lily, resting on a liquid bed, and warmed by the midsummer sunbeams. It may seem a contradiction, but Arthur gathered a certain carelessness and confidence from his timidity: it was an entirely different state of mind from what he had expected in such a meeting with Hetty; and full as he was of vague feeling, there was room, in those moments of silence, for the thought that his previous debates and scruples were needless.

"You are quite right to choose this way of coming to the Chase," he said at last, looking down at Hetty, "it is so much prettier as well as shorter than coming by either of the lodges."

"Yes, sir," Hetty answered, with a tremulous, almost whispering voice. She didn't know one bit how to speak to a gentleman like Mr Arthur, and her very vanity made her more coy of speech.

"Do you come every week to see Mrs Pomfret?"

"Yes, sir, every Thursday, only when she's got to go out with Miss Donnithorne."

"And she's teaching you something, is she?"

"Yes, sir, the lace-mending as she learnt abroad, and the stocking-mending—it looks just like the stocking, you can't tell it's been mended; and she teaches me cutting-out too."

"What,[7] are *you* going to be a lady's-maid?"

"I should like to be one very much indeed." Hetty spoke more audibly now, but still rather tremulously; she thought, perhaps she seemed as stupid to Captain Donnithorne as Luke Britton did to her.

"I suppose Mrs Pomfret always expects you at this time?"

"She expects me at four o'clock. I'm rather late to-day, because my aunt couldn't spare me; but[8] the regular time is four, because that gives us time before Miss Donnithorne's bell rings."

"Ah, then, I must not keep you now, else I should like to show you the Hermitage. Did you ever see it?"

"No, sir."

"This is the walk where we turn up to it. But we must not go now. I'll show it you some other time, if you'd like to see it."

"Yes, please, sir."

"Do you always come back this way in the evening, or are you afraid to come so lonely a road?"

"O no, sir, it's never late; I always[9] set out by eight o'clock, and it's so light now in the evening[1]. My aunt would be angry with me if I[2] didn't get home before nine."

"Perhaps Craig[3], the gardener, comes to take care of you?"

A deep blush overspread Hetty's face and neck. "I'm sure he doesn't; I'm sure he never did; I wouldn't let him; I don't like him," she said hastily, and the tears of vexation had come so fast, that before she had done speaking a bright drop rolled down her hot cheek. Then she felt ashamed to death that she was crying, and for one long instant her happiness was all gone. But in the next she felt an arm steal round her, and a gentle voice said,

"Why, Hetty, what makes you cry? I didn't mean to vex you. I wouldn't vex you for the world, you little blossom. Come, don't cry; look at me, else I shall think you won't forgive me."

Arthur had laid his hand on the soft arm that was nearest to him, and was stooping towards Hetty with a look of coaxing entreaty. Hetty lifted[4] her long dewy lashes, and met the eyes that were bent towards her with a sweet, timid, beseeching look[5]. What a space of time those three moments[6] were, while their eyes met and his arms touched her! Love is such a simple thing

[7] "What,] "What! *Cabinet*   [8] me; but] me. But *MS*
[9] always ⟨set out before⟩ set *MS*   [1] evening] evenings *MS*
[2] I ⟨stayed⟩ didn't *MS*   [3] Perhaps Craig] Perhaps Mr. Craig *MS*
[4] lifted ⟨the⟩ her *MS*   [5] sweet, timid, beseeching look] sweet spaniel-like look *MS*
[6] moments ⟨seemed⟩ were *MS*

when we have only one- and-twenty summers and a sweet girl of seventeen trembles under our glance, as if she were a bud[7] first opening her heart with wondering rapture to the morning. Such young unfurrowed souls roll[8] to meet each other like two velvet peaches that touch softly and are at rest; they mingle as easily as two brooklets that ask for nothing but to entwine themselves and ripple with ever-interlacing curves in the leafiest hiding-places. While Arthur gazed into Hetty's dark beseeching eyes, it made no difference to him what sort of English she spoke; and even if hoops and powder had been in[9] fashion, he would very likely[1] not have been sensible just then that Hetty wanted those signs of high breeding.

But they started asunder with beating hearts: something had fallen on the ground with a rattling noise; it was Hetty's basket; all her little work-woman's matters were scattered on the path, some of them showing a capability of rolling to great lengths. There was much to be done in picking up,[2] and not a word was spoken;[3] but when Arthur hung the basket over her arm again, the poor child felt a strange difference in his look and manner. He just pressed her hand[4], and said with a look and tone that were almost[5] chilling to her,

"I have been hindering you; I must not keep you any longer now. You will be expected at the house. Good-by."

Without waiting for her to speak, he turned away from her and hurried back towards the road that led to the Hermitage, leaving Hetty to pursue her way in a strange dream, that seemed to have begun in bewildering delight, and was now passing into contrarieties and sadness. Would he meet her again as she came home? Why had he spoken almost as if he were displeased with her? and then run away so suddenly? She cried, hardly knowing why.

Arthur too was very uneasy, but his feelings were lit up for him by a more distinct consciousness. He hurried to the Hermitage, which stood in the heart of the wood, unlocked the door with a hasty wrench, slammed it after him, pitched *Zeluco* into the most distant corner, and, thrusting his[6] right hand into his pocket, first walked four or five times up and down the scanty length of the little room, and then seated himself on the ottoman in an uncomfortable, stiff way[7], as we often do when we wish not to abandon ourselves to feeling.

He was getting in love with Hetty—that was quite plain. He was ready to pitch everything else—no matter where—for the sake of surrendering himself to this delicious feeling which had just disclosed itself. It was no

---

[7] bud {first} opening her heart {with} wondering *MS*   [8] roll ⟨together⟩ to *MS*

[9] been in] been then in *MS*   [1] likely ⟨he would⟩ not have *MS*

[2] up, ⟨but⟩ and *MS*   [3] spoken, ⟨&⟩ but *MS*   [4] hand] hands *MS*

[5] almost] *added in MS*   [6] his {right} hand⟨s⟩ into his pocket⟨s⟩ first *MS*

[7] himself on the ottoman in an uncomfortable, stiff way] himself in an uncomfortable, stiff ⟨[?in]⟩ way on the ottoman *MS*

use blinking the fact now—they would get too fond of each other, if he went on taking notice of her—and what would come of it? He should have to go away in a few weeks, and the poor little thing would be miserable. He *must not* see her alone[8] again; he must keep out of her way. What a fool he was for coming back from Gawaine's!

He got up and threw open the windows, to let in the soft breath of the afternoon, and the healthy scent of the firs that made a belt round the Hermitage. The soft air did not help his resolutions, as he leaned out and looked into the leafy distance. But he considered his resolution sufficiently fixed: there was no need to debate with himself any longer. He had made up his mind not to meet Hetty again; and now he might give himself up to thinking how immensely agreeable it would be if circumstances were different—how pleasant it would have been to meet her this evening as she came back, and put his arm round her again and look into her sweet face. He wondered if the dear little thing were thinking of him too—twenty to one she was. How beautiful her eyes[9] were with the tear on their lashes! He would like to satisfy his soul for a day with looking at them, and[1] he *must* see her again:—he must see her, simply to remove any false impression from her mind about his[2] manner to her just now. He would behave in a quiet, kind way to her—just to prevent her from going home with her head full of wrong fancies. Yes, that would be the best thing to do, after all.

It was a long while—more than an hour—before Arthur had brought his meditations to this point; but once arrived there, he could stay no longer at the Hermitage. The time must be filled up with movement until he should see Hetty again. And it was[3] already late enough to go and dress for dinner, for his grandfather's dinner-hour was six.

---

[8] alone] *added in MS*   [9] eyes ⟨looked⟩ were *MS*
[1] them, and] them. And *MS*   [2] his ⟨behaviour⟩ manner to her *MS*
[3] was ⟨time⟩ already late enough *MS*

CHAPTER XIII.

EVENING IN THE WOOD.

It happened that Mrs Pomfret had had a[1] slight quarrel with Mrs Best, the housekeeper, on this Thursday morning—a fact which had two consequences highly convenient to Hetty. It caused Mrs Pomfret to have tea sent up to her own room, and it inspired that exemplary lady's-maid with so lively a recollection of former passages in Mrs Best's conduct, and of dialogues in which Mrs Best had decidedly the inferiority as an interlocutor with Mrs Pomfret, that Hetty required no more presence of mind than was demanded for using her needle and throwing in[2] an occasional "yes" or "no." She would have wanted to put on her hat earlier than usual; only she had told Captain Donnithorne that she usually set out about eight o'clock, and if he *should* go to the Grove again expecting to see her, and she should be gone! Would he come? Her little butterfly-soul[3] fluttered incessantly between memory and dubious expectation. At last the minute-hand of the old-fashioned brazen-faced timepiece was on the last quarter to eight, and there was every reason for its being time to get ready for departure. Even Mrs Pomfret's preoccupied mind did not prevent her from noticing what looked like a new flush of beauty in the little thing as she tied on her hat before the looking-glass.

"That child gets prettier and prettier every day, I do believe," was her inward comment. "The more's the pity. She'll get neither a place nor a husband any the sooner for it. Sober well-to-do men don't like such pretty wives. When I was a girl, I was more admired than if I had[4] been so very pretty. However, she's reason to be grateful to me for teaching her something to get her bread with, better than farm-house work. They always told me I was good-natured—and that's the truth, and to my hurt, too, else there's them in this house that wouldn't be here now to lord it over me in the housekeeper's room."

Hetty walked hastily across the short space of pleasure-ground which she had to traverse, dreading to meet Mr Craig, to whom she could hardly have spoken civilly. How relieved she was when she had got safely under the oaks and among the fern of the Chase! Even then she was as ready to be startled as the deer that leaped away at her approach. She thought nothing

---

[1] Pomfret had had a] Pomfret had a *MS*   [2] in] *added in MS*
[3] butterfly-soul] butterfly soul *MS 1* butterfly{-}soul *8*   [4] I had] I'd *MS 1*

of the evening light that lay gently in the grassy alleys between the fern, and made the beauty of their living green more visible than it had been in the overpowering flood of noon: she thought of nothing that was present. She only saw something that was possible: Mr Arthur Donnithorne coming to meet her again along the Fir-tree Grove. That was the foreground of Hetty's picture; behind it lay a bright hazy something—days that were not to be as the other days of her life had been. It was as if she had been wooed by a river-god, who might any time take her to his wondrous halls below a watery heaven. There was no knowing what would come, since[5] this strange entrancing delight had come. If a chest full of lace and satin and jewels had been sent her from some unknown source, how could she[6] but have thought that her whole lot was going to change, and that to-morrow some still more bewildering joy would befall her? Hetty had never read a novel; if[7] she had ever seen one, I think the words would have been too hard for her: how then could she find a shape for her expectations? They were as formless as the sweet languid odours of the garden at the Chase, which had floated past her as she walked by the gate.

She is at another gate now—that leading into Fir-tree Grove. She enters the wood, where it is already twilight, and at every step she takes, the[8] fear at her heart becomes colder. If he[9] should not come! O how dreary it was—the thought of going out at the other end of the wood, into the unsheltered road, without having seen him. She reaches the first turning towards the Hermitage, walking slowly—he is not there. She hates the leveret that runs across the path: she hates everything that is not what she longs for. She walks on, happy whenever she is coming to a bend in the road, for perhaps he is behind it. No. She is beginning to cry: her heart has swelled so, the tears stand in her eyes; she gives one great sob, while the corners of her mouth quiver, and the tears roll down.

She doesn't know that there is another turning to the Hermitage, that she is close against it, and that Arthur Donnithorne is only a few yards from her, full of one thought, and a thought of which she only is[1] the object. He is going to see Hetty again: that[2] is the longing which has been growing through the last three hours to a feverish thirst. Not, of course, to speak in the caressing way into which he had unguardedly[3] fallen before dinner, but to set things right with her by a kindness which would have the air of friendly civility, and prevent her from running away with wrong notions about their mutual relation.

If Hetty had known he was there, she would not have cried; and it would have been better, for[4] then Arthur would perhaps have behaved as wisely as

[5] come, since] come since *MS 1* come {,} since *8*   [6] she ⟨think⟩ but have thought *MS*
[7] novel; if] novel: if *MS 1* novel⟨:⟩{;} if *8*   [8] takes, the] takes the *1* takes {,} the *8*
[9] he should⟨n't⟩ not *MS*   [1] is ⟨the⟩ object *MS*
[2] again: that] again—that *MS 1* again⟨—⟩{:} that *8*   [3] unguardedly] *added in MS*
[4] better, for] better. For *MS* better; for *1*

he had intended. As it was, she started when he appeared at the end of the side-alley, and looked up at him with two great drops rolling down her cheeks. What else could he do but speak to her in a soft, soothing tone, as if she were a bright-eyed spaniel with a thorn in her foot?

"Has something frightened you, Hetty? Have you seen anything in the wood? Don't be frightened—I'll take care of you now."

Hetty was blushing so, she didn't know whether she was happy or miserable. To be crying again—what did gentlemen think of girls who cried in that way? She felt unable even to say "no," but could only look away from him, and wipe the tears from her cheek. Not before a great drop had fallen on her rose-coloured strings: she knew that quite well.

"Come, be cheerful again. Smile at me, and tell me what's the matter. Come, tell me."

Hetty turned her head towards him, whispered, "I thought you wouldn't come," and slowly got courage to lift her eyes to him. That look was too much: he must have had eyes of Egyptian granite not to look too lovingly in return.

"You little frightened bird! little tearful rose! silly pet! You won't cry again, now I'm with you, will you?"

Ah, he doesn't know in the least what he is saying. This is not what he meant to say. His arm is stealing round the waist again, it is tightening its clasp;[5] he is bending his face nearer and nearer to the round cheek, his lips are meeting those pouting child-lips, and for a long moment time has vanished. He may be a shepherd in Arcadia for aught he knows, he may be the first youth kissing the first maiden, he may be Eros himself, sipping the lips of Psyche—it is all one.

There was no speaking for minutes after. They walked along with beating hearts till they came within sight of the gate at the end of the wood. Then they looked at each other,[6] not quite as they had looked before, for in their eyes there[7] was the memory of a kiss.

But already something bitter had begun to mingle itself with the fountain of sweets: already Arthur was uncomfortable. He took his arm from Hetty's waist, and said,

"Here we are, almost at the end of the Grove. I wonder how late it is," he added, pulling out his watch. "Twenty minutes past eight—but my watch is too fast. However, I'd better not go any farther[8] now. Trot along quickly with your little feet, and get home safely. Good-by."

He took her hand, and looked at her half sadly, half with a constrained smile. Hetty's eyes seemed to beseech him not to go away yet; but he patted her cheek and said "Good-by" again. She was obliged to turn away from him, and go on.

---

[5] clasp; ⟨your⟩ he *MS*   [6] other, ⟨but⟩ not *MS*   [7] there] *added in MS*
[8] farther] further *Cabinet*

As for Arthur, he rushed back through the wood, as if he wanted to put a wide space between himself and Hetty. He would not go to the Hermitage again; he remembered how he had debated with himself there before dinner, and it had all come to nothing—worse than nothing. He walked right on into the Chase, glad to get out of the Grove, which surely was haunted by his evil genius. Those beeches and smooth limes—there was something enervating in the very sight of them; but the strong knotted old oaks had no bending languor in them—the sight of them would give a man some energy. Arthur lost himself among the narrow openings in the fern, winding about without seeking any issue, till the twilight deepened almost to night under the great boughs, and the hare looked black as it darted across his path.

He was feeling much more strongly than he had done in the morning: it was as if his horse had wheeled round from a leap, and dared to dispute his mastery. He was dissatisfied with himself, irritated, mortified. He no sooner fixed his mind on the probable consequences of giving way to the emotions which had stolen over him to-day—of continuing to notice Hetty, of allowing himself any opportunity for such slight caresses as he had been betrayed into already—than he refused to believe such a future possible for himself. To flirt with Hetty was a very different affair from flirting with a pretty girl of his own station: that[9] was understood to be an amusement on both sides; or, if it became serious, there was no obstacle to marriage. But this little thing would be spoken ill of directly, if she happened to be seen walking with him; and then those excellent people, the Poysers, to whom a good name was as precious as if they had the best blood in the land in their veins—he should hate himself if he made a scandal of that sort, on the estate that was to be his own some day, and among tenants by whom he liked, above all, to be respected. He could no more believe that he should so fall in his own esteem than that he should break both his legs and go on crutches all the rest of his life. He couldn't imagine himself in that position; it[1] was too odious, too unlike him.

And even if no one knew anything about it, they might get too fond of each other, and then there could be nothing but the misery of parting, after all. No gentleman, out of a ballad, could marry a farmer's niece. There must be an end to the whole thing at once. It was too foolish.

And yet he had been so determined this morning, before he went to Gawaine's; and while he was there something had taken hold of him and made him gallop back. It seemed, he[2] couldn't quite depend on his own resolution, as he had thought he could: he almost wished his arm would get painful again, and then he should think of nothing but the comfort it would

[9] station: that] MS 1 station⟨—⟩{:} that 8

[1] position; it] position: it MS position—it 1 position⟨—⟩{;} it 8

[2] seemed, he] MS seemed he 1 seemed {that}⟨that⟩{,} he 8

be to get rid of the pain. There was no knowing what impulse might seize him to-morrow, in this confounded place, where there was nothing to occupy him imperiously through the live-long day. What could he do to secure himself from any more of this folly?

There was but one resource. He would go and tell Irwine—tell him everything. The mere act of telling it would make it seem trivial; the temptation would vanish, as the charm of fond words vanishes when one repeats them to the indifferent. In every way it would help him, to tell Irwine. He would ride to Broxton Rectory the first thing after breakfast to-morrow.

Arthur had no sooner come to this determination than he began to think which of the paths would lead him home, and made as short a walk thither as he could. He felt sure he should sleep now: he[3] had had enough to tire him, and there was no more need for him to think.

---

[3] now: he] now—he *MS 1* now⟨—⟩{:} he *8*

CHAPTER XIV.

THE RETURN HOME.

While that parting in the wood was happening, there was a parting in the cottage too, and Lisbeth had stood with Adam at the door, straining her aged eyes to get the last glimpse of Seth and Dinah, as they mounted the opposite slope.

"Eh, I'm loath to see the last on her," she said to Adam, as they turned into the house again. "I'd ha' been willin' t' ha' her about me till I died and went to lie by my old man. She'd make[1] it easier dyin'—she spakes so gentle an' moves about so still. I could be fast sure that pictur was drawed for her i' thy new Bible—th' angel a-sittin' on the big stone by the grave. Eh, I wouldna mind ha'in' a daughter like that; but nobody ne'er marries them as is good for aught."

"Well, mother, I hope thee *wilt*[2] have her for a daughter; for Seth's got a liking for her, and I hope she'll get a liking for Seth in time."

"Where's the[3] use o' talkin' a-that'n? She[4] caresna for Seth. She's goin'[5] away twenty mile aff. How's she[6] to get a likin' for him[7], I'd like to know[8]? No more nor the cake 'ull come wi'out the[9] leaven.[1] Thy figurin' books might ha' tould thee better nor that, I should think, else thee mightst as well read the commin print, as Seth allays[2] does."

"Nay, mother," said Adam, laughing, "the figures tell us a fine deal, and we couldn't go far without 'em, but they don't[3] tell us about folks's feelings. It's a nicer job to calculate *them*. But Seth's as good-hearted a lad as ever handled a tool, and plenty o'[4] sense, and good-looking too; and he's got the same way o' thinking as Dinah. He deserves to win her, though[5] there's no denying she's a rare bit o' workmanship. You don't see such women turned off the wheel[6] every day."

---

[1] She'd make] Shey'd ma' *MS*   [2] *wilt*] wilt *MS* wilt *1* ⟨wilt⟩ <u>wilt</u> *8*
[3] the] th' *MS 1* ⟨th'⟩ the *8*   [4] She] Shey *MS*
[5] She's goin'] Shey's gooin' *MS*   [6] How's she] Hoo's shey *MS*
[7] him] 'm *MS 1* ⟨'m⟩ him *8*   [8] know] knoo *MS*   [9] the] th' *MS 1* ⟨th'⟩ the *8*
[1] No more nor the cake 'ull come wi'out the leaven.] Thee mut as well say as the cake 'ud come wi'out th' leaven. *MS*
[2] allays] alys *MS*   [3] they ⟨donna⟩ don't *MS*   [4] o'] of *MS*
[5] though ⟨I think myself⟩ there's no denying *MS*   [6] the wheel] *added in MS*

"Eh, thee't allays[7] stick up for thy brother. Thee'st been just the[8] same, e'er sin' ye[9] war little uns together. Thee wart allays[1] for halving iverything wi' him[2]. But what's Seth got to do with marryin'[3], as is on'y three-an'-twenty? He'd more[4] need to[5] learn an' lay by sixpence. An' as for his desarvin'[6] her—she's[7] two 'ear older nor Seth: she's[8] pretty near as old as thee. But that's[9] the way; folks mun allays[1] choose by contrairies, as if they must be sorted like the pork[2]—a bit o' good meat wi' a bit o' offal."

To the feminine mind in some of its moods, all things that might be, receive a temporary charm from comparison with what is; and since Adam did not want to marry Dinah himself, Lisbeth felt rather peevish on that score—as peevish as she would have been if he *had* wanted to marry her, and so shut himself out from Mary Burge and the partnership as effectually as by marrying Hetty.

It was more than half past eight when Adam and his mother were talking in this way, so that when, about ten minutes later,[3] Hetty reached the turning of the lane that led to the farm-yard gate, she saw Dinah and Seth approaching it from the opposite direction, and waited for them to come up to her. They, too, like Hetty, had lingered a little in their walk, for Dinah was trying to speak words of comfort and strength to Seth in these parting moments. But when they saw Hetty, they paused and shook hands: Seth turned homewards, and Dinah came on alone.

"Seth Bede would have come and spoken to you, my dear," she said, as she reached Hetty, "but he's very full of trouble to-night."

Hetty answered with a dimpled smile, as if she did not quite know what had been said; and it made a strange contrast to see that sparkling self-engrossed loveliness looked at by Dinah's calm pitying face, with its open glance which told that her heart lived in no cherished secrets of its own, but in feelings which it longed to share with all the world. Hetty liked Dinah as well as she had ever liked any woman; how was it possible to feel otherwise towards one who[4] always put in a kind word for her when her aunt was finding fault, and who was always ready to take Totty off her hands—little tiresome Totty, that was made such a pet of by every one, and that Hetty could see no interest in at all? Dinah[5] had never said anything disapproving or reproachful to Hetty during her whole visit to the Hall Farm; she had talked to her a great deal in a serious way, but Hetty didn't mind that much, for she never listened: whatever Dinah might say, she almost always

[7] allays] alys *MS*   [8] Thee'st been just the] Thee'st alys been the *MS*
[9] ye] yey *MS*   [1] allays] alys *MS*   [2] him] 'm *MS 1* ⟨'m⟩ him *8*
[3] with marryin'] wi' marr'in *MS* with marr'in' *1* with ⟨marr'in'⟩ marryin' *8*
[4] He'd more] Hey'd moor *MS*   [5] to] t' *MS 1* ⟨t'⟩ to *8*
[6] desarvin'] *MS 1* desarving *8*   [7] she's] shey's *MS*   [8] she's] shey's *MS*
[9] that's ⟨they⟩ the *MS*   [1] allays] alys *MS*   [2] pork {,} ⟨meats⟩ a *MS*
[3] about ten minutes later] *added in MS*   [4] who ⟨was⟩ always *MS*
[5] all? Dinah] all. Dinah *MS*

stroked Hetty's cheek after it, and wanted to do some mending for her. Dinah was a riddle to her;[6] Hetty looked at her much in the same way as one might imagine a little perching bird that could only flutter from bough to bough, to look at the swoop of the swallow or the mounting of the lark; but she did not care to solve such riddles, any more than she cared to know what was meant by[7] the pictures in the "Pilgrim's Progress," or in the old folio Bible that Marty and Tommy always plagued her about on a Sunday.

Dinah took her hand now and drew it under her own arm.

"You look very happy to-night, dear child," she said. "I shall think of you often when I'm at Snowfield, and see your face before me as it is now. It's a strange thing—sometimes when I'm quite alone, sitting in my room with my eyes closed, or walking over the hills, the people I've seen and known, if it's only been for a few days, are brought before me, and I hear their voices and see them look and move almost plainer than I ever did when they were really with me so as I could touch them. And then my heart is drawn out towards them, and I feel their lot as if it was my own, and I take comfort in spreading it before the Lord and resting in His love,[8] on their behalf as well as my own. And so I feel sure you will come before me."

She paused a moment, but Hetty said nothing.

"It has been a very precious time to me," Dinah went on, "last night and to-day—[9]seeing two such good sons as Adam and Seth Bede. They are so tender and thoughtful for their aged mother. And she has been telling me what Adam has done, for these many years, to help his father and his brother; it's wonderful what a spirit of wisdom and knowledge he has, and how he's ready to use it all in behalf of them that are feeble. And I'm sure he has a loving spirit too. I've noticed it often among my own people round Snowfield, that the strong, skilful men are often the gentlest to the women and children; and it's pretty to see 'em carrying the little babies as if they were no heavier than little birds. And the babies always seem to like the strong arm best. I feel sure it would be so with Adam Bede. Don't you think so, Hetty?"

"Yes," said Hetty, abstractedly, for her mind had been all the while in the wood, and she would have found it difficult to say what she was assenting to.[1] Dinah saw she was not inclined to talk, but there would not have been time to say much more, for they were now at the yard-gate.

The[2] still twilight, with its dying[3] western red, and its few faint struggling stars, rested on the farm-yard, where there was not a sound to be heard but the stamping of the cart-horses in the stable. It was about twenty

---

[6] her; ⟨she⟩ Hetty *MS*   [7] was meant by] *added in MS*

[8] love, ⟨for their behalf⟩ ⟨sake⟩ on their behalf as *MS*   [9] to-day—⟨the⟩ seeing *MS*

[1]   for her mind had been all the while in the wood, & she would have found it difficult to say what she was assenting to] *added in MS*

[2] The ⟨soft early⟩ still *MS*   [3] dying ⟨red in the west⟩ western red *MS*

minutes after sunset:[4] the[5] fowls were all gone to roost, and the bull-dog lay stretched on the straw outside his kennel, with the black-and-tan terrier by his side, when the falling-to of the gate disturbed them, and set them barking, like good officials, before they had any distinct knowledge of the reason.

The barking had its effect in the house, for, as Dinah and Hetty approached, the doorway was filled by a[6] portly figure, with a ruddy black-eyed face, which bore in it the possibility of looking extremely acute, and occasionally contemptuous, on market-days, but had now a predominant after-supper expression of hearty good-nature. It is well known that great scholars who have shown the most pitiless acerbity in their criticism of other men's scholarship,[7] have yet been of a relenting and indulgent temper in private life; and I have heard of a learned man meekly[8] rocking the twins in the cradle with his left hand, while with his[9] right he inflicted the most lacerating sarcasms on an opponent who had betrayed a brutal ignorance of Hebrew. Weaknesses and errors must be forgiven—alas! they are not alien to us—but the man who takes the wrong side on the momentous subject of the Hebrew points must be treated as the enemy of his race. There was the same sort of antithetic mixture in Martin Poyser: he was of so excellent a disposition that he had been kinder and more respectful than ever to his old father since he had made a deed of gift of all his property, and no man judged his neighbours more charitably on all personal matters; but for a farmer, like Luke Britton, for example, whose[1] fallows were not well cleaned, who didn't know the rudiments of hedging and ditching, and showed but a small share of judgment in the purchase of winter stock, Martin Poyser was as hard and implacable as the north-east wind. Luke Britton could not make a remark, even on the weather, but Martin Poyser detected in it a taint of that unsoundness and general ignorance which was palpable in all his farming operations. He hated to see the fellow lift the pewter pint to his mouth in the bar of the Royal George on market day, and the mere sight of him on the other side of the road brought a severe and critical expression into his black eyes, as different as possible from the fatherly glance he bent on his two nieces as they approached the door. Mr Poyser had smoked his evening pipe, and now held[2] his hands in his pockets, as the only resource of a man who continues to sit up after the day's business is done.

"Why, lasses, ye're rather late to-night," he said, when they reached the little gate leading into the causeway. "The mother's begun to fidget about you, an' she's got the little un ill. An' how did you leave the[3] old woman

[4] It was about twenty minutes after sunset:] *added in MS*   [5] sunset: ⟨T⟩the *MS*
[6] a ⟨ruddy⟩ portly *MS*   [7] scholarship ⟨& yet⟩ have *MS*
[8] meekly] *added in MS*   [9] his ⟨write⟩ right *MS*
[1] example, whose] *MS 1* example {,} whose *8*   [2] and now held] & held *MS*
[3] the] th' *MS 1*

Bede, Dinah? Is she much down about the[4] old man? He'd been but a poor bargain to her this five year."

"She's been greatly distressed for the loss of him," said Dinah; "but she's seemed more comforted to-day. Her son Adam's been at home all day, working at his father's coffin, and she loves to have him at home. She's been talking about him to me almost all the day. She[5] has a loving heart, though she's sorely given to fret and be fearful. I wish she had a surer trust to comfort her[6] in her old age."

"Adam's sure enough," said Mr Poyser, misunderstanding Dinah's wish. "There's no fear but he'll yield well i' the threshing. He's not one o' them as is all straw and no[7] grain. I'll be bond for him any day, as he'll be a good son to the last. Did he say he'd be coming to see us soon? But come in, come in," he added, making way for them; "I hadn't need keep y' out any longer."

The tall buildings round the yard shut out[8] a good deal of the sky, but the large window[9] let in abundant light to show every corner of the house-place.

Mrs Poyser, seated in the[1] rocking-chair, which had been brought out of the "right-hand parlour," was trying to soothe Totty to sleep. But Totty was not disposed to sleep; and when her cousins entered, she raised herself up, and showed a pair of flushed cheeks, which looked fatter than ever now they were defined by the edge of[2] her linen night-cap.

In the large wicker-bottomed arm-chair in the left-hand[3] chimney-nook sat old Martin Poyser, a hale but shrunken and bleached image of his portly black-haired son—his head hanging forward a little, and his elbows pushed backward[4] so as to allow the whole of his fore-arm to rest on the arm of the chair. His blue handkerchief was spread over his knees, as was usual in-doors, when it was not hanging over his head; and he sat watching what went forward with the quiet *outward* glance of healthy old age, which, disengaged from any interest in an inward drama, spies out pins upon the floor, follows one's minutest motions with an unexpectant purposeless tenacity, watches the flickering of the flame or the sun-gleams on the wall, counts the quarries on the floor, watches even the hand of the clock, and pleases itself with detecting a rhythm in the[5] tick.

"What a time o' night this is to come home, Hetty,"[6] said Mrs Poyser. "Look at the clock, do; why, it's going on for half past nine, and[7] I've sent

    [4] the] th' *MS 1*   [5] day. She] day: she *MS*   [6] to comfort her] *added in MS*
    [7] no ⟨ear⟩ grain *MS*
    [8] out ⟨some of the evening light, & there was no candle lit in the kitchen⟩ a good deal of the sky, but the large window *MS*
    [9] window ⟨of the house-place⟩ let *MS*   [1] the ⟨large⟩ rocking-chair *MS*
    [2] the edge of] *added in MS*   [3] left hand ⟨of the⟩ chimney nook *MS*
    [4] backward] backwards *Cabinet*   [5] the] its *MS*   [6] Hetty,"] Hetty!" *Cabinet*
    [7] and] & *MS* an' *1*

the gells to bed this half-hour, and late enough too,[8] when they've[9] got to get up at half after four, and the mowers' bottles to fill, and the baking; and[1] here's this blessed child wi' the fever for what I know, and[2] as wakeful as if it was dinner-time, and[3] nobody to help me to give her the physic but your uncle, and[4] fine work there's been, and half of it spilt on her night-gown— it's well if she's swallowed more nor 'ull make her worse istead o' better. But folks as have no mind to be o' use have allays[5] the luck to be out o' the road when there's anything to be done."

"I did set out before eight, aunt," said Hetty, in a pettish tone, with a slight toss of her head. "But this clock's so much before the clock at the Chase, there's no telling what time it'll be when I get here."[6]

"What![7] you'd be wanting the clock set by gentle-folks's time, would you? an' sit up burnin' candle, an' lie a-bed wi' the sun a-bakin' you like a cowcumber i' the frame? The clock hasn't been put forrard for the first time to-day, I reckon."

The fact was, Hetty had really forgotten the difference of the clocks when she told Captain Donnithorne that she set out at eight, and this, with her lingering pace, had made her nearly half an hour later than usual. But here[8] her aunt's attention was diverted from this tender subject by Totty, who, perceiving[9] at length that the arrival of her cousins was not likely to bring anything satisfactory to her in particular, began to cry, "Munny, munny," in an explosive manner.

"Well, then, my pet, mother's got her, mother won't leave her; Totty be a good dilling, and go to sleep now," said Mrs Poyser, leaning back and rocking the chair, while she tried to make Totty nestle against her. But Totty only cried louder, and said, "Don't yock!" So[1] the mother, with that wondrous patience which love gives to the quickest temperament, sat up again, and pressed her cheek against the linen night-cap and kissed it, and forgot to scold Hetty any longer.

"Come, Hetty," said Martin Poyser, in a conciliatory tone, "go and get your supper i' the pantry, as the things are all put away; an'[2] then you can come an' take the little un while your aunt undresses herself, for she won't lie down in bed without her mother. An' I reckon *you* could eat a bit, Dinah, for they don't keep much of a house down there."

"No, thank you, uncle," said Dinah; "I[3] ate a good meal before I came away, for Mrs Bede would make a kettle-cake for me."

[8] too,] *MS 1* too; *8*   [9] when they've] & them's *MS*   [1] an⟨'⟩{d} *MS*

[2] an⟨'⟩{d} *MS*   [3] an⟨'⟩{d} *MS*   [4] an⟨'⟩{d} *MS*

[5] allays] alys *MS*   [6] here."⟨It's only a quarter to nine by the night⟩ *MS*

[7] "What!] "What, *MS*

[8] here ⟨Totty created a diversion in⟩ her aunt's attention was diverted *MS*

[9] perceiving ⟨that nothing⟩ at length that the arrival of her cousins was not likely to bring anything *MS*

[1] yock!" So] yock!" so *MS*   [2] an'] & *MS*   [3] Dinah; "I] Dinah. "I *MS*

"I don't want any supper," said Hetty, taking off her hat. "I can hold Totty now, if aunt wants me."

"Why, what nonsense that is to talk!"[4] said Mrs Poyser. "Do you think you can live wi'out eatin', an' nourish your inside wi' stickin' red ribbins[5] on your head? Go an' get your supper this minute, child;[6] there's a nice bit o' cold pudding i' the safe—just what you're fond of[7]."

Hetty complied silently by going towards the pantry, and Mrs Poyser went on,[8] speaking to Dinah.

"Sit down, my dear, an'[9] look as if you knowed what it was to make yourself a bit comfortable i' the world. I warrant the[1] old woman was glad to see you, since you[2] stayed so long."[3]

"She seemed to like having me there at last; but her sons say she doesn't like young women about her commonly[4]; and I thought just at first she was almost angry with me for going."

"Eh, it's a poor look-out when[5] th' ould foulks doesna like the[6] young uns," said old Martin, bending his head down lower, and seeming to trace the pattern of the quarries with his eye.

"Ay, it's ill livin' in a hen-roost for them as doesn't like fleas," said Mrs Poyser. "We've all had our turn at bein' young, I reckon, be't good luck or ill."

"But she must learn to 'commodate herself to young women," said Mr Poyser[7], "for it isn't to be counted on as Adam and Seth[8] 'ull keep bachelors for the next ten year[9] to please their mother. That 'ud be unreasonable[1]. It isn't right for old nor young nayther to make a bargain all o' their own side. What's good for one's good all round i' the long run. I'm no friend to young fellows a-marrying[2] afore they know the difference atween a crab an' a apple; but they may wait o'er long."

"To be sure," said Mrs Poyser; "if you go past your dinner-time, there'll be little relish o' your meat. You turn it o'er an' o'er wi' your fork, an' don't eat it after all.[3] You find faut wi' your meat, an' the faut's all i' your own stomach."

Hetty now came back from the pantry, and said, "I can take Totty now, aunt, if you like."

⁴ talk!"] talk," *MS 1*   ⁵ ribbins] ribbons *Cabinet*

⁶ child; ⟨—an' let us have no nonsense"⟩ there's a nice bit o' cold pudding *MS*

⁷ of] on *MS 1* ⟨on⟩ of *8*   ⁸ on,] *MS 1* on *8*   ⁹ an'] & *MS*

¹ the] th' *MS*   ² you ⟨staid⟩ stayed *MS*   ³ long."] long?" *MS 1*

⁴ her commonly] her much, commonly *MS* her, commonly *1*

⁵ when] whan *MS*   ⁶ the] th' *MS*   ⁷ Mr Poyser] Martin Poyser *MS*

⁸ Seth ⟨'ll⟩ 'ull *MS*   ⁹ year] 'ear *MS*

¹ unreasonable] onreasonable *MS 1* ⟨onreasonable⟩ unreasonable *8*

² a-marrying] a-marr'ing *MS 1* ⟨a-marr'ing⟩ a-marrying *8*

³ all. ⟨An' it's the way wi' them puts love⟩ You find faut wi' your meat, an' *MS*

"Come, Rachel," said Mr Poyser, as his wife seemed to hesitate, seeing that Totty was at last nestling quietly, "thee'dst better let Hetty carry her upstairs, while thee tak'st thy things off. Thee't tired. It's time thee wast in bed. Thee't bring on the pain in thy side again."

"Well, she may hold her if the child 'ull[4] go to her," said Mrs Poyser.

Hetty went close to the rocking-chair, and stood without her usual smile, and without any attempt to entice Totty, simply waiting for her aunt to give the child into her hands.

"Wilt go to cousin Hetty, my dilling, while mother gets ready to go to bed?[5] Then Totty shall go into mother's bed and sleep there all night."

Before her mother had done speaking, Totty had given her answer in an unmistakeable manner, by knitting her brow, setting her tiny teeth against her underlip, and leaning forward to slap Hetty on the arm with her utmost force. Then, without speaking, she nestled to her mother again.

"Hey, hey," said Mr Poyser, while Hetty stood without moving, "not go to cousin Hetty? That's like a babby: Totty's a little woman, an' not a babby."

"It's no use trying[6] to persuade her," said Mrs Poyser. "She allays[7] takes against Hetty when she isn't well. Happen she'll go to Dinah."

Dinah, having taken off her bonnet and shawl, had hitherto kept quietly seated in the background, not liking to thrust herself between Hetty and what was considered Hetty's proper work. But now she came forward, and, putting out her arms, said, "Come Totty, come and let Dinah carry her upstairs along with mother: poor, poor mother! she's[8] so tired—she wants to go to bed."

Totty turned her face towards Dinah, and looked at her an instant, then lifted herself up, put out her little arms, and let Dinah lift her from her mother's lap. Hetty turned away without any sign of ill-humour, and, taking her hat from the table, stood waiting with an air of indifference, to see if she should be told to do anything else.

"You may make the door fast now, Poyser; Alick's been come in this long while," said Mrs Poyser, rising with an appearance of relief from her low chair. "Get me the matches down, Hetty, for I must have the rushlight burning i' my room. Come, father."

The heavy wooden bolts began to roll in the house door[9], and[1] old Martin prepared to move, by gathering up his blue handkerchief, and reaching his bright knobbed walnut-tree stick from the corner. Mrs Poyser then led the way out of the kitchen, followed by the grandfather, and Dinah with Totty in her arms—all going to bed by twilight, like the birds. Mrs

⁴ 'ull] 'ill *MS* 'll *1* ⟨'ll⟩ 'ull *8*   ⁵ bed?] bed. *MS*   ⁶ trying] tryin' *MS 1*
⁷ allays] alys *MS*   ⁸ mother! she's] mother! She's *MS*   ⁹ door] *MS* doors *1 8*
¹ The heavy wooden bolts began to roll in the house-door, &] *added in MS*

Poyser, on her way, peeped into the room where her two boys lay, just to see their[2] ruddy round cheeks on the pillow, and to hear for a moment their light regular breathing.

"Come, Hetty, get to bed," said Mr Poyser, in a soothing tone, as he himself turned to go upstairs. "You didna[3] mean to be late, I'll be bound, but your aunt's been worrited to-day. Good night, my wench, good night."

---

[2] their ⟨heads⟩ ruddy *MS*   [3] didna] didn't *MS*

CHAPTER XV.

THE TWO BED-CHAMBERS.

Hetty and Dinah both slept in the[1] second story, in rooms adjoining each other, meagrely-furnished rooms, with no blinds to shut out the light, which was now beginning to gather new strength from the rising of the moon—more than enough strength to enable Hetty to move about and undress with perfect comfort. She could see quite well the pegs in the old painted linen-press on which she hung her hat and gown; she could see the head of every pin on her red cloth pin-cushion; she could see a reflection of herself in the old-fashioned looking-glass, quite as distinct as was needful, considering that she had only to brush her hair and put on her night-cap. A queer old looking-glass! Hetty got into an ill-temper with it almost every time she dressed. It had been considered a handsome glass in its day, and had probably been bought into the Poyser family a quarter of a century before, at a sale of genteel household furniture. Even[2] now an auctioneer could say something for it: it had a great deal of tarnished gilding about it; it had a firm mahogany base, well supplied with drawers, which opened with a decided jerk, and sent the contents leaping out from the farthest corners, without giving you the trouble of reaching them; above all, it had a brass candle-socket on each side, which would give it an aristocratic air to the very last. But Hetty objected to it because it had numerous dim blotches sprinkled over the mirror, which no rubbing would remove, and because, instead of swinging backwards and forwards, it was fixed in an upright position, so that she could only get one good view of her head and neck, and that was to be had only by[3] sitting down on a low chair before her dressing-table. And the dressing-table was no dressing-table at all, but a small old chest of drawers, the most awkward thing in the world to sit down before, for the big brass handles quite hurt her knees, and she couldn't get near the glass at all comfortably. But devout worshippers never allow inconveniences to prevent them from performing their religious rites, and Hetty this evening was more bent on her peculiar form of worship than usual.

Having taken off her gown and white kerchief, she drew a key from the large pocket that hung outside her petticoat, and, unlocking one of the lower drawers in the chest,[4] reached from it two short bits of wax candle—secretly bought at Treddleston—and stuck them in the two brass sockets.

---

[1]   slept in the] slept ⟨in⟩ on the *MS*
[2]   furniture. Even] furniture; even *MS*
[3]   was to be had only by] was by *MS*
[4]   chest, ⟨drew⟩ reached *MS*

Then she drew forth a[5] bundle of matches, and lighted the candles; and last
of all, a small red-framed shilling looking-glass, without blotches. It was
into this small glass that she chose to look first after seating herself. She[6]
looked into it, smiling, and turning her head on one side, for a minute, then
laid it down and took out her brush and comb from an upper drawer. She
was going to let down her hair, and make herself look like that picture of a
lady in Miss Lydia Donnithorne's dressing-room. It was soon done, and
the dark hyacinthine curves fell on her neck. It was not heavy, massive,
merely rippling hair, but soft and silken, running at every opportunity into
delicate rings. But she pushed it all backward to look like the picture, and
form a dark curtain, throwing into relief her round white neck. Then she
put down her brush and comb, and looked at herself, folding her arms
before her, still like the picture. Even the old mottled glass couldn't help
sending back a lovely image, none the less lovely because Hetty's stays were
not of white satin—such as I feel sure heroines must generally wear—but of
a dark greenish cotton texture.

O yes! she was very pretty: Captain Donnithorne thought so. Prettier
than anybody about Hayslope—prettier than any of the ladies she had ever
seen visiting at the Chase—indeed it seemed fine ladies were rather[7] old
and ugly—and prettier than Miss Bacon, the miller's daughter, who was
called the beauty of Treddleston. And Hetty looked at herself to-night[8]
with quite a different sensation from what she had ever felt before; there
was an invisible spectator whose eye rested on her like morning on the
flowers. His soft voice was saying over and over again those pretty things
she had heard in the wood; his arm was round her, and the delicate rose-
scent of his hair was with her still. The vainest woman is never thoroughly[9]
conscious of her own beauty till she is loved by the man who sets her own
passion vibrating in return.

But Hetty seemed to have made up her mind that something was
wanting, for she got up and reached an old black lace scarf out of the
linen-press, and a pair of large ear-rings out of the sacred drawer from
which she had taken her candles. It was an old, old scarf, full of rents, but it
would make a becoming border round her shoulders, and set off the
whiteness of her upper arm. And she would take out the little ear-rings
she had in her ears—[1]oh, how her aunt had scolded her for having her ears
bored!—and put in those large ones: they were but coloured glass and
gilding; but if you didn't know what they were made of, they looked just as
well as what the ladies wore. And so she sat down again, with the large ear-
rings in her ears, and the black lace scarf adjusted round her shoulders. She

[5] a ⟨box⟩ bundle *MS*   [6] herself. She] herself: she *MS*
[7] were rather] were generally rather *MS*   [8] tonight] *added in MS*
[9] thoroughly] *added in MS*
[1] ears—⟨she dared not wear larger ones or any more conspicuous, for⟩ oh, *MS*

looked down at her arms: no arms could be prettier down to a little way below the elbow—they were white and plump, and dimpled to match her cheeks; but towards the wrist, she thought with vexation that they were coarsened by butter-making, and other work that ladies never did.

Captain Donnithorne couldn't like her to go on doing work: he would like to see her in nice clothes, and thin shoes and white stockings, perhaps with silk clocks to them; for he must love her very much—no one else had ever put his arm round her and kissed her in that way. He would want to marry her, and make a lady of her; she[2] could hardly dare to shape the thought—yet how else could it be? Marry her quite secretly, as Mr James, the Doctor's assistant, married the Doctor's niece, and nobody ever found it out for a long while after, and then it was of no[3] use to be angry. The Doctor had told her aunt all about it in Hetty's hearing. She didn't know how it[4] would be, but it was quite plain the old Squire could never be told anything about it, for Hetty was ready to faint with awe and fright if she came across him at the Chase. He might have been earth-born, for what she knew: it had never entered her mind that he had been young like other men; he[5] had always been the old Squire at whom everybody was frightened. O it was impossible to think how it would be! But Captain Donnithorne would know; he was a great gentleman, and could have his way in everything, and could buy everything he liked. And nothing could be as it had been again: perhaps some day she should be a grand lady, and ride in her coach, and dress for dinner in a brocaded silk, with feathers in her hair, and her dress sweeping the ground, like Miss Lydia and Lady Dacey, when she saw them going into the dining-room one evening, as she peeped through the little round window in the lobby; only[6] she should not[7] be old and ugly like Miss Lydia, or all the same thickness like Lady Dacey, but very pretty, with her hair done in a great many different ways, and sometimes in a pink dress, and sometimes in a white one—she didn't know which she liked best; and[8] Mary Burge and everybody would perhaps see her going out in her carriage—or rather,[9] they would *hear*[1] of it: it was impossible to imagine these things happening at Hayslope in sight of her aunt. At the thought of all this splendour, Hetty got up from her chair, and in doing so caught the little red-framed glass with the edge of her scarf, so that it fell with a bang on the floor; but she was too eagerly occupied with her vision to care about picking it up; and after a momentary start, began to pace[2] [3] with a pigeon-

---

[2] her; she] her: she *MS* her—she *1* her ⟨—⟩ {;} she *8*   [3] was of no] was no *MS*
[4] it ⟨could⟩ would *MS*   [5] men; he] men—he *MS 1* men ⟨—⟩ {;} he *8*
[6] lobby; only] lobby. Only *MS*   [7] should not] shouldn't *MS*
[8] best; and] best. And *MS*   [9] or rather,] at least *MS*   [1] *hear*] hear *MS*
[2] & in doing so caught the little red-framed glass with the edge of her scarf, so that it fell with a bang on the floor; but she was too eagerly occupied with her vision to care about picking it up, & after a momentary start, began to pace] *added on verso of MS 1. 239*
[3] pace ⟨& paced⟩ with *MS*

like stateliness backwards and forwards along her room, in her coloured
stays and coloured skirt, and the old black lace scarf round her shoulders,
and the great glass ear-rings in her ears.

How pretty the little puss looks in that odd dress![4] It would be the easiest
folly in the world to fall in love with her: there is such a sweet baby-like
roundness about her face and figure; the delicate dark rings of hair lie so
charmingly about her ears and neck; her great dark eyes with their long
eyelashes touch one so strangely, as if an imprisoned frisky sprite looked
out of them.

Ah, what a prize the man gets who wins a sweet bride like Hetty![5] How
the men envy him who come to the wedding breakfast, and see her hanging
on his arm in her white lace and orange blossoms. The dear, young, round,
soft, flexible thing! Her heart must be just as soft, her temper just as free
from angles, her character just as pliant. If anything ever goes wrong,
it must be the husband's fault there: he can make her what he likes—
that[6] is plain. And the lover himself thinks so too: the little darling is so fond
of him, her little vanities are so bewitching, he wouldn't consent to her
being a bit wiser; those kitten-like glances and movements are just what one
wants to make one's hearth a paradise. Every man under such circumstances is conscious of being a great physiognomist. Nature[7], he knows, has
a language of her own, which she uses with strict veracity, and he considers
himself an adept in the language. Nature[8] has written out his bride's
character for him in those exquisite lines of cheek and lip and chin, in
those eyelids delicate as petals, in those long lashes curled like the stamen of
a flower, in the dark liquid depths of those wonderful eyes. How she will
dote on her children! She is almost a child herself, and the little pink round
things will hang about her like florets round the central flower; and[9] the
husband will look on, smiling benignly, able, whenever he chooses, to
withdraw into the sanctuary of his wisdom, towards which his sweet wife
will look reverently, and never lift the curtain. It is a marriage such as they
made in the golden age, when the men were all wise and majestic, and the
women all lovely and loving.

[1]It was very much in this way that our friend Adam Bede thought about
Hetty; only he put his thoughts into different words. If ever she behaved
with cold vanity towards him, he said to himself, it is only because she
doesn't love me well enough; and he was sure that her love, whenever she
gave it, would be the most precious thing a man could possess on earth.

[4] dress! I{t} ⟨can hardly help falling in love with her myself⟩ would be the easiest folly in
the world to fall in love with her: *MS*
[5] Hetty!] Hetty. *MS*   [6] likes—that] likes, that *MS 1* likes ⟨,⟩ {—} that *8*
[7] physiognomist. Nature] physiognomist: Nature *MS*
[8] language. Nature] language; Nature *MS*   [9] flower; and] flower. And *MS*
[1] {It was very much in this way that} Our friend Adam Bede thought ⟨very much in this
way⟩ about *MS*

Before you despise Adam as deficient in penetration, pray ask yourself if you were ever predisposed to believe evil of any pretty woman—if you ever *could*, without hard head-breaking demonstration, believe evil of the *one* supremely pretty woman who has bewitched you. No: people who love downy peaches are apt not to think of the stone, and sometimes jar their teeth terribly against it.

Arthur Donnithorne, too, had the same sort of notion about Hetty, so far as he had thought of her nature at all. He felt sure she was a dear, affectionate, good little thing. The man who awakes the wondering tremulous passion of a young girl always thinks her affectionate; and if he chances to look forward to future years, probably imagines himself being virtuously tender to her, because the poor thing is so clingingly fond of him. God made these dear women so—and it is a convenient arrangement in case of sickness.

After all, I believe the wisest of us must be beguiled in this way sometimes, and must think both better and worse of people than they deserve. Nature has her language, and she is not unveracious; but we don't know[2] all the intricacies of her syntax just yet, and in a hasty reading we may happen to extract the very opposite of her real meaning. Long dark eyelashes, now: what can be more exquisite? I find it impossible not to expect some depth of soul behind a deep grey eye with a long dark eyelash, in spite of an experience which has shown me that they may go along with deceit, peculation, and stupidity. But if, in the reaction of disgust,[3] I have betaken myself to a fishy eye, there has been a surprising similarity of result. One begins to suspect at length that there is no direct correlation between eyelashes and morals; or else, that the eyelashes express the disposition of the fair one's grandmother, which is on the whole less important to us.

No eyelashes could be more beautiful than Hetty's; and[4] now, while she walks with her pigeon-like stateliness along the room and looks down on her shoulders bordered by the old black lace, the dark fringe shows to perfection on her pink cheek. They are but dim ill-defined pictures that her narrow bit of an imagination can make of the future; but of every picture she is the central figure, in fine clothes; Captain Donnithorne is very close to her, putting his arm round her, perhaps kissing her, and everybody else is admiring and envying her—especially Mary Burge, whose new print dress looks very contemptible by the side of Hetty's resplendent toilette. Does any sweet or sad memory mingle with this dream of the future—any loving thought of her second parents—of the children she had helped to tend—of any youthful companion, any pet animal, any relic of her own childhood

---

[2] know {all ⟨of⟩} the *MS*

[3] disgust, {I} ⟨one betakes oneself⟩ {have betaken myself} to a fishy eye, there ⟨may⟩ {has} be{en} a *MS*

[4] Hetty's; and] Hetty's, & *MS* Hetty's, and *1* Hetty's⟨,⟩ {;} and *8*

even? Not one. There are some plants that have hardly any roots: you may tear them from their native nook of rock or wall, and just lay them over your ornamental flower-pot, and they blossom none the worse. Hetty could have cast all her past life behind her and never cared to be reminded of it again. I think she had no feeling at all towards the old house,[5] and did not like the Jacob's Ladder and the long row of hollyhocks[6] in the garden better than other flowers—perhaps not so well. It was wonderful how little she seemed to care about waiting on her uncle, who had been a good father to her: she hardly ever remembered to reach him his pipe at the right time without being told, unless a visitor happened to be there, who would have a better opportunity of seeing her as she walked across the hearth. Hetty did not[7] understand how anybody could be very fond of middle-aged people. And as for those tiresome children, Marty and Tommy and Totty, they had been the very nuisance of her life—as bad as buzzing insects that will come teasing you on a hot day when you want to be quiet. Marty, the eldest, was a baby when she first came to the farm, for the children born before him had died, and so Hetty had had them all three, one after the other, toddling by her side in the meadow, or playing about her on wet days in the half-empty rooms of the large old house. The boys were out of hand now, but Totty was still a day-long plague, worse than either of the others had been, because there was more fuss made about her. And there was no end to the making and mending of clothes. Hetty would have been glad to hear that she should never see a child again; they were worse than the nasty little lambs that the shepherd was always bringing in to be taken special care of in lambing time; for the lambs *were* got rid of sooner or later. As for the young chickens and turkeys, Hetty would have hated the very word "hatching," if her aunt had not bribed her to attend to the young poultry by promising her the proceeds of one out of every brood. The round downy[8] chicks peeping out from[9] under their mother's wing never touched Hetty with any pleasure; that was not the sort of prettiness she cared about, but she did care about the prettiness of the new things she would buy for herself at Treddleston fair with the money they fetched. And yet she looked so dimpled, so charming, as she stooped down to put the soaked bread under the hen-coop, that you must have been a very acute personage indeed to suspect her of that hardness. Molly, the housemaid, with a turn-up nose and a protuberant jaw, was really a tender-hearted girl, and, as Mrs Poyser said, a jewel to look after the poultry, but her stolid face showed nothing of this maternal delight, any more than a brown earthenware pitcher will show the light of the lamp within it.

[5] had no feeling at all towards the old house,] didn't mind about the old house at all, *MS*
[6] hollyhocks] Holyoaks *MS*   [7] did not] didn't *MS*
[8] downy ⟨chickens⟩ chicks *MS*   [9] out from] *added in MS*

It is generally a feminine eye that first[1] detects the moral deficiencies hidden under the "dear deceit" of beauty: so it is not surprising that Mrs Poyser, with her keenness and abundant opportunity for observation, should have formed a tolerably fair estimate of what might be expected from Hetty in the way of feeling, and in moments of indignation she had sometimes spoken with great openness on the subject to her husband.

"She's no better than a peacock, as 'ud strut about on the wall, and spread its tail when the sun shone if all the folks i' the parish was dying: there's nothing seems to give her a turn i' th' inside, not even when we thought Totty had tumbled into the pit. To think o' that dear cherub! And we found her wi' her little shoes stuck i' the mud an' crying fit to break her heart by the far horse-pit. But Hetty niver[2] minded it, I could see, though she's been at the nussin' o' the child ever[3] since it was a babby. It's my belief her heart's as hard as a pebble[4]."

"Nay, nay," said Mr Poyser, "thee mustn't judge Hetty too hard. Them young gells are like th'[5] unripe grain; they'll make good meal by-and-by, but they're squashy as yet[6]. Thee't see,[7] Hetty'll be all right when she's got a good husband and[8] children of her own."

"*I* don't want to be hard upo' the gell. She's got cliver fingers of her own, and can be useful enough when she likes, and[9] I should miss her wi' the butter, for she's got a cool hand. An' let be what may, I'd strive to do my part by a niece o' yours, an' *that*[1] I've done: for I've taught her everything as belongs to a house, an' I've told her her duty often enough, though, God knows, I've no breath to spare, an' that catchin' pain comes on dreadful by times. Wi' them three gells in the house[2] I'd need have twice the strength, to keep 'em up to their work. It's like having roast meat at three fires; as soon as you've basted one, another's burnin'."

Hetty stood sufficiently in awe of her aunt to be anxious to conceal from her so much of her vanity as could be hidden without too great a sacrifice. She could not resist spending her money in bits of finery which Mrs Poyser disapproved; but she would have been ready to die with shame, vexation, and fright, if her aunt had this moment opened the door, and seen her with her bits of candle lighted, and strutting about decked in her scarf and ear-rings. To prevent such a surprise, she always bolted her door, and she had not forgotten to do so to-night. It was well: for there now came a light tap, and Hetty, with a leaping heart, rushed to blow out the candles and throw them into the drawer. She dared[3] not stay to take out her ear-rings, but she threw off her scarf, and let it fall on the[4] floor, before the light tap came

[1] first] *added in MS*   [2] niver] never *Cabinet*   [3] ever] iver *MS 1* ⟨iver⟩ ever *8*
[4] pebble] pibble *MS 1* ⟨pibble⟩ pebble *8*   [5] th'] the *Cabinet*
[6] yet] yit *MS 1* ⟨yit⟩ yet *8*   [7] see,] *MS 1* see *8*   [8] and] an' *MS 1*
[9] and] an' *MS*   [1] that] that *MS 1* ⟨that⟩ that *8*
[2] house ⟨it 'ud take⟩ I'd need have *MS*   [3] dared] dare *MS 1* dare{d} *8*
[4] the ⟨ground⟩ floor *MS*

again. We shall know how it was that the light tap came, if we leave Hetty
for a short time, and return to Dinah, at the moment when she had
delivered Totty to her mother's arms, and was come up-stairs to her
bedroom, adjoining Hetty's.

Dinah delighted in her bedroom window. Being on the second story of
that tall house, it gave her a wide view over the fields. The thickness of the
wall formed a broad[5] step about a yard below the window, where she could
place her chair. And now the first thing she did, on entering her room, was
to seat herself in this chair, and look out on the peaceful fields beyond which
the large moon was rising, just above the hedgerow elms. She liked the
pasture best, where the milch cows were lying, and next to that the meadow
where the grass was half mown, and lay in silvered sweeping lines. Her
heart was very full, for there was to be only one more night on which she
would look out on those fields for a long time to come; but she thought little
of leaving the mere scene, for[6], to her, bleak Snowfield had just as many
charms: she thought of all the dear people whom she had learned to care for
among these peaceful fields, and who would now have a place in her loving
remembrance for ever. She thought of the struggles and the weariness that
might lie before them in the rest of their life's journey, when she would be
away from them, and know nothing of what was befalling them; and the
pressure of this thought soon became too strong for her to enjoy the
unresponding stillness of the[7] moonlit fields. She closed her eyes, that
she might feel more intensely the presence of a Love and Sympathy deeper
and more tender than was breathed from the earth and sky. That was often
Dinah's mode of praying in solitude. Simply[8] to close her eyes, and to feel
herself enclosed by the Divine Presence; then gradually her fears, her
yearning anxieties for others, melted away like ice-crystals in a warm
ocean. She had sat in this way perfectly still, with her hands crossed on
her lap, and the pale light resting on her calm face, for at least ten minutes,
when she was startled by a loud sound, apparently of something falling in
Hetty's room. But like all sounds that fall on our ears in a state of abstraction, it had no distinct character, but was simply loud and startling, so that
she[9] felt uncertain whether she had interpreted it rightly. She rose and
listened, but all was quiet afterwards, and she reflected that Hetty might[1]
merely have knocked something down in getting into bed. She began
slowly to undress; but now, owing to the suggestions of this sound, her
thoughts became concentrated on Hetty: that[2] sweet young thing, with life
and all its trials before her—the solemn daily duties of the wife and
mother—and her mind so unprepared for them all; bent merely on little
foolish, selfish pleasures, like a child hugging its toys in the beginning of a

[5] broad] *added in MS*   [6] for ⟨bleak⟩ to *MS*
[7] the ⟨earth & sky⟩ moonlit fields *MS*   [8] solitude. Simply] solitude: simply *MS*
[9] she ⟨still⟩ felt *MS*   [1] might] *added in MS*   [2] Hetty: that] Hetty. That *MS*

long[3] toilsome journey, in which it will have to bear hunger and cold and unsheltered darkness. Dinah felt a double[4] care for Hetty, because she shared Seth's anxious interest in his brother's lot, and she had not come to the conclusion that Hetty did not love Adam well enough to marry him. She saw too clearly the absence of any warm, self-devoting love in Hetty's nature, to regard the coldness of her behaviour towards Adam as any indication that he was not the man she would like to have for a husband. And this blank in Hetty's nature, instead of exciting Dinah's dislike, only touched her with a deeper pity: the lovely face and form affected her as beauty always affects a pure and tender mind, free from selfish jealousies: it was an excellent divine gift, that gave a deeper pathos to the need, the sin, the sorrow with which it was mingled, as the canker in a lily-white bud is more grievous to behold than in a common pot-herb.

By the time Dinah had undressed and put on her night-gown, this feeling about Hetty had gathered a painful intensity; her imagination had created a thorny thicket of sin and sorrow, in which she saw the poor thing struggling torn and bleeding, looking with tears for rescue and finding none[5]. It was in this way that Dinah's imagination and sympathy acted and reacted habitually, each heightening the other. She felt a deep longing to go now and pour into Hetty's ear all the words of tender warning and appeal that rushed into her mind. But perhaps Hetty was already asleep. Dinah[6] put her ear to the partition, and heard still some slight noises, which convinced her that Hetty was not yet in bed.[7] Still she hesitated; she was not quite certain of a divine direction; the voice that told her to go to Hetty seemed no stronger than the other voice which said that Hetty was weary, and that going to her now in an unseasonable moment would only tend to close her heart more obstinately. Dinah was not satisfied without a more unmistakeable guidance than those[8] inward voices. There was light enough for her, if she opened her Bible, for her to discern the text sufficiently to know what it would say to her. She knew the physiognomy of every page, and could tell on what book she opened, sometimes on what chapter, without seeing title or number. It was a small thick Bible, worn quite round at the edges. Dinah[9] laid it sideways on the window-ledge, where the light was strongest, and then opened it with her forefinger. The first words she looked at were those at the top of the left-hand page: "And they all wept sore, and fell on Paul's neck and kissed him." That was enough for Dinah; she had opened on that memorable parting at Ephesus, when Paul had felt bound to open his heart in a last exhortation and warning. She

---

[3] long ⟨painful⟩ toilsome *MS*   [4] double ⟨interest in⟩ care for *MS*
[5] looking with tears for rescue and finding none] while she looked with tears for rescue & found none *MS*
[6] asleep. Dinah] asleep: Dinah *MS*   [7] bed. ⟨But⟩ Still *MS*
[8] those] these *MS*   [9] edges. Dinah] edges; Dinah *MS*

hesitated no longer, but, opening her own door gently, went and tapped at Hetty's. We know she had to tap twice, because Hetty had to put out her candles and throw off her black lace scarf; but after the second tap the door was opened immediately. Dinah said, "Will you let me come in, Hetty?" and Hetty, without speaking, for she was confused and vexed, opened the door wider and let her in.

What a strange contrast the two figures made! Visible enough in that mingled twilight and moonlight. Hetty, her cheeks flushed and her eyes glistening from her imaginary drama, her beautiful neck and arms bare, her hair hanging in a curly tangle down her back, and the baubles in her ears. Dinah, covered with her long white dress, her pale face full of subdued emotion, almost like a lovely corpse into which the soul has returned charged with sublimer secrets and a sublimer love. They were nearly of the same height; Dinah evidently a little the taller as she put[1] her arm round Hetty's waist, and kissed[2] her forehead.

"I knew you were not in bed, my dear," she said, in her sweet clear voice, which was irritating to Hetty, mingling with her own peevish vexation like music with jangling chains, "for I heard you moving; and[3] I longed to speak to you again to-night, for it is the last but one that I shall be here, and we don't know what may happen to-morrow to keep us apart. Shall I sit down with you while you do up your hair?"

"O yes," said Hetty, hastily turning round and reaching the second chair in the room, glad that Dinah looked as if she did[4] not notice her ear-rings.

Dinah sat down, and Hetty began to brush together her hair before twisting it up, doing it with that air of excessive indifference[5] which belongs to confused self-consciousness. But the expression of Dinah's eyes gradually relieved her; they seemed unobservant of all details.

"Dear Hetty," she said, "it has been borne in upon my mind to-night that you may some day be in trouble—trouble is appointed for us all here below, and there comes a time when we need more comfort and help than the things of this life can give. I want to tell you that if ever you are in trouble, and need a friend that will always feel for you and love you, you have got that friend in Dinah Morris at Snowfield; and[6] if you come to her, or send for her, she'll never forget this night and the words she is speaking to you now. Will you remember it, Hetty?"

"Yes," said Hetty, rather frightened. "But why should you think I shall be in trouble? Do you know of anything?"

Hetty had seated herself as she tied on her cap, and now Dinah leaned forwards and took her hands as[7] she answered—

<hr />

[1]   put] puts *MS*   [2]   kissed] kisses *MS*   [3]   moving; and] moving. And *MS*
[4]   if she did] if did *MS*
[5]   with that air of excessive indifference] with excessive air of indifference *MS*
[6]   Snowfield; and] Snowfield. And *MS*   [7]   hands as] hands ⟨as⟩ while *MS*

"Because, dear, trouble comes to us all in this life: we set our hearts on things which it isn't God's will for us to have, and then we go sorrowing; the people we love are taken from us, and we can joy in nothing because they are not with us; sickness comes, and we faint under the burthen of our feeble bodies; we go astray and do wrong, and bring ourselves into trouble with our fellow-men. There is no man or woman born into this world to whom some of these trials do not fall, and so I feel that some of them must happen to you; and I desire for you, that while you are young you should seek for strength from your Heavenly Father, that you may have a[8] support which will not fail you in the evil day."

Dinah paused and released Hetty's hands, that she might not hinder her. Hetty[9] sat quite still; she felt no response within herself to Dinah's anxious affection; but Dinah's[1] words, uttered with solemn pathetic distinctness, affected her with a chill fear. Her flush had died away almost to paleness; she had the timidity of a luxurious pleasure-seeking nature, which shrinks from the hint of pain. Dinah saw the effect, and her tender anxious pleading became the more earnest, till Hetty, full of a vague fear that something evil was sometime to befall her, began to cry.

It is our habit to say that while the lower nature can never understand the higher, the higher nature commands a complete view of the lower. But I think the higher nature has to learn this comprehension, as we learn the art of vision, by a good deal of hard experience, often with bruises and gashes incurred in taking things up by the wrong end, and fancying our space wider than it is. Dinah had never seen Hetty affected in this way before, and, with her usual benignant hopefulness, she trusted it was the stirring of a divine impulse. She kissed the sobbing thing, and began to cry with her for grateful joy. But Hetty was simply in that excitable state of mind in which there is no calculating what turn the feelings may take from one moment to another, and for the first time she became irritated under Dinah's caress. She pushed her away impatiently, and said with a childish sobbing voice,—

"Don't talk to me so, Dinah. Why do you come to frighten me? I've never done anything to you. Why can't you let me be?"

Poor Dinah felt a pang. She was too wise to persist, and only said mildly, "Yes, my dear, you're tired; I won't hinder you any longer. Make haste and get into bed. Good night."

She went out of the room almost as quietly and quickly as if she had been a ghost; but once by the side of her own bed, she threw herself on her knees, and poured out in deep silence all the passionate pity that filled her heart.

As for Hetty, she was soon in the wood again[2]—her waking dreams being merged in a sleeping life scarcely more fragmentary and confused.

[8] a ⟨refuge⟩ support *MS*   [9] her. Hetty] her. But Hetty *MS*
[1] Dinah's] her *MS*   [2] again ⟨, &⟩ —her *MS*

CHAPTER XVI.

LINKS.

Arthur Donnithorne, you remember, is under an engagement with himself to go and see Mr Irwine this Friday morning, and he is awake and dressing so early, that he determines to go before breakfast, instead of after. The Rector, he knows, breakfasts alone at half past nine, the ladies of the family having a different breakfast hour; Arthur will have an early ride over the hill and breakfast with him. One can say everything best over a meal.

The progress of civilization has made a breakfast or a dinner an easy and cheerful substitute for more troublesome and disagreeable ceremonies. We[1] take a less gloomy view of our errors now our father confessor listens to us over his egg and coffee. We[2] are more distinctly conscious that rude penances are out of the question for gentlemen in an enlightened age, and that mortal sin is not incompatible with an appetite for muffins. An[3] assault on our pockets, which in more barbarous times would have been made in the brusque form of a pistol-shot, is quite a well-bred and smiling procedure now it has become a request for a loan thrown in as an easy parenthesis between the second and third glasses of claret.

Still, there was this advantage in the old rigid forms, that they committed you to the fulfilment of a resolution by some outward deed: when you have put your mouth to one end of a hole in a stone wall, and are aware that there is an expectant ear at the other end, you are more likely to say what you came out with the intention of saying, than if you were seated with your legs in an easy attitude under the mahogany, with a companion who will have no reason to be surprised if you have nothing particular to say.

However, Arthur Donnithorne, as he winds among the pleasant lanes on horseback in the morning sunshine, has a sincere determination to open his heart to the Rector, and the swirling sound of the scythe as he passes by the meadow is all the pleasanter to him because of this honest purpose. He is glad to see the promise of settled weather now, for getting in the hay, about which the farmers have been fearful; and there is something so healthful in the sharing of a joy that is general and not merely personal, that this thought about the hay-harvest reacts on his state of mind, and makes his resolution seem an easier matter. A man about town might perhaps consider that these influences were not to be felt out of a child's story-book; but when you are

---

[1] ceremonies. We] ceremonies: we *MS*   [2] coffee. We] coffee, we *MS*
[3] muffins. An] muffins; ⟨while⟩ an *MS* muffins; an *1* muffins⟨;⟩{.} ⟨a⟩An *8*

among the fields and hedgerows, it is impossible to maintain a consistent superiority to simple natural pleasures.

Arthur had passed the village of Hayslope, and was approaching the Broxton side of the hill, when, at a turning in the road, he saw a figure about a hundred yards before him which it was impossible to mistake for any one else than Adam Bede, even if there had been no grey, tailless[4] shepherd-dog at his heels. He was striding along at his usual rapid pace; and Arthur pushed on his horse to overtake him, for he retained too much of his boyish feeling for Adam to miss an opportunity of chatting with him. I will not say that his love for that good fellow did not owe some of its force to the love of patronage: our friend Arthur liked to do everything that was handsome, and to have his handsome deeds recognized.

Adam looked round as he heard the quickening clatter of the horse's heels, and waited for the horseman, lifting his paper cap from his head with a bright smile of recognition. Next to his own brother Seth, Adam would have done more for Arthur Donnithorne than for any other young man in the world. There was hardly anything he would not rather have lost than the two-feet ruler which he always carried in his pocket; it was Arthur's present, bought with his pocket-money when he was a fair-haired lad of eleven, and[5] when he had profited so well by Adam's lessons in carpentering and turning[6], as to embarrass every female in the house with gifts of superfluous thread-reels and round boxes. Adam had quite a pride in the little squire in those early days, and the feeling had only become slightly modified as the fair-haired lad had grown into the whiskered young man. Adam, I confess, was very susceptible to the influence of rank, and quite ready to give an extra amount of respect to every one who had more advantages than himself, not being a philosopher, or a proletaire with democratic ideas, but simply a stout-limbed clever carpenter with a large fund of reverence in his nature, which inclined him to admit all established claims unless he saw very clear grounds for questioning them. He had no theories about setting the world to rights, but he saw there was a great deal of damage done by building with[7] ill-seasoned timber,[8] by ignorant men in fine clothes making plans for outhouses and workshops and the like, without knowing the bearings of things,[9] by slovenly joiners' work, and by hasty contracts that could never be fulfilled without ruining somebody; and he resolved, for his part, to set his face against such doings. On[1] these points he would have maintained his opinion against the largest landed proprietor in Loamshire or Stonyshire either; but he felt that beyond these it would be

---

[4] tailless] *MS* tailless, *1 8*
[5] & ⟨Adam had taught him⟩ when he had profited so well by Adam's lessons in *MS*
[6] turning ⟨with so much success⟩ as to embarass every *MS*
[7] with ⟨un⟩ {ill}seasoned *MS*   [8] timber,] *MS* timber,— *1* timber— *8*
[9] things,] *MS* things,— *1* things— *8*
[1] On ⟨such⟩ {these} points ⟨as these⟩, he *MS*

better for him to defer to people who were more knowing than himself.[2] He saw as plainly as possible how ill the woods on the estate were managed, and the shameful state of the farm-buildings; and if old Squire Donnithorne had asked him the effect of this mismanagement, he would have spoken his opinion without flinching, but the impulse to a respectful demeanour towards a "gentleman" would have been strong within him all the while. The word "gentleman" had a spell for Adam, and,[3] as he often said, he "couldn't[4] abide a fellow who thought he made himself fine by being coxy to 's betters." I must remind you again that Adam had the blood of the peasant in his veins, and that since he was in his prime half a century ago, you must expect[5] some of his characteristics to be obsolete.

Towards the young squire this instinctive reverence of Adam's was assisted by boyish memories and personal regard; so you may imagine that he thought far more of[6] Arthur's good qualities, and attached far more value to very slight actions of his, than if they had been the qualities and actions of a common workman like himself. He felt sure it would be a fine day for everybody about Hayslope when the young squire came into the estate—such a generous open-hearted disposition as he had, and an "uncommon" notion about improvements and repairs, considering he was only just coming of age. Thus there was both respect and affection in the smile with which he raised his paper cap as Arthur Donnithorne rode up.

"Well, Adam, how are you?" said Arthur, holding out his hand. He never shook hands with any of the farmers[7], and Adam felt the honour keenly. "I could swear to your back a long way off. It's just[8] the same back, only broader, as when you used to carry me on it. Do you remember?"

"Ay, sir, I remember. It 'ud[9] be a poor look-out if folks didn't remember what they did and said when they were lads. We should think no more about old friends than we do about new uns[1], then."

"You're going to Broxton, I suppose?" said Arthur, putting his horse on at a slow pace while Adam walked by his side. "Are you going to the Rectory?"

"No, sir, I'm going to see about Bradwell's barn. They're afraid of the roof pushing the walls out; and I'm going to see what can be done with it before we send the stuff and the workmen."

"Why, Burge trusts almost everything to you now, Adam, doesn't he? I should think he will make you his partner soon. He will, if he's wise."

[2] himself. ⟨He felt as⟩ He *MS*   [3] & ⟨there was nothing⟩, as *MS*
[4] he "couldn't] "he couldn't *MS*   [5] expect ⟨him⟩ some *MS*
[6] of ⟨the⟩ Arthur's *MS*
[7] hands with any of the farmers] hands with any other workman, or with any of the farmers *MS*
[8] just] *added in MS*   [9] 'ud] would *MS*   [1] uns] ones *MS*

"Nay, sir, I don't see as he'd be[2] much the better off for that. A foreman, if he's got a conscience, and delights in his work, will do his business as well as if he was a partner. I wouldn't give a penny for a man as 'ud drive a nail in slack because he didn't get extra pay for it."

"I know that, Adam; I know you work for him as well as if you were working for yourself. But you would have more power than you have now, and could turn the business to better account perhaps. The old man must give up his[3] business some time, and he has no son; I suppose he'll want a son-in-law who can take to[4] it. But he[5] has rather grasping fingers of his own, I fancy: I dare say he wants a man who can put some money into the business. If I were not as poor as a rat, I would gladly invest some money in that way, for the sake of having you[6] settled on the estate. I'm sure I should profit by it in the end. And perhaps I shall be better off in a year or two. I shall have a larger allowance now I'm of age; and when I've paid off a debt or two, I shall be able to look about me."

"You're very good to say so, sir, and I'm not unthankful. But"—Adam continued in a decided tone—"I shouldn't like to make any offers to Mr Burge, or t'[7] have any made for me. I see no clear road to a partnership. If he should ever want to dispose of[8] the business, that 'ud[9] be a different matter. I should be glad of some money at a fair interest then, for I feel sure I could pay it off in time."

"Very well, Adam," said Arthur, remembering what Mr Irwine had said about a probable hitch in the love-making between Adam and Mary Burge, "we'll say no more about it at present. When is your father to be buried?"

"On Sunday, sir; Mr[1] Irwine's coming[2] earlier on purpose. I shall be glad when it's over, for I think my mother 'ull[3] perhaps get easier then. It cuts one sadly to see the grief of old people; they've no way o'[4] working it off; and the new spring brings no new shoots out on[5] the withered tree."

"Ah, you've had a good deal of trouble and vexation in your life, Adam. I don't think you've ever been hare-brained and light-hearted, like other youngsters. You've always had some care on your mind."[6]

"Why, yes, sir; but[7] that's nothing to make a fuss about. If we're men, and have men's feelings, I reckon we must have men's troubles. We can't be like the birds, as[8] fly from their nest as soon as they've got their wings, and never know their kin when they see 'em, and get a fresh lot every year. I've had enough to be thankful for: I've allays[9] had health and strength and brains to give me a[1] delight in my work; and I count it a great thing as I've

---

[2] be ⟨any⟩ much *MS*   [3] his] *added in MS*   [4] to] *added in MS*
[5] he ⟨'s⟩ has *MS*   [6] you] *added in MS*   [7] t'] to *MS*
[8] of] o' *1*   [9] 'ud] would *MS*   [1] sir; Mr] Sir. Mr. *MS*
[2] coming ⟨before the morning service at Broxton⟩ earlier *MS*
[3] 'ull] will *MS*   [4] o'] of *MS 1* ⟨of⟩ o' *8*   [5] on] in *MS*
[6] mind."] mind?" *MS 1*   [7] sir; but] Sir. But *MS*   [8] birds, as] birds that *MS*
[9] allays] always *MS*   [1] a] *added in MS*

had Bartle Massey's night-school to go to. He's helped me to knowledge I could never ha'[2] got by myself."

"What a rare fellow you are, Adam!" said Arthur, after a pause, in which he had looked musingly at the big fellow walking by his side. "I could hit out better than most men at Oxford, and yet I believe you would knock me into next week if I were to have a battle with you."

"God forbid I should ever do that, sir," said Adam, looking round at Arthur, and smiling. "I used to fight for fun; but I've never done that since I was the cause o'[3] poor Gil[4] Tranter being laid up for a fortnight. I'll never fight any man again, only when he behaves like a scoundrel. If you get hold of a chap that's got no shame nor conscience to stop him, you must try what you can do by bunging his eyes up."

Arthur did not laugh, for he was preoccupied with some thought that made him say presently,

"I should think now, Adam, you never have any struggles within yourself. I[5] fancy you would master a wish that you had made up your mind it[6] was not quite right to indulge, as easily as you would knock down a drunken fellow who was quarrelsome with you. I mean, you are[7] never shilly-shally, first making up your mind that you won't do a thing, and then doing it after all?"

"Well," said Adam slowly, after a moment's hesitation—"no. I don't remember ever being see-saw in that way, when I'd made my mind up, as you say, that a thing was wrong. It takes the taste out o' my mouth for things, when I know I should have a heavy conscience after 'em. I've seen pretty clear, ever since I could cast up a sum, as you can never do what's wrong without breeding sin and[8] trouble more than you can ever see. It's like a bit o' bad workmanship—you never see th' end o' the mischief it'll do. And it's a[9] poor look-out to come into the world to make your fellow-creaturs[1] worse off instead o'[2] better. But there's a difference between the things folks call wrong. I'm not for making a sin of every little fool's trick, or bit o'[3] nonsense[4] anybody may be let into, like some o'[5] them dissenters. And a man may have two minds whether it isn't worth while to get a bruise or two for the sake of a bit o' fun. But it isn't my way to be see-saw about anything: I think my fault lies th'[6] other way. When I've said a thing, if it's only to myself, it's hard for me to go back."

"Yes, that's just what I expected of you," said Arthur. "You've got an iron will, as well as an iron arm. But however strong a man's resolution may

---

[2] ha'] have *MS*   [3] o'] of *MS*   [4] Gil] Gill *MS*
[5] yourself. I] yourself—I *MS*   [6] it] *added in MS*   [7] you are] you're *MS*
[8] & ⟨mischief⟩ trouble *MS*   [9] a] *added in MS*
[1] fellow-creaturs] fellow-creatures *MS*   [2] o'] of *MS*   [3] o'] of *MS*
[4] nonsense ⟨a man⟩ anybody *MS*   [5] o'] of *MS*   [6] th'] the *MS*

be, it costs[7] him something to carry it out, now and then. We may
determine not to gather any cherries, and keep our hands sturdily in our
pockets, but we can't[8] prevent our mouths from watering."

"That's true, sir; but there's nothing like settling with[9] ourselves as[1]
there's a deal[2] we must do without i'[3] this life. It's no use looking on life as if
it was Treddles'on[4] fair, where folks only go to see shows and get fairings. If
we do, we[5] shall find it different. But where's the use o'[6] me talking to you,
sir? You know better than I do[7]."

"I'm not so sure of that, Adam.[8] You've had four or five years of
experience more than I've had, and I think your life has been a better school
to you than college has been to me."

"Why, sir, you seem to think o'[9] college something like what Bartle
Massey does. He says college mostly makes people like bladders—just good
for nothing but t'[1] hold the stuff as is[2] poured into 'em. But he's got a tongue
like a sharp blade, Bartle has: it never touches anything but it[3] cuts. Here's
the turning, sir. I must bid you good morning, as you're going to the
Rectory."

"Good-by, Adam, good-by."

Arthur gave his horse to the groom at the Rectory gate, and walked along
the gravel towards the door which opened on the garden. He knew that the
Rector always breakfasted in his study, and the study lay on the left hand of
this door, opposite the dining-room. It was a small low room, belonging to
the old part of the house—dark with the sombre covers of the books that
lined the walls; yet it looked very cheery this morning as Arthur reached the
open window. For the morning sun fell aslant on the great glass globe with
gold fish in it, which stood on a scagliola pillar in front of the ready-spread
bachelor breakfast-table, and by the side of this breakfast-table was a group
which would have made any room enticing. In the crimson damask easy
chair sat Mr Irwine, with that radiant freshness which he always had when
he came from his morning toilette[4]; his finely-formed plump white hand
was playing along Juno's brown[5] curly back; and close to Juno's tail, which
was wagging with calm[6] matronly pleasure, the two brown pups were
rolling over each other in an ecstatic duet of worrying noises. On a cushion
a little removed sat Pug, with the air of a maiden lady who looked on these
familiarities as animal weaknesses, which she made as little show as possible
of observing. On the table, at Mr Irwine's elbow, lay the first volume of the

[7] costs ⟨some⟩ him *MS*   [8] cant ⟨help⟩ prevent *MS*
[9] with ⟨yourself⟩ ourselves *MS*   [1] as] that *MS*   [2] deal ⟨you⟩ we *MS*
[3] i'] in *MS*   [4] Treddles'on] Treddleston *MS*   [5] we] *added in MS*
[6] o'] of *MS*   [7] better than I do] it as well as I do *MS*
[8] Adam. You'⟨re⟩{ve} ⟨five years older than I am,⟩ had four or five years *MS*
[9] o'] of *MS*   [1] t'] to *MS*   [2] as is] that's *MS*   [3] it⟨s⟩ cuts *MS*
[4] toilette] toilet *Cabinet*   [5] brown] *added in MS*   [6] calm] *added in MS*

Foulis Æschylus, which Arthur knew well by sight; and the silver[7] coffee-pot, which Carroll[8] was[9] bringing in, sent forth a fragrant steam which completed the delights of a bachelor breakfast.

"Hallo, Arthur, that's a good fellow! You're just in time," said Mr Irwine, as Arthur paused[1] and stepped in over the low window-sill. "Carroll[2], we shall want more coffee and eggs, and haven't you got some cold fowl for us to eat with that ham? Why, this is like old days, Arthur; you haven't been to breakfast with me these five years."[3]

"It was a tempting morning for a ride before breakfast," said Arthur, "and I used to like breakfasting with you so when I was reading with you. My grandfather is always a few degrees colder at breakfast than at any other hour in the day. I[4] think his morning bath[5] doesn't agree with him."

Arthur was anxious not to imply that he came with any special purpose. He had no sooner found himself in Mr Irwine's presence than the confidence which he had thought quite easy before, suddenly appeared the most difficult thing in the world to him, and at the very moment of shaking hands he saw his purpose in quite a new light. How could he make Irwine understand his position unless he told him those little scenes in the wood; and how could he tell them without looking like a fool? And then his weakness in coming back from Gawaine's, and doing the very opposite of what he intended! Irwine would think him a shilly-shally fellow ever after. However, it[6] must come out in an unpremeditated way; the conversation might lead up to it.

"I like breakfast-time better than any other moment in the day," said Mr Irwine. "No dust has settled on one's mind then, and it presents a clear mirror to the rays of things. I always have a favourite book by me at breakfast, and I enjoy the bits I pick up then so much, that regularly every morning it seems to me as if I should certainly become studious again. But presently Dent brings up a poor fellow who has killed a hare, and when I've got through my 'justicing,' as Carroll[7] calls it, I'm inclined for a ride round the glebe, and on my way back I meet with the master of the workhouse, who has got a long story of a mutinous pauper to tell me; and so the day goes on, and I'm always the same lazy fellow before evening sets in. Besides, one wants the stimulus of sympathy, and I have never had that since poor D'Oyley left Treddleston. If you had stuck to your books well, you rascal, I should have had a pleasanter prospect before me. But scholarship doesn't run in your family blood."

"No indeed. It's well if I can remember a little inapplicable Latin to adorn my maiden speech in Parliament six or seven years hence. 'Cras

[7] silver] *added in MS*   [8] Carroll] Carrol *MS*   [9] was ⟨placing⟩ bringing *MS*
[1] paused ⟨before the window⟩ & stepped in *MS*   [2] Carroll] Carrol *MS*
[3] years."⟨I thought⟩ *MS*   [4] day. I] day—I *MS*   [5] bath] toilette *MS*
[6] it ⟨might⟩ must *MS*   [7] Carroll] Carrol *MS*

ingens iterabimus æquor,' and a few shreds of that sort, will perhaps stick to me, and I shall arrange my opinions so as to introduce them. But I don't think a knowledge of the classics is a pressing want to a country gentleman; as far as I can see, he'd much better have a knowledge of manures. I've been reading your friend[8] Arthur Young's books lately, and there's nothing I should like better than to carry out some of his ideas in putting the farmers on a better management of their land; and, as he says, making what was a wild country, all of the same dark hue, bright and variegated with corn and cattle. My grandfather will never let me have any power while he lives; but there's nothing I should like better than to undertake the Stonyshire side of the estate—it's in a dismal condition—and set improvements on foot, and gallop about from one place to another and overlook them. I should like to know all the labourers, and see them touching their hats to me with a look of goodwill."

"Bravo, Arthur! a[9] man who has no feeling for the classics[1] couldn't make a better apology for coming into the world than[2] by increasing the quantity of food to maintain scholars—and rectors who[3] appreciate scholars. And whenever you[4] enter on your career of model landlord may I be there to see. You'll want a portly rector to complete the picture, and take his tithe of all the respect and honour you get by your hard work. Only don't set your heart too strongly on the goodwill you are to get in consequence. I'm not sure that men are the fondest of those who try to be useful to them. You know Gawaine has got the curses of the whole neighbourhood upon him about that enclosure. You must make it quite clear to your mind which you are most bent upon, old boy—popularity or usefulness—else you may happen to miss both."

"O! Gawaine is harsh in his manners; he doesn't make himself personally agreeable to his tenants. I don't believe there's anything you can't prevail on people to do with kindness. For my part, I couldn't live in a neighbourhood where I was not respected and beloved; and it's[5] very pleasant to go among the tenants here, they[6] seem all so well inclined to me. I[7] suppose it seems only the other day to them since I was a little lad, riding on a pony about as big as a sheep. And if fair allowances were made to them, and their buildings attended to, one could persuade them to farm on a better plan, stupid as they are."

"Then mind you fall in love in the right place, and don't get a wife who will drain your purse and make you niggardly in spite of yourself. My mother and I have a little discussion about you sometimes: she says, 'I'll never risk a single prophecy on Arthur until I see the woman he falls in love

[8] your friend] *added in MS*   [9] Arthur! a] Arthur: a *MS* Arthur; a *1*
[1] who has no feeling for the classics] *added in MS*   [2] than ⟨that,⟩ by *MS*
[3] who ⟨admire⟩ appreciate *MS*   [4] you ⟨are⟩ enter *MS*   [5] it's] it is *MS*
[6] here, they] here. They *MS*   [7] me. I] me—I *MS*

with.' She thinks your lady-love will rule you as the moon rules the tides. But I feel bound to stand up for you, as my pupil, you know; and I maintain that you're not of that watery quality. So mind you don't disgrace my judgment."

Arthur winced under this speech, for keen[8] old Mrs Irwine's opinion about him had the disagreeable effect of a sinister omen. This, to be sure, was only another reason for persevering in his intention, and getting an additional security against himself. Nevertheless, at this point in the conversation, he was conscious of increased disinclination to tell his story about Hetty.[9] He was of an impressible[1] nature, and lived a great deal in other people's opinions and feelings concerning himself; and the mere fact that he was in the presence of an intimate friend, who had not the slightest notion that he had had any such serious internal[2] struggle as he came to confide, rather shook his own belief in the seriousness of the struggle. It was not, after all, a thing to make a fuss about; and what could Irwine do for him that he could not do for himself? He would go to Eagledale in spite of Meg's lameness—go on Rattler, and let Pym follow as well as he could on the old hack. That was his thought as he sugared his coffee; but the next minute, as he was lifting the cup to his lips, he remembered how thoroughly he had made up his mind last night[3] to tell Irwine. No! he would not be vacillating again—he *would* do what he had meant to do, this time. So it would be well not to let the personal tone of the conversation altogether drop. If they went to quite indifferent topics, his difficulty would be[4] heightened. It had required no noticeable pause for[5] this rush and rebound of feeling, before he answered,—

"But I think it is hardly an argument against a man's general strength of character, that he should be apt to be mastered by love. A fine constitution doesn't insure one against small-pox or any other of those inevitable diseases. A man may be very firm in other matters, and yet be under a sort of witchery from a woman."

"Yes; but there's this difference between love and small-pox, or bewitchment either—that if you detect the disease at an early stage and try change of air, there is every chance of complete escape, without any further development of symptoms. And there are certain alterative doses which a man may administer to himself by keeping unpleasant consequences before his mind: this[6] gives you a sort of smoked glass through which you may look at the resplendent fair one and discern her true outline; though[7] I'm afraid, by the by, the smoked glass is apt to be missing just at

[8] keen] *added in MS*   [9] Hetty. ⟨You perceive⟩ ⟨h⟩He *MS*
[1] impressible] impressionable *MS 1* ⟨impressionable⟩ impressible *8*
[2] internal] *added in MS*   [3] last night] *added in MS*
[4] be ⟨increased⟩ heightened *MS*
[5] for ⟨him to think about this,⟩ this rush & rebound of feeling *MS*
[6] this] that *MS 1* ⟨that⟩ this *8*   [7] outline; though] outline. Though *MS*

the moment it is most wanted. I dare say, now, even a man fortified with a knowledge of the classics[8] might be lured into an imprudent marriage, in spite of the warning given him by the chorus in the Prometheus."

The smile that flitted across Arthur's face was a faint one, and instead of following Mr Irwine's playful lead, he said quite seriously—"Yes, that's the worst of it. It's a desperately vexatious thing, that after all one's reflections and quiet determinations, we should be ruled by moods that one can't calculate on beforehand. I don't think a man ought to be blamed so much if he is betrayed into doing things in that way, in spite of his resolutions."

"Ah, but the moods lie in his nature[9], my boy, just as much as his reflections did, and more. A man can never do anything at variance with his own nature[1]. He carries within him the germ of his most exceptional action; and[2] if we wise people make eminent fools of ourselves on any particular occasion, we must endure the legitimate conclusion that we carry a few grains of folly to our ounce of wisdom."

"Well, but one may be betrayed into doing things by a combination of circumstances, which one might never have done otherwise."

"Why, yes, a man can't very well steal a bank-note unless the bank-note lies within convenient reach; but he won't make us think him an honest man because he begins to howl at the bank-note for falling in his way."

"But surely you don't think a man who struggles against a temptation into which he falls at last, as bad as the man who never struggles at all?"

[3]"No, certainly; I pity him[4] in proportion to his struggles, for they foreshadow the inward suffering which is the[5] worst form of Nemesis[6]. Consequences are unpitying. Our deeds carry their terrible consequences, quite apart from any fluctuations that went before—consequences that are hardly ever confined to ourselves[7]. And it is best to fix our minds on that certainty, instead of considering what may be the elements of excuse for us. But I never knew you so inclined for moral discussion, Arthur? Is it some danger of your own that you are considering in this philosophical, general way?"

In asking this question, Mr Irwine pushed his plate away, threw himself back in his chair, and looked straight at Arthur. He really suspected that Arthur wanted to tell him something, and thought of smoothing the way for him by this direct question. But he was mistaken. Brought suddenly and

---

[8] classics, ⟨may⟩ might *MS*

[9] nature] character *MS*   [1] nature] character *MS*

[2] action; and] action. And *MS*

[3] "No, certainly; I] "No, my boy. I *MS 1* "No, ⟨my boy,⟩ {certainly;} I *8*

[4] him ⟨—such a tendency [?foretells] his⟩ {one that} ⟨one that⟩ {in proportion to his struggles, for they foreshadow} the *MS*

[5] which is the] which ⟨is⟩ will be the *MS*   [6] of Nemesis] of the Nemesis *MS*

[7] —consequences that are hardly ever confined to ourselves] *added in MS*

involuntarily to the brink of confession, Arthur shrank back, and felt less disposed towards it than ever. The conversation had taken a more serious tone than he had intended—it would[8] quite mislead Irwine—he would imagine there was a deep passion for Hetty, while there was no such thing. He was conscious of colouring, and was annoyed at his boyishness.

"O no, no danger," he said, as indifferently as he could. "I don't know that I am[9] more liable to irresolution than other people; only[1] there are little incidents now and then that set one speculating on what might happen in the future."

Was there a motive at work under this strange reluctance of Arthur's which had a sort of backstairs influence, not admitted to himself? Our mental business is carried on much in the same way as the business of the State: a great deal of hard work is done by agents who are not acknowledged. In a piece of machinery, too, I believe there is often a small unnoticeable wheel which has a great deal to do with the motion of the large obvious ones. Possibly there was some such unrecognized agent secretly busy in Arthur's mind at this moment—possibly it was the fear lest he might hereafter find the fact of having made a confession to the Rector a serious annoyance, in case he should *not* be able quite to carry out his good resolutions? I dare not assert that it was not so. The human soul is a very complex thing.

The idea of Hetty had just crossed Mr Irwine's mind as he looked inquiringly at Arthur, but his disclaiming, indifferent answer confirmed the thought which had quickly followed—that there could be nothing serious in that direction. There was no probability that Arthur ever saw her except at church, and at her own home under the eye of Mrs Poyser; and the hint he had given Arthur about her the other day had no more serious meaning than to prevent him from noticing her so as[2] to rouse the little chit's vanity, and in this way perturb the rustic drama of her life. Arthur would soon join his regiment, and be far away: no, there could be no danger in that quarter, even if Arthur's character had not been a strong security against it. His honest, patronizing pride in the goodwill and respect of everybody about him was a safeguard even against foolish romance, still more against a lower kind of folly. If there had been anything special on Arthur's mind in the previous conversation,[3] it was clear he was not inclined to enter into details, and Mr Irwine was too delicate to imply even a friendly curiosity. He perceived[4] a change of subject would be welcome, and said—

"By the way, Arthur, at your colonel's birthday fête[5] there were some transparencies that made a great effect in honour of Britannia, and Pitt, and

---

[8] would ⟨have⟩ quite ⟨misled⟩ mislead *MS*

[9] I am] I'm *MS*   [1] people; only] people. Only *MS*   [2] so as] in a way *MS*

[3] conversation, ⟨he⟩ it *MS*   [4] perceived ⟨in⟩ a *MS*   [5] fête] *fête Cabinet*

the Loamshire Militia, and, above all, the 'generous youth,' the hero of the day. Don't you think you should get up something of the same sort to astonish our weak minds?"

The opportunity was gone. While Arthur was hesitating, the rope to which he might have clung had drifted away—he must trust now to his own swimming.

In ten minutes from that time, Mr Irwine was called for on business, and Arthur, bidding him good-by, mounted his horse again with a sense of dissatisfaction, which he tried to quell by determining to set off for Eagle-dale without an hour's delay.

BOOK SECOND

*

CHAPTER XVII.

IN WHICH THE STORY PAUSES A LITTLE.

"This Rector of Broxton is little better than a pagan!" I hear one of my readers[1] exclaim. "How much more edifying it would have been if you had made him give Arthur some truly spiritual advice.[2] You might have put into his mouth the most beautiful things—quite as good as reading a sermon."

Certainly I could, if I held it the highest vocation of the novelist to represent things as they never have been and never will be. Then, of course, I might refashion life and character entirely after my own liking; I might select the most unexceptionable type of clergyman, and put my own admirable opinions into his mouth on all occasions. But it happens, on the contrary, that my strongest effort is to avoid any such arbitrary picture, and to give a faithful[3] account of men and things as they have mirrored

---

[1] readers] lady-readers *MS* lady readers *1* ⟨lady⟩ readers *8*

[2] advice.] advice! *Cabinet*

[3] Certainly, I could, if I held it the highest vocation of the novelist to represent things as they never have been and never will be. Then, of course, I might refashion life and character entirely after my own liking; I might select the most unexceptionable type of clergyman, and put my own admirable opinions into his mouth on all occasions. But it happens, on the contrary, that my strongest effort is to avoid any such arbitrary picture, and to give a faithful] *MS 1 read* Certainly I could, my fair critic, if I were a clever novelist, not obliged to creep servilely after nature and [*MS*: &] fact, but able to represent things as they never have been and [*MS*: &] never will be. Then, of course, my characters would be entirely of my own choosing, and [*MS*: &] I could select the most unexceptionable type of clergyman, and [*MS*: &] put my own admirable opinions into his mouth on all occasions. But you must have perceived long ago that I have no such lofty vocation, and [*MS*: &] that I aspire to give no more than a faithful *First revised within the printed text on 1. [259] of the marked 8th edition, thus* Certainly I could, ⟨my fair critic⟩, if I ⟨were a clever⟩ {held it the highest vocation of the} novelist, ⟨not obliged to creep servilely after nature and fact, but able⟩ to represent things as they never have been and never will be. Then, of course, ⟨my characters would {might} be entirely of my own choosing, and I could⟩ {I might refashion life & character entirely after my own liking; I might} select the most unexceptionable type of clergyman, and put my own admirable opinions into his mouth on all occasions. But ⟨you must have perceived long ago that I have no such lofty vocation, and that I aspire⟩ {it happens} {, on the contrary, ⟨it is⟩ that my strongest desire is to avoid any such arbitrary picture ⟨of the people & things⟩ &} to give ⟨no more than⟩ a faithful *Rewritten in George Eliot's hand on blank page 1.[258], facing the opening of chapter 17 of the marked 8th edition as* Certainly I could, if I held it the highest vocation of the novelist to represent things as they never have been & never will be. Then, of course, I might refashion life & character entirely after my own liking; I might select the most unexceptionable type of clergyman, & put my own admirable opinions into his mouth on all occasions. But it happens, on the contrary, that my strongest effort is to avoid any such arbitrary picture, & to give a faithful &c.

themselves in my mind. The mirror is doubtless defective; the outlines will sometimes be disturbed, the reflection faint or confused; but I feel as much bound to tell you as precisely as I can what that reflection is, as if I were in the witness-box narrating my experience on oath.

Sixty years ago—it is a long time, so no wonder things have changed—all clergymen were not zealous; indeed there is reason to believe that the number of zealous clergymen was small, and it is probable that if one among the small minority had owned the livings of Broxton and Hayslope in the year 1799, you would have liked him no better than you like Mr Irwine. Ten to one, you would have thought him a tasteless, indiscreet, methodistical man. It is so very rarely that facts hit that nice medium required by our own enlightened opinions and refined taste! Perhaps you will say, "Do improve the facts a little, then; make them more accordant with those correct views which it is our privilege to possess. The world is not just what we like; do touch it up with a tasteful pencil, and make believe it is not quite such a mixed entangled affair. Let all people who hold unexceptionable opinions act unexceptionably. Let your most faulty characters always be on the wrong side, and your virtuous ones on the right. Then we shall see at a glance whom we are to condemn, and whom we are to approve. Then we shall be able to[4] admire, without the slightest disturbance of our prepossessions:[5] we shall hate and despise with that true ruminant relish which belongs to undoubting confidence."

But, my good friend, what will you do then with your fellow-parishioner[6] who opposes your husband in the vestry?—with[7] your newly-appointed vicar, whose style of preaching you find painfully below that of his regretted predecessor?—with[8] the honest servant who worries your soul with her one failing?—with[9] your neighbour, Mrs Green, who was really kind to you in your last illness, but has said several ill-natured things about you since your convalescence?—nay[1], with your excellent husband himself, who has other irritating habits besides that of not wiping his shoes? These fellow-mortals, every one, must be accepted as they are: you can neither straighten their noses, nor brighten their wit, nor rectify their dispositions;[2] and it is these people—amongst whom your life is passed—that it is needful you should tolerate, pity, and love: it is these more or less ugly, stupid, inconsistent people, whose movements of goodness you should be able to admire—for whom you should cherish all possible hopes, all possible patience. And I would not, even if I had the

---

[4] be able to] *added in MS*   [5] prepossessions: ⟨&⟩ we *MS*
[6] fellow-parishioner⟨s⟩ who *MS*   [7] vestry?—with] vestry; with *MS*
[8] predecessor?—with] predecessor; with *MS*
[9] failing?—with] failing; with *MS*
[1] convalescence?—nay] convalescence; nay *MS*
[2] noses, nor brighten their wit, nor rectify their dispositions;] *revised in MS from* straighten their noses, nor rectify their dispositions, nor brighten their wit;

choice, be the[3] clever novelist who could create a world so much better than
this, in which we get up in the morning[4] to do our daily work, that you
would be likely to turn a harder, colder eye on the dusty streets and the
common green fields—on the real breathing men and women, who can be
chilled by your indifference or injured by your prejudice;[5] who can be[6]
cheered and helped onward by your fellow-feeling, your forbearance, your
outspoken, brave justice.

So I am content to tell my simple story, without trying to make things
seem better than they were; dreading nothing, indeed, but falsity, which, in
spite of one's best efforts, there is reason to dread. Falsehood is so easy,
truth so difficult. The pencil is conscious of a delightful facility in drawing a
griffin—the longer the claws, and the larger the wings, the better; but that
marvellous facility which we mistook for genius is apt to forsake us when we
want to draw a real unexaggerated lion. Examine your words well, and you
will find that even when you have no motive to be false, it is a very hard
thing to say the exact[7] truth, even about your own immediate feelings—
much harder than to say something fine about them which is *not* the exact
truth.

It is for this rare, precious quality of truthfulness that I delight in many
Dutch paintings, which lofty-minded[8] people despise. I find a source of[9]
delicious sympathy in these faithful pictures of a monotonous[1] homely
existence, which has been the fate[2] of so many more among my fellow-
mortals than a life of pomp or of absolute indigence,[3] of tragic suffering or
of world-stirring actions. I turn, without[4] shrinking, from cloud-borne
angels, from prophets, sibyls, and heroic warriors, to an old woman bending over her flower-pot, or[5] eating her solitary dinner, while the noonday
light, softened perhaps by a screen of leaves, falls on her mob-cap, and just
touches the rim of her spinning-wheel, and her stone jug, and all those
cheap common things which are the precious necessaries of life to her;—or
I turn to[6] that village wedding, kept between four brown walls,[7] where an
awkward bridegroom opens the dance with a high-shouldered, broad-faced
bride, while elderly and middle-aged friends look on, with very irregular

   [3] the] a *MS*   [4] in the morning] *added in MS*
   [5] by your indifference or injured by your prejudice;] or thwarted or injured by your
indifference, your bigotry, your prejudice, *MS*
   [6] be ⟨warmed &⟩ cheered *MS*   [7] exact ⟨& whole⟩ truth {even} about *MS*
   [8] in many Dutch paintings, which lofty-minded] in ⟨Flemish⟩ Dutch paintings, which so
many lofty-minded *MS*
   [9] of ⟨solemn⟩ delicious ⟨pleasure⟩ {sympathy} in *MS*
   [1] monotonous] *added in MS*   [2] fate] lot *MS*
   [3] of absolute indigence,] *added in MS*
   [4] turn, without] turn without *MS 1* turn{,} without *8*
   [5] bending over her flower-pot, or] *added in MS*
   [6] her;—or I turn to] her⟨;⟩—or to *MS*
   [7] kept between four brown walls,] *added in MS*

noses and lips, and probably with quart-pots in their hands, but with an expression of unmistakeable contentment and good-will. "Foh!"[8] says my idealistic friend, "what vulgar details! What good is there in taking all these pains to give an exact likeness of old women and clowns? What a low phase of life!—what[9] clumsy, ugly people!"

But, bless us, things may be lovable that are not altogether handsome, I hope? I am not at all sure that the majority of the human race have not been ugly, and even among those "lords of their kind," the British, squat figures, ill-shapen nostrils, and dingy complexions are not startling exceptions. Yet there is a great deal of family love amongst us. I have a friend or two whose class of features is such that the Apollo curl on the summit of their brows would be decidedly trying; yet to my certain knowledge tender hearts have beaten for them, and their miniatures—flattering, but still not lovely—are kissed in secret by motherly lips. I have seen many an excellent matron, who could never in her best days have been handsome, and yet she had a packet of yellow love-letters in a private drawer, and sweet children showered kisses on her sallow cheeks. And I believe there[1] have been plenty of young heroes, of middle stature and feeble beards, who have felt quite sure they could never love anything more insignificant than a Diana, and yet have found themselves[2] in middle life happily settled with a wife who waddles. Yes! thank God; human feeling is like the mighty rivers that bless the earth: it does not wait for beauty—it flows with resistless force and brings beauty with it.

All honour[3] and reverence to the divine beauty of form! Let us cultivate it to the utmost in men, women, and children—in our gardens and in our houses. But let us love that other beauty too, which lies in no secret of proportion, but in the secret of deep human sympathy. Paint[4] us an angel, if you can, with a floating violet robe, and a face paled by the celestial light; paint[5] us yet oftener a Madonna, turning her mild face upward and opening her arms[6] to welcome the divine glory; but do not impose on us any aesthetic rules which shall banish from the region of Art those old women scraping carrots with their work-worn hands, those heavy clowns taking holiday in a dingy pot-house, those rounded backs and stupid weather-beaten faces that have bent over the spade and done the rough work of the world—those homes with their tin pans, their brown pitchers, their rough curs, and their clusters of onions. In this world there are so many of these common, coarse[7] people, who have no picturesque senti-mental wretchedness! It is so needful we should remember their existence,

[8] good will. "⟨Ba⟩ Foh!" *MS*   [9] life!—what] life! What *MS*

[1] there ⟨are⟩ have been *MS*   [2] themselves ⟨ha⟩ in *MS*

[3] honour ⟨to the⟩ & reverence *MS*   [4] Paint ⟨me⟩ us *MS*

[5] paint ⟨me⟩ us *MS*

[6] arms ⟨in rapt submission to the divine influence⟩ to welcome the divine glory *MS*

[7] common, coarse] *transposed in MS from* coarse common

else we may happen to leave them quite out of our religion and philosophy, and frame lofty theories which only fit a world of extremes. Therefore let Art always remind us of them; therefore let us always have men ready to give the loving pains of a life to the faithful representing of commonplace[8] things—men who see beauty in these commonplace things, and delight in showing how kindly the light of heaven falls on them. There are few prophets in[9] the world; few sublimely beautiful women; few heroes. I[1] can't afford to give all my love and reverence to such rarities: I want a great deal of those feelings for my every-day fellow-men, especially for the[2] few in the foreground of the great multitude, whose faces I know, whose hands I touch, for whom I have to make way with kindly courtesy. Neither are picturesque lazzaroni or romantic criminals half so frequent as your common labourer[3], who gets his[4] own bread, and eats it vulgarly but creditably with his own pocket-knife. It is more needful that I should have a fibre of sympathy connecting me with that vulgar citizen who weighs out my sugar in a vilely-assorted cravat and waistcoat, than with the handsomest rascal in red scarf and green feathers;—more needful that my heart should swell with loving admiration at some trait of gentle goodness in the faulty people who sit at the same hearth with me, or in[5] the clergyman of my own parish, who is perhaps rather too corpulent, and in other respects is not an Oberlin or a Tillotson, than at the deeds of heroes whom I shall never know except by hearsay, or at the sublimest abstract of all clerical graces that was ever conceived by an able novelist.

And so I come back to Mr Irwine, with whom I desire you to be in perfect charity, far as he may be from satisfying your demands on the clerical character. Perhaps you think he was not—as he ought to have been—a living demonstration of the benefits attached to a national church? But I am not sure of that; at[6] least I know that the people in Broxton and Hayslope would have been very sorry to part with their clergyman, and that most faces brightened at his approach; and until it can be proved that hatred is a better thing for the soul than love, I must believe that Mr Irwine's influence in his parish was a more wholesome one than that of[7] the zealous Mr Ryde, who came there twenty[8] years afterwards, when Mr Irwine had been gathered to his fathers. It is true Mr Ryde insisted strongly on the doctrines of the Reformation, visited his flock a great deal in their own homes, and was severe in rebuking the aberrations of the flesh—put a stop, indeed, to the Christmas rounds of the church singers, as promoting[9] drunkenness, and too light a handling of sacred things. But I gathered from Adam Bede,

---

[8] place] *added in MS*   [9] in ⟨the [one word] world, few sub-⟩ the *MS*

[1] heroes. I] heroes; I *MS*   [2] the] those *MS*   [3] labourer] citizen *MS*

[4] his {own} bread ⟨honestly⟩ & eats it ⟨with his own pocket knife.⟩ vulgarly *MS*

[5] me, or in] me, in *MS*   [6] that; at] that. At *MS*   [7] of ⟨his⟩ the *MS*

[8] there twenty] there more than twenty *MS*   [9] promoting ⟨of⟩ drunkenness *MS*

to whom I talked of these matters in his old age, that few clergymen could be less successful in winning the hearts of their parishioners than Mr Ryde. They learned[1] a great many notions about doctrine from him, so that almost every church-goer under fifty began to distinguish as well between the genuine gospel and what did not come precisely up to that standard, as if he had been born and bred a Dissenter; and for some time after his arrival there seemed to be quite a religious movement in that quiet rural district. "But," said Adam, "I've seen pretty clear, ever since I was a young un, as religion's something else besides notions. It isn't notions sets people doing the right thing—it's feelings. It's the same with the notions in religion as it is with math'matics,—a man may be able to work problems straight off in's head as he sits by the fire and smokes his pipe; but if he has to make a machine or a building, he must have a will and a resolution, and love something else better than his own ease. Somehow, the congregation began to fall off, and people began to speak light o' Mr Ryde. I believe he meant right at bottom; but, you see, he was sourish-tempered, and was for beating down prices with the people as worked for him; and his preaching wouldn't go down well with that sauce. And[2] he wanted to be like my lord judge i'[3] the parish, punishing folks for doing wrong; and[4] he scolded 'em from the pulpit as if he'd been a Ranter, and yet he couldn't abide the Dissenters, and was a deal more set against 'em than Mr Irwine was. And then he didn't keep within his income, for he seemed to think at first go-off that six hundred a year was to make him as big a man as Mr Donnithorne: that's a sore mischief I've often seen with the poor curates jumping into a bit of a living all of a sudden. Mr Ryde was a deal thought on at a distance, I believe, and he wrote books; but as for math'matics and the natur[5] o' things, he was as ignorant as a woman. He was very knowing about doctrines, and used to call 'em[6] the bulwarks of the Reformation; but I've always mistrusted that sort o' learning as leaves folks foolish and unreasonable about business. Now Mester Irwine was as different as could be: as quick!—he understood what you meant in a minute; and he knew all about building, and could see when you'd made a good job. And he behaved as much like a gentleman to the farmers, and th' old women and the labourers, as he did to the gentry. You never saw *him* interfering and scolding, and trying to play th' emperor. Ah! he was a fine man as ever you set eyes on; and so kind to's mother and sisters. That[7] poor sickly Miss Anne[8]—he seemed to think more of her than of[9] anybody else in the world. There wasn't a soul in the parish had[1] a word to say against him; and his servants stayed with him till they were so old and pottering, he had to hire other folks to do their work."

---

[1] learned] gathered *MS 1* ⟨gathered⟩ learned *8*   [2] sauce. And] sauce; & *MS*
[3] i'] in *MS*   [4] wrong; and] wrong. And *MS*   [5] natur] nature *MS*
[6] and used to call 'em] that he used to say were *MS*   [7] sisters. That] sisters—that *MS*
[8] Anne] Ann *MS*   [9] of] *added in MS*   [1] had ⟨an ill⟩ a *MS*

"Well," I said, "that was an excellent way of preaching in the week-days; but I dare say, if your old friend Mr Irwine were to come to life again, and get into the pulpit next Sunday, you would be rather ashamed that he didn't preach better after all your praise of him."

"Nay, nay," said Adam, broadening his chest and throwing himself back in his chair, as if he were ready to meet all inferences,[2] "nobody has ever heard me say Mr Irwine was much of a preacher. He didn't go into deep,[3] speritial experience[4]; and I know there's a deal in a man's inward life as you can't measure by the square, and say, 'do this and that'll follow,' and[5], 'do that and this'll follow.' There's things go on in the soul, and times when feelings come into you like a rushing mighty wind, as the Scripture says, and[6] part your life in two a'most, so as you look back on yourself as if[7] you was somebody else. Those are things as you can't bottle up in a 'do this' and 'do that;' and I'll go so far with the strongest Methodist ever you'll find. That shows me there's deep, speritial things in religion. You[8] can't make much out wi' talking about it, but you feel it. Mr Irwine didn't go into those things[9]: he preached short moral sermons, and that was all. But then he acted pretty much up to what he said; he didn't set up for being so different from other folks one day, and then be as like 'em as two[1] peas the next. And he made folks love him and respect him, and that was better nor[2] stirring up their gall wi'[3] being over-busy. Mrs Poyser used to say—you know she would have her word about everything—she said, Mr Irwine was like a good meal o' victual, you were the better for him without thinking on it, and Mr Ryde was like a dose o' physic, he griped you and worreted you, and after all he left you much the same."

"But didn't Mr Ryde preach a great deal more about that spiritual part of religion that you talk of, Adam? Couldn't you get more out of his sermons than out of Mr Irwine's?"

"Eh, I knowna. He preached a deal about doctrines. But I've seen pretty clear ever since I was a young un, as religion's something else besides doctrines and notions. I look at it as if the doctrines was like finding names for your feelings, so as you can talk of 'em when you've never known 'em, just as a man may talk o' tools when he knows their names, though he's never so much as seen 'em, still less handled 'em. I've heard a deal o' doctrine i' my time, for I used to go after the dissenting preachers along wi' Seth[4], when I was a lad o' seventeen, and got puzzling myself a deal about th' Arminians and the[5] Calvinists. The Wesleyans, you know, are strong Arminians; and Seth, who could never abide anything harsh, and

---

[2] inferences⟨.⟩, "⟨I never⟩ nobody *MS*   [3] deep,] *MS 1* deep *8*
[4] experience ⟨—good moral sermons, & short, that was all⟩. And *MS*
[5] and] an' *MS*   [6] and] an' *MS*   [7] if] *added in MS*
[8] religion. You] religion: you *MS*   [9] things ⟨at all⟩ —he *MS*
[1] two peas⟨e⟩ the *MS*   [2] nor] than *MS*   [3] wi'] with *MS*
[4] along wi' Seth] *added in MS*   [5] the] *added in MS*

was always for hoping the best, held fast by the Wesleyans from the very first; but I thought I could pick a hole or two[6] in their notions, and I got disputing wi' one o' the class leaders down at Treddles'on, and harassed him so, first o' this side and then o' that, till at last he said, 'Young man, it's the devil making use o' your pride and conceit as a weapon to war against the simplicity o' the truth.' I couldn't help laughing then, but as I was going home, I thought the man wasn't far wrong. I began to see as all this weighing and sifting what this text means and that text means, and whether folks are saved all by God's grace, or whether there goes an ounce o' their own will to 't, was no part o' real religion at all. You may talk o' these things for hours on end, and you'll only be all the more coxy and conceited for 't[7]. So I took to going nowhere but to church, and hearing nobody but Mr Irwine, for he said nothing but what was good, and what you'd be the[8] wiser for remembering. And I found it better for my soul to be humble before the mysteries o' God's dealings, and not be making a clatter about what I could never understand. And they're poor foolish questions after all; for[9] what have we got either inside or outside of us but what comes from God? If[1] we've got a resolution[2] to do right, He gave it us, I reckon, first or last; but[3] I see plain enough we shall never do it without a resolution, and that's enough for me."

Adam, you perceive, was[4] a warm admirer, perhaps a partial judge, of Mr Irwine, as, happily, some of us still are of the people we have known familiarly. Doubtless it will be despised as a weakness by that lofty order of minds who pant after the ideal, and are oppressed by a general sense that their emotions are of too exquisite a character to find fit objects among their everyday fellow-men. I have often been favoured with the confidence of these select natures, and find them concur in the experience that great men are over-estimated and small men are insupportable;[5] that if you would love a woman without ever looking back on your love as a folly, she must die while you are courting her; and if you would maintain the slightest belief in human heroism, you must never make a pilgrimage to see the hero. I confess I have often meanly shrunk from confessing to these accomplished and acute gentlemen[6] what my own experience has been. I am afraid I have often smiled with hypocritical assent, and gratified them with an epigram

---

[6] or two] *added in MS*   [7] 't] it *MS*   [8] the ⟨better⟩ wiser *MS*
[9] all; for] all. For *MS*   [1] God? If] God: if *MS*
[2] resolution ⟨& a love⟩ to *MS*   [3] reckon, first or last; but] reckon; but *MS*
[4] was ⟨rather⟩ {a warm admirer perhaps} a partial judge of Mr. Irwine, as, Thank Heaven! ⟨[?many still are]⟩ ⟨some of the people who have loved & who have befriended us in our need.⟩ {Some of us still are of the people we have known familiarly.} ⟨& who have lived in the same parish with us⟩ Doubtless it ⟨is⟩ {will be despised as} a weakness ⟨which will be despised⟩ by that ⟨imperial⟩ {lofty} order⟨s⟩ of *MS*
[5] insupportable, ⟨&⟩ that *MS*
[6] gentlemen ⟨that⟩ what my own experience has been ⟨precisely opposite⟩: I *MS*

on the fleeting nature of our illusions, which any one moderately acquainted with French literature can command at a moment's notice. Human converse, I think some wise man has remarked, is not rigidly sincere. But I herewith discharge my conscience, and declare, that I have had quite enthusiastic movements of admiration towards old gentlemen who spoke the worst English, who were occasionally fretful in their temper, and who had never[7] moved in a higher sphere of influence than that of parish overseer;[8] and that the way in which I have come to the conclusion that human nature is lovable—the way I have learnt something of its deep pathos, its sublime mysteries—[9]has been by living a great deal among people more or less commonplace and vulgar, of whom you would perhaps hear nothing very surprising if you were to inquire about them in the neighbourhoods where they dwelt. Ten to one most of the small shop-keepers in their vicinity saw nothing at all in them. For I have observed this remarkable coincidence, that the select natures who pant after the ideal, and[1] find nothing in pantaloons or petticoats great enough to command their reverence and love, are curiously in unison with the narrowest and[2] pettiest. For example, I have often heard Mr Gedge, the landlord of the Royal Oak, who used to turn a bloodshot eye on his neighbours in the village of Shepperton, sum up his opinion of the people in his own parish—and they were all the people he knew—in these emphatic words: "Ay, sir, I've said it often, and I'll say it again, they're a poor lot i' this parish—a poor lot, sir, big and little." I think he had a dim idea that if he could migrate to a distant parish, he might find neighbours worthy of him, and indeed he did subsequently transfer himself to the Saracen's Head, which was doing a thriving business in the back street of a neighbouring market-town. But, oddly enough, he has found the people up that back street of precisely the same stamp as the inhabitants of Shepperton—"a poor lot, sir, big and little, and them as comes for a go o' gin are no better than them as comes for a pint o' twopenny—a poor lot."

---

[7] never ⟨held⟩ moved in *MS*   [8] overseer; ⟨I have⟩ & *MS*
[9] the way I have learnt something of its deep pathos, its sublime mysteries—] *added in MS*
[1] & find⟨ing⟩ nothing *MS*   [2] & ⟨?coarsest⟩ pettiest *MS*

CHAPTER XVIII.

CHURCH.

"Hetty, Hetty, don't you know church begins at two, and it's gone half after one a'ready? Have you got nothing better to think on this good Sunday, as poor old Thias Bede's to be put into the ground, and him drownded i' th'[1] dead o' the night, as it's enough to make one's back run cold, but you must be 'dizening yourself as if there was a wedding istid[2] of a funeral?"

"Well, aunt," said Hetty, "I can't be ready so soon as everybody else, when I've got Totty's things to put on. And I'd ever such work to make her stand still."

Hetty was coming downstairs, and[3] Mrs Poyser, in her plain bonnet and shawl, was standing below. If ever a girl looked as if she had been made of roses, that girl was Hetty in her Sunday hat and frock. For her hat was trimmed with pink, and her frock had pink spots, sprinkled on a white ground. There[4] was nothing but pink and white about her, except in her dark hair and eyes and her little buckled shoes. Mrs Poyser was provoked at herself, for she could hardly keep from smiling, as any mortal is inclined to do at the sight of pretty round things. So she turned without speaking,[5] and joined the group outside the house door, followed by Hetty, whose heart was fluttering so at the thought of some one she expected to see at church, that she hardly felt the ground she trod on.

And now the little procession set off. Mr Poyser was in[6] his Sunday suit of drab, with a red and green waistcoat, and a green watch-ribbon having a large cornelian[7] seal attached, pendent like a plumb-line from that promontory where his watch-pocket was situated; a silk handkerchief of a yellow tone round his neck; and excellent grey ribbed stockings, knitted by Mrs Poyser's own hand, setting off the proportions of his leg. Mr Poyser had no reason to be ashamed of his leg, and suspected that the growing abuse of top-boots and other fashions tending to disguise the nether limbs, had their origin in a pitiable degeneracy of the human calf. Still less had he reason to be ashamed of his round jolly face, which was good-humour itself as he said, "Come, Hetty—come, little uns!" and, giving his arm to his wife, led the way through the causeway gate into the yard.

---

[1] th'] the *MS 1*   [2] istid] i'stid *1*   [3] & ⟨Hetty⟩ Mrs. *MS*
[4] ground. There] ground: there *MS*   [5] speaking, ⟨followed by Hetty⟩ & *MS*
[6] Poyser was in] Poyser in *MS*   [7] cornelian] coppery-looking *MS*

The "little uns" addressed were Marty and Tommy, boys of nine and seven, in little fustian[8] tailed coats[9] and knee-breeches, relieved by rosy cheeks and black eyes; looking as much like their father as a very small elephant is like a very large one. Hetty walked between them, and behind came patient Molly, whose task it was to carry Totty through the yard, and over all the wet places on the road; for Totty, having speedily recovered from her threatened fever, had insisted on going to church to-day, and especially on wearing her red-and-black necklace outside her tippet. And there were many wet places for her to be carried over this afternoon, for there had been heavy showers in the morning, though now the clouds had rolled off and lay in towering[1] silvery masses on the horizon.

You might have known it was Sunday if you had only waked up in the farm-yard. The cocks and hens seemed to know it, and made only crooning subdued noises; the very bull-dog looked less savage, as if he would have been satisfied with a smaller bite than usual. The sunshine seemed to call all things to rest and not to labour; it was asleep itself on the moss-grown cow-shed; on the group of white ducks nestling together with their bills tucked under their wings; on the old black sow stretched languidly on the straw, while her largest young one found an excellent spring-bed on his mother's fat ribs; on Alick, the shepherd, in his new smock-frock, taking an uneasy siesta, half-sitting half-standing on the granary steps. Alick was of opinion that church, like other luxuries, was not to be indulged in often by a foreman who had the weather and the ewes on his mind. "Church! nay— I'n gotten summat else to think on," was an answer which he often uttered in a tone of bitter significance that silenced further question. I feel sure Alick meant no irreverence; indeed, I know that his mind was not of a speculative, negative cast, and he would on no account have missed going to church on Christmas Day, Easter Sunday, and "Whissuntide." But he had a general impression that public worship and religious ceremonies, like other non-productive employments, were intended for people who had leisure.

"There's father a-standing at the yard-gate," said Martin Poyser. "I reckon he wants to watch us down the field. It's wonderful what sight he has, and him turned seventy-five."

"Ah, I often think it's wi' th' old folks as it is wi' the babbies," said Mrs Poyser; "they're satisfied wi' looking, no matter what they're looking at. It's God A'mighty's way o' quietening 'em, I reckon, afore they go to sleep."

Old Martin opened the gate as he saw the[2] family procession approaching, and held it wide open, leaning on his stick—pleased to do this bit of work; for, like all old men whose life has been spent in labour, he liked to feel that he was still useful—that there was a better crop of onions in the

---

[8] in little fustian] in fustian *MS*　　　[9] tailed coats] coat tails *MS*
[1] towering] *added in MS*　　　[2] the ⟨little⟩ family *MS*

garden because he was by at the sowing—and that the cows would be milked the better if he staid at home on a Sunday afternoon to look on. He always went to church on Sacrament Sundays, but not very regularly at other times; on wet Sundays, or whenever he had a touch of rheumatism, he used to read the three first chapters of Genesis instead.

"They'll ha' putten Thias Bede i' the ground afore ye get to the churchyard," he said, as his son came up. "It 'ud ha' been better luck if they'd ha' buried him i' the forenoon when the rain was fallin'; there's no likelihoods of a drop now; an' the moon lies like a boat there, dost see? That's a sure sign o' fair weather—there's a many³ as is false, but that's sure."

"Ay, ay," said the son, "I'm in hopes it'll hold up now."

"Mind what the parson says, mind what the parson says, my lads," said Grandfather to the black-eyed youngsters in knee-breeches, conscious of a marble or two in their pockets, which they looked forward to handling a little, secretly, during the sermon.

"Dood-by, dandad," said Totty. "Me doin to church. Me dot my netlace on. Dive me a peppermint."

Grandad, shaking with laughter at this "deep little wench," slowly transferred his stick to his left hand which held the gate open, and slowly thrust his finger into the waistcoat pocket on which Totty had fixed her eyes with a confident look of expectation.

And when they were all gone, the old man leaned on the gate again, watching them across the lane along the Home Close, and through the far gate, till they disappeared behind a bend in the hedge. For the hedgerows in those days shut out one's view, even on the better-managed farms; and this afternoon, the dog-roses were tossing out their pink wreaths, the nightshade was in its yellow and purple glory, the pale honeysuckle grew out of reach, peeping high up out of a holly bush, and over all, an ash or a sycamore every now and then threw its shadow across the path.

There were acquaintances at other gates who had to move aside and let them pass: at the gate of the Home Close there was half the dairy of cows standing one behind the other, extremely slow to understand that their large bodies might be in the way; at the far gate there was the mare holding her head over the bars, and beside her the liver-coloured foal with its head towards its mother's flank, apparently still much embarrassed by its own straddling existence. The way lay entirely through Mr Poyser's own fields till they reached the main road leading to the village, and he turned a keen eye on the stock and the crops as they went along, while Mrs Poyser was ready to supply a running commentary on them all. The woman who manages a dairy has a large share in making the rent, so she may well be allowed to have her opinion on stock and their "keep"—an exercise which

³ many] maeny *MS*

strengthens her understanding so much that she finds herself able to give her husband advice on most other subjects.

"There's that short-horned Sally," she said, as they entered the Home Close, and she caught sight of the meek beast that lay chewing the cud, and looking at her with a sleepy eye. "I[4] begin to hate the sight o' the cow; and I say now what I said three weeks ago, the sooner we get rid of her the better, for there's that little yellow cow as doesn't give half the milk, and yet[5] I've twice as much butter from her."

"Why, thee't not like the women in general," said Mr Poyser; "they like the short-horns, as give such a lot o' milk. There's Chowne's wife wants him to buy no other sort."

"What's it sinnify what Chowne's wife likes?—a poor soft thing, wi' no more head-piece nor a sparrow. She'd take a big cullender to strain her lard wi', and then wonder as the scratchins run through. I've seen enough of her to know as I'll niver take a servant from her house again—all hugger-mugger—and you'd niver know, when you went in, whether it was Monday or Friday, the wash draggin' on to th' end o' the week; and as for her cheese, I know well enough it rose like a loaf in a tin last year. And[6] then she talks o' the weather bein' i' fault, as there's folks 'ud stand on their heads and then say the fault was i' their boots."

"Well, Chowne's been wanting[7] to buy Sally, so we can get rid of her if thee lik'st," said Mr Poyser, secretly proud of his wife's superior power of putting two and two together; indeed, on recent market days he had more than once boasted of her discernment in this very matter of short-horns.

"Ay, them as choose a soft for a wife may's well buy up the short-horns, for if you get your head stuck in a bog your[8] legs may's well go after it. Eh! talk o' legs, there's legs for you," Mrs Poyser continued, as Totty, who had been set down now the road was dry, toddled on in front of her father and mother. "There's shapes! An' she's got such a long foot, she'll be her father's own child."

"Ay, she'll be welly such a one as Hetty i' ten years'[9] time, on'y she's got *thy* coloured eyes. I niver remember a blue eye i' my family; my mother had eyes as black as sloes, just like Hetty's."

"The child 'ull be none the worse for having summat as isn't like Hetty. An' I'm none for having her so over pretty. Though, for the matter o' that, there's people wi' light hair an' blue eyes as pretty as them wi' black. If Dinah had got a bit o' colour in her cheeks, an' didn't stick that Methodist cap on her head, enough to frighten the crows[1], folks 'ud think her as pretty as Hetty."

---

4 eye. "I] eye, "I *MS*   5 yet] yit *MS*   6 And] An' *MS*
7 wanting] wantin' *MS 1*   8 your] you're *1*   9 years'] years *1*
1 crows] cows *Cabinet*

"Nay, nay," said Mr Poyser, with rather a contemptuous emphasis, "thee dostna know the pints of a woman. The men 'ud niver run after Dinah as they[2] would after Hetty."

"What care I what the men 'ud run after? It's well seen what choice the most of 'em know how to make, by the poor draggle-tails o' wives you see, like bits o' gauze ribbin, good for nothing when the colour's gone."

"Well, well, thee canstna say but what I knowed[3] how to make a choice when I married thee," said Mr Poyser, who usually settled little conjugal disputes by a compliment of this sort; "and[4] thee wast twice as buxom as Dinah ten year ago."

"I niver said as a woman had need to be ugly to make a good missis of a house. There's Chowne's wife ugly enough to turn the milk an' save the rennet, but she'll niver save nothing any other way. But as for Dinah, poor child, she's niver likely to be buxom as long as she'll make her dinner o' cake and water, for the sake o' giving to them as want. She provoked me past bearing sometimes; and, as I told her, she went clean again' the Scriptur, for that says, 'Love your neighbour as yourself;' 'but,' I said, 'if you loved your[5] neighbour no better nor you do yourself, Dinah, it's little enough you'd do for him. You'd be thinking he might do well enough on a half-empty stomach.' Eh, I wonder where she is this blessed Sunday!—sitting by that sick woman,[6] I dare say, as she'd set her heart on going to all of a sudden."

"Ah, it was a pity she should take such megrims into[7] her head, when she might ha' stayed wi' us all summer,[8] and eaten twice as much as she wanted,[9] and it 'ud niver ha' been missed. She made no odds in th'[1] house at all, for she sat as still at her sewing as a bird on the nest,[2] and was uncommon nimble at running to fetch anything. If Hetty gets married, thee'dst[3] like to[4] ha' Dinah wi' thee constant."

"It's no use thinking o' that," said Mrs Poyser. "You might as well beckon to the flying[5] swallow, as ask Dinah to come an' live here comfortable, like other folks. If anything could turn her, I[6] should ha' turned her, for I've talked to her for a hour on end, and scolded her too; for she's my own sister's child, and it behoves me to do what I can for her. But eh, poor thing,[7] as soon as she'd said us 'good-by,' an' got into the cart, an' looked

---

[2] they ⟨do⟩ would *MS*   [3] knowed] know'd *MS 1*

[4] sort; "and] sort. "And *MS*

[5] yourself;' 'but,' I said, 'if you loved your] yourself," but I said, "if you you [*sic*] loved your *MS* yourself;' but I said, 'If you loved your *1* yourself;' {'}but{,} I said, ⟨'I⟩ {i}f you love{d} your *8*

[6] woman, ⟨as⟩ I *MS*   [7] into] *MS* int' *1* ⟨int'⟩ into *8*

[8] summer, an⟨'⟩d eaten *MS*   [9] wanted, an⟨'⟩d it *MS*   [1] th'] the *MS*

[2] nest, an⟨'⟩d was *MS*   [3] thee'dst] *MS 1* ⟨thee'st⟩ thee'dst *8* theed'st *Cabinet*

[4] to] t' *MS 1* ⟨t'⟩ to *8*   [5] flying] flyin' *MS 1*   [6] I] I *MS*

[7] thing, ⟨near⟩ as *MS*

back at me with her pale face, as is welly like her aunt Judith come[8] back
from heaven, I begun to be frightened[9] to think o' the set-downs I'd given
her; for it comes over you sometimes as if she'd a way o' knowing the rights
o' things more nor other folks have. But I'll niver give in as that's[1] 'cause
she's a Methodist, no more nor a white calf's white 'cause it eats out o' the
same bucket wi' a black un[2]."

"Nay," said Mr Poyser, with as near an approach to a snarl as his good-
nature would allow; "I'n[3] no opinion o' the[4] Methodists.[5] It's on'y tradesfolks as turn Methodists; you niver knew a farmer bitten wi' them maggots.
There's maybe a workman now an' then, as isn't over clever[6] at 's work,
takes to preachin' an' that, like Seth Bede. But you see[7] Adam, as has got
one o' the best head-pieces hereabout, knows better; he's a good Churchman, else I'd never[8] encourage him for a sweetheart for Hetty."

"Why, goodness me," said Mrs Poyser, who had looked back while her
husband was speaking, "look where[9] Molly is with them lads.[1] They're the
field's length behind us. How _could_ you let 'em do so, Hetty? Anybody
might as well set a pictur to watch the children as you.[2] Run back,[3] and tell
'em to come on."

Mr and Mrs Poyser were now at the end of the[4] second field, so they set
Totty on the top of one of the large stones forming the true Loamshire stile,
and awaited the loiterers; Totty observing with complacency, "Dey
naughty, naughty boys—me dood."

The fact was that this Sunday walk through the fields was fraught with
great excitement to Marty and Tommy, who saw a perpetual drama going
on in the hedgerows, and could no more refrain from stopping and peeping
than if they had been a couple of spaniels or terriers. Marty was quite sure
he saw a yellowhammer on the boughs of the great ash, and while he was
peeping, he missed the sight of a white-throated stoat, which had run[5]
across the path and was described with much fervour by the junior
Tommy. Then there was a little greenfinch, just fledged, fluttering along
the[6] ground, and it seemed quite possible to catch it, till[7] it managed to

[8] like her aunt Judith come] _MS reads_ like ⟨Mother⟩ {her aunt Mary} come
[9] frightened ⟨at the [?things] I'd⟩ ⟨set-downs I'd given her for bein' a Methodist. But I
thought soon after as I'd been in the right on't⟩ to think o' the set-downs I'd given her, _MS_
[1] that's ⟨be⟩{'}cause she's a Methodist, ⟨for she's no more like the rest o' the Meth-
odist⟨⟨s⟩⟩ women as I've seen⟩, no _MS_
[2] un] 'un _MS_   [3] allow; "I'n] allow. "I'n _MS_   [4] the] _added in MS_
[5] Methodists. ⟨I niver knowed a farmer as⟩ It's on'y tradesfolks as _MS_
[6] over clever] over-cliver _MS 1_   [7] see Adam{,} ⟨'s a good churchman⟩ as _MS_
[8] never] niver _MS 1_   [9] where ⟨Hetty⟩ Molly _MS_   [1] lads.] lads! _Cabinet_
[2] How <u>could</u> you let 'em do so Hetty? Anybody might as well set a pictur to watch the
children, as you.] _added in MS_
[3] back, ⟨Molly⟩, and _MS_
[4] the ⟨last⟩ {second} field, ⟨before entering the road⟩, so _MS_
[5] had run] ran _MS_   [6] the ⟨path⟩ ground _MS_   [7] till ⟨all at once⟩ it _MS_

flutter under the blackberry bush. Hetty could not be got to give any heed to these things, so Molly was called on[8] for her ready sympathy, and peeped with open mouth wherever she was told, and said "Lawks!" whenever she was expected to wonder.

Molly hastened on with some alarm when Hetty[9] had come back and called to them that her aunt was angry; but Marty ran on first, shouting, "We've found the speckled turkey's nest, mother!" with the instinctive confidence that people who bring good news are never in fault.

"Ah," said Mrs Poyser, really forgetting all discipline in this pleasant surprise,[1] "that's a good lad; why, where is it?"

"Down in ever such a hole, under the hedge. I[2] saw it first, looking after the greenfinch, and[3] she[4] sat on th'[5] nest."

"You didn't frighten her, I hope," said the mother, "else she'll forsake it."

"No, I went away as still as still, and whispered to Molly—didn't I, Molly?"

"Well, well, now come on," said Mrs Poyser, "and walk before[6] father and mother, and take your little sister by the hand. We must go straight on now. Good boys don't look after the birds[7] of a Sunday."

"But, mother," said Marty,[8] "you said you'd give half-a-crown to find the speckled turkey's nest. Mayn't I have the half-crown put into my money-box?"

"We'll see about that, my lad, if you walk along now, like a good boy."

The father and mother exchanged a significant glance of amusement at their eldest-born's acuteness; but on Tommy's round[9] face there was a cloud.

"Mother," he said, half crying, "Marty's got ever so much more money in his box nor I've got in mine."

"Munny, *me* want half-a-toun in *my* bots," said Totty.

"Hush, hush, hush," said Mrs Poyser, "did ever anybody hear such naughty children? Nobody shall[1] ever see their money-boxes any more, if they don't make haste and go on to church."

This dreadful threat had the desired effect, and through the two remaining fields the three pair of small legs trotted on without any serious interruption, notwithstanding a small pond full of tadpoles, alias[2] "bull-heads," which the lads looked at wistfully.

[8] on ⟨to give⟩ for *MS*   [9] Hetty ⟨came⟩ had come *MS*

[1] really forgetting all discipline in this pleasant surprise,] *added in MS*

[2] I] I *MS*   [3] greenfinch, and] greenfinch. And *MS*   [4] she ⟨sits⟩ sat *MS*

[5] th'] the *MS*   [6] before ⟨your⟩ father *MS*   [7] birds ⟨on⟩ of *MS*

[8] Marty, ⟨looking round, after they had set off in the⟩ ⟨you said that whoever⟩ "you *MS*

[9] round] *added in MS*

[1] shall ⟨have any money in their boxes⟩ ever see their money boxes any more *MS*

[2] alias] *alias Cabinet*

The[3] damp hay that must be scattered and turned afresh to–morrow was not a cheering sight to Mr Poyser, who during hay and corn harvest had often some mental struggles as to the[4] benefits of a day of rest; but no temptation would have induced him to carry on any field-work, however early in the morning, on a Sunday; for had not Michael Holdsworth[5] had a pair of oxen "sweltered" while he was ploughing on Good Friday? That was a demonstration that work on sacred days was a wicked thing; and with wickedness of any sort Martin Poyser was quite clear that he would have nothing to do, since money got by such means would never prosper.[6]

"It a'most makes[7] your fingers itch to be at the hay now the sun shines so," he observed, as they passed through the "Big Meadow." "But it's poor foolishness to think o' saving by going against your conscience. There's that Jim Wakefield, as they used to call 'Gentleman Wakefield,' used to do the same of a Sunday as o' weekdays, and took no heed to right or wrong, as if there was nayther God nor devil. An' what's he come to? Why, I saw him myself last market day a–carrying a basket wi' oranges in't."

"Ah, to be sure," said Mrs Poyser, emphatically, "you make but a poor trap to catch luck if you go and bait it wi' wickedness. The money as is got so 's like to burn holes i' your pocket. I'd niver wish us to leave our lads a sixpence but what was got i' the rightful way. And as for the weather, there's One above makes it, and we must put up wi't: it's nothing of a plague to what the wenches are."[8]

Notwithstanding the interruption in their walk, the excellent habit[9] which Mrs Poyser's clock had of[1] taking time by the forelock, had secured their arrival at the village while it was still[2] a quarter to two,[3] though almost every one who meant to go to church was already within the churchyard gates. Those who staid at home were chiefly[4] mothers, like Timothy's Bess, who stood at her own door[5] nursing her baby, and feeling as women feel in that position—that nothing else[6] can be expected of them.

---

[3] The ⟨hay lay⟩ damp hay, ⟨cocks, which⟩ {that} must *MS*

[4] the ⟨advantages of Sunday⟩ {benefits of a day of rest}: but ⟨neither he nor any other farmer in the neighbourhood⟩ {no temptation} would have ⟨ventured⟩ {induced him} to carry on any field work {,} ⟨even⟩ {however} early *MS*

[5] Holdsworth ⟨lost⟩ had *MS*

[6] prosper. ⟨He made a remark to this effect as they were passing through "the Big Meadow", & Mrs. Poyser, ⟨⟨who liked "a right thing to go forrard on all occasions⟩⟩ as usual, gave her hearty concurrence⟩ "It *MS*

[7] makes ⟨one's⟩ your *MS*

[8] are." ⟨Now then, get ⟨⟨under this puzzle-lock⟩⟩ over the stile and let us through the gates"⟩ ¶ *MS*

[9] habit ⟨of⟩ which *MS*   [1] of ⟨keeping the later⟩ taking time *MS*

[2] still ⟨not ⟨⟨later⟩⟩ more than⟩ a *MS*   [3] two, ⟨by the church clock⟩ though *MS*

[4] chiefly ⟨young women who⟩ mothers, like *MS*

[5] door ⟨with the⟩ {nursing her} baby ⟨in her arms & felt⟩ {& feeling} as *MS*

[6] else] *added in MS*

It was not entirely to see Thias Bede's funeral that the people were standing about the churchyard so long before service began; that[7] was their common practice. The women, indeed, usually entered the church at once, and the farmers' wives[8] talked in an under-tone to each other, over the tall pews, about their illnesses and the total failure of doctor's stuff, recommending[9] dandelion-tea, and other home-made specifics, as far preferable—about the servants, and their[1] growing exorbitance as to wages, whereas the quality of their services declined from year to year, and there was no girl nowadays to be trusted any further than you could see her—about the bad price Mr Dingall, the Treddleston grocer, was giving for butter[2], and the reasonable doubts that might be held as to his solvency, notwithstanding that Mrs Dingall was a sensible woman, and they were all sorry for *her*, for she had very good kin. Meantime the men lingered outside, and hardly any of them except the singers, who had a[3] humming and fragmentary rehearsal to go through, entered the church until Mr Irwine was in the desk. They saw no reason for that premature entrance,—what could they do in church, if they were there before service began?—and they did not conceive that any power in the universe could take it ill of them if they staid out and talked a little about "bus'ness[4]."[5]

Chad Cranage[6] looks like quite a new acquaintance to-day, for he has got his clean Sunday face, which always makes his little granddaughter cry at him as a stranger. But[7] an experienced eye would have fixed on him at once as the village blacksmith, after seeing the humble deference with which the big saucy fellow took off his hat and stroked his hair to the farmers; for Chad was accustomed to say[8] that a working-man must hold a candle to——a personage understood to be as black as he was himself on weekdays; by which evil-sounding rule of conduct he meant what was, after all, rather virtuous than otherwise, namely, that[9] men who had horses to be shod must be treated with respect. Chad and the rougher sort of workmen kept aloof from the grave under the white thorn, where the burial was going forward; but Sandy Jim, and several of the farm-labourers, made a group round it, and stood with their hats off, as fellow-mourners with the mother and sons.

---

[7] began; that] began. That *MS*   [8] wives ⟨whispered⟩ talked in an under tone *MS*

[9] recommending ⟨home-made⟩ {dandelion} tea *MS*   [1] their] there *Cabinet*

[2] butter ⟨so that you might almost as well hire a man to sell the milk in pints to the town-folks⟩ & the reasonable doubts that might be held as to his solvency, notwithstanding that Mrs. Dingall *MS*

[3] a ⟨slight⟩ humming *MS*   [4] bus'ness] bis'ness *MS 1*

[5] What could they do in church, if they were there ⟨,⟩ before service began? & {they} did not conceive that any power in the universe could take it ill of them if they staid out & talked a little about "bis'ness".] *added on verso of MS 11.29*

[6] Cranage {the blacksmith} ⟨the blacksmith⟩ looks *MS*

[7] stranger. But] stranger: but *MS*   [8] say ⟨of himself⟩ that *MS*

[9] otherwise, namely, that] otherwise, that *MS*

Others held a midway position, sometimes watching the group at the grave, sometimes listening to the conversation of the farmers, who stood in a knot near the church door, and were now joined by Martin Poyser, while his family passed into the church. On the outside of this knot stood Mr Casson, the landlord of the Donnithorne Arms[1], in his most striking attitude—that is to say, with the forefinger of his right hand thrust[2] between the buttons of his waistcoat, his left hand in his breeches pocket, and his head very much on one side; looking, on the whole, like an actor who has only a mono-syllabic part entrusted to him, but feels sure that the audience discern his fitness for the leading business; curiously in contrast with old Jonathan Burge, who held his hands behind him, and[3] leaned forward coughing asthmatically, with an inward scorn of all[4] knowingness that could not be turned into cash. The talk was in rather a lower tone than usual to-day, hushed a little by the sound of Mr Irwine's voice reading the final prayers of the burial-service. They had all had their word of pity for poor Thias, but now they had got upon the nearer subject of their own grievances against Satchell, the Squire's bailiff, who played the part of steward so far as it was not performed by old Mr Donnithorne himself,[5] for that gentleman had the meanness to receive his own rents and make bargains about his own timber. This subject of conversation was an additional reason for not being loud, since Satchell himself[6] might presently be walking up the paved road to the church door. And soon they became suddenly silent; for[7] Mr Irwine's voice had ceased, and the group round the white thorn was dispersing itself towards the church.

They all moved aside, and stood with their hats off, while Mr Irwine passed[8]. Adam and Seth were coming next, with their mother between them; for Joshua Rann officiated as head sexton as well as clerk, and was not yet ready to follow the rector into the vestry. But there was a pause before the three mourners came on:[9] Lisbeth had turned round to look again towards the grave![1] Ah! there was nothing now but the brown earth under the white thorn. Yet[2] she cried less to-day than she had done any day since her husband's death: along with all her grief there was mixed an unusual sense of her own importance in having a "burial," and in[3] Mr Irwine's

---

[1] the landlord of the Donnithorne Arms] *added in MS*
[2] thrust ⟨into⟩ between *MS*   [3] & ⟨coughed⟩ leaned *MS*
[4] all ⟨pretensions to⟩ knowingness *MS*
[5] himself, ⟨who had⟩ for that gentleman had *MS*
[6] himself ⟨would perhaps soon be coming⟩ might presently be walking *MS*
[7] for ⟨the⟩ Mr. *MS*
[8] passed; ⟨followed by Joshua Rann with that same air of self-importance⟩ Adam *MS*
[9] on: ⟨figh⟩ Lisbeth {had} turned *MS*
[1] grave!] grave. *MS 1*   [2] Yet ⟨Lisbeth⟩ she *MS*
[3] in] *added in MS*

reading a special service for her husband; and[4] besides, she knew the funeral psalm was going to be sung for him.[5] She felt this counter-excitement to her sorrow still more strongly as she walked with her sons towards the church door, and saw the friendly sympathetic nods of their fellow-parishioners.[6]

The mother and sons passed into the church, and one by one the loiterers followed, though some still lingered without; the sight of Mr Donni-thorne's carriage, which was winding slowly up the hill, perhaps helping to make them feel that there was no need for haste.

But presently the sound of the bassoon and the key-bugles burst forth; the evening hymn, which always opened the service, had begun, and every one must now enter and take his place.

I cannot say that the interior of Hayslope Church was remarkable for anything except for the grey age of its oaken[7] pews—great square pews mostly, ranged on each side of a narrow aisle. It was free, indeed, from the modern blemish of galleries. The choir had two narrow pews to themselves in the middle of the right-hand row, so that it was a short process for Joshua Rann to take his place among them as principal bass, and return to his desk after the singing was over. The pulpit and desk, grey and old as the pews, stood on one side of the arch[8] leading into the chancel, which also had its grey square pews for Mr Donnithorne's family and servants. Yet I assure you these grey pews, with the buff-washed walls, gave a very pleasing tone to this shabby interior, and[9] agreed extremely well with the ruddy faces and bright waistcoats. And there were liberal touches of crimson towards[1] the chancel, for the pulpit and Mr Donnithorne's own pew had handsome crimson cloth cushions; and, to close the vista, there was a crimson altar-cloth, embroidered with golden rays by Miss Lydia's own hand.

But even without the crimson cloth,[2] the effect must have been warm and cheering when Mr Irwine was in the desk,[3] looking benignly round on that simple congregation—on the hardy old men, with bent knees and shoulders, perhaps, but with vigour left for much hedge-clipping and thatching; on the tall stalwart frames and roughly-cut bronzed faces of the stone-cutters and carpenters; on the half-dozen well-to-do farmers, with their apple-cheeked families; and on the[4] clean old women, mostly

---

[4] husband; and] husband. And *MS*

[5] And besides, she knew the funeral psalm was going to be sung for him.] *added in MS*

[6] fellow-parishioners. ⟨¶⟩ ⟨"Mrs. Bede," said Mr. Poyser, ⟨⟨"⟩⟩ who stood nearest the church door, "ye must keep up your heart: husbands & wives mun be thankful when they'n lived to see ⟨⟨each other's⟩⟩ {one another's} hair grey. Adam, I shall look for you to come and see us soon."⟩ *MS*

[7] oaken] *added in MS*   [8] arch] *MS 1* arch, *8*

[9] & ⟨made an excellent background for⟩ agreed extremely well with *MS*

[1] towards] *MS* toward *1 8*   [2] cloth, ⟨I think⟩ the *MS*

[3] desk ⟨with his fine face⟩ looking *MS*   [4] the] those *MS*

farm-labourers' wives, with their bit of snow-white cap-border under their black bonnets, and with their[5] withered arms, bare from the elbow,[6] folded passively over their chests. For none of the old people held books— why should they? not[7] one of them could read. But[8] they knew a few "good words" by heart, and their withered lips[9] now and then moved silently, following the service without any very clear comprehension indeed, but with a simple faith in its efficacy to ward off harm and bring blessing. And now all faces were visible, for all were standing up—the little children on the seats peeping over the edge of the grey pews, while[1] good[2] Bishop Ken's evening hymn was being sung to one of those lively[3] psalm-tunes which[4] died out with the last generation of rectors and choral parish clerks. Melodies die out, like the pipe of Pan, with the ears that love them and listen for them. Adam was not in his usual place among the singers to-day, for he sat with his mother and Seth, and[5] he noticed with surprise that Bartle Massey was absent too: all the more agreeable for Mr Joshua Rann, who[6] gave out his bass notes with unusual complacency, and threw an extra ray of severity into the glances he sent over his spectacles at the recusant Will Maskery.

I beseech you to imagine Mr Irwine looking round on this scene, in his ample white surplice, that became him so well, with his powdered hair thrown back, his rich brown complexion, and his finely-cut nostril and upper lip; for there was a certain virtue in that benignant yet keen countenance, as there is in all human faces from which a generous soul beams out. And over all streamed the delicious June sunshine through the old windows, with their desultory patches of yellow, red, and blue, that threw pleasant touches of colour on the opposite wall.

I think, as Mr Irwine looked round to-day, his eyes rested an instant longer than usual on the square pew occupied by Martin Poyser and his family. And there was another pair of dark eyes that found it impossible not to wander thither, and rest on that round pink-and-white figure. But Hetty was at that moment quite careless of any glances—she was absorbed in the thought that Arthur Donnithorne would soon be coming into church, for the carriage must surely be at the church gate by this time. She had never seen him since she parted with him in the wood on Thursday evening, and oh! how long the time had seemed[7]! Things had gone on just the same as

---

    [5] and with their] and their *MS*   [6] elbow, fold{ed} ⟨over⟩ passively *MS*
    [7] they? not] they? Not *MS*   [8] read. But] read: but *MS*
    [9] lips ⟨followed in silent motion⟩ now & then moved *MS*   [1] while ⟨the⟩ good *MS*
    [2] good Bishop] good old Bishop *MS 1* good ⟨old⟩ Bishop *8*
    [3] lively ⟨old⟩ psalm tunes *MS*   [4] which ⟨went⟩ died *MS*
    [5] & ⟨there was another member of the choir whose baritone [?is] absent too⟩ {he noticed with surprize that Bartle Massey was absent too.} All *MS*
    [6] who ⟨had the pleasure of leading⟩ gave out his bass notes with *MS*
    [7] seemed ⟨since then⟩! Things *MS*

ever since that evening; the[8] wonders that had happened then had brought
no changes after them; they were already like a dream. When she heard the
church door swinging, her heart beat so, she[9] dared not look up. She felt
that her aunt was curtsying; she curtsied herself. That[1] must be old Mr
Donnithorne—he always came first, the wrinkled small old man, peering
round with short-sighted glances at the bowing and curtsying congregation; then she knew Miss Lydia was passing, and though Hetty liked so
much to[2] look at her[3] fashionable little coal-scuttle bonnet, with the wreath
of small roses round it, she didn't mind it to-day. But there were no more
curtsies—no, he was not come; she felt sure there was nothing else passing
the pew door but the housekeeper's black bonnet, and the lady's-maid's
beautiful straw that had once been Miss Lydia's, and then the powdered
heads of the butler and footman. No, he was not there; yet she would look
now—she might be mistaken—for, after all, she had not looked. So she
lifted up her eyelids and glanced timidly at the cushioned pew in the
chancel:—there was no one but old Mr Donnithorne rubbing his spectacles
with his white handkerchief, and Miss Lydia opening the large gilt-edged
prayer-book. The chill disappointment was too hard to bear: she felt herself
turning pale, her lips trembling; she was ready to cry. Oh, what *should* she
do? Everybody would know the reason; they would know she was crying
because Arthur was not there. And Mr Craig, with the wonderful hot-
house plant in his button-hole, was staring at her, she knew. It was dreadfully long before the General Confession began, so that she could kneel
down. Two great drops *would* fall then, but no one saw them except good-
natured Molly[4], for her aunt and uncle knelt with their backs towards her.
Molly, unable to imagine any cause for tears in church except faintness, of
which she had a vague traditional knowledge, drew out of her pocket a
queer little flat blue smelling-bottle, and after much labour in pulling
the cork out, thrust the narrow neck against Hetty's nostrils. "It donna
smell," she whispered, thinking this was a great advantage which old salts
had over fresh ones: they did you good without biting your nose. Hetty
pushed it away peevishly; but this little flash of temper did what the salts
could[5] not have done—it roused her to wipe away the traces of her tears,
and try with all her might not to shed any more. Hetty had a certain
strength in her vain little nature: she would have borne anything rather
than be laughed at, or pointed at[6] with any other feeling than admiration;
she would have pressed her own nails into her tender flesh rather than
people[7] should know a secret she did not[8] want them to know.

---

[8] the ⟨wonderful things⟩ wonders *MS*   [9] so, she] so she *MS 1* so{,} she *8*
[1] herself. That] herself: that *MS*   [2] so much to] so to *MS*
[3] her {fashionable little coal scuttle} bonnet, ⟨& silk scarf⟩ with *MS*
[4] Molly{.}⟨,⟩ {for her aunt & uncle knelt with their backs towards her.} ⟨who⟩ Molly *MS*
[5] could] would *MS*   [6] pointed at] have people pointing at her *MS*
[7] people] they *MS*   [8] did not] didn't *MS*

What fluctuations there were in her busy thoughts and[9] feelings, while Mr Irwine was pronouncing the solemn "Absolution" in her deaf ears, and through all the tones of petition that followed![1] Anger lay very close to disappointment, and soon won the victory over the conjectures her small ingenuity could devise to account for Arthur's absence on the supposition that[2] he really wanted to come, really wanted to see her again. And by the time she rose from her knees mechanically, because all the rest were rising, the colour had returned to her cheeks even with a heightened glow, for she was framing little indignant speeches to herself, saying she hated Arthur for giving her[3] this pain—she would like him to suffer too. Yet while this selfish tumult was going on in her soul, her eyes were bent down on her prayer-book, and the eyelids with their dark fringe looked as lovely as ever. Adam Bede thought so, as he glanced at her for a moment on rising from his knees.

But Adam's thoughts of Hetty did not deafen him to the service; they rather blended with all the other deep feelings for which the church service was a channel to him this afternoon, as a certain consciousness of our entire past and our imagined future blends itself with all our moments of keen sensibility. And to Adam the church service was the best channel he could have found for his mingled regret, yearning, and resignation; its interchange of beseeching cries for help, with outbursts of faith and praise—its recurrent responses and the familiar rhythm of its collects, seemed to speak for him as no other form of worship[4] could have done; as, to those early Christians who had worshipped from their childhood upward in catacombs, the torchlight and shadows must have seemed nearer the Divine presence than the heathenish daylight of the streets. The secret of our emotions never lies in the bare object, but in its subtle relations to our own past: no wonder the secret escapes the unsympathizing[5] observer, who might as well put on his spectacles to discern odours.

But there was one reason why even a chance comer would have found the service in Hayslope Church more impressive than in[6] most other village nooks in the kingdom—a reason, of which I am sure you have not the slightest suspicion. It was the reading of our friend Joshua Rann. Where that good shoemaker got his notion of reading from, remained a mystery even to his most intimate acquaintances. I believe, after all, he got it chiefly from Nature, who had poured some of her music into this honest conceited soul, as she had been known to do into other narrow souls before his. She had given him, at least, a fine bass voice and a musical ear; but I cannot positively say whether these alone had sufficed to inspire him with the rich

---

[9] thoughts &] *added in MS*   [1] followed!] followed. *MS*

[2] that ⟨A⟩ he *MS*   [3] her] *added in MS*

[4] worship ⟨would⟩ could *MS*   [5] unsympathizing ⟨critic⟩ observer *MS*

[6] in ⟨any⟩ most *MS*

chant in which he delivered the responses. The way he rolled from a rich deep forte into a melancholy cadence, subsiding, at the end of the last word, into a sort of faint resonance, like the lingering vibrations of a fine violoncello, I can compare to nothing for its strong calm melancholy but the rush and cadence of the wind among the autumn boughs. This may seem a strange[7] mode of speaking about the reading of a parish clerk—a man[8] in rusty spectacles, with stubbly hair, a large occiput, and a prominent crown. But that is Nature's way: she will allow a[9] gentleman of splendid physiognomy and poetic aspirations to sing woefully out of tune, and not give him the slightest hint of it; and takes care that some narrow-browed[1] fellow, trolling a ballad in the corner of a pot-house, shall be as true to his intervals as a[2] bird.

Joshua himself was less proud of his reading than of his singing, and it was always with a sense of heightened importance that[3] he passed from the desk to the quire. Still more to-day:[4] it was a special occasion; for an old man familiar to all the parish, had died a sad death—not in his bed, a circumstance the most painful to the mind of the peasant—and now the funeral psalm was to be sung in memory of his sudden departure. Moreover, Bartle Massey was not at church, and[5] Joshua's importance in the choir suffered no eclipse. It was a solemn minor strain they sang. The[6] old psalm-tunes have many a wail among them, and the words—

> "Thou sweep'st us off as with a flood;
> We vanish hence like dreams"—

seemed to have a closer application than usual, in the death of poor Thias. The mother and sons listened,[7] each with peculiar feelings. Lisbeth had a vague belief that the psalm was doing her husband good; it was part of that decent burial which she would have[8] thought it a greater wrong to withhold from him than to have caused him many unhappy days while he was living. The more there was said about her husband, the more there was done for him, surely the safer he would be. It[9] was poor Lisbeth's blind way of feeling that human love and pity are a ground of faith in some other love. Seth, who was easily touched, shed[1] tears, and tried to recall, as he had done

---

7 strange ⟨way⟩ mode *MS*   8 man ⟨with⟩ in *MS*

9 a ⟨man⟩ gentleman *MS*   1 narrow-browed ⟨man⟩ fellow *MS*

2 a ⟨black⟩bird *MS*   3 that ⟨the⟩ he *MS*

4 today: ⟨which was made⟩ {it was} a special occasion; ⟨not only because the funeral psalm was to be sung⟩ for *MS*

5 and Joshua{'s} ⟨reasserted his place as leader of the⟩ importance in the *MS*

6 sang. The] sang—the *MS*

7 listened ⟨with swelling hearts. Adam had never been unable to join in the psalm before.⟩ each with peculiar feelings. Lisbeth had a vague belief that the psalm *MS*

8 have ⟨held⟩ thought *MS*   9 be. It] be: it *MS*   1 shed ⟨some⟩ tears *MS*

continually since his father's death, all that he had heard of the possibility that a single moment of consciousness at the last might be a moment of pardon and reconcilement; for was it not written in the very psalm they were singing, that the divine dealings were not measured and circumscribed by time? Adam had never been unable to join in a psalm before.[2] He had known plenty of trouble and vexation since he had been a lad; but this was the first sorrow that had hemmed in his voice, and strangely enough it was sorrow because[3] the chief source of his past trouble and vexation was for ever gone out of his reach. He[4] had not been able to press his father's hand before their parting, and say, "Father, you know it was all right between us; I never forgot what I owed you when I was a lad; you forgive me if I have[5] been too hot and hasty now and then!" Adam thought but little to-day of the hard work and the earnings he had spent on his father: his thoughts ran constantly on what the old man's feelings had been in moments of humiliation, when he had held down his head before the rebukes of his son.[6] When our indignation is borne in submissive silence, we are apt to feel twinges of doubt afterwards as to our own generosity, if not justice; how much more when the object of our anger has gone into everlasting silence, and we have seen his face for the last time in the meekness of death![7]

"Ah, I was[8] always too hard," Adam said to himself. "It's a sore fault in me as[9] I'm so hot and out o' patience with people when they do wrong, and my heart gets shut up against 'em, so as I can't bring myself to forgive 'em.[1] I see clear enough there's more pride nor love in my soul, for I could sooner make a thousand strokes with th' hammer for my father than[2] bring myself to say a kind word to him. And there went plenty o' pride and temper to the strokes, as the devil *will*[3] be having his finger in what we call our duties as well as our sins. Mayhap the best thing I ever did in my life was only doing what was easiest for[4] myself. It's allays[5] been easier[6] for me to work nor to sit still, but the real tough job for me 'ud be to master my own will and temper, and go right against my own pride. It seems to me now,[7] if I was to find father at home to-night, I should behave different; but there's no knowing—perhaps nothing 'ud be a lesson to us if it didn't come too late. It's well we should feel as life's a reckoning we can't make twice over;

---

[2] before:—⟨it was the first time he had had a sadness which hemmed⟩ he *MS*
[3] sorrow because] *MS 1* sorrow⟨,⟩ because *8*
[4] He ⟨could never⟩ had not been able to *MS*   [5] I have] I've *MS 1*
[6] son. ⟨The⟩ When⟨ever⟩ our *MS*   [7] death!] death? *MS 1*
[8] Ah, I was] Ah, I⟨'m⟩ was *MS* Ah! I was *Cabinet*   [9] as I ⟨get⟩ 'm *MS*
[1] 'em. ⟨till it's too late.⟩ I see clear *MS*
[2] than ⟨keep from saying a sharp word to him⟩ bring *MS*
[3] *will*] will *MS*   [4] for] to *MS*   [5] allays] always *MS*
[6] easier ⟨to⟩ for *MS*   [7] to me now,] now as, *MS*

there's no real making amends in this world, any more nor you can mend a wrong subtraction by doing your addition right."

This was the key-note to which Adam's thoughts had perpetually returned since his father's death, and the solemn wail of the funeral psalm was only an influence that brought back the old thoughts with stronger emphasis. So was the sermon, which Mr Irwine had chosen with reference to Thias's funeral. It spoke briefly and simply of the words, "In the midst of life we are in death"—how the present moment is all we can call our own for works of mercy, of righteous dealing, and of family tenderness. All very old truths—but what we thought the oldest truth becomes the most startling to us in the week when we have looked on the dead face of one who has made a part of our own lives. For when men want to impress us with the effect of a new and wonderfully vivid light, do they not let it fall on the most familiar objects, that we may measure its intensity by remembering the former dimness?[8]

Then came the moment of the final blessing, when the for-ever[9] sublime words, "The peace of God, which passeth all understanding," seemed to blend with the calm afternoon sunshine that fell on the bowed heads of the congregation; and then the quiet rising, the mothers tying on the bonnets of the little maidens who had slept through the sermon, the fathers collecting the prayer-books, until all streamed out through the old archway into the green churchyard, and began their neighbourly talk, their simple civilities, and their invitations to tea; for on a Sunday every one was ready to receive a guest—it was the day when[1] all must be in their best clothes and their best humour.

Mr and Mrs Poyser paused a minute at the church gate: they were waiting for Adam to come up, not being contented to go away without saying a kind word to the widow and her sons.

"Well, Mrs Bede," said Mrs Poyser, as they walked on together[2], "[3]you must keep up your heart; husbands and wives must be content when they've lived to[4] rear their children and see one another's hair grey."[5]

"Ay, ay," said Mr Poyser; "they wonna have long to wait for one another then, anyhow. And[6] ye've got two o' the strapping'st sons i' th'[7] country; and well you may, for I remember poor Thias as fine a broad-shouldered fellow as need to be; and as for you, Mrs Bede, why you're straighter i' the back nor half the young women now."

[8] dimness?] dimness?⟨(")⟩ 8   [9] for-ever] for ever *MS 1* for{-}ever *8*
[1] when ⟨every one⟩ all *MS*   [2] as they walked on together] *added in MS*
[3] together, "⟨ye⟩ you *MS*
[4] to ⟨see each other's ⟨⟨one another's⟩⟩ hair grey⟩ rear *MS*
[5] *This paragraph is a slightly different version of one cancelled on MS II. 32 (p. 183 n. 6, above), which Eliot apparently decided was more fitting for conversation after church than before.*
[6] And ⟨you⟩ {ye}'ve *MS*   [7] th'] the *MS*

"Eh," said Lisbeth, "[8] it's poor luck for the platter to wear well when it's broke i' two. The sooner I'm laid under the thorn the better. I'm[9] no good to nobody now."

Adam[1] never took notice of his mother's little unjust plaints; but Seth said, "Nay, mother, thee mustna say so. Thy sons 'ull never get another mother."

"That's true, lad, that's true," said Mr Poyser; "and[2] it's wrong on us to give way to grief, Mrs Bede; for it's like the children cryin' when the fathers and mothers take things from 'em. There's One above knows better nor us."

"Ah," said Mrs Poyser, "[3]an' it's poor work allays settin' the dead above the livin'. We shall all on us be dead sometime, I reckon—it 'ud be better if folks 'ud make much on us beforehand, istid o' beginnin' when we're gone.[4] It's but little good you'll do a-watering the last year's crop."

"Well, Adam," said Mr Poyser, feeling that his wife's words were, as usual, rather incisive than soothing, and that it would be well to change the subject[5], "you'll come and see us again now, I hope. I hanna[6] had a talk with you this long while, and[7] the missis here wants[8] you to see what can be done with her[9] best spinning-wheel, for it's got broke, and it'll be a nice job to mend it—there'll want a bit o' turning.[1] You'll come as soon as you can, now, will you?"

Mr Poyser paused and looked round[2] while he was speaking, as if to see where Hetty was; for the children were running on before. Hetty was not without a companion, and she had,[3] besides, more pink and white about her than ever; for she held in her hand the wonderful pink-and-white hot-house plant[4], with a very long name—a Scotch name, she supposed, since people said Mr Craig the gardener was Scotch. Adam took the opportunity of looking round too; and I am sure you will not require of him that he should feel any vexation in observing a pouting expression on Hetty's face

---

[8] Lisbeth, "⟨where's that use to bein' so strong when them's gone as⟩ {it's poor luck} ⟨to wear well;⟩ {for the} platter *MS*

[9] better. I'm] better: I'm *MS*

[1] Adam ⟨never⟩ {never} took ⟨no⟩ notice of ⟨these⟩ his mother's little {unjust} plaints, *MS*

[2] Poyser; "and] Poyser. "And *MS*

[3] Poyser, "⟨It's sad there's folks as are⟩ {an' it's poor work,} ⟨when⟩ alys *MS*

[4] gone. ⟨You canna water the last year's crop—naethin' about to water⟩ It's but little good you'll do, a-watering *MS*

[5] & that it would be well to change the subject] *added in MS*

[6] hanna] haven't *MS*   [7] while, and] while. And *MS*   [8] wants ⟨to⟩ you *MS*

[9] her ⟨cheese [one word] shelves⟩ best spinning wheel *MS*

[1] turning{.} ⟨doing."⟩ You'll *MS*

[2] round ⟨as he finished⟩ {while he was} speaking ⟨to⟩ {as if to} see where {⟨if⟩} Hetty ⟨& the children were close behind⟩ {was, for the children were running} on *MS*

[3] had, ⟨moreover⟩ besides *MS*   [4] plant ⟨to which⟩ with *MS*

as she listened to the gardener's small-talk. Yet in her secret heart she was glad to have him by her side, for she would perhaps learn from him how it was Arthur had not come to church. Not that she cared[5] to ask him the question, but she hoped the information would be given spontaneously; for Mr Craig, like a superior man, was very fond of giving information.

Mr Craig was never aware that his conversation and advances were received coldly, for to shift one's point of view beyond certain limits is impossible to the most liberal and expansive mind; we are none of us aware of the impression we produce on Brazilian monkeys of feeble understanding—it is possible they see hardly anything in us. Moreover, Mr Craig was a man of sober passions, and was already in his tenth year of hesitation as to the relative advantages of matrimony and bachelorhood. It is true that, now and then, when he had been a little heated by an extra glass of grog, he had been heard to say of Hetty that the "lass was well enough," and that "a man might do worse;" but on convivial occasions men are apt to express themselves strongly.

Martin Poyser held Mr Craig in honour, as a man who "knew his business," and who had great lights concerning soils and compost; but he was less of a favourite with Mrs Poyser, who[6] had more than once said in confidence to her husband, "You're mighty fond o' Craig; but for my part, I think he's welly like a cock as thinks the sun's rose o' purpose to hear him crow." For the rest, Mr Craig was an estimable gardener, and was not without reasons[7] for having a high opinion of himself. He[8] had also high shoulders and high cheek-bones, and hung his head forward a little, as he walked along with his hands in his breeches pockets. I think it was his pedigree only that had the advantage of being Scotch, and not his "bringing up;" for except that he had a stronger burr in his accent, his speech differed little from that of the Loamshire people about him. But a gardener is Scotch, as a French teacher is Parisian.

"Well,[9] Mr Poyser," he said, before the good slow farmer had time to speak, "ye'll not be carrying your hay to-morrow, I'm thinking: the glass sticks at 'change,' and ye may rely upo' my word as we'll ha' more downfall afore twenty-four hours is past. Ye see that darkish blue[1] cloud there upo' the 'rizon—ye[2] know what I mean by the 'rizon, where the land and sky seems to meet?"[3]

[5] cared] dared *MS*

[6] who ⟨saw in him considerable resemblance to a certain cock as thought⟩ {had more than once ⟨been heard to say⟩ said in confidence to her husband, "<u>You're</u> mighty fond o' Craig, but for my part I think he's welly like ⟨the⟩ a cock as thinks} the *MS*

[7] reasons] grounds *MS*   [8] himself. He] himself: He *MS*

[9] Well, ⟨M^rs⟩Mr. *MS*   [1] darkish blue] *added in MS*

[2] ye] you *MS 1* ⟨you⟩ ye *8*   [3] meet?"] meet ... *MS* meet." *1*

"Ay, ay,[4] I see the cloud," said Mr Poyser, "'rizon or no 'rizon. It's right o'er[5] Mike Holdsworth's fallow, and a foul fallow it is."

"Well, you mark my words, as that cloud 'ull spread o'er the sky[6] pretty nigh as quick as you'd spread a tarpaulin over one o' your hayricks. It's a great thing to ha' studied the look o' the clouds.[7] Lord bless you! th'[8] met'orological almanecks can learn me nothing, but there's a pretty sight o' things I could let *them* up to, if they'd just come to me. And how are *you*, Mrs Poyser?—thinking[9] o'[1] getherin' the red currants soon, I reckon. You'd a deal better gether 'em afore they're o'er-ripe, wi' such weather as we've got to look forward[2] to. How do ye do,[3] Mistress Bede?" Mr Craig continued, without a pause, nodding by the way to Adam and Seth. "I hope y' enjoyed them spinach and gooseberries as I sent[4] Chester[5] with th' other day. If ye[6] want vegetables while ye're[7] in trouble, ye[8] know where to come to[9]. It's well known I'm not giving[1] other folks's[2] things away; for when I've supplied the house, the garden's my own spekilation, and it isna every man th' old Squire could get as 'ud be equil to th'[3] undertaking, let alone asking whether he'd be willing. I've got to run my calkilation fine, I can tell you, to make sure o' getting[4] back[5] the money as I pay the Squire. I should like to see some o' them fellows as make[6] th'[7] almanecks looking as far[8] before their noses as I've got to do every year as comes."

"They look pretty fur, though," said Mr Poyser, turning his head on one side, and speaking in rather a subdued reverential tone. "Why[9], what could come truer nor that pictur o' the cock wi' the big spurs, as has got its[1] head knocked down wi' th' anchor, an' th'[2] firin', an'[3] the ships behind? Why, that pictur was made afore Christmas, and yit it's come as true as th' Bible. Why, th' cock's France, an' th' anchor's Nelson—an' they told us that beforehand."

"Pee—ee-eh!" said Mr Craig. "A man doesna want to see fur to know as th' English 'ull beat the French. Why, I know upo' good authority as it's a big Frenchman[4] as reaches five foot high, an' they live upo' spoon-meat mostly. I knew a man as his father had a particular knowledge o' the

---

[4] ay, ⟨" said Mr. Poyser⟩ "I *MS*   [5] o'er ⟨the Binton Hills⟩ Mike *MS*
[6] o'er the sky] *added in MS*
[7] clouds. ⟨Now I've studied 'em⟩ Lord bless you! The met' *MS*
[8] th'] The *MS* the *1*
[9] Poyser?—thinking] Poyser? Thinkin' *MS* Poyser?—thinkin' *1*
[1] o' ⟨getting⟩ gethering *MS*   [2] forward] forrard *MS*
[3] do, ⟨Mester Adam⟩ Mistress *MS*   [4] I sent] *added in MS*
[5] Chester] Kester *MS*   [6] ye] you *MS*   [7] ye're] you're *MS*
[8] ye] you *MS*   [9] to{.} ⟨, for⟩ ⟨i⟩It's *MS*
[1] giving] givin' *MS*   [2] folks's] *MS 1* folk's *8* folks' *Cabinet*
[3] th'] *MS 1* the *8*   [4] getting] gettin' *MS*   [5] back ⟨my⟩ the *MS*
[6] make ⟨the⟩ th' ⟨?House's⟩ Almanecks *MS*   [7] th'] ⟨the⟩ th' *MS* th' *1* the *8*
[8] far] fur *MS*   [9] tone. "Why] tone, "Why *MS*   [1] its] it's *MS 1*
[2] th'] the *MS*   [3] an'] & *MS* and *1*   [4] Frenchman ⟨is o⟩ {as} ⟨is⟩ reaches *MS*

French.[5] I should like to[6] know what them grasshoppers are to do against such fine fellows as our young Captain Arthur. Why, it 'ud astonish a Frenchman only to look at him; his arm's thicker nor a Frenchman's body, I'll be bound, for they pinch theirsells[7] in wi' stays; and it's easy enough, for they've got nothing i' their insides."

"Where *is*[8] the Captain, as he wasna[9] at church to-day?" said Adam. "I was talking to him o' Friday, and he said nothing[1] about his going away."

"Oh, he's only gone to[2] Eagledale for a bit o' fishing; I reckon he'll be back again afore many days are o'er, for he's to be at all th' arranging and preparing o' things for the comin' o' age o' the thirtieth[3] o' July. But he's fond o' getting away for a bit, now and then. Him and th' old Squire fit one another like frost and flowers."

Mr Craig smiled and winked slowly as he made this last observation, but the subject was not developed farther[4], for now they had reached the turning in the road where Adam and his companions[5] must say "good-by." The gardener, too, would have had to turn off in[6] the same direction if he had not accepted Mr Poyser's invitation to tea. Mrs Poyser duly seconded the invitation, for she would have held it a deep disgrace not to make her neighbours welcome to her house: personal likes and dislikes must not interfere with that sacred custom. Moreover, Mr Craig had always been full of civilities to the family at the Hall Farm, and Mrs Poyser was scrupulous in declaring that she had "nothing to say again' him, on'y it was a pity he couldna[7] be hatched o'er again, an' hatched different."

So Adam and Seth, with their mother between them, wound their way down to[8] the valley and up again to the old house, where[9] a saddened memory had taken the place of a long, long anxiety—where Adam would never have to ask again as he entered, "Where's father?"

And the other family party, with Mr[1] Craig for company, went back to the pleasant bright house-place at the Hall Farm—all with quiet minds, except Hetty, who knew now where Arthur was gone, but was[2] only the more puzzled and uneasy.[3] For it appeared that his absence was quite voluntary; he need not have gone—he would not have gone if he had wanted to see her. She had a sickening sense that no lot could ever be

<hr />

⁵ I knew a man as his father had a particular knowledge o' the French.] *added in MS*
⁶ to] t' *MS*   ⁷ theirsells] theirselves *MS 1*   ⁸ *is*] is *MS* is *1* ⟨is⟩ is *8*
⁹ wasna] wasn't *MS* was'n *1* ⟨was'n⟩ wasna *8*   ¹ nothing ⟨as t⟩ about $\overline{M}$*S*
² to] t' *MS*   ³ thirtieth] thirt'eth *MS* 30th *Cabinet*   ⁴ farther] further *MS*
⁵ & his companions] *added in MS*   ⁶ in ⟨that⟩ the same *MS*
⁷ couldna] couldn't *MS*   ⁸ to] *added in MS*
⁹ where ⟨the darkened bedchamber was empty now,⟩ a saddened memory had taken the *MS*
¹ Mr.] *added in MS*   ² was ⟨as⟩ only the more *MS*
³ uneasy{.} ⟨& [?alarmed at]⟩ ⟨The reason for this voluntary absence—⟩ {For it appeared that his absence was quite voluntary—} he *MS*

pleasant to her again if her Thursday night's vision was not to be fulfilled;
and in[4] this moment of chill, bare, wintry disappointment and doubt, she
looked towards the possibility of[5] being with Arthur again, of meeting[6] his
loving glance, and hearing[7] his soft words, with that eager yearning which
one may call the "growing pain" of passion.

[4] fulfilled; and in] fulfilled. And ⟨from⟩ in *MS*   [5] of ⟨seeing⟩ being with *MS*
[6] meeting ⟨that⟩ his *MS*   [7] hearing ⟨those⟩ his *MS*

CHAPTER XIX.

[1]ADAM ON A WORKING DAY.

Notwithstanding Mr Craig's[2] prophecy, the dark-blue cloud[3] dispersed itself without having produced the threatened consequences. "The weather," as he observed the next morning—"the weather, you see, 's a ticklish thing, an' a fool 'ull hit on't sometimes when a wise man misses; that's why th'[4] almanecks gets[5] so much credit. It's one o' them chancy things as fools thrive on[6]."

This unreasonable[7] behaviour of the weather, however, could[8] displease no one else in Hayslope besides Mr Craig. All hands were to be out in the meadows[9] this morning as soon as the dew had risen; the[1] wives and daughters did double work in every farm-house, that the maids might give their help in tossing the hay; and when Adam[2] was marching along the lanes, with his basket of tools over his shoulder, he caught the sound of jocose talk and ringing laughter from behind the hedges. The jocose talk of haymakers is best at a distance;[3] like those clumsy bells round the cows' necks, it has rather a coarse sound when it comes[4] close, and may even grate on your ears painfully; but heard from far off, it mingles very prettily with the other joyous sounds of nature.[5] Men's muscles move better when their souls are making merry music, though their merriment is of a poor[6] blundering sort, not at all like the merriment of birds.

And perhaps there is no time in a summer's day more cheering, than when the warmth of the sun is just beginning to triumph over the freshness of the morning—when there is just a lingering hint of early coolness to keep

---

¹ ⟨Adam visits the Hall Farm.⟩ Adam on a Working Day. *MS*
² Craig's ⟨threatening⟩ prophecy *MS*
³ the dark-blue cloud] the ⟨black⟩ {blue} cloud *MS*
⁴ th'] *MS 1* the *8*   ⁵ gets] *MS 1* get *8*
⁶ on{."} ⟨, for if anything ⟨⟨nothing⟩⟩ was to [two or three words] rain able men could calkilate it,⟩ ¶ This *MS*
⁷ unreasonable ⟨character⟩ behaviour *MS*
⁸ could dis⟨appoint⟩{please} no one {else} in *MS*
⁹ meadows ⟨the first thing in the morning⟩ this morning as soon as the dew had risen *MS*
¹ the ⟨men's work was hurried on⟩ wives & daughters did double work in *MS*
² Adam ⟨whose way, ⟨⟨lay⟩⟩ over back⟩ was *MS*
³ distance; ⟨it is⟩ like *MS*   ⁴ comes ⟨near⟩ close *MS*
⁵ nature. ⟨It is good that men should be merry over their work⟩ Men's muscles move better when their souls are making merry music *MS*
⁶ poor] *added in MS*

off languor under the delicious influence of warmth. The reason Adam was
walking along the lanes at this time was because his work for the rest of the
day lay at a country house[7] about three miles off, which[8] was being put in
repair for the son of a neighbouring squire; and he had been busy since early
morning[9] with the packing of panels, doors, and chimney-pieces, in a
waggon which was now gone on before him, while Jonathan Burge himself
had ridden to the spot on horseback, to await its arrival and direct the
workmen.

This little walk was a rest to Adam, and he[1] was unconsciously under the
charm of the moment. It was summer morning in his heart, and he saw
Hetty in[2] the sunshine: a sunshine without glare—with slanting rays that
tremble between the delicate shadows of the leaves. He thought, yesterday,
when he put out his hand to her as they came out of church, that there was a
touch of melancholy kindness in her face, such as he had not seen before,
and he took it as a sign that she had some sympathy with his family trouble.
Poor fellow! that touch of melancholy came from quite another source; but
how was he to know? We look at the one little woman's face we love, as we
look at the face of our mother earth, and see all sorts of answers to our own
yearnings. It was impossible for Adam not to feel that what had happened in
the last week had brought the prospect of marriage nearer to him. Hitherto
he had felt keenly the danger that some other man might step in and get
possession of Hetty's heart and hand[3], while he himself[4] was still in a
position that made him shrink from asking her to accept him. Even if he
had had a strong hope that she was fond of him—and his hope was far from
being strong—he[5] had been too heavily burthened with other claims to
provide a home for himself and Hetty—a home such as he could expect her
to be content with after the comfort and plenty of the Farm. Like all strong
natures, Adam had confidence in his ability to achieve something in the
future; he felt sure he should some day, if he lived, be able to maintain a
family, and make a good broad path for himself; but he had too cool a head
not to estimate to the full the obstacles that were to be overcome.[6] And the
time would be so long! And there was Hetty, like[7] a bright-cheeked apple
hanging over the orchard wall, within sight of everybody, and everybody
must long for her! To be sure, if she loved him very much, she would be
content to wait for him: but *did* she love him? His hopes had never risen so
high that he had dared to ask her. He was clear-sighted enough to be aware
that her uncle and aunt would have looked kindly on his suit, and indeed
without this encouragement he would never have persevered in going to

---

[7] house ⟨which⟩ about three miles off, that *MS*
[8] which] that *MS*   [9] morning ⟨in⟩ with the *MS*
[1] he ⟨felt the charm of the⟩ was unconsciously under the charm⟨ing⟩ of *MS*
[2] in ⟨that delicious⟩ the sunshine *MS*   [3] hand ⟨before⟩ while *MS*
[4] himself] *added in MS*   [5] he ⟨was⟩ had been *MS*
[6] overcome. ⟨But⟩ And *MS*   [7] like ⟨an ap⟩ a *MS*

the Farm; but it was impossible to come to any but fluctuating conclusions about Hetty's feelings[8]. She was like a kitten, and had the same distractingly pretty looks, that meant nothing, for everybody that came near her.

But now he could not help saying to himself that[9] the heaviest part of his burden was removed, and that even before the end of another year[1] his circumstances might be brought into a shape that would allow him to think of marrying. It would always be a hard struggle with his mother, he knew: she would be jealous of any wife he might choose, and she had set her mind especially against Hetty—perhaps for no other reason than that[2] she suspected Hetty to be the woman he *had* chosen. It would never do, he feared, for his mother to live in the same house with him when he was married; and yet how[3] hard she would think it if he asked her to leave him![4] Yes, there was a great deal of pain to be gone through with his mother, but it was a case in which he must make her feel that his will was strong—it would be better for her in the end. For[5] himself, he would have liked that they should all live together till Seth was married, and they might have built a bit themselves to the old house, and made more room. He did not[6] like "to part wi' th' lad:" they had[7] hardly ever been separated for more than a day since they were born.

But Adam had no sooner caught his imagination leaping forward in this way—making arrangements for an uncertain future—than he checked himself. "A pretty building I'm making, without either bricks or timber. I'm up in[8] the garret a'ready[9], and haven't so much as dug the foundation." Whenever Adam was strongly convinced of any proposition, it took the form of a principle in his mind: it was knowledge to be acted on, as much as the knowledge that damp will cause rust. Perhaps here lay the secret of the hardness he had accused himself of: he had too little fellow-feeling with the weakness that errs in spite of foreseen consequences. Without this fellow-feeling, how are we to get enough patience and charity towards our stumbling, falling companions in the long and changeful journey? And there is but one way in which a strong determined soul can learn it—by getting his heart-strings bound round the weak and erring, so that he must share not only the outward consequence of their error, but their inward suffering. That is a long and hard lesson, and Adam had at present only learned the alphabet of it in his father's sudden death, which, by annihilating in an instant all that had stimulated his indignation, had sent a sudden

---

[8] feelings] feeling *MS*

[9] that ⟨some of his burdens were⟩ the heaviest part of his burden was *MS*

[1] year ⟨things might⟩ his *MS*   [2] that ⟨she was⟩ she suspected Hetty to be *MS*

[3] how ⟨cruel⟩ hard she would think ⟨him⟩ it *MS*

[4] him! ⟨Even though she might still live with Seth, who did not seem likely to marry yet.⟩ Yes, there was a great deal of pain to be gone through with his mother, but it was *MS*

[5] For ⟨his own part⟩ himself *MS*   [6] did not] didn't *MS*

[7] had ⟨never⟩ hardly ever *MS*   [8] in] i' *Cabinet*   [9] a'ready] already *MS*

rush of thought and memory over what had claimed his pity and tenderness.

But it was Adam's strength, not its correlative hardness, that influenced
his meditations this morning. He had long made up his mind that it would
be wrong as well as foolish for him to marry a blooming young girl, so long
as he had no other prospect than that of growing poverty with a growing
family. And his savings had been so constantly[1] drawn upon (besides the
terrible sweep of paying for Seth's substitute in the militia), that he had not
enough money beforehand to furnish even a small cottage, and keep something in reserve against a rainy day. He had good hope that he should be
"firmer on his legs" by-and-by; but he could not be satisfied with a vague
confidence in his arm and brain; he must have definite plans, and set about
them at once. The partnership with Jonathan Burge was not to be thought
of at present[2]—there were things implicitly tacked to it that he could not
accept; but Adam thought that he and Seth might carry on a little business
for themselves in addition to their journeyman's work, by buying a small
stock of superior wood and making articles of household furniture, for
which Adam had no end of contrivances.[3] Seth might gain more by working
at separate jobs under Adam's direction than by his journeyman's work,
and Adam, in his over-hours, could do all the "nice" work, that required
peculiar skill. The money gained in this way, with the good wages[4] he
received as foreman, would soon enable them to get beforehand with the
world, so sparingly as they would[5] all live now.[6] No sooner had this little
plan shaped itself in his mind than he began to be busy with[7] exact
calculations about the wood to be bought, and the particular article of
furniture that should be[8] undertaken first—a kitchen cupboard of his own[9]
contrivance, with such an ingenious arrangement of sliding doors and
bolts, such convenient nooks for stowing household provender, and such
a symmetrical result to the eye, that every good housewife would be in
raptures with it, and fall[1] through all the gradations of melancholy longing
till her husband promised to buy it for her. Adam pictured to himself Mrs
Poyser examining it with her keen eye, and trying in vain to find out a
deficiency; and, of course, close to Mrs Poyser stood Hetty, and Adam was

---

¹ constantly ⟨drained⟩ drawn upon—(besides the terrible sweep of paying for Seth's
substitute in the Militia) *MS*

² at present] *added in MS*

³ contrivances. ⟨They could work at these things in over hours, Adam doing all the "nice"
work that required peculiar skill, &⟩ Seth might gain more by working at separate jobs under
Adam's direction than by his journeyman's work, & Adam {in his over hours} could do all the
"nice" work that required peculiar skill{.} ⟨in his over hours⟩ ⟨t⟩The *MS*

⁴ wages ⟨Adam⟩ he *MS*   ⁵ would] should *MS*

⁶ now. ⟨Then Adam⟩ ⟨This⟩ No *MS*

⁷ with ⟨the⟩ exact⟨est⟩ calculations about the wood⟨s⟩ to *MS*

⁸ be ⟨set about⟩ undertaken *MS*   ⁹ own contrivance⟨s⟩ with *MS*

¹ fall ⟨into⟩ through *MS*

again beguiled from calculations and contrivances into dreams and hopes. Yes, he would go and see her this evening—it was so long since he had been at the Hall Farm. He would have liked to go to the night-school, to see why Bartle Massey had not been at church yesterday, for he feared his old friend was ill[2]; but[3], unless he could manage both visits, this last must be put off till to-morrow—the desire to[4] be near Hetty, and to speak to her again, was too strong.

[5]As[6] he made up his mind to this, he was coming very near to the end of his walk, within the sound of the hammers at work on the refitting of the old house. The sound of tools to a clever workman who loves his work is like the tentative[7] sounds of the orchestra to the violinist who has to bear his part in the overture: the strong fibres begin their accustomed thrill, and[8] what was a moment before joy, vexation, or ambition, begins its change into energy. All passion becomes strength when it has an outlet from the narrow limits of our personal lot in the labour of our right arm, the cunning of our right hand, or the still, creative activity of our thought. Look at Adam through the rest of the day, as he[9] stands on the scaffolding with the two-feet ruler in his hand, whistling low while he considers how a difficulty about a floor-joist or a window-frame is to be overcome; or as he pushes one of the younger workmen aside, and takes his place in upheaving a weight of timber, saying, "Let alone, lad! thee'st got too much gristle i' thy bones yet;" or as he fixes his keen black eyes on the motions of a workman on the other side of the room, and warns him that his distances are not right. Look at this broad-shouldered man with the bare muscular arms, and the thick firm black hair tossed about like trodden meadow-grass whenever he takes off his paper cap, and with the strong barytone voice bursting every now and then into loud and solemn psalm-tunes, as if seeking an[1] outlet for superfluous strength, yet[2] presently checking himself, apparently crossed by some thought which[3] jars with the singing. Perhaps, if you had not been already in the secret, you might not have guessed what sad memories, what warm affection, what tender fluttering hopes, had their home in this athletic body with the broken finger-nails—in this rough man, who knew no better lyrics[4] than he could find in the Old and New Version and an occasional hymn; who knew the smallest possible amount of profane

---

[2] to see why Bartle Massey had not been at church yesterday, for he feared his old friend was ill] *cancelled and then restored in MS*

[3] but ⟨that⟩ {unless he could manage both visits, this last} must *MS*

[4] to ⟨see⟩ be near Hetty {& to speak to her again,} was *MS*

[5] *Paragraph division added in 1.* [6] As ⟨Adam had⟩ he *MS*

[7] tentative] *added in MS*

[8] & ⟨that passion which the moment before has been absorbed in his⟩ what *MS*

[9] he ⟨stood⟩ stands *MS* [1] an] some *MS 1* ⟨some⟩ an *8*

[2] strength, yet] strength, & yet *MS* [3] which jar⟨red⟩{s} with *MS*

[4] lyrics] poetry *MS*

history; and for whom the motion and shape of the earth, the course of the sun, and the changes of the seasons, lay in the region of mystery just made visible by fragmentary knowledge. It had cost Adam a great deal of trouble, and work in over-hours, to know what he knew over and above[5] the secrets of his handicraft, and that acquaintance with mechanics and figures, and the nature of the materials[6] he worked with, which was made easy to him by inborn inherited faculty—to get the mastery of his pen, and write a plain hand, to spell without any[7] other mistakes than[8] must in fairness be attributed to the unreasonable character of orthography rather than to any deficiency in the speller, and, moreover, to learn his musical notes and part-singing. Besides all this, he had read his Bible, including the apocryphal books; "Poor Richard's Almanac[9]," Taylor's "Holy Living and Dying," "The Pilgrim's Progress," with Bunyan's Life and "Holy War," a great deal of Bailey's Dictionary,[1] "Valentine and Orson," and part of[2] a "History of Babylon," which Bartle Massey had lent him. He might have had many more books from Bartle Massey, but he had no time for reading "the commin print," as Lisbeth called it, so busy as he was with figures in all the leisure moments which he did not fill up with extra carpentry.

Adam, you perceive, was by no means a marvellous man, nor, properly speaking, a genius, yet I will not pretend that his was[3] an ordinary character among workmen; and it would not be at all a safe conclusion that the next best man you may happen to see with a basket of tools over his shoulder and a paper cap on his head has the strong conscience and the strong sense, the blended susceptibility and self-command of our friend Adam. He was not an average man. Yet such men as he are reared here and there in every generation of our peasant artisans—with an inheritance of[4] affections nurtured by a simple family life of common need and common industry, and an inheritance of faculties trained in skilful courageous labour: they make their way upward, rarely as geniuses, most commonly as painstaking honest men, with the skill and conscience to do well the tasks that lie before them. Their lives have no discernible echo[5] beyond the neighbourhood where they dwelt, but you are almost sure to find there some good piece of road, some building, some[6] application of mineral produce, some improvement in farming practice, some reform of[7] parish abuses, with which their names are associated by one or two generations after them. Their employers were the richer for them, the work of their hands has worn well, and the work of their brains has guided well the hands of other men. They went

---

[5] over and above] besides *MS*   [6] materials ⟨with⟩ he *MS*
[7] any ⟨worse⟩ other *MS*   [8] than ⟨might⟩ must *MS*
[9] Almanac] Almanack *MS*
[1] Dictionary, ⟨the Life of⟩ "Valentine *MS*   [2] part of] *added in MS*
[3] was ⟨a common⟩ an ordinary *MS*   [4] of ⟨faculties⟩ affections *MS*
[5] no discernible echo] no echo *MS*
[6] some ⟨mine,⟩ application of mineral produce *MS*   [7] reform of] *added in MS*

about in their youth in flannel or paper caps, in coats black with coal-dust or streaked with lime and red paint; in old age their white hairs are seen in a place of honour at church and at market, and they tell their well-dressed sons and daughters, seated round the bright hearth on winter evenings, how pleased they were when they first earned their twopence a day. Others there are who die poor, and never put off the workman's coat on weekdays: they have not had the art of getting rich; but they are men of trust, and when they die before the work is all out of them, it is as if some main screw had got loose in a machine; the master who employed them says, "Where shall I find their like?"

CHAPTER XX.

ADAM VISITS THE HALL FARM.

Adam came back from his work in the empty[1] waggon; that was why he had changed his clothes, and was ready to set out to the Hall Farm[2] when it still wanted a quarter to seven.

"What's[3] thee got thy Sunday cloose[4] on for?" said Lisbeth, complainingly, as he came downstairs. "Thee artna[5] goin' to th' school i' thy best coat?"

"No, mother," said Adam, quietly. "I'm going to the[6] Hall Farm, but mayhap I may go to the school after, so[7] thee mustna wonder if I'm a bit late. Seth 'ull be at home in half an hour—he's only gone to the village;[8] so thee wutna[9] mind."

"Eh, an' what's[1] thee got thy best cloose[2] on for to[3] go to th' Hall Farm? The Poyser folks see'd thee in 'em yesterday[4], I warrand. What dost mean[5] by turnin' worki'day into Sunday a-that'n?[6] It's poor keepin'[7] company wi' folks as donna[8] like to see thee i' thy workin' jacket."

"Good-by, mother, I can't stay,"[9] said Adam, putting on his hat and going out.

But he had no sooner gone a few paces beyond the door than Lisbeth became uneasy at the thought that she had vexed him. Of course, the secret of her objection to the best clothes was her[1] suspicion that they were put on for Hetty's sake; but deeper than all her peevishness lay the need that her son should love her. She hurried after him, and laid hold of his arm before he had got half-way down to the brook, and said, "Nay, my lad, thee wutna[2] go away[3] angered wi' thy mother, an' her got nought to do but to sit by hersen an' think on thee?"

---

[1] empty] *added in MS*

[2] Farm ⟨as early⟩ ⟨when it still wanted a quarter to seven⟩ ⟨as early as seven o'clock that evening⟩ when it still wanted a quarter to seven. *MS*

[3] What's] What'n *MS*   [4] *MS shows* clothes *written above the uncancelled* cloose.

[5] artna] artn't *MS*   [6] the] th' *MS*   [7] so ⟨you⟩ thee must⟨na⟩n't wonder *MS*

[8] in half an hour—he's only gone to the village;] *added in MS*

[9] wutna] wotn't *MS* wotna *1* ⟨wotna⟩ wutna *8*   [1] what's] what'n *MS*

[2] cloose] cloos *MS*   [3] on for to] on to *MS*   [4] yesterday] yisterday *MS*

[5] mean] mane *MS*   [6] a-that'n? ⟨An' then, thee't go to th' school⟩ It's *MS*

[7] keepin'] keeping *MS*   [8] donna] doesn't *MS*   [9] I can't stay,"] *added in MS*

[1] her ⟨knowledge of the fact that he was courting Hetty⟩ suspicion that they were put on for Hetty's sake; *MS*

[2] wutna] wotna *MS 1* ⟨wotna⟩ wutna *8*   [3] away ⟨angry⟩ angered *MS*

"Nay, nay, mother," said Adam, gravely, and standing still while he put his arm on her shoulder, "I'm not angered. But[4] I wish, for thy own sake, thee'dst be more contented to let me do what I've made up my mind to do. I'll never be no other than a good son to thee as long as we live. But a man has other feelings besides what he owes to's father and mother; and thee oughtna[5] to want to rule over me body and soul. And thee must make up thy mind, as I'll not give way to thee where I've a right to do what I like. So let us have no more words about it."

"Eh," said Lisbeth, not willing to show that she felt the real bearing of Adam's words, "an' who likes to see thee i' thy best cloose[6] better nor[7] thy mother? An' when thee'st got thy face washed as clean as the smooth white pibble[8], an' thy hair combed so nice, an'[9] thy eyes a-sparklin'—what else is there as thy old mother should like to look at half so well? An' thee sha't put on thy Sunday cloose[1] when thee lik'st for me—I'll ne'er plague thee no moor about'n."

"Well, well; good-by, mother," said Adam, kissing her, and hurrying away. He saw there was no other means of putting an end to the dialogue.[2] Lisbeth stood still on the spot, shading her eyes and looking after him till he was quite out of sight. She[3] felt to the full all the meaning that had lain in Adam's words, and, as she lost sight of him and turned back slowly into the house, she said aloud to herself—for it was her way to speak her thoughts aloud in the long days when her husband and sons were at their work— "Eh, he'll be tellin' me as he's goin' to bring her home one o' these[4] days; an' she'll be missis o'er me, an'[5] I mun look on, belike, while[6] she uses the blue-edged platters, an'[7] [8] breaks 'em, mayhap, though there's ne'er been one broke sin' my old man an' me bought 'em at the[9] fair twenty 'ear come[1] next Whissuntide. Eh!" she went on, still louder, as she caught[2] up her knitting from the table, "but she'll ne'er knit the lads'[3] stockins, nor foot 'em nayther, while I live; an' when I'm gone, he'll bethink him as nobody 'ull ne'er fit's leg an' foot as his old mother did.[4] She'll know[5] nothin' o' narrowin' an' heelin', I warrand, an' she'll make a long toe as he canna get's boot on. That's what comes o' marr'in' young wenches. I[6] war gone thirty, an' th' feyther too, afore we[7] war married; an' young enough too.

---

4 But ⟨thee⟩ I *MS*   5 oughtna] ought'stnt *MS*   6 cloose] cloos *MS*
7 nor ⟨me⟩ thy *MS*   8 as ⟨a⟩ the smooth {white} pibble *MS*
9 an'] *MS 1 and 8*   1 cloose] clothes *MS*   2 dialogue. ⟨She⟩ Lisbeth *MS*
3 She ⟨was⟩ felt *MS*   4 these] they *MS*   5 an'] *MS 1 and 8*
6 while she⟨'ll⟩ use{s} the *MS*   7 an'] *MS 1 and 8*
8 an' ⟨'ull⟩ break{s} 'em *MS*   9 the] th' *MS*
1 come ⟨next E'ster⟩ next *MS*   2 caught ⟨sight of⟩ {up} her knitting ⟨on⟩ {from}
the *MS*   3 the lads'] th' lad's *MS*   4 did. ⟨Them young wenches now-a-days⟩
She'll *MS*
5 know] knoo *MS*   6 wenches. I] wenches: I *MS*   7 we ⟨war⟩ was *MS*

She'll be a poor dratchell by then *she's* thirty, a-marr'in' a-that'n, afore her teeth's all come."

Adam walked so fast that he was at the yard gate before seven.[8] Martin Poyser and the grandfather were[9] not yet come in from the meadow: every one was in the meadow, even to the black-and-tan terrier—no[1] one kept watch in the yard but the bull-dog;[2] and when Adam reached the house-door, which stood wide open, he saw there was no one in the bright clean house-place. But he guessed where Mrs Poyser and some one else would be, quite within hearing; so he knocked on the door and said in his strong voice, "Mrs Poyser within?"

"Come in, Mr Bede, come in,"[3] Mrs Poyser called out from the dairy. She always gave Adam this title when she received him in her own house. "You may come into the dairy if you will, for I canna[4] justly leave the cheese."

Adam walked into the dairy, where Mrs Poyser and Nancy were crushing the first evening cheese.

"Why, you might think you war come to a dead-house," said Mrs Poyser, as he stood in the open doorway; "they're all i' the meadow; but Martin's sure to be in afore long, for they're leaving the hay[5] cocked to-night, ready for carrying first thing to-morrow. I've been forced[6] t' have Nancy in, upo' 'count[7] as Hetty must gether the red currants to-night; the fruit allays[8] ripens so contrairy, just when every[9] hand's wanted. An' there's no trustin' the children to gether it, for they put more into their own mouths nor into the basket; you[1] might[2] as well set the wasps to gether the fruit."

Adam longed to say he would go into the garden till Mr Poyser came in, but he was not quite courageous enough, so he said, "I could be looking at your spinning-wheel, then, and see what wants doing to it. Perhaps it stands in the house, where I can find it?"

"No, I've put it away in the right-hand parlour; but let it be till I can fetch it an'[3] show it you. I'd be glad now, if you'd go into the garden, and tell Hetty to send Totty in. The child 'ull run in if she's told, an' I know Hetty's lettin' her eat[4] too many currans[5]. I'll be much obliged to you, Mr Bede, if

[8] seven. ⟨Mr.⟩ Martin *MS*

[9] were ⟨still out in the hay-field⟩ not yet come in from the *MS*

[1] terrier—no] terrier, & no *MS*

[2] every one was in the meadow, even to the black & tan terrier, & no one kept watch in the yard but the bull dog;] *added in MS*

[3] in," ⟨Mrs. Poyser⟩ {Mrs. Poyser called out from the dairy. She} always *MS*

[4] canna] can't *MS*   [5] hay ⟨ready⟩ cocked tonight, {ready} for *MS*

[6] forced ⟨to⟩ t' *MS*   [7] count ⟨o'⟩ as *MS*   [8] allays] alys *MS*

[9] every] ivery *MS 1* ⟨ivery⟩ every *8*

[1] basket; you] basket. You *MS*   [2] might] mut *MS*

[3] an'] *MS 1* and *8*   ⁀   [4] eat ⟨the⟩ too many *MS*   [5] currans] currants *MS*

you'll go an'[6] send her in; an' there's the York an'[7] Lankester roses beautiful in the garden now—you'll like to see 'em. But you'd like a drink[8] o' whey first, p'r'aps; I know you're fond o' whey, as most folks is when they hanna got[9] to crush it out."

"Thank you, Mrs Poyser," said Adam; "a drink o' whey's allays[1] a treat to me. I'd rather[2] have it than beer any day."

[3]"Ay, ay," said Mrs Poyser, reaching a small white basin that stood on the shelf, and dipping it into the whey-tub, "the smell o' bread's sweet t' everybody but the baker.[4] The Miss Irwines allays[5] say, 'O Mrs Poyser, I envy you your dairy; and I envy you your chickens; and what a beautiful thing a farmhouse is, to be sure!' An' I say, 'Yes[6] [7]; a farm-house is a fine thing for them as look on, an' don't know the liftin', an' the stannin', an' the worritin' o' th' inside, as belongs to't.' "

"Why, Mrs Poyser, you wouldn't like to live anywhere else but in a farm-house, so well as you manage it," said Adam, taking the basin; "and there can be nothing to look at pleasanter nor[8] a fine milch cow[9], standing up to 'ts knees in pasture, and the new milk frothing in the pail[1], and the fresh butter ready for market[2], and the calves, and the poultry. Here's[3] to your health, and may you allays[4] have strength to look after your own dairy,[5] and set a pattern t'[6] all the farmers' wives in the county[7]."

Mrs Poyser was not to be caught in the weakness of smiling at a compliment, but[8] a quiet complacency overspread her face like a stealing sunbeam, and gave a milder[9] glance than usual to her blue-grey eyes, as she looked at Adam drinking the whey. Ah! I think I taste that whey now—with a flavour so delicate that one can hardly distinguish it from an odour, and with that soft gliding warmth that fills[1] one's imagination with a still,[2] happy dreaminess. And the light[3] music of the dropping whey is in my[4] ears, mingling with the twittering of a bird outside the[5] wire network

---

[6] an'] MS 1 and 8   [7] an'] MS 1 and 8

[8] MS shows basin written above the uncancelled drink.

[9] got ⟨the crushing on't⟩ to crush it MS

[1] allays] always MS   [2] rather] rether MS   [3] ⟨That's⟩ "Ay MS

[4] baker. ⟨That's what⟩ The MS   [5] allays] alys MS

[6] Yes] Yis MS 1 ⟨Yis⟩ Yes 8   [7] Yis, ⟨ma'am⟩ a MS   [8] nor] than MS

[9] a fine milch cow] added in MS   [1] frothing in the pail] added in MS

[2] ready for market] added in MS   [3] poultry. Here's] poultry:—here's MS

[4] allays] always MS

[5] dairy, ⟨for there isn't a woman in the county can match you for a farmer's wife⟩ & set a pattern to all the farmers' wives in the county." MS

[6] t'] to MS   [7] county] MS country 1 8   [8] but ⟨there⟩ a MS

[9] milder ⟨look⟩ glance MS   [1] fills ⟨your⟩ one's MS

[2] still ⟨softness⟩ happy MS   [3] light] added in MS

[4] whey is in my] whey in one's MS   [5] the ⟨open window⟩ wire MS

window—the window overlooking the garden, and shaded by tall
Gueldres[6] roses.

"Have a little more, Mr Bede?" said Mrs Poyser, as Adam set down the
basin.

"No, thank you; I'll go into the garden now, and send in the little lass."

"Ay, do; and tell her to come to her mother in the dairy."

Adam walked round by the rick-yard, at present empty of ricks, to the
little wooden gate leading into the garden—once the well-tended kitchen-
garden[7] of a manor-house; now, but for the handsome[8] brick wall with
stone coping that ran along one side of it,[9] a true farm-house garden, with
hardy perennial flowers, unpruned fruit-trees, and kitchen vegetables
growing together in careless, half-neglected abundance. In that leafy,
flowery, bushy time, to look for any one in this garden was like playing at
"hide-and-seek." There were the tall hollyhocks[1] beginning to flower, and
dazzle the eye with their pink, white, and yellow; there were the syringas
and Gueldres[2] roses, all large and disorderly for want of trimming; there
were leafy walls of scarlet beans and late peas; there was a row of bushy
filberts in one direction, and in another a huge apple-tree making a barren
circle under its low-spreading boughs. But what signified a barren patch or
two? The garden was so large. There was always a superfluity of broad
beans—it took nine or ten of Adam's strides to get to the end of the
uncut grass walk that ran by the side of them; and as for other
vegetables, there was so much more room than was necessary for them,
that in the rotation of crops a large flourishing bed of groundsel was of
yearly occurrence on one spot or other. The very rose-trees, at which Adam
stopped to pluck one, looked as if they grew wild; they were all huddled
together in bushy masses, now flaunting with wide open petals, almost all of
them of the streaked pink-and-white kind, which doubtless dated from the
union of the houses of York and Lancaster[3]. Adam was wise enough to
choose a compact Provence rose that peeped out half-smothered by its
flaunting scentless neighbours, and held it in his hand—he thought he
should be more at ease holding something in his hand—as he walked on to
the[4] far end of the garden, where he remembered there was the largest row
of currant-trees, not far off from the great yew-tree arbour.

But he had not gone many steps[5] beyond the roses, when he heard the
shaking of a bough, and a[6] boy's voice saying,

"Now, then, Totty, hold out your pinny—there's a duck."

---

    [6] Gueldres] gueldre *MS 1* ⟨gueldre⟩ Gueldres *8*   [7] kitchen-] *added in MS*
    [8] handsome ⟨stone⟩ brick *MS*   [9] it, ⟨facing the south⟩ a *MS*
    [1] hollyhocks] holyoaks *MS*   [2] Gueldres] *Cabinet* gueldre *MS 1 8*
    [3] Lancaster{.} ⟨and had lost their poetry and their scent in the moment of compromise⟩
Adam *MS*   [4] the ⟨end⟩ far *MS*
    [5] gone many steps] gone steps *MS*   [6] a ⟨small⟩ boy's *MS*

[7]The voice came from the boughs of a tall cherry-tree, where Adam had no difficulty in discerning a small[8] blue-pinafored figure perched in a commodious position where the fruit was thickest. Doubtless Totty was below, behind the screen of peas. Yes—with her bonnet hanging down her back, and her fat face, dreadfully smeared with red juice, turned up towards the cherry-tree, while she held her little round hole of a mouth and her red-stained pinafore to receive the promised downfall. I am sorry to say, more than half the cherries that fell were hard and yellow instead of juicy and red; but Totty spent no time in useless regrets, and she was already sucking the third juiciest when Adam said, "There now, Totty, you've got your cherries. Run into the house with[9] 'em to mother—she wants you—she's in the dairy. Run in this minute—there's a good little girl."

He lifted her up in his strong arms and kissed her as he spoke, a ceremony which Totty regarded as a tiresome interruption to cherry-eating; and when he set her down she trotted off quite silently towards the house, sucking her cherries as she went along.

"Tommy, my lad, take care you're not shot for a little thieving bird," said Adam, as he walked on towards the currant-trees.

He could see there was a large basket at the end of the row: Hetty would not be far off, and Adam already felt as if she were looking at him. Yet when he turned the corner she was standing with her back towards him, and stooping to gather the low-hanging fruit. Strange that she had not heard him coming! perhaps it was because she was[1] making the leaves rustle. She started when she became conscious that some one was near—started so violently that she dropped the basin with the currants in it, and then, when she saw it was Adam, she turned from pale to deep red. That blush made his heart beat with a new happiness. Hetty[2] had never blushed at seeing him before.

"I frightened you," he said, with a delicious sense that it didn't signify what he said, since Hetty seemed to feel as much as he did; "let[3] me pick the currants up."

That was soon done, for they had only fallen in a tangled mass on the grass-plot, and Adam, as he rose and gave her the basin again, looked straight into her eyes with the subdued tenderness that belongs to the first moments of hopeful love.

Hetty did not turn away her eyes;[4] her blush had subsided, and she met his glance with a quiet sadness, which contented Adam, because it was so unlike anything he had seen in her before.

---

[7] *Paragraph division added in 1.*
[8] small ⟨drab figure⟩ blue-pinafored *MS*   [9] with ⟨them⟩ 'em *MS*
[1] was ⟨rustling⟩ making *MS*
[2] happiness. Hetty] happiness: Hetty *MS*   [3] did; "let] did. "Let *MS*
[4] eyes: ⟨she met his glance with⟩ her blush had subsided *MS*

"There's not many more currants to get," she said; "I shall soon ha'[5] done now."

"I'll help you," said Adam; and he fetched the large basket which was nearly full of currants, and set it close to them.

Not a word more was spoken as they gathered the currants. Adam's heart was too full to speak, and he thought Hetty knew all that was in it. She was not indifferent to his presence after all; she had blushed when she saw him, and then there was that touch of sadness about her which must surely mean love, since it was the opposite of her usual manner, which had often impressed him as indifference. And he could glance at her continually as she bent over the fruit, while the level evening sunbeams stole through the thick apple-tree boughs, and rested on her round cheek and neck as if they too were in love with her. It was to Adam the time that a man can least forget in after-life—the time when he believes that the first woman he has ever loved betrays by a slight something, a word, a tone, a glance, the quivering of a lip or an eyelid, that she is at least beginning to love him in return. The sign is so slight, it is scarcely perceptible to the ear or eye—he could describe it to no one—it is a mere feather-touch, yet it seems to have changed his whole being, to have merged an uneasy yearning into a delicious unconsciousness of everything but the present moment. So much of our early gladness vanishes utterly from our memory: we can never recall the joy with which we laid our heads on our mother's bosom or rode on our father's back in childhood; doubtless that joy is wrought up into our nature, as the sunlight of long-past mornings is wrought up in the soft mellowness of the apricot; but it is gone for ever from our imagination, and we can only *believe* in the joy of childhood. But the first glad moment in our first love is a vision which returns to us to the last, and brings with it[6] a thrill of feeling intense and special as the recurrent sensation of a sweet odour breathed in a far-off hour of happiness. It is a memory that gives a more exquisite touch to tenderness, that feeds the madness of jealousy, and adds the last keenness to the agony of despair.

Hetty bending over the red bunches, the level rays piercing the screen of apple-tree boughs,[7] the length of bushy garden beyond, his own emotion as he looked at her and believed that she was thinking of him, and that there was no need for them to talk—Adam remembered it all to the last moment of his life.

And Hetty? You know quite well that Adam was mistaken about her. Like many other men[8], he[9] thought the signs of love for another were signs of love towards himself. When Adam was approaching unseen by her, she was absorbed as usual in thinking and wondering about Arthur's possible

[5] ha'] have *MS*   [6] with it] *added in MS*   [7] boughs, ⟨his own emotion as he looked⟩ the length of bushy garden *MS*
[8] other men] another man *MS 1* ⟨an⟩other ⟨man⟩ men *8*   [9] he ⟨mist⟩ thought *MS*

return: the sound of any man's footstep would have affected her just in the same way—she would have *felt* it might be Arthur before she had time to see, and the blood that forsook her cheek in the agitation of that momentary feeling would have rushed back again at the sight of any one else just[1] as much as at the sight of Adam. He was not wrong in thinking that a change had come over Hetty: the anxieties and fears of a first passion, with which she was trembling, had become stronger than vanity, had given her for the first time that sense of helpless dependence on another's feeling which awakens the clinging deprecating womanhood even in the shallowest girl that can ever experience it, and creates in her a sensibility to kindness which found her quite hard before. For the first time Hetty felt that there was something soothing to her in Adam's timid yet manly tenderness: she wanted to be treated lovingly—O, it was very hard to bear this blank of absence, silence, apparent indifference, after those moments of glowing love! She was not afraid that Adam would tease her with love-making and flattering speeches like her other admirers: he had always been so reserved to her: she could enjoy without any fear the sense that this strong brave man loved her, and was[2] near her. It never entered into her mind that Adam was pitiable too—that Adam, too, must suffer one day.

Hetty, we know, was not the first woman that had behaved more gently to the man who loved her in vain, because she had herself begun to love another. It was a very old story; but Adam knew nothing about it, so he drank in the sweet delusion.

"That'll do," said Hetty, after a little while. "Aunt wants me to leave some on the trees. I'll take 'em in now."

"It's very well I came to carry the basket," said Adam, "for it 'ud ha' been too heavy for your little arms."

"No; I could ha' carried it with both hands."

"O, I dare say," said Adam, smiling, "and been as long getting into the house as a little ant carrying a caterpillar. Have you ever seen those tiny fellows carrying things four times as big as themselves?"

"No," said Hetty,[3] indifferently, not caring to know the difficulties of ant-life.

"O, I used to watch 'em often when I was a lad. But now, you see, I can carry the basket with one arm, as if it was an empty nutshell, and give you th' other arm to lean on. Won't you? Such big arms as mine were made for little arms like yours[4] to lean on."

Hetty smiled faintly, and put her arm within his. Adam looked down at her, but her eyes were turned dreamily towards another corner of the garden.

"Have you ever been to Eagledale?" she said, as they walked slowly along.

<hr>

[1] just] *added in MS*   [2] was near⟨er⟩ her *MS*
[3] Hetty, ⟨carelessly⟩ indifferently *MS*   [4] like yours] *added in MS*

"Yes," said Adam, pleased to have her ask a question about himself; "ten years ago, when I was a lad, I went with father to see about some work there. It's a wonderful sight—rocks and caves such as you never saw in your life. I never had a right notion o' rocks till I went there."

"How long did it take to get there?"

"Why, it took us the best part o' two days' walking. But it's nothing of a day's journey for anybody as has got a first-rate nag. The Captain 'ud get there in[5] nine or ten hours, I'll be bound, he's such a rider. And I shouldn't wonder if he's back again to-morrow; he's[6] too active to rest long in that lonely place, all by himself, for there's nothing but a bit of a[7] inn i' that part where he's gone to fish. I wish he'd got th' estate in his hands; that 'ud be the right thing for him, for it 'ud give him plenty to do, and he'd do 't well too[8], for all he's so young; he's got better notions o' things than many a man twice his age. He spoke very handsome to me th' other day about lending me money to set up i' business; and if things came round that way, I'd rather be beholding to him nor to any man i' the world."

Poor Adam was led on to speak about Arthur because he thought Hetty would be pleased to know that the young squire was so ready to befriend him; the fact entered into his future prospects, which he would like to seem promising in her eyes. And it was true that Hetty listened with an interest which brought a new light into her eyes and a half smile upon her lips.

"How pretty the roses are now!" Adam[9] continued, pausing to look at them. "See! I stole the prettiest, but I didna[1] mean to keep it myself. I think these as are all pink, and have got a finer sort o' green leaves, are prettier than the striped uns, don't you?"

He set down the basket, and took the rose from his button-hole.

"It smells very sweet," he said; "those striped uns have no smell. Stick it in your frock, and then you can put it in water after. It 'ud be a pity to let it fade."

Hetty took the rose, smiling as she did so at the pleasant thought that Arthur could so soon get back if he liked. There was a flash of hope and happiness in her mind, and with a sudden impulse of gaiety she did what she had very often done before—stuck the rose in her hair a little above[2] the left ear. The tender admiration in Adam's face was slightly shadowed by reluctant disapproval. Hetty's love of finery was just the thing that would most provoke his mother, and he himself disliked it as much as it was possible for him to dislike anything that belonged to her.

"Ah," he said, "that's like the ladies in the pictures at the Chase; they've mostly got flowers or feathers or gold things i' their hair, but somehow I don't like to see 'em; they allays[3] [4] put me i' mind o'[5] the painted women

[5] in ⟨eight or⟩ nine {or ten} hours *MS*
[6] to-morrow; he's] to-morrow, for he's *MS*   [7] a] an *MS*
[8] too] *MS 1 to 8*   [9] now!" Adam] now," Adam *MS*   [1] didna] didn't *MS*
[2] little above] little way above *MS*   [3] allays] always *MS*
[4] always ⟨remind me⟩ put me i' mind *MS*   [5] o'] of *MS*

outside the shows at Treddles'on fair. What can a woman have[6] to set her off better than her own hair,[7] when it curls so, like yours?[8] If a woman's young and pretty, I think you can see her[9] good looks all the better for her being plain-dressed. Why, Dinah Morris looks very[1] nice, for all she wears such a plain cap and gown. It seems to me[2] as a woman's face[3] doesna want flowers; it's almost like a flower itself.[4] I'm sure yours is."

"O, very well," said Hetty, with a little playful[5] pout, taking the rose out of her hair. "I'll put one o' Dinah's caps on when we go in, and you'll see if I look better in it. She left one behind, so I can take the pattern."

"Nay, nay, I don't want you to wear a Methodist cap like Dinah's. I dare say it's a very ugly cap, and I used to think when I saw her here, as it was nonsense for her to dress different t'[6] other people; but I never rightly noticed her till she came to see mother last week, and then I thought the cap seemed to fit her face somehow[7] as th' acorn-cup fits th' acorn, and I shouldn't like to see her so well without it. But you've got another sort o' face; I'd have you just as you are now, without anything t' interfere with your own looks. It's like when a man's singing a good tune, you don't want t' hear bells tinkling and interfering wi' the sound."

He took her arm and put it within his again, looking down on her fondly. He was afraid she should think he had lectured her; imagining, as we are apt to do, that she had perceived all the thoughts he had only half expressed. And the thing he dreaded most was lest any cloud should come over this evening's happiness. For the world he would not have spoken of his love to Hetty yet, till this commencing kindness towards him should have grown into unmistakeable love. In his imagination he saw long years of his future life stretching before him, blest with the right to call Hetty his own: he could be content with very little at present. So he took up the basket of currants[8] once more, and they went on towards the house.

The scene had quite changed in the half-hour that Adam had been in the garden. The yard was full of life now: Marty was letting the screaming geese through the gate, and wickedly provoking the gander by hissing at him; the granary door was groaning on its hinges as Alick shut it, after dealing out the corn; the horses were being let[9] out to watering, amidst much barking of all the three dogs, and many "whups" from Tim the ploughman, as if the heavy animals who held down their meek, intelligent heads, and lifted their shaggy feet so deliberately, were likely to rush wildly

[6] have ⟨prettier⟩ to set her off better *MS*   [7] hair, ⟨&⟩ when *MS*
[8] yours? ⟨it's a pity to put anything in it, I think⟩ If ⟨When⟩ a woman's young & pretty, I think *MS*
[9] her ⟨prettiness⟩ good looks *MS*   [1] very ⟨pretty⟩ nice *MS*
[2] me ⟨somehow⟩ as *MS*   [3] face ⟨is⟩ doesn't want flowers; it's *MS*
[4] flower {itself.} ⟨and yours looks all the better⟩ I'm sure yours is." *MS*
[5] playful] *added in MS*   [6] t'] from *MS*   [7] somehow ⟨as well⟩ as th' *MS*
[8] of currants] *added in MS*   [9] let] *MS 1* led *8*

in every direction but the right. Everybody was come back from the meadow; and when Hetty and Adam entered the house-place, Mr Poyser was seated in the three-cornered chair, and the grandfather in the large arm-chair opposite, looking on with pleasant expectation while the supper was being laid on the oak table. Mrs Poyser had laid the cloth herself—a cloth made of homespun linen, with a shining chequered pattern on it, and of an agreeable whitey-brown hue, such as all sensible housewives like[1] to see—none[2] of your bleached "shop-rag" that would wear into holes in no time, but good homespun that would last for two generations. The cold veal, the fresh lettuces, and the stuffed chine, might well look tempting to hungry men who had dined at half past twelve o'clock. On the large deal table against the wall there were bright pewter plates and spoons and cans, ready for Alick and his companions; for the master and servants ate their supper not far off each other; which was all the pleasanter, because if a remark about to-morrow morning's work occurred to Mr Poyser, Alick was at hand to hear it.

"Well, Adam, I'm glad to see ye[3]," said Mr Poyser. "What! ye've[4] been helping Hetty to gether the currans, eh ? Come, sit ye down, sit ye down. Why, it's pretty near a three-week since y'[5] had your supper with[6] us; and[7] the missis has got one of her rare stuffed chines. I'm glad ye're[8] come."

"Hetty," said Mrs Poyser, as she looked into the basket of currants to see if the fruit was fine, "run upstairs, and send Molly down. She's putting Totty to bed, and I want her to draw th' ale, for Nancy's busy yet i' the dairy. You can see to the child. But whativer did you let her run away from you along wi' Tommy for, and stuff herself wi' fruit as she can't eat a bit o' good victual?"

This was said in a lower tone than usual, while her husband was talking to Adam; for Mrs Poyser was strict in adherence to her own rules of propriety, and she considered that a young girl was not to be treated sharply in the presence of a respectable man who was courting her. That would not be fair play: every[9] woman was young in her turn, and had her chances of matrimony, which it was a point of honour for other women not to spoil—just as one market-woman who has sold her own eggs must not try to balk another of a customer.

Hetty made haste to run away upstairs, not easily finding an answer to her aunt's question, and Mrs Poyser went out to see after[1] Marty and Tommy, and bring them in to[2] supper.

Soon they were all seated—the two rosy lads,[3] one on each side, by the pale mother, a place being left for Hetty between Adam and her uncle.

[1] like] liked *MS 1*   [2] see—none] see—it was none *MS*
[3] ye] you *MS*   [4] ye've] you've *MS*   [5] y'] ye *MS*
[6] with] wi' *MS 1* ⟨wi'⟩ with *8*   [7] us; and] us. And *MS*   [8] ye're] you're *MS*
[9] play: every] play. Every *MS*   [1] after ⟨the⟩ Marty *MS*
[2] in to] into *Cabinet*   [3] lads ⟨were seated⟩ one on each side *MS*

Alick too was come in, and was seated in his far corner, eating cold broad beans out of a large dish with his pocket-knife, and finding a flavour in them which he would not have exchanged for the finest pineapple.

"What a time that gell is drawing th' ale, to be sure," said[4] Mrs Poyser, when she was dispensing her slices of stuffed chine. "I think she sets the jug under and forgets to turn the tap, as there's nothing you can't believe o' them wenches: they'll set th'[5] empty kettle o' the fire, and then come an hour after to see if the water boils."

"She's drawin'[6] for the men too," said Mr Poyser. "Thee[7] shouldst ha' told her to bring our jug up first."

"Told her?" said Mrs Poyser: "yes[8], I might spend all the wind i' my body, an' take the bellows too, if I was to tell them gells everything as their own sharpness wonna[9] tell 'em. Mr Bede, will[1] you take some vinegar with your lettuce? Ay, you're i' the right not. It spoils the flavour o' the chine, to my thinking. It's poor eating where the flavour o' the meat lies i' the cruets. There's folks as make bad butter, and trusten to the salt t' hide it."

Mrs Poyser's attention was here diverted by the appearance of Molly, carrying a large jug, two small mugs, and four drinking-cans, all full of ale or small beer—an interesting example of the prehensile power possessed by the human hand. Poor Molly's mouth was rather wider open than usual, as she walked along with her eyes fixed on the double cluster of vessels in her hands, quite innocent of the expression in her mistress's eye.

"Molly, I niver knew your equils—to think o' your poor mother as is a widow, an' I took you wi' as good as no character, an' the times an' times I've told you" . . . .

Molly had not seen the lightning, and the thunder shook her nerves the more for the want of that preparation. With a vague alarmed sense that she must somehow comport herself differently, she hastened her step a little towards the far deal table, where she might set down her cans—caught her foot in her apron, which had become untied, and fell with a crash and a splash into a pool of beer; whereupon a tittering explosion from Marty and Tommy, and a serious "Ello!" from Mr Poyser, who saw his draught of ale unpleasantly deferred.

"There you go!" resumed Mrs Poyser, in a cutting tone, as she rose and went towards the cupboard while Molly began dolefully to pick up the fragments of pottery. "It's what I told you 'ud come, over and over again; and[2] there's your month's wage gone, an'[3] more, to pay for that jug as I've had i' the house this ten year, and nothing ever happened to 't before; but the crockery you've broke sin' here in th' house you've been 'ud make a

[4] sure," said] sure!" said *Cabinet*   [5] th'] the *Cabinet*
[6] drawin'] drawing *MS*   [7] Poyser. "Thee] Poyser, "Thee *MS*
[8] yes] Yis *MS* yis *1* ⟨yis⟩ yes *8*   [9] wonna] wont *MS*   [1] will] wont *MS*
[2] and] an *MS*   [3] an'] and *Cabinet*

parson swear—God forgi' me for saying so; an' if it had been boiling wort out o' the copper, it 'ud ha' been the same, and you'd ha' been scalded, and very like lamed for life, as there's no knowing but what you will be some day if you go on; for anybody 'ud think you'd got the St Vitus's Dance, to see the things you've throwed down. It's[4] a pity but what the bits was stacked up for you to see, though it's neither seeing nor hearing as 'ull make much odds to you—anybody 'ud think you war case-hardened."

Poor Molly's tears were dropping fast by this time, and in her desperation at the lively movement of the beer-stream towards Alick's legs, she was[5] converting her apron into a mop, while Mrs Poyser,[6] opening the cupboard, turned a blighting eye upon her.

"Ah," she went on, "you'll do no good wi' crying an'[7] making more wet to wipe up. It's all your own wilfulness, as I tell you, for there's nobody no call to break anything if they'll only go the right way to work. But wooden folks had need ha' wooden things t' handle. And here must I take the brown-and-white jug, as it's never[8] been used three times this year, and go down i' the cellar myself, and belike catch my death, and be laid up wi' inflammation". . . .

Mrs Poyser had turned round from the cupboard with the brown-and-white jug in her hand, when she caught sight of something at the other end of the kitchen; perhaps[9] it was because she was already trembling and nervous that the apparition had so strong an effect on her; perhaps jug-breaking, like other crimes, has a contagious influence. However[1] it was, she stared and started like a ghost-seer, and the precious brown-and-white jug fell to the ground, parting for ever with its spout and handle.

"Did ever anybody see the like?" she said, with a suddenly-lowered tone, after a moment's bewildered glance round the room. "The jugs are bewitched, *I* think. It's them nasty glazed handles—they slip o'er the finger like a snail."

"Why, thee'st let thy own whip fly i' thy face," said her husband, who had now joined in the laugh of the young ones.

"It's all very fine to look on and grin," rejoined Mrs Poyser; "but there's times when the crockery seems alive, an' flies out o' your hand like a bird. It's like the glass, sometimes, 'ull crack as it stands. What is to be broke *will* be broke, for I never dropped a thing i' my life for want o' holding it, else I should never ha' kept the crockery all these 'ears as I bought at my own wedding. And Hetty, are you mad? Whatever do you mean by coming down i' that way, and making one think as there's a ghost a-walking i' th' house?"

A new outbreak of laughter, while Mrs Poyser was speaking, was caused, less by her sudden conversion to a fatalistic view of jug-breaking, than by

⁴ down. It's] down—it's *MS*   ⁵ was ⟨turning⟩ converting *MS*
⁶ Poyser, ⟨as she⟩ open⟨ed⟩ {ing} the *MS*   ⁷ an'] & *MS*
⁸ never] niver *Cabinet*   ⁹ perhaps ⟨pe⟩ {it} was *MS*
¹ influence. However] influence—however *MS*

that strange appearance of Hetty, which had startled her aunt.[2] The little
minx had found a black gown of her aunt's, and pinned it close round her
neck to look like Dinah's, had made her hair as flat as she could, and had tied
on one of Dinah's high-crowned,[3] borderless net caps. The thought of
Dinah's pale grave face and mild grey eyes, which the sight of the gown and
cap brought with it, made it a laughable surprise enough to see them
replaced by Hetty's round rosy cheeks and coquettish dark eyes. The
boys got off their chairs and jumped round her, clapping their hands, and
even Alick gave a low ventral laugh as he looked up from his beans. Under
cover of the noise,[4] Mrs Poyser went into the back kitchen to send Nancy
into the cellar with the great pewter measure, which had some chance of
being free from bewitchment.

"Why, Hetty, lass, are ye turned Methodist?" said Mr Poyser, with that
comfortable slow enjoyment of a laugh which one only sees in stout people.
"You[5] must[6] pull your face a deal longer before you'll do for one; mustna[7]
she, Adam? How come you to put them things on, eh?"

"Adam said he liked Dinah's cap and gown better nor my clothes," said
Hetty, sitting down demurely. "He says folks look better in ugly clothes."

"Nay, nay," said Adam, looking at her admiringly; "I only said they
seemed to suit Dinah. But if I'd said you'd look pretty in 'em, I should ha'[8]
said nothing but what was true."

"Why, thee thought'st Hetty war a ghost, didstna?" said Mr Poyser to
his wife, who now came back and took her seat again. "Thee look'dst as
scared as scared."

"It little sinnifies how I looked," said Mrs Poyser; "looks 'ull mend no
jugs, nor laughing neither, as I see. Mr Bede, I'm sorry you've to wait so
long for your ale, but it's coming in a minute. Make yourself at home wi'
th'[9] cold potatoes; I[1] know you like 'em. Tommy, I'll send you to bed this
minute, if you don't give over laughing. What is there to laugh at, I should
like to know? I'd sooner cry nor laugh at the sight o' that poor thing's cap;
and there's them as 'ud be better if they could make[2] theirselves like her i'
more ways nor putting on her cap. It little becomes anybody i' this house to
make fun o' my sister's child, an' her just gone away from us, as it went to
my heart to part wi' her: an' I know one thing, as if trouble was to come, an' I
was[3] to be laid up i' my bed, an' the children was to die—as there's no
knowing but what they will—an' the murrain was to come among the cattle
again, an' everything went to rack an' ruin—I say we might be glad to get
sight o' Dinah's cap again, wi' her own face under it, border or no border.

---

[2] aunt. ⟨Hetty now⟩ The *MS*   [3] high-crowned,] *MS* high-crowned *1 8*
[4] Under cover of the noise,] *added in MS*   [5] people. "You] people, "You *MS*
[6] must ⟨put⟩ pull *MS*   [7] mustna] mustn't *MS*   [8] ha'] have *MS*
[9] th'] the *MS 1*   [1] I ⟨see⟩ know *MS*   [2] make ⟨themselves⟩ theirselves *MS*
[3] was] war *MS 1* ⟨war⟩ was *8*

For she's one o' them things as looks the brightest[4] on a rainy day,[5] and loves you the best when you're most i' need on't."

[6]Mrs Poyser, you perceive, was aware that nothing would be so likely to expel the comic as the terrible.[7] Tommy, who was of a susceptible disposition, and very fond of his mother, and who had, besides, eaten so many cherries as to have his feelings less under command than usual, was so affected by[8] the dreadful picture she had made of the possible future, that he began to cry; and the good-natured father, indulgent to all weaknesses but those of negligent farmers, said to Hetty,

"[9]You'd better take the things off again, my lass;[1] it hurts your aunt to see 'em."

Hetty went upstairs again, and the arrival of the ale made an agreeable diversion; for Adam had to give his opinion of the new tap, which could not be otherwise than complimentary to Mrs Poyser; and then followed a discussion on the secrets of good brewing, the folly of stinginess in "hopping," and the doubtful economy of a farmer's making his own malt. Mrs Poyser had so many opportunities of expressing herself with weight on these subjects, that by the time supper was ended, the ale-jug refilled, and Mr Poyser's pipe alight, she was once more in high good humour, and ready, at Adam's request, to fetch the broken spinning-wheel for[2] his inspection.

"Ah," said Adam, looking at it carefully, "here's a nice bit o' turning wanted. It's[3] a pretty wheel. I must have it up at the turning-shop in the village, and do it there, for I've no[4] convenence for turning at home. If you'll send it to Mr Burge's shop i' the morning, I'll get it done for you by Wednesday. I've been turning it over in my mind," he continued,[5] looking at Mr Poyser, "to make a bit more convenence at home for nice jobs o' cabinet-making. I've always done a deal at such little things in odd hours, and[6] they're profitable, for there's more workmanship nor material in 'em. I look for me and Seth to get a[7] little business for ourselves i' that way, for I know a man at Rosseter as 'ull take as many things as we should make, besides what we could get orders for round about."

Mr Poyser entered with interest into a project which seemed a step towards Adam's becoming a "master-man;" and Mrs Poyser gave her approbation to the scheme of the movable[8] kitchen cupboard, which was

---

[4] brightest ⟨when nigh⟩ on *MS*

[5] day, ⟨& folks [two words] [?this] dark world sometimes⟩ & loves you the best when you're most i' need on't." *MS*

[6] ¶ Mrs. Poyser, you perceive, was aware that nothing would be so likely to expel the comic as the terrible{.} ⟨, & the necessity for recovering her dignity⟩] *added on verso of MS 11. 86*

[7] terrible.] *New paragraph in MS 1*   [8] by] *added in MS*   [9] "⟨T⟩You'd *MS*

[1] lass; ⟨your⟩ it *MS*   [2] for ⟨its⟩ his *MS*   [3] wanted. It's] wanted—it's *MS*

[4] no ⟨convenience⟩ convenence *MS*   [5] continued, ⟨"to make a⟩ looking *MS*

[6] and ⟨their⟩ they're *MS*   [7] a ⟨good bit⟩ little *MS*   [8] moveable] *added in MS*

to be capable of containing grocery, pickles, crockery, and house-linen, in the utmost compactness, without confusion. Hetty, once more in her own dress, with her neckerchief pushed a little backwards on[9] this warm evening, was seated picking currants near the window, where Adam could see her quite well. And so the[1] time passed pleasantly till[2] Adam got up to go. He was pressed to come again soon, but not to stay longer, for at this busy time sensible people would not run the risk of being sleepy at five o'clock in the morning.

"I shall take a step farther," said Adam, "and go on to see[3] Mester Massey, for he wasn't at church[4] yesterday, and I've not seen him for a week past. I've never hardly known him to miss church before."

"Ay," said Mr Poyser, "we've heared nothing about him, for it's the boys' hollodays now, so we can give you no account."

"But you'll niver think o' going there at this hour o' th'[5] night?" said Mrs Poyser, folding up her knitting.

"O, Mester Massey sits up late," said Adam. "An' the night-school's[6] not over yet. Some o' the men don't come till late—they've got so far to walk. And Bartle himself 's never in bed till it's gone eleven."

"I wouldna[7] have him to live wi' me, then," said Mrs Poyser, "a-dropping candle-grease about, as you're like to tumble down o' the floor the first thing i' the morning."

"Ay, eleven o'clock's late—it's late," said old Martin. "I ne'er sot up so i' *my* life, not to say as it warna a marr'in', or a christenin', or a wake, or th' harvest supper. Eleven o'clock's late."

"Why, I sit up till after twelve often," said Adam, laughing, "but it isn't t' eat and drink extry, it's to work extry. Good night, Mrs Poyser; good night[8], Hetty."

Hetty[9] could only smile and not shake hands, for hers were dyed and damp with currant-juice; but all the rest gave a hearty shake to the large palm that was held out to them, and said, "Come again, come again!"

"Ay, think o' that now," said Mr Poyser, when Adam was out on the causeway. "Sitting up till past twelve to do extry work! Ye'll not find many men o' six-an'-twenty as 'ull do to put i' the shafts wi' him. If you can catch

---

[9] backwards on] backwarder ⟨in⟩ on *MS*
[1] the ⟨next half hour⟩ time passed pleasantly *MS*
[2] till ⟨the forward clock declared it to be half past nine &⟩ Adam *MS*
[3] see ⟨Mr.⟩ Mester *MS*
[4] church ⟨on Sunday—I doubt he's⟩ yesterday, & I've not seen *MS*   [5] th'] the *Cabinet*
[6] night-] *added in MS*   [7] wouldna] wouldn't *MS*
[8] Poyser; good night] Poyser. Good night *MS*
[9] Hetty could⟨n't⟩ only smile & not *MS*

Adam for a husband, Hetty, you'll ride i'[1] your own spring-cart some day, I'll be your warrant."

Hetty was moving across the kitchen with the currants, so her uncle did not see the little toss of the head with which she answered him. To ride in a spring-cart seemed a very miserable lot indeed to her now.

[1] i'] in *MS*

CHAPTER XXI.

THE NIGHT-SCHOOL AND THE SCHOOLMASTER.

Bartle Massey's was one of[1] a few scattered houses on the edge of a common, which was divided by the road to Treddleston. Adam reached it in a quarter of an hour after leaving the Hall Farm; and when he had his hand on the door-latch, he could see, through the curtainless window,[2] that there were eight or nine heads bending over the desks, lighted by thin dips.

When he entered, a reading lesson was going forward, and Bartle Massey merely nodded[3], leaving him to take his place where he pleased. He had not come for the sake of a lesson to-night, and his mind was too full of personal matters, too full of the last two hours he had passed in Hetty's presence, for him to amuse himself with a book till school was over; so he sat down in a corner, and looked on with an absent mind. It was a sort of scene which Adam had beheld almost weekly for years; he knew by heart every arabesque flourish in the framed specimen of Bartle Massey's handwriting which hung over the schoolmaster's head, by way of keeping a lofty ideal before the minds of his pupils; he knew the backs of all the books on the shelf running along the whitewashed wall above the pegs for the slates; he knew exactly how many grains were gone out of the ear of Indian corn that hung[4] from one of the rafters; he had long ago exhausted the resources of[5] his imagination in trying to think how the bunch of leathery sea-weed had[6] looked and grown in its native element; and from the place where he sat, he could make nothing of the old map of England that hung against the opposite wall, for age had turned it of a fine yellow brown, something like that of a well-seasoned meerschaum. The drama that was going on was almost as familiar as[7] the scene, nevertheless habit had not made him indifferent to it, and even in his present self-absorbed mood, Adam felt a momentary stirring of the old fellow-feeling, as he looked at the rough men painfully holding pen or pencil with their cramped hands, or humbly labouring through their reading lesson.

The reading class now seated on the form in front of the schoolmaster's desk, consisted of the three most backward pupils. Adam would have known it,[8] only by seeing Bartle Massey's face as he looked over his

[1] of ⟨the⟩ a *MS*   [2] window ⟨he could see⟩ that *MS*
[3] nodded ⟨to Adam⟩, leaving *MS*   [4] hung ⟨from ⟨⟨over⟩⟩ the rafters⟩ from one *MS*
[5] the resources of] *added in MS*   [6] had] *added in MS*
[7] familiar as] *added in MS*   [8] it,] that *MS*

spectacles, which he had shifted to the ridge of his nose, not requiring them for present purposes. The face wore its mildest expression: the grizzled bushy eyebrows had taken their more acute angle of compassionate kindness, and the mouth, habitually compressed with a pout of the lower lip, was relaxed so as to be ready to speak a helpful word or syllable in a moment. This gentle expression was the more interesting because the schoolmaster's nose, an irregular aquiline twisted a little on one side, had rather a formidable character; and his brow, moreover, had that peculiar tension which always impresses one as a sign of a keen impatient temperament: the blue veins stood out like cords under the transparent yellow skin, and this intimidating brow was softened by no tendency to baldness, for the grey bristly[9] hair, cut down to about an inch in length, stood round it in as close ranks as ever.[1]

"Nay, Bill, nay," Bartle was saying, in a kind tone, as he nodded to Adam, "begin that again, and then perhaps it'll come to you what d, r, y, spells. It's the same lesson you read last week, you know."

"Bill" was a sturdy fellow, aged four-and-twenty, an excellent stone-sawyer, who could get as good wages as any man in the trade of his years; but he found a[2] reading lesson in words of one syllable[3] a harder matter to deal with than the hardest stone he had ever had to saw. The letters, he complained, were so "uncommon alike[4], there was no tellin' 'em one from another," the[5] sawyer's business not being concerned with minute differences such as exist between a letter with its tail turned up and a letter with its tail turned down. But Bill had a firm determination that he would learn to read, founded chiefly on two reasons: first, that Tom Hazelow, his cousin, could read anything "right off," whether it was print or writing, and Tom had sent him a letter from twenty miles off, saying how he was prospering in the world, and had got an overlooker's place; secondly, that Sam Phillips, who sawed with him, had learned to read when he was turned twenty; and what could be done by a little fellow like Sam Phillips, Bill considered, could be done by himself, seeing that he could pound Sam into wet clay if circumstances required it. So here he was, pointing his big finger towards three words at once, and turning his head on one side that he might keep better hold with his eye of the one word which was to be discriminated out of the group. The amount of knowledge Bartle Massey must possess was something so dim and vast that Bill's imagination recoiled before it: he

---

[9] bristly] *added in MS*

[1] ever. ⟨Perhaps too the fact that the proud man sat forward in that ⟨⟨a⟩⟩ painful way which indicated that there was a slight hump between the [?broad &] [?pain] shoulders, made the gentle encouraging look more impressive as anyone will believe [?so], who has ever been surprised by a glance of selfforgetful kindness where he expected to see the lines of bitter sadness,⟩ ¶ "Nay *MS*

[2] a] *added in MS*   [3] syllable a⟨s⟩ hard{er} ⟨a⟩ matter *MS*

[4] alike⟨"⟩, there was no tellin⟨g⟩{'} 'em *MS*   [5] the ⟨stonesawyer's⟩ sawyer's *MS*

would hardly have ventured to deny that the schoolmaster might have something to do in bringing about the regular return of daylight and the changes in the weather.

The man seated next to Bill was of a very different type: he was a Methodist brickmaker, who, after spending thirty years of his life in perfect satisfaction with his ignorance, had lately "got religion," and along with it the desire to read the Bible. But with him, too, learning was a heavy business, and on his way out to-night he had offered as usual a special prayer for help, seeing that he had undertaken this hard task with a single eye to the nourishment of his soul—that he might have a greater abundance of texts and hymns wherewith to banish evil memories and the temptations of old habit; or, in brief language, the devil. For the brickmaker had been a notorious poacher, and was suspected, though there was no good evidence against him, of being the man who had shot[6] a neighbouring gamekeeper in the leg. However that might be, it is certain that shortly after the accident referred to, which was coincident with the arrival of an awakening Methodist preacher at Treddleston, a great change had been observed in the brickmaker; and though he was still known in the neighbourhood by his old sobriquet[7] of "Brimstone," there was nothing he held in so much horror as any farther[8] transactions with that evil-smelling element. He was a broad-chested fellow with a fervid temperament, which[9] helped him better in[1] imbibing religious ideas than in the dry process of acquiring the mere human knowledge of the alphabet. Indeed, he had been already a little shaken in his resolution by a brother Methodist, who assured him that the letter was a mere obstruction to the Spirit, and expressed a fear that Brimstone was too eager for the knowledge that puffeth up.

The third beginner was a much more promising pupil. He was a tall[2] but thin and wiry man, nearly as old as Brimstone, with a very pale face, and hands stained a deep blue. He was a dyer, who in the course of dipping homespun wool and old women's petticoats, had got fired with the ambition to learn a great deal more about the strange secrets of colour. He had already a high reputation in the district for his dyes, and he was bent on discovering some method by which he could reduce the expense of crimsons and scarlets. The druggist at Treddleston had given him a notion that he might save himself a great deal of labour and expense if he could learn to read, and so he had[3] begun to give his spare hours to the night-school,

---

[6] shot ⟨M^r. Donnithorne's⟩ a neighbouring *MS*

[7] sobriquet] soubriquet *MS soubriquet Cabinet*

[8] farther] further *MS*   [9] which ⟨had⟩ helped *MS*

[1] in ⟨dangerous expeditions on "a shiny night"⟩ imbibing religious ideas than in the dry *MS*

[2] tall ⟨wiry man⟩, but *MS*

[3] had ⟨set to work at this task very heartily in his⟩ begun *MS*

resolving that his "little chap" should lose no time in coming to Mr Massey's day-school as soon as he was old enough.

It was touching to see these three big men, with the marks of their hard labour about them, anxiously bending over the worn books, and painfully making out, "The grass is green," "The sticks are dry," "The corn is ripe"—a very hard lesson to pass to after[4] columns of single words all alike except in the first letter. It was almost as if three rough animals were making humble efforts to learn how they might become human. And it touched the tenderest fibre in Bartle Massey's nature, for such full-grown children as these were the only pupils for whom he had no severe epithets, and no impatient tones. He was not gifted with an imperturbable temper, and on music-nights it was apparent that patience could never be an easy virtue to him; but this evening, as he glances over his spectacles at Bill Downes, the sawyer, who is turning his head on one side with a desperate sense of blankness before the letters d, r, y, his eyes shed their mildest and most encouraging light.

After the reading class, two youths, between sixteen and nineteen, came up with imaginary bills of parcels, which they had been writing out on their slates, and were now required to calculate "off-hand"—a test which they stood with such imperfect success that Bartle Massey, whose eyes had been glaring at them ominously through his spectacles for some minutes, at length burst out in a bitter, high-pitched tone, pausing between every sentence to rap the floor with a knobbed stick which rested between his legs.

"Now, you see, you don't do this thing a bit better than you did a fortnight ago; and I'll tell you what's the reason. You want to learn accounts; that's well and good. But you think all you need do to learn accounts is to come to me and do sums for an hour or so, two or three times a week; and no sooner do you get your caps on and turn out of doors again, than you sweep the whole thing clean out of your mind. You go whistling about, and take no more care what you're thinking of than if your heads were gutters for any rubbish to swill through that happened to be in the way; and if you get a good notion in 'em, it's pretty soon washed out again. You think knowledge is to be got cheap—you'll come and pay Bartle Massey sixpence a week, and he'll make you clever at figures without your taking any trouble. But knowledge isn't to be got with paying sixpence, let me tell you: if you're to know figures, you must turn[5] 'em over in your own heads[6], and keep your thoughts fixed on 'em. There's nothing you can't turn into a sum, for there's nothing but what's got number in it—even a fool. You may say to yourselves, 'I'm one fool, and Jack's another; if my fool's head weighed four pound, and Jack's three pound three ounces and three quarters, how many pennyweights heavier[7]

---

[4] after ⟨a⟩ column{s} of *MS*   [5] turn ⟨th⟩{'}em over *MS*
[6] your own heads] your heads *Cabinet*   [7] heavier] *added in MS*

would my head[8] be than Jack's?' A man that had got his heart in learning figures would make sums for himself, and work 'em in his head: when he sat at his shoemaking, he'd count his stitches by fives, and then put a price on his stitches, say half a farthing, and then see how much money he could get in an hour; and then ask himself how much money he'd get in a day at that rate; and then how much ten workmen would get working three, or twenty, or a hundred years at that rate—and all the while his needle would be going just as fast as if he left his head empty for the devil to dance in. But the long and the short of it is—I'll have nobody in my night-school that doesn't strive to learn what he comes to learn, as hard as if he was striving to get out of a dark hole into broad daylight. I'll send no man away because he's stupid: if Billy Taft, the idiot, wanted to learn anything, I'd not refuse to teach him. But I'll not throw away good knowledge on people who think they can get it by the sixpenn'orth[9], and carry it away with 'em as they would an ounce of snuff. So never come to me again, if you can't show that you've been working with your own heads, instead of thinking you can pay for mine to work for you. That's the last word I've got to say to you."

With this final sentence, Bartle Massey gave a sharper rap than ever with his knobbed stick, and the discomfited lads got up to go with a sulky look. The other pupils had happily only their writing-books to show, in various stages of progress from pot-hooks to round text; and mere pen-strokes, however perverse, were less exasperating to Bartle than false arithmetic. He was a little more severe than usual on Jacob Storey's Z's, of which poor Jacob[1] had written a pageful, all with their tops turned the wrong way, with a puzzled sense that they were not right "somehow." But he[2] observed in apology, that it was a letter you never wanted hardly, and he thought it had only been put there "to finish off th' alphabet, like, though ampus-and (&) would ha' done as well, for what he could see."

At last the pupils had all taken their hats and said their "Good-nights," and Adam, knowing his old master's habits, rose and said, "Shall I put the candles out, Mr Massey?"

"Yes, my boy, yes, all but this, which I'll carry into the house; and just lock the outer door, now you're near it," said Bartle, getting his stick in the fitting[3] angle to help him in descending from his stool. He was no sooner on the ground than it became obvious why the stick was[4] necessary—the left leg was much shorter than the right. But the schoolmaster was so active with his lameness, that it was hardly thought of as a misfortune; and if you had seen him make his way along the schoolroom floor, and up the step into his kitchen, you would perhaps have understood why the naughty boys

---

[8] my head] my ⟨hea⟩ fool's head *MS*   [9] sixpenn'orth] sixpennorth *MS*
[1] poor Jacob] he *MS*   [2] he] Jacob *MS*   [3] fitting] right *MS*
[4] was ⟨so⟩ necessary *MS*

sometimes felt that his pace might[5] be indefinitely quickened, and that he and his stick might overtake them even in their swiftest run.

The moment he appeared at the kitchen door with the candle in his hand, a faint whimpering began in the chimney-corner, and a brown-and[6]-tan-coloured bitch, of that wise-looking breed with short legs and long body, known to an unmechanical generation as turnspits, came creeping along the floor, wagging her tail, and hesitating at every other step, as if her affections were painfully divided between the hamper in the chimney-corner and the master, whom she could not leave without a greeting.

"Well, Vixen, well[7] then, how are the babbies?" said the schoolmaster, making haste towards the chimney-corner, and holding the candle over the low hamper, where two extremely blind puppies lifted up their heads towards the light, from a nest of flannel and wool. Vixen could not[8] even see her master look at them without painful excitement: she got into the hamper and got out again the next moment, and behaved with true feminine folly, though looking all the while as wise as a dwarf with a large old-fashioned head and body on the most abbreviated[9] legs.

"Why, you've got a family, I see, Mr Massey?" said Adam, smiling, as he came into the kitchen. "How's that? I thought it was against the law here."

"Law? What's the use o'[1] law when a man's once such a fool as to let a woman into his house?" said Bartle, turning away from the hamper with some bitterness. He always called Vixen a woman, and seemed to have lost all consciousness that he was using a figure of speech. "If I'd known Vixen was a woman, I'd never have held the boys from drowning her; but when I'd got her into my hand, I was forced to take to her. And now you see what she's brought me to—the sly, hypocritical wench"—Bartle spoke these last words in a rasping tone of reproach, and looked at Vixen, who poked down her head and turned up her eyes towards him with a keen sense of opprobrium—"and contrived to be brought to bed on a Sunday at church-time. I've wished again and again I'd been a bloody-minded man, that I could have strangled the mother and the brats with one cord."

"I'm glad it was no worse a cause kept you from church," said Adam. "I was afraid you must be ill for the first time i'[2] your life. And I was particular sorry not to have you at church yesterday."

"Ah, my boy, I know why, I know why," said Bartle, kindly, going up to Adam, and raising his hand up to the shoulder that was almost on a level with his own head. "You've had a rough bit o' road to get over since I saw you—a rough bit o' road. But I'm in hopes there are better times coming for you. I've got some news to tell you. But I must get my supper first, for I'm hungry, I'm hungry. Sit down, sit down."

⁵ might] *added in MS*   ⁶ brown &] *added in MS*   ⁷ well ⟨say⟩ then *MS*
⁸ could not] couldn't *MS*   ⁹ abbreviated ⟨hind⟩ legs *MS*   ¹ o'] of *MS*
² i'] in *MS*

Bartle went into his little pantry, and brought out[3] an excellent home-baked loaf; for it was his one extravagance in these dear times to eat bread once a day instead of oat-cake; and he justified it by observing, that what a schoolmaster wanted was brains, and oat-cake ran too much to bone instead of brains. Then came a piece of cheese and a quart jug with a crown of foam upon it. He placed them all on the round deal table which stood against his large arm-chair in the chimney-corner, with Vixen's hamper on one side of it, and a window shelf with a few books piled up in it on the other. The table was as clean as if Vixen had been an excellent housewife in a chequered apron; so was the quarry floor; and the old carved oaken press, table, and chairs, which in these days would be bought at a high price in aristocratic houses, though, in that period of spider-legs and inlaid cupids, Bartle had got them for an old song, were as free from dust as things could be at the end of a summer's day.

"Now, then, my boy, draw up, draw up. We'll not talk about business till[4] we've had our supper. No man can be wise on an empty stomach. But," said Bartle, rising from his chair again, "I must give Vixen her supper too, confound her! though[5] she'll do nothing with it but nourish those un-necessary babbies. That's the way with these women, they've got no head-pieces to nourish, and so their food all runs either to fat or to brats."

He brought out of the pantry a dish of scraps, which Vixen at once fixed her eyes on, and jumped out of her hamper to lick up with the utmost despatch.

"I've had my supper, Mr Massey," said Adam, "so I'll look on while you eat yours. I've been at the Hall Farm, and they always have their supper betimes, you know: they don't keep your late hours."

"I know little about their hours," said Bartle, dryly, cutting his bread and not shrinking from the crust. "It's[6] a house I seldom go into, though I'm fond of the boys, and Martin Poyser's a good fellow. There's too many women in the house for me: I hate the sound of women's voices; they're always either a-buzz or a-squeak, always either a-buzz or a-squeak. Mrs Poyser keeps at the top o'[7] the talk, like a fife; and as for the young lasses, I'd as soon look at water-grubs—I know what they'll turn to—stinging gnats, stinging gnats. Here, take some ale, my boy: it's been drawn for you, it's been drawn for you."

"Nay, Mr Massey," said Adam, who took his old friend's whim more seriously than usual to-night, "don't be so hard on the creaturs[8] God has made to be companions for us. A working man 'ud be badly off without a wife to see to th'[9] house and the victual, and make things clean and comfortable."

---

[3] out ⟨first⟩ an MS   [4] till we'⟨re⟩ve had MS   [5] her! though] her; though MS
[6] crust. "It's] MS 1 crust. {"}It's 8   [7] o'] of MS   [8] creaturs] creatures MS
[9] th'] the MS

"Nonsense! It's the silliest lie a sensible man like you ever believed, to say a woman makes a house comfortable. It's a story got up, because the women are there, and something must be found for 'em to do.[1] I tell you there isn't a thing under the sun that needs to be done at all, but what a man can do better than a woman, unless it's bearing children, and they do that in a poor make-shift way; it had better ha'[2] been left to the men—it had better ha'[3] been left to the men. I tell you, a woman 'ull[4] bake you a pie every week of her life, and never come to see that the hotter th' oven the shorter the time. I tell you, a woman 'ull[5] make your porridge every day for twenty years, and never think of measuring the proportion between the meal and the milk—a little more or less, she'll think, doesn't signify: the porridge *will* be awk'ard now and then: if it's wrong, it's summat in the meal, or it's summat in the milk, or it's summat in the water. Look at me! I make my own bread, and there's no difference between one batch and another from year's end to year's end; but if I'd got any other woman besides Vixen in the house, I must pray to the Lord every baking to give me patience if the bread turned out heavy. And as for cleanliness, my house is cleaner than any other house on the Common, though the[6] half of 'em swarm with women. Will Baker's lad comes to help me in a morning, and we get as much cleaning done in one hour without any fuss, as a woman 'ud get done in three, and all the while be sending buckets o' water after your ankles, and let the fender and the fire-irons stand in the middle o'[7] the floor half the day, for you to[8] break your shins against 'em. Don't tell me about God having made such creatures to be companions for us! I don't say but He might make Eve to be a companion to Adam in Paradise—there was no cooking to be spoilt there, and no other woman to cackle with and make mischief; though you see what mischief she did as soon as she'd an opportunity. But it's an impious, unscriptural opinion to say a woman's a blessing to a man now; you might as well say adders and wasps, and bugs[9] and wild beasts, are a blessing, when they're only the evils that belong to this state o'[1] probation, which it's lawful for a man to keep as clear of as he can in this life, hoping to get quit of 'em for ever in another—hoping to get quit of 'em for ever in another."

Bartle had become so excited and angry in the course of his invective that he had forgotten his supper, and only used the knife for the purpose of rapping the table with the haft. But towards the close, the raps became[2] so sharp and frequent, and his voice so quarrelsome, that Vixen felt it incumbent on her to jump out of the hamper and bark vaguely.

[1] do.] do—something must be found for 'em to do. *MS*   [2] ha'] have *MS*
[3] ha'] have *MS*   [4] 'ull] will *MS*   [5] 'ull] will *MS*   [6] the] they *MS*
[7] o'] of *MS*   [8] for you to] that you might *MS*
[9] bugs] *MS* hogs *1* ⟨hogs⟩ foxes *8*   [1] o'] of *MS*   [2] became] *MS 1* because *8*

"Quiet, Vixen!" snarled Bartle, turning round upon her. "You're like the rest o' the women—always putting in *your* word before you know why."

Vixen returned to her hamper again in humiliation, and her master continued his supper in a silence which Adam did not choose to interrupt; he knew the old man would be in a better humour when he had had his supper and lighted his pipe. Adam was used to hear him talk in this way, but had never learned so much of Bartle's past life as to know whether his view of married[3] comfort was founded on experience. On that point Bartle was mute; and it was even a secret where he had lived previous to the twenty years in which, happily for the peasants and artisans of this neighbourhood, he had been settled among them as their only schoolmaster. If anything like a question was ventured on this subject, Bartle always replied, "O, I've seen many places—I've been a deal in the south"—and the[4] Loamshire men would as soon have thought[5] of asking for a particular town or village in Africa as in "the south."

"Now then, my boy," said Bartle, at last, when he had poured out his second mug of ale and lighted his pipe—"now then, we'll have a little talk. But tell me first, have you heard any particular news to-day?"

"No," said Adam, "not as I remember."

"Ah, they'll keep it close, they'll keep it close, I dare say.[6] But I found it out by chance; and it's news that may concern you, Adam, else I'm a man that don't know a superficial square foot from a solid."

Here Bartle gave a series of fierce and rapid puffs, looking earnestly the while at Adam. Your impatient loquacious man has never any notion of keeping his pipe alight by gentle measured puffs; he is always letting it go nearly out, and then punishing it for that negligence. At last he said,

"Satchell's got a paralytic stroke. I[7] found it out from the lad they sent to Treddleston for the doctor, before seven o'clock this morning. He's a good way beyond sixty, you know; it's much if he gets over it."

"Well," said Adam, "I dare say there'd be more rejoicing than sorrow in the parish at his being laid up. He's been a selfish, tale-bearing, mischievous fellow; but, after all, there's nobody he's done so much harm to as to th' old Squire. Though it's the Squire himself as is to blame—making a stupid fellow like that a[8] sort o' man-of-all-work, just to save th' expense of having a proper steward to look after th' estate. And he's lost more by ill-management o' the woods, I'll be bound, than 'ud pay for two stewards.[9]

---

[3] married ⟨life⟩ comfort *MS*   [4] the ⟨inhabitants of⟩ Loamshire {men} would *MS*
[5] thought ⟨have⟩ of *MS*
[6] say. ⟨When the fox has got lamed, his wife doesn't send word of it to the cocks & hens.⟩ But *MS*
[7] stroke—I ⟨got ⟨⟨it⟩⟩ from⟩ found *MS*   [8] a ⟨man⟩ sort *MS*
[9] stewards. ⟨But as⟩ If *MS*

If he's laid on the shelf, it's to be hoped he'll make way for a better man, but I don't see how it's like to make any difference to me."

"But I see it, but I see it," said Bartle; "and others besides me. The Captain's coming of age now—you know that as well as I do—and it's to be expected he'll have a little more voice in things. And I know, and you know too, what 'ud be the Captain's wish about the woods, if there was a fair opportunity for making a change.[1] He's said in plenty of people's hearing that he'd make you manager of the woods to-morrow, if he'd the power. Why, Carroll[2], Mr Irwine's butler, heard him say so to the parson not many days ago. Carroll[3] looked in when we were smoking our pipes o' Saturday[4] night at Casson's, and he told us about it; and whenever[5] anybody says a good word for you, the parson's ready to back it, that I'll answer for. It was pretty well talked over, I can tell you, at Casson's, and one and another had their fling at you; for if donkeys set to work to sing, you're pretty sure what the tune 'll be."

"Why, did they talk it over before Mr Burge?" said Adam; "or wasn't he there o' Saturday?"

"O, he went away before Carroll[6] came; and Casson[7]—he's always for setting other folks right, you know—[8]would have it Burge was the[9] man to have the management of the woods. 'A[1] substantial man,' says he, 'with pretty near sixty years' experience o' timber: it 'ud be all very well for Adam Bede to act under him, but it isn't to be supposed the Squire 'ud appoint a young fellow like[2] Adam, when there's his elders and betters at hand!' But[3] I said, 'That's a pretty notion o'[4] yours, Casson. Why[5], Burge is the man to *buy*[6] timber; would you put the woods into his hands, and let him make his own bargains? I think you don't leave your customers to score their own drink, do you? And as for[7] age, what that's worth depends on the quality o' the liquor. It's pretty well known who's the backbone of Jonathan Burge's business.'"

"I thank you for your good word, Mr Massey," said Adam. "But, for all that, Casson was partly i' the right for once. There's not much likelihood that th' old Squire 'ud ever consent t' employ me: I offended him about two years ago, and he's never forgiven me."

"Why, how was that? You never told me about it," said Bartle.

---

[1] change{.} ⟨, as there's a good chance⟩ He's said in plenty of *MS*
[2] Carroll] Carrol *MS*   [3] Carroll] Carrol *MS*   [4] Saturday ⟨evening⟩ night *MS*
[5] whenever] wherever *MS*   [6] Carroll] Carrol *MS*
[7] Casson ⟨, who's⟩—he's *MS*   [8] you know—] *added in MS*
[9] the ⟨right⟩ man *MS*   [1] woods. 'A] woods—'a *MS*
[2] like ⟨him over the ⟨⟨h⟩⟩ heads of his elders⟩ Adam when there's his elders & betters *MS*
[3] hand!' But] hand.' But *MS*
[4] o'] of *MS*   [5] Casson. Why] Casson; why *MS*   [6] buy ⟨half o' the⟩ timber *MS*
[7] for ⟨experience⟩ age *MS*

"O, it was a bit o' nonsense. I'd made a[8] frame for a screen for Miss Lyddy—she's allays[9] making something with her worsted-work, you know—and she'd given me particular orders about this screen, and there was as much talking and measuring as if we'd been planning a house. However, it was a nice bit o' work, and I liked doing it for her. But, you know, those little friggling things take a deal o' time. I[1] only worked at it in over-hours—often late at night—and I had to go to Treddleston over an' over again, about little bits o' brass nails and such gear; and I turned the little knobs and the legs, and carved th' open work, after a pattern, as nice as could be. And I was uncommon pleased with it when it was done. And when I took it home, Miss Lyddy[2] sent for me to bring it into her drawing-room[3], so as she might give me directions about fastening on the work—very fine needlework,[4] Jacob and Rachel a-kissing one another among the sheep[5], like a picture—and th' old Squire was sitting there, for he mostly sits with her. Well, she was mighty pleased with the screen, and then she wanted to know what pay she was to give me. I didn't speak at random—you know it's not my way; I'd calculated pretty close, though I hadn't made out a bill, and I said, one[6] pound thirteen. That was paying for the mater'als and paying me, but none too much, for my work. Th' old Squire looked up at this, and peered in his way at the screen, and said, 'One pound thirteen for a gimcrack like that! Lydia, my dear, if you must spend money on these things, why don't you get them at Rosseter, instead of paying double price for clumsy work here? Such[7] things are not work for a carpenter like Adam. Give him a guinea, and no more.' Well, Miss Lyddy[8], I reckon, believed what he told her, and she's not over-fond o' parting with the money herself—she's not a bad woman at bottom, but she's been brought up under his thumb; so she began fidgeting with her purse, and turned as red as her ribbon. But I made a bow, and[9] said, 'No, thank you, madam; I'll make you a present o' the screen, if you please. I've charged the regular price for my work, and I know it's done well; and I know, begging his honour's pardon, that you couldn't get such a screen at Rosseter under two guineas. I'm willing to give you my work—it's been done in my own time, and nobody's got anything to do with it but me; but if I'm paid, I can't take a smaller price than I asked, because that 'ud be like saying, I'd asked more than was just. With your leave, madam, I'll bid you good morning.' I made my bow and went out before she'd time to say any more, for she stood with the purse in her hand, looking almost foolish. I didn't mean to be disrespectful, and I spoke as polite as I could; but I can give in to no man, if he

[8] a ⟨bit of a⟩ frame *MS*   [9] allays] alys *MS*   [1] time. I] time: I *MS*

[2] Lyddy] Lydia *MS*   [3] drawing-room] sitting-room *MS*

[4] needlework, ⟨a lady & gentleman⟩ Jacob & Rachel *MS*

[5] among the sheep] *added in MS*   [6] said, one] *MS 1* said one *8*

[7] here? Such] here. Such *MS 1*   [8] Lyddy] Lydia *MS*   [9] & ⟨side⟩ said *MS*

wants to make it out as I'm trying t'[1] overreach him. And in the[2] evening the footman brought me the one pound thirteen wrapped in paper. But since then I've seen pretty clear as th' old Squire can't abide me."

"That's likely enough, that's likely enough," said Bartle, meditatively. "The only way to bring him round would be to show him what was for his own interest, and that the Captain may do—that the Captain may do."

"Nay, I don't know," said Adam; "the[3] Squire's 'cute enough, but it takes something else besides 'cuteness to make folks see what'll be their interest in the long run. It takes some conscience and belief in right and wrong, I see that pretty clear. You'd hardly ever bring round th' old Squire to believe he'd gain as much in a straitfor'ard[4] way as by tricks and turns. And, besides, I've not much mind to work under him: I don't want to quarrel with any gentleman, more particular an old gentleman turned eighty, and I know we couldn't agree long. If the Captain was master o' th' estate, it 'ud be different: he's got a conscience and a will to do right, and I'd sooner work for him nor for any man living."

"Well, well, my boy, if good luck knocks at your door, don't you put your head out at window and tell it to be gone about its business, that's all. You must learn to deal with odd and even in life, as well as in figures. I tell you now, as I told you ten years ago, when you pommelled young Mike Holdsworth for wanting to pass a bad shilling, before you knew whether he was in jest or earnest—you're over-hasty and proud, and apt to set your teeth against folks that don't square to your notions. It's no harm for me[5] to be a bit fiery and stiff-backed: I'm an old schoolmaster, and shall never want to get on to a higher perch. But where's the use of all the time I've spent in teaching you writing and mapping and mensuration, if you're not to get for'ard in the world, and show folks[6] there's some advantage in having a head on your shoulders, instead of a turnip? Do you mean[7] to go on turning up[8] your nose at every opportunity, because it's got a bit of a smell about it that nobody[9] finds out but yourself? It's as foolish as that notion o' yours that a wife is to make a working man comfortable. Stuff and nonsense!— stuff[1] and nonsense![2] Leave that to fools that never got beyond a sum in simple addition. Simple addition enough! Add one fool to another fool, and in six years' time six fools more—they're all of the same denomination, big and little's nothing to do with the sum!"

During this rather heated exhortation to coolness and discretion the pipe had gone out, and Bartle[3] gave the climax to his speech[4] by striking a light

[1] t'] to *Cabinet*   [2] the] th' *MS*   [3] Adam; "the] Adam. "The *MS*

[4] straitfor'ard] strait forrard *MS* straightfor'ard *Cabinet*

[5] *me*] *MS 1* ⟨me⟩ me *8*   [6] folks] *MS 1* ⟨folk's⟩ folks *8*

[7] mean ⟨you⟩ to $\overline{MS}$ [8] up] *added in MS*   [9] nobody ⟨foun⟩ finds *MS*

[1] nonsense!—stuff] nonsense! Stuff *MS*   [2] nonsense! ⟨Its⟩ Leave *MS*

[3] Bartle ⟨found a⟩ gave the *MS*   [4] speech ⟨in⟩ by *MS*

furiously, after[5] which he puffed with fierce resolution, fixing his eye still on Adam, who was trying not to laugh.

"There's a good deal o' sense in what you say, Mr Massey," Adam began, as soon as he felt quite serious, "as there always is. But you'll give in that it's no business o' mine to be building on chances that may never happen. What I've got to do is to work as well as I can with the tools and mater'als I've got in my hands. If a good chance comes to me, I'll think o' what you've been saying; but till then, I've got nothing to do but to trust to my own hands and my own head-piece. I'm turning over a little plan for Seth and me to go into the cabinet-making a bit by ourselves, and win a[6] extra pound or two in that way. But it's getting late now—it'll be pretty near eleven[7] before I'm at home, and mother may happen to lie awake; she's more fidgety nor usual now. So I'll bid you good night."

"Well, well, we'll go to the gate with you—it's a fine night," said Bartle, taking up his stick. Vixen was at once on her legs, and without further words the three walked out into the starlight, by the side of Bartle's potato-beds, to the little gate.

"Come to the music o'[8] Friday night, if you can, my boy," said the old man, as he closed the gate after Adam, and leaned against it.

"Ay, ay," said Adam, striding along towards the streak of pale road. He was the only object moving on the wide common. The two grey donkeys, just visible in front of the gorse bushes,[9] stood as still as limestone images— as still as the grey-thatched roof of the mud cottage a little farther[1] on. Bartle kept his eye on the moving figure till it passed into the darkness, while Vixen, in a state of divided affection, had twice run back to the house to bestow a parenthetic lick on her puppies.

"Ay, ay," muttered the schoolmaster, as Adam disappeared; "there you go, stalking along—stalking along; but you wouldn't have been what you are if you hadn't had a bit of old lame Bartle inside you. The strongest calf must have something to suck at. There's plenty of these big, lumbering fellows 'ud never have known their A B C, if it hadn't been for Bartle Massey. Well, well, Vixen, you foolish wench, what is it, what is it? I must go in, must I? Ay, ay, I'm never to have a will o' my own any more. And those pups, what do you think I'm to do with 'em, when they're twice as big as you?—for[2] I'm pretty sure the father was that hulking bull-terrier of Will Baker's—wasn't he now, eh, you sly hussey?" (Here Vixen tucked her tail

---

[5] by striking a light furiously,] by lighting a match furiously against the hob, *MS 1* by {striking a} light⟨ing a match⟩ furiously ⟨against the hob⟩ {between the [?brass]} ⟨between the [?brass]⟩, *8*

[6] a] an *MS*   [7] pretty near eleven] pretty eleven *MS*   [8] o'] on *MS*

[9] bushes ⟨were⟩ stood *MS*   [1] farther] further *MS*   [2] you?—for] you? For *MS*

between her legs, and ran forward into the house.[3] Subjects are sometimes
broached which a well-bred female will ignore.)

"But where's the use of talking to a woman with babbies?" continued
Bartle: "she's[4] got no conscience—no conscience—it's all run to milk."[5]

[3] house. ⟨There are some⟩ ⟨s⟩Subjects *MS*
[4] babbies?" continued Bartle: "she's] babbies? She's *MS*
[5] milk."] milk!" *MS 1*

BOOK THIRD

*

CHAPTER XXII.

GOING TO THE BIRTHDAY FEAST.

The[1] thirtieth of July was come, and it was one of those half-dozen warm days which sometimes occur in the middle of a rainy English summer. No rain had fallen for the last three or four days, and the weather was perfect for that time of the year: there was less dust than usual on the dark-green hedgerows, and on the wild camomile that starred the roadside, yet the grass was dry enough for the little children to roll on it, and there was no cloud but a long dash of light, downy ripple, high, high up in the far-off blue sky. Perfect weather for an outdoor July[2] merrymaking, yet surely not[3] the best time of year to be born in. Nature seems to make a hot pause just then—all the loveliest flowers are gone; the sweet time of early growth and vague hopes is past; and yet the time of harvest and ingathering is not come, and we tremble at the possible storms that may[4] ruin the precious fruit in the moment of its ripeness. The woods are all one dark monotonous green; the waggon-loads of hay no longer creep along the lanes, scattering[5] their sweet-smelling fragments on the blackberry branches; the[6] pastures are often[7] a little tanned, yet the corn has not got its last splendour of red and gold; the lambs and calves have lost all traces of their innocent frisky prettiness, and have become stupid young sheep and cows.[8] But it is a time of leisure on the farm—that pause between hay and corn-harvest, and so the farmers and labourers in Hayslope and Broxton thought the Captain did well to come of age just then, when they could give their undivided minds to the flavour of the great cask of ale which had been brewed the autumn after "the heir" was born, and was to be tapped on his twenty-first birthday.[9] The air had been merry with the ringing of church-bells very

[1] The ⟨thirtieth⟩ ⟨twenty fifth⟩ thirtieth of July was come ⟨.⟩ {& it was one of those ⟨hot⟩ {half dozen warm} days which sometimes occur in the middle of a rainy English summer.} No *MS*

[2] July] *added in MS*   [3] not ⟨a lovely⟩ the best *MS*

[4] may ⟨break down⟩ {ruin} the precious fruit ⟨& ruin it⟩ in *MS*

[5] scattering ⟨delicious scents & delicious morsels for⟩ their sweet smelling fragments on *MS*

[6] the ⟨shorn meadows⟩ pastures *MS*   [7] often] *added in MS*

[8] cows. ⟨Yet it⟩ But *MS*

[9] when they could give their undivided minds to the flavour of the great cask of ale which had been brewed ⟨when⟩ the autumn after "the heir" was born & was to be tapped on his twenty first birthday.] *added on verso of MS 11. 116*

early this morning, and every one had made haste to get through[1] the
needful work before[2] twelve, when it would be time to think of[3] getting
ready to go to the Chase.

The mid-day sun was streaming into Hetty's bed-chamber, and there
was no blind to temper the heat with which it fell on her head as she looked
at herself in the old specked glass. Still, that was the only glass she had in
which she could see her neck and arms, for the small hanging glass she had
fetched out of the next room—the room that had been Dinah's—would
show her nothing below her little chin, and that beautiful bit of neck where
the roundness of her cheek[4] melted into another roundness shadowed by
dark delicate curls. And to-day she thought more than usual about her neck
and arms; for at the dance this evening she was not to wear any neckerchief,
and she had been busy yesterday with her spotted pink-and-white frock,
that she might make the sleeves either long or short at will. She was dressed
now just as she was to be in the evening, with a tucker made of "real" lace,
which her aunt had lent her for this unparalleled occasion, but with no
ornaments besides; she had even taken out her small round ear-rings which
she wore every day. But there was something more to be done, apparently,
before she put on her neckerchief and long sleeves, which she was to wear in
the day-time, for now she unlocked the drawer that held her private
treasures. It is more than a month since we saw her unlock that drawer
before, and now it holds new treasures, so much more precious than the old
ones that these are thrust into the corner. Hetty would not care to put the
large coloured glass ear-rings into her ears now; for see! she[5] has got a
beautiful pair of gold and pearls and garnet, lying snugly in a pretty little
box lined with white satin. O the delight of taking out that little box and
looking at the ear-rings![6] Do not reason about it, my philosophical reader,[7]
and say that Hetty, being very pretty,[8] must have known that it did not
signify whether she had on any ornaments or not; and that, moreover, to
look at ear-rings which she could not possibly wear out of her bedroom
could hardly be a satisfaction,[9] the essence of vanity being a reference to the
impressions produced on others; you will never understand women's
natures if you are so excessively rational. Try rather to divest yourself of
all your rational prejudices, as much as if you were studying the psychology
of a[1] canary-bird, and only watch the movements of this pretty round
creature as she turns her head on one side with an unconscious smile at the
ear-rings nestled in the little box. Ah, you think, it is for the sake of the

[1] through ⟨all⟩ the MS   [2] before ⟨half past eleven⟩ twelve, MS
[3] of ⟨putting⟩ getting MS   [4] of her cheek] added in MS
[5] see! she] see, she MS   [6] ear-rings! ⟨Please⟩ {Do} not to reason MS
[7] my philosophical reader,] added in MS   [8] pretty, ⟨might⟩ must MS
[9] satisfaction, ⟨vanity⟩ the MS
[1] a ⟨?golden nigh[t]⟩ ⟨humming⟩ ⟨or a⟩ canary-bird MS

person who has given them to her, and her thoughts are gone back now to the moment when they were put into her hands. No; else why should she have[2] cared to have ear-rings rather than anything else? and I know that she had longed for ear-rings from among all the ornaments she could imagine.

[3]"Little, little ears!" Arthur had said, pretending to pinch them one evening, as Hetty sat beside him on the grass without her hat. "I wish I had some pretty ear-rings!" she said in a moment, almost before she knew what she was saying—the wish lay so close to her lips, it *would* flutter past them at the slightest breath. And the next day—it was only last week—Arthur had ridden over to Rosseter on purpose to buy them. That little wish so naïvely[4] uttered, seemed to him the prettiest bit of childishness; he[5] had never heard anything like it before; and he had wrapped the box up in a great many covers, that he might see Hetty unwrapping it with growing curiosity, till at last her eyes flashed back[6] their new delight into his.

No,[7] she was not thinking most of the giver when she smiled at the ear-rings, for[8] now she is taking them out of the box, not to press them to her lips, but to fasten them in her ears,—only for one moment, to see how pretty they look, as she peeps at[9] them in the glass against the wall, with first one position of the head and then another, like a listening bird. It is impossible to be wise on the subject of ear-rings as one looks at her; what should those delicate pearls and crystals be made for, if not for such ears? One cannot even find fault with the tiny round hole which they leave when they are taken out; perhaps water-nixies, and such lovely[1] things without souls, have these little round holes in their ears by nature, ready to hang jewels in. And Hetty must be one of them: it is too painful to think that she is a woman, with a woman's destiny before her—a woman spinning in[2] young ignorance a light web of folly and vain hopes which may one day close round her and press upon her, a rancorous poisoned garment, changing all at once her fluttering, trivial butterfly sensations into a life of deep human anguish.

But she[3] cannot keep in the ear-rings long, else she[4] may make her uncle and aunt wait. She puts them quickly into the box again, and shuts them up. Some day she will be able to wear any ear-rings she likes, and already she lives in an invisible world of brilliant costumes, shimmering gauze, soft satin, and velvet, such as the lady's-maid at the Chase has shown her in

[2] have ⟨chosen⟩ cared *MS*   [3] *Paragraph division added in 1.*
[4] naïvely ⟨?express⟩ uttered *MS*
[5] childishness; he] childishness—he *MS 1* childishness ⟨—⟩ {;} he *8*
[6] back ⟨into his all the⟩ their new *MS*
[7] No, ⟨it was not merely for the sake of the giver⟩ she was not thinking most of the giver *MS*
[8] for ⟨she presently took⟩ now she is taking *MS*   [9] at ⟨herself⟩ them *MS*
[1] lovely ⟨summer-like⟩ things *MS*
[2] in ⟨sad⟩ young *MS*   [3] she ⟨cannot⟩ ⟨could not⟩ ⟨cannot⟩ cannot *MS*
[4] she ⟨may keep⟩ ⟨might⟩ may make her uncle & aunt wait⟨ing⟩. She *MS*

Miss Lydia's wardrobe: she feels the bracelets on her arms, and treads on a soft carpet in front of a tall mirror. But she has[5] one thing in the drawer which she can venture to wear to-day, because she can hang it on the chain of dark-brown berries which she has been used to wear on grand days, with a tiny flat scent-bottle at the end of it tucked inside her frock; and she *must* put on her brown berries—her neck would look so unfinished without it. Hetty was not quite as fond of the locket as of the ear-rings, though it was a handsome large locket, with enamelled flowers at the back and a beautiful gold border round the glass, which showed a light brown, slightly-waving lock, forming a background for two little dark rings. She must keep it under her clothes, and no one would see it. But[6] Hetty had another passion; only a little less strong than her love of finery[7], and that other passion made her like to wear the locket even hidden in her bosom. She would always have worn it, if she had dared to encounter her aunt's questions about a ribbon round her neck. So now she[8] slipped it on along her chain of dark-brown berries, and snapped the chain round her neck.[9] It was not a very long chain, only allowing the locket to hang a little way below the edge of her frock. And now she had nothing to do but to put on her long sleeves, her new white[1] gauze neckerchief, and her straw hat[2] trimmed with white to-day instead of the[3] pink, which had become rather faded under the July sun. That hat made the drop of bitterness in Hetty's cup to-day, for it was not quite new—everybody would see that it was a little tanned against the white ribbon—and Mary Burge, she felt sure, would have a new hat or bonnet on. She looked for consolation at her fine white cotton stockings: they really were very nice indeed, and she had given almost all her spare money for them. Hetty's dream of the future could not make her insensible to triumph in[4] the present: to be sure,[5] Captain Donnithorne loved her so, that he would never care about looking at other people, but then those other people didn't know how he loved her, and she was not satisfied to appear shabby and insignificant in their eyes even for a short space.

[6]The whole party was assembled in the house-place when Hetty went down, all of course in their Sunday clothes; and the bells had been ringing so this morning in honour of the Captain's twenty-first[7] birthday, and the

---

[5] has ⟨something else⟩ one thing *MS*   [6] it. But] it; but *MS*

[7] finery ⟨things, & she would tell one person that she had it on⟩ ⟨the locket round⟩ ⟨on⟩ & that other passion made her like to wear the locket even hidden in her bosom. *MS*

[8] she ⟨strung⟩ slipped it on {along} her *MS*

[9] neck. ⟨The locket was a great deal heavier than the little scent bottle, so much heavier that it dragged down the chain in an uncomfortable way, & so Hetty took ⟨⟨taking⟩⟩ it off again and doubled the chain so that the locket might not sink so low. It was just within her frock.⟩ It was not a very long chain ⟨&⟩ only allow⟨ed⟩ {ing} the locket to hang a little way below the edge of her frock. And now she had nothing to do but to ⟨fasten⟩ put *MS*

[1] white] *added in MS*   [2] & her straw hat] *added in MS*   [3] the] *added in MS*

[4] triumph in] *added in MS*   [5] sure, ⟨Arthur⟩ Captain Donnithorne *MS*

[6] ⟨She hastened down into⟩ The *MS*   [7] twenty first] *added in MS*

work had all been got done so early, that Marty and Tommy were not quite easy in their minds until their mother had assured them that going to church was not part of the day's festivities. Mr Poyser had once suggested that the house should be shut up, and left to take care of itself;[8] "for," said he, "there's no danger of anybody's breaking in—everybody[9] 'll be at the Chase, thieves an' all. If we lock th' house up,[1] all the men can go: it's a day they wonna[2] see twice i' their lives." But Mrs Poyser answered with great decision: "I never[3] left th' house to take care of itself since I was a missis, and I never[4] will. There's been ill-looking tramps[5] enoo' about the[6] place this last week, to carry off every[7] ham an' every[8] spoon we'n got;[9] and they all collogue together, them tramps, as it's a[1] mercy they hanna come and pisoned[2] the dogs and murdered us all in our beds afore we knowed, some Friday night when[3] we'n got the money in th' house to pay the men. And it's like enough the tramps know where we're going as well as we do oursens; for if[4] Old Harry wants any work done, you may be sure he'll find the means."

"Nonsense about murdering us in our beds," said Mr Poyser; "I've got a gun i'[5] our room, hanna[6] I? and thee'st got ears as 'ud find it out[7] if a mouse was gnawing the bacon. Howiver, if thee[8] wouldstna be easy,[9] Alick can stay at home i' the fore-part o' the day,[1] and Tim can come back tow'rds[2] five o'clock, and let[3] Alick have his turn. They may let Growler loose if anybody offers to do mischief, and there's Alick's dog, too, ready enough to set his tooth in a tramp if Alick gives him a wink."

Mrs Poyser accepted this compromise, but thought it advisable to bar and bolt to the utmost; and now, at the last moment before starting, Nancy, the dairymaid, was closing the shutters of the house-place, although the[4] window, lying under the immediate observation of Alick and the dogs, might have been supposed the least likely to be selected for a burglarious attempt.

The covered cart, without springs, was standing ready to carry the whole family except the men-servants: Mr Poyser and the grandfather sat on the seat in front, and within there was room for all the women and children; the

[8] & left to take care of itself,] *added in MS*
[9] everybody] iverybody *MS 1* ⟨iverybody⟩ everybody *8*
[1] up, ⟨[?then all the servants]⟩ all the men *MS*   [2] wonna] wont *MS*
[3] never] niver *MS 1* ⟨niver⟩ never *8*   [4] never] niver *MS 1*
[5] tramps ⟨anoo⟩ enoo *MS*   [6] the ⟨house⟩ place *MS*
[7] every] ivery *MS 1* ⟨ivery⟩ every *8*   [8] every] ivery *MS* every *1* ⟨ivery⟩ every *8*
[9] got; ⟨about⟩ and *MS*
[1] a ⟨massy⟩ mercy they ⟨haven't⟩ hanna come and ⟨murdered us⟩ pisoned *MS*
[2] pisoned] poisoned *Cabinet*   [3] when ⟨you'n⟩ we'n *MS*
[4] if ⟨the divil⟩ Old Harry *MS*   [5] i' ⟨my⟩ our *MS*   [6] hanna] ⟨ha'nt⟩ hadn't *MS*
[7] find it out] find out welly *MS*   [8] thee ⟨wouldstn't⟩ wouldstna *MS*
[9] easy, ⟨Nancy &⟩ Alick *MS*   [1] day, ⟨& Molly⟩ & *MS*   [2] tow'rds] tow'rts *MS*
[3] let ⟨th' others⟩ Alick have ⟨their⟩ his *MS*   [4] the] that *MS 1* ⟨that⟩ the *8*

fuller the cart the better, because then the jolting would not hurt so much, and Nancy's broad person and thick arms were an excellent cushion to be pitched on. But Mr Poyser drove at no more than a walking pace, that there might be as little risk of jolting as possible on this warm day; and there was time to exchange greetings and remarks with the foot-passengers who were going the same way, specking[5] the paths between the green meadows and the golden cornfields with bits of movable bright colour—a scarlet waist-coat to match the poppies that nodded a little too thickly among the corn, or a dark-blue neckerchief with ends flaunting[6] across a bran-new white smock-frock. All Broxton and all Hayslope were to be at the Chase, and make merry there in honour of "th' heir;" and the old men and women, who had never been so far down this side of the hill for the last twenty years, were being brought from Broxton and Hayslope in one of the farmer's[7] waggons, at Mr Irwine's suggestion. The church-bells had struck up again now—a last tune, before the ringers came down the hill to have their share in[8] the festival; and before the bells had finished, other music was heard approaching, so that even Old Brown, the sober horse that was drawing Mr Poyser's cart, began to prick up his ears. It was the band of the Benefit Club, which had mustered in all its glory; that is to say, in bright-blue scarfs and blue favours, and carrying its banner with the motto, "Let brotherly love continue," encircling a picture of a stone-pit.

The carts, of course, were not to enter the Chase. Every one must get down at the lodges, and the vehicles must be sent back.

"Why, the Chase is like a fair a'ready," said[9] Mrs Poyser, as she got down from the cart, and saw the groups scattered under the great oaks, and the boys running about in the hot sunshine to survey the tall poles surmounted by the fluttering garments that were to be the prize of the successful climbers. "I should ha' thought there wasna[1] so many people i' the two parishes. Mercy[2] on us! how hot it is out o' the shade! Come here, Totty, else your little face 'ull be burnt to a scratchin'! They might ha' cooked the dinners i' that open space, an' saved the fires. I shall go to Mrs Best's room an'[3] sit down."

"Stop a bit, stop a bit," said Mr Poyser. "There's th'[4] waggin coming wi' th' old folks in't; it'll be such a sight as wonna[5] come o'er again, to see 'em get down an'[6] walk along all together. You remember some on 'em i' their prime, eh[7], father?"

"Ay, ay," said old Martin, walking slowly under the shade of the lodge porch, from which he could see the aged party descend. "I remember Jacob

⁵ specking] speckling *MS*   ⁶ flaunting ⟨against⟩ across *MS*
⁷ farmer's] farmers' *MS*   ⁸ in] of *MS*
⁹ a'ready," said] *MS 1* a'ready,{"} said *8*   ¹ wasna] wasn't *MS*
² Mercy] Massy *MS 1* ⟨Massy⟩ Mercy *8*   ³ an'] & *MS*   ⁴ th'] the *MS*
⁵ wonna] wont *MS*   ⁶ an'] & *MS*   ⁷ eh] dont you *MS*

Taft walking fifty mile after the Scotch raybels, when they turned back
from Stoniton."

He felt himself quite a youngster, with a long life before him, as he saw
the Hayslope patriarch, old Feyther Taft, descend from the waggon and
walk towards him, in his brown nightcap, and leaning on his two sticks.

"Well, Mester Taft," shouted old Martin, at the utmost stretch of his
voice,—for though he knew the old man was stone deaf, he could not omit
the propriety of a greeting,—"you're[8] hearty yet[9]. You can enjoy yoursen
to-day, for-all[1] you're ninety an' better."

"Your sarvant, mesters, your sarvant," said Feyther Taft in a treble
tone, perceiving that he was in company.

The aged group, under care of sons or daughters, themselves worn and
grey, passed on along the least-winding carriage-road towards the house,
where a special table was prepared for them; while the Poyser party wisely
struck across the grass under the shade of the great trees, but not out of view
of the house-front, with its sloping lawn and flower-beds, or of the pretty
striped marquee at the edge of the lawn, standing at right angles with two
larger marquees on each side of the open green space where the games were
to be played. The house would have been nothing but a plain square
mansion of Queen Anne's time, but for the remnant of an old abbey to
which it was united at one end, in much the same way as one may sometimes
see a new farm-house rising high and prim at the end of older and lower
farm-offices. The fine old remnant stood a little backward and under the
shadow of tall beeches, but the sun was now[2] on the[3] taller and more
advanced front, the blinds were all down, and the house seemed asleep in
the hot midday: it made Hetty quite sad to look at it: Arthur must be
somewhere in the back rooms, with the grand company, where he could not
possibly know that she was come, and she should not see him for a long,
long while—not till after dinner, when they said he was to come up and
make a speech.

But Hetty was wrong in part of her conjecture. No grand company was
come except the Irwines, for whom the carriage had been sent early, and
Arthur was at that moment not in a back room, but walking with the Rector
into the broad stone cloisters of the old abbey, where the long tables were
laid for all the cottage tenants and the farm-servants. A very handsome
young Briton he looked to-day, in high spirits and a bright-blue frock-coat,
the highest mode—his arm no longer in a sling. So open-looking and
candid, too; but candid people have their secrets,[4] and secrets leave no
lines in young faces.

[8] greeting,—"you're] greeting. "You're *MS*   [9] yet] yit *MS 1* ⟨yit⟩ yet *8*
[1] for-all] for all *MS 1* for{-}all *8*   [2] was now] was just now *MS*
[3] the ⟨stately stone⟩ taller & more advanced *MS*   [4] secrets, ⟨which⟩ & secrets *MS*

"Upon my word," he said, as they entered the cool cloisters, "I think the cottagers have the best of it: these cloisters make a delightful dining-room on a hot day. That was capital advice of yours, Irwine, about the dinners—to let them be as orderly and comfortable as possible, and only for the tenants: especially as I had only a limited sum after all; for though my grandfather talked of a⁵ *carte blanche*, he couldn't make up his mind to trust me, when it came to the point."

"⁶Never mind, you'll give more pleasure in this quiet way," said Mr Irwine. "In this sort of thing people are constantly confounding liberality with riot and disorder. It sounds very grand to say that so many sheep and oxen were⁷ roasted whole, and everybody ate who liked to come; but in the end it generally happens that no one has had an enjoyable meal. If the people get a good dinner and a moderate quantity of ale in the middle of the day, they'll be able to enjoy the games as the day cools. You can't hinder some of them from getting too much towards evening, but drunkenness and darkness go better together than drunkenness and daylight."

"Well, I hope there won't be much of it. I've kept the Treddleston people away, by having a feast for them in the town; and I've got Casson and Adam Bede, and some other good fellows, to look to the giving out of ale in the booths, and to take care things don't go too far. Come, let us go up above now, and see the dinner-tables for the large tenants."

They went up the stone staircase leading simply to the long gallery above the cloisters, a gallery where all the dusty worthless old pictures had been banished for the last three generations—mouldy portraits of Queen Elizabeth and her ladies, General Monk with his eye knocked out, Daniel very much in the dark among the lions,⁸ and Julius Cæsar on horseback, with a high nose and laurel crown, holding his Commentaries in his hand.

"What a capital thing it is⁹ that they saved this piece of the old abbey," said¹ Arthur. "If I'm ever master here, I shall do up the gallery in first-rate style: we've got no room in the house a third as large as this. That second table is for the farmers' wives and children: Mrs Best said it would be more comfortable for the mothers and children to be by themselves. I was determined to have the children, and make a regular family thing of it. I shall be 'the old squire' to those little lads and lasses some day, and they'll tell their children what a much finer young fellow I was than my own son. There's a table for the women and children below as well. But you will see them all—you will come up with me after dinner, I hope?"

"Yes, to be sure," said Mr Irwine. "I² wouldn't miss your maiden speech to the tenantry."

---

⁵ a] *added in MS*   ⁶ "⟨Well⟩ Never mind *MS*   ⁷ were ⟨killed⟩ roasted *MS*
⁸ Daniel very much in the dark among the lions,] *added in MS*
⁹ thing it is] *added in MS*   ¹ abbey," said] abbey!" said *Cabinet*
² Irwine. "I] *MS 1* Irwine. {"}I *8*

"And there will be something else you'll like to hear," said Arthur. "Let us go into the library and I'll tell you all about it while[3] my grandfather is in the drawing-room with the ladies. Something that will surprise you," he continued, as they sat[4] down. "My grandfather has come round after all."

"What, about Adam?"

"Yes; I should have ridden over to tell you about it, only I was so busy. You know I told you I had quite given up arguing the matter with him—I thought it was hopeless; but yesterday morning he asked me to come in here to him before I went out, and astonished me by saying that he had decided on all the new arrangements he should make in consequence of old Satchell being obliged to lay by work, and that he intended to employ Adam in superintending the woods at a salary of a guinea a week, and the use of a pony to be kept here. I believe the secret of it is, he saw from the first it would be a profitable plan, but he had some particular dislike of Adam to get over—and besides, the fact that I propose a thing is generally a reason with him for rejecting it. There's the most curious contradiction in my grandfather: I know he means to leave me all the money he has saved, and he is likely enough to have cut off poor aunt Lydia, who has been a slave to him all her life, with only five hundred a year, for the sake of giving me all the more; and yet I sometimes think he positively hates me because I'm his heir. I believe if I were to break my neck, he would feel it the greatest misfortune that could befall him, and yet it seems a pleasure to him to make my life a series of petty annoyances."

"Ah, my boy, it is not only woman's[5] love that is $\dot{\alpha}\pi\acute{\epsilon}\rho\omega\tau o\varsigma\ \ddot{\epsilon}\rho\omega\varsigma$, as old Æschylus calls it. There's plenty of 'unloving love' in the world of a masculine kind. But tell me about Adam. Has he accepted the post? I don't see that it can be much more profitable than his present work, though, to be sure, it will leave him a good deal of time on his own hands."

"Well, I felt some doubt about it when I spoke to him, and he seemed to hesitate at first. His[6] objection was, that he thought he should not be able to satisfy my grandfather. But I begged him as a personal favour to me not to let any reason prevent him from accepting the place, if he really liked the employment, and would not be giving up anything that was more profitable to him. And he assured me he should like it of all things;—it would be a great step forward for him in business, and it would enable him to do what he had long wished to do—to give up working for Burge. He says he shall have plenty of time to superintend a little business of his own, which he and Seth will carry on, and will perhaps be able to enlarge by degrees. So he has agreed at last, and I[7] have arranged that he shall dine with the large tenants to-day; and I mean to announce the appointment to them, and ask them to drink Adam's health. It's a little drama I've got up in honour of my friend

---

[3] about it while] about while *MS*   [4] sat ⟨"Som⟩ down *MS*
[5] woman's] women's *MS*   [6] first. His] first; but his *MS*   [7] I ⟨mean⟩ have *MS*

Adam. He's a fine fellow, and I like the opportunity of letting people know that I think so."

"A drama in which friend Arthur piques himself on having a pretty part to play," said Mr Irwine, smiling. But when he saw Arthur colour, he went on relentlessly, "My part, you know, is always that of the old Fogy who sees nothing to admire in the young folks. I don't like to admit that I'm proud of my pupil when he does graceful things. But I must play the amiable old gentleman for once, and second your toast in honour of Adam.[8] Has your grandfather yielded on the other point too, and agreed to have a respectable man as steward?"

"O no," said Arthur, rising from his chair with an air of impatience, and walking along the room with[9] his hands in his pockets. "He's got some project or other about letting the Chase Farm, and bargaining for a supply of milk and butter for the house. But I ask no questions about it—it makes me too angry. I believe he means to do all the business himself, and have nothing in the shape of a steward. It's amazing what energy he has, though."

"Well, we'll go to the ladies now," said Mr Irwine, rising too. "I want to tell my mother what a splendid throne you've prepared for her under the marquee."

"Yes, and we must be going to luncheon too," said Arthur. "It must be two o'clock, for there is the gong beginning to sound for the tenants' dinners."

CHAPTER XXIII.

DINNER-TIME.

When Adam heard that he was to dine upstairs with the large tenants, he felt rather uncomfortable at the idea of being exalted in this way above his mother and Seth, who were to dine in the cloisters below. But Mr Mills, the butler, assured him that Captain Donnithorne had given particular orders about it, and would be very angry if Adam was not there.

Adam nodded, and went up to Seth, who was standing a few yards off. "Seth, lad," he said, "the Captain has sent to say I'm to dine upstairs—he wishes it particular, Mr Mills says, so I suppose it 'ud be behaving ill for me not to go. But I don't like sitting up above[1] thee and mother, as if I was better than my own flesh and blood.[2] Thee't not take it unkind, I hope?"

"Nay, nay, lad," said Seth, "thy honour's our honour; and[3] if thee get'st respect, thee'st won it by thy own deserts. The further I see thee above me, the better, so long as thee feel'st like a brother to me. It's because o' thy being appointed over the woods, and it's nothing but what's right. That's a place o' trust, and thee't above a common workman now."

"Ay," said Adam, "but nobody knows a word about it yet. I haven't given notice to Mr Burge about leaving him, and I don't like to tell anybody else about it before[4] he knows, for he'll be a good bit hurt, I doubt. People 'ull be wondering to see me there, and they'll like enough be guessing the reason, and asking questions, for there's been so much talk up and down about my having the place, this last three weeks[5]."

"Well, thee canst say thee wast ordered to come without being told the reason. That's the truth. And mother 'ull be fine and joyful about it.[6] Let's go and tell her."

Adam was not the only guest invited to come upstairs on other grounds than the amount he contributed to the rent-roll. There were other people in the two parishes who derived dignity from their functions rather than from their pocket, and of these Bartle Massey was one. His lame walk was rather slower than usual on this warm day, so[7] Adam lingered behind when the bell rang for dinner, that he might walk up with his old friend; for[8] he was a little too shy to join the Poyser party on this public occasion.[9]

---

[1] above ⟨you⟩ ⟨thee⟩ thee *MS*   [2] blood. ⟨You'll⟩ Thee't *MS*
[3] honour; and] honour. And *MS*   [4] before ⟨him⟩ he *MS*   [5] weeks] week *MS*
[6] it. ⟨I'll⟩ Let's *MS*   [7] so] & *MS*   [8] for ⟨Adam⟩ he *MS*
[9] occasion. ⟨He should have o⟩Opportunities *MS*

Opportunities of getting to Hetty's side would be sure to turn up in the course of the day, and[1] Adam contented himself with that, for he disliked any risk of being "joked" about Hetty;—the big, outspoken, fearless man was very shy and diffident[2] as to his love-making.

"Well, Mester Massey," said Adam, as Bartle came up, "I'm going to dine upstairs with you to-day: the Captain's sent me orders."

"Ah!" said[3] Bartle, pausing, with one hand on his back. "Then[4] there's something in the wind—there's something in the wind. Have you heard anything about what the old Squire means to do?"

"Why, yes," said Adam; "I'll tell you what I know, because I believe you can keep a still tongue in your head if you like; and[5] I hope you'll not let drop a word[6] till it's common talk, for I've particular reasons against its[7] being known."

"Trust to me, my boy, trust to me. I've got no wife to worm it out of me, and then run out and[8] cackle[9] it in everybody's hearing. If you trust a man, let him be a bachelor—let him be a bachelor."

"Well, then, it was so far settled yesterday, that I'm to take the management o' the woods. The Captain[1] sent for me, t' offer it me, when I was seeing to the poles and things here, and I've agreed to 't. But if anybody asks any questions[2] upstairs, just you take no notice, and turn the talk to something else, and I'll be obliged to you. Now, let us go on, for we're pretty nigh the last, I think."

"I know what to do, never fear," said Bartle, moving on. "The news will be good sauce to my dinner. Ay, ay, my boy, you'll get on. I'll back you for an eye at measuring, and a head-piece for figures, against any man in this county; and you've had good teaching—you've had good teaching."

When they got upstairs, the question which Arthur had left unsettled[3], as to who was to be president, and who vice,[4] was still under discussion, so that Adam's entrance passed without remark.

"It stands to sense,"[5] Mr Casson was saying, "as old Mr Poyser,[6] as is th' oldest man i' the room, should sit at[7] top o' the table.[8] I wasn't butler fifteen year without learning the rights and the wrongs about dinner[9]."

---

[1] & ⟨she had promised to dance with him in the evening⟩ Adam *MS*
[2] diffident ⟨about⟩ as to *MS*   [3] "Ah!" said] "Ah?" said *MS*
[4] back. "Then] back, "Then *MS*   [5] like; and] like. And *MS*
[6] word ⟨today,⟩ till it's common talk *MS*   [7] its] it's *MS*
[8] run out &] *added in MS*   [9] cackle ⟨it over the parish⟩ it in everybody's hearing *MS*
[1] Captain ⟨came [?out] t'offer it me⟩ sent for me *MS*
[2] questions ⟨when⟩ upstairs *MS*   [3] which Arthur had left unsettled] *added in MS*
[4] vice{,} ⟨president⟩ was *MS*   [5] sense," ⟨said⟩ Mr *MS*
[6] Poyser, ⟨who⟩ as *MS*   [7] at ⟨the⟩ top *MS*   [8] table. I'⟨ve not been⟩ wasn't *MS*
[9] dinners.{"} ⟨He's no 'casion to do hanything &⟩ ⟨his⟩ ⟨there's plenty can do the carving & the helping. But on a day like this, iverybody hes to be in their places."⟩ ¶ "Nay, *MS*

"Nay, nay," said old Martin, "I'n gi'en[1] up to my son; I'm no tenant now: let my son take my place. Th' ould foulks ha' had their turn: they mun make way for the young uns."

"I should ha' thought the biggest tenant had the best right, more nor th' oldest," said Luke Britton, who was not fond of the critical Mr Poyser; "there's Mester Holdsworth has more land nor anybody else on th' estate."

"Well," said[2] Mr Poyser, "suppose we say the man wi' the foulest land shall sit at top; then whoever[3] gets th' honour, there'll be no envying on him."

"Eh, here's Mester Massey," said Mr Craig, who, being a neutral[4] in the dispute, had no interest but in conciliation; "the schoolmaster ought to be able to tell you what's right. Who's to sit at top o' the table, Mr Massey?"

"Why, the broadest man," said Bartle; "and[5] then he won't take up other folks'[6] room; and[7] the next broadest must sit at bottom."

This happy mode of settling the dispute produced much laughter—a[8] smaller joke would have sufficed for that. Mr Casson, however, did not feel it compatible with his dignity and superior knowledge to join in the laugh, until it turned out that he was fixed on as the second broadest man. Martin Poyser, the younger, as the broadest, was to be president, and Mr Casson, as next broadest, was to be vice.

Owing to this arrangement, Adam, being, of course, at the bottom of the table, fell under the immediate observation of Mr Casson, who, too much occupied with the question of precedence, had not hitherto noticed his entrance. Mr Casson, we have seen, considered Adam "rather lifted up and peppery-like:" he thought the gentry made more fuss about this young carpenter than was necessary; they made no fuss about Mr Casson, although he had been an excellent butler for fifteen years.

"Well, Mr Bede, you're one o' them as mounts hup'ards[9] apace," he said, when Adam sat down. "You've niver dined here before, as I remember."

"No, Mr Casson," said Adam, in his strong voice, that could be heard along the table; "I've never dined here before, but I come by Captain Donnithorne's wish, and I hope it's not disagreeable to anybody here."

"Nay, nay," said several voices at once, "we're glad ye're come. Who's got anything to say again[1] it?"

"And ye'll sing us 'Over the hills and far away,' after dinner, wonna ye?" said Mr Chowne. "That's a song I'm uncommon fond on."

[1] gi'en] gen *MS*   [2] said ⟨Martin⟩ Mr Poyser, ⟨the younger⟩, "suppose *MS*
[3] whoever] whoiver *MS*   [4] neutral ⟨person⟩ in *MS*
[5] Bartle; "and] Bartle. "And *MS*   [6] folks'] folks's *MS* folk's *1* ⟨folk's⟩ folks' *8*
[7] room; and] room. And *MS*   [8] a ⟨much⟩ smaller *MS*
[9] mounts hup'ards] mount{s} up'ards *MS*   [1] again'] agen *MS*

"Peeh!" said Mr Craig; "it's² not to be named by side³ o' the Scotch tunes. I've never cared about singing myself; I've had something better to do. A man that's got the names and the natur o' plants in's head isna likely to keep a hollow place t' hold tunes in. But a second cousin o' mine, a drovier, was a rare hand at remembering the Scotch tunes. He'd got nothing else to think on."

"The Scotch tunes!" said Bartle Massey, contemptuously; "I've heard enough o' the Scotch tunes to last me while I live. They're fit for nothing but to frighten the birds with—that's to say, the English birds, for the Scotch birds may sing Scotch for what I know. Give the lads a bagpipes instead of a rattle, and I'll answer for it the corn 'll be safe."

"Yes, there's folks as find a pleasure in undervallying what they know but little about," said Mr Craig.

"Why, the Scotch tunes are just like a scolding, nagging woman," Bartle went on, without deigning to notice Mr Craig's remark. "They go on with the same thing over and over again, and never come to a reasonable end. Anybody 'ud think the Scotch tunes had⁴ always been⁵ asking a question of somebody as deaf as old Taft, and had never got an answer yet."

Adam minded the less about sitting by Mr Casson, because this position enabled him to see Hetty, who was not far off him at the next table. Hetty, however, had not even⁶ noticed his presence yet, for she was giving angry attention to Totty, who insisted on drawing up her feet on to the bench in antique fashion, and thereby threatened to make dusty marks on Hetty's pink-and-white frock. No sooner were the little fat legs pushed down than up they came again, for Totty's eyes were too busy in staring at the large dishes to see where the plum-pudding was, for her to retain any conscious-ness of her legs. Hetty got quite out of patience, and at last, with a frown and pout, and gathering tears, she said,

"O dear, aunt, I wish you'd speak to Totty, she keeps putting her legs up so, and messing my frock."

"What's the matter wi' the child? She can niver please you," said the mother. "Let her come by the side o' me, then: *I* can put up wi' her."

Adam was looking at Hetty, and saw the frown and pout, and the dark eyes seeming to grow larger with pettish half-gathered tears. Quiet Mary Burge, who sat near enough to see that Hetty was cross, and that⁷ Adam's eyes were fixed on her, thought that so sensible a man as Adam must be reflecting on the small value of beauty in a woman whose temper was bad. Mary was a good girl, not given to indulge in evil feelings, but she said to herself, that, since Hetty had a bad temper, it was better Adam should know

  ² Craig; "it's] Craig. "It's *MS*
  ³ by side] ⟨beside⟩ biside *MS* beside *1* ⟨beside⟩ by side *8*
  ⁴ Scotch tunes had] Scotch had *MS*   ⁵ been] being *MS*   ⁶ even] *added in MS*
  ⁷ that Adam{'s} ⟨was looking at her⟩ {eyes were fixed on} her *MS*

it. And it was quite true, that if Hetty had been plain she would have looked very ugly and unamiable at that moment, and no one's moral judgment upon her would have been in the least beguiled. But[8] really there was something quite charming in her pettishness: it looked so much more like innocent distress than ill-humour; and the severe Adam felt no movement of disapprobation; he only felt a sort of amused pity, as if he had seen a kitten setting up its[9] back, or a little bird with its feathers ruffled. He could not gather what was vexing her, but it was impossible to him to feel otherwise than that she was the prettiest thing in the world, and that if he could have his way, nothing should ever vex her any more. And presently, when Totty was gone, she caught his eye, and her face broke into one of its brightest smiles, as she nodded to him. It was a bit of flirtation: she knew Mary Burge was looking at them. But the smile was like wine to Adam.

[8] beguiled. But] beguiled; but *MS*   [9] its] it's *MS*

CHAPTER XXIV.

THE HEALTH-DRINKING.

When the dinner was over, and the first draughts from the great cask of birthday ale were brought up, room was made for the broad Mr Poyser at the side of the table, and two chairs were placed at the head. It had been settled very definitely what Mr Poyser was to do when the young Squire should appear, and for the last five minutes he had been in a state of abstraction, with his eyes fixed on the dark picture opposite, and his hands busy with the loose cash and other articles in his breeches pockets.

When the young Squire entered, with Mr Irwine by his side, every one stood up, and this moment of homage was very agreeable to Arthur. He liked to feel his own importance, and besides that, he cared a great deal for the goodwill of these people: he was fond of thinking that they had a hearty, special regard for him. The pleasure he felt was in his face as he said,

"My grandfather and I hope all our friends here[1] have enjoyed their dinner, and find my birthday ale good. Mr Irwine and I are come to taste it with you, and I'm sure we shall all like anything the better that the Rector shares with us."

All eyes were now turned on Mr Poyser, who, with his hands still busy in his pockets, began with the deliberateness of a slow-striking clock. "Captain[2], my neighbours have put it upo' me to speak for 'em to-day, for where folks think pretty much alike, one spokesman's as good as a score. And though we've mayhappen got contrairy ways o' thinking about a many things—one man lays down his land one way, an' another another—an' I'll not take it upon me to speak to no man's farming[3] but my own—this I'll say, as we're all o' one mind about our young Squire. We've pretty nigh all on us known you when you war a little un, an' we've niver known anything on you but what was good an' honourable. You speak fair an' y' act fair, an' we're joyful when we look forrard to your being our landlord, for we b'lieve you mean to do right by everybody, an' 'ull make no man's bread bitter to him if you can help it. That's what I mean, an' that's what we all mean; an'[4] when a man's said what he means, he'd better stop, for th' ale 'ull be none the better for stannin'. An' I'll not say how we like th' ale yet[5], for we couldna well[6]

---

[1] here] *added in MS*   [2] clock. "Captain] clock: "Captain *MS*

[3] farming] *MS 1* farming, *8*   [4] an'] *MS 1* and *8*

[5] yet] yit *MS 1* ⟨yit⟩ yet *8*

[6] couldna well] warna goin' to *MS 1* ⟨warna goin' to⟩ couldna well *8*

taste it till we'd drunk your health in it; but the dinner was good, an' if there's anybody hasna enjoyed it, it must be the fault of his own inside. An' as for the Rector's company, it's well known as that's welcome t' all the parish wherever he may be; an' I hope, an' we all hope, as he'll live to see us old folks, an' our[7] children grown to men an' women, an' your honour a family man. I've no more to say as concerns the present time, an'[8] so we'll drink our young Squire's health—three times three."

Hereupon a glorious shouting,[9] a rapping, a jingling, a clattering, and a shouting, with plentiful *da capo*,[1] pleasanter than a strain of sublimest music in the ears that receive such a tribute for the first time.[2] Arthur had felt a twinge of conscience during Mr Poyser's speech, but it was too feeble to nullify the pleasure he felt in being praised. Did he not deserve what was said of him, on the whole? If there was something in his conduct that Poyser wouldn't have liked if he had known it, why, no man's conduct will bear too close an inspection; and Poyser was not likely to know it; and, after all, what had he done? Gone a little too[3] far perhaps in flirtation, but another man in his place would have acted much worse; and[4] no harm would come—no harm *should* come, for the next time he was alone with Hetty, he would explain to her that she must not think seriously of him or of what had passed. It was necessary to Arthur, you perceive, to be satisfied with himself: uncomfortable thoughts must be got rid of by good intentions for the future, which can be formed so rapidly, that he had time to be[5] uncomfortable and to become easy again before Mr Poyser's slow speech was finished, and when[6] it was time for him to speak he was quite light-hearted.

"I thank you all, my good friends and neighbours," Arthur said, "for the good opinion of me, and the kind feelings towards me which Mr Poyser has been expressing on your behalf and on his own, and it will always be my heartiest wish to deserve them. In the course of things we may expect that, if I live, I shall one day or other[7] be your landlord; indeed it is on the ground of that expectation that my grandfather has wished me to celebrate this day and to come among you now; and I look forward to this position, not merely as one of power and pleasure for myself, but as a means of benefiting my neighbours. It hardly becomes so young a man as I am, to talk much about farming to you, who are most of you so much older, and are men of experience; still, I have interested myself a good deal in such matters, and learned as much about them as my opportunities have allowed; and when

---

[7] our] wer *MS 1* ⟨wer⟩ our *8*   [8] time, an'] time. An' *MS*
[9] shouting, ⟨worthy of ⟨⟨brave⟩⟩ ⟨⟨Britons⟩⟩ men descended from those brave (but noisy) Teutons who delighted to shout⟩ a *MS*
[1] capo,—⟨dear to young ears that receive this tribute for the first time⟩ pleasanter *MS*
[2] time. ⟨And perhaps there lurks an⟩ Arthur *MS*   [3] too] *added in MS*
[4] worse; and] worse. And *MS*   [5] be ⟨comfortable⟩ uncomfortable *MS*
[6] when ⟨Arthur⟩ it *MS*   [7] or other] *added in MS*

the course of events shall place the estate in my hands, it will be my first desire to afford my tenants all the encouragement a landlord can give[8] them, in improving their land, and trying to bring about a better practice of husbandry. It will be my wish to be looked on by all my deserving tenants as their best friend, and nothing would make me so happy as to be able to respect[9] every man on the estate, and to be respected by[1] him in return. It is not my place at present to enter into particulars; I only meet your good hopes concerning me by telling you that my own hopes correspond to them—that what you expect from me I desire to fulfil; and I am quite of Mr Poyser's opinion, that when a man has said what he means, he had better stop. But the pleasure I feel in having my own health drunk by you would not be perfect if we did not drink the health of my grandfather, who has filled the place of both parents to me. I will say no more, until you have joined me in drinking his health on a day when he has wished me to appear among you as the future representative of his name and family."

Perhaps there was no one present except Mr Irwine who thoroughly understood and approved Arthur's graceful mode of proposing his grand-father's health. The farmers thought[2] the young Squire knew well enough that they hated the old Squire,[3] and Mrs Poyser said, "he'd better not ha' stirred a kettle o' sour broth." The bucolic mind does not readily appre-hend the refinements of good taste. But the toast could not be rejected, and when it had been drunk, Arthur said,

"I thank you, both for my grandfather and myself; and now there is one more thing I wish to tell you, that you may share my pleasure about it, as I hope and believe you will. I think there can be no man here who has not a respect, and some of you, I am sure, have a very high regard, for my friend Adam Bede. It is well known to every one in this neighbourhood that there is no man whose word can be more depended on than his; that whatever he undertakes to do, he does well, and is as careful for the interests of those who employ him as for his own. I'm proud to say that I was very fond of Adam when I was a little boy, and I have never lost my old feeling for him— I think that shows that I know a good fellow when I find him. It has long been my wish that he should have the management of the woods on the estate, which happen to be very valuable; not only because I think so highly of his character, but because he has the knowledge and the skill which fit him for the place. And I am happy to tell you that it is my grandfather's wish too, and it is now settled that Adam shall manage the woods—a change which I am sure will be very much for the advantage of the estate; and[4] I hope you will by-and-by join me in drinking his health, and in wishing him

---

[8] give {them} in ⟨the improvement of⟩ improving *MS*
[9] respect ⟨not only my tenants but⟩ every man ⟨employed⟩ on *MS*
[1] by ⟨them⟩ him *MS*   [2] thought ⟨that⟩ the *MS*
[3] squire, ⟨& that [two or three words]⟩ & *MS*   [4] estate; and] estate. And *MS*

all the prosperity in life that he deserves. But there is a still older friend of mine than Adam Bede present, and I need not tell you that it is[5] Mr Irwine. I'm sure you will agree with me that we must drink no other person's health until we have drunk his. I know you have all reason to love him, but no one of his parishioners has so much reason as I. Come, charge your glasses, and let us drink to our excellent Rector—three times three!"

This toast was drunk with all the enthusiasm that was wanting to the last, and it certainly was the most picturesque moment in the scene when Mr Irwine got up to speak, and all the faces in the room were turned towards him. The superior refinement of his face was much more striking than that of Arthur's when seen in comparison with the people round them. Arthur's was a much commoner British face, and the splendour of his new-fashioned clothes was more akin to the young farmer's taste in costume than Mr Irwine's powder, and the well-brushed[6] but well-worn black, which seemed to be his chosen suit for great occasions; for he had the mysterious secret of never wearing a new-looking coat.

"This is not the first time, by a great many," he said, "that I have had to thank my parishioners for giving me tokens of their goodwill, but neighbourly kindness is among those things that are the more precious the older they get. Indeed, our pleasant meeting to-day is a proof that when what is good comes of age and is likely to live, there is reason for rejoicing, and the relation between us as clergyman and parishioners came of age two years ago, for it is three-and-twenty years since I first came among you, and I see some tall, fine-looking young men here, as well as some blooming young women, that were far from looking as pleasantly at me when I christened them, as I am happy to see them looking now. But I'm sure you will not wonder when I say, that among all those young men, the one in whom I have the strongest interest is my friend Mr Arthur Donnithorne, for whom you have just expressed your regard. I had the pleasure of being his tutor for several years, and have naturally had opportunities of knowing him intimately which cannot have occurred to any one else who is present; and I have some pride as well as pleasure in assuring you that I share your high hopes concerning him, and your confidence in his possession of those qualities which will make him an excellent landlord when the time shall come for him to take that important position among you. We feel alike on most matters on which a man who is getting towards fifty can feel in common with a young man of one-and-twenty, and he has just been expressing a feeling which I share very heartily, and I[7] would not willingly omit the opportunity of saying so. That feeling is his value and respect for Adam Bede. People in a high station are of course more thought of and talked about, and have their virtues more praised, than those whose lives

---

[5] that it is] that is *MS*   [6] well-brushed ⟨&⟩ but *MS*   [7] I] *added in MS*

are passed in humble everyday work; but every sensible man knows how[8] necessary that humble everyday work is, and how important it is to us that it should be done well. And I agree with my friend Mr Arthur Donnithorne in feeling that when a man whose duty lies in that sort of work shows a character which would make him an example in any station, his merit should be acknowledged. He is one of those to whom honour is due, and his friends should delight to honour him. I know Adam Bede well—I know what he is as a workman, and what he has been as a son and brother—and I am saying the simplest truth when I say that I respect him as much as I respect any man living. But I am not speaking to you about a stranger; some of you are his intimate friends, and I believe there is not one here who does not know enough of him to join heartily in drinking his health."

As Mr Irwine paused, Arthur jumped up, and filling his glass, said, "A bumper to Adam Bede, and may he[9] live to have sons as faithful and clever as himself!"

No hearer, not even Bartle Massey, was so delighted with this toast as Mr Poyser: "tough work" as his first speech had been, he would have started up to make another if he had not known the extreme irregularity of such a course. As it was, he found an outlet for his feeling in drinking his ale unusually fast, and setting down his glass with a swing of his arm and a determined rap. If Jonathan Burge and a few others felt less comfortable on the occasion, they tried their best to look contented, and so the toast was drunk with a goodwill apparently unanimous.

Adam was rather paler than usual when he got up to thank his friends. He was a good deal moved by this public tribute—very naturally, for he was in the presence of all his little world, and it was uniting to do him honour. But he felt no shyness about speaking, not being troubled with small vanity or lack of words; he looked neither awkward nor embarrassed, but[1] stood in his usual firm upright attitude, with his head thrown a little backward and his hands perfectly still, in that rough dignity which is peculiar to intelligent, honest, well-built workmen, who are never wondering what is their business in the world.

"I'm quite taken by surprise," he said. "I didn't expect anything o' this sort, for it's a good deal more than my wages. But I've the more reason to be grateful to you, Captain, and to you, Mr Irwine, and to all my friends here, who've drunk my health and wished me well. It 'ud be nonsense for me to be saying, I don't at all deserve th' opinion you have of me; that 'ud be poor thanks to you, to say that you've known me all these years, and yet haven't sense enough to find out a great[2] deal o' the truth about me. You think, if I undertake to do a bit o' work, I'll do it well,[3] be my pay big or little—and

[8] how ⟨important it is to us⟩ necessary *MS*   [9] he ⟨have⟩ live *MS*
[1] but ⟨held⟩ stood *MS*   [2] great] good *MS*   [3] well, ⟨by⟩ ⟨be⟩ be *MS*

that's true. I'd be ashamed to stand before you here if it wasna[4] true. But it seems to me, that's a man's plain duty, and nothing to be conceited about, and it's pretty clear to me[5] as[6] I've never done more than my duty; for let us do what we will, it's only making use o' the sperrit and the powers that ha'[7] been given to us. And so this kindness o' yours, I'm sure, is no debt you owe me, but a free gift, and as such I accept it and am thankful. And as to this new employment I've taken in hand, I'll only say that I took it at Captain Donnithorne's desire, and that I'll try to fulfil his expectations. I'd wish for no better lot than to work under him, and to know that while I was getting my own bread I was taking care of his int'rests. For I believe he's one o' those gentlemen[8] as wishes to do the right thing, and to leave the world[9] a bit better than he found it, which it's my belief every man may do, whether he's gentle or simple, whether he sets a good[1] bit o' work going and finds the money, or whether he does the work with his own hands. There's no occasion for me to say any more about what I feel towards him: I hope to show it through the rest o' my life in my actions."

There were various opinions about Adam's speech: some of the women[2] whispered that he didn't show himself thankful enough,[3] and seemed to speak as proud as could be; but most of the men were of opinion that nobody could speak more straitfor'ard[4], and that Adam was as fine a chap as need to be. While such observations were being buzzed about, mingled with wonderings as to what the old Squire meant to do for a bailiff, and whether he was going to have a steward, the two gentlemen had risen, and were walking round to the table where the wives and children sat. There was none of the strong ale here, of course, but wine and dessert—sparkling gooseberry for the young ones, and some good sherry for the mothers. Mrs Poyser was at the head of this table, and Totty was now seated in her lap, bending her small nose deep down into a wine-glass in search of the nuts floating there.

"How do you do, Mrs Poyser?" said Arthur. "Weren't you pleased to hear your husband make such a good speech to-day?"

"O, sir, the men are mostly so tongue-tied—you're forced partly to guess what they mean, as you do wi' the dumb creaturs."

"What! you[5] think you could have made it better for him?" said[6] Mr Irwine, laughing.

"Well, sir, when I want to say anything, I can mostly find words to say it in, thank God. Not as I'm a-finding faut wi' my husband, for if he's a man o' few words, what he says he'll stand to."

4 wasna] wasn't *MS* 5 to me] *added in MS* 6 as] that *MS*
7 ha'] have *MS* 8 gentlemen ⟨that⟩ as *MS* 9 world ⟨better⟩ a *MS*
1 good] *added in MS* 2 women] *added in MS* 3 enough, ⟨but⟩ and *MS*
4 straitfor'ard] strait-forrard *MS* straightfor'ard *Cabinet*
5 "What! you] "What, you *MS* 6 him?" said] him, eh?" said *MS*

"I'm sure I never saw a prettier party than this,"[7] Arthur said, looking round at the apple-cheeked children. "My aunt and the Miss Irwines will come up and see you[8] presently. They were afraid of the noise of the toasts, but it would be a shame for them not to see you at table."

He walked on, speaking to the mothers and patting the children, while Mr Irwine satisfied himself with standing still, and nodding at a distance, that no one's attention might be disturbed from the young Squire, the hero of the day. Arthur did not venture to stop near Hetty, but merely bowed to her as he passed along the opposite side. The foolish child felt her heart swelling with discontent; for what woman[9] was ever satisfied with [1]apparent neglect, even when she knows it to be the mask of love? Hetty thought this was going to be the most miserable day she had had for a long while; a moment of chill daylight and reality came across her dream: Arthur, who had seemed so near to her only a few hours before, was separated from her, as the hero of a great procession is separated from a small outsider in the crowd.

---

[7] this," ⟨said⟩ Arthur {said}, looking *MS*   [8] you ⟨when we⟩ presently *MS*
[9] woman] women *MS*   [1] with ⟨the⟩ apparent *MS*

CHAPTER XXV.

THE GAMES.

The great dance was not to begin until eight o'clock; but for any lads and lasses who liked to dance on the shady grass before then, there was music always at hand; for was not the band of the Benefit Club capable of playing excellent jigs, reels, and hornpipes? And, besides this, there was a grand band hired from Rosseter, who, with their wonderful wind-instruments and puffed-out cheeks, were themselves a delightful show to the small boys and girls. To say nothing of Joshua Rann's fiddle, which, by an act of generous forethought, he had provided himself with, in case any one should be of sufficiently pure taste to prefer dancing to a solo on that instrument.

Meantime, when the sun had moved off the great open space in front of the house, the games began. There were of course well-soaped poles to be climbed by the boys and youths, races to be run by the old women, races to be run in sacks, heavy weights to be lifted by the strong men, and a long list of challenges to such ambitious attempts as that of walking as many yards as possible on one leg—feats in which it was generally remarked that Wiry Ben, being "the lissom'st, springest fellow i' the country," was sure to be pre-eminent. To crown all, there was to be a donkey race—that sublimest of all races, conducted on the grand socialistic idea of everybody encouraging everybody else's donkey, and the sorriest donkey winning.

And soon after four o'clock, splendid old Mrs Irwine, in her damask satin and jewels and black lace, was led out by Arthur, followed by the whole family party, to her raised seat under the striped marquee, where she was to give out the prizes to the victors. Staid, formal Miss Lydia had requested to resign that queenly office to the royal old lady, and[1] Arthur was pleased with this opportunity of gratifying his godmother's taste for stateliness. Old Mr Donnithorne, the delicately-clean, finely-scented, withered old man, led out Miss Irwine, with his air of punctilious, acid politeness; Mr Gawaine brought Miss Lydia, looking neutral and stiff in an elegant peach-blossom silk; and Mr Irwine came last with his pale sister Anne[2]. No other friend of the family, besides Mr Gawaine, was invited to-day; there was to be a grand dinner for the neighbouring gentry on the

---

[1] and Arthur⟨s⟩ was *MS*   [2] Anne] Ann *MS*

morrow, but to-day all the forces were required for the entertainment of the tenants.

There was a[3] sunk fence in front of the marquee, dividing the lawn from the park,[4] but a temporary bridge had been made for the passage of the victors, and the groups of people[5] standing, or seated here and there on benches, stretched on each side of the open space from the[6] white marquees up to the[7] sunk fence.

"Upon my word it's a pretty sight," said the old lady, in her deep voice, when she was seated, and looked round on the bright scene with its dark-green background; "and it's the last fête-day I'm likely to see, unless you make haste and get married, Arthur. But take care you get a charming bride, else I would rather die without seeing her."

"You're so terribly fastidious, godmother," said Arthur, "I'm[8] afraid I should never satisfy you with my choice."

"Well, I won't forgive you if she's not handsome. I can't be put off with amiability, which is always the excuse people are making for the existence of plain people. And she must not be silly; that will never do, because you'll want managing, and a silly woman can't manage you. Who is that tall young man, Dauphin, with the mild face? There, standing without his hat, and taking such care of that tall old woman by the side of him—his mother, of course. I like to see that."

"What, don't you know him, mother?" said Mr Irwine. "That is Seth Bede, Adam's brother—a Methodist, but a very good fellow. Poor Seth has looked rather down-hearted of late; I thought it was because of his father's[9] dying in that sad way; but Joshua Rann tells me he[1] wanted to marry that sweet little Methodist preacher who was here about a month ago, and I suppose she refused him."

"Ah, I remember hearing about her: but there are no end of people here that I don't know, for[2] they're grown up and altered so since I used to go about."

"What excellent sight you have!" said old Mr Donnithorne, who was holding a double glass up to his eyes, "to see the expression of that young man's face so far off. His face is nothing but a pale blurred[3] spot to me. But I fancy I have the advantage of you when we come to look close. I can read small print without spectacles."

    [3] a ⟨light wire⟩ sunk *MS*
    [4] park, ⟨with a little gate which was to admit the victors⟩ but a temporary bridge had been made ⟨admitting⟩ {for the} the [*sic*] {passage of the} victors; & *MS*
    [5] people ⟨stretched down each side the⟩ standing, or seated here & there on benches, stretched on each side of the *MS*
    [6] the ⟨large⟩ white *MS*   [7] the ⟨wire⟩ sunk *MS*
    [8] Arthur, "I'm] Arthur. I'm *MS*   [9] father's ⟨sudden⟩ dying in *MS*
    [1] he ⟨was in love with⟩ wanted to marry *MS*   [2] for ⟨their⟩ they're *MS*
    [3] blurred ⟨speck⟩ ⟨spot⟩ spot *MS*

"Ah, my dear sir, you began with being very near-sighted, and those near-sighted eyes always wear the best. I want very strong spectacles to read with, but then I think[4] my eyes get better and better for things at a distance. I suppose if I could live another fifty years, I should be blind to everything that wasn't out of other people's sight, like a man who stands in a well, and sees nothing but the stars."

"See," said Arthur, "the old women are ready to set out on their race now. Which do you bet on, Gawaine?"

"The long-legged one, unless they're going to have several heats, and then the little wiry one may win."

"There are the Poysers, mother,[5] not far off on the right hand," said Miss Irwine. "Mrs Poyser is[6] looking at you. Do[7] take notice of her."

"To be sure I will," said the old lady, giving a gracious bow to Mrs Poyser. "A woman who sends me such excellent cream-cheese is not to be neglected. Bless me! what a fat child that is she is holding on her knee! But who is that pretty girl with dark eyes?"

"That is Hetty Sorrel," said Miss Lydia Donnithorne, "Martin Poyser's niece—a very[8] likely young person, and well-looking too. My maid has taught her fine needlework, and she has mended some lace of mine very respectably indeed—very respectably."

"Why, she has lived with the Poysers six or seven years, mother; you must have seen her," said Miss Irwine.

"No, I've never seen her, child; at least not as she is now," said Mrs Irwine, continuing to look at Hetty. "Well-looking, indeed![9] She's a perfect beauty! I've never seen anything so pretty since my young days. What a pity such beauty as that should be thrown away among the farmers, when it's wanted so terribly among the good families without fortune! I dare say, now, she'll marry a man who would have thought her just as pretty if she had had round eyes and red hair."

Arthur dared[1] not turn his eyes towards Hetty while Mrs Irwine was speaking of her. He feigned not to hear, and to be occupied with something on the opposite side. But he saw her plainly enough without looking; saw her in heightened beauty, because he heard her beauty praised—for other men's opinion, you know, was like a native climate to Arthur's feelings: it was the air on which they thrived the best, and grew strong. Yes! she *was* enough to turn any man's head: any man in his place would have done and felt the same. And to give her up after all, as he was determined to do, would be an act that he should always look back upon with pride.[2]

---

[4] think ⟨the⟩ my *MS*   [5] mother, ⟨close to the fence⟩ not far off *MS*
[6] is ⟨nodding to you⟩ looking *MS*   [7] Do ⟨nod to⟩ take notice of *MS*
[8] very ⟨we⟩ likely *MS*   [9] indeed! — ⟨why⟩ She's a perfect beauty: I've *MS*
[1] dared] dare *MS 1*
[2] ¶ Arthur dare not turn his eyes towards Hetty while Mrs. Irwine was speaking of her. He feigned not to hear & to be ⟨looking at⟩ {occupied with} something on the opposite side. But he

"No, mother," said Mr Irwine, replying to her last words;[3] "I can't agree with you there. The[4] common people are not quite so stupid as you imagine. The commonest man, who has his ounce of sense and feeling, is conscious of the difference between a lovely, delicate woman, and a coarse one. Even a dog feels a difference in their presence. The man may be no[5] better able than the dog to explain the influence the more refined beauty has on him, but he feels it."

"Bless me, Dauphin, what does an old bachelor like you know about it?"

"O, that is one of the matters in which old bachelors are wiser than married men, because they have time for more general contemplation. Your fine critic of women must never shackle his judgment by calling one woman his own. But, as an example of what I was saying, that pretty Methodist preacher I mentioned just now, told me that she had preached to the roughest miners, and had never been treated with anything but the utmost respect and kindness by them. The reason is—though she doesn't know it—that there's so much[6] tenderness, refinement, and purity about her. Such a woman as that brings with her 'airs from heaven' that the coarsest fellow is not insensible to."

"Here's a delicate bit of womanhood, or girlhood, coming to receive a prize, I suppose," said Mr Gawaine. "She must be one of the racers in the sacks, who had set off before we came."

The "bit of womanhood" was our old acquaintance Bessy Cranage, otherwise Chad's Bess, whose large red cheeks and blowsy person had undergone an exaggeration of colour, which, if she had happened to be a heavenly body, would have made her sublime. Bessy, I am sorry to say, had taken to her ear-rings again since Dinah's departure, and was otherwise decked out in such small finery as she could muster. Any one who could have looked into poor Bessy's heart would have seen a striking resemblance between her little hopes and anxieties and Hetty's. The[7] advantage, perhaps, would have been on Bessy's side in the matter of feeling. But then, you see, they were so very different outside! You would have been inclined to box Bessy's ears, and you would have longed to kiss Hetty.

Bessy had been tempted to run the arduous race, partly from mere hoydenish gaiety, partly because of the prize. Some one had said there were to be cloaks and other nice clothes for prizes, and she approached the

---

saw her plainly enough without looking—saw her in heightened beauty because he heard her beauty praised—for other men's opinion, you know, was like a native climate to Arthur's feelings: it was the air on which they thrived the best, & grew strong. Yes! she was enough to turn any man's head—any man in his place would have done & felt the same. And to give her up after all, as he was determined to do, would be an act that he should always look back upon with pride.] *added on verso of MS* '11. *158*

   [3] replying to her last words,] *added in MS*   [4] The ⟨country⟩ common *MS*
   [5] no ⟨more⟩ better *MS*   [6] so much] such *MS*
   [7] Hetty's. The] Hetty's: the *MS*

marquee, fanning herself with her handkerchief, but with exultation sparkling in her round eyes.

"Here is the prize for the first sack race," said Miss Lydia, taking a large
parcel from the table where the prizes were laid, and giving it to Mrs Irwine
before Bessy came up; "an excellent grogram gown and a piece of flannel."

"You didn't think the winner was to be so young, I suppose,[8] aunt?" said
Arthur. "Couldn't you find something else for this girl, and save that grim-
looking gown for one of the older women?"

"I have bought nothing but what is useful and substantial," said Miss
Lydia, adjusting her own lace; "I should not think of encouraging a love of
finery in young women of that class. I have a scarlet cloak, but that is for the
old woman who wins."

[9]This speech of Miss Lydia's produced rather a mocking expression in
Mrs Irwine's face as she looked at Arthur, while Bessy came up and
dropped a series of curtsies.

"This is Bessy Cranage, mother," said Mr Irwine kindly, "Chad Cranage's daughter. You remember Chad Cranage, the blacksmith?"

"Yes, to be sure," said Mrs Irwine. "Well, Bessy, here is your prize—
excellent warm things for winter. I'm[1] sure you have had hard work to win
them this warm day."

Bessy's lip fell, as she saw the ugly, heavy gown,—which felt so hot and
disagreeable, too, on this July day, and was[2] such a great ugly thing to carry.
She dropped her curtsies again, without looking up, and with a growing
tremulousness about the corners of her mouth, and then turned away.

"Poor girl," said Arthur; "I[3] think she's disappointed. I wish it had been
something more to her taste."

"She's a bold-looking young person," observed Miss Lydia. "Not at all
one I should like to encourage."

Arthur silently resolved that he would make Bessy a present of money
before the day was over, that she might buy something more to her mind;
but she, not aware of the consolation in store for her, turned out of the open
space, where she was visible from the marquee, and throwing down the
odious bundle under a tree, began to cry—very much tittered at the while
by the small boys. In this situation she was descried by her discreet
matronly cousin, who lost no time in coming up, having just given the
baby into her husband's charge.

"What's the matter wi' ye?" said[4] Bess the matron, taking up the bundle
and examining it. "Ye'n sweltered yoursen, I reckon, running that fool's
race. An' here, they'n gi'en you lots o' good grogram an'[5] flannel, as should

  [8] I suppose,] *added in MS*
  [9] ⟨There was⟩ {This speech of Miss Lydia's produced} rather *MS*
  [1] winter. I'm] winter: I'm *MS*   [2] and was] & it was *MS*
  [3] Arthur; "I] Arthur. "I *MS*   [4] said ⟨the matronly Bess,⟩ Bess, the matron, *MS*
  [5] an'] and *Cabinet*

ha' been gi'en by good rights to them as had[6] the sense to keep away from
such foolery. Ye might spare me a bit o' this grogram to make clothes for the
lad—ye war ne'er ill-natured[7], Bess; I ne'er said that on ye[8]."

"Ye may take it all, for what I care," said Bess the maiden, with a pettish
movement, beginning to wipe away her tears and recover herself.

"Well, I could do wi't, if so be ye[9] want to get rid on't," said the
disinterested cousin, walking quickly away with the bundle, lest Chad's
Bess should change her mind.

But that bonny-cheeked lass was blest with an elasticity of spirits that
secured her from any rankling grief; and by the time the grand climax of the
donkey race came on, her disappointment was entirely lost in the[1] delightful excitement of attempting to stimulate the last donkey by hisses, while
the boys applied the argument of sticks. But the strength of the donkey
mind lies in adopting a course inversely as the arguments urged, which,
well-considered, requires as great a mental force as the direct sequence; and
the present donkey proved the first-rate order of his intelligence by coming
to a dead stand-still just when the blows were thickest. Great was the
shouting of the crowd, radiant the grinning of Bill Downes the stone-
sawyer[2] and the fortunate rider of this superior beast, which stood calm and
stiff-legged in the midst of its triumph.

Arthur himself had provided the prizes for the men, and Bill was made
happy with a splendid pocket-knife, supplied with blades and gimlets
enough to make a man at home on a desert island. He had hardly returned
from the marquee with the prize in his hand, when it began to be understood that Wiry Ben proposed to amuse the company, before the gentry
went to dinner, with an impromptu and gratuitous performance—namely,
a hornpipe, the main idea of which was doubtless borrowed; but this was to
be developed[3] by the dancer in so peculiar and complex a manner that no
one could deny him the praise of originality. Wiry Ben's pride in his
dancing—an accomplishment productive of great effect at the yearly
Wake—had needed only slightly elevating by an extra quantity of good
ale, to convince him that the gentry would be very much struck with his
performance of the hornpipe; and he had been decidedly encouraged in this
idea by Joshua Rann, who observed that it was nothing but right to do
something to please the young Squire, in return for what he had done for
them. You will be the less surprised at this opinion in so grave a personage
when you learn that Ben had requested Mr Rann to accompany him on the
fiddle, and Joshua felt quite sure that though there might not be much in

 [6] had] hed *MS*   [7] ill-natured] ill-natur'd *MS 1*   [8] ye] you *MS*
 [9] ye] you *MS*
 [1] the ⟨delightful excitement⟩ ⟨exciting⟩ delightful excitement of attempting *MS*
 [2] stone sawyer ⟨who was the⟩ & the *MS*
 [3] this was to be developed] this was ⟨to be⟩ developed *MS*

the dancing, the music would make up for it. Adam Bede, who was present in one of the large marquees, where the plan was being discussed, told Ben he had better not make a fool of himself—a remark which at once fixed Ben's determination: he was not going to let anything alone because Adam Bede turned up his nose at it.

"What's this, what's this?" said old Mr Donnithorne. "Is it something you've arranged, Arthur? Here's the clerk coming with his fiddle, and a smart fellow with a nosegay in his button-hole."

"No," said Arthur; "I[4] know nothing about it. By Jove, he's going to dance! It's one of the carpenters—I forget his name at this moment."

"It's Ben Cranage—Wiry Ben, they call him," said Mr Irwine; "rather a loose fish, I think. Anne[5], my dear, I see that fiddle-scraping is too much for you: you're getting tired. Let me take you in now, that you may rest till dinner."

Miss Anne[6] rose assentingly, and the good brother took her away, while Joshua's preliminary scrapings burst into the "White Cockade," from which he intended to pass to a variety of tunes, by a series of transitions which his good ear really taught him to execute with some skill. It would have been an exasperating fact to him, if he had known it, that the general attention was too thoroughly absorbed by Ben's dancing for any one to give much heed to the music.

Have you ever seen a real English rustic perform a solo dance? Perhaps you have only seen a ballet rustic, smiling like a merry countryman in crockery, with graceful turns of[7] the haunch and insinuating movements of the head. That is as much like the real thing as the "Bird Waltz" is like the song of birds. Wiry Ben never smiled: he looked as serious as a dancing monkey—as serious as if he had been an experimental philosopher ascertaining in his own person the amount of shaking and the varieties of angularity that could be given to the human limbs.

To make amends for the abundant laughter in the striped marquee, Arthur clapped his hands continually and cried "Bravo!" But Ben had one admirer whose eyes followed his movements with a fervid gravity that equalled his own. It was Martin Poyser, who was seated on a bench, with Tommy between his legs.

"What dost think o' that?" he said to his wife. "He goes as pat to the music as if he was made o' clockwork. I used to be a pretty good un at dancing myself when I was lighter, but I could niver ha' hit it just to th' hair like that."

"It's little matter what his limbs are, to my thinking," returned Mrs Poyser. "He's empty enough i' the[8] upper story, or he'd niver come jigging

---

[4] Arthur; "I] Arthur. "I *MS*   [5] Anne] Ann *MS*   [6] Anne] Ann *MS*
[7] of ⟨his⟩ the *MS*   [8] the] th' *MS*

an' stamping i' that way, like a mad grasshopper, for the gentry to look at him. They're fit to die wi' laughing, I can see."

"Well, well, so much the better, it amuses 'em," said Mr Poyser, who did not easily take an irritable view of things. "But they're going away now, t' have their dinner, I reckon. We'll move about a bit, shall we? and see what Adam Bede's doing. He's got to look after the drinking and things: I doubt he hasna had much fun."

CHAPTER XXVI.

THE DANCE.

Arthur had chosen the entrance-hall for the ball-room: very wisely, for no other room could have been so airy, or would have had the advantage of the wide doors opening into the garden, as well as a ready entrance into the other rooms. To be sure, a stone floor was not the pleasantest to dance on, but then, most of the dancers had known what it was to enjoy a Christmas dance on kitchen quarries. It was one of those entrance-halls which make the surrounding rooms look like closets—with[1] stucco angels, trumpets, and flower-wreaths on the lofty ceiling, and great medallions of miscellaneous heroes on the walls, alternating with statues in niches. Just the sort of place to be ornamented well with green boughs, and Mr Craig had been proud to show his taste and his hot-house plants on the occasion. The broad steps of the stone staircase were covered with cushions to serve as seats for the children, who were to stay till half-past nine with the servant-maids, to see the dancing; and as this dance was confined to the chief tenants, there was abundant room for every one. The lights were charmingly disposed in coloured-paper lamps, high up among green boughs, and the farmers' wives and daughters, as they peeped in,[2] believed no scene could be more splendid; they knew now quite well in what sort of rooms the king and queen lived, and their thoughts glanced with some pity towards cousins and acquaintances who had not this fine opportunity of knowing how things went on in the great world. The lamps were already lit[3], though the sun had not long set, and there was that calm light out of doors in which we seem to see all objects more distinctly than in the broad day.

It was a pretty scene outside the house: the farmers and their families were moving about the lawn, among the flowers and shrubs, or along the broad straight road leading from the east front, where a carpet of mossy grass spread on each side,[4] studded here and there with a dark flat-boughed[5] cedar, or a grand[6] pyramidal fir sweeping the ground with its[7] branches, all tipped with a fringe of paler green. The groups of cottagers in the park were gradually diminishing,[8] the young ones being attracted

---

[1] closets—with] closets; with *MS* closets, with *1* closets {—} with *8*
[2] in, ⟨thought⟩ believed *MS*   [3] lit] alight *MS*
[4] side, ⟨with⟩ {studded} here & there {with} a *MS*
[5] flat-boughed] level-boughed *MS*   [6] grand] *added in MS*
[7] its ⟨lowest⟩ branches *MS*   [8] diminishing, ⟨the young ones⟩ the young ones *MS*

towards the lights that were beginning to gleam from the windows of the gallery in the[9] abbey, which was to be their dancing-room, and[1] some of the sober[2] elder ones thinking it time to go home quietly. One of these was Lisbeth Bede, and[3] Seth went with her—not[4] from filial attention only, for his conscience would not let him join in dancing. It had been rather a melancholy day to Seth:[5] Dinah had never been more constantly present with him than[6] in this scene, where everything was so unlike her. He saw her all the more vividly[7] after looking at the thoughtless faces and gay-coloured dresses of the young women—just as one feels the beauty and the greatness of a pictured Madonna the more, when it has been for a moment screened from us by a vulgar head in a bonnet.[8] But this presence of Dinah in his mind only helped him to bear the better with his mother's mood, which had[9] been becoming more and more querulous[1] for the last hour. Poor Lisbeth was suffering from a strange conflict of feelings.[2] Her joy and pride in the honour paid to her darling son Adam[3] was beginning to be worsted in the conflict with[4] the jealousy and fretfulness which had revived when Adam came to tell her that Captain Donnithorne desired him to join the dancers in the hall. Adam was getting more and more out of her reach;[5] she wished all the old troubles[6] back again, for then it mattered more to Adam what his mother said and did.

"Eh, it's[7] fine talkin' o' dancin'," she said, "an' thy father not a five week in's grave. An' I wish I war there too, istid o' bein' left to take up merrier folks's room above ground."

"Nay, don't look at it i'[8] that way, mother," said Adam, who was determined to be gentle to[9] her to-day. "I don't mean to dance—I shall only look on. And since the Captain wishes me to be there, it 'ud look[1] as if I thought I knew better than him, to say as I'd rather not stay. And thee know'st how he's behaved[2] to me to-day."

[9] the ⟨old⟩ abbey *MS*   [1] & ⟨many⟩ some *MS*   [2] sober] *added in MS*
[3] & ⟨her⟩ Seth ⟨was⟩ went *MS*
[4] not ⟨only⟩ from filial attention {only;} ⟨but because⟩ {for} his *MS*
[5] It had been rather a melancholy day to Seth:] *added in MS*
[6] than ⟨to-day⟩ in *MS*
[7] vividly ⟨when he looked⟩ after looking at the ⟨vacant⟩, thoughtless *MS*
[8] bonnet. ⟨Therefore⟩ But *MS*   [9] had {been} becom⟨e⟩{ing} more *MS*
[1] querulous ⟨during⟩ for *MS*
[2] feelings. ⟨The joyful pride at⟩ Her joy & pride in *MS*
[3] darling son Adam] darling Adam *MS*
[4] with ⟨her⟩ the jealousy {& fretfulness} ⟨when Adam next shared⟩ which had ⟨been⟩ revived *MS*
[5] reach: ⟨she wished⟩ she wished *MS*   [6] troubles ⟨&⟩ back *MS*
[7] "Eh, it's] "Eh! It's *MS 1*   [8] i'] in *MS*   [9] to ⟨his mother⟩ her today *MS*
[1] look ⟨I⟩ as *MS*
[2] thee know'st how he's behaved] you know ⟨what he's done⟩ how he's behaved *MS*

"Eh, thee't do as thee lik'st, for thy old[3] mother's got no right t' hinder thee. She's nought but th' old husk, and thee'st slipped away from her, like the ripe nut."[4]

"Well, mother," said Adam, "[5]I'll go and tell the Captain as it hurts thy feelings for me to stay, and I'd rather go home[6] upo' that account: he won't take it ill then, I dare say, and I'm willing." He said this with some effort, for he really longed to be[7] near Hetty this evening.

"Nay, nay,[8] I wonna ha' thee do that—the young Squire 'ull be angered. Go an' do what thee't ordered to do, an' me an'[9] Seth 'ull go whome. I know it's a grit honour for thee to be so looked on—an' who's to be prouder on it nor thy mother? Hadna she the cumber o'[1] rearin' thee an' doin' for thee all these 'ears?"

"Well, good-by, then, mother—good-by, lad—[2]remember Gyp when you get home," said Adam, turning away towards the gate of the pleasure-grounds, where he hoped he might be able to join the Poysers, for he had been so occupied throughout the afternoon that he had had no time to speak to Hetty. His eye soon detected a distant group, which he knew to be the right one,[3] returning to the house along the broad gravel road, and he hastened on to meet them.

"Why, Adam, I'm glad to get sight on y'[4] again," said Mr Poyser, who was carrying Totty[5] on his arm. "You're going t' have a bit o' fun[6], I hope, now your work's all done. And here's Hetty has[7] promised no end o' partners, an' I've just been askin' her if she'd agreed to dance wi' you, an' she says no."

"Well, I didn't think o' dancing to-night," said Adam, already[8] tempted to change his mind, as he looked at Hetty.

"Nonsense!" said Mr Poyser. "Why, everybody's goin'[9] to dance to-night, all but th' old Squire and Mrs Irwine[1]. Mrs Best's been tellin'[2] us as Miss Lyddy[3] and Miss Irwine 'ull dance, an' the young Squire 'ull pick[4] my wife for his first[5] partner, t' open the ball[6]: so she'll be forced to dance,

[3] old] *added in MS*

[4] She's nought but an old husk, an' thee'st slipped away from her, like the ripe nut."] *added in MS*

[5] Adam, "⟨perhaps if I was to tell the⟩ I'll go and tell the *MS*

[6] home ⟨on⟩ upo' *MS*   [7] be ⟨with⟩ near *MS*

[8] nay, ⟨thee mustna do aught t' offend thy betters⟩ I wonna ha' thee do that—th' young *MS*

[9] an'] *MS 1 and 8*   [1] o' ⟨rearing⟩ rearin' *MS*

[2] lad—⟨& head home⟩ remember Gyp when you get home, *MS*

[3] which he knew to be the right one,] *added in MS*   [4] y'] you *MS*

[5] Totty ⟨, to save her from being overtired⟩ on his arm. You're going t' have *MS*

[6] fun ⟨now⟩, I hope *MS*   [7] has] *added in MS*

[8] already ⟨inclined⟩ tempted *MS*   [9] goin'] going *MS*

[1] & Mrs. Irwine] *added in MS*   [2] tellin'] telling *MS*   [3] Lyddy] Lydia *MS*

[4] 'ull dance, an' the young Squire 'ull pick] are going to dance, an' the young squire's going to ⟨dance⟩ pick *MS*

[5] first] *MS* furst *1* ⟨furst⟩ first *8*   [6] t' open the ball] to lead the dance *MS*

though she's laid by ever sin' the Christmas afore the little[7] un was born. You canna[8] for shame stand still, Adam, an' you a fine young fellow, and[9] can dance as well as anybody."

"Nay, nay," said Mrs Poyser, "it 'ud be unbecomin'. I know the dancin's nonsense; but if you stick at everything because it's nonsense, you wonna[1] go far[2] i' this life. When your broth's ready-made for you, you mun[3] swallow the thickenin'[4], or else let the broth alone."[5]

"Then if Hetty 'ull[6] dance with me," said Adam, yielding either to Mrs Poyser's argument or to something else, "I'll dance whichever dance she's free."

"I've got no partner for the fourth dance," said Hetty; "I'll dance that with you, if you like."

"Ah," said Mr Poyser, "but you mun[7] dance the first dance, Adam, else it'll look[8] partic'ler. There's plenty o' nice partners to pick an' choose from, an' it's hard for the gells when the men stan'[9] by and don't ask 'em."

Adam felt the justice of Mr Poyser's observation: it would not do for him to dance with no one besides Hetty; and remembering that Jonathan Burge had some reason to feel hurt to-day, he resolved to ask Miss Mary to dance with him the first dance, if she had no other partner.

"There's the big clock strikin'[1] eight," said Mr Poyser; "we must make haste in now, else the Squire and the ladies 'ull be in afore[2] us, an' that wouldna look well."

When they had entered the hall, and the three children under Molly's charge had been seated on the stairs, the folding doors of the drawing-room were thrown open, and Arthur entered in his regimentals, leading Mrs Irwine to a carpet-covered dais ornamented with hot-house plants, where she and Miss Anne were to be seated with old Mr Donnithorne, that they might look on at the dancing, like the kings and queens in the plays. Arthur had put on his uniform to please the tenants, he said, who thought as much of his militia dignity as if it had been an elevation to the premiership. He had not the least objection to gratify them in that way: his uniform was very advantageous to his figure.

The old Squire, before sitting down, walked round the hall to greet the tenants and make polite speeches to the wives: he was always polite; but the farmers had found out, after long puzzling, that this polish was one of

[7] Christmas afore the little] Christmas {before} the ⟨little⟩ little *MS*
[8] canna] cant *MS*   [9] and] an' *MS*   [1] wonna] wont *MS*   [2] far] fur *MS*
[3] mun] must *MS*   [4] thickenin'] thickening *MS*
[5] "Nay, nay . . . broth alone."] *deleted MS version on verso of II. 171 reads* "Nay, nay, it 'ud be unbecomin' ", said Mrs. Poyser. "The dancin's nonsense I know, but if you stick at things because they're nonsense, you won't go fur i' this life. When your broth's ready made for you, you must swallow the thickenin', or else let the broth alone."
[6] 'ull] will *MS*   [7] mun] must *MS*   [8] look ⟨partickler⟩ partic'ler *MS*
[9] stan'] stand *MS*   [1] strikin'] striking *MS*   [2] afore] before *MS*

the signs of hardness. It was observed that he gave his most elaborate civility to Mrs Poyser to-night, inquiring particularly about her health, recommending her to strengthen herself with cold water as he did, and avoid all drugs. Mrs Poyser curtsied and thanked him with great self-command, but when he had passed on, she whispered to her husband, "I'll lay my life he's brewin'[3] some nasty turn against us. Old Harry doesna[4] wag his tail so for nothin'[5]." Mr Poyser had no time to answer, for now Arthur came up and said, "Mrs Poyser, I'm come to request the favour of your hand for the first dance; and, Mr Poyser, you must let me take you to my aunt, for she claims you as her partner."

The wife's pale[6] cheek flushed with a nervous sense of unwonted honour as Arthur led her to the top of the[7] room; but Mr Poyser, to whom an extra glass had restored his youthful confidence in his good looks and good dancing, walked along with them quite proudly, secretly flattering himself that Miss Lydia had never had a partner in *her* life who could lift her off the ground as he would. In order to balance the honours given to the two parishes, Miss Irwine danced with Luke Britton, the largest Broxton farmer, and Mr[8] Gawaine led out Mrs Britton. Mr Irwine, after seating his sister Anne, had gone to the abbey gallery, as he had agreed with Arthur beforehand, to see how the merriment of the cottagers was prospering. Meanwhile, all the less distinguished couples had taken their places:[9] Hetty was led out by the inevitable Mr Craig, and Mary Burge[1] by Adam; and now the music struck up, and the glorious country-dance, best of all dances, began.

Pity it was not a boarded floor! Then the rhythmic stamping of the thick shoes would have been better than any drums. That merry stamping, that gracious nodding of the head, that waving bestowal of the hand—where can we see them now? That simple dancing of well-covered matrons, laying aside for an hour the cares of house and dairy, remembering but not affecting youth, not jealous but proud[2] of the young maidens by their side—[3]that holiday sprightliness of portly husbands[4] paying little compliments to their wives, as if their courting days were come again—those lads and lasses a little confused and awkward with their partners, having nothing to say—it would be a pleasant variety to see all that sometimes, instead of low dresses and large skirts, and scanning glances exploring

---

[3] brewin'] brewing *MS*   [4] doesna] doesn't *MS*   [5] nothin'] nothing *MS*
[6] pale cheek⟨ed⟩ flushed *MS*   [7] the ⟨dance⟩ room, *MS*
[8] Mr ⟨Irwine⟩ Gawaine *MS*
[9] Meanwhile, all the less distinguished couples had taken their places:] *added in MS*
[1] Burge ⟨&⟩ by *MS*
[2] youth, not jealous but proud] youth⟨—⟩{,} proud not jealous *MS*
[3] side—⟨their holiday spirits express⟩ that holiday sprightliness *MS*
[4] husbands ⟨hearkened ⟨⟨reminding⟩⟩ their wives of the days when they⟩ paying little compliments to their *MS*

costumes, and languid men[5] in lacquered boots smiling with double meaning.

There was but one thing to mar Martin Poyser's pleasure in this dance: it was, that he was always in close contact with Luke Britton, that slovenly farmer. He thought of throwing a little[6] glazed coldness into his eye in the crossing of hands; but then, as Miss Irwine was opposite to him instead of the offensive Luke,[7] he might freeze the wrong person. So he gave his face up to hilarity, unchilled by moral judgments.

How Hetty's heart beat as Arthur approached her! He had hardly looked at her to-day: now he *must* take her hand. Would he press it? would he look at her? She thought she should[8] cry if he gave her no sign of feeling. Now he was there—he had taken her hand—yes, he was pressing it. Hetty turned pale as she looked up[9] at him for an instant and met his eyes, before the dance carried him away. That pale look came upon Arthur like the beginning of a dull pain, which clung to him, though he must dance and smile and joke all the same. Hetty would look so, when he told her what he had to tell her; and he should never be able to bear it—he should be a fool, and give way again. Hetty's look did not really mean so much as he thought: it was only the sign of a struggle between the desire for him to notice her, and the dread lest she should betray the desire to others. But[1] Hetty's face had a language that transcended her feelings. There are faces which nature charges with a meaning and[2] pathos not belonging to the single human soul that flutters beneath them, but speaking the joys and sorrows of foregone generations—eyes that tell of deep love which doubtless has been and is somewhere, but not paired with these eyes—perhaps paired with pale eyes that can say nothing; just[3] as a national language may be instinct with poetry unfelt by the lips that use it. That look of Hetty's oppressed Arthur with a dread which yet had something of a terrible unconfessed delight in it, that[4] she loved him too well.[5] There was a hard task before him, for at that moment he felt he would have given up three years of his youth for the happiness of abandoning himself without remorse to his passion for Hetty.

These were the incongruous thoughts in his mind, as he led Mrs Poyser, who was panting with fatigue, and secretly resolving that neither judge nor jury should force her to dance another dance, to take a quiet rest in the

---

[5] men ⟨with [?faces faintly] smiling with doubtful meaning⟩ in lacquered boots smiling with double meaning *MS*

[6] little ⟨sternness⟩ glazed coldness *MS*

[7] Luke, ⟨the object of this⟩ he might freeze the *MS*   [8] should] would *Cabinet*

[9] up] *added in MS*   [1] others. But] others; but *MS*

[2] meaning &] *added in MS*   [3] nothing; just] nothing. Just *MS*

[4] that ⟨Hetty⟩ she *MS*

[5] well{.} ⟨, that he should never be able to carry out⟩ There was a hard task before him, for ⟨now⟩ {at that moment he felt he} would *MS*

dining-room, where supper was laid out for the guests to come and take it as
they chose.

"I've desired Hetty to remember as she's got to dance[6] wi' you, sir," said
the good innocent woman; "for she's[7] so thoughtless, she'd be like enough
to go an'[8] engage herself for ivery[9] dance. So I told her not to promise too
many."

"Thank you, Mrs Poyser," said Arthur, not without a twinge. "Now, sit
down in this comfortable chair, and here is Mills ready to give you what you
would like best."

He hurried away to seek another matronly partner, for due honour must
be paid to the married women before he asked any of the young ones; and
the country dances, and the stamping, and the gracious nodding, and the
waving of the hands, went on joyously.

At last the time had come for the fourth dance—longed for by the strong,
grave Adam, as if he had been a delicate-handed youth of eighteen; for we
are all very much alike when we are in our first love; and[1] Adam had hardly
ever[2] touched Hetty's hand for more than a transient greeting—had never
danced with her but once before. His eyes had followed her eagerly to-night
in spite of himself, and had taken in deeper draughts of love. He[3] thought
she behaved so prettily[4], so quietly; she did not seem to be flirting at all, she
smiled less than usual; there was almost a sweet sadness[5] about her. "God
bless her!" he said inwardly; "I'd make her life a happy[6] un, if a strong arm
to work for her, and a heart to love her, could do it."

And then there stole over him delicious thoughts[7] of coming home from
work, and drawing Hetty to his side, and feeling her cheek softly pressed
against his, till he forgot where he was, and the music and the tread of feet
might have been the falling of rain and the roaring of the wind, for what he
knew.

But now the[8] third dance was ended, and he might go up to her and claim
her hand. She was at the far end of the hall near the staircase, whispering
with Molly, who had[9] just given the sleeping Totty into her arms,[1] before
running to fetch shawls and bonnets from the landing. Mrs Poyser had
taken the two boys away into the dining-room to give them some cake

---

[6] dance ⟨some dance⟩ with *MS*   [7] she's ⟨that⟩ so *MS*   [8] an'] and *MS*
[9] ivery] every *MS*   [1] love; and] love. And *MS*   [2] ever] *added in MS*
[3] love. He] love: he *MS*   [4] prettily ⟨tonight⟩, so *MS*
[5] sadness ⟨in her⟩ about her. ⟨With ⟨⟨p⟩⟩ Plenty of work for hand & brain, & Hetty near him
⟨⟨to fill his heart⟩⟩ that he might love her unspeakably & pour out on her all the yearning
tenderness of his soul—life seemed a blessed gift shone upon by that hope!⟩ "God *MS*
[6] happy ⟨one⟩ un *MS*   [7] delicious thoughts] *added in MS*
[8] the ⟨time was come for him to dance with her⟩ third dance was ended, & he might go up to
MS
[9] had ⟨Totty fast⟩ just *MS*   [1] arms, ⟨that⟩ before *MS*

before they went home in the cart with grandfather,[2] and Molly was to follow as fast as possible.

"Let me hold her," said Adam, as Molly turned upstairs: "the children are so heavy when they're asleep."

Hetty was glad of the relief, for to hold Totty in her arms,[3] standing, was not at all a pleasant variety to her. But this second transfer had the unfortunate effect of rousing Totty, who was not behind any child of her age in peevishness at an unseasonable awaking. While Hetty was in the act of placing her in Adam's arms, and had not yet withdrawn her own, Totty opened her eyes, and forthwith fought out with her left fist at Adam's arm, and with her right caught at the string of brown beads round Hetty's neck. The locket leaped out from her frock, and the next moment the string was broken, and Hetty, helpless, saw beads and locket scattered wide on the floor.

"My locket, my locket!" she said, in a loud frightened whisper to Adam; "never[4] mind the beads."

Adam had already seen where the locket fell, for it had attracted his glance as it[5] leaped out of her frock. It had fallen on the raised wooden dais where the band sat, not on the stone floor; and as Adam picked it up,[6] he saw the glass with the dark and light locks of hair under it. It[7] had fallen that side upwards, so the glass was not broken. He[8] turned it over on his hand, and saw the enamelled gold back.[9]

"It isn't hurt," he said, as he[1] held it towards Hetty, who was unable to take it because both her hands were occupied with Totty.

"O, it doesn't matter, I don't mind about it," said Hetty, who had been pale and was now red.

"Not matter?" said Adam, gravely. "You seemed very frightened about it. I'll hold it till you're ready to take it," he added, quietly closing his hand over it, that she might not think he wanted to look at it again.

By this time Molly had come with bonnet and shawl, and as soon as she had taken Totty, Adam placed the locket in Hetty's hand. She took it with an air of indifference, and put it in her pocket; in her heart vexed and angry with Adam, because he had seen it, but determined now that she would show no more signs of agitation.

"See," she said, "they're taking their places to dance; let us go."

    [2] in the cart with grandfather,] *added in MS*   [3] in her arms,] *added in MS*
    [4] Adam; "never] Adam. "Never *MS*   [5] it ⟨fell⟩ leaped *MS*
    [6] up, ⟨he looked at it to assure himself that it was not broken. As it lay on the floor⟩ he saw the ⟨enamelled gold back,⟩ ⟨as he picked it up, he saw the enamelled⟩ glass with the {with the [*sic*] dark & light locks of} hair under it: it had fallen that side upwards, so the *MS*
    [7] it. It] it: it *MS*   [8] broken. He] broken: ⟨in taking⟩ he *MS*
    [9] back. ⟨It was all the work of an instant,⟩ *MS*   [1] he ⟨put⟩ held *MS*

Adam assented silently. A puzzled alarm had taken possession of him. Had Hetty a lover he didn't know of?—for[2] none of her relations, he was sure, would give her a locket like that; and none of her admirers, with whom he was acquainted, was in the position of an accepted lover, as the giver of that locket must be. Adam was lost in the utter impossibility of finding any person for his fears to alight on: he could only feel with a terrible pang that there[3] was something in Hetty's life unknown to him; that while he had been rocking himself in[4] the hope that she would come to love him, she[5] was already loving another. The pleasure of the dance with Hetty was gone; his eyes, when they rested on her, had an uneasy questioning expression in them; he could think of nothing to say to her; and she, too, was out of temper and disinclined to speak. They were both glad when the dance was ended.

Adam was determined to stay no longer; no one wanted him, and no one would notice if he slipped away. As soon as he got out of doors, he began to walk[6] at his habitual rapid pace, hurrying along without knowing why, busy with the painful thought that the memory of this day, so full of honour and promise to him, was poisoned for ever. Suddenly, when he was far on through the Chase, he stopped, startled by a[7] flash of reviving hope. After all, he might be a fool, making a great misery out of a trifle. Hetty, fond of finery as she was, might have bought the thing herself. It looked too expensive for that—it looked like the things on white satin in the great jeweller's shop at Rosseter. But Adam had very imperfect notions of the value of such things, and he thought it could certainly not cost more than a guinea. Perhaps Hetty had had as much as that in Christmas-boxes, and there was no knowing but she might have been childish enough to spend it in that way; she was such a young thing, and she couldn't help loving finery! But then, why had she been so frightened about it at first, and changed colour so, and afterwards pretended not to care? O, that was because she was ashamed of his seeing that she had such a smart thing—she was conscious that it was wrong for her to spend her money on it, and she knew that Adam disapproved of finery. It was a proof she cared about what he[8] liked and disliked. She must have thought from his silence and gravity afterwards that he was very much displeased with her, that he was inclined to be harsh and severe towards her foibles. And as he walked on more quietly, chewing the cud of this new hope,[9] his only uneasiness was that he had behaved in a way which might chill Hetty's feeling towards him. For

---

[2] of?—for] of? For *MS*   [3] there ⟨might be⟩ was *MS*
[4] in ⟨flattering hopes,⟩ the hope that *MS*
[5] she ⟨had⟩ was *MS*   [6] walk ⟨in⟩ at *MS*   [7] a flash⟨ed⟩ of *MS*
[8] he ⟨thought⟩ liked & disliked *MS*
[9] hope, ⟨he began to be angry with himself for behaving⟩ his only uneasiness was that he had behaved in a way ⟨that⟩ which *MS*

this last view of the matter *must* be the true one. How could Hetty have an accepted lover, quite unknown to him? She was[1] never away from her uncle's house for more than a day; she could have no acquaintances that did not come there, and no intimacies unknown to her uncle and aunt. It would be folly to believe that the locket was given to her by a lover. The little ring of[2] dark hair he felt sure was her own;[3] he could form no guess about the light hair under it, for he had not seen it very distinctly. It might be a bit of her father's or mother's, who had died when she was a child, and she would naturally put a bit of her own along with it.

And so Adam went to bed comforted, having woven for himself an ingenious web of probabilities—the surest screen a wise[4] man can place between himself and the truth. His last waking thoughts melted into a dream that he was with Hetty again at the Hall Farm, and that he was asking her to forgive him for being so cold and silent.

[5]And while he was dreaming this, Arthur was leading Hetty to the dance, and saying to her in low hurried tones,[6] "I shall be in the wood the day after to-morrow at seven; come as early as you can." And[7] Hetty's foolish joys and hopes, which had flown away for a little space, scared by a mere nothing[8], now all came fluttering back, unconscious of the real peril. She was happy for the first time this long day, and wished that dance would last for hours. Arthur wished it too;[9] it was the last weakness he meant to indulge in; and a man never lies with more delicious languor under the influence of a passion, than when he has[1] persuaded himself that he shall subdue it to-morrow.

But Mrs Poyser's wishes were quite the reverse of this, for her mind was filled with dreary forebodings as to the retardation of to-morrow morning's cheese in consequence of these late hours. Now that Hetty had done her duty and danced one dance with the young Squire, Mr Poyser must go out and see if the cart was come back to fetch them, for it was half-past ten o'clock, and notwithstanding a mild suggestion on his part that it would be bad manners for them to be the first to go, Mrs Poyser was resolute on the point, "manners or no manners."

"What! going[2] already, Mrs Poyser?" said old Mr Donnithorne, as she came to curtsy and take leave; "I thought we should not part with any of our

---

[1] was] *added in MS* [2] little ring of] *added in MS* [3] own; ⟨& the⟩ he *MS*
[4] wise] *added in MS* [5] ⟨While⟩ And *MS* [6] tones, ⟨while⟩ "I *MS*
[7] And Hetty{'s} ⟨, happy again for the first time this long day,⟩ foolish joys & hopes which had flown away *MS*
[8] a mere nothing] a nothing *MS*
[9] too; ⟨though he looked beyond the night [?& the sign of the] [two or three words], & from it [?he was] to step into the [?serious world]⟩ ⟨but in his thoughts this dance was⟩ it was the last weakness he meant to indulge in, & a man never lies with *MS*
[1] has] *added in MS* [2] "What! going] "What, going *MS*

guests till eleven: Mrs Irwine and I, who are elderly people, think of sitting out the dance till then."

"O your honour, it's all right and proper for gentlefolks to stay up by candle-light—they've got no cheese on their minds. We're late enough as it is, an' there's no lettin'[3] the cows know as they mustn't want to be milked so early to-morrow mornin'[4].[5] So, if you'll please t' excuse us, we'll take our leave."

"Eh!" she said to her husband, as they set off in the cart, "I'd sooner ha' brewin'[6] day and washin'[7] day together than one o' these pleasurin'[8] days. There's no work so tirin'[9] as danglin'[1] about an' starin' an' not rightly knowin' what you're goin' to do next; an'[2] keepin' your face i' smilin' order[3] like a grocer o' market day[4] for fear people shouldna think you civil enough. An' you've nothing to show for't when it's done, if it isn't a yellow face wi' eatin'[5] things as disagree."

"Nay, nay," said Mr Poyser, who was in his merriest mood, and felt that he had had a great day, "a bit o' pleasuring's good for thee sometimes. An' thee danc'st as well as any of 'em, for I'll back thee against all the wives i' the parish for a light foot an' ankle. An' it was a great honour for th'[6] young Squire to ask thee first—I reckon it was because I sat at th' head o' the table an' made the speech. An' Hetty too—*she* never had such a partner before— a fine young gentleman in reg'mentals. It'll serve you to talk on, Hetty, when you're an old woman—how you danced wi' th' young Squire the day he come o'[7] age."

---

[3] lettin'] letting *MS*   [4] mornin'] morning *MS*
[5] morning.⟨"⟩ ⟨[several words]⟩ So if you'll please t' excuse us we'll take *MS*
[6] brewin'] brewing *MS*   [7] washin'] washing *MS*
[8] pleasurin'] pleasuring *MS*   [9] tirin'] tiring *MS*   [1] danglin'] dangling *MS*
[2] an'] ⟨&⟩ an' *MS* an' *1 8* and *Cabinet*   [3] order ⟨because⟩ like *MS*
[4] market day, ⟨because⟩ for *MS*   [5] eatin'] eating *MS*   [6] th'] the *Cabinet*
[7] o'] of *MS*

ADAM BEDE

BY

GEORGE ELIOT

AUTHOR OF

"SCENES OF CLERICAL LIFE"

EIGHTH EDITION

IN TWO VOLUMES

VOL. II.

WILLIAM BLACKWOOD AND SONS
EDINBURGH AND LONDON
MDCCCLX

BOOK FOURTH

*

CHAPTER XXVII.

A CRISIS.[1]

It was beyond[2] the middle of August—nearly[3] three weeks after the birth-day feast. The reaping of the wheat had begun in our north midland county of Loamshire, but the harvest was likely still to be retarded by the heavy rains, which were causing inundations and much damage throughout the country. From this last trouble the Broxton and Hayslope farmers, on their pleasant uplands, and in their brook-watered valleys, had not suffered, and as I cannot pretend that they were such exceptional farmers as to love the general good better than their own, you will infer that they were not in very low spirits about the rapid rise in the price of bread, so long as there was hope of gathering in their own corn undamaged; and[4] occasional days of sunshine and drying winds[5] flattered this hope.

The[6] eighteenth of August was one of these days, when the sunshine looked brighter in all eyes for the gloom that went before. Grand masses of cloud were hurried across the blue, and the great round hills behind the Chase seemed alive with their flying shadows; the sun was hidden for a moment, and then shone out warm again like a recovered joy; the leaves, still green, were tossed off the hedgerow trees by the wind; around[7] the farm-houses there was a sound of clapping doors; the[8] apples[9] fell in the orchards; and[1] the stray horses on the green sides of the lanes and on the common had their manes blown about their faces. And yet the wind seemed only part of the general gladness because the sun was shining. A merry day for the children, who ran and shouted to see if they could top the wind with[2] their voices; and the grown-up people, too, were in good spirits, inclined to believe in yet finer days, when the wind had fallen. If only the corn were not ripe enough to be blown out of the husk and scattered as untimely seed!

And yet a day on which a blighting sorrow may fall upon a man. For if it be true that Nature at certain moments seems charged with a presentiment of one individual lot, must it not also be true that she seems[3] unmindful,

---

[1] ⟨In the Wood Again⟩ A Crisis *MS*   [2] beyond] *added in MS*
[3] nearly] *added in MS*   [4] undamaged; and] undamaged. And *MS*
[5] & drying winds] *added in MS*   [6] The ⟨fifteenth⟩ eighteenth *MS*
[7] around] about *MS*   [8] doors; the] doors, the *MS 1* doors⟨,⟩ {;} the *8*
[9] the apples] the small apples *MS*
[1] orchards; and] orchards, and *MS 1* orchards⟨,⟩ {;} and *8*   [2] with] *added in MS*
[3] seems ⟨insensible⟩ unmindful *MS*

unconscious of another? For there is no hour that has not its births of gladness and despair, no morning brightness that does not bring new sickness to desolation as well as new forces to genius and love. There are so many of us, and our lots are so different: what[4] wonder that Nature's mood is often in harsh contrast with the great crisis of our lives? We are children of a large family, and must learn, as such children do, not to expect that our hurts will be made much of—to be content with little nurture and caressing, and help each other the more.

It was a busy day with Adam, who of late had done almost double work; for he was continuing to act as foreman for Jonathan Burge, until some satisfactory person could be found to supply his place, and Jonathan was slow to find that person. But he had done the extra work cheerfully, for his hopes were buoyant again about Hetty. Every time she had seen him since the birthday, she had seemed to make an effort to behave all the more kindly to him, that she might make him understand she had forgiven his silence and coldness during the dance. He had never mentioned the locket to her again; too happy that she smiled at him—still happier because he observed in her a more subdued air, something that he interpreted as the growth of womanly tenderness and seriousness. "Ah!" he thought, again and again, "she's only seventeen; she'll be thoughtful enough after a while. And her aunt allays[5] says how clever she is at the work. She'll make a wife as mother'll have no occasion to grumble at, after all." To be sure, he had only seen her at home[6] twice since the birthday; for one Sunday, when he was intending to go from church to the Hall Farm, Hetty had joined the party of upper servants from the Chase, and had gone home with them— almost as if she were inclined to encourage Mr Craig. "She's takin'[7] too much likin' to them folks i' the[8] housekeeper's room," Mrs Poyser remarked. "For my part, I was never over-fond o' gentlefolks's ser-vants—they're mostly like the fine ladies' fat dogs, nayther good for barking nor[9] butcher's meat, but on'y[1] for show." And another evening she was gone to Treddleston to buy some things; though[2], to his great surprise, as he was returning home, he saw her at a distance getting over a stile quite out of the Treddleston road. But, when he hastened to her, she was very kind,[3] and asked him to go in again when he had taken her to the yard gate. She[4] had gone a little farther into the fields after coming from Treddleston, because she didn't want to go in, she said: it was so nice to be out of doors, and her aunt always made such a fuss about it if she wanted to go out. "O do come in with me[5]!" she said, as he was going to shake hands

---

[4] different: what] different⟨?⟩: What *MS*   [5] allays] always *MS*
[6] home ⟨three times⟩ twice since the Birthday *MS*   [7] takin'] taking *MS*
[8] the] th' *MS*   [9] nor ⟨kicking⟩ butcher's meat *MS*   [1] on'y] only *MS*
[2] things; though] things, though *MS 1* things⟨,⟩ {;} though *8*
[3] kind, ⟨to him & shook⟩ & *MS*   [4] gate. She] gate: she *MS*
[5] me, ⟨Adam⟩ !" she *MS*

with her at the gate, and he could not resist that. So he went in, and Mrs Poyser was contented with only a slight remark on Hetty's being later than was expected; while Hetty, who had looked out of spirits when he met her, smiled, and talked, and waited on them all with unusual promptitude.

That was the last time he had seen her; but he meant to make leisure for going to the Farm to-morrow. To-day, he knew, was her day for going to the Chase to sew with the lady's-maid, so he would get as much work done as possible this evening, that the next might be clear.

One piece of work that Adam was superintending was some slight repairs at the Chase Farm, which had been hitherto occupied by Satchell, as bailiff, but which it was now rumoured that the old Squire was going to let to a smart man in top-boots, who had been seen to ride over it one day. Nothing but the desire to get a tenant could account for the Squire's undertaking repairs, though the Saturday-evening party at Mr Casson's agreed over their pipes that[6] no man in his senses would take the Chase Farm unless there was a bit more ploughland laid to it. However that might be, the repairs were ordered to be executed with all despatch; and Adam, acting for Mr Burge, was carrying out the order with his usual energy. But to-day, having been occupied elsewhere, he had not been able to arrive at the Chase Farm till late in the afternoon; and he then discovered that some old roofing, which he had calculated on preserving, had given way. There was clearly no good to be done with this part of the building without pulling it all down; and Adam immediately saw in his mind a plan for building it up again, so as to make the most convenient of[7] cow-sheds and calf-pens, with a hovel for implements; and all without any great expense for materials. So, when the workmen were gone, he sat down, took out his pocket-book, and busied himself with sketching a plan, and making a specification of the expenses, that he might show it to Burge the next morning, and set him on persuading the Squire to consent. To "make a good job" of anything, however small, was always a pleasure to Adam; and he sat on a block, with his book resting on a planing-table, whistling low every now and then, and turning his head on one side with a just perceptible smile of gratification— of pride, too, for if Adam loved a bit of good work, he loved also to think, "I[8] did it!" And I[9] believe the only people who are free from that weakness are those who have no work to call their own. It was[1] nearly seven before he had finished and put on his jacket again; and on[2] giving a last look round, he[3]

---

[6] that ⟨it wo⟩ no *MS*

[7] of ⟨back sheds with [three words] & places ⟨⟨for⟩⟩ to put⟩ cow sheds & calf pens with a hovel for implements *MS*

[8] I]I̲ *MS*

[9] And I ⟨dont know why any of us should dislike⟩ believe the only people who ⟨will deserve⟩ {are free from} that ⟨disposition, unless⟩ weakness, are *MS*

[1] was ⟨after⟩ nearly *MS*   [2] on ⟨looking⟩ giving a last look *MS*

[3] he ⟨saw⟩ observed *MS*

observed that Seth, who had been working here to-day, had left his basket of tools behind him. "Why, th' lad's forgot his tools," thought Adam, "and he's got to work up at the shop to-morrow. There never was such a chap for wool-gathering; he'd leave his head behind him, if it was loose. However, it's lucky I've seen 'em; I'll carry 'em home."

The buildings of the Chase Farm lay at one extremity of the Chase, at about ten minutes' walking distance from the Abbey. Adam had come thither on his pony, intending to ride to the stables, and put up his nag on his way home. At the stables he encountered Mr Craig, who had come to look at the Captain's new horse, on which he was to ride away the day after to-morrow; and Mr Craig detained him to tell how all the servants were to collect at the gate of the courtyard to wish the young Squire luck as he rode out; so that, by the time Adam had got into the Chase, and was striding along with the basket of tools over his shoulder, the sun was on the point of setting, and was sending level crimson rays among the great trunks of the old oaks, and touching every bare patch of ground[4] with a transient glory, that made it look like a jewel[5] dropt upon the grass. The wind had fallen now, and there was only enough breeze to stir the delicate-stemmed leaves. Any one who had been sitting in the house all day would have been glad to walk now; but Adam had been quite enough in the open air to wish to shorten his way home; and he bethought himself that he might do so by striking across the Chase and going through the Grove, where he had never been for years.[6] He hurried on across the Chase,[7] stalking along the narrow paths between the fern, with Gyp at his heels, not lingering to watch the magnificent changes of the light—hardly once[8] thinking of it—yet feeling its presence in a certain calm happy awe which mingled itself with his busy working-day[9] thoughts. How could he help feeling it? The very deer felt it, and were more timid.

Presently Adam's thoughts recurred to what Mr Craig had said about Arthur Donnithorne, and pictured his going away, and the changes that might take place before he came back;[1] then they travelled back affectionately over the old scenes of boyish companionship, and dwelt on Arthur's good qualities, which Adam had a pride in, as we all have in the virtues of the superior who honours us. A nature like Adam's, with a great need of

[4] ground] gound *Cabinet*   [5] jewel ⟨fallen among⟩ dropt upon *MS*

[6] years. ⟨It would be as well, he thought, for him to have a look at the Grove, for though it was on the demesne where {there was to be} no {falling of} timber{,} ⟨⟨was to be⟩⟩ the underwood ought to be made worth something. He should do a bit of business as well as shorten his way by going through the Grove, & when he got home he should have time to finish an estimate he was making for Burge, so that to-morrow evening he would be free to go & see Hetty.⟩ He *MS*

[7] Chase, ⟨not lingering to watch⟩ stalking *MS*   [8] once] *added in MS*

[9] working-day] workaday *MS*

[1] back; {then} they ⟨lingered⟩ {travelled back} affectionately *MS*

love and reverence in it, depends for so much of its happiness on what it can believe and feel about others! And he had no ideal world of dead heroes; he knew little of the life of men in the past; he must find the beings to whom he could cling with loving admiration among those who came within speech of him. These[2] pleasant thoughts about Arthur brought a milder expression than usual into his keen rough face: perhaps they were the reason why, when he opened the old green gate leading into the Grove, he paused to pat Gyp, and say a kind word to him.

After that pause, he strode on again along the broad winding path through the Grove. What grand beeches! Adam[3] delighted in a fine tree of all things; as the fisherman's sight is keenest on the sea, so Adam's perceptions were more at home with trees than with other objects. He[4] kept them in his memory, as a painter does, with all the flecks and[5] knots in their bark, all the curves and angles of their boughs; and[6] had often calculated the height and contents of a trunk to a nicety, as he stood looking at it. No wonder that, notwithstanding his desire to get on,[7] he could not help pausing to look at a curious large beech which he had seen standing before him at a turning in the road, and convince himself that it was not two trees[8] wedded together, but only one. For the rest of his life he remembered that moment when he was calmly examining the beech, as a man remembers his last glimpse of the home where his youth was passed, before the road[9] turned, and he saw it no more. The beech stood at the last turning before the Grove ended in an archway of boughs that let in the eastern light; and as Adam stepped away from the tree to continue his walk, his eyes fell on two figures about twenty yards before him.

He remained as motionless as a statue, and turned almost as pale. The two figures were standing opposite to each other, with clasped hands, about to part; and while they were bending to kiss, Gyp, who had been running among the brushwood, came out, caught sight of them, and gave a sharp bark. They separated with a start—one hurried through the gate out of the Grove, and the other, turning round, walked slowly, with a sort of saunter, towards Adam, who still stood transfixed and pale, clutching tighter the stick with which he held the basket of tools over his shoulder, and looking at the approaching figure with eyes in which amazement was fast turning to fierceness.

[2] him. These] him. And these *MS*
[3] Grove. What grand beeches! Adam] Plenty of underwood & what grand beeches! ⟨There the⟩ Adam *MS*
[4] objects. He] objects; he *MS*   [5] & ⟨?fractures⟩ knots *MS*
[6] & ⟨could⟩ {had often} calculate{d} the {height &} contents *MS*
[7] that notwithstanding his desire to get on,] *added in MS*
[8] two trees {wedded together}, but {only} one. {For the rest of his life} He *MS*
[9] road ⟨bends⟩ turned *MS*

Arthur Donnithorne looked flushed and excited; he had[1] tried to make
unpleasant feelings more bearable by drinking a little more wine than usual
at dinner to-day, and was still enough under its flattering influence to think
more lightly of this unwished-for rencontre with Adam than he would
otherwise have done. After all, Adam was the best person who could have
happened to see him and Hetty together: he was a sensible fellow, and
would not babble about it to other people. Arthur felt confident that he
could laugh the thing off, and explain it away. And so he sauntered forward
with elaborate carelessness—his flushed face, his evening dress of fine cloth
and fine linen, his hands[2] half thrust into his waistcoat pockets, all shone
upon by the strange evening light which the light clouds[3] had caught up
even to the zenith, and were now shedding down between the topmost
branches above him.

Adam was still motionless, looking at him as he came up. He understood
it all now—the locket, and everything else that had been doubtful to him: a
terrible scorching light showed him the hidden letters that changed the
meaning of the past. If he had moved a muscle, he must inevitably have
sprung upon Arthur like a tiger; and in the conflicting emotions that filled
those long moments, he had told himself that he would not give loose to
passion, he would only speak the right thing. He stood as if petrified by an
unseen force, but the force was his own strong will.

"Well, Adam," said Arthur, "you've been looking at the fine old
beeches, eh? They're not to be come near by the hatchet, though; this is a
sacred grove. I overtook pretty[4] little Hetty Sorrel as I was coming to my
den—the Hermitage, there. She ought not to come home this way so late.
So[5] I took care of her to the gate, and asked for a kiss for my pains. But I
must get back now, for this road is confoundedly damp. Good night, Adam:
I shall see you to-morrow—to say good-by, you know."

Arthur was too much preoccupied with the part he was playing himself
to be thoroughly aware of the expression in Adam's face. He did not look
directly at Adam, but glanced carelessly round at the trees, and then lifted
up one foot to look at the sole of his boot. He cared to say no more; he had
thrown quite dust enough into honest Adam's eyes; and as he spoke the last
words, he walked on.

"Stop a bit, sir," said Adam, in a hard peremptory voice,[6] without
turning round. "I've got a word to say to you."

Arthur paused in[7] surprise. Susceptible persons are more affected by a
change of tone than by unexpected words, and Arthur had the suscepti-

---

[1] had ⟨drunk⟩ {tried to make ⟨uncomfortable⟩ unpleasant feelings more bearable by
drinking} a MS
[2] his hands] his white jewelled hands MS 1 his ⟨white jewelled⟩ hands 8
[3] the light clouds] the clouds MS   [4] pretty] added in MS
[5] late. So] late; so MS
[6] voice, ⟨but⟩ without MS   [7] in ⟨startled⟩ surprise: susceptible MS

bility of a nature at once affectionate and vain. He was still more surprised when he saw that Adam had not moved, but stood with his back to him, as if summoning him to return. What did he mean? He was going to make a serious business of this affair. Arthur[8] felt his temper rising. A patronizing disposition always has its meaner side, and in the confusion of his irritation and alarm there entered the feeling that a man to whom he had shown so much favour as to Adam, was not in a position to criticise his conduct. And yet he was dominated, as one who feels himself in the wrong always is, by the man whose good opinion he cares for. In spite of pride and temper, there was as much deprecation as anger in his voice when he said,

"What do you mean, Adam?"

"I mean, sir," answered Adam, in the same harsh voice, still without turning round,—"I mean, sir, that you don't deceive me by your light words. This is not the first time you've met Hetty Sorrel in this grove, and this is not the first time you've kissed her."

Arthur felt a startled uncertainty how far Adam was speaking from knowledge, and how far from mere inference. And this uncertainty, which prevented him from contriving a prudent answer, heightened his irritation. He said in a high sharp tone,

"Well, sir, what then?"

"Why, then, instead of acting like the[9] upright, honourable man we've all believed you to be, you've been acting the part of a selfish,[1] light-minded scoundrel. You know, as well as I do, what it's to lead to, when a gentleman like you kisses and makes love to a young woman like Hetty, and gives her presents as she's frightened for other folks to see. And I say it again, you're acting the part of a selfish, light-minded scoundrel, though it cuts me to th' heart to say so, and I'd rather ha' lost my right hand."

"Let me tell you, Adam," said Arthur, bridling his growing anger, and trying to recur to his careless tone, "you're not only devilishly impertinent, but you're talking nonsense. Every pretty girl is not such a fool as you, to suppose that when a gentleman admires her beauty, and pays her a little attention, he must mean something particular. Every man likes to flirt with a pretty girl, and every pretty girl likes to be flirted with. The wider the distance between them the less harm there is, for then she's not likely to deceive herself."

"I don't know what you mean by flirting," said Adam, "but if you mean behaving to a woman as if you loved her, and yet not loving her all the while, I say that's not th' action of an honest man, and what isn't honest does come t'[2] harm. I'm not a fool, and you're not a fool, and you know better than what you're saying. You know it couldn't be made public as you've behaved

---

[8] affair. Arthur] affair. Confound the fellow!—Arthur *MS* affair. Confound the fellow! Arthur *1* affair. ⟨Confound the fellow!⟩ Arthur *8*

[9] the] th' *MS 1*   [1] selfish,] *MS 1* selfish *8*   [2] t'] to *MS*

to Hetty as y' have done without her losing her character, and bringing shame and trouble on her and her relations. What if you meant nothing by your kissing and your presents? Other folks won't believe as you've meant nothing; and[3] don't tell me about her not deceiving herself. I tell you as you've filled her mind so with the thought of you as it'll mayhap poison her life; and she'll never love another man as 'ud make her a good husband."

Arthur had felt a sudden relief while Adam was speaking; he perceived that Adam had no positive knowledge of the past, and that there was no irrevocable damage done by this evening's unfortunate rencontre. Adam could still be deceived. The candid Arthur had brought himself into[4] a position in which successful lying was his only hope. The hope allayed his anger a little.

"Well, Adam," he said, in a tone of friendly concession, "you're perhaps right. Perhaps I've gone a little too far in taking notice of the pretty little thing, and stealing a kiss now and then. You're such a grave, steady fellow, you don't understand the temptation to such trifling. I'm sure I wouldn't bring any trouble or annoyance on her and the good Poysers on any account if I could help it. But I think you look a little too seriously at it. You know I'm going away immediately, so I shan't make any more mistakes of the kind. But let us say good night,"—Arthur here turned round to walk on—[5] [6] "and talk no more about the matter. The whole thing will soon be forgotten."

"No, by God!" Adam burst out with rage that could be controlled no longer, throwing down the basket of tools, and striding forward till he was right in front of Arthur. All his jealousy and sense of personal injury, which he had been hitherto trying to keep under, had leaped up and mastered him. What man of us, in the first moments of a sharp agony, could ever[7] feel that the fellow-man who has been the medium of inflicting it,[8] did not mean to hurt us?[9] In our instinctive rebellion against pain, we are children again, and demand an active will to wreak our vengeance on. Adam at this moment could only feel that he had been robbed of Hetty—robbed treacherously by the man in whom he had trusted; and he stood close in front of Arthur, with fierce eyes glaring at him, with pale lips and clenched hands, the hard[1] tones in which he had hitherto been constraining himself to express no more than a just indignation, giving way to a deep agitated voice that seemed to shake him as he spoke.

"No, it'll not be soon forgot[2], as you've come in between her and me, when she might ha' loved me—it'll not soon[3] be forgot as you've robbed me

---

[3] nothing; and] nothing. And *MS*   [4] into ⟨that⟩ a *MS*
[5] —Arthur here turned round to walk on—] *added in MS*
[6] on—] *MS 1* on,— *8*   [7] ever ⟨see in⟩ feel that *MS*
[8] it, ⟨[?had] no motive in hurting us⟩ did not mean to hurt us *MS*
[9] us? ⟨On⟩ In *MS*   [1] hard ⟨voice⟩ tones *MS*   [2] forgot] forgotten *MS*
[3] soon] *added in MS*

o' my happiness, while I thought you was my best friend, and a noble-minded man[4], as I was proud to work for. And you've been kissing her and meaning nothing, have you? And I never kissed her i' my life—but[5] I'd ha' worked hard for years for the right to kiss her. And you make light of it. You think little o' doing what may damage other folks, so as you get your bit o' trifling, as means nothing. I throw back your favours, for you're not the man I took you for. I'll never count you my friend any more. I'd rather you'd act as my enemy, and fight me where I stand- -it's all th' amends you can make me."

Poor Adam, possessed by rage that could find no other vent, began to throw off his coat and his cap, too blind with passion to notice the change that had taken place in Arthur while he was speaking. Arthur's lips were now as pale as Adam's; his heart was beating violently. The discovery that Adam loved Hetty, was a shock which made him for the moment see himself in the light of Adam's indignation, and regard Adam's suffering as not[6] merely a consequence, but an element of his error.[7] The words of hatred and contempt—the first he had ever heard in his life—seemed like scorching missiles that were making ineffaceable scars on him. All screening self-excuse, which rarely falls quite away while others respect us, forsook him for an instant, and he stood face to face with the first[8] great irrevocable evil he had ever committed. He was only twenty-one—and three months ago—nay, much later—he had thought proudly that no man should ever be able to reproach him justly. His first impulse, if there had been time for[9] it, would perhaps have been to utter words of propitiation; but Adam had no sooner thrown off his coat and cap, than he became aware that Arthur was standing pale and motionless, with his hands still thrust in his waistcoat pockets.

"What!" he said,[1] "won't you fight me like a man? You know I won't strike you while you stand so."

"Go away, Adam," said Arthur,[2] "I don't want to fight you."

"No," said Adam, bitterly; "you don't want to fight me,—you think I'm a common man, as you can injure without answering for it."

"I never meant to injure you," said Arthur, with returning anger. "I didn't know you loved her."

---

[4] man] *added in MS*   [5] life—but] life, but *MS* 1 life⟨,⟩ {—}but *8*
[6] not ⟨only⟩ merely *MS*
[7] error. ⟨All screening self-excuse, which rarely falls quite away while others respect us, forsook him for an instant⟩ The words of hatred & contempt—the first he had ever heard in his life—seemed like scorching missiles *MS*
[8] the first] the {consciousness of the} first *MS*
[9] for ⟨an active impulse,⟩ it, would perhaps *MS*
[1] said, ⟨"are you a coward then?⟩ Wont *MS*   [2] Arthur, ⟨rousing himself⟩ "I *MS*

"But you've made her love *you*," said Adam.[3] "You're a double-faced man—I'll never believe a word you say again.[4]"

"Go away, I tell you," said Arthur, angrily, "or we shall both repent."

"No," said Adam, with a convulsed voice, "I swear I won't go away without fighting you. Do you want provoking any more? I tell you you're a coward and a scoundrel, and I despise you."

The colour had all rushed back to Arthur's face: in a moment his right hand[5] was clenched, and dealt a blow like lightning, which sent Adam staggering backward. His blood was as thoroughly up as Adam's now, and the two men, forgetting the emotions that had gone before, fought with the instinctive fierceness of panthers in the deepening twilight darkened by the trees. The delicate-handed gentleman was a match for the workman in everything but strength, and Arthur's skill enabled[6] him to protract the struggle for some long moments. But between unarmed men the battle is to the strong, where the strong is no blunderer, and Arthur must sink under a well-planted blow of Adam's, as a steel rod is broken by an iron bar. The blow soon came, and Arthur fell,[7] his head lying concealed in a tuft of fern, so that Adam could only discern his darkly-clad body.

He stood still in the dim light waiting for Arthur to rise.

[8]The blow had been given now, towards which he had been straining all the force of nerve and muscle—and what was the good of it? What had he done by fighting? Only satisfied his own passion, only wreaked his own vengeance. He had not rescued Hetty, not[9] changed the past—there it was just as it had been, and he sickened at the[1] vanity of his own rage.

But why did not Arthur rise? He was perfectly motionless, and the time seemed long to Adam. . . . Good God! had the blow been too much for him? Adam shuddered at the thought of his own strength, as with the on-coming of this dread he knelt down by Arthur's side and lifted his head from among the fern. There was no sign of life: the eyes and teeth were set. The horror that rushed over Adam completely mastered him, and forced upon him its own belief. He could feel nothing but that death was in Arthur's face, and that he was helpless before it. He[2] made not a single movement, but knelt like[3] an image of despair gazing at an image of death.

³ But you've made her love you," said Adam.] *added in MS*
⁴ again. ⟨" said Adam⟩ ¶ "Go *MS*
⁵ his right hand] his white right hand *MS 1* his ⟨white⟩ right hand *8*
⁶ skill enabled] skill in parrying enabled *MS 1* skill ⟨in parrying⟩ enabled *8*
⁷ fell{,} ⟨with⟩ his head {lying concealed} in *MS*   ⁸ *Paragraph division added in 8.*
⁹ not] nor *Cabinet*   ¹ the ⟨thought⟩ vanity *MS*   ² He ⟨thought⟩ made *MS*
³ like ⟨the⟩ an *MS*

CHAPTER XXVIII.

A DILEMMA.

It was[1] only a few minutes measured by the clock—though Adam always thought it had been a long while—before he perceived a gleam of consciousness in Arthur's face and a slight shiver through his frame. The intense joy that flooded his soul brought back some of the old affection with it.

"Do you feel any pain, sir?" he said, tenderly, loosening Arthur's cravat.

Arthur turned his eyes on Adam with a vague[2] stare which gave way to a slightly startled motion as if from the shock of returning memory. But he only shivered again and said nothing.

"Do you feel any hurt, sir?" Adam said again, with a trembling in his voice.

Arthur put his hand up to his waistcoat buttons, and[3] when Adam had unbuttoned it, he took a longer breath. "Lay my head down," he said, faintly, "and get me some water if you can."

Adam laid the head down gently on the fern again, and emptying the tools out of the flag-basket,[4] hurried through the trees to the edge of the Grove bordering on the Chase, where[5] a brook ran below the bank. When he returned with his basket leaking, but still half-full, Arthur looked at him with a more thoroughly reawakened consciousness.[6]

"Can you drink a drop out o' your hand, sir[7]?" said Adam, kneeling down again to lift up Arthur's head.

"No,"[8] said Arthur, "dip my cravat in and[9] souse it on my head."

The water seemed to do him some good, for he presently[1] raised himself a little higher, resting on Adam's arm.

"Do you feel any hurt inside, sir?" Adam asked again.

"No—no hurt," said Arthur, still faintly, "but rather done up."

---

[1] was ⟨[?merely] ⟨⟨but⟩⟩ moments⟩ only a few minutes MS

[2] vague ⟨expression⟩ stare MS

[3] & {when} Adam ⟨understanding the sign, began to unbutton⟩ had unbuttoned MS

[4] flag-basket— ⟨the only vessel at hand—he⟩ hurried MS   [5] where ⟨the⟩ a MS

[6] When . . . consciousness] *Revised in MS from* Arthur looked at him with a more {thoroughly re-} awakened consciousness when he returned with his basket leaking but still half full.

[7] out o' your hand, sir] out of ⟨my hand⟩ your hand, Sir MS

[8] "No," ⟨I can take it with my own⟩ {said Arthur, ⟨beginning to⟩} ⟨take some in the bottom of his own hand⟩, "dip MS

[9] & ⟨drip⟩ souse MS   [1] presently] *added in MS*

After a while he said, "I suppose I fainted away when you knocked me down."

"Yes, sir, thank God," said Adam. "I thought it was worse."

"What! you[2] thought you'd done for me, eh? come[3], help me on my legs."[4]

"I feel terribly shaky and dizzy," Arthur said, as he stood leaning on Adam's arm; "that blow of yours must have come against me like a battering-ram. I don't believe I can walk alone."

"Lean on me, sir; I'll get you along," said Adam. "Or, will you sit down a bit longer, on my coat here? and I'll prop y'[5] up. You'll perhaps be better in a minute or two."

"No," said Arthur. "I'll go to the Hermitage—I think I've got some brandy there. There's a short road to it a little further on, near the gate. If you'll just help me on."

They walked slowly, with frequent pauses, but without speaking again. In both of them, the concentration in the present which had attended[6] the first moments of Arthur's revival, had now given way to a vivid recollection of the previous scene. It was nearly dark in the narrow path among the trees, but within the circle of fir-trees round the Hermitage there was room for the growing moonlight to enter in at the windows. Their steps were noiseless on the thick carpet of fir-needles, and the outward stillness seemed to heighten their inward consciousness, as Arthur took the key out of his pocket and placed it in Adam's hand, for him to open the door. Adam had not known before that Arthur had furnished the old Hermitage and made it a retreat for himself, and it was a surprise to him when he opened the door to see a snug room with all the signs of frequent habitation.

Arthur loosed Adam's arm and threw himself on the ottoman. "You'll see my hunting-bottle somewhere," he said. "A leather case with a bottle and glass in."

Adam was not long in finding the case. "There's very little brandy in it, sir," he said,[7] turning it downwards over the glass, as he held it before the window[8], "hardly this little glassful."

"Well, give me that," said Arthur, with the peevishness of physical depression. When he had taken some sips, Adam said, "Hadn't I better run to th' house, sir, and get some more brandy? I can be there and back pretty soon. It'll be a stiff walk home for you, if you don't have something to revive you."

"Yes—go. But don't say I'm ill. Ask for my man Pym, and tell him to get it from Mills, and not to say I'm at the Hermitage. Get some water too."

---

[2] "What! you] "What, you *MS*   [3] eh? come] eh? Come *MS*

[4] on my legs."] on to my legs." *MS*   [5] y'] you *MS*

[6] attended ⟨Arthur's first return to consciousness,⟩ the first moments of Arthur's revival, *MS*

[7] said, ⟨emptying⟩ turning *MS*   [8] as he held it before the window—] *added in MS*

Adam was relieved to have an active task—both of them[9] were relieved to be apart from each other for a short[1] time. But Adam's swift pace could not still the eager pain of thinking—of living again with concentrated suffering through the last wretched hour, and looking out from it over all the new, sad future.

Arthur lay still for some minutes after Adam was gone, but presently he rose feebly from the ottoman and peered about slowly in the broken moonlight, seeking something. It was a short bit of wax candle that stood amongst a confusion of writing and drawing materials. There was more searching for the means of lighting the candle, and when that was done, he went cautiously round the room as if wishing to assure himself of the presence or absence of something. At last he had found a slight thing, which he put first in his pocket, and then, on a second thought, took out again, and thrust deep down into a waste-paper basket. It was a woman's little pink silk neckerchief. He set the candle on the table, and threw himself down on the ottoman again, exhausted with the effort.

When Adam came back with his supplies, his entrance awoke Arthur from a doze.

"That's right," Arthur said; "I'm[2] tremendously in want of some brandy-vigour."

"I'm glad to see you've got a light, sir," said Adam. "I've been thinking I'd better have asked for a lanthorn."

"No, no; the candle will last long enough—I shall soon be up to walking home now."

"I can't go before I've seen you safe home, sir," said Adam, hesitatingly.

"No: it will be better for you to stay—sit down."

Adam sat down, and they remained opposite to each other in uneasy silence, while Arthur slowly drank brandy-and-water, with visibly reno-vating effect. He began to lie in a more voluntary position, and looked as if he were less overpowered by bodily sensations. Adam was keenly alive to these indications, and as his anxiety about Arthur's condition began to be allayed, he felt more of that impatience which every one knows who has had his just indignation suspended by the physical state of the culprit. Yet there was one thing on his mind to be done before he could recur to remon-strance: it was to confess what had been unjust in his own words. Perhaps he longed all the more to make this confession, that his indignation might be free again; and as he saw the signs of returning ease in Arthur, the words again and again came to his lips and went back, checked by the thought that it would be better to leave everything till to-morrow. As long as they were silent they did not look at each other, and a foreboding came across Adam that if they began to speak as[3] though they remembered the past—if they

[9] of them] *added in MS*   [1] short ⟨space⟩ time *MS*

[2] said; "I'm] said. "I'm *MS* said, "I'm *1*   [3] as ⟨if⟩ though *MS*

looked at each with full recognition—they must take fire again. So they sat in silence till the bit of wax candle[4] flickered low in the socket; the silence all the while becoming more irksome to Adam. Arthur had just poured out some more brandy-and-water, and he threw one arm behind his head and drew up one leg in an attitude of recovered ease, which was an irresistible temptation to Adam to speak what was on his mind.

"You begin to feel more yourself again, sir," he said, as the candle went out, and they were half-hidden from each other in the faint moon-light.

"Yes: I don't feel good for much—very lazy, and not inclined to move; but I'll go home when I've taken this dose."

There was a slight pause before Adam said,

"My temper got the better of me, and I said things as[5] wasn't true. I'd no right to speak as if you'd known you was doing me an injury: you'd[6] no grounds for knowing it; I've[7] always kept what I felt for her as secret as I could."

He paused again before he went on.

"And perhaps I judged you too harsh—I'm apt to be harsh; and you may have acted out o' thoughtlessness more than I should ha' believed was possible for a man with a heart and a conscience. We're not all put together alike, and we may misjudge one another. God knows, it's all the joy I could have now, to think the best of you."

Arthur[8] wanted to go home without saying any more—he was too painfully embarrassed in mind, as well as too weak in body, to wish for any further explanation to-night. And yet it was a relief to him[9] that Adam reopened the subject in[1] a way the least difficult for him to answer. Arthur was in the wretched position of an open, generous man, who has committed an error which makes deception seem a necessity. The native impulse to give truth in return for truth, to meet[2] trust with frank confession, must be suppressed, and duty was become a question of tactics. His deed was reacting upon him—was already governing him tyrannously, and forcing him into a course that jarred with his habitual feelings. The only aim that seemed admissible to him now was to deceive Adam to the utmost: to make Adam think better of him than he deserved. And when he heard the words of honest retractation—when he heard the sad appeal with which Adam ended—he was obliged to rejoice in the remains of ignorant confidence it implied. He did not answer immediately, for he had to be judicious, and not truthful.

---

[4] candle ⟨burned⟩ flickered *MS*   [5] as] that *MS*
[6] injury: you'd] injury. You'd *MS*   [7] it; I've] it. I've *MS*
[8] Arthur ⟨felt⟩ wanted *MS*   [9] him ⟨when⟩ that *MS*   [1] in ⟨this⟩ a *MS*
[2] meet ⟨truth⟩ trust *MS*

"Say no more about your[3] anger, Adam," he said, at last, very languidly, for the labour of speech was unwelcome to him[4]; "I forgive your momentary injustice—it was quite natural, with the exaggerated notions you had in your mind. We shall be none[5] the worse friends in future, I hope, because we've fought: you had the best of it, and that was as it should be, for I believe I've been most in the wrong of the two. Come, let us shake hands."

Arthur held out his hand, but Adam sat still.

"I don't like to say 'No' to that, sir," he said, "but I can't shake hands till it's clear what we mean by't. I was wrong when I spoke as if you'd done me an injury knowingly, but I wasn't wrong in what I said before, about your behaviour t'[6] Hetty, and I can't shake hands with you as if I held you my friend the same as ever, till you've cleared that up better."

Arthur swallowed his pride and resentment as he drew back his hand. He was silent for some moments, and then said, as indifferently as he could,

"I don't know what you mean by clearing up, Adam. I've told you already that you think too seriously of a little flirtation. But if you are right in supposing there is any danger in it—I'm going away on Saturday, and there will be an end of it. As for the pain it has given you, I'm heartily sorry for it. I can say no more."

Adam said nothing, but rose from his chair, and stood with his face towards one of the windows, as if looking at the[7] blackness of the moonlit fir-trees; but[8] he was in reality conscious of nothing but the conflict within him. It was of no use now—his resolution not to speak till to-morrow: he must speak there and then. But it was several minutes before he turned round and stepped nearer to Arthur, standing and looking down on him as he lay.

"It'll be better for me to speak plain," he said, with evident effort, "though it's hard work. You see, sir, this isn't a trifle to me, whatever it may be to you. I'm none[9] o' them men as can go making love first to one woman and then t' another, and don't think it much odds which of 'em I take. What I feel for Hetty's[1] a different sort o' love, such as I believe nobody can know much about but them as feel it, and God as has given it to 'em. She's more nor[2] everything else to me, all but my conscience and my good name. And if it's true what you've been saying all along—and if it's only been trifling and flirting as you call it, as'll be put an end to by[3] your going away—why, then, I'd wait, and hope her heart 'ud turn to me after all. I'm loath to think you'd speak false to me, and I'll believe your word, however things may look."

---

³ your] MS our 1 8
⁴ very languidly, for the labour of speech was unwelcome to him,] *added in MS*
⁵ shall be none] shall none MS   ⁶ t'] to MS   ⁷ the ⟨visible⟩ blackness MS
⁸ fir-trees; but] fir-trees. But MS   ⁹ I'm none] I'm not one MS
¹ Hetty's] Hetty is MS   ² nor] than MS   ³ to by] to you by MS

"You would be wronging Hetty more than me not to believe it," said Arthur, almost violently[4], starting up from the ottoman,[5] and moving away. But he threw himself into a chair again directly, saying,[6] more feebly, "You seem to forget that, in suspecting me, you are casting imputations upon her."

"Nay, sir," Adam said, in a calmer voice, as if he were[7] half relieved—for he was too straightforward to make a distinction between a direct falsehood and an indirect one—"Nay[8], sir, things don't lie level[9] between Hetty and you. You're acting with your eyes[1] open, whatever you may do; but how do you know what's been in her mind? She's all but a child—as any man with a conscience in him ought to feel bound to take care on[2]. And whatever you may think, I know you've disturbed her mind. I[3] know she's been fixing her heart on you; for[4] there's a many things clear to me now as I didn't understand before. But you seem to make light o' what *she* may feel—you don't think o' that."

"Good God, Adam, let me alone!" Arthur burst out impetuously; "I feel it enough without your worrying me."

He was aware of his indiscretion as soon as the words had escaped him.

"Well, then, if you feel it," Adam rejoined, eagerly; "if you feel as you may ha' put false notions into her mind, and made her believe as you loved her, when all the while you meant nothing, I've this demand to make of you;—I'm[5] not speaking for myself, but for her.[6] I ask you t' undeceive her before you go away. Y'aren't[7] going away for ever; and if you leave her behind with a notion in her head o' your feeling about her the[8] same as she feels about you, she'll be hankering after you, and the mischief may get worse. It may be a smart to her now, but it'll save her pain i' th' end. I ask you to write a letter—you may trust to my seeing as she gets it: tell her the truth, and take blame to yourself for behaving as you'd no right to do to a young woman as isn't your equal. I speak plain, sir. But[9] I can't speak any other way. There's nobody can take care o'[1] Hetty in this thing but me."

"I can do what I think needful in the matter," said Arthur, more and more irritated by mingled distress and perplexity, "without giving promises to you. I shall take what measures I think proper."

   [4] almost violently] *added in MS*

   [5] ottoman {& moving away.} ⟨,⟩ ⟨as if some sudden feeling had made him forget his languor,⟩ ⟨& getting as far away from Adam as possible⟩ ⟨moving away⟩. But he threw himself into *MS*

   [6] saying, ⟨in a lower tone⟩ more feebly *MS*

   [7] were ⟨{now} reassured⟩ half relieved *MS*

   [8] one—"Nay] one. "Nay *MS*   [9] level] even *MS*   [1] eyes] *added in MS*

   [2] on] of *MS*   [3] mind. I] mind—I *MS*   [4] you; for] you. For *MS*

   [5] you;—I'm] you. I'm *MS*   [6] her. ⟨If yo⟩ I *MS*   [7] Y'aren't] You're not *MS*

   [8] behind with a notion in her head o' your feeling about her the] behind with the notion that you feel about her ⟨as⟩ the *MS*

   [9] sir. But] Sir. But *MS* sir; but *Cabinet*   [1] o'] of *MS*

"No," said Adam, in an abrupt decided tone, "that[2] won't do. I must know what ground I'm treading on. I must be safe as[3] you've put an end to what ought never to ha' been begun. I don't forget what's owing to you as a gentleman; but in this thing we're man and man, and I can't give up."

There was no answer for some moments. Then Arthur said, "I'll see you to-morrow. I can bear no more now; I'm[4] ill." He rose as he spoke, and reached his cap,[5] as if intending to go.

"You won't see her again!" Adam exclaimed, with a flash of recurring anger and suspicion, moving towards the door and placing his back against it. "Either tell me she can never be my wife—tell me you've been lying—or else promise me what I've said."

Adam, uttering this alternative, stood like a terrible fate before Arthur, who had moved forward a step or two, and now stopped, faint, shaken, sick in mind and body. It seemed long to both of them—that inward struggle of Arthur's—before he said, feebly, "I promise; let[6] me go."

Adam moved away from the door and opened it, but when Arthur reached the step, he stopped again and leaned against the door-post.

"You're not well enough to walk alone, sir," said Adam. "Take my arm again."

Arthur made no answer, and presently walked on, Adam following. But, after a few steps, he stood still again, and said coldly, "I believe I must trouble you. It's getting late now, and there may be[7] an alarm set up about me at home."

Adam gave his arm, and they walked on without uttering a word, till they came where the basket and the tools lay.

"I must pick up the tools, sir," Adam said. "They're my brother's. I[8] doubt they'll be rusted. If you'll please to wait a minute."

Arthur stood still without speaking,[9] and no other word passed between them till they were at the side entrance, where[1] he hoped to get in without being seen by any one. He said then, "Thank you; I[2] needn't trouble you any further."

"What time will it be conven'ent[3] for me to see you to-morrow, sir?" said Adam.

---

[2] tone, "that] tone. "That *MS*
[3] must be safe as] must ⟨have security⟩ {be safe that} *MS*
[4] now; I'm] now. I'm *MS* [5] cap, ⟨which he had thrown on the table⟩, as *MS*
[6] promise; let] promise. Let *MS* promise: let *1*
[7] be ⟨some inquiries⟩ an alarm set up *MS* [8] brother's. I] brother's—I *MS*
[9] speaking— ⟨he said nothing till⟩ & no {other} word passed between them till they ⟨got to⟩ were at *MS*
[1] where ⟨Arthur⟩ he *MS* [2] you; I] you. I *MS*
[3] conven'ent] convenient *MS*

"You may send me word that[4] you're here at five o'clock," said Arthur; "not[5] before."

"Good night, sir," said Adam. But he heard no reply; Arthur[6] had turned into the house.

[4] that] *added in MS*   [5] Arthur; "not] Arthur. "Not *MS*
[6] reply; Arthur] reply. Arthur *MS*

CHAPTER XXIX.

THE NEXT MORNING.

Arthur did not pass a sleepless night; he slept long and well. For sleep comes to the perplexed—if the perplexed are only weary enough. But at seven he rang his bell and astonished Pym by declaring he[1] was going to get up, and must have breakfast brought to him at eight.

"And see that my mare is saddled at half past eight, and tell my grand-father when he's down that I'm better this morning, and am gone for a ride."

He had been awake an hour, and could rest in bed no longer. In bed our yesterdays are too oppressive: if a man can only get up, though it be[2] but to whistle or to smoke, he has a present which offers some resistance to the past—sensations which assert themselves against tyrannous memories. And if there were such a thing as taking averages of feeling, it would certainly be found that in the hunting and shooting seasons regret, self-reproach, and mortified pride, weigh lighter on country gentlemen than in late spring and summer. Arthur felt that he should be more of a man on horseback. Even the presence of Pym, waiting on him with the usual deference, was a reassurance to him after the scenes of yesterday. For, with Arthur's sensitiveness to opinion, the loss of Adam's respect was a shock to his self-contentment which suffused his imagination with the sense that he had sunk in all eyes; as a sudden shock of fear from some real peril makes a nervous woman afraid even to step, because all her perceptions are suffused with a[3] sense of danger.

Arthur's, as you know, was a loving nature. Deeds of kindness were as easy to him as a bad habit: they were the common issue of his weaknesses and good qualities, of his egoism and his sympathy. He didn't like to witness pain, and he liked to have grateful eyes beaming on him as the giver of pleasure. When he was a lad of seven, he one day kicked down an old gardener's pitcher of broth, from no motive but a kicking impulse, not reflecting that it was the old man's dinner; but on learning that sad fact, he took his favourite pencil-case and a silver-hafted knife out of his pocket and offered them as compensation. He had been the same Arthur ever since, trying to make all offences forgotten in benefits. If there were any bitterness in his nature, it could only show itself against the man who refused to be

---

[1] declaring he] declaring that he *MS*   [2] be] is *MS*   [3] a] the *MS*

conciliated by him. And perhaps the time was come for some of that bitterness to rise. At the first moment, Arthur had felt pure distress and self-reproach at discovering that Adam's happiness was involved in his relation to Hetty: if there had been a possibility of making Adam tenfold amends—if deeds of gift, or any other deeds, could have restored Adam's contentment and regard for him as a benefactor, Arthur would not only have executed them without hesitation, but would have felt bound all the more closely to Adam, and would never have been weary of making retribution. But Adam could receive no amends; his suffering could not be cancelled; his respect and affection could not be recovered by any prompt deeds of atonement[4]. He stood like an immovable obstacle against which no pressure could avail; an embodiment of what Arthur most shrank from believing in—the irrevocableness of his own wrong-doing. The words of scorn, the refusal to shake hands, the mastery asserted over him in their last conversation in the Hermitage—above all, the sense of having been knocked down, to which a man does not very well reconcile himself, even under the most heroic circumstances—[5]pressed on him with a galling pain which was stronger than compunction. Arthur would so gladly have persuaded himself that he had done no harm! And if no one had told him the contrary, he could have persuaded himself so much better. Nemesis can seldom forge a sword for herself out of our consciences—out of the suffering we feel in the suffering we may have caused: there is rarely metal enough there to make an effective weapon. Our moral sense learns the manners of good society, and smiles when others smile; but when some rude person gives rough names to our actions, she is apt to take part against us. And so it was with Arthur: Adam's judgment of him, Adam's grating words, disturbed his self-soothing arguments.

Not that Arthur had been at ease before Adam's discovery. Struggles and resolves had transformed themselves into compunction and anxiety. He was distressed for Hetty's sake, and distressed for his own, that he must leave her behind. He had always, both in making and breaking resolutions, looked beyond his passion, and seen that it must speedily end in separation; but his nature was too ardent and tender for him not to suffer at this parting; and on Hetty's account he was filled with uneasiness. He had found out the dream in which she was living—that she was to be a lady in silks and satins; and when he had first talked to her about his going away, she had asked him tremblingly to let her go with him and be married. It was his painful knowledge of this which had given the most exasperating sting to Adam's reproaches. He had said no word with the purpose of deceiving her, her vision was all spun by her own childish fancy; but he was obliged to confess

---

[4] atonement⟨,⟩ {.} ⟨h⟩He *MS*
[5] Hermitage—above all the sense of having been knocked down, to which a man does not very well reconcile himself even under the most heroic circumstances—] *added in MS*

to himself that it was spun half out of his own actions. And to increase the mischief, on this last evening he had not dared to hint the truth to Hetty: he had been[6] obliged to soothe her with tender, hopeful words, lest he should throw her into violent distress. He felt the situation acutely; felt the sorrow of the dear thing in the present, and thought with a darker anxiety of the tenacity which her feelings might have in the future. That was the one sharp point which pressed against him; every other he could evade by hopeful self-persuasion. The whole thing had been secret; the Poysers had not the shadow of a suspicion. No one, except Adam, knew anything of what had passed—no one else was likely to know; for Arthur had impressed on Hetty that it would be fatal to betray, by word or look, that there had been the least intimacy between them; and Adam, who knew half their secret, would rather help them to keep it than betray it. It was an unfortunate business altogether, but there was no use in making it worse than it was, by imaginary exaggerations and forebodings of evil that[7] might never come. The temporary sadness for Hetty was the worst consequence: he resolutely turned away his eyes from any[8] bad consequence that was not demonstrably inevitable. But—but Hetty might have had the trouble in some other way if not in this. And perhaps hereafter he might be able to do a great deal for her, and make up to her for all the tears she would shed about him. She would owe the advantage of his care for her in future years to the sorrow she had incurred now. *So*[9] good comes out of evil. Such[1] is the beautiful arrangement of things!

Are you inclined to ask whether this can be the same Arthur who, two months ago, had that freshness of feeling, that delicate honour which shrinks from wounding even a sentiment, and does not contemplate any more positive offence as possible for it?—who[2] thought that his own self-respect was a higher tribunal than any external opinion? The same, I assure you, only under[3] different conditions. Our deeds determine us, as much as we determine our deeds; and until[4] we know what has been or will be the peculiar combination of[5] outward with inward facts, which constitutes a man's critical actions, it will be better not to think ourselves wise about his character. There is a terrible coercion in our deeds which may first turn the honest man into a deceiver, and then reconcile him to the change; for this[6] reason—that the second wrong presents itself to him in the guise of the only practicable right. The action which before commission has been seen with that blended common sense and fresh untarnished feeling which is the healthy eye of the soul, is looked at afterwards[7] with the lens of apologetic ingenuity, through which all things that men call beautiful and ugly are

---

[6] been] felt *MS*   [7] that ⟨would⟩ might *MS*   [8] any ⟨other⟩ bad *MS*
[9] *So*] So *MS*   [1] evil. Such] evil; Such *MS*   [2] it?—who] it—who *MS*
[3] under ⟨other⟩ different *MS*   [4] until ⟨you⟩ we *MS*   [5] of ⟨the⟩ outward *MS*
[6] this] the *MS*   [7] afterwards ⟨through⟩ with *MS*

seen to be made up of[8] textures very much alike. Europe adjusts itself to a
fait accompli, and so does an individual character,—until the placid adjust-
ment is disturbed by a convulsive retribution.

No man can escape this vitiating effect of an offence against his own
sentiment of right, and the effect was the stronger in Arthur because of that
very need of self-respect which, while his conscience was still at ease, was
one of his best safeguards. Self-accusation was too painful to him—he
could not face it. He must persuade himself that he had not been very much
to blame; he began even to pity himself for the necessity he was under of
deceiving Adam: it was a course so opposed to the honesty of his own
nature. But then, it was the only right thing to do.

Well, whatever had been amiss in him, he was miserable enough in
consequence: miserable about Hetty: miserable about this letter[9] that he
had promised to write, and that seemed at one moment to be a gross
barbarity, at another perhaps the greatest kindness he could do to her.
And across all this reflection would dart every now and then a sudden
impulse of passionate defiance towards all consequences: he would carry
Hetty away, and all other considerations might go to . . . . .

In this state of mind the four walls of his room made[1] an intolerable
prison to him; they seemed to hem in and press down upon him all the
crowd of contradictory thoughts and conflicting feelings, some of
which would fly away in the open air. He had only an hour or two to
make up his mind in, and he must get clear and calm. Once on Meg's back,
in the fresh air of that fine morning, he should be more master of the
situation.

The pretty creature arched her bay neck in the sunshine, and pawed the
gravel, and trembled with pleasure when her master stroked her nose, and
patted her, and talked to her even in a more[2] caressing tone than usual. He
loved her the better because she knew nothing of his secrets. But Meg was
quite as well acquainted with her master's mental state as many others[3] of
her sex with the mental condition of the nice young gentlemen towards
whom their hearts are in a state of fluttering expectation.

Arthur cantered for five miles beyond the Chase, till he was at the foot of
a hill where there were no hedges or trees to hem in the road. Then he threw
the bridle on Meg's neck, and prepared to make up his mind.

Hetty knew that their meeting yesterday must be the last before Arthur
went away; there was no possibility of their contriving another without
exciting suspicion; and she was[4] like a frightened child,[5] unable to think of
anything,[6] only able to cry at the mention of parting, and then put her face

[8] of ⟨tissues⟩ textures *MS*
[9] Hetty: miserable about this letter] Hetty—about this This [*sic*] letter *MS*
[1] made] were *MS*   [2] more ⟨soothing⟩ caressing *MS*   [3] others] *added in MS*
[4] was ⟨so⟩ like *MS*   [5] child, ⟨so⟩ unable *MS*   [6] anything, ⟨but⟩ only *MS*

up to have the tears kissed away. He *could* do nothing but comfort her, and[7] lull her into dreaming on. A letter would be a dreadfully abrupt[8] way of awakening her! Yet there was truth in what Adam said—that it would[9] save her from a lengthened delusion,[1] which might be worse than a sharp immediate pain. And it was the only way of satisfying Adam, who *must* be satisfied, for[2] more reasons than one.[3] If he could have seen her again! But that was impossible; there was such a thorny hedge of hindrances between them, and an imprudence[4] would be fatal. And[5] yet, if he *could* see her again, what good would it do? Only cause him to suffer more from the sight of her distress and the remembrance of it. Away from him, she was surrounded by all the motives to self-control.

A sudden dread here fell like a shadow across his imagination—the dread lest she should do something violent in her grief; and close upon that dread came another, which deepened the shadow. But he shook them off with the force of youth and hope. What was the ground for painting the future in that dark way? It was just as likely to be the reverse. Arthur told himself,[6] he did not deserve that things should turn out badly—he had never meant beforehand to do anything his conscience disapproved—he had been led on by circumstances. There was a sort of implicit confidence in him that he was really such a good fellow at bottom, Providence would not treat him harshly.

At all events, he couldn't help what would come now: all he could do was to take what seemed the best course at the present moment. And he persuaded himself that that course was to make the way open between Adam and Hetty. Her heart might really turn to Adam, as he said, after a while; and in that case[7] there would have been no great harm done, since it was still Adam's ardent wish to make her his wife. To be sure, Adam was deceived—deceived in a way that Arthur would have resented as a deep wrong if it had been practised on himself. That was a reflection that marred the consoling prospect. Arthur's cheeks even burned in mingled shame and irritation at the thought. But what could a man do in such a dilemma? He was bound in honour to say no word that could injure Hetty: his first duty was to guard *her*.[8] He would never have told or acted a lie on his own account. Good God! what a miserable fool he was to have brought himself into such a dilemma; and yet, if ever a man had excuses, he had. (Pity that consequences are determined not by excuses but[9] by actions!)

---

[7] & ⟨encourage⟩ {lull her} in{to} dream⟨s⟩ {ing on}. A *MS*
[8] abrupt ⟨cold⟩ way *MS*   [9] would ⟨prevent⟩ save *MS*
[1] delusion ⟨that⟩ which *MS*   [2] satisfied, for] satisfied for *MS 1* satisfied {,} for *8*
[3] one{.} ⟨who must be satisfied⟩ If he could have seen *MS*
[4] them, and an imprudence] them—⟨the⟩ {an} imprudence *MS*
[5] fatal. And] fatal. . . . And *MS*   [6] himself, ⟨that⟩ he *MS*
[7] and in that case] & then, after all, *MS*   [8] *her*] her *MS*   [9] but] *added in MS*

Well, the letter must be written; it was the only means that promised a solution of the difficulty. The tears came into Arthur's eyes as he thought of Hetty reading it; but it would be almost as hard for him to write it: he was not doing anything easy to himself; and[1] this last thought[2] helped him to arrive at a conclusion. He could never deliberately have taken a step which inflicted pain on another and left himself at ease. Even a movement of jealousy at the thought of giving up Hetty to Adam, went to convince him that he was making a sacrifice.

When once he had come to this conclusion, he turned Meg round, and set off home again in a canter. The letter should be written the first thing, and the rest of the day would be filled up with other business: he should have no time to look behind him. Happily Irwine and Gawaine were coming to dinner, and by twelve o'clock the next day he should have left the Chase miles behind him. There was some security in this constant occupation against an uncontrollable impulse seizing him to rush to Hetty, and thrust into her hand some mad proposition that would undo everything. Faster and faster went the sensitive Meg, at every slight sign from her rider, till the canter had passed into a swift gallop.

"I thought they said th' young mester war took ill last night," said sour old John, the groom, at dinner-time in the servants' hall. "He's been ridin' fit to split the mare i' two this forenoon."

"That's happen one o' the symptoms, John," said the facetious coachman.

"Then I wish he war let blood for 't, that's all," said John, grimly.

Adam had been early at the Chase to know how Arthur was, and had been relieved from all anxiety about the effects of his blow by learning that he was gone out for a ride. At five o'clock he was punctually there again, and sent up word of his arrival. In a few minutes Pym came down with a letter in his hand, and gave it to Adam, saying that the Captain was too busy to see him, and had written everything he had to say. The letter was directed to Adam, but he went out of doors again before opening it. It contained a sealed enclosure directed to Hetty. On the inside of the cover Adam read:—

"In the enclosed letter I have written everything you wish. I leave it to[3] you to decide whether you will be doing best to deliver it to Hetty or to return it to me. Ask yourself once more whether you are not taking a measure which may pain her more than mere silence.

"There is no need for our seeing each other again now. We shall meet with better feelings some months hence.   "A.D."

"Perhaps he's i' th' right on 't not to see me," thought Adam. "It's no use meeting to say more hard words, and it's no use meeting to shake hands and

---

[1] himself; and] himself, and *MS 1* himself⟨,⟩ {;} and *8*
[2] this last thought] this thought *MS*   [3] to ⟨her⟩ you *MS*

say we're friends again. We're not friends, an'[4] it's better not to[5] pretend it. I know forgiveness is a man's duty, but, to my thinking, that can only mean as you're to give up all thoughts o' taking revenge: it can never mean as you're t' have[6] your old feelings back again, for that's not possible. He's not the same man to me, and I can't *feel*[7] the same towards him. God help me! I[8] don't know whether I feel the same towards anybody: I seem as if I'd been measuring my work from a false line, and had got it all to measure over[9] again."

But the question about delivering the letter to Hetty soon absorbed Adam's thoughts. Arthur had procured some relief to himself by[1] throwing the decision on Adam with a warning; and Adam, who was not given to hesitation, hesitated here. He determined to feel his way—to ascertain as well as he could what was Hetty's state of mind before he decided on delivering the letter.

[4] an'] & *MS* an *1*   [5] to] *added in MS*   [6] have ⟨the⟩ your *MS*
[7] *feel*] feel *MS*   [8] me! I] me, I *MS*   [9] over] *MS* o'er *1* ⟨o'er⟩ over *8*
[1] by ⟨thus expressly⟩ throwing *MS*

CHAPTER XXX.

THE DELIVERY OF THE LETTER.[1]

The next Sunday Adam joined the Poysers on their way out of church, hoping for an invitation to go home with them. He had the letter in his pocket, and was anxious to have an opportunity of talking to Hetty alone. He could not see her face at church, for she had changed her seat, and when he came up to her to shake hands, her manner was doubtful and constrained. He expected this, for it was the first time she had met him since she had been aware that he had[2] seen her with Arthur in the Grove.

"Come, you'll go on with[3] us, Adam," Mr Poyser said when they reached the turning; and as soon as they were in the fields, Adam ventured to offer his arm to Hetty. The children soon gave them an opportunity of lingering behind a little, and then Adam said,

"Will you contrive for me to walk out in the garden a bit with you this evening, if it keeps fine, Hetty? I've something partic'lar[4] to talk to you about."

Hetty said, "Very well." She was really as anxious as Adam was that she should have some private talk with him: she wondered what he thought of her and Arthur: he must have seen them kissing, she knew, but she had no conception of the scene that had taken place between Arthur and Adam. Her first feeling had been that Adam would be very angry with her, and perhaps would tell her aunt and uncle; but it never entered her mind that he would dare to say anything to Captain Donnithorne. It was a relief to her that he[5] behaved so kindly to her to-day, and wanted to speak to *her* alone; for she had trembled when she found he was going home with them lest he should mean "to tell." But, now he wanted to talk to her by herself, she should learn what he thought, and what he meant to do. She felt[6] a certain confidence that she could persuade him not to do anything she did not want him to do; she could perhaps even make him believe that she didn't care for Arthur; and[7] as long as Adam thought[8] there was any hope of her having him, he would do just what she liked, she knew. Besides,[9] she *must* go on

---

[1] *MS reads* <u>The delivery of ⟨a⟩ {the} letter {.} ⟨; & the reading of a letter.⟩</u>

[2] had ⟨since⟩ seen *MS*   [3] with] *MS* wi' *1* ⟨wi'⟩ with *8*

[4] partic'lar] particular *MS*   [5] he ⟨spoke⟩ behaved *MS*

[6] felt ⟨assured⟩ a certain confidence *MS*   [7] Arthur; and] Arthur. And *MS*

[8] thought ⟨he had⟩ there was *MS*   [9] Besides ⟨if⟩ she ⟨could⟩ {must} go *MS*

seeming to encourage Adam,[1] lest her uncle and aunt should be angry, and suspect her of having some secret lover.

Hetty's little brain was busy with this combination, as she hung on Adam's arm, and said "yes" or "no" to some slight observations of his about the[2] many hawthorn-berries there would be for the birds this next winter, and the low-hanging clouds that would hardly hold up till morning. And when they rejoined[3] her aunt and uncle, she could pursue her thoughts without interruption, for Mr Poyser held, that though a young man might like to have the woman he was courting on his arm, he would nevertheless be glad of a little reasonable talk about business the while; and, for his own part, he was curious to hear the most recent news about the Chase Farm. So,[4] through the rest of the walk, he claimed Adam's conversation for himself; and Hetty laid her small plots, and imagined her little scenes of cunning blandishment, as she walked along by[5] the hedgerows on honest Adam's arm, quite as well as if she had been an elegantly clad coquette alone in her boudoir. For if a country beauty in clumsy shoes be only shallow-hearted enough, it is astonishing how closely her mental processes may resemble those of a lady in society and crinoline, who applies her refined intellect to the problem of committing indiscretions without compromising herself. Perhaps the resemblance was not much the less because Hetty felt very unhappy all the while. The parting with Arthur was a double pain to her; mingling with the tumult of passion and vanity, there was a dim undefined fear that the future might shape itself in some way quite unlike her dream. She clung to the comforting hopeful words Arthur had uttered in their last meeting—"I shall come again at Christmas, and then we will see what can be done."[6] She clung to the belief that he was so fond of her, he would never be happy without her; and she still hugged her secret—that a great gentleman loved her—with gratified pride, as a superiority over all the girls she knew. But the uncertainty of the future, the possibilities to which she could give no shape,[7] began to press upon her like the invisible weight of air; she was alone on her little island of dreams, and all round[8] her was the dark unknown water where Arthur was gone. She

---

[1] Adam, ⟨that would be a way of preventing all suspicion in her uncle & aunt that she had ⟨⟨any secret⟩⟩ another lover⟩ lest her uncle & aunt should be angry, & suspect her of having some secret lover. ¶ ⟨That was the combination arrived at by Hetty's small⟩ Hetty's little brain was busy with this combination as she *MS*

[2] the ⟨children⟩ many *MS*

[3] rejoined ⟨Mr. & Mrs. Poyser⟩ {her ⟨uncle⟩ aunt & uncle} she *MS*

[4] So ⟨he kept Adam in conversa-⟩ through the rest of the walk *MS*

[5] by] *added in MS*

[6] meeting—"I shall . . . done."] meeting—that he would come again at Christmas, & then they would see what could be done. *MS*

[7] possibilities to which she could give no shape,] possibilities of which she knew nothing, *MS*

[8] round] *MS 1* around *8*

could gather no elation of spirits now by looking forward, but only by looking backward to build confidence on past words and caresses. But occasionally, since Thursday evening, her dim anxieties had been almost lost behind the more definite fear that Adam might betray what he knew to her uncle and aunt, and his sudden proposition to talk with her alone had set her thoughts to work in a new way. She was eager not to lose this evening's opportunity; and after tea, when the boys were going into the garden, and Totty begged to go with them, Hetty said, with an alacrity that surprised Mrs Poyser—

"I'll go with her, aunt."

It did not seem at all surprising that Adam said he would go too; and soon he and Hetty were left alone together on the walk[9] by the filbert trees, while the boys were busy elsewhere gathering the large unripe nuts to play at "cob-nut" with, and Totty was watching them with a puppy-like air of contemplation. It was but a short time—hardly two months—since Adam had had his mind filled with delicious hopes, as he stood by Hetty's side in this garden. The remembrance of that scene had often been with him since Thursday evening: the sunlight through the apple-tree boughs, the red bunches, Hetty's sweet blush. It[1] came importunately now, on this sad evening, with the low-hanging clouds; but he tried to suppress it, lest some emotion should impel him to say[2] more than was needful for Hetty's sake.

"After what I saw on Thursday night, Hetty," he began, "you won't think me making too free in[3] what I'm going to say. If you was being courted by any man as 'ud make you[4] his wife, and I'd known you was fond of him, and meant to have him, I should have no right to speak a word to you about it; but[5] when I see you're being made love to by a gentleman as can never marry you, and doesna[6] think o' marrying you, I feel bound t' interfere for you. I can't speak about it to them as are i' the place o'[7] your parents, for that might bring worse trouble than's needful."

Adam's words relieved one of Hetty's fears, but they also carried a meaning which sickened her with a strengthened foreboding. She was pale and trembling, and yet she would have angrily contradicted Adam, if she had dared to betray her feelings. But she was silent.

"You're so young, you know, Hetty," he went on, almost tenderly, "and y' haven't[8] seen much o' what goes on in the world. It's right for me to do what I can to save you from getting into trouble for want o'[9] your knowing where you're being led to. If anybody besides me knew what I know about

[9] walk ⟨between⟩ by *MS*   [1] blush. It] blush; it *MS*   [2] say ⟨what⟩ more than *MS*
[3] in] i' *MS* *1* ⟨i'⟩ in *8*   [4] make you] make you *MS* make y' *1* ⟨mak y'⟩ make you *8*
[5] it; but] it. But *MS*   [6] doesna] doesn't *MS*
[7] i' the place o'] *added in MS*   [8] and y' haven't] & haven't *MS*
[9] for want o'] without *MS*

your meeting a gentleman, and having fine presents from him, they'd speak light on[1] you, and you'd lose your character. And besides that, you'll have to suffer in your feelings, wi'[2] giving your love to a man as can never marry you, so[3] as he might take care of you all your life."

Adam paused, and looked at Hetty, who was plucking the leaves from the filbert trees, and tearing them up in her hand. Her little plans and preconcerted speeches had all forsaken her, like an ill-learnt lesson, under the terrible agitation produced by Adam's words. There was a cruel force in their calm certainty which threatened to grapple and crush her flimsy hopes and fancies. She wanted to resist them—she wanted to throw them off with angry contradiction; but the[4] determination to conceal what she felt still governed her. It was nothing more than a blind prompting now, for she was unable to calculate the effect of her words.

"You've no right to say as I love him," she said, faintly, but impetuously,[5] plucking another rough leaf and tearing it up. She[6] was very beautiful in her paleness and agitation, with her dark childish eyes dilated, and her breath shorter than usual. Adam's heart yearned over her as he looked at her. Ah,[7] if he could but comfort her, and soothe her, and save her from this pain; if he had but some sort of strength that would enable him to rescue her poor troubled mind, as he would have rescued her body in the face of all danger!

"I doubt it must be so, Hetty," he said, tenderly; "for[8] I canna[9] believe you'd let any man kiss you by yourselves, and[1] give you a gold box with his hair, and go a-walking i' the Grove to meet[2] him, if you didna[3] love him. I'm not blaming you, for I know it 'ud begin by little and little, till at last you'd not be able to throw it off. It's him I blame for stealing your love i' that way, when he knew he could never make you the right amends. He's been trifling with you, and making a plaything of you, and caring nothing about you as a man ought to care."

"Yes, he does care for me; I know better nor[4] you," Hetty burst out[5]. Everything was forgotten but the pain and anger she felt at Adam's words.

"Nay, Hetty," said Adam, "if he'd cared for you rightly he'd never ha' behaved so. He told me himself he meant nothing by his kissing and presents,[6] and he wanted to make me believe as you thought light of 'em

---

[1] on] of *MS*	[2] wi'] with *MS*	[3] marry you, so] marry, so *MS*
[4] the ⟨recollection that she had⟩ determination *MS*
[5] impetuously, ⟨tearing⟩ plucking *MS*	[6] She ⟨looked⟩ was *MS*
[7] her. Ah,] her:—ah, *MS*	[8] tenderly; "for] tenderly. "For *MS*
[9] canna] cant *MS*	[1] kiss you by yourselves, and] kiss you, & *MS*
[2] go a-walking i' the Grove to meet] go {awalking} to meet *MS*
[3] didna] didn't *MS*	[4] nor] than *MS*
[5] out—⟨the great tears starting from her eyes⟩ ⟨tears were starting⟩ Everything *MS*
[6] by his kissing & presents,] *added in MS*

too.[7] But I know better nor that. I can't help thinking as you've been trusting to his[8] loving you well enough to marry you, for all he's a gentleman. And that's why I must speak to you about it, Hetty,—for fear you should be deceiving yourself. It's never entered his head, the thought o' marrying you."

"How do you know? How durst[9] you say so?" said Hetty, pausing in her walk and[1] trembling. The terrible decision of Adam's tone shook her with fear. She[2] had no presence of mind left[3] for the reflection that Arthur would have his reasons for not telling the truth to Adam. Her words and look were enough to determine Adam: he must give her the letter.

"Perhaps you[4] can't believe me, Hetty; because you think too well of him—because you think he loves you better than he does. But I've got a letter i'[5] my pocket, as he wrote himself for me to give you. I've not read the letter, but he says he's told you the truth in it. But before I give you the letter, consider, Hetty, and don't let it take too much hold on[6] you. It wouldna ha'[7] been good for you if he'd wanted to do such a mad thing as marry you: it 'ud ha'[8] led to no happiness i' th' end."

Hetty said nothing: she felt a revival of hope at the mention of a letter which Adam had not read. There would be something quite different in it from what he thought.

Adam took out the letter, but he held it in his hand still, while he said, in a tone of tender entreaty—

"Don't you bear me ill-will, Hetty, because I'm the means o' bringing you this pain. God knows I'd ha' borne a good deal worse for the sake o' sparing it you. And think—there's nobody but me knows about this; and I'll take care of you as if I was your brother. You're the same as ever to me, for I don't believe you've done any wrong knowingly."

Hetty had laid her hand on[9] the letter, but Adam did not loose it till he had done speaking. She took no notice of what he said—she had not listened; but when he loosed the letter, she put it into her pocket, without opening it, and then began to walk more quickly, as if she wanted to go in.

"You're in the right not to read it just yet," said Adam. "Read it when you're by yourself. But stay out a little bit longer, and let us call the children: you look so white and ill; your aunt may take notice of it."

---

[7] too. ⟨But I knew better than that to think he'd a kiss of you because you're a pretty girl, & you knew that very well, & he was going away, & it 'ud soon be all forgot.⟩ ⟨He said it had been only a [?bit o' fun]. But I cant believe that. I know {of} [two words] been brought up.⟩ {But I know better than that. I cant help thinking as you've been trusting to his loving} you *MS*

[8] to his] *MS* t's *1* ⟨t's⟩ to his *8*   [9] know? How durst] know—how can *MS*

[1] pausing in her walk &] *added in MS*   [2] fear. She] fear: she *MS*

[3] left ⟨to⟩ {for the} reflect{ion} that *MS*

[4] Perhaps you] You perhaps *MS 1* ⟨You, perhaps,⟩ Perhaps you *8*   [5] i'] in *MS*

[6] on] of *MS*   [7] wouldna ha'] wouldn't have *MS*   [8] ha'] have *MS*

[9] hand on] hand too on *MS*

Hetty heard the warning. It[1] recalled to her the necessity of[2] rallying her native powers[3] of concealment, which had half given way under the shock of Adam's words. And she had the letter in her pocket: she was sure there was comfort in that letter, in spite of Adam. She ran to find Totty, and soon reappeared with recovered colour, leading Totty[4], who was making a sour face, because she had been obliged to throw away an unripe apple that she had set her small teeth in.

"Hegh, Totty," said Adam, "come[5] and ride on my shoulder—ever so high—you'll touch the tops o' the trees."

What little child ever refused to be comforted by that glorious sense of being seized strongly and swung upward? I[6] don't believe Ganymede cried when the eagle carried him away, and perhaps deposited him on Jove's shoulder at the end. Totty smiled down complacently from her secure height, and[7] pleasant was the sight to the mother's eyes, as she stood at the house-door and saw Adam coming with his small burthen.

"Bless your sweet face, my pet," she said, the mother's strong love[8] filling her keen eyes with mildness, as Totty leaned forward and put out her arms. She had no eyes for Hetty at that moment, and only said, without looking at her, "You go and draw some ale, Hetty: the gells are both at the cheese."

After the ale had been drawn and[9] her uncle's pipe lighted, there was Totty to be taken to bed, and brought down again in her night-gown, because she would cry instead of going to sleep. Then there was supper to be got ready, and[1] Hetty must be continually in the way to give help. Adam stayed till he knew Mrs Poyser expected him to go, engaging her and her husband in talk as constantly as he could, for the sake of leaving Hetty more at ease. He lingered, because he wanted to see her safely through that evening, and he was delighted to[2] find how much self-command she showed. He knew she had not had time to read the letter, but he did not know[3] she was buoyed up by a secret hope that the letter would contradict everything he had said. It was hard work for him to leave her—hard to think that he should not know for days how she was bearing her trouble. But he must go at last, and all he could do was to press her hand gently as he said "Good-by," and hope she would take that as a sign that if his love could

---

[1] warning. It] warning: it *MS*   [2] of ⟨exerting⟩ rallying *MS*
[3] powers] power *MS*   [4] Totty ⟨by the hand⟩ who *MS*
[5] Adam, "come] Adam. "Come *MS*   [6] upward? I] upward. I *MS*
[7] & ⟨Mrs. Poyser who was standing near, & who⟩ ⟨Mrs. Poyser was standing⟩ {⟨when they came near the house⟩ pleasant was the sight to the mother's} eyes *MS*
[8] love ⟨shedding mildness over her keen face⟩ filling her keen eyes with mildness *MS*
[9] & ⟨the⟩ her *MS*
[1] & ⟨constant demands on Hetty's attention.⟩ Hetty must be continually in the way to give help. *MS*
[2] to ⟨see⟩ find *MS*   [3] know ⟨that⟩ she *MS*

ever be a refuge for her, it was there the same as ever. How busy his
thoughts were, as he walked home, in devising[4] pitying excuses for her
folly; in referring all her weakness to the sweet lovingness of her nature; in
blaming Arthur,[5] with less and less inclination to admit that *his* conduct
might be extenuated too! His[6] exasperation at Hetty's suffering—and also
at the sense that she was possibly thrust for ever out of his own reach—
deafened him to any plea for the[7] miscalled friend who had wrought this
misery. Adam was a clear-sighted, fair-minded man—a fine fellow, indeed,
morally as well as physically. But if Aristides the Just was ever in love and
jealous, he was at that moment not perfectly magnanimous. And I cannot
pretend that Adam, in these painful days, felt nothing but righteous
indignation and loving pity. He[8] was bitterly jealous; and in proportion
as his love made him indulgent in his judgment of Hetty, the bitterness
found a vent in his feeling towards Arthur.

"Her head was allays[9] likely to be turned," he thought, "when a gentleman, with his fine manners, and fine clothes,[1] and his white hands, and that
way o' talking gentlefolks have, came about her, making up to her in a bold
way, as a man couldn't do that was only her equal; and[2] it's much if she'll
ever like a common man now." He could not help drawing his own hands
out of his pocket, and looking at them—at the hard palms and the broken
finger-nails. "I'm a roughish fellow, altogether: I[3] don't know, now I come
to think on't, what there is much for a woman to like about me; and[4] yet I
might ha' got another wife easy enough, if I hadn't set my heart on her. But
it's little matter what other women think about me, if she can't love me. She
might ha' loved me,[5] perhaps, as likely as any other man—there's nobody
hereabouts as I'm afraid of, if *he* hadn't come between us; but now I shall
belike be hateful to her because I'm so different to him. And yet there's no
telling—she may turn round the[6] other way, when she finds[7] he's made
light of her all the while. She may come to feel the vally of a man as[8] 'ud be
thankful to be bound to her all his life. But I must put up with it whichever
way it is—I've only to be thankful it's been no worse:[9] I'm[1] not th' only man
that's got to do without much happiness i' this life. There's many a good bit
o' work done with a sad heart. It's God's will, and that's enough for us:[2] we
shouldn't know better how things ought to be than He does, I reckon, if we

---

[4] devising] *added in MS*   [5] Arthur ⟨&⟩ with *MS*   [6] too! His] too. His *MS*
[7] the ⟨once⟩ ⟨too⟩ ⟨well-loved⟩ {miscalled} friend *MS*   [8] pity. He] pity: he *MS*
[9] allays] always *MS*   [1] clothes, ⟨& that⟩ & his *MS*
[2] equal; and] equal. And *MS*   [3] altogether: I] altogether. I *MS*
[4] me; and] me. And *MS*   [5] me, ⟨belike⟩ perhaps *MS*   [6] the] th' *MS*
[7] finds ⟨the gentleman was making⟩ he's made light of her all the while. *MS*
[8] as ⟨'ud never expect so much as a kiss from her if he didn't⟩ 'ud be thankful to be bound to
her all his life. But I must *MS*
[9] worse. ⟨I can bear what comes as a man & my back's broad enough⟩ I'm *MS*
[1] I'm] I am *Cabinet*   [2] us: ⟨it's not likely⟩ we should{n't} know *MS*

was[3] to[4] spend our lives i' puzzling. But it 'ud ha'[5] gone near to spoil my work for me, if I'd seen her brought to sorrow and shame, and through[6] the man as I've always[7] been proud to think on. Since I've been spared that, I've no right to grumble. When a man's got his limbs whole, he can bear a smart cut or two."

As Adam was getting over a stile at this point in his reflections, he perceived a man walking along the field before him. He knew it was Seth, returning from an evening preaching, and made haste to overtake him.

"I thought thee'dst be at home before me," he said, as Seth turned round to wait for him, "for I'm later[8] than usual to-night."

"Well, I'm later too, for I got into talk, after[9] meeting, with John Barnes, who has lately professed himself in a state of perfection, and[1] I'd a question to ask him about his experience. It's one o' them subjects that lead you further than y' expect—they don't lie along the straight road."

They walked along together in silence[2] two or three minutes. Adam was not inclined to[3] enter into the subtleties of religious experience, but he *was* inclined to interchange a word or two of brotherly affection and confidence with Seth. That was a rare impulse in him, much as the brothers loved each other. They hardly ever spoke of personal matters, or uttered more than an allusion to their family troubles. Adam was by nature reserved in all matters of feeling, and Seth felt a certain timidity towards his more practical brother.

"Seth, lad," Adam said, putting his arm on his brother's shoulder, "hast heard anything from Dinah Morris since she went away?"

"Yes," said Seth. "She[4] told me I might write her word after a while, how we went on, and how mother bore up under her trouble. So I wrote to her a[5] fortnight ago, and told her about thee having a new employment, and how mother was more contented; and[6] last Wednesday, when I called at the post at Treddles'on, I found a letter from her. I think thee'dst perhaps like to read it; but I didna[7] say anything about it, because thee'st seemed so full of other things. It's quite easy t' read—she writes wonderful for a woman."

Seth had drawn the letter from his pocket and held it out to Adam, who said, as he took it,

---

[3] was] were *MS*   [4] to ⟨puzzle⟩ spend *MS*   [5] ha'] have *MS*
[6] through ⟨him⟩ the man *MS*   [7] always] *added in MS*
[8] later ⟨then⟩ than *MS*   [9] after ⟨the⟩ meeting *MS*
[1] & ⟨that's an experience⟩ I'd a question to *MS*   [2] silence ⟨a few⟩ two or three *MS*
[3] to ⟨pursue a difficult question⟩ {enter into the subtleties of} religious {experience}, but ⟨the pain he had been enduring in his affections, for the last few days made his heart go out to Seth's⟩ he <u>was</u> inclined to ⟨speak⟩ interchange a word or two of brotherly affection & confidence with Seth ⟨to whom his heart [one word] [?went] with new tenderness as towards the friend who⟩. {That was a rare impulse in him, well as the brothers loved each other. They hardly ever} spoke of personal matters, ⟨[?&] never⟩ {or} uttered *MS*
[4] Seth. "She] Seth, "She *MS*   [5] a ⟨three-week⟩ fortnight *MS*
[6] contented; and] contented. And *MS*   [7] didna] didn't *MS*

"Ay, lad, I've got a tough load to carry just now—thee mustna take it ill if I'm a bit silenter and crustier nor[8] usual. Trouble doesna[9] make me care the less for thee. I know we shall stick together to the[1] last."

"I take nought ill o'[2] thee, Adam: I[3] know well enough what it means if thee't a bit short wi'[4] me now and then."

"There's mother opening the door to look out for us," said Adam, as they mounted the slope. "She's been sitting i' the dark as usual. Well, Gyp, well! art glad to see me?"

Lisbeth went in again quickly and lighted a candle, for she had heard the welcome rustling of footsteps on the grass, before Gyp's joyful bark.

"Eh, my lads! th' hours war ne'er so long sin' I war born as they'n been this blessed Sunday night. What can ye both ha' been doin' till this time?"

"Thee shouldstna sit i' the[5] dark, mother," said Adam; "that[6] makes the time seem longer."

"Eh, what am I to[7] do wi' burnin' candle of a Sunday, when there's on'y me, an' it's sin to do a bit o' knittin'? The daylight's long enough for me to stare i' th'[8] booke as I canna read. It 'ud be a fine way o' shortenin' the time, to make it waste the good candle. But which on you's for ha'ing[9] supper? Ye mun ayther[1] be clemmed or full, I should think, seein' what time o' night it is."[2]

"I'm hungry, mother," said Seth, seating himself at the little table, which had been spread ever since it was light.

"I've had my supper," said Adam. "Here, Gyp," he added, taking some cold potato from the table, and rubbing the rough grey head that looked up towards him.

"Thee needstna be gi'in' th'[3] dog," said Lisbeth: "I'n[4] fed him well a'ready. I'm not like to forget him, I reckon, when he's all o' thee I can get sight on."

"Come, then, Gyp," said Adam, "we'll[5] go to bed. Good night, mother; I'm very tired."

"What ails him, dost know?" Lisbeth said to Seth, when Adam was gone upstairs. "He's like as if he was struck for death this day or two—he's so cast down. I found him i' the shop this forenoon, arter thee wast gone, a-sittin' an' doin' nothin'[6]—not so much as a booke[7] afore him."

"He's a deal o' work upon him just now, mother," said Seth, "and I think he's a bit troubled in his mind. Don't you take notice of it, because it hurts

---

[8] nor] than *MS*   [9] doesna] doesn't *MS*   [1] the] th' *MS*   [2] o'] of *MS*
[3] Adam: I] Adam. I *MS*   [4] wi'] with *MS*   [5] the] th' *MS*
[6] Adam; "that] Adam. "That *MS*   [7] to] t' *MS 1* ⟨t'⟩ to *8*
[8] th'] the *Cabinet*   [9] ha'ing] ha'in' *Cabinet*   [1] ayther] eyther *MS*
[2] think, seein' what time o' night it is."] think—an' look at the clock." *MS*
[3] th'] the *MS*   [4] Lisbeth: "I'n] Lisbeth. "I'n *MS*
[5] Adam, "we'll] Adam. "We'll *MS*   [6] nothin'] nothing *MS 1* ⟨nothing⟩ nothin' *8*
[7] booke ⟨be⟩{a}fore *MS*

him when you do. Be as kind to him as you can, mother, and don't say anything to vex him."

"Eh, what dost talk o' my vexin' him? an' what am I like to be but kind? I'll ma' him a kettle-cake for breakfast i' the[8] mornin'.'"

Adam, meanwhile, was reading[9] Dinah's letter by the light of his dip candle.

"DEAR BROTHER SETH,—Your letter lay three days beyond my knowing of it at the Post, for I had not money enough by me to pay the carriage, this being a time of great need and sickness here, with the rains that have fallen, as if the windows of heaven were opened again; and[1] to lay by money, from day to day, in such a time, when there are so many in present need of all things, would be a want of trust like the laying up of the manna. I speak of this, because I would not have you think me slow to answer, or that I had small[2] joy in your rejoicing at the worldly good that has befallen your brother Adam. The honour and love you bear him is nothing but meet, for God has given him great gifts, and he uses them as the patriarch Joseph did, who, when he was exalted to a place of power and trust, yet yearned with tenderness towards his parent and his younger brother.

"My heart is knit to your aged mother since it was granted me to be near her in the day of trouble. Speak to her of me, and tell her I often bear her in my thoughts at evening time, when I am sitting in the dim light as I did with her, and we held one another's hands, and I spoke the[3] words of comfort that were given to me. Ah, that is a blessed time, isn't it, Seth, when the outward light is fading, and the body is a little wearied with its work and its labour. Then the inward light shines the brighter, and we have a deeper sense of resting on the Divine strength. I sit on my chair in the dark room and close my eyes, and it is as if I was out of the body and could feel no want for evermore. For then, the very hardship, and the sorrow, and the blindness, and the sin, I have beheld and been ready to weep over,—yea, all the anguish of the children of men, which sometimes wraps me round like sudden darkness—I can bear with a willing pain, as if I was sharing the Redeemer's cross. For I feel it, I feel it—infinite love is suffering[4] too—yea, in the fullness of knowledge it suffers, it yearns, it mourns; and that is a blind self-seeking which wants to be freed from the sorrow wherewith the whole creation groaneth and travaileth. Surely it is not true blessedness to be free from sorrow, while there is sorrow and sin in the world: sorrow is

    [8] the] th' MS
    [9] Adam, meanwhile, was reading] Adam had thrown off his coat & waistcoat & was reading MS 1 Adam ⟨had thrown off his coat and waistcoat, and⟩ {, meanwhile,} was reading 8
    [1] again; and] again. And MS   [2] small ⟨rejoicing⟩ joy MS
    [3] the word{s} ⟨the⟩ of MS
    [4] I feel it—infinite love is suffering] I feel it—the Infinite Love is suffering MS I feel it—Infinite Love is suffering 1

then a part of love, and love does not seek to throw it off. It is not the spirit only that tells me this—I see it in the whole work and word of the gospel. Is there not pleading in heaven? Is not the Man of Sorrows there in that crucified body wherewith he ascended? And is He not one with the Infinite Love itself—as our love is one with our sorrow?

"These thoughts have been much borne in on me of late, and I have seen with new clearness the meaning of those words, 'If any man love me, let him take up my cross.' I have heard this enlarged on as if it meant the troubles and persecutions we bring on ourselves by confessing[5] Jesus. But surely that is a narrow thought. The true cross of the Redeemer was the sin and sorrow of this world—[6]*that* was what[7] lay heavy on his heart—and that is the cross we shall share with him, that is the cup we must drink of with him, if we would have any part in that Divine Love which is one with his sorrow.

"In my outward lot, which you ask about, I have all things and abound. I have had constant work in the mill, though some of the other hands have been turned off for a time; and my body is greatly strengthened, so that I feel little weariness after long walking and speaking. What you say about staying in your own country with your mother and brother shows me that you have a true guidance: your lot is appointed there by a clear showing, and to seek a greater blessing elsewhere would be like laying a false offering on the altar and expecting the fire from heaven to kindle it. My work and my joy are here among the hills, and I sometimes think I cling too much to my life among the people here, and should be rebellious if I was called away.

"I was thankful for your tidings about the dear friends at the Hall Farm; for though I sent them a letter, by my aunt's desire, after I came back from my sojourn among them, I have had no word from them. My aunt has not the pen of a ready writer, and the work of the house is sufficient for the day, for she is weak in body. My heart cleaves to her and her children as the nearest of all to me in the flesh; yea, and to all in that house. I am carried away to them continually in my sleep, and often in the midst of work, and even of speech, the thought of them is borne in on me as if they were in need and trouble, which yet is dark to me. There may be some leading here; but I wait to be taught. You say they are all well.

"We shall see each other again in the body, I trust,—though, it may be, not for a long while; for the brethren and sisters at Leeds are desirous to have me for a short space among them, when I have a door opened me again to leave Snowfield.

"Farewell, dear brother—and yet not farewell. For those children of God[8] whom it has been granted to see each other face to face and to hold communion together and to feel the same spirit working in both, can never more be sundered, though the hills may lie between. For their souls are

---

[5] confessing ⟨the Saviour⟩ Jesus *MS*   [6] world—⟨it was⟩ that *MS*
[7] was what] *added in MS*   [8] of God] *added in MS*

enlarged for evermore by that union, and they bear one another about in their thoughts continually as it were a new strength.—Your faithful Sister and fellow-worker in Christ,

"DINAH MORRIS."[9]

"I have not skill to write the words so small as you do, and my pen moves slow. And so I am straitened, and say but little of what is in my mind. Greet your mother for me with a kiss. She asked me to kiss her twice when we parted."

Adam had refolded the letter, and was sitting meditatively[1] with his head resting on his arm at the head of the bed, when Seth came upstairs.

"Hast read the letter?" said Seth.

"Yes," said Adam. "I don't know what I should ha' thought of her and her letter if I'd never seen her: I dare say I should ha' thought a preaching woman hateful. But she's one as[2] makes everything seem right she says and does, and I seemed to see her and hear her speaking when I read the letter. It's wonderful how I remember her looks and her voice. She'd make thee rare and happy, Seth; she's just the woman for thee."

"It's no use thinking o' that," said Seth, despondingly. "She spoke so firm, and she's not the woman to say one thing and mean another."

"Nay, but her feelings may grow different. A woman may get to love by degrees—the best fire doesna flare up the soonest. I'd have thee go and see her by-and-by: I'd make it convenient for thee to be away three or four days, and it 'ud be no walk for thee—only between twenty and thirty mile."

"I should[3] like to see her again, whether or no, if she wouldna be[4] displeased with me for going," said Seth.

"She'll be none[5] displeased," said Adam, emphatically, getting up and[6] throwing off his coat. "It might be a great happiness to us all, if she'd have thee, for mother took to her so wonderful, and seemed so contented to be with her."

"Ay," said Seth, rather timidly, "and Dinah's fond o' Hetty too; she thinks a deal about her."

Adam made no reply to that, and no other word but "good night" passed between them.

---

9 strength.—Your faithful Sister and fellow-worker in Christ, ¶ [flush right] "DINAH MORRIS."] strength. ¶ [centred] Your faithful Sister & fellowworker in Christ, ¶ [centred] Dinah Morris. *MS*
1 meditatively] *added in MS*   2 one as] one o' them people as *MS*
3 should ⟨be thankful to see her again⟩ like to see her again, whether or no *MS*
4 be ⟨angry⟩ displeased with me for going *MS*
5 none ⟨angry⟩ displeased *MS*   6 getting up &] *added in MS*

CHAPTER XXXI.

IN HETTY'S BED-CHAMBER.

It was no longer light enough to go to bed without a candle, even in Mrs Poyser's early household, and Hetty carried one with her as she went up at last to her bedroom soon[1] after Adam was gone, and bolted the door behind her.

Now[2] she would read her letter. It must—it must have comfort in it. How was Adam to know the truth? It was always likely he should say what he did say.

She set down the candle, and took out the letter. It had a faint scent of roses, which made her feel as if Arthur were close to her. She put it to her lips, and a rush of remembered sensations for a moment or two swept away all fear. But her heart began to flutter strangely, and her hands to tremble as she broke the seal. She read slowly; it was not easy for her to read a gentleman's handwriting, though Arthur had taken pains to write plainly.

"DEAREST HETTY,—I have spoken truly when I have said that I loved you, and I shall never forget our love. I shall be your true friend as long as life lasts, and I hope to prove this to you in many ways. If I say anything to pain you in this letter, do not believe it is for want of love and tenderness towards you, for there is nothing I would not do for you, if I knew it to be really for your happiness. I cannot bear to think of my little Hetty shedding tears when I am not there to kiss them away; and if I followed only my own inclinations, I should be with her at this moment instead of writing. It is very hard for me to part from her—harder still for me to write words which may seem unkind, though they spring from the truest kindness.

"Dear, dear Hetty, sweet as our love has been to me, sweet[3] as it would be to me for you to love me always, I feel that it would have been better for us both if we had never had that happiness, and that it is my duty to ask you to love me and care for me as little as you can. The fault has all been mine, for though I have been unable to resist the longing to be near you, I have felt all the while that your affection for me might cause you grief. I ought to have resisted my feelings. I[4] should have done so, if I had been a better fellow than I am; but now,[5] since the past cannot be altered, I am bound to save

---

[1] soon] *added in MS*   [2] *Now*] Now *MS*
[3] as our love has been to me, sweet] *added in MS*
[4] feelings. I] feelings—I *MS*   [5] now, ⟨that⟩ since *MS*

you[6] from any evil that I have power to prevent. And I feel it would be a great evil for you if your affections continued so fixed on me that you could think of no other man who might be able to make you happier by his love than I ever can, and if you continued to look towards something in the future which cannot possibly happen. For, dear Hetty, if I were to do what you one day spoke of, and make you my wife, I should do what you yourself would come to feel was for your misery instead of your[7] welfare. I know you can never be happy except by marrying a man in your own station; and if I were to marry you now, I should only be adding to any wrong I have done, besides offending against my duty in the other relations of life. You know nothing, dear Hetty, of the world in which I must always live, and you would soon begin to dislike me, because there would be so little[8] in which we should be alike.

"And since I cannot marry you, we must part—we must try not to feel like lovers any more. I am miserable while I say this, but nothing else can be. Be angry with me, my sweet one, I deserve it; but[9] do not believe that I shall not always care for you—always be grateful to you—always remember my Hetty; and[1] if any trouble should come that we do not now foresee, trust in me to do everything that lies in my power.

"I have told you where you are to direct a letter to, if you want to write, but I put it down below lest you should have forgotten. Do not write unless there is something I can really do for you; for, dear Hetty, we must try to think of each other as little as we can. Forgive me, and[2] try to forget everything about me, except that I shall be, as long as I live, your affectionate friend,

"ARTHUR DONNITHORNE."

Slowly Hetty had read this letter; and when she looked up from it there was the reflection of a blanched face in the old dim glass—a white[3] marble face with rounded childish forms, but with something sadder than a child's pain in it. Hetty did not see the face—she saw nothing—she only felt that she was cold and sick and trembling. The letter shook and rustled in her hand. She laid it down. It was a horrible sensation—this cold and trembling: it swept away the very ideas that produced it, and Hetty got up to reach a warm cloak from her clothes-press, wrapped it round her, and sat as if she were thinking of nothing but getting warm. Presently she took up the letter[4] with a firmer hand, and began to read it through again. The tears came this time—great rushing tears, that blinded her and[5] blotched the paper. She felt nothing but that Arthur was cruel—cruel to write so, cruel

---

[6] you ⟨to the utmost of my power⟩ from *MS*   [7] your ⟨happiness in life⟩ welfare *MS*
[8] little ⟨that⟩ in which *MS*   [9] it; but] it. But *MS*
[1] Hetty; and] Hetty. And *MS*   [2] & ⟨?dear Hetty [one word]⟩ try *MS*
[3] white] *added in MS*   [4] letter ⟨again⟩ with *MS*   [5] blinded her &] *added in MS*

not to marry her. Reasons why he could not marry her had no existence for her mind; how could she believe in any misery that could come to her from the fulfilment of all she had been[6] longing for and dreaming of? She had not the ideas that could make up the notion of that misery.

As she threw down the letter again, she caught sight of her face in the glass; it was reddened now, and wet[7] with tears; it was almost like a companion that she might complain to—that would pity her. She leaned forward on her elbows, and looked into those dark overflooding eyes, and at that quivering mouth, and saw how the tears came thicker and thicker, and how the mouth became convulsed with sobs.

The shattering of all her little dream-world, the crushing blow[8] on her new-born passion, afflicted her pleasure-craving nature with an overpowering pain that annihilated all impulse to resistance, and suspended her anger. She sat sobbing till the candle went out, and then wearied, aching, stupefied with crying, threw herself on the bed without undressing, and went to sleep.

There was a feeble dawn in the room when Hetty awoke, a little after four o'clock, with a sense of dull misery, the cause of which broke upon her gradually, as she began to discern the objects round her in the dim light. And then came the frightening thought that she had to conceal her misery, as well as to bear it, in this dreary daylight that was coming. She could lie no longer: she got up and went towards the table: there lay the letter; she opened her treasure-drawer: there lay the ear-rings and the locket—the signs of all her short happiness—the signs[9] of the life-long dreariness that was to follow it. Looking at the little trinkets which she had once eyed and fingered so fondly as the earnest of her future paradise of finery, she lived back in the moments when they had been given to her with such tender caresses, such strangely pretty words, such glowing looks, which filled her with a bewildering delicious surprise—they were so much sweeter than she had thought anything could be. And the Arthur who had spoken to her and looked at her in this way, who was present with her now—whose arm she felt round[1] her, his cheek against hers, his very breath upon her[2]—was the cruel, cruel Arthur who had written that letter:—that letter which she snatched and crushed and then opened again, that she might read it once more.[3] The half-benumbed mental condition which was the effect of the last night's violent crying, made it necessary to her to look again and see if[4] her wretched thoughts were actually true—if the letter was really[5] so

---

[6] she had been] she been *MS*   [7] & wet] *added in MS*   [8] blow ⟨to⟩ on *MS*
[9] signs] sign *MS*   [1] now—whose arm she felt round] now—she felt his arm round *MS*
[2] her—⟨& looked at her in that way, under whose very breath she had loved to be continually⟩ *MS. The published version of this cancelled passage is squeezed below the bottom line of MS II. 255 (recto). The cancellation appears on II. 256 (recto).*
[3] more{.} ⟨; for t⟩The *MS*   [4] if ⟨it ⟨⟨this⟩⟩ was really⟩ her *MS*
[5] really ⟨that⟩ so *MS*

cruel. She had to hold it close to the window, else she could not have read it by the faint light. Yes! it was worse—it was more cruel. She crushed it up again in anger. She hated the[6] writer of that letter—hated him[7] for the very reason that[8] she hung upon him with all her love—all the girlish passion and vanity that made up her love.

She had no tears this morning. She had wept them all away last night, and now she felt that dry-eyed morning misery,[9] which is worse than the first shock, because it has the future in it as well as the present. Every morning to come, as far as her imagination could stretch, she would have to get up and feel that the day would have no joy for her. For there is no despair so absolute as that which comes with the first moments of our first great sorrow, when we have not yet known what it is to have suffered and be healed, to have despaired and to have recovered hope. As Hetty began languidly to take off the clothes she had worn all the night, that she might wash herself and brush her hair, she had a sickening sense that her life would go on in this way: she should always be doing things she had no pleasure in, getting up to[1] the old tasks of work, seeing people she cared nothing about, going to church, and to Treddleston, and to tea[2] with Mrs Best, and carrying no happy thought with her. For[3] her short poisonous delights had spoiled for ever all the little joys that had once made the sweetness of her life—the[4] new frock ready for Treddleston fair, the party at Mr Britton's at Broxton wake, the beaux that she would say "No" to for a long while, and the prospect of the wedding that was to come at last[5] when she would have a silk gown and a great many clothes all at once. These things were all flat and dreary to her now: everything would be a weariness: and she would[6] carry about for ever a hopeless thirst and longing.

She paused in the midst of her languid undressing, and leaned against the dark old clothes-press.[7] Her neck and arms were bare, her hair hung down in delicate rings[8]; and they were just as beautiful as they were that night two months ago, when she walked up and down this[9] bed-chamber glowing with vanity and hope. She was not thinking of her neck and arms now; even[1] her own beauty was[2] indifferent to her. Her eyes wandered

---

[6] the ⟨Arthur who wrote⟩ writer of *MS*

[7] him ⟨in the very moment⟩ for the very reason *MS*

[8] that ⟨she⟩ ⟨all her love⟩ she *MS*

[9] misery ⟨which⟩ {which is wors⟨t⟩e than the first shock because it} has *MS*

[1] to ⟨do⟩ the *MS*   [2] tea ⟨at⟩ with *MS*   [3] For ⟨the⟩ her *MS*

[4] the ⟨having a⟩ new *MS*

[5] last ⟨with the choosing of the clothes & the having a great many at once⟩ when she would have a silk gown & a great many clothes all at once. *MS*

[6] would ⟨have⟩ carry *MS*

[7] clothes press. ⟨She thought nothing of her⟩ {Her neck & arms were bare}, her ⟨beautiful⟩ hair *MS*

[8] rings, ⟨as it did⟩ and *MS*   [9] this ⟨very⟩ bedchamber *MS*

[1] even] *added in MS*   [2] was ⟨for the moment⟩ indifferent *MS*

sadly over the dull old chamber, and then looked out vacantly towards the growing dawn. Did[3] a remembrance of Dinah come across her mind?—of her foreboding[4] words, which had made her angry?—of[5] Dinah's affectionate entreaty to think of her as a friend in trouble? No, the impression had been too slight to recur. Any affection or comfort Dinah could have given her would have been as indifferent to Hetty[6] this morning as everything else was[7] except her bruised[8] passion. She was only thinking[9] she could never stay here and go on with the old life—she could better bear something quite new than sinking back into the old everyday round. She would like to run away that very morning, and never see any of the old faces again. But Hetty's was not a nature to face difficulties—[1]to dare to loose her hold on the familiar, and rush blindly on[2] some unknown condition. Hers was a luxurious and vain nature, not a passionate one; and if she were ever to take any violent measure, she must be urged to it by the desperation of terror. There was not much room for her thoughts to travel in the narrow circle of her imagination, and she soon fixed on the one thing she would do to get away from her old life: she would ask her uncle to let her go and[3] be a lady's-maid. Miss Lydia's maid would help her to get a situation, if she knew Hetty had her uncle's leave.

When she had thought of this, she[4] fastened up her hair and began to wash: it seemed more possible to her to go downstairs and try to behave as usual. She would ask her uncle this very day. On Hetty's blooming health it would take a great deal of such mental suffering as hers to leave any deep impress; and when she was dressed as neatly as usual in her working dress, with her hair tucked up under her little cap, an indifferent observer would have been more struck with the young roundness of her cheek and neck, and the darkness of her eyes and[5] eyelashes, than with any signs of sadness about her. But when she took up the crushed letter and put it in her drawer, that she might lock it out of sight, hard smarting tears, having no relief in

---

[3] Did ⟨the⟩ a *MS*

[4] mind?—of her foreboding] mind? Of ⟨Dinah's⟩ the foreboding *MS* mind? Of her foreboding *1*

[5] angry?—of] angry—of *MS 1*   [6] Hetty ⟨at⟩ this *MS*

[7] was ⟨but⟩ except *MS*   [8] bruised ⟨vanity⟩ passion *MS*

[9] thinking ⟨how impossible it would be for her⟩ she could never stay here and go on *MS*

[1] difficulties ⟨, unless⟩ to *MS*

[2] on ⟨the⟩ {some} unknown {condition}. Hers was a luxurious & vain nature{,} ⟨rather than⟩ not a passionate one & if she {were} ever ⟨took⟩ {to take} any ⟨desperate step⟩ {violent measure} she must be urged to it by ⟨a⟩ {the} desperat⟨e⟩{ion} {of} terror. ⟨Her thoughts have⟩ There ⟨were⟩ {was} not ⟨many resources in the narrow⟩ {much room for her thoughts to travel in the narrow} circle of her imagination, & she soon fixed on the one ⟨resource⟩ {thing} she would ⟨?to⟩ do *MS*

[3] go and] go & *MS* go to *1 8*

[4] she ⟨went on with her washing & dressing⟩ fastened up her hair, & began *MS*

[5] eyes &] *added in MS*

them as the great drops had that fell last night, forced their way into her eyes.[6] She wiped them away quickly: she must not cry in the day-time: nobody should find out[7] how miserable she was, nobody should know she was disappointed about anything; and the thought[8] that the eyes of her aunt and uncle would be upon her, gave her the self-command which often accompanies a great dread. For Hetty looked out from her secret misery towards the possibility of their ever knowing what had happened, as the sick and weary prisoner might think of the possible pillory. They would think her conduct shameful; and shame was torture. That was poor little Hetty's conscience.

So she locked up her drawer and went away to her early work.

In the evening, when[9] Mr Poyser was smoking his pipe, and his good nature was therefore at its superlative moment, Hetty seized the opportunity of her aunt's absence to say,

"Uncle, I wish you'd let me go for a lady's-maid."

Mr Poyser took the pipe from his mouth, and looked at Hetty in mild surprise for some moments. She was sewing, and went on with her work industriously.

"Why, what's put that into your head, my wench?" he said at last, after he had given one conservative puff.

"I should like it—I should like it better than farm-work."

"Nay, nay; you fancy so because you donna know it, my wench. It wouldn't be half so good for your health, nor for your luck i' life. I'd like you to stay wi' us till you've got a good husband: you're my own niece, and I wouldn't have you go to service, though it was a gentleman's house, as long as I've got a home for you."

Mr Poyser paused, and puffed away at his pipe.

"I like the needlework," said Hetty, "and I should get good wages."

"Has[1] your aunt been a bit sharp wi' you?" said Mr Poyser, not noticing Hetty's further argument. "You mustna[2] mind that, my wench—she does it for your good. She wishes you well; an'[3] there isn't many aunts as are no kin to you 'ud ha' done by you as she has."

"No, it isn't my aunt," said Hetty, "but I should like the work better."

"It was all very well for you to learn the work a bit—an' I gev[4] my consent to that fast enough, sin' Mrs Pomfret[5] was willing to teach you. For if anything was t' happen, it's well to know how to turn your hand to different sorts o' things. But I niver meant you to go to service, my wench; my

---

[6] eyes. ⟨But s⟩{S}he MS
[7] out ⟨her misery & her mortification⟩ how miserable she was, nobody MS
[8] thought ⟨of⟩ {that the eyes of} her aunt & uncle⟨'s⟩ would MS
[9] when ⟨her uncle⟩ Mr. Poyser MS   [1] "Has ⟨thy⟩ your MS
[2] mustna] mustn't MS   [3] an'] & MS
[4] bit—an' I gev] bit—I ⟨gave⟩ gev MS
[5] sin' Mrs. Pomfret] sin' Mrs. G. [space left for name] MS

family's ate[6] their own bread and cheese as fur back as anybody knows, hanna they, father? You wouldna like your grandchild to take wage?"

[7]"Na-a-y," said old Martin, with an elongation of the word, meant to make[8] it bitter as well as negative, while he leaned forward and looked down on the floor. "But the wench takes arter her mother. I'd[9] hard work t' hould *her* in, an'[1] she married i' spite o' me—a feller wi' on'y two head o' stock when there should ha' been ten on's farm—she might[2] well die o' th' inflammation afore she war thirty."

It was seldom the old man made so long a speech; but his son's question had fallen like a bit of dry fuel on the embers of a long unextinguished resentment, which had always made the grandfather more indifferent to Hetty than to his son's children. Her mother's fortune had been spent by that good-for-nought Sorrel, and Hetty had Sorrel's blood in her veins.

"Poor thing, poor thing!" said Martin the younger, who was sorry to have provoked this retrospective harshness. "She'd but bad luck. But Hetty's got as good a chanche[3] o' getting a solid, sober husband as any gell i' this country."

After throwing out this pregnant hint, Mr Poyser recurred to his pipe and his silence, looking at Hetty to see if she did not give some sign of having renounced her ill-advised wish. But instead of that, Hetty, in spite of herself, began to cry, half out of ill-temper at the denial, half out of the day's repressed sadness.

"Hegh, hegh!" said Mr Poyser, meaning to check her playfully, "don't let's have any crying. Crying's for them as ha'[4] got no home, not for them as want to get rid o' one. What dost think?" he continued to his wife, who now came back into the house-place, knitting with fierce rapidity, as if that movement were a necessary function, like the twittering of a crab's antennæ.

"Think?—why, I think we shall have the fowl stole before we are[5] much older, wi' that gell forgetting to lock the pens up o' nights. What's the matter, now, Hetty? What are you crying at?"

"Why, she's been wanting to go for a lady's-maid," said Mr Poyser. "I tell her we can do better for her nor that."

"I thought she'd got some maggot in her head, she's gone about wi' her mouth buttoned up so all day. It's all wi' going so among them servants at the Chase, as we war fools for letting her. She thinks it 'ud be a finer life than being wi' them as are akin to her, and ha' brought her up sin'[6] she war no bigger nor Marty. She thinks there's nothing belongs to being a lady's-maid, but wearing finer clothes nor she was born to, I'll be bound.[7] It's what

---

[6] ate] eat *MS*   [7] "⟨Nay⟩ Na-a-y *MS*   [8] make ⟨the negative⟩ it bitter *MS*
[9] mother. I'd] mother: I'd *MS*   [1] in, an'] in. An' *MS*   [2] might] mut *MS*
[3] chanche ⟨as⟩ o' *MS*   [4] ha'] have *MS*   [5] we are] we're *MS*   [6] sin'] since *MS*
[7] bound. ⟨As I often ask her if she wouldnt like to be the⟩ It's what rag she can get to *MS*

rag she can get to stick on her as she's thinking on from morning till night; as I often ask her if she wouldn't like to be the mawkin i'[8] the field, for then she'd be made o' rags inside an'[9] out. I'll never gi'[1] my consent to her going for a lady's-maid, while she's got good friends to take care on her till she's married to somebody better nor[2] one o' them[3] valets, as is neither a common man nor a gentleman, an' must live on the fat o' the land, an's like enough to stick his hands under his coat tails and[4] expect his wife to work for him."

"Ay, ay," said Mr Poyser, "we must have a better husband for her nor[5] that, and there's better at hand. Come, my wench,[6] give over crying, and get to bed. I'll do better for you nor letting you go for a lady's-maid. Let's hear no more on't[7]."

When Hetty was gone upstairs he said,

"I canna[8] make it out as she should want to go away, for I thought she'd got a mind t' Adam Bede. She's looked like it o' late."

"Eh, there's no knowing what she's got a liking to, for things take no more hold on her than if she was a dried pea. I believe that gell, Molly—as is aggravatin'[9] enough, for the matter o' that—but I believe she'd care more about leaving[1] us[2] and the children, for all she's been here but a year come Michaelmas, nor[3] Hetty would. But she's got this notion o' being a lady's-maid wi' going among them servants—we might ha' known what it 'ud lead to when we let her go to learn the fine work. But I'll put a stop to it[4] pretty quick."

"Thee'dst be sorry to part wi' her, if it wasn't for her good," said Mr Poyser. "She's useful to thee i' the[5] work."

"Sorry? yes[6]; I'm fonder on her nor[7] she deserves—a little hard-hearted hussy, wanting to[8] leave us i' that way. I can't ha' had her about me these seven year, I reckon, and done for her, and taught her everything, wi'out caring about her. An' here I'm having linen spun, an' thinking all the while it'll make sheeting and table-clothing for her when she's married, an' she'll live i' the parish wi' us, and never go out of our sights—like[9] a fool as I am for thinking aught about her, as is no better nor a[1] cherry wi' a hard stone inside it."

"Nay, nay, thee mustna make much of a trifle," said Mr Poyser, soothingly. "She's fond on us, I'll be bound; but she's young, an' get's things in

---

[8] i'] in *MS*   [9] an'] and *Cabinet*   [1] gi'] give *MS*   [2] nor] than *MS*
[3] them ⟨gentleman's⟩ valets as ⟨are⟩ {is} neither ⟨like⟩ {a} common ⟨men⟩ {man} nor {a} gentlemen [*sic*] *MS*
[4] and] an' *MS*   [5] nor] than *MS*   [6] wench, ⟨dry up your⟩ give over crying *MS*
[7] on't] of it *MS*   [8] canna] can't *MS*   [9] aggravatin'] aggravating *MS*
[1] leaving] leavin' *MS*   [2] us an⟨'⟩d the *MS*   [3] nor] than *MS*
[4] it] 't *MS*   [5] the] th' *MS*   [6] yes] *MS* yis *1* ⟨yis⟩ yes *8*
[7] nor] than *MS*   [8] to ⟨be⟩ ⟨go away⟩ leave *MS*
[9] sights—like] sights, like *MS 1* sights⟨,⟩ {—} like *8*   [1] a ⟨white-heart⟩ cherry *MS*

her head as she can't rightly give account on. Them young fillies 'ull run away often wi'out knowing why."

Her uncle's answers, however, had had another effect on Hetty besides that of disappointing her and making her cry. She knew quite well whom he had in his mind in his allusions to marriage, and to a sober, solid husband; and when she was in her bedroom again,[2] the possibility of her marrying Adam presented itself to her in a new light. In a mind where no strong sympathies are at work, where there is no supreme sense of right to which the agitated[3] nature can cling and steady itself to quiet endurance, one of the first results of sorrow is a desperate vague clutching after any deed that will change the actual condition. Poor Hetty's vision of consequences,[4] at no time more than a narrow fantastic calculation of her own probable pleasures and pains, was now quite shut out by reckless irritation under[5] present suffering, and she was ready for one of those convulsive, motiveless actions by which wretched men and women leap from a temporary sorrow into a life-long misery.

Why should she not marry Adam? She did not[6] care what she did, so that it made some change in her life. She felt confident that he would still want to marry her, and any further thought about Adam's happiness in the matter had never yet visited her.

"Strange!" perhaps you will say, "this rush of impulse towards a course that might have seemed the most repugnant[7] to her present state of mind, and in only the second night of her sadness!"

Yes, the actions of a little trivial soul like Hetty's,[8] struggling amidst the serious, sad destinies of a human being, *are* strange. So[9] are the motions[1] of a little vessel without ballast tossed about on a stormy sea. How pretty it looked with its particoloured sail in the sunlight, moored in the quiet bay!

"Let that man bear the loss who loosed it from its moorings."

But that will not save the vessel—the pretty thing that might have been a lasting[2] joy.

[2] again, ⟨her thoughts & mind turned with new feeling towards⟩ the possibility of her marrying Adam presented *MS*

[3] agitated ⟨suffering⟩ nature *MS*

[4] consequences, ⟨most times⟩ {at no time} {⟨nothing⟩ more than a} narrow⟨ed to a⟩ fantastic *MS*

[5] now quite shut out by reckless irritation under] *MS reads* now ⟨dimmed for her⟩ quite shut out by ⟨a⟩ the reckless irritation of *MS*

[6] did not] didn't *MS*

[7] "Strange!" perhaps you will say, "this rush of impulse towards a course that might have seemed the most repugnant] *MS reads* "Strange!" ⟨that at the very time her⟩ {this rush of impulse towards} a course that might have seemed the ⟨very⟩ most ⟨opposed⟩ repugnant

[8] Hetty's, ⟨responding to the destinies⟩ struggling amidst the serious, sad *MS*

[9] strange. So] strange—so *MS*   [1] motions] *MS 1* ⟨emotions⟩ motions *8*

[2] lasting] life-long *MS 1* ⟨life-long⟩ lasting *8*

CHAPTER XXXII.

MRS POYSER "HAS HER SAY OUT."

The next Saturday evening there was much excited discussion at the Donnithorne Arms concerning an incident which had occurred that very day—no less than a second appearance of the smart man in top-boots, said by some to be a mere farmer in treaty for the Chase Farm, by others to be the future steward; but by Mr Casson himself, the personal witness to the stranger's visit, pronounced contemptuously to be nothing better than a bailiff, such as Satchell had been before him. No one had thought of denying Mr Casson's testimony to the fact that he had seen the stranger, nevertheless he proffered various corroborating circumstances.

"I see him myself," he said; "I see him coming along by the Crab-tree meadow on a bald-faced hoss. I'd just been t' hev a pint—it was half after ten i' the forenoon, when I hev my pint as reg'lar as the clock—and I says to Knowles, as druv up with his waggon, 'You'll get a bit o' barley to-day, Knowles,' I says, 'if you look about you;' and then I went round by the rick-yard, and towart the Treddles'on road; and just as I come up by the big ash tree, I see the man i' top-boots coming along on a bald-faced hoss—I wish I may never[1] stir if I didn't. And I stood still till[2] he come up, and I says, 'Good morning, sir,' I says, for I wanted to hear the turn of his tongue, as I might know whether he was a this-country-man; so I says, 'Good morning, sir: it'll 'old hup for the barley this morning, I think. There'll be a bit got hin, if we've good-luck.' And he says, 'Eh, ye may be raight,[3] there's noo tallin',' he says; and I knowed[4] by that"—here Mr Casson gave a wink—"as he didn't come from a hundred mile off. I dare say he'd think me a hodd talker, as you Loamshire folks allays[5] does hany one[6] as talks the right language."

"The right language!" said Bartle Massey, contemptuously. "You're[7] about as near the right language as a pig's squeaking is like a tune played on a key-bugle."

"Well, I don't know," answered Mr Casson, with an angry smile. "I[8] should think a man as has lived among the gentry from a by, is likely to know what's the right language pretty nigh[9] as well as a schoolmaster."

---

[1] never] niver *MS*   [2] till] *added in MS*   [3] ye may be raight,] *added in MS*
[4] knowed] know'd *MS 1*   [5] allays] aly's *MS*   [6] one] wonn *MS 1* ⟨wonn⟩ one *8*
[7] contemptuously. "You're] contemptuously, "You're *MS*
[8] smile. "I] smile, "I *MS*   [9] pretty nigh] *added in MS*

"Ay, ay, man," said Bartle, with a tone of sarcastic consolation, "you talk the right language for *you*. When Mike Holdsworth's goat says ba-a-a, it's all right—it 'ud be unnatural for it to make any other noise."

The rest of the party being Loamshire men, Mr Casson had the laugh strongly against him, and wisely fell back on the previous question, which, far from being exhausted in a single evening, was renewed in the church-yard, before service, the next day, with the fresh interest conferred on all news when there is a fresh person to hear it; and[1] that fresh hearer was Martin Poyser, who, as his wife said, "never went boozin'[2] with that set at Casson's, a-sittin' soakin'-in[3] drink, and looking as wise as a lot o' cod-fish wi' red faces."

It was probably owing to the conversation she had had with her husband on their way from church, concerning this problematic stranger, that Mrs Poyser's thoughts immediately reverted to him when, a day or two after-wards, as she was standing at the house-door with her knitting, in that eager leisure which came to her when the afternoon cleaning was done, she saw the old Squire enter the yard on his black pony, followed by John the groom. She always cited it afterwards as a case of prevision, which really had something more in it than her own remarkable penetration, that the moment she set eyes on the Squire, she said to herself, "I shouldna[4] wonder if he's come about that man as is a-going to take the Chase Farm, wanting Poyser to do something for him without pay. But Poyser's a fool if he does."

Something unwonted must clearly be in the wind, for the old Squire's visits to his tenantry were rare; and though Mrs Poyser had during the last twelvemonth recited many imaginary speeches, meaning even more than met the ear, which she was quite determined to make to him the next time he appeared within the gates of the Hall Farm, the speeches had always remained imaginary.[5]

"Good day, Mrs Poyser," said the old Squire, peering at her with his short-sighted eyes—a mode of looking at her which, as Mrs Poyser observed, "allays[6] aggravated her: it was as if you was a insect, and he was going to dab his finger-nail on you."

However, she said, "Your servant, sir," and curtsied with an air of perfect deference as she advanced towards him: she was not the woman to misbehave towards her betters, and fly in the face of the catechism, without severe provocation.

[1] it; and] it. And *MS*   [2] boozin'] boozing *MS*
[3] a-sittin' soakin'-in] a-sitting soaking in *MS*   [4] shouldna] shouldn't *MS*
[5] ¶ Something unwonted must clearly be in the wind, for the old Squire's visits to his tenantry were rare & though Mrs. Poyser had during the last twelvemonth recited many imaginary speeches meaning even more than met the ear, which she was quite determined to make to him the next time he appeared within the gates of the Hall Farm, the speeches had always remained imaginary.] *added on verso of MS 11. 268*
[6] allays] always *MS*

"Is your husband at home, Mrs Poyser?"

"Yes, sir; he's only i' the rick-yard. I'll[7] send for him in a minute, if you'll please to get down and step in."

"Thank you; I will do so.[8] I want to consult him about a little matter; but you are quite as much concerned in it, if not more. I must have your opinion too."

"Hetty, run and tell your uncle to come in," said Mrs Poyser, as they entered the house, and the old gentleman bowed low in answer to Hetty's curtsy; while Totty, conscious of a pinafore stained with[9] gooseberry jam, stood hiding her face against the clock, and peeping round furtively.

"What a fine old kitchen this is!" said Mr Donnithorne, looking round admiringly. He always spoke in the same deliberate, well-chiselled, polite way, whether his words were sugary or venomous. "And you keep it so exquisitely clean, Mrs Poyser. I like these premises, do you know, beyond any on the estate."

"Well, sir, since you're fond of 'em, I should be glad if you'd let a bit o' repairs be done to 'em, for the boarding's i' that state, as we're like to be eaten up wi' rats and mice; and the cellar, you may stan' up to your knees i' water in't, if you like to go down; but perhaps you'd rather[1] believe my words. Won't you please to sit down, sir?"

"Not yet; I must see your dairy. I have not seen it for years, and I hear on all hands about your fine cheese and butter," said the Squire, looking politely unconscious that there could be any question on which he and Mrs Poyser might happen to disagree. "I think I see the door open, there: you[2] must not be surprised if I cast a covetous eye on your cream and butter. I don't expect that Mrs Satchell's cream and butter will bear comparison with yours."

"I can't say, sir, I'm sure. It's seldom I see other folks's butter, though there's some on it as one's no need to see—the smell's enough."

"Ah, now this I like," said Mr Donnithorne, looking round at the damp temple of cleanliness, but keeping near the door. "I'm sure I should like my breakfast better if I knew the butter and cream came from this dairy. Thank you, that really is a pleasant sight. Unfortunately, my slight tendency to rheumatism makes me afraid of damp: I'll[3] sit down in your comfortable kitchen. Ah, Poyser, how do you do?[4] In the midst of business, I see, as usual. I've been looking at your wife's beautiful dairy—the best manager in the parish, is she not?"

---

[7] rick-yard. I'll] rickyard: I'll *MS*   [8] so. ⟨But⟩ I *MS*

[9] with ⟨the⟩ gooseberry jam, ⟨which was boiling under Hetty's superintendence,⟩ stood *MS*

[1] rather] rether *MS*   [2] there: you] there. You *MS*

[3] damp: I'll] damp. I'll *MS*   [4] do? ⟨"Hard at work⟩ In the midst of business *MS*

Mr Poyser had just entered in shirt-sleeves and open waistcoat, with a face a shade redder than usual, from the exertion of "pitching." As he stood, red, rotund, and radiant before the small, wiry, cool, old gentleman, he looked like a prize apple by the side of a withered crab.

"Will you please to take this chair, sir?" he said, lifting his father's arm-chair[5] forward a little: "you'll[6] find it easy."

"No, thank you, I never sit in easy chairs," said the old gentleman, seating himself on a small chair near the door. "Do you know, Mrs Poyser—sit down, pray, both of you—I've been far from contented, for some time, with Mrs Satchell's dairy management. I think she has not a good method, as you have."

"Indeed, sir, I can't speak to that," said Mrs Poyser, in a hard voice, rolling and unrolling her knitting, and looking icily out of the window, as she continued to stand opposite the Squire. Poyser might sit down if he liked, she thought: *she* wasn't going to sit down, as if she'd give in to any such smooth-tongued palaver. Mr Poyser, who looked and felt the reverse of icy, did sit down in his three-cornered chair.[7]

"And now, Poyser, as Satchell is laid up, I am intending to let the Chase Farm to a respectable tenant. I'm tired of having a farm on my own hands—nothing is made the best of in such cases, as you know. A satisfactory bailiff is hard to find; and[8] I think you and I, Poyser, and your excellent wife here, can enter into a little arrangement in consequence, which will be to our mutual advantage."

"Oh," said Mr Poyser, with a good-natured blankness of imagination as to the nature of the arrangement.

"If I'm called upon to speak, sir," said Mrs Poyser, after glancing at her husband with pity at his softness, "you know better than me; but I don't see what the Chase Farm is t'[9] us—we've cumber enough wi'[1] our own farm. Not but what I'm glad to hear o' anybody respectable coming into the parish: there's some as ha' been brought in as hasn't been looked on[2] i' that character."

"You're likely to find Mr Thurle an excellent neighbour, I assure you: such a one as you will feel[3] glad to have accommodated by the little plan I'm going to mention; especially[4] as I hope[5] you will find it as much to your own advantage as his."

"Indeed, sir, if it's anything t' our advantage, it'll be the first offer o' the sort I've heared on. It's them as take advantage that get advantage i'

[5] arm-chair ⟨away from the fire⟩ forward a little *MS*
[6] little: "you'll] little. "You'll *MS*
[7] chair ⟨, with an air of fearless good nature, which added to his wife's irritation as she glanced at him⟩. ¶ "And *MS*
[8] find; and] find. And *MS*   [9] t'] to *MS*   [1] wi'] with *MS*
[2] on] *MS* in *1* ⟨in⟩ on *8*   [3] feel] be *MS*
[4] mention; especially] mention. Especially *MS*   [5] I hope] *added in MS*

this world[6], *I* think: folks have to wait long enough afore[7] it's brought to 'em."

"The fact is, Poyser[8]," said the Squire, ignoring Mrs Poyser's theory of worldly prosperity, "there is too much dairy land, and too little plough land, on the Chase Farm, to suit Thurle's purpose—indeed, he will only take the farm on condition of some change in it[9]: his wife, it appears, is not a clever dairy-woman, like yours. Now, the plan I'm thinking of is to effect a little exchange. If[1] you were to have the Hollow Pastures, you might increase your dairy, which must be so profitable under your wife's management; and I should request you, Mrs Poyser, to supply my house with milk, cream, and butter at the market prices. On the other hand, Poyser, you might let Thurle have the Lower and Upper Ridges, which really, with our wet seasons, would be a good riddance for you. There is much less risk in dairy land than corn land."

Mr Poyser was leaning forward, with his elbows on his knees, his head on one side, and his mouth screwed up—apparently absorbed in making the tips of his fingers meet so as to represent with perfect accuracy the ribs of a ship. He was much too acute a man not to see through the whole business, and to foresee perfectly what would be his wife's view of the subject;[2] but he disliked giving unpleasant answers: unless[3] it was on a point of farming practice, he would rather give up than have a quarrel, any day; and,[4] after all, it mattered more to his wife than to him. So after a few moments' silence, he looked up at her and said mildly, "What dost say?"

Mrs Poyser had had her eyes fixed on her husband with cold severity during his silence, but now she turned away her head with a toss, looked icily at the opposite roof of the cow-shed, and spearing her knitting together with the loose pin, held it firmly between her clasped hands.

"Say? Why, I say you may do as you like about giving up any o' your corn land afore your lease is up, which it won't be for a year come next Michaelmas[5], but I'll not consent to take more dairy work into my hands, either for love or money; and there's nayther[6] love nor money here, as I can see, on'y other folks's love o' theirselves, and the money as is to go into other folks's pockets. I know there's them as is born t' own the land, and them as is born to sweat on't"—here Mrs Poyser paused to gasp a little—"and[7] I know it's christened folks's duty to submit to their betters as fur as flesh and

---

[6] i' this world] *added in MS*   [7] afore] before *MS*

[8] Poyser, ⟨as you know⟩," said *MS*

[9] indeed, he will only take the farm on condition of some change in it] *added in MS*

[1] exchange. If] exchange: if *MS*   [2] subject. ⟨For him⟩ But he *MS*

[3] answers: unless] answers. Unless *MS*   [4] day; and,] day. And *MS*

[5] Michaelmas] Michaelmas Lady Day *MS 1* ⟨Michaelmas Lady Day⟩ {Michaelmas} *8*

[6] nayther] neyther *MS*

[7] on't"—here Mrs Poyser paused to gasp a little—"and] on 't, & *MS*

blood 'ull bear it; but[8] I'll not make a martyr o' myself, and wear myself to skin and bone, and worret myself as if I was a churn wi' butter a-coming in't, for no landlord in England, not if he was King George himself."

"No, no, my dear Mrs Poyser, certainly not," said the Squire, still confident in his own powers of persuasion, "you[9] must not overwork yourself; but don't you think your work will rather be lessened than increased in this way? There is so much milk[1] required at the Abbey, that you will have[2] little increase of cheese and butter making from the addition to your dairy; and I believe selling the milk is the most profitable way of disposing of dairy produce, is it not?"

"Ay, that's true," said Mr Poyser, unable to repress an opinion on[3] a question of farming profits, and forgetting that it was not in this case a purely abstract question.

"I dare say," said Mrs Poyser bitterly, turning her head half-way towards her husband, and looking at the vacant arm-chair—"I[4] dare say it's true for men as sit i' th'[5] chimney-corner and make[6] believe as everything's cut wi' ins an'[7] outs to fit int' everything else. If you could make a pudding wi' thinking o' the batter, it 'ud be easy getting dinner. How do I know[8] whether the milk 'ull be wanted constant? What's to make me sure as the house won't be put o' board-wage afore we're many months older, and then I may have to lie awake o' nights wi' twenty gallons o' milk on my mind—and Dingall 'ull take no more butter, let alone paying for it; and we must fat pigs till we're obliged to beg the butcher on our knees to buy 'em, and lose half[9] of 'em wi' the measles. And there's the fetching and carrying, as 'ud be welly half a day's work for a man an' hoss—*that's* to be took[1] out o' the profits, I reckon? But there's folks 'ud hold a sieve under the pump and expect to carry away the water."

"That difficulty—about the fetching and carrying—you will not have, Mrs Poyser," said the Squire, who thought that this entrance into particulars indicated a distant inclination to compromise on Mrs Poyser's part—"Bethell[2] will do that regularly with the cart and pony."

"O, sir, begging your pardon, I've never been used t'[3] having gentlefolks's servants coming about my back places, a-making love to both the gells at once, and keeping 'em with their hands on their hips listening to all manner o' gossip when they should be down on their knees a-scouring. If we're to go to ruin, it shanna[4] be wi' having our back kitchen turned into a public."

---

[8] it; but] it. But *MS*   [9] persuasion, "you] persuasion. "You *MS*

[1] milk ⟨& butter⟩ required *MS*   [2] have ⟨no h⟩ little *MS*   [3] on ⟨far⟩ a *MS*

[4] arm-chair—"I] arm-chair. "I *MS*   [5] th'] the *MS*   [6] make ⟨out⟩ believe *MS*

[7] an'] & *MS*   [8] know ⟨what⟩ whether *MS*   [9] half ⟨on⟩ of *MS*

[1] man an' hoss—*that's* to be took] man and horse—that's to be taken *MS*

[2] part—"Bethell] part. "Bethell *MS*   [3] t'] to *MS*   [4] shanna] shan't *MS*

"Well, Poyser," said the Squire, shifting his tactics, and looking as if he thought Mrs Poyser had suddenly withdrawn from the proceedings and left the room, "you can turn the Hollows into feeding-land. I can easily make another arrangement about supplying my house. And I shall not forget your readiness to accommodate your landlord as well as[5] a neighbour. I know you will be glad to have your lease renewed for three years, when the present one expires; otherwise, I dare say Thurle, who is a man of some capital, would be glad to take both the farms, as they[6] could be worked so well together. But I don't want to part with an old tenant like you."

[7]To be thrust out of the discussion in this way would have been enough to complete Mrs Poyser's exasperation, even without the final threat. Her husband, really alarmed at the possibility of their leaving the old place where he had been bred and born—for he believed the old Squire had small spite enough for anything—was beginning a mild remonstrance explanatory of the inconvenience he should find in having to buy and sell more stock, with—

"Well, sir, I think as it's rether hard" . . . . when Mrs Poyser burst in with the desperate determination to have her say out this once, though it were to rain notices to quit, and the only shelter were the workhouse.

"Then, sir, if I may speak—as, for all I'm a woman, and there's folks as thinks[8] a woman's fool enough to stan' by an'[9] look on while the men sign her soul away, I've[1] a right to speak, for I make one quarter o' the rent, and save another[2] quarter—I say, if Mr Thurle's so ready to take farms under you, it's a pity but what he should take this, and see if he likes to live in a house wi' all the plagues o' Egypt in't[3]—wi' the cellar full o' water, and frogs[4] and toads hoppin'[5] up the steps by dozens—and the floors rotten, and the rats and mice gnawing every bit o' cheese, and runnin' over our heads as we lie i' bed till we expect 'em to eat us up alive—as it's a mercy they hanna[6] eat the[7] children long ago. I should like to see if there's another tenant besides Poyser as 'ud put up wi' never having a bit o' repairs done till a place tumbles down—and not then, on'y[8] wi' begging and praying, and having to pay half—and being strung up wi' the rent as it's much if he gets enough out o' the land to pay, for all he's put his own money into the ground beforehand. See if you'll get a stranger to lead such a life here as that: a

---

[5] your landlord as well as] *added in MS*   [6] they ⟨lie⟩ could be worked *MS*

[7] ¶⟨This sudden ignoring of her & the final threat just completed⟩ {To be thrust out of the discussion in this way would have been enough to complete} Mrs. Poyser's exasperation {even without the final threat.} Her *MS*

[8] thinks] *MS 1* ⟨think's⟩ thinks *8*   [9] an'] & *MS*

[1] I've ⟨as much to do with⟩ a right to *MS*

[2] another] th' other *MS 1* ⟨th' other⟩ another *8*   [3] in't] in it *MS*

[4] and frogs] & the frogs *MS*   [5] hoppin'] hopping *MS*

[6] hanna] haven't *MS*   [7] the ⟨little⟩ children *MS*   [8] on'y] only *MS*

maggot must be born i' the rotten cheese to like it, I reckon. You may run
away from my words, sir," continued Mrs Poyser, following the old Squire
beyond the door—for after the first moments of stunned surprise he had
got up, and, waving his hand towards her with a smile, had walked out
towards his pony. But it was impossible for him to get away immediately,
for John was walking the pony up and down the yard, and was some
distance from the causeway when his master beckoned.

"You may run away from my words, sir, and you may go spinnin'[9]
underhand ways o' doing us a mischief, for you've got Old Harry to your
friend, though nobody else is, but I tell you for once as we're not dumb
creaturs[1] to be abused and made money on[2] by them as ha' got the lash i'
their hands, for want o' knowing how t' undo the tackle. An'[3] if I'm th' only
one as speaks my mind, there's plenty[4] o' the same way o' thinking i' this
parish and the next to 't, for your name's no better than a brimstone match
in everybody's nose—if it isna[5] two-three old folks as you think o' saving
your soul by giving 'em a bit o' flannel and a drop o' porridge. An' you may
be right i' thinking it'll take but little to save your soul, for it'll be the
smallest savin' y'[6] iver made, wi' all your scrapin'[7]."

There are occasions on which two servant-girls and a waggoner may be a
formidable audience, and as the Squire rode away on his black pony, even
the gift of short-sightedness did not prevent him from being aware that
Molly and Nancy and Tim were grinning not far from him. Perhaps he
suspected that sour old John was grinning behind him—which was also the
fact. Meanwhile the bull-dog, the black-and-tan terrier, Alick's sheep-dog,
and the gander hissing at a safe distance from the pony's heels, carried out
the idea of Mrs Poyser's solo in an impressive quartett.

Mrs Poyser, however, had no sooner seen the pony move off than she
turned round, gave[8] the two[9] hilarious damsels a look which drove them
into the back kitchen, and unspearing her knitting, began to knit again with
her usual rapidity, as she re-entered the house.

"Thee'st done it now," said Mr Poyser, a little alarmed and uneasy, but
not without some triumphant amusement at his wife's outbreak.

"Yes[1], I know I've done it," said Mrs Poyser; "but I've had my say
out, and I shall be th' easier for't[2] all my life. There's no pleasure i' living,
if you're to be corked up for ever[3], and only[4] dribble your mind out by
the sly, like a leaky barrel. I shan't repent saying[5] what I think, if I live to
be as old as th' old Squire; and[6] there's little likelihoods—for it seems as[7]

[9] spinnin'] spinning *MS*   [1] creaturs] creatures *Cabinet*   [2] on] of *MS*
[3] An'] And *MS*   [4] mind, there's plenty] mind, it isn't because there isn't plenty *MS*
[5] isna] isn't *MS*   [6] y' ⟨ever⟩ iver *MS*   [7] scrapin'] scraping *MS*
[8] gave ⟨her⟩ the *MS*   [9] two] too *MS*   [1] Yes] *MS* Yis *1* ⟨Yis⟩ Yes *8*
[2] for't] for it *MS*   [3] ever] *MS* iver *1* ⟨iver⟩ ever *8*
[4] only ⟨leak⟩ dribble *MS*   [5] repent saying] repent o' saying *MS*
[6] Squire; and] squire. And *MS*   [7] as ⟨it's only⟩ if *MS*

if them as[8] aren't wanted here are th' only folks as aren't wanted i' th' other world."

"But thee wutna[9] like moving from th' old place, this[1] Michaelmas twelvemonth," said Mr Poyser, "and going into a strange parish, where thee know'st nobody. It'll be hard upon us both, and upo' father too."

"Eh, it's no use worreting; there's plenty o' things may happen between this and Michaelmas twelvemonth. The Captain may be master afore[2] then, for what we know," said Mrs[3] Poyser, inclined to take an unusually hopeful view of an embarrassment which had been brought about by her own merit, and not by other people's fault.

"*I'm* none[4] for worreting," said Mr Poyser, rising from his three-cornered chair, and walking slowly towards the door; "but[5] I should be loath to leave th' old place, and the parish where I was bred and born, and father afore[6] me. We should leave our[7] roots behind us, I doubt, and niver[8] thrive again."

---

[8] as ⟨arena⟩ aren't *MS*   [9] wutna] wotn't *MS* wotna *1* ⟨wotna⟩ wutna *8*
[1] this ⟨Michaelmas⟩ {Lady} ⟨Lady⟩ Michaelmas *8*   [2] afore] before *MS*
[3] said ⟨Mr.⟩ Mrs. *MS*   [4] none] not *MS*   [5] door; "but] door. "But *MS*
[6] afore] before *MS*   [7] our] wer *MS*   [8] niver] never *MS*

CHAPTER XXXIII.

MORE LINKS.

The barley was all carried at last, and the harvest suppers went by without waiting for the dismal black crop of beans. The[1] apples and nuts were gathered and stored; the scent of whey departed from the farm-houses, and the scent of brewing came in its stead. The[2] woods behind the Chase, and all the hedgerow trees, took on a solemn splendour under the dark[3] low-hanging skies. Michaelmas[4] was come, with its fragrant basketfuls of purple damsons, and its paler purple daisies, and its lads and lasses leaving or seeking service, and winding along between the yellow hedges, with their bundles under their arms. But though Michaelmas was come, Mr Thurle, that desirable tenant, did not come to the Chase Farm, and the old Squire, after all, had been obliged to put in a new bailiff. It was known throughout the two parishes that the Squire's plan had been frustrated because the Poysers had refused to be "put upon," and Mrs Poyser's outbreak was discussed in[5] all the farmhouses with a zest which was only heightened by frequent repetition. The news that "Bony" was come back from Egypt was comparatively insipid, and the repulse of the French in Italy was nothing to Mrs Poyser's repulse of the old Squire. Mr Irwine had heard a version of it in every parishioner's house, with the one exception of the Chase. But since he had always, with marvellous skill, avoided any quarrel with Mr Don-nithorne, he could not allow himself the pleasure of laughing at[6] the old gentleman's discomfiture with any one besides his mother, who declared that if she were rich she should like to allow Mrs Poyser a pension for life, and wanted to invite her to the parsonage, that she might hear an account of the scene from Mrs Poyser's own lips.

"No, no, mother," said Mr Irwine; "it[7] was a little bit of irregular justice on Mrs Poyser's part, but a magistrate like me must not countenance irregular justice. There must be no report spread that I have taken notice of the quarrel, else I shall lose the little good influence I have over the old man."

---

[1] beans. The] beans; the *MS*   [2] stead. The] stead; the *MS*
[3] dark ⟨purple⟩ low-hanging *MS*   [4] skies. Michaelmas] skies: Michaelmas *MS*
[5] in ⟨every⟩ {all the} farm-house{s} with *MS*
[6] at ⟨his⟩ ⟨the⟩ ⟨gen⟩ {the old} gentleman's *MS*
[7] Irwine; "it] Irwine. "It *MS*

"Well, I like that woman even better than her cream-cheeses," said Mrs Irwine.[8] "She has the[9] spirit of three men, with that pale face of hers; and she says such sharp things too."

"Sharp! yes, her tongue is like a new-set razor. She's[1] quite original in her talk, too; one of those untaught wits that help to stock a country with proverbs. I told you that capital thing[2] I heard her say about Craig—that he was like a cock who thought the sun had risen to hear him crow. Now that's an Æsop's fable in a sentence."

"But it will be a bad business if the old gentleman turns them out of the farm next Michaelmas, eh?" said Mrs Irwine.

"O that must not be; and Poyser is such a good tenant, that Donnithorne is likely to think twice, and digest his spleen rather than turn them out. But if he should give them notice at Lady Day, Arthur and I must move heaven and earth to mollify him. Such[3] old parishioners as they are must not go."

"Ah, there's no knowing what may happen before Lady Day," said Mrs Irwine. "It struck me on Arthur's birthday that the old man was a little shaken: he's eighty-three, you know. It's really an unconscionable age. It's only[4] women who have a right to live as long as that."

"When they've got old-bachelor sons who would be forlorn without them," said Mr Irwine,[5] laughing, and kissing his[6] mother's hand.

Mrs Poyser, too, met her husband's occasional forebodings of a notice to quit with "There's no knowing what may happen before Lady Day:"—one of those[7] undeniable general propositions which are usually intended to convey a particular meaning very far from undeniable. But it is really too hard upon human nature[8] that it should be held a criminal offence to imagine the death even of the king when he is turned eighty-three. It is not to be believed that any but the dullest Britons can be good subjects under that hard condition.

Apart from this foreboding, things went on much as usual in the Poyser household. Mrs Poyser thought she noticed a surprising improvement in Hetty. To be sure, the girl got "closer tempered, and sometimes she seemed as if there'd be no drawing a word from her with cart-ropes;" but she thought much less about her dress, and went after the work quite eagerly, without any telling. And it was wonderful how she never wanted to go out now—indeed, could hardly be persuaded to go; and she bore her aunt's putting a stop to her weekly lesson in fine-work at the Chase, without

[8] Irwine. "⟨What a spirit she must have &⟩ She *MS*   [9] the] *added in MS*
[1] razor. She's] razor; she's *MS*   [2] thing ⟨she said⟩ I heard her say *MS*
[3] him. Such] him—such *MS*   [4] It's only] {It's} Only *MS*
[5] Irwine, ⟨kissing his hands⟩ laughing *MS*
[6] his ⟨handsome old mother's smooth forehead⟩ mother's hand. *MS*
[7] those ⟨wide⟩ undeniable {general} propositions *MS*
[8] nature ⟨to⟩ that *MS*

the least grumbling or pouting. It must be, after all, that she had set her heart on Adam at last, and[9] her sudden freak of wanting to be a lady's-maid must have been caused by some little pique or misunderstanding between them, which had passed by. For whenever Adam came to the Hall Farm, Hetty seemed to be in better spirits, and to talk more than at other times, though she was almost sullen when Mr Craig or any other admirer happened to pay a visit there.

Adam himself watched her at first with trembling anxiety, which gave way to surprise and delicious hope.[1] Five days after delivering Arthur's letter[2], he had ventured to go to the Hall Farm again—not without dread lest the sight of him might be painful to her. She was not in the house-place when he entered, and he sat talking to Mr and Mrs Poyser for a few minutes with a heavy fear on his heart that they might presently tell him Hetty was ill. But[3] by-and-by there came a light step that he knew, and when Mrs Poyser said, "Come, Hetty, where have you been?" Adam was obliged to turn round, though he was afraid to see the changed look there must be in her face. He almost started when he saw her smiling as if she were pleased to see him—looking the same as ever at a first glance, only that she had her cap on, which he had never seen her in before when he came of an evening. Still, when he looked at her again and again as she moved about or sat at her work, there was a change: the cheeks were as pink as ever, and she smiled as much as she had ever done of late, but there was something different in her eyes, in the expression of her face, in all her movements, Adam thought—something harder, older, less child-like. "Poor thing!" he said to himself, "that's allays[4] likely. It's because she's had her first heart-ache. But she's got a spirit to bear up under it. Thank God for that."

As the weeks went by and he saw her always looking pleased to see him—turning up her lovely face towards him as if she meant him to understand that she was glad for him to come—and going about her work in the same equable way, making no sign of sorrow, he began to[5] believe that her feeling towards Arthur[6] must have been much slighter than he had imagined in his first indignation and alarm, and that she had been able to think of her girlish fancy that Arthur was in love with her, and would marry her, as a folly of which she was timely cured. And it perhaps was, as he had sometimes, in his more cheerful moments, hoped it would be—her heart[7] was really turning with all the more[8] warmth towards the man she knew to have a serious love for her.

---

[9] & ⟨that⟩ her *MS*   [1] hope. ⟨When ten⟩ Five *MS*   [2] letter ⟨to her⟩, he *MS*
[3] But ⟨presently⟩ by & bye *MS*   [4] allays] always *MS*   [5] to ⟨think⟩ believe *MS*
[6] Arthur ⟨was⟩ must have been *MS*
[7] sometimes, in his more cheerful moments, hoped it would be—her heart] sometimes hoped in {his} more cheerful moments—her heart *MS*
[8] more ⟨force⟩ warmth *MS*

Possibly[9] you think that Adam was not at all sagacious in his[1] interpretations, and that it was altogether extremely unbecoming in a sensible man to behave as he did—falling in love with a girl who really had nothing more than her beauty to recommend her, attributing imaginary virtues to her, and even condescending to cleave to her after she had fallen in love with another man, waiting for her kind looks as a patient trembling dog waits for his master's eye to be turned upon him. But in so complex a thing as human nature, we must consider, it[2] is hard to find rules without exceptions. Of course, I know that[3], as a rule, sensible men fall in love with the most sensible women[4] of their[5] acquaintance, see through all the pretty deceits of coquettish beauty, never[6] imagine themselves loved when they are not loved, cease loving on all proper occasions, and marry the woman most fitted for them in every respect—indeed, so as to compel the approbation of all the maiden ladies in their neighbourhood. But even to this rule an exception will occur now and then in the lapse of centuries, and my friend Adam was one. For my own part, however, I respect him none the less: nay, I think the deep love he had for that sweet, rounded,[7] blossom-like, dark-eyed Hetty, of whose inward self he was really very ignorant, came out of the very strength of his nature, and not out of any inconsistent weakness. Is it any weakness, pray, to be wrought on by exquisite music?—to feel its wondrous harmonies searching the subtlest windings of your soul, the delicate fibres of life where no memory can penetrate, and binding together your whole being past and present in one unspeakable vibration: melting you in one moment with all the tenderness, all the love that has been scattered through the toilsome years, concentrating in one emotion of heroic courage or resignation all the hard-learnt lessons of self-renouncing sympathy, blending your present joy with past sorrow, and your present sorrow with all your past joy? If not, then neither is it a weakness to be so wrought upon by the exquisite curves of a woman's cheek and neck and arms, by the liquid depths of her beseeching eyes, or the sweet childish pout of her lips. For the beauty of a lovely woman is like music: what can one say more? Beauty has an expression beyond and far above the one woman's soul that it clothes, as the words of genius have a wider meaning than the thought that prompted them: it is more than a woman's love that moves

---

[9] Possibly] Perhaps *MS*

[1] his interpretation{s}, ⟨of Hetty's smiles⟩ & that it was {altogether} extremely unbecoming in a sensible man to behave as he did ⟨altogether⟩—falling *MS*

[2] nature, we must consider, it] nature {we must consider} it *MS* nature we must consider it *1* nature{,} we must consider{,} it *8*

[3] that] *added in MS*   [4] women] woman *MS*

[5] their ⟨neighbourhood⟩ acquaintance *MS*

[6] never ⟨mistake any woman's admiration⟩ {imagine⟨d⟩ themselves loved when they are not loved, cease loving on all proper occasions,} & *MS*

[7] sweet, rounded,] sweet little rounded, *MS*

us in a woman's eyes—it seems to be a far-off mighty love that has come near to us, and made speech for itself there; the rounded neck, the dimpled arm, move us by something more than their prettiness—by their close kinship with all we have known of tenderness and peace. The noblest nature sees the most of this *impersonal* expression in beauty (it is needless to say that there are gentlemen with whiskers dyed and undyed who see none of it whatever), and for this reason, the noblest nature is often the most blinded to the character of the one woman's soul that the beauty clothes. Whence, I fear, the tragedy of human life is likely to continue for a long time to come, in spite of mental philosophers who are ready with the best receipts for avoiding all mistakes of the kind.

Our good Adam had no fine words into which he could put his feeling for Hetty: he could not disguise mystery in this way with the appearance of knowledge; he called his love frankly a mystery, as you have heard him. He only knew that the sight and memory of her moved him deeply, touching the spring of all love and tenderness, all faith and courage within him. How[8] could he imagine narrowness, selfishness, hardness in her? He created the mind he believed in out of his own, which was large, unselfish, tender.

The hopes he felt about Hetty softened a little his feeling towards Arthur.[9] Surely his attentions to Hetty must have been of a slight kind; they were altogether wrong, and such as no man in Arthur's position ought to have allowed himself, but they must have had an air of playfulness about them, which had probably blinded him to their danger, and had prevented them from laying any strong hold on Hetty's heart. As the new promise of happiness rose for Adam, his indignation and jealousy began to die out: Hetty was not made unhappy; he almost believed that she liked him best; and the thought sometimes crossed his mind that the friendship which had once seemed dead for ever might revive in[1] the days to come, and he would not have to say "good-by" to the grand old woods, but would like them better because they were Arthur's. For this new promise of happiness,[2] following so quickly on the[3] shock of pain, had an intoxicating effect on the sober Adam,[4] who had all his life been used to much hardship and moderate hope. Was he really going to have an easy lot after all? It seemed so; for at the beginning of November,[5] Jonathan Burge, finding it impossible to replace Adam, had at last made up his mind to offer him a share in the business,[6] without further condition than that he should continue to give his energies to it, and[7] renounce all thought of having a separate business of his own.

[8] him. How] him: how *MS*   [9] Arthur. ⟨After all⟩ Surely, *MS*
[1] in ⟨years⟩ the days *MS*   [2] happiness ⟨which had risen⟩ following *MS*
[3] the ⟨time⟩ {shock} of ⟨darkness & despondence⟩ {pain} had *MS*
[4] Adam, ⟨changing his judgment of things which themselves had not changed⟩ who had all his life been used to much hardship & moderate hope. *MS*
[5] November ⟨had⟩ Jonathan *MS*   [6] business, ⟨if he would⟩ without *MS*
[7] & ⟨give⟩ renounce all thought of {having} a *MS*

Son-in-law or no son-in-law, Adam had made himself too necessary to be parted with, and his headwork was so much more important to Burge than his skill in handicraft, that his having the management of the woods made little difference in the value of his services; and as to the bargains about the Squire's timber, it would be easy to call in a third person. Adam[8] saw here an opening into a broadening path of prosperous work, such as he had thought of with ambitious longing ever since he was a lad: he might come to build a bridge, or a town-hall, or a factory, for he had always said to himself that Jonathan Burge's building business was like an acorn, which might be the[9] mother of a great tree. So he gave his hand to Burge on that bargain, and went home with his mind full of happy visions, in which (my refined reader will perhaps be shocked when I say it) the image of Hetty hovered and smiled over plans for seasoning timber at a trifling expense, calculations as to the cheapening of bricks per thousand by water-carriage, and a favourite scheme for the strengthening of roofs and walls with a peculiar form of iron girder. What then? Adam's enthusiasm lay in these things; and our[1] love is inwrought in our enthusiasm as electricity is inwrought in the air, exalting its power by a subtle presence.

Adam would be able to take a separate house now, and provide for his mother in the old one; his prospects would justify his marrying very soon, and if[2] Dinah consented to have Seth, their[3] mother would perhaps be more[4] contented to live apart from Adam. But he told himself that he would not be hasty—he would not try Hetty's feeling for him until it had had time to grow strong and firm. However, to-morrow, after church, he would go to the Hall Farm and tell them the news. Mr Poyser, he knew, would[5] like it better than a five-pound note, and he should see if Hetty's eyes brightened at it.[6] The months would be short with all he had to fill his mind, and this foolish eagerness which[7] had come over him of late must not[8] hurry him into any premature words. Yet when he got home and told his mother the good news, and[9] ate his supper, while she sat by almost crying for joy, and wanting him to eat twice as much as usual because of this good luck, he could not help preparing her gently for the coming change, by talking of the old house being too small for them all[1] to go on living in it always[2].

---

[8] services; and as to the bargains about the Squire's timber, it would be easy to call in a third person. Adam] services {& as to the bargains with Burge for timber—why, it would be easy to call in a third person.} Adam *MS*   [9] the ⟨father⟩ mother *MS*

[1] things; and our] & things, and I am not sure that enthusiasm cannot give a grander poetry to bricks & timber than all the poets have found in nightingales & roses. And our *MS*

[2] if ⟨Seth⟩ Dinah *MS*   [3] their] his *MS*   [4] more] *added in MS*

[5] would ⟨the⟩ like *MS*   [6] it. ⟨But⟩ The *MS*   [7] which] that *MS*

[8] not ⟨lead⟩ hurry *MS*   [9] & ⟨said⟩ ate *MS*   [1] all] *added in MS*

[2] always{.} ⟨, & asking her if she wouldn't like to live with Dinah & have her for a daughter-in-law, while he himself would {could} ⟨⟨could⟩⟩ take another cottage here in the village.⟩ *MS*

CHAPTER XXXIV.

THE BETROTHAL.

It was a dry Sunday, and really a pleasant day for the 2nd of November. There was no sunshine, but the clouds were high, and the wind was so still that the yellow leaves which fluttered down from the hedgerow elms must have fallen from pure decay. Nevertheless, Mrs Poyser did not go to church, for she had taken a cold too serious to be neglected; only two winters ago she had been laid up for weeks with a cold; and[1] since his wife did not go to church, Mr Poyser considered that on the whole it would be as well for him to stay away too[2] and "keep her company." He[3] could perhaps have given no precise form to the reasons that determined this conclusion; but it is well known to all experienced minds that our firmest convictions are often dependent on subtle impressions for which words are quite too coarse a medium. However it was, no one from the Poyser family went to church that afternoon except Hetty and the boys; yet Adam was bold enough to join them after church, and say that he would walk home with them, though all the way through the village he appeared to be chiefly occupied with Marty and Tommy, telling them about the squirrels in Binton Coppice, and promising to take them there some day. But when they came to the fields he said to the boys, "Now, then, which is the stoutest walker? Him as gets to th'[4] home-gate first shall be the first to go with me to Binton Coppice on the donkey. But Tommy must have the start up to the next stile, because he's the smallest."

Adam had never behaved so much like a determined lover before. As soon as the boys had both set off, he looked down at Hetty, and said, "Won't you hang on my arm, Hetty?" in a pleading tone, as if he had already asked her and she had refused. Hetty looked up at him smilingly and put her round arm through his in a moment. It was nothing to her—putting her arm through Adam's; but she knew he cared a great deal about having her arm through his, and she wished him to care. Her heart beat no faster, and she looked at the half-bare hedgerows and the ploughed field with the same sense of oppressive dulness as before. But Adam scarcely[5] felt that he was walking; he thought Hetty must know that he was pressing her arm a little—a very little; words rushed to his lips that he[6] dared

---

[1] cold; and] cold. And *MS*   [2] too] *added in MS*
[3] company." He] company": he *MS*   [4] th'] the *MS*
[5] scarcely ⟨knew⟩ felt *MS*   [6] he ⟨was determined⟩ ⟨must⟩ dared *MS*

not utter[7]—that he had made up his mind not to utter yet; and so he was silent for the length of that field. The calm patience with which he had once waited for Hetty's love, content only with her presence and the thought of the future, had forsaken him since that terrible shock nearly three months ago. The agitations of jealousy had given a new restlessness to his passion— had made fear and uncertainty too hard almost to bear. But though he might not speak to Hetty of his love, he would tell her about his new prospects, and see if she would be pleased. So when he was enough master of himself to talk, he said—

"I'm going to tell your uncle some news that'll surprise him, Hetty; and I think he'll be glad to hear it too."

"What's that?" Hetty said, indifferently.

"Why, Mr Burge has offered me a share in his business, and I'm going to take it."

There was a[8] change in Hetty's face, certainly not produced by any agreeable impression from this news. In fact she felt a momentary annoyance and alarm; for she had so often heard it hinted by her uncle that Adam might have Mary Burge and a share in the business any day if he liked, that she associated the two objects now, and the thought immediately occurred that perhaps Adam had given her up because of what had happened lately, and had[9] turned towards Mary Burge. With that thought, and before she had time to remember any reasons why it could not be true,[1] came a new sense of forsakenness and disappointment[2]: the one thing[3]—the one person—her mind had rested on in its dull weariness, had slipped away from her, and peevish misery filled her eyes with tears. She was looking on the ground, but Adam saw her face, saw the tears, and before he had finished saying, "Hetty, dear Hetty, what are you crying for?" his eager rapid thought had flown through all the causes conceivable to him, and had at last alighted on half the true one. Hetty thought he was going to marry Mary Burge—she didn't like him to marry—perhaps[4] she didn't like him to marry any one but herself? All caution was swept away—all reason for it was gone, and Adam could feel nothing but trembling joy. He leaned towards her and took her hand, as he said—

"I could afford to be married now, Hetty—I could make a wife comfortable; but I shall never want to be married if you won't have me."

Hetty looked up at him, and smiled through her tears as she had done to Arthur that first evening in the wood, when she had thought he was not

---

[7] utter ⟨yet⟩—that *MS*   [8] a ⟨slight⟩ change *MS*
[9] had ⟨made up his mind to have⟩ ⟨turned in [one word] towards⟩ turned towards *MS*
[1] & before she had time to remember any reasons why it could not be true,] *added in MS*
[2] forsakenness and disappointment] *revised in MS from* forsakenness ⟨& misery⟩ disappointment *to read* disappointment forsakenness
[3] thing—⟨she had⟩ the *MS*   [4] marry—perhaps] marry—that was, perhaps *MS*

coming, and yet he came. It was a feebler relief, a feebler triumph she felt now, but the great dark eyes and the sweet lips were as beautiful as ever, perhaps more beautiful, for there was a more luxuriant womanliness about Hetty of late. Adam could hardly believe in the happiness of that moment. His right hand held her left, and[5] he pressed her arm close against his heart as he leaned down towards her.

"Do you really love me, Hetty? Will you be my own wife, to love and take care of as long as I live?"

Hetty did not speak, but Adam's face was very close to hers, and she put up her round cheek against his, like a kitten. She wanted to be caressed—she wanted to feel as if Arthur were with her again.

Adam cared for no words after that, and they hardly spoke through the rest of the walk. He only said, "I may tell your uncle and aunt, mayn't I, Hetty?" and she said, "Yes."

The red fire-light on the hearth at the Hall Farm shone on joyful faces that evening, when Hetty was gone upstairs and Adam took the opportunity of telling Mr and Mrs Poyser and the grandfather that he saw his way to maintaining a wife now, and that Hetty had consented to have him.

"I hope you have[6] no objections against me for her husband," said Adam; "I'm a poor man as yet, but she shall want nothing as I can work for."

"Objections?" said Mr Poyser, while the grandfather leaned forward and brought out his long "Nay, nay." "What[7] objections can we ha'[8] to you, lad? Never mind your being poorish as yet; there's money in your head-piece as there's money i'[9] the sown field, but it must ha' time. You'n got enough to begin on, and we can do a deal tow'rt the bit o' furniture you'll want. Thee'st got feathers and linen to spare—plenty, eh?"

This question was of course addressed to Mrs Poyser, who was wrapped up in a warm shawl, and was too hoarse to speak with her usual facility. At first she only nodded emphatically, but she was presently unable to resist the temptation to be more explicit.

"It 'ud be a poor tale if I hadna[1] feathers and linen," she said, hoarsely, "when I never sell a fowl but what's plucked, and the wheel's a-going every day o' the week."

"Come, my wench," said Mr Poyser, when Hetty came down, "come and kiss us, and let us wish you luck."

Hetty went very quietly and kissed the big good-natured man.

"There!" he said, patting her on the back, "go and kiss your aunt and your grandfather. I'm as wishful t'[2] have you settled well as if you was my

---

[5] & ⟨his other arm stole round her waist; he didn't kiss her⟩ he pressed her arm close against his heart as he leaned down MS

[6] you have] you've MS 1   [7] nay." "What] nay," "What MS

[8] ha'] have MS   [9] i'] in MS   [1] hadna] hadn't MS   [2] t'] to MS

own daughter; and so's your aunt, I'll be bound, for she's done by you this seven 'ear[3], welly[4], as if you'd been her own. Come, come, now," he went on, becoming jocose, as soon as Hetty had kissed her aunt and the old man, "Adam wants a kiss too, I'll[5] warrant, and he's a right to one now."

Hetty turned away, smiling, towards her empty chair.

"Come, Adam, then, take one," persisted Mr Poyser, "else y' arena half a man."

Adam got up, blushing like a small maiden—great strong fellow as he was—and, putting his arm round Hetty, stooped down and gently kissed her lips.

It was a pretty scene in the red fire-light: for[6] there were no candles; why should there be, when the fire was so bright, and was reflected from all the pewter and the polished oak? No one wanted to work on a Sunday evening. [7]Even Hetty felt something like contentment in the midst of all this love. Adam's attachment to her, Adam's caress, stirred no passion in her, were no longer enough to satisfy her vanity; but they were the best her life offered her now—they promised her some change.

There was a great deal of discussion before Adam went away, about the possibility of his finding a house that would do for him to settle in.[8] No house was empty except the one next to Will Maskery's in the village, and that was too small for Adam now. Mr Poyser insisted that the best plan would be for Seth and his mother to move, and leave Adam in the old home, which might be enlarged after a while, for there was plenty of space in the wood-yard and garden; but Adam objected to turning his mother out.

"Well, well," said Mr Poyser at last, "we needna[9] fix everything[1] to-night. We must take time to consider. You canna[2] think o' getting married afore[3] Easter. I'm not for long courtships, but there must be a bit o' time to make things comfortable."

"Ay, to be sure," said Mrs Poyser, in a hoarse whisper; "Christian folks can't be married like cuckoos, I reckon."

"I'm a bit daunted, though," said Mr Poyser, "when I think as we may have notice to quit, and belike be forced to take a farm twenty mile off."

"Eh," said the old man,[4] staring at the floor, and lifting his hands up and down, while his arms rested on the elbows of his chair, "it's a poor tale if I mun leave th' ould spot, an'[5] be buried in a strange parish. An' you'll happen[6] ha' double rates to pay," he added, looking up at his son.

---

[3] 'ear] year *MS*   [4] welly] *MS* Hetty *1 8*   [5] I'll ⟨be bound⟩ warrant *MS*
[6] fire-light: for] firelight. For *MS*   [7] *Paragraph division added in MS.*
[8] in. ⟨There was n⟩ {N}o house {was} empty *MS*   [9] needna] needn't *MS*
[1] everything] *MS* iverything *1* ⟨iverything⟩ everything *8*
[2] canna] ⟨canna⟩ can't *MS*   [3] afore] before *MS*
[4] man, ⟨looking vaguely⟩ staring *MS*   [5] an'] & *MS* an *Cabinet*
[6] happen ⟨have⟩ ha' *MS*

"Well, thee mustna fret beforehand[7], father," said Martin the younger. "Happen[8] the Captain 'ull come home and make our peace wi' th' old Squire. I build upo' that, for I know the Captain 'll[9] see folks righted if he can."

---

[7] beforehand] *added in MS*   [8] younger. "Happen] younger, "Happen *MS*
[9] 'll] 'ull *MS 1*

CHAPTER XXXV.

THE HIDDEN DREAD.

It was a busy time for Adam—the time between the beginning of November and the beginning of February, and he could see little of Hetty, except on Sundays. But a happy time, nevertheless; for it was taking him nearer and nearer to March, when they were to be married; and all the little preparations for[1] their new housekeeping marked the progress towards the longed-for day. Two new rooms had been "run up" to the old house, for his mother and Seth were to live with them after all. Lisbeth[2] had cried so piteously at the thought of leaving Adam, that he had gone to Hetty and asked her if,[3] for the love of him, she would put up with his mother's ways, and consent to live with her. To his great delight, Hetty said, "Yes; I'd as soon she lived with us as not." Hetty's mind was oppressed at that moment with a worse difficulty than poor Lisbeth's ways, she could not[4] care about them. So Adam was consoled for the disappointment he had felt when Seth had come back from his visit to Snowfield and said "it was no use[5]— Dinah's heart wasna[6] turned towards marrying." For[7] when he told his mother that Hetty was willing they should all live together, and there was no more need of[8] them to think of parting, she said, in a more contented tone than he had heard her speak in since it had been settled that he was to be married, "Eh, my lad, I'll be as still as th' ould tabby, an'[9] ne'er want to do aught but th' offal work, as *she* wonna like t' do. An' then, we needna part the[1] platters an' things, as ha' stood on the shelf together sin' afore thee wast born."

There was only one cloud that now and then came across Adam's sunshine: Hetty seemed unhappy sometimes. But to all his anxious, tender questions, she replied with an assurance that she was quite contented and wished nothing different; and the next time he saw her she was more[2] lively than usual. It might be that she was a little overdone with work and anxiety now, for soon after Christmas Mrs Poyser had taken another cold, which had brought on inflammation, and this illness had confined her to her room all through January. Hetty had to manage everything downstairs,

[1] for ⟨that⟩ their MS   [2] all. Lisbeth] all: Lisbeth MS
[3] if, ⟨she⟩ for MS   [4] could not] couldn't MS
[5] and said "it was no use] & told him "it was of no use MS
[6] wasna] was not MS   [7] marrying." For] marrying;" for MS   [8] of] for MS
[9] an'] & MS   [1] the] MS th' *1* ⟨th'⟩ the 8   [2] was more] would be more MS

and half supply Molly's place too, while that good damsel waited on her mistress; and she seemed to throw herself so entirely into her new functions, working with a grave steadiness[3] which was new in her, that Mr Poyser often told Adam she was wanting to show him what a good housekeeper he would have; but he "doubted the lass was o'er-doing[4] it—she must have a bit o' rest when her aunt could come down-stairs."

This desirable event of Mrs Poyser's coming downstairs happened in the early part of February, when some mild weather thawed the last patch of snow on the Binton Hills. On one of these days, soon after her aunt came down, Hetty went to Treddleston to buy some of the wedding things[5] which were wanting, and[6] which Mrs Poyser had scolded her for neglect-ing, observing that she supposed "it was because they were[7] not for th' outside, else she'd ha' bought 'em fast enough."

It was about ten o'clock when Hetty set off, and the slight hoar-frost that had whitened the hedges in the early morning had disappeared as the sun mounted the cloudless sky. Bright February days have a stronger charm of hope about them than any other days in the year. One likes to pause in the mild rays of the sun, and look over the gates at the patient plough-horses turning at the end of the furrow, and think that the beautiful year is all before one. The birds seem to feel just the same: their notes are as clear as the clear air. There are no leaves on the trees and hedgerows, but how green all the grassy fields are! and the dark purplish brown of the ploughed earth and of the[8] bare branches is beautiful too. What a glad world this looks like, as one drives or rides along the valleys and over the hills! I have often thought so when, in foreign countries, where the fields and woods have looked to me like our English Loamshire—the rich land tilled with just as much care, the woods rolling down the gentle slopes to the green meadows—I have come on something by the roadside which has reminded me that I am not in Loamshire: an image of a great agony—the agony of the Cross. It has stood perhaps by the clustering apple-blossoms, or in the broad sunshine by the cornfield, or at a turning by the wood where a clear brook was gurgling below; and surely, if there came a traveller to this world who knew nothing of the story of man's life upon it, this image of agony would seem to him strangely out of place in the midst of this joyous nature. He would not know that hidden behind the apple-blossoms, or among the golden corn, or under the shrouding boughs of the wood, there might be a human heart beating heavily with anguish—[9]perhaps a young blooming girl, not knowing where to turn for refuge from swift-advancing shame; understanding no more of this life of ours than a foolish lost lamb wander-

---

[3] steadiness ⟨that⟩ which *MS*   [4] o'er-doing] over-doing *MS*
[5] things ⟨that⟩ which *MS*   [6] & ⟨that⟩ which *MS*   [7] were ⟨for⟩ not for *MS*
[8] and of the] and the *MS 1* and {of} the *8*   [9] anguish—] *MS* anguish: *1* anguish; *8*

ing farther and farther in the nightfall on the lonely heath; yet tasting the bitterest of life's bitterness.

Such things are sometimes hidden among the sunny fields and behind the blossoming orchards; and the sound of the gurgling brook, if you came close to one spot behind a small bush, would be mingled for your ear with a despairing human[1] sob. No wonder man's religion has much sorrow in it: no wonder he needs a Suffering God.

Hetty, in her red cloak and warm bonnet, with her basket in her hand, is turning towards a gate by the side of the Treddleston road, but not that she may have a more lingering enjoyment of the sunshine, and think with hope of the long unfolding year. She hardly knows that the sun is shining; and for weeks[2] now, when she has hoped at all, it has been for something at which she herself trembles and shudders. She only wants to be out of the high road, that she may walk slowly, and not care how her face looks, as she dwells on wretched thoughts; and through this gate she can get into a field-path behind the wide thick hedgerows. Her great dark eyes wander blankly over the fields like the eyes of one who is desolate, homeless, unloved, not the promised bride of a brave, tender man. But there are no tears in them: her tears were[3] all wept away in the weary night, before[4] she went to sleep. At the next stile the pathway branches off: there are two roads before her—one along by the hedgerow, which will by-and-by lead her into the road again; the other across the fields, which will take her much farther out of the way into the Scantlands, low shrouded pastures where she will see nobody. She chooses this, and begins to walk a little faster, as if she had suddenly thought of an object towards which it was worth while to hasten. Soon she is in the Scantlands, where the grassy land slopes gradually downwards, and she leaves the level ground to follow the slope. Farther on there is a clump of trees on the low ground, and she is making her way towards it. No[5], it is not a clump of trees, but a dark shrouded pool, so full with the wintry rains that the under boughs of the elder-bushes lie low beneath the water. She sits down on the grassy bank, against the[6] stooping stem of the great oak that hangs over the dark pool. She has thought of this pool often in the nights of the month that has[7] just gone by, and now at last she is come to see it. She clasps her hands round her knees and leans forward, and looks earnestly at it, as if trying to guess what sort of bed it would make for her young round limbs.

No, she has not courage to jump into that cold watery bed, and if she had, they might find her—they might find out why she had drowned herself. There is but one thing left to her: she must go away, go where they can't find her.

---

[1] human] *added in MS*   [2] weeks] *MS 1* weeks, *8*   [3] were] have been *MS*
[4] night, before] night before *MS 1* night {,} before *8*   [5] it. No] it: no *MS*
[6] the ⟨leaning⟩ stooping *MS*   [7] has] is *MS*

After the first on-coming of her great dread, some weeks after her betrothal to Adam, she had waited and waited, in the blind vague hope that something would happen to set her free from her terror; but she could wait no longer. All the force of her nature had been concentrated on the one effort of concealment, and she had shrunk with irresistible dread from every course that could tend towards a betrayal of her miserable secret. Whenever the thought of writing to Arthur had occurred to her, she had rejected it: he could do nothing for her that would shelter her from discovery and scorn among the relatives and neighbours who once more made all her world, now her airy dream had vanished. Her imagination no longer saw happiness with Arthur, for he could do nothing that would satisfy or soothe her pride. No, something else would happen—something *must* happen—to set her free from this dread. In young, childish, ignorant souls there is constantly this blind trust in some unshapen chance: it is as hard to a boy or girl to believe that a great wretchedness will actually befall them, as to believe that they will die.

But now necessity was pressing hard upon her—now the time of her marriage was close at hand—she could no longer rest in this blind trust. She must run away; she must hide herself where no familiar eyes could detect her; and *then*[8] the terror of wandering out into the world, of which she knew nothing, made the possibility of going to Arthur a thought which brought some comfort with it. She felt so helpless now, so unable to fashion the future for herself, that the prospect of throwing herself on him had a relief in it which was stronger than her pride. As she sat by the pool, and shuddered at the dark cold water, the hope that he would receive her tenderly—that he would care for her and think for her—was like a sense of lulling warmth, that made her for the moment indifferent to everything else; and she began now to think of nothing but the scheme by which she should get away.

She had had a letter from Dinah lately, full of kind words about the[9] coming marriage, which she had heard of[1] from Seth; and when Hetty had[2] read this letter aloud to her uncle, he had said, "I wish Dinah 'ud come again now, for she'd be a comfort to your aunt when you're gone. What do you think, my wench, o' going to see her as soon as you can be spared, and persuading her to come back wi'[3] you? You might happen persuade her wi' telling her as her aunt[4] wants her, for all she writes o' not being able to come." Hetty had not liked the thought of going to Snowfield, and felt no longing to see Dinah, so she only said, "It's so far off,[5] uncle." But now she

---

[8] *then*] then, *MS* then *1* ⟨then⟩ then *8*   [9] the] her *MS*
[1] heard of] learned *MS*   [2] had] *added in MS*   [3] wi'] with *MS*
[4] You might happen persuade her wi' telling her as her aunt] You might persuade her with telling her her aunt *MS*
[5] far off,] far, *MS*

thought this proposed visit would serve as a pretext for going away. She would tell her aunt when she got home again, that she should like the change of going to Snowfield for a week or ten days. And then, when she got to Stoniton, where nobody knew her, she would ask for the coach that would take her on the way to Windsor. Arthur was at Windsor, and she would go to him.

As soon as Hetty had determined on this scheme, she rose from the grassy bank of the pool, took up her basket, and went on her way to Treddleston, for she must buy the wedding things she had come out for, though she would never want them. She must be careful not to raise any suspicion that she was going to run away.

Mrs Poyser was quite agreeably surprised that Hetty wished to go and see Dinah, and try to bring her back to stay over the wedding. The sooner she went the better, since the weather was pleasant now; and Adam, when he came in the evening, said, if Hetty could set off to-morrow, he would make time to go with her to[6] Treddleston, and see her safe into the Stoniton coach.

"I wish I could go with you and take care of you, Hetty," he said, the next morning, leaning in at the coach door; "but you won't stay much beyond a week—the time 'll[7] seem long."

He was looking at her fondly, and his strong hand held hers in its grasp. Hetty felt a sense of protection in his presence—she was used to it now: if she could have had the past undone, and known no other love than her quiet liking for Adam! The tears rose as she gave him the last look.

"God bless her for loving me," said Adam, as he went on his way to work again, with Gyp at his heels.

But Hetty's tears were not for Adam—not for the anguish that would come upon him when he found she was gone from him for ever. They were for the misery of her own lot, which took her away from this brave tender man who offered up his whole life to her, and threw her, a poor helpless suppliant, on the man who would think it a misfortune that she was obliged to cling to him.

At three o'clock that day, when Hetty was on the coach that was to take her, they said, to Leicester—part of the long, long way to Windsor—she felt dimly that she might be travelling all this weary journey towards the beginning of new misery.

Yet Arthur was at Windsor; he would surely not be angry with her. If he did not mind about her as he used to do, he had promised to be good to her.

[6] to ⟨Stoniton⟩ Treddleston *MS*   [7] 'll] 'ull *Cabinet*

BOOK FIFTH

*

CHAPTER XXXVI.

THE JOURNEY IN HOPE.

A long, lonely journey, with sadness in the heart; away from the familiar to the strange: that[1] is a hard and dreary thing even to the rich, the strong, the instructed: a hard thing, even when we are called by duty, not urged by dread.

What was it then to Hetty? With her poor narrow thoughts, no longer melting into vague hopes, but pressed upon by the chill of definite fear; repeating again and again the same small round of memories—shaping again and again the same childish, doubtful images of what was to come— seeing nothing in this wide world but the little history of her own pleasures and pains; with so little money in her pocket, and the way so long and difficult. Unless she could afford always to go in the coaches—and she felt sure she could not, for the journey to Stoniton was more expensive than she had expected—it[2] was plain that she must trust to carriers' carts or slow waggons; and what a time it would be before she could get to the end of her journey! The burly old coachman from Oakbourne, seeing such a pretty young woman among the outside passengers, had invited her to come and sit beside him; and feeling that it became him as a man and a coachman to open the dialogue with a joke, he applied himself as soon as they were off the stones to the elaboration of one suitable in all respects. After many cuts with his whip and glances at Hetty out of the corner of his eye, he lifted his lips above the edge of his wrapper and said,

"He's pretty nigh six foot, I'll be bound, isna he, now?"

"Who?" said Hetty, rather startled.

"Why, the sweetheart as you've left behind, or else him as you're goin'[3] arter—which is it?"

Hetty felt her face flushing and then turning pale. She thought this coachman must know something about her. He must know Adam, and might tell him where she was gone, for it is difficult to country people to believe that those who make a figure in their own parish are not known everywhere else, and it was equally difficult to Hetty to understand that chance words could happen to apply closely to her circumstances. She was too frightened to speak.

---

[1] strange: that] strange. That *MS*
[2] expected—it] expected. It *MS* expected,—it *1*   [3] goin'] going *MS*

"Hegh, hegh!" said the coachman, seeing that his joke was not so gratifying as he had expected, "you munna take it too ser'ous; if he's behaved ill, get another. Such a pretty lass as you can get a sweetheart any day."

Hetty's fear was allayed by-and-by, when she found that the coachman made no further allusion to her personal concerns; but it still had the effect of preventing her from asking him what were the places on the road to Windsor. She told him she was only going a little way out of Stoniton, and when she got down at the inn where the coach stopped, she hastened away with her basket to another part of the town. When she had formed her plan of going to Windsor, she had not foreseen any difficulties except that of getting away; and after she had overcome this by proposing the visit to Dinah, her thoughts flew to the meeting with Arthur, and the question how he would behave to her—not resting on any probable incidents of the journey. She was too entirely ignorant of travelling to imagine any of its details, and with all her store of money—her three guineas—in her pocket,[4] she thought herself amply provided. It was not until she found how much it cost her to get to Stoniton that she began to be alarmed about the journey, and then, for the first time, she felt her ignorance as to the places that must be passed on her way. Oppressed with this new alarm, she walked along the grim Stoniton streets, and at last turned into a shabby little inn, where she hoped to get a cheap lodging for the night. Here she asked the landlord if he could tell her what places she must go to, to get to Windsor.

"Well, I can't rightly say. Windsor[5] must be pretty nigh London, for it's where the king lives," was the answer. "Anyhow, you'd best go t' Ashby next—that's south'ard. But there's as many places from here to London as there's houses in Stoniton, by what I can make out. I've never been no traveller myself. But how comes a lone young woman like you, to be thinking o' taking such a journey as that?"

"I'm going to my brother—he's a soldier at Windsor," said Hetty, frightened at the landlord's questioning look. "I[6] can't afford to go by the coach; do you think there's a cart goes[7] towards[8] Ashby in the morning?"

"Yes, there may be carts[9] if anybody knowed where they started from; but you might run over the town before you found out. You'd best set off and walk, and trust to summat overtaking you."

Every word sank like lead on Hetty's spirits; she saw the journey stretch bit by bit before her now; even to get to[1] Ashby seemed a hard thing: it might take the day, for what she knew, and that was[2] nothing to the rest of

---

[4] pocket, ⟨besides what her uncle had given her for her expenses to Snowfield & back,⟩ she *MS*

[5] say. Windsor] say: Windsor *MS*   [6] look. "I] *MS 1* look. {"} I *8*

[7] goes to{wards} ⟨Leicester⟩ Ashby *MS*   [8] towards] *MS* toward *1 8*

[9] carts, ⟨but⟩ if *MS*   [1] to ⟨Leicester⟩ Ashby *MS*   [2] was ⟨only⟩ nothing *MS*

the journey. But it must be done—she must get to Arthur: oh, how she yearned to be again[3] with somebody who would care for her! She who had never got up in the morning without the certainty of seeing familiar faces, people on whom she had an acknowledged claim; whose farthest journey had been to Rosseter on the pillion with her uncle; whose thoughts had always been taking holiday in[4] dreams of pleasure, because all the business of her life was managed for her:—this kitten-like Hetty, who till[5] a few months ago had never felt any other grief than that of envying Mary Burge a new ribbon, or being girded at by her aunt for neglecting Totty, must now make her toilsome way in loneliness, her peaceful home left behind for ever, and nothing but a tremulous hope of distant refuge before her. Now for the first time, as she lay down to-night in the strange hard bed, she felt that her home had been a happy one, that her uncle had been very good to her, that her quiet lot at Hayslope among the things and people she knew, with her little pride in her one best gown and bonnet, and nothing to hide from any one, was what she would like to wake up to as a reality, and find that all the feverish life she had known besides was[6] a short nightmare. She thought of all she had left behind with yearning regret for her own sake: her own misery filled her heart: there was no room in it for other people's sorrow. And yet, before the cruel letter, Arthur had been so tender and loving: the memory of that had still a charm for her, though it was no more than a soothing draught that just made pain bearable. For Hetty could conceive no other existence for herself in future than a hidden one, and a hidden life, even with love, would have had no delights for her; still less a life mingled with shame. She knew no romances, and had only a feeble share in the feelings which are the source of romance, so that well-read ladies may find it difficult to understand her state of mind. She was too ignorant of every-thing beyond the simple notions and habits in which she had been brought up, to have any more definite idea of her probable future than that Arthur would take care of her somehow, and shelter her from anger and scorn. He would not marry her and make her a lady; and apart from that she could think of nothing he could give towards which she looked with longing and ambition.

The next morning she rose early, and taking only some milk and bread for her breakfast, set out to walk on the road towards Ashby, under a leaden-coloured sky, with a narrowing streak of yellow, like a departing hope on the edge of the horizon. Now in her faintness of heart at the length and difficulty of her journey, she was most of all afraid of spending her money, and becoming so destitute that she would have to ask people's charity; for Hetty had the pride not only of a proud nature but of a proud class—the class that pays the most poor-rates, and most shudders at the

---

[3] again] *added in MS*   [4] in ⟨little⟩ dreams *MS*   [5] till] til *MS*
[6] besides was] besides that, was *MS*

idea of profiting by a poor-rate. It had not yet occurred to her that she might get money for her locket and ear-rings which she carried with her, and she applied all her small arithmetic and knowledge of prices to calculating how many meals and how many rides were contained in her two guineas, and the odd shillings, which had a melancholy look, as if they were the pale ashes of the other bright-flaming coin.

For the first[7] few miles out of Stoniton she walked on bravely, always fixing on some tree or gate or projecting bush at the most distant visible point in the road as a goal, and feeling a faint joy when she had reached it. But when she came to the fourth milestone, the first she had happened to notice among the long grass by the road-side, and read that she was still only four miles beyond Stoniton, her courage sank. She had come only this little way, and yet felt tired, and almost hungry again in the keen morning air; for though Hetty was accustomed to much movement and exertion in-doors, she was not used to long walks, which produce[8] quite a different sort of fatigue from that of household activity. As she was looking at the milestone she felt some drops falling on her face—it was beginning to rain. Here was a new trouble which had not entered into her sad thoughts before; and quite weighed down by this sudden addition to her burthen, she sat down on the step of a stile and began to sob hysterically. The beginning of hardship is like the first taste of bitter food—it seems for a moment unbearable; yet, if there is nothing else to satisfy our hunger, we take another bite and find it possible to go on. When Hetty recovered from her burst of weeping, she rallied her fainting courage: it was raining, and she must try to get on[9] to a village where she might find rest and shelter. Presently, as she walked on wearily, she heard the rumbling of heavy wheels behind her, a covered waggon was coming, creeping slowly along with a slouching driver cracking his whip beside the horses. She waited for it, thinking that if the waggoner were not a very sour-looking man, she would ask him to take her up. As the waggon approached her, the driver had fallen behind, but there was something in the front of the big vehicle which encouraged her. At any previous moment in her life she would not have noticed it; but now, the new susceptibility that suffering had awakened in her caused this object to impress her strongly. It was only a small white-and-liver coloured spaniel which sat on the front ledge of the waggon, with large timid eyes, and an incessant trembling in the body, such as you may have seen in some of these small creatures. Hetty cared little for animals, as you know, but at this moment she felt as if the helpless timid creature had some fellowship with her, and without being quite aware of the reason, she was less doubtful about speaking to the driver, who now came forward—a large ruddy man, with a sack over his shoulders by way of scarf or mantle.

---

7 first ⟨two or three⟩ few *MS*   8 produce] produced *Cabinet*
9 on] *added in MS*

"Could you take me up in your waggon, if you're going towards Ashby?" said Hetty. "I'll pay you for it."

"Aw," said the big fellow, with that slowly-dawning smile which belongs to heavy faces, "I can take y' up fawst enough wi'out bein'[1] paid for't if you dooant mind lyin'[2] a bit closish a-top o' the wool-packs. Where do you coom from? and what do you want at Ashby?"

"I come from Stoniton. I'm going a long way—to Windsor."

"What, arter some service, or what?"

"Going to my brother—he's a soldier there."

"Well, I'm going no furder nor Leicester—and fur enough too—but I'll take you, if you dooant mind being a bit long on the road. Th' hosses wooant[3] feel *your* weight no more nor they feel the little doog there, as I puck up on the road a fortni't agoo. He war lost, I b'lieve, an's been all of a tremble iver sin'. Come, gi' us your basket, an'[4] come behind and let me put y' in."

To lie on the wool-packs, with a cranny left between the curtains of the awning to let in the air, was luxury to Hetty now, and she half slept away the hours till the driver came to ask her if she wanted to get down and have "some victual;" he himself was going to eat his dinner at this "public." Late at night they reached Leicester, and so this second day of Hetty's journey was past. She had spent no money except what she had paid for her food, but she felt that this slow journeying would be intolerable for her another day, and in the morning she found her way to a coach-office to ask about the road to Windsor, and see if it would cost her too much to go part of the distance by coach again. Yes! the distance was too great—the coaches were too dear—she must give them up; but the elderly clerk at the office, touched by her pretty anxious face, wrote down for her the names of the chief places she must pass through. This was the only comfort she got in Leicester, for the men stared at her as she went along the street, and for the first time in her life Hetty wished no one would look at her. She set out walking again; but this day she was fortunate, for she was soon overtaken by a carrier's cart which carried her to Hinckley, and by the help of a return chaise, with a drunken[5] postilion,—who frightened her by driving like Jehu the son of Nimshi, and shouting hilarious remarks at her, twisting himself backwards on his saddle,—she was before night in the heart of woody Warwickshire: but[6] still almost a hundred miles from Windsor, they told her. O what a large world it was, and what hard work for her to find her way in it! She[7] went by mistake to Stratford-on-Avon, finding Stratford set down in her list of places, and then she was told she had come a long way out of the right

---

[1] bein'] being *MS*   [2] lyin'] lying *MS*   [3] wooant] woont *MS*
[4] an'] & *MS* an *1*   [5] drunken ⟨driver⟩ postilion *MS*
[6] Warwickshire: but] Warwickshire. But *MS* Warwickshire; but *1*
[7] it! She] it. She *MS*

road. It was not till the fifth day that she got to Stony[8] Stratford. That seems but a slight journey[9] as you look at the map, or remember your own pleasant travels to and from the meadowy banks of the Avon. But how wearily long it was to Hetty! It seemed to her as if this country of flat[1] fields and hedge-rows, and dotted houses, and villages, and market-towns—all so much alike to her indifferent eyes—must have no end, and she must go on wandering among them for ever, waiting tired at toll-gates for some cart to come, and then finding the cart went only a little way—a very little way—to the miller's a mile off perhaps; and[2] she hated going into the public houses, where she must go to get food and ask questions, because there were always men lounging there, who stared at her and joked her rudely. Her body was very weary too with these days of new fatigue and anxiety; they had made her look more pale[3] and worn than all the time of hidden dread she had gone through at home. When at last she reached Stony[4] Stratford, her impatience and weariness had become too strong for her economical caution; she determined to take the coach for the rest of the way, though it should cost her all her remaining money. She would need nothing at Windsor but to find Arthur. When she had paid the fare for the last coach, she had only a shilling; and as she got down at the sign of the Green Man in Windsor at twelve o'clock in the middle of the seventh day, hungry and faint, the coachman came up, and begged her to "remem-ber" him.[5] She put her hand in her pocket, and took out the shilling, but the tears came with the sense of exhaustion and the thought that she was giving away her last means of getting food, which she really required before she could go in search of Arthur. As she held out the shilling, she lifted up her dark tear-filled eyes to the coachman's face and said, "Can you give me back sixpence?"

"No, no," he said gruffly, "never mind—put the shilling up again."

[6]The landlord of the Green Man had stood near enough to witness this scene, and he was a man whose abundant feeding served to keep his good-nature, as well as his person, in high condition. And that lovely tearful face of Hetty's would have found out the sensitive fibre in most men.

"Come, young woman, come in," he said, "and have a drop o' some-thing; you're[7] pretty well knocked up: I can see that."

He took her into the bar and said to his wife, "Here, missis, take this young woman into the parlour; she's a little overcome,"—for Hetty's tears were falling fast. They were merely hysterical tears: she thought she had no reason for weeping now, and was vexed that she was too weak and tired to help it. She was at Windsor at last, not far from Arthur.

[8] Stony] Stoney *MS*   [9] journey, ⟨easily⟩ as *MS*   [1] flat] *added in MS*
[2] perhaps; and] perhaps. And *MS*   [3] pale] paled *MS*   [4] Stony] Stoney *MS*
[5] "remember" him.] *MS* "remember him." *1 8*   [6] *Paragraph division added in 1.*
[7] something; you're] something. You're *MS*

She looked with eager, hungry eyes at the bread and meat and beer that the landlady brought her, and for some minutes she forgot everything else in the delicious sensations of[8] satisfying hunger[9] and recovering from exhaustion. The landlady sat opposite to her as she ate, and looked at her earnestly. No wonder: Hetty had thrown off her bonnet, and her curls had fallen down: her face was all the more touching in its youth and beauty because of its weary look; and the good woman's eyes presently wandered to her figure, which in[1] her hurried dressing on her journey she had taken no pains to conceal; moreover, the[2] stranger's eye detects what the familiar unsuspecting eye[3] leaves unnoticed.

"Why, you're not very fit for travelling," she said, glancing while she spoke at Hetty's ringless hand. "Have you come far?"

"Yes," said Hetty, roused by this question to exert more self-command, and feeling the better for the food she had taken. "I've come a good long way, and it's very tiring. But I'm better now. Could you tell me which way to go to this place?" Here Hetty took from her pocket a bit of paper: it was the end of Arthur's letter on which he had written his address.

While she was speaking, the landlord had come in, and had begun to look at her as earnestly as his wife had done. He took up the piece of paper which Hetty handed across the table, and read the address.

"Why, what do you want at this house?" he said. It is in the nature of innkeepers, and all men who have no pressing business of their own, to ask as many questions as possible before giving any information.

"I want to see a gentleman as is there," said Hetty.

[4]"But there's no gentleman there," returned the landlord. "It's shut up—been shut up this fortnight. What gentleman is it you want? Perhaps I can let you know where to find him."

"It's Captain Donnithorne," said Hetty, tremulously, her heart beginning to beat painfully at this disappointment of her hope that she should find Arthur at once.

"Captain Donnithorne? Stop a bit," said the landlord, slowly. "Was he in the Loamshire Militia? A tall young officer with a fairish skin and reddish whiskers—and had a servant by the name o' Pym?"

"O yes," said Hetty; "you know him—where is he?"

"A fine sight o' miles away from here: the Loamshire Militia's gone to Ireland; it's been gone this fortnight."

"Look there! she's fainting," said the landlady, hastening to support Hetty, who had lost her miserable consciousness and looked like a beautiful corpse. They carried her to the sofa and loosened her dress.

---

[8] of ⟨quelling⟩ satisfying *MS*   [9] hunger ⟨of⟩ & *MS*   [1] in ⟨the⟩ her *MS*
[2] conceal; moreover, the] conceal{.} ⟨, &⟩ ⟨t⟩The *MS*   [3] eye ⟨passes⟩ leaves *MS*
[4] *Paragraph division added in 1.*

"Here's a bad business, I suspect[5]," said the landlord, as he brought in some water.

"Ah, it's plain enough what sort of[6] business it is," said the wife. "She's not a common flaunting dratchell, I can see that. She looks like a respectable country girl, and she comes from a good way off, to judge by her tongue. She talks something like that ostler we had that come from the north: he was as honest a fellow[7] as we ever had about the[8] house—they're all honest folks in the north."

"I never saw a prettier young woman in my life," said the husband. "She's like a pictur in a shop-winder. It goes to one's 'eart to look at her."

"It 'ud have been a good deal better for her if she'd been uglier and had more conduct," said the landlady, who on any charitable construction[9] must have been supposed to have more "conduct" than beauty. "But she's coming to again. Fetch a drop more water."

---

[5] suspect] doubt *MS* [6] of] o' *MS* [7] as honest a fellow] an honest fellow *MS*
[8] the ⟨h⟩'ouse—they're *MS* [9] construction ⟨would be⟩ must have been *MS*

CHAPTER XXXVII.

THE JOURNEY IN DESPAIR.

Hetty was too ill through the rest of that day for any questions to be addressed to her—too[1] ill even to think[2] with any distinctness of[3] the evils that were to come. She only felt that all her hope was crushed, and that instead of having found a refuge she had only reached the borders of a new wilderness where no goal lay before her.[4] The sensations of bodily sickness, in a comfortable bed, and with the tendance of the good-natured landlady, made a sort of respite[5] for her; such a respite as there is in the faint weariness which obliges a man to[6] throw himself on the sand, instead of toiling onward under the scorching sun.

But when sleep and rest had brought back the strength necessary[7] for the keenness of mental suffering,—when she lay the next morning looking at the growing light which was like a cruel taskmaster returning to urge from her a fresh round of hated hopeless labour,—she began to think what course she must take, to remember that all her money was gone, to look at the prospect of further wandering among strangers with the new clearness[8] shed on it by the experience of her journey to Windsor. But which way could she turn? It was impossible for her to[9] enter into any service, even if she could obtain it:[1] there was nothing but immediate beggary before her. She thought of a young woman who had been found[2] against the church wall at Hayslope one[3] Sunday, nearly dead with cold and hunger—a tiny infant in her arms: the woman was rescued and taken to the parish. "The parish!"[4] You can perhaps hardly understand the effect of that word on a mind like Hetty's, brought up among people who were

---

[1] too] to *MS*   [2] even to think] even for her to think *MS*
[3] of ⟨her⟩ the ⟨lengthening path of misery that lay before her⟩ evils that were to come. *MS*
[4] her. ⟨But⟩ ⟨t⟩The *MS*
[5] respite ⟨or lull, compared with⟩ ⟨from the⟩ {for her—such} a respite as there is in the faint⟨ness with⟩ {weariness} which *MS*
[6] to thro⟨ugh⟩{w} himself *MS*   [7] necessary ⟨to the⟩ for *MS*
[8] clearness ⟨that⟩ shed on it by *MS*
[9] to ⟨take⟩ {enter} into any service, ⟨if⟩ even {if} she *MS*
[1] it: ⟨; & away from her own friends there was nothing⟩ there was nothing but {immediate} beggary before her. She *MS*
[2] found ⟨by the roadside⟩ against the Church wall *MS*
[3] one ⟨morning⟩ Sunday *MS*
[4] parish!" ⟨It is difficult for people with culture enough⟩ You can perhaps hardly understand the effect of *MS*

somewhat hard in their feelings even towards[5] poverty, who lived among the fields, and had little pity for want and rags as a cruel[6] inevitable fate such as they sometimes seem in cities, but[7] held them a mark of idleness and vice—and it was idleness and vice that brought burthens on the parish.[8] To Hetty the "parish" was next to the prison in obloquy; and to ask anything of strangers—to beg—lay in the same far-off hideous region of intolerable shame that[9] Hetty had all her life thought it impossible she could ever come near. But now the remembrance of that[1] wretched woman whom she had seen herself, on her way[2] from church, being carried into Joshua Rann's, came back upon her with the new terrible sense that there was very little now to divide her[3] from the same lot. And the dread of bodily hardship mingled with the dread of shame; for Hetty had the luxurious nature of a round, soft-coated pet animal.

How she yearned to be back in her safe home again, cherished and cared for as she had always been! Her aunt's scolding about trifles would have been music to her ears now: she longed for it: she[4] used to hear it in a time when she had only trifles to hide. Could she be the same Hetty that used to make up the butter in the dairy with the Gueldres[5] roses peeping in at the window—she,[6] a runaway whom her friends would not open their doors to again, lying in this strange bed, with the knowledge that she had no money to pay for what she received, and must offer those strangers some of the clothes in her basket? It was then she thought of her locket and ear-rings, and seeing her pocket lie near, she[7] reached it and spread the contents on the bed before her. There were the locket and ear-rings in the little velvet-lined boxes, and with them there was a beautiful silver thimble which Adam had bought her, the words "Remember me" making the ornament of the border;[8] a steel purse, with her one shilling in it, and a small red-leather case fastening with a strap. Those beautiful little ear-rings with their delicate pearls and garnet, that she had tried in her ears with such longing in the bright sunshine on the 30th of July! She had no longing to put them in her ears now: her head with its dark rings of hair lay back languidly on the pillow, and the sadness that[9] rested about her brow and eyes was something too hard for[1] regretful memory. Yet she put her hands up to her ears: it was

---

[5] towards ⟨mere⟩ poverty, ⟨never looking on want & rags⟩ ⟨& never looked on want & rags as⟩ who lived among the fields & had little pity for want & rags as MS

[6] cruel] hard MS 1 ⟨hard⟩ cruel 8   [7] but ⟨as⟩ held them MS

[8] parish. {To Hetty,} The ⟨word⟩ 'parish' was ⟨only⟩ next to the prison in obloquy ⟨to Hetty⟩; & to ⟨beg⟩ ask MS

[9] shame that] shame, that MS 1 shame⟨,⟩ that 8   [1] that ⟨young⟩ wretched MS

[2] way ⟨to⟩ from MS   [3] her] her MS   [4] it: she] it, for she MS

[5] Gueldres] Gueldres MS Gueldre 1 ⟨Gueldre⟩ Gueldres 8   [6] she{,} ⟨who⟩ a MS

[7] she ⟨got out of bed to⟩ reached MS

[8] border; ⟨Besides these, there was a small red leather case fastening with a strap⟩ a steel purse, with her one shilling in it, & a small red leather case fastening MS

[9] that ⟨lay⟩ rested MS   [1] for ⟨any⟩ regretful memor⟨ies⟩{y}. Yet MS

because there were[2] some thin gold rings in them, which were also worth a little money. Yes, she[3] could surely get some money for[4] her ornaments: those Arthur had given her must have cost[5] a great deal of money. The landlord and landlady had been good to her; perhaps[6] they would help her to get the money for these things.

But this money would not keep her long: what should she do when it was gone? Where should she go? The horrible thought of want and beggary drove her once to think she would go back to her uncle and aunt, and ask them to forgive her and have pity on her. But she shrank from that idea again, as[7] she might have shrunk from scorching metal: she could never endure that shame before her uncle and aunt, before Mary Burge, and the[8] servants at the Chase, and the people at Broxton, and everybody who knew her. They should never know what had happened to her. What *could* she do? She would go away from Windsor—travel again as she had done the last week, and get among the flat green fields with the high hedges round them, where nobody could see her or know her; and there, perhaps, when there was nothing else she could do, she should get courage to drown herself in some pond like that in the Scantlands. Yes, she would get away from Windsor as soon as[9] possible: she didn't like these people at the inn to know about her, to know that she had come to look for Captain Donnithorne: she must think of some reason to tell them why she had asked for him.

With this thought she began to put the things back into her pocket, meaning to get up and dress before the landlady came to her. She had her hand on the red-leather case, when it occurred to her that there might be something in this case which she had forgotten—something worth selling; for without knowing what she should do with her life,[1] she craved the means of living as long as possible; and when we desire eagerly to find something, we are apt to search for it in[2] hopeless places. No, there was nothing but common needles and pins, and dried tulip-petals between the paper leaves where she had written down her little money-accounts. But on one of these leaves there was a name, which,[3] often as she had seen it before, now flashed on Hetty's mind like[4] a newly-discovered message. The name was—*Dinah Morris, Snowfield*. There was a text above it, written, as well as the name, by Dinah's own hand with a[5] little pencil,[6] one evening that they

[2] were] *MS 1* ⟨was⟩ were *8*   [3] Yes, she] Yes! she *MS*
[4] for ⟨these⟩ her *MS*   [5] cost ⟨him⟩ a *MS*
[6] her; perhaps] her—perhaps *MS 1* her⟨—⟩{;} perhaps *8*
[7] as ⟨if she had touched⟩ she might have shrunk from *MS*
[8] the ⟨people⟩ servants *MS*   [9] as ⟨she⟩ possible *MS*
[1] life ⟨of getting⟩ she *MS*   [2] in ⟨impossible⟩ hopeless *MS*
[3] which, ⟨for the first time flashed on Hetty's mind⟩ often as she had seen it before, now *MS*
[4] like] likely *MS*   [5] a] the *MS 1*   [6] pencil, ⟨belonging to the⟩ one *MS*

were sitting together and Hetty happened to have the red case lying open before her. Hetty did not read the text now: she was only arrested by the name. Now, for the first time, she remembered without indifference[7] the affectionate kindness Dinah had shown her, and those words of Dinah in the bed-chamber—that Hetty must think of her as a friend in trouble. Suppose she were to go to Dinah, and ask her to help her? Dinah did not think about things as other people did: she was a mystery to Hetty, but Hetty knew she was always kind. She couldn't imagine Dinah's face turning away from her in dark reproof or scorn, Dinah's voice willingly speaking[8] ill of her, or rejoicing in her misery as a punishment. Dinah did not seem to belong to that world of Hetty's, whose glance she dreaded like scorching fire. But even to[9] her Hetty shrank from beseeching and confession: she could not prevail on herself to say, "I will go to Dinah;" she only thought of that as a possible alternative, if she had not courage for death.

The good landlady was amazed when she saw Hetty come downstairs soon after herself, neatly dressed, and looking resolutely self-possessed. Hetty told her she was quite well this morning: she had only been very tired and overcome with her journey, for she had come a long way to ask about her brother who had run[1] away, and they thought he was gone for a soldier, and Captain Donnithorne might know, for he had been very kind to her brother once. It was a lame story, and the landlady looked doubtfully at Hetty as she told it; but there was a resolute air of self-reliance about her this morning, so different from the helpless prostration of yesterday, that the landlady hardly knew how to make a remark that might seem like prying into other people's affairs. She only invited[2] her to sit down to breakfast with them, and in the course of it Hetty brought out her ear-rings and locket, and asked the landlord if he could help her to get money for them: her journey, she said, had[3] cost her much more than she expected, and now she had no money to get back to her friends, which she[4] wanted to do at once.

It was not the first time the landlady had seen the ornaments, for she had examined the contents of Hetty's pocket yesterday, and she and her husband had discussed the fact of a country girl having these[5] beautiful things, with a stronger conviction than ever that Hetty had been miserably deluded by the fine young officer.

"Well," said the landlord, when Hetty had spread the precious trifles before him, "we might take 'em to the jeweller's shop, for there's one not far off; but Lord bless you, they wouldn't give you a quarter o' what the things

---

[7] she remembered without indifference] *added in MS*

[8] willingly speaking] speaking willing *MS*   [9] to ⟨Dinah⟩ her *MS*

[1] run {away} ⟨& gone for a soldier & they didn't know where he was,⟩ & they thought {he was gone for a soldier &} Captain *MS*

[2] invited ⟨Hetty⟩ her *MS*   [3] journey, she said, had] journey had *MS*

[4] she ⟨desired⟩ wanted *MS*   [5] these ⟨elegant⟩ beautiful *MS*

are worth. And you wouldn't like to part with 'em?" he added, looking at her inquiringly.

"O, I don't mind," said Hetty, hastily, "so as I can get money to go back."

"And they might think the things were stolen[6], as you wanted to sell 'em," he went on; "for it isn't usual[7] for a young woman like you to have fine jew'llery like that."

The blood rushed to Hetty's face with anger. "I belong to respectable folks," she said; "I'm[8] not a thief."

"No, that you aren't, I'll be bound," said the landlady; "and[9] you'd no call to say that," looking indignantly at her husband. "The things were gev to her: that's plain enough to be seen."

"I didn't mean as I[1] thought so," said the husband, apologetically, "but I said it was what the jeweller might think, and so he wouldn't be offering much money for 'em."

"Well," said the wife, "suppose you were[2] to advance some money on the things yourself, and then if she liked to redeem 'em when she got home, she could. But if we heard nothing from her[3] after two months, we might do as we liked with 'em."

I will not say that in this accommodating proposition the landlady had no[4] regard whatever to the possible reward of her good nature in the ultimate possession of the locket and ear-rings: indeed[5], the effect they would have in that case on the mind of the grocer's wife had presented itself with remarkable vividness to her rapid imagination. The landlord took up the ornaments and pushed out his lips in a meditative manner. He[6] wished Hetty well, doubtless; but pray, how many of your well-wishers would decline to make a little gain out of you? Your landlady is sincerely affected at parting with you, respects you highly, and will really rejoice if any one else is generous to you; but at the same time she hands you a bill by which she gains as high a per-centage as possible.

"How much money do you want to get home with, young woman?" said the[7] well-wisher, at length.

"Three[8] guineas," answered Hetty, fixing on the sum she set out with, for want of any other standard, and afraid of asking too much.

"Well, I've no objections to advance you three[9] guineas," said the landlord; "and if you like to send it me back and get the jew'llery[1] again, you can, you know: the[2] Green Man isn't going to run away."

---

⁶ stolen] stole *MS*   ⁷ usual] usial *MS*   ⁸ said; "I'm] said. "I'm *MS*
⁹ landlady; "and] landlady. "And *MS*   ¹ I] I *MS*   ² were] was *MS*
³ her ⟨for⟩ after *MS*   ⁴ no ⟨eye⟩ regard *MS*
⁵ ear-rings: indeed] ear-rings. Indeed *MS*   ⁶ manner. He] manner: he *MS*
⁷ the ⟨host⟩ well-wisher *MS*   ⁸ Three ⟨pounds⟩ guineas *MS*
⁹ three ⟨pound⟩ guineas *MS*   ¹ jew'llery] *MS* jewellery *1 8*
² know: the] know. The *MS*

"O yes,[3] I'll be very glad if you'll give me that," said Hetty, relieved at the thought that she would not have to go to the jeweller's, and be stared at and questioned.

"But if you want the things again, you'll write before long," said the landlady, "because when two months are up, we shall make up our minds as you don't want 'em."

"Yes," said Hetty, indifferently.

The husband and wife were equally content with this arrangement. The husband thought, if the[4] ornaments were not redeemed, he could make a good thing of it by taking them to London and selling them: the wife thought she would coax the good man into letting her keep them. And they were accommodating Hetty, poor thing![5]—a pretty, respectable-looking young woman, apparently in a sad case. They declined to take anything for her food and bed: she was quite welcome. And at eleven o'clock Hetty said "Good-by" to them, with the same quiet, resolute air she had worn all the morning, mounting the coach that was to take her twenty miles back along the way she had come.

There is a strength of self-possession which is the sign that the last hope has departed. Despair no more leans on others than perfect contentment, and in despair[6] pride ceases to be counteracted by the sense of[7] dependence.

Hetty felt that no one could deliver her from the evils that would[8] make life hateful to her; and no one, she said to herself, should ever know her misery and humiliation. No; she would not confess even to Dinah: she would wander out of sight, and drown herself where[9] her body would never be found, and no one should know what had become of her.

When she got off this coach, she began to walk again, and take cheap rides in carts, and get cheap meals, going on and on without distinct purpose, yet strangely, by some fascination, taking the way she had come, though she was determined not to go back to her own country. Perhaps it was because she had fixed her mind on the grassy Warwickshire fields, with the bushy tree-studded hedgerows that made a[1] hiding-place even in this leafless season. She went more slowly than she came, often getting over the stiles and sitting for hours under the hedgerows, looking before her with blank, beautiful eyes; fancying herself at the edge of a hidden pool, low down, like that in the Scantlands; wondering if it were very painful to be drowned, and if there would be anything worse after death than what she dreaded in life. Religious doctrines had taken no hold on Hetty's mind: she was one of those numerous people who have[2] had godfathers and godmothers, learned their

[3] yes," ⟨said Hetty⟩ , "I'll *MS* [4] the ⟨jewels⟩ ornaments *MS*
[5] thing!] *MS 1* thing: *8* [6] in despair] *added in MS* [7] the sense of] *added in MS*
[8] would] *added in MS* [9] where ⟨no ev⟩ her *MS* [1] a] *added in MS*
[2] have] *added in MS*

catechism, been confirmed, and gone to church every Sunday, and yet, for any practical[3] result of strength in life[4], or trust in death, have never appropriated a single Christian idea or Christian feeling. You would misunderstand her thoughts[5] during these wretched days, if you imagined that they were influenced either by religious fears or religious hopes.

She chose to go[6] to Stratford-on-Avon again, where she had gone before[7] by mistake; for she remembered some grassy fields on her former way[8] towards it—fields among which she thought she might find just the sort of pool she had in her mind. Yet she took care of her money still; she carried her basket: death seemed still a long way off, and life was so strong in her! She craved food and rest—she hastened towards them at the very moment she was picturing to herself the bank from which she would leap towards death. It was already five days since she had left Windsor, for she had wandered about, always avoiding speech or questioning looks, and recovering her air of proud self-dependence whenever she was under observation, choosing her decent lodging at night, and dressing herself neatly in the morning, and setting off on her way steadily, or remaining under shelter if it rained, as if she had a happy life to cherish.

And yet, even in[9] her most self-conscious moments,[1] the face was sadly different from that which had smiled at itself in the old specked glass[2], or smiled at others when they glanced at it admiringly. A hard and even fierce look had come in the eyes, though their[3] lashes were as long as ever, and they had[4] all their dark brightness. And[5] the cheek was never dimpled with smiles now. It was the same rounded, pouting, childish[6] prettiness, but with all love and belief in love departed from it—the sadder for its[7] beauty, like that wondrous Medusa-face, with the passionate, passionless lips.

At last she was among the fields she had been dreaming of, on a long narrow pathway leading towards a wood. If there should be a pool in that wood! It would be better hidden than one in the fields.[8] No, it was not a wood, only a wild brake, where there had once been gravel-pits, leaving mounds and hollows studded with brushwood and small trees. She roamed up and down, thinking there was perhaps a pool in every hollow before she

---

[3] practical ⟨purpose⟩ result *MS*   [4] in life] *added in MS*
[5] thoughts ⟨in⟩ during *MS*
[6] go to⟨wards⟩ Stratford on Avon again ⟨which⟩ ⟨whither⟩ where *MS*
[7] had gone before] *revised in MS from* had before gone
[8] way ⟨there where⟩ {towards it—fields ⟨in⟩ among which} she *MS*
[9] yet, even in] yet in *MS*
[1] moments, ⟨she ⟨⟨looked⟩⟩ was no longer the same Hetty⟩ the face was sadly different from that *MS*
[2] specked glass] specked ⟨looking⟩-glass *MS* speckled glass *1* ⟨speckled⟩ specked glass *8*
[3] their] the *MS*   [4] had ⟨still had⟩ all *MS*
[5] brightness. And] brightness; & *MS*   [6] childish ⟨beauty⟩ prettiness *MS*
[7] its ⟨loveliness⟩ beauty *MS*
[8] fields. ⟨It was not a thick wood, she found⟩ No, it was not a wood *MS*

came to it, till her limbs were weary, and she sat down to rest. The afternoon was far advanced, and the leaden sky was darkening, as if the sun[9] were setting behind it. After a little while Hetty started up again, feeling that darkness would soon come on; and she must put off finding the pool till to-morrow, and make her way to some shelter for the night. She had quite lost her way in the fields, and might as well go in one direction as another, for aught she knew. She walked through field after field, and no village, no house was in sight; but *there*, at [1] the corner of this pasture, there was a break in the hedges; the land seemed to dip down a little, and two trees leaned towards each other across the opening. Hetty's heart gave a great beat as she thought[2] there must be a pool there. She walked towards it heavily over the tufted grass, with pale lips and a sense of trembling: it was as if the thing were come in spite of herself, instead of being the object of her search.

There it was, black under the darkening sky: no motion, no sound near. She set down her basket, and then sank down herself on the grass, trembling.[3] The pool had its wintry depth now:[4] by the time it got shallow, as she remembered the pools did at Hayslope, in the summer, no one could find out that[5] it was her body. But then there was her basket—she must hide that too: she must throw it into the water—make it heavy with stones first, and then throw it in. She got up to look about for stones, and soon brought five or six, which she laid down beside her basket, and then sat down again. There was no need to hurry—there was all the night to drown herself in. She sat leaning her elbow on the basket. She was weary, hungry. There were some buns in her basket—three, which she had supplied herself with at the place where she ate her dinner. She took them out now, and ate them eagerly, and then sat still again, looking at the pool. The soothed sensation that came over her from the satisfaction of her hunger, and this fixed dreamy attitude, brought on drowsiness, and presently her head sank down on her knees. She[6] was fast asleep.

When she awoke it was deep night, and she felt chill. She was frightened at this darkness—frightened at the long night before her. If she *could* but throw herself into the water! No, not yet. She began to walk about that she might get warm again, as if she would have more resolution then. O how long the time was in that darkness! The bright hearth and the warmth and the voices of home,—the secure uprising and lying down,—the familiar fields, the familiar people, the Sundays and holidays with their simple joys

---

[9] sun ⟨had set⟩ were setting *MS*

[1] and no village, no house was in sight; but *there*, at] & there was no village, no house in sight; but there, at *MS*

[2] thought ⟨this was⟩ there *MS*   [3] trembling. ⟨It⟩ The pool *MS*

[4] now: ⟨before⟩ by the time *MS*

[5] that {it was} her body. ⟨She was too inobservant to reflect that her body⟩ But then there was her basket—she must hide *MS*

[6] knees. She] knees: she *MS*

of dress and feasting,—all the sweets of her young life rushed before her now, and she seemed to be stretching her arms towards them across a great gulf. She set her teeth when she thought of Arthur: she cursed him, without knowing what her cursing would do: she wished he too might know desolation, and cold, and a life of shame that he dared not end by death.

The horror of this cold, and darkness, and solitude—out of all human reach—became greater every long minute: it was almost as if she were dead already, and knew that she was dead, and longed to get back to life again. But no: she was alive still; she had not taken the dreadful leap. She felt a strange contradictory wretchedness and exultation: wretchedness, that she did not dare to face death; exultation, that she was still in life—that she might yet know[7] light and warmth again. She walked backwards and forwards to warm herself, beginning to discern something of the objects around her, as her eyes became accustomed to the night: the darker line of the hedge, the rapid motion of some living creature—perhaps a field-mouse—rushing across the grass. She no longer felt as if the darkness hedged her in: she thought she could walk back across the field, and get over the stile; and then, in the very[8] next field, she thought she[9] remembered there was a hovel of furze near a sheepfold. If she could get into that hovel, she would be warmer; she could pass the night there, for that was what[1] Alick did at Hayslope in lambing time. The thought of this hovel brought the energy of a new hope: she took up her basket and walked across the field, but it was some time before she[2] got in the right direction for the stile. The exercise and the occupation of finding the stile were a stimulus to her, however, and lightened the horror of the darkness and solitude. There were sheep in the next field, and she startled a group[3] as she set down her basket and got over the stile; and the sound of their movement comforted her, for it assured her that her impression was right: this *was* the field where she had seen the hovel, for it was the field where the sheep were. Right on along the path, and she would get to it. She reached the opposite gate, and felt her way along its rails, and the rails of the sheepfold, till her hand encountered the pricking of the gorsy wall. Delicious sensation! She had found the shelter: she groped her way, touching the prickly gorse, to the door, and pushed it open. It was an ill-smelling close place, but warm, and there was straw on the ground: Hetty sank down on the straw with a sense of escape. Tears came—she had never shed tears before since she left Windsor—tears and sobs of hysterical joy that she had still hold of life, that she was still on the familiar earth, with the sheep near her. The[4] very consciousness of her

---

[7] might yet know] might know *MS*　　　　[8] very] *added in MS*
[9] thought she] *added in MS*　　　[1] what ⟨the shepherd⟩ Alick *MS*
[2] she ⟨could⟩ got *MS*
[3] field, and she startled a group] field; ⟨&⟩ she startled ⟨one⟩ a group *MS*
[4] her. The] her: the *MS*

own limbs was a delight to her: she turned up her sleeves, and kissed her arms with the passionate love of life. Soon warmth and weariness lulled her in the midst of her sobs, and she fell continually into dozing, fancying herself at the brink of the pool again—fancying that she had jumped into the water, and then awaking with a start, and wondering where she was. But at last[5] deep dreamless sleep came; her head, guarded by her bonnet, found a pillow against the gorsy wall; and the poor soul, driven to and fro between two equal terrors, found the one relief that was possible to it—the relief of unconsciousness.

[6]Alas! that relief seems to end the moment it has begun.[7] It seemed to Hetty as if those dozing[8] dreams had only passed into another dream—that she was in the hovel, and her aunt was standing over her with a candle in her hand. She trembled under her aunt's glance, and opened her eyes. There was no candle, but there was light in the hovel—the light of early morning through the open door. And there was[9] a face looking down on her; but it was an unknown face, belonging to an elderly man in a smock-frock.

"Why, what[1] do you do here, young woman?" the man said roughly.

Hetty trembled still worse[2] under this real fear and shame than she had done in her momentary[3] dream under her aunt's glance. She felt that she was like a beggar already—found sleeping in that place. But in spite of her trembling, she was so eager[4] to account to the man for her presence here, that she found words at once.

"I lost my way," she said. "I'm travelling—north'ard, and I got away from the road into the fields, and was overtaken by the dark.[5] Will you tell me the way to the nearest village?"

She got up as she was speaking, and put her hands to her bonnet to adjust it, and then laid hold of her basket.

The man looked at her with a slow bovine gaze, without giving her any answer, for some seconds. Then he turned[6] away and walked towards the door of the hovel, but it was not till he got there that he stood still, and turning his shoulder half round towards her, said,

"Aw, I can show you[7] the way to Norton, if you[8] like. But what do you do gettin'[9] out o' the high road?" he added, with a tone of gruff reproof. "Y'ull[1] be gettin' into mischief, if you[2] dooant mind."

"Yes," said Hetty, "I won't do it again. I'll keep in the road, if you'll be so good as show me how to get to it."

[5] last ⟨real⟩ deep {dreamless} sleep *MS*
[6] *Paragraph division added in MS.*   [7] begun. ⟨Hetty opened her eyes⟩ It *MS*
[8] dozing] dozen *Cabinet*   [9] was ⟨some one standing over⟩ a face looking down on *MS*
[1] what ⟨are⟩ {do} you ⟨doing⟩ do *MS*   [2] worse ⟨with⟩ under *MS*
[3] momentary] *added in MS*   [4] eager ⟨the⟩ to *MS*   [5] dark. ⟨Could⟩ Will *MS*
[6] turned ⟨round⟩ away *MS*   [7] you] yer *MS*   [8] you] yer *MS*
[9] gettin'] getting *MS*   [1] Y'ull] Yer'll *MS*   [2] you] yer *MS*

"Why dooant you[3] keep where there's finger-poasses an'[4] folks to ax the way on?" the man said, still more gruffly. "Anybody 'ud think you[5] was a wild woman, an' look at yer."

Hetty was frightened at this gruff old man, and still more at this last suggestion that she looked like a wild woman. As she followed him out of the hovel she thought she would give him a sixpence for telling her the way, and then he would not suppose she was wild. As he stopped to point out the road to her, she put her hand in her pocket to get the sixpence ready, and when he was turning away, without saying good morning, she held it out to him and said, "Thank you; will you please to take something for your trouble?"

He looked slowly at the sixpence, and then said, "I want none o' your money. You'd better take care on't, else you'll get it stool from yer, if you go[6] trapesin' about the fields like a mad woman a-that-way[7]."

The man left her without further speech, and Hetty held on her way. Another day had risen, and she must wander on. It was no use to think of drowning herself—she could not[8] do it, at least while she had money left to buy food, and strength to[9] journey on. But the incident on her waking this morning heightened her dread of that time when her money would be all gone; she would have to sell her basket and clothes then, and she would really look like a beggar or a wild woman, as the man had said. The passionate joy in life she had felt in the night, after escaping from the brink of the black cold death in the pool, was gone now. Life[1] now, by the morning light, with the impression of that man's hard wondering look at her, was as full of dread as death:—it was worse; it was a dread to which she felt chained, from which she shrank and shrank as she did from the black pool, and yet could find no refuge from it.

She took out her money from her purse, and looked at it; she had still two-and-twenty shillings; it would serve her for many days more, or it would help her to get on faster to Stonyshire, within reach of Dinah. The thought of Dinah urged itself more strongly now, since the experience of the night had driven her shuddering imagination away from the pool. If[2] it had been only going to Dinah—if nobody besides Dinah would ever know—Hetty could have made up her mind to go to her. The soft voice, the pitying eyes, would have drawn her. But afterwards[3] the other people must know, and she could no more rush on that shame than she could rush on death.

---

3 you] yer *MS*   4 finger-poasses an'] ⟨finger-poses⟩ finger-poces & *MS*
5 you] yer *MS*   6 go ⟨round⟩ trapesin' *MS*
7 a-that-way] a-that'n *MS* 1 ⟨a-that'n⟩ a-that-way 8
8 could not] couldn't *MS*   9 to ⟨walk &⟩ journey {on}. But *MS*
1 Life ⟨was only languid misery,⟩ now, by the morning light, *MS*
2 If ⟨she could have gone⟩ {it had been} only {going} to *MS*
3 afterwards] after that, *MS*

She must wander on and on, and wait for a lower depth of despair to give her courage. Perhaps death would come to her, for she was getting less and less able to bear the day's weariness. And yet—such is the strange action of our souls, drawing us by a lurking desire towards the very ends we dread— Hetty, when she set out again from Norton, asked the straightest road northward towards Stonyshire, and kept it all that day.

Poor wandering Hetty, with the rounded[4] childish face, and the hard unloving despairing soul looking out of it—with the narrow heart and narrow thoughts, no room in them for any sorrows but her own, and tasting that sorrow with the more intense bitterness! My[5] heart bleeds for her as I see her toiling along on her weary feet, or seated in a cart, with her eyes fixed vacantly on the road before her, never thinking or caring whither it tends, till hunger comes and makes her desire that a village may be near.

What will be the end?—the end of her[6] objectless wandering, apart from all love, caring for human beings only through her pride, clinging to life only as the hunted wounded brute clings to it?

God preserve you and me from being the beginners of such misery!

---

[4] rounded ⟨childs⟩ childish *MS*   [5] bitterness! My] bitterness. My *MS*
[6] her] this *MS*

CHAPTER XXXVIII.

THE QUEST.

The first ten days after Hetty's departure passed as quietly as any other days with the family at the Hall Farm, and with Adam at his daily work. They had expected Hetty to stay away a week or ten days at least, perhaps a little longer if Dinah came back with her, because there might then be something to detain them at Snowfield. But when a fortnight had passed they began to feel a little surprise that Hetty did not return; she must surely have found it pleasanter to be[1] with Dinah than any one could have supposed. Adam, for his part, was getting very impatient to see her, and he resolved that, if she did not appear the next day (Saturday), he would set out on Sunday morning to[2] fetch her. There was no coach on a Sunday; but by setting out before it was light, and perhaps getting a lift in a cart by the way, he would arrive pretty early at Snowfield, and bring back Hetty the next day—Dinah too, if she were coming. It was quite time Hetty came home, and he would afford to lose his Monday for the sake of bringing her.

His project was quite approved at the Farm when he went there on Saturday evening. Mrs Poyser desired him emphatically not to come back without Hetty, for she had been quite too long away, considering the things she had to get ready by the middle of March, and a week was surely enough for any one to go out for their health. As for Dinah, Mrs Poyser had small hope of their bringing her, unless they could make her believe the folks at Hayslope were twice as miserable as the folks at Snowfield. "Though," said Mrs Poyser, by way of conclusion, "you might tell her she's got but one aunt left, and *she's* wasted pretty nigh to a shadder; and we shall p'rhaps[3] all be gone twenty mile further off her next Michaelmas, and shall die o' broken hearts among strange folks, and leave the children fatherless and motherless."

"Nay, nay," said Mr Poyser, who certainly had the air of a man perfectly heart-whole, "it isna so bad as that. Thee't looking rarely now, and getting flesh every day. But I'd be glad for Dinah t' come, for she'd help thee wi' the little uns: they took t' her wonderful."

So at daybreak, on Sunday, Adam set off. Seth went with him the first mile or two, for the thought of Snowfield, and the possibility that Dinah

---

[1] be ⟨at Snowfield⟩ with Dinah *MS*   [2] to ⟨Snowfield⟩ fetch her *MS*
[3] p'rhaps] perhaps *MS*

might come again, made him restless, and the walk with Adam in the cold morning air, both in their best clothes, helped to give him a sense of Sunday calm. It was the last morning in February, with a low grey sky, and a slight hoar-frost on the green border of the road and on the black hedges. They heard the gurgling of the full brooklet hurrying down the hill, and the faint twittering of the early birds. For they walked in silence, though with a pleased sense of companionship.

"Good-by, lad," said Adam, laying his hand on Scth's shoulder, and looking at him affectionately as thcy were about to part, "I wish thee wast going all the way wi' me, and as happy as I am."

"I'm content, Addy, I'm content," said Seth, cheerfully. "I'll be an old bachelor, belike, and make a fuss wi' thy children."

They turned away from each other, and Seth walked leisurely homeward, mentally repeating one of his favourite hymns—he was very fond of hymns:

> "Dark and cheerless is the morn
>   Unaccompanied by thee:
> Joyless is the day's return
>   Till thy mercy's beams I see:
> Till thou inward light impart,
> Glad my eyes and warm my heart.

> Visit, then, this soul of mine,
>   Pierce the gloom of sin and grief,—
> Fill me, Radiancy Divine,
>   Scatter all my unbelief.
> More and more thyself display,
> Shining to the perfect day."

Adam walked much faster, and any one coming along the Oakbourne road at sunrise that morning must have had a pleasant sight in this tall broad-chested man, striding along with a carriage as upright and firm as any soldier's, glancing with keen glad eyes at the[4] dark-blue hills as they began to show themselves on his way. Seldom in Adam's life had his face been so free from any cloud of anxiety as it was this morning; and this freedom from care, as is usual with constructive practical minds like his, made him all the more observant of the objects round him, and all the more ready to gather suggestions from them towards his own favourite plans and ingenious contrivances. His happy love—the knowledge that his steps were carrying him nearer and nearer to Hetty, who was so soon to be his—was to his thoughts what the sweet morning air was to his sensations: it gave him a consciousness of well-being that made activity delightful. Every now and then there was a rush of more intense feeling towards her, which chased away other images than Hetty; and along with that would come a wondering

---

[4] the ⟨distant⟩ dark blue *MS*

thankfulness that all this happiness was given to him—that this life of ours had such sweetness in it. For Adam[5] had a devout mind, though he was perhaps rather impatient[6] of devout words; and his tenderness lay very close to his reverence, so that the one could hardly be stirred without the other. But after feeling had welled up and poured itself out in this way, busy thought would come back with the greater vigour; and this morning it was intent on schemes by which the roads might be improved that were so imperfect all through the country, and on[7] picturing all the benefits that might come from the exertions of a single country gentleman, if he would set himself to getting the roads made good in his own district.

It seemed a very short walk, the ten miles to Oakbourne, that pretty town within sight of the blue hills, where he breakfasted. After this, the country grew[8] barer and barer: no more rolling woods, no more wide-branching trees near frequent homesteads, no more bushy hedgerows; but grey stone walls intersecting the meagre pastures, and dismal wide-scattered grey stone houses on broken lands where mines had been and were no[9] longer. "A hungry land," said Adam to himself. "I'd[1] rather go[2] south'ard, where they say it's as flat as a table, than come to live here; though if Dinah likes to live in a country where she can be the most comfort to folks, she's i' the right to live o' this side; for she must look as if she'd come straight from heaven, like th'[3] angels in the desert, to strengthen them as ha' got nothing t' eat." And when at last he came in sight of Snowfield, he thought it looked like a town that was "fellow to the country," though the stream through the valley where the great mill stood gave a pleasant greenness to the lower fields. The town[4] lay, grim, stony, and unsheltered, up the side of a steep hill, and Adam did not go forward to it at present, for Seth had told him where to find Dinah. It was at a thatched cottage outside the town, a little way from the mill—an old cottage, standing sideways towards the road,[5] with a little bit of potato-ground before it. Here Dinah lodged with an elderly couple; and if she and Hetty happened to be out, Adam could learn where they were gone, or when they would be at home again. Dinah might be out on some preaching errand, and perhaps she would have left Hetty at home. Adam could not help hoping this, and as he recognized the cottage by the roadside before him, there shone out in his face that involuntary smile which belongs to the expectation of a near joy.

He hurried his step along the narrow causeway, and rapped at the door. It was opened by a very clean old woman, with a slow palsied shake of the head.

[5]　For Adam] For our friend Adam *MS 1* For ⟨our friend⟩ Adam *8*

[6]　was perhaps rather impatient] was ⟨not much given to⟩ perhaps rather too impatient *MS*

[7]　on ⟨a⟩ picturing *MS*　　　　[8]　grew ⟨more dreary⟩ barer & barer *MS*

[9]　no] *added in MS*　　　[1]　himself. "I'd] himself, "I'd *MS*　　　[2]　go ⟨to⟩ south'ard *MS*

[3]　th'] *added in MS*　　　[4]　town ⟨stood⟩ lay *MS*

[5]　standing sideways towards the road,] *added in MS*

"Is Dinah Morris at home?" said Adam.

"Eh? . . . no," said the old woman, looking up at this tall stranger with a wonder that made her slower of speech than usual. "Will ye[6] please to come in?" she added, retiring from the door, as if recollecting herself. "Why, ye're brother to the[7] young man as come afore, arena ye?"

"Yes," said Adam, entering. "That was Seth Bede. I'm his brother Adam. He told me to give his respects to you and your good master."

"Ay, the same t' him: he was a gracious young man. An' ye feature him, on'y ye're darker. Sit ye down i' th' arm-chair. My man isna come home from meeting."

Adam sat down patiently, not liking to hurry the shaking old woman with questions, but looking eagerly towards the narrow twisting stairs in one corner, for he thought it was possible Hetty might have heard his voice, and would come down them.

"So[8] you're come to see Dinah Morris?" said the old woman, standing opposite to him. "An' you didna know she was away from home, then?"

"No," said Adam, "but[9] I thought it likely she might be away, seeing as it's Sunday. But the other young woman—is she at home, or gone along with Dinah?"

The old woman looked at Adam with a bewildered air.

"Gone along wi' her?" she said. "Eh, Dinah's gone to Leeds, a big town ye may ha' heared on, where there's a many o' the Lord's people. She's been gone sin' Friday was a[1] fortnight: they sent her the money for her journey. You may see her room here," she went on, opening a door, and not noticing the effect of her words on Adam. He rose and followed her, and darted an eager glance into the little room, with its narrow bed, the portrait of Wesley on the wall, and the few books lying on the large Bible. He had had an irrational hope that Hetty might be there. He could not speak[2] in the first moment after seeing that the room was empty; an undefined fear had seized him—something had happened to Hetty on the journey. Still,[3] the old woman was so slow of speech and[4] apprehension, that Hetty might be at Snowfield after all.

"It's a pity[5] ye didna know," she said. "Have ye[6] come from your own country o' purpose to see her?"

"But Hetty—Hetty Sorrel," said Adam, abruptly; "where[7] is *she*?"

"I know nobody by that name," said the old woman, wonderingly. "Is it anybody ye've heared on at Snowfield?"

[6] ye] you *MS*   [7] the] th' *MS*   [8] "So ⟨you'n⟩ you're *MS*
[9] Adam, "but] *MS 1* Adam, {"}but *8*   [1] a ⟨week⟩ fortnight *MS*
[2] speak ⟨to the old woman⟩ in *MS*   [3] Still,] *MS 1* Still *8*
[4] speech &] *added in MS*   [5] pity ⟨you⟩ ye *MS*
[6] Have ye] Han ⟨you⟩ ye *MS*   [7] abruptly; "where] abruptly. "Where *MS*

"Did there come no young woman here—very young and pretty—[8]
Friday was a fortnight, to see Dinah Morris?"

"Nay; I'n seen no young woman."

"Think; are you quite sure? A girl, eighteen years old, with dark eyes and
dark curly hair, and a red cloak on, and a basket on her arm? You couldn't
forget her if you saw her."

"Nay;[9] Friday was a fortnight—it was the day as Dinah went away—
there[1] come nobody. There's ne'er been nobody asking for her till you
come, for the folks about know as she's gone. Eh dear, eh dear, is there
summat the matter?"

The old woman had seen the ghastly look of fear in Adam's face. But he
was not stunned or confounded: he was thinking eagerly where he could
inquire about Hetty.

"Yes; a young woman started from our country to see Dinah,[2] Friday
was a fortnight. I came to fetch her back. I'm[3] afraid something has
happened to her. I can't stop. Good-by."

He hastened out of the cottage, and the old woman followed him[4] to the
gate, watching him sadly with her shaking head, as he almost ran towards
the town. He was going to inquire at the place where the Oakbourne coach
stopped.

No! no young woman like Hetty had been seen there. Had any accident
happened to the coach[5] a fortnight ago? No. And there was no coach to take
him back to Oakbourne that day. Well, he would walk: he couldn't stay
here, in wretched inaction. But the innkeeper, seeing that Adam was in
great anxiety,[6] and entering into this new incident with the eagerness of a
man who passes[7] a great deal of time with his hands in his pockets looking
into an obstinately monotonous street, offered to take him back to Oakbourne in his own "taxed cart" this very evening. It was not five o'clock;
there was plenty of time for Adam to take a meal, and yet to get to
Oakbourne before ten o'clock.[8] The innkeeper declared that he really
wanted to go to Oakbourne, and might as well go to-night; he should
have all Monday before him then. Adam, after making an ineffectual
attempt to eat, put the food in his pocket, and[9], drinking a draught of ale,

---

[8] pretty—⟨yesterday week, & ask for⟩ Friday was a fortnight, to see *MS*

[9] "Nay. ⟨Yesterday⟩ Friday was a ⟨week⟩ fortnight—it was the day ⟨after⟩ as *MS*

[1] away—there] away. There *MS*   [2] Dinah ⟨yesterday week⟩ Friday was a fortnight
MS

[3] back. I'm] back: I'm *MS*   [4] him ⟨there⟩ to *MS*

[5] coach ⟨yesterday week⟩ a fortnight ago *MS*

[6] anxiety, ⟨offered to take him back to Oakbourne⟩ & entering into this new incident with
the *MS*

[7] passes ⟨his⟩ a *MS*

[8] o'clock. ⟨But Adam, after making⟩ The innkeeper declared that he *MS*

[9] & ⟨contenting himself with⟩ drinking *MS*

declared himself ready to set off.[1] As they approached the cottage, it occurred to him that he would do well to learn from the old woman where Dinah was to be found in Leeds: if there was trouble at the Hall Farm—he only half admitted the foreboding that there would be—the Poysers might like to send for Dinah. But Dinah had not left any address, and the old woman, whose memory for names was infirm, could not recall the name of the "blessed woman" who was Dinah's chief friend in the Society at Leeds.

During that long, long journey in the taxed cart, there was time for all the conjectures of importunate fear and struggling hope. In the very first shock of discovering that Hetty had not been to Snowfield, the thought of Arthur had darted through Adam like a[2] sharp pang: but he tried for some time to ward off its return by busying himself with modes of accounting for the alarming fact, quite apart from that intolerable thought. Some accident had happened. Hetty[3] had, by some strange chance, got into a wrong vehicle from Oakbourne: she had been taken ill, and did not want to frighten them by letting them know. But this frail fence of vague improbabilities was soon hurled down by a rush of distinct agonizing fears. Hetty had been deceiving herself in thinking that she could love and marry him: she had been loving Arthur all the while: and now, in her desperation at the nearness of their marriage, she had run away. And she was gone to *him*. The old indignation and jealousy rose again, and prompted the suspicion that Arthur had been dealing falsely—had written to Hetty—had tempted her to come to him— being unwilling, after all, that she should belong to another man besides himself. Perhaps the whole thing had been contrived by him, and he had given her directions how to follow him to Ireland: for Adam knew[4] that Arthur had been gone thither three weeks ago, having recently learnt it at the Chase. Every sad look of Hetty's, since she had been engaged to Adam, returned upon him now with all the exaggeration of painful retrospect. He[5] had been foolishly sanguine and confident. The[6] poor thing hadn't perhaps known her own mind for a long while; had thought that she could forget Arthur; had been momentarily[7] drawn towards the man who offered her a protecting, faithful love. He couldn't bear to blame her: she never meant to cause him this dreadful pain. The[8] blame lay with that man who had selfishly played with her heart—had perhaps even[9] deliberately lured her away.

---

[1] off. ⟨But⟩ As *MS*   [2] a {sharp} pang ⟨of sharp [one word],⟩ but *MS*
[3] happened. Hetty] happened—Hetty *MS*
[4] knew ⟨by this time⟩ that Arthur ⟨was⟩ {had been} gone thither {three weeks ago,} having learnt *MS*
[5] retrospect. He] retrospect: he *MS*   [6] confident. The] confident; the *MS*
[7] momentarily] *added in MS*   [8] pain. The] pain: the *MS*
[9] even ⟨drawn⟩ deliberately lured *MS*

At Oakbourne, the ostler at the Royal Oak remembered such a young woman as Adam described getting[1] out of the Treddleston coach more than a[2] fortnight ago—wasn't likely to forget such a pretty lass as that in a hurry—was[3] sure she had not gone on by the[4] Buxton coach that went through Snowfield, but[5] had lost sight of her[6] while he went away with the horses, and had never set eyes on her again. Adam then[7] went straight to the[8] house from which the Stoniton coach started: Stoniton was the most obvious place for Hetty to go to first, whatever might be her destination, for she would hardly venture on any but the chief coach-roads.[9] She had been noticed here too, and was remembered to have sat on the box by the coachman; but the coachman could not be seen,[1] for another man had been driving on that road in his stead the last three or four days: he[2] could probably be seen at Stoniton, through inquiry at the inn where the coach put up. So the anxious, heart-stricken Adam must of necessity wait and try to rest till morning—nay, till eleven o'clock, when the coach started.

At Stoniton another delay occurred, for the old coachman who had driven Hetty would not be in the town again till night. When[3] he did come, he remembered Hetty well, and remembered[4] his own joke addressed to her, quoting it many times to Adam, and observing with equal frequency that he thought there was something more than common, because Hetty had not laughed[5] when he joked her. But he declared, as the people had done at the inn, that he had lost sight of Hetty directly she got down. Part of the next morning was consumed in inquiries at every house in the town from which a coach started—(all in vain; for you know Hetty did not start from Stoniton by coach, but on foot in the grey morning)—[6] and then in walking out to the first toll-gates on the different lines of road, in the forlorn hope of finding some recollection of her there. No, she was not to be traced any farther[7]; and the next hard task for Adam was to go home[8], and carry the wretched tidings to the Hall Farm.[9] As to what he should do beyond that, he had come to two distinct resolutions amidst the tumult of

[1] getting {out} of⟨f⟩ the *MS*   [2] a ⟨week⟩ fortnight *MS*
[3] hurry—was] hurry, but was *MS*   [4] the {Buxton} ⟨c⟩Coach *MS*
[5] Snowfield, but] Snowfield, ⟨for⟩ {but} he *MS*   [6] her] *added in MS*
[7] then ⟨wh⟩ went *MS*   [8] the ⟨place⟩ house *MS*
[9] coach roads. ⟨Hetty⟩ {She} had been ⟨seen⟩ {noticed} here {too}, & was remembered to have sat {on the box} by *MS*
[1] seen, ⟨till⟩ for ⟨it was another coachman⟩ ⟨he had⟩ {another man} had been {driving} on *MS*
[2] days: he] days. He *MS*   [3] When ⟨at last⟩ he {did} ⟨came⟩ come, *MS*
[4] remembered ⟨equally well⟩ his *MS*   [5] laughed ⟨at his⟩ when he *MS*
[6] morning—⟨No, she was not to be traced any further⟩ & then in walking out to the first toll-gates on *MS*
[7] farther] further *MS*   [8] home ⟨again⟩ & *MS*
[9] Farm. {As to what he should do beyond that, he had come to} ⟨T⟩two *MS*

thought and feeling which was going on within him[1] while he went to and[2] fro. He would not mention what he knew of Arthur Donnithorne's behaviour to Hetty till there was a clear necessity for it: it[3] was still possible Hetty might come back, and the disclosure might be an injury or an offence to her. And as soon as he had been home,[4] and done what was necessary there to prepare for his further absence, he would start off to Ireland: if he found no trace of Hetty on the road, he would go straight to Arthur Donnithorne, and make himself certain how far he was acquainted with her movements.[5] Several times the thought occurred to him that he would consult Mr Irwine; but that would be useless, unless he told him all, and so betrayed the secret about Arthur. It seems strange that Adam, in the incessant occupation of his mind about Hetty, should never have alighted on the probability that she had gone to Windsor, ignorant that Arthur was no longer there. Perhaps the reason was, that he could not conceive Hetty's throwing herself on Arthur uncalled; he imagined no cause that could have driven her to such a step, after that letter written in August. There were but two alternatives in his mind: either Arthur had written to her again and enticed her away, or she had simply fled from her approaching marriage with himself, because she found, after all, she could not love him well enough, and yet was afraid of her friends' anger if she retracted.

With this last determination on his mind, of going straight to Arthur, the thought that he had spent two days in inquiries which had proved to be almost useless, was torturing to Adam; and yet, since he would not tell the Poysers his conviction as to where Hetty was gone, or his intention to follow her thither, he must be able to say to them that he had traced her as far as possible.

It was after twelve o'clock on Tuesday night when Adam reached Treddleston; and unwilling to disturb his mother and Seth, and also to encounter their questions at that hour, he threw himself without undressing on a bed at the "Waggon Overthrown," and slept hard from pure weariness. Not more than four hours, however; for before five o'clock he set out on his way home in the faint morning twilight. He always kept a key of the workshop door in his pocket, so that he could let himself in; and he wished to enter without awaking his mother, for he was anxious to avoid telling her the new trouble himself by seeing Seth first, and asking him to tell her when it should be necessary. He walked gently along the yard, and turned the key gently in the door; but, as he expected, Gyp, who lay in the workshop, gave a sharp bark. It subsided when he saw Adam, holding up his finger at him to impose silence; and in his dumb, tailless joy he must content himself with rubbing his body against his master's legs.

[1] him ⟨as⟩ while *MS*   [2] & fro⟨:⟩{.} ⟨h⟩He *MS*   [3] it: it] it. It *MS*
[4] home ⟨& told⟩ & done *MS*
[5] movements. ⟨When now & again,⟩ ⟨Again⟩Several times *MS*

Adam was too heart-sick to take notice of Gyp's fondling. He threw himself on the bench, and stared dully at the wood and the signs of work around him, wondering if he should ever come to feel pleasure in them again; while Gyp, dimly aware that there was something wrong with his master, laid his rough grey head on Adam's knee, and wrinkled his brows to look up at him. Hitherto, since Sunday afternoon, Adam had been constantly among strange people and in strange places, having no associations with the details of his daily life; and now that by the light of this new morning he was come back to his home, and surrounded by the familiar objects that seemed for ever robbed of their charm, the reality—the hard, inevitable reality of his trouble[6] pressed upon him with a new weight. Right before him was an unfinished chest of drawers, which he had been making in spare moments for Hetty's use, when his home should be hers.

Seth had not heard Adam's entrance, but he had been roused by Gyp's bark, and Adam heard him moving about in the room above, dressing himself. Seth's[7] first thoughts were about his brother: he would come home to-day, surely, for the business would be wanting him sadly by to-morrow, but it was pleasant to think he had had a longer holiday than he had[8] expected. And would Dinah come too? Seth felt that that[9] was the greatest happiness he could look forward to for himself, though he had no hope left that she would ever love him well enough to marry him; but[1] he had often said to himself, it was better to be Dinah's friend and brother than any other woman's husband. If he could but be always near her, instead of living so far off!

He came downstairs and opened the inner door leading from the kitchen[2] into the workshop, intending to let out Gyp; but he stood still in the doorway, smitten with a sudden shock at the sight of Adam seated listlessly on the bench, pale, unwashed, with sunken blank eyes, almost like a drunkard in the morning. But Seth felt in an instant what the marks meant: not drunkenness, but some great calamity. Adam looked up at him without speaking, and Seth moved forward towards the bench, himself trembling so that speech did not come readily.

"God have mercy on us, Addy," he said, in a low voice, sitting down on the bench beside Adam[3], "what is it?"

---

[6] trouble] trouble⟨s⟩ *MS* troubles *1 8*
[7] Seth's {first} thoughts were about his brother ⟨all the while⟩: he *MS*
[8] had ⟨himself⟩ expected *MS*   [9] that ⟨would⟩ was *MS*
[1] but ⟨it was better, Seth⟩ he *MS*
[2] kitchen] houseplace *MS* house-place *1* ⟨house-place⟩ kitchen *8*
[3] sitting down on the bench beside Adam] *revised in MS from* sitting down beside Adam on the bench

Adam was unable to speak: the strong man, accustomed to suppress the signs of sorrow, had felt his heart swell like a child's at this first approach of sympathy. He[4] fell on Seth's neck and sobbed.[5]

Seth was prepared for the worst now, for, even in his recollections of their boyhood, Adam had never sobbed before.

"Is it death, Adam? Is she dead?" he asked, in a low tone, when Adam raised his head and was recovering himself.

"No, lad; but she's gone—gone away from us. She's never been to Snowfield. Dinah's been gone to Leeds ever since last Friday was a fortnight, the very day Hetty set out. I can't find out where she went after she got to Stoniton."

Seth was silent from utter astonishment: he[6] knew nothing that could suggest to him a reason for Hetty's going away.

"Hast any notion what she's done it for?" he said, at last.

"She can't ha' loved me: she didn't like our marriage when it came nigh—that must be it," said Adam. He had determined to mention no further reason.

"I hear mother stirring," said Seth. "Must we tell her?"

"No, not yet," said Adam, rising from the bench, and pushing the hair from his face, as if he wanted to rouse himself. "I can't have her told yet; and[7] I must set out on another journey directly, after I've been to the village and th'[8] Hall Farm. I can't tell thee where I'm going, and thee must say to her I'm gone on business as nobody is to know anything about. I'll go and wash myself now." Adam moved towards the door of the workshop, but after a step or two, he turned round, and meeting Seth's eyes with a calm sad glance, he said, "I must take all the money out o' the tin box, lad; but if anything happens to me, all the rest'll be thine, to take care o' mother with."

Seth was pale and trembling: he felt there was some terrible secret under all this. "Brother," he said, faintly—he never called Adam "brother" except in solemn moments—"I don't believe you'll do anything as you can't ask God's blessing on."

"Nay, lad," said Adam, "don't be afraid. I'm for doing nought but what's a man's duty."

The thought that if he betrayed his trouble to his mother, she would only distress him by words, half of blundering affection, half of irrepressible triumph that Hetty proved as unfit to be his wife[9] as she had always foreseen, brought back some of his habitual firmness and self-command. He had felt ill on his journey home—he told her when she came down,— had stayed all night at Treddleston for that reason; and a bad headache, that

---

[4] sympathy. He] sympathy: he *MS*   [5] sobbed.] *MS 1* sobbed{.} *8*
[6] astonishment: he] astonishment. He *MS*   [7] yet; and] yet. And *MS*
[8] th'] the *MS*
[9] Hetty proved as unfit to be his wife] Hetty was proved to be as unfit for Adam's wife *MS*

still hung about him this morning, accounted for his paleness and heavy eyes.

He determined to go to the village, in the first place; attend to his business for an hour, and give notice to Burge of his being obliged to go on a journey, which he must beg him not to mention to any one; for[1] he wished to avoid going to the Hall Farm near breakfast-time, when the children and servants would be in the house-place, and there must be exclamations in their hearing about his having returned without Hetty. He waited until the clock struck nine before he left the work-yard at the village, and set off, through the fields, towards the Farm. It was an immense relief to him, as he came near the Home Close, to see Mr Poyser advancing towards him, for this would spare him the pain of going to the house. Mr Poyser was walking briskly this March morning, with a sense of Spring business on his mind: he was going to cast the master's eye on the shoeing of a new cart-horse, carrying his spud as a useful companion by the way. His surprise was great when he caught sight of Adam, but he was not a man given to presentiments of evil.

"Why, Adam, lad, is't[2] you? Have[3] ye been all this time away, and not brought the lasses back, after all? Where are they?"

"No, I've not brought 'em," said Adam, turning round, to indicate that he wished to walk back with Mr Poyser.

"Why," said Martin, looking with sharper attention at Adam, "ye[4] look bad. Is there anything happened?"

"Yes," said Adam heavily. "A sad thing's happened. I didna[5] find Hetty at Snowfield."

Mr Poyser's good-natured face showed signs of troubled astonishment. "Not find her? What's happened to her?" he said, his thoughts flying at once to bodily accident.

"That I can't tell, whether anything's happened to her. She never went to Snowfield—she took the coach to Stoniton, but I can't learn nothing of her after she got down from the Stoniton coach."[6]

"Why, you donna[7] mean she's run away?" said Martin, standing still,[8] so puzzled and bewildered that the fact did not yet make itself felt as a trouble by him.

"She must ha' done," said Adam. "She didn't like our marriage when it came to the point—that must be it. She'd mistook her feelings."

Martin was silent for a minute or two, looking on the ground, and rooting up the grass with his spud, without knowing what he was doing. His usual slowness was always trebled when the subject of speech was painful. At last he looked up, right in Adam's face, saying,

---

[1] one; for] one. For *MS*   [2] is't] is it *MS*   [3] Have] Han *MS 1* ⟨Han⟩ Have *8*
[4] ye] You *MS*   [5] didna] didn't *MS*   [6] coach."] coach?" *MS*
[7] donna] dont *MS*   [8] standing still,] *added in MS*

"Then she didna deserve t' ha' ye[9], my lad. An' I feel i' fault myself, for she was my niece, and I was allays[1] hot for her marr'ing ye[2]. There's no amends I can make ye, lad—the more's the pity: it's a sad cut-up for ye, I doubt."

Adam could say nothing; and Mr Poyser, after pursuing his walk for a little while, went on:—

"I'll be bound she's gone after trying to get a lady's-maid's place, for she'd got that in her head half a year ago, and wanted me to gi' my consent. But I'd thought better on her," he added, shaking his head slowly and sadly—"I'd thought better on her, nor to look for this, after she'd gi'en y' her word, an' everything[3] been got ready."[4]

Adam had the strongest motives for encouraging this supposition[5] in Mr Poyser, and he even tried to believe that it might possibly be true. He had no[6] warrant for the *certainty* that she was gone to Arthur.

"It was better it should be so," he said, as quietly as he could, "if she felt she couldn't like me for a husband. Better run away before than repent after. I hope you won't look harshly on her if she comes back, as she may do if she finds it hard to get on away from home."

"I canna look on her as I've[7] done before," said Martin, decisively. "She's acted bad by you, and by all of[8] us. But I'll not turn my back on her: she's but a young un, and it's the first harm I've[9] knowed on her. It'll be a hard job for me to tell her aunt. Why didna Dinah come back wi' ye?— she'd ha' helped to pacify her aunt a bit."[1]

"Dinah wasn't at Snowfield. She's been gone to Leeds this fortnight; and[2] I couldn't learn from th' old woman any direction[3] where she is at Leeds, else I should ha' brought it you."

"She'd a deal better be staying wi' her own kin," said Mr Poyser, indignantly, "than going preaching among strange folks a-that'n."

"I must leave you now, Mr Poyser," said Adam, "for I've a deal to see to."

"Ay, you'd best be after your business, and[4] I must tell the missis when I go home. It's a hard job."

"But," said Adam, "I beg particular, you'll keep what's happened quiet for a week or two. I've not told my mother yet, and there's no knowing how things may turn out."

[9] ye] you *MS*   [1] allays] allys [*sic*] *MS*   [2] ye] you *MS*
[3] everything] ⟨e⟩iverything *MS* iverything *1* ⟨iverything⟩ everything *8*
[4] got ready."] got ready welly." *MS*
[5] supposition {in Mr. Poyser} & ⟨it even appeared not impossible to himself⟩ he even tried to believe *MS*   [6] no ⟨right to be⟩ {warrant for the} certain{ty} that *MS*
[7] I've] I'n *MS 1* ⟨I'n⟩ I've *8*   [8] of] on *MS 1* ⟨on⟩ of *8*
[9] I've] I'n *MS 1* ⟨I'n⟩ I've *8*   [1] bit."] bit?" *MS*
[2] fortnight; and] fortnight. And *MS*   [3] direction] directions *MS*
[4] business, and] business. And *MS*

"Ay, ay; least said, soonest mended. We'n no need to say why the match is broke off, an' we may hear of her after a bit. Shake hands wi' me, lad: I wish I could make thee amends."

There was something in Martin Poyser's throat at that moment which caused him to bring out those scanty words in rather a broken fashion. Yet Adam knew what they meant all the better; and the two honest men grasped each other's hard hands in mutual understanding.

There was nothing now to hinder Adam from setting off. He had told Seth to go to the Chase, and leave a message for the Squire, saying that Adam Bede had been obliged to start off suddenly on a journey,—and to say as much, and no more, to any one else who made inquiries about him. If the Poysers learned that he was gone away again, Adam knew they would infer that he was gone in search of Hetty.

He had intended to go right on his way from the Hall Farm; but[5] now the impulse which had frequently visited him before—to go to Mr Irwine, and make a confidant of him—recurred with the new force which belongs to a last opportunity. He was about to start on a long journey—a difficult one— by sea—and no soul would know where he was gone. If anything happened to him? or, if he absolutely needed help in any matter concerning Hetty? Mr Irwine was to be trusted; and the feeling which made Adam shrink from telling anything which was *her* secret, must give way before the need there was that she should have some one else besides himself, who would be prepared to defend her in the worst extremity. Towards Arthur, even though he might have incurred no new guilt, Adam felt that he was not bound to keep silence when Hetty's interest called on him to speak.

"I must do it," said Adam, when these thoughts, which had spread themselves through hours of his sad journeying, now rushed upon him in an instant, like a wave that had been slowly gathering; "it's the right thing. I can't stand alone in this way any longer."

---

[5] Farm; but] Farm. But *MS*

CHAPTER XXXIX.

THE TIDINGS.

Adam turned his face towards Broxton and walked with his swiftest stride, looking at his watch with the fear that Mr Irwine might be gone out— hunting, perhaps. The fear and haste together produced a state of strong excitement before he reached the Rectory gate; and outside it he saw the deep marks of a recent hoof on the gravel.

But the hoofs were turned towards the gate, not away from it; and though there was a horse against the stable door, it was not Mr Irwine's: it had evidently had a journey this morning, and must belong to some one who had come on business. Mr Irwine was at home, then; but Adam could hardly[1] find breath and calmness to tell Carroll[2] that he wanted to speak to the Rector. The double suffering of certain and uncertain sorrow had begun to shake the strong man. The butler looked at him wonderingly, as he threw himself on a bench in the passage and[3] stared absently at the clock on the opposite wall: the master had somebody with him, he said, but he heard the study door open—the stranger seemed to be coming out, and as Adam[4] was in a hurry, he would let the master know at once.

Adam sat[5] looking at the clock: the[6] minute-hand was hurrying along the last five minutes to ten, with a loud hard indifferent tick, and Adam watched the movement and listened to the sound as if he had had some reason for doing so. In our times of bitter suffering, there are almost always these pauses, when our consciousness[7] is benumbed to everything but some trivial perception or sensation. It is[8] as if semi-idiocy came to give us rest from the memory and the dread which refuse to leave us in our sleep.

Carroll[9], coming back, recalled Adam to the sense of his burthen. He was to go into the study immediately. "I can't think what that strange person's come about," the butler added, from mere incontinence of remark, as he preceded Adam to the door, "he's gone i' the dining-room. And master looks unaccountable—as if he was frightened." Adam took no notice of the

---

[1] hardly ⟨muster⟩ find breath & *MS*

[2] Carroll] Carroll *MS* Carrol *1* ⟨Carrol⟩ Carroll *8*

[3] and ⟨looked⟩ {stared absently} at the clock on the opposite wall ⟨with an absent stare⟩: the *MS*

[4] Adam ⟨seemed to be⟩ was *MS*　　　　[5] sat ⟨opposite the clock⟩ looking at the *MS*

[6] the ⟨creeping⟩ minute hand *MS*　　　　[7] consciousness ⟨numb⟩ is benumbed *MS*

[8] is ⟨almost⟩ as *MS*　　　[9] Carroll] Carroll *MS* Carrol *1* ⟨Carrol⟩ Carroll *8*

words: he could not care about other people's business. But when he
entered the study and looked in Mr Irwine's face, he felt in an instant
that there was a new expression in it, strangely different from the warm
friendliness it had always worn for him before. A letter lay open on the
table, and Mr Irwine's hand was on it; but the changed glance he cast on
Adam could not be owing entirely to preoccupation with some disagreeable
business, for he was looking eagerly towards the door,[1] as if Adam's
entrance were a matter of poignant anxiety to him.

"You want to speak to me, Adam," he said, in that low, constrainedly
quiet[2] tone which a man uses when he is determined to suppress agitation.
"Sit down here." He pointed to a chair just opposite to him, at no more than
a yard's distance from his own, and Adam sat down with a sense that this
cold manner of Mr Irwine's gave[3] an additional unexpected difficulty to
his[4] disclosure. But when Adam had made up his mind to a measure, he was
not the man to renounce it for any but imperative reasons.

"I come to you, sir," he said, "as the[5] gentleman I look up to most of
anybody. I've something very painful to tell you—something as it'll pain
you to hear, as well as me to tell. But if I speak o' the wrong other people
have done, you'll see I didn't speak till I'd good reason."

Mr Irwine nodded slowly[6], and Adam went on rather tremulously.[7]

"You was t' ha' married me and Hetty Sorrel, you know, sir, o' the
fifteenth o' this month. I thought she loved me, and I was th'[8] happiest man
i' the parish. But a dreadful blow's come upon me."

Mr Irwine started up from his chair, as if involuntarily, but then,
determined to control himself, walked to the window and looked out.

"She's gone away, sir, and we don't know where. She said she was going
to Snowfield o' Friday was a[9] fortnight, and I went last Sunday to fetch her
back; but she'd never been there, and she took the coach to Stoniton, and
beyond that I can't trace her. But now I'm going a long journey to look for
her, and I can't trust t'[1] anybody but you where I'm going."

Mr Irwine came back from the window and sat down.

"Have you no idea of the reason why she went away?" he said.

"It's plain enough she didn't want to marry me, sir," said Adam. "She
didn't like it when it came so near. But that isn't all, I doubt. There's
something else I must tell you, sir. There's somebody else concerned
besides me."[2]

[1] door ⟨& fixed his eyes with a keen searching ⟨⟨glance⟩⟩ look on Adam as he entered.⟩ as if
Adam's entrance were a matter of poignant anxiety to him. *MS*
[2] quiet ⟨way⟩ tone *MS*   [3] gave ⟨a new &⟩ an additional, *MS*
[4] his ⟨confidential⟩ disclosure *MS*   [5] the ⟨man⟩ gentleman *MS*
[6] slowly ⟨without speaking⟩, & *MS*   [7] tremulously.] tremulously, *MS*
[8] th'] the *MS*   [9] was a] *added in MS*   [1] t'] to *MS*
[2] me."¶ ⟨There was a⟩ A *MS*

A gleam of something—it was almost like relief or joy—came[3] across the eager anxiety of Mr Irwine's face at that moment. Adam was looking on the ground, and paused a little: the next words were hard to speak. But when he went on, he lifted up his head and looked straight at Mr Irwine[4]. He would do the thing he had resolved to do, without flinching.

"You know who's the man I've reckoned my greatest friend," he said, "and used to be proud to think as I should pass my life i' working for him, and had felt so ever since we were lads" . . .

Mr Irwine, as if all self-[5]control had forsaken him, grasped Adam's arm, which lay on the table, and, clutching it tightly like a man in[6] pain, said, with pale lips and a low[7] hurried voice,

"No, Adam, no—don't say it, for God's sake!"

Adam,[8] surprised at the violence of Mr Irwine's feeling, repented of the words that had passed his lips, and sat in distressed silence. The grasp on his arm gradually relaxed, and Mr Irwine threw himself back in his chair, saying, "Go on—I must know it."

"That man played with Hetty's feelings, and[9] behaved to her as he'd no right to do to a girl in her station o' life—made her presents, and used to go and meet her out a-walking: I found it out only two days before he went away—found him a-kissing[1] her as they were parting in the Grove. There'd been nothing said between me and Hetty then, though I'd loved her for a long while, and she knew it. But I reproached him with his wrong actions, and words and blows passed between us; and he said solemnly to me, after that, as it had been all nonsense, and no more than a bit o' flirting. But I made him write a letter to tell Hetty he'd meant nothing; for I saw clear enough, sir, by several things as I hadn't understood at the time, as he'd got hold of her heart, and I thought she'd belike go on thinking of him, and never come to love another man as wanted to marry her. And I gave her the letter, and she seemed to bear it all after a while better than I'd expected . . . and she behaved kinder and kinder to me . . . I dare say she didn't know her own feelings then, poor thing, and they came back upon her when[2] it was too late . . . I don't want to blame her . . . I can't think as she meant to deceive me. But I was encouraged to think she loved me[3], and—you know the rest, sir. But it's on my mind as he's been false to me, and 'ticed[4] her away, and she's gone to him—and I'm going now to see; for I can never go to work again till I know what's become of her."

During Adam's narrative, Mr Irwine had had time to recover his self-mastery in spite of the painful thoughts that crowded upon him. It was a

---

[3] came] added in MS   [4] Irwine, ⟨with the air of a man who will⟩ He would MS
[5] self-] added in MS   [6] in ⟨agonizing⟩ pain MS
[7] lips and a low] lips, & low MS   [8] Adam, ⟨amazed & distressed⟩ surprized MS
[9] & ⟨showed her⟩ behaved MS   [1] a-kissing] kissing MS
[2] when ⟨she⟩ it MS   [3] me ⟨best⟩ & MS   [4] 'ticed] enticed MS

bitter remembrance to him now—that morning when Arthur breakfasted with him[5], and seemed as if he were on the verge of a confession. It was plain enough *now*[6] what he had wanted to confess. And if their words had taken another turn ... if he himself had been less fastidious about intruding on another man's secrets ... it was cruel to think how thin a film had shut out rescue from all this guilt and misery.[7] He saw the whole history now by[8] that terrible[9] illumination which the present sheds back upon the past. But every other feeling as it rushed upon him was thrown into abeyance by pity, deep respectful pity, for the man who sat before him,—already so bruised,[1] going forth with sad blind resignedness to an unreal sorrow, while a real one was close upon him, too far beyond the range of common trial for him ever to have feared it. His own agitation was quelled by a certain awe that comes over us in the presence of a great anguish; for the anguish he must inflict on Adam was already present to him. Again he put his hand on the arm that lay on the table, but very gently this time, as he said solemnly,

"Adam, my dear friend, you have had some hard trials in your life. You can bear sorrow manfully, as well as act manfully: God requires both tasks at our hands. And there is a heavier sorrow coming upon you than any you have yet known. But you are not guilty—you have not the worst of all sorrows. God help him who has!"

The two pale faces looked at each other; in Adam's there was trembling suspense, in Mr Irwine's hesitating, shrinking pity. But he went on.[2]

"I have had news of Hetty this morning. She is not gone to *him*. She is in Stonyshire—at Stoniton."

Adam started up from his chair, as if he thought he could have leaped to her that moment. But Mr Irwine laid hold of his arm again, and said, persuasively, "Wait, Adam, wait." So he sat down.

"She is in a very unhappy position—one which will make it worse for you to find her, my poor friend, than to have lost her for ever."

Adam's lips moved tremulously, but no sound came. They moved again, and he whispered, "Tell me."

"She has been arrested .... she is in prison."

It was as if an insulting blow had brought back the spirit of resistance into Adam. The blood rushed to his face, and he said, loudly and sharply,

---

[5] him] *added in MS*   [6] *now*] now MS

[7] misery. ⟨He saw everything now⟩ ⟨He seemed to see⟩ He saw MS

[8] by ⟨this⟩ that MS   [9] terrible ⟨flash as Arthur's wretched⟩ illumination which MS

[1] bruised, ⟨yet already [?instructed by dread] &⟩ going forth ⟨blindly towards something that his imagination pictured as the worst of sorrows to be able⟩ {with sad blind resignedess to an unreal sorrow, while a real one was close upon him too far beyond the range of common trial} for him ever to have feared it. ⟨There is nothing as subduing & quieting as the presence of supreme suffering—agitation subsides⟩ His own agitation was quelled by a certain awe that comes over us in the presence of a great MS

[2] on.] on, MS

"For what?"

"For a great crime—the murder of her child."

"It *can't be!*" Adam almost shouted, starting up from his chair, and making a stride towards the door; but he turned round again, setting his back against the bookcase, and looking fiercely at Mr Irwine. "It isn't possible. She never had a child.[3] She can't be guilty. *Who* says it?"[4]

"God grant she may be innocent, Adam. We can still hope she is."

"But who says she is guilty?" said Adam, violently. "Tell me every-thing."

"Here is a letter from the magistrate before whom she was taken, and the constable who[5] arrested her is in the dining-room. She will not confess her name or where she comes from; but I fear, I fear there can be no doubt it is Hetty. The description of her person corresponds, only that she is said to look very pale and ill. She had a small red-leather pocket-book in her pocket, with two names written in it—one at the beginning, 'Hetty Sorrel, Hayslope,' and the other near the end, 'Dinah Morris, Snowfield.' She will not say which is her own name—she denies everything, and will answer no questions; and application has been made to me, as a magistrate[6], that I may take measures for identifying her,[7] for it was thought probable that the name which stands first is her own name."

"But what proof have they got against her, if it *is*[8] Hetty?" said Adam, still violently,[9] with an effort that seemed to shake his whole frame. "I'll[1] not believe it. It couldn't ha'[2] been, and none of us know it."

"Terrible proof that she was under the temptation to commit the crime;[3] but we have room to hope that she did not really commit it. Try and read that letter, Adam."

Adam took the letter[4] between his shaking hands, and tried to fix his eyes steadily on it. Mr Irwine meanwhile went[5] out to give some orders. When he came back, Adam's eyes were still on the first page—he couldn't read—he could not put the words together, and make out what they meant. He threw it down at last, and clenched his fist.

"It's *his* doing," he said; "if there's been any crime, it's at his door, not at hers. *He* taught her to deceive—*he* deceived me first. Let 'em put *him* on his trial—[6]let him stand in court beside her, and I'll tell 'em how he got hold of

[3] She never had a child.] *added in MS*   [4] it?"¶ ⟨"Let us hope⟩ God grant *MS*
[5] who ⟨?must⟩ arrested *MS*   [6] magistrate ⟨in Hayslope⟩ that *MS*
[7] her, ⟨the probability being⟩ for it was thought probable *MS*
[8] *is*] is *MS*   [9] violently, ⟨but⟩ with *MS*   [1] frame. "I'll] frame—"I'll *MS*
[2] ha'] have *MS*   [3] crime—⟨that she was⟩ but *MS*
[4] letter ⟨Mr. Irwine gave him⟩ between *MS*
[5] went ⟨into the dining-room to say a few words to the man waiting there⟩ out to give some orders *MS*
[6] trial—⟨Is he to go free⟩ let *MS*

her heart, and 'ticed her t' evil, and[7] then lied to me.[8] Is *he* to go free, while they lay all the punishment on her . . . . so weak and young?"

The image called up by these last words gave a new direction to poor Adam's maddened feelings. He was silent, looking at the corner of the room as if he saw something there. Then he burst out again, in a tone of appealing anguish,

"I *can't* bear it . . . . O God, it's too hard to lay upon me—it's too hard to think she's wicked."

Mr Irwine had sat down again in silence: he was too wise to utter soothing words at present, and indeed the sight of Adam before him, with that look of sudden age which sometimes comes over a young face in moments of terrible emotion—the hard bloodless look of the skin, the deep lines about the quivering mouth, the furrows in the brow—the sight of this strong firm man shattered by the invisible stroke of sorrow, moved him so deeply that speech was not easy. Adam stood motionless, with his eyes vacantly fixed in this way for a minute or two; in that short space he was living through all his love again.

"She can't ha' done it," he said, still without moving his eyes, as if he were only talking to himself: "it was fear made her hide it . . . . I forgive her for deceiving me . . . . I forgive thee, Hetty . . . . thee wast deceived too . . . . it's gone hard wi' thee, my poor Hetty . . . . but they'll never make me believe it."

He was silent again for a few moments, and then he said[9] with fierce abruptness,

"I'll go to him—I'll bring him back—I'll make him go and look at her in her misery—he shall look at her till he can't forget it—it shall follow him night and day—as long as he lives it shall follow him—he shan't escape wi' lies this time—I'll fetch him, I'll drag him myself."

In the act of going towards the door, Adam paused automatically and looked about for his hat, quite unconscious where he was, or who was present with him. Mr Irwine had followed him, and now took him by the arm, saying in a quiet but decided tone,

"No, Adam, no; I'm sure you will wish to stay and see what good can be done for *her*, instead of going on a useless errand of vengeance. The punishment will surely fall without your aid. Besides, he is no longer in Ireland: he must be on his way home—or would be, long before you arrived[1]; for his grandfather, I know, wrote for him to come at least ten days ago. I want you now to go with me to Stoniton. I have ordered a horse for you to ride with us, as soon as you can compose yourself."

---

[7] & ⟨how he⟩ then *MS*
[8] me{.} ⟨& made as [two or three words] everything⟩ Is <u>he</u> to go free, while they lay *MS*
[9] said ⟨abruptly,⟩ with fierce abruptness *MS*
[1] or would be, long before you arrived] *added in MS*

While Mr Irwine was speaking, Adam recovered his consciousness of the actual scene: he rubbed his hair off his forehead and listened.

"Remember," Mr Irwine went on, "there are others to think of, and act for, besides yourself, Adam: there are Hetty's friends, the good Poysers, on whom this stroke will fall more heavily than I can bear to think. I expect it from your strength of mind, Adam—from your sense of duty to God and man—that you will try to act as long as action can be of any use."

In reality, Mr Irwine proposed this journey to Stoniton for Adam's own sake. Movement, with some object before him, was the best means of counteracting the violence of suffering in these first hours.

"You *will* go with me to Stoniton, Adam?" he said again, after a moment's pause. "We have to see if it is really Hetty who is there, you know."

"Yes, sir," said Adam, "I'll do what you think right. But the folks at th'[2] Hall Farm?"

"I wish them not to know till I return to tell them myself. I shall have ascertained things then which I am uncertain about now, and I shall return as soon as possible. Come now, the horses are ready."

[2] th'] the *MS*

CHAPTER XL.

THE BITTER WATERS SPREAD.

Mr Irwine returned from Stoniton in a post-chaise that night, and the first words Carroll[1] said to him, as he entered the house, were,[2] that Squire Donnithorne was dead—found dead in his bed at ten o'clock that morning—and that Mrs Irwine desired him to say she should be awake when Mr Irwine came home, and she begged him not to go to bed without seeing her.

"Well, Dauphin," Mrs Irwine said, as her son entered her room, "you're come at last. So the old gentleman's fidgetiness and low spirits, which made him send for Arthur in that sudden way, really meant something. I suppose Carroll[3] has told you that Donnithorne was found dead in his bed this morning. You will believe my prognostications another time, though I dare say I shan't live to prognosticate anything but my own death."

"What have they done about Arthur?" said Mr Irwine. "Sent[4] a messenger to await him at Liverpool?"

"Yes, Ralph[5] was gone before the news was brought to us. Dear Arthur, I shall live now to see him master at the Chase, and making good times on the estate, like a generous-hearted fellow[6] as he is. He'll be as happy as a king now[7]."

Mr Irwine could not help giving a slight groan: he was worn with anxiety and exertion, and his mother's light words were almost intolerable.

"What[8] are you so dismal about, Dauphin? Is there any bad news? Or are you thinking of the danger for Arthur in crossing that frightful Irish Channel at this time of year?"

"No, mother, I'm not thinking of that; but I'm not prepared to rejoice just now."

---

[1] Carroll] Carrol *1*
[2] were, {that} ⟨¶ "⟩ Squire Donnithorne⟨'s⟩ {was} dead, ⟨if you please, Sir, to see⟩ found dead in his bed at ten o'clock ⟨this⟩ that morning, and {that} Mrs. Irwine desired ⟨me⟩ {him} to say ⟨to you⟩ she should be awake when ⟨you⟩ {Mr. Irwine} came home, & she begged ⟨you⟩ {him} not to go to bed without seeing her.⟨"⟩ *MS*
[3] Carroll] Carrol *1*   [4] Irwine. "Sent] Irwine, "sent *MS*   [5] Ralph] Ralphs *MS*
[6] fellow] Tradgett *MS*
[7] now{."} ⟨—if he doesn't get drowned in that frightful Irish channel. It's just the time for vessels to be lost."⟩ ¶ Mr. Irwine ⟨had⟩ could not help giving a slight groan: he was worn with anxiety & exertion, & his mother's *MS*
[8] What ⟨do⟩ are *MS*

"You've been worried by this law business that you've been to Stoniton about. What in the world is it, that you can't tell me?"

"You will know by-and-by, mother. It would not be right for me to tell you at present. Good-night: you'll sleep now you have no longer anything to listen for."

Mr Irwine gave up his intention of sending a letter to meet Arthur, since it would not now hasten his return: the news of his grandfather's death would bring him as soon as he could possibly come. He could go to bed now and get some needful rest, before the time came for the morning's heavy duty of carrying his sickening news to the Hall Farm and to Adam's home.

Adam himself was not come back from Stoniton, for though he shrank from seeing Hetty, he could not bear to go to a distance from her again.

"It's no use, sir," he said to the Rector—"it's no use for me to go back. I can't go to work again while she's here; and I couldn't bear the sight o' the things and folks round home. I'll take a bit of a room here, where I can see the prison walls, and perhaps I shall get, in time, to bear seeing *her*."

Adam had not been shaken in his belief that Hetty was innocent of the crime she was charged with, for Mr Irwine, feeling that the belief in her guilt would be a crushing addition to Adam's load, had kept from him the facts which left no hope in his own mind. There was not any reason for thrusting the whole burthen on Adam at once, and Mr Irwine, at parting, only said, "If the evidence should tell too strongly against her, Adam, we may still hope for a pardon. Her youth and other circumstances will be a plea for her."

"Ah, and it's right people should know how she was tempted into the wrong way," said Adam, with bitter earnestness. "It's right they should know it was a fine gentleman made love to her, and turned her head wi'[9] notions. You'll remember, sir, you've promised to tell my mother, and Seth, and the people at the Farm, who it was as led her wrong, else they'll think harder of her than she deserves. You'll be doing her a hurt by sparing him, and I hold him the guiltiest before God, let her ha'[1] done what she may. If you spare him, I'll expose him!"

"I think your demand is just, Adam," said Mr Irwine, "but when you are calmer, you will judge Arthur more mercifully. I say nothing now, only that his punishment is in other hands than ours."

Mr Irwine felt it hard upon him that he should have to tell of Arthur's sad part in the story of sin and sorrow—he who cared for Arthur with fatherly affection—who had cared for him with fatherly pride. But[2] he saw clearly that the secret must be known before long, even apart from Adam's determination,[3] since it was scarcely[4] to be supposed that Hetty would

[9] wi'] with *MS*   [1] ha'] have *MS*   [2] pride. But] pride; but *MS*
[3] determination, ⟨for⟩ since *MS*   [4] scarcely] hardly *MS*

persist to the end in her obstinate silence. He made up his mind to[5] withhold nothing from the Poysers, but to tell them the worst at once, for there was no time to rob the tidings of their suddenness. Hetty's trial must come on at the Lent assizes, and they were to be held at Stoniton the next week.[6] It was scarcely to be hoped that Martin Poyser could escape the pain of being called as a witness, and it was better he should know everything as long beforehand as possible.

Before ten o'clock on Thursday morning the home at the[7] Hall Farm was a house of mourning for a misfortune felt to be worse than death. The sense of family dishonour was too keen even in the kind-hearted Martin Poyser the younger, to leave room for any compassion towards Hetty. He and his father were simple-minded farmers, proud of their untarnished character, proud that they came of a family which had held up its head and paid its way as far back as its name was in the parish register; and Hetty had brought disgrace on them all—disgrace that could never be wiped out. That was the all-conquering feeling in the mind both of father and son—the scorching sense of disgrace, which neutralized all other sensibility; and Mr Irwine was struck with surprise to observe that Mrs Poyser was less severe than her husband. We are often startled by the severity of mild people on exceptional occasions; the reason is, that mild people are most liable to be under the yoke of traditional impressions.

"I'm willing to pay any money as is wanted towards trying to bring her off," said Martin the younger when Mr Irwine was gone, while the old grandfather was crying in the opposite chair, "but I'll not go nigh her, nor ever see her again, by my own will. She's made our bread bitter to us for all our lives to come, an' we shall ne'er hold up our heads i' this parish nor i' any other. The parson talks o' folks pitying [8] us: it's poor amends pity 'ull[9] make us."

"Pity?" said the grandfather sharply. "I ne'er wanted folks's pity i' *my* life afore . . . an' I mun begin to be looked down on now, an' me turned seventy-two last St Thomas's[1], an' all th' under-bearers an'[2] pall-bearers as I'n picked for my funeral are i' this parish an'[3] the next to 't . . . . It's[4] o' no use now . . . I mun be ta'en to the grave by strangers."

"Don't fret so, father," said Mrs Poyser, who had spoken very little, being almost[5] overawed by her husband's unusual hardness and decision.[6]

⁵ to ⟨tell⟩ withhold *MS*

⁶ week: {it was scarcely to be hoped that} Martin Poyser ⟨could scarcely be saved⟩ {could escape} the pain of being called as a witness, ⟨& it was desirable that all possible measures should be⟩ & it was better he should know everything as long before *MS*

⁷ home at the] *added in MS*   ⁸ pitying] pityin' *1*   ⁹ 'ull] 'll *MS 1*

¹ Thomas's] Thomas *MS*   ² an'] *MS* and *1 8*   ³ an'] *MS 1* and *8*

⁴ 't . . . . It's] 't . . . . . it's *MS*   ⁵ little, being almost] little, almost *MS*

⁶ decision. "⟨There's the lads⟩ you'll *MS*

"You'll have your children wi' you; an'[7] there's the lads[8] and the little un 'ull grow up in a new parish as well as i' th' old un."

"Ah, there's no staying i' this country for us now," said Mr Poyser, and the hard tears trickled slowly down his round cheeks. "We[9] thought it 'ud be bad luck if the[1] old Squire gave us notice this Lady Day, but I must gi' notice myself now, an' see if there can anybody be got to come an' take to the crops as I'n put i' the ground; for[2] I wonna stay upo' that man's land a day longer nor I'm forced to 't.[3] An' me, as thought him such a good upright young man, as I should be glad when he come to be our landlord. I'll ne'er lift my hat to him[4] again, nor sit i' the same church wi' him[5] . . . a man as has brought shame on respectable folks . . . an' pretended to be such a friend t' everybody . . . . Poor Adam there . . . a fine friend he's been t' Adam, making speeches an' talking so fine, an' all the while poisoning the lad's life, as it's much if he[6] can stay i' this country any more nor we can."

"An' you t' ha' to go into court and own you're akin t' her," said the old man. "Why,[7] they'll cast it up to the little un, as isn't four 'ear old[8], some day—they'll cast it up t' her as she'd a cousin tried at the 'sizes for murder."

"It'll be their own wickedness, then," said Mrs Poyser, with a sob in her voice. "But[9] there's One above 'ull take care o' the[1] innicent[2] child, else it's but little truth they tell us at church. It'll be harder nor ever to die an' leave the little uns, an' nobody to be a mother to 'em[3]."

[4]"We'd better ha' sent for Dinah, if we'd known where she is," said Mr Poyser; "but Adam said she'd left no direction where she'd be at Leeds."

"Why, she'd be wi' that woman as was a friend t'[5] her[6] aunt Judith[7]," said Mrs Poyser[8], comforted a little by this suggestion of her husband's. "I've[9] often heard Dinah talk of her, but I can't remember what name she called her by. But there's Seth Bede; he's like enough to know, for she's a preaching woman as the Methodists think a deal on."

"I'll send to Seth," said Mr Poyser. "I'll[1] send Alick to tell him to come, or else to send us word o' the woman's name, an' thee canst write a letter ready to send off to Treddles'on as soon as we can make out a direction."

"It's poor work writing letters when you want folks to come to you i' trouble," said Mrs Poyser. "Happen it'll be ever so long on the road, an' never reach her at last."

---

[7] an'] & *MS* and *1*   [8] lads an⟨'⟩ {d} the *MS*   [9] cheeks. "We] cheeks, "We *MS*

[1] the] th' *MS 1*   [2] ground; for] ground. For *MS*   [3] to 't.] to. *MS*

[4] to him] to 'm *MS 1* ⟨to 'm⟩ to him *8*

[5] wi' him] wi' 'm *MS 1* ⟨wi' 'm⟩ wi' him *8*   [6] he ⟨'ll⟩ can *MS*

[7] man. "Why,] man, "why *MS*   [8] four 'ear old] four old *MS*

[9] voice. "But] voice, "but *MS*   [1] the] th' *MS 1*   [2] innicent] innocent *MS*

[3] to 'em] to 'em *MS* to 'm *1* ⟨to 'm⟩ to 'em *8*   [4] "We'd] "Why, we'd *MS*

[5] a friend to] *added in MS*   [6] t' her] to her *MS*

[7] Judith] Mary *MS 1* ⟨Mary⟩ Judith *8*   [8] said Mrs Poyser] said Poyser *MS*

[9] husband's. "I've] husband's; "I've *MS*   [1] Poyser. "I'll] Poyser, "I'll *MS*

Before Alick arrived with the message[2], Lisbeth's thoughts too had already flown to Dinah, and she had said to Seth,

"Eh, there's no comfort for us i' this world any more, wi'out thee couldst get Dinah Morris to come to us, as she did when my old man died. I'd like her to come in an' take me by th' hand again, an' talk to me: she'd tell me the rights on't, belike—she'd happen know some good i' all this trouble an' heart-break comin' upo' that poor lad, as ne'er done a bit o' wrong in's life, but war better nor anybody else's son, pick the country round. Eh, my lad . . . Adam, my poor lad!"

"Thee wouldstna like me to leave thee, to go and fetch Dinah?" said Seth, as his mother sobbed, and rocked herself to and fro.

"Fetch her?" said Lisbeth, looking up, and pausing from her grief, like a crying child[3] who hears some promise of consolation. "Why, what place is't[4] she's at, do they say?"

"It's a good way off, mother—Leeds, a big town. But I could be back in three days, if thee couldst spare me."

"Nay, nay, I canna spare thee. Thee[5] must go an' see thy brother, an' bring me word what he's a-doin'. Mester Irwine said he'd come an' tell me, but I canna make out so well what it means when he tells me. Thee must go thysen, sin' Adam wonna let me go to him[6]. Write a letter to Dinah, canstna? Thee't[7] fond enough o' writin' when nobody wants thee."

"I'm not sure where she'd be i' that big town," said Seth. "If I'd gone myself, I could ha' found out by asking the members o' the Society. But perhaps, if I put Sarah Williamson, Methodist preacher, Leeds, o' th' outside, it might get to her; for[8] most like she'd be wi' Sarah Williamson."

Alick came now with the message, and Seth, finding that Mrs Poyser was writing to Dinah, gave up the intention of writing himself; but he went to the Hall Farm to tell them all he could suggest about the address of the letter, and warn them that there might be some delay in the delivery, from his not knowing an exact direction.

On leaving Lisbeth, Mr Irwine had gone to Jonathan Burge,[9] who had also a claim to be acquainted with what was likely to keep Adam away from business for some time; and before six o'clock that evening there were few people in Broxton and Hayslope who had not heard the sad news. Mr Irwine had not mentioned Arthur's name to Burge, and yet the story of his conduct towards Hetty, with all the dark shadows cast upon it by its terrible consequences, was presently as well known[1] as that his grandfather was dead, and that he[2] was come into the estate. For Martin Poyser felt no

[2] message ⟨to Seth⟩, Lisbeth's *MS*   [3] child] *MS 1* child, *8*   [4] is't] is it *MS*
[5] thee. Thee] thee—thee *MS*   [6] to him] {to 'm} *MS* to 'm *1* ⟨to 'em⟩ to him *8*
[7] canstna? Thee't] canstna?—. [*sic*] thee't *MS*
[8] her; for] her, for *MS 1* her⟨,⟩ {;} for *8*   [9] Burge, ⟨when⟩ who *MS*
[1] known] *added in MS*   [2] and that he] & he *MS* and he *1* and {that} he *8*

motive to keep silence towards the[3] one or two neighbours who ventured to come and shake him sorrowfully by the hand on[4] the first day of his trouble; and Carroll[5], who kept his ears open to all that passed at the Rectory, had framed an inferential version of the story, and found early opportunities of communicating it.

One of those neighbours who came to Martin Poyser and shook him by the hand without speaking for some minutes, was Bartle Massey. He had shut up his school, and was on his way to the Rectory, where he arrived about half past seven in the evening, and, sending his duty to Mr Irwine, begged pardon for troubling him at that hour, but had something particular on his mind. He was shown into the study, where Mr Irwine soon joined him.

"Well, Bartle?" said Mr Irwine, putting out his hand. That was not his usual way of saluting the schoolmaster, but trouble makes us treat all who feel with us very much alike. "Sit down."

"You know what I'm come about as well as I do, sir, I dare say," said Bartle.

"You wish to know the truth about the sad news that has reached you . . . about Hetty Sorrel?"

"Nay, sir, what I wish to know is about Adam Bede. I understand you left him at Stoniton, and I beg the favour of you to tell me what's the state of the poor lad's mind, and what he means to do. For as for that bit o' pink-and-white they've taken the trouble to put in gaol, I don't value[6] her a rotten nut—not a rotten nut—only for the harm or good that may come out of her to an honest man—a lad I've set such store by—trusted to, that[7] he'd make my bit o' knowledge go a good way in the world . . . . Why[8], sir, he's the only scholar I've had[9] in this stupid country that ever had the will or the head-piece for mathematics. If he hadn't had so much hard work to do, poor fellow, he might have gone into the higher branches, and then this might never have happened—might never have happened."

Bartle was heated by the exertion of walking fast in an agitated frame of mind, and was not able to check himself on this first occasion of venting his feelings. But he paused now to rub his moist forehead, and probably his moist eyes also.

"You'll excuse me, sir," he said, when this pause had given him time to reflect, "for running on in this way about my own feelings, like that foolish dog of mine, howling in a storm, when there's nobody wants to listen to me. I came to hear you speak, not to talk myself; if you'll[1] take the trouble to tell me what the poor lad's doing."

---

[3] motive to keep silence towards the] motive for keeping silence ⟨on this man's deed⟩ to the *MS*

[4] on ⟨this⟩ the *MS*   [5] Carroll] Carrol *1*   [6] value] vally *MS*

[7] to, that] *MS* to that *1* to {,} that *8*   [8] world. . . . Why] world . . . why *MS*

[9] had ⟨that ever had⟩ in *MS*   [1] you'll ⟨be⟩ take *MS*

"Don't put yourself under any restraint, Bartle," said Mr Irwine. "The fact is, I'm very much in the same condition as you just now; I've a great deal that's painful on my mind, and I find it hard work to be quite silent about my own feelings and only[2] attend to others. I share your concern for Adam, though he is not the only one whose sufferings I care for in this affair. He intends to remain at Stoniton till after the trial: it will come on probably a week to-morrow. He has taken a room there, and I encouraged him to do so, because I think it better he should be away from his own home at present; and[3], poor fellow, he still believes Hetty is innocent—he wants to summon up courage to see her if he can; he is[4] unwilling to leave the spot where she is."

"Do you think the creatur's guilty, then?" said Bartle. "Do you think they'll hang her?"

"I'm afraid it will go hard with her: the evidence is very strong. And one bad symptom is that she denies everything—denies that she has had a child, in the face of the most positive evidence. I saw her myself, and she was obstinately silent to me; she shrank up like a frightened animal when she saw me. I was never so shocked in my life as at the change in her. But I trust that, in the worst case, we may obtain a pardon for the sake of the innocent who are involved."

"Stuff and nonsense!" said Bartle, forgetting in his irritation to whom he was speaking—"I beg your pardon, sir; I mean it's stuff and nonsense for the[5] innocent to care about her being hanged. For my own part, I think the sooner such women are put out o' the world the better; and the men that help 'em to do mischief had better go along with 'em for that matter. What good will you do by keeping such vermin alive? eating the victual that 'ud feed rational[6] beings. But if Adam's fool enough to care about it, I don't want him to suffer more than's needful . . . . Is he very much cut up, poor fellow?" Bartle[7] added, taking out his spectacles and putting them on, as if they would assist his imagination.

"Yes, I'm afraid the[8] grief cuts very deep," said Mr Irwine. "He looks terribly shattered, and a certain violence came over him now and then yesterday, which made me wish I could have remained near him. But I shall go to Stoniton again to-morrow, and I have[9] confidence enough in the strength of Adam's principle to trust that he will be able to endure the worst without being driven to anything rash."

Mr Irwine, who was involuntarily[1] uttering his own thoughts[2] rather than addressing Bartle Massey in the last sentence, had in his mind the

    [2] only] *added in MS*   [3] present; and] present. And *MS*
    [4] he is] he's *MS*   [5] the] th' *MS*   [6] rational ⟨creaturs⟩ beings *MS*
    [7] Bartle ⟨, as he said this, took⟩ {added, taking} out his spectacles & put{ting} them *MS*
    [8] the ⟨pain⟩ grief *MS*   [9] have ⟨such⟩ confidence *MS*
    [1] involuntarily] *added in MS*   [2] thoughts] thought *MS*

possibility that the spirit of vengeance[3] towards Arthur, which was the form Adam's anguish was continually taking, might make him seek an encounter that was likely to end more fatally than the one in the Grove. This possibility heightened the anxiety with which he looked forward to Arthur's arrival. But Bartle thought Mr Irwine was referring to suicide, and his face wore a new alarm.

"I'll tell you what I have in my head, sir," he said, "and I hope you'll approve of it. I'm going to shut up my school: if the scholars come, they must go back again, that's all: and I shall go to Stoniton and look after Adam till this business is over. I'll pretend I'm come to look on at the assizes; he can't object to that. What do you think about it, sir?"

"Well," said Mr Irwine, rather hesitatingly, "there would be some real advantages in that . . . and I honour you for your friendship towards him, Bartle. But . . . you must be careful what you say to him, you know. I'm afraid you have too little fellow-feeling in what you consider his weakness about Hetty."

"Trust to me, sir—trust to me. I know what you mean. I've been a fool myself in my time, but that's between you and me. I shan't thrust[4] myself on him—only keep my eye on him, and see that he gets some good food, and put in a word here and there."

"Then," said Mr Irwine, reassured a little as to Bartle's discretion, "I think you'll be doing a good deed; and it will be well for you to let Adam's mother and brother know that you're going."

"Yes, sir, yes," said Bartle, rising, and taking off his spectacles, "I'll do that, I'll do that; though the mother's a whimpering thing—I don't like to come within earshot of her; however, she's a straight-backed, clean woman, none of your slatterns. I wish you good-by, sir, and thank you for the time you've spared me. You're everybody's friend in this business—everybody's friend. It's a heavy weight you've got on your shoulders."

"Good-by, Bartle, till we meet at Stoniton, as I dare say we shall."

Bartle hurried away from the Rectory, evading Carroll's[5] conversational advances, and saying in an exasperated tone to Vixen, whose short legs pattered beside him on the gravel,

"Now, I shall be obliged to take you with me, you good-for-nothing woman. You'd go fretting yourself to death if I left you—you know you would, and perhaps get snapped up by some tramp; and[6] you'll be running into bad company, I expect, putting your nose in every hole and corner where you've no business! but[7] if you do anything disgraceful, I'll disown you—mind that madam, mind that!"

---

[3] vengeance ⟨against⟩ towards *MS*   [4] thrust] trust *Cabinet*
[5] Carroll's] Carrol's *1*   [6] tramp; and] tramp. And *MS*
[7] business! but] business. But *MS* business; but *1*

CHAPTER XLI.

THE EVE OF THE TRIAL.

An upper room in a dull Stoniton street, with two beds in it—one laid on the floor. It is ten o'clock[1] on Thursday night, and the dark wall opposite the window shuts out the moonlight that might have struggled with the light of the one dip candle by which Bartle Massey is pretending to read, while he is really looking over his spectacles at Adam Bede, seated near the dark window.

You would hardly have known it was Adam without being told. His face has got thinner this last week: he has the sunken eyes, the neglected beard of a man just risen from a sick-bed. His heavy black hair hangs over his forehead, and there is no active impulse in him which inclines him to push it off, that he may be more awake to what is around him. He has one arm over the back of the chair, and he seems to be looking down at his clasped hands. He is roused by a knock at the door.

"There he is," said Bartle Massey, rising hastily and unfastening the door. It was Mr Irwine.

Adam rose from his chair with instinctive respect, as Mr Irwine approached him and took his hand.

"I'm late, Adam," he said, sitting down on the chair which Bartle placed for him; "but[2] I was later in setting off from Broxton than I intended to be, and I have been incessantly occupied since I arrived. I have[3] done everything now, however—everything that[4] can be done to-night, at least. Let us all sit down."

Adam took his chair again mechanically, and Bartle, for whom there was no chair remaining, sat on the bed in the background.

"Have you seen her, sir?" said Adam, tremulously.

"Yes, Adam; I and the chaplain have both been with her this evening."

"Did you ask her, sir . . . did you say anything about me?"

"Yes," said Mr Irwine, with some hesitation, "I[5] spoke of you. I said you wished to see her before the trial, if she consented."

As Mr Irwine paused, Adam looked at him with eager, questioning eyes.

"You know she shrinks from seeing any one, Adam. It is not only you—some[6] fatal influence seems to have shut up her heart against her fellow-

---

[1] o'clock ⟨at n⟩ on *MS*   [2] him; "but] him. "But *MS*   [3] I have] I've *MS*
[4] however—everything that] however—that *MS*
[5] hesitation, "I] hesitation. "I *MS*   [6] you—some] you. Some *MS*

creatures. She has scarcely said anything more than 'No,' either to me or the chaplain. Three or four days ago, before you were mentioned to her, when[7] I asked her if there was any one of her family whom she would like to see—to whom she[8] could open her mind, she said, with a violent shudder, 'Tell them not to come near me—I[9] won't see any of them.'"

Adam's head was hanging down again, and he did not speak. There was silence for a few minutes, and then Mr Irwine said:

"I don't like to advise you against your own feelings, Adam, if they now urge you strongly to go and see her to-morrow morning, even without her consent. It is just possible, notwithstanding appearances to the contrary, that the interview might affect her favourably. But I grieve to say[1] I have scarcely any hope of that. She didn't seem agitated when I mentioned your name; she only said 'No,' in the same cold, obstinate way as usual. And if the meeting had no good effect on her, it would be pure, useless suffering to you—[2]severe suffering, I fear. She is very much changed" . . .

Adam started up from his chair, and seized his hat which lay on the table. But he stood still then, and looked at Mr Irwine, as if he had a question to ask, which it was yet difficult to utter. Bartle Massey rose quietly, turned the key in the door, and put it in his pocket.

"Is he come back?" said Adam at last.

"No, he is not," said Mr Irwine, quietly. "Lay down your hat, Adam, unless you like to walk out with me for a little fresh air. I fear you have not been out again to-day."

"You needn't deceive me, sir," said Adam, looking hard at Mr Irwine, and speaking in a tone of angry suspicion. "You needn't be afraid of me. I only want justice. I want him to feel what she feels. It's his work . . . she was a child as it 'ud ha' gone t' anybody's heart to look at . . . I don't care what she's done . . . it was him brought her to it. And he shall know it . . . he shall feel it . . . if there's a just God, he shall feel what it is t' ha' brought a child like her to sin and misery" . . .

"I'm not deceiving you, Adam," said Mr Irwine. "Arthur Donnithorne is not come back—was not come back when I left. I have left a letter for him: he will know all as soon as he arrives."

"But you don't mind about it," said Adam, indignantly. "You think it doesn't matter as she lies there in shame and misery, and he knows nothing about it—he suffers nothing."

"Adam, he *will* know—he *will* suffer, long and bitterly. He has a heart and a conscience: I can't be entirely deceived in his character. I am convinced—I am sure he didn't fall under temptation without a struggle. He may be weak, but he is not callous, not coldly selfish. I am persuaded that this will be a shock of which he will feel the effects all his life. Why do

[7] when] *added in MS*   [8] she ⟨would⟩ could *MS*   [9] me—I] me. I *MS*
[1] say ⟨the probability seems⟩ ⟨there seem⟩ I *MS*   [2] you—⟨very⟩ severe *MS*

you crave vengeance in this way? No amount of torture that you could inflict on *him* could benefit *her*[3]."

"No—O God, no," Adam groaned out, sinking on his chair again; "but then, that's the deepest curse of all . . . that's what makes the blackness of it . . . *it can never be undone*. My poor Hetty . . . she can never be my sweet Hetty again . . . the prettiest thing God had made—smiling up at me . . . I thought she loved me . . . and was good" . . .

Adam's voice had been gradually sinking into a hoarse under-tone, as if he were only talking to himself; but now he said abruptly, looking at Mr Irwine,

"But she isn't as guilty as they say? You don't think she is, sir? She can't ha' done it."

"That perhaps can never be known with certainty, Adam," Mr Irwine answered, gently. "In these cases we sometimes form our judgment on what seems to us strong evidence, and yet, for want of knowing some small fact, our judgment is wrong. But suppose the worst: you have no right to say that the guilt of her crime lies with him, and that he ought to bear the punishment. It is not for us men to apportion the shares of moral guilt and retribution. We find it impossible to avoid mistakes even in determining who has committed a single criminal act, and[4] the problem how far a man is to be held responsible for the unforeseen consequences of his own deed, is[5] one that might well make[6] us tremble to look into it. The evil consequences that may lie folded in a single act of selfish indulgence[7], is a thought so awful that it ought surely to awaken some feeling less presumptuous than a rash desire to punish. You have a mind that can understand this fully, Adam, when you are calm. Don't[8] suppose I can't enter into the anguish that drives you into this state of revengeful hatred; but think of this: if you were to obey your passion—for it *is* passion, and you deceive yourself in calling it justice—it might be with you precisely as it has been with Arthur; nay, worse; your passion might lead you yourself into a horrible crime."

"No—not worse," said Adam, bitterly; "I[9] don't believe[1] it's worse— I'd sooner do it—I'd sooner do a wickedness as I could suffer for by myself, than ha' brought *her* to do wickedness and then stand by and see 'em punish her while they let me alone; and[2] all for a bit o' pleasure, as, if he'd had a man's heart in him, he'd ha' cut his hand off sooner than he'd ha' taken it. What if he didn't foresee what's happened? He foresaw enough: he'd no right to expect[3] anything but harm and shame to her. And then he wanted to smooth it off wi'[4] lies. No—there's plenty o' things folks are hanged for,

[3] on *him* could benefit *her*] on him could benefit her *MS*
[4] act, and] act. And *MS*   [5] is ⟨a problem⟩ one *MS*   [6] make ⟨me⟩ us *MS*
[7] of selfish indulgence] *added in MS*   [8] calm. Don't] calm: dont *MS*
[9] bitterly; "I] bitterly. "I *MS*   [1] believe it{'s} ⟨'ud be⟩ worse{.} I'd *MS*
[2] alone; and] alone. And *MS*   [3] to] t' *1*   [4] wi'] with *MS*

not half so hateful as that: let a man do what he will, if he knows he's to bear the punishment himself, he isn't half so bad as a mean selfish coward as makes things easy t'[5] himself, and knows all the while the punishment 'll[6] fall on somebody else."

"There again you partly deceive yourself, Adam.[7] There is no sort of wrong deed of which a man can bear the punishment alone; you can't isolate yourself, and say that the evil which is in you shall not spread. Men's lives are as thoroughly blended with each other as the air they breathe: evil spreads as necessarily as disease.[8] I know, I feel the terrible extent of suffering this sin of Arthur's has caused to others; but so does every sin cause suffering[9] to others besides those who commit it. An act of vengeance on your part against Arthur would simply be another evil added to those we are suffering under: you could not bear the punishment alone; you would entail the worst sorrows on every one who loves you.[1] You would have committed an act of blind fury, that would leave all[2] the present evils just as they were, and[3] add worse evils to them. You may tell me that you meditate no fatal[4] act of vengeance: but the feeling in your mind is what gives birth to such actions, and as long as you indulge it, as long as you do not see that to fix your mind on Arthur's punishment is revenge, and not[5] justice, you are in danger of being led on to the commission of some great wrong. Remember what you told me about your feelings after you had given that blow to Arthur in the Grove."

Adam was silent: the last words had called up a vivid image of the past, and Mr Irwine left him to his thoughts, while he spoke to Bartle Massey about[6] old Mr Donnithorne's funeral and other matters of an indifferent kind. But at length Adam turned round and said, in a more subdued tone,

"I've not asked about 'em at th'[7] Hall Farm, sir. Is Mr Poyser coming?"

"He is come; he is in Stoniton to-night. But I could not advise him to see you, Adam. His own mind is in a very perturbed state, and it is best he should not see you till you are calmer."[8]

"Is Dinah Morris come to 'em, sir? Seth said they'd sent for her."

"No. Mr[9] Poyser tells me she was not come when he left. They're[1] afraid the letter has not reached her. It seems they had no exact address."

---

[5] t'] to *MS*   [6] 'll] '{u}ll *MS* 'ull *1*

[7] Adam. ⟨You talk as if those near⟩ There is no sort of *MS*

[8] disease. ⟨I know that⟩ {I know, I feel the terrible extent of suffering} ⟨t⟩ This *MS*

[9] suffering ⟨beyond⟩ to others besides *MS*   [1] you{.}⟨, &⟩ ⟨y⟩ You *MS*

[2] all ⟨other⟩ the *MS*   [3] & add⟨ed⟩ worse *MS*   [4] fatal] *added in MS*

[5] not ⟨desire⟩ justice *MS*   [6] about ⟨some⟩ old *MS*   [7] th'] the *MS*

[8] calmer.{"} ⟨He & his wife have been looking anxiously for Dinah Morris to come to them⟩ ⟨it seems they⟩ ⟨they've written to her at Leeds, but ⟨⟨Mrs Poyser⟩⟩ it seems they dont know her exact address & they are afraid the letter has not reached her.⟩ ¶ {"Is Dinah . . . . They are} afraid *MS*

[9] "No. Mr] "No, Mr. *MS*   [1] They're] They are *MS 1*

Adam sat ruminating a little while, and then said,

"I wonder if Dinah 'ud ha'[2] gone to see her. But perhaps the Poysers would ha'[3] been sorely against it, since[4] they won't come nigh her themselves. But I think she would, for the Methodists are great folks for going into the prisons; and Seth said he thought she would. She'd a very tender way with her, Dinah had; I wonder if she could ha'[5] done any good. You never saw her, sir, did you?"

"Yes, I did: I had a conversation with her—she pleased me a good deal. And now you mention it, I wish she would come; for it is possible that a[6] gentle, mild woman like her might[7] move Hetty to open her heart. The gaol chaplain is rather harsh in his manner."

"But it's o' no use if she doesn't come," said Adam, sadly.

"If I'd[8] thought of it earlier, I would have taken some measures for finding her out[9]," said Mr Irwine, "but it's too late now, I fear . . . Well, Adam, I must go now. Try to get some rest to-night. God bless you. I'll[1] see you early to-morrow morning."

[2] ha'] have *MS*   [3] ha'] have *MS*   [4] since] as *MS*   [5] ha'] have *MS*
[6] possible that a] possible a *MS*   [7] might ⟨touch⟩ move *MS*
[8] I'd ⟨known⟩ thought *MS*   [9] out{,"} {said Mr. Irwine}—{"}but *MS*
[1] you. I'll] you—I'll *MS*

CHAPTER XLII.

THE[1] MORNING OF THE TRIAL.

At one o'clock the next day, Adam was alone in his dull upper room; his watch lay before him on the table, as if he were counting the long minutes. He had no knowledge of what was likely to be said by the witnesses on the trial, for he had shrunk from all the particulars connected with Hetty's arrest and accusation. This brave active man, who would have hastened towards any danger or toil to rescue Hetty from an apprehended wrong or misfortune, felt himself powerless to contemplate irremediable evil and suffering. The susceptibility which would have been an impelling force where there was any possibility of action, became helpless anguish when he was obliged to be passive; or else sought an active outlet in the thought of inflicting justice on Arthur. Energetic natures, strong for all strenuous deeds, will often rush away from a hopeless sufferer, as if they were hard-hearted. It[2] is the overmastering sense of pain that drives them. They[3] shrink by an ungovernable instinct, as they would shrink from laceration. Adam had brought himself to think of seeing Hetty, if she would consent to see him, because he thought the meeting might possibly be a good to her— might help to melt away this terrible hardness they told him of. If[4] she saw he bore her no ill-will for what she had done to him, she might open her heart to him. But this resolution had been an immense effort; he trembled at the thought of seeing her changed face, as a timid woman trembles at the thought of the surgeon's knife; and he chose now to bear the long hours of suspense, rather than[5] encounter what seemed to him the more intolerable agony of witnessing her trial.

Deep, unspeakable suffering may well be called a baptism, a regeneration, the initiation into a new state. The yearning memories, the bitter regret, the agonized sympathy, the struggling appeals to the Invisible Right—all the intense emotions which had filled the days and nights of the past week, and were compressing themselves again like an eager crowd into the hours of this single morning, made Adam look back[6] on all the previous years as if they had been a dim sleepy existence, and he had only now awaked to full consciousness. It seemed to him as if he had always

---

[1] The {morning of the} Trial ⟨morning⟩. *MS*
[2] hard-hearted. It] hardhearted: it *MS*   [3] them. They] them; they *MS*
[4] of. If] of: if *MS*   [5] than encounter⟨ed⟩ what *MS*
[6] back ⟨on all⟩ {on all} the *MS*

before thought it a light thing that men should suffer; as if all that he had himself endured and called sorrow before, was only a moment's stroke that had never left a bruise. Doubtless a great anguish may do the work of years, and we may come out from that[7] baptism of fire with a soul full of new awe and[8] new pity.

"O God," Adam groaned, as he leaned on the table, and looked blankly at the face of the watch, "and men have suffered like this before . . . and poor helpless young things have suffered like her . . . . Such a little while ago,[9] looking so happy and so pretty . . . kissing 'em all, her grandfather and all of 'em, and they wishing her luck . . . O my poor, poor Hetty . . . dost think on it now?"

Adam started and looked round towards the door. Vixen had begun to whimper, and there was the[1] sound of a stick and a lame walk on the stairs. It was Bartle Massey come back. Could[2] it be all over?

Bartle entered quietly, and, going up to Adam, grasped his hand and said, "I'm just come to look at you, my boy, for the folks are gone out of court for[3] a bit."

Adam's heart beat so violently, he was unable to speak—[4]he could only return the pressure of his friend's hand; and Bartle,[5] drawing up the other chair, came and sat in front of him, taking off his hat and his spectacles.

"That's a thing never happened to me before," he observed—"to go out o' door with my spectacles on. I clean forgot to take 'em off."

The old man made this trivial remark, thinking it better not to respond at all to Adam's agitation: he would gather, in an indirect way, that there was nothing decisive to communicate at present.

"And now," he said, rising again, "I must see to your having a bit of the loaf, and some of that wine Mr Irwine sent this morning. He'll be angry with me if you don't have it. Come, now," he went on, bringing forward the bottle and the loaf, and pouring some wine into a cup, "I must have a bit and a sup myself. Drink a drop with me, my lad—drink with me."

Adam pushed the cup gently away, and said entreatingly, "Tell me about it, Mr Massey—tell me all about it. Was she there? Have they begun?"[6]

"Yes, my boy, yes—it's taken all the time since I first went; but they're slow, they're slow; and there's the counsel they've got for her puts a spoke in the wheel whenever he can, and makes a deal to do with cross-examining the witnesses, and quarrelling with the other lawyers. That's all he can do for the money they give him; and it's a big sum—it's a big sum. But he's a 'cute fellow, with an eye that 'ud pick the needles out of the hay in no time.

[7] that ⟨per⟩ baptism *MS*   [8] & ⟨of⟩ new *MS*   [9] ago,] *MS 1* ago *8*
[1] the] a *Cabinet*   [2] back. Could] back—could *MS*
[3] for ⟨an hour⟩ a bit *MS*   [4] speak; ⟨bu⟩ he *MS*   [5] Bartle, ⟨taking⟩ drawing *MS*
[6] begun?"] begun." *MS*

If a man had got no feelings, it 'ud be as good as a demonstration to listen to what goes on in court; but a tender heart makes one stupid. I'd have given up figures for ever only to have had some good news to bring to you[7], my poor lad."

"But does it seem to be going against her?" said Adam. "Tell me what they've said. I must know it now—I must know what they have to bring against her."

"Why, the chief evidence yet has been the doctors; all but Martin[8] Poyser—poor Martin. Everybody in court felt for him—it was like one sob, the sound they made when he came down again. The worst was, when they told him to look at the prisoner at the bar. It was hard work, poor fellow—it was hard work. Adam, my boy, the blow falls heavily on him as well as you: you must help poor Martin; you must show courage. Drink some wine now, and show me you mean to bear it like a man."

Bartle had made the right sort of appeal. Adam, with an air of quiet obedience, took up the cup, and drank a little.

"Tell me how *she* looked," he said, presently.

"Frightened, very frightened, when they first brought her in; it was the first sight of the crowd and the judge, poor creatur. And there's a lot o' foolish women in fine clothes, with gewgaws all up their arms and feathers on their heads, sitting near the judge: they've dressed themselves out in that way, one 'ud think, to be scarecrows and warnings against any man ever meddling with a woman again; they put up their glasses, and stared and whispered. But after that[9] she stood like a white image, staring down at her hands, and seeming neither to hear nor see anything. And she's as white as[1] a sheet. She didn't speak when they asked her if she'd plead 'guilty' or 'not guilty,' and they pled 'not guilty' for her. But when she heard her uncle's name, there seemed to go a shiver right through her; and when they told him to look at her, she hung her head down, and cowered, and[2] hid her face in her hands. He'd much ado to speak, poor man, his voice trembled so. And the counsellors,—who look as hard as nails mostly,—I saw, spared him as much as they could. Mr Irwine put himself near him, and went with him out o'[3] court. Ah, it's a great thing in a man's life to be able to stand by a neighbour, and uphold him in such trouble as that."

"God bless him, and you too,[4] Mr Massey," said Adam, in a low voice, laying his hand on Bartle's arm.

"Ay, ay, he's good metal; he gives the right ring when you try him, our parson does. A man o' sense—says no more than's needful. He's not one of those that think they can comfort you with chattering, as if folks who stand

[7] bring to you] bring you *MS*   [8] doctors; all but Martin] doctors; only Martin *MS*
[9] that ⟨she stood like a statue⟩ she stood like a white image *MS*
[1] as ⟨marble⟩ a sheet *MS*   [2] & ⟨her⟩ hid *MS*   [3] o'] of *MS*
[4] too, ⟨Bartle⟩ Mr. Massey *MS*

by and look on knew a deal better what the trouble was than those who have to bear it. I've had to do with such folks in my time—in the south, when I was in trouble myself. Mr Irwine is to be a witness himself, by-and-by, on her side, you know, to speak to her character and bringing up."

"But the other evidence ... does it go hard against her?" said Adam. "What do you think, Mr Massey? Tell me the truth."

"Yes, my lad, yes: the truth is the best thing to tell. It must come at last. The doctors' evidence is heavy on her—is heavy. But she's gone on denying she's had a child from first to last: these poor silly women-things—they've not the sense to know it's no use denying what's proved. It'll make against her with the jury, I doubt, her being so obstinate: they may be less for recommending her to mercy, if the verdict's against her[5]. But Mr Irwine 'll[6] leave no stone unturned with the judge—you may rely upon that, Adam."

"Is there nobody to stand by her, and seem to care for her, in the court?" said Adam.

"There's the chaplain o' the gaol sits near her, but he's a sharp ferrety-faced man—another sort o' flesh and blood to Mr Irwine. They say the gaol chaplains are mostly the fag-end o'[7] the clergy."

"There's one man as ought to be there," said Adam, bitterly. Presently he drew himself up, and looked fixedly out of the window, apparently turning[8] over some new idea in his mind.

"Mr Massey," he said at last, pushing the hair off his forehead, "I'll go back with you. I'll go into court. It's cowardly of me to keep away. I'll stand by her—I'll own her—for all[9] she's been deceitful. They oughtn't to cast her off—her own flesh and blood. We hand folks over to God's mercy, and show none ourselves. I used to be hard sometimes: I'll never be hard again. I'll go, Mr Massey—I'll go with you."

There was a decision in Adam's manner which would have prevented Bartle from opposing him, even if he had wished to do so. He only said,

"Take a bit, then, and another sup, Adam, for the love of me. See, I must stop and eat a morsel. Now, you take some."

Nerved by an active resolution, Adam took a morsel of bread, and drank some wine. He was haggard and unshaven, as he had been yesterday, but he stood upright again, and looked more like the[1] Adam Bede of former days.

---

[5] if the verdict's against her] *added in MS*   [6] 'll] 'ill *MS* 'ull *Cabinet*
[7] o'] of *MS*   [8] window, apparently turning] window, as if he was turning *MS*
[9] all ⟨she may have been wicked⟩ she's been deceitful *MS*
[1] the] *added in MS*

CHAPTER XLIII.

THE VERDICT.

The place fitted up that day as a court of justice was a grand old hall, now destroyed by fire. The[1] mid-day light that fell on the close pavement of human heads, was shed through a line of high pointed windows, variegated with the mellow tints of old painted glass. Grim[2] dusty armour hung in high relief in front of the dark oaken gallery at the farther end; and under the broad arch of the great mullioned window opposite was spread a curtain of old tapestry, covered with dim melancholy figures, like a dozing indistinct dream of the past. It was a place that through the rest of the year was haunted with the shadowy memories of old kings and queens, unhappy, discrowned, imprisoned; but to-day all those shadows had fled, and not a soul in the vast hall felt the presence of any but a living sorrow, which was quivering in warm hearts.

But that sorrow seemed to have made itself feebly felt hitherto, now when Adam Bede's tall figure was suddenly seen, being ushered to the side of the prisoner's dock. In the broad sunlight of the great hall, among the sleek shaven faces of other men, the marks of suffering in his face were startling even to Mr Irwine, who had last seen him in the dim light of his small room; and the neighbours from Hayslope who were present, and who told Hetty Sorrel's story[3] by their firesides in their old age, never forgot to say how it moved them when Adam Bede, poor fellow, taller by the head than most of the people round him, came into court, and took his place by her side.

But Hetty did not see him. She was standing in the same position Bartle Massey had described, her hands crossed over each other[4], and her eyes fixed on them. Adam had not dared to look at her in the first moments, but at last, when the attention of the court was withdrawn by the proceedings, he turned his face towards her with a resolution not to shrink.

Why did they say she was so changed? In the corpse we love, it is the *likeness* we see—it is the likeness, which makes itself felt the more keenly because[5] something else *was* and *is not*[6]. There they were—the sweet face and neck, with the dark tendrils of hair, the long dark lashes, the rounded cheek and the pouting lips: pale and thin—yes—but like Hetty, and only

---

[1] fire. The] fire: the *MS*   [2] glass. Grim] glass; grim *MS*
[3] story ⟨in⟩ by *MS*   [4] other ⟨& not even⟩, & *MS*
[5] because ⟨there is⟩ something *MS*   [6] *was* and *is not*] was & is not *MS*

Hetty. Others thought she looked as if some demon had cast a blighting glance upon her, withered up the woman's soul in her, and left only a hard despairing obstinacy. But the mother's yearning, that completest type of the life in another life which is the essence of real human love, feels the presence of the cherished child even in the debased, degraded man; and to Adam, this pale hard-looking culprit was the Hetty who had smiled at him in the garden under the apple-tree boughs—[7]she was that Hetty's corpse, which he had trembled to look at the first time, and then was unwilling to turn away his eyes from.

But presently he heard something that compelled him to listen, and made the sense of sight less absorbing. A woman was in the witness-box, a middle-aged woman, who spoke in a firm distinct voice. She said,

"My name is Sarah Stone. I am a widow, and keep a small shop licensed to sell tobacco, snuff, and tea, in Church Lane, Stoniton. The prisoner at the bar is the same young woman who came, looking ill and tired, with a basket on her arm, and asked for a lodging at my house on Saturday evening, the 27th of February. She had taken the house for a public, because there was a figure against the door. And when I said I didn't take in lodgers, the prisoner began to cry, and said she was too tired to go anywhere else, and she only wanted a bed for one night. And her prettiness, and her condition, and something respectable about her clothes and looks, and the trouble she seemed to be in, made me as I couldn't find in my heart to send her away at once. I asked her to sit down, and gave her some tea, and asked her where she was going, and where her friends were. She said she was going home to her friends: they were farming folks a good way off, and she'd had a long journey that had cost her more money than she expected, so as she'd hardly any money left in her pocket, and was afraid of going where it would cost her much. She[8] had been obliged to sell most of the things out of her basket[9]; but she'd thankfully give a shilling for a bed. I saw no reason why I shouldn't take the young woman in for the night. I had only one room, but there were two beds in it, and I told her she might stay with me. I thought she'd been led wrong, and got into trouble, but if she was going to her friends, it would be a good work to keep her out of further harm."

The witness then stated that in the night a child was born, and she identified[1] the baby-clothes then shown to her as those in which she had herself dressed the child.

"Those are the clothes. I made them myself, and had kept them by me ever since my last child was born. I took a deal of trouble both for the child and the mother. I couldn't help taking to the little thing and being anxious about it. I didn't send for a doctor, for there seemed no need. I told the mother in the day-time she must tell me the name of her friends, and where they lived, and let me write to them. She said, by-and-by she would write herself, but not to-day. She would have no nay, but she would get up and be dressed, in spite of everything I could say. She said she felt quite strong enough; and it was wonderful what spirit she showed. But I wasn't quite easy what I should do about her, and towards evening I made up my mind I'd go, after Meeting was over, and speak to our minister about it. I left the house about half past eight o'clock. I didn't[2] go out at the shop door, but at the back door, which opens into a narrow[3] alley. I've only got the ground floor of the house, and the kitchen and bedroom both look into the alley. I left the prisoner sitting up by the fire in the kitchen with the baby on her lap. She hadn't cried or seemed low at all, as she did the night before. I thought she had a strange look with her eyes, and she got a bit flushed towards evening. I was afraid of the fever, and I thought I'd call and ask an acquaintance of mine, an experienced woman, to come back with me when I went out. It was a very dark night. I didn't fasten the door behind me: there was no lock: it was a latch with a bolt inside, and when there was nobody in the house I always went out at the shop door. But I thought there was no danger in leaving it unfastened that little while. I was longer than I meant to be, for I had to wait for the woman that came back with me[4]. It was an hour and a half before we got back, and when we went in, the candle was standing burning just as I left it, but the prisoner and the baby were both gone. She'd taken her cloak and bonnet, but she'd left the basket and the things in it . . . . I was dreadful frightened, and angry with her for going. I didn't go to give information, because I'd no thought she meant to do any harm, and I knew she had money in her pocket to buy her food and lodging. I didn't like to set the constable after her, for she'd a right to go from me if she liked."

The effect of this evidence on Adam was electrical; it gave him new force. Hetty could not be guilty of the crime—[5]her heart must have clung to her baby—else why should she have taken it with her? She might have left it behind. The little creature had died naturally, and then she had hidden it: babies were so liable to death—and there might be the strongest suspicions without any proof of guilt. His mind was so occupied with imaginary arguments against such suspicions, that he could not listen to the cross-examination by Hetty's counsel, who tried, without result, to elicit evidence that the prisoner had shown some movements of maternal affection towards the child. The whole time this witness was[6] being examined, Hetty had stood as motionless as before: no word seemed to arrest her ear. But the

---

[2] didn't] did not *MS*   [3] narrow ⟨back street⟩ alley *MS*
[4] me{.} ⟨and she didn't come after all⟩. It *MS*   [5] crime—⟨she⟩ her heart *MS*
[6] this witness was] this prisoner ⟨had⟩ was *MS*

sound of the next witness's voice touched a chord that was still sensitive; she gave a start and a frightened look towards him, but immediately turned away her head and looked down at her hands as before. This witness was a man, a rough peasant. He said:

"My name is John Olding. I am a labourer, and live at Tedd's Hole, two miles out of Stoniton. A week last Monday, towards[7] one o'clock in the afternoon, I was going towards Hetton Coppice, and about a quarter of a mile from the coppice I saw the prisoner, in a red cloak, sitting under a bit of a haystack not far off the stile. She got up when she saw me, and seemed as if she'd be walking on the other way. It was a regular road through the fields, and nothing very[8] uncommon to see a young woman there, but I took notice of her because she looked white and scared. I should have thought she was a beggar-woman, only for her good clothes. I thought she looked a bit crazy, but it was no business of mine. I stood and looked back after her, but she went right on while she was in sight. I had to go to the other side of the coppice to look after some stakes. There's a road right through it, and bits of openings here and there, where the trees have been cut down, and some of 'em not carried away. I didn't go straight along the road, but turned off towards the middle, and took a shorter way[9] towards the spot I wanted to get to. I hadn't got far out of the road into one of the open[1] places, before I heard a strange cry. I thought it didn't come from any animal I knew, but I wasn't for stopping to look about just then. But it went on, and seemed so strange to me in that place, I couldn't help stopping to look. I began to think I might make some money of it, if it was a new thing. But I had[2] hard work to tell which way it came from, and for a good while I kept looking up at the boughs. And then I thought it came from the ground; and there was a lot of timber-choppings lying about, and loose pieces of turf, and a trunk or two. And I looked about among them, but could find nothing; and at last the cry stopped. So I was for giving it up, and I went on about my business. But when I came back the same way pretty nigh an hour after, I couldn't help[3] laying down my stakes[4] to have another look. And just as I was stooping and[5] laying down the stakes, I saw something odd and round and whitish lying on the ground under a nut-bush by the side of me. And I stooped down on hands and knees to pick it up. And I saw it was a little baby's hand."

At these words a thrill ran through the court. Hetty was visibly trembling: now, for[6] the first time, she seemed to be listening to what a witness said.

---

[7] towards ⟨four⟩ one *MS*   [8] very] *added in MS*   [9] way ⟨to⟩ towards *MS*
[1] open ⟨spaces⟩ places *MS*   [2] I had] I'd *MS 1*   [3] help] *added in MS*
[4] stakes ⟨& having⟩ to have *MS*   [5] stooping &] *added in MS*
[6] hand."¶ At these words a thrill ran through the court. Hetty was visibly trembling: now, for] hand."¶ Hetty was visibly trembling: for *MS*

"There was a lot of timber-choppings put together just where the ground went hollow, like, under the bush, and the hand came out from among them. But there was a hole left in one place, and I could see down it, and see the child's head; and[7] I made haste and did away the turf and the choppings, and took out the child. It had got comfortable clothes on, but its body was cold, and I thought it must be dead. I made haste back with it out of the wood, and took it home to my wife. She said it was dead, and I'd better take it to the parish and tell the constable. And I said, 'I'll lay my life it's that young woman's child as I met going to the coppice.' But she seemed to be gone clean[8] out of sight. And I took the child on to Hetton parish and told the constable, and we went on to Justice Hardy. And then we went looking after the young woman till dark at night, and we went and gave information at Stoniton, as they might stop her. And the next morning, another constable came to me, to go with him to the spot where I found the child. And when we got there, there was the prisoner a-sitting against the bush where I found the child; and she cried out when she saw us, but she never offered to move. She'd got a big piece of bread on her lap."

Adam had given a faint groan of despair while this witness was speaking. He had hidden his face on his arm, which[9] rested on the boarding in front of him. It was the supreme moment of his suffering: Hetty was guilty: and he was silently calling to God for help. He heard no more of the evidence, and was unconscious when the case for the prosecution had closed—unconscious that Mr Irwine was in the witness-box, telling of Hetty's unblemished character in her own parish, and of the virtuous habits in which she had been brought up. This testimony could have no influence on the verdict, but it was given as part of that plea for mercy which her own counsel would have made if he had been allowed to speak for her—a favour not granted to criminals in those stern times.

At last Adam lifted up his head, for there was a general movement round him. The judge had addressed the jury, and they were retiring. The decisive moment was not far off. Adam felt a shuddering horror that would not let him look at Hetty, but she had long relapsed into her blank hard indifference. All eyes were strained to look at her, but she stood like a statue of dull despair.

There was a mingled rustling, whispering, and low buzzing throughout the court during this interval. The desire to listen was suspended, and every one had some feeling or opinion to express in under-tones. Adam sat looking blankly before him, but he did not see the objects that were right in front of his eyes—the counsel and attorneys talking with an air of cool business, and Mr Irwine in low earnest conversation with the judge: did not see Mr Irwine sit down again in agitation, and shake his head mournfully

---

[7] head; and] head. And *MS*   [8] gone clean] clean gone *MS*
[9] which] that *MS*

when somebody whispered to him. The inward action was too intense for
Adam[1] to take-in[2] outward objects, until some strong sensation roused
him.

It was not very long, hardly more than a quarter of an hour, before the
knock which told that the jury had come to their decision, fell as a signal for
silence on every ear. It is sublime—that sudden pause of a great multitude,
which tells that one soul moves in them all. Deeper and deeper the silence
seemed to become, like the deepening night,[3] while the jurymen's names
were called over, and the prisoner was made to hold up her hand, and the
jury were asked for their verdict.

"Guilty."

It was the verdict every one expected, but there was a sigh of disappointment from some hearts, that it was followed by no recommendation to
mercy. Still the sympathy of the court was not with the prisoner: the
unnaturalness of her crime stood out the more harshly by the side of[4] her
hard immovability and obstinate silence. Even the verdict, to distant eyes,
had not appeared to move her; but those who were near saw her trembling.

The stillness was less intense until the judge put on his black cap, and the
chaplain in his canonicals was observed behind him. Then it deepened
again, before the crier had had time to command silence. If any sound were
heard, it must have been the sound of beating hearts. The judge spoke:

"Hester Sorrel." . . .

The blood rushed to Hetty's face, and then fled back again, as she looked
up at the judge, and kept her wide-open eyes fixed on him, as if fascinated
by fear. Adam had not yet turned towards her: there was a deep horror, like
a great gulf, between them. But at the words—"and then to be hanged by
the neck till you be dead," a piercing shriek rang through the hall. It was
Hetty's shriek. Adam started to his feet and stretched out his arms towards
her; but the arms could not reach her: she had fallen down in a fainting fit,
and was carried out of court.

---

[1] Adam] him *MS*   [2] take-in] take in *MS 1* take {-} in *8*
[3] night, ⟨till⟩ while *MS*   [4] of ⟨the⟩ her *MS*

CHAPTER XLIV.

ARTHUR'S RETURN.

When Arthur Donnithorne landed at Liverpool, and read the letter from his aunt Lydia, briefly announcing his grandfather's death, his first feeling was, "Poor grandfather! I wish I could have got to him to be with him when he died. He might have felt or wished something at the last that I shall never know now. It was a lonely death."

It is impossible to say that his grief was deeper than that. Pity and softened memory took place of the old antagonism, and in his busy thoughts about the future, as the chaise carried him rapidly along towards the home where he was now to be master,[1] there was a continually recurring effort to remember anything by which he could show a regard for his grandfather's wishes, without counteracting his own cherished aims for the good of the tenants and the estate. But it is not in human nature—only in human pretence—for a young man like Arthur,[2] with a fine constitution and fine spirits, thinking well of himself, believing that others think well of him, and having a very ardent intention to give them more and more reason for that good opinion,—it is not possible for such a young man, just coming into a splendid estate through the death of a very old man whom he was not fond of, to feel anything very different from exultant joy. *Now* his real life was beginning; now he would have room and opportunity for action, and he would use them. He would show the Loamshire people what a fine country gentleman was; he would not exchange that career for any other under the sun. He felt himself riding over the hills in the breezy autumn days, looking after favourite plans of drainage and enclosure; then admired on sombre mornings[3] as the best rider on the best horse in the hunt; spoken well of on market days as a first-rate landlord; by-and-by making speeches at election dinners, and showing a wonderful knowledge of agriculture; the patron of new ploughs and drills, the severe upbraider of negligent landowners, and withal a jolly fellow that everybody must like,—happy faces greeting him everywhere on his own estate, and the neighbouring families on the best terms with him. The Irwines should dine with him every week, and have their own carriage to come in, for[4] in some very delicate way that Arthur

---

[1] and in his busy . . . master,] *revised in MS from* & {as the chaise carried him rapidly along towards the home where he was now to be master,} ⟨Arthur⟩ in his busy thoughts about the future,

[2] Arthur, ⟨who has lost nothing that he loves⟩ with a fine constitution & fine spirits, *MS*

[3] mornings ⟨for⟩ as *MS*   [4] for ⟨Irwine should⟩, in *MS*

would devise,[5] the lay impropriator of the Hayslope tithes would insist on paying a couple of hundreds more to the Vicar; and his aunt should be as comfortable as possible, and go on living at the Chase, if she liked, in spite of her old-maidish ways,—at[6] least until he was married; and that event lay in the indistinct background, for Arthur had not yet seen the woman who would play the lady-wife to the first-rate country gentleman.

These were Arthur's chief thoughts, so far as a man's thoughts through hours of travelling can be compressed into a few sentences, which are[7] only like the list of names telling you what are the scenes in a long, long panorama, full of colour, of detail, and of life. The happy faces Arthur saw greeting him were not pale abstractions, but real ruddy faces, long familiar to him: Martin Poyser was there—the whole Poyser family.

What—Hetty?

Yes; for Arthur was at ease about Hetty: not quite at ease about the past, for a certain burning of the ears would come whenever he thought of the scenes with Adam last August,—but at ease about her present lot. Mr Irwine, who had been a[8] regular correspondent, telling him all the news about the old places and people, had sent him word nearly three months ago that Adam Bede was not to marry Mary Burge, as he had thought, but pretty Hetty Sorrel. Martin[9] Poyser and Adam himself had both told Mr Irwine all about it—[1]that Adam had been deeply in love with Hetty these two years, and that now it was agreed they were to be married in March. That stalwart rogue Adam was more susceptible than the Rector had thought; it was really quite an idyllic love-affair; and if it had not been too long to tell in a letter, he would have liked to describe to Arthur the blushing[2] looks and the simple strong words with which the fine honest fellow told his secret. He knew Arthur would like to hear that[3] Adam had this sort of happiness in prospect.

Yes, indeed! Arthur[4] felt there was not air enough in the room to satisfy his renovated life, when he had read that passage in the letter. He threw up the windows, he rushed out of doors into the December air, and greeted every one who spoke to him with an eager gaiety, as if there had been news of a[5] fresh Nelson victory. For the first time that day since he had come to Windsor, he was in true boyish spirits: the load that had been

---

[5] devise, ⟨should get a couple of hundreds more for the Hayslope living⟩ the lay impropriator of the Hayslope tithes would insist on paying a couple of hundreds more to the Vicar. *MS*

[6] ways,—at] ways. At *MS*   [7] are ⟨as pale &⟩ only like *MS*

[8] a ⟨constant⟩ regular *MS*   [9] Sorrel. Martin] Sorrel: Martin *MS*

[1] it—] *MS* it:—*1* it;—*8*

[2] blushing ⟨way in which good Adam⟩ looks & the simple strong words with which the fine honest fellow *MS*

[3] that ⟨his favourite⟩ Adam *MS*   [4] indeed! Arthur] indeed: Arthur *MS*

[5] a ⟨new⟩ fresh *MS*

pressing upon him was gone; the haunting fear had vanished. He thought he could conquer his bitterness towards Adam now—could offer him his hand, and[6] ask to be his friend again, in spite of that painful memory which would still make his ears burn. He had been knocked down, and he had been forced to tell a lie: such things make a scar, do what we will. But if Adam were the same again as in the old days,[7] Arthur wished to be the same too, and to have Adam mixed up with his business and his future, as he had always desired before that accursed meeting in August. Nay, he would do a great deal more for Adam than he should otherwise have done, when he came into the estate;[8] Hetty's husband had a special claim on him—Hetty herself should feel that any pain she had suffered through Arthur in the past, was compensated to her a hundredfold. For really,[9] she could not have felt much, since she had so soon made up her mind to marry Adam.

You perceive clearly what[1] sort of picture Adam and Hetty made in the panorama of Arthur's thoughts on his journey homeward. It was March now; they were soon to be married: perhaps they were already married. And *now* it was actually in his power to do a great deal for them. Sweet—sweet little Hetty! The little puss hadn't cared for him half as much as he cared for her; for he was a great fool about her still—was almost afraid of seeing her—indeed, had not cared much to look at any other woman since he parted from her. That little figure coming towards him in the Grove, those dark-fringed childish eyes, the lovely lips put up to kiss him—that picture had[2] got no fainter with the lapse of months. And she would look just the same. It was impossible to think how he could meet her: he should certainly tremble.[3] Strange, how long this sort of influence lasts; for he was certainly not in love with Hetty now: he had been earnestly desiring, for months, that she should marry Adam, and there was nothing that contributed more to[4] his happiness in these moments than the thought of their marriage. It was the exaggerating effect of imagination that made his heart still beat a little more quickly at the thought of her. When he saw the little thing again as she really was, as Adam's wife, at work quite prosaically in her new home, he should perhaps wonder at the possibility of his past feelings. Thank heaven it had turned out so well! He should have plenty of affairs and interests to fill his life now, and not be in danger of playing the fool again.

Pleasant the crack of the post-boy's whip! Pleasant the sense of being hurried along[5] in swift ease through English scenes, so like those round his own home, only not quite so charming. Here was a market town[6]—very

[6] & ⟨be ⟨⟨his⟩⟩ friend⟨⟨s⟩⟩ the same⟩ ask to be his *MS*
[7] as in the old days,] *added in MS*   [8] estate; ⟨& he &⟩ Hetty{'s} husband *MS*
[9] really,] *MS 1* really *8*   [1] clearly what] clearly {now} what *MS*
[2] had] *added in MS*   [3] tremble. ⟨It was⟩ Strange, *MS*   [4] to ⟨thes⟩ his *MS*
[5] along ⟨with⟩ in *MS*
[6] charming. Here was a market town] charming. A market town *MS*

much like Treddleston—where the arms of the neighbouring lord of the
manor were borne on the sign of the principal inn: then mere fields and
hedges, their vicinity to a market town carrying an agreeable suggestion of
high rent, till the land began to assume a trimmer look, the woods were
more frequent, and at length a white or red mansion looked down from a
moderate eminence, or allowed him to be aware of its parapet and chimneys
among the dense-looking masses of oaks and elms—masses reddened now
with early buds. And close at hand came the village: the small church, with
its red-tiled roof, looking humble even among the faded half-timbered
houses; the old green gravestones with nettles round them; nothing fresh
and bright but the children, opening round eyes at the swift post-chaise;
nothing noisy and busy but the yapping[7] curs of mysterious pedigree. What
a much prettier village Hayslope was! And it should not be neglected like
this place: vigorous repairs should go on everywhere among farm-buildings and cottages, and travellers in post-chaises, coming along the Rosseter
road, should do nothing but admire as they went, and[8] Adam Bede[9] should
superintend all the repairs, for he had a share in Burge's business now, and,
if he liked, Arthur would put some money into the concern, and buy the old
man out in another year or two. That was an ugly fault in Arthur's[1] life, that
affair last summer; but the future should make amends. Many men would
have retained a feeling of vindictiveness towards Adam; but *he* would not—
he would resolutely overcome all littleness of that kind, for he had certainly
been very much in the wrong; and though Adam had been harsh and
violent, and had thrust on him a painful dilemma, the poor fellow was in
love, and had[2] real provocation. No; Arthur had not an evil feeling in his
mind towards any human being: he was happy, and would make every one
else happy that came within his reach.

And here was dear old Hayslope at last,[3] sleeping on the hill, like a quiet
old place as it was, in the late afternoon sunlight; and opposite to it the great
shoulders of the Binton Hills, below them the purplish blackness of the
hanging woods, and at last the pale front of the Abbey, looking out from
among the oaks of the Chase, as if anxious for the heir's return. "Poor
grandfather! and he lies dead there. *He* was a young fellow once, coming
into the estate, and making his plans. So the world goes round! Aunt[4] Lydia

---

[7] yapping] *MS* gaping *1 8*   [8] went, and] went. And *MS 1*
[9] Bede ⟨should superintend all the repairs now and would probably soon have the whole
in his hands, for Arthur, if Adam liked⟩ ⟨had a share in Burge's business⟩
⟨sh⟩{w}ould superintend all the repairs, for he had a share in Burge's business now, & if he
liked *MS*
[1] Arthur's] his *MS*
[2] had ⟨certainly⟩ real *MS*
[3] last⟨;⟩ {,} ⟨he could see the outline of the church & village quite well against the late sunlit
sky⟩ sleeping *MS*
[4] round! Aunt] round. Aunt *MS*

must feel very desolate, poor thing; but she shall be indulged as much as she indulges her fat Fido."

The wheels of Arthur's chaise had been anxiously listened for at the Chase, for to-day was Friday, and the funeral had already been deferred two days. Before it drew up on the gravel of the courtyard, all the servants in the house were assembled to receive him with a grave, decent welcome, befitting a house of death. A month ago, perhaps, it would have been difficult for them to have maintained a suitable sadness in their faces, when Mr Arthur was come to take possession; but the hearts of the head-servants were heavy that day for another cause than the death of the old squire, and more than one of them was longing to be twenty miles away, as Mr Craig was, knowing what was to become of Hetty Sorrel—pretty Hetty Sorrel—whom they used to see every week. They had the partisanship of household servants who like their places, and were not inclined to go the full length of the severe indignation felt against him by the farming tenants, but rather to make excuses for him; nevertheless, the upper servants who had been on terms of neighbourly intercourse with the Poysers for many years, could not help feeling that the longed-for event of the young Squire's coming into[5] the estate had been robbed of all its pleasantness.[6]

To Arthur it was nothing surprising that the servants looked grave and sad: he himself was very much touched on[7] seeing them all again, and feeling that he was in[8] a new relation to them. It was that sort of pathetic emotion which has more pleasure than pain in it—which[9] is perhaps one of the most delicious of all states to a good-natured man, conscious of the power to satisfy his good nature. His heart swelled agreeably as he said,

"Well, Mills, how is my aunt?"

But now Mr Bygate, the lawyer, who had been in the house ever since the death, came forward to give deferential greetings and answer all questions, and Arthur walked with him towards the library, where his aunt Lydia was expecting him. Aunt Lydia was the only person in the house who knew nothing about Hetty: her[1] sorrow as a maiden daughter was unmixed with any other thoughts than those of anxiety about funeral arrangements and her own future lot; and, after the manner of women, she mourned[2] for the father who had made her life important, all the more because she had a secret sense that there was little mourning for him in other hearts.

But Arthur kissed her[3] tearful face more tenderly than he had ever done in his life before.

---

[5] into] in to *MS*   [6] pleasantness. ¶ {To} Arthur ⟨felt⟩ it {was} nothing *MS*

[7] he himself was very much touched on] he was very much touched himself on *MS*

[8] feeling that he was in] feeling himself in *MS*

[9] which ⟨indeed⟩ is perhaps ⟨is⟩ one *MS*

[1] her ⟨maiden sorrow entirely⟩ sorrow as a maiden *MS*

[2] mourned ⟨the more⟩ for *MS*   [3] her ⟨weeping⟩ tearful *MS*

"Dear aunt," he said affectionately, as he held her hand, "*your*[4] loss is the greatest of all, but you must tell me how to try and make it up to you all the rest of your life."

"It was so sudden and so dreadful, Arthur," poor Miss Lydia began, pouring out her little plaints; and Arthur sat down to listen with impatient patience. When a pause came, he said,

"Now, aunt, I'll leave you for a quarter of an hour, just to go to my own room, and then I shall come and give full attention to everything."

"My room is all ready for me, I suppose, Mills," he[5] said to the butler, who seemed to be lingering uneasily about the entrance-hall.

"Yes, sir, and there are letters for you; they are all laid on the writing-table in your dressing-room."

On entering the small ante-room, which was called a dressing-room, but which Arthur really used only to lounge and write in, he just cast his eyes on the writing-table, and saw that there were several letters and packets lying there; but he was in the uncomfortable dusty[6] condition of a man who has had a long hurried journey, and he must really refresh himself by attending to his toilette a little, before he read his letters. Pym was there, making everything ready for him—and soon, with a delightful freshness about him, as if he were prepared[7] to begin a new day, he went back into his dressing-room to open his letters. The level rays of the low afternoon sun entered directly at the window, and as Arthur seated himself in his velvet chair with their pleasant warmth upon him, he was conscious of that quiet well-being which perhaps you and I have felt on a sunny afternoon, when, in our brightest youth and health, life has opened a[8] new vista for us, and long to-morrows of activity have stretched before us like a lovely plain which[9] there was no need for hurrying to look at, because[1] it was all our own.

The top letter was placed with its address upwards: it was in Mr Irwine's handwriting, Arthur saw at once; and below the address was written, "To be delivered as soon as he arrives." Nothing could have been less surprising to[2] him than a letter from Mr Irwine at that moment: of course there[3] was something he wished Arthur to know earlier than it was possible for them to see each other. At such a time as that it was quite natural that Irwine should have something pressing to say. Arthur broke the seal with an agreeable anticipation of soon seeing the writer.

"I send this letter to meet you on your arrival, Arthur, because I may then be at Stoniton, whither I am called by the most painful duty it has ever been given me to perform; and it is right that you should know what I have to tell you without delay.

4 *your*] your *MS*   5 Mills," he] *MS 1* Mills?" he *8*   6 dusty] adust *MS*
7 prepared] ready *MS*   8 opened a] opened on a *MS 1* opened ⟨on⟩ a *8*
9 which] that *MS*   1 at, because] *MS 1* at{,} because *8*   2 to ⟨Arthur⟩ him *MS*
3 moment: of course there] moment:—there *MS*

"I will not attempt to add by one word of reproach to the retribution that is now falling on you: any other words that I could write at this moment must be weak and unmeaning by the side of those in which I must tell you the simple fact.

"Hetty Sorrel is in prison, and will be tried[4] on Friday for the crime of child-murder." . . .

Arthur read no more. He started up from his chair, and stood for a single minute with a sense of violent convulsion in his whole frame, as if the life were going out of him with horrible throbs; but the next minute he had rushed out of the room, still clutching the letter—he was hurrying along the corridor, and down the stairs into the hall. Mills was still there, but Arthur did not see him, as he passed like a hunted man across the hall and out along the gravel. The butler hurried out after him as fast as his elderly limbs could run: he guessed, he knew, where the young Squire was going.

When Mills got to the stables, a horse was being saddled, and Arthur was forcing himself to read the remaining words of the letter. He thrust it into his pocket as the horse was led up to him, and at that moment caught sight of Mills'[5] anxious face in front of him.

"Tell them I'm gone—gone to Stoniton," he said in a muffled tone of agitation—sprang into the saddle, and set off at a gallop.

---

[4] tried ⟨on Friday next⟩ ⟨to-morrow⟩ {on Friday} ⟨the 12ᵗʰ⟩ for *MS*
[5] Mills'] Mills's *MS 1*

CHAPTER XLV.

IN THE PRISON.

Near sunset that evening an elderly gentleman was standing with his back against the smaller entrance-door of Stoniton gaol, saying a few last words to the departing chaplain. The chaplain walked away, but the elderly gentleman stood still, looking down on the pavement, and stroking his chin with a ruminating air, when[1] he was roused by a sweet clear woman's voice, saying,

"Can I get into the prison, if you please?"

He turned his head, and looked fixedly at the speaker for a few moments without answering.

"I have seen you before," he said, at last. "Do you remember preaching on the village green at Hayslope in Loamshire?"

"Yes, sir, surely. Are you the gentleman that staid to listen on horse-back?"[2]

[3]"Yes. Why[4] do you want to go into the prison?"

"I want to go to Hetty Sorrel, the young woman who has been con-demned to death—and to stay with her, if I may be permitted. Have you power in the prison, sir?"

"Yes; I am a magistrate, and can get admittance for you. But did you know this criminal, Hetty Sorrel?"

"Yes, we are kin: my own aunt married her uncle, Martin Poyser. But I was away at Leeds, and didn't know of this great trouble in time to get here before to-day. I entreat you, sir, for the love of our heavenly Father, to let me go to her and stay with her."

"How did you know she was condemned to death, if you are only just come from Leeds?"

"I have seen my uncle since the trial[5], sir. He is gone back to his home now, and the poor sinner is forsaken of all. I beseech you to get leave for me to be with her."

"What! have[6] you courage to stay all night in the prison? She is very sullen, and will scarcely make answer when she is spoken to."

"O, sir, it may please God to open her heart still. Don't let us delay."

---

[1] when {he was roused by} a sweet ⟨clear⟩ {clear} woman's voice, ⟨said to him⟩ saying *MS*

[2] horseback?"] horseback." *MS*   [3] *Paragraph division added in 1.*

[4] "Yes. Why] "Yes: why *MS*   [5] since the trial] *added in MS*

[6] "What! have] "What, have *MS*

"Come, then," said the elderly gentleman, ringing, and gaining admission; "I[7] know you have a key to unlock hearts."

Dinah mechanically took off her bonnet and shawl as soon as they were within the prison court, from the habit she had of throwing them off when she preached or prayed, or visited the sick; and when they entered the gaoler's[8] room, she laid them down on a chair unthinkingly. There was no agitation visible in her[9], but a deep concentrated calmness, as if, even when she was speaking, her soul was in prayer reposing on an unseen support.

After speaking to the gaoler, the magistrate turned to her and said, "The turnkey will take you to the prisoner's cell, and leave you there for the night, if you desire it; but[1] you[2] can't have a light during the night—it is contrary to rules. My name is Colonel Townley: if I can help you in anything, ask the gaoler for my address, and come to me. I take some interest in this Hetty Sorrel, for the sake of that fine fellow, Adam Bede: I happened to see him at Hayslope the same evening I heard you preach, and recognized him in court to-day,[3] ill as he looked."

"Ah, sir, can you tell me anything about him? Can you tell me where he lodges? For my poor uncle was too much weighed down with trouble to remember."

"Close by here. I inquired all about him of Mr Irwine.[4] He lodges over a tinman's shop, in the street on the right hand as you entered the prison. There is an old schoolmaster with him. Now, good-by: I wish you success."

"Farewell, sir. I am grateful to you."

As Dinah crossed the prison court with the turnkey, the solemn evening light seemed to make the walls higher than they were by day, and the sweet pale face in the cap was more than ever like a white flower on this background of gloom. The turnkey looked askance at her all the while, but never spoke: he somehow felt that the sound of his own rude voice would be grating just then. He struck a light as they entered the dark corridor leading to the condemned cell, and then said in his most civil tone, "It'll be pretty nigh dark in the cell a'ready; but I can stop with my light a bit, if you like."

"Nay, friend, thank you," said Dinah. "I wish to go in alone."

[5]"As you like," said the gaoler,[6] turning the harsh key in the lock, and opening the door[7] wide enough to admit Dinah.[8] A jet of light from his lanthorn fell on the opposite corner of the cell, where Hetty was sitting on her straw pallet with her face buried in her knees. It seemed as if she were asleep, and yet the grating of the lock would have been likely to waken her.

[7] admission; "I] admission. "I *MS*   [8] the ⟨turnkey's⟩ gaoler's *MS*
[9] her ⟨manner⟩ , but *MS*   [1] it; but] it. But *MS*   [2] you ⟨cannot⟩ can't *MS*
[3] today, ⟨though⟩ ill *MS*   [4] Irwine{.} ⟨, the clergyman⟩ He lodges *MS*
[5] *Paragraph division added in 1.*   [6] gaoler, ⟨setting down his lanthorn⟩ turning *MS*
[7] door ⟨just⟩ wide *MS*   [8] Dinah.] *added in MS*

The door closed again, and the only light in the cell was that of the evening sky, through the small high grating—enough to discern human faces by. Dinah stood still for a minute, hesitating to speak, because Hetty might be asleep; and looking at the motionless heap with a yearning heart. Then she said, softly,

"Hetty!"

There was a slight movement perceptible in Hetty's frame—a start such as might have been produced by a feeble electrical shock; but she did not look up. Dinah spoke again, in a tone made stronger by irrepressible emotion:

"Hetty . . . it's Dinah."

Again there was a slight, startled movement through Hetty's frame, and without uncovering her face, she raised her head a little, as if listening.

"Hetty . . . Dinah is come to you."

After a moment's pause, Hetty lifted her head slowly and timidly from her knees, and raised her eyes. The two pale faces were looking at each other: one with a wild hard despair in it, the other full of sad, yearning love. Dinah unconsciously opened her arms and stretched them out.

"Don't you know me, Hetty? Don't you remember Dinah? Did you think I wouldn't come to you in trouble?"

Hetty kept her eyes fixed on Dinah's face,—at first like an animal that gazes, and gazes, and keeps aloof.

"I'm come to be with you, Hetty—not to leave you—to stay with you— to be your sister to the last."

Slowly, while Dinah was speaking, Hetty rose, took a step forward, and was clasped in Dinah's arms.

They stood[9] so a long while, for neither of them felt the impulse to move apart again. Hetty, without any distinct thought of it, hung on this something that was come to clasp her now, while she was sinking helpless in a dark gulf; and Dinah felt a deep joy in the first sign that her love was welcomed by the wretched lost one. The light got fainter as they stood, and when at last they sat down on the straw pallet together, their faces had become indistinct.

Not a word was spoken. Dinah waited, hoping for a spontaneous word from Hetty; but she sat in the same dull despair, only clutching the hand that held hers, and leaning her cheek against Dinah's. It was the human contact she clung to, but[1] she was not the less sinking into the dark gulf.

Dinah began to doubt whether Hetty was conscious who it was that sat beside her. She[2] thought suffering and fear might have driven the poor sinner out of her mind. But it was borne in upon her, as she afterwards said, that she must not hurry God's work: we are over-hasty to speak—as if God did not manifest himself by our silent feeling, and make his love felt

---

[9] stood ⟨a⟩ so *MS*   [1] but ⟨her⟩ she *MS*   [2] her. She] her: she *MS*

through ours. She did not know how long they sat in that way, but it got darker and darker, till there was only a pale patch of light on the opposite wall: all the rest was darkness. But she felt the Divine presence more and more,—nay, as if she herself were a part of it, and it was the Divine pity that was beating in her heart, and[3] was willing the rescue of this helpless one. At last she was prompted to speak, and find out how far Hetty was conscious of the present.

"Hetty," she said gently, "do you know who it is that sits by your side?"

"Yes," Hetty answered, slowly, "it's Dinah."

"And do you remember the time when we were at the Hall Farm together, and that night when I told you to be sure and think of me as a friend in trouble?"

"Yes," said Hetty. Then, after a pause, she added, "But you can do nothing for me. You can't make 'em do anything. They'll hang me o' Monday—it's Friday now."

As Hetty said the last words, she clung closer to Dinah, shuddering.

"No, Hetty, I can't save you from that death. But isn't the suffering less hard when you have somebody with you, that feels for you—that you can speak to, and say what's in your heart?. . . Yes, Hetty: you lean on me: you are glad to have me with you."

"You won't leave me, Dinah? You'll keep close to me?"

"No, Hetty, I won't leave you. I'll stay with you to the last. . . . But, Hetty, there is some one else in this cell besides me, some one close to you."

Hetty said in a frightened whisper, "Who?"

"Some one who has been with you through all your hours of sin and trouble—who has known every thought you have had—has seen where you went, where you lay down and rose up again, and all the deeds you have tried to hide in darkness. And on Monday, when I can't follow you,—when my arms can't reach you,—when death has parted us,—He who is with us now, and knows all, will be with you then. It makes no difference—whether we live or die, we are in the presence of God."

"O, Dinah, won't nobody do anything for me? *Will* they hang me for certain? . . . I wouldn't mind if they'd let me live."

"My poor Hetty, death is very dreadful to you. I[4] know[5] it's dreadful. But if you had a friend to take care of you after death—in that other world—some one whose love is greater than mine—who can do everything. . . . If God our Father was[6] your friend, and was willing to save you from sin and suffering, so as you should neither know wicked feelings nor pain again? If you could believe he loved you and would help you, as you believe I love you and will help you, it wouldn't be so hard to die on Monday, would it?"

---

[3] heart, and] heart—that *MS*   [4] you. I] you—I *MS*
[5] know ⟨it is⟩ it's *MS*   [6] was] were *MS*

"But I can't know anything about it," Hetty said, with sullen sadness.

"Because, Hetty, you are shutting up your soul against him, by trying to hide the truth. God's love and mercy can overcome all things—our ignorance, and weakness, and all the burthen of our past wickedness—all things but our wilful sin; sin that we cling to, and will not give up. You believe in my love and pity for you, Hetty; but if you had not let me come near you, if you wouldn't[7] have looked at me or[8] spoken to me, you'd have shut me out from helping you: I couldn't have made you feel my love; I couldn't have told you what I felt for you. Don't[9] shut God's love out in that way, by clinging to sin. . . . He can't[1] bless you while you have one falsehood in your soul; his pardoning mercy can't[2] reach you until you open your heart to him, and say, 'I have done this great wickedness; O God, save me, make me pure from sin.' While you cling to one sin and will not part with it, it must drag you down to misery after death, as it has dragged you to misery here in this world, my poor, poor Hetty. It is sin that brings dread, and darkness, and despair: there is light and blessedness for us as soon as we cast it off: God enters our souls then, and teaches us, and brings us strength and peace. Cast it off now, Hetty—now: confess the wickedness you have done—the sin you have been guilty of against your heavenly Father[3]. Let us kneel down together, for we are in the presence of God."

Hetty obeyed Dinah's movement, and sank on her knees. They still held each other's hands, and there was long silence. Then Dinah said,

"Hetty, we are before God: he is waiting for you to tell the truth."

Still there was silence. At last Hetty spoke, in a tone of beseeching,

"Dinah . . . help me . . . I can't feel anything like you . . . my heart is hard."

Dinah held the clinging hand, and all her soul went forth in her voice:[4]

"Jesus, thou present Saviour! Thou hast known the depths of all sorrow: thou[5] hast entered that black darkness where God is not, and hast uttered the cry of the forsaken. Come, Lord, and gather of the fruits of thy travail and thy pleading: stretch forth thy hand, thou who art mighty to save to the uttermost, and rescue this lost one. She is clothed round with thick darkness: the fetters of her sin are upon her, and she cannot stir to come to thee: she can only feel her heart is hard, and she is helpless. She cries to me, thy weak creature. . . . Saviour! it is a blind cry to thee. Hear it! Pierce the darkness! Look[6] upon her with thy face of love and sorrow, that thou didst turn on him who denied thee; and melt her hard heart."

---

[7] wouldn't] would not *MS*   [8] or] & *MS*   [9] Don't] Do not *MS*
[1] can't] cannot *MS*   [2] can't] cannot *MS*
[3] against your heavenly Father] against God your heavenly Father *MS 1* against ⟨God⟩ your heavenly Father *8*
[4] voice:] voice. *MS*   [5] sorrow: thou] sorrow. Thou *MS*
[6] darkness! Look] darkness—look *MS*

[7]"See, Lord,—I bring her, as they of old brought the sick and helpless, and thou didst heal them: I bear her on my arms and carry her before thee. Fear and trembling have taken hold on her; but she trembles only at the pain and death of the body: breathe upon her thy life-giving Spirit, and put a new fear within her—the fear of her sin. Make her dread to keep the accursed thing within her soul: make her feel the presence of the living God, who beholds all the past, to whom the darkness is as noonday; who is waiting now, at the eleventh hour, for her to turn to him, and confess her sin, and cry for mercy—now, before the night of death comes, and the moment of pardon is for ever[8] fled, like yesterday that returneth not.

[9]"Saviour! it is yet time—time to snatch this poor soul from everlasting darkness. I believe—I believe in thy infinite love. What[1] is *my* love or *my* pleading? It is quenched in thine. I can only clasp her in my weak[2] arms, and urge her with my weak pity. Thou—thou wilt breathe on the dead soul, and it shall arise from the unanswering sleep of death.

[3]"Yea, Lord, I see thee, coming through the darkness, coming, like the morning, with healing on thy wings. The marks of thy agony are upon thee—I see, I see thou art able and willing to save—thou wilt not let her perish for ever.

[4]"Come, mighty Saviour! let the dead hear thy voice; let the eyes of the blind be opened: let her see that God encompasses her; let her tremble at nothing but at the sin that cuts her off from him. Melt the hard heart; unseal the closed lips: make her cry with her whole soul, 'Father, I have sinned.[5] . . .'"

"Dinah," Hetty sobbed out, throwing her arms round Dinah's neck, "I will speak . . . I will tell . . . I won't[6] hide it any more."

But the tears and sobs were too violent. Dinah raised her gently from her knees, and seated her on the pallet again, sitting down by her side. It was a long time[7] before the convulsed throat was quiet, and even then they sat some time in stillness and darkness, holding each other's hands. At last Hetty whispered,

"I did do it, Dinah . . . I buried it in the wood . . . the little baby . . . and it cried . . . I heard it cry . . . ever such a way off . . . all night . . . and I went back because it cried."

She paused, and then spoke hurriedly[8] in a louder, pleading tone.

"But I thought perhaps it wouldn't die—there might somebody find it. I[9] didn't kill it—I didn't kill it myself. I[1] put it down there and covered it

---

[7] *Paragraph division added in 1.*   [8] ever ⟨past⟩ fled *MS*
[9] *Paragraph division added in 1.*   [1] love. What] Love—what *MS*
[2] weak] *added in MS*   [3] *Paragraph division added in 1.*
[4] *Paragraph division added in 1.*
[5] sinned {. . .} ⟨against heaven & before thee⟩' . . . . *MS*
[6] won't] will not *MS*   [7] time] while *MS*   [8] hurriedly] *added in MS*
[9] it. I] it—I *MS*   [1] myself. I] myself—I *MS*

up, and when I came back it was gone. . . . It was because I was so very
miserable, Dinah . . . I didn't know where to go . . . and I[2] tried to kill myself
before, and I couldn't. O, I tried so to drown myself in the pool, and
I couldn't. I went to Windsor—I ran away—did you know? I went to find
him, as he might take care of me; and he was gone; and then I didn't know
what to do. I daredn't go back home again—I couldn't bear it. I[3] couldn't
have bore to look at anybody, for they'd have scorned me. I thought o' you
sometimes, and thought I'd come to you, for I didn't think you'd be cross
with me, and cry shame on me: I thought I could tell you. But then the other
folks 'ud come to know it at last, and I couldn't bear that. It was partly
thinking o' you made me come toward Stoniton; and, besides, I was so
frightened at going wandering about till I was a beggar-woman, and had
nothing; and sometimes it seemed as if I must go back to the Farm sooner
than that. O, it was so dreadful, Dinah . . . I was so miserable . . . I wished I'd
never been born into this world. I should never like to go into the green
fields again—I hated 'em so in my misery."

Hetty paused again, as if the sense of the past were too strong upon her
for words.

"And then I got to Stoniton, and I began to feel frightened that night,
because I was so near home. And then the little baby was born, when
I didn't expect it; and the thought came into my mind that I might get rid
of it, and go home again. The thought came all of a sudden, as I was lying
in the bed, and it got stronger and stronger . . . I longed so to go back
again . . . I couldn't bear being so lonely, and coming to beg for want. And
it gave me strength and resolution to get up and dress myself. I felt I must
do it . . . I didn't know how . . . I thought I'd find a pool, if I could, like that
other, in the corner of the field, in the dark. And when the woman went out,
I felt as if I was strong enough to do anything . . . I thought I should get rid
of all my misery, and go back home, and never let 'em know why I ran away.
I put on my bonnet and shawl, and went out into the dark street, with the
baby under my cloak; and I walked fast till I got into a street a good way off,
and there was a public, and I got some warm stuff to drink and some bread.
And I walked on and on, and I hardly felt the ground I trod on; and it got
lighter, for there came the moon—O, Dinah, it frightened me when it first
looked at me out o' the clouds—it never looked so before; and I turned out
of the road into the fields, for I was afraid o' meeting anybody with the
moon shining on me. And I came to a haystack, where I thought I could lie
down and keep myself warm all night. There was a place cut into it, where I
could make me a bed; and I lay comfortable, and the baby was warm against
me; and I must have gone to sleep for a good while, for when I woke it was
morning, but not very light, and the baby was crying. And I saw a wood a
little way off . . . I thought there'd perhaps be a ditch or a pond there . . . and

² I] I'd MS   ³ it. I] it: I MS

it was so early I thought I could hide the child there, and get a long way off before folks was[4] up. And then I thought I'd go home—I'd get rides in carts and go home, and tell 'em I'd been to try and see for a place, and couldn't get one. I longed so for it, Dinah, I longed so to be safe at home. I don't know how I felt about the baby. I seemed to hate it—it was like a heavy weight hanging round my neck; and yet its crying went through me, and I daredn't look at its little hands and face. But I went on[5] to the wood, and I walked about, but there was no water"...

Hetty shuddered. She was silent for some moments, and when she began again, it was in a whisper.

"I came to a place where there was lots of chips and turf, and I sat down on the trunk of a tree to think what I should do. And all of a sudden I saw a hole under the nut-tree, like a little grave. And it darted into me like lightning—I'd[6] lay the baby there, and cover it with the grass and the chips. I couldn't kill it any other way. And I'd done it in a minute; and, O, it cried so, Dinah—I *couldn't* cover it quite up—I thought perhaps[7] somebody 'ud come and take care of it, and then it wouldn't die. And I made haste out of the wood, but I could hear it crying all the while; and when I got out into the fields, it was as if I was held fast—I couldn't go away, for all I wanted so to go. And I sat against the haystack to watch if anybody 'ud come[8]: I was very hungry, and I'd only a bit of bread left; but I couldn't go away. And after ever such a while—hours and hours—[9]the man came—him in a smock-frock, and he looked at me so, I was frightened, and I made haste and went on. I thought he was going to the wood, and would perhaps find the baby. And I went right on, till I came to a village, a[1] long way off from the wood; and I was very sick, and faint, and hungry. I got something to eat there, and bought a loaf. But I was frightened to stay. I heard the baby crying, and thought the other folks heard it too,—and I went[2] on. But I was so tired, and it was getting towards dark. And at last, by the roadside there was a barn—ever such a way off any house—like the barn in Abbot's Close; and I thought I could go in there and hide myself among the hay and straw, and nobody 'ud[3] be likely to come. I went in, and it was half full o' trusses of straw, and there was some hay, too. And I made myself a bed, ever so far behind, where nobody could find me; and[4] I was so tired and weak, I went to sleep.... But[5] O, the baby's crying kept waking me; and I thought that man as looked at me so was come and laying hold of me. But I must have slept a long while at last, though I didn't know; for when I got up and went out of

<hr />

[4] was] were *MS*   [5] on] *added in MS*
[6] I'd ⟨bury⟩ {lay} the baby {there} & *MS*
[7] perhaps] *added in MS*   [8] 'ud come] came *MS*
[9] hours—⟨there came a labouring⟩ the man came—him *MS*
[1] a ⟨good bit⟩ long *MS*
[2] went ⟨away into the fields again⟩ on. But I was so tired, *MS*   [3] 'ud] would *MS*
[4] me; and] me. And *MS*   [5] sleep.... But] sleep.... but *MS*

the barn, I didn't know whether it was night or morning. But it was morning, for it kept getting lighter; and[6] I turned back the way I'd come. I[7] couldn't help it, Dinah; it was the baby's crying made me go: and yet I was frightened to death. I[8] thought that man in the smock-frock 'ud see me, and know I put the baby there. But I went on, for all that: I'd left off thinking about going home—it had gone out o' my mind. I saw nothing but that place in the wood where I'd buried the baby . . . I see it now. O Dinah! shall[9] I allays[1] see it?"

Hetty clung round Dinah, and shuddered again. The silence seemed long before she went on.

"I met nobody, for it was very early, and I got into the wood. . . . I knew the way to the place . . . the place against the nut-tree; and[2] I could hear it crying at every step. . . . I thought it was alive. . . . I don't know whether I was frightened or glad . . . I don't know what I felt. I only know I was in the wood, and heard the cry. I don't know what I felt till I saw the baby was gone. And when I'd put it there, I thought I should like somebody to find it, and save it from dying; but when I[3] saw it was gone, I was struck like a stone, with fear. I never thought o' stirring, I felt so weak. I[4] knew I couldn't run away, and everybody as saw me 'ud know about the baby. My heart went like a stone: I couldn't wish or try for anything; it seemed like as if I should stay there for ever, and nothing 'ud ever change. But they came and took me away."

Hetty was silent, but she shuddered again, as if there were still something behind; and Dinah waited, for her heart was so full, that tears must come before words. At last Hetty burst out, with a sob,

"Dinah, do you think God will take away that crying and the place in the wood, now I've told everything?"

"Let us pray, poor sinner: let us fall on our knees again, and pray to the God of all mercy."

---

[6] lighter; and] lighter. And *MS*   [7] come. I] come: I *MS*
[8] death. I] death: I *MS*   [9] Dinah! shall] Dinah, shall *MS*
[1] allays] al'ays *MS*   [2] nut-tree; and] nut tree. And *MS*
[3] I ⟨was⟩ saw *MS*   [4] weak. I] weak, I *MS*

CHAPTER XLVI.

THE HOURS OF SUSPENSE.

On Sunday morning, when the church bells[1] in Stoniton were ringing for morning service, Bartle Massey re-entered Adam's room, after a short absence, and said,

"Adam, here's a visitor wants to see you."

Adam was seated with his back towards the door, but he started up and turned round instantly, with a flushed face and an eager look. His face was even thinner and more worn than we have seen it before, but he was washed and shaven this Sunday morning.

"Is it any news?" he said.

"Keep yourself quiet, my lad," said Bartle; "keep quiet. It's not what you're thinking of: it's[2] the young Methodist woman come[3] from the prison. She's[4] at the bottom o' the stairs, and wants to know if you think well to see her, for she has something to say to you about that poor castaway; but she wouldn't come in without your leave, she said. She thought you'd perhaps like to go out and speak to her. These[5] preaching women are not so back'ard commonly," Bartle muttered to himself.

"Ask her to come in," said Adam.

He was standing with his face towards the door, and as Dinah entered, lifting up her mild grey eyes towards him, she saw at once the great change that had come since the day when she had looked up at the tall man in the cottage. There was a trembling in her clear voice as she put her hand into his, and said,

"Be comforted, Adam Bede: the Lord has not forsaken her."

"Bless you for coming to her," Adam said. "Mr Massey brought me word yesterday as you was come."

They could neither of them say any more just yet, but stood before each other in silence; and Bartle Massey, too, who had put on his spectacles, seemed transfixed, examining Dinah's face. But he recovered himself first, and said, "Sit down, young woman, sit down," placing the chair for her, and retiring to his old[6] seat on the bed.

"Thank you, friend; I won't sit down," said Dinah, "for I must hasten back: she entreated me not to stay long away. What I came for, Adam Bede,

---

[1] bells ⟨were⟩ in MS   [2] of: it's] of. It's MS   [3] come] added in MS
[4] She's ⟨on⟩ at the bottom o' MS   [5] These] Those MS 1
[6] old ⟨place⟩ seat MS

was to pray you to go and see the poor sinner, and bid her farewell. She desires to ask your forgiveness, and it is meet you should see her to-day, rather than in the early morning, when the time will be short."

Adam stood trembling, and at last sank down on his chair again.

"It won't be," he said: "it'll be put off—there'll perhaps come a pardon. Mr[7] Irwine said there was hope: he said, I needn't quite give it up."

"That's a blessed thought to me," said Dinah, her eyes filling with tears. "It's[8] a fearful thing hurrying her soul away so fast."

"But let what will be," she added, presently, "you will surely come, and let her speak the words that are in her heart. Although her poor soul is very dark, and discerns little beyond the things of the flesh, she is no longer hard: she is contrite—she has confessed all to me. The pride of her heart has given way, and she leans on me for help, and desires to be taught. This fills me with trust; for I cannot but think that the brethren sometimes err in measuring the Divine love by the sinner's knowledge. She is going to write a letter to the friends at the Hall Farm for me to give them when she is gone; and when I told her you were here, she said, 'I should like to say good-by to Adam, and ask him to forgive me.' You will come, Adam?—perhaps you will even now come back with me."

"I can't," Adam said: "I can't say good-by, while there's any hope. I'm listening, and listening—I can think o' nothing but that. It can't be as she'll die that shameful death—I can't bring my mind to it."

He got up from his chair again, and looked away out of the window, while Dinah stood with compassionate patience. In a minute or two he turned round and said,

"I *will* come, Dinah . . . to-morrow morning . . . if it must be. I may have more strength to bear it, if I know it *must*[9] be. Tell her, I forgive her; tell her I will come—at the very last."

"I will not urge you against the voice of your own heart," said Dinah. "I must hasten back to her, for it is wonderful how she clings now, and was not willing to let me out of her sight. She used never to make any return to my affection before, but now tribulation has opened her heart. Farewell, Adam[1]: our heavenly Father comfort you, and strengthen you to bear all things." Dinah put out her hand, and Adam pressed it in silence.[2]

Bartle Massey was getting up to lift the stiff[3] latch of the door for her, but before he could reach it, she had said, gently, "Farewell, friend," and was gone, with her light step, down the stairs.

"Well," said Bartle, taking off his spectacles, and putting them into his pocket, "if there must be women to make trouble in the world, it's but fair

---

[7] pardon. Mr] pardon: Mr. *MS*   [8] tears. "It's] tears, "It's *MS*
[9] *must*] must *MS*   [1] Adam] Adam Bede *MS*
[2] Dinah put out her hand, & Adam pressed it in silence.] *added in MS*
[3] stiff] hard *MS*

there should be women to be comforters under it; and[4] she's one—she's one. It's a pity she's a Methodist; but there's no getting a woman without some foolishness or other."

Adam never went to bed that night: the excitement of suspense, heightening with every hour that brought him nearer the fatal moment, was too great; and in spite of his entreaties, in spite of his promises that he would be perfectly quiet, the schoolmaster watched too.

"What does it matter to me, lad?" Bartle said: "a night's sleep more or less? I shall sleep long enough, by-and-by, underground. Let me keep thee company in trouble while I can."

It was a long and dreary night in that small chamber. Adam[5] would sometimes get up, and tread backwards and forwards along the short space from wall to wall; then he would sit down and hide his face, and no sound would be heard but the ticking of the watch on the table, or the falling of a cinder from the fire which[6] the schoolmaster carefully tended. Sometimes he would burst out into vehement speech.

"If I could ha' done anything to save her—if my bearing anything would ha' done any good . . . but t'[7] have to sit still, and know it, and do nothing . . . it's hard for a man to bear . . . and to think o' what might ha' been now, if it hadn't been for *him*[8]. . . . O God, it's the very day we should ha' been married."

"Ay, my lad," said Bartle, tenderly, "it's heavy—it's heavy. But you must remember this: when you thought of marrying her, you'd a notion she'd got another sort of a nature inside her. You didn't think she could have got hardened in that little while to do what she's done."

"I know—I know that," said Adam. "I[9] thought she was loving and tender-hearted, and wouldn't tell a lie, or act deceitful. How could I think any other way? And if he'd never come near her, and I'd married her, and been loving to her, and took care of her, she might never ha' done anything bad. What would it ha' signified—my having a bit o' trouble with her? It 'ud ha'[1] been nothing to this."

"There's no knowing, my lad—there's no knowing what might have come. The smart's bad for you to bear now: you must have time—you must have time. But I've that opinion of you, that you'll rise above it all, and be a man again; and there may good come out of this that we don't see."

"Good come out of[2] it!" said Adam, passionately. "That doesn't alter th' evil: *her*[3] ruin can't be undone. I hate that talk o' people, as if there was a way o' making amends for everything. They'd more need be brought to see as the wrong they do can never be altered. When a man's spoiled his

[4] it; and] it. And *MS*   [5] Adam {would} sometimes ⟨got⟩ get *MS*
[6] which] that *MS*   [7] good . . . but t'] good. But to *MS*   [8] *him*] him *MS*
[9] Adam. "I] *MS 1* Adam. {"}I *8*   [1] ha'] have *MS*
[2] come out of] come of *MS*   [3] evil: *her*] evil. Her *MS*

fellow-creatur's life, he's no right to comfort himself with thinking good may come out of it: somebody[4] else's good doesn't alter her shame and misery."

"Well, lad, well," said Bartle, in a gentle tone, strangely in contrast with his usual peremptoriness and impatience of contradiction, "it's likely enough I talk foolishness: I'm an old fellow, and it's a good many years since I was in trouble myself. It's easy finding reasons why other folks should be patient."

"Mr Massey," said Adam, penitently, "I'm very hot and hasty. I owe you something different; but you mustn't take it ill of me."

"Not I, lad—not I."

So the night wore on in agitation, till the chill dawn and the growing light brought the tremulous quiet that comes on the brink of despair. There would soon be no more suspense.

"Let us go to the prison now, Mr Massey," said Adam, when he saw the hand of his watch at six. "If[5] there's any news come, we shall hear about it."

The people were astir already, moving rapidly, in one direction, through the streets. Adam tried not to think where they were going, as they hurried past him in that short space between his lodging and the prison gates. He was thankful when the gates shut him in from[6] seeing those eager people.

No; there was no news come—no pardon—no reprieve.

Adam lingered in the court half an hour, before he could bring himself to send word to Dinah that he was come. But a voice caught his ear: he could not shut out the words.[7]

"The cart is to set off at half past seven."

It must be said—the last good-by: there was no help.

In ten minutes from that time, Adam was at the door of the cell. Dinah had sent him word that she could not come to him, she could not leave Hetty one moment; but Hetty was prepared[8] for the meeting.

He could not see her when he entered, for agitation deadened his senses, and the dim cell was almost dark to him. He stood a moment after the door closed behind him, trembling and stupefied.

But he began to see through the dimness—to see the dark eyes lifted up to him once more, but with no smile in them. O[9] God, how sad they looked! The last time they had met his was when he parted from her with his heart full of joyous, hopeful love, and they looked out with a tearful smile from a pink, dimpled, childish face. The face was marble now; the sweet lips were pallid and half-open, and quivering; the dimples were all gone—all but one, that never went; and the eyes—O! the[1] worst of all was the likeness

---

[4] it: somebody] it. Somebody *MS*   [5] six. "If] *MS* six. ¶ "If *1* six. ⟨¶⟩ "If *8*

[6] from ⟨the sight of⟩ seeing *MS*   [7] words.] words: *MS 1*

[8] prepared ⟨to see⟩ {for} ⟨him⟩ the *MS*   [9] them. O] them—O *MS*

[1] O! the] O the *MS*

they had to Hetty's. They were Hetty's eyes looking at him with that mournful gaze, as if she had come back to him from the dead to tell him of her misery.

She was clinging close to Dinah; her cheek was against Dinah's. It seemed as if her last faint strength and hope lay in that contact; and the pitying love that shone out from Dinah's face looked like a visible pledge of the Invisible Mercy.

When the sad eyes met—when Hetty and Adam looked at each other, she felt the change in *him*[2] too, and it seemed to strike her with fresh fear. It was the first time she had seen any being whose face seemed to reflect the change in herself: Adam was a new image of the dreadful past and the dreadful present. She trembled more as she looked at him.

"Speak to[3] him, Hetty," Dinah said,[4] "tell him what is in your heart."

Hetty obeyed her, like a little child.

"Adam . . . I'm very sorry . . . I behaved very wrong to you . . . will you forgive me . . . before I die?"

Adam answered with a half-sob: "Yes, I forgive thee, Hetty: I forgave thee long ago."

It had seemed to Adam as if his brain would burst with the anguish of meeting Hetty's eyes in the first moments; but the sound of her voice uttering these penitent words touched a chord which had been less strained: there was a sense of relief from what was becoming unbearable, and the rare tears came—they had never come before, since he had hung on Seth's neck in the beginning of his sorrow.

Hetty made an involuntary movement towards him; some of the love that she had once lived in the midst of was come near her again. She kept hold of Dinah's hand, but she went up to Adam and said, timidly,

"Will you kiss me again, Adam, for all I've been so wicked?"

Adam[5] took the blanched wasted hand she put out to him, and they gave each other the solemn unspeakable kiss of a life-long parting.

"And tell him," Hetty said, in rather a stronger voice, "tell him . . . for there's nobody else to tell him . . . as I went after him and couldn't find him . . . and I hated him and cursed him once . . . but Dinah says, I should forgive him . . . and I try . . . for else God won't forgive me."

There was a noise at the door of the cell[6] now—the key was being turned in the lock, and when the door opened, Adam saw indistinctly that there were several faces there: he was too agitated to see more—even to see that Mr Irwine's face was one of them. He felt that the last preparations were beginning, and he could stay no longer. Room was silently made for him to depart, and he went to his chamber in loneliness, leaving Bartle Massey to watch and see the end.

---

² *him*] him *MS 1* ⟨him⟩ him *8*   ³ to ⟨Adam⟩ him *MS*
⁴ said,] *MS 1* said; *8*   ⁵ Adam] Arthur *MS*   ⁶ of the cell] *added in MS*

CHAPTER XLVII.

THE LAST MOMENT.

It was a sight that some people remembered better even than their own sorrows—the sight in that grey clear morning, when the fatal cart with the two young women in it was descried by the waiting watching multitude, cleaving its way towards the hideous symbol of a deliberately-inflicted sudden death.

All Stoniton had heard of Dinah Morris, the young Methodist woman who had brought the obstinate criminal to confess, and there was as much eagerness to see her as to see the wretched Hetty.

But Dinah was hardly conscious of the multitude. When Hetty had caught sight of the vast crowd in the distance, she had clutched Dinah convulsively.

"Close your eyes, Hetty," Dinah said, "and let us pray without ceasing to God."

And in a low voice, as the cart went slowly along through the midst of the gazing crowd, she poured forth her soul[1] with the wrestling intensity of a last pleading, for the trembling creature that clung to her and clutched her as the only[2] visible sign of love and pity.

Dinah did not know that the crowd was silent, gazing at her with a sort of awe—she did not even know how near they were to the fatal spot, when the cart stopped, and she shrank appalled at a loud shout hideous to her ear, like a vast yell of demons. Hetty's shriek mingled with the sound, and they clasped each other in mutual horror.

But it was not a shout of execration—not a yell of exultant cruelty.

It was a shout of sudden excitement at the appearance of a horseman cleaving the crowd at full gallop. The horse is hot and distressed, but answers to the desperate spurring; the rider looks as if his eyes were glazed by madness, and he saw nothing but what was unseen by others. See, he has something in his hand—he is holding it up as if it were a signal.

The Sheriff knows him: it is Arthur Donnithorne, carrying in his hand a[3] hard-won release from death.

---

[1] soul ⟨in⟩ with *MS*
[2] only ⟨sign that there may be love & pity for⟩ {visible sign of love & pity.} {¶} Dinah *MS*
[3] a] the *MS* *1*

CHAPTER XLVIII.

ANOTHER MEETING IN THE WOOD.

The next day, at evening, two men were walking from opposite points towards the same scene, drawn thither by a common memory. The scene was the Grove by Donnithorne Chase: you know who the men were.

The old Squire's funeral had taken place that morning, the will had been read, and now, in the first breathing-space, Arthur Donnithorne had come out for a lonely walk, that he might look fixedly at the new future before him, and confirm himself in a sad resolution. He thought he could do that best in the Grove.

Adam, too, had come from Stoniton on Monday evening, and to-day he had not left home, except to go to the family at the Hall Farm, and tell them everything that Mr Irwine had left untold. He had agreed with the Poysers that he would follow them to their new neighbourhood, wherever that might be; for he meant to give up the management of the woods, and, as soon as[1] it was practicable, he would wind up his business with Jonathan Burge, and settle with his mother and Seth in a home within reach of the friends to whom he felt bound by a mutual sorrow.

"Seth and me are sure to find work," he said. "A man that's got our trade at his finger ends is at home everywhere; and we must make a new start. My mother won't stand in the way, for she's told me, since I came home, she'd made up her mind to being buried in another parish, if I wished it, and if I'd be more comfortable elsewhere. It's wonderful how quiet she's been ever since I came back. It seems as if the very greatness o' the trouble had quieted and calmed her. We shall all be better in a new country; though there's some I shall be loth to leave behind. But I won't part from you and yours, if I can help it, Mr Poyser. Trouble's made us kin."

"Ay, lad," said Martin. "We'll[2] go out o' hearing o' that man's name. But[3] I doubt we shall ne'er go far[4] enough for folks not[5] to find out as we've got them belonging to us as are transported o'er the seas, and were[6] like to be hanged. We shall have that flyin' up in our faces, and our children's after us."

That was a long visit to the Hall Farm, and drew too strongly on Adam's energies for him to think of seeing others, or re-entering on his old

[1] as ⟨might be⟩ it was practicable *MS*   [2] Martin. "We'll] Martin, "We'll *MS*
[3] name. But] name; but *MS*   [4] far] fur *MS*   [5] not] *added in MS*
[6] were] war *MS 1* ⟨war⟩ were *8*

occupations till the morrow. "But to-morrow," he said to himself, "I'll go
to work again. I shall learn to like it again some time, maybe[7]; and it's right,
whether I like it or not."

This evening was the last he would allow to be absorbed by sorrow:
suspense was gone now, and he must bear the unalterable.[8] He was resolved
not to see Arthur Donnithorne again, if it were possible to avoid him. He
had no message to deliver from Hetty now, for Hetty had[9] seen Arthur; and
Adam distrusted himself: he had learned to dread the violence of his own
feeling. That word of Mr Irwine's—that he must remember what he had
felt after giving the last blow to Arthur in the Grove—had remained with
him.[1]

These thoughts about Arthur, like all thoughts that are charged with
strong feeling, were continually recurring, and they always called up the
image of the Grove—of that spot under the overarching boughs where he
had caught sight of the two bending figures, and had been possessed by
sudden rage.

"I'll go and see it again to-night for the last time," he said; "it'll[2] do me
good; it'll make me feel over again what I felt when I'd knocked him down. I
felt what poor empty work it was, as soon as I'd done it, *before* I began to
think he might be dead."

In this way it happened that Arthur and Adam were walking towards the
same spot at the same time.

Adam had on his working dress again, now,—for he had thrown off the
other with a sense of relief as soon as he came home; and if he had had the
basket of tools over his shoulder, he might have been taken,[3] with his pale[4]
wasted face, for the spectre of the Adam Bede who[5] entered the Grove on
that August[6] evening eight months ago. But he had no basket of tools, and
he was not walking with the old erectness, looking keenly round him; his
hands were thrust in his side-pockets, and his eyes rested chiefly on the
ground. He had not long entered the Grove, and now he paused before a
beech. He[7] knew that tree well; it was the boundary mark of his youth—the
sign, to him, of[8] the time when some of his earliest, strongest feelings had
left him. He felt sure they would never return. And yet, at this moment,
there was a stirring of affection at the remembrance of that Arthur Donnithorne whom he had believed in before he had come up to this beech eight
months ago. It was affection for the dead: *that*[9] Arthur existed no longer.

---

[7] maybe] perhaps *MS*   [8] unalterable. ⟨But on⟩ He *MS*
[9] had ⟨herself⟩ seen *MS*
    [1] him. ⟨"They say he looks miserable enough," Adam thought, "& if he's got a conscience, I
ought to bring myself to pity him."⟩ ¶ These *MS*
    [2] said; "it'll] said. "It'll *MS*   [3] taken{,} ⟨for⟩ with *MS*   [4] pale] paled *MS*
    [5] who ⟨had walked through⟩ entered *MS*   [6] August] *added in MS*
    [7] beech. He] beech.—⟨h⟩He *MS*   [8] of ⟨that moment⟩ the time *MS*
    [9] *that*] that *MS*

He was disturbed by the sound of approaching footsteps, but the beech stood at a turning in the road, and he could not see who was coming, until the tall slim figure in deep mourning suddenly stood before him at only two yards' distance. They both started, and looked at each other in silence. Often, in the last fortnight, Adam had imagined himself as close to Arthur as this,[1] assailing him with words that should be as harrowing as the voice of remorse, forcing upon him a just share in the misery he had caused; and often, too, he had told himself that such a meeting had better not be. But in imagining[2] the meeting he had always seen Arthur as he had met him on that evening in the Grove, florid, careless, light of speech; and the figure before him touched him with the signs of suffering. Adam knew what suffering was—he could not lay a cruel finger on a bruised man. He felt no impulse[3] that he needed to resist: silence was more just than reproach. Arthur was the first to speak.

"Adam," he said, quietly, "it may be a good thing that we have met here, for I wished to see you. I[4] should have asked to see you to-morrow."

He paused, but Adam said nothing.

"I know it is painful to you to meet me," Arthur went on, "but it is not likely to happen again for years to come."

"No, sir," said Adam, coldly, "that was what I meant to write to you to-morrow, as it would be better all dealings should be at an end between us[5], and somebody else put in my place."

Arthur felt the answer keenly, and it was not without an effort that he spoke again.

"It was partly on that subject I wished to speak to you. I don't want to lessen your indignation against me, or ask you to do anything for my sake. I only wish to ask you if you will help me to lessen the evil consequences of the past, which is unchangeable. I don't mean consequences to myself, but to others. It is but little I can do, I know. I[6] know the worst consequences will[7] remain; but something may be done, and you can help me. Will you listen to me patiently?"

"Yes, sir," said Adam, after some hesitation; "I'll[8] hear what it is. If I can help to mend[9] anything, I will. Anger 'ull mend nothing, I know. We've had enough o' that."

"I was going to the Hermitage," said Arthur. "Will you go there with me and sit down? We[1] can talk better there."

The Hermitage had never been entered since they left it together, for Arthur had locked up the key in his desk. And[2] now, when he opened the

---

[1] this, ⟨stinging⟩ assailing *MS*   [2] imagining ⟨that⟩ the *MS*
[3] impulse ⟨in him⟩ that *MS*   [4] you. I] you—I *MS*   [5] us] *added in MS*
[6] know. I] know—I *MS*   [7] will] *added in MS*
[8] hesitation; "I'll] hesitation. "I'll *MS*
[9] help to mend] help mend *MS 1* help {to} mend *8*   [1] We ⟨may⟩ can *MS*
[2] desk. And] desk, & *MS*

door, there was the candle burnt out in the socket; there was the chair in the
same place where Adam remembered sitting; there was the waste-paper
basket full of scraps, and deep down in it, Arthur felt in an instant, there was
the little pink silk handkerchief. It would have been painful to enter this
place if their previous thoughts had been less painful.

They sat down opposite each other in the old places, and Arthur said,
"I'm going away, Adam; I'm going into the army."[3]

Poor Arthur felt that Adam ought to be affected by this announcement—
ought to have a movement of sympathy towards him. But Adam's lips
remained firmly closed, and the expression of his face unchanged.

"What I want to say to you," Arthur continued, "is this: one of my
reasons for going away is, that no one else may leave Hayslope—may leave
their home on my account. I would do anything, there is no sacrifice I would
not make, to prevent any further injury to others through my—through
what has happened."

Arthur's words had precisely the opposite effect to[4] that he had anticipated[5]. Adam thought he perceived in them that notion of compensation
for irretrievable wrong, that self-soothing attempt to make evil bear the
same fruits as good, which most of all roused his indignation. He was as
strongly impelled to look painful facts right in the face as Arthur was to turn
away his eyes from them. Moreover, he had the wakeful suspicious pride of
a poor man in the presence of a rich man. He felt his old severity returning
as he said,

"The time's past for that, sir. A man should make sacrifices to keep clear
of doing a wrong; sacrifices won't[6] undo it when it's done. When people's
feelings have got a deadly wound, they can't be cured with favours."

"Favours!" said Arthur, passionately; "no; how can you suppose I
meant[7] that? But the Poysers—Mr Irwine tells me the Poysers mean to
leave the place where they have lived so many years—for generations.
Don't you see, as Mr Irwine does, that if they could be persuaded to
overcome the feeling that drives them away, it would be much better for
them in the end to remain on the old spot, among the friends and neighbours who know them?"

"That's true," said Adam, coldly. "But then, sir, folks's feelings are not
so easily[8] overcome. It'll be hard for Martin Poyser to go to a strange place,
among strange faces, when he's been bred up on the Hall Farm, and his
father before him; but then it 'ud be harder for a man with his feelings to
stay. I don't see how the thing's to be made any other than hard. There's a
sort o' damage, sir, that can't be made up for."

---

[3] army."] regulars." ⟨Whatever they may say about this peace, it is sure not to last long &
there will be harder service for our army than ever⟩." *MS*

[4] to] from *MS*   [5] had anticipated] anticipated *MS*

[6] wont ⟨alter⟩ undo *MS*   [7] meant] mean *MS*   [8] easily] easy to *MS*

Arthur was silent some moments. In spite of other feelings, dominant in him this evening, his pride winced under Adam's mode of treating him. Wasn't he himself suffering? Was not he too obliged to renounce his most cherished hopes? It was now as it had been eight months ago— Adam was forcing Arthur to feel more intensely the irrevocableness of his own wrong-doing: he was presenting the sort of resistance that was the most irritating to Arthur's eager, ardent nature. But his anger was subdued by the same influence that had subdued Adam's when they first confronted each other—by the marks of suffering in a long-familiar face. The momentary struggle ended in the feeling that he could bear a great deal from Adam, to whom he had been the occasion of bearing so much; but there was a touch of pleading, boyish vexation in his tone as he said,

"But people may make injuries worse by unreasonable conduct—by giving way to anger and satisfying that for the moment, instead of thinking what will be the effect in the future.

"If I were going to stay here and act as landlord," he added, presently, with still more eagerness[9]—"if I were careless about what I've done—what I've been the cause of, you would have some excuse, Adam, for going away and encouraging others to go. You would have some excuse then for trying to make the evil worse. But when I tell you I'm going away for years—when you know what that means for me, how it cuts off every plan of happiness I've ever formed—it is impossible for a sensible man like you to believe that there is any real ground for the Poysers[1] refusing to remain. I know their feeling about disgrace[2],—Mr Irwine has told me all; but he is of opinion that they might be persuaded out of this idea that they are disgraced in the eyes of their neighbours, and that they can't remain on my estate, if you would join him in his efforts,—if you would stay yourself, and go on managing the old woods."

Arthur paused a moment, and then added, pleadingly, "You know that's a good work to do for the sake of other people, besides the owner. And you don't know but that they may have a better owner soon, whom you will like to work for. If I die, my cousin Tradgett will have the estate, and take my name. He is a good fellow.[3]"

Adam could not help being moved: it was impossible for him not to feel that this was the voice of the honest, warm-hearted Arthur whom he had loved and been proud of in old days; but nearer memories would not be thrust away. He was silent; yet Arthur saw an answer in his face that induced him to go on, with growing earnestness.

---

[9] he added, presently, with still more eagerness,] *added in MS*
[1] Poysers' ⟨going away⟩ refusing *MS*   [2] disgrace ⟨, but⟩—Mr. *MS*
[3] If I die my cousin Tradgett will have the estate, & take my name. He is a good fellow.] *added in MS*

"And then, if you would talk to the Poysers—if you would talk the matter over with Mr Irwine—he means to see you to-morrow—and then if you would[4] join your arguments to his to prevail on them not to go. . . . I[5] know, of course, that they would not accept any favour[6] from me: I mean nothing of that kind: but I'm sure they would suffer less in the end. Irwine thinks so too; and[7] Mr Irwine is to have the chief authority on the estate— he has consented to undertake that. They will really be under no man, but one whom they respect and like. It would be the same with you, Adam; and it could be nothing but a desire to give me worse pain that could incline you to go."

Arthur was silent again for a little while, and then said, with some agitation in his voice,

"I wouldn't act so towards you, I know. If you were in my place and I in yours, I should try to help you to do the best."

Adam made a hasty movement on his chair, and looked on the ground. Arthur went on:

"Perhaps[8] you've never done anything you've had bitterly to repent of in your life, Adam; if you had, you would be more generous. You would know then that it's worse for me than for you."

Arthur rose from his seat[9] with the last words, and went to one of the windows, looking out and turning his back on Adam, as he[1] continued passionately,

"Haven't I[2] loved her too? Didn't I see her yesterday? Shan't I carry the thought of her about with me as much as you will? And don't you think you would suffer more if you'd been in fault?"

There was silence for several minutes, for the struggle in Adam's mind was not easily decided. Facile natures, whose emotions have little permanence, can hardly understand how much inward resistance he overcame before he rose from his seat and turned towards Arthur. Arthur heard the movement, and turning round, met the sad but softened look with which Adam said,

"It's true what you say, sir: I'm hard—it's in my nature. I was too hard with my father[3] for doing wrong. I've been a bit hard t'[4] everybody but *her*. I felt as if nobody pitied her enough—her suffering cut into me so; and when I thought the folks at the Farm were too hard with her, I said I'd never be hard to anybody myself again. But feeling overmuch about her has perhaps made me unfair to you. I've known what it is in my life to repent and feel it's too late: I felt I'd been too harsh to my father when he was gone from me—I

---

[4] if you would] *added in MS*   [5] go. . . . I] go. I *MS*   [6] favour] favours *MS*
[7] too; and] too. And *MS*
[8] ground. Arthur went on: ¶ "Perhaps] ground. ¶ "Perhaps *MS*
[9] seat ⟨as he said⟩ with *MS*   [1] he ⟨said⟩ continued *MS*   [2] I] I I *MS*
[3] father] *MS* *1* father, *8*   [4] t'] to *MS*

feel it now, when I think of him. I've no right to be hard towards them as have done wrong and repent."

Adam spoke these words with the firm distinctness of a man who is resolved to leave nothing unsaid that he is bound to say; but he went on with more hesitation.

"I wouldn't shake hands with you once, sir, when you asked me—but if you're willing to do it now, for all I refused then" ...

Arthur's white hand was in Adam's large grasp in an instant, and with that action there was a strong rush, on both sides, of the old, boyish affection.

"Adam," Arthur said, impelled to full confession now, "it would never have happened if I'd known you loved her. That would have helped to save me from it. And I *did* struggle: I never meant to injure her. I deceived you afterwards—and that led on to worse; but I thought it was forced upon me, I thought it was the best thing I could do. And in that letter I told her to let me know if she were in any trouble: don't think I would not have done everything I could. But I was all wrong from the very first, and horrible wrong has come of it. God knows, I'd give my life if I could undo it."

They sat down again opposite each other, and Adam said, tremulously, "How did she seem when you left her, sir?"

"Don't ask me, Adam," Arthur said;[5] "I feel sometimes as if I should go mad with thinking of her looks and what she said to me, and[6] then, that I couldn't get a full pardon—that I couldn't save her from that wretched fate of being transported—that[7] I can do nothing for her all those years; and she may die under it, and never know comfort any more."

"Ah, sir," said Adam, for the first time feeling his own pain merged in sympathy for Arthur, "you and me'll[8] often be thinking o' the same thing, when we're a long way off one another. I'll pray God to help you, as I pray him to help me."

"But there's that sweet woman—that Dinah Morris," Arthur said, pursuing his own thoughts, and not knowing what had been the sense of Adam's words, "she says she shall stay with her to the very last moment—till she goes; and[9] the poor thing clings to her as if she found some comfort in her. I could worship that woman; I don't know what I should do if she were not there. Adam, you will see her when she comes back: I could say nothing to her yesterday—nothing of what I felt towards her. Tell her," Arthur went on hurriedly, as if he wanted to hide the emotion with which he spoke, while he took off his chain and watch—"tell her I asked you to

---

[5] said, ⟨leaning his head on his hand & looking as if he saw a sight of unforgetable painfulness,⟩ ⟨looking & speaking like a man in torturing pain. "I think I shall go mad with thinking⟩ "I *MS*

[6] me, and] me. And *MS*   [7] fate of being transported—that] fate—that *MS*

[8] me'll] me {'}⟨u⟩ill *MS*   [9] goes; and] goes. And *MS*

give her this in remembrance of me—of the man[1] to whom she is the one source of comfort, when he thinks of . . . I know she doesn't care about such things—or anything else I can give her for its own sake. But she will use the watch—I shall like to think of her using it."

"I'll give it to her, sir," Adam said, "and tell her your words. She told me she should come back to the people at the Hall Farm."

"And you *will* persuade the Poysers to stay, Adam?" said Arthur, reminded of the subject which both of them had forgotten in the first interchange of revived friendship. "You *will* stay yourself, and help Mr Irwine to carry out the repairs and improvements on the estate?"

"There's one thing, sir, that perhaps you don't take account of," said Adam, with hesitating gentleness, "and that was what made me hang back longer. You see, it's the same with both me and the Poysers: if we stay, it's for our own worldly interest, and it looks as if we'd put up with anything for the sake o' that. I know that's what they'll feel, and I can't help feeling a little of it myself. When folks have got an honourable, independent spirit, they don't like to do anything that might make 'em seem base-minded."

"But no one who knows you will think that, Adam: that is not a reason strong enough[2] against a course that is really more generous, more unselfish than the[3] other. And it will be known—it shall be made known, that both you and[4] the Poysers stayed at my entreaty. Adam, don't try to make things worse for me; I'm punished enough without that."

"No, sir, no," Adam said, looking at Arthur with mournful affection. "God forbid I should make things worse for you. I used to wish I could do it, in my passion;—but that was when I thought you didn't feel enough. I'll stay, sir: I'll do the best I can. It's all I've got to think of now—to do my work well, and make the world a bit better place for them as can enjoy it."

"Then we'll part now, Adam. You will see Mr Irwine to-morrow, and consult with him about everything."

"Are you going soon, sir?" said Adam.

"As soon as possible—after I've made the necessary arrangements. Good-by, Adam. I shall think of you going about the old place."

"Good-by, sir. God bless you."

The hands were clasped once more, and Adam left the Hermitage, feeling that sorrow was more bearable now hatred was gone.

As soon as the door was closed behind him, Arthur went to the wastepaper basket and took out the little pink silk handkerchief.

---

[1] man ⟨she has been⟩ {to whom she is} the one source of comfort{,} ⟨to⟩ when *MS*

[2] reason strong enough] *revised in MS from* strong reason enough

[3] the ⟨opposite⟩ other *MS*   [4] both you &] *added in MS*

BOOK SIXTH

*

CHAPTER XLIX.

AT THE HALL FARM.

The first autumnal afternoon sunshine of 1801—more than eighteen months after that parting of Adam and Arthur in the Hermitage—was on the yard at the Hall Farm, and the bulldog was in one of his most excited moments; for it was that hour of the day when the cows were being driven into the yard for their afternoon milking. No wonder the patient beasts ran confusedly into the wrong places, for the alarming din of the bulldog was mingled with more distant sounds which the timid feminine creatures, with pardonable superstition, imagined also to have some relation to their own movements—with the tremendous crack of the waggoner's whip, the roar of his voice, and the booming thunder of the waggon, as it left the rick-yard empty of its golden load.

The milking of the cows was[1] a sight Mrs Poyser loved, and at this hour on mild days she was usually standing at the house door, with her knitting in her hands, in quiet contemplation, only heightened to a keener interest when the vicious yellow cow, who had once kicked over a pailful of precious milk, was about to undergo the preventive punishment of having her hinder-legs strapped.

To-day, however, Mrs Poyser gave but a divided attention to the arrival of the cows, for she was in eager discussion with Dinah, who was stitching Mr Poyser's shirt-collars, and had borne patiently to have her thread broken three times by Totty pulling at her arm with a sudden insistance that she should look at "Baby," that is, at a large wooden doll with no legs and a long skirt, whose bald head Totty, seated in her small chair at Dinah's side, was caressing and pressing to her fat cheek with much fervour. Totty is larger by more than two years' growth than when you first saw her, and she has on a black frock under her pinafore: Mrs Poyser too has on a black gown, which seems to heighten the family likeness between her and Dinah. In other respects there is little outward change now discernible in our old friends, or in the pleasant house-place, bright with polished oak and pewter.

"I never saw the like to you, Dinah," Mrs Poyser was saying, "when you've once took anything into your head: there's no more moving you than the rooted tree. You may say what you like, but I don't believe *that's*[2]

---

[1] was] *added in MS*   [2] *that's*] that's *MS*

religion; for what's the Sermon on the Mount about, as you're so fond o'
reading to the boys, but doing what other folks 'ud have you do? But if it was
anything unreasonable they wanted you to do, like taking your cloak off and
giving it to 'em, or letting 'em slap you i' the face, I dare say you'd be ready
enough: it's only when one 'ud have you do what's plain common sense and
good for yourself, as you're obstinate th' other way."

"Nay, dear aunt," said Dinah, smiling slightly as she went on with her
work, "I'm sure your wish 'ud be a reason for me to do anything that I
didn't feel it was wrong to do."

"Wrong! You drive me past bearing. What is there wrong, I should like
to know, i' staying along wi' your own friends, as are th' happier for having
you with 'em, an' are willing to provide for you, even if your work didn't
more nor pay 'em for the bit o' sparrow's victual y' eat, and the bit o' rag you
put on? An' who is it, I should like to know, as you're bound t' help and
comfort i' the world more nor your own flesh and blood—an' me th' only
aunt you've got[3] above-ground, an' am brought to the brink o' the grave
welly every winter as comes, an' there's the child as sits beside[4] you 'ull[5]
break her little heart when you go, an' the grandfather not been dead a
twelvemonth,[6] an' your uncle 'ull[7] miss you so as never was—a-lighting his
pipe an' waiting on him, an' now I can trust you wi' the butter, an' have had
all the trouble o' teaching you, an'[8] there's all the sewing to be done, an' I
must have a strange gell out o' Treddles'on to do it—an' all because you
must[9] go back to that bare heap o' stones as the very crows fly over an' won't
stop at."

"Dear aunt Rachel," said Dinah, looking up in Mrs Poyser's face, "it's
your kindness makes you say I'm useful to you. You don't really want me
now; for Nancy and Molly are clever at their work, and you're in good
health now, by the blessing of God, and my uncle is of a cheerful countenance again, and you have neighbours and friends not a few—some of them
come to sit with my uncle almost daily. Indeed, you will not miss me; and at
Snowfield there are brethren and sisters in great need, who have none of
those comforts you have around you. I feel that I am called back to those
amongst whom my lot was first cast: I feel drawn again towards the hills
where I used to be blessed in carrying the word of life to the sinful and
desolate."

"You feel! yes[1]," said Mrs Poyser, returning from a parenthetic glance at
the cows. "That's[2] allays[3] the reason I'm to sit down wi'[4], when you've a
mind to do anything contrairy. What do you want to be preaching for more

³   got ⟨i' the⟩ above-ground *MS*   ⁴   beside] besides *1*   ⁵   'ull] 'ill *MS*
⁶   an' the grandfather not been dead a twelvemonth,] *added in MS*
⁷   'ull] 'ill *MS*   ⁸   an'] *MS 1* and *8*   ⁹   must] *added in MS*
ᴵ   feel! yes] feel—yes *MS*   ²   cows. "That's] cows, "That's *MS*
³   allays] al'ays *MS*   ⁴   wi'] with *MS*

than you're preaching now? Don't you go off, the Lord knows where, every Sunday a-preaching and praying? an' haven't you got Methodists enow at Treddles'on to go and look at, if church folks's faces are too handsome to please you? an' isn't there them i' this parish as you've got under hand, and[5] they're like[6] enough to make friends wi'[7] Old Harry again as soon as your back's turned? There's that Bessy Cranage—she'll be flaunting i' new finery three weeks after you're gone, I'll be bound: she'll no more go on in her new ways without you, than a dog 'ull stand[8] on its hind legs when there's nobody looking. But I suppose it doesna[9] matter so much about folks's souls i' this country, else you'd be for staying with your own aunt, for she's none so good but what you might help her to be better."

There was a certain something in Mrs Poyser's voice just then, which she did not wish to be noticed, so she turned round hastily to look at the clock, and said: "See there! It's tea-time; an' if Martin's i' the rick-yard, he'll like a cup. Here, Totty, my chicken, let mother put your bonnet on, and then you go out into the rick-yard and see if father's there, and tell him he mustn't go away again without coming t' have a cup o' tea; and tell your brothers to come in too."

Totty trotted off in her flapping bonnet, while Mrs Poyser set out the bright oak table, and reached down the tea-cups.

"You talk o' them gells Nancy and Molly being clever i' their work," she began again;—"it's fine talking. They're all the same, clever or stupid—one can't trust 'em out o' one's sight a minute. They want somebody's eye on 'em constant if they're to be kept to their work. An' suppose I'm ill again this winter, as I was the winter before last, who's to look after 'em then, if you're gone? An' there's that blessed child—something's sure t' happen to her—they'll let her tumble into the fire, or get at the kettle wi' the boiling lard in't, or some mischief as 'ull lame her for life; an'[1] it'll be all your fault, Dinah."

"Aunt," said Dinah, "I promise to come back to you in the winter if you're ill. Don't think I will ever stay away from you if you're in real want of me. But indeed it is needful for my own soul that I should go away from this life of ease and luxury,[2] in which I have all things too richly to enjoy—at least that I should go away for a short space. No one can know but myself what are my inward needs, and the besetments I am most in danger from. Your wish for me to stay is not a call of duty which I refuse to hearken to because it is against my own desires; it is a temptation that I must resist, lest the love of the creature should become like a mist in my soul shutting out the heavenly light."

"It passes my cunning to know what you mean by ease and luxury," said Mrs Poyser, as she cut the bread and butter. "It's true there's good victual enough about you, as nobody shall ever say I don't provide enough and to

[5] and] an' MS [6] like] likely MS [7] wi'] with MS [8] stand] stan' MS
[9] doesna] doesn't MS [1] life; an'] life. An' MS [2] luxury ⟨for⟩ in MS

spare, but if there's ever a bit o' odds an' ends as nobody else 'ud eat, you're
sure to pick it out . . . but look there! there's Adam Bede a-carrying the little
un in. I wonder how it is he's come so early."

Mrs Poyser hastened to the door for the pleasure of looking at her darling
in a new position, with love in her eyes but reproof on her tongue.

"O for shame, Totty! Little gells o' five year old should be ashamed to be
carried. Why, Adam, she'll break your arm, such a big gell as that; set her
down—for shame!"

"Nay, nay," said Adam, "I can lift her with my hand, I've no need to take
my arm to it."

Totty, looking as serenely unconscious of remark as a fat white puppy,
was set down at the door-place, and the mother enforced her reproof with a
shower of kisses.

"You're surprised to see me at this hour o'[3] the day," said Adam.

"Yes, but come in," said Mrs Poyser, making way for him; "there's no
bad news, I hope?"

"No, nothing bad," Adam answered, as he went up to Dinah and put out
his hand to her. She had laid down her work and stood up, instinctively, as
he approached her. A faint blush died away from her pale cheek as she put
her hand in his, and looked up at him timidly.

"It's an errand to you brought me, Dinah," said Adam, apparently
unconscious that he was holding her hand all the while; "mother's a bit
ailing, and she's set her heart on your coming to stay the night with her, if
you'll be so kind. I told her I'd call and ask you as I came from the village.
She overworks herself, and I can't persuade her to have a little girl t'[4] help
her. I don't know what's to be done."

Adam released Dinah's hand as he ceased speaking, and was expecting an
answer; but before she had opened her lips Mrs Poyser said,

"Look there now! I told you there was[5] folks enow t'[6] help i' this parish,
wi'out[7] going further off. There's Mrs Bede getting as old and cas'alty as
can be, and she won't let anybody but you go a-nigh her hardly. The folks at
Snowfield have learnt by this time to do better wi'out[8] you nor[9] she can."

"I'll put my bonnet on and set off directly, if you don't want anything
done first, aunt," said Dinah, folding up her work.

"Yes, I do want something done. I want you t' have your tea, child; it's all
ready; and[1] you'll have a cup, Adam, if y' arena[2] in too big a hurry."

"Yes, I'll[3] have a cup, please; and then I'll walk with Dinah. I'm going
straight home, for I've got a lot o' timber valuations to write out."

"Why, Adam lad, are you here?" said Mr Poyser, entering warm and
coatless, with the two black-eyed boys behind him, still looking as much

³ o'] of MS   ⁴ t'] to MS   ⁵ was] were MS   ⁶ t'] to MS
⁷ wi'out] without MS   ⁸ wi'out] without MS   ⁹ nor] than MS
¹ ready; and] ready. And MS   ² y' arena] you⟨'re not⟩ aren't MS
³ I'll] I will MS

like him as two small elephants are like a large one. "How is it we've got sight o' you so long before foddering-time?"

"I came on an errand for mother," said Adam. "She's got a touch of her old complaint, and she wants Dinah to go and stay with her a bit."

"Well, we'll spare her for your mother a little while," said Mr Poyser. "But we wonna spare her for anybody else, on'y her husband."

"Husband!" said Marty, who was at the most prosaic and literal period of the boyish mind. "Why, Dinah hasn't got a husband."

"Spare her?" said Mrs Poyser, placing a seed-cake on the table, and then seating herself to pour out the tea. "But we must spare her, it seems, and not for a husband neither, but for her own megrims. Tommy, what are you doing to your little sister's doll? making[4] the child naughty, when she'd be good if you'd let her. You shanna[5] have a morsel o' cake if you behave so."

Tommy, with true brotherly sympathy, was amusing himself by turning Dolly's skirt over her bald head, and exhibiting her truncated body to the general scorn—an indignity which cut Totty to the heart.

"What do you think Dinah's been a-telling me since dinner-time?" Mrs Poyser continued, looking at her husband.

"Eh! I'm[6] a poor un at guessing," said Mr Poyser.

"Why, she means to go back to Snowfield again, and work i'[7] the mill, and starve herself, as she used to do, like a creatur as has got no friends."

Mr Poyser did not readily find words to express his unpleasant astonishment; he only looked from his wife to Dinah, who had now seated herself beside Totty, as a bulwark against brotherly playfulness, and was busying herself with the children's tea. If he had been given to making general reflections, it would have occurred to him that there was certainly a change come over Dinah, for she never used to change colour; but, as it was, he merely observed that her face was flushed at that moment. Mr Poyser thought she looked the prettier for it: it was a flush no deeper than the petal of a monthly rose. Perhaps it came because her uncle was looking at her so fixedly; but there is no knowing; for just then Adam was saying, with quiet surprise,

"Why, I hoped Dinah was settled among us for life. I thought she'd[8] given up the notion o' going back to her old country."

"Thought! yes[9]," said Mrs Poyser; "and so would anybody else ha' thought, as had got their right end up'ards. But I suppose you must *be* a Methodist to know what a Methodist 'ull do. It's ill guessing what the bats are flying after."

"Why, what have[1] we done to you, Dinah, as you must go away from us?" said Mr Poyser, still pausing over his tea-cup. "It's like breaking your

[4] making ⟨her⟩ the *MS*   [5] shanna] shant *MS*   [6] "Eh! I'm] "Eh, I'm *MS*
[7] i'] in *MS*   [8] she'd ⟨never⟩ {given up the notion o'} go{ing} back *MS*
[9] Thought! yes] Thought? Yes *MS* Thought! yis *1* Thought! ⟨yis⟩ yes *8*
[1] have] han *MS*

word, welly; for your aunt never had no thought but you'd make this your home."

"Nay, uncle," said Dinah, trying to be quite calm. "When[2] I first came, I said it was only for a time, as long as I could be of any comfort to my aunt."

"Well, an' who said you'd ever left off being a comfort to me?" said Mrs Poyser. "If you didna[3] mean to stay wi' me, you'd better never ha' come. Them as ha' never had a cushion don't miss it."

"Nay, nay," said Mr Poyser, who objected to exaggerated views. "Thee[4] mustna say so; we should ha' been ill off wi'out her, Lady[5] Day was a twelvemont': we mun be thankful for that, whether she stays or no. But I canna think what she mun leave a good home for, to go back int'[6] a country where the land, most on't, isna worth ten shillings an acre, rent and profits."

"Why, that's just the reason she wants to go, as fur as she can give a reason," said Mrs Poyser. "She says this country's too comfortable, an' there's too much t' eat, an' folks arena[7] miserable enough. And she's going next week: I canna[8] turn her, say what I will. It's allays[9] the way wi' them meekfaced people; you may's well pelt a bag o' feathers as talk to 'em. But I[1] say it isna[2] religion, to be so obstinate—is it now, Adam?"

Adam saw that Dinah was more disturbed than he had ever seen her by any matter relating to herself, and anxious to relieve her, if possible, he said, looking at[3] her affectionately,

"Nay, I can't find fault with anything Dinah does. I[4] believe her thoughts are better than our guesses, let 'em be what they may. I should ha' been thankful for her to stay among us; but if she thinks well to go, I wouldn't cross her, or make it hard to her by objecting. We[5] owe her something different to that."

As it often happens, the words intended to relieve her were just too much for Dinah's susceptible feelings at this moment. The tears came into the grey eyes too fast to be hidden; and she got up hurriedly, meaning it to be understood that she was going to put on her bonnet.

"Mother, what's Dinah crying for?" said Totty. "She isn't a naughty dell."

"Thee'st gone a bit too fur," said Mr Poyser. "We've no right t' interfere with her doing as she likes. An' thee'dst be as angry as could be wi' me, if I said a word against anything she did."

"Because you'd very like be finding fault wi'out reason," said Mrs Poyser. "But there's reason i' what I say, else I shouldna[6] say it. It's easy talking for them as can't love her so well as her own aunt does. An'[7] me got

² calm. "When] calm, "When *MS*   ³ didna] didn't *MS*
⁴ views. "Thee] views, "Thee *MS*   ⁵ her, Lady] her Lady *MS* *1* her {,} Lady *8*
⁶ int'] into *MS*   ⁷ arena] aren't *MS*   ⁸ canna] cant *MS*   ⁹ allays] al'ays
MS   ¹ *I*] I *MS*   ² isna] isn't *MS*   ³ look{ing} at *8*
⁴ does. I] does: I *MS*   ⁵ objecting. We] objecting: we *MS*
⁶ shouldna] shouldn't *MS*   ⁷ does. An'] does—an' *MS*

so used to her! I[8] shall feel as uneasy as a new-sheared sheep when she's gone from me. An' to think of her leaving a parish where she's so looked on. There's[9] Mr Irwine makes as much of her as if she was a lady, for all her being a Methodist, an' wi' that maggot o' preaching in her head;—God forgi'e[1] me if I'm i' the wrong to call it so."

"Ay," said Mr Poyser, looking jocose; "but thee dostna tell Adam what he said to thee about it one day. The missis was saying, Adam, as the preaching was th' only fault to be found wi'[2] Dinah, and Mr Irwine says, 'But you mustn't find fault with her for that, Mrs Poyser; you forget she's got[3] no husband to preach to. I'll answer for it, you give Poyser many a good sermon.' The parson had thee there," Mr Poyser added, laughing unctuously. "I told Bartle Massey on it, an' he laughed too."

"Yes, it's a small joke sets men laughing when they sit a-staring at one another with a pipe i' their mouths," said Mrs Poyser.[4] "Give Bartle Massey his way, and he'd have all the sharpness to himself. If the chaff-cutter had the making of us, we should all be straw, I reckon. Totty, my chicken, go upstairs to cousin Dinah, and see what she's doing, and give her a pretty kiss."

This errand was devised for Totty[5] as a means of checking certain threatening symptoms about the corners of the mouth; for Tommy, no longer expectant of cake, was lifting up his eyelids with his forefingers, and turning his eyeballs towards Totty, in a way that she felt to be disagreeably personal.

"You're rare and busy now—eh, Adam?" said Mr Poyser. "Burge's getting so bad wi' his asthmy, it's[6] well if he'll ever do much riding about again."

"Yes, we've got a pretty bit o' building on hand now," said Adam: "what with the repairs on th' estate, and the new houses at Treddles'on."

"I'll bet a penny that new house Burge is building on his own bit o' land is for him and Mary to go to," said Mr Poyser. "He'll be for laying by business soon, I'll warrant, and be wanting you to take to it[7] all, and pay him so much by th' 'ear[8]. We shall see you living on th' hill before another twelvemont's over."

"Well," said Adam, "I should like t'[9] have the business in my own hands. It isn't as I mind much about getting any more money: we've enough and to spare now, with only our two selves and mother; but I should like t'[1] have my own way about things: I[2] could try plans then, as I can't do now."

[8] her! I] her, I *MS*   [9] on. There's] on: there's *MS*
[1] forgi'e] forgi' *MS*   [2] wi'] with *MS*   [3] got] *added in MS*
[4] Poyser. ⟨Let⟩ Give *MS*   [5] Totty ⟨by way⟩ as a means *MS*
[6] Burge's getting so bad wi' his asthmy, it's] Burge's asmy's getting so bad—it's *MS*
[7] to it] to 't *MS*   [8] 'ear] year *MS*   [9] t'] to *MS*
[1] t'] to *MS*   [2] things: I] things. I *MS*

"You get on pretty well wi' the new steward, I reckon?" said Mr Poyser.

"Yes, yes; he's a sensible man enough: understands farming—he's carrying on the draining, and all that, capital. You[3] must go some day towards the Stonyshire side, and see what alterations they're making. But he's got no notion about buildings: you can so seldom get hold of a man as can turn his brains to more nor[4] one thing; it's just as if they wore blinkers like th'[5] horses, and could see nothing o' one side of 'em. Now, there's Mr Irwine has got notions o' building more nor[6] most architects; for as for th' architects, they set up to be fine fellows, but the[7] most of 'em don't know where to set a chimney so as it shan't be quarrelling with a door. My notion is, a practical builder, that's got a bit o' taste,[8] makes the best architect for common things; and I've ten times the pleasure i' seeing[9] after the work when I've made the plan myself."

Mr Poyser listened with an admiring interest[1] to Adam's discourse on building;[2] but perhaps it suggested to him that the building of his corn-rick had been proceeding a little too long without the control of the[3] master's eye; for when Adam had done speaking,[4] he got up and said,

"Well, lad, I'll bid you good-by now, for I'm off to the rick-yard again."

Adam rose too, for he saw Dinah entering,[5] with her bonnet on, and a little basket in her hand, preceded by Totty.[6]

"You're ready, I see, Dinah," Adam said; "so[7] we'll set off, for the sooner I'm at home the better."

"Mother," said Totty, with her treble pipe, "Dinah was saying her prayers and crying ever so."

"Hush, hush," said the mother: "little[8] gells mustn't chatter."

Whereupon the father, shaking with silent laughter, set Totty on the white deal table, and desired her to kiss him. Mr and Mrs Poyser, you perceive, had no correct principles of education.

"Come back to-morrow, if Mrs Bede doesn't want you, Dinah," said Mrs Poyser: "but[9] you can stay, you know, if she's ill."

So, when the good-byes had been said, Dinah and Adam left the Hall Farm together.

---

[3] capital. You] capital—you *MS*   [4] nor] than *MS*   [5] th'] the *MS*
[6] nor] than *MS*   [7] the] they *MS*   [8] taste, ⟨'ud⟩ make{s} the *MS*
[9] pleasure i' seeing] pleasure seeing *MS*   [1] interest ⟨that made him⟩ to Adam's *MS*
[2] building{;} ⟨, which made him forget the building of his corn rick⟩ but perhaps it suggested to him that the building of his *MS*
[3] control of the] *added in MS*   [4] when Adam had done speaking,] *added in MS*
[5] entering ⟨in⟩ with *MS*   [6] Totty{.} ⟨, who said⟩ ¶ "You're *MS*
[7] said; "so] said. "So *MS*   [8] mother: "little] mother. "Little *MS*
[9] Poyser: "but] Poyser. "But *MS* Poyser; "but *1*

CHAPTER L.

[1]IN THE COTTAGE.

Adam did not ask Dinah to take his arm when they got out into the lane. He had never yet done so, often as they had walked together; for he had observed that she never walked arm-in-arm with Seth, and he thought, perhaps[2], that kind of support was not agreeable to her. So they walked apart, though side by side, and the close poke of her little black bonnet hid her face from him.

"You can't be happy, then, to make the Hall Farm your home, Dinah?" Adam said, with the[3] quiet interest of a brother, who has no anxiety for himself in the matter. "It's a pity, seeing they're so fond of you."

"You know, Adam, my heart is as their heart, so far as love for them and care for their welfare goes; but they are in[4] no present need, their sorrows are healed, and I feel that I am[5] called back to my old work, in which I found a blessing that I have missed of late in the midst of too abundant worldly good. I know it is a vain thought to flee from the work that God appoints us, for the sake of finding a greater blessing to our own souls, as if we could choose for ourselves where we shall find the fulness of the Divine Presence, instead of seeking it where alone it is to be found, in loving obedience. But now, I believe, I have a clear showing that my work lies elsewhere—at least for a time. In the years to come, if my aunt's health should fail, or she should otherwise need me, I shall return."

"You know best, Dinah," said Adam. "I don't believe you'd go against the wishes of them that love you, and are akin to you, without a good and sufficient reason in your own conscience. I've no right to say anything about my being sorry: you know well enough what cause I have to put you above every other friend I've got; and if it had been ordered so that you could ha' been my sister, and lived with us all our lives, I should ha' counted it the greatest blessing[6] as could happen to us now; but[7] Seth tells me there's no hope o' that: your feelings are different; and perhaps I'm taking too much upon me to speak about it."

Dinah made no answer, and they walked on in silence for some yards, till they came to the[8] stone stile; where, as Adam had passed through first, and

---

[1] ⟨Evening⟩ In the Cottage. *MS*　　[2] perhaps] *added in MS*　　[3] the] *added in MS*
[4] in] *added in MS*　　[5] that I am] *added in MS*
[6] blessing ⟨life has to bring me now⟩ as *MS*　　[7] now; but] now. But *MS*
[8] the {stone} ⟨style⟩ {stile}, where, {as} Adam ⟨having⟩ {had} passed *MS*

turned round to give her his hand[9] while she mounted the unusually high step, she could not prevent him from seeing her face. It struck him with surprise; for the grey eyes, usually so mild and grave, had the bright uneasy glance which accompanies suppressed agitation, and the slight flush in her cheeks, with which she had come downstairs, was heightened to a deep rose-colour. She looked as if she were only sister to Dinah. Adam was silent with surprise and conjecture for some moments, and then he said:

"I hope I've not hurt or displeased you by what I've said, Dinah: perhaps[1] I was making too free. I've no wish different from what you see to be best; and I'm satisfied for you to live[2] thirty mile off, if you think it right. I shall think of you just as much as I do now; for you're bound up with what I can no more help remembering, than I can help my heart beating."

Poor Adam! Thus do men blunder. Dinah made no answer, but she presently said,

"Have you heard any news from that poor young man since we last spoke of him?"

Dinah always called Arthur so; she had never lost the image of him as she had seen him in the prison.

"Yes," said Adam. "Mr Irwine read me part of a letter from him yesterday. It's pretty certain, they say, that there'll be a peace soon, though nobody believes it'll last long; but he says he doesn't mean to come home. He's no heart for it yet;[3] and it's better for others that he should keep away. Mr Irwine thinks he's in the right not to come:—it's a sorrowful letter. He asks about you and the Poysers, as he always does. There's one thing[4] in the letter cut me a good deal:—'You[5] can't think what an old fellow I feel,' he says; 'I make no schemes now. I'm the best when I've a good day's march or fighting before me.'"

"He's of a rash,[6] warm-hearted nature, like Esau, for whom I have always felt great pity," said Dinah. "That meeting between the brothers, where Esau is so loving and generous, and Jacob so timid and distrustful, notwithstanding his sense of the Divine favour, has always touched me greatly. Truly, I have been tempted sometimes to say, that Jacob was of a mean spirit. But that is our trial:—we must learn to see the good in the midst of much that is unlovely."

"Ah," said Adam, "I like to read about Moses best, in th' Old Testament. He carried a hard business well through, and died when other folks[7] were going to reap the fruits: a man must have courage to look at his life so, and think what'll come of it after he's dead and gone. A good solid bit[8] o'

---

[9] hand ⟨as⟩ while *MS*   [1] Dinah: perhaps] Dinah. Perhaps *MS*
[2] live] *MS 1* ⟨life⟩ live *8*   [3] yet; ⟨he says,⟩ & *MS*
[4] thing ⟨he says⟩ in the letter *MS*   [5] deal:—'You] deal. 'You *MS*
[6] rash, ⟨hearted⟩ warm-hearted *MS*   [7] folks] people *MS*
[8] good solid bit] good bit *MS*

work lasts: if it's only laying a floor down, somebody's the better for it[9] being done well, besides the man as does it."

They were both glad to talk of subjects that were not personal, and in this way they went on till they passed the bridge across the Willow Brook, when Adam turned round and said,

"Ah, here's Seth. I thought he'd be home soon. Does he know of your going, Dinah?"

"Yes, I told him last Sabbath."

Adam remembered now that Seth had come home much depressed on Sunday evening, a circumstance which had been very unusual with him of late, for the happiness he had in seeing Dinah every week seemed long to have outweighed the pain of knowing she would never marry him. This evening he had his habitual air of dreamy benignant contentment, until he came quite close to Dinah, and saw the traces of tears on her delicate eyelids and eyelashes. He gave one rapid glance at his brother; but Adam was evidently quite outside the current of emotion that had shaken Dinah: he wore his everyday look of unexpectant calm. Seth tried not to let Dinah see that he had noticed her face, and only said,

"I'm thankful you're come, Dinah, for mother's been hungering after the sight of you all day. She began to talk of you the first thing in the morning."

When they entered the cottage, Lisbeth was seated in her arm-chair, too tired with setting out the evening meal, a task she always performed a long time beforehand, to go and meet them at the door as usual, when she heard the approaching footsteps.

"Coom, child, thee't coom at last," she said, when Dinah went towards her. "What[1] dost mane by lavin'[2] me a week[3], an' ne'er coomin' a-nigh me?"

"Dear friend," said Dinah, taking her hand, "you're not well. If I'd known it sooner, I'd have come."

"An' how's thee t' know if thee dostna coom? Th' lads on'y know what I tell 'em: as long as ye can stir hand and foot the men think ye're hearty. But I'm none so bad, on'y a bit of a cold sets me achin'. An' th' lads tease me so t' ha' somebody wi' me t' do the work—they make me ache worse[4] wi' talkin'[5]. If thee'dst come and stay wi' me, they'd let me alone. The[6] Poysers canna want thee so bad as I do. But take thy bonnet off, an' let me look at thee."

Dinah was moving away, but Lisbeth held her fast, while she was taking off her bonnet, and looked at her face, as one looks into a newly-gathered snowdrop, to renew the old impressions of purity and gentleness.

---

9 it] its *MS*   1 her. "What] her, "what *MS*   2 lavin'] laving *MS*
3 week] wick *MS*   4 worse] wuss *MS 1* ⟨wuss⟩ worse *8*
5 talkin'] talking *MS*   6 The] Th' *MS*

"What's the[7] matter wi' thee?" said Lisbeth, in astonishment; "thee'st been a-cryin'[8]."

"It's only a grief that'll[9] pass away," said Dinah, who did not wish just now to call forth Lisbeth's remonstrances by disclosing her intention to leave Hayslope. "You shall know about it shortly—we'll[1] talk of it to-night. I shall stay with you to-night."

Lisbeth was pacified by this prospect; and she had the whole evening to talk with Dinah alone; for there was a new room in the cottage, you remember, built nearly two years ago, in the expectation of a new inmate; and here Adam always sat when he had writing to do, or plans to make. Seth sat there too this evening, for he knew his mother would like to have Dinah all to herself.

There were two pretty pictures on the two[2] sides of the wall in the cottage.[3] On one side there was the broad-shouldered, large-featured, hardy old woman, in her blue jacket and buff kerchief, with her dim-eyed anxious looks turned continually on the lily face and the slight form in the black dress that were either moving lightly about in helpful activity, or seated close by the old woman's arm-chair, holding her withered hand,[4] with eyes lifted up[5] towards her to speak a language which Lisbeth understood far better than the[6] Bible or the hymn-book. She would scarcely listen to reading at all to-night. "Nay, nay, shut the[7] book," she said. "We mun talk. I[8] want t' know what thee wast[9] cryin'[1] about. Hast got troubles o' thy own, like other folks?"

On the other side of the wall there were the two brothers, so like each other in the midst of their unlikeness: Adam, with knit brows, shaggy hair, and dark vigorous colour, absorbed in his "figuring;" Seth, with large rugged features, the close copy of his brother's, but with thin wavy brown hair and blue dreamy eyes, as often as not looking vaguely out of the window instead of at his book, although it was a newly-bought book— Wesley's abridgment of Madame Guyon's life, which was full of wonder and interest for him. Seth had said to Adam, "Can I help thee with anything in here to-night? I don't want to make a noise in the shop."

"No, lad," Adam answered, "there's nothing but what I must do myself. Thee'st got thy new book to read."

And often, when Seth was quite unconscious, Adam, as he paused after drawing a line with his ruler, looked at his brother with a kind smile dawning in his eyes. He knew "th'[2] lad liked to sit full o' thoughts he could give no account of; they'd never come t' anything, but they made him

---

⁷ the] th' *MS*   ⁸ a-cryin'] crying *MS*   ⁹ that'll] which will *MS*
¹ we'll] we will *MS*   ² two] *added in MS*   ³ cottage. On⟨e⟩ one *MS*
⁴ hand, ⟨&⟩ with *MS*   ⁵ up ⟨, perhaps from the book,⟩ towards her *MS*
⁶ the ⟨book⟩ Bible *MS*   ⁷ the] th' *MS*   ⁸ talk. I] talk: I *MS*
⁹ wast] was *Cabinet*   ¹ cryin'] crying *MS*   ² th'] the *MS*

happy;" and in the last year or so, Adam had been[3] getting more and more
indulgent to Seth. It was part of that growing tenderness which came from
the sorrow at work within him.

For Adam, though you see him quite master of himself, working hard
and delighting in his work after his inborn inalienable nature, had not
outlived his sorrow[4]—had not felt it slip from him as a temporary burthen,
and[5] leave him the same man again. Do any of us? God forbid. It would be a
poor result of all our anguish and our wrestling, if we won nothing but our
old selves at the end of it—if we could return to the same blind loves, the
same self-confident blame, the same light thoughts of human suffering,
the same frivolous gossip over blighted human lives, the same feeble sense
of that Unknown[6] towards which we have sent forth irrepressible cries in
our loneliness. Let us rather be thankful[7] that our sorrow lives in us as an
indestructible force, only changing its form, as forces do, and passing from
pain into sympathy—the one poor word which includes all our best insight
and our best love. Not that this transformation of pain into sympathy had
completely taken place in Adam yet: there was still a great remnant of pain,
and this he[8] felt would subsist as long as *her* pain was not a memory, but an
existing thing, which he must think of as renewed with the light of every
new morning. But we get[9] accustomed to mental as well as bodily[1] pain,
without, for all that, losing our sensibility to it: it becomes a habit of our
lives, and we cease to imagine a condition of perfect ease as possible for us.
Desire[2] is chastened into submission; and we are contented with our day
when we have been able to bear our grief in silence, and act as if we were not
suffering. For it is at such periods that the sense of our lives having visible
and invisible relations beyond any of which either our present or prospective self is the centre, grows like a muscle that we are obliged to lean on and
exert.

That was Adam's state of mind in this second autumn of his sorrow. His[3]
work, as[4] you know, had always been part of his religion, and from very
early days he saw clearly that good carpentry was God's will—was that
form of God's will that most immediately concerned him[5]; but now there
was no margin of dreams for him[6] beyond this daylight reality, no holiday-
time in the working-day world;[7] no moment in the distance when duty
would take off her iron glove and breastplate, and clasp him gently[8] into

[3] been ⟨becoming⟩ getting *MS*   [4] sorrow, ⟨or cast it⟩ had not *MS*
[5] & ⟨become⟩ leave him *MS*   [6] Unknown ⟨to⟩ towards *MS*
[7] be thankful] thank heaven *MS*
[8] pain, and this he] pain, which he *MS 1* pain, ⟨which⟩ {and this} he *8*
[9] get] become *MS*   [1] bodily] to bodily *MS*   [2] us. Desire] us: desire *MS*
[3] sorrow. His] sorrow: his *MS*   [4] as] *added in MS*
[5] —was that form of God's will that most immediately concerned him] *added in MS*
[6] for him] *added in MS*
[7] world; ⟨no moment when duty⟩ no moment in the distance *MS*
[8] gently {in} to rest. He ⟨made⟩ conceived *MS*

rest. He conceived no picture of the future but one made up of hard-working days such as he lived through, with growing contentment and intensity of interest, every fresh week: love, he thought, could never be anything to him but a living memory—a limb lopped off, but not gone from consciousness. He did not know that the power of loving was[9] all the while gaining new force within him; that the new sensibilities brought[1] by a deep experience were so many new fibres by which it was possible, nay, necessary[2] to him, that his nature should intertwine with another. Yet he was aware that[3] common affection and friendship were more precious to him than they used to be,—that he clung more to his mother and Seth, and had an unspeakable satisfaction in the sight or imagination of any small addition to their happiness. The Poysers, too—hardly three or four days passed but he felt the need of seeing them, and interchanging words and looks of friendliness with them: he would have felt this[4], probably, even[5] if Dinah had not been with them; but he had only said the simplest truth in telling Dinah that he put her above all other friends in the world. Could anything be more natural? For in the darkest moments of memory the thought of her always came as the first ray of returning comfort: the early days of gloom at the Hall Farm had been gradually turned into soft moonlight by her presence; and in the cottage, too,—for she had come at every spare moment to soothe and cheer poor Lisbeth, who had been stricken[6][7] with a fear that subdued even her querulousness, at the sight of her darling Adam's grief-worn face. He had become used to watching her light quiet movements, her pretty loving ways to the children, when he went to the Hall Farm; to listen for her voice as for a recurrent music; to think everything she said and did was just right, and could not have been better. In spite of his wisdom, he could not find fault with her for her over-indulgence of the children, who had managed to convert Dinah the preacher, before whom a circle of rough men had often trembled a little, into a convenient household slave[8]; though Dinah herself was rather ashamed of this weakness, and had some inward conflict as to her departure from the precepts of Solomon. Yes, there was one thing that might have been better; she might have loved Seth, and consented to marry him. He felt a little vexed, for his brother's sake; and he could not help thinking regretfully how Dinah, as Seth's wife, would have made their home as happy as it could be for them all—how she was the one being that would have soothed their mother's last days into peacefulness and rest.

"It's wonderful she doesn't love th' lad," Adam had said sometimes to himself; "for anybody 'ud think he was just cut out for her. But her heart's

[9] was ⟨only⟩ all *MS*   [1] brought] *MS* bought *1 8*
[2] nay, necessary] *MS 1* nay{,} necessary *8*
[3] that ⟨the⟩ common affection⟨s⟩ & *MS*   [4] this] that *MS*
[5] even] *added in MS*   [6] Lisbeth, who had been stricken] Lisbeth, stricken *MS*
[7] stricken ⟨& sub⟩ with *MS*   [8] slave⟨.⟩ {, though} Dinah *MS*

so taken up with other things. She's one o' those women that feel no drawing towards having a husband and children o' their own. She thinks she should be filled up with her own life then; and she's been used so to living in other folks's cares, she can't bear the thought of her heart being shut up from 'em. I see how it is, well enough. She's cut out o' different stuff from most women: I saw that long ago. She's never easy but when she's helping somebody, and marriage 'ud interfere with her ways,—that's true. I've no right to be contriving and thinking it 'ud be better if she'd have Seth, as if I was wiser than she is;—or than[9] God either, for He made her what she is, and that's one o' the greatest blessings I've ever had from His hands, and others besides me."

This self-reproof had recurred strongly to Adam's mind, when he gathered from Dinah's face that he had wounded her by referring to his wish that she had accepted Seth, and so he had endeavoured to put into the strongest words his confidence in her decision as right—his resignation even to her going away from them, and ceasing to make part of their life otherwise than by living in their thoughts, if that separation were chosen by herself. He felt sure she knew quite well enough how much he cared to see her continually—to talk to her with the silent consciousness of a mutual great remembrance. It[1] was not possible she should hear anything but self-renouncing affection and respect in his assurance that he was contented for her to go away; and[2] yet there remained an uneasy feeling in his mind that he had not said quite the right thing—that, somehow, Dinah had not understood him.

Dinah must have risen a little before the sun the next morning, for she was downstairs about five o'clock. So was Seth; for, through Lisbeth's obstinate refusal to have any woman-helper in the house, he had learned to make himself, as Adam said, "very handy in the housework," that he might save his mother from too great weariness; on which ground I hope you will not think him unmanly, any more than you can have thought the gallant Colonel Bath unmanly when he made the gruel for his invalid sister. Adam, who had sat up late at his writing, was still asleep, and was not likely, Seth said, to be down till breakfast-time.[3] Often as Dinah had visited Lisbeth during the last eighteen months, she had never slept in the cottage since that night after Thias's death, when, you remember, Lisbeth praised her deft movements, and even gave a modified approval to her porridge. But in that long interval Dinah had made great advances in household[4] cleverness: and this morning, since Seth was there to help, she was bent on bringing everything[5] to a[6] pitch of cleanliness and order that would have satisfied her

---

[9] than] *added in MS*   [1] remembrance. It] remembrance: it *MS*
[2] away; and] away. And *MS*   [3] breakfast time{.} ⟨at half past six⟩. Often *MS*
[4] household] *added in MS*   [5] everything ⟨downstairs⟩ to *MS*
[6] a ⟨pictu⟩ pitch *MS*

aunt Poyser. The[7] cottage was far from that standard at present, for Lisbeth's rheumatism had forced her to give up her old habits of dilettante scouring and polishing. When the kitchen[8] was to her mind, Dinah went into the new room, where Adam had been writing the night before, to see what sweeping and dusting were needed there. She opened the window and let in the fresh morning air, and the smell of the sweetbrier, and the bright low-slanting rays of the early sun,[9] which made a glory about her pale face and pale auburn hair as she held the long brush, and swept, singing to herself in a very low tone—like a sweet summer murmur that you have to listen for very closely—one of Charles Wesley's hymns:

> "Eternal Beam of Light Divine,
>   Fountain of unexhausted love,
> In whom the Father's glories shine,
>   Through earth beneath and heaven above;
>
> Jesus! the weary wanderer's rest,
>   Give me thy easy yoke to bear;
> With steadfast patience arm my breast
>   With spotless love and holy fear.[1]
>
> Speak to my warring passions, 'Peace!'
>   Say to my trembling heart, 'Be still!'
> Thy power my strength and fortress is,
>   For all things serve thy sovereign will."

She laid by the brush and took up the duster; and if you had ever lived in Mrs Poyser's household, you would know how the duster behaved in Dinah's hand—how it went into every small corner, and on every ledge in and out of sight—how it went again and again round every bar of the chairs, and every leg, and under and over everything that lay on the table, till it came to Adam's papers and rulers, and the open desk near them. Dinah dusted up to the very edge of these, and then hesitated, looking at them with a longing but timid eye. It was painful to see how much dust there was among them. As she was looking in this way[2], she heard Seth's step just outside the open door, towards which her back was turned, and said, raising her clear treble,

"Seth, is your brother wrathful when his papers are stirred?"

---

[7] Poyser. The] Poyser; & the *MS*
[8] kitchen] house-place *MS* 1 ⟨house-place⟩ kitchen 8   [9] sun, ⟨that⟩ which *MS*
[1] *Stanza cancelled in MS*:
    ⟨"Thankful I take the cup from thee,
        Prepared & mingled by thy skill;
    Though bitter to the taste it be,
        Powerful the wounded soul to heal.⟩
[2] way{,} ⟨with her back towards the door⟩, she *MS*

"Yes, very, when they are not put back in the right places," said a deep strong voice, not Seth's.

It was as if Dinah had put her hands unawares on a vibrating chord; she was shaken with an intense thrill, and for the instant felt nothing else; then she knew her cheeks were glowing, and dared[3] not look round, but stood still, distressed because she could not say good-morning in a friendly way. Adam, finding that she did not look round so as to see the smile on his face, was afraid she had thought him serious about his wrathfulness, and went up to her, so that she was obliged to look at him.

"What! you[4] think I'm a cross fellow at home, Dinah?" he said, smilingly.

"Nay," said Dinah, looking up with timid eyes, "not so. But you might be put about by finding things meddled with; and even the man Moses, the meekest of men, was wrathful sometimes."

"Come, then," said Adam, looking at her affectionately, "I'll help you move the things, and put 'em back again, and then they can't get wrong. You're getting to be your aunt's own niece, I see, for particularness."

They began their little task together, but Dinah had not recovered herself sufficiently to think of any remark, and Adam looked at her uneasily. Dinah, he thought, had seemed to disapprove him somehow lately; she had not been so kind and open to him as she used to be. He wanted her to look at him, and be as pleased as he was himself with doing this bit of playful work. But Dinah did not look at him—it was easy for her to avoid looking at the tall man; and when at last there was no more dusting to be done, and no further excuse for him to linger near her, he could bear it no longer, and said, in rather a pleading tone,

"Dinah, you're not displeased with me for anything, are you? I've not said or done anything to make you think ill of me?"

The question surprised her, and relieved her by giving a new course to her feeling. She looked up at him now, quite earnestly, almost with the tears coming, and said,

"O, no, Adam! how[5] could you think so?"

"I couldn't bear you not to feel as much a friend to me as I do to you," said Adam. "And you don't know the value I set on the very thought of you, Dinah. That was what I meant yesterday, when I said I'd be content for you to go, if you thought right. I meant, the thought of you was worth so much to me, I should feel I ought to be thankful, and not grumble, if you see right to go away. You know I do mind parting with you, Dinah?"

"Yes, dear friend," said Dinah, trembling, but trying to speak calmly, "I[6] know you have a brother's heart towards me, and[7] we shall often be with one another in spirit; but[8] at this season I am in heaviness through manifold

3 dared] dare MS   4 "What! you] "What, you MS
5 Adam! how] Adam: how MS   6 calmly, "I] calmly. "I MS
7 me, and] me. And MS   8 spirit; but] spirit. But MS

temptations: you must not mark me. I feel called to leave my kindred for a while; but it is a trial: the flesh is weak."

Adam saw that it pained her to be obliged to answer.

"I hurt you by talking about it, Dinah," he said: "I'll⁹ say no more. Let's see if Seth's ready with breakfast now."

That is a simple scene, reader. But it is almost certain that you, too, have been in love—perhaps, even, more than once, though you may not choose to say so to all your feminine friends.¹ If so, you will no more think the slight words, the timid looks, the tremulous touches, by which two human souls approach each other gradually, like two little² quivering rain-streams, before they mingle into one—you will no more think these things trivial than you will think the first-detected signs of coming spring trivial, though they be but a faint, indescribable something in the air and in the song of the birds, and the tiniest perceptible budding on the hedgerow branches. Those slight words and looks and touches are part of the soul's language; and the finest language, I believe, is chiefly made up of unimposing words, such as "light," "sound," "stars," "music,"—words really not worth looking at, or hearing, in themselves, any more than "chips" or "sawdust:" it³ is only that they happen to be the signs of something unspeakably great and beautiful. I am of opinion that love is a great and beautiful thing too; and if you agree with me, the smallest signs of it will not be chips and sawdust to you: they will⁴ rather be like those little words, "light" and "music," stirring the long-winding fibres of your memory, and enriching your present with your most precious past.

---

⁹ said: "I'll] said. "I'll *MS*

¹ That is a simple scene, reader. But it is almost certain that you, too, have been in love— perhaps, even, more than once, though you may not choose to say so to all your ⟨lady⟩ feminine friends.] *8* That is a simple scene, I confess; & now I have written it, I am alarmed at the recollection that these "immense nothings" of a growing, half-conscious love have seldom been thought worth writing or reading, unless they have had the adjuncts of expensive upholstery & millinery, & very refined language, if not abundant literary allusion. But after all, reader, if you had demanded these conditions of interest, you would long ago have ceased to follow Adam Bede's fortunes: you must have perceived at a much earlier stage than this, that you had mistaken your road & got into a rugged lane, where you could meet with no elegant equipages, no delicately shod ladies, ⟨not⟩ {no} trim villas with hothouses beside them, & you would have ⟨made your way⟩ {turned} out of this unpromising, rustic by-way with all speed. Since you have come with him so far, you must care more for the man than for his clothes or his grammar, & drapery, whether of the tailoring or literary kind must be a small thing in your esteem. It is almost certain, too, that you have been in love—perhaps, even, more than once, though you may not choose to say so to all your lady friends. *MS* That is a simple scene, reader. But it is almost certain that you, too, have been in love—perhaps, even, more than once, though you may not choose to say so to all your lady friends. *1*

² little] *added in MS*

³ in themselves, any more than "chips" or "sawdust:" it] in themselves: it *MS*

⁴ will ⟨stir⟩ rather *MS*

CHAPTER LI.

SUNDAY MORNING.

Lisbeth's touch of rheumatism could not be made to appear serious enough to detain Dinah another night from the Hall Farm, now she had made up her mind to leave her aunt so soon; and at evening the friends must part. "For a long while," Dinah had said; for she had told Lisbeth of her resolve.

"Then it'll be for all my life, an' I shall ne'er see thee again," said Lisbeth. "Long while! I'n got no[1] long while t' live. An' I shall be took bad an' die, an' thee canst ne'er come a-nigh me, an' I shall die a-longing for thee."

That had been the key-note of her wailing talk all day; for Adam was not in the house, and so she put no restraint on her complaining. She had tried poor Dinah by returning again and again to the question, why she must go away; and refusing to accept reasons, which seemed to her nothing but whim and "contrairiness;" and still more, by regretting that she "couldna[2] ha'[3] one o' the[4] lads," and be her daughter.

"Thee couldstna put up wi' Seth," she said: "he isna cliver[5] enough for thee, happen; but he'd[6] ha' been very good t' thee—he's[7] as handy as can be at doin'[8] things for me when I'm bad; an'[9] he's as fond o' the[1] Bible an' chappellin'[2] as thee art[3] thysen. But happen, thee'dst like a husband better as isna just the cut o' thysen:[4] the runnin' brook isna athirst for th' rain. Adam 'ud ha' done for thee—I know he would; an' he[5] might[6] come t' like thee well enough, if thee'dst stop. But he's[7] as stubborn as th' iron bar—there's no bendin'[8] him no way but's own. But he'd[9] be a fine husband for anybody, be they[1] who they will[2], so looked-on an' so cliver as he[3] is. And he'd[4] be rare an' lovin'[5]: it does me good on'y a look o' the[6] lad's eye, when he[7] means kind tow'rt me."

---

[1] got no] gotna no *MS*   [2] she "couldna] *1* she "couldn't *MS* she {"}couldna *8*
[3] ha'] have *MS*   [4] the] th' *MS*
[5] he isna cliver] hey ⟨'d⟩ isna ⟨good⟩ cliver *MS*   [6] he'd] hey'd *MS*
[7] he's] hey's *MS*   [8] doin'] doing *MS*   [9] an' ⟨as⟩ hey's *MS*
[1] the] th' *MS*   [2] chappellin'] chappelling *MS*   [3] art] a't *MS 1* ⟨a't⟩ art *8*
[4] thysen: ⟨I know I did. I liked Thias 'cause he was cliver at things. I knowed nothin' [?then] an'⟩ th' runnin' brook isna athirst for th' rain. Adam 'ud ha' done for thee—I *MS*
[5] he] hey *MS*   [6] might ⟨be⟩ come *MS*   [7] he's] hey's *MS*
[8] bendin'] *MS 1* bending *8*   [9] he'd] hey'd *MS*   [1] they] the' *MS*
[2] they will] the' wull *MS*   [3] he] hey *MS*   [4] And he'd] An' hey'd *MS*
[5] lovin'] loving *MS*   [6] the] th' *MS*   [7] he] hey *MS*

Dinah tried to escape from Lisbeth's closest looks and questions by finding little tasks of housework, that kept her moving about; and as soon as Seth came home in the evening she put on her bonnet to go. It touched Dinah keenly to say the last good-by, and still more to look round on her way across the fields, and see the old woman still standing at the door,[8] gazing after her till she must have been the faintest speck in the dim aged eyes. "The God of love and peace be with them," Dinah prayed, as she looked back from the last stile. "Make them glad according to the days wherein thou hast afflicted them, and the years wherein they have seen evil. It is thy will that I should part from them; let me have no will but thine."

Lisbeth turned into the house at last, and sat down in the workshop near Seth, who was busying himself there with fitting some bits of turned wood he had brought from the village, into a small work-box which he meant to give to Dinah before she went away.

"Thee't see her again o' Sunday afore she goes," were her first words. "If thee wast good for anything, thee'dst make her come in again o' Sunday night wi' thee, an'[9] see me once more."

"Nay, mother," said Seth, "Dinah 'ud be sure to come again if she saw right to come. I should have no need to persuade her. She only thinks it 'ud be troubling thee for nought, just to come in to say good-by over again."

"She'd[1] ne'er go away, I know, if Adam 'ud be fond on her an' marry her; but everything's so[2] contrary," said Lisbeth, with a burst of vexation.

Seth paused a moment, and looked up, with a slight blush, at his mother's face. "What! has[3] she said anything o' that sort to[4] thee, mother?" he said, in a lower tone.

"Said? nay, she'll[5] say nothin'. It's on'y the men as have to wait till folks say things afore they find 'em out."

"Well, but what makes[6] thee think so, mother? What's put it into thy head?"

"It's no matter what's put it into my head: my[7] head's[8] none so hollow as it must get in, an' nought[9] to put it there. I know she's fond on him,[1] as I know th' wind's comin' in at th'[2] door, an' that's anoof. An' he[3] might be willin' to marry her if he know'd she's[4] fond on him, but he'll[5] ne'er think on't if somebody doesna put it into's head."

His mother's suggestion about Dinah's feeling towards Adam was not quite a new thought to Seth, but her last words alarmed him, lest she should

---

[8] door, ⟨looking⟩ gazing MS   [9] an'] and Cabinet   [1] She'd] Shey'd MS
[2] so] soo MS   [3] "What! has] "What, has MS   [4] to ⟨you⟩ thee MS
[5] she'll] shey'll MS   [6] makes ⟨you⟩ thee MS   [7] head: my] head. My MS
[8] head's ⟨not⟩ none MS   [9] nought ⟨t'⟩ to MS
[1] him, ⟨an' that's anoof⟩ ⟨know shey isna fond o' thee, an' that's anoof⟩ {as ⟨well as⟩ I know th' wind's comin' in at th' door, an' that's anoof.} An' MS
[2] th'] MS 1 the 8   [3] he] hey MS   [4] he know'd she's] hey knoo'd shey's MS
[5] he'll] hey'll MS

herself undertake to open Adam's eyes. He was not[6] sure about Dinah's feeling, and he thought he *was* sure about Adam's.

"Nay, mother, nay," he said, earnestly, "thee[7] mustna think o' speaking o' such things to Adam. Thee'st no right to say what Dinah's feelings are if she hasna[8] told thee; and[9] it 'ud do nothing but mischief to say such things to Adam: he feels very grateful and affectionate toward Dinah, but he's no thoughts towards[1] her[2] that 'ud incline him to make her his wife; and[3] I don't believe Dinah 'ud marry him either. I[4] don't think she'll marry at all."

"Eh," said Lisbeth, impatiently. "Thee[5] think'st so 'cause she wouldna ha' thee. She'll[6] ne'er marry thee; thee mightst as well like her t' ha' thy brother."

Seth was hurt. "Mother," he said, in a remonstrating tone, "don't think that of me. I should be as thankful t' have her for a sister as thee wouldst t' have her for a daughter. I've no more thoughts about myself in that thing,[7] and I shall take it hard if ever thee say'st it[8] again."

"Well, well, then thee shouldstna cross me wi' sayin' things arena as I say they[9] are."

"But, mother," said Seth, "thee'dst be doing Dinah a wrong by telling Adam what thee think'st about her. It 'ud do nothing but mischief; for it 'ud make Adam uneasy if he doesna feel[1] the same to[2] her. And I'm pretty sure he feels nothing o' the sort."

"Eh, donna tell me[3] what thee't sure on; thee know'st nought about it. What's he allays[4] goin' to the Poysers' for, if he[5] didna want t' see her? He[6] goes twice where he[7] used t' go once. Happen he[8] knowsna as he[9] wants t' see her; he[1] knowsna as I put salt in's broth, but he'd[2] miss it pretty quick if it warna there. He'll[3] ne'er think o' marrying[4] if it isna put into's head; an' if thee'dst any love for thy mother, thee'dst put him up to't, an' not let her go away out o' my sight, when I might ha' her to make a bit o' comfort for me afore I go to bed to my old man under the white thorn."

"Nay, mother," said Seth, "thee mustna think me unkind; but I should be going against my conscience if I took upon me to say what Dinah's feelings are. And besides that, I think I should give offence to Adam by speaking to him at all about marrying; and[5] I counsel thee not to do't. Thee

---

[6] not ⟨at all⟩ sure *MS*   [7] earnestly, "thee] earnestly. "Thee *MS*
[8] hasna] hasn't *MS*   [9] thee; and] thee. And *MS*   [1] towards] toward *MS*
[2] her ⟨or anybody else,⟩ that *MS*   [3] wife; and] wife. And *MS*
[4] either. I] either: I *MS*   [5] impatiently. "Thee] impatiently, "Thee *MS*
[6] She'll] Shey'll *MS*   [7] thing; ⟨an'⟩ and *MS*
[8] if ever thee say'st it] if ⟨you⟩ thee ever say{st} it *MS*
[9] they] the' *MS*   [1] feel ⟨if he⟩ the *MS*   [2] to] t' *MS*   [3] me] mey *MS*
[4] he allays] hey al'ays *MS*   [5] he] he{y} *MS*   [6] He] Hey *MS*
[7] he] hey *MS*   [8] he] hey *MS*   [9] he] hey *MS*   [1] he] hey *MS*
[2] he'd] hey'd *MS*   [3] He'll] Hey'll *MS*
[4] marrying] marr'in' *MS 1* ⟨marr'ing⟩ marrying *8*
[5] marrying; and] marrying. And *MS*

may'st be quite deceived about Dinah; nay, I'm pretty sure, by words she said to me last Sabbath, as she's no mind to marry."

"Eh, thee't as contrairy as the rest on 'em. If it war summat I didna want, it 'ud be done fast enough."

Lisbeth rose from the bench at this, and went out of the workshop, leaving Seth in much anxiety lest she should disturb Adam's mind about Dinah. He consoled himself after a time with reflecting that, since Adam's trouble, Lisbeth had been very timid about speaking to him on matters of feeling[6], and that she would hardly dare to approach this tenderest of all subjects. Even if she did, he hoped Adam would not take much notice of what she said.

Seth was right in believing that Lisbeth would be held in restraint by timidity; and during the next three days, the intervals in which she had an opportunity of speaking to Adam were too rare and short to cause her any strong temptation. But in her long solitary hours she brooded over her regretful thoughts about Dinah, till they had grown very near that point of unmanageable strength[7] when thoughts are apt to take wing out of their secret nest[8] in a startling manner. And on Sunday morning, when Seth went away to chapel at Treddleston, the dangerous opportunity came.

Sunday morning was the happiest time in all the week to Lisbeth; for as there was no service at Hayslope church till the afternoon, Adam was always at home, doing nothing but reading, an occupation in which she could venture to interrupt him. Moreover, she had always a better dinner than usual to prepare for her sons—very frequently for Adam and herself alone, Seth being often away the entire day[9]; and the smell of the roast meat before the clear fire in the clean kitchen,[1] the clock ticking in a peaceful Sunday manner, her darling Adam seated near her in his best clothes, doing nothing very important, so that she could go and stroke her hand across his hair if she liked, and see him look up at her and smile, while Gyp, rather jealous, poked his muzzle up between them—all these things made poor Lisbeth's earthly paradise.

The book Adam most often read on a Sunday morning was his large pictured Bible,[2] and this morning it lay open before him on the round white deal table in the kitchen; for he sat there in spite of the fire, because he knew his mother liked[3] to have him with her, and it was the only day in the week when he could indulge her in that way. You would have liked to see Adam reading his Bible: he never opened it on a weekday, and so[4] he came to it as a

---

[6] to him on matters of feeling] *added in MS*   [7] strength] growth *MS*

[8] out of their secret nest] *added in MS*

[9] very frequently, for Adam & herself alone, Seth being often away the entire day] *added on verso of MS III. 193*

[1] kitchen, ⟨with⟩ the *MS*   [2] Bible, ⟨which he⟩ & *MS*   [3] liked ⟨it⟩ to *MS*

[4] so ⟨he read it with⟩ he came to *MS*

holiday book, serving him for history, biography, and poetry. He held one hand thrust between his waistcoat buttons, and the other ready to turn the pages; and in the course of the morning[5] you would have seen many changes in his face. Sometimes[6] his lips moved in semi-articulation—it was when he came to a speech that he could fancy himself uttering, such as Samuel's dying speech to the people; then his eyebrows would be raised, and the corners of his mouth would quiver a little with sad sympathy— something, perhaps old Isaac's meeting with his son, touched him closely;[7] at other times, over the New Testament, a very solemn look would come upon his face, and he would every now and then shake his head in serious assent, or just lift up his hand and let it fall again; and on some mornings, when he read in the Apocrypha, of which he was very fond, the son of Sirach's keen-edged words would bring a delighted smile, though he also enjoyed the freedom of occasionally differing from[8] an Apocryphal writer. For Adam knew the Articles quite well, as became a good Churchman.

Lisbeth, in the pauses of attending to her dinner, always sat opposite to him and watched him, till she could rest no longer without going up to him and giving him a caress, to call his attention to her. This morning he was reading the Gospel according to St Matthew, and Lisbeth had been standing close by him for some minutes, stroking his hair, which was smoother than usual this morning, and looking down at the large page with silent wonderment[9] at the mystery of letters. She was encouraged to continue this caress, because, when she first went up to him, he had thrown himself back in his chair to look at her affectionately and say, "Why, mother, thee look'st rare and hearty this morning. Eh, Gyp wants me t' look at him: he can't abide to think I love thee the best." Lisbeth said nothing, because she wanted to say so many things. [1]And now there was a new leaf to be turned over, and it was a picture—that of the angel seated on the great stone that has been rolled away from the sepulchre.[2] This picture had one strong association in Lisbeth's[3] memory, for she had been reminded of it when she first saw Dinah; and Adam had no sooner turned the page, and lifted the book sideways that they might look at the angel, than she said, "That's her—that's Dinah."

Adam smiled, and looking more intently at the angel's face, said,

"It *is* a bit like her; but Dinah's prettier, I think."

"Well, then, if thee think'st her so pretty, why arn't[4] fond on her?"

---

[5] the morning] one ⟨halfhour⟩ morning *MS*

[6] Sometimes, ⟨when he came to some passage⟩ his lips moved in semi-articulation *MS*

[7] closely; ⟨& on some mornings, when he read in the Apocrypha, of which he was very fond, the Son of Sirach's⟩ at other times, over the New Testament, a very solemn look would come ⟨over⟩ upon his face & he would every now *MS*

[8] from ⟨him, as⟩ an *MS*   [9] wonderment ⟨that⟩ at *MS*

[1] *Paragraph division added in MS.*   [2] sepulchre{.} ⟨, & the⟩ This *MS*

[3] Lisbeth's ⟨mind⟩ memory *MS*   [4] arn't] atn't *MS 1* ⟨atn't⟩ arn't *8*

[5]Adam looked up in surprise. "Why, mother, dost think I don't set store by Dinah?"

"Nay," said Lisbeth, frightened at her own courage, yet feeling that she had broken the ice, and the waters must flow, whatever mischief they might do. "What's th' use o' settin' store by things as are thirty mile off[6]? If thee wast fond enough on her, thee wouldstna let her go away."

"But I've no right t' hinder her, if she thinks well," said Adam, looking at his book as if he wanted to go on reading. He foresaw a series of complaints tending to nothing. Lisbeth sat down again in the chair opposite to him, as she said,

"But she wouldna think well if thee wastna so[7] contrary." Lisbeth dared[8] not venture beyond a vague phrase yet.

"Contrary, mother?" Adam said, looking up again in some anxiety. "What have I done? What dost mean?"

"Why, thee't never look at nothin', nor think o' nothin', but thy figurin' an' thy work," said Lisbeth, half crying. "An'[9] dost think thee canst go on so all thy life, as if thee wast a man cut out o' timber? An' what wut do when thy mother's gone, an' nobody to take care on thee as thee gett'st[1] a bit o' victual comfortable i' the mornin'?"

"What hast got i' thy mind, mother?" said Adam, vexed at this whimpering. "I canna see what thee't[2] driving at. Is there anything I could do for thee as I don't do?"

"Ay, an' that there is. Thee might'st do so as I should ha' somebody wi' me to comfort me a bit, an' wait on me when I'm bad, an' be good to me."

"Well, mother, whose fault is it there isna[3] some tidy body i' th' house t' help thee? It isna[4] by my wish as[5] thee hast a stroke o' work to do. We can afford it—I've told thee often enough. It 'ud be a deal better for us."

"Eh, what's th'[6] use o' talkin'[7] o' tidy bodies, when thee mean'st one o' th' wenches out o' th' village, or somebody from Treddles'on as I ne'er set eyes on i' my life? I'd sooner make a shift an' get into my own coffin afore I die, nor ha' them folks to put me in."

Adam was silent, and tried to go on reading. That was the utmost severity he could show towards his mother on a Sunday morning. But Lisbeth had gone too far now to check herself, and after scarcely a minute's quietness she began again.

"Thee mightst know well[8] enough who 'tis I'd like t' ha' wi' me. It isna many folks I send for t' come an' see me, I reckon. An' thee'st had the fetchin' on her times enow[9]."

---

[5] *Paragraph division added in MS.*   [6] off] aff *MS*   [7] so] soo *MS*

[8] dared] dare *MS*   [9] crying. "An'] crying, "An' *MS*   [1] gett'st] getst *MS*

[2] thee't] thee'rt *MS*   [3] isna] isn't *MS*   [4] isna] isn't *MS*   [5] as] that *MS*

[6] th'] *MS 1* the *8*   [7] talkin'] talking *Cabinet*

[8] well ⟨enough⟩ {anoogh} who ⟨it is⟩ 'tis *MS*   [9] enow] anoo *MS 1* ⟨anoo⟩ enow *8*

"[1]Thee mean'st Dinah, mother, I know," said Adam. "But it's no use setting thy mind on what can't be. If Dinah 'ud be willing to stay at Hayslope, it isn't likely she can come away from her aunt's house, where they hold her like a daughter, and where she's more bound than she is to us. If [2] it had been so that she could ha' married Seth, that 'ud ha' been a great blessing to us, but we can't have things just as we like in this life. Thee must try and make up thy mind to do without her."

"Nay, but I canna ma' up my mind, when she's just cut out for thee; an' nought shall ma' me believe as God didna make her an' send her there o' purpose for thee. What's it sinnify about her bein' a Methody? It 'ud happen wear out on her wi' marryin'."

Adam threw himself back in his chair and looked at his mother. He understood now what she had been aiming at from the beginning of the conversation. It was as unreasonable, impracticable a wish as she had ever urged, but he could not help being moved by so entirely new an idea. The chief point, however, was to chase away the notion from his mother's mind as quickly as possible.

"Mother," he said, gravely, "thee't talking wild. Don't let me hear thee say such things again. It's no good talking o' what can never be. Dinah's not for marrying; she's fixed her heart on a different sort o' life."

"Very like," said Lisbeth, impatiently, "very like she's none for marr'ing, when them as she'd be willin' t' marry wonna ax her. I shouldna[3] ha' been for marr'ing thy feyther if he'd ne'er axed me; an' she's as fond o' thee as e'er I war o' Thias, poor fellow."

The blood rushed to Adam's face, and for a few moments he was not quite conscious where he was: his mother and the kitchen had vanished for him, and he saw nothing but Dinah's face turned up towards his[4]. It seemed as if there were a resurrection of his dead joy. But he woke up very speedily from that dream (the waking was chill and sad); for it would have been very foolish in him to believe his mother's words; she could have no ground for them. He was prompted to express his disbelief very strongly—perhaps that he might call forth the proofs, if there were any to be offered.

"What dost say such things for, mother, when thee'st got no foundation for 'em? Thee know'st nothing as[5] gives thee a right to say that."

"Then I knowna nought as gi'es me a right to say as the[6] year's turned, for all I feel it[7] fust thing when I get up i' th' mornin'. She[8] isna fond o' Seth, I reckon, is she? She[9] doesna want to[1] marry *him*? But I can see as she doesna

[1] "⟨You mean{st}⟩ Thee mean'st *MS*   [2] If ⟨she'd⟩ it *MS*
[3] shouldna] shouldn' *MS*   [4] towards his] to him *MS*   [5] as] that *MS*
[6] the] th' *MS*   [7] it] 't *MS 1* ⟨'t⟩ it *8*   [8] She] She{y} *MS*
[9] She] She{y} *MS*   [1] to] t' *MS 1*

behave tow'rt thee as she does tow'rt Seth. She makes no more o' Seth's comin'[2] a-nigh her nor if he war Gyp, but she's all of a tremble when thee't a-sittin' down by her at breakfast, an' a-lookin'[3] at her. Thee think'st thy mother knows nought, but she war alive afore thee wast born."

"But thee canstna be sure as the trembling means love?" said Adam, anxiously.

"Eh, what else should it mane? It isna hate, I reckon. An' what should she do but love thee? Thee't made to be loved—for where's there a straighter, cliverer man? An' what's it sinnify her bein' a Methody? It's on'y the marigold[4] i' th'[5] parridge."

Adam had thrust his hands in his pockets, and was looking down at the book on the table, without seeing any of the letters. He was trembling like a[6] gold-seeker, who sees the strong promise of gold, but sees in the same moment a sickening vision of disappointment. He could not trust his mother's insight; she had seen what she wished to see. And yet—and yet, now the suggestion had been made to him, he remembered so many things, very slight things, like the stirring of the water by an imperceptible breeze, which seemed to him some confirmation of his mother's words.

Lisbeth noticed that he was moved. She went on:[7]

"An' thee't find out as thee't poorly aff when she's gone. Thee't fonder on her nor thee know'st. Thy eyes follow her about, welly as Gyp's follow thee."

Adam could sit still no longer. He rose, took down his hat, and went out into the fields.

The sunshine was on them: that early autumn sunshine which we should know was not summer's, even if there were not the touches of yellow on the lime and chesnut: the Sunday sunshine, too, which has more than autumnal calmness for the working man: the morning sunshine, which still leaves the dew-crystals on the fine gossamer webs in the shadow of the bushy hedgerows.

Adam needed the calm influence; he was amazed at the way in which this new thought of Dinah's love had taken possession of him, with an over-mastering power that made all other feelings give way before the impetuous desire to know that the thought was true. Strange, that till that moment the possibility of their ever being lovers had never crossed his mind, and yet now, all his longing suddenly went out towards that possibility; he had no more doubt or hesitation as to his own wishes than the bird that flies towards the opening through which the daylight gleams and the breath of heaven enters.

---

² comin'] *MS 1* coming *8*   ³ a-lookin'] *MS 1* a-looking *8*
⁴ the marigold] th' ⟨yarbs⟩ herbs *MS* th' marigold *1* ⟨th'⟩ the marigold *8*
⁵ th' ⟨porridge⟩ parridge *MS*   ⁶ a ⟨man who⟩ gold-seeker *MS*
⁷ on:] on. *MS 1* on—*Cabinet*

The autumnal Sunday[8] sunshine soothed him; but not by preparing him with resignation to the disappointment if his mother—if he himself,[9] proved to be mistaken about Dinah: it soothed him by gentle encouragement of his hopes. Her love was so like that calm sunshine that they seemed to make one presence to him, and he believed in them both alike. And Dinah was so bound up with the sad memories of his first passion, that he was not forsaking them, but rather giving them a new sacredness by loving her. Nay, his love for her had grown out of that past: it was the noon of that morning.

But Seth? Would the lad be hurt? Hardly;[1] for he had seemed quite contented of late, and there was no selfish jealousy in him; he had never been jealous of his mother's fondness for Adam. But had *he* seen anything of what their mother talked about? Adam longed to know this[2], for he thought he could trust Seth's observation better than his mother's. He must talk to Seth before he went to see Dinah; and, with this intention in his mind, he walked back to the cottage and said to his mother,

"Did Seth say anything to thee about when he was coming home? Will he be back to dinner?"[3]

"Ay, lad; he'll[4] be back for a wonder. He[5] isna gone to Treddles'on. He's[6] gone somewhere else a-preachin'[7] and[8] a-prayin'."

"Hast any notion which way he's gone?" said Adam.

"Nay, but he[9] aften goes to th' Common. Thee know'st more o's goings nor I do."

Adam wanted to go and meet Seth, but he must content himself with walking about the near fields and getting sight of him as soon as possible. That would not be for more than an hour to come, for Seth would scarcely be at home much before their dinner-time, which was twelve o'clock. But Adam could not sit down to his reading again, and he sauntered along by the brook and stood leaning against the stiles, with eager, intense eyes, which looked as if they saw something very vividly; but it was not the brook or the willows, not the fields or the sky. Again and again his vision was interrupted by wonder at the strength of his own feeling, at the strength and sweetness of this new love—almost like the wonder a man feels at the added power he finds in himself for an art which he had laid aside for a space. How is it that the poets have said so many fine things about our first love, so few about our later love? Are their first poems their best? or are not those the best which come from their fuller thought, their larger experience, their deeper-rooted affections?[1] The boy's flute-like voice has its own spring charm; but the man should yield a richer, deeper music.

[8] autumnal Sunday] *revised in MS from* Sunday autumnal
[9] himself ⟨were⟩ proved to be *MS*   [1] Hardly; ⟨Adam thought,⟩ for *MS*
[2] this] that *MS*   [3] dinner?"] dinner." *MS*   [4] he'll] hey'll *MS*
[5] He] Hey *MS*   [6] He's] Hey's *MS*   [7] a-preachin'] *MS 1* a-preachin', *8*
[8] and] an' *MS*   [9] he] he{y} *MS*
[1] affections? ⟨The first love is like⟩ ⟨t⟩The boy's flute-like voice ⟨& it⟩ has *MS*

At last, there was Seth, visible at the farthest stile, and Adam hastened to meet him. Seth was surprised, and thought something unusual must have happened: but when Adam came up, his face said plainly enough that it was nothing alarming.

"Where hast been?" said Adam, when they were side by side.

"I've been to the[2] Common," said Seth. "Dinah's been speaking the Word to a little company of hearers at Brimstone's, as they call him. They're folks as never go to church hardly—them on the Common—but they'll go and hear Dinah a bit. She's[3] been speaking with power this forenoon from the words, 'I came not to call the righteous, but sinners to repentance.' And there was a little thing happened as was pretty to see. The women mostly bring their children with 'em, but to-day there was one stout curly-headed fellow about three or four year old, that I never saw there before. He was as naughty as could be at the beginning while I was praying, and while we was[4] singing, but when we all sat down and Dinah began to speak, th' young un stood stock still all at once, and began to look at her with's mouth open, and presently he run[5] away from's mother and went up to Dinah, and pulled at her, like a little dog, for her to take notice of him. So Dinah lifted him up and held th' lad on her lap, while she went on speaking; and he was as good as could be till he went t'[6] sleep—and the mother cried to see him."

"It's a pity she shouldna[7] be a mother herself," said Adam, "so fond as the children are of her. Dost think she's quite fixed against marrying, Seth? Dost think nothing 'ud turn her?"

There was something peculiar in his brother's tone, which made Seth steal a glance at his face before he answered.

"It 'ud be wrong of me to say nothing 'ud turn her," he answered. "But if thee mean'st[8] it about myself, I've given up all thoughts as she can ever be *my* wife. She calls me her brother, and that's enough."

"But dost think she might ever get fond enough of anybody else to be willing to marry 'em?" said Adam, rather shyly.

"Well," said Seth,[9] after some hesitation, "it's crossed my mind some-times o' late as she might; but Dinah 'ud let no fondness for the creature draw her out o' the path as[1] she believed God had marked out for her[2]. If she thought the leading was not from Him, she's not one to be brought under the power of it. And she's[3] allays seemed clear[4] about that—as her[5] work was to minister t' others, and make no home for herself i' this world."

  [2] "I've been to the] "I've been to th' *MS 1* "⟨Ive⟩ I've been to ⟨th'⟩ the *8*
  [3] She's] And truly she's *MS*   [4] was] war *MS*   [5] run] ran *Cabinet*
  [6] t'] to *Cabinet*   [7] shouldna] shouldn't *MS*
  [8] mean'st ⟨, do I think she'd⟩ it about myself, *MS*
  [9] Seth, ⟨with⟩ after *MS*   [1] as] *added in MS*   [2] her] *added in MS*
  [3] she's ⟨always⟩ al'ays *MS*   [4] clear] *added in MS*
  [5] her ⟨heart was too full of her work for her t' marry. She spoke her mind about that to me only last Sabbath."⟩ work was to minister t' others⟨.⟩{,}⟨"⟩ and make no ⟨abiding place⟩ {home} for herself i' this world." *MS*

"But suppose," said Adam, earnestly, "suppose there was[6] a man as 'ud let her do just the same[7] and not interfere with her,—she might do a good deal o' what she does now, just as well when she was[8] married as when she was single. Other women of her sort have married—that's to say, not just[9] like her, but women[1] as preached and attended on the sick and needy. There's Mrs Fletcher as she talks of."

A new light had broken in on Seth. He turned round, and laying his hand on Adam's shoulder, said, "Why, wouldst[2] like her to marry *thee*, brother?"

Adam looked doubtfully at Seth's inquiring eyes, and said, "Wouldst be hurt if she was to be fonder o' me than o' thee?"

"Nay," said Seth, warmly, "how canst think it? Have I felt thy trouble so little, that[3] I shouldna feel thy joy?"

There was silence a few moments as they walked on,[4] and then Seth said, "[5]I'd no notion as thee'dst ever think of her for a wife."

"But is it o' any use to think of her?" said Adam—"what[6] dost say? Mother's[7] made me as I hardly know where I am, with what she's been saying to me this forenoon. She says she's sure Dinah feels for me more than common,[8] and 'ud be willing t' have me. But I'm afraid she speaks without book. I want to know if thee'st seen anything."

"It's a nice point to speak about," said Seth, "and I'm afraid o' being wrong; besides,[9] we've no right[1] t' intermeddle with people's feelings when they[2] wouldn't tell 'em themselves."

Seth paused.

"But thee mightst ask her," he said, presently. "She took no offence at *me*[3] for asking; and thee'st more right than I had, only thee't not in the Society. But Dinah doesn't hold wi' them as are for keeping the Society so strict to themselves. She doesn't mind about making folks[4] enter the Society, so as they're fit t' enter the kingdom o' God. Some o' the brethren at Treddles'on are displeased with her for that."

"Where will she be the rest o' the day?" said Adam.

"She said she shouldn't leave the Farm again to-day," said Seth, "because it's her last Sabbath there, and she's going t' read out o' the big Bible wi' the children."

Adam thought—but did not say—"Then I'll go this afternoon; for if I go to church, my thoughts 'ull be with her all the while. They must sing th' anthem without me to-day."

[6] was] wa *MS*   [7] same ⟨as she does now⟩, and *MS*

[8] when she was] *added in MS*   [9] just] *added in MS*   [1] women ⟨that⟩ as *MS*

[2] wouldst ⟨thee⟩ like {her} to *MS*   [3] that] as *MS*

[4] as they walked on,] *added in MS*   [5] "⟨But⟩ I'd *MS*

[6] Adam—"what] Adam. "What *MS*   [7] say? Mother's] say. Mother's *MS*

[8] common, ⟨"She's⟩ & 'ud *MS*   [9] besides,] besides as *MS*

[1] right t{'}⟨o meddle⟩ intermeddle *MS*   [2] they ⟨'ve never told⟩ wouldn't tell *MS*

[3] at *me*] with me, *MS*   [4] folks ⟨Methodists⟩ enter *MS*

CHAPTER LII.

ADAM AND DINAH.

It was about three o'clock when Adam entered the farm-yard and roused Alick and the dogs from their Sunday dozing. Alick said everybody was gone to church but "th' young missis"[1]—so he called Dinah; but this did not disappoint Adam, although the "everybody" was[2] so liberal[3] as to include Nancy,[4] the dairymaid, whose works of necessity were not unfrequently incompatible with church-going.

There was perfect stillness about the house: the doors were all closed, and the very stones and tubs seemed quieter than usual. Adam heard the water gently dripping from the pump—that was the only sound; and he knocked at the house-door rather softly, as was suitable in that stillness.

The door opened and Dinah stood before him, colouring deeply with the great surprise of seeing Adam at this hour, when she knew it was his regular practice to be at church. Yesterday he would have said to her without any difficulty, "I came to see you, Dinah: I knew the rest were not at home." But to-day something prevented him from saying that, and he put out his hand to her in silence. Neither of them spoke, and yet both wished they could speak, as Adam entered, and they sat down. Dinah took the chair she had just left; it was at the corner of the table near the window, and there was a book lying on the table, but it was not open: she had been sitting perfectly still, looking at the small bit of clear fire in the bright grate. Adam sat down opposite her, in Mr Poyser's three-cornered chair.

"Your mother is not ill again, I hope, Adam?" Dinah said, recovering herself. "Seth said she was well this morning."

"No, she's very hearty to-day," said Adam, happy in the signs of Dinah's feeling at the sight of him, but shy.

"There's nobody at home, you see," Dinah said; "but you'll wait. You've been hindered from going to church to-day, doubtless."

"Yes," Adam said, and then paused, before he added, "I was thinking about you: that was the reason."

This confession was very awkward and sudden, Adam felt; for he thought Dinah must understand all he meant. But the frankness of the words caused her immediately to interpret them into a renewal of his brotherly regrets that she was going away, and she answered calmly,

---

[1] but "th' young missis"] "but th' young missis" *Cabinet*   [2] was ⟨quite⟩ so *MS*
[3] liberal] literal *MS*   [4] Nancy,] *MS 1* Nancy *8*

"Do not be careful and troubled for me, Adam. I have all things and abound at Snowfield. And my mind is at rest, for I am not seeking my own will in going."

"But if things were different, Dinah," said Adam, hesitatingly—"if you knew things that perhaps you don't know now" . . .

Dinah looked at him inquiringly, but instead of going on, he[5] reached a chair and brought it near the corner of the table where she was sitting. She wondered, and was afraid—and the next moment her thoughts flew to the past: was it something about those distant unhappy ones that she didn't know?

Adam looked at her: it was so sweet to look at her eyes, which had now a self-forgetful questioning in them,—for[6] a moment he forgot that he wanted to say anything, or that[7] it was necessary to tell her what he meant.

"Dinah," he said suddenly, taking both her hands between his, "I love you with my whole heart and soul. I love you next to God who made me."

Dinah's lips became pale, like her cheeks, and she trembled violently under the shock of painful joy. Her hands were cold as death between Adam's. She could not draw them away, because he held them fast.

"Don't tell me you can't love me, Dinah. Don't tell me we must part, and pass our lives away from one another."

The tears were trembling in Dinah's eyes, and they fell before she could answer. But she spoke in a quiet low voice.

"Yes, dear Adam, we must submit to another Will. We must part."

"Not if you love me, Dinah—not if you love me," Adam said, passionately. "Tell me—tell me if you can love me better than a brother?"[8]

Dinah was too entirely reliant on the Supreme guidance[9] to attempt to achieve any end by a deceptive concealment. She was recovering now from the first shock of emotion, and she looked at Adam with simple sincere eyes as she said,

"Yes, Adam, my heart is drawn strongly towards you; and of my own will, if I had no clear showing to the contrary, I could find my happiness in being near you, and ministering to you continually. I fear I should forget to rejoice and weep with others; nay, I fear I should forget the Divine presence, and seek no love but yours."

Adam did not speak immediately. They sat looking at each other in delicious silence,—for the first sense of mutual love excludes other feelings; it will have the soul all to itself.

"Then, Dinah," Adam said at last, "how can there be anything contrary to what's right in our belonging to[1] one another, and spending our lives

---

[5] he ⟨searched⟩ reached *MS*   [6] them,—for] them, that, for *MS*
[7] anything, or that] anything, that *MS*   [8] brother?"] brother." *MS*
[9] Supreme guidance] divine will *MS* Divine will *1* ⟨Divine will⟩ Supreme guidance *8*
[1] to ⟨eac⟩ one *MS*

together? Who put this great love into our hearts? Can anything be holier
than that? For we can help one another in everything as is good.² I'd never
think o' putting myself between you and God³, and saying you oughtn't to
do this, and you oughtn't to do that. You'd follow your conscience as much
as you do now."

"Yes, Adam," Dinah said, "I know marriage is a holy state for those who
are truly called to it, and have no other drawing; but⁴ from my childhood
upward I have been led towards another path; all my peace and my joy have
come from having no life of my own, no wants, no wishes for myself, and
living only in God and those of his creatures whose sorrows and joys he has
given me to know. Those have been very blessed years to me, and I feel that⁵
if I was to listen to any voice that would draw me aside from that path, I
should⁶ be turning my back on the light that has shone upon me, and
darkness and doubt would take hold of me. We could not bless each other,
Adam, if there were doubts in my soul, and if I yearned, when it was too
late, after that better part which had once been given me and I had put⁷
away from me."

"But if a new feeling has come into your mind, Dinah, and if you love me
so as to be willing to be nearer to me than to other people, isn't that a sign
that⁸ it's right for you to change your life? Doesn't the love make it right
when nothing else would?"

"⁹Adam, my mind is full of questionings about that; for now, since you
tell me of your strong love towards me,¹ what was clear to me has become
dark again. I felt before that my heart was too strongly drawn towards
you, and that your heart was not as mine; and the thought of you had taken
hold of me, so that my soul had lost its freedom, and was becoming enslaved
to an earthly affection, which made me anxious and careful about what
should befall myself. For in all other affection I had been content with
any small return, or with none; but my heart was beginning to hunger after
an equal love from you. And I had no doubt² that I must wrestle against that
as a great temptation; and the command was clear that I must go away."

"But now, dear, dear Dinah, now you know I love you better than you
love me . . . it's all different now. You³ won't think o' going: you'll⁴ stay, and

² For we can help one another in everything as is good.] For we can ask God to be with us
continually, & we'll help one another in ⟨all that's⟩ {everything as is} good. *MS This sentence
appears in 1 to 8. It is deleted and replaced in 8 with* For we can help one another in everything as is
good.
³ God] your conscience *substituted for* God *and then cancelled in 8*.
⁴ drawing; but] drawing. But *MS*   ⁵ that ⟨I⟩ if *MS*   ⁶ I should] it would *MS*
⁷ put ⟨it⟩ away *MS*   ⁸ sign that] sign to you that *MS*
⁹ "⟨That is a question⟩ Adam, my mind *MS*
¹ me, ⟨things are not as⟩ what was clear *MS*
² doubt ⟨but⟩ that I must ⟨cast⟩ wrestle *MS*
³ now. You] now—you *MS*   ⁴ going: you'll] going? You'll *MS*

be my dear wife, and I shall thank God for[5] giving me my life[6] as I never thanked him before."

"Adam, it's hard to me to turn a deaf ear . . . you know it's hard; but[7] a great fear is upon me. It seems to me as if you were stretching out your arms to me, and beckoning me to come and take my ease, and live for my own delight, and Jesus, the Man of Sorrows, was standing looking towards me, and pointing to the sinful,[8] and suffering, and afflicted. I have seen that again and again when I have been sitting in stillness and darkness, and a great terror[9] has come upon me lest[1] I should become hard, and a lover of self, and no more bear willingly the Redeemer's cross."

Dinah had closed her eyes, and a faint shudder[2] went through her. "Adam," she went on, "you wouldn't[3] desire that we should seek a good through any unfaithfulness to the light that is in us; you wouldn't believe that could be a good. We are of one mind in that."

"Yes, Dinah," said Adam, sadly, "I'll never be the man t'[4] urge you against your conscience. But I can't give up the hope that you may come to see different. I don't believe your loving me could shut up your heart; it's only adding to what you've been before, not taking away from it; for[5] it seems to me[6] it's the same with love and happiness as with sorrow—the more we know of it the better we can feel what other people's lives are or might be, and so we shall only be more tender to 'em, and wishful to[7] help 'em. The more knowledge a man has, the[8] better he'll do's work; and feeling's a sort o' knowledge."

Dinah was silent; her eyes were fixed in contemplation of something visible only to herself. Adam went on presently with his pleading:[9]

"And you can do almost as much as you do now. I won't ask you to go to church with me of a Sunday; you shall go where you like among the people, and teach 'em; for though I like church best, I don't put my soul above yours, as if my words was[1] better for you to[2] follow than your own conscience. And you can help the sick just as much, and you'll have more means o' making 'em a bit comfortable; and[3] you'll be among all your own friends as love you, and can help[4] 'em and be a blessing to 'em till their dying day.[5] Surely, Dinah, you'd be as near to God as if you was[6] living lonely and away from me."

---

[5] for] *added in MS*   [6] me my life] me life *MS 1* me {my} life *8*
[7] hard; but] hard. But *MS*   [8] sinful ⟨& afflicted⟩ & suffering *MS*
[9] terror ⟨is⟩ has come *MS*   [1] lest ⟨my heart⟩ I *MS*   [2] shudder ⟨was⟩ went *MS*
[3] wouldn't] would not *MS*   [4] t'] to *MS*   [5] it; for] it. For *MS*
[6] me, ⟨the more we know o'⟩ it's the same with *MS*   [7] to] t' *MS*
[8] has, the] *MS* has the *1* has{,} the *8*   [9] pleading:] pleading. *MS*
[1] was] were *MS*   [2] to] t' *MS 1*
[3] comfortable; and] comfortable. And *MS*   [4] and can help] & help *MS*
[5] day. Sure{ly}, Dinah, ⟨that life would⟩ you'd *MS*   [6] was] were *MS 1* ⟨were⟩ was *8*

Dinah made no answer for some time. Adam was still holding her hands, and looking at her with almost trembling anxiety, when she turned her grave loving eyes on his, and said in rather a sad voice[7],

"Adam, there is truth in what you say, and there's[8] many of the brethren and sisters[9] who have greater strength than I have, and find their hearts enlarged by the cares of husband and kindred. But I have not faith that it would be so with me, for since my affections have been set above measure on you, I have had less peace and joy in God; I have felt as it were[1] a division in my heart. And think how it is with me, Adam:—that life I have led is like a land I have trodden in blessedness[2] since my childhood; and if I long for a moment to follow the voice which[3] calls me to another land that I know not, I cannot but fear that my soul might hereafter yearn for that early blessedness which I had forsaken; and[4] where doubt enters, there is not perfect love. I must wait for clearer guidance: I must go from you, and we must submit ourselves entirely to the Divine Will. We are sometimes required to lay our natural, lawful affections on the altar."

Adam dared not plead again, for Dinah's was not the voice of caprice or insincerity. But it was very hard for him; his eyes got dim as he looked at her.

"But you may come to feel satisfied . . . to feel that you may come to me again, and we may never part, Dinah?"

"We must submit ourselves, Adam. With time, our duty will be made clear.[5] It may be, when[6] I have entered on my former life, I shall find all[7] these new thoughts and wishes vanish[8], and become as things that were not. Then I shall know that my calling is not towards marriage. But we must wait."

"Dinah," said Adam, mournfully, "you can't love me so well as I love you, else you'd have no doubts. But it's natural you shouldn't; for I'm not so good as you. I can't doubt it's right for me to love the best thing God's ever given me to know."

"Nay, Adam; it seems to me that my love for you is not weak; for my heart waits on your words and looks, almost as a little child waits on the help and tenderness of the strong on whom it depends. If the thought of you took slight hold of me, I should not fear that it would be an idol in the temple. But you will strengthen me—you will not hinder me in seeking to obey to the uttermost."

[7] in rather a sad voice] in a pure, sad voice *MS*

[8] say, and there's] say. And there are *MS*

[9] the brethren and sisters] God's servants *MS 1* ⟨God's servants⟩ {children} ⟨children⟩ the brethren & sisters *8*

[1] were] *added in MS*   [2] blessedness ⟨all⟩ since *MS*   [3] which] that *MS*

[4] forsaken; and] forsaken. And *MS*   [5] clear. ⟨For⟩ It *MS*

[6] be, when] be that when *MS*   [7] find all] find that all *MS*

[8] wishes vanish] wishes will vanish *MS*

"Let us go out into the sunshine, Dinah, and walk together. I'll speak no word to disturb you."

They went out and walked towards the fields, where they would meet the[9] family coming from church. Adam said, "Take my arm, Dinah," and she took it.[1] That was the only change in their manner to each other since they were last walking together. But no sadness in the prospect of her going away—in the uncertainty of the issue—could rob the[2] sweetness from Adam's sense that Dinah loved him. He thought he would stay at the Hall Farm all that evening. He would be near her as long as he could.

"Heyday! there's[3] Adam along wi' Dinah," said Mr Poyser, as he opened the far gate into the Home Close. "I[4] couldna think how he happened away from church. Why," added good Martin, after a moment's pause, "what dost think has just jumped into my head?"

"Summat[5] as hadna[6] far to jump, for it's just under our nose. You mean as Adam's fond o' Dinah."

"Ay! hast[7] ever had any notion of it before?"

"To be sure I have," said Mrs Poyser, who always declined, if possible, to be taken by surprise. "I'm not one o' them[8] as can see the cat i' the dairy, an' wonder what she's come after."

"Thee never saidst a word to me about it."

"Well, I aren't[9] like a bird-clapper, forced to make a rattle when the wind blows on me. I can keep my own counsel when there's no good i' speaking."

"But Dinah 'll ha' none o' him; dost think she will?"

"Nay," said Mrs Poyser, not sufficiently on her guard against a possible surprise; "she'll never marry anybody, if he isn't a Methodist and a cripple."

"It 'ud ha' been a pretty thing though for 'em t' marry," said Martin, turning his head on one side, as if in pleased contemplation of his new idea. "Thee'dst ha' liked it too, wouldstna?"

"Ah! I should. I[1] should ha' been sure of her then, as she wouldn't go away from me to Snowfield, welly thirty mile[2] off, and me not got a creatur to look to, only neighbours, as are no kin to me, an' most of 'em women as I'd be ashamed to show my face, if my[3] dairy things war like their'n. There may well be streaky butter i' the market. An' I should be glad to see the poor thing settled like a Christian woman, with a house of her own over her head; and we'd stock her well wi' linen and feathers; for I love her next to my own children. An' she makes one feel safer when she's i' the house; for she's like the driven snow: anybody might sin for two as had her at their elbow."

9 the ⟨farm⟩ family *MS*   1 & she took it.] *added in MS*
2 the ⟨sense⟩ sweetness *MS*   3 "Heyday! there's] "Heyday, there's *MS*
4 Close. "I] Close, "I *MS*   5 Summat] Some 'at *MS*   6 hadna] hadn't *MS*
7 "Ay! hast] "Ay, hast *MS*   8 them] *MS* those *1 8*   9 aren't] arn't *MS*
1 "Ah! I should. I] "Ah⟨,⟩ {I should:} I *MS*   2 mile] miles *MS*   3 my] my *MS*

"Dinah," said Tommy, running forward to meet her, "mother says you'll never marry anybody but a Methodist cripple. What a silly you must be!" a comment which Tommy followed up by seizing Dinah with both arms, and dancing along by her side with incommodious fondness.

"Why, Adam, we missed you i' the singing to-day," said Mr Poyser. "How was it?"

"I wanted to see Dinah: she's going away so soon," said Adam.

"Ah, lad! can[4] you persuade her to stop somehow? Find her a good husband somewhere i' the parish. If[5] you'll do that, we'll forgive you for missing church. But, anyway, she isna going before the[6] harvest supper o' Wednesday, and you must come then. There's Bartle Massey comin',[7] an' happen Craig. You'll be sure an' come, now, at seven? The missis wunna[8] have it a bit later."

"Ay," said Adam, "I'll come, if I can. But I can't often say what I'll do beforehand, for the work often holds me[9] longer than I expect. You'll stay till the[1] end o' the week, Dinah?"

"Yes, yes!" said[2] Mr Poyser; "we'll have no nay."

"She's no call to be in a hurry," observed Mrs Poyser. "Scarceness o' victual 'ull keep: there's no need to be hasty[3] wi' the cooking. An' scarceness is what there's the biggest stock of i' that country."

Dinah smiled, but gave no promise to stay, and they talked of other things through the rest of the walk,[4] lingering in the sunshine to look at the great flock of geese grazing, at[5] the new corn-ricks, and at the surprising abundance of fruit on the old pear-tree; Nancy and Molly having already hastened home, side by side, each holding, carefully wrapped in her pocket-handkerchief, a prayer-book, in which[6] she could read little beyond the large letters and the Amens.

Surely all other leisure is hurry compared with a sunny walk through the fields from "afternoon church,"—as such walks used to be in those old leisurely times, when the boat, gliding sleepily along the canal, was the newest locomotive wonder; when Sunday books had most of them old brown-leather covers, and opened with remarkable precision always in one place. Leisure is gone—gone where the spinning-wheels are gone, and the pack-horses, and the slow waggons[7], and the pedlars who brought bargains to the door on sunny afternoons.[8] Ingenious philosophers tell you, perhaps, that the great work of the steam-engine is to create leisure for mankind. Do not believe them: it only creates a vacuum for eager thought to rush in.

---

[4] lad! can] lad, can *MS*   [5] parish. If] parish: if *MS*   [6] the] th' *MS 1*

[7] comin', ⟨&⟩ an' *MS*   [8] wunna] wonna *MS 1* ⟨wonna⟩ wunna *8*

[9] me] *added in MS*   [1] the] th' *MS*   [2] yes!" said] yes," said *MS*

[3] hasty] in a hurry *MS*   [4] walk, ⟨walking slowly⟩ lingering *MS*

[5] grazing, at] *MS 1* grazing{,} at *8*   [6] which ⟨they⟩ she *MS*

[7] and the slow waggons] *added in MS*   [8] afternoons. ⟨Do⟩ ⟨i⟩Ingenious *MS*

Even idleness is eager now—eager for amusement: prone to excursion-trains, art-museums, periodical literature, and exciting novels: prone even to scientific theorizing, and cursory peeps through microscopes. Old Leisure was quite a different personage: he[9] only read one newspaper, innocent of leaders, and was free from that periodicity of sensations which we call post-time. He[1] was a contemplative, rather stout gentleman, of excellent digestion,—of quiet perceptions, undiseased by hypothesis: happy in his inability to know the causes of things, preferring the things themselves. He lived chiefly in the country, among pleasant seats and homesteads, and was fond of sauntering by the fruit-tree wall, and scenting the apricots when they were warmed by the morning sunshine, or of sheltering himself under the orchard boughs at noon, when the summer pears were falling. He[2] knew nothing of weekday services, and thought none the worse of the Sunday sermon if it allowed him to sleep from the text to the blessing—liking the afternoon service best, because the prayers were the shortest, and not ashamed to say so; for[3] he had an easy, jolly con-science, broad-backed like himself, and able to carry a great deal of beer or port-wine,—not being made squeamish by doubts and qualms and lofty aspirations. Life was not a task to him but a sinecure: he fingered the guineas in his pocket, and ate his dinners, and slept the sleep of the irresponsible; for[4] had he not kept up his charter by going to church on the Sunday afternoons?

Fine old Leisure! Do not be severe upon him, and judge him by our modern standard: he never went to Exeter Hall, or heard a popular preacher, or read *Tracts for the Times*[5] or *Sartor Resartus*.

[9] personage: he] personage. He *MS*   [1] post-time. He] post time: he *MS*
[2] falling. He] falling; he *MS*   [3] so; for] so. For *MS*
[4] irresponsible; for] irresponsible. For *MS*
[5] *Tracts for the Times*] Tracts for the Times *MS*

CHAPTER LIII.

THE HARVEST SUPPER.

As Adam was going homewards, on Wednesday evening[1], in the six o'clock sunlight, he saw in the distance the last load of barley winding its way towards the yard-gate of the Hall Farm, and heard the chant of "Harvest Home!" rising and sinking like a wave. Fainter and fainter, and more musical through the growing distance, the falling, dying sound still reached him, as he neared the Willow Brook. The low westering sun shone right on the shoulders of the old Binton Hills, turning the unconscious sheep into bright spots of light; shone on the windows of the cottage too, and made them aflame with a glory beyond that of amber or amethyst. It was enough to make Adam feel that he was in a great temple, and that the distant chant was a sacred song.

"It's wonderful," he thought, "how that sound goes to one's heart almost like a funeral bell, for all it tells one o' the joyfullest time o' the year, and the time when men are mostly the thankfullest. I suppose it's a bit hard to us to think anything's over and gone in our lives; and there's a parting at the root of all our[2] joys. It's like what I feel about Dinah: I should never ha' come to know that her[3] love 'ud be the greatest o' blessings to me, if what I counted a blessing hadn't been wrenched and torn away from me, and left me with a greater need, so as I could crave and hunger for a greater and a better comfort."

He expected to see Dinah again this evening, and get leave to accompany her as far as Oakbourne; and then he would ask her to fix some time when he might go to Snowfield, and learn whether the last best hope that had been born to him must be resigned like the rest. The work he had to do at home, besides putting on his best clothes, made it[4] seven before he was on his way again to the Hall Farm, and it was questionable whether, with his longest and quickest strides, he should be there in time even[5] for the roast beef, which came after the plum-pudding; for Mrs Poyser's supper would be punctual.

Great was the clatter of knives and pewter plates and tin cans[6] when Adam entered the house[7], but there was no hum of voices to this accom-

---

[1] on Wednesday evening] *added in MS*   [2] our] wer *MS*
[3] know that her] know her *MS*   [4] it ⟨nearly⟩ seven *MS*
[5] there in time even] *revised in MS from* there even in time
[6] & tin cans] *added in MS*   [7] house] house-place *MS 1* ⟨house-place⟩ house *8*

paniment: the eating of excellent roast beef, provided free of expense, was too serious a business to those good farm-labourers to be performed with a divided attention, even if they had had anything to say to each other,—which they had not; and Mr Poyser, at the head of the table, was too busy with his carving to listen to Bartle Massey's or Mr Craig's ready talk.

"Here, Adam," said Mrs Poyser, who was standing and looking on to see that Molly and Nancy did their duty as waiters, "here's a place kept for you between Mr Massey and the boys. It's a poor tale you couldn't come to see the pudding when it was whole."

Adam looked anxiously round for a fourth woman's figure; but Dinah was not there. He was almost afraid of asking about her; besides, his attention was claimed by greetings, and there remained the hope that Dinah was in the house, though perhaps disinclined to festivities on the eve of her departure.

It was a goodly sight—that table, with Martin Poyser's round good-humoured face and large person[8] at the head of it, helping his servants to the fragrant roast beef, and pleased when the empty plates came again. Martin, though usually blest with a good appetite, really forgot to finish his own beef to-night—it was so pleasant to him to look on in the intervals of carving, and see how the others enjoyed their supper; for[9] were they not men who, on all the days of the year except Christmas Day and Sundays, ate their cold[1] dinner, in a make-shift manner, under the hedgerows, and drank their beer out of wooden bottles—with relish certainly, but with their mouths towards the zenith, after a fashion more endurable to ducks than to human bipeds. Martin Poyser had some faint conception of the flavour such men must find in hot roast beef and fresh-drawn ale. He held his head on one side, and screwed up his mouth, as he nudged Bartle Massey, and watched half-witted Tom Tholer, otherwise known as "Tom Saft," receiving his second plateful of beef. A[2] grin of delight broke[3] over Tom's face as the plate was set down before him, between his knife and fork, which he held erect, as if they had been sacred tapers; but the delight was too strong to continue smouldering in a grin—it burst out the next instant in a long-drawn "haw, haw!" followed by a sudden collapse into utter gravity, as the knife and fork darted down on the prey. Martin Poyser's large person shook with his silent unctuous laugh: he[4] turned towards Mrs Poyser to see if she, too, had been observant of Tom, and the eyes of husband and wife met in a glance of good-natured amusement.

"Tom Saft" was a great favourite on the farm, where he played the part of the old jester,[5] and made up for his practical deficiencies by his[6] success

---

[8] & large person] *added in MS*   [9] supper; for] supper. For *MS*
[1] cold] *added in MS*   [2] beef. A] beef: a *MS*   [3] broke ⟨out⟩ over *MS*
[4] he ⟨looked⟩ turned *MS*   [5] jester, ⟨making⟩ & made *MS*
[6] his ⟨skill⟩ success *MS*

in repartee. His hits, I imagine, were those of the flail, which falls quite at random, but nevertheless smashes an insect now and then. They were much quoted at sheep-shearing and haymaking times; but I refrain from recording them here, lest Tom's wit should prove to be like that of many other bygone jesters eminent in their day—rather of a temporary nature, not dealing with the deeper and more lasting relations of things.

Tom excepted, Martin Poyser had some pride in his servants and labourers, thinking with satisfaction that they were the best worth their pay of any set on the estate. There was[7] Kester Bale, for example (Beale, probably, if the truth were known, but he was called Bale, and was not conscious of any claim to a fifth letter),—the old man with the close leather cap, and the network of wrinkles on his sun-browned face. Was there any man in Loamshire who knew better the "natur" of all farming work? He was one[8] of those invaluable labourers who can not only turn their hand to everything, but excel in everything they turn their hand to. It is true Kester's knees were much bent outward by this time, and he walked with a perpetual curtsy, as if he were among the most reverent of men. And so he was; but I am obliged to admit that the object of his reverence was his own skill,[9] towards which he performed some rather affecting acts of worship. He always thatched the ricks; for if anything were his forte more than another, it was thatching; and when the last touch had been put to the last beehive rick, Kester, whose home lay at some distance from the farm, would take a walk to the rick-yard[1] in his best clothes on a Sunday morning, and stand in the lane, at a due distance, to contemplate his own thatching,—walking about to get each rick[2] from the proper point of view. As he curtsied along, with his eyes upturned to the straw knobs imitative of golden globes at the summits of[3] the beehive ricks, which indeed were gold of the best sort, you might have imagined him to be engaged in some pagan act of adoration. Kester was an old bachelor, and reputed to have stockings full of coin, concerning which his master cracked a joke with him every pay-night: not a[4] new, unseasoned joke, but a good old one, that had been tried many times before, and had worn[5] well.[6] "Th' young measter's a merry mon," Kester frequently remarked; for[7] having begun his career by frightening away the crows under the last Martin Poyser but one, he could never cease to account the reigning Martin a young master. I am not ashamed of commemorating old Kester: you and I are indebted to the hard hands of such men—hands that have long ago mingled with the soil

[7] was ⟨old⟩ Kester MS
[8] work? He was one] work? One MS 1 work? {He was} ⟨O⟩one 8
[9] skill, to{wards} which MS   [1] to the rick-yard] added in MS
[2] rick ⟨at⟩ from MS   [3] of ⟨each⟩ the beehive rick{s}, which MS
[4] a ⟨ready⟩ new MS   [5] and had worn] & worn MS
[6] well. "Th{'} young measter{'s} ⟨was a⟩ {a} merry MS
[7] for ⟨so he always called the present⟩ having begun his career by frightening MS

they tilled so faithfully, thriftily making the best they could of the earth's fruits, and receiving the smallest share as their own wages.

Then, at the end of the table, opposite his master, there was Alick, the shepherd and head man, with the ruddy face and broad shoulders, not on the best terms with old Kester: indeed, their intercourse was confined to an occasional snarl, for though they probably differed little concerning hedging and ditching and the treatment of ewes, there was a profound difference of opinion between them as to their own respective merits. When Tityrus and Melibœus happen to be on the same farm, they are not sentimentally polite to each other. Alick, indeed, was not by any means a honeyed man:[8] his speech had usually something of a snarl in it, and his broad-shouldered aspect something of the bull-dog expression—"Don't you meddle with me, and I won't meddle with you;" but he was honest even to the splitting of an oat-grain rather than he would take beyond his acknowledged share, and[9] as "close-fisted" with his master's property as if it had been his own,—throwing very small handfuls of damaged barley to the chickens, because a large handful affected his imagination painfully with a sense of profusion. Good-tempered Tim, the waggoner, who loved his horses,[1] had his grudge against Alick in the matter of corn: they rarely spoke to each other, and never looked at each other, even over their dish of cold potatoes; but then, as this was their usual mode of behaviour towards all mankind, it would be an[2] unsafe conclusion that[3] they had more than transient fits of unfriendliness. The bucolic character at Hayslope, you perceive, was not of that entirely genial, merry, broad-grinning sort, apparently observed[4] in most districts visited by artists. The mild radiance of a smile was a rare sight on a field-labourer's face, and there was seldom any gradation between bovine gravity and a laugh. Nor was every labourer so honest as our friend Alick. At this very table, among Mr Poyser's men, there is that big[5] Ben Tholoway, a very powerful thresher, but detected more than once in carrying away his master's corn in his pockets: an action which, as Ben was not a philosopher, could hardly be ascribed to absence of mind.[6] However, his master had forgiven him, and continued to employ him; for the Tholoways had lived on the Common, time out of mind, and had always worked for the Poysers. And on the whole, I dare say, society was not much the worse because Ben had not six months of it at the

[8] man; ⟨but⟩ his MS

[9] than he would take beyond his acknowledged share, and] than {he would} ⟨he would⟩ take ⟨more than⟩ beyond his ⟨avowed⟩ acknowledged share{,} ⟨of things⟩ & MS than take beyond his acknowledged share, and 1 than {he would} take beyond his acknowledged share, and 8

[1] horses{,} ⟨so well that⟩ had his grudge MS   [2] an] added in MS

[3] that ⟨their⟩ they MS   [4] observed ⟨by⟩ in MS   [5] that big] added in MS

[6] mind{:} ⟨, & in those days when to steal by grains was not sufficiently understood⟩ however, his master had forgiven him & continued to employ him, for MS

treadmill; for[7] his views of depredation were narrow, and the House of Correction might have enlarged them. As it was, Ben ate his roast beef to-night with a serene sense of having stolen nothing more than a few peas and beans, as seed for his garden, since the last harvest supper, and felt warranted in thinking that Alick's suspicious eye, for ever upon him, was an injury to his innocence.

But *now* the roast beef was finished and the cloth was drawn, leaving a fair large deal table for the bright drinking-cans, and the foaming brown jugs, and the bright[8] brass candlesticks, pleasant to behold. *Now*, the great ceremony of the evening was to begin—the harvest song, in which every man must join: he might be in tune, if he liked to be singular, but he must not sit with closed lips. The movement[9] was obliged to be in triple time; the rest was *ad libitum*.

As to the origin of this song—whether it came in its actual state from the brain of a single rhapsodist, or was gradually perfected by a school or succession of rhapsodists, I am ignorant. There is a stamp of unity, of individual genius, upon it, which inclines me to the former hypothesis, though I am not blind to the consideration that this[1] unity may rather have arisen from that consensus of many minds which was a condition of primitive thought, foreign to our modern consciousness. Some will perhaps think that they detect in the first quatrain an indication of a lost line, which later rhapsodists, failing in[2] imaginative vigour, have supplied[3] by the feeble device of iteration: others, however, may rather maintain that this very iteration is an original felicity, to which none but the most prosaic minds can be insensible.

The ceremony connected with the song was a drinking ceremony. (That is perhaps a painful fact, but then, you know, we cannot reform our forefathers.) During the first and second quatrain, sung decidedly *forte*, no can was filled.

"Here's a health unto our master,
    The founder of the feast;
Here's a health unto our master
    And to our mistress!

And may his doings prosper
    Whate'er he takes in hand,
For we are all his servants,
    And are at his command."

But now, immediately before the third quatrain or chorus, sung *fortissimo*, with emphatic raps of the table, which gave the effect of cymbals and drum

[7] for ⟨Ben's⟩ his *MS*   [8] bright] *added in MS*
[9] movement ⟨must be⟩ was obliged to be *MS*
[1] this ⟨very⟩ unity *MS*   [2] in ⟨imagination⟩ imaginative vigour *MS*
[3] supplied ⟨with⟩ by *MS*

together, Alick's can was filled, and he was bound to empty it before the chorus ceased.

"Then drink, boys, drink!
And see ye do not spill,
For if ye do, ye shall drink two,
For 'tis[4] our master's will."

When Alick had gone[5] successfully through this test of steady-handed manliness, it was the turn of old Kester, at his right hand,—and so on, till every man had drunk his initiatory pint under the stimulus of the chorus. Tom Saft—the rogue—took care to spill a little by accident; but Mrs Poyser[6] (too officiously, Tom thought) interfered to prevent the exaction of the penalty.

To any listener outside the door it would have been the reverse of obvious why the "Drink, boys, drink!" should have such an immediate and often-repeated encore; but once entered, he would have seen that all faces were at present sober, and most of them serious: it was the regular and respectable thing for those excellent farm-labourers to do, as much as for elegant ladies and gentlemen to smirk and bow over their wine-glasses. Bartle Massey, whose ears were rather sensitive, had gone out to see what sort of evening it was, at an early stage in the ceremony; and had not finished his contemplation until a silence of five minutes declared that "Drink, boys, drink!" was not likely to begin again for the next twelvemonth. Much to the regret of the boys and Totty:[7] on them the stillness fell rather flat, after that glorious thumping of the table, towards which Totty, seated on her father's knee, contributed with her small might and small fist.

When Bartle re-entered, however, there appeared to be a general desire for solo music after the choral. Nancy declared that Tim the waggoner knew a song, and was "allays[8] singing like a lark i' the stable;" whereupon Mr Poyser said encouragingly, "Come, Tim, lad, let's hear it." Tim looked sheepish, tucked down his head, and said he couldn't sing; but this encouraging invitation of the master's was echoed all round the table. It[9] was a conversational opportunity: everybody could say "Come, Tim,"— except Alick, who never relaxed into the frivolity of unnecessary speech. At last, Tim's next neighbour, Ben Tholoway, began to give emphasis to his speech by nudges, at which Tim, growing rather savage, said, "Let me alooan, will ye? else I'll ma' ye sing a[1] toon ye wonna like." A good-tempered waggoner's patience has limits, and Tim was not to be urged further.

---

[4] 'tis] it is *MS*   [5] gone] *added in MS*
[6] Poyser, ⟨who considered Tom's sobriety was in her charge⟩ (too officiously, Tom thought) interfered to prevent the exaction *MS*
[7] Totty{:} ⟨, to whom⟩ on them *MS*   [8] allays] al'ays *MS*
[9] table. It] table; it *MS 1* ⟨table; it⟩ table. It *8*   [1] a ⟨song⟩ ⟨tune⟩ toon *MS*

"Well, then, David, ye're the lad to sing," said Ben, willing to show that he was not discomfited by this check. "Sing 'My[2] loove's a roos wi'out a thorn.'"

The amatory David was a young man of an unconscious abstracted expression, which was due probably to a squint of superior intensity rather than to any mental characteristic; for he was not[3] indifferent to Ben's invitation, but blushed and laughed and rubbed his sleeve over his mouth in a way that was regarded as a symptom of yielding. And for some time the company appeared to be much in earnest about the desire to hear David's song. But in vain. The lyrism of the evening was in the cellar at present, and was not to be drawn from that retreat just yet.

Meanwhile the conversation at the head of the table had taken a political turn. Mr Craig was not above talking politics occasionally, though he piqued himself rather on a wise insight than on specific information. He saw so far beyond the mere facts of a case, that really it was superfluous to know them.

"I'm no reader o' the paper myself," he observed to-night, as he filled his pipe,[4] "though I might read it fast enough if I liked, for there's Miss Lyddy has 'em,[5] and 's done with 'em i' no time; but there's Mills, now, sits i' the chimney-corner[6] and reads the paper pretty nigh from morning to night, and when he's got to th' end on't he's more addleheaded than he was at the beginning. He's full o' this peace now, as they talk on; he's[7] been reading and reading, and thinks he's got to the bottom on't. 'Why, Lor' bless you, Mills,' says I, 'you see no more into this thing nor you can see into the middle of a potato. I'll tell you what it is: you think it'll be a fine thing for the country; and I'm not again' it—mark my words—I'm not again' it. But it's my opinion as there's them at th'[8] head o' this country as are worse enemies to[9] us nor Bony and all the mounseers he's got at 's back; for as for the mounseers, you may skewer half-a-dozen of 'em at once as if they war frogs.'"

"Ay, ay," said Martin Poyser, listening with an air of much intelligence and edification, "they ne'er ate a bit o' beef i' their lives. Mostly sallet, I reckon."

"And says I to Mills," continued Mr Craig, "'will[1] *you* try to make me believe as furriners like them can do us half th' harm them ministers do with[2] their bad government? If King George 'ud turn 'em all away and govern by himself, he'd see everything righted. He might take on Billy Pitt again if he liked; but I don't see myself what we want wi' anybody besides

[2] My] M' *MS* 1 ⟨M'⟩ My 8   [3] not ⟨untouched by⟩ indifferent to *MS*
[4] as he filled his pipe,] *added in MS*   [5] 'em, an⟨'⟩{d} 's *MS*
[6] chimney corner an⟨'⟩{d} reads *MS*   [7] on; he's] on—{he}'s *MS*
[8] th'] the *Cabinet*   [9] to] t' *MS* 1 ⟨t'⟩ to 8   [1] will] Ull *MS* Will *Cabinet*
[2] with] wi' *MS*

King and Parliament. It's that nest o' ministers does the mischief, I tell you.' "

"Ah, it's fine talking," observed Mrs Poyser, who was now seated near her husband, with Totty on her lap—"it's fine talking. It's hard work to tell which is Old Harry when everybody's got boots on."

"As for this peace," said Mr Poyser, turning his head on one side in a dubitative manner, and giving a precautionary puff to his pipe between each sentence,[3] "I don't know. Th'[4] war's a fine thing for the country, an' how'll you keep up prices wi'out it? An' them French are a wicked sort o' folks, by what I can make out; what can you do better nor fight 'em?"

"[5]Ye're partly right there, Poyser," said Mr Craig, "but I'm not again' the peace—to make a holiday for a bit. We can break it when we like, an' *I'm* in[6] no fear o' Bony, for all they talk so much o' his[7] cliverness. That's what I says to Mills this morning. Lor' bless you, he sees no more through Bony! . . . why, I put him up to more in three minutes than he gets from 's paper[8] all the year round. Says I, 'Am I a gardener as knows his business, or arn't I, Mills? answer me that.' 'To be sure y' are, Craig,' says he—he's not a bad fellow, Mills isn't, for a butler, but weak i' the[9] head. 'Well,' says I, 'you talk o' Bony's cliverness; would[1] it be any use my being a first-rate[2] gardener if I'd got nought but a quagmire to work on?' 'No,' says he. 'Well,' I says, 'that's just what it is wi' Bony. I'll not deny but he may be a bit cliver—he's no Frenchman born, as I understand[3]; but[4] what's he got at's back but mounseers?' "

Mr Craig paused a moment with an emphatic stare after this triumphant specimen of Socratic argument, and then added, thumping the table rather fiercely,

"Why, it's a sure thing—and there's them 'ull bear witness to't—as i' one regiment where there was[5] one man a-missing, they put the regimentals on a big monkey, and they fit him as the shell fits the walnut, and you couldn't tell the monkey from the mounseers!"

"Ah! think[6] o' that, now!" said Mr Poyser, impressed at once with the political bearings of the fact, and with its striking interest as an anecdote in natural history.

"Come, Craig," said Adam, "that's a little too strong. You don't believe that. It's all nonsense about the French being such poor sticks. Mr Irwine's seen 'em in their own country, and he says they've plenty o' fine fellows among 'em. And as for knowledge, and contrivances, and manifactures[7],

---

[3] & giving a precautionary puff to his pipe between each sentence,] *added in MS*
[4] Th'] The *MS*   [5] "⟨You're⟩ Ye're *MS*   [6] *I'm* in] I'm i' *MS*
[7] o' his] o's *MS*   [8] paper] papers *MS*   [9] the] th' *M̄S 1*
[1] cliverness; would] cliverness. Would *MS*   [2] first-rate] fust-rate *MS*
[3] as I understand] *added in MS*   [4] understand; but] understand. But *MS*
[5] was ⟨a⟩ one {man} a-missing *MS*   [6] "Ah! think] "Ah, think *MS*
[7] manifactures] manufactures *Cabinet*

there's a many things as we're a fine sight behind 'em in. It's poor foolishness to run down your enemies. Why[8], Nelson and the rest of 'em 'ud have no merit i' beating 'em, if they were[9] such offal as folks pretend."

Mr Poyser looked doubtfully at Mr Craig, puzzled by this opposition of authorities. Mr Irwine's[1] testimony was not to be disputed; but, on the other hand, Craig was a knowing fellow, and his view was less startling. Martin had never "heard tell" of the French being good for much. Mr Craig had found no answer but such as was implied in taking a long draught of ale, and then looking down[2] fixedly at the proportions of his own leg, which he turned a little outward for that purpose[3], when Bartle Massey returned from the fire-place, where he had been smoking his first pipe in quiet, and broke the silence by saying, as he thrust his forefinger into the canister,

"Why, Adam, how happened you not to be at church on Sunday? answer[4] me that, you rascal. The anthem went limping without you. Are you going to disgrace your schoolmaster in his old age?"

"No, Mr Massey," said Adam. "Mr and Mrs Poyser can tell you where I was. I was in no bad company."

"She's gone, Adam—gone to Snowfield," said Mr Poyser, reminded of Dinah for the first time this evening. "I thought you'd ha' persuaded her better. Nought 'ud hold her, but she must go yesterday forenoon. The missis has hardly got over it. I[5] thought she'd ha' no sperrit for th' harvest supper."

Mrs Poyser had thought of Dinah several times since Adam had come in, but she had had "no heart" to mention the bad news.

"What!" said Bartle, with an air of disgust. "Was[6] there a woman concerned? Then I give you[7] up, Adam."

"But it's a woman you'n spoke well on, Bartle," said Mr Poyser. "Come, now, you canna draw back; you[8] said once as women wouldna ha' been a bad invention if they'd all been like Dinah."

"I meant her voice, man—I meant her voice, that was all," said Bartle. "I can bear to hear her speak without wanting to put wool in my ears.[9] As for other things, I dare say she's like the rest o' the women—thinks two and two'll come to make five, if she cries and bothers enough about it."

"Ay, ay!'" said Mrs Poyser; "one 'ud think, an' hear some folks talk, as the men war 'cute enough to count the corns in a bag o' wheat wi' only

[8] enemies. Why] enemies: why *MS*   [9] were] war *MS*
[1] Irwine's ⟨evidence⟩ testimony *MS*   [2] down] *added in MS*
[3] which he turned a little outward for that purpose] *added in MS*
[4] Sunday? answer] Sunday? Answer *MS*   [5] it. I] it: I *MS*
[6] disgust. "Was] disgust, "Was *MS*   [7] you] y' *MS*
[8] back; you] back. You *MS*
[9] ears. ⟨Her voice isn't quite so much like a creaking hinge as most.⟩ As *MS*
[1] ay!] ay, *MS*

smelling at it. They can see through a barn-door, *they* can. Perhaps[2] that's the reason they can see so little o' this side on't."

Martin Poyser shook with delighted laughter, and winked at Adam, as much as to say the schoolmaster was in for it now.

"Ah!"[3] said Bartle, sneeringly, "the women are quick enough—they're quick enough. They know the rights of a story before they hear it, and can tell a man what his thoughts are before he knows 'em himself."

"Like enough," said Mrs Poyser; "for the men are mostly so slow, their thoughts overrun 'em, an' they can only catch 'em by the tail. I can count a stocking-top[4] while a man's getting's tongue ready; an' when he outs wi' his speech at last, there's little broth to be made on't. It's your dead chicks take the longest hatchin'. Howiver, I'm not denyin' the women are foolish: God Almighty[5] made 'em to match the men."

"Match!"[6] said Bartle; "ay, as vinegar matches one's teeth. If a man says a word, his wife'll match it with a contradiction; if he's a mind for hot[7] meat, his wife'll match it with cold bacon; if he laughs, she'll match him with whimpering. She's such a match as the[8] horse-fly is to th' horse: she's got the right venom to sting him with—the right venom to sting him with."

"Yes[9]," said Mrs Poyser, "I know what the men like—a poor soft, as 'ud simper at 'em like the pictur o' the sun, whether they did right or wrong, an' say thank you for a kick, an' pretend she didna know which end she stood uppermost, till her husband told her. That's what a man wants in a wife, mostly: he wants to make sure o' one fool as 'ull[1] tell him he's wise. But there's some men can do wi'out that—they think so much o' themselves a'ready; an' that's[2] how it is there's old bachelors."

"Come, Craig," said Mr Poyser, jocosely, "you mun get married pretty quick, else you'll be set down for an old bachelor; an' you see what the women 'ull think on you."

"Well," said Mr Craig, willing to conciliate Mrs Poyser, and setting a high value on his own compliments, "*I* like a cleverish[3] woman—a woman o' sperrit—a managing woman."

"You're out there, Craig," said Bartle, dryly; "you're out there. You judge o' your garden-stuff on a better plan than that: you pick the things for what they can excel in—for what they can excel in. You[4] don't value[5] your peas for their roots, or your carrots for their flowers. Now, that's the way you should choose women: their cleverness 'll never come to much—never come to much; but they make excellent simpletons, ripe and strong-flavoured."

---

[2] can. Perhaps] can: perhaps *MS*   [3] "Ah!"] "Ah," *MS*
[4] stocking ⟨& in⟩ top *MS*   [5] Almighty] Amighty *MS*
[6] "Match!"] "Match?" *MS*   [7] hot] cold *MS*   [8] the] th' *MS*
[9] Yes] Yis *MS*   [1] 'ull] 'll *MS 1*   [2] that's ⟨the reason⟩ how *MS*
[3] cleverish] cliverish *MS*   [4] in. You] in: you *MS*   [5] value] vally *MS*

"What dost say to that?" said Mr Poyser, throwing himself back and looking merrily at his wife.

"Say!" answered[6] Mrs Poyser, with dangerous fire kindling in her eye; "why[7], I say as some folks'[8] tongues are like the clocks as run on strikin', not to tell you the time o' the day, but because there's summat[9] wrong i' their own inside" ...

Mrs Poyser would probably have brought her rejoinder to a further climax, if every one's attention had not at this moment been called to the other end of the table, where the lyrism, which had at first only manifested itself by David's *sotto voce* performance of "My love's a rose without a thorn," had gradually assumed a rather deafening and complex character. Tim, thinking slightly of David's vocalization, was impelled to supersede that feeble buzz by a spirited commencement of "Three Merry Mowers;" but David was not to be put down so easily, and showed himself capable of a copious crescendo, which[1] was rendering it doubtful whether the rose would not predominate over the mowers, when old Kester, with an entirely unmoved and immovable aspect, suddenly set up a quavering treble,—as if he had been an alarum, and the time was come for him to go off.

The company at Alick's end of the table took this form of vocal entertainment very much as a matter of course, being free from musical prejudices; but Bartle Massey laid down his pipe and put his fingers in his ears; and Adam, who had been longing to go, ever since he had heard Dinah was not in the house, rose and said he must bid good-night.

"I'll go with you, lad," said Bartle; "I'll[2] go with you before my ears are split."

"I'll go round by the Common, and see you home, if you like, Mr Massey," said Adam.

"Ay, ay!" said[3] Bartle; "then[4] we can have a bit o' talk together. I never get hold of you now."

"Eh! it's[5] a pity but you'd sit it out," said Martin Poyser. "They'll all go soon; for th' missis niver lets 'em stay past ten."

But Adam was resolute, so the good-nights were said, and the two friends turned out on their starlight walk together.

"There's that poor fool, Vixen, whimpering for me at home," said Bartle. "I can never bring her here with me for fear she should be struck with Mrs Poyser's eye, and the poor bitch might go limping for ever after."

"I've never any need to drive Gyp back," said Adam, laughing. "He always turns back of his own head when he finds out I'm coming here."

---

   [6] "Say!" answered] "Say?" answered *MS*   [7] eye; "why] eye, "Why *MS*

   [8] folks'] folks's *MS*   [9] summat] some'at *MS*   [1] which ⟨lef⟩ was *MS*

   [2] Bartle; "I'll] Bartle. "I'll *MS*   [3] ay!" said] ay," said *MS*

   [4] Bartle; "then] Bartle. "Then *MS*   [5] "Eh! it's] "Eh, it's *MS*

"Ay, ay," said[6] Bartle. "A terrible woman!—[7]made of needles—made of needles. But I stick to Martin—I shall always stick to Martin. And he likes the needles, God help him! He's[8] a cushion made on purpose for 'em."[9]

"But she's a downright good-natur'd[1] woman, for all that," said Adam, "and as true as the daylight. She's a bit cross wi' the dogs when they offer to come in th' house, but if they depended on her, she'd take care and have 'em well fed. If her tongue's keen, her heart's tender: I've seen that in times o' trouble. She's one o' those women as are better than their word."

"Well, well," said Bartle, "I don't say th' apple isn't sound at the core; but it sets my teeth on edge, it sets my teeth on edge."

[6] ay," said] ay!" said *1*
[7] Bartle. "A terrible woman!—] Bartle, "a terrable woman— *MS*
[8] him! He's] him: he's *MS*
[9] *Chapter LIII ends here in MS; the final two paragraphs were added in the first edition.*
[1] good-natur'd] good-natured *1* ⟨good-natured⟩ good-natur'd *8*

CHAPTER LIV.

THE MEETING ON THE HILL.

Adam understood Dinah's haste to go away, and drew hope rather than discouragement from it. She was fearful lest the strength of her feeling towards him should hinder her from waiting and listening faithfully for the ultimate guiding voice from within.

"I wish I'd asked her to write to me, though," he thought. "And yet even that might disturb her a bit, perhaps. She wants to be quite quiet in her old way for a while. And I've no right to be impatient and interrupting her with my wishes. She's told me what her mind is; and she's not a woman to say one thing and mean another. I'll wait patiently."

That was Adam's wise resolution, and it throve excellently for the first two or three weeks on the nourishment it got from the remembrance of Dinah's confession that Sunday afternoon. There is a wonderful amount of sustenance in the first few words of love. But towards the middle of October the resolution began to dwindle perceptibly, and showed dangerous symptoms of exhaustion. The weeks were unusually long: Dinah must surely have had more than enough time to make up her mind. Let a woman say what she will after she has once told a man that she loves him, he is a little too[1] flushed and exalted with that first draught she offers him to care much about the taste of the second: he treads the earth with[2] a very elastic step as he walks away from her, and makes light of all difficulties. But that sort of glow dies out: memory gets sadly diluted with time, and is not strong enough to revive us. Adam was no longer so confident as he had been: he began to fear that[3] perhaps Dinah's old life would have too strong a grasp upon her for any new feeling to triumph. If she had not felt this, she would surely have written to him to give him some comfort; but it appeared that she[4] held it right to discourage him. As Adam's confidence waned, his patience waned with it, and he thought he must write himself; he must ask Dinah not to leave him in painful doubt longer than was needful. He sat up late one night to write her a letter, but the next morning he burnt it,[5] afraid of its effect. It would be worse to have a discouraging answer by letter than from her own lips, for her presence reconciled him to her will.

---

[1] too ⟨much⟩ flushed *MS*   [2] with] *added in MS*
[3] he began to fear that] *added in MS*   [4] she ⟨felt⟩ ⟨thought⟩ held *MS*
[5] he burnt it,] {he} tore it up, *MS*

[6]You perceive how it was: Adam was hungering for the sight of Dinah; and when that sort of hunger reaches a certain stage, a lover is likely to still it though he may have to put his future in pawn.

But what harm could he do by going to Snowfield? Dinah could not be displeased with him for it: she had not forbidden him to go: she must surely expect that he would go before long. By the second Sunday in October this view of the case had become so clear to Adam, that he was already on his way to Snowfield; on horseback this time, for his hours were precious now, and he had borrowed Jonathan Burge's good nag for the journey.

What keen memories went along the road with him! He had often been to Oakbourne and back since that first journey to Snowfield, but beyond Oakbourne the grey stone walls, the broken country, the meagre trees, seemed to be telling him afresh the story of that painful past which he knew so well by heart. But no story is the same to us after a lapse of time; or rather, we who read it are no longer the same interpreters: and Adam this morning brought with him new thoughts through that grey country—thoughts which gave an altered significance to its story of the past.

That is a base and selfish, even a blasphemous, spirit, which rejoices and is thankful over the past evil that has blighted or crushed another, because it has been made a source of unforeseen good to ourselves: Adam could never cease to mourn over that mystery of human sorrow which had been brought so close to him: he could never thank God for another's misery. And if I were capable[7] of that narrow-sighted joy in Adam's behalf, I should still know he was not the man to[8] feel it for himself: he would have shaken his head at such a sentiment, and said, "Evil's evil, and sorrow's sorrow, and you can't alter its[9] natur by wrapping it up in other words. Other folks were not created for my sake, that I should think all square when things turn out well for me."

But it is not ignoble to feel that the fuller life which a sad experience has brought us is worth our own personal share of pain: surely it is not possible to feel otherwise, any more than it would be possible for a man with cataract to[1] regret the painful process by which his dim blurred sight of men as trees walking had been exchanged for clear outline and effulgent day. The growth of higher feeling within us is like the growth of faculty, bringing with it a sense of added strength: we can no more wish to return to a narrower sympathy, than a painter or a musician can wish to return to his cruder manner, or a philosopher to his less complete formula.

Something like this sense of enlarged being was in Adam's mind this Sunday morning, as he rode along in vivid recollection of the past. His

[6] *Paragraph division added in 1.*   [7] capable ⟨myself⟩ of *MS*
[8] to ⟨share it⟩ feel *MS*   [9] its] it's *MS*
[1] possible for a man with cataract to] possible {for a man} to *MS*

feeling towards Dinah, the hope of passing his life with her, had been the distant unseen point towards which that hard journey from Snowfield eighteen months ago had been leading him. Tender and deep as his love for Hetty had been—so deep that the roots of it would never be torn away—his love for Dinah was better and more precious to him; for it was the outgrowth of that fuller life which had come to him from his acquaintance with deep sorrow. "It's like as if it was a new strength to me," he said to himself, "to love her, and know as she loves me. I shall look t' her to help me to see things right. For she's better than I am—there's less o' self in her, and pride. And it's a feeling as gives you a sort o' liberty, as if you could walk more fearless, when you've more trust in another than y' have in yourself. I've always been thinking I knew better than them as belonged to me, and that's a poor sort o' life, when you can't look to them nearest to you t' help you with a bit better thought than what you've got inside you a'ready."

It was more than two o'clock in the afternoon when Adam came in sight of the grey town on the hill-side, and looked searchingly towards the green valley below, for the first glimpse of the old thatched roof near the ugly red mill. The scene looked less harsh in the soft October sunshine than it had done in the eager time of early spring; and the one grand charm it possessed in common with all wide-stretching woodless regions—that it filled you with a new consciousness of the overarching sky—had a milder, more soothing influence than usual, on this almost cloudless day. Adam's doubts and fears melted under this influence as the delicate web-like clouds had gradually melted away into the clear blue above him. He seemed to see Dinah's gentle face assuring him, with its looks alone, of all he longed to know.

He did not expect Dinah to be at home at this hour, but he got down from his horse and tied it[2] at the little gate, that he might ask where she was gone to-day. He had set his mind on following her and bringing her home. She was gone to Sloman's End, a hamlet about three miles off, over the hill, the old woman told him: had set off directly after morning chapel, to preach in a cottage there, as her habit was. Anybody at the town would tell him the way to Sloman's End. So Adam got on his horse again and rode to the town, putting up at the old inn, and taking a hasty dinner there in the company of the too chatty landlord, from whose friendly questions and reminiscences he was glad to escape as soon as possible, and set out towards Sloman's End. With all his haste, it was nearly four o'clock before he could set off, and he thought that as Dinah had gone so early, she would perhaps already be near returning. The little[3] grey, desolate-looking hamlet[4], unscreened by sheltering trees, lay in sight long before he reached it; and as he came near he could hear the sound of voices singing a hymn. "Perhaps that's the last

---

[2] it ⟨to⟩ at *MS*   [3] little] *MS 1* little, 8
[4] desolate{-looking} hamlet *MS*

hymn before they come away," Adam thought: "I'll walk back a bit, and turn again to meet her, further off the village." He walked back till he got nearly to the top of the hill again, and seated himself[5] on a loose stone, against the low wall, to watch till he should see the little black figure[6] leaving the hamlet and winding up the hill. He chose this spot, almost at the top of the hill, because it was away from all eyes—no house, no cattle, not even a nibbling sheep near—no presence but the still lights and shadows, and the great embracing sky.

She was much longer coming than he expected: he waited an hour at least,[7] watching for her and thinking of her, while the afternoon shadows lengthened, and the light grew softer. At last he saw the little black figure coming from between the grey houses, and gradually approaching the foot of the hill. Slowly, Adam thought; but Dinah was really walking at her usual pace, with a light quiet step. Now she was beginning to wind along the path up the hill, but Adam would not move yet: he would not meet her too soon; he had set his heart on meeting her in this assured loneliness. And now he began to fear lest he should startle her too much; "Yet," he thought, "she's not one to be over-startled; she's always so calm and quiet, as if she was prepared for anything."

What was she thinking of as she wound up the hill? Perhaps she had found complete repose without him, and had ceased to feel any need of his love. On the verge of a decision we all tremble: hope pauses with fluttering wings.

But now at last she was very near, and Adam rose from the stone wall. It happened that just as he walked forward, Dinah had paused and turned round to look back at the village: who does not pause and look back in mounting a hill? Adam was glad; for, with the fine instinct of a lover, he felt that it would be best for her to hear his voice before she saw him. He came within three paces of her and then said, "Dinah!" She started without looking round, as if she connected the sound with no place. "Dinah!" Adam said again. He knew quite well what was in her mind. She was so accustomed to think of impressions as purely spiritual monitions, that she looked for no material visible[8] accompaniment of the voice.

But this second time she looked round. What a look of yearning love it was that the mild grey eyes turned on the strong dark-eyed man! She did not start again at the sight of him; she said nothing, but moved towards him so that his arm could clasp her round.

And they walked on so in silence, while the warm tears fell. Adam was content, and said nothing. It was Dinah who spoke first.

[5] himself ⟨out of sight⟩ {on a loose stone} against the low ⟨stone⟩ wall *MS*
[6] figure ⟨with⟩ leaving *MS*   [7] least,] *MS 1* least *8*
[8] material visible] *revised in MS from* visible material

"Adam," she said, "it is the Divine Will. My soul is so knit to yours that it is but a divided life I live without you. And this moment, now you are with me, and I feel that our hearts are filled with the same love, I have a fullness of strength to bear and do our heavenly Father's Will, that I had lost before."

Adam paused and looked into her sincere eyes[9].

"Then we'll never part any more, Dinah, till death parts us."

[1]And they kissed each other with a deep joy.

[2]What greater thing is there for two human souls, than to feel that they are joined for life—to strengthen each other in all labour, to rest on each other in all sorrow, to minister to each other in all pain, to be one with each other in silent unspeakable memories at the moment of the last parting?

---

[9] sincere eyes] sincere loving eyes *MS 1* sincere ⟨loving⟩ eyes *8*
[1] *Paragraph division added in 1.*   [2] *Paragraph division added in 1.*

CHAPTER LV.

¹MARRIAGE BELLS.

In little more than a month after that meeting on the hill—on a rimy morning in departing November—Adam and Dinah were married.

It was an event much thought of in the village. All Mr Burge's men had a holiday, and all Mr Poyser's; and most of those who had a holiday appeared in their best clothes at the wedding. I think there was hardly an inhabitant of Hayslope specially mentioned in this history and still resident in the parish on this November morning, who was not either in church to see Adam and Dinah married, or near the church door to greet them as they came forth. Mrs Irwine and her daughters were waiting at the churchyard gates in their carriage (for they had a carriage now) to shake hands with the bride and bridegroom,² and wish them well; and in the absence of Miss Lydia Donnithorne at Bath, Mrs Best, Mr Mills, and Mr Craig had felt it incumbent on them to represent "the family" at the Chase on the occasion. The churchyard walk was quite lined with familiar faces, many of them faces that had first looked at Dinah when she preached on the Green; and³ no wonder they showed this eager interest on her marriage morning, for nothing like Dinah and the history which had brought her and Adam Bede together had been known at Hayslope within the memory of man.

Bessy Cranage, in her neatest cap and frock, was crying, though she did not exactly know why; for, as her cousin Wiry Ben, who stood near her, judiciously suggested, Dinah was not going away, and if Bessy was in low spirits, the best thing for her to do was to follow Dinah's example, and marry an honest fellow who was ready to have her. Next to Bessy, just within the church door, there were the Poyser children, peeping round the corner of the pews to get a sight of the mysterious ceremony; Totty's face wearing an unusual air of anxiety at the idea of seeing cousin Dinah come back looking rather old, for in Totty's experience no married people were young.

I envy them all the sight they had when the marriage was fairly ended and Adam led Dinah out of church. She was not in black this morning; for her

---

¹ ⟨Conclusion.⟩ Marriage Bells *MS*

² waiting at the churchyard gates in their carriage (for they had a carriage now) to shake hands with the bride and bridegroom,] *revised in MS from* waiting in their carriage (for they had a carriage now) to shake hands with the bride & bridegroom at the churchyard gates

³ Green; and] Green. And *MS*

aunt Poyser would by no means allow such a risk of incurring bad luck, and had herself made a present of the wedding dress, made all of grey, though in the usual Quaker form, for on this point Dinah could not give way. So the lily face looked out with sweet gravity from under a[4] grey Quaker bonnet, neither smiling nor blushing, but with lips trembling a little under the weight of solemn feelings. Adam, as he pressed her arm to his side, walked with[5] his old erectness and his head thrown rather backward as if to face all the world better;[6] but it was not because he was particularly proud this morning, as is the wont of bridegrooms, for his happiness was of a kind that had little reference to men's opinion of it. There was a tinge of sadness in his deep joy: Dinah knew it, and did not feel aggrieved.

There were three other couples, following the bride and bridegroom: first[7], Martin Poyser, looking as cheery as a bright fire on this rimy morning, led quiet Mary Burge, the bridesmaid; then came Seth,[8] serenely happy, with Mrs Poyser on his arm; and last of all Bartle Massey, with Lisbeth—Lisbeth in a new gown and bonnet, too busy with her pride in her son, and her delight in possessing the one daughter she had desired, to devise a single[9] pretext for complaint.

Bartle Massey had consented to attend[1] the wedding at Adam's earnest request, under protest against marriage in general, and the marriage of a sensible man in particular. Nevertheless, Mr Poyser had a joke against him after the wedding dinner, to the effect that in the vestry he had given the bride one more kiss than was necessary.

Behind this last couple came Mr Irwine, glad at heart over this good morning's work of joining Adam and Dinah. For he had seen Adam in the worst moments of his sorrow; and what better harvest from that painful seed-time could there be than this? The love that had[2] brought hope and comfort in the hour of despair, the love that had found its way to the dark prison cell and to poor Hetty's darker soul—this strong, gentle love was to be Adam's companion and helper till death.

There was much shaking of hands mingled with "God bless you's," and other good wishes to[3] the four couples, at the churchyard gate, Mr Poyser answering for[4] the rest with unwonted vivacity of tongue, for he had all the appropriate wedding-day jokes at his command. And the women, he observed, could never do anything but put finger in eye at a wedding. Even Mrs Poyser could not trust herself to speak as the neighbours shook hands with her; and Lisbeth began to cry in the face of the very first person who told her she was getting young again.

---

⁴ a ⟨little⟩ grey *MS*   ⁵ with ⟨the⟩ his *MS*   ⁶ better; ⟨yet he⟩ but *MS*
⁷ bridegroom: first] bridegroom⟨;⟩ First *MS*   ⁸ Seth,] *MS 1* Seth *8*
⁹ single ⟨ground⟩ pretext *MS*   ¹ attend] *MS 1* atten⟨t⟩d *8*
² had ⟨shed rays of⟩ brought *MS*   ³ to ⟨all⟩ the *MS*
⁴ for ⟨every one⟩ {⟨all⟩ the rest} with *MS*

Mr Joshua Rann, having a slight touch of rheumatism, did not join in the ringing of the bells this morning, and,[5] looking on with some contempt at these informal greetings which required no official co-operation from the clerk, began to hum in his musical bass, "O what a joyful thing it is," by way of preluding a little to the effect he intended to produce in the wedding psalm next Sunday.

"That's a bit of good news to cheer Arthur," said Mr Irwine to his mother, as they drove off. "I shall write to him the first thing when we get home."

[5] &, ⟨looked⟩ looking *MS*

EPILOGUE.

It is near the end of June, in 1807. The workshops have been shut up half an hour or more in Adam Bede's timber-yard, which used to be Jonathan Burge's, and the mellow evening light is falling on the pleasant house with the buff walls and the soft grey thatch, very much as it did when we saw Adam bringing in the keys on that June evening nine years ago.

There is a figure we know well, just come out of the house, and shading her eyes with her hands as she looks for something in the distance; for the rays that fall on her white borderless cap and her pale auburn hair are very dazzling. But now she turns away from the sunlight and looks towards the door. We[1] can see the sweet pale face quite well now: it is scarcely at all altered—only a little fuller, to correspond to her more matronly figure, which still seems light and active enough in the plain black dress.

"I see him, Seth," Dinah said, as she looked into the house. "Let[2] us go and meet him. Come, Lisbeth, come with mother."

The last call was answered immediately by a small fair creature with pale auburn hair and grey eyes, little more than four years old, who ran out silently and put her hand into her mother's.

"Come, uncle Seth," said Dinah[3].

"Ay, ay, we're coming,"[4] Seth answered from within, and presently appeared stooping under the doorway, being taller than usual by the black head of a sturdy two-year-old nephew, who had caused some delay by demanding to be carried on uncle's shoulder.

"Better take him on thy arm, Seth," said Dinah, looking fondly at the stout black-eyed fellow. "He's[5] troublesome to thee so."

"Nay, nay: Addy likes a ride on my shoulder. I can carry him so for a bit." A kindness which young Addy acknowledged by drumming his heels with promising force against uncle Seth's chest. But to walk by Dinah's side, and be tyrannized over by Dinah's[6] and Adam's children, was uncle Seth's earthly happiness.[7]

---

[1] door. We] door. ¶ We *Cabinet*   [2] house. "Let] house, "Let *MS*
[3] Dinah {.} ⟨again⟩. *MS*
[4] coming," ⟨answered Seth, who⟩ Seth answered from within, & *MS*
[5] fellow. "He's] fellow, "He's *MS*   [6] Dinah's] Dinah *MS* / Dinah{'s} *8*
[7] But to walk by Dinah's side & be tyrannized over by Dinah & Adam's children, was uncle Seth's earthly happiness.] *added in MS*

"Where didst see him?" asked Seth, as they walked on into the adjoining field. "I can't catch sight of him anywhere."

"Between the hedges by the roadside," said Dinah. "I saw his hat and his shoulder. There he is again."

"Trust thee for catching sight of him if he's anywhere to be seen," said Seth, smiling. "Thee't like poor mother used to be. She was always on the look-out for Adam, and could see him sooner than other folks, for all her eyes got dim."

"He's been longer than he expected," said Dinah, taking[8] Arthur's watch from a small side-pocket and looking at it; "it's nigh upon seven now."

"Ay, they'd have a deal to say to one another," said Seth, "and[9] the meeting 'ud touch 'em both pretty closish. Why, it's[1] getting on towards eight year since they parted."

"Yes," said Dinah, "Adam was greatly moved this morning at the thought of the change he should see in the poor young man, from the sickness he has undergone, as well as the years which have changed us all. And the death of the poor wanderer, when she was coming back to us, has been sorrow upon sorrow."

"See, Addy," said Seth, lowering the young one to his arm now, and pointing,[2] "there's father coming—at the far stile."

Dinah hastened her steps, and little Lisbeth ran on at her utmost speed till she clasped her father's leg. Adam patted her head and lifted her up to kiss her, but Dinah could see the marks of agitation on his face as she approached him, and he put her arm within his in silence.

"Well, youngster, must I take you?" he said, trying to smile, when Addy stretched out his arms—ready, with the usual baseness of infancy, to give up his uncle Seth at once, now there was some rarer patronage at hand.

"It's cut me a good deal, Dinah," Adam said at last, when they were walking on.

"Didst find him greatly altered?" said Dinah.

"Why, he's altered and yet not altered. I should ha' known him any-where. But his colour's changed, and he looks sadly. However, the doctors say he'll soon be set right in his own country air. He's all sound in th' inside; it's only the fever shattered him so. But he speaks just the same, and smiles at me just as he did when he was a lad. It's wonderful how he's always had just the same sort o' look when he smiles."

"I've never seen him smile, poor young man," said Dinah.

"But thee *wilt* see[3] him smile, to-morrow," said Adam. "He asked after thee the first thing when he began to come round, and we could talk to one

---

[8] taking ⟨a gold⟩ Arthur's *MS*   [9] Seth, "and] Seth. "And *MS*
[1] it's ⟨seven year & a quarter as nigh as can be⟩ getting on towards eight year *MS*
[2] & pointing,] *added in MS*   [3] see ⟨it⟩ him *MS*

another. 'I hope she isn't altered,' he said, 'I remember her face so well.'
I told him, 'no,'" Adam continued, looking fondly at the eyes that were
turned up towards his, "only a bit plumper, as thee'dst a right to be after
seven year. 'I may come and see her to-morrow, mayn't I?' he said; 'I long to
tell her how I've thought of her all these years.'"

"Didst tell him I'd always used the watch?" said Dinah.

"Ay; and we talked a deal about thee, for he says he never saw a woman a
bit like thee. 'I shall turn Methodist some day,' he said, 'when she preaches
out of doors, and go to hear her.' And I said, 'Nay, sir, you can't do that, for
Conference has forbid the women preaching, and she's given it up, all but
talking to the people a bit in their houses.'"

"Ah," said Seth, who could not repress a comment on this point, "and a
sore pity it was o' Conference; and[4] if Dinah had seen as I did, we'd ha' left
the Wesleyans and joined a body that 'ud put no bonds on Christian
liberty."

"Nay, lad, nay," said[5] Adam, "she was right and thee wast wrong.
There's no rule so wise but what it's a pity for somebody or other. Most
o' the women do more harm nor good with their preaching—they've not
got Dinah's gift nor her sperrit; and she's seen that, and she thought it right
to set th' example o' submitting, for she's not held from other sorts o'
teaching. And I agree with her, and approve o' what she did."

Seth was silent. This was a standing subject of difference rarely alluded
to, and Dinah, wishing to[6] quit it at once, said,

"Didst remember, Adam, to speak to Colonel Donnithorne the words
my uncle and aunt entrusted to thee?"

"Yes, and he's going to the[7] Hall Farm with Mr Irwine the day after
to-morrow. Mr Irwine came in while we were talking about it, and he
would have it as the Colonel must see nobody but thee to-morrow:
he said—and he's in the right of it—as it'll be bad for him t' have[8] his
feelings stirred with seeing many people one after another. 'We must get
you strong and hearty,' he said, 'that's the first thing to be done, Arthur,
and then you shall have your own way. But I shall keep you under your old
tutor's thumb till then.' Mr Irwine's fine and joyful at having him home
again."

Adam was silent a little while, and then[9] said:

"It was[1] very cutting when we first saw one another. He'd never heard
about poor Hetty till Mr Irwine met him in London, for the letters missed
him on his journey. The first thing he said to me, when we'd got hold o' one
another's hands, was, 'I could never do anything for her, Adam—she lived
long enough for all the suffering—and I'd thought so of the time when

  [4] Conference; and] Conference. And *MS*   [5] nay," said] *MS 1* nay⟨.⟩{,}" said *8*
  [6] to ⟨change⟩ quit *MS*   [7] the] th' *MS*   [8] t' have] to ⟨see⟩ have *MS*
  [9] then ⟨add⟩ said, *MS*   [1] was ⟨fir⟩ very *MS*

I might do something for her. But you told me the truth when you said to me once, 'There's a sort of wrong that can never be made up for.'"

"Why, there's Mr and Mrs Poyser coming in at the yard gate," said Seth.

"So there is," said Dinah. "Run, Lisbeth, run to meet aunt Poyser. Come in, Adam, and rest; it has been a hard day for thee."

EXPLANATORY NOTES

Writing *Adam Bede* did not require the extensive background research and reading that were part of George Eliot's preparation for *Romola* and, to a lesser extent, *Daniel Deronda*. Nonetheless, as *A Writer's Notebook* demonstrates, she read the lives of John Wesley and George Stephenson and consulted the *Gentleman's Magazine* and other historical documents for detailed information about the late eighteenth century. She also drew upon her memory of her reading and study of the Bible in her youth for the extensive biblical quotations and allusions found in Dinah's speeches and sermon, and she incorporated her knowledge of the visual arts, enhanced by her travels in Germany in summer 1858, and her reading or rereading of classical literature and the poetry of Wordsworth. The following explanatory notes show how that reading entered the text. Where appropriate, the notes give not only the source of a reference but a brief commentary on the way in which the reference enriches and deepens the novel. Biblical quotations are cited from the King James Version, although Eliot's 'quotations' are not always exact, presenting instead the text as she remembered it or as she chose to have Dinah adapt it to her preaching. As befits a scholarly rather than a classroom edition, I have omitted all but a few references of the kind that can be found in well-known and easily accessible sources, such as the *Oxford English Dictionary*.

2 *'So that ye may . . . may attend'*: as discussed in the Introduction, the epigraph is a quotation from the *Excursion*, book VI, 'The Churchyard among the Mountains', lines 651–8, by Wordsworth.

7 *'Awake my soul . . . the noonday clear'*: the morning hymn of Thomas Ken (1637–1711), bishop of Bath and Wells from 1685 to 1691, and fearless preacher. His hymns were published in 1695 in his *Manual for the Use of Winchester Scholars*. 'Awake, my soul' is one of the best-known English hymns, and is especially appropriate for Adam, as a staunch member of the Church, to sing at his work—although he seems unsusceptible to 'dull sloth'.

10 *What come ye out for to see . . . a uncommon pretty young woman*: Wiry Ben's irreverent paraphrase of Matthew 11: 9 sparks a discussion of religion that leads to the novel's first characterization of Adam as a man more interested in the technological advances of the eighteenth century, which are evidence of God's 'put[ing] his sperrit into the work-man', than in the theological controversies of his time.

dissenters: members of Protestant religious groups outside the Church of England. In many nineteenth-century novels, they were subjects for ridicule. For a comprehensive discussion of the portrayal of Dissent in the Victorian novel, see Cunningham.

11 *Arkwright's mills . . . at Cromford*: the spinning frame invented by Sir Richard Arkwright (1732–92) revolutionized the production of thread. His water-powered spinning mills, along with the aqueducts, canals, and steam engines used in the coal mines, were major technological innovations of the eighteenth century and were often invented by self-taught mechanics and artisans like Adam, such as George Stephenson and Richard Arkwright, who studied at night to learn the mathematics they needed in their work. The narrator describes Adam's work ethic and values at greater length in Chapter XIX, 'Adam on a Working Day'.

15 *'spotty globe'*: Milton, *Paradise Lost*, I. 291.

16 *But you've not got many Methodists about here . . . You're all farmers, aren't you? The Methodists can seldom lay much hold on them*: Eliot recorded in her notebook that 'The class Wesley liked least were the farmers. The agricultural part of the people were least susceptible of Methodism, for Methodism could be kept alive only by associations & frequent meetings; & it is difficult, or impossible, to arrange these among a scattered population. Where converts were made, & the discipline could not be introduced among them, & the effect kept up by constant preaching & inspection, they soon fell off' (*A Writer's Notebook*, 27). Bess Cranage, induced by the power of Dinah's sermon to throw down her earrings, 'falls off' after Dinah returns to Snowfield, but when Dinah remains in Hayslope after Hetty's transportation, Bess again responds to her message, as we find out when Mrs Poyser predicts that if Dinah leaves again Bess will be 'flaunting i'' new finery three weeks after you're gone' (Chapter XLIX).

17 *lick the French*: this reference to England's war with France, which began in February 1793, is one of several details that set the Napoleonic background for *Adam Bede*. Adam has had to use his savings to pay for a substitute for Seth in the militia, as Seth reminds his mother in Chapter IV; Arthur leaves the militia and goes into the regular army in Chapter XLVIII; and, in Chapter L, a year and a half later, Adam relates to Dinah Arthur's intention to remain away from Hayslope, quoting his letter to Mr Irwine, 'I'm the best when I've a good day's march or fighting before me.' In Chapter LIII, some of the guests at the harvest supper discuss the French in derisive language and exaggerated anecdotes; and in the epilogue Arthur has returned to Hayslope as a colonel, recovering from an unspecified kind of 'fever' after seven years of service.

20 '*Sehon, King of the Amorites: for His mercy endureth for ever; and Og the King of Basan: for His mercy endureth for ever*': Psalm 136: 19–20.

22 *boguy*: this term for an apparition or ghost appears in several forms in different English dialects. Neither the cancelled form, *buggat*, nor the substituted form, *boguy*, is listed in Joseph Wright's *English Dialect Dictionary* (Oxford, 1970), which gives *boggart* as the usage in Derbyshire and Staffordshire; *buggart*, which is closest to the cancelled form, is found in Lancashire.

23–4 *a poor woman, . . . and yet Thou wast ready to give her that blessing which she had never sought*: John 4: 5–26.

24 *they see Thee in the night-watches*: Psalm 63: 6.

and their hearts burn within them as Thou talkest with them by the way: Luke 24: 32.

'*Ye will not come unto me that ye might have life*': John 5: 40.

'*Father, forgive them, for they know not what they do*': Luke 23: 34.

see Thee as Thou wilt come again in Thy glory to judge them at the last: Matthew 24: 30; Luke 21: 27.

'*The spirit of the Lord is upon me, because he hath anointed me to preach the gospel to the poor*': Luke 4: 18.

entered into his rest: John Wesley (b. 1703) died in 1791.

'*Gospel*' meant '*good news*': Old English, *gód+spel*, i.e. good+story.

26 '*in the image of the Father*': 2 Corinthians 4: 4 refers to 'the glorious gospel of Christ, who is the image of God'.

'*I came to seek and to save that which was lost*': Luke 19: 10.

'*I came not to call the righteous, but sinners to repentance*': Mark 2: 17; Luke 5: 32.

27 *Ranter*: originally a reference to members of a sect of Antinomians in 1645, but later applied to the Primitive Methodists. In this specific application, the observation, which appears to be that of the stranger on horseback (a magistrate named Colonel Townley, the reader discovers in Chapter XLV), is anachronistic if it applies to the latter, to whom 'Ranter' was not applied until the nineteenth century. The locale, however, is appropriate. The *OED* quotes the *Penny Cyclopedia* (1839) as noting that the Primitive Methodists originated in Staffordshire.

28 '*eat an egg, an apple, or a nut*': M. P. Tilley's *Dictionary of the Proverbs in England in the Sixteenth and Seventeenth Centuries* (Ann Arbor, 1950) cites the proverb as 'Apples, eggs, and nuts you may eat though dressed by sluts.' Among Tilley's citations, a definition from the Roxburghe Ballads, II. 186 (1656) gives the clearest sense of the meaning that Bess

is a slovenly woman: 'My wife is such a beastly slut, Unlesse it be an egge or a nut, I in the house dare nothing eat.'

29 '*How often would I have gathered you* [thy children together] *as a hen gathereth her chickens under her wings, and ye would not!*': Matthew 23: 37.

the print of the nails on his dear hands and feet: John 20: 25.

agony . . . and the great drops of sweat fell like blood to the ground: Luke 22: 44.

'*Father, forgive them, for they know not what they do*': see note to p. 24.

great darkness: 'darkness over all the land', Matthew 27: 45; also Mark 15: 33; Luke 23: 44.

cup of bitterness: an allusion to Jesus' prayer the night before his Crucifixion. Matthew 26: 39; Mark 14: 36; Luke 22: 42.

'*My God, my God! . . . why hast Thou forsaken me?*': Matthew 27: 46. Cf. also Psalm 22: 1.

30 '*Come to me that you may have life*': Matthew 11: 28 and John 10: 10; image also found in John 5: 40.

'*Depart from me into everlasting fire!*': Matthew 25: 41.

And one day when she put her new cap on and looked in the glass, she saw a bleeding Face crowned with thorns: as noted in the Introduction, this image comes from a story related by Eliot's aunt Elizabeth Tomlinson Evans, the model for Dinah Morris.

31 '*Its streams the whole creation reach . . . Enough for all, enough for each, Enough for evermore*': Cunningham notes that 'Dinah reinforces her sermon's optimistic proclamation of the Arminian gospel with a verse from Charles Wesley ("Enough for all, enough for each").' His annotation cites 'Stanza 4 of No. 241, in *A Collection of Hymns* (2nd edn., 1781), from the section "For Believers Rejoicing"' (165, 165 n. 3).

32 '*And after we had seen the vision, immediately we endeavoured to go into Macedonia*': Acts 16: 10. Later in this chapter Dinah argues against Seth's view that his marriage proposal might indicate 'a leading of Providence': 'when I've opened the Bible for direction, I've always lighted on some clear word to tell me where my work lay'—i.e. in her ministry, and not in marriage. David Leon Higdon discusses the Methodists' practice of opening the Bible for direction in 'Sortes Biblicae in *Adam Bede*', *Papers on Language and Literature*, 9 (1973), 396–405. He notes that this passage and two others from *Adam Bede* are part of a tradition going back to St Augustine. The second passage, also in Chapter III, is the one noted immediately above. In the third example, in Chapter XV, however, Dinah is less successful. (See note to p. 149.) Higdon points out that 'The *sortes biblicae* characterize

Dinah in the same way that witty sayings, misogyny, and John Moore's novels do Mrs. Poyser, Bartle Massey, and Arthur Donnithorne. "Opening the Bible" contributes to the creation of a unique personality as do her Methodist rhetoric and severe manner of dress' (400).

33   *'And Jacob served seven years for Rachel; and they seemed to him but a few days for the love he had to her'*: Genesis 29: 20. The image emphasizes Seth's patience in awaiting a favourable answer from Dinah. In *George Eliot's Mythmaking*, Wiesenfarth posits that the 'tragic and comedic complexity . . . in Adam's life [is] mirrored in the Old Testament story of Jacob and Rachel'. Whereas Jacob's love for Rachel never wavers, 'Adam first loves Hetty, then Dinah. He must come to find his true Rachel' (91). Just as 'Jacob's relation to Rachel is defined by love and work', so too 'the relation between work and love is undeniable in Adam's connection with Hetty. But that work finds its fruition in love only when the true Rachel appears in Dinah. . . . So just as Jacob finds the blessing of his labors in finally winning Rachel, Adam finds his in winning Dinah' (92–3). A second reference to Jacob and Rachel is harder to fit into the symbolic structure. In Chapter XXI, Adam describes a frame he built for a piece of needlework done by Miss Lydia Donnithorne, which depicted 'Jacob and Rachel a-kissing one another among the sheep'. Eliot apparently considered the introduction of the biblical image carefully: in manuscript she cancelled the phrase 'a lady and gentleman', and inserted 'Jacob and Rachel' above the line. Adam's diction and the needlework's pastoral setting are echoed, tragically and ironically, in Chapter XXXIX when Adam describes his discovery of Arthur 'a-kissing [Hetty] as they were parting in the Grove'.

'She that's married careth for the things of the world, how she may please her husband': 1 Corinthians 7: 34.

'I will that the younger women marry, bear children, guide the house, give none occasion to the adversary to speak reproachfully': 1 Timothy 5: 14.

'two are better than one': Ecclesiastes 4: 9.

serve the same Master: Matthew 6: 24.

33–4   *as God has distributed to every man, as the Lord hath called every man, so let him walk*: 1 Corinthians 7: 17.

34   *rejoice with them that do rejoice, and to weep with those that weep*: Romans 12: 15.

from my rising up till my lying down: images from Psalm 139: 2–3; Lamentations 3: 63.

to endure as seeing Him who is invisible: Hebrews 11: 27.

passing the love of women: 2 Samuel 1: 26.

35 *'In darkest shades if she appear, . . . And she my rising sun'*: Cunningham points out that in fitting hymns to her artistic purposes, 'Eliot lets Seth bear the blame for her most blatant and daring alteration. He apologizes, as well he might, for improving on Watts's "My God, the spring of all my joys." ' Quoting the novel's version of this hymn, Cunningham compares 'the change of pronouns' to 'the blasphemous inscription (*Illumina Tenebr[as] Nostras Domina*) on the portrait of Donne'. Considering the narrator's comment that love like Seth's 'is hardly distinguishable from religious feeling', he concludes, 'Clearly the hymns have a face value in the novel, they are to signal the Methodist mentality; but they are also tailored to serve the novel, especially its humanism' (166).

land of Goshen: that part of Egypt in which 'all the souls of the house of Jacob' came to dwell. Cf. Genesis 46: 27–28 and *passim*.

36 *sensibility to the three concords*: in the context of the narrator's comment that 'it is impossible for me to represent their diction as correct, or their instruction as liberal', the reference is almost certainly to the concept of concord in grammar. The final part of the sentence referring to 'very erroneous theories and very sublime feelings' rounds out the parallel by addressing the question of their 'instruction'. Although there are four 'concords' (case, number, gender, and person), Eliot may have forgotten 'person' as it relates to substantives, an excusable error given that even Lindley Murray in his famous *English Grammar*, used extensively in the nineteenth century, originally listed only three concords for substantives, the inflections of which had been much reduced by his time. The 1795 edition of *English Grammar, Adapted to the Different Classes of Learners* states simply 'To substantives belong gender, number, and case.' When he revised the work early in the nineteenth century in response to objections (from classics scholars in particular), Murray added after 'case': 'and they are all of the third person when spoken *of*, and of the second when spoken *to*: as, "Blessings attend us on every side; be grateful, children of men!" that is, *ye* children of men' (*English Grammar, Adapted to the Different Classes of Learners*, 44th edn., 1830, 47).

39 *Thee't allays stay till the last child's born*: although Mrs Poyser is the usual originator of folk proverbs, Lisbeth Bede may have produced an original proverb here; I have been unable to locate it in proverb dictionaries.

41 *and if Solomon was as wise as he is reputed to be, I feel sure that when he compared a contentious woman to a continual dropping on a very rainy day*: Proverbs 27: 15.

44 *God distributes talents... as He sees good*: cf. parable of the talents in Matthew 25: 14–30.

Take no thought for the morrow: Matthew 6: 31, 34.

45 '*God helps them as helps theirsens*': the man that Seth calls the 'knowing' but 'over-worldly' author is Ben Franklin, whose witty, wise, and sometimes worldly sayings differ from the speech of the earnest Seth. In Chapter XIX, the narrator lists Franklin's *Poor Richard's Almanack* as one of the books that Adam has read. 'God helps them that help themselves' is among the aphorisms for June 1736.

we must be workers together with God: 2 Corinthians 6: 1.

all the days of her pilgrimage: life's journey as a pilgrimage, a major motif in the literature and practices of the Middle Ages, is the allegorical basis for Bunyan's *Pilgrim's Progress* (1678), which, in Chapter XIX, is listed as one of the books Adam has read. The image also appears in Exodus 6: 4.

47 *when my doings are cast up at the last*: a reference to the Last Judgement.

'*They that are strong ought to bear the infirmities of those that are weak, and not to please themselves*': Romans 15: 1.

52 *pluralist*: a clergyman who held more than one living in the Church of England. Mr Irwine holds three. The practice came under increasing criticism in the nineteenth century. See note to p. 64.

53 *Ceres*: Roman goddess of agriculture.

Dauphin: Mrs Irwine's habit of calling her son by the title of the heir to the French throne not long after the guillotining of the King and Queen of France is in keeping with her 'queenly' nature emphasized later in this chapter, where she is referred to as 'an Olympian goddess', and in Chapter XXV, where the narrator calls her 'the royal old lady', a slightly ironic appellation, given Mrs Irwine's psychological and philosophical distance from the working-class characters and the realism of the novel.

Juno: Mr Irwine has named his dog after the Roman goddess (Greek: Hera), the wife of Jupiter. This is one of many details in the novel that attest to Mr Irwine's taste for the classical.

56 *blind Pharisee*: Pharisees were members of a strict Jewish sect whose pride is criticized in the parable of the Pharisee and the publican (Luke 18: 9–14). The image of the 'blind [Pharisee] leading the blind' is found in Matthew 15: 12–14.

'*dumb dog*': Isaiah 56: 10.

'idle shepherd': following immediately the reference to 'dumb dog', Isaiah 56: 11 refers to 'greedy dogs' and 'shepherds that cannot understand'. Will Maskery's exact phrase is found in Zechariah 11: 17.

57 *An' he said as our Christmas singin' was no better nor the cracklin' o' thorns under a pot. . . . it turns a man's stomach t' hear the Scripture misused i' that way*: Ecclesiastes 7: 6: 'For as the crackling of thorns under a pot, so is the laughter of the fool: this also is vanity.' Like 'dumb dog' and 'idle shepherd', this passage is another example of what Joshua Rann finds objectionable in Will Maskery. Mr Irwine, both tolerant and self-aware, declines to punish the Methodist wheelwright (from his perspective, Methodism has served well in changing Maskery from a drunken wife-beater into a responsible husband and worker), and later in the chapter he admits the justice of the 'aspersions'.

60 *St Catherine*: Wiesenfarth identifies Dinah in the early parts of the novel with St Catherine of Alexandria: a woman 'beautiful, learned, and with oratorical skill, who steadfastly refused to marry, recognizing Christ alone as her spouse. Dinah has to move from this exclusive position and accept Adam's love' (91).

62 *'Lyrical Ballads'*: published anonymously in 1798 by William Wordsworth and Samuel Taylor Coleridge. In keeping with his tendency not to see the farmers and labourers in Hayslope—and particularly the dairymaid Hetty—as they are, Arthur calls Wordsworth's poems 'twaddle' and is drawn instead to Coleridge's fabulous tale of the Ancient Mariner. But he seems not to have absorbed that poem's moral regarding human responsibility toward all creatures.

Antinomianism and Evangelicalism: Antinomianism is a belief system that rejected Mosaic moral law, including the Ten Commandments, believing that faith alone is necessary for salvation. Evangelicalism refers to the eighteenth-century movement that called for increased moral seriousness in clergy and laity. It began outside the Church of England but became a force for reform in the Established Church in the nineteenth century. Cunningham notes that 'Arthur's unconcern about the theological debate is ironic: his antinomianism had all too obviously evil results; he lacked, and fatally, Dinah's "inward holiness"' (149). George Eliot as a young woman was a fervently Evangelical member of the Church of England.

63 *the King's health*: since 1788 George III had suffered attacks of what was perceived as insanity. The cause of his condition has recently been thought to be porphyria. After several months, he recovered and did not experience a repetition of the problem until 1801, so perhaps his subjects were simply concerned about the health of an ageing monarch.

63 *the news from Egypt*: after the battle of the Nile in August 1798, in which
the British navy under Admiral Horatio Nelson defeated the French,
Bonaparte invaded Syria, but was forced to return to Egypt in May
1799 after the failure of his two-month siege of Acre, in the defence of
which the British navy played a leading role. The *Gentleman's Magazine* published its first report of the siege of Acre in July 1799, quoting a
letter from Captain Sir William Sidney Smith, dated 'March 23, Tigre
off St. John d'Acre', in which Smith notes that having had intelligence
of 'the incursion of Gen. Buonaparte's army into [the] province [of
Syria], and his approach to its capital Acre', he 'hastened with a portion
of the naval force under [his] orders to its relief' and arrived two days
before the French general (69: 612).

64 *Mr Roe, the 'travelling preacher'*: a temporary, local preacher who, like
the Methodist wheelwright Will Maskery, uses the Bible to attack Mr
Irwine.

lusts of the flesh and the pride of life: 1 John 2: 16.

*asking what shall we eat, and what shall we drink, and wherewithal shall we
be clothed?*: Matthew 6: 31. For another use of Matthew 6: 31 and 34, cf.
the dialogue between Seth and Lisbeth Bede (notes to pp. 44-5)

*trafficking in the souls of men by receiving money for discharging the pastoral
office . . . making statements scarcely less melancholy than that of Mr Roe*:
the opposition of clerical duty and money payment suggests the story of
Christ's expelling the moneychangers from the temple (Matthew 21:
12; Mark 11: 15). The complaint that Church of England clergy held
more than one living and did not serve their parishioners adequately
was the subject of increasing public discussion in the late eighteenth
century. By 1838, during the debate that led to an Act of Parliament that
year in which the number of benefices that could be held simultaneously was limited to two, a pamphlet by an anonymous 'Clergyman',
titled 'Pluralism and Non-Residence Unnecessary, Injurious, and
Indefensible; and Their Entire Prohibition Practical and Indispensible
to the Security, Extension, and Efficiency of the National Church; with
Statistical Tables Founded on Public Documents', reminded readers
of the long debate on these issues, pointed to the continued existence of
abuses, and argued that pluralism, which resulted in the Church of
England's failure to provide adequate religious instruction to a growing
population, promoted the growth of Dissent (London: James Nisbet
and Company, 1838).

65 *Sophocles or Theocritus*: Sophocles, fifth-century Athenian playwright,
and Theocritus, pastoral poet from Syracuse in the early third century
BC, are examples of Mr Irwine's love for the classics. As noted in the
Introduction, when Eliot argued to John Blackwood that treatment of a

subject, not the subject itself, determined whether a work was suitable for readers, she defended her view by citing Sophocles' play *The Philoctetes*.

Isaiah or Amos: Old Testament writers.

declined to give his body to be burned . . . he had that charity which has sometimes been lacking to very illustrious virtue: 1 Corinthians 13: 3.

70 *Martha and Mary*: Luke 10: 38–42. The ever-busy Mrs Poyser is the image of Martha, who is 'cumbered about much serving' and is 'careful and troubled about many things'. Dinah is like Mary, who 'hath chosen that good part, which shall not be taken away from her'. Although she works hard, Dinah is not 'cumbered' and 'careful'. Like Seth, she has little money saved; in Chapter XXX, she has been unable to collect Seth's letter, because she cannot pay the postage, having used all her spare money to help those in need.

Michaelmas: see note to p. 93.

Dantean picture: Mrs Poyser's picture, which is limited to the first part of Dante's *Divine Comedy*, 'The Inferno', is typical of her tendency to dire admonition. She uses another gloomy Dantean picture effectively in silencing the laughter at her expense in Chapter XX, when she breaks a jug herself after scolding the servant girl, Molly, for this offence.

73 *Catechism and the Prayer-book*: Mrs Poyser rests her faith on the Catechism and Book of Common Prayer of the Church of England, in contrast to Dinah's reliance on the Bible.

83 *O that the good seed might fall on that soil, for it would surely flourish*: parable of the sower, Matthew 13: 3–9, Mark 4: 3–20.

a good land, wherein they eat bread without scarceness: Deuteronomy 8: 9.

84 *Methodist—a Wesleyan*: Irwine corrects himself, showing that he knows that there are two branches of Methodism by 1799, the followers of Wesley, who were Arminians, practising an inclusive kind of Christianity, such as Eliot saw in her aunt, and the Calvinistic followers of George Whitefield. Seth describes Dinah's inclusiveness to Adam in Chapter LI: 'Dinah doesn't hold wi' them as are for keeping the Society so strict to themselves. She doesn't mind about making folks enter the Society, so as they're fit t' enter the kingdom o' God.' See also notes to p. 170.

Mrs Fletcher . . . first woman to preach in the Society . . . was Miss Bosanquet: Mary Bosanquet Fletcher (1739–1815). Cunningham notes that George Eliot read 'Henry Moore's Life of Mrs. Mary [Bosanquet] Fletcher', having borrowed it in March 1839 from her aunt. He suggests that 'Dinah's channel image' in this same paragraph 'perhaps relates to Mrs. Fletcher's seeing herself as a "pipe" through which God's blessing flows' (158). (I am grateful to Dr Peter Nockles of the Methodist Archives and Research Centre, John Rylands University Library of Manchester, for confirming, among contradictory print and online sources I consulted, Mrs Fletcher's death date as 9 December 1815.)

84 *there have been evil-doers among us who have sought to deceive the brethren*: Matthew 24: 24.

and some there are who deceive their own selves: James 1: 22.

the brethren and sisters watch for each other's souls as they that must give account: Hebrews 13: 17.

They don't go every one his own way: Isaiah 53: 6.

'Am I my brother's keeper?': Genesis 4: 9.

had my heart enlarged: Psalm 25: 17.

85 *sheep without a shepherd*: image in both Old and New Testament, e.g. Numbers 27: 17; Matthew 9: 36.

the heavens stretched out like a tent: Isaiah 40: 22.

the everlasting arms: Deuteronomy 33: 27.

watching and praying: Matthew 26: 41.

Word of Life: 1 John 1: 1.

86 *the burning bush*: Exodus 3: 2–4.

87 *patriarch Joseph*: Genesis 37–50. Eliot's manuscript cancellation in Chapter VIII ('I know both Seth & his brother Adam well' became 'I know Seth well & his brother Adam a little') emphasizes the slight knowledge Dinah has of Adam at this point, in contrast to her closer association with his Methodist brother. By Chapter XXX, when she again compares Adam with the Jewish patriarch, she had expanded her acquaintance with him in her conversations in the Bede cottage in Chapters X and XI. Her regard for Adam expressed in both references to him as Joseph foreshadows the 'ultimate relation' between them which George Henry Lewes had suggested to George Eliot during the composition of the novel.

88 *Pyrrhic dance*: a war dance of the ancient Greeks, done in armour and imitating the actions of battle.

worldly Sadducee: a member of the Jewish elite who collaborated with the Romans in the time of Christ. Like Will Maskery who regards Mr Irwine, a priest in the Established Church, as a 'blind Pharisee', Dinah had thought of him as one of the enemies of true professing Christians, but in this first meeting she alters her views.

91 *We do not hear that Memnon's statue gave forth its melody at all under the rushing of the mightiest wind*: a reference to one of the colossi of Memnon, 'two seated statues of Amenophis III on the west bank of the Nile at Thebes.... One of them, damaged by earthquake, regularly emitted a sound at dawn until repaired by Septimus Severus' (*Oxford Classical Dictionary*, 3rd edn., ed. Simon Hornblower and Antony Spawforth (1996), 955).

93 *Lady Day or Michaelmas*: Lady Day is 25 March, the date of the Annunciation to the Virgin Mary that she was to be the mother of Jesus. Michaelmas, the feast of St Michael, is 29 September. Michaelmas and Lady Day were traditional times for giving notice to labourers or tenants and for hiring farm labour. In Chapter VI, Mrs Poyser refers to having hired the servant girl Molly 'last Michaelmas'. After 'Mrs Poyser has her say out' (Chapter XXXII; late August 1799), the Poysers fear that the old Squire will give them notice to quit their farm next 'Michaelmas twelvemonth'. That this notice would come on the following Lady Day is alluded to in Chapter XXXIII, where Mrs Irwine reflects that 'there's no knowing what may happen before Lady Day'. In Chapter XL, having heard of Arthur's seduction of his niece and its fatal consequences, Mr Poyser says, 'We thought it 'ud be bad luck if th' old Squire gave us notice this Lady Day, but I must gi' notice myself now.'

95 *Olympian god*: this reference to Arthur as one of the Greek gods on Mount Olympus suggests Hetty's blindness to the realities of the working life around her. In Chapter V Arthur refers to his godmother, Mrs Irwine, as an 'Olympian goddess'. These allusions are part of the structure of references to a classical pastoral world in which Hetty and Arthur anticipate no unfortunate consequences for their relationship. The world in which they live, however, is a version of the Wordsworthian pastoral, where consequences can involve great suffering.

96 *Hebe*: the daughter of Juno and cupbearer to the gods who handed round the nectar at their feasts. In this same chapter Arthur is compared to an 'Olympian god' in his effect on 'a simple farmer's girl' like Hetty.

97 *Socrates*: Athenian philosopher (470–399 BC), famous for his technique of asking people questions to force them to defend their views to themselves and others.

107 *the children of this world and the children of light*: Luke 16: 8.

107–8 *Do you remember what David did ... 'I shall go to him, but he shall not return to me'*: 2 Samuel 12: 14–23.

110 *bear the burthen and heat of the day*: Matthew 20: 12.

117 *Pharaoh's daughter ... Moses*: Exodus 2: 1–10.

117 *'When the heart of a man is oppressed with care'*: Arthur misquotes the opening line of a song from *The Beggar's Opera*, II. iii, which reads 'If the heart of a man is depressed with cares'. The imagery of the stanza, suggesting the sensual nature of Arthur's attraction to Hetty, fore-shadows events to come, 'The mist is dispelled when a woman appears . . . Roses and lilies her cheeks disclose, But her ripe lips are more sweet than those. Press her, caress her with blisses, her kisses Dissolve us in pleasure and soft repose.' The cancelled passage above which these lines are written, the entirety of which is difficult to distinguish with certainty, concludes with words from the famous song 'Believe me if all those endearing young charms' by Thomas Moore (1779–1852). From the format of the cancellation, it appears that Eliot thought it was from *The Beggar's Opera*, and then realized that it was not (and perhaps that the reference was anachronistic). She replaced the cancelled lines with those of a more sensual song that suggests a temporary infatuation rather than lasting love.

121 *Centaurs*: half-man and half-horse, the centaurs, although not always regarded negatively, were often remembered (and visualized in art) for the battle of the Lapithae and the Centaurs, after the latter attempted the rape of the bride and other women at the wedding of Pirithous and Hippodamia, establishing the basis for 'their bad repu-tation in history'. Sculptures on the temple of Zeus in Olympia and on the Parthenon on the Acropolis in Athens depict scenes from this battle.

122 *Zeluco*: a novel by John Moore, MD, published in 2 vols. in 1789 under the title *Zeluco: Various Views of Human Nature, Taken from Life and Manners*. The portrayal of Zeluco, a heartless seducer, is at odds with Arthur's image of himself as he sets out on the first step to the seduction of Hetty Sorrel, throughout which he persuades himself that he means no harm and is not such a bad fellow at heart.

129 *Arcadia*: a mythical place in pastoral poetry and prose from Virgil to Sidney. Remote from the 'business' of the real world, Arcadia is associated with love apart from conventional mores. Since Arthur is not a shepherd or even a farmer, but instead the heir to the Donnithorne estate, and Hetty is not a mythical shepherdess but a hard-working dairymaid, the classical allusion signals the dangerous territory into which they are entering.

Eros . . . Psyche: Eros (Roman: Cupid), the son of Aphrodite (Venus), loved Psyche, the daughter of a king, but because of the jealousy of his mother, he could visit Psyche only in secret and could not allow her to know who her lover was. The necessity of secrecy and Psyche's suffering provide parallels with Hetty's story. However, unlike Hetty and Arthur, Eros and Psyche are finally united through the intercession of Zeus. The story is another indicator that Hetty and Arthur's relationship could thrive only in a mythical world.

134 *'Pilgrim's Progress'*: by John Bunyan (1628–88). Richard Altick, describing English reading habits between 1800 and 1900, places *Pilgrim's Progress* second to the Bible among works read in England during that period (*English Common Reader* (Chicago, 1957), 255). He also notes that in 1743 John Wesley, as 'a pioneer popularizer of literature, ... condensed ... *Pilgrim's Progress* into a pocket-size booklet selling for 4d.' (36). Wesley's version would, of course, not have been the edition found in the household of Mr and Mrs Poyser, whose antipathy to Methodism is strongly expressed.

135 *Hebrew points*: the diacritical marks used in Hebrew (and similarly in other Semitic alphabets) to indicate vowels, stress, accent, etc.

149 *'And they all wept sore, and fell on Paul's neck and kissed him'*: Acts 20: 37. Dinah's habit of opening the Bible for directions is discussed in the note to p. 32.

158 *Foulis Æschylus*: Robert Foulis (1707–76) was a Glasgow printer whose press produced Greek texts renowned for their excellence. He was printer to the University of Glasgow. As noted in the Introduction, Eliot was reading Aeschylus' *Oresteia* during the composition of *Adam Bede*, and its debate on justice and revenge underlies the novel. Wiesenfarth details several of the elements *Adam Bede* shares with the Greek trilogy, and notes that 'Adam narrowly avoids entering into the pattern of tragedy. He seeks to revenge himself on Arthur, and only the intervention of Irwine—who understands Aeschylus all too well—prevents him. Consequently, the revenge element of the *Oresteia* works itself out in the novel with a moral wisdom not unlike that which Athena brings to the *Eumenides* itself. Trial by one's peers replaces a cycle of personal revenge. Hetty is judged guilty by a court, and Arthur becomes an exile from a community that cannot tolerate his presence' (82–3).

158–9 *'Cras ingens iterabimus æquor'*: tomorrow we shall go forth again on the vast sea. Horace, *Odes* 1. 7. 32.

159 *Arthur Young*: Young (1741–1820) was a noted agriculturalist whose monthly periodical *Annals of Agriculture* appeared from 1784 to 1809. He also wrote numerous books on agricultural reform, incorporating his own experience as a farmer. This reference demonstrates Eliot's careful plotting. Here she establishes Mr Irwine's interest in practical matters of farming, anticipating the end of the novel, when he becomes manager for the Donnithorne estate in the absence of its owner. Arthur's naming Young 'your friend' is probably a reference to Irwine's reading, rather than a suggestion of personal acquaintance.

Although Young travelled extensively, his properties were in the south-east, and in his tour of the north he passed to the west of the north Staffordshire–Derbyshire locale in which the novel is set. Eliot made two entries on Young in her notebook, both from *A Six Months Tour through the North of England*, published in 1770 in 4 volumes (*A Writer's Notebook*, 20, 29, 156, 161).

161 *Prometheus*: Mr Irwine refers Arthur to Aeschylus' *Prometheus Bound*, which has more specific application than he realizes. Wiesenfarth points out that although they refer explicitly to Zeus and Io, the 'chorus's words bear directly on the story of Arthur and Hetty:

> Wise was the man who declared, "like is fitly coupled
>   with like, and let equal pair with equal."
> Not for grimy craftsman the hand of a rich man's
>   daughter, nor must
> Simple maid plight troth with purse-proud nobleman. . . .
> For me a match within my own degree,
> Not the glance from eyes invisible
> Weaving around me inescapably
> Magical miseries and miracles of wrong,
> Caught in the irresistible
> Cunning of Zeus Almighty.' (80–1)

Wiesenfarth also sees Prometheus as a figure for Adam, in 'his action and his suffering'. Like Prometheus, Adam cannot act, he can only suffer. 'Prometheus's rage against Zeus is ineffectual, and so is Adam's against Arthur. Were it to be effectual—with individual and societal justice colliding head-on—*Adam Bede* would have been a tragedy, not a tragicomedy' (81–2).

Nemesis: goddess of vengeance, representing the righteous anger of the gods, Nemesis is a favourite image in Eliot, who used the word not only in her fiction but in her essays. See, for example, her review of Harriet Beecher Stowe's *Dred: or A Tale of the Great Dismal Swamp* (Pinney, 328). Nemesis is also referred to in *Adam Bede* Chapter XXIX: 'Nemesis can seldom forge a sword for herself out of our consciences—out of the suffering we feel in the suffering we may have caused.'

167 *Apollo curl*: the Apollo Belvedere, a Roman copy of an antique Greek statue, depicts the god with abundant curly hair. Apollo, or Phoebus Apollo, was the god of the sun.

Diana: Roman goddess of the hunt, and twin sister of Apollo (Greek: Artemis).

168   *lazzaroni*: 'one of the lowest class at Naples, who lounge about the streets, living by odd jobs, or by begging' (*OED*). The *OED* includes this passage from *Adam Bede* among the citations.

   Oberlin: Jean Frédéric Oberlin (1740–1826), Lutheran pastor and philanthropist.

   Tillotson: John Tillotson (1630–94), Archbishop of Canterbury and noted preacher.

170   *Arminians*: followers of the tenets of Jacobus Arminius (1560–1609), Dutch theologian. Arminians emphasized the role of the individual in saving his or her own soul and believed in the efficacy of good works. See also notes to pp. 31, 84.

   Calvinists: followers of the tenets of John Calvin (1509–64), French theologian, who believed in predestination. See also note to p. 84.

172   *Shepperton*: Eliot connects the setting of *Adam Bede* with that in her previous work, *Scenes of Clerical Life*, whose first story opens with a description of Shepperton, fictional name for Chilvers Coton, not far from Nuneaton, Warwickshire, which is perhaps the 'neighbouring market-town' to which Mr Gedge 'transfer[s] himself'.

174   *'Whissuntide'*: dialect form for Whitsuntide, the season of Pentecost. Whit Sunday, the seventh Sunday after Easter, celebrates the descent of the Holy Ghost (Acts 2).

175   *Sacrament Sundays*: Sundays on which Holy Eucharist, or Communion, was celebrated in the Church of England.

180   *taking time by the forelock*: a folk proverb, 'Take Time (Occasion) by the forelock, for she is bald behind' (*The Oxford Dictionary of English Proverbs*, 3rd edn., rev. F. P. Wilson, 1970).

184   *evening hymn*: like Bishop Ken's morning hymn (see note to p. 7), his evening hymn, 'Glory to Thee, my God, this night', is among the most famous Anglican hymns.

   Pan: god of nature, flocks, and shepherds, who pursued one of Diana's nymphs, Syrinx. When he neared her and threw his arms around her, he found that he grasped only a handful of reeds. His sighs sounding through the reeds produced a melody, and from the reeds he made a musical instrument called the syrinx, or, more popularly, the panpipe.

185   *General Confession*: the public confession of sin in the Anglican service.

187   *'Thou sweep'st us off as with a flood . . . dreams'*: This 'old psalm-tune' is a setting of Psalm 90: 5, 'Thou carriest them away as with a flood.' Its 'closer application than usual' lies, of course, in the fact that Thias Bede died by drowning in the flooded Willow Brook.

189   *'In the midst of life we are in death'*: Mr Irwine speaks from the words of the Burial Service, which he has just performed.

192 *Nelson*: see note to p. 63.

199 *Old and New Version*: two verse settings of the Psalms, the old, from the sixteenth century, by Thomas Sternhold and John Hopkins, and the new by Nahum Tate and Nicholas Brady (1696).

200 *'Poor Richard's Almanac'*: by American printer, inventor, statesman, and writer Benjamin Franklin (1706–90), published as a series from 1732 to 1757.

   Taylor's 'Holy Living and Dying': by Anglican clergyman Jeremy Taylor (1613–67), *The Rule and Exercises of Holy Living* was first published in 1650 and *The Rule and Exercises of Holy Dying* in 1651.

   'The Pilgrim's Progress': by John Bunyan (1628–88). See also note to p. 45.

   Bunyan's Life and 'Holy War': first published in 1682.

   Bailey's Dictionary: by Nathan, or Nathaniel, Bailey (d. 1742). His *An Universal Etymological English Dictionary* was first published in 1721.

   'Valentine and Orson': a story about two brothers, *Valentine and Orson*, published in French in the fifteenth century, was translated and frequently reprinted in English as well as other European languages.

206 *streaked pink-and-white . . . the union of the houses of York and Lancaster*: the roses blend the colours of the white rose of the house of York and the red rose of the house of Lancaster, which were united after the defeat of Richard III at the battle of Bosworth Field.

214 *St Vitus's Dance*: popular name for Sydenham's chorea, or rheumatic chorea. It affects the part of the brain that controls motor coordination.

221 *'Brimstone'*: nickname referring to the devil, from the 'lake of fire burning with brimstone' described in Revelation 19: 20.

229 *Jacob and Rachel*: see note to p. 33.

235 *a rancorous poisoned garment*: the image suggests Medea's revenge on Jason's new bride Creusa, princess of Corinth, to whom Medea sent a poisoned robe. Like Medea, who kills her sons by the faithless Jason, Hetty will kill her own child by Arthur Donnithorne. However, it is Hetty, not a new bride, who will wear the rancorous poisoned garment she has made from her 'web of folly and vain hopes'.

237 *Old Harry*: folk usage for the devil, which was the word (in dialect form: *divil*) originally used and then cancelled in manuscript. Perhaps Eliot recalled the folk superstition against naming the devil, and substituted instead the euphemism *Old Harry*.

238 *Benefit Club*: an organization in which working people contributed a monthly sum as a kind of insurance which could be drawn upon in sickness or old age.

239 *Scotch raybels*: during the Jacobite rebellion of 1745, the rebels under Bonnie Prince Charlie reached 'Stoniton', i.e. Derby, in December that year, when they turned back after failing to receive the support of English Jacobites.

240 *General Monk*: General George Monck (1608–70), one of Cromwell's supporters during the Civil War. He became first Duke of Albemarle after switching his support to Charles II following Cromwell's death.

   Daniel . . . among the lions: Daniel 6: 16–23.

   Julius Cæsar . . . his Commentaries: Caesar's *Commentaries* are his narratives of the Gallic Wars (58–50 BC) and the Civil War (50–47 BC).

241 ἀπέρωτος ἔρως: unloving love, from Aeschylus' *Choephoroe*, line 576. Eliot recorded the Greek phrase in her notebook (*A Writer's Notebook*, 20 and 155 n. 13). As discussed in the Introduction, Eliot and Lewes were reading the *Oresteia* during the composition of *Adam Bede*. Wiesenfarth notes that the Greek phrase not only describes 'Squire Donnithorne's relation to his grandson Arthur, but it also accurately describes Arthur's relation to Hetty' (80 n. 6).

245 *'Over the hills and far away'*: traditional folksong, *c.*1620.

255 *Benefit Club*: see note to p. 238.

260 *yearly Wake*: an annual village festival, in earlier times on the feast day of the patron saint of the parish church of the village, an occasion for dancing, games, and other forms of merriment.

261 *'White Cockade'*: a Jacobite folksong.

   'Bird Waltz': a popular piece of music written by Francis Panormo (1765–1844), which went through more than forty editions by the time *Adam Bede* was published. The earliest date to which I have been able to trace this work, in an arrangement for pianoforte or harp, is 1818 when a third edition was published. Although the allusion at first may seem to be one of the anachronisms to which the *Times* reviewer referred, the voice is that of the narrator speaking to the reader, continuing the discussion of realism in fiction. In it one can detect the voice of George Eliot, the critic for various periodicals in the early and mid-1850s. In her review of Wilhelm Heinrich von Riehl's 'The Natural History of German Life', published in the *Westminster Review*, 66 (July 1856), 51–79, she seems to exempt music from the requirements of realism: 'Opera peasants . . . are surely too frank an idealization to be misleading; and since popular chorus is one of the most effective elements of the opera, we can hardly object to lyric rustics in elegant laced boddices and picturesque motley, unless we are prepared to advocate a chorus of colliers in their pit costume, or a ballet of char-women and stocking-weavers' (Pinney, 270). In *Adam*

Bede, the narrator contrasts 'ballet rustics' whom readers might have seen on stage with Wiry Ben who dances like a true rustic, reinforcing the point by noting the difference between a popular drawing room song called 'The Bird Waltz' and the music of birds in nature.

296 *Nemesis*: See note to p. 161.

307 *Ganymede*: a beautiful Trojan prince, who was seized by Zeus in the form of an eagle and carried to Mount Olympus, where he became the cupbearer to the gods, replacing Hebe. The image is a curious one. Except in terms of physical position on Adam's shoulder, it is unlikely that Eliot envisioned a parallel between Totty and Ganymede, nor is Adam associated with any figures from classical myth, much less Zeus, the abductor of the youth. The description is strongly visual, and at least two visual images representing the abduction of Ganymede have survived from ancient Greece, one of the eagle with Ganymede (a copy after Leochares, in the Vatican Museum), and the other a half-size polychrome terracotta of Zeus with Ganymede under his arm, in the Olympia Museum.

308 *Aristides the Just*: fifth-century Athenian statesman, hero of Marathon and founder of the Delian league.

309 *state of perfection*: in *A State of Christian Perfection*, John Wesley explored the doctrine of perfection, the belief that it was possible to reach a state of perfection and be delivered from sin. Seth's questioning of John Barnes is consonant with the question and answer structure of both Wesley's *A Plain Account of Christian Perfection* and his *Further Thoughts on Christian Perfection*.

311 *the windows of heaven were opened again*: Genesis 7: 11.

a want of trust like the laying up of the manna: Exodus 16.

patriarch Joseph: see note to p. 87.

wherewith the whole creation groaneth and travaileth: Romans 8: 22.

312 *'If any man love me, let him take up my cross'*: images from Matthew 10: 38 and 16: 24; Mark 8: 34; Luke 9: 23.

the cup we must drink of with him: Matthew 20: 23.

I have all things and abound: Philippians 4: 18.

laying a false offering on the altar and expecting the fire from heaven to kindle it: 1 Kings 18: 19–40.

sufficient for the day: Matthew 6: 34. Another allusion to the text 'take no thought', to which Lisbeth Bede objected in Chapter IV.

317 *Broxton wake*: see note to p. 260.

327 *Michaelmas*: see note to p. 93.

329 *plagues o' Egypt . . . frogs and toads*: Exodus 8: 2–14.

330 *Old Harry*: see note to p. 237.

331 *Michaelmas*: see note to p. 93.

332 *'Bony' was come back from Egypt*: Bonaparte left Egypt on 23 August 1799, slipped through the British blockade, and reached Paris on 16 October. In November, a *coup d'état* overthrew the Directory and he became First Consul.

  the repulse of the French in Italy: the French in Italy suffered heavy losses in the summer of 1799, culminating in the battle of Novi on 15 August 1799 in which the respected French general Joubert was killed.

333 *Lady Day*: see note to p. 93.

341 *Christian folks can't be married like cuckoos*: this has the ring of a proverb, but I have been unable to locate it in proverb dictionaries. It is probably one of those Mrs Poyser originals that impressed early readers. Mrs Poyser could not, of course, be aware of its applicability to Hetty's situation or to the tragedy about to unfold.

352 *Jehu the son of Nimshi*: 2 Kings 9: 20.

362 *Medusa-face*: Eliot had seen and admired the Medusa Rondanini in the Glyptothek in Munich during the summer of 1858 while she was writing *Adam Bede*. She copied into her notebook a description of this work from Ludwig Stahr's *Torso, Kunst, Künstler und Kunstwerke der Alten* (which she had reviewed for the *Leader* on 17 March 1855; Pinney, 458). Wiesenfarth notes that 'Stahr's lyric description ... impressed itself on her mind—impressed itself so much so that in *Adam Bede* when Hetty, the beautiful sinner, is caught between life and death on her Journey in Despair, she appears as the Medusa Rondanini' (43–4).

369 *'Dark and cheerless is the morn ... perfect day'*: the second and third stanzas of Charles Wesley's hymn 'Christ, Whose Glory Fills the Skies'.

388 *Bitter Waters Spread*: Exodus 15: 23. Like Moses, whom God inspires to make the bitter waters sweet (Exodus 15: 25), Dinah returns to Loamshire in Chapter XLV to bring Hetty to confess and repent. She also gives consolation to Arthur before he leaves for the army, and, for the Poyser and the Bede families during the next eighteen months, she helps change the bitter waters to sweet.

392 *Sarah Williamson, Methodist preacher*: a fictional name, but one that may derive from the Methodist preacher Sarah Crosby, a friend of Mary Bosanquet Fletcher. Cunningham notes that Crosby 'was probably "the first authorised woman preacher in Methodism"' and the model for the fictional Sarah Williamson (158–9, quoting A. W.

Harrison). Sarah Williamson is probably the unnamed 'holy woman who preaches' in Leeds in Chapter VIII.

401 *upper room*: imagery in this chapter—the upper room as well as the bread and wine that Adam partakes of before he goes to the trial that is his as well as Hetty's—suggests an identification of Adam with Christ. Wiesenfarth points out that this identification begins in Chapter XLI, where the 'eve of the trial finds Adam a haggard and worn man, bearing within himself the sorrow of his friend's deceit and his beloved's wickedness.... Adam's face—like the sad face of a Christ which George Eliot saw in Nürnberg—makes the Man of Sorrows [an image in Dinah's letter in Chapter XXX] seem "a very close thing— not a faint hearsay"', as Eliot wrote in her journal. He also notes the connection between Adam and the risen Christ in Chapter LI (Wiesenfarth, 89–90).

403 *took up the cup, and drank*: an allusion to Matthew 26: 27.

422 *pure from sin*: Proverbs 20: 9. Proverbs 20: 11 provides an answer to Adam's view of Hetty as an innocent child in Chapter XLI: 'she was a child as it 'ud ha' gone t' anybody's heart to look at ... I don't care what she's done.'

the cry of the forsaken: see note to p. 29.

Look upon her with thy face of love and sorrow, that thou didst turn on him who denied thee: Luke 22: 61.

423 *I bring her, as they of old brought the sick and helpless, and thou didst heal them*: Matthew 4: 24.

darkness is as noonday: Isaiah 58: 10.

the eleventh hour: Matthew 20: 6, 9.

coming, like the morning, with healing on thy wings: Malachi 4: 2.

let the dead hear thy voice: John 5: 25, and cf. Isaiah 35: 5.

let the eyes of the blind be opened: Isaiah 35: 5.

'Father, I have sinned': Luke 15: 18.

425 *it was like a heavy weight hanging round my neck*: Matthew 18: 6. This use of the biblical reference to the millstone is complex. By the mere fact of its existence, the infant was the millstone round Hetty's neck. Its death at her hands, however, has not eliminated the dread of censure on the tongues of her Hayslope neighbours that led Hetty to commit the crime. Rather, the crime has made the dead infant a greater 'millstone' than it was living, subjecting her now not only to social death in the censure of her neighbours but to the ultimate doom of the state, death as a condemned murderer. Unlike Hetty, Dinah is concerned not with social death or the death of the body, but with the death of the soul. Cunningham suggests, however, that Hetty never

does grasp the supernatural dimension that Dinah seeks to impress upon her. 'She leans on Dinah as a human being, rather than on a Divine source of comfort... Hetty repents superficially to God, but most movingly to Adam: the human connection is the most prominent' (169). The image of the weight round the neck also recalls Arthur's reading of *The Ancient Mariner* (Chapter V); his punishment is social banishment for a period that coincides with Hetty's sentence of seven years, one of the customary terms of transportation. She is returning to England when she dies seven years after her trial.

432   *pray without ceasing*: 1 Thessalonians 5: 17.

433   *transported o'er the seas*: transportation to Australia began in 1787; the first shipload of convicts arrived there in 1788. It continued until late in the nineteenth century, being abolished at different times in different parts of the country. See Robert Hughes, *The Fatal Shore* (New York, 1986).

442   *Sermon on the Mount*: Matthew 5–7. Mrs Poyser provides her own individualistic gloss on the text in the remainder of her speech.

like taking your cloak off and giving it to 'em: Matthew 5: 40.

or letting 'em slap you i' the face, I dare say you'd be ready enough: Matthew 5: 39.

443   *all things too richly to enjoy*: 1 Timothy 6: 17.

443–4   *enough and to spare*: Luke 15: 17.

450   *there'll be a peace soon, though nobody believes it'll last long*: Arthur is surprisingly well informed. Serious peace negotiations began in September 1801 (when the activities of Chapter L take place), and on 1 October preliminaries of peace were signed. The signing of the Peace of Amiens concluded the negotiations on 25 March 1802. 'Nobody' was correct; the peace lasted about a year.

That meeting... where Esau is so loving and generous, and Jacob so timid and distrustful: Genesis 32–3.

Moses... carried a hard business well through, and died when other folks were going to reap the fruits: Deuteronomy 34: 1–5.

452   *Wesley's abridgment of Madame Guyon's life*: 'John Wesley, *An Extract of the Life of Madam Guion* (1776): entry No. 314 in Richard Green's Bibliography of Wesley's works (1896), 186' (Cunningham, 160 n. 3).

454   *precepts of Solomon*: Dinah is thinking of texts like Proverbs 13: 24.

455   *Colonel Bath*: in Henry Fielding's *Amelia* (1751), book 3, chapter viii. Bath (who is a major at this point) cares for his sister during her illness

and, trying to explain away his seemingly unmanly position, provokes a vigorous defence of manly tenderness in the narrator Mr Booth.

456 *'Eternal Beam of Light Divine . . . For all things serve thy sovereign will'*: Dinah sings stanzas 1, 2, and 5, the last having particular application to the conflict between her love for Adam and her desire to submit herself to God's will.

457 *the man Moses, the meekest of men*: Numbers 12: 3.

was wrathful sometimes: 'and Moses' anger waxed hot, and he cast the tables out of his hands', Exodus 32: 19.

457–8 *in heaviness through manifold temptations*: 1 Peter 1: 6.

458 *the flesh is weak*: Matthew 26: 41.

460 *The God of love and peace be with them*: 2 Corinthians 13: 11.

It is thy will . . . let me have no will but thine: Luke 22: 42; also Matthew 26: 42; Mark 14: 36.

463 *Samuel's dying speech*: 1 Samuel 12.

old Isaac's meeting with his son: Genesis 27: 1–40.

son of Sirach's keen-edged words: 'Wisdom of Jesus Son of Sirach', part of the Old Testament Apocrypha.

the angel seated on the great stone that has been rolled away from the sepulchre: Matthew 27: 60, 28: 2; Mark 16: 4–5.

466 *the marigold i' th' parridge*: not a proverbial expression, but a reference to the use of marigold flowers for colour. *The English Dialect Dictionary*, vol. IV, ed. Joseph Wright, gives *marigold* in the combination marigold-cheese: 'cheese made of skim-milk, having the petals of marigold-flowers strewn amongst the uncoloured curd.' Lisbeth's image suggests that she sees Dinah's Methodism as an incidental matter, not central to her being.

468 *'I came not to call the righteous, but sinners to repentance'*: Mark 2: 17; Luke 5: 32.

469 *Mrs Fletcher*: see note to p. 84.

471 *I have all things and abound*: see note to p. 312.

474 *where doubt enters, there is not perfect love*: 1 John 4: 18.

477 *Exeter Hall*: a large public building constructed in 1829–31 on the Strand, London, where concerts and religious (especially Evangelical), scientific, and political meetings were held.

Tracts for the Times: a series of pamphlets published between 1833 and 1841 by Anglican clergymen at Oxford, including J. H. Newman, E. B. Pusey, John Keble, and others, who endeavoured to bring a new spirit into the Church of England.

Sartor Resartus: by Thomas Carlyle, first published serially in *Fraser's Magazine* in 1833–4.

481 *Tityrus and Melibœus*: two rustics who converse on their pastoral delights and the changing times in Virgil's Eclogue 1. Their polite, measured speech stands in contrast to that of the Hall Farm labourers, particularly Alick, who is 'not by any means a honeyed man' but whose 'speech had usually something of a snarl in it'.

The bucolic character at Hayslope, you perceive, was not of that entirely genial, merry, broad-grinning sort, apparently observed in most districts visited by artists: in her review of Riehl's 'The Natural History of German Life' (see note to p. 261), Eliot argued against false depictions of peasants in art: 'even those among our painters who aim at giving the rustic type of features . . . treat their subjects under the influence of traditions and prepossessions rather than of direct observation' (Pinney, 268–9). In countering the idyllic picture of peasant life that predominates in the arts, she points to 'the still lingering mistake, that an unintelligible dialect is a guarantee for ingenuousness, and that slouching shoulders indicate an upright disposition. It is quite true that a thresher is likely to be innocent of any adroit arithmetical cheating, but he is not the less likely to carry home his master's corn in his shoes and pocket' (Pinney, 269–70). When she came to write Chapter LIII, Eliot took her own advice, showing precisely this thresher in Ben Tholoway and the other decidedly unidyllic labourers, who nonetheless have the respect of their master and the narrator.

482–3 *'Here's a health unto our master . . . For 'tis our master's will'*: a traditional Harvest Home drinking song. Two versions appear in an undated pamphlet, *The Harvest Songster*, issued by J. Pitts, of Great St Andrew Street, Seven Dials, one of which matches the rhythm and some of the words in the version Eliot gives to the merrymakers.

484 *He's full o' this peace now*: the peace of Amiens. See note to p. 450.

take on Billy Pitt again: William Pitt the Younger (1759–1806), who resigned as Prime Minister in March 1801, but re-entered office in May 1804.

485 *It's hard work to tell which is Old Harry when everybody's got boots on*: the devil's cloven hoof cannot be seen if everyone is wearing boots.

Socratic argument: see note to p. 97.

488 *'Three Merry Mowers'*: I have been unable to locate a reference to this song.

497 *wedding psalm*: the Solemnization of Marriage in the Book of Common Prayer gives either of two psalms to be said or sung after the joining of the couple and the minister's blessing: *Beati omnes*, Psalm 128, or *Deus*

misereatur, Psalm 67. Neither, however, includes the phrase that Joshua Rann is humming. The reference fits closely a verse setting of Psalm 133. Rann's 'O what a joyful thing it is' condenses two lines ('O what a happy thing it is, And joyful for to see') that George Eliot first quoted in *Scenes of Clerical Life*, in the midst of a discussion of the singing of 'the wedding psalm for a newly-married couple' at Shepperton Church. Mr Hackit describes it as 'as pretty a psalm an' as pretty a tune as any's in the prayer-book'. Thomas A. Noble's note to this reference in the Clarendon edition of *Scenes of Clerical Life* (Oxford, 1995) reads: 'Metrical version of Psalm 133, as rendered in Sternhold and Hopkins ("Old Version")' (Noble, 13 n. 5). The reference to a psalm in the Old Version suggests that Rann, while present like other Hayslope inhabitants to celebrate the wedding of Adam and Dinah, nonetheless feels, as he had at Dinah's sermon in Chapter II, a need to assert the traditions of the Church of England against the new religious movements, just as Mr Hackit in *Scenes of Clerical Life* breaks 'into [traditional] melody' as he objects to the new hymns that Amos Barton wishes to introduce at Shepperton Church.

500 *Conference has forbid the women preaching*: Cunningham notes that 'the Wesleyan Conference forbade [women preachers] "in general" in 1803' (159). Eliot recorded this date in her notebook (*A Writer's Notebook*, 29), but, as Wiesenfarth points out in his notes (as discussed in the Introduction), her representation in the Epilogue is not strictly accurate.